Revel enables students to read and interact with course material on the devices they use, **anywhere** and **anytime**. Responsive design allows students to access Revel on their tablet devices, with content displayed clearly in both portrait and landscape view.

Highlighting, **note taking**, and a **glossary** personalize the learning experience. Educators can add **notes** for students, too, including reminders or study tips

Revel's variety of **writing** activities and assignments develop and assess concept **mastery** and **critical thinking**.

Superior assignability and tracking

Revel's assignability and tracking tools help educators make sure students are completing their reading and understanding core concepts.

Revel allows educators to indicate precisely which readings must be completed on which dates. This clear, detailed schedule helps students stay on task and keeps them motivated throughout the course.

Revel lets educators monitor class assignment completion and individual student achievement. It offers actionable information that helps educators intersect with their students in meaningful ways, such as points earned on quizzes and time on task.

THE STRUGGLE FOR DEMOCRACY

2018 Elections and Updates Edition

THE STRUGGLE FOR DEMOCRACY

2018 Elections and Updates Edition

Edward S. GREENBERG
University of Colorado, Boulder

Benjamin I. PAGE
Northwestern University

with assistance by
David Doherty
Loyola University Chicago

Scott L. Minkoff
SUNY New Paltz

Josh M. Ryan
Utah State University

 Pearson

Executive Portfolio Manager: Jeff Marshall
Content Producer: Mary Donovan
Content Developer: Allison Collins
Portfolio Manager Assistant: Christina Winterburn
Product Marketer: Candice Madden
Field Marketer: Alexa Macri
Content Producer Manager: Amber Mackey
Content Development Manager: Rebecca Green
Art/Designer: Lumina Datamatics, Inc.

Digital Studio Course Producer: Tina Gagliostro
Full-Service Project Manager: Lumina Datamatics, Inc.
Compositor: Lumina Datamatics, Inc.
Printer/Binder: LSC Communications, Inc.
Cover Printer: LSC Communications, Inc.
Cover Design: Lumina Datamatics, Inc.
Cover Credit: José Miguel Hernández Hernández/ Moment Open/Getty Images

Acknowledgements of third party content appear on page 645, which constitutes an extension of this copyright page.

Library of Congress Cataloging-in-Publication Data

Names: Greenberg, Edward S., 1942– author. | Page, Benjamin I., author.
Title: The struggle for democracy / Edward S. Greenberg, Benjamin I. Page ;
   with assistance by David Doherty, Scott L. Minkoff.
Description: 12th edition, 2018 elections and updates edition. | Hudson
   Street, N.Y., NY : Pearson, 2020. | Includes bibliographical references and index.
Identifiers: LCCN 2018040806 | ISBN 9780135246429 | ISBN 0135246423
Subjects: LCSH: United States—Politics and government—Textbooks. |
   Democracy—United States—Textbooks.
Classification: LCC JK276 .G74 2020 | DDC 320.473—dc23
LC record available at https://lccn.loc.gov/2018040806

1 18

Access Code Card
ISBN-10:   0-13-520276-0
ISBN-13: 978-0-13-520276-0

Revel Combo Card
ISBN-10:   0-13-558193-1
ISBN-13: 978-0-13-558193-3

Rental Edition
ISBN-10:   0-13-524642-3
ISBN-13: 978-0-13-524642-9

Loose Leaf Edition
ISBN-10:   0-13-522948-0
ISBN-13: 978-0-13-522948-4

Instructor's Review Copy:
ISBN-10:   0-13-524690-3
ISBN-13: 978-0-13-524690-0

Brief Contents

PART V **What Government Does**

Contents

18   Foreign and National Defense Policies   529

Why study American government and politics, and why read this textbook to do it? Here's why: Only by understanding how our complex political system operates and how government works can you play a role in deciding what government does. Only by understanding the obstacles that stand in your way as you enter the political fray, as well as the abundant opportunities you have to advance your ideas and values in the political process, can you play an effective role.

You can learn this best, we believe, by studying what political scientists have discovered about American politics and government. Political science is the systematic study of the role that people and groups play in determining what government does; how government goes about implementing its policy decisions; and what social, economic, and political consequences flow from government actions. The best political science research is testable, evidence-based, and peer-reviewed—as free as possible from ideological and partisan bias as it can be.

The Struggle for Democracy not only introduces you to that research but also gives you tools to decode the American political system, analyze its pieces, consider its linkages, and identify opportunities to make a difference. A simple but powerful framework will guide you in discovering how government, politics, and the larger society are intertwined and how government policies are a product of the interactions of actors and institutions across these domains.

Our hope and expectation is that *The Struggle for Democracy* will enable your success in your introduction to American government and politics course. But we are interested in more than your classroom experiences. We believe that knowing how politics and government work and how closely they conform to our democratic values will also enable a lifetime of productive choices. Put all naïveté aside, however. Making a mark on public policies is never easy. Like-minded individuals need to do more than vote. Those who gain the most from government policies have, after all, substantial resources to make certain that government treats them well.

But you have resources to make changes, too. Beyond voting, opportunities for affecting change may come from your involvement in political campaigns, from using social media to persuade others of your views or to organize meetings and demonstrations, from participating in social movements, from contributing to groups and politicians who share your views, and from many more such avenues. So, much like waging war, making your voice heard requires that you know the "lay of the land," including the weapons you have at your disposal (we would call them political tools) and the weapons of those arrayed against you. But, much like peacemaking, you need to know how and when compromises can be reached that serve the interests of all parties.

Lest all of the above seems too daunting, we also have tried to make this book enjoyable, accessible, and fun. If your experience in reading *The Struggle for Democracy* comes close to the pleasure we had in writing it, we have come as near as possible to achieving our goal.

Meet Your Author

EDWARD S. GREENBERG is Professor Emeritus of Political Science and Research Professor of Behavioral Science at the University of Colorado, Boulder. Ed's research and teaching interests include American government and politics, domestic and global political economy, and democratic theory and practice, with a special emphasis on workplace issues. His multi-year longitudinal panel study, funded by the NIH, examining the impact of technological change and the globalization of production on Boeing managers and employees, is reported in more than a dozen journal articles and in his book *Turbulence: Boeing and the State of American Workers and Managers* (Yale University Press, 2010, co-authored with Leon Grunberg, Sarah Moore, and Pat Sikora). He is currently doing research on the global competition between Boeing and Airbus and its impact on people who work in these firms.

Ben Page and I decided to write this book because, as instructors in introductory American government courses, we could not find a book that provided students with usable tools for critically analyzing our political system and making judgments about how well our government works. *The Struggle for Democracy* does not simply present facts about government and politics—it also provides several analytical and normative frameworks for putting the flood of facts we ask our students to absorb into a more comprehensible form. By doing so, I believe we have made it easier and more satisfying for instructors to teach the introductory course.

Our goal all along was to create a textbook that treats students as adults, engages their intellectual and emotional attention, and encourages them to be active learners. Every element in this text is designed to promote the kind of critical thinking skills scholars and instructors believe students need to become the engaged, active, and informed citizens that are so vital to any democracy. Over the next several sections, I show the elements we created to meet these objectives.

Features

APPROACH *The Struggle for Democracy* provides several analytical and normative frameworks for putting the flood of facts teachers ask their students to absorb into a more comprehensible form. Although all topics that are common and expected in the introductory American government and politics course are covered in this textbook, the two main focal points—an analytical framework for understanding how politics and government work and the normative question "How democratic are we?" (addressed in concluding remarks at the end of each chapter under the "Using the Democracy Standard" headline)—allow for a fresh look at traditional topics.

This book pays great attention to *structural factors*—which include the American economy, social and demographic change in the United States, technological innovations and change, the American political culture, and changes in the global system—and examines how they affect politics, government, and public policy. These factors are introduced in Chapter 4—a chapter unique among introductory texts—and they are brought to bear on a wide range of issues in subsequent chapters.

The Struggle for Democracy attends very carefully to issues of *democratic political theory*. This follows from a critical thinking objective, which asks students to assess the progress of, and prospects for, democracy in the United States and from a desire to present American history as the history of the struggle for democracy. For instance, *Struggle* examines how the evolution of the party system has improved democracy in some respects in the United States, but hurt it in others.

Struggle also includes more *historical perspective* because it provides the necessary context for thinking comprehensively and critically about contemporary political debates. It shows, for example, how the expansion of civil rights in the United States is tied to important historical events and trends.

Comparisons of developments, practices, and institutions in the United States with those in other nations add another dimension to our understanding. We can better comprehend how our system of social welfare works, for example, when we see how other rich democratic countries deal with the problems of poverty, unemployment, and old age.

COVERAGE In an effort to build a ground-up understanding of American politics and the policy outcomes it does (and does not) produce, the chapters in *Struggle* mirror the structure of our analytical pyramid framework. Part 1 includes an introduction to the textbook, its themes, and the critical thinking tools used throughout the book. Part 2 covers the *structural foundations* of American government and politics, addressing subjects such as the U.S. economy and political culture and its place in the international system; the constitutional framework of the American political system; and the development of federalism. Part 3 focuses on *political linkage* institutions such as parties, elections, public opinion, social movements, and interest groups that convey the wants, needs, and demands of individuals and groups to public officials. Part 4 concentrates on the central institutions of the national government, including the presidency, Congress, and the Supreme Court. Part 5 describes the kinds of policies the national government produces and analyzes how effective government is at solving pressing social and economic problems. The analytical framework used in this book also means that the subjects of *civil liberties* and *civil rights* are not treated in conjunction with the Constitution in Part 2, which is the case with many introductory texts, but in Part 5, on public policy. This is because we believe that the real-world status of civil liberties and civil rights, while partly determined by specific provisions of the Constitution, is better understood as the outcome of the interaction of structural, political, and governmental factors. For example, the status of civil rights for gays, lesbians, and transgendered people depends not only on constitutional provisions but also on the state of public opinion, degrees of support from elected political leaders, and the decisions of the Supreme Court.

PEDAGOGY *The Struggle for Democracy* offers unique features that help students better understand, interpret, and critically evaluate American politics and government.

- **Chapter-opening** stories provide useful frames of reference for defining why the principal topic of each chapter matters to the citizens of our American democracy.
- A unique visual tool that maps out the many influences in the American political process and how they shape political decisions and policies, the **Applying the Framework** model makes clear that government, politics, and society are deeply intertwined in recognizable patterns. The framework simplifies complex associations, builds on the "deep structures" that underlay American politics and government—the economy, society, political culture, and the constitutional rules—and encourages holistic comprehension of American politics.
- More than one hundred **figures and tables** strengthen the narrative and help students extract meaning and insights from data that drive political decision making and government action.
- **Timelines** appear throughout this book to help students develop a sense of historical context and to clarify the chronology of a particular period. Timeline topics include federalism milestones and a history of the civil rights movement.
- Every chapter includes a **marginal glossary of key terms** to support students' understanding of new and important concepts at first encounter. For easy reference, key terms from the marginal glossary are repeated at the end of each chapter and in the end-of-book glossary.
- Every chapter includes a **Using the Democracy Standard** section to help students consolidate their thinking about the American political system as a whole by using a normative democracy "yardstick" that asks students to assess the degree to which the United States has become more or less democratic.
- **Review the Chapter** sections organized around chapter learning objectives is included at the end of each chapter to help students better understand and retain information and to think critically about the material.

New to This Edition

Key updates to *The Struggle for Democracy* include the following:

- Substantial coverage of the contentious 2018 national midterm elections with special attention to the partisan aspects of the election in Chapter 9, the voting and campaign aspects in Chapter 10, the consequences for Congress in Chapter 11, and the impact on the presidency in Chapter 12.

- Coverage throughout, but especially in Chapters 3, 10, 14, 15, 16, and 17, on **important rulings by the Supreme Court** on religious liberty, LGBTQ rights, congressional district gerrymandering, voting rights, and presidential powers.

- Consideration, especially in Chapter 12, "The Presidency," and Chapter 18, "Foreign Policy and National Defense," on the changing relationships with America's traditional allies, efforts to tame the nuclear weapons and missile programs in North Korea and Iran, China's emergence as a competing world power, and Russia's growing military aggressiveness in Europe and the Middle East, as well as its continuing interference in the politics of democratic countries.

- Increased attention to the **growing partisan bitterness** in Washington and across much of the nation that affects how government addresses or fails to address virtually every major problem facing the nation whether it be energy, illegal immigration, climate change, or the shrinking middle class (Chapters 5, 9, 10, 11, and 17).

- Questions of whether and to what degree income and wealth inequality has increased, and if it has, with what political and public policy consequences were thoroughly considered during this revision. We also look closely at **globalization and technological change and their impact on Americans**, with extensive research and analysis of particular note evident in Chapters 4 and 18.

- The ways in which social, economic, and technological trends shape government action are also considered, including executive orders increasing border security, tightening immigration asylum processing, intensifying the expulsion of undocumented immigrants, and rolling back financial industry and environmental regulations (Chapters 4, 15, 17, and 18).

- **Photos** in this edition were selected not only to capture major events from the last few years but to illustrate the relevancy of politics in our daily lives. They show political actors and processes as well as people affected by politics, creating a visual narrative that enhances rather than repeats the text. Each includes critical thinking questions that allow readers to engage with the material more intensely.

- The data in all of the **figures and tables** have been updated throughout with the intention of helping users think critically not only about political decisions in retrospect but also about pending government action.

Revel™

Revel is an interactive learning environment that deeply engages students and prepares them for class. Media and assessment integrated directly within the authors' narrative lets students read, explore interactive content, and practice in one continuous learning path. Thanks to the dynamic reading experience in Revel, students come to class prepared to discuss, apply, and learn from instructors and from each other.

Learn more about Revel at www.pearson.com/revel.

- Chapter-opening **Current Events Bulletins** feature author-written articles that put breaking news and current events into the context of American government. Examples include the 2016 elections in context, the strained relationship between the U.S. and Russia, and how Democratic turnout in the 2016 election helps to explain Trump's victory.

> # Chapter 10
> # Voting, Campaigns, and Elections
>
> ## Current Events Bulletin
>
> > Current Events Bulletin
> >
> > **The 2018 House Elections and Partisan Redistricting** ≡
> >
> > July 2018
> >
> > As you will learn in this chapter, congressional elections are held every two years, when all seats in the House of Representatives, and approximately one-third of Senate seats, are contested. Currently, both the House and Senate are controlled by the Republican Party, which holds a small majority in each. Typically, the president's party does poorly in midterm elections for a variety of reasons. After two years, the honeymoon period is over, and as a natural result of trying to govern, presidents have accumulated broken promises and failures, which in turn anger different constituencies. Voters are ready for a change, and send that message through congressional elections. In fact, since World War II, only in 1998 and 2002 did the president's party gain seats in the House in a midterm election. The president's party typically loses between 15 and 30 seats in the House, with losses minimized when a president's approval rating is high, generally considered to be over 50 percent.
> >
> > Donald Trump was historically unpopular when elected as compared to other new presidents; his campaign was highly divisive, he lost the popular vote, and many believe he never reached

- Captivating **videos** bring to life chapter content and key moments in American government. Videos are incorporated into the chapters, where pertinent, and can also be easily accessed from the instructor's Resources folder within Revel.

  - *ABC News footage* and *Smithsonian short documentary videos* provide examples from both current and historical events. Examples of footage include FDR visiting the newly completed Boulder Dam (Hoover Dam), an NRA lobbyist's proposition to put guns in schools one week after the Sandy Hook tragedy, important events in African Americans' struggle for equality, how war and the preparation for war increased the role of the federal government, and President Obama's struggle to make a case for air strikes in Syria.

  - *Pearson Originals for Political Science* are compelling stories about contemporary issues. These short-form documentaries contextualize the complex social and political issues impacting the world today. In addition to helping students better understand core concepts, *Pearson Originals* inspire students to think critically as empowered citizens who can inspire social and political change. Explaining complex political issues in a simplified and entertaining way, *Pearson Originals for Political Science* help students become informed members of society. Videos in these short-form documentary series include Marijuana and Federalism: Who's in Charge?; Who Should Be Allowed to Call Themselves "American"?; and What Is the Emoluments Clause and Why Should I Care About It?

  - Pearson's *Politics Hidden in Plain Sight video series* does exactly that—provides students with concrete examples of how politics influences the activities of their daily lives—from using their cellphones to going to a convenience store—in ways they likely had not previously noticed.

  - In addition, each chapter concludes with an *author-narrated video* subtitled "Why It Matters," helping students to put chapter content in a real-world context. For example, Chapter 16, "Civil Rights: The Struggle for Political Equality," concludes with a discussion of the real-life implications of affirmative action in college admission and on campus—a topic immediately relevant to today's undergraduate students.

Watch the Video CIVIL RIGHTS: WHY IT MATTERS

Watch the Video THE NEW DEAL AT WORK

- **Shared Media activities** all allow instructors to assign and grade both pre-written and their own prompts that incorporate video, weblinks, and visuals and ask students to respond in a variety of formats, in writing or by uploading their own video or audio responses. Pre-written assignments around the *Pearson Originals for Political Science videos* are available.

- **Interactive maps, figures, and tables** featuring innovative Social Explorer technology allow for inputting the latest data, toggling to illustrate movement over time, and clicking on hot spots with pop-ups of images and captions. Examples include Figure 12.2: Trends in Presidential Job Approval, 1946–2018 (line graph); Figure 9.2: Presidential Elections, 1960 and 2012 (map); and Figure 11.2: Women and Minorities in the U.S. Congress (bar chart).

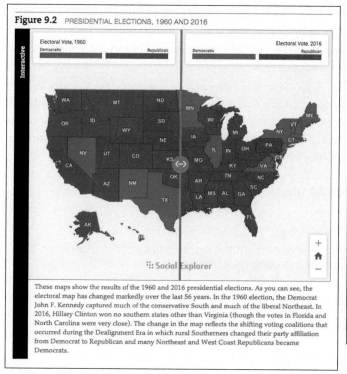

Figure 9.2 PRESIDENTIAL ELECTIONS, 1960 AND 2016

These maps show the results of the 1960 and 2016 presidential elections. As you can see, the electoral map has changed markedly over the last 56 years. In the 1960 election, the Democrat John F. Kennedy captured much of the conservative South and much of the liberal Northeast. In 2016, Hillary Clinton won no southern states other than Virginia (though the votes in Florida and North Carolina were very close). The change in the map reflects the shifting voting coalitions that occurred during the Dealignment Era in which rural Southerners changed their party affiliation from Democrat to Republican and many Northeast and West Coast Republicans became Democrats.

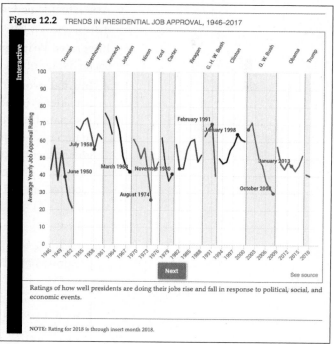

Figure 12.2 TRENDS IN PRESIDENTIAL JOB APPROVAL, 1946–2017

Ratings of how well presidents are doing their jobs rise and fall in response to political, social, and economic events.

NOTE: Rating for 2018 is through insert month 2018.

- **Interactive simulations** in every chapter (beginning with Chapter 2) allow students to explore critical issues and challenges that the country's Founders faced and that elected officials, bureaucrats, and political activists still face today. Students apply key chapter concepts in realistic situations. For example, in Chapter 3, students have the opportunity to imagine themselves as federal judges; in Chapter 8, they lead a social movement; and in Chapter 15, they are police officers.

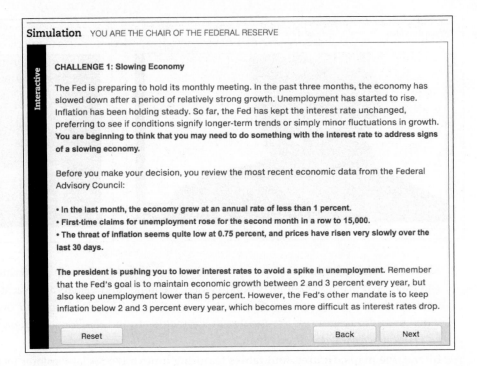

- Interactive **Conclusion and Review** summaries using video, learning objectives, image galleries, and flashcards featuring key terms and definitions allow students to review chapter content. In addition, a common, recent events bulletin called "The Stuggle for Democracy in Context" appears in every chapter and briefly examines how recent events relate to the material presented in the text.
- **Assessments** tied to primary chapter sections, as well as full chapter exams, allow instructors and students to track progress and get immediate feedback.
- **Integrated Writing Opportunities** To help students reason and write more clearly, each chapter offers two varieties of writing prompts:
  - **Journal prompts** in nearly every section across the narrative ask students to consider critical issues that are first presented in a relevant photograph and associated photo caption. These questions are designed to reinforce one of the material's primary goals: to equip students to engage critically with American government and thereby ensure a healthy, thriving democracy.

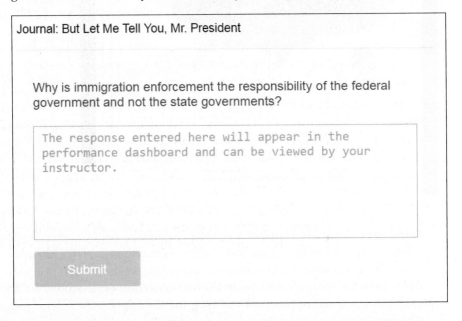

- **Shared writing prompts,** following each chapter's Conclusion and Review section, encourage students to consider how to address the challenges described in the chapter in an essay format. For example, in Chapter 3, students must argue for or against the proposition that the federal government should not provide funds to support large infrastructure projects, such as the construction and expansion of interstate highways. Through these shared writing prompts, instructors and students can address multiple sides of an issue by sharing their own views and responding to each other's viewpoints.

Shared Writing: Federalism: States and Nation

Worth 20 Points: ❶

The federal interstate highway system is so much a part of our lives and has been for so many years that it is hard to imagine a time in America when long-distance car and truck travel was limited to two-lane roads.

Before the interstate, car travel and commercial truck transportation was painfully slow and fairly dangerous. Accidents at crossroads were frequent. Innumerable access points to and from businesses, schools, and homes continually disrupted the flow of traffic. Congestion increased in population centers, where stoplights and stop signs were common.

Legislation for a new federal transportation system of limited-access multilane highways was proposed by Republican president Dwight Eisenhower and passed by Congress in 1956. Planned construction was completed in the early 1980s, but more miles of interstate have been added each year since.

Today the length of the U.S. interstate system is nearly 48,000 miles and it carries about one-fourth of all traffic in the United States. The system is funded by a tax of 18.4 cents per gallon on gasoline—unchanged since 1993—with most outlays paying for maintenance and repair.

Now construct a brief argument for or against this proposition: The federal government should not provide funds to support large infrastructure projects, such as the construction and expansion of interstate highways.

A minimum number of characters is required to post and earn points. After posting, your response can be viewed by your class

---

- **Essay prompts** are from Pearson's *Writing Space*, where instructors can assign both automatically graded and instructor-graded prompts. *Writing Space* is the best way to develop and assess concept mastery and critical thinking through writing. *Writing Space* provides a single place within Revel to create, track, and grade writing assignments; access writing resources; and exchange meaningful, personalized feedback quickly and easily to improve results. For students, *Writing Space* provides everything they need to keep up with writing assignments, access assignment guides and checklists, write or upload completed assignments, and receive grades and feedback—all in one convenient place. For educators, *Writing Space* makes assigning, receiving, and evaluating writing assignments easier. It's simple to create new assignments and upload relevant materials, see student progress, and receive alerts when students submit work. *Writing Space* makes students' work more focused and effective, with customized grading rubrics they can see and personalized feedback. *Writing Space* can also check students' work for improper citation or plagiarism by comparing it against the world's most accurate text comparison database available from Turnitin.

- **Learning Management Systems** Pearson provides Blackboard Learn™, Canvas™, Brightspace by D2L, and Moodle integration, giving institutions, instructors, and students easy access to Revel. Our Revel integration delivers streamlined access to everything your students need for the course in these learning management system (LMS) environments. *Single Sign-on*: With single sign-on, students are ready on their first day. From your LMS course, students have easy access to an interactive blend of authors' narrative, media, and assessment. *Grade Sync:* Flexible, on-demand grade synchronization capabilities allow you to control exactly which Revel grades should be transferred to the LMS gradebook.

- **Revel Combo Card** The Revel Combo Card provides an all-in-one access code and loose-leaf print reference (delivered by mail).

Supplements

Make more time for your students with instructor resources that offer effective learning assessments and classroom engagement. Pearson's partnership with educators does not end with the delivery of course materials; Pearson is there with you on the first day of class and beyond. A dedicated team of local Pearson representatives will work with you to not only choose course materials but also integrate them into your class and assess their effectiveness. Our goal is your goal—to improve instruction with each semester.

Pearson is pleased to offer the following resources to qualified adopters of *The Struggle for Democracy*. Several of these supplements are available to instantly download on the Instructor Resource Center (IRC); please visit the IRC at www.pearsonhighered.com/irc to register for access.

TEST BANK   Evaluate learning at every level. Reviewed for clarity and accuracy, the Test Bank measures this book's learning objectives with multiple choice, true/false, fill-in-the-blank, short answer, and essay questions. You can easily customize the assessment to work in any major learning management system and to match what is covered in your course. Word, BlackBoard, and WebCT versions available on the IRC and Respondus versions available upon request from www.respondus.com.

PEARSON MYTEST   This powerful assessment generation program includes all of the questions in the Test Bank. Quizzes and exams can be easily authored and saved online and then printed for classroom use, giving you ultimate flexibility to manage assessments anytime and anywhere. To learn more, visit, www.pearsonhighered.com/mytest.

INSTRUCTOR'S MANUAL   Create a comprehensive roadmap for teaching classroom, online, or hybrid courses. Designed for new and experienced instructors, the Instructor's Manual includes a sample syllabus, lecture and discussion suggestions, activities for in or out of class, and essays on teaching American Government. Available on the IRC.

POWERPOINT PRESENTATION   Make lectures more enriching for students. The PowerPoint Presentation includes a full lecture outline and full-color images of maps and art. All PowerPoints are ADA compliant.

LIVESLIDES   Social Explorers are data-rich interactive maps and figures that enable students to visually explore demographic data to understand how local trends impact them while improving data and statistical literacy. LiveSlides are dynamic lecture slides, which give you a direct path to all the Social Explorers within your Revel course. Available within Revel and on the IRC.

Acknowledgments

Heartfelt thanks and gratitude go to Ben Page, friend and long-time collaborator, who co-authored many editions of this book, though not this one. For over a year after I first broached the idea about our doing a textbook together, we hashed out whether it was possible to write a textbook that would be consistent with our standards as teachers and scholars, offer a perspective on American government and politics that was unique in the discipline, and do well in the marketplace. Once we concluded that it was possible to produce a textbook that hit these benchmarks and that we passionately wanted to make happen, we spent more than two years writing what became the First Edition of *The Struggle for Democracy*. When Ben and I started this process, we were only acquaintances. Over the years, in the process of collaborating on the publication of several editions of this textbook, we became and remain very good friends.

Though Ben has not been an active co-author on this edition of *Struggle*, his brilliant insights, analytical approach, and elegant writing are visible on virtually every page, and it is why his name sits next to mine on the cover and the title page. Ben Page, of course, is one of the most brilliant, cited, visible, and admired political scientists in the world, and hardly needs additional praise from me. But, I will say that I feel extraordinarily lucky to have worked with him for a good part of my academic career.

This edition of *Struggle* has been refreshed by and has benefited from the work of three extremely talented and energetic young political scientists, all former teaching assistants of mine in the large introductory course on American government and politics at the University of Colorado, Boulder, and all now launched on their own academic careers as teachers and scholars. David Doherty of Loyola University Chicago, Josh Ryan of Utah State University, and Scott Minkoff of SUNY New Paltz, took on a substantial portion of the burden of producing this new edition of *Struggle*, each taking responsibility for updating three chapters and each responsible for creating or modernizing chapter features that make this book such an exciting tool for student learning. I am grateful to each of them and hope and trust we will work together on future editions.

I also want to thank the many students, teaching assistants, and faculty at the University of Colorado and other universities, colleges, and two-year institutions who have used this book over the years as a learning and teaching tool and who have let me know what worked and what didn't work in previous editions. I appreciate their insight and candor.

My thanks also go to my editor at Pearson Higher Education, Jeff Marshall, who has been a champion of this book and my principal guide into the brave new world of textbooks in the digital age. To Jeff and to all of his very smart and very capable colleagues at Pearson, I express my very special appreciation. Allison Collins, our developmental editor, who heroically kept David, Josh, Scott, and me on track, offered compelling suggestions for content updates, helped with everything from photo selection to the design of line art, and acted as liaison with the many people involved in the complex process of getting this book out the door and into the hands of teachers and students. My thanks also go to Anju Joshi and her team at Lumina Datamatics; Megan Vertucci, Jennifer Jacobson, and Rebecca Green at Ohlinger Studios; the magnificent team at Social Explorer; and Tara Cook at Metrodigi. The shrewd and judicious contributions of these individuals to the production of *Struggle* are apparent on every printed page and on every digital screen.

Thanks go to John Aughenbaugh, of Virginia Commonwealth University, Leslie Baker, of Mississippi State University, Anita Chadha, of the University of Houston, Downtown, Lisa Iyer, of Riverside City College, Stephanie Paul, of the University of Alabama, and Kevin Wagner, of Florida Atlantic University, who reviewed our work and supplied insights and expertise on this revision.

We also wish to thank the many professors who gave their time to provide invaluable input during the following conferences and Pearson events:

Spring 2018 Revel Editorial Workshops Christopher Hallenbrook, Bloomsburg University; Ben Christ, Harrisburg Area Community College; Laci Hubbard–Mattix, Spokane Falls Community College–Pullman; Shobana Jayaraman, Savannah State University; Jeneen Hobby, Cleveland State University; John Arnold, Midland College; Reed Welch, West Texas A&M; Amanda Friesen, IUPUI; Thomas Ambrosio, North Dakota State; Ted Vaggalis, Drury University; Coyle Neal, Southwest Baptist University; Hanna Samir Kassab, Northern Michigan University; Julie Keil, Saginaw Valley State University; Henry Esparza, University of Texas at San Antonio; Sierra Powell, Mount San Antonio College; Edgar Bravo, Broward College; Alicia Andreatta, Angelina College; Robert Sterken, The University of Texas at Tyler; Jessica Anderson, University of Louisiana Monroe; Pat Frost, San Diego Miramar College; Scott

Robinson, Houston Baptist University; Cessna Winslow, Tarleton State; Carrie Currier, Texas Christian University; Paul Jorgensen, University of Texas Rio Grande Valley; Steve Lem, Kutztown University; Meng Lu, Sinclair Community College; James Pearn, Southern State Community College; Blake Farrar, Texas State University; Carlin Barmada, NVCC; Michael Chan, California State University, Long Beach; Mehwish, SUNY Buffalo State; Daniel Tirone, Louisiana State University; Richard Haesly, California State University, Long Beach; Hyung Park, El Paso Community College; Jesse Kapenga, UTEP; Stephanie A. Slocum–Schaffer, Shepherd University; Augustine Hammond, Augusta University; Shawn Easley, Cuyahoga Community College; Darius Smith, Community College of Aurora; Robert Glover, University of Maine; Carolyn Cocca, State University of NY, College at Old Westbury; Benjamin Arah, Bowie State University; Ahmet Turker, Pima Community College; Eric Loepp, UW–Whitewater; Holly Lindamod, University of North Georgia; Denise Robles, San Antonio College; Asslan Khaligh, Alamo–San Antonio College; Brandy Martinez, San Antonio College; Andrew Sanders, Texas A&M University, San Antonio; Mohsen Omar, Northeast Lakeview College; Heather Frederick, Slippery Rock University; Heather Rice, Slippery Rock University; Leslie Baker, Mississippi State University; Jamie Warner, Marshall University; Will Jennings, University of Tennessee; Arjun Banerjee, University of Tennessee, Knoxville; Jonathan Honig, University of Tennessee; Rachel Fuentes, University of Tennessee, Knoxville; Andrew Straight, University of Tennessee, Knoxville; Margaret Choka, Pellissippi State Community College; Christopher Lawrence, Middle Georgia State University; LaTasha Chaffin, College of Charleston; Jeff Worsham, West Virginia University; Cigdem Sirin–Villalobos, University of Texas at El Paso; Lyle Wind, Suffolk Community College; Marcus Holmes, College of William & Mary; Kurt Guenther, Palm Beach State College; Kevin Wagner, Florida Atlantic University; Eric Sands, Berry College; Shari MacLachlan, Palm Beach State College; Sharon Manna, North Lake College; Tamir Sukkary, American River College; Willie Hamilton, Mt. San Jacinto College; Linda Trautman, Ohio University–Lancaster; Dr. William H, Kraus, Motlow State Community College; Kim Winford, Blinn College; Lana Obradovic, University of Nebraska at Omaha; Doug Schorling, College of the Sequoias; Sarah Lischer, Wake Forest University; Ted Clayton, Central Michigan University; Steven Greene, North Carolina State University; Sharon Navarro, University of Texas at San Antonio; Curtis Ogland, San Antonio College; Henry Esparza, UT San Antonio; Mario Salas, UTSA; Robert Porter, Ventura College; Will Jennings, University of Tennessee; Haroon Khan, Henderson State University; Brenda Riddick, Houston Community College; Julie Lantrip, Tarrant County College; Kyle C. Kopko, Elizabethtown College; Kristine Mohajer, Austin Community College (ACC); Dovie D. Dawson, Central Texas College; Joycelyn Caesar, Cedar Valley College; Daniel Ponder, Drury University

APSA TLC 2018   Mujahid Nyahuma, Community College of Philadelphia; Tahiya Nyahuma, NCAT; Christopher Lawrence, Middle Georgia State University; Jason Robles, University of Colorado; Tim Reynolds, Alvin Community College; Marilyn C. Buresh, Lake Region State College; Frances Marquez, Gallaudet University; Natasha Washington, Liberal Arts and Communications; Jonathan Honig, University of Tennessee–Knoxville; Ayesha Ahsanuddin, University of Tennessee–Knoxville; Arjun Banerjee, The University of Tennessee–Knoxville; Jesse R. Cragwall, Tusculum College and Pellissippi State Community College; Ms. Amnah H. Ibraheem, University of Tennessee–Knoxville; Karl Smith, Delaware Technical Community College; Richard Waterman, University of Kentucky; Peggy R. Wright, ASU–Jonesboro; Christopher Hallenbrook, Bloomsburg University; Eric Loepp, UW–Whitewater; Robert Glover, University of Maine; Heather Rice, Slippery Rock University; Shawn Easley, Cuyahoga Community College; Benjamin Arah, Bowie State University; Andrew Straight, University of Tennessee; Rachel Fuentes, University of Tennessee at Knoxville; Stephanie A. Slocum–Schaffer, Shepherd University; Will Jennings, University of Tennessee

APSA 2017 Jooeun Kim, Georgetown; Leonard L. Lira, San José State University; Abigail Post, University of Virginia; Jamilya Ukudeeva, Chabot College; Shannon Jenkins, University of Massachusetts–Dartmouth; Matthew Platt, Morehouse College; Sara Angevine, Whittier College; Andy Aoki, Augsburg University; Stephen Meinhold, University of North Carolina–Wilmington; Manoutchehr Eskandari–Qajar, Santa Barbara City College; Clayton Thyne, University of Kentucky; Alice Jackson, Morgan State University; Mark Rom, Georgetown University; Krista Wiegand, University of Tennessee; Geoffrey Wallace, University of Washington; Precious Hall, Truckee Meadows Community College; Patrick Larue, University of Texas at Dallas; Margot Morgan, Indiana University Southeast; Patrick Wohlfarth, University of Maryland; Christian Grose, University of Southern California; Clinton Jenkins, George Washington University; Jeffrey W. Koch, US Air Force Academy and SUNY Geneseo; Albert Ponce, Diablo Valley College; Justin Vaughn, Boise State University; Joe Weinberg, University of Southern Mississippi; Cindy Stavrianos, Gonzaga University; Kevan M. Yenerall, Clarion University; Katherine Barbieri, University of South Carolina; Elsa Dias, Metropolitan State University of Denver; Maria Gabryszewska, Florida International University; Erich Saphir, Pima Community College; Mzilikazi Kone, College of the Desert; Mary McHugh, Merrimack College; Joel Lieske, Cleveland State University; Joseph W. Roberts, Roger Williams University; Eugen L. Nagy, Central Washington University; Henry B. Sirgo, McNeese State University; Brian Newman, Pepperdine University; Bruce Stinebrickner, DePauw University; Amanda Friesen, IUPUI; LaTasha Chaffin, College of Charleston; Richard Waterman, University of Kentucky

MPSA 2018 Adam Bilinski, Pittsburg State University; Daniel Chand, Kent State University; Agber Dimah, Chicago State University; Yu Ouyang, Purdue University Northwest; Steven Sylvester, Utah Valley University; Ben Bierly, Joliet Junior College; Mahalley Allen, California State University, Chico; Christian Goergen, College of DuPage; Patrick Stewart, University of Arkansas, Fayettville; Richard Barrett, Mount Mercy University; Daniel Hawes, Kent State University; Niki Kalaf–Hughes, Bowling Green State University; Gregg R. Murray, Augusta University; Ryan Reed, Bradley University; Kimberly Turner, College of DuPage; Peter Wielhouwer, Western Michigan University; Leena Thacker Kumar, University of Houston–DTN; Debra Leiter, University of Missouri Kansas City; Michael Makara, University of Central Missouri; Ola Adeoye, University of Illinois–Chicago; Russell Brooker, Alverno College; Dr. Royal G. Cravens, Bowling Green State University; Vincent T. Gawronski, Birmingham–Southern College; Benjamin I. Gross, Jacksonville State University; Matthew Hitt, University of Northern Colorado; Megan Osterbur, New England College; Pamela Schaal, Ball State University; Edward Clayton, Central Michigan University; Ali Masood, California State University, Fresno; Joel Lieske, Cleveland State University; Patrick Wohlfarth, University of Maryland; Steven Greene, NC State; Will Jennings, University of Tennessee; Haroon Khan, Henderson State University; Kyle Kopko, Elizabethtown College; Hyung Lae Park, El Paso Community College; Linda Trautman, Ohio University–Lancaster

AT LONG LAST, THE RIGHT TO VOTE

The 1965 Voting Rights Act allowed African Americans in the Deep South to vote for the first time without fear. In this photo from the period, African Americans wait to enter the Haywood County Courthouse to register to vote, unimpeded by the brutalities and humiliations of Jim Crow. Passage of the act, an example of the struggle for democracy at work in American politics, put an end to a long history of refusing to protect the voting rights of minorities.

Do measures such as voter ID requirements for voting, recently implemented in a number of states, and which mostly affect the youngest and oldest voters, rural people, and racial and ethnic minorities, suggest that the struggle for democracy must continue? Or does it mean that our democracy has matured and we no longer need worry about access to the voting booth?

DEMOCRACY AND AMERICAN POLITICS

CHAPTER OUTLINE AND LEARNING OBJECTIVES

WHAT IS DEMOCRACY?

1.1 Explain democracy as the standard by which American government and politics can be evaluated.

HOW DO GOVERNMENT AND POLITICS WORK?

1.2 Construct an analytical framework for examining how government and politics work.

The Struggle for Democracy

ROBERT MOSES AND THE STRUGGLE OF AFRICAN AMERICANS FOR VOTING RIGHTS

Although the right to vote is fundamental to democracy, African Americans in the South were not able to vote in any numbers until after 1965, despite passage of the Fifteenth Amendment in 1870, which prohibited discrimination in voting on the basis of race, color, or previous condition of servitude.

In Mississippi in the early 1960s, only 5 percent of African Americans were registered to vote, and none held elective office. In Walthall County, not a single African American was registered, although roughly three thousand were eligible.[1] A combination of exclusionary voting registration rules, economic pressures, hard and stubborn racial discrimination, and violence kept them from the polls.

When the Student Non-Violent Coordinating Committee (SNCC) launched its Voter Education Project in 1961 with the aim of ending black political powerlessness in the Deep South, its first step was to create "freedom schools" in the segregated counties of Mississippi, Alabama, and Georgia. The first freedom school was founded in McComb, Mississippi, by a remarkable young man named Robert Parris Moses. Shrugging off repeated threats to his life, vicious assaults, arrests, fines, and public recriminations, Moses taught African American citizens about their rights under the law and sent them in droves to county registrars' offices.

Despite the voter registration efforts of Moses and other SNCC volunteers, African Americans in the Deep South would have to wait four more years—for the passage of the 1965 Voting Rights Act—to exercise their constitutional right to elect representatives to govern in their names.[2] The Voter Education Project, a key building block of a powerful and growing civil rights movement, along with many moral and political acts of defiance, did eventually force federal action to support the citizenship rights of African Americans in the South. Robert Moses and many other African Americans were willing to risk all they had, including their lives, to gain full and equal citizenship in the United States. They would, most assuredly, have been gratified by the election of Barack Obama in 2008 as the nation's forty-fourth president.

* * * * *

The struggle for democracy is happening in many countries today, where people often fight against all odds for the right to govern themselves and to control their own destinies even as the rise of authoritarian nationalism in places such as Hungary, Poland, and Turkey has made their efforts more difficult.[3] In the United States, democracy, although honored and celebrated, remains an unfinished project and may even be threatened. The continuing struggle to protect and expand democracy is a major feature of American history and a defining characteristic of our politics today. It is also a central theme of this book.

WHAT IS DEMOCRACY?

1.1 Explain democracy as the standard by which American government and politics can be evaluated.

Why should there not be a patient confidence in the ultimate justice of the people? Is there any better, or equal, hope in the world?

—ABRAHAM LINCOLN, FIRST INAUGURAL ADDRESS

anarchist
One who believes that people are natural cooperators capable of creating free and decent societies without the need for government.

Anarchists believe that people can live in harmony without any form of authority; however, most people believe that when living together in groups and communities, there is a need for an entity of some sort to provide law and order; to protect against external aggressors; and to provide essential public goods such as roads, waste disposal, education, and clean water. It is safe to say that most people do not want to live in places where there is effectively no government to speak of, as in Somalia, or where there is a failed state, as in Haiti and Yemen. If government is both necessary and inevitable, certain questions are unavoidable: Who is to govern? How are those who govern encouraged to serve the best interests of society? How can governments be induced to make policies and laws that citizens consider legitimate and worth obeying? How can citizens ensure that those who govern carry out both laws and policies that the people want and do so effectively? In short, what is the best form of government? For a majority of Americans, the answer is clear: democracy.

Democracy's central idea is that ordinary people want to rule themselves and are capable of doing so.[4] This idea has proved enormously popular, not only with Americans, but with people all over the world.[5] To be sure, some people would give top priority to other things besides self-government as a requirement for good society, including such things as safety and security, the widespread availability of good jobs, or the need to have religious law and values determine what government does. Nevertheless, the appealing notion that ordinary people can and should rule themselves has spread to all corners of the globe, and the number of people living in democratic societies increased significantly for several decades[6] until its recent setbacks in countries such as Hungary, Poland, Turkey, and Venezuela where more autocratic governments have come to power, and in the United states and Western Europe where disillusionment with democracy has increased some.[7]

It is no wonder that a form of government based on the notion that people are capable of ruling themselves has enjoyed widespread popularity, especially compared with government by the few (by the Communist Party in China and in Cuba, for example) or by a single person (by dictator Kim Jong-un in North Korea). Some political thinkers argue that democracy is the form of government that best protects human rights because it is the only one based on a recognition of the intrinsic worth and equality of human beings. Others believe that democracy is the form of government most likely to produce rational policies because it can count on the pooled knowledge and expertise of a society's entire population: a political version, if you will, of the wisdom of crowds, something like the wiki phenomenon.[8] Still others claim that democracies are more stable and long-lasting because their leaders, elected by and answerable to voters, enjoy a strong sense of legitimacy among citizens. Many others suggest that democracy is the form of government most conducive to economic growth and material well-being, a claim with substantial scholarly support.[9] (In the years ahead, the relative economic growth of India, a democracy, and China, a one-party-state, will be a real-world test of this proposition.) Still others believe that democracy is the form of government under which human beings, because they are free, are best able to develop their natural capacities and talents.[10] There are many compelling reasons, then, why so many people have preferred democracy.

Americans have supported the idea of self-government and have helped make the nation more democratic over the course of its history.[11] Nevertheless, democracy in America remains an aspiration rather than a finished product. The goal behind this book is to help you think carefully about the quality and progress of democracy in the United States. We want to help you reach your own judgments about the degree to which politics and government in the United States make the country more or less democratic. You can then draw your own conclusions about which political practices and institutions in the United States encourage and sustain popular self-rule and which ones discourage and undermine it. To help you do this, we must be clear about the meaning of democracy.

The Origins of Democracy

Many of our ideas about democracy originated with the ancient Greeks. The Greek roots of the word *democracy* are *demos*, meaning "the people," and *kratein*, meaning "to rule." Greek philosophers and rulers, however, were not uniformly friendly to the

DEMOCRACY AND ECONOMIC GROWTH

Some scholars assert that fully functioning democracies are a prerequisite to economic growth, a claim that is supported by fast-growing India—symbolized in the top photo by the skyscraper boom in Mumbai's business district—but belied by the Chinese example in the bottom photo. China, whose economic growth is without precedent—note the gleaming high-speed train and visually captivating skyline in Shanghai—is anything but a democracy ruled as it is by the Central Committee of the Communist Party and its paramount leader, Xi Jinping.

Can you think of other examples that address the question of the relationship between economic growth in a society and its form of government? Were Britain, France, Germany, and Japan democracies when they were in their most dynamic periods of economic activity? Or, do you believe that the relationship is the other way around, that economic growth makes it more likely that a society will become more democratic as its middle classes insist that they have a greater say in society's affairs? If so, will China become more democratic in the long run?

democracy

A system of government in which the people rule; rule by the many as opposed to rule by one, or rule by the few.

oligarchy

Rule by the few, where a minority holds power over a majority, as in an aristocracy or a clerical establishment.

monarchy

Rule by the one, such as where power rests in the hands of a king or queen.

idea that the *many* could and should rule themselves. Most believed that governing required the greatest sophistication, intelligence, character, and training—certainly not the province of ordinary people. Aristotle expressed this view in his classic work *Politics*, in which he observed that democracy "is a government in the hands of men of low birth, no property, and vulgar employments."

Instead, the Greeks preferred rule either by a select *few* (by an aristocracy, in which a hereditary nobility rules, or by a clerical elite, as in Iran today) or by an enlightened *one*, somewhat akin to the philosopher-king described by Plato in his *Republic* or as in England in the time of Elizabeth I. **Democracy**, then, is "rule by the people" or, to put it as the Greeks did, self-government by the many, as opposed to **oligarchy** (rule by the *few*) or **monarchy** (rule by the *one*). The idea that ordinary people might rule themselves represents an important departure from most historical beliefs.[12] In practice, throughout human history, most governments have been quite undemocratic.

Inherent in the idea of self-rule by ordinary people is an understanding that government must serve *all* its people and that ultimately none but the people themselves can be relied on to know, and hence to act in accordance with, their own values and interests.[13]

In this sense, democracy is more a set of utopian ideas than a description of real societies. Until recently, examples of democracies or near-democracies over the course of human history have been few.[14] Athens of the 5th century BCE is usually cited as the purest form of democracy that ever existed. There, all public policies were decided in periodic assemblies of Athenian citizens, though women, slaves, and immigrants were excluded from participation.[15] Nevertheless, the existence of a society where "a substantial number of free, adult males were entitled as citizens to participate freely in governing"[16] proved to be a powerful example of what was possible for those who believed that rule by the people was the best form of government. A handful of other cases of popular rule kept the democratic idea alive across the centuries. Beginning in the 5th century BCE, for example, India enjoyed long periods marked by spirited and broadly inclusive public debate and discourse on public issues. In the Roman Republic, male citizens elected the consuls, the chief magistrates of the powerful city-state. In the Middle Ages, some European cities were governed directly by the people (at least by men who owned property) rather than by nobles, church, or crown. During the Renaissance, periods of popular control of government (again, limited to male property holders) occurred in the city-states of Venice, Florence, and Milan.

Direct Versus Representative Democracy

To the ancient Greeks, democracy meant **direct democracy**, rule by the common people exercised *directly* in open assemblies. They believed that democracy implied face-to-face deliberation and decision making about the public business. Direct democracy requires, however, that all citizens be able to meet together regularly to debate and decide the issues of the day.[17] Such a thing was possible in 5th century BCE Athens, which was small enough to allow all male citizens to gather in one place. Men had time to meet and to deliberate because women provided household labor and slaves accounted for most production.

Because direct (participatory) democracy is possible only in small communities where citizens with abundant leisure time can meet on a face-to-face basis, it is an unworkable arrangement for a large and widely dispersed society such as the United States.[18] Democracy in large societies must take the representative form, since millions of citizens cannot meet in open assembly. **Representative democracy** is a system in which the people select others, called *representatives*, to act on their behalf.

The Benchmarks of Representative Democracy

Democracy is rule by the many. What does this mean in a large society where representatives of the people make government policies? How can we know that the many are in charge when they are not themselves making decisions in public assemblies, as the ancient Athenians did? What features must exist in representative systems to ensure that those who govern do so on behalf of and in the interest of the people? This involves more than the existence of elections.[19] After all, autocratic states such as Turkey, Egypt, and Russia hold elections.

Three additional benchmarks are necessary to clarify our understanding of representative democracy in large societies: *popular sovereignty*, *political equality*, and *political liberty*, with the latter two being necessary for the first (that is to say, for popular sovereignty to work, political equality and political liberty must exist). A society in which all three flourish, we argue, is a healthy representative democracy. A society in which any of the three is absent or impaired falls short of the representative democratic ideal.

RULE BY THE FEW

Although the elected president of Iran is influential in determining what the Iranian government does, real power in the country is exercised by an unelected clergy and the Revolutionary Guards, the country's leading security force with considerable influence in the political sphere. The mullahs (or clerics), the ideological custodians of all Iranian institutions and debates, listen to presidential addresses for any slackening in ideological commitment. *Is a system that is responsive, in theory, to the many but run, in reality, by the few likely to retain legitimacy over the long term? How might the people of Iran move their system to one where the majority rules rather than the few?*

direct democracy

A form of political decision making in which policies are decided by the people themselves, rather than by their representatives, acting either in small face-to-face assemblies or through the electoral process as in initiatives and referenda in the American states.

representative democracy

Indirect democracy, in which the people rule through elected representatives; see liberal democracy.

DIRECT DEMOCRACY

In small towns throughout New England, local policies and budgets are decided at regular town meetings, in which the entire town population is invited to participate.

What are some advantages of town meetings? What might be the drawbacks? What other kinds of forums might there be where direct democracy is possible?

popular sovereignty

The basic principle of democracy that the people are the ultimate source of government authority and of the policies that government leaders make.

autocracy

General term that describes all forms of government characterized by rule by a single person or by a group with total power, whether a monarchy, a military tyranny, or a theocracy.

POPULAR SOVEREIGNTY   **Popular sovereignty** means that people are the ultimate source of government authority and that what the government does is determined by what the people want. If ultimate authority resides not in the hands of the *many* but in the hands of the *few* (as in an aristocratic order) or of the *one* (whether a benevolent sovereign or a ruthless dictator), democracy does not exist. Nor does it exist if government consistently fails to follow the preferences and to serve the interests of the people. The following six conditions are especially important for popular sovereignty to flourish.

Leaders Are Selected in Competitive Elections   The existence of a close match between what the people want and what government does, however, does not necessarily prove that the people are sovereign. In an **autocracy**, for example, the will of the people can be shaped through coercion or propaganda to correspond to the wishes of the leadership. For influence to flow from the people to the leadership, some mechanism must ensure responsiveness and accountability to the people. The best mechanism ever invented to achieve these goals is the contested election, in which both existing and aspiring government leaders periodically face the people for judgment. Elections in which voters choose among competing candidates and political parties is one of the hallmarks of democratic political systems.

Elections Are Free and Fair   If elections are to be useful as a way to keep government leaders responsive and responsible, they must be conducted in a fashion that is free and fair. By free, we mean there is no coercion of voters or election officials and no serious barriers that prevent people from running for office and voting. By fair, we mean, among other things, that election rules do not favor some parties and candidates over others, that ballots are accurately counted, and that there is no outside interference by other countries.

People Participate in the Political Process   A process is useful in conveying the will of the people and in keeping leaders responsive and responsible only if the people participate. If elections and other forms of political participation attract only a minority of the eligible population, they cannot serve as a way to understand what the broad public wants or as an instrument forcing leaders to pay attention to what the people want. Widespread participation in politics—including voting in elections, contacting public officials, working with others to bring matters to public attention, joining associations that work to shape government actions, and more—is necessary to ensure not only that responsive representatives will be chosen, but that they will also have continuous incentives to pay attention to the people. Because widespread participation is so central to popular sovereignty, we *can* say that the less political participation there is in a society, the weaker the democracy.

High-Quality Information Is Available   If people are to form authentic and rational attitudes about public policies and political leaders, they must have access to accurate political information, insightful interpretations, and vigorous debate. These are the responsibility of government officials, opposition parties, opinion leaders, and the news media. If false or biased information is provided, if policies are not challenged and debated, or if misleading interpretations of the political world (or none at all) are offered, the people cannot form opinions in accordance with their values and interests, and popular sovereignty cannot be said to exist.

The Majority Rules   How can the opinions and preferences of many individual citizens be combined into a single binding decision? Because unanimity is unlikely—so the insistence that new policies should require unanimous agreement for them to be adopted would simply enshrine the status quo—reaching a decision requires a decision rule of some sort. If the actions of government are to respond to all citizens, and each citizen is counted equally, the only decision rule that makes sense is **majority rule**, which means that the government adopts the policy that the *most* people want.[20] The only alternative to majority rule is minority rule, which would unacceptably elevate the preferences and the interests of the *few* over the *many*.

VOTING IN A DANGEROUS PLACE

In a burqa that completely covers her, a woman shows, by her inked finger, that she had cast a ballot in the April 2014 presidential election in Afghanistan. Voter turnout was very high—more than 60 percent of eligible voters went to the polls—an outcome that surprised many observers because of Taliban threats to bomb polling places. *Is voting, clearly important to people in Afghanistan and in other troubled spots around the globe, a sufficient condition for democracy, or must other conditions exist to ensure that political leaders act as representatives of the people?*

Government Policies Reflect the Wishes of the People   The most obvious sign of popular sovereignty is the existence of a close correspondence between what government does and what the people want it to do. It is hard to imagine a situation in which the people rule but government officials continuously make policies contrary to the expressed wishes of the majority of the people; sovereign people would most likely react by removing such officials from power.

But does the democratic ideal require that government officials always do exactly what the people want, right away, responding to every whim and passing fancy of the public? This question has troubled many democratic theorists, and most have answered that democracy is best served when representatives and other public officials respond to the people after the people have had the opportunity to deliberate among themselves about the issues.[21] We might, then, want to speak of democracy as a system in which government policies conform to what the people want over some period of time.

POLITICAL EQUALITY   The second benchmark of representative democracy and a necessary condition for popular sovereignty to exist is **political equality**, the idea that each person, having an intrinsic value that is equal to that of other human beings, carries the same weight in voting and other political decision making.[22] Imagine, if you will, a society in which one person could cast a hundred votes in an election, another person fifty votes, and still another twenty-five votes, while many unlucky folks had only one vote each—or none at all. Democracy is a way of making decisions in which each person has one, and only one, voice.

Most people know this intuitively. Our sense of what is fair is offended, for instance, when some class of people is denied the right to vote in a society that boasts the outer trappings of democracy. The denial of citizenship rights to African Americans in the South before the passage of the **1965 Voting Rights Act** is such an example. We count it as a victory for democracy when previously excluded groups win the right to vote.

Political equality also involves what the Fourteenth Amendment to the Constitution calls "equal protection," meaning that everyone in a democracy is treated the same by government. Government programs, for example, cannot favor one group

majority rule
The form of political decision making in which policies are decided on the basis of what a majority of the people want.

political equality
The principle that each person carries equal weight in the conduct of the public business.

1965 Voting Rights Act
A law that banned racial discrimination in voting across the United States; it gave the federal government broad powers to register voters in a set of states, mostly in the South, that had long practiced election discrimination, and required that such states pre-clear any changes in its election laws with the Department of Justice.

WORTH THE WAIT

In the top photo, African Americans wait outside a polling station at a rural grocery store in Alabama in order to vote in the 1966 national election, something that was only possible because of the passage of the 1965 Voting Rights Act that invalidated many practices by state governments designed to keep African Americans from voting. About 50 years later, African Americans voters helped to elect the first black U.S. president, Barack Obama. In the bottom photo, voters line up early to participate in the 2016 general elections in Raleigh, NC.

Are voting rights for African Americans in any danger today? If so, what role should the federal government take in ensuring that voting rights are protected?

over another or deny benefits or protections to identifiable groups in the population, such as racial and religious minorities. Nor should people be treated better or worse than others by law enforcement agencies and the courts. Taken together, political equality and equal treatment are sometimes called **civil rights**.

But does political equality require that people be equal in ways that go beyond having a voice in decision making and treatment by government? In particular, does democracy require that inequalities in the distribution of income and wealth not be too extreme? While many do not think this is the case, thinkers as diverse as Aristotle, Rousseau, and Jefferson thought so, believing that great inequalities in economic circumstances almost always translate into political inequality.[23] Political scientist Robert Dahl describes the problem in the following way:

> If citizens are unequal in economic resources, so are they likely to be unequal in political resources; and political equality will be impossible to achieve. In the extreme case, a minority of rich will possess so much greater political resources than other citizens that they will control the state, dominate the majority of citizens, and empty the democratic process of all content.[24]

civil rights

Guarantees of equal treatment by government officials regarding political rights, the judicial system, and public programs.

POLITICAL EQUALITY UNDER THE FLAG

Although Americans enjoy formal political equality, some Americans, clearly, are more equal than others in their ability to mobilize resources that enable the exercise of real political influence. A homeless person sleeping on a park bench in Brooklyn, New York, though probably eligible to vote, is less likely than better off Americans to register, cast a ballot, circulate a petition, make a campaign contribution, or petition members of Congress or the administration.
What, if anything, can be done to ensure that policy makers hear from more than a limited number of better-educated and more affluent Americans?

Later chapters will show that income and wealth are distributed in a highly unequal way in the United States, that the scale of this inequality has become dramatically more pronounced over the past four decades, and that this inequality more often than not translates into great inequalities among people and groups in the political arena. For example, powerful groups representing the most privileged sectors of American society shape elections and legislation more than other Americans do.[25] In such circumstances, the political equality benchmark is in danger of being violated.

POLITICAL LIBERTY   A third benchmark of democracy in representative systems, and a necessary condition for popular sovereignty to exist, is **political liberty**. Political liberty refers to basic freedoms essential to the formation and expression of majority opinion and its translation into public policies. These essential liberties include the freedoms of speech, of conscience and religion, of the press, and of assembly and association embodied in the First Amendment to the U.S. Constitution, for example. Philosopher John Locke thought that individual rights and liberties were so fundamental to the good society that their preservation was the central responsibility of any legitimate government and that their protection was the very reason people agreed to enter into a **social contract** to form government in the first place.

Without these First Amendment freedoms, as well as those freedoms involving protections against arbitrary arrest and imprisonment, the other fundamental principles of democracy could not exist. Popular sovereignty cannot be guaranteed if people are prevented from participating in politics or if authorities crush any opposition to the government. Popular sovereignty cannot prevail if the voice of the people is silenced and if citizens are not free to argue and debate, based on their own ideas, values, and personal beliefs, and to form and express their political opinions.[26] Political equality is violated if some people can speak out but others cannot. Voting without liberty can lead to elected autocrats such as Vladimir Putin in Russia and Abdel Fattah el-Sisi in Egypt, an outcome that is clearly undemocratic because, among other things, opposition voices have been silenced.

For most people today, democracy and liberty are inseparable. The concept of *self-government* implies not only the right to vote and to run for public office, but also the right to speak one's mind, to petition the government, and to join with others in political parties, interest groups, or social movements.

political liberty

The principle that citizens in a democracy are protected from government interference in the exercise of a range of basic freedoms such as the freedoms of speech, association, and conscience.

social contract

The idea that government is the result of an agreement among people to form one, and that people have the right to create an entirely new government if the terms of the contract have been violated by the existing one.

Over the years, a number of political philosophers and practitioners have viewed liberty as *threatened* by democracy rather than as essential to it. It is our position that self-government and political liberty are inseparable, in the sense that the former is impossible without the latter.[27] It follows that a majority cannot deprive an individual or a minority group of its political liberty without violating democracy itself.

Objections to Representative Democracy

liberal democracy
Representative democracy characterized by popular sovereignty, liberty, and political equality; see representative democracy.

majority tyranny
Suppression of the rights and liberties of a minority by the majority.

What we have been describing—a system of representative government characterized by popular sovereignty, political equality, and liberty—commonly is called **liberal democracy**. Not everyone is convinced that liberal democracy is the best form of government. What are the main criticisms that have been leveled against representative, or liberal, democracy as we have defined it?

THE THREAT OF "MAJORITY TYRANNY"   James Madison and the other Founders of the American republic feared that majority rule was bound to undermine freedom and threaten the rights of the individual. They created a constitutional system designed to protect certain liberties against the unwelcome intrusions of the majority. The fears of the Founders were not without basis. What they called the "popular passions" have sometimes stifled the freedoms of groups and individuals who have dared to be different. In the 1950s, for example, many people in the movie industry lost their jobs because of anticommunist hysteria whipped up by Senator Joseph McCarthy and others.[28] For a time after the 9/11 attacks on the United States, and after the attack in San Bernardino, California in 2015, Muslims became targets of popular hostility. Mexican American immigrants are routinely derided for taking jobs from others, especially in periods of high unemployment or when popular political leaders label them criminals.

FEAR CAN UNDERMINE DEMOCRACY

Political hysteria has periodically blemished the record of American democracy. Fear of communism, captured in this editorial cartoon, was widespread in the United States for much of the 20th century and led to the suppression of anti-establishment political groups by federal and state authorities who were acting, in their view, in the name of a majority of Americans.
Why was such hysteria able to take hold in the United States? Can such political hysteria happen again?

Although there have been instances in our history of **majority tyranny**, when, as in the South after Reconstruction, the majority has violated the citizenship rights of a minority, there is no evidence that the *many* consistently threaten liberty more than the *few* or the *one*. To put it another way, the majority does not seem to be a special or unique threat to liberty. Violations against freedom seem as likely to come from powerful individuals, powerful groups, or government officials responding to vocal and narrow interests as from the majority of the people.

Liberty is essential to self-government, and all who value democracy must guard against threats to liberty, whatever their origin. But we firmly reject the view that majority rule inevitably or uniquely threatens liberty. Majority rule is unthinkable, in fact, without the existence of basic political liberties.[29]

THE THREAT OF THE PEOPLE'S IRRATIONALITY AND INCOMPETENCE   Political scientists have spent decades studying the attitudes and behaviors of U.S. citizens, and some of the findings are not encouraging. For the most part, the evidence shows that individual Americans do not care a great deal about politics and are rather poorly informed, unstable in their views, and not much interested in participating in the political process.[30] These findings have led some observers to assert that citizens are not well equipped for the responsibility of self-governance and that public opinion (the will of the majority) should not be the ultimate determinant of what government does.

Is the American public uninformed, unsophisticated, and unstable in its views? This is a serious charge that is addressed in various places throughout this book. We suggest that much of the evidence about individual opinions often has been misinterpreted and that the American public, taken in aggregate, is more informed, sophisticated, and stable in its views than it is generally given credit for, though there remains considerable room for improvement.

THE THREAT OF MAJORITARIAN DEMOCRACY TO MINORITIES   We have suggested that, when rendering a decision in a democracy, the majority must prevail. In most cases, the minority on the losing side of an issue need not worry unduly about its well-being because many of its members are likely to be on the winning side in future decisions about other matters. Thus, people on the losing side of one issue, such as welfare reform, may be part of the majority and winning side on another issue, such as how much to spend on education. In most policy decisions in a democracy, what prevents majority tyranny over a minority is that the composition of the majority and the minority is always shifting, depending on the issue.

However, what happens in cases that involve race, ethnicity, religion, or sexual orientation, for example, where minority status is fixed? Many people worry about the possibility that the majority would then pose a threat.[31] The worry that unbridled majority rule leaves no room for the claims of minorities has some historical foundations because majorities have trampled on minority rights with alarming frequency. Majorities long held, for example, that Native Americans and African Americans were inferior and undeserving of full citizenship. Irish, Eastern European, Asian, and Latin American immigrants to our shores, among others, have been subjected to long periods of intolerance, as have Catholics, Jews, and now Muslims. Gays and lesbians have been violently victimized.

As Robert Dahl has convincingly argued, however, no evidence supports the belief that the rights of minorities are better protected under alternative forms of government, whether rule by the *few* (note the persecution of the Christian minority in China by the Communist ruling party) or by the *one* (note the persecution of Shia Muslims under the rule of Saddam Hussein in Iraq). Dahl affirms that, given its other benefits, majority rule democracy is to be preferred.[32]

In any case, democracy, as we have defined it, requires the protection of crucial minority rights. Recall that majority rule is only one of the defining conditions of popular sovereignty and that popular sovereignty is only one of the three basic benchmarks of democracy, the others being political equality and political liberty. The position of minorities is protected in fully developed representative liberal democracies, in our view, by the requirements of equal citizenship (the right to vote, to hold public office, to be safe from violence, and to enjoy the equal protection of the law) and access to the full range of civil liberties (speech, press, conscience, and association). To the extent that a majority violates the citizenship rights and liberties of minorities, society falls short of the democratic ideal.

* * * * *

So, how democratic are we? After reading this chapter, it should be easy to see how and why the democratic ideal can be used as a measuring stick with which to evaluate American politics. We have learned that the fundamental attributes of liberal representative democracy are popular sovereignty, political equality, and political liberty. Each suggests a set of questions that will be raised throughout this book to encourage critical thinking about American political life.

About popular sovereignty, we should ask:

- Do citizens participate in politics?
- Can citizens be involved when they choose to be, and are political leaders responsive?
- Do institutions, such as political parties, elections, interest groups, and social movements, effectively transmit what citizens want to political leaders?
- What is the quality of the public deliberation on the major public policy issues of the day?

- Do the news media and political leaders provide accurate and complete information?
- Does government do what citizens want it to do?
- Does government effectively carry out the policies they have instituted in response to what the people want?

About political equality, we should ask:

- Do some individuals and groups have persistent and substantial advantages over other individuals and groups in the political process?
- Is the political game open to all equally?
- Do government decisions and policies benefit some individuals and groups more than others?

About political liberty, we should ask:

- Are citizens' rights and liberties universally available, protected, and used?
- Are people free to vote?
- Can people speak openly and form groups freely to petition their government?
- Do public authorities, private groups, or the members of the majority threaten liberty or the rights of minorities?

These questions will help us assess where we are and where we are going as a democracy. They will help us go past superficial evaluations based on the existence or nonexistence of this institution or that institution—for example, an elected legislature—and allow us to raise questions about the quality of democracy in the United States and its prospects. Of popular sovereignty, political equality, and political liberty, none are attainable, of course, in perfect form. They are, rather, ideals to which our nation can aspire and standards against which we can measure everyday reality. Throughout this book, we will revisit these questions about the quality of democracy in the United States.

* * * * *

Throughout *Struggle for Democracy*, we will regularly revisit these topics. And, as a conclusion to each chapter, you will find a formal assessment for weighing how well American government and politics measure up to the democratic ideal. Jump forward to the "Using the Democracy Standard" section at the end of Chapter 2 for a preview.

HOW DO GOVERNMENT AND POLITICS WORK?

1.2 Construct an analytical framework for examining how government and politics work.

In addition to helping you answer questions about the quality and development of democracy in the United States, this text offers an analytical framework for examining how American government and politics work.

Identifying the Factors That Influence Government and Politics

If we are to understand why things happen in government and politics—for example, the passage of the 1965 Voting Rights Act—we must begin with what biologists call *taxonomy*: placing things in their proper categories. Refer to the analytical framework in Figure 1.1. We believe that each and every actor, institution, and process that influences what our politics are like and what our national government does can be placed into four main categories: (1) structure, (2) political linkage, (3) government, and (4) government action.

STRUCTURE Structural factors play key roles in determining what issues become important in politics and government, how political power is distributed in the population,

FIGURE 1.1 THE ANALYTICAL FRAMEWORK

Various actors, institutions, and processes interact to influence what government does. *Structural factors*—the economy, society, the political culture, the international system, and constitutional rules—play a foundational role in shaping government actions. They may influence the government directly, or, as is more often the case, they may exercise influence through *political linkage*—public opinion, the news media, interest groups, social movements, political parties, and elections. In a democratic society, government institutions—the presidency, Congress, the Supreme Court, and the federal bureaucracy—should reflect these influences both in the policies they create and in the actions they take.

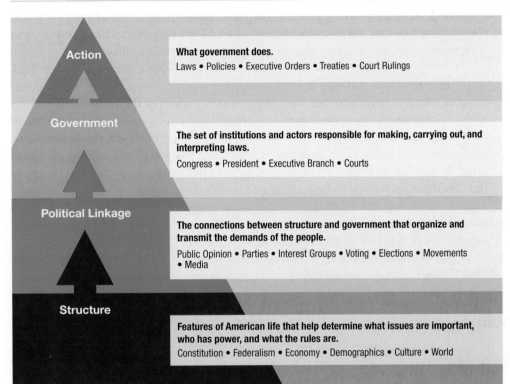

Action

What government does.
Laws • Policies • Executive Orders • Treaties • Court Rulings

Government

The set of institutions and actors responsible for making, carrying out, and interpreting laws.
Congress • President • Executive Branch • Courts

Political Linkage

The connections between structure and government that organize and transmit the demands of the people.
Public Opinion • Parties • Interest Groups • Voting • Elections • Movements • Media

Structure

Features of American life that help determine what issues are important, who has power, and what the rules are.
Constitution • Federalism • Economy • Demographics • Culture • World

© Edward S. Greenberg

and what attitudes and beliefs guide the behavior of citizens and public officials. This category includes the economy and society, the constitutional rules, the political culture, and the international system. These are the most fundamental and enduring factors that influence government and politics. They form the foundation on which all else is built. They are the most enduring parts of the American system, and the slowest to change.[33]

POLITICAL LINKAGE Political linkage factors transmit the wants and demands of people and groups in our society to government officials and together help shape what government officials do and what policies they adopt. These include public opinion, political parties, interest groups, the news media, and elections. While not a formal part of government, they directly influence what sorts of people are chosen to be government officials and what these officials do once they are in office.

GOVERNMENT Government factors include all public officials and institutions that have formal, legal responsibilities for making public policy for the United States. These include Congress, the president and the executive branch, the federal bureaucracy, and the federal courts, including the Supreme Court.

GOVERNMENT ACTION This is about what government does. This category includes the wide range of actions carried out by government: making laws, issuing rules and regulations, waging war and providing national defense, settling civil disputes, providing order, and more.

Connecting the Factors That Influence Government and Politics: An Application

To understand how government and politics work in the United States, we must appreciate the fact that the *structural*, *political linkage*, and *governmental* categories interact with one another in a particular kind of way to determine what actions government takes. One way to see this is to look at these categories in action, using the passage of the 1965 Voting Rights Act as an example (see Figure 1.2). The Voting Rights Act, which transformed the politics of the South, offered federal protection for African Americans who wished to vote and run for public office. Connecting and considering together the main factors of political life—*structure*, *political linkage*, and *government*—can help explain why government takes certain actions.

A conventional analysis of the passage of the 1965 Voting Rights Act might look solely at *government*, focusing attention on Congress and its members, on President Lyndon Johnson (who was the most vigorous proponent of the legislation) and his advisers, and on the Supreme Court, which was becoming increasingly supportive of civil rights claims in the mid-1960s. Knowing these things, however, would not tell us all that we need to know. To understand why Congress, the president, and the Court acted as they did in 1965, we would want to pay attention to the pressures brought to bear on them by *political linkage* actors and institutions: public opinion (increasingly supportive of civil rights), the growing electoral power of African Americans in states outside the South, and most important, the moral power of the civil rights movement inspired by people like Robert Moses and Martin Luther King Jr.

Even knowing these things, however, would not tell us all. Our inquiry into the 1965 Voting Rights Act would have to go deeper to include *structural* factors: economic,

FIGURE 1.2   APPLYING THE FRAMEWORK: PASSAGE OF THE 1965 VOTING RIGHTS ACT

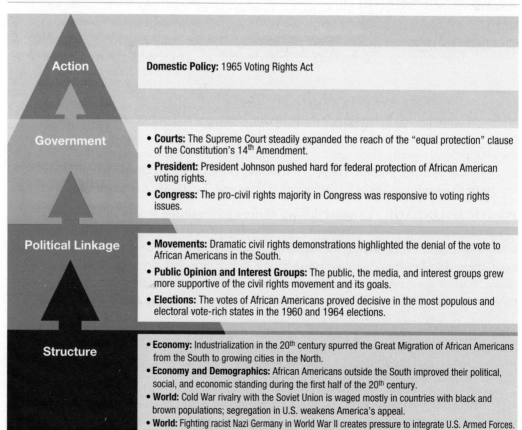

cultural, and social change; constitutional rules; and the international position of the United States. For example, economic changes in the nation over the course of many decades had triggered a "great migration" of African Americans from the rural South to the urban North. Over the long run, this population shift to states with large blocs of Electoral College votes, critical to the election of presidents, increased the political power of African Americans. Cultural change increased the number of Americans bothered by the second-class citizenship of African Americans, even as combat service in World War II and the Korean War led many black Americans to insist on full citizenship rights. Finally, the Cold War struggle of the United States against the Soviet Union played an important role. Many American leaders, recognizing the contradiction between asking for the support of people of color in Third World countries in the struggle against communism while treating African Americans in the United States as second-class citizens, sought an end to the system of official segregation in the South (known as **Jim Crow**).[34]

We see, then, that a full explanation of why the 1965 Voting Rights Act happened (government action) requires that we take into account how *governmental, political linkage*, and *structural* factors interacted with one another to bring about significant change in American politics. Modeling complex government actions can be a challenging task, but application of an analytical framework can help. The framework developed for *Struggle for Democracy* (see Figure 1.1) is just such a tool.

Jim Crow

Popular term for the system of legally sanctioned racial segregation that existed in the American South from the end of the 19th century until the middle of the 20th century.

Understanding Government and Politics Holistically

This way of looking at things—that what government does can only be understood by considering *structural, political linkage*, and *governmental* factors—will be used throughout this book and will help bring order to the information presented. We will suggest that action by public officials is the product not simply of their personal desires (although these are important), but also of the influences and pressures brought to bear by other governmental institutions and by individuals, groups, and classes at work in the political linkage sphere. Political linkage institutions and processes, in turn, can often be understood only when we see how they are shaped by the larger structural context, including such things as the national and global economies and the political culture.

Keep in mind that, as in all complex systems, influence sometimes flows in the opposite direction, from government to political linkage actors and institutions to structural factors. For example, federal tax laws influence the distribution of income and wealth in society, government regulations affect the operations of corporations, and decisions by the courts may determine what interest groups and political parties are able to do. We will want to pay attention, then, to these sorts of influences in our effort to understand how the American political system works.

Keep in mind as well that government actions do not necessarily hold for all time. Even laws can change, whether by passage of new laws or reinterpretation of existing ones. For example, after the Supreme Court in 2013 overturned an important section of the Voting Rights Act, a number of states controlled by Republicans quickly passed laws that shortened the period for early voting and required IDs for access to the ballot in the name of stopping voter fraud. Critics pointed out that these statutes would lower turnout among the poor, racial and ethnic minorities, and younger voters, all of whom tend to vote for Democrats. The courts in 2016 sided with the critics of these restrictive laws in a series of decisions in the Fifth, Sixth, and Seventh Circuit Courts of Appeal.

Do not worry about remembering exactly which actors and influences belong to which category in our model; the book's chapters are organized into sections corresponding to the categories. Do not worry, either, about exactly how the people and institutions in different categories interact with one another. This will become clear as you become more familiar with the American political process.

REVIEW THE CHAPTER

WHAT IS DEMOCRACY?

1.1 Explain democracy as the standard by which American government and politics can be evaluated.

Democracy is a system of rule by the people, rooted in three fundamental principles: popular sovereignty (meaning that the people ultimately rule), political equality (meaning that each person has an equal say in determining what government does), and political liberty (meaning that the people are protected from government interference in exercising their rights).

Ensuring that all three aspects of democracy are available and practiced has played an important role in American history and remains an important theme in our country—as well as many other parts of the world—today.

The United States is a liberal representative democracy—meaning that the people do not rule directly but through elected representatives and have broad civil and political rights, but the majority does not always get its way.

Because democracy holds a very special place in Americans' constellation of values and is particularly relevant to judging political processes, it is the standard used throughout this text to evaluate the quality of our politics and government.

HOW DO GOVERNMENT AND POLITICS WORK?

1.2 Construct an analytical framework for examining how government and politics work.

The organizing framework presented in this chapter visualizes the world of American politics as a set of interrelated *actors* and *influences*—institutions, groups, and individuals—that operate in three interconnected realms: the *structural, political linkage,* and *governmental* sectors. This way of looking at American political life as an ordered, interconnected whole will be used throughout the remainder of the book.

LEARN THE TERMS

1965 Voting Rights Act A law that banned racial discrimination in voting across the United States; it gave the federal government broad powers to register voters in a set of states, mostly in the South, that had long practiced election discrimination, and required that such states pre-clear any changes in its election laws with the Department of Justice.

anarchist One who believes that people are natural cooperators capable of creating free and decent societies without the need for government.

autocracy General term that describes all forms of government characterized by rule by a single person or by a group with total power, whether a monarchy, a military tyranny, or a theocracy.

civil rights Guarantees of equal treatment by government officials regarding political rights, the judicial system, and public programs.

democracy A system of government in which the people rule; rule by the many as opposed to rule by one, or rule by the few.

direct democracy A form of political decision making in which policies are decided by the people themselves, rather than by their representatives, acting either in small face-to-face assemblies or through the electoral process as in initiatives and referenda in the American states.

Jim Crow Popular term for the system of legally sanctioned racial segregation that existed in the American South from the end of the 19th century until the middle of the 20th century.

liberal democracy Representative democracy characterized by popular sovereignty, liberty, and political equality.

majority rule The form of political decision making in which policies are decided on the basis of what a majority of the people want.

majority tyranny Suppression of the rights and liberties of a minority by the majority.

monarchy Rule by the one, such as where power rests in the hands of a king or queen.

oligarchy Rule by the few, where a minority holds power over a majority, as in an aristocracy or a clerical establishment.

political equality The principle that each person carries equal weight in the conduct of the public business.

political liberty The principle that citizens in a democracy are protected from government interference in the exercise of a range of basic freedoms such as the freedoms of speech, association, and conscience.

popular sovereignty The basic principle of democracy that the people are the ultimate source of government authority and of the policies that government leaders make.

representative democracy Indirect democracy, in which the people rule through elected representatives; see liberal democracy.

social contract The idea that government is the result of an agreement among people to form one, and that people have the right to create an entirely new government if the terms of the contract have been violated by the existing one.

THE IRAN NUCLEAR DEAL
Secretary of State John Kerry and the lead negotiators from Iran, Great Britain, France, Germany, Russia, and the European Union pose for photographers after reaching an international agreement to limit Iran's nuclear weapons program for a minimum of ten years in trade for the end to international economic sanctions. Whether the agreement was a good or bad deal for the United States and its allies became a central issue in the 2016 presidential campaign, with Republican Donald Trump strongly against it, and Democrat Hillary Clinton strongly for it. In 2018, President Trump withdrew the United States from the agreement.

Did the agreement slow the Iran nuclear weapons program while it was in effect? Would it have been better had President Obama entered into a formal treaty requiring Senate approval rather than settle for an agreement that was easy for President Trump to withdraw from?

THE CONSTITUTION

CHAPTER OUTLINE AND LEARNING OBJECTIVES

THE AMERICAN REVOLUTION AND THE DECLARATION OF INDEPENDENCE

2.1 Assess the enduring legacies of the American Revolution and the Declaration of Independence.

THE ARTICLES OF CONFEDERATION: OUR FIRST CONSTITUTION

2.2 Describe the system of government established by our first constitution.

FACTORS LEADING TO THE CONSTITUTIONAL CONVENTION

2.3 Analyze the developments that led to the Constitutional Convention.

THE CONSTITUTIONAL CONVENTION AND A NEW FRAMEWORK FOR GOVERNMENT

2.4 Describe and evaluate the framework for government that the Constitutional Convention created.

THE STRUGGLE TO RATIFY THE CONSTITUTION

2.5 Outline the arguments for and against ratification of the Constitution.

THE CHANGING CONSTITUTION, DEMOCRACY, AND AMERICAN POLITICS

2.6 Describe the processes by which the Constitution can be altered.

The Struggle for Democracy

DOES THE "ADVICE AND CONSENT" OF THE SENATE MATTER?

In July 2015, the Obama administration reached an agreement with Iran, the European Union, Russia, China, Great Britain, and Germany to limit Iran's nuclear program in return for lifting economic sanctions against the Islamic Republic. The president did not submit the agreement to the Senate for ratification even though the Constitution specifies that the Senate must approve international treaties entered into by the president. Afterward, speaking in defense of the Obama administration's actions at a Senate committee hearing, Secretary of State John Kerry stated that the Iran nuclear agreement was not a treaty requiring the "advice and consent" of the Senate, but simply a legally nonbinding international agreement entered into by the president on behalf of the United States, whose terms would be enforced by the signatories to the agreement.

Republicans, as well as some Democrats in Congress, were strongly opposed to the Iran nuclear deal arguing that it would only limit—not end—Iranian nuclear ambitions and would provide the regime additional financial resources to do mischief in the Middle East once economic sanctions were lifted. In an historically unprecedented step, taken several weeks before the agreement was signed by negotiators, a group of forty-seven Republican senators went over the head of the president and expressed its opposition to the deal in an open letter to the leaders of Iran. The letter warned the Iranians that any international agreement negotiated by the president without the approval of the Senate could and likely would be nullified by a future Republican president with the stroke of a pen. In fact, during the 2016 presidential campaign, Donald Trump lambasted the Iran nuclear deal, promising to withdraw from it if elected. Once he became president, President Trump refused on several occasions to certify that the Iranians were in compliance with the terms of the agreement, signaled on several occasions his intention to withdraw the United States from it entirely, which he did on May 8, 2018.

*   *   *   *   *

Presidents throughout our history have entered into many international agreements without asking the Senate's permission to do so. Legally non-binding international agreements and legally binding executive agreements have evolved over time into powerful instruments of presidential foreign and national defense policy making: the U.S.-brokered agreement with Russia to rid Syria of chemical weapons (2013) is an example of the former; Richard Nixon's recognition of the Peoples' Republic of China (1972) is an example of the latter. The practice of entering into international agreements without Senate consent has increased substantially in modern times for many reasons—a subject we examine in detail in a later chapter on the presidency. Divided government plays a role, especially in an era of hyper-partisanship like the present one when presidents wish to bypass a recalcitrant Senate. It is likely that the dim prospect of gaining treaty approval for an Iran nuclear deal in a hostile Republican-controlled Senate persuaded President Obama to pursue an international agreement with Iran, not a treaty.

Constitutional scholars vary widely in their assessments of whether the Obama administration had the power, without Senate approval, to enter into an international agreement of this importance. It is easy to see why. Article II, Section 2, of the Constitution, the portion that describes presidential powers, is only 223 words long and leaves a great deal of room for interpretation. Over the course of our history, presidents of both parties have interpreted the powers of the office quite expansively, resulting in a steady amplification of the primacy of the president's role in a wide range of areas, but most especially in the conduct of foreign affairs and national defense. This change in the definition of the powers of the office has happened, even though the wording of Article II, Section 2 has not been amended in any way. This is one reason why many scholars describe our Constitution as a "living constitution," one that changes with the times and the needs of the United States. It is one of the ways our Constitution changes, in addition to formal amendments and Supreme Court decisions about the meaning of the document's various provisions.

One of the enduring debates in the United States is whether the Constitution's meaning is unambiguous and unchanging, or whether many of its provisions are open to interpretation and the precedents created by the practices of public officials. We suggest in this chapter that the latter interpretation of the Constitution is closer to what has actually unfolded over the years.

THINKING CRITICALLY **ABOUT THIS CHAPTER**

This chapter is about the founding of the United States and the formulation of the constitutional rules that structure American politics to this day.

APPLYING THE **FRAMEWORK**

In this chapter, you will see how structural factors, such as the American political culture, economic developments, and the composition of the Constitutional Convention, shaped the substance of our Constitution. You will also see how the Constitution itself is an important structural factor that helps us understand how American government and politics work today.

USING THE **DEMOCRACY STANDARD**

Using the concept of democracy outlined in Chapter 1, you will be able to see how and why the framers were uneasy about democracy and created a republican form of government that, although based on popular consent, placed a number of roadblocks in the path of popular rule.

THE AMERICAN REVOLUTION AND THE DECLARATION OF INDEPENDENCE

2.1 Assess the enduring legacies of the American Revolution and the Declaration of Independence.

Initially, the American Revolution (1775–1783) was waged more to preserve an existing way of life than to create something new. By and large, American colonists in the 1760s and 1770s were proud to be affiliated with Great Britain and satisfied with the general prosperity that came with participation in the British commercial empire.[1] When revolution broke out, the colonists at first wanted only to preserve their traditional rights as British subjects. These traditional rights of life, liberty, and property seemed threatened by British policies on trade and taxation. For example, rather than allowing American colonists to trade freely with whomever they pleased and to produce whatever goods they wanted, England restricted their freedom to do either in order to protect its own manufacturers. To pay for protection against raids by Native Americans and their French allies, England imposed taxes on a number of items, including sugar, tea, and stamps (required for legal documents, pamphlets, and newspapers). The imposition of these taxes without the colonists' consent seemed an act of tyranny to many English subjects in America.

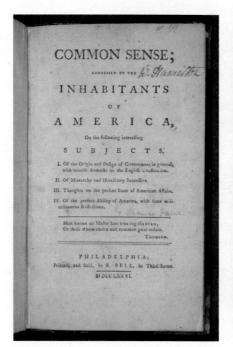

Although the initial aims of the American Revolution were quite modest, like most revolutions, it did not stay on the track planned by its leaders. It was sparked by a concern for liberty—understood as the preservation of traditional rights against the intrusions of a distant government—but it also stimulated the development of sentiments for popular sovereignty and political equality. As these sentiments grew, so did the likelihood that American colonies would split from their British parent and form a system of government more to their liking.

When the Second Continental Congress began its session on May 10, 1775—the First had met only briefly in 1774 to formulate a list of grievances to submit to the British Parliament—the delegates did not have independence in mind, even though armed conflict with Britain had already begun with the battles of Lexington and Concord. By the end of spring, pushed by the logic of armed conflict, an unyielding British government, and Thomas Paine's incendiary call for American independence in his wildly popular pamphlet *Common Sense*, the delegates concluded that separation and independence were inescapable.[2] In early June, the Continental Congress appointed a special committee, composed of Thomas Jefferson, John Adams, and Benjamin Franklin, to draft a declaration of independence. The document, mostly Jefferson's handiwork, was adopted unanimously on July 4, 1776. (See the timeline in Figure 2.1 for a review of the key events in the history of the American Revolution and the early republic.)

Key Ideas in the Declaration of Independence

The ideas in the Declaration of Independence are so familiar that we may easily miss their revolutionary importance. In the late 18th century, most of the world's societies were ruled by kings with authority purportedly derived from God, subject to little or no control by the populace. Closely following John Locke's ideas in *The Second Treatise on Government,* Jefferson's ideas about legitimate government sparked a responsive chord in people everywhere when they were first presented in the Declaration, and they remain extremely popular all over the world today. Jefferson argued the following points:

1. People possess rights that cannot be legitimately given away or taken from them: We hold these truths to be self-evident, that all men are created equal, that they are endowed by their Creator with certain unalienable Rights, that among these are Life, Liberty, and the Pursuit of Happiness.

FIGURE 2.1 TIMELINE OF THE FOUNDING OF THE UNITED STATES, 1774–1791

The British need for revenue to finance the operations of an empire created a crisis in America that eventually sparked a war for independence. After the Americans overthrew British rule, a new government and political system emerged.

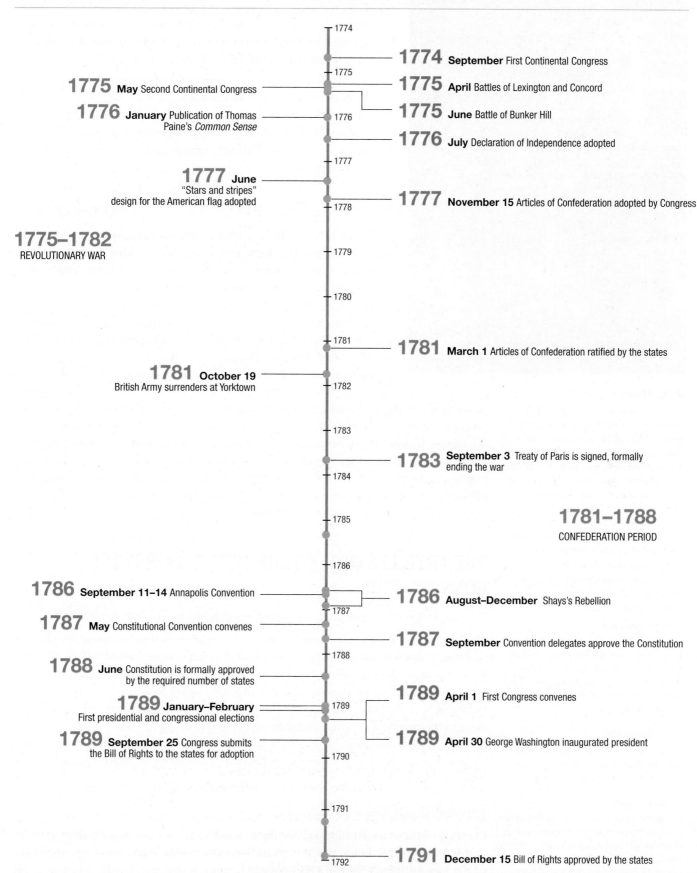

1774 September First Continental Congress

1775 May Second Continental Congress

1775 April Battles of Lexington and Concord

1776 January Publication of Thomas Paine's *Common Sense*

1775 June Battle of Bunker Hill

1776 July Declaration of Independence adopted

1777 June "Stars and stripes" design for the American flag adopted

1777 November 15 Articles of Confederation adopted by Congress

1775–1782
REVOLUTIONARY WAR

1781 March 1 Articles of Confederation ratified by the states

1781 October 19 British Army surrenders at Yorktown

1783 September 3 Treaty of Paris is signed, formally ending the war

1781–1788
CONFEDERATION PERIOD

1786 September 11–14 Annapolis Convention

1786 August–December Shays's Rebellion

1787 May Constitutional Convention convenes

1787 September Convention delegates approve the Constitution

1788 June Constitution is formally approved by the required number of states

1789 January–February First presidential and congressional elections

1789 April 1 First Congress convenes

1789 September 25 Congress submits the Bill of Rights to the states for adoption

1789 April 30 George Washington inaugurated president

1791 December 15 Bill of Rights approved by the states

© Edward S. Greenberg

UNALIENABLE RIGHTS

Thomas Jefferson was the principal author of the Declaration of Independence, although he received a great deal of editorial help in writing the final document from John Adams and Benjamin Franklin. Despite the contradictions in his own life on matters of liberty and equality—he was, after all, a slave owner—the words in the Declaration have been instrumental in advancing the cause of freedom and democracy both in the United States and abroad. *Do Jefferson's words, as expressed in the Declaration of Independence, still matter to many today?*

social contract

The idea that government is the result of an agreement among people to form one, and that people have the right to create an entirely new government if the terms of the contract have been violated by the existing one.

confederation

A loose association of states or territorial units in which very little or no power is lodged in a central government.

constitution

The basic framework of law for a nation that prescribes how government is to be organized, how government decisions are to be made, and what powers and responsibilities government shall have.

2. People create government to protect these rights:

That to secure these rights, Governments are instituted among Men, deriving their just powers from the consent of the governed.

3. If government fails to protect people's rights or itself becomes a threat to them, people can withdraw their consent from that government and form a new one; that is, people may void the existing **social contract** and agree to a new one:

That whenever any Form of Government becomes destructive of these ends, it is the Right of the People to alter or to abolish it, and to institute new Government, laying its foundation on such principles, and organizing its powers in such form, as to them shall seem most likely to effect their Safety and Happiness.

Key Omissions in the Declaration of Independence

The Declaration of Independence carefully avoided addressing several controversial subjects, including slavery. Jefferson's initial draft denounced the Crown for violating human rights by "captivating and carrying Africans into slavery," but this language was considered too inflammatory and was dropped from subsequent versions. The contradiction between the institution of slavery and the Declaration's sweeping defense of self-government, "unalienable" individual rights, and equality ("all men are created equal") was obvious to many observers at the time and is glaringly apparent to us today. The Declaration was also silent about the political status of women and the inalienable rights of Native Americans (referred to in the Declaration as "merciless Indian savages") and African Americans, even those who were not slaves. Indeed, it is safe to assume that neither Jefferson, the main author of the Declaration, nor the other signers of the document had women, Native Americans, free blacks, or slaves in mind when they were fomenting revolution and calling for a different kind of political society. Interestingly, free blacks and women would go on to play important roles in waging war against Britain.[3]

THE ARTICLES OF CONFEDERATION: OUR FIRST CONSTITUTION

2.2 Describe the system of government established by our first constitution.

The leaders of the American Revolution almost certainly did not envision the creation of a single, unified nation. At most, they had in mind a loose **confederation** of states. This should not be surprising. In the late 18th century, most Americans believed that a government based on popular consent and committed to the protection of individual rights was possible only in small, homogeneous republics, where government was close to the people and where fundamental conflicts of interest among the people did not exist. Given the great geographic expanse of the colonies, as well as their varied ways of life and economic interests, the formation of a single, unified republic seemed unworkable.

Provisions of the Articles

Our first written **constitution**—a document specifying the basic organization, powers, and limits of government passed by the Second Continental Congress in the midst of the Revolutionary War in 1777—created a nation that was hardly a nation at all.

The **Articles of Confederation** created in law what had existed in practice from the time of the Declaration of Independence: a loose confederation of independent states with little power vested in a central government, much like the United Nations today. Under the Articles, most important decisions were made in state legislatures.

The Articles of Confederation provided for a central government of sorts, but it had few responsibilities and virtually no power. It could make war or peace but had no power to levy taxes (even customs duties). It could not regulate interstate commerce nor deny states the right to collect customs duties. It had no independent chief executive to ensure that laws passed by Congress would be enforced, nor a national court system to settle disputes between states, nor the means to provide for a sound national money system. The rule requiring that all national laws be approved by nine of the thirteen states, with each state having one vote in Congress, made lawmaking almost impossible, and defects were difficult to remedy because amending the Articles required unanimous approval.

Shortcomings of the Articles

Although the Articles of Confederation did what most of its authors intended—preserved the power, independence, and sovereignty of the states and ensured that the central government would not encroach on the liberty of the people—the confederation was not well equipped to handle many problems.

Most important, the new central government could not finance its activities and was forced to rely on each state's willingness to pay its annual tax assessment. Few states were eager to cooperate. As a result, confederation bonds and notes became almost worthless, dramatically undermining the creditworthiness of the new country.

The central government was also unable to defend American interests in foreign affairs. Without a chief executive or a standing army, and with the states holding veto power over actions of the central government, the confederation lacked the capacity to reach binding agreements with other nations or to deal with a wide range of foreign policy problems. These included the continuing presence of British troops in western lands ceded to the new nation by Britain at the end of the Revolutionary War, violent clashes with Native Americans on the western frontier, and piracy on the high seas.

Articles of Confederation
The first constitution of the United States, adopted during the last stages of the Revolutionary War, created a system of government with most power lodged in the states and little in the central government.

STARVING AT WINTER QUARTERS
The principal reason why American military forces suffered so much at their winter encampment at Valley Forge, Pennsylvania, is that Congress, dependent on the voluntary willingness of states to pay taxes to the national government under the Articles of Confederation, could not provide adequate funds for the purchase of supplies and munitions. As a consequence, George Washington led his battered army to take up winter quarters at a strategically defensible location where he could forage for food and hang on to fight the British another day.
How much does the well-being of any army, that of Washington or of any other general, owe to good governance?

The government also was unable to prevent the outbreak of commercial warfare between the states. As virtually independent nations with the power to levy customs duties, many states became intense commercial rivals and sought every possible advantage over neighboring states. New York and New Jersey, for instance, imposed high tariffs on goods that crossed their borders. This level of competition was an obstacle to the expansion of commercial activities and economic growth.

FACTORS LEADING TO THE CONSTITUTIONAL CONVENTION

2.3 Analyze the developments that led to the Constitutional Convention.

Most of America's economic, social, and political leaders were convinced by 1787 that the new nation and its experiment in self-government were in great peril. These concerns helped convince leaders in the states to select seventy-three delegates to attend a convention in Philadelphia, with the goal of creating a new government capable of providing both energy and stability. Only fifty-five delegates actually showed up.

The convention officially convened on May 25, 1787, with George Washington presiding. It met in secret for a period of almost four months. By the end of their deliberations, the delegates had hammered out a new constitutional framework that has served as one of the structural foundations of American government and politics to the present day.

What Worried American Notables and Why

Historians now generally agree that the failings of the Articles of Confederation led most of the leading citizens of the confederation to believe that a new constitution was desperately needed for the fledgling nation. What is left out of many accounts of the Constitutional Convention, however, is the story of the growing concern among many of the most influential men in the confederation that the passions for democracy and equality among the common people set loose by the American Revolution were getting out of hand. During the American Revolution, the people often saw appeals for the defense of freedom and for the spread of the blessings of liberty as inevitable rights to the means of government and to better livelihoods.[4] The common people were convinced that overthrow of British rule would bring substantial improvements in their lives.[5]

THE FOUNDERS' BELIEFS ABOUT REPUBLICANISM Fervor for popular participation and greater equality is not what most of the leaders of the American Revolution had in mind.[6] The Founders were believers in a theory of government known as **republicanism**. (This is not a reference to the Republican Party or its members and supporters.)[7] Like all republicans of the 18th century, the framers were seeking a form of government that would not only be based on the consent of the governed but would prevent **tyranny**, whether tyranny came from the misrule of a single person (such as a king or military dictator), a small group of elites (an aristocracy, a clerical theocracy, or a moneyed merchant class), or even the majority of the population.

The solution to the problem of tyranny for 18th-century republican thinkers was threefold:

1. to elect government leaders
2. to limit the power of government
3. to place roadblocks in the path of the majority

The election of representatives to lead the government, in their view, would keep potentially tyrannical kings and aristocratic

---

republicanism

A political doctrine advocating limited government based on popular consent, protected against majority tyranny.

tyranny

The abuse of the inalienable rights of citizens by government.

RULE BY THE ONE

The one-man rule of repressive autocrats like Kim Jong-un, whose North Korean regime detains, tortures, and kills political opponents with impunity, is a form of tyranny that deeply worried the framers of the Constitution. The framers also tried to guard against tyranny by the few and by the many. *What are the consequences for North Korean society that no mechanism ensures responsiveness and accountability of Kim's leadership to the people?*

factions from power while ensuring popular consent. Limiting the power of government, both by writing in a constitution what government could and could not do and by fragmenting governmental power, would prevent tyranny no matter who eventually won control, including the majority of the people. The influence of the majority could be limited by making only a portion of government subject to election by the people.

Although 18th-century republicans believed in representative government—a government whose political leaders are elected by the people—they were not sympathetic to what we might today call popular democracy. For the most part, they thought that public affairs ought to be left to men from the "better" parts of society. The conduct of the public business was, in their view, the province of individuals with wisdom and experience, capacities associated mainly with people of social standing, substantial financial resources, and high levels of education. They expected that voters would cast their ballots in accordance with this view. 18th-century republicans believed that elected representatives, once in office, should not be overly responsive to public opinion; representatives were to exercise independent judgment about how best to serve the public interest, taking into account the needs and interests of society rather than the moods and opinions of the people. They believed that such a deliberative approach would not only protect liberty but result in better government decisions and policies.[8]

THE FOUNDERS' BELIEFS ABOUT THE PROBLEMS OF DEMOCRACY Eighteenth-century republicans, then, did not believe that the people could or should rule directly. While they favored a system that allowed the common people to play a larger role in public life than existed under other political systems of the day, they wanted to limit the role of the people far more than we would find acceptable today. They worried that too much participation by the people would have a bad outcome. As James Madison put it in *The Federalist* No. 10, "[Democracies] have ever been spectacles of turbulence and contention; have ever been found incompatible with personal security or the rights of property; and have in general been as short in their lives as they have been violent in their deaths."[9] (See Table 2.1 for a summary of the differences between 18th-century republicanism and democracy as defined in Chapter 1.)

An Excess of Democracy in the States Worries that untamed democracy was on the rise were not unfounded.[10] In the mid-1780s, popular assemblies (called conventions) in several states kept tabs on state legislatures and issued instructions to legislatures concerning which bills to pass. Both conventions and instructions struck directly

TABLE 2.1 A COMPARISON OF 18TH-CENTURY REPUBLICANISM AND THE DEMOCRATIC IDEAL

	Eighteenth-Century Republicanism	The Democratic Ideal
Government	Based on popular consent	Based on popular consent
	Has limited mandate	Has unlimited mandate (does whatever the people want)
	Safeguards rights and liberties, with a special emphasis on property rights	Safeguards rights and liberties, with no special emphasis on property rights
Rule by the people	Indirect, through layers of representatives	Direct or indirect, through layers of representatives
The *people* defined	Narrowly defined, by education, property holding, and social standing	Broadly defined
Eligibility for elective office	Narrow eligibility, confined to a privileged stratum of the population	Broad eligibility
Model for elective representatives	"Trustees" of the public good	"Delegates" of the people's wishes
Majority rule	Barriers to majority rule exist	Majority rule prevails

© Edward S. Greenberg

at the heart of the republican conception of the legislature as a deliberative body made up of representatives shielded from popular opinion.[11]

The constitution of the state of Pennsylvania was also an affront to republican principles. Benjamin Rush, a signatory to the Declaration of Independence, described it as "too much upon the democratic order."[12] This constitution replaced the property qualification to vote with a very small tax (thus allowing many more people to vote), created a unicameral (single-house) legislative body whose members were to be elected in annual elections, mandated that legislative deliberations be open to the public, and required that proposed legislation be widely publicized and voted on only after a general election had been held (making the canvassing of public opinion easier).

To many advocates of popular democracy, including Thomas Paine, the Pennsylvania constitution was the most perfect instrument of popular sovereignty. To others, like James Madison, the Pennsylvania case was a perfect example of popular tyranny exercised through the legislative branch of government.[13]

The Threat to Property Rights in the States   One of the freedoms that 18th-century republicans wanted to protect against the intrusions of a tyrannical government was the right of the people to acquire and enjoy private property. Developments toward the end of the 1770s and the beginning of the 1780s seemed to put this freedom in jeopardy. For one thing, the popular culture was growing increasingly hostile to privilege of any kind, whether of social standing, education, or wealth. Writers derided aristocratic airs; expressed their preference for unlettered, plain-speaking leaders; and pointed out how wealth undermined equal rights.[14] In addition, legislatures were increasingly inclined to pass laws protecting debtors. For example, Rhode Island and North Carolina issued cheap paper money, which note holders were forced to accept as payment for debts. Other states passed stay acts, which forbade farm foreclosures for nonpayment of debts. Popular opinion, while strongly in favor of property rights (after all, most of the debtors in question were owners of small farms), also sympathized with farmers, who were hard-pressed to pay their debts with increasingly tight money, and believed—with some reason—that many creditors had accumulated notes speculatively or unfairly and were not, therefore, entitled to full repayment.

One reason American notables wanted a new constitutional order was their belief that an excess of democracy in the states under the Articles of Confederation was leading to a devaluation of the money supply. As several states began to print cheap paper money, they may have had good cause to worry. More than a few historical examples of hyperinflation (what happens when money loses its value) suffice. In Germany after World War I, where currency became almost worthless, grocers were obliged to accept wheelbarrows full of bills for the purchase of small tins of oatmeal.

What ultimately pushed American notables over the edge was the threat of insurrection. Shays's Rebellion, named for its leader, Daniel Shays, occurred in western Massachusetts in 1786, when armed men took over courthouses in order to prevent judges from ordering the seizure of farms and the incarceration of their owners in debtors' prison for the nonpayment of state taxes.

The crisis in western Massachusetts was the result of a near "perfect storm" of developments: plummeting prices for crops, a dramatic increase in state taxes to pay off Revolutionary War debts, and Governor James Bowdoin's insistence that note-holders be paid in full by the state (mostly financial speculators who had bought up the state debt for pennies on the dollar). Unlike most other states in similar circumstances, Massachusetts did not take action to help its debt-ridden farmers. While other states passed legislation postponing tax and mortgage payments, Massachusetts instead raised taxes and insisted on full and timely payment with forfeiture of farms and jail penalties for noncompliance. Although the state succeeded in putting down the rebellion and reopening the courts, it required the dispatch of the state militia, two pitched battles, and arrests of most of the leaders of the insurrection.

THE CONSTITUTIONAL CONVENTION AND A NEW FRAMEWORK FOR GOVERNMENT

2.4 Describe and evaluate the framework for government that the Constitutional Convention created.

Most of the new nation's leading citizens were alarmed by the apparent inability of state governments to maintain public order under the Articles of Confederation.[15] Shays's Rebellion confirmed national leaders' worst fears about the dangers of ineffective state governments and popular democracy spinning out of control, unchecked by a strong national government. As George Washington said, "If government cannot check these disorders, what security has a man?"[16] It was in this climate of crisis in 1786 that twelve delegates from five states meeting in Annapolis issued a call for a convention to correct the flaws in our first constitution. Rather than amend the Articles of Confederation, however, the delegates who gathered at the subsequent convention in Philadelphia in the summer of 1787 did a very surprising thing: they wrote an entirely new constitution.

Who Were the Framers?

Most of America's economic, social, and political leaders were convinced by 1787 that the new nation and the experiment in self-government were in great peril. These concerns helped convince leaders in the states to select seventy-three delegates to attend the Constitutional Convention in Philadelphia (only fifty-five actually showed up for its deliberations). The goal was to create a new government capable of providing both energy and stability.

The convention officially convened in Philadelphia on May 25, 1787, with George Washington presiding. It met in secret for a period of almost four months. By the end of their deliberations, the delegates had hammered out a constitutional framework that has served as one of the structural foundations of American government and politics to the present day.

The delegates to the convention were not common folk. There were no common laborers, skilled craftspeople, small farmers, women, or racial minorities in attendance. Most delegates were wealthy men: holders of government bonds, real estate investors, successful merchants, bankers, lawyers, and owners of large plantations worked by slaves. They were, for the most part, far better educated than the average American and solidly steeped in the classics. The journal of the convention debates kept by James Madison of Virginia shows that the delegates were conversant with the great works of Western philosophy and political science. With great facility and frequency, they quoted Aristotle, Plato, Locke, and Montesquieu. Finally, they were a group with broad experience in American politics—most had served in their state legislatures—and many were veterans of the Revolutionary War.[17]

Judgments about the framers, their intentions, and what they produced vary widely. Historian Melvin Urofsky writes that "few gatherings in the history of this or any other country could boast such a concentration of talent."[18] On the other hand, Supreme Court Justice Thurgood Marshall, the first African American member of the Court, once claimed that the Constitution was "defective from the start" because the convention at which it was written did not include women or blacks.[19]

The most influential criticism of the framers and what they created was mounted in 1913 by Progressive historian Charles Beard in his book *An Economic Interpretation of the Constitution*.[20] Beard boldly claimed that the framers were engaged in a conspiracy to protect their immediate and personal economic interests. He suggested that those

VENERATING THE CONSTITUTION

Americans generally believe that the U.S. Constitution, fashioned by the framers in Philadelphia in 1788, is one of the main reasons the American system of government has proved so enduring. Here, a family looks at the original document at the National Archives.

What reasons other than the Constitution might explain why our system has endured?

who controlled the convention and the ratification process after the convention were owners of government bonds and notes who were interested in a government that could pay its debts, merchants interested in protections of commerce, and land speculators interested in the protection of property rights.

Beard has had legions of defenders and detractors.[21] Historians today generally agree that Beard overemphasized the degree to which the framers were driven by desires to "line their own pockets," failed to credit their more noble motivations, and even got many of his facts wrong. So a simple self-interest analysis is not supportable. But Beard was probably on the mark when he suggested that broad economic and social-class motives were at work in shaping the actions of the framers. This is not to suggest that they were not concerned about the national interest, economic stability, or the preservation of liberty. It does suggest, however, that the ways in which they understood these concepts were fully compatible with their own positions of economic and social eminence. It is fair to say that the Constitutional Convention was the work of American notables who were authentically worried about the instability and economic chaos of the confederation as well as the rise of a democratic and equalitarian culture among the common people.[22]

However, we must also acknowledge that the framers were launched on a novel and exciting adventure, trying to create a form of government that existed nowhere else during the late 18th century. The success of their efforts was not guaranteed. They were, in effect, sailing in uncharted waters, guided by their reading of history and of republican philosophy, by their understanding of the nature of the unwritten English constitution, and by their experience with colonial governments before the Revolution and state governments after the Revolution.

Consensus and Conflict at the Constitutional Convention

The delegates to the convention were of one mind on many fundamental points. Most important, they agreed that the Articles of Confederation had to be replaced with a new constitution.

Most of the delegates also agreed about the need for a substantially strengthened national government to protect American interests in the world, provide for social order, and regulate interstate commerce. Such a government would diminish the power and sovereignty of the states. Supporters of the idea of a strong, centralized national government—such as Alexander Hamilton—had long argued this position. By the time of the convention, even such traditional opponents of centralized governmental power as James Madison had changed their minds. As Madison put it, some way must be found "which will at once support a due supremacy of the national authority, and leave in force the local authorities so far as they can be subordinately useful."[23]

But the delegates also believed a strong national government was potentially tyrannical and should not be allowed to fall into the hands of any particular interest or set of interests, particularly the majority of the people, referred to by Madison as the "majority faction." The delegates' most important task became finding a formula for creating a republican government based on popular consent but a government not unduly swayed by public opinion and popular democracy. As Benjamin Franklin put it, "We have been guarding against an evil that old states are most liable to, excess of power in the rulers; but our present danger seems to be a defect of obedience in the subjects."[24]

THE GREAT COMPROMISE   By far, the most intense disagreements at the convention concerned the issue of representation in Congress, especially whether large or small states would wield the most power in the legislative branch. The **Virginia Plan**, drafted by James Madison, proposed the creation of a strong central government dominated by a powerful bicameral (two-house) Congress controlled by the

Virginia Plan
Proposal by the large states at the Constitutional Convention to create a strong central government with power in the government apportioned to the states on the basis of population.

most populous states: Virginia, Massachusetts, and Pennsylvania. The Virginians proposed that seats in the national legislature be apportioned to the states on the basis of population and that the legislature be vested with the power to appoint executive and judiciary branches and to veto state laws. The smaller states countered with a set of proposals drafted by William Paterson of New Jersey (thereafter known as the **New Jersey Plan**), the central feature of which was a unicameral national legislature with seats equally apportioned among the states and with representatives selected by state legislatures. The New Jersey Plan envisioned a slightly more powerful national government than the one that existed under the Articles of Confederation, but one that was to be organized on representational lines not unlike those in the Articles, in which each of the states remained sovereign and equal. The Virginia Plan, by contrast, with its strong national government run by a popularly elected legislature, represented a fundamentally different kind of national union, one in which national sovereignty was superior to state sovereignty.[25]

Debate was so intense that no decision could be reached on the floor of the convention. As a way out of this impasse, the convention appointed a committee to hammer out a compromise. The so-called Committee of Eleven met over the Fourth of July holiday while the convention was adjourned. It presented its report, sometimes called the Great Compromise and sometimes the **Connecticut Compromise** (because it was drafted by Roger Sherman of that state), on July 5, 1787. Adopted on July 16, the compromise broke the deadlock at the convention and allowed the delegates to turn their attention to other matters.[26]

The key part of the Connecticut Compromise established a two-chamber legislative branch, with each chamber based on a different principle of representation. Each state's representation in the House of Representatives would be based on its relative population size, with the proviso that no state would have fewer than one representative. Representation in the House, because it very nearly mirrors the distribution of the American population among the states, can fairly be called democratic, based on the principle of one person, one vote. The Senate, on the other hand, would be based on equal representation—each state would have two senators regardless of its population size—giving disproportionate political power to low-population states. In 2010, for example, more than 37 million people lived in California, while about 560,000 people lived in Wyoming—yet each state had then, as always, two senators. Each California senator represented, therefore, more than 18.5 million people, while each Wyoming senator represented only about 280,000. In terms of representation in 2010, when the last census of the American population occurred, each person in Wyoming had sixty-six times the power in the Senate as each person in California had. This divergence from the democratic ideal for representation in the U.S. Senate is shown dramatically in two cartograms (see Figure 2.2).

SLAVERY Despite great distaste for the institution of slavery among many delegates—it is said that Benjamin Franklin wanted to insert a provision in the Constitution condemning slavery and the slave trade but was talked out of it for fear of splintering the convention[27]—slavery was ultimately condoned in the Constitution, although only indirectly; the word *slavery*, in fact, does not appear in the Constitution at all. But even without using the word, the legal standing of slaves is affirmed in the Constitution in three places. First, the delegates agreed, after much heated debate, to count three-fifths of a state's slave population (referred to as "three-fifths of all other Persons") in the calculation of how many representatives a state was entitled to in the House of Representatives (Article I, Section 2, paragraph 3). Much harm came of this; counting noncitizen slaves for purposes of representation in the House increased the power of the slave states in Congress as well as the number of their electoral votes in presidential elections. This imbalance would continue until 1865, when the Civil War and the Thirteenth Amendment, ratified after the war, ended slavery in the United States.

New Jersey Plan

Proposal of the smaller states at the Constitutional Convention to create a government with slightly more power in a central government than under the Articles, with the states equally represented in a unicameral national legislature.

Connecticut Compromise

Also called the Great Compromise; the compromise between the New Jersey and Virginia plans formulated by the Connecticut delegates at the Constitutional Convention; called for a lower legislative house based on population size and an upper house based on equal representation of the states.

FIGURE 2.2 PRINCIPLES OF REPRESENTATION IN CONGRESS

The cartogram on the left shows states drawn in proportion to the number of representatives each has in the House of Representatives. Because representation in the House is based roughly on population, the largest numbers of representatives come from more populous states—California, Texas, Florida, Ohio, Illinois, New York, and Pennsylvania—as one would expect in a democratic system. Equal representation of each state in the Senate, combined with vast population differences among the states, however, leads to serious representational distortions, from a democratic theory point of view. The cartogram on the right shows the representational power of the people in each state in the Senate, measured as the number of senators—always two—divided by state population size. The most populous states—California, New York, Texas, and Florida—almost disappear, while less populous states—Wyoming, Montana, Delaware, and the two Dakotas—loom large.

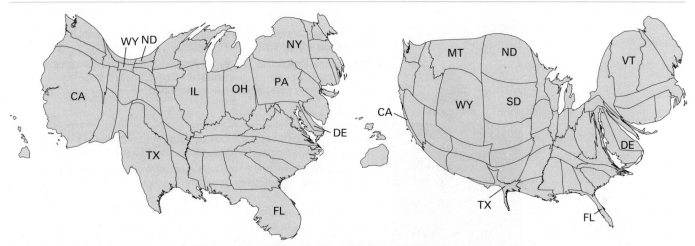

States in Proportion to Number of U.S. Representatives Each Has   States in Proportion to Number of Residents per Senator

SOURCE: U.S. Census Bureau, Census Apportionment Results, December 2010.

Second, it forbade enactments against the slave trade until the year 1808 (Article I, Section 9). Third, it required nonslave states to return runaway slaves to their owners in slave states (Article IV, Section 2, paragraph 3).

Today, many Americans are bothered by the fact that a significant number of the delegates to a convention whose goal was to build a nontyrannical republic were themselves slaveholders (although a few, including George Washington, had provisions in their wills freeing their slaves). To understand more fully why the delegates not only did not abolish slavery but fashioned provisions that would protect the institution, apply the framework (see Figure 2.3).

THE PRESIDENCY   The Virginia Plan called for a single executive, while the New Jersey Plan called for a multi-person executive. In the spirit of cooperation that pervaded the convention after the Connecticut Compromise, the delegates quickly settled on the idea of a single executive. They could not agree, however, on how this executive should be selected. Both sides rejected direct election of the chief executive by the people, of course, because this would be "too much upon the democratic order," but they locked horns over the Virginia Plan's method of selection: by the vote of state legislatures. The compromise that was eventually struck involved a provision for an **Electoral College** that would select the president. In the Electoral College, each state would have votes equal in number to its total of representatives and senators in Congress. Selection of electors was left to state legislatures. (Electoral College votes are determined today by popular vote in each state.) Elected members of the Electoral College would then cast votes for president. Should the Electoral College fail to give a majority to any person, which most framers assumed would usually

Electoral College
Representatives selected in each of the states, their numbers based on each state's total number of its senators and representatives; a majority of Electoral College votes elects the president.

THE FRAMERS RETAIN SLAVERY

One of the framers' great shortcomings was their inability or unwillingness to include language in the Constitution that would abolish slavery.

What were some of the consequences that stemmed from the framers allowing slavery in our new nation?

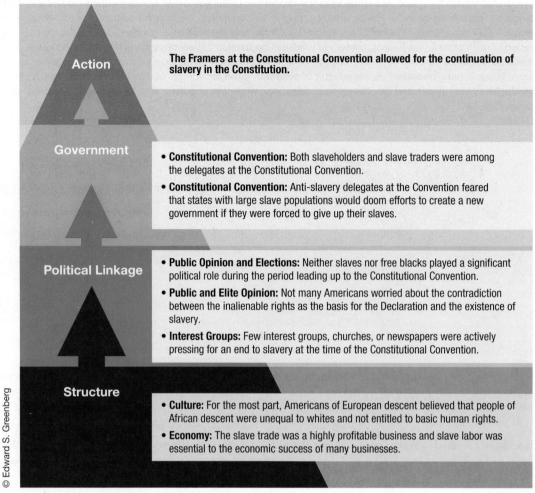

FIGURE 2.3 APPLYING THE FRAMEWORK: CONDONING SLAVERY IN THE CONSTITUTION

Action

The Framers at the Constitutional Convention allowed for the continuation of slavery in the Constitution.

Government

- **Constitutional Convention:** Both slaveholders and slave traders were among the delegates at the Constitutional Convention.
- **Constitutional Convention:** Anti-slavery delegates at the Convention feared that states with large slave populations would doom efforts to create a new government if they were forced to give up their slaves.

Political Linkage

- **Public Opinion and Elections:** Neither slaves nor free blacks played a significant political role during the period leading up to the Constitutional Convention.
- **Public and Elite Opinion:** Not many Americans worried about the contradiction between the inalienable rights as the basis for the Declaration and the existence of slavery.
- **Interest Groups:** Few interest groups, churches, or newspapers were actively pressing for an end to slavery at the time of the Constitutional Convention.

Structure

- **Culture:** For the most part, Americans of European descent believed that people of African descent were unequal to whites and not entitled to basic human rights.
- **Economy:** The slave trade was a highly profitable business and slave labor was essential to the economic success of many businesses.

© Edward S. Greenberg

happen given the likelihood of three or more candidates, the House of Representatives would choose the president, with each state having one vote (Article II, Section 1, paragraphs 2 and 3).

What the Framers Created at the Constitutional Convention

The Constitution of the United States deserves a careful reading. Each word and phrase tells something important about how American government works. If you keep in mind how the document is organized, it will help you understand the structure of the Constitution, locate specific provisions, and understand what kind of government the framers created. (A brief outline of constitutional provisions is provided in Table 2.2.)

A REPUBLICAN FORM OF GOVERNMENT   Recall that 18th-century republican doctrine advocated a form of government that, while based on popular consent and some popular participation, places obstacles in the path of majoritarian democracy and limits the purposes and powers of the government to prevent tyranny.

Elections and Representation   Republican government is based on the principle of representation, meaning that public policies are made not by the people directly but by the people's elected representatives acting in their stead. Under the rules of the Constitution, the people elect the president and members of Congress, although in the case of the presidency and the Senate, they are elected indirectly (through the Electoral College and state legislatures, respectively). The upshot, then, is that government policies at the national level are mostly made either directly or

TABLE 2.2 READING THE CONSTITUTION

Article	What It's About	What It Does
Preamble	The Purpose of the Constitution	• Declares that "we the people" (not just the separate states) establish the Constitution
Article I	The Legislative Branch	• Provides for a House of Representatives, elected by the people and apportioned according to population
		• Provides for a Senate, with equal representation for each state
		• Discusses various rules and procedures, including the presidential veto
		• Enumerates specific powers of the Congress, concluding with the necessary and proper clause
		• Limits the powers of Congress
		• Limits the powers of the states
Article II	The Executive Branch	• Vests executive power in a single president
		• Describes the Electoral College scheme for electing presidents indirectly (changed, in effect, by the development of a party system)
		• Describes the qualifications, removal, compensation, and oath of office for the presidency
		• Describes presidential powers and duties
		• Provides for impeachment
Article III	The Judicial Branch	• Vests judicial power in a Supreme Court, letting Congress establish other courts, if desired
		• Provides for a limited original jurisdiction and (subject to congressional regulation) for broader appellate jurisdiction (i.e., jurisdiction to review lower court decisions)
		• Specifies a right to jury trials
		• Defines treason, ruling out certain punishments for it
Article IV	Interstate and Federal Relations	• Requires that full faith and credit be given other states
		• Requires that fugitives (slaves) be delivered to authorities
		• Provides for the admission of new states and the regulation of new territories
		• Guarantees a republican form of government to the states
Article V	Amending the Constitution	• Provides two ways of proposing amendments to the Constitution and two ways of ratifying them
		• Forbids amendments that would attempt to change equal state suffrage in the Senate, that would (before 1808) prohibit the slave trade, or that would change the apportionment of taxes
Article VI	Miscellaneous	• Assumes the debts of the Confederation
		• Makes the Constitution, laws, and treaties of the United States the supreme law of the land
		• Requires an oath by U.S. and state officials
Article VII	Ratification of the Constitution	• Provides that the Constitution will be established when ratified by nine state conventions

© Edward S. Greenberg

indirectly by elected officials. (The Seventeenth Amendment, ratified in 1913, transferred election of senators from state legislatures to the people.) This filters the voices of the people by encouraging the election to office of those "whose enlightened views and virtuous sentiments render them superior to local prejudices and to schemes of injustice."[28] This guarantees a degree of popular consent and some protection against the possibilities of tyrannical government arising from misrule by the *one* or by the *few*, given the electoral power of the *many*, but the many are still several steps removed from direct influence over officials.

Federalism The Articles of Confederation envisioned a nation structured as a loose union of politically independent states with little power in the hands of the central government. The Constitution fashioned **federalism**, a system in which some powers are left to the states, some powers are shared by the states and the central government, and some powers are granted to the central government alone.

The powers in the Constitution tilt toward the center, however.[29] This recasting of the union from a loose confederation to a more centralized federal system is boldly stated in Article VI, Section 2, commonly called the **supremacy clause**:

federalism

A system in which significant governmental powers are divided between a central government and smaller territorial units, such as states.

supremacy clause

The provision in Article VI of the Constitution that states that the Constitution and the laws and treaties of the United States are the supreme law of the land, taking precedence over state laws and constitutions when they are in conflict.

This Constitution and the Laws of the United States which shall be made in Pursuance thereof; and all Treaties made, or which shall be made, under the Authority of the United States, shall be the supreme Law of the Land; and the Judges in every State shall be bound thereby, any Thing in the Constitution or Laws of any State to the Contrary notwithstanding.

The tilt toward national power is also enhanced by assigning important powers and responsibilities to the national government: to regulate commerce, to provide a uniform currency, to provide uniform laws on bankruptcy, to raise and support an army and a navy, to declare war, to collect taxes and customs duties, to provide for the common defense of the United States, and more. (See Article I, Section 8.) Especially important for later constitutional history is the last of the clauses in Section 8, which states that Congress has the power to "make all laws which shall be necessary and proper" to carry out its specific powers and responsibilities. We shall see later how this **elastic clause** (also known as the necessary and proper clause) became one of the foundations for the growth of the federal government in the 20th century.

The Constitution left it up to each of the states, however, to determine qualifications for voting within their borders. This left rules in place in all the states that denied the right to vote to women, slaves, and Native Americans; it left rules untouched in many states that denied the vote to free blacks and to white males without property. Most states removed property qualifications by the 1830s, establishing universal white male suffrage in the United States. It would take many more years and constitutional amendments to remove state restrictions on the voting rights of women and racial minorities.

elastic clause

Article I, Section 8, of the Constitution, also called the necessary and proper clause; gives Congress the authority to make whatever laws are necessary and proper to carry out its enumerated responsibilities.

Limited Government The basic purpose of the U.S. Constitution, like any written constitution, is to define the purposes and powers of government. Such a definition of purposes and powers automatically places a boundary between what is permissible and what is impermissible. By listing the specific powers of the national government (as in Article I, Section 8) and specifically denying others to the national government (as in Article I, Section 9, and in the first ten amendments to the Constitution, known as the **Bill of Rights**), the Constitution limited what government may legitimately do.

Bill of Rights

The first ten amendments to the U.S. Constitution, concerned with the protection of basic liberties.

Checks on Majority Rule Afraid of unbridled democracy, the framers created a constitution by which the people rule only indirectly, barriers are placed in the path of majorities, and deliberation is prized over conformity to majority opinion. As political philosopher Robert Dahl writes, "To achieve their goal of preserving a set of inalienable rights superior to the majority principle ... the framers deliberately created a framework of government that was carefully designed to impede and even prevent the operation of majority rule."[30] James Madison, often called the father of the Constitution because of his prominent role at the convention and his reportage and commentaries on the debates there, wrote in *The Federalist # 63* that the key feature of the new form of government the Constitution created was "... the total exclusion of the people in their collective capacity from any share" in deciding specific government policies.[31] Let us see what the framers did to try to dilute the power of the majority in the national government.

Of the three branches of government, the framers made only a part of one of them subject to election by the direct vote of the people: the House of Representatives (Article I, Section 2, paragraph 1). They left the election of the president to an Electoral College, whose members were selected by state legislatures and not by the direct vote of the people. They gave the responsibility of electing senators to state legislatures (since changed by the Seventeenth Amendment). They placed selection of federal judges in the hands of the president and the Senate. They arranged, as well, that representatives, senators, and presidents would serve for different terms (two years for representatives, four years for presidents, and six years for senators), and be beholden to different constituencies. These incongruities in terms of office, constituencies, and

FIGURE 2.4   AMENDING THE CONSTITUTION

With two ways of proposing a constitutional amendment and two ways of ratifying one, there are four routes to changing the Constitution. In all but one case (the Twenty-First Amendment, which repealed Prohibition), constitutional amendments have been proposed by Congress and then ratified by state legislatures.

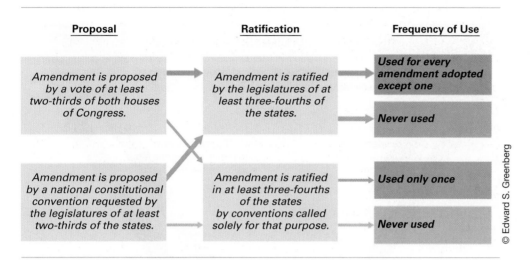

methods for selecting members of each of the branches were intended to ensure that popular majorities, at least in the short run, would be unlikely to overwhelm those who govern. Finally, the framers rejected the advice of radical democrats, such as Thomas Paine, Samuel Adams, and Thomas Jefferson, to allow the Constitution to be easily amended. Instead, they created an amending process that is exceedingly cumbersome and difficult (see Figure 2.4). Thus, the framers designed a system in which majority opinion, although given some play (more than anywhere in the world at the time),[32] was largely deflected and slowed, allowing somewhat insulated political leaders to deliberate at their pleasure.

Separation of Powers and Checks and Balances   During the American Revolution, American leaders worried mainly about the misrule of executives (kings and governors) and judges. As an antidote, they substituted legislative supremacy in state constitutions and in the Articles of Confederation, thinking that placing power in an elected representative body would make government effective and nontyrannical. By 1787, the men who drafted the Constitution, though still leery of executive and judicial power, were more concerned about the danger of legislative tyranny. To deal with this problem, the framers turned to the ancient notion of balanced government, popularized by the French philosopher Montesquieu. The central idea of balanced government is that concentrated power of any kind is dangerous and that the way to prevent tyranny is first to fragment governmental power into its constituent parts—executive, legislative, and judicial—and then place each into a separate and independent branch. In the U.S. Constitution, Article I (on the legislative power), Article II (on the executive power), and Article III (on the judicial power) designate separate spheres of responsibility and enumerate specific powers for each branch. We call this the **separation of powers** (see Figure 2.5).

To further ensure that power would not be exercised tyrannically, the framers arranged for the legislative, executive, and judicial powers to check one another in such a way that "ambition…be made to counteract ambition."[33] They did this by ensuring that no branch of the national government would be able to act entirely on its own without the cooperation of the others. To put it another way, each branch has ways of blocking the actions of the others. We call the constitutional provisions that accomplish this objective **checks and balances**. Figure 2.5 shows in detail how each

separation of powers

The distribution of government legislative, executive, and judicial powers to separate branches of government.

checks and balances

The constitutional principle that each of the separate branches of government has the power to hinder the unilateral actions of the other branches as a way to restrain an overreaching government and prevent tyranny.

FIGURE 2.5 SEPARATION OF POWERS AND CHECKS AND BALANCES

The framers of the Constitution believed that tyranny might be avoided if the powers of government were fragmented into executive, legislative, and judicial components and if each component resided in a separate branch of government. To further protect against tyranny, they created mechanisms by which the actions of any single branch could be blocked by either or both of the other branches.

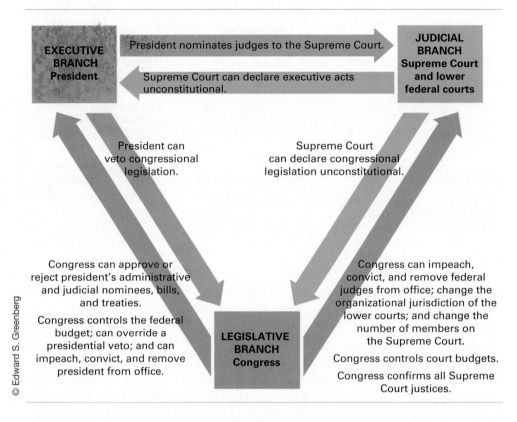

separate branch of the federal government can be checked by the other two. In this constitutional scheme, each branch has power, but none is able to exercise all of its powers on its own, without some concurrence and cooperation from the other two.

THE FOUNDATIONS FOR A NATIONAL FREE ENTERPRISE ECONOMY   The framers believed that **property rights**—the right to accumulate, use, and transfer private property—was one of the fundamental and inalienable rights that governments were instituted to defend, so they looked for ways to protect it. They also believed that the obstacles to trade allowed under the Articles of Confederation were threatening the emergence of a vibrant national economy in which most of them were involved.

Property rights are protected in several places in the Constitution. Article I, Section 10, forbids states to impair the obligation of contracts, to coin money, or to make anything but gold and silver coin a tender in payment of debts. In other words, the states could no longer help debtors by printing inflated paper money, forgiving debts, or otherwise infringing on the property of creditors, as had happened in such places as Rhode Island and North Carolina under the Articles of Confederation. Article IV, Section 1, further guarantees contracts by establishing that states must give "full faith and credit" to the public acts, records, and judicial proceedings of every other state, which means that one could no longer escape legal and financial obligations in one state by moving to another. In addition, the Constitution guaranteed that the U.S. government would pay all debts contracted under the Articles of Confederation (Article VI, Section 1). Article IV, Section 2, paragraph 3, even protected private property in slaves by requiring states to deliver escaped slaves back to their owners.

Besides protecting private property, the framers took additional steps to encourage the emergence of a national economy based on **free enterprise**. Article I, Section 8, grants Congress the power to regulate interstate commerce (thus ending the chaos of

property rights

The freedom to use, accumulate, and dispose of a valuable asset subject to rules established by government.

free enterprise

An economic system characterized by competitive markets and private ownership of a society's productive assets; a form of capitalism.

individual state regulations), to coin money and regulate its value (thus establishing a uniform national currency), to establish uniform laws of bankruptcy, and to protect the financial fruits of invention by establishing patent and copyright laws. At the same time, Article I, Sections 9 and 10, broke down barriers to trade by forbidding states from imposing taxes or duties on other states' exports, entering into foreign treaties, coining money, or laying any imposts or duties on imports or exports.

It took a little while for a national free enterprise system to emerge and flower in the United States because of the existence of an entirely different sort of economy in the slave South. Although free enterprise was thriving in the northern and western states by the 1820s, it took the destruction of slavery during and after the Civil War to create a free enterprise economy for the country as a whole.

THE IDEAL ECONOMIC MODEL
In this artist's conception of commerce on the Delaware River looking west from Camden, New Jersey, to East Philadelphia, circa 1836, we see the emergence of a national free enterprise system based on trade. The framers recognized that the obstacles to trade allowed under the Articles of Confederation were an impediment to their own economic futures as well as that of America.
What did the framers envision as the ideal economic model for the new republic? An urban model that thrived on industry, commerce, and new technology or one that used slave labor to produce agricultural staples? Or, a combination of both?

THE STRUGGLE TO RATIFY THE CONSTITUTION

2.5 Outline the arguments for and against ratification of the Constitution.

Congress had instructed the delegates to the convention to propose changes to the Articles of Confederation. Under the provisions of the Articles of Confederation, such alterations would have required the unanimous consent of the thirteen states. To follow such a course would have meant instant rejection of the new constitution, because Rhode Island, never friendly to the deliberations in Philadelphia, surely would have voted against it, and one or two additional states may well have joined Rhode Island. Acting boldly, the framers decided that ratification would be based on guidelines specified in Article VII of the unratified document they had just written, namely, approval by nine states meeting in special constitutional conventions. Congress agreed to this procedure, voting on September 28, 1787, to transmit the Constitution to the states for their consideration.

The battle over ratification was heated, and the outcome was far from certain. That the Constitution eventually carried the day may be partly attributed to the fact that the **Federalists** (those who supported the Constitution) did a better job of making their case than did the **Anti-Federalists** (those who opposed the Constitution). Their intellectual advantages were nowhere more obvious than in the eighty-five articles written for New York newspapers by Alexander Hamilton, James Madison, and John Jay (under the common pen name "Publius") in defense of the Constitution. Later collected and published as the Federalist Papers (which Thomas Jefferson judged to be "the best commentary on the principles of government which ever was written"),[34] these articles strongly influenced the debate over ratification and remain among the most impressive commentaries ever written about the U.S. Constitution.

Anti-Federalist opposition to the Constitution was based on fear of centralized power and concern about the absence of a bill of rights.[35] Although the Federalists firmly believed that a bill of rights was unnecessary because of the protection of individual rights in existing state constitutions and the many safeguards against tyranny in the federal Constitution, they promised to add one during the first session of Congress. Without this promise, ratification would probably not have happened. (The Federalists kept their word. The 1st Congress passed a bill of rights in the form of ten amendments to the Constitution (see Table 2.3), and the amendments were eventually ratified by the required number of states by 1791.)

Federalists
Proponents of the Constitution during the ratification fight; later, also the political party of Hamilton, Washington, and Adams.

Anti-Federalists
Opponents of the Constitution during the fight over ratification; the political orientation of people like Patrick Henry.

TABLE 2.3   THE BILL OF RIGHTS

Amendment	Freedoms, Rights, Protections, Guarantees
Amendment I	Freedom of religion, speech, press, and assembly
Amendment II	The right to bear arms
Amendment III	Prohibition against quartering of troops in private homes
Amendment IV	Prohibition against unreasonable searches and seizures
Amendment V	Rights guaranteed to the accused: requirement for grand jury indictment; protections against double jeopardy and self-incrimination; guarantee of due process
Amendment VI	Right to a speedy and public trial before an impartial jury, to cross-examine witnesses, and to have counsel
Amendment VII	Right to a trial by jury in civil suits
Amendment VIII	Prohibition against excessive bail and fines and against cruel and unusual punishment
Amendment IX	Traditional rights not listed in the Constitution are retained by the people
Amendment X	Powers not denied to them by the Constitution or given solely to the national government are retained by the states or the people

© Edward S. Greenberg

Even with the promise of a Bill of Rights, ratification of the Constitution was a close call. Most of the small states quickly approved it, attracted by the formula of equal representation in the Senate, and the Federalists orchestrated a victory in Pennsylvania before the Anti-Federalists realized what had happened. After that, ratification became a struggle. Rhode Island voted no. North Carolina abstained because of the absence of a bill of rights and did not vote its approval until 1790. In the largest and most important states, the vote was exceedingly close. Massachusetts approved

JAMES MADISON, *PUBLIUS*

During the fight to ratify the Constitution, James Madison helped publish a series of essays with the purpose of persuading the voters of New York to endorse the Constitution.

by a vote of 187–168; Virginia, by 89–79; and New York, by 30–27. The struggle was especially intense in Virginia, where prominent, articulate, and influential men were involved on both sides of the ratification decision. The Federalists could call on George Washington, James Madison, John Marshall, and Edmund Randolph. The Anti-Federalists countered with George Mason, Richard Henry Lee, and Patrick Henry. Patrick Henry was particularly passionate, saying that the Constitution "squints towards monarchy." Although New Hampshire technically put the Constitution over the top, being the ninth state to vote approval, proponents of ratification did not rest easily until Virginia and New York, the two most populous states, approved it.

THE CHANGING CONSTITUTION, DEMOCRACY, AND AMERICAN POLITICS

2.6 Describe the processes by which the Constitution can be altered.

The Constitution is the basic rulebook for the game of American politics. Constitutional rules apportion power and responsibility among governmental branches, define the fundamental nature of the relationships among governmental institutions, specify how individuals are to be selected for office, and tell how the rules themselves may be changed. Every aspiring politician who wants to attain office, every citizen who wants to influence what government does, and every group that wants to advance its interests in the political arena must know the rules and how to use them to their best advantage. Because the Constitution has this character, we understand it to be a fundamental *structural* factor influencing all of American political life. It is why we have placed it in the structural base of our pyramid-shaped analytical model (see Figure 1.1).

Like all rules, however, constitutional rules can and do change over time, which is why we sometimes speak of the "living Constitution." Constitutional changes come about in three specific ways: (1) formal amendment, (2) judicial interpretation, and (3) enduring political practices.

Changing the Constitution Through Formal Amendment

The Constitution may be formally amended by use of the procedures outlined in Article V (again, refer to Figure 2.4). This method has resulted in the addition of twenty-seven amendments since the founding, the first ten of which (the Bill of Rights) were added within three years of ratification. That only seventeen more amendments have been added since 1791 suggests that this method of changing the Constitution is extremely difficult. Over the years, proponents of constitutional amendments that would guarantee equal rights for women, ban same-sex marriages, and ban the burning of the American flag have learned how difficult it is to formally amend the Constitution; none of these amendments were added, despite public opinion polls reporting majorities in favor of them. Seen in this light, the cumbersome method for formally amending the Constitution is an important barrier to democracy.[36] On the other hand, several formal amendments have played an important role in expanding democracy in the United States by ending slavery; extending voting rights to African Americans, women, and young people between the ages of 18 and 20; and making the selection of senators the business of voters, not state legislatures.

Changing the Constitution Through Judicial Review

The Constitution is also changed by decisions and interpretations of the U.S. Supreme Court found in the written opinions of the justices. In *Marbury v. Madison* (1803), the Court claimed the power of **judicial review**—the right to declare the actions of the other branches of government null and void if they are contrary to the Constitution— even though such a power is not specifically mentioned in the Constitution. In two more

judicial review

The power of the Supreme Court to declare actions of the other branches and levels of government unconstitutional.

The Constitution has evolved over
the years in three ways: through the
amendment process, through evolving
political practices, and through the
Supreme Court's changing interpretation of the Constitution's meaning.
Here, antiabortion protesters demonstrate in front of the Supreme Court
building on the anniversary of the
Court's 1973 *Roe v. Wade* decision to
demand a reversal of that landmark
decision.

*How does the Constitution protect both
the Supreme Court's decision and these
people's public protest of it? How likely
is it that the present Supreme Court will
listen to these and other voices and overturn* Roe?

examples, *Griswold v. Connecticut* (1965) and *Roe v. Wade* (1973), the Court supported a
claim for the existence of a fundamental right to privacy even though such a right is not
explicitly mentioned in the Constitution. Many conservatives believe that such actions
by the Supreme Court are illegitimate because they go beyond the original intentions
of the framers or cannot be justified in the written provisions of the Constitution. Many
others disagree, believing that the Court has and must interpret the Constitution in light
of changing circumstances that the framers could not have envisioned.

Changing the Constitution Through Political Practices

The meaning of the Constitution also changes through changing political practices which
end up serving as precedents for political actors. Political parties, party primaries, and presidential nominating conventions are not mentioned in the Constitution, for example, but
it would be hard to think about American politics today without them. It is also fair to
say that the framers would not recognize the modern presidency, which is now a far more
important office than they envisioned, a change that has been brought about largely by the
political and military involvement of the United States in world affairs, tied to vigorous
assertion of the office's diplomatic and commander-in-chief powers by many presidents,
and the widespread demand that the president do something during economic crises. The
Constitution does not specify, for example, that the Treasury secretary, acting for the president, can force the merger of failing financial firms as was done in the last months of the
George W. Bush presidency in the depths of a recession. Nor would the framers have predicted the increasing use of **signing statements**, by which a president can alter the meaning
of a bill even while signing it into law. Nor did they envision the flood of executive orders
from Presidents Obama and Trump, many of which were issued to bypass the legislative
process in Congress. Needless to say, all three ways of changing the Constitution are politically contentious, meaning that not all Americans necessarily agree with particular changes
in the meaning of the Constitution, and sometimes they have taken to the streets, the voting
booth, and the courts to express their displeasure.

Throughout this book you will see many examples of these three forms of constitutional change that have shaped our current understanding of the meaning of the
Constitution and its many provisions. You also will learn that the third factor, changing
political practices—itself a product of social and cultural change and pressure from the
American people, as shown in our pyramid-style analytical model (Figure 1.1)—is at least
as important as amendments and judicial rulings in adjusting the Constitution to its times.[37]

signing statement
A document sometimes issued by the
president in connection with the signing
of a bill from Congress that sets out the
president's understanding of the new
law and how executive branch officials
should carry it out.

THE CONSTITUTION: HOW DEMOCRATIC?

Scarred by the failings of the Articles of Confederation, the framers endeavored to create a republic that would offer representative democracy without the threat of majority tyranny. Consequently, they wrote a number of provisions into the Constitution to control the purported excesses of democracy. These include the separation of powers into executive, legislative, and judicial branches; checks and balances to prevent any of the branches from governing on its own; federalism to fragment government powers between a national government and the states; an appointed federal judiciary with life tenure charged with, among other things, protecting private property; selection of the president by the Electoral College; election of members of the Senate by state legislatures with each state having two senators no matter the size of states; and a process for changing the Constitution that makes it exceedingly easy for small numbers of people in Congress and a very few states to block amendments favored by a majority of Americans.

Although the framers had every intention of creating a republic and of holding democracy in check, the tide of democracy has gradually transformed the original constitutional design. For example, the Seventeenth Amendment created a Senate whose members are elected directly by the people. In addition, the Supreme Court has extended civil rights protections to racial and ethnic minorities, and the presidency has become both more powerful and more attentive to majority opinion. By formal amendment, through judicial interpretations, and through changing political practices, government has been fashioned into a more responsive set of institutions that often—but not always—heed the voice of the people.

Yet despite these changes, the American system of government remains essentially "republican" in nature, with the majority finding it very difficult to prevail. Provisions of the Constitution, designed to keep the majority in check, effectively provide minorities with disproportionate power in government. Five times in our history, presidents have taken office without having won a majority of the popular vote (John Quincy Adams, 1825; Rutherford B. Hayes, 1877; Benjamin Harrison, 1889; George W. Bush, 2001; Donald Trump, 2016). And while the Seventeenth Amendment has made the election of senators more democratic, the Senate itself—which provides equal representation to all states regardless of population—remains skewed toward smaller population states, thus serving as a major barrier in the translation of what the American people want into what government does.[38] As we will see in later chapters, the ability of private and privileged groups to use the many blocking points provided by the Constitution has grown, often frustrating majority interests and demands.

"REPUBLICAN" IN NATURE

The Electoral College, whatever its virtues might be, is an important anti-democratic feature of our Constitution. Five times during our history, it has enabled a candidate to be elected president who has had fewer popular votes than his opponent. George W. Bush celebrated his Electoral College victory in the disputed 2000 presidential election with 500,000 fewer popular votes than Al Gore. In 2016, Republican Donald Trump was elected president, though he received almost 3 million fewer votes nationally than his Democratic opponent Hillary Clinton. *Why would the framers consider it desirable that a professed democracy keep the majority in check?*

REVIEW THE CHAPTER

THE AMERICAN REVOLUTION AND THE DECLARATION OF INDEPENDENCE

2.1 Assess the enduring legacies of the American Revolution and the Declaration of Independence.

The American Revolution and the Declaration of Independence helped establish the ideas of self-government and inalienable individual rights as the core of the American political ideology.

THE ARTICLES OF CONFEDERATION: THE FIRST CONSTITUTION

2.2 Describe the system of government established by our first constitution.

The first constitution joining the American states was the Articles of Confederation. Under its terms, the states were organized into a loose confederation in which the states retained full sovereignty and the central government had little power.

FACTORS LEADING TO THE CONSTITUTIONAL CONVENTION

2.3 Analyze the developments that led to the Constitutional Convention.

Defects in the Articles of Confederation, along with fears that democratic and egalitarian tendencies were beginning to spin out of control, prompted American leaders to gather in Philadelphia to amend the Articles. The delegates chose instead to formulate an entirely new constitution.

THE CONSTITUTIONAL CONVENTION AND A NEW FRAMEWORK FOR GOVERNMENT

2.4 Describe and evaluate the framework for government that the Constitutional Convention created.

The framers created a constitutional framework for republican government, including representative elections, separation of powers, checks and balances, and federalism.

The Connecticut Compromise settled the tensions between large and small states by giving states equal representation in the Senate and representation based on population in the House of Representatives. The framers condoned and protected slavery in several constitutional provisions. The framers created the legal foundations for a thriving commercial republic.

THE STRUGGLE TO RATIFY THE CONSTITUTION

2.5 Outline the arguments for and against ratification of the Constitution.

The Constitution was ratified in an extremely close vote of the states after a hard-fought struggle between the Federalists, who wanted a more centralized republicanism, and the Anti-Federalists, who wanted small-scale republicanism.

The promise by the Federalists to introduce amendments specifying the rights of Americans in the 1st Congress helped swing the vote in favor of ratification in a number of key states.

Despite its "close shave," the Constitution became very popular among the American people within only a few years of the ratification fight.

THE CHANGING CONSTITUTION, DEMOCRACY, AND AMERICAN POLITICS

2.6 Describe the processes by which the Constitution can be altered.

The Constitution changes by three processes: amendments to the document, judicial interpretations of the meaning of constitutional provisions, and the everyday political practices of Americans and their elected leaders. Because the American people continue to struggle for democracy, the Constitution has become far more democratic over the years than was originally intended by the framers.

LEARN THE TERMS

Anti-Federalists Opponents of the Constitution during the fight over ratification; the political orientation of people like Patrick Henry.

Articles of Confederation The first constitution of the United States, adopted during the last stages of the Revolutionary War, created a system of government with most power lodged in the states and little in the central government.

Bill of Rights The first ten amendments to the U.S. Constitution, concerned with the protection of basic liberties.

checks and balances The constitutional principle that each of the separate branches of government has the power to hinder the unilateral actions of the other branches as a way to restrain an overreaching government and prevent tyranny.

confederation A loose association of states or territorial units in which very little or no power is lodged in a central government.

Connecticut Compromise Also called the Great Compromise; the compromise between the New Jersey and Virginia plans formulated by the Connecticut delegates at the Constitutional Convention; called for a lower legislative house based on population size and an upper house based on equal representation of the states.

constitution The basic framework of law for a nation that prescribes how government is to be organized, how government decisions are to be made, and what powers and responsibilities government shall have.

elastic clause Article I, Section 8, of the Constitution, also called the necessary and proper clause; gives Congress the authority to make whatever laws are necessary and proper to carry out its enumerated responsibilities.

Electoral College Representatives selected in each of the states, their numbers based on each state's total number of its senators and representatives; a majority of Electoral College votes elects the president.

federalism A system in which significant governmental powers are divided between a central government and smaller territorial units, such as states.

Federalists Proponents of the Constitution during the ratification fight; later, also the political party of Hamilton, Washington, and Adams.

free enterprise An economic system characterized by competitive markets and private ownership of a society's productive assets; a form of capitalism.

judicial review The power of the Supreme Court to declare actions of the other branches and levels of government unconstitutional.

New Jersey Plan Proposal of the smaller states at the Constitutional Convention to create a government with slightly more power in a central government than under the Articles, with the states equally represented in a unicameral national legislature.

property rights The freedom to use, accumulate, and dispose of a valuable asset subject to rules established by government.

republicanism A political doctrine advocating limited government based on popular consent, protected against majority tyranny.

separation of powers The distribution of government legislative, executive, and judicial powers to separate branches of government.

signing statement A document sometimes issued by the president in connection with the signing of a bill from Congress that sets out the president's understanding of the new law and how executive branch officials should carry it out.

social contract The idea that government is the result of an agreement among people to form one, and that people have the right to create an entirely new government if the terms of the contract have been violated by the existing one.

supremacy clause The provision in Article VI of the Constitution that states that the Constitution and the laws and treaties of the United States are the supreme law of the land, taking precedence over state laws and constitutions when they are in conflict.

tyranny The abuse of the inalienable rights of citizens by government.

Virginia Plan Proposal by the large states at the Constitutional Convention to create a strong central government with power in the government apportioned to the states on the basis of population.

CHAPTER
3

California Governor Jerry Brown (D) speaks at the 2017 World Climate Conference in Bonn, Germany. Brown, a strong advocate for environmental protection, opposed President Trump's decision to leave the Paris Climate Accord and has responded by advocating for more state-level environmental regulations that help meet global climate change goals. *What are some of the challenges of having conflicting environmental policies at the state and federal levels?*

FEDERALISM: STATES AND NATION

CHAPTER OUTLINE AND LEARNING OBJECTIVES

FEDERALISM AS A SYSTEM OF GOVERNMENT

3.1 Define federalism and explain why we have it.

FEDERALISM IN THE CONSTITUTION

3.2 Explain the constitutional foundations of federalism.

THE EVOLUTION OF AMERICAN FEDERALISM

3.3 Trace the evolution of American federalism.

FISCAL FEDERALISM

3.4 Analyze how federal grants structure national and state government relations.

STRONG STATES VERSUS A STRONG NATIONAL GOVERNMENT

3.5 Evaluate the arguments for and against a strong national government.

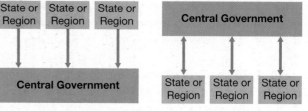

The Struggle for Democracy

A PATCHWORK OF POLICIES

The term **federalism** describes the relationship between the federal (or national) government and all the state governments. The unique system of federalism in the United States provides each state with a certain amount of autonomy. The precise amount of autonomy that states have has been the source of considerable debate since the country's founding. While this debate rarely makes headlines, it has profound implications for the laws Americans are subject to. Questions related to federalism have been central to slavery, civil rights, social policy, economic policy, and many other aspects of American life and liberty. Today, the country faces a set of questions about federalism that are impacting everything from immigration to public health to the protection of the environment.

Consider the case of marijuana. The U.S. Controlled Substances Act of 1970 makes it illegal to possess or distribute marijuana. However, in recent years public opinion on marijuana has shifted—as of October 2017, 61 percent of Americans support legalization compared to 36 percent just a decade ago—and some states have sought alternative policies. Nine states and Washington, DC, have fully legalized marijuana (in some cases via state-wide vote), and many others have legalized it for medical use. Citizens and lawmakers in these states have argued that its widespread use and medicinal effects justify legalization. Legalization advocates also say that arresting small-time marijuana users is not worth the resources, and the ability to tax the sale of marijuana creates a lucrative revenue stream for the states. Opponents of legalization argue that no public health benefit comes from increased access to drugs and that marijuana has the potential to lead to more serious drug abuse.

The states that have legalized marijuana (see Figure 3.0) are now operating in direct contradiction to federal law. During the Obama administration, these states were allowed to continue their policies so long as there was no evidence that marijuana was ending up in the hands of minors or crossing state lines. But this was a choice made by the Obama administration, and early in the Trump administration there were indications that things would change. Trump, though, has elected to continue the Obama-era approach—in part on the counsel of fellow Republican, Senator Cory Gardner, who represents Colorado where marijuana was legalized for recreational use in 2012. Colorado raised over $247 million in taxes on marijuana in 2017 alone—almost all of that money will go to help fund public education in the state.

federalism

A system in which significant governmental powers are divided between a central government and smaller territorial units, such as states.

FIGURE 3.0 MARIJUANA LEGALIZATION MAP

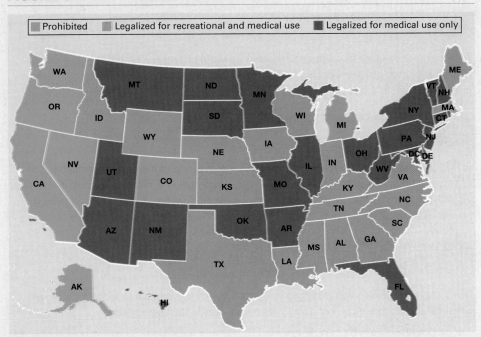

■ Prohibited ■ Legalized for recreational and medical use ■ Legalized for medical use only

Now consider the case of climate change. Since taking office in January 2017, President Trump and his administration have taken actions to reverse the environmental policy trajectory of the Obama administration. The most public of those actions was Trump's decision to withdraw the United States from the Paris Climate Accord—a 2015 agreement among 195 countries to reduce carbon emissions to combat global climate change. But the actions have gone beyond leaving the Paris Accord. According to the *New York Times*, the Trump administration has rolled back at least 25 environmental rules created during the Obama presidency with many more rollbacks in the pipeline. These overturned rules include regulations that restricted oil drilling in the Atlantic and Arctic oceans, restricted coal mining on public lands, required oil and gas companies to report their methane emissions, funded UN programs to reduce carbon emissions in developing countries, and required federal agencies to mitigate environmental impacts on new projects among many others.

As you will learn later in the book, decisions about this type of environmental policy making are generally understood to be within the authority of the president. However, states also have a range of policy tools at their disposal for combating climate change. These include funding the development of clean energy, forcing companies to increase their use of clean energy, and setting certain pollution emissions standards. Following Trump's decision to leave the Paris Accord, the governors of Washington State, New York, and California responded by announcing a "US Climate Alliance" aimed at upholding the Paris Accord plus additional reductions—they have since been joined by additional states. California, in particular, has long used its economic power (alone it has an economy roughly as big as France) to be a state-level environmental leader willing to challenge the federal government.

California officials have vowed to fight many of the Trump administration's regulatory rollbacks in court and continue to set their own ambitious environmental goals. Since 2009, California has operated under a waiver from the federal government that allows it to set its own vehicle carbon emissions standards. These standards (which require auto manufacturers to almost double the fuel efficiency of their vehicles by 2025) are substantially more aggressive than the Trump administration would prefer and, because California is such a large market, tend to impact vehicles sold nationwide. The President and his administration retain the authority to revoke that waiver if they so choose.

The patchwork of policies and the federal-state tensions that exist under federalism are on full display in both of the above examples. Where you live impacts the drug laws you are subject to, and who the president is impacts how drug laws are enforced. Likewise, different states are making different commitments to dealing with climate change, commitments that may even be at odds with national economic priorities.[1]

THINKING CRITICALLY **ABOUT THIS CHAPTER**

This complex mixture of state and national government authority and responsibilities highlighted in the chapter-opening story is an important characteristic of American federalism today and in the past.

APPLYING THE **FRAMEWORK**

In this chapter, you will learn how and why federalism is one of the most important *structural factors* that affect American politics and government and shape public policy. You will learn how federalism influences our entire system, from the divisions in Congress to presidential decisions. You will also learn how federalism itself has changed over time.

USING THE **DEMOCRACY STANDARD**

Using the evaluative tools introduced in Chapter 1, you will be able to judge for yourself whether federalism enriches or diminishes democracy in the United States.

FEDERALISM AS A SYSTEM OF GOVERNMENT

3.1 Define federalism and explain why we have it.

The United States has lots of governments. We not only have a federal (or national) government, but also governments in each of the fifty states and in each of thousands of smaller governmental units such as counties, cities, towns, and school districts. Each level of government has its own governing system. Just as the national government has a legislature (Congress), an executive (the President), a bureaucracy, and a court system so too does each state have its own legislature (sometimes called the state assembly), bureaucracy, executive (governor), and court system responsible for making, executing, and interpreting state laws.

State governments play a particularly important role in the American political system owing to their prominent place in the Constitution—that role is discussed throughout this chapter. Local governments are legal creations of state governments: They can be created, changed, or abolished by state legislatures. Despite being subsidiary to their respective state government, local governments also play a critical role: They are frequently responsible for (or involved with) providing services essential to our daily lives—services such as roads, trash collection, parks, schools, and policing.

All these levels of government are organized and related to one another in a particular way and together form what is known as a "federal system." The federal system is part of the basic structure of U.S. government, deeply rooted in our Constitution and history. As a *structural* part of our analytical framework introduced in Chapter 1, you should understand the federal system as helping to form the foundation on which all American policy actions are built.

Federalism Defined

Federalism is a system under which significant government powers are divided between the central government and smaller units of government, such as states or provinces. Neither one completely controls the other; each has some room for independent action. A federal system can be contrasted with two other types of government: a confederation and a unitary government. In a **confederation**, the constituent states get together for certain common purposes but retain ultimate individual authority and can veto major central governmental actions. The United Nations and the American government under the Articles of Confederation are examples of confederations. In a **unitary system**, the central government has all the power and can change its constituent units or tell them what to do. China, Japan, Turkey, Iran, and France have unitary governments, as do a substantial majority of nations around the world. These three different types of governmental systems are contrasted in Figure 3.1.

confederation

A loose association of states or territorial units in which very little power or no power at all is lodged in a central government.

unitary system

A system in which a central government has complete power over its constituent units or states.

Comparing American Federalism

Some of the elements of federalism go back in history at least as far as the Union of Utrecht in the Netherlands in 1579, but federalism as it exists today is largely an American invention.[2] American federalism emerged from the way in which the states declared independence from Britain—first becoming, in effect, separate countries, then joining to form a confederation, and then uniting as a single nation. Recall that the framers of the Constitution turned to federalism as a middle-ground solution between a confederation form of government (which was deemed a failed model based on their experience under the Articles of Confederation) and a unitary form of government (which, owing to their disparate interests and time as colonies, a majority of states found unacceptable). Federalism was consistent with the 18th-century republicanism of the framers in that it fragmented government power.

FIGURE 3.1 TYPES OF POLITICAL SYSTEMS

A majority of countries have unitary systems (A), in which the central government controls state and regional governments. The United States, however, has a federal system (C), in which the central government has power on some issues, the states have power on other issues, and the central and state governments share power on yet others. In a confederation (B), the central institutions have only a loose coordinating role, with real governing power residing in the constituent states or units.

A. UNITARY SYSTEM

The central government controls all subunit governments (e.g., states, regions, localities)

Examples: Japan, France

B. CONFEDERAL SYSTEM

The central government exercises no control over subunit governments and acts at the sufferance of the subunits.

Examples: European Union, United Nations, the United States under the Articles of Confederation

C. FEDERAL SYSTEM

The central government and subunit governments share power.

Examples: United States, Mexico, India, Canada

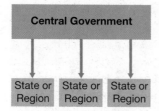

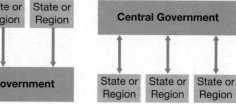

Federalism tends to be found in nations that are large in territory and in which the various geographical regions are fairly distinctive from one another in terms of religion, ethnicity, language, and forms of economic activity. Such is the case with the United States. From the early days of the republic, the slave-holding and agriculture-oriented South was quite distinct from the mercantile Northeast, and many important social, economic, and political differences persist today. Illinois is not Louisiana; the farmers of Iowa differ from defense and tech workers in California. States today also vary in their approaches to public policy, their racial and ethnic composition, and their political cultures. In *Federalist* No. 10, Madison argued that this size and diversity made federalism especially appropriate for the United States.

While the American system of federalism was truly exceptional at the founding, other large and diverse countries have adopted federalism in the years since. Canada also has a federal system. In Canada, the farmers of the central plains are not much like the fishers of Nova Scotia, and the French-speaking (and primarily Catholic) residents of Quebec differ markedly from the mostly English-speaking Protestants of the rest of the country. Spain's federal system has helped the country to deal with deep divisions along ethnic and language lines (as in the distinctive Basque and Catalán regions).[3] Other important federal systems include such large and richly diverse countries as India, Pakistan, Russia, and Brazil. In all of these countries, the central government remains the most powerful governing force, but federalism gives diverse and geographically concentrated groups the degree of local autonomy they want by providing them with the authority to pursue some of their own policies.

Federalist **No. 10**

One of a series on essays written by James Madison (others were written by Alexander Hamilton and John Jay), urging the people of New York to support ratification of the Constitution. In No. 10, Madison defended republican government for large states with heterogeneous populations and expressed his fear of majorities and his abhorrence of political parties.

FEDERALISM IN THE CONSTITUTION

3.2 Explain the constitutional foundations of federalism.

Federalism is embodied in the U.S. Constitution in three main ways: (1) the powers expressly given to the national government, (2) the powers expressly given to the states, and (3) the role given to states in shaping and choosing national officials and in

TABLE 3.1   CONSTITUTIONAL UNDERPINNINGS OF FEDERALISM

Federalism Issue	Constitutional Provision	Meaning
The Powers of the Federal Government		
Supremacy of the national government	Article VI (supremacy clause)	Federal laws and the Constitution take precedence over state laws and state constitutions.
Enumerated powers of the national government	Article I, Section 8	Powers of the federal government are laid out specifically in the Constitution.
Limitations on the powers of the national government	Article I, Section 9 Article IV, Section 3 Eleventh Amendment	Strict limitations on the power of the federal government are laid out specifically in the Constitution (e.g., no suspension of habeas corpus).
The Powers of the States		
Original limitations on the powers of the states	Article I, Section 10	The Constitution places strict limitations on the power of states in particular areas of activity (e.g., states can't coin money).
Amended limitations on the powers of the states	Thirteenth through Fifteenth Amendments (Civil War Amendments)	States are compelled to uphold civil liberties and civil rights of people living within their borders.
Reservation of powers to the states	Tenth Amendment	Powers not specifically spelled out are reserved to the states or to the people (e.g., police powers).
Ratification of the Constitution	Article VII	The role of states in national affairs is clearly laid out. Rules for voting and electing representatives, senators, and the president are defined so that state governments play a part.
Amendment of the Constitution	Article V	
Election of congressional representatives	Article I, Sections 2 and 4	
Election of senators	Article I, Section 3, and Seventeenth Amendment	
Election of president	Article II, Section 1 (however, see Twelfth Amendment)	
Relations Among the States		
Full faith and credit among states	Article IV, Section 1 (full faith and credit clause)	Constitutional rules ensure that states must respect each other's legal actions and judgments (e.g., states can't reopen cases closed in other states).
The rights of state citizens	Article IV, Section 2 (privileges and immunities clause)	Citizens from other states have the same rights and privileges as a state's own citizens (e.g., evading financial obligations).

amending the Constitution. For a summary of the provisions in the Constitution that address federalism issues, see Table 3.1.

Federal, State, and Concurrent Powers

Although the Constitution makes the central government supreme in certain matters, it also makes clear that state governments have independent powers. The **supremacy clause** in Article VI states that the Constitution, laws, and treaties of the United States shall be the "supreme law of the land." According to a doctrine known as **preemption**, states cannot act in certain matters when the national government has authority.[4] However, Article I, Section 8, enumerates what kinds of laws Congress has the power to pass, and the Tenth Amendment declares that the powers not delegated to the central government by the Constitution or prohibited by the Constitution to the states are *"reserved to the states* [emphasis added] respectively, or to the people." This provision is known as the **reservation clause**.

The Constitution specifically enumerates the national (federal) government's powers, including the authority to levy taxes, regulate interstate commerce, establish post offices, declare war, and to make laws "necessary and proper" for carrying out those powers. The Constitution then declares that all other legitimate government functions may be performed by the states, except for a few things, such as coining money or conducting foreign policy (which are forbidden by Article I, Section 10). This leaves a great deal in the hands of state governments, including licensing law-yers, doctors, and drivers; regulating businesses within their boundaries; chartering

supremacy clause

The provision in Article VI of the Constitution states that the Constitution and the laws and treaties of the United States are the supreme law of the land, taking precedence over state laws and constitutions when they are in conflict.

preemption

Exclusion of the states from actions that might interfere with federal authority or statutes.

reservation clause

Part of the Tenth Amendment to the Constitution that says those powers not given to the federal government and not prohibited to the states by the Constitution are reserved for the states and the people.

FIGURE 3.2 FEDERAL, STATE, AND CONCURRENT POWERS

The Constitution makes the federal government supreme in certain matters and grants independent powers to the states, but the federal government and the states also share powers. Powers that both the federal government and the states hold are called concurrent powers.

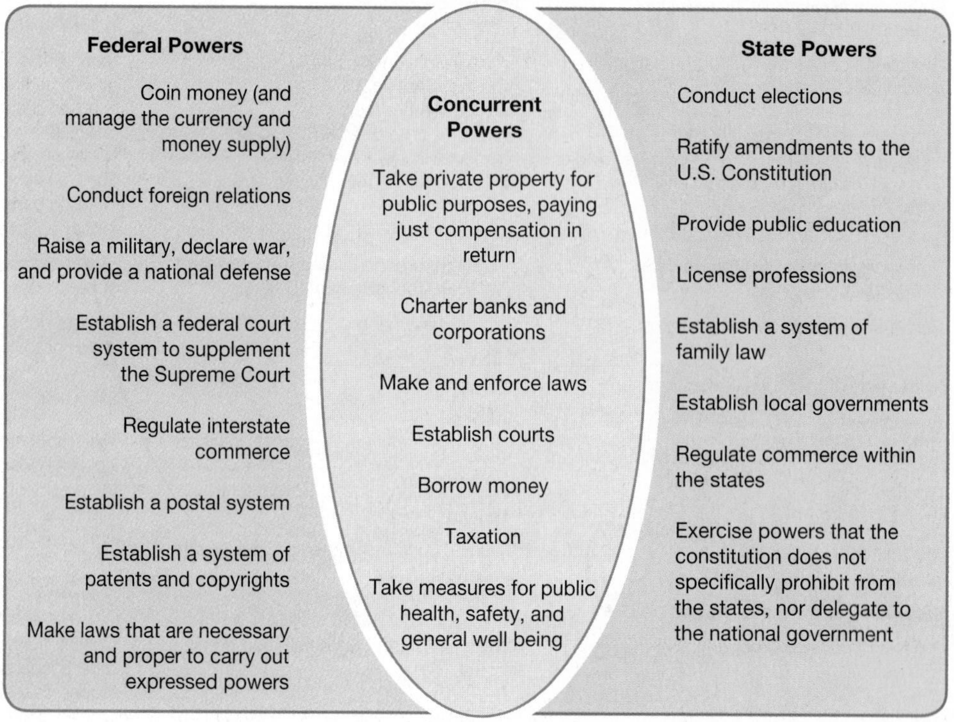

Federal Powers

Coin money (and manage the currency and money supply)

Conduct foreign relations

Raise a military, declare war, and provide a national defense

Establish a federal court system to supplement the Supreme Court

Regulate interstate commerce

Establish a postal system

Establish a system of patents and copyrights

Make laws that are necessary and proper to carry out expressed powers

Concurrent Powers

Take private property for public purposes, paying just compensation in return

Charter banks and corporations

Make and enforce laws

Establish courts

Borrow money

Taxation

Take measures for public health, safety, and general well being

State Powers

Conduct elections

Ratify amendments to the U.S. Constitution

Provide public education

License professions

Establish a system of family law

Establish local governments

Regulate commerce within the states

Exercise powers that the constitution does not specifically prohibit from the states, nor delegate to the national government

---

police powers

Powers of a government to protect the health, safety, and general well-being of its people.

concurrent powers

Powers under the Constitution that are shared by the federal government and the states.

banks and corporations; providing a system of family law; providing a system of public education; and assuming the responsibility for building roads and highways, and registering cars. Under terms of the reservation clause, states exercise what are called their **police powers** to protect the health, safety, and general well-being of people living in their states. Police powers have allowed states to make decisions independent of the federal government and other states on matters such as stem-cell research, the death penalty, emissions of greenhouse gases, the regulation of abortion services, and financial regulations.

Powers that both the federal and state governments hold are called **concurrent powers**. Some of these concurrent powers include the power to levy taxes, to borrow money for public purposes, and to spend money for the protection and well-being of their populations. With both independent national and state powers and responsibilities, as well as concurrent powers and responsibilities, the Constitution is not crystal clear about the exact shape of federalism, leaving ample room for the meaning of federalism to change with the times, the preferences of the American people, and the calculations of political leaders. Figure 3.2 shows which powers and responsibilities go with which level of government.

The Roles of States in the National Government

Various provisions in the Constitution assign a special position for the states in the national government. Article VII declares that the Constitution was "done in Convention by the unanimous consent of the *states* present" (emphasis added) and stipulates that the Constitution would go into effect, not when a majority of all Americans voted for it, but when the conventions of nine *states* ratified it. Article V similarly addresses the distinct role of states in amending the Constitution. Only when three-quarters of states ratify (via state convention or state legislature) an amendment is the Constitution duly amended. Article IV, Section 3 makes clear that no states can be combined or divided into new states without the consent of the state legislatures concerned.

The Constitution also provides special roles for the states in the selection of national officials. The states decide who can vote for members of the U.S. House of Representatives (Article I, Section 2) and who draws the boundaries of House districts. Each state is given two senators (Article V) who were, until 1913, to be chosen by state legislatures rather than by the voters until altered by the Seventeenth Amendment, which puts the election of senators in the hands of the people. States also play a key part in the complicated Electoral College system of choosing a president in which each state has votes equal to the number of its senators and representatives combined, with the president elected by a majority of electoral votes, not by a majority of popular votes (Article II, Section 1).

Relations Among the States

The Constitution also regulates relations among the states. These state-to-state relations are sometimes called **horizontal federalism**. Article IV of the Constitution is particularly important in regard to relations among states (refer again to Table 3.1). For example, each state is required to give "full faith and credit" to the public acts, records, and judicial proceedings of every other state. This means that private contractual or financial agreements among people or companies in one state are valid in all the other states and that civil judgments by the courts of one state must be recognized by the others. Because of the **full faith and credit clause**, people in one state cannot evade financial obligations—for example, credit card debts and alimony or child support payments—by moving to another state.

horizontal federalism
Term used to refer to relationships among the states.

full faith and credit clause
The provision in Article IV, Section 1 of the Constitution which provides that states must respect the public acts, laws, and judicial rulings of other states.

Prior to the Supreme Court declaring same-sex marriage legal nationwide, in *Obergefell v. Hodges* (2015), same-sex marriage was an example of a policy that varied by state with significant consequences. Some states had enacted laws legalizing it, others had been forced into accepting it by way of court rulings, and still others had banned it. During the pre-*Obergefell* period, questions persisted about whether same-sex marriages should be legally recognized in states without same-sex marriage and whether same-sex partners would be eligible for federal benefits entitled to spouses. Worried about the contestability of these questions, Congress passed the Defense of Marriage Act (DOMA) in 1996 denying federal benefits (e.g., Social Security) to spouses in same-sex marriages and allowing states to decide whether to recognize their marriages. Later, in *U.S. v. Windsor* (2013), the Supreme Court struck down the portion of DOMA that denied federal benefits to those in same-sex marriages. In its *Obergefell* decision, which affirms that same-sex marriage is a constitutional right, the Supreme Court ruled that it was not even up to states to make a determination about whether same-sex couples could marry.[5] As a result, the debate about whether states must accept other states' same-sex marriages based on the Constitution's "full faith and credit" clause was rendered moot.

Article IV also specifies that the citizens of each state are entitled to all the "privileges and immunities" of the citizens in the several states. That means that whatever citizenship rights a person has in one state apply in the other states as well. For example, out-of-state residents have the same access to state courts as in-state residents as well as an equal right to own property and to be protected by the police. However, the Supreme Court has never clearly defined the meaning of "privileges and immunities" nor has it been entirely consistent in applying them in practice.

Agreements among a group of states to solve mutual problems, called **interstate compacts**, require the consent of Congress. The framers inserted this provision (Article I,

interstate compacts
Agreements among states to cooperate on solving mutual problems; requires approval by Congress.

THE GEORGE WASHINGTON BRIDGE, NEW YORK CITY

The George Washington Bridge spans the Hudson River and connects New York City with New Jersey. With over 106 million cars crossing it every year, it is among the world's busiest bridges. It is owned and operated by the Port Authority of New York and New Jersey—a special government, created via an interstate compact, which manages major transportation infrastructure throughout the New York Metropolitan Area, including bridges, tunnels, airports, bus stations, and trains.

What is the benefit of states creating interstate compacts to manage infrastructure?

Section 10) into the Constitution as a way to prevent the emergence of coalitions of states that might threaten federal authority or the union itself. Interstate compacts in force today cover a wide range of cooperative state activities. For example, New York and New Jersey entered into and Congress approved a compact to establish the Port Authority of New York & New Jersey. Similarly, seven Western states formed the Colorado River Compact in 1922 to allocate water rights to the states along the river's basin. Other compacts among states include agreements to cooperate on pollution control, crime prevention, regional transportation needs, and disaster planning.

THE EVOLUTION OF AMERICAN FEDERALISM

3.3   Trace the evolution of American federalism.

From the very beginnings of the United States, two political philosophies have contended with one another over the nature of American federalism and the role of the central government. Tension between these two philosophies, which are generally referred to as the nationalist position and the states' rights position, has been and remains a critical aspect of American democracy. The United States initially adhered largely to a states' rights position but it has transitioned to a more nationalist approach.

THE NATIONALIST POSITION   Proponents of the **nationalist position** believe that the Constitution represents a compact among the states that creates a single national community of the people and their government. They point to the words in the preamble and to the clear expression of the purposes for which the *people* formed a new government:

> We the People of the United States, in Order to form a more perfect Union, establish Justice, ensure domestic Tranquility, provide for the common defense, promote the general Welfare, and secure the Blessings of Liberty to ourselves and our Posterity, do ordain and establish this Constitution for the United States of America.

The nationalist position also embraces the provisions in the Constitution that endow the central government with expansive responsibilities, including the commerce clause, the supremacy clause, and the **necessary and proper clause** (also

nationalist position

The view of American federalism that holds that the Constitution created a system in which the national government is supreme, relative to the states, and that it granted government a broad range of powers and responsibilities.

necessary and proper clause

Article I, Section 8, of the Constitution; also known as the *elastic clause*; gives Congress the authority to make whatever laws are necessary and proper to carry out its enumerated powers and the responsibilities mentioned in the Constitution's preamble.

known as the elastic clause). Proponents of the nationalist position, such as Alexander Hamilton, Chief Justice John Marshall, Abraham Lincoln, Woodrow Wilson, Teddy Roosevelt, and Franklin Roosevelt, advocated for an active national government with the capacity and the will to tackle whatever problems might emerge to threaten the peace and prosperity of the United States or the general welfare of its people.[6]

THE STATES' RIGHTS POSITION Proponents of the **states' rights position** argue that the Constitution was framed as a compact among the states, with the states and the national government as coequal. Proponents of states' rights note, for instance, that the Constitution was written by representatives of the states, that it was ratified by the states and not by a vote of the public, and that the process for amending the Constitution requires the affirmative votes of three-fourths of the states, not three-fourths of the people. They also point to the Tenth Amendment's reservation clause, which stipulates that powers not given to the national government nor denied to the states reside in the states and in the people.[7]

Proponents of the states' rights position have argued that the Constitution created a form of government in which the national government is strictly limited in size and responsibility and in which states retain broad autonomy in the conduct of their own affairs. Popular among states' rights proponents is the concept of **dual federalism**, which suggests that each level of government is sovereign in its own sphere. Thomas Jefferson, John C. Calhoun, Southern secessionists, the Southern resistors to the civil rights movement, and members of today's House Freedom Caucus are associated with this view of American federalism. Despite the success of the nationalist position (discussed in more depth below), the states' rights view has always been and remains a vital position from which to oppose power concentrated in Washington.

Traditionally, conservatives in the United States have tended to support states' rights, while liberals have been more supportive of a strong national government. But the reality is that federalism is a political issue just like any other and people aim to leverage it to achieve their desired policy goals. Liberals used federal power over the states to help achieve civil rights and national environmental regulation in the 1960s and 1970s. In the Trump era, liberals are trying to leverage state's rights arguments to pursue more aggressive climate change policies and protect undocumented immigrants. Likewise, conservatives have long fought for states' rights on education and social policy but in the post-9/11 era champion federal power on many national security and immigration issues.

The Ascendant Power of the National Government

It took a long time after the adoption of the Constitution for the present federal system to emerge. Ebbs and flows in the nature of the relationship between the states and the national government and in the relative power of the states and the national government have been present since the founding.[8] However, economic crises, national security needs, and the Supreme Court's support for national policies eventually led to the national government becoming the more dominant governmental power.[9]

ECONOMIC CRISES LEAD TO NATIONAL POWER One reason the national government has established primacy is that economic crises put pressure on the federal government to do something to fix the national economy. The Great Depression in the 1930s is the primary example, but even today, most expect the president, Congress, and the Federal Reserve Bank to manage national economic affairs—something the states cannot do for themselves. More recently, most Americans expected the national government to do something to solve the financial crisis, Great Recession, and jobless recovery of 2008–2012. Presidents George W. Bush and Barack Obama responded by

states' rights position

The view of American federalism that holds that the Constitution created a system of dual sovereignty in which the national government and the state governments are sovereign in their own spheres.

dual federalism

A system of federalism in which state and national powers are neatly divided between the national and state governments. Most powers of the national government are not shared with the states, and most powers of the states are not shared with the national government.

CONGRESSIONAL OVERSIGHT HEARINGS ON TARP BAILOUT

Treasury Secretary Timothy Geithner (right), called to testify in front of the TARP Congressional Oversight Panel (left), played an important role in managing the national response to the financial crisis. The Troubled Asset Relief Program (TARP), created under the Bush administration and continued under Obama, was established to ensure that major financial institutions did not collapse during the Great Recession. Before her election to the Senate in 2012, Elizabeth Warren (left) served as chair of the TARP Congressional Oversight Panel.

What role should the federal government play in ensuring that major banks remain in business during difficult economic times?

using federal dollars to bail out troubled banks and create government programs to boost economic growth.

NATIONAL SECURITY DEMANDS LEAD TO NATIONAL POWER   A second reason that the national government has, over time, increased its authority over states is that preparing for war, waging war, and ensuring national security spur national-level actions. Only the national government can raise an army, generate sufficient revenues to pay for military campaigns, engage in intelligence collection, and coordinate the resources of the nation to make sustained war possible. It is no accident, then, that each of our major wars has served to enhance the power of government in Washington.

SUPREME COURT SUPPORT LEADS TO NATIONAL POWER   A third reason for the ascension of federal power is that the Supreme Court has tended to support the federal government's efforts to solve complex national problems. Over the course of the country's history, a number of problems emerged that most political leaders and the public believed could be solved more effectively by the national government rather than by fifty separate state governments. Some of these problems included:

* Anti-competitive practices of corporations
* Unsafe foods, drugs, and consumer products
* Persistent poverty
* Air and water pollution
* Denial of civil rights

For much of American history, these problems were not understood to be the domain of the national government. In the late 19th century, the U.S. Supreme Court resisted the growth in federal power to regulate business. In 1895, for example, the Court ruled that the Sherman Antitrust Act could not forbid monopolies in manufacturing, since manufacturing affected interstate commerce only "indirectly." In 1918, the Court struck down as unconstitutional a national law regulating child labor. During the 1930s, the Court declared unconstitutional such important New Deal measures as the National Recovery Act and the Agricultural Adjustment Act.[10]

The balance began to shift in 1937, when the Court became a centralizing force, upholding essential elements of the New Deal, including the Social Security Act (which created Social Security) and the National Labor Relations Act. In *Wickard v. Filburn* (1942), the Court said that Congress has very broad powers under the commerce clause to regulate the economic activities of states, even if such activities are only indirectly related to interstate commerce. Since that time, almost all acts of Congress to make nationwide policy changes—such as making federal highway construction grants to states contingent on states raising their drinking age to 21—have been upheld by the Supreme Court or gone unchallenged.

Federalism Before the Civil War

In the late 1790s, when John Adams was president, Thomas Jefferson's party, the Democratic Republicans, deeply resented the Alien and Sedition Acts, which the Federalists used to punish political dissent. In response, Jefferson and Madison secretly authored the Virginia and Kentucky Resolutions, which declared that the states did not have to obey unconstitutional national laws and left it to the states to decide what was unconstitutional. In this case, the Democratic Republicans, representing the more agricultural South, were advocating states' rights and the principle of dual federalism against a national government run by the more merchant-oriented Federalists of the Northeast. About a decade later, however, the merchants of New England used the Southerners' own arguments to oppose President Madison's War of 1812 against Britain, which they felt interfered with their trade. Neither of these efforts at **nullification** prevailed.

In the early years of the United States, one crucial question about federalism concerned who, if anyone, would enforce the supremacy clause. Who would make sure that federal laws and the Constitution were actually the "supreme law of the land"? The U.S. Supreme Court gradually and haltingly settled this question. Only after the strong-willed and subtle John Marshall became chief justice and, in 1803, established the Supreme Court's authority to declare national laws unconstitutional (called "judicial review"; discussed in detail in Chapter 14) did the Supreme Court turn to the question of national power relative to the states. In *Fletcher v. Peck* (1810), it established the power of judicial review over states: the ability to hold a state law unconstitutional under the U.S. Constitution. Chief Justice Marshall cleverly avoided explicit discussion of the Court's power of judicial review over state laws. He simply took it for granted and used it.[11]

The Supreme Court also provided crucial legal justification for the expansion of federal power in the historic case of *McCulloch v. Maryland* (1819), which affirmed the supremacy clause and asserted that Congress had broad powers under the "necessary and proper" clause. *McCulloch* involved action by the state of Maryland to impose a tax on a federal institution, the Bank of the United States. The state of Maryland argued that the creation of the bank had been unconstitutional, exceeding the powers of Congress, and that, in any case, states could tax whatever they wanted within their own borders. But Chief Justice Marshall upheld the constitutionality of the bank's charter and its immunity from state taxation and, in the process, made a major statement justifying extensive national authority.[12] In his majority opinion, Marshall declared that the Constitution emanated from the sovereign people who had made their national government supreme to all rivals within the sphere of its powers, and those powers must be construed generously if they were to be sufficient for the "various crises" of the age to come. Congress, declared Marshall, had the power to charter the bank under Article I, Section 8, which authorized Congress to make all laws "necessary and proper" for carrying into execution its named powers. Moreover, Maryland's tax was invalid because "the power to tax involves the power to destroy," which would defeat the national government's supremacy. Justice Marshall's broad reading of the necessary and proper clause laid the foundation for an expansion of what the national government could do in the years ahead. He made it clear that states would not be allowed

nullification

An attempt by states to declare national laws or actions null and void.

OUR CIVIL WAR
Confederate General Robert E. Lee (front left) surrenders to Union General Ulysses S. Grant (right), bringing an end to the Civil War in 1865. The Civil War settled an important principle of American federalism: The nation is indissoluble and no state or group of states can decide on its own to withdraw from it.

Why is this principle of an indissoluble nation, established over 150 years ago, still essential for understanding federalism in the United States?

Civil War Amendments
The Thirteenth, Fourteenth, and Fifteenth Amendments to the Constitution, adopted immediately after the Civil War, each of which represented the imposition of a national claim over that of the states.

due process clause
The section of the Fourteenth Amendment that prohibits states from depriving anyone of life, liberty, or property "without due process of law," a guarantee against arbitrary government action.

to interfere. (See Figure 3.3 for a timeline of critical turning points that contributed to the rise in power of the national government relative to the states.)

Expansion of National Power Following the Civil War

The Civil War profoundly affected the relationship between the states and the national government. First, the unconditional Southern surrender decisively established that the Union was indissoluble; states could not withdraw or secede.

Second, passage of the **Civil War Amendments** resulted in constitutional changes that subordinated the states to certain new national standards, enforced by the central government. For example, the Thirteenth Amendment abolished slavery and the Fifteenth gave former male slaves and their descendants a constitutional right to vote. (This right was enforced by the national government for a short time after the Civil War; it was then widely ignored until passage of the 1965 Voting Rights Act.)

Most importantly, the Fourteenth Amendment (1868) included broad language limiting state power in a number of areas: it declared that no state shall "deprive any person of life, liberty, or property, without due process of law, nor deny to any person within its jurisdiction the equal protection of the laws." The **due process clause**

FIGURE 3.3 TIMELINE: LANDMARKS IN THE HISTORY OF U.S. FEDERALISM

Over the course of American history, the power of the national government over the states has slowly increased. This timeline documents many of the major court cases, laws, crises, and events in the history of federalism that contributed to this transition.

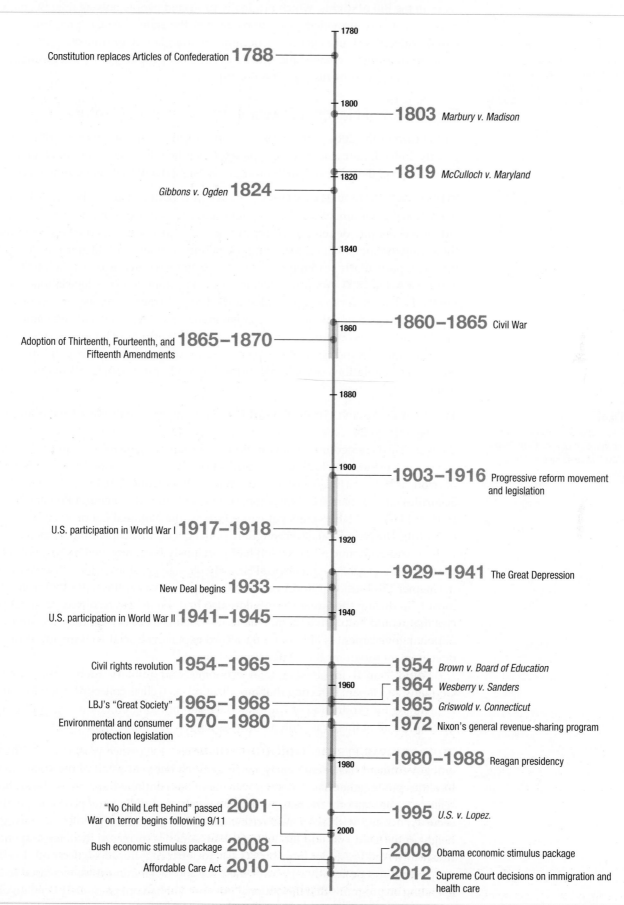

Constitution replaces Articles of Confederation **1788**

— 1780

— 1800

1803 *Marbury v. Madison*

— 1820

1819 *McCulloch v. Maryland*

Gibbons v. Ogden **1824**

— 1840

1860–1865 Civil War

— 1860

Adoption of Thirteenth, Fourteenth, and **1865–1870** Fifteenth Amendments

— 1880

— 1900

1903–1916 Progressive reform movement and legislation

U.S. participation in World War I **1917–1918**

— 1920

1929–1941 The Great Depression

New Deal begins **1933**

U.S. participation in World War II **1941–1945**

— 1940

Civil rights revolution **1954–1965**

1954 *Brown v. Board of Education*

— 1960

1964 *Wesberry v. Sanders*

LBJ's "Great Society" **1965–1968**

1965 *Griswold v. Connecticut*

Environmental and consumer **1970–1980** protection legislation

1972 Nixon's general revenue-sharing program

1980–1988 Reagan presidency

— 1980

"No Child Left Behind" passed **2001** War on terror begins following 9/11

1995 *U.S. v. Lopez.*

— 2000

Bush economic stimulus package **2008**

2009 Obama economic stimulus package

Affordable Care Act **2010**

2012 Supreme Court decisions on immigration and health care

equal protection clause

The section of the Fourteenth Amendment that provides for equal treatment by government of people residing within the United States and each of its states.

eventually became the vehicle by which the Supreme Court ruled that many civil liberties in the Bill of Rights, which originally protected people only against the national government, also provided protections against the states (see Chapter 15). And the **equal protection clause** eventually became the foundation for protecting the rights of African Americans, women, and other categories of people against discrimination by state or local governments (see Chapter 16).

Expansion of National Power in the Twentieth Century

At the turn of the 20th century, the activities of the national government expanded greatly. Indeed, national powers expanded so much that they now touch on almost every aspect of daily life and are thoroughly entangled with state government activities.

THE TURN OF THE 20TH CENTURY AND WORLD WAR I   During the late 19th century, the national government was increasingly active in administering western lands, subsidizing economic development (granting railroads enormous tracts of land along their transcontinental lines, for example), helping farmers, and beginning to regulate business, particularly through the Interstate Commerce Act of 1887 and the Sherman Antitrust Act of 1890. Woodrow Wilson's New Freedom domestic legislation—including the Federal Reserve Act of 1913 and the Federal Trade Commission Act of 1914—spurred even greater national government involvement in social and economic issues, as did the great economic and military effort of World War I. During that war, for example, the War Industries Board engaged in a form of economic planning whose orders and regulations covered a substantial number of the nation's manufacturing firms.

New Deal

The social and economic programs of the administration of President Franklin D. Roosevelt in response to the Great Depression.

THE NEW DEAL AND WORLD WAR II   Franklin Roosevelt's **New Deal** of the 1930s was essential to the expansion of national power. In response to the Great Depression, the New Deal created many new national regulatory agencies to supervise various aspects of business, including communications (the Federal Communications Commission, or FCC), airlines (the Civil Aeronautics Board, or CAB), financial markets (the Securities and Exchange Commission, or SEC), utilities (the Federal Power Commission, or FPC), and labor–management relations (the National Labor Relations Board, or NLRB). The New Deal also brought national government spending to such areas as welfare and economic relief, which had previously been reserved almost entirely to the states, and established the Social Security old-age pension system (discussed more in Chapter 17). President Roosevelt saw that in many cases, the states that needed the most help during the Great Depression also had the fewest resources to enact policies that would help solve them. Due to its much larger tax base than the states, the national government is able to better afford expensive social welfare and economic development programs that states simply cannot.[13]

World War II involved a total economic and military mobilization to fight Germany and Japan. Directing that mobilization, as well as collecting taxes to support it, planning for production of war materials, and bringing on board the employees to accomplish all of this, was centered in Washington, DC—not in the states.

THE POST-WAR PERIOD THROUGH THE 1970S   Ever since World War II, the federal government has spent nearly twice as much per year as all of the states and all localities put together. The federal government has continued to increase its authority relative to the states for the reasons mentioned above: funding and protecting national security, dealing with economic crises, and solving complex problems. During the height of the Cold War and the Vietnam War, America increased its defense spending drastically. And President Johnson's Great Society programs, designed both to alleviate poverty and politically empower the poor and racial minorities, increased federal spending on programs that the national government had not previously been involved with and created a more complex entanglement between the national government and

FIGURE 3.4 FEDERAL EXPENDITURES ON NATIONAL DEFENSE AND HEALTH CARE (IN MILLIONS OF 2016 DOLLARS)

Federal defense spending has been on a steady rise since the end of World War II and the same can be said of expenditures on health. This increasing level of spending has contributed to the primacy of the national government over the states.

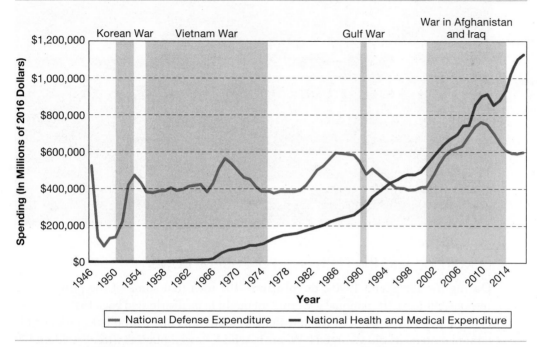

SOURCE: Data from White House, Office of Management and Budget, Historical Tables, Table 3.1, Outlays by Superfunction and Function: 1940–2021.

the states. Federal expenditures on defense and on programs like Medicare (health insurance for the elderly) and Medicaid (health insurance for the poor) have trended consistently upward since the end of World War II (see Figure 3.4). The long-term success of many of the Great Society programs has been a source of considerable debate, but one thing is for sure: they positioned the national government as the primary source of policy for tackling deeply-rooted socioeconomic problems.

Two other trends during this period involved the imposition of national standards on the states. The first trend was the regulatory revolution of the 1960s and 1970s. During the regulatory revolution, Congress passed laws mandating state action on myriad issues, including new environmental standards (e.g., Clean Air Act of 1970, Clean Water Act of 1972) and new consumer protection standards (e.g., Truth in Lending Act of 1968, Fair Credit Reporting Act of 1970).

The second trend in the centralization of federal authority was also critical for the preservation of democratic values: the passage of the **The Civil Rights Act of 1964**. In the Civil Rights Act, the national government asserted a power to forbid discrimination in restaurants and other places of public accommodation across the country. The power for the national government to do this was premised on a very broad reading of the commerce clause which allows the national government to regulate interstate commerce. Supporters argued that people involved in transactions are engaged in interstate commerce (for example, restaurants serve food imported from out of state; hotels buy bedding, towels, flooring, and bathroom fixtures from companies in a variety of states) and thus that national government could regulate them. State economies are so closely tied to each other that by this standard, practically every economic transaction everywhere affects interstate commerce and is therefore subject to national legislative power. This understanding of the commerce clause is a major *structural* part of American federalism and created the foundation for government action.

The Civil Rights Act of 1964

A law that banned discrimination based on race, sex, or national origin in public accommodations such as hotels, restaurants, and conveyances and gave the Attorney General the power to sue local and state governments that maintained racially segregated schools.

SIGNING THE CIVIL RIGHTS ACT OF 1964

Lyndon Johnson signs the Civil Rights Act of 1964, with Dr. Martin Luther King Jr. by his side. The Civil Rights Act, a seminal legislative accomplishment in American history, established equal opportunities for African Americans. Many of the law's provisions relied on a broad conception of national power under American federalism.

In what way did the federal government's enactment of national civil rights legislation pose a challenge to the previously understood distributions of power between the state and federal governments?

Devolution and the Rethinking of Federal Power

During the 1980s and 1990s, **devolution**—the idea that some of the powers and responsibilities of the national government ought to be distributed back to the states—became popular. President Ronald Reagan made this one of the hallmarks of his administration, as did George H. W. Bush, who followed him in office. President Bill Clinton, a former governor of the state of Arkansas, was also an enthusiastic devotee of devolution. The public seemed to be on board with this change at the time too. Polls showed, for example, that a substantial majority of Americans believed that state governments were more effective and more trustworthy than the government in Washington and more likely to be responsive to the people. And Americans said that they wanted state governments to do more and the federal government to do less.[14]

devolution

The delegation of authority over government programs from the federal government down to state and/or local governments.

THE CLINTON ADMINISTRATION The hallmark moment in devolution occurred when President Clinton worked with the Republican majority in 1995 and 1996 to completely overhaul the nation's welfare system. America's traditional welfare system, created in 1935 almost as an afterthought to Social Security, had grown to the point that it provided cash payments to families of one in nine children in the United States by 1995. Although the program, Aid to Families with Dependent Children (AFDC), did not supplement family incomes by much and represented but a tiny portion of the federal government's budget, AFDC was never very popular with the public and grew even less popular in the 1980s and the 1990s. The new welfare program, **Temporary Assistance for Needy Families (TANF),** gave states responsibility for their own welfare programs and provided them with much of the money necessary to operate them. However, the federal government imposed some requirements on state programs, such as requiring recipients to find work within a certain period. The analytical framework in Figure 3.5 examines the *structural, political linkage, and governmental factors* that contributed to this major policy change—an important moment for federalism.

Temporary Assistance for Needy Families (TANF)

Federal welfare program that provides income and services to poor families via state block grants. The program has benefit time limits and a work requirement.

THE REHNQUIST COURT During the height of devolution's popularity, the Supreme Court, led by Chief Justice William Rehnquist, also supported increasing the power of the states and decreasing that of the national government. It overruled a number of federal actions and laws on the grounds that Congress had exceeded its constitutional powers, reversing more than half a century of decisions favoring an

FIGURE 3.5 APPLYING THE FRAMEWORK: WELFARE REFORM

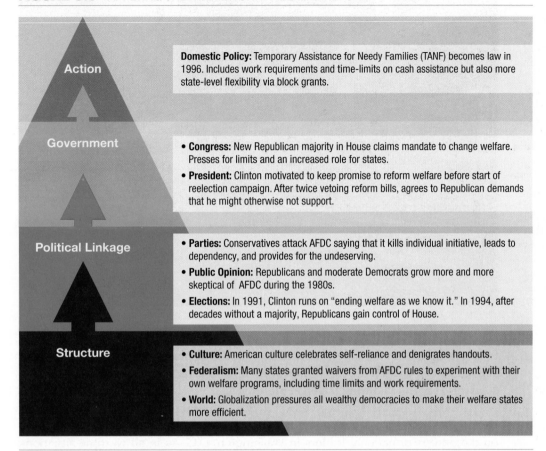

Action

Domestic Policy: Temporary Assistance for Needy Families (TANF) becomes law in 1996. Includes work requirements and time-limits on cash assistance but also more state-level flexibility via block grants.

Government

- **Congress:** New Republican majority in House claims mandate to change welfare. Presses for limits and an increased role for states.
- **President:** Clinton motivated to keep promise to reform welfare before start of reelection campaign. After twice vetoing reform bills, agrees to Republican demands that he might otherwise not support.

Political Linkage

- **Parties:** Conservatives attack AFDC saying that it kills individual initiative, leads to dependency, and provides for the undeserving.
- **Public Opinion:** Republicans and moderate Democrats grow more and more skeptical of AFDC during the 1980s.
- **Elections:** In 1991, Clinton runs on "ending welfare as we know it." In 1994, after decades without a majority, Republicans gain control of House.

Structure

- **Culture:** American culture celebrates self-reliance and denigrates handouts.
- **Federalism:** Many states granted waivers from AFDC rules to experiment with their own welfare programs, including time limits and work requirements.
- **World:** Globalization pressures all wealthy democracies to make their welfare states more efficient.

increased federal government role. For example, in *United States v. Lopez* (1995), the Supreme Court overturned federal legislation banning guns from the area around schools and legislation requiring background checks for gun buyers, arguing that both represented too broad a use of the commerce power in the Constitution. The Court used similar language in 2000 when it invalidated part of the Violence Against Women Act (*United States v. Morrison*) and in 2001 when it did the same to the Americans with Disabilities Act (*Board of Trustees of the University of Alabama v. Garrett*).

In the last years of Rehnquist's leadership the Court retreated a bit from this states' rights position, supporting federal authority over that of the states on issues ranging from the use of medical marijuana to the juvenile death penalty, affirmative action, and gay rights. In each of these areas, several states wanted to go in more liberal directions than the rest of the country—such as using affirmative action to create diversity in government hiring and contracting—but the Court affirmed the more restrictive federal statutes.

The Reassertion of Federal Power After 2000

Talk of devolution subsided after the Clinton presidency ended in 2000. Republican George W. Bush, who followed Clinton into the Oval Office in January 2001, had signaled during the presidential campaign that he was willing to use the federal government to serve conservative ends. He termed his position "compassionate conservatism," suggesting that he would use the power of the office to try to, among other things, end abortion, protect family values, enhance educational performance, and do more to move people from welfare to jobs. While preserving his traditional Republican conservative credentials on a number of fronts—cutting taxes, for example, and pushing for looser environmental regulations on businesses—Bush gave a big boost to the power, cost, and scope of the federal government.[15] Most important was his support of the No Child Left Behind educational reform legislation, which imposed

THE FEDERAL ROLE IN PUBLIC EDUCATION

For most of American history, education was understood to be entirely the responsibility of state and local governments. This began to change with the Elementary and Secondary Education Act of 1965, which distributed federal money to states which they were to allocate to public schools in need. Since 1965, the role of the federal government in education has expanded considerably, with more funding and more requirements going along with that funding. With the well-known No Child Left Behind Act of 2001, federal involvement in public education reached new heights. That federal role was then reduced some in the 2015 Every Student Succeeds Act. *What are the pros and cons of the federal government setting educational standards that apply to the whole country?*

testing mandates on the states, and a prescription drug benefit under Medicare, which substantially increased the cost of the program. Mandatory Medicaid spending by the states also expanded during the Bush presidency.

The terrorist attacks of September 11, 2001, the subsequent global "war on terrorism," and the wars in Iraq and Afghanistan further focused the nation's attention on the powers of national leaders in Washington, D.C. As in all wartime situations during our country's history, war and the mobilization for war require centralized coordination and planning. This tendency to embrace nationalism during times of war has been further exaggerated by the need for enhancing homeland security post-9/11. Since 9/11, the national government in Washington is playing a larger role in law enforcement, intelligence gathering, bank oversight (to track terrorist money), public health (to protect against possible bioterrorism), and more. Many of these federal activities were continued by Barack Obama when he assumed office in 2008 and will remain in place for the foreseeable future.

The economic crisis that began in 2008, sometimes called the Great Recession, generated an expanded role for the national government relative to the states in economic affairs. In the last months of the Bush presidency, Congress passed a $700 billion rescue package for financial institutions that gave the Treasury secretary broad powers to rescue and reorganize banks and investment firms even as the Federal Reserve (the Fed), under the leadership of Ben Bernanke, undertook its own rescue and reorganization efforts. This rescue greatly expanded the role of the federal government in managing the economy. When Barack Obama became president, he not only continued to support the efforts of the Treasury and the Fed to bolster the national economy, but insisted on the sale of Chrysler and the managed bankruptcy of General Motors as conditions of the rescue. Within 30 days of Obama's inauguration, Congress passed a new $787 billion stimulus bill, which did a great deal to shore up state budgets, almost all of which were, by that time, in crisis. Obama's stimulus was a combination of tax cuts and new expenditures on programs that, among other things, extended benefits for the unemployed; funded new research and development into alternative energy sources; put money into school construction (and, thereby, kept teachers on the job); massively increased spending on infrastructure projects for roads, bridges, and canals; and helped the states pay for some of their rising Medicaid outlays.

President Barack Obama tours a Michigan plant that manufactures diesel transmissions. Preventing the collapse of the American auto industry was an important part of President Obama's effort to bring an end to the Financial Crisis and begin an economic recovery.

From a federalism perspective, why would the federal government providing help to auto companies that are on the brink of bankruptcy be controversial?

Recent Pushback Against National Power

There has been considerable pushback against recent increases in national power, suggesting that the states remain significant actors in the American system. The anti-tax, anti–big government Tea Party movement was a major force in local, state, and national elections through the Obama presidency. Republican governors even turned down federal grants to fund high-speed rail and other infrastructure projects in their states.[16] While Tea Party voices in the Republican Party have gotten less attention amid Trump's populist and nationalist rhetoric, they remain a critical faction within the Republican Party—particularly in the House of Representatives.

The recent pushback against national power is most evident at the Supreme Court. In 2012 the Supreme Court struck down a provision of the Affordable Care Act (also known as Obamacare) that forced states to expand their Medicaid programs or face a drastic cut in federal funding. Writing for the majority, Chief Justice John Roberts ruled that there is a limit to how coercive Congress can be with the states using its spending power.[17] The decision had important real-world consequences as eighteen states have since opted not to expand their Medicaid programs. Estimates indicated that more than 3 million low-income people are not eligible for government-funded health insurance as a result.[18]

As you read in the opening story of the chapter, the flow of power to Washington over time has recently triggered a reaction among the public and in statehouses across the country. Regulatory burdens, intensifying budgetary demands, and a sense that important national problems are being ignored and mishandled has led to a rather extraordinary revitalization of innovation at the state level.[19] Over the last decade, several states passed laws allowing, and sometimes subsidizing, new kinds of biomedical research. Others passed minimum wage legislation, while others legislated gas mileage requirements for cars and trucks. Many legislated incentives for companies and consumers to use energy more efficiently and find alternative fuel sources.

FISCAL FEDERALISM

3.4 Analyze how federal grants structure national and state government relations.

As you learned in the previous section, today's federalism is very different from what it was in the 1790s or early 1800s.[20] One major difference is that the national government is dominant in many policy areas; it calls many shots for the states. Another difference

cooperative federalism

Federalism in which the powers and responsibilities of the states and the national government are intertwined and in which they work together to solve common problems; said to have characterized the 1960s and 1970s.

fiscal federalism

That aspect of federalism having to do with federal grants to the states.

grants-in-aid

Funds from the national government to state and local governments to help pay for programs created by the national government.

is that state and national government powers and activities have become deeply intertwined and entangled. The old, simple metaphor for federalism was a "layer cake"—a system of dual federalism in which state and national powers were neatly divided into separate layers, with each level of government going its own way, unencumbered by the other. A much more accurate metaphor for today's federalism is a "marble cake" in which elements of national and state responsibilities swirl around each other, without clear boundaries. This intermixing of responsibilities is frequently referred to as "**cooperative federalism**."[21]

Much of this "swirling" of federal and state governments is a product of **fiscal federalism**: the financial links among the national and state governments, primarily via **grants-in-aid** that transfer money from the national government to state governments. These grants-in-aid have been used to increase national government influence over what the states and localities do. The grants have grown from small beginnings to form a substantial part of state government budgets. In the following sections, you will learn how and why this trend began, what kinds of grants have and are being made, and how they affect national–state relationships.

Origin and Growth of Federal Grants

National government grants to the states began at least as early as the 1787 Northwest Ordinance. The U.S. government granted land for government buildings, schools, and colleges in the Northwest Territory and imposed various regulations, such as forbidding slavery there. During the early 19th century, the federal government provided some land grants to the states for roads, canals, and railroads, as well as a little cash for militias; after 1862, it helped establish agricultural colleges. Some small cash-grant programs were begun around 1900 for agriculture, vocational education, and highways.[22]

However, it was during the 1950s, 1960s, and 1970s, under both Republican and Democratic administrations, that federal grants to the states really took off. Such programs as President Dwight Eisenhower's interstate highway system and President Lyndon Johnson's Great Society poured money into the states.[23] After a pause during the Reagan presidency, grants began to increase again in the 1990s (see Figure 3.6). Federal grants to the states increased because presidents and Congress sought to deal with many nationwide problems—especially transportation, education, HIV/AIDS, poverty, crime, and air and water pollution—by setting policy at the national level and providing money from national tax revenues, while having state and local officials carry out the policies. The spike in grants in 2010 was tied to various efforts by the federal government to stimulate the economy during the Great Recession, including assistance to states for Medicaid, unemployment insurance, education, and infrastructure.[24]

Types of Federal Grants

categorical grants

Federal aid to states and localities clearly specifying what the money can be used for.

Over the years, many of the new programs were established through **categorical grants**, which give the states money but also clearly specify the category of activity for which the money has to be spent and define how the program should work. For example, Lyndon Johnson's antipoverty initiatives—in the areas of housing, job training, medical assistance, and more—funneled substantial federal money to states and localities but attached strict rules on how the money could be used.

block grants

Federal grants to the states to be used for general activities.

Responding to complaints from the states and seeking to reduce federal government power to better fit their ideas about the proper role of government, Republican presidents Nixon and Ford succeeded in convincing Congress to loosen centralized rules and oversight, first instituting **block grants** (which give money for more general purposes, such as secondary education, and with fewer rules than categorical grant programs). In 1972, Congress enacted President Nixon's general revenue sharing plan, which distributed money to the states with no federal controls and allowed states to use the money as they saw fit. Revenue sharing ended in 1987 when even proponents

FIGURE 3.6 THE GROWTH IN FEDERAL GRANTS-IN-AID TO STATES AND LOCALITIES AS A PERCENT OF
TOTAL FEDERAL SPENDING

Federal grants-in-aid to state and local governments as a percentage of federal spending have grown steadily since 1970, except
during the Reagan presidency in the first half of the 1980s. Grants to states peaked in 2010 and 2011 as federal assistance to the states
increased to address problems caused by financial collapse and economic recession.

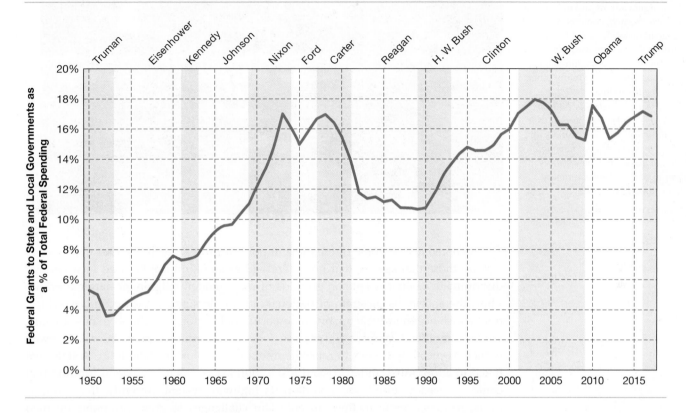

SOURCE: Budget of the United States Government, Fiscal Year 2019: Historical Tables, Table 12.1.

of a smaller federal government realized that giving money to the states with "no
strings attached" meant that elected officials in the federal government were losing
influence over policies in which they wanted to have a say.[25]

Categorical and block grants often provide federal money under an automatic
formula related to the statistical characteristics of each state or locality (thus the term
"formula grant"), such as the number of needy residents, the total size of the population, or the average income level. Disputes frequently arise when these formulas benefit one state or region rather than another. Because statistical counts by the Census
affect how much money the states and localities get, Census counts themselves have
become the subject of political conflict.

Federal Grants: Money and Control

Most contemporary conflicts about fiscal federalism concern money and control.
Below, we frame the principal arguments that fuel these debates in terms of conditions
on aid, mandates, and preemption.

CONDITIONS ON AID Categorical grant-in-aid programs require that states spend federal money only in certain restricted ways. Even block grants have conditions attached to
them. Indeed, both types of grants are frequently referred to as **conditional grants**. In theory, these conditions are "voluntary" because states can refuse to accept the aid. But in practice, there is no clear line between incentive and coercion. Because states cannot generally
afford to give up federal money, they normally must accept the conditions attached to it.

conditional grants

Federal grants with provisions requiring
that state and local governments follow
certain policies in order to obtain funds.

President Lyndon Johnson signs a bill creating the National Endowment for the Humanities (NEH) and the National Endowment for the Arts (NEA) into law in 1965. These programs were part of Johnson's Great Society initiative. They provide federal funds to organizations and individuals to produce research, complete original work, facilitate teaching, and develop institutions focused on furthering our understanding of history, language, literature, and art among many other topics and endeavours.

In the last several decades, the NEH and the NEA have become controversial with liberals in support and conservatives in opposition to their continued funding. Why would liberals and conservatives disagree about the federal government's support of the NEH and NEA?

As noted above, some of the most important provisions of the 1964 Civil Rights Act are those that specify that no federal aid of any kind can be used in ways that discriminate against people on grounds of race, gender, religion, or national origin. Thus, the enormous program of national aid for elementary and secondary education, which began in 1965, became a powerful tool for forcing schools to desegregate. To take another example, in 1984 the federal government used federal highway money to encourage states to raise the minimum age for drinking to 21. A state that failed to adopt this standard risked losing billions of dollars in federal funding that could be used to build and maintain its highway system. Recently, the Supreme Court has been more inclined to entertain challenges to grant programs deemed unduly coercive.

mandate
A formal order from the national government that the states carry out certain policies.

MANDATES   The national government often imposes a **mandate**, or demand, that states carry out certain policies even when little or no national government aid is offered. (An "unfunded mandate" involves no aid at all or less aid than compliance

WISCONSIN STATE EMPLOYEES PROTEST PLAN TO REDUCE UNION POWER

At the state capitol in Madison, Wisconsin, thousands protested Republican Governor Scott Walker's plan to strip public-sector unions of their collective bargaining rights. In the end, Walker's plan prevailed and the state's public-sector unions (which represent teachers and other government workers) lost considerable power.

What is the connection between fiscal federalism and concerns from state employees about their ability to collectively negotiate their wages, benefits, hours, and conditions with the state?

will cost.) Mandates have been especially important in the areas of civil rights and the environment. Most civil rights policies flow from the
equal protection clause of the Fourteenth Amendment to the U.S. Constitution or from national
legislation that imposes uniform national standards. Environmental regulations also flow from
the national government since problems of dirty
air, polluted water, and acid rain spill across state
boundaries. The Supreme Court ruled in *EPA v.
EME Homer City Generation* (2013) that the EPA
has the authority to set standards that account
for how air pollution travels from one state to
another. National legislation and regulations have
required state governments to provide costly special facilities for the disabled, to set up environmental protection agencies, and to limit the kinds
and amounts of pollutants that can be discharged.
The states often complain bitterly about federal
mandates that require state spending without
providing the money necessary to carry them out.

Cutting back on these **"unfunded mandates"**
was one of the main promises in the Republicans'
1994 Contract with America.[26] The congressional
Republicans delivered on their promise early in
1995 with a bill that had bipartisan support in
Congress and that President Clinton signed into law.
However, unfunded mandates have continued to proliferate because the law did not ban
them but only forced Congress to monitor them (e.g., requiring cost–benefit analyses).

Today's governors continue to be concerned by the substantial costs imposed on
the states by the rising cost of supporting Medicaid and testing requirements that began
under the No Child Left Behind Act (some of these testing pressures were relaxed in the
Every Student Succeeds Act, which replaced No Child Left Behind in 2015). Pressures on
state budgets became especially pronounced during the Great Recession when revenues
from sales and other taxes plummeted because of the national economic downturn.
In 2013, hard-fought budget agreements between Congress and President Obama to
address the problem of federal deficits cut federal spending across a wide range of programs, including money to keep teachers and first responders from being laid off and to
help with Medicaid. These federal cuts plunged many states even farther into the red.
Many responded by making deep cuts in education, in social programs for the poor, and
in programs for maintaining and improving infrastructure (roads, bridges, and dams,
for example). Several governors, such as Governor Walker of Wisconsin, tried to tame
public employee unions or rescind the collective bargaining rights of state workers.

PREEMPTION The doctrine of preemption, based on the supremacy clause in the
Constitution and supported by a series of Supreme Court decisions, says that federal
treaties, statutes, and rules must prevail over state statutes and rules when the two
are in conflict. For example, in *U.S. v. Arizona* (2012), the Supreme Court preempted
the portions of Arizona's tough immigration law, including one that required immigrants to carry documentation of their legal residency at all times, ruling that immigration enforcement is the responsibility of the federal government. However, even
when national laws preempt state laws, the national government may still choose not
to interfere. As you read in the opening story of this chapter, this has been the case in
states that have decided to legalize marijuana use despite federal laws prohibiting it.

**BUT LET ME TELL YOU,
MR. PRESIDENT**

State governors and presidents have
not always seen eye-to-eye on the
issues. During the Obama administration, the level of conflict among
Republican state leaders and the president reached a fever pitch over health
care and immigration reform. Here,
Arizona governor Jan Brewer, whose
state passed harsh anti-immigration
measures in 2010 designed to purge
undocumented immigrants from
the state, defended the legislation as
a state-level response to a problem
that the federal government was, in
Brewer's estimation, neglecting. The
Supreme Court later overturned most
of the measures as an unconstitutional
state intrusion on federal authority in
U.S. v. Arizona (2012).
*Why is immigration enforcement the
responsibility of the federal government
and not the state governments?*

unfunded mandates
Requirements imposed by the federal
government on the states to perform
certain actions, with not enough money
provided to fulfill the requirements.

STRONG STATES VERSUS A STRONG NATIONAL GOVERNMENT

3.5 Evaluate the arguments for and against a strong national government.

From the framing of the U.S. Constitution to the present day, people have offered many strong arguments for different power balances under federalism. Federalism is not just about abstract theories, it is also about who wins and who loses valuable benefits. People's opinions about federalism often depend on their interests, their ideologies, and the kinds of things they want government to do. The following discussion presents arguments in favor of strong state governments and arguments in favor of a strong national government.

Strong States: Diversity of Needs

The oldest and most important argument in favor of decentralized government is that in a large and diverse country, needs and wants and conditions differ from one place to another. Why not let different states enact different policies to meet their own needs? The border state of Arizona, feeling overwhelmed by illegal immigrants, has tried to pursue its own policy agenda on immigration (though some of its efforts have been preempted). And social welfare policies vary considerably by state, with more liberal states tending to offer a larger safety net than conservative states on programs such as cash assistance (TANF) and Medicaid.

Strong National Government: The Importance of National Standards

The needs or desires that different states pursue may not be worthy ones. Political scientist William Riker has pointed out that, in the past, one of the main effects of federalism was to let white majorities in the Southern states enslave and then discriminate against black people, without interference from the North.[27] Additionally, when large states like California make certain policy changes (such as vehicle emissions standards), they can impact national companies who are then forced to adjust nationwide. Perhaps it is better, in some cases, to insist on national standards that apply everywhere.

Strong States: Closeness to the People

It is sometimes claimed that state governments are closer to ordinary citizens, who have a better chance to know their officials, to be aware of what they are doing, to contact them, and to hold them responsible for what they do.

Strong National Government: Low Visibility of State Officials

Geographic closeness may not be the real issue. More Americans are better informed about the federal government than they are about state governments, and more people participate in national than in state elections. When more people know what the government is doing and more people vote, they are better able to insist that the government do what they want. For that reason, responsiveness to ordinary citizens may be greater in national government.

Strong States: Innovation and Experimentation

When the states have independent power, they can try out new ideas. Individual states can be **"laboratories of democracy"** If the experiments work, other states or the nation as a whole can adopt their ideas, as has happened on such issues as allowing women and 18-year-olds to vote, fighting air pollution, reforming welfare, and

laboratories of democracy
The ability of states in the U.S. federal system to experiment with policy ideas; the success or failure of state policies can then be a template for national policy action.

SPEWING POLLUTION
Industrial pollution, such as these untreated emissions from this coal-burning power plant in Tennessee, often affects people of more than one state and requires the participation of the national government to clean up the mess and prevent recurrences. *What role should the federal government take in environmental issues in situations where pollution spreads from one state into other states?*

dealing with water pollution. In 2006, California passed a law committing itself to reducing greenhouse gas emissions to 1990 levels by 2020, and that law eventually became the basis of the EPA's national regulations.[28] Similarly, Massachusetts passed a law in 2006 mandating health insurance coverage for every person in the state, and that became the model for the Affordable Care Act. And many states have also acted on gun control in ways that the national government has not: such as those that force domestic abusers to surrender their guns.[29]

Likewise, when the national government is controlled by one political party, federalism allows the states with majorities favoring a different party to compensate by enacting different policies. This aspect of diversity in policymaking is related to the Founders' contention that tyranny is less likely when government's power is dispersed. Multiple governments reduce the risks of bad policy or the blockage of the popular will; if things go wrong at one governmental level, they may go right at another.

Strong National Government: Spillover Effects and Competition

Diversity and experimentation in policies may not always be good. Divergent regulations can cause bad effects that spill over from one state to another. When factories in the Midwest spew out oxides of nitrogen and sulfur that fall as acid rain in the Northeast, the northeastern states acting on their own can do nothing about it. Only nationwide rules can solve such problems. Similarly, it is very difficult for cities or local communities in the states to do much about poverty or other social problems. If a city raises taxes to pay for social programs, businesses and the wealthy may move out of town and poorer residents may move in, impoverishing the city and reducing the government's ability to pay for those programs in the first place.[30]

AMERICAN FEDERALISM: HOW DEMOCRATIC?

Federalism is one of the basic foundations of the Constitution of the United States and key *structural* attributes of American government. Along with the separation of powers and checks and balances, its purpose, from the framers' point of view, was to make it impossible for any person or group (and, most especially, the majority faction) to monopolize the power of government and use it for tyrannical purposes. By fragmenting government power among a national government and fifty state governments and by giving each of the states some say on what the national government does, federalism makes it difficult for any faction, minority, or majority, to dominate government. On balance, federalism has served the intentions of the framers by toning down the influence of majoritarian democracy in determining what the national government does—even while maintaining the principle of popular consent.

Federalism constrains democracy in at least five ways:

1. It adds complexity to policymaking and makes it difficult for citizens to know which elected leaders to hold responsible for government actions.

2. Many policy areas, including education and voting eligibility, are mainly the responsibility of the states, where policymakers are insulated from national majorities, although not from majorities in their own states.

3. Small-population states play a decisive role in the constitutional amending process, where states of all sizes count equally.

4. Small and large states have equal representation in the Senate, meaning that senators representing a minority of the population can block actions favored by senators representing the majority.

5. State politics are much less visible to the public; citizens are much less informed about what goes on in state governments where many important policies are made, and thus, popular participation tends to be lower.

All of this makes state-level politics especially vulnerable to the influence of special interests and those with substantial political resources. Because the well-organized and the affluent have extra influence, political equality and popular sovereignty face pretty tough challenges in many of the states.

In the end, the story of federalism is not entirely about the persistence of the framer's initial 18th-century republican constitutional design. The democratic aspirations of the American people have also shaped federalism and turned it into something that might not be entirely familiar to the framers. We noted in this chapter how the nature of federalism has changed over the course of American history, with the national government assuming an ever-larger role relative to the states. Much of this, we have suggested, has been brought about by the wishes of the American people as expressed through *linkage factors* such as elections, public opinion polls, and social movements. Repeatedly, Americans have said they want a national government capable of taking policy actions on a broad range of problems, including economic difficulties (such as depressions, recessions, and inflation); persistent poverty; environmental degradation; unsafe food, drugs, and other consumer products; racial and ethnic discrimination; and foreign threats to the United States. Over the years, public officials and candidates have responded to these popular aspirations, altering federalism in the process.

FEDERALISM AS A SYSTEM OF GOVERNMENT

3.1 Define federalism, and explain why we have it.

Federalism is a system under which political powers are divided and shared between the state and federal governments and is a key *structural* aspect of American politics.

Federalism in the United States was the product of both important compromises made at the Constitutional Convention and 18th-century republican doctrines about the nature of good government.

FEDERALISM IN THE CONSTITUTION

3.2 Explain the constitutional foundations of federalism.

There is no section of the Constitution where federalism is described in its entirety. Rather, federalism is constructed from scattered clauses throughout the document that describe what the federal government may do and not do, how relations among the states are structured, the role of the states in amending the Constitution and electing the president, and how the states are represented in the national government.

The U.S. Constitution specifies the powers of the national government and reserves all others (except a few that are specifically forbidden) to the states. Concurrent powers fall within the authority both of the national government and the states.

THE EVOLUTION OF AMERICAN FEDERALISM

3.3 Trace the evolution of American federalism.

The story of American federalism is the story of the increasing power of the federal government relative to the states.

The trend toward national power is lodged in the "supremacy," "elastic," and "commerce" clauses in the Constitution and propelled by war and national security demands, economic troubles and crises, and a range of problems that no state could handle alone.

FISCAL FEDERALISM

3.4 Analyze how federal grants structure national and state government relations.

Contemporary federalism involves complex "cooperative" relations among the national and state governments in which federal grants-in-aid play an important part. Except for the Reagan years, grant totals have grown steadily; they took a big jump upward as the country battled the Great Recession and jobless recovery in the 2008–2012 period, then leveled out after the anti-tax, anti-government, deficit-reducing agenda came to dominate congressional politics.

The national government also influences or controls many state policies through mandates and through conditions placed on aid. Coercive conditions on grants to states have recently been reconsidered by the Supreme Court.

STRONG STATES VERSUS A STRONG NATIONAL GOVERNMENT

3.5 Evaluate the arguments for and against a strong national government.

Arguments in favor of a strong national government are based on a need for national standards, resources to provide respond to social problems, and needs for uniformity.

Arguments in favor of strong states are based on a diversity of needs, closeness to the people, experimentation, and innovation.

Affordable Care Act (ACA)   The far-reaching health care reform law passed in 2010. The Act was aimed at increasing access to health insurance for all Americans and driving down the rising, burdensome cost of health care in the United States.

block grants   Federal grants to the states to be used for general activities.

categorical grants   Federal aid to states and localities clearly specifying what the money can be used for.

Civil Rights Act of 1964   A law that banned discrimination based on race, sex, or national origin in public accommodations such as hotels, restaurants, and conveyances and gave the Attorney General the power to sue local and state governments that maintained racially segregated schools.

Civil War Amendments   The Thirteenth, Fourteenth, and Fifteenth Amendments to the Constitution, adopted immediately after the Civil War, each of which represented the imposition of a national claim over that of the states.

concurrent powers   Powers under the Constitution that are shared by the federal government and the states.

conditional grants   Federal grants with provisions requiring that state and local governments follow certain policies in order to obtain funds.

confederation   A loose association of states or territorial units in which very little power or no power at all is lodged in a central government.

cooperative federalism   Federalism in which the powers and responsibilities of the states and the national government are intertwined and in which they work together to solve common problems; said to have characterized the 1960s and 1970s.

devolution   The delegation of authority over government programs from the federal government down to state and/or local governments.

dual federalism   A system of federalism in which state and national powers are neatly divided between the national and state governments. Most powers of the national government are not shared with the states, and most powers of the states are not shared with the national government.

due process clause   The section of the Fourteenth Amendment that prohibits states from depriving anyone of life, liberty, or property "without due process of law," a guarantee against arbitrary government action.

equal protection clause   The section of the Fourteenth Amendment that provides for equal treatment by government of people residing within the United States and each of its states.

federalism   A system in which significant governmental powers are divided between a central government and smaller territorial units, such as states.

Federalist No. 10   One of a series on essays written by James Madison (others were written by Alexander Hamilton and John Jay), urging the people of New York to support ratification of the Constitution. In No. 10, Madison defended republican government for large states with heterogeneous populations and expressed his fear of majorities and his abhorrence of political parties.

fiscal federalism   That aspect of federalism having to do with federal grants to the states.

full faith and credit clause   The provision in Article IV, Section 1 of the Constitution which provides that states must respect the public acts, laws, and judicial rulings of other states.

grants-in-aid   Funds from the national government to state and local governments to help pay for programs created by the national government.

horizontal federalism   Term used to refer to relationships among the states.

interstate compacts   Agreements among states to cooperate on solving mutual problems; requires approval by Congress.

laboratories of democracy   The ability of states in the U.S. federal system to experiment with policy ideas; the success or failure of state policies can then be a template for national policy action.

mandate   A formal order from the national government that the states carry out certain policies.

nationalist position   The view of American federalism that holds that the Constitution created a system in which the national government is supreme, relative to the states, and that it granted government a broad range of powers and responsibilities.

necessary and proper clause   Article I, Section 8, of the Constitution, also known as the *elastic clause*; gives Congress the authority to make whatever laws are necessary and proper to carry out its enumerated powers and the responsibilities mentioned in the Constitution's preamble.

New Deal   The social and economic programs of the administration of President Franklin D. Roosevelt in response to the Great Depression.

nullification   An attempt by states to declare national laws or actions null and void.

police powers   Powers of a government to protect the health, safety, and general well-being of its people.

preemption   Exclusion of the states from actions that might interfere with federal authority or statutes.

reservation clause   Part of the Tenth Amendment to the Constitution that says those powers not given to the federal government and not prohibited to the states by the Constitution are reserved for the states and the people.

states' rights position   The view of American federalism that holds that the Constitution created a system of dual sovereignty in which the national government and the state governments are sovereign in their own spheres.

supremacy clause   The provision in Article VI of the Constitution states that the Constitution and the laws and treaties of the United States are the supreme law of the land, taking precedence over state laws and constitutions when they are in conflict.

Temporary Assistance for Needy Families (TANF)   Federal welfare program that provides income and services to poor families via state block grants. The program has benefit time limits and a work requirement.

unfunded mandates   Requirements imposed by the federal government on the states to perform certain actions, with not enough money provided to fulfill the requirements.

unitary system   A system in which a central government has complete power over its constituent units or states.

CHAPTER 4

GLOBAL BOEING
Two new Boeing 787 Dreamliners await delivery to Air India and All Nippon Airways. Indian and Japanese companies are not only customers for the new aircraft but also suppliers and partners in its design and production.

Do such global arrangements cause jobs to depart the United States or help to create new ones? What should government do to encourage further job growth in the United States?

THE STRUCTURAL FOUNDATIONS OF AMERICAN GOVERNMENT AND POLITICS

CHAPTER OUTLINE AND LEARNING OBJECTIVES

AMERICA'S POPULATION

4.1 Describe the effect of recent demographic trends on American politics.

AMERICA'S ECONOMY

4.2 Discuss how the American economy shapes government and politics.

AMERICA'S POLITICAL CULTURE

4.3 Describe the values and beliefs that make up American political culture and how they affect politics and government.

The Struggle for Democracy

Fifty-six thousand jobs is a lot of leverage, and Boeing executives were anxious to use it to influence elected officials in Washington state and labor unions at the company. The jobs were tied to the newly announced Boeing 777X, a stretched and more fuel-efficient version of the Boeing 777, at the time, the most popular best-selling twin-aisle big jet ever produced. Airline carriers were so impressed with the new plane that they placed more than 300 orders for the 777X at the 2013 Dubai air show before Boeing had built a single plane.

But where would Boeing choose to assemble the new plane? Where would the good engineering and production jobs land, so to speak? According to most observers, the logical place would be Boeing's plant in Everett, Washington, where the current 777 and the 787 Dreamliners are assembled. Everett has a highly educated and trained workforce with extensive experience in design, engineering, building, final assembly, and testing. Everett also has the advantage of being near the Port of Seattle, where parts and sections from Boeing's main Japanese supplier enter the country. But before agreeing to manufacture the 777X in Everett, Boeing wanted special subsidies from the state of Washington and major concessions from the International Association of Machinists (IAM), Local 751, which represents most of its production employees in the Puget Sound area. Unless satisfied on both counts, Boeing spokespersons said they would look elsewhere to assemble the new plane.

Washington complied. In a one-day special session of the legislature, the state agreed to grant Boeing, among other things, almost $9 billion in tax breaks over sixteen years, the most generous series of tax subsidies ever granted to an American corporation by a state—even though Boeing was very profitable at the time (and remains so).

Though the IAM had a contract in effect until 2016, Boeing insisted that the union revise it on a "take it or leave it" basis. Boeing's proposal, sweetened by a one-time $10,000 payment to each employee, would stretch to 2024, increase employee health insurance premiums, freeze pensions, and limit pay increases to 1 percent every other year, regardless of company profitability or the inflation rate. Boeing said these contract changes were required if the company was to keep its long-term labor costs down and remain competitive with Airbus, the other major commercial aircraft producer. While Boeing had been rapidly increasing the efficiency of airplane production and lowering its costs through automation, the rapid introduction of computer technology and robots to the production line, and global sourcing and partnering with companies in other countries—especially on the 787 Dreamliner—rival Airbus was doing the same things, so executives felt justified in demanding more from their production employees.

After IAM District 751 members voted down the proposal by a two-to-one margin, Boeing made good on its threat, inviting other states and communities to bid for the 777X assembly operation. Many did. Scared by the prospect of permanently losing jobs in the Puget Sound area, local Democratic leaders and state officials pressed Local 751 to reconsider its contract vote. It refused to do so until a second vote on the contract was ordered by officials from the national office of the machinists union. The contract was approved by a very narrow margin on the second vote.

Under the terms of the new contract, machinists at Boeing are worse off than before Boeing made its bold threat to leave Everett. Boeing was able to take on one of the most powerful remaining unions in the United States and win. It not only gained a more favorable contract with the IAM that stretched to the year 2024, but it proceeded to shift much of the work on the 787 model to its nonunion plants in North Charleston, South Carolina. And, despite the subsidies from the state of Washington and contract concessions by the IAM to keep the 777X in the state, Boeing announced in late 2013 that much of the engineering and design work on the new 777X would happen outside the Puget Sound area, with nonunion South Carolina among the main winners of these new jobs. The machinists who assemble airplanes are among the last production workers in the United States who, because of their unions and the generous wages and benefits that come with union protection, have been able to live middle-class lifestyles. This may now be at risk as Boeing has every incentive to employ the same bargaining tactics in the future when it comes to decisions about where to assemble new or upgraded airplane models. Whatever one thinks of unions, whether for them or against them in terms of economic efficiency, it is undeniable that the decline of labor unions in the private sector—now only about 6 percent of private-sector workers, down from 33 percent in the mid-1950s—is one of the main reasons why the middle class is being steadily hollowed out.[1]

*   *   *   *   *

Many Americans rightly are worried about whether the nation's high standard of living can be maintained and whether they can continue to provide for themselves and their families. Many at Boeing and other companies are worried that the opportunity to live a middle-class lifestyle is threatened by jobs that are disappearing because of global and domestic (such as the shift of many activities to nonunion South Carolina) sourcing, automation, and the increased sophistication and use of computer technology and robots in the workplace.[2] When they are worried about such matters, Americans tend to turn to their elected officials and candidates for solutions. Some want outsourcing to be stopped or regulated. Others want government to provide health insurance so that they will not be left in the lurch when companies downsize their workforces. Still others want more retraining and education assistance. Others want lower taxes and fewer regulations to help the competitiveness of American companies like Boeing. Still others want their government to be tougher with economic competitors in Europe and Asia and to do a better job of keeping low-wage immigrants out of the country. Whatever the particulars might be, it is inevitably the case that big economic and technological changes, and the choices corporations make in the face of such changes, find expression in the political arena and shape what government does.[3] What to do about such things is part of the continuing debate between Democrats and Republicans and liberals and conservatives.

What can and should government do to encourage further job growth in the United States, especially jobs that can provide wages that are high enough to provide the foundation for solid middle class lifestyles? It is evident that a number of forces are at work in the United States today, ranging from globalization to technological change, corporate labor and production policies, and government actions, that are shrinking the middle class. We can see the rising threat to the middle class even among the highly trained and skilled employees at Boeing, one of the nation's most successful and visible companies.

THINKING CRITICALLY **ABOUT THIS CHAPTER**

Many changes in American society, culture, economy, and our place in the world are shaping and reshaping American politics and government. Tracking change at the structural level of our analytical model and examining how change is influencing American politics and what government does is the focus of this chapter.

APPLYING THE **FRAMEWORK**

In this chapter, you will learn about the most important demographic characteristics of the American population (race, ethnicity, geographical location, occupation, and income), about the U.S. economy and how it is evolving and changing, and about the core beliefs of Americans—sometimes referred to as the American political culture. Together with the constitutional rules you have learned about in previous chapters, you will see how these structural factors have a great deal to do with what issues dominate the political agenda, how political power is distributed in the population, and what ideas Americans bring to bear when grappling with complex public policy issues.

> ## USING THE **DEMOCRACY STANDARD**
>
> Popular sovereignty, political equality, and liberty require a supportive economic and social environment. These include (but are not confined to) such things as a well-educated population; a sizable middle class with access to resources, allowing its members to participate in public affairs; and a culture that values and protects liberty. In this chapter, you will begin to learn whether or not such an environment exists.

AMERICA'S POPULATION

4.1 Describe the effect of recent demographic trends on American politics.

Where we live, how we work, our racial and ethnic composition, and our average age and standard of living have all changed substantially over the course of our history. Each change, it goes without saying, has influenced and continues to influence American government and politics. A discussion of the most important of these **demographic** characteristics follows.

demographic
Pertaining to the statistical study and description of a population.

America's Population Is Growing

Unlike most other rich democracies, the United States continues to experience significant population growth. According to the U.S. Census Bureau, the U.S. population grew almost 11 percent between 2000 and 2015, to a total of almost 325 million people. This leaves the United States as the third most populous country in the world, trailing only China at 1.41 billion and India at 1.34 billion. During the same period, other countries experienced stagnant growth—Germany did not grow at all—or their populations actually declined, as in Japan and Russia. U.S. population growth has been the product both of a higher-than-replacement birthrate (more people are being born than dying)[4] and of immigration. The Census estimates that we will continue to grow for a long time into the future (see Figure 4.1). (However, the Trump administration's crackdown on both legal and illegal immigration will affect projections about what the American population might look like by mid-century.) Both births and immigration are important for economic growth and fiscal health. When a country's population grows, most economists believe, more people become part of the working, tax-paying population, helping to cushion the burden on national budgets of those who have retired, and more businesses are formed to service the needs of new and growing households.

Some worry, however, that population growth in a rich country like the United States must at some point run up against the limits of available resources, such as oil, and that the natural environment will be hurt as more people invariably produce more pollutants, perhaps contributing to global climate change. Of course, an increase in population need not lead to such outcomes if businesses and consumers use more efficient and less polluting forms of energy, such as natural gas, which is in generous supply because of the revolution in fracking, and use and dispose of other resources in more environmentally friendly ways. How to do this and what the relative roles government and the private sector should play in accomplishing these outcomes is a recurring element of political debate in the United States today.

FIGURE 4.1 CHANGE IN TOTAL POPULATION: 2014–2060

Unlike many of our political and economic partners and rivals, the U.S. population is projected to continue to grow at a healthy clip in the coming decades. This growth is a product of above replacement-rate fertility among the native-born population and an increase in the number of immigrants to the United States. By and large, economists, social scientists, and policy makers believe a growing population is a good thing for a country because it is considered a necessary condition for a growing and dynamic economy. If Donald Trump's policies to slow down both legal and illegal immigration are successful, net international migration and total change in the U.S. population may be somewhat lower than shown here.

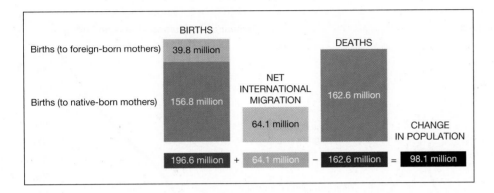

SOURCE: Sandra L. Colby and Jennifer M. Ortman, "Projections of the Size and Composition of the U.S. Population: 2014 to 2060, *Current Population Reports* (Washington, DC: U.S. Census Bureau, March, 2015), 3.

America's Population Is Becoming More Diverse

Based on a long history of immigration, ours is an ethnically, religiously, and racially diverse society.[5] White European Protestants, African slaves, and Native Americans, who made up the bulk of the U.S. population when the first census was taken in 1790, were joined by Catholic immigrants from Ireland and Germany in the 1840s and 1850s (see Figure 4.2) and the Chinese in the 1870s, drawn by jobs in railroad construction. Around the turn of the 20th century, immigrants from eastern, central, and southern Europe raised the ethnic, linguistic, and religious diversity of America. Today, most immigrants are from Asia and Latin America, with people from Mexico representing the largest single component (25 percent of all immigrants between 1965 and 2015 came from Mexico[6]). Starting in the 1990s, the number of immigrants from the Middle East and other locations with Muslim populations has been significant. More than 1 million people from predominantly Muslim countries in the Middle East, Africa, and Asia immigrated to the United States between 2000 and 2015, bringing their total to about 2.8 million.[7] The number of immigrants from majority Muslim countries declined sharply after Donald Trump became president in 2017.

As a result of these immigration streams, the percentage of foreign-born people residing in the United States has more than quadrupled since 1965, reaching almost 15 percent of the population in 2015, about 45 million people.[8] This is very close to the 15 percent foreign born population in the United States in the early part of the 20th century. Although the foreign-born population is concentrated in a handful of states—mainly California, New York, New Jersey, Florida, Illinois, New Mexico, Arizona, and Texas—and in a handful of cities and localities—mainly Miami, New York, Los Angeles–Long Beach, Orange County, Oakland, and Houston—the presence of new immigrants is felt almost everywhere in America, including the Midwest (Ohio, Michigan, and Wisconsin) and the Deep South (North Carolina and Georgia, especially).

The natural outcome of this history of immigration is substantial racial and ethnic diversity in the American population. Although the largest segment of the population in the United States is still overwhelmingly non-Hispanic white (61.3 percent in 2016, as shown in Figure 4.3), diversity is growing every year because of continuing

FIGURE 4.2 IMMIGRANTS IN THE UNITED STATES, BY DECADE, 1820–2010

Measuring how many immigrants reside in the United States in different ways gives rise to quite different interpretations of its scale. Measured in total numbers, the country has more immigrants today than at any time in its history. However, looking at immigrants as a percentage of the total population is a much more revealing statistic. As the figure demonstrates, immigrants as a percentage of the population was highest in the middle and late 19th century and in the early part of the 20th century but fell after that as stringent immigration laws came into force. Even with the high numbers of immigrants who have come into the country in the 1990s and 2000s, the number of immigrants as a percentage of population remains historically lower than its high point in the early 20th century (though it has been increasing steadily from its low point in the 1930s). Donald Trump was elected President in part on his plans to reduce both illegal and legal immigration, so this graph may begin to look different in the coming years if his promises to build a wall on the U.S.–Mexico border and to deport more undocumented people from the United States actually become policy.

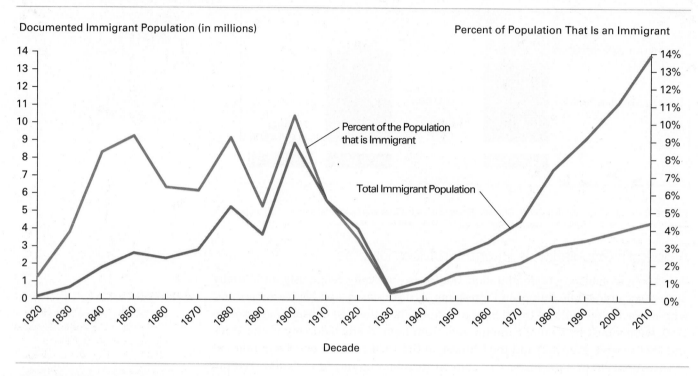

SOURCE: Source: Data from U.S. Department of Homeland Security, Yearbook of Immigration Statistics, "Table 1: Persons Obtaining Lawful Permanent Resident Status: Fiscal Years 1820 To 2014".

immigration (though this has slowed substantially since the 2007 financial collapse) and differential birthrates among population groups. Immigrants are younger than the resident population and tend to have larger families. In 2013, for the first time, births among non-Hispanic whites fell below 50 percent of total births in the United States.[9] Hispanics are now the nation's largest minority group, accounting for 17.8 percent of the U.S. population—with most of the recent growth coming from births rather than immigration—and are projected to account for almost 27.5 percent by 2060.[10] The African American population is the second largest minority group at 13.3 percent of people in the United States and will grow to about 15 percent by 2060. Asian Americans are the fastest-growing group in percentage terms; they make up 5.7 percent of the population, a figure projected to increase to 9.7 percent by 2060. Demographers predict that these trends will continue and that current minority groups, taken together, will become the majority of the U.S. population by 2050, though non-Hispanic whites will remain the largest single group for a long time after that.[11]

The most recent wave of immigration, like all previous ones, has added to our rich linguistic, cultural, and religious traditions; it has also helped revitalize formerly poverty-stricken neighborhoods in cities such as Los Angeles, New York, and Chicago. Immigrants from Asia and Europe especially have also made a mark in science and technology, earning a disproportionate share of PhDs in the sciences as

FIGURE 4.3 ESTIMATED CHANGES IN THE RACIAL AND ETHNIC COMPOSITION OF
THE U.S. POPULATION, PERCENTAGES

Non-Hispanic whites will remain the largest segment of the U.S. population for the foreseeable future,
though this segment will fall below 50 percent in the 2040s.

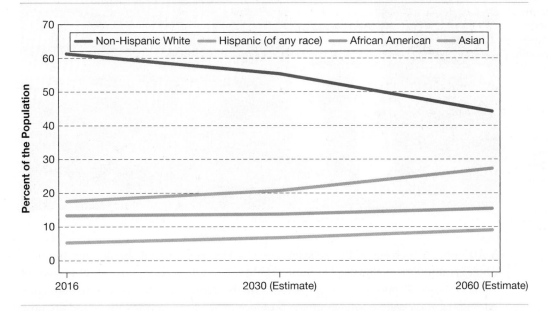

SOURCE: Sandra L. Colby and Jennifer M. Ortman, Projections of the Size and Composition of the U.S. Population: 2014 to
2060 (Washington, DC: U.S. Census Bureau, March, 2015), Table 2, http://www.census.gov/population/projections/data
/national/2015/summarytables.html.

well as technology patents, and are responsible for creating some of the most innovative high-technology companies (e.g., Comcast, Google, SpaceX, WhatsApp, Yahoo!,
and YouTube). Because immigrants tend to be younger and have more children
than non-immigrants, they have slowed the rate at which the American population
is aging, particularly when compared with the rapidly aging populations of Japan,
Russia, China, and most of Europe.

But immigration also has generated political and social tensions at various times
in our history, including today. The arrival of immigrants who are different from the
majority population in significant ways has often sparked anti-immigration agitation
and demands that public officials stem the tide. Nativist (antiforeign) reactions
to Irish Catholic immigrants were common throughout the 19th century. Anti-
Chinese agitation swept the western states in the 1870s and 1880s. Alarm at the
arrival of waves of immigrants from eastern, southern, and central Europe in
the early part of the last century led Congress virtually to close the doors of the
United States in 1921 and keep them closed until the 1950s.

Hispanic immigration—about one-half of immigrants to the United States are
from Latin America—has caused unease among some Americans, even though it
has slowed dramatically since 2007. In 2015, according to a Pew survey, 50 percent
of Americans said that immigrants today are making the economy and crime worse
(but improving food, music, and the arts). When comparing different immigrant
groups, 37 percent of Americans expressed negative views about immigrants from
Latin America compared to only 9 percent for those from Europe and 11 percent for
those from Asia.[12] (Immigrants from the predominantly Muslim Middle East are
viewed even more negatively than those from Latin America).

Republicans especially say they are worried about illegal immigration from
Mexico and Central America (though the number of illegal immigrants living in the
United States reached its peak in 2005 and has been declining steadily since then[13])
and strongly oppose a pathway to citizenship for undocumented immigrants. In

URBAN RENEWAL

Immigrants to the United States have
revitalized urban neighborhoods across
the country, as this street scene in
Flushing, Queens, New York, affirms.
*Can national legislation help to harness
the energies and skills of immigrant populations, or is the cultivation of newcomers
as a potential component of economic
development strictly a local matter?*

MAKING READY FOR DEPORTATION

Suspected undocumented immigrants are gathered together at the U.S. Customs and Border Protection Headquarters in Tucson for possible deportation back to Mexico. Deportations reached record numbers under the Obama administration but nonetheless failed to quell Republican critics despite the fact that the number of immigrants from Mexico living in the United States has declined steadily since 2007. As a result, immigration reform legislation went nowhere during the Obama's presidency or Trump's presidency. Deportations increased after Donald Trump came to office, as he had promised during the presidential campaign.

What other levers of government might the Obama administration have pulled to push immigration reform forward?

a 2015 poll, 63 percent of Republicans said the U.S. government should stop the flow of illegal immigrants and deport those who are living here, compared to 29 percent of Democrats and 39 percent of independents.[14] In the Republican Party, concerns about illegal immigration were once mainly the province of Tea Party conservatives and are now more widespread. One 2018 poll showed, for example, that 77 percent of Republicans wanted a wall built on the Southern border to keep undocumented immigrants out of the country compared to only 10 percent of Democrats.[15] By a margin of 55-35, declared Republicans even supported President Donald Trump's policy of separating children from their parents among people trying to illegally enter the U.S. at the southern border, a policy overwhelmingly rejected by declared Democrats and Independents.[16]

Donald Trump made the discomfiture about immigration a central element in his campaign to win the GOP nomination for president. He jumped to a lead among likely Republican voters at the start of the GOP nomination process in 2015 by demeaning illegal Mexican immigrants, claiming that he would build a wall across the entire border, when he became president, and get Mexico to pay for it. Proposing that people here illegally be deported also helped him stay ahead in the GOP polls. Strikingly, none of the Republican presidential aspirants was willing, during the 2015–2016 nomination cycle, to support a so-called "pathway to citizenship" for illegal immigrants, though several said they would agree to a pathway to legal status of some sort.

After he became president, Donald Trump carried through. He announced, for example, that he was ending President Obama's Deferred Action on Childhood Arrivals (DACA) program created in 2012 that protected against deportation roughly 700,000 children brought to the country illegally by their parents. Trump gave Congress six months to create a successor program that would protect "Dreamer" children so long as Congress also provided funding for a border wall to stop the flow of immigrants as well as additional resources to deport non-DACA individuals in the country illegally. To no one's surprise, Congress failed to pass a new DACA bill but the program held on for some time under court order as the issue played out in the federal courts with the issue bound to be ruled on by the Supreme Court.

The Trump administration did a number of other things to prevent further immigration and to decrease the number of undocumented aliens living in the United States. Attorney General Jeff Sessions, for example, ordered immigration judges to increase the number of cases they processed annually and made how they performed in this aspect of their jobs a factor in determining their salaries. Trump also ordered Immigration and Customs Enforcement (ICE) to be more vigorous in its activities. It worked. During the first nine months of the new administration, ICE arrests for immigration violations rose 42 percent above Obama-era arrests. Arrests of undocumented immigrants who had committed no other crime save that of being here illegally tripled under Trump. Finally, the Trump administration cut back substantially on the number of refugee applications it processed and how many were granted refugee status, reaching a forty year low in 2017.[17]

In addition to a wide split between Republicans and Democrats on what to do about illegal immigration and what the status of undocumented immigrants should be in the future, where immigrants settle is also very important for American politics and government policies. For example, states and localities with high concentrations of immigrants must find additional monies for social services, health care, and education in order to serve a growing and changing population, though the taxes paid by immigrants, whether legal or illegal, help pay for these things. A less well-known impact of immigrant populations is the increase that destination states gain in Congress, where apportionment of seats in the House of Representatives is calculated on the basis of a state's entire adult population regardless of legal status. And, because each state's Electoral College vote is the sum of the number of its representatives in the House and its two senators, high-immigration states play a larger role in presidential elections than they might if only adult citizens and legal aliens were counted in population surveys.

America's Population Is Moving West and South

During the first decade of the 21st century, Americans continued a decades-long trend of moving to the South and West (see Figure 4.4). The Great Recession slowed down this process a bit—Americans had trouble selling their homes and moving elsewhere because of the housing market collapse—but did not stop them. While the Northeast and Midwest still grew from 2000 to 2010—3 percent and 4 percent, respectively—these regions were outpaced by the South and the West, each

---

FIGURE 4.4   THE CENTER OF AMERICAN POPULATION

The mean center of the American population has gradually moved west and south over the course of our history, from near the Chesapeake Bay in Maryland in 1790 to near Plato, Missouri, in the most recent census. This change in the center of population has given western and southern states more power in the Senate and in the Electoral College.

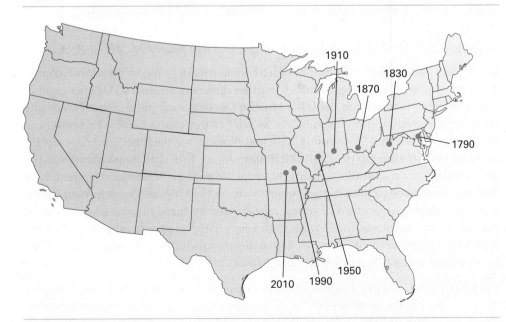

SOURCE: U.S. Census Bureau, "Mean Center of Population for the United States: 1790 to 2010."

of which expanded by 14 percent. The population shift to the South and West has led to changes in the relative political power of the states. Following each census from 1950 to 2000, states in the East and the upper Midwest lost congressional seats and presidential electoral votes. States in the West and the South—often referred to as the Sun Belt because of their generally pleasant weather—gained at the expense of those other regions. After the 2010 census, Missouri, Ohio, Pennsylvania, New York, Massachusetts, Louisiana, New Jersey, Illinois, and Michigan lost House seats and electoral votes; Florida, Georgia, Texas, South Carolina, Arizona, Utah, Washington, and Nevada picked up seats and electoral votes, and Texas was the big winner with four.

America's Population Is Growing Older

One of the most significant demographic trends in the United States and in other industrialized countries is the aging of the population. In 1800, the median age of the United States was just under 16; today, it is a bit more than 35. By 2030, it will be about 38. The proportion of the population older than age 65 has been growing, while the proportion between the ages of 18 and 64 has been shrinking. Today, 13 percent of Americans are elderly. In addition, the number of the very aged—older than 85— is the fastest-growing age segment of all. By 2030, this figure is likely to rise to about 20 percent.[18] Meanwhile, the proportion of the population in the prime working years is likely to fall from 62 percent today to about 58 percent in 2030. Thus, an increasing proportion of Americans is likely to be dependent and in need of services, and a shrinking proportion is likely to comprise taxpaying wage or salary earners, though, to be sure, more Americans who are older than 65 are staying employed, both for financial reasons and to stay active and engaged.[19] The United States is aging much less rapidly, however, than other countries and regions, primarily because of the younger age profile and higher fertility of its minority group populations. Aging is happening much more rapidly in Japan, South Korea, Italy, Russia, China, and much of Europe, for example.[20]

Because the population is aging, the question of how to finance Social Security and Medicare is likely to remain important politically for the foreseeable future. The voting power of the elderly is likely to make it difficult for elected officials to substantially reduce social insurance programs for Americans who are older than 65. Meanwhile, the tax load on those still in the workforce may feel increasingly burdensome. Also, more and more middle-aged people are trying to figure out how to finance assisted-living and nursing home care for their elderly parents. How these issues will play out in the political arena in the near future will be interesting.

America's Population Is Becoming Economically More Unequal

gross domestic product (GDP)
Monetary value of all goods and services produced in a nation each year, excluding income residents earn abroad.

The United States enjoys one of the highest standards of living in the world, consistently ranking among the top countries in **gross domestic product (GDP)** per capita[21] and ranked tenth in 2016 on the UN's Human Development Index, which takes into account education and life expectancy as well as per capita GDP.[22] Luxembourg, Denmark, Switzerland, Singapore, Qatar, and Norway are the other countries always in the running for the top per capita GDP spot. Along with the United States, Australia, Canada, France, Ireland, Germany, Norway, Iceland, the Netherlands, Japan, New Zealand, and Sweden rank highest every year on the Human Development Index. However, the high standard of living represented by these numbers is not shared equally by all Americans. Indeed, we rank very poorly relative to other high income, high human development countries on the degree to which our high standard of living is shared across different groups and classes.

median household income
The midpoint of all households ranked by income.

INCOME INEQUALITY Overall, **median household income** in the United States— the household in the exact middle of the income distribution of all households measured in constant dollars—has grown only modestly over the past four decades, even as the size of the American economy has grown substantially.[23] While the overall

FIGURE 4.5 MEDIAN HOUSEHOLD INCOME AND GDP (IN CONSTANT 2016 DOLLARS), 1967–2016

While the size of the American economy increased by over 1,300 percent between 1967 and 2016, median household income increased by only 130 percent; that is, the overall economy grew at ten times the pace as the income of the median household. The only significant increases in median household income—defined as the household in the exact middle of the income distribution—came in the second half of the 1960s, the mid-to-late 1980s, and the 1990s. The combination of a growing economy and stagnant median household income leads to growing inequality as the fruits of growth go to the top income earners. *How might the slow gains in household income for most Americans and growing income inequality affect how people act politically and what they may want from government?*

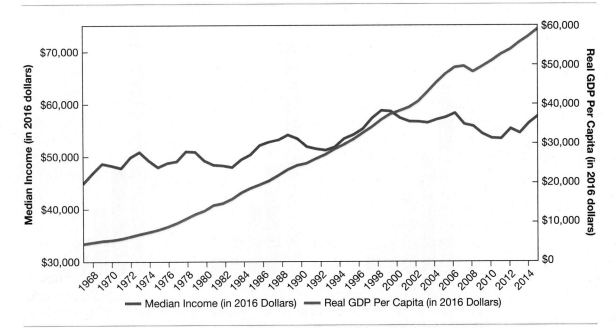

SOURCE: U.S. Census Bureau, Historical Income Tables (Table H-5), U.S. Department of Commerce, Bureau of Economic Analysis.

economy has grown substantially, median household income is about where it was in 1998 (see Figure 4.5). This growing gap suggests that households in the middle have not been reaping the rewards of America's economic growth despite a recent uptick in median family income starting in 2015. A growing economy paired with a relatively stagnant median household income suggests that incomes across American society must be becoming more unequal. Research shows that this is indeed the case.

To be sure, the degree of income inequality has always been higher in the United States than in other rich democracies, but it has become even more pronounced over the past four decades or so.[24] By 2016, the top quintile (the top 20 percent) of households took home 51.5 percent of national income (see Figure 4.6), the second highest share ever recorded. Also noticeable is the drop in the share of national income enjoyed by the bottom 60 percent of the population, and the stagnation of the second highest quintile. The winners are the upper 20 percent. But the real winners, however—not shown in this quintiles graph—are the households at the very, very top. In 2016, the top 1 percent of households took home almost 24 percent of national income, the highest share in the U.S. since pre–Great Depression 1928.[25]

The median household incomes of African Americans and Hispanics (any race) increased significantly between 2015 and 2016 to $39,490 for the former and $47,675 for the latter, though each was well below the median household incomes of Asian Americans ($81,431) and non-Hispanic Whites ($65,041). Meanwhile, white non-college-educated men were hit hard for reasons we will explore below. Men working full time in 2014 made on average and in constant dollars less than they made in the mid-1970s.[26]

WEALTH INEQUALITY Wealth (assets such as real estate, stocks and bonds, art, bank accounts, cash-value insurance policies, and so on) is even more unequally

FIGURE 4.6 U.S. HOUSEHOLD INCOME DISTRIBUTION BY QUINTILES, 1970 VERSUS 1996 VERSUS 2016

Income inequality has been increasing in the United States, reaching levels not seen since the 1920s. A standard way to measure income inequality is to compare the proportion of national income going to each 20 percent (quintile) of households in the population. Especially striking is the shrinking share of the bottom 60 percent, the lack of improvement among the second highest quintile over four-and-a-half decades, and the increasing share of the top 20 percent.

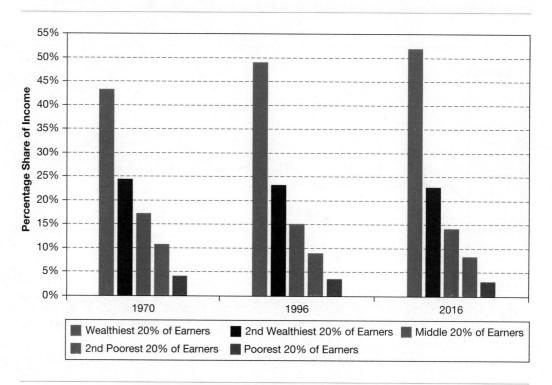

SOURCE: Bernadette D. Proctor, Jessica L. Semega, and Melissa A. Kollar, *Income and Poverty in the United States* (Washington, DC: US Census Bureau, Current Population Reports), September 2016.

distributed than income though harder to pin down. As far as scholars and government statisticians have been able to determine, wealth distribution became slightly more equal during the Great Recession when stocks, mostly owned by upper-income groups, took a beating. But since the recovery, the wealthy have regained their pre-recession share of national economic and financial assets. Thomas Piketty and Emmanuel Saez, the leading scholars on income and wealth inequality, show that the upper 5 percent of wealth holders controlled over 35 percent of all privately held assets in the United States in 2016, the highest level since the 1920s (see Figure 4.7). The top 1 percent controlled almost 20 percent of national wealth almost reaching levels last seen in the 1920s. The top 0.1 percent held about 8 percent of national wealth, near record levels as well. The wealthier are getting wealthier, particularly in the United States.[27]

POVERTY In 1955, almost 25 percent of Americans fell below the federal government's official **poverty line**. Things improved a great deal after that, dropping to 11.1 percent in 1973. During the first decade of the 21st century, however, things took a dramatic turn for the worse. By 2012, 15 percent of Americans were officially below the government's poverty line, the highest since 1993.[28] There was marked improvement in the overall poverty rate during the last two years of the Obama administration. By 2016, the poverty rate fell to 12.7 percent. (See Figure 4.8.)[29]

Is poverty a problem? Here is why many people think so:

- A distressingly large number of Americans live in poverty—using the standard government poverty line measure, almost 40.6 million in 2016, a record number.

poverty line

The federal government's calculation of the amount of income families of various sizes need to stay out of poverty. In 2016, it was $24,300 for a family of four.

FIGURE 4.7 PERCENTAGE OF WEALTH HELD BY THE WEALTHIEST AMERICANS (TOP 5%, 1%, AND .1%) 1917–2015.

At various times in American history, the wealthiest Americans have controlled different percentages of the country's total wealth. This graph shows these changes over time, focusing on the richest 5 percent, 1 percent, and 0.1 percent of the population. The more wealth held by the top earners, the less is held in a proportional sense by everyone else (the 95, 99, and 99.9 percent). As the graph demonstrates, the wealthiest Americans hold more of the nation's wealth than at any time since the 1920s.

Do you think this is a fair outcome of a properly functioning economy? If not, what should we do about it? Should government be more involved in solving this problem or has it helped create the current problem?

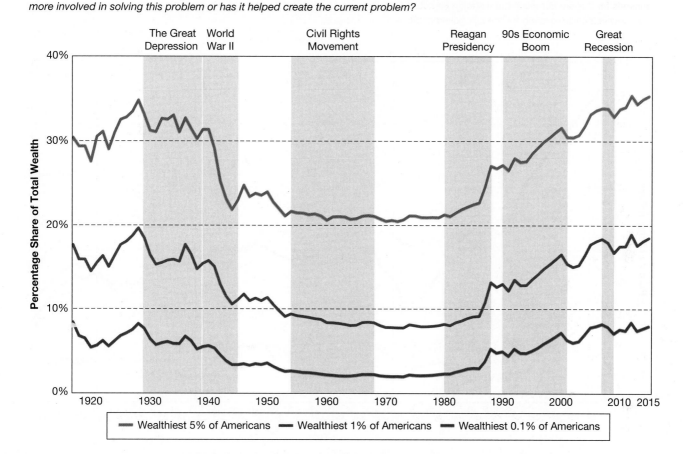

SOURCE: Thomas Piketty and Emmanuel Saez, "Income Inequality in the United States, 1913–1998," *Quarterly Journal of Economics* 118, no. 1 (2003), pp. 1–39; (tables and figures updated to 2015, June 2016).

- The poverty rate is unlikely to fall much unless there is sustained job growth, especially in jobs that will be available to low-skill workers who make up the bulk of the poor. This seems unlikely.

- The poverty rate in the United States remains substantially higher than in other rich democracies.

The distribution of poverty is not random. As evidenced in Figure 4.8, poverty is concentrated among racial minorities and single-parent, female-headed households, and their children.[30] For example, in 2016, more than 22 percent of African Americans and 19.4 percent of Hispanic Americans lived in poverty (although a sizable middle class has emerged in both communities), compared with 8.8 percent of non-Hispanic whites and 10.1 percent of Asians. Of children under the age of 18, 18 percent lived in poverty, as do 26.6 percent of single-parent, female-headed households.[31]

Poverty in the United States has proved to be surprisingly persistent. After a period of improvement after Lyndon Johnson's "War on Poverty" was launched, the rate rebounded steadily to its current level by 1992 and has stayed there for quite some time. Most importantly, there have been few federal government initiatives, other than the Child Nutrition Program or the Earned Income Tax Credit, to solve the problem. The reason why government has paid little attention to poverty reduction

FIGURE 4.8 POVERTY BY RACE

In 2016, a family of four making less than $24,000 per year (this amount is adjusted based on family size) was considered by the federal government to be living poverty. Currently, more than four million Americans (roughly 12 percent) are living on wages that put them below the poverty line. As the graph below shows, poverty rates are much lower now than in the 1960s, when nearly one-quarter of the U.S. population lived in poverty. However, two additional things should also stand out in this graph. First, following significant declines in poverty rates in 1960s, the percentage of the population that lives in poverty has remained fairly steady. Second, black and Hispanic people are about twice as likely as white people to be living in poverty in present day America. The reasons for this are complex, but it should be noted that compared to the middle and upper classes, those living in poverty have very few voices advocating for them in government.

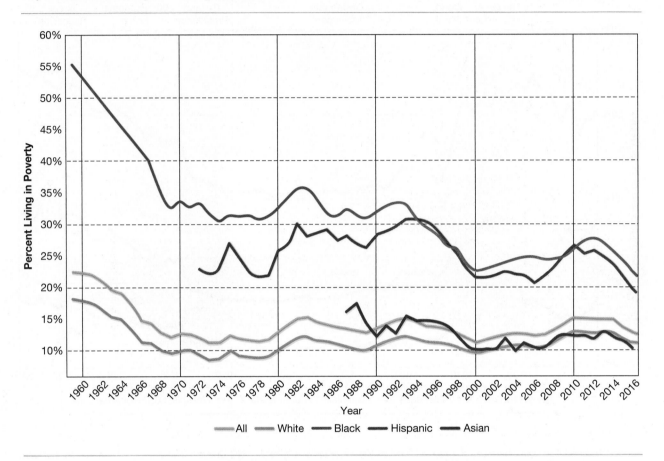

SOURCE: United States Census Bureau, Historical Poverty Tables (Table 2), https://www.census.gov/hhes/www/poverty/data/historical/people.html

has to do with certain cultural notions about poverty, changes in manufacturing jobs, the almost nonexistent political influence of the poor and those who advocate for them, and a political environment that focuses on the problems of the middle class. To sharpen and extend your understanding of the problem of persistent poverty in America, turn to Figure 4.9, an application of our analytical framework.

SOME POLITICAL IMPLICATIONS OF RISING ECONOMIC INEQUALITY A number of problems have become more salient as overall economic inequality has increased.

- When the economic situation of average Americans is improving, Americans tend to express satisfaction with their situation and confidence in elected leaders. This was true for much of the three-decade long period from the end of World War II in 1945. When economic times become more difficult for average Americans, their satisfaction with the status quo, confidence in the political system, and trust in government declined. In the weeks just prior to the November 2016 presidential election, 67 percent of Americans said they believed the nation "was generally headed in the wrong direction."[32] In this context, it is hardly surprising that non-mainstream, populist GOP candidate Donald Trump won the presidential

FIGURE 4.9 APPLYING THE FRAMEWORK: WHY GOVERNMENT DOES LITTLE TO REDUCE POVERTY

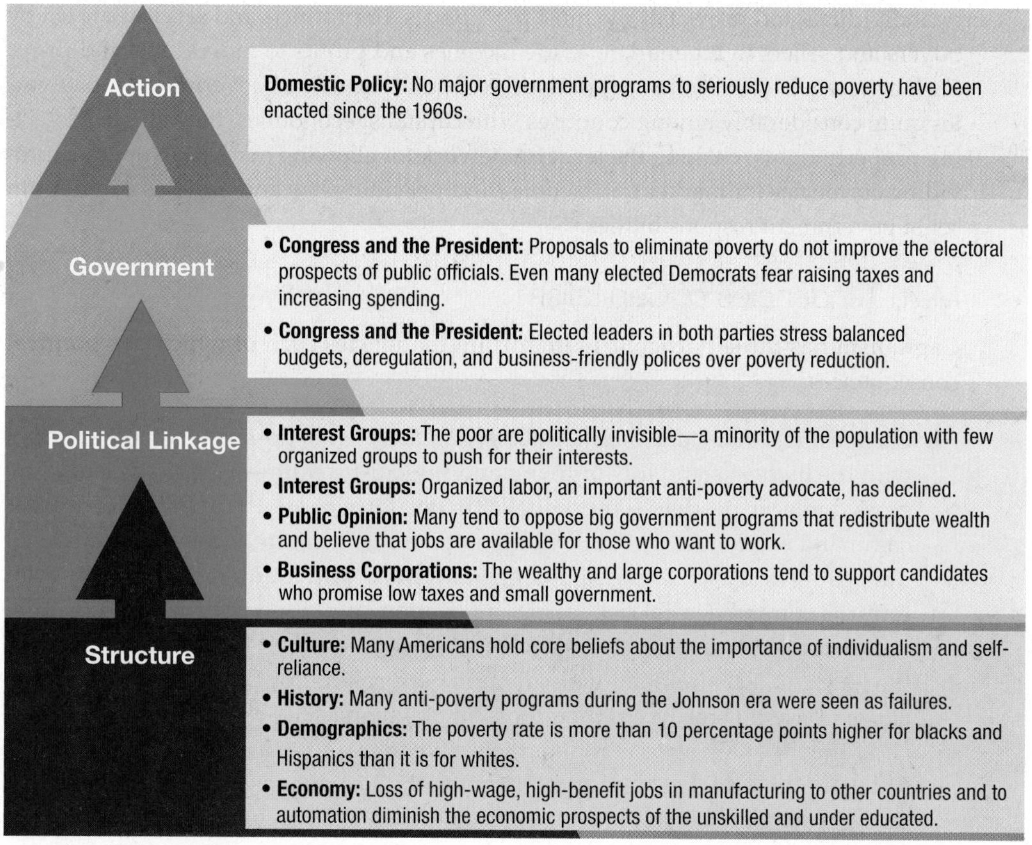

Action

Domestic Policy: No major government programs to seriously reduce poverty have been enacted since the 1960s.

Government

- **Congress and the President:** Proposals to eliminate poverty do not improve the electoral prospects of public officials. Even many elected Democrats fear raising taxes and increasing spending.
- **Congress and the President:** Elected leaders in both parties stress balanced budgets, deregulation, and business-friendly polices over poverty reduction.

Political Linkage

- **Interest Groups:** The poor are politically invisible—a minority of the population with few organized groups to push for their interests.
- **Interest Groups:** Organized labor, an important anti-poverty advocate, has declined.
- **Public Opinion:** Many tend to oppose big government programs that redistribute wealth and believe that jobs are available for those who want to work.
- **Business Corporations:** The wealthy and large corporations tend to support candidates who promise low taxes and small government.

Structure

- **Culture:** Many Americans hold core beliefs about the importance of individualism and self-reliance.
- **History:** Many anti-poverty programs during the Johnson era were seen as failures.
- **Demographics:** The poverty rate is more than 10 percentage points higher for blacks and Hispanics than it is for whites.
- **Economy:** Loss of high-wage, high-benefit jobs in manufacturing to other countries and to automation diminish the economic prospects of the unskilled and under educated.

© Edward S. Greenberg

election, probably helped by the fact that many Democrats who favored populist Senator Bernie Sanders over Hilary Clinton did not turn out to vote.

- High poverty levels also are politically consequential. While the poor have little voice in the American political system, poverty tends to be linked to a range of socially undesirable outcomes, including crime, drug use, and family disintegration,[33] which draws the attention of other citizens who want government to do something about these problems. The cause of poverty reduction has also drawn the attention of many Americans who are offended on moral and religious grounds by the extent of the poverty that exists in what is still the world's largest economy.

- Money is important in how different people and groups bring influence to bear in American politics and in shaping what government does. It is quite troubling, then, to see the extent to which income and wealth are flowing in such a manner that rich are becoming richer. We shall examine how the rich are playing an ever more important role in our political and government system in Chapters 7 and 10.

AMERICA'S ECONOMY

4.2 Discuss how the American economy shapes government and politics.

Virtually everything discussed so far in this chapter is shaped by the nature of the American economy. The growth, diversification, and geographic dispersion of the American population, for example, can be traced directly to economic changes. The way we earn our livings, our standard of living, and the distribution of income and wealth in our nation are closely connected to the operations of our economic institutions. Even important elements of American political culture, as we shall soon see, are associated with our economy and how it works.

capitalism

An economic system characterized by private ownership of productive assets where most decisions about how to use these assets are made by individuals and firms operating in a market rather than by government.

America's economy is one in which the productive assets of society (e.g., land, machinery, factories and offices, financial capital, and so on) are privately owned and where most decisions about how to use them are made, not by the government, but by individuals and firms. For the most part, prices for products and services are set by buyers and sellers in the market, as are incomes and profits to individuals and firms. Such a system is often called **capitalism**. Although the role of government today varies quite considerably among countries with capitalist economies, they all see protecting property rights, creating the legal framework for allowing markets to operate, providing currencies for market transactions, and providing law and order as a minimum set of government responsibilities.[34]

Main Tendencies of Capitalism

Capitalism has three particularly important tendencies each of which has political consequences.

1. *Capitalist economies are tremendously productive.*   It is no mystery that societies with the highest standards of living and the most wealth—usually measured by gross domestic product—are capitalist in one form or another. Unlike the former command economies of the Soviet Union and its Eastern European satellites of the post–World War II era, and China and India until quite recently, capitalism rewards entrepreneurial risk-taking, innovation, and responsiveness to consumer preferences. Productivity gains and economic growth tend to follow, at least over the long run. The tremendous economic performance of China and India in the current period is related to their loosening of many state controls on individuals and firms, opening up to world markets, and doing more to protect property rights (though China still has a long way to go on this last dimension). One result is that by every measure of well-being, people in the United States and in most of the rest of the world are better off than they have ever been before in human history.[35]

2. *Capitalist economies tend to produce substantial income and wealth inequalities.*   Capitalism is a system that rewards those who win in the marketplace. It is an economic system that tends to pay off for those with high skills, entrepreneurs and firms that successfully innovate, and those who satisfy consumers. Big income gains over time are converted by individuals into property assets such as residential and commercial real estate, jewelry and art, and stocks and bonds. Over the long run, as economist Thomas Piketty has demonstrated, property grows at a faster pace than the overall economy and average incomes, meaning that inequality of property ownership grows inexorably over time.[36] The wealthy not only generate additional income for themselves and their families from their holdings but give their heirs a leg up in the next round by passing on their estates, their greater access to quality education, and their social and economic connections. Where there are winners, of course, there are also losers—that is, individuals and firms who do not do well in the competitive market. It is not surprising, then, that fast-growing capitalist economies such as China and India are experiencing a rising tide of income and wealth inequality. Inequality is also characteristic of the United States, western Europe, Australia, and New Zealand. Where capitalist countries differ considerably, of course, is the degree to which government acts to alter this situation by redistributing income and wealth, by imposing high tax rates on high-income earners and delivering programs that provide generous educational, unemployment, retirement, and medical benefits for all. The United States does less of this than any other rich capitalist country.[37]

3. *Capitalist economies are unstable.*   Capitalist economies are subject to business cycles, alternating periods of high and low (or even negative) economic growth. In the former, firms, investors, and those who have jobs all tend to gain, to one degree or another; in the latter down period, rewards to firms, investors, and

workers grow only slowly, stagnate, or even decline. Historically, capitalism has experienced these fluctuations around a general upward trend of economic growth. One reason for this overall growth, despite periods of negative growth, seems to be that in bad times, inefficient and ineffective firms fall by the wayside and innovative and nimble firms emerge better positioned for the next phase of growth. During the Great Depression, for example, big technical advances were made in radio, television, and automobiles.[38]

At times, the up and down cycles can become quite extreme, a so-called boom-and-bust pattern. The biggest bust of the 20th century in American capitalism was the Great Depression of the 1930s, when industrial production fell by half and unemployment at one point reached 31 percent. The Great Recession of 2008 and 2009, which represents the biggest economic downturn since the Great Depression and whose effects still trouble the American economy, followed the bursting of a gigantic real estate bubble (fueled by a flood of easy credit) and the collapse of the financial industry.

Globalization, Technological Change, and Hypercompetition

For roughly three decades following the end of World War II in 1945, the American version of capitalism enjoyed unparalleled and unchallenged success. By 1975, for example, eleven of the largest fifteen corporations in the world were American; by 1981, 40 percent of the world's total foreign direct investment was accounted for by the United States.[39]

During this period, most major industries in the United States were dominated by three or four firms—such as GM, Ford, and Chrysler, known as the "Big Three," in autos—that mass-produced commodities such as steel, cars, and refrigerators. Facing little domestic or foreign competition in the U.S. market and protected in their market dominance by federal regulators, major companies enjoyed substantial and stable profits over many years. Because they could easily pass on their costs in the prices they charged consumers, corporations were happy to enter into contracts with **labor unions** that provided good wages and benefits for their employees as well as employment stability and predictability for themselves. One result was an impressive expansion of the middle class and a general rise in the American standard of living.

labor union
An organization representing employees that bargains with employers over wages, benefits, and working conditions.

THE NEW AMERICAN ECONOMY   The relatively protected and stable world of the post–World War II corporation is gone, replaced by a form of capitalism where

ENERGY INNOVATION
Although the practice is controversial, primarily because of environmental concerns, hydraulic fracturing, or fracking, has helped make possible an oil and natural gas production boom in the United States after decades of worry about importing more and more energy to meet U.S. demand for power.
Why is innovation an important characteristic of capitalist economies, and does government have a role in encouraging it? These workers in Mead, Colorado, might have a one-word answer for you—jobs. Are there other explanations?

GLOBALIZATION

Production and distribution of most manufactured products is now global, a trend that has been accelerated by a wide range of technological changes, including containerization, an example of which is shown in this massive container shipping complex in Hamburg, Germany.

How does globalization shape the issues that concern the American public, and how does it affect what government does?

major companies face intense and unrelenting competition at home and abroad. Their changed situation was brought about by a set of near-simultaneous transformations across a broad front that accelerated the introduction of labor-saving technologies and the pace of **globalization**. For example, the digital revolution brought advances in computer hardware and software and the explosive growth in the Internet. Dramatic improvements in the speed and costs of moving raw materials and commodities here and abroad included containerized trucking and shipping, bigger and faster jet planes, high-speed trains, and improved highways. A strong move in the United States, beginning in the 1970s and picking up steam after that, deregulated a broad range of industries (including shipping, banking, securities, and telecommunications, among others) in hopes of fighting inflation and improving American competitiveness in the face of the galloping economies of Japan, the so-called Asian Tigers, and the European Union. And, finally, a number of international agreements came into force that diminished barriers to trade and investment across national borders.

Globalization[40] is the term often used to describe this new world where goods, services, and money flow easily across national borders. In this new world, companies can and must produce and sell almost anywhere and seek hard-working and talented employees where they can find them. They can also find subcontractors and partner companies in diverse geographical locations to supply them with parts, as Boeing does for the airplanes it assembles, or with finished products, as Walmart does to supply its many stores. With the infrastructure provided by global financial markets and services, investors can move money to those places and into those companies wherein they believe they can get the highest rate of return. Customers, having a wider range of choices, increasingly insist on the best possible products at the lowest possible prices and will switch where they shop with breathtaking speed to make sure this happens.[41]

With many emerging markets, new industry-spawning technologies, fickle investors and customers, and ample investment capital for new companies, large companies everywhere face fierce competition. Growth and profitability, even survival, for many of them, are no longer routine as they were for much of the postwar period. Some formerly powerful companies simply disappeared (including TWA, Eastern, and Pan Am among American airlines), giving way to more innovative and nimble

challengers (e.g., JetBlue and Southwest), while others were forced to dramatically change their business model (e.g., Kodak shifting from film to digital photography and IBM focusing on IT services after offloading its computer manufacturing division to the Chinese company Lenovo). Even the most powerful companies today dare not stand pat for fear of losing out to new competitors. Microsoft, for example, must figure out how to compete with Apple in the smartphone, laptop, and tablet markets and with Google and Amazon in cloud-based software model for enterprise computing. Apple cannot afford to rest on its considerable laurels when Amazon is pushing hard to become the main supplier of cloud computing capacity. Amazon is pushing hard to become the place where people everywhere do their shopping, battling not only Walmart but several giant Chinese firms. Amazon, Netflix, HBO, Disney, and others are in intense competition to be the main suppliers of original content for streaming. Big coal companies such as Peabody Energy must rise to the challenge of natural gas, which is cleaner and cheaper than coal.

To a great extent, globalization and rapid technological innovation have been good for Americans (and for people generally around the world).[42] For example, they have helped drop prices for consumer goods, ranging from consumer electronics to computers, furniture, and clothing, and brought new, exciting, and useful products to market. But globalization and hypercompetition, in association with the introduction of labor-saving technologies, also have had negative impacts. In a global economy where companies are fighting for advantages over other companies, costs become a factor, and many choose to become "lean and mean." What this means for companies is trimming or eliminating health care and retirement plans and shedding employees as part of their competitive strategies. Because of costs, they feel they must do so; because of productivity-enhancing technological changes that allow them to produce more with fewer employees, they can do so. For example, Google announced in late 2013 that it was investing heavily in robotics to make supply-chain distribution channels faster and more efficient, with need for fewer and fewer workers. As the engineer in charge of the project noted with some amazement, "There are still people who walk around in factories and pick things up in distribution centers and work in the back rooms of grocery stores."[43]

Some companies believe they must outsource to lower-cost suppliers and shift some operations to other locations to be closer to overseas customers. This happened first with basic manufacturing (think cars and steel), then with back-office low-skilled

WHERE DID ALL THE WORKERS GO?

Polls show that a majority of Americans believe that jobs losses in manufacturing are the product of globalization and trade. However, a majority of economists believe that automation and computerization have decreased the need for as many workers as before, as can be seen in this modern Amazon fulfillment center where product orders are filled for shipping.

Where do you stand on this extremely important debate? Do you believe there are public policies that might allow us to enjoy the benefits of globalization, trade, automation, and computerization, yet create plentiful and well-paying jobs at the same time?

service activities (think call centers and mortgage processing services), and increasingly today with highly skilled work in design engineering, research and development, advanced manufacturing,[44] and some medical services (medical records, radiology, and the like). Faced with this combination of labor-saving, computer-based technologies and globalization, jobs have been lost and employees have lost much of their bargaining power with employers.[45]

President Donald Trump has long believed that globalization, as embodied in free trade agreements, globally distributed manufacturing, and the extensive movement of labor across national boundaries to fill available jobs, has hurt Americans. Carrying out his pledge to "make America great again," he began a tariff fight in 2018 raising rates against foreign steel and aluminum products imported from Canada, Mexico, and the European Union, and against a wide range of products imported to the United States from China. It is too early to tell whether these changes in tariff policies will fundamentally change the nature of globalization as each country raises tariff rates against American products or whether it will represent but a bump on the road to fuller global economic integration.

THE TROUBLED MIDDLE CLASS   Because of these transformations, the American middle class is in trouble.[46] This is true no matter how we define the middle class, whether strictly **by income** (say the middle three quintiles shown in Figure 4.6), **occupation** (say blue-collar manufacturing and extractive industry workers and white-collar and service workers in either the private or public sectors), or **lifestyle**, say those who live in safe neighborhoods with good public schools, hold relatively steady jobs, make enough to take an occasional vacation, purchase or lease a late model new or used car, put a little away for retirement, and pay for college for their children. This lifestyle concept of middle class is what has traditionally been called the American Dream.

In terms of income, as you learned, the three middle quintiles have actually fallen behind where they were in the middle 1970s. In terms of occupation, a wide variety of popular news outlets, government reports, and scholarly articles have pointed to the diminished prospects for blue-collar workers and white-collar workers whose jobs can and have been reduced by automation and robotization. Average wages and salaries for the middle class have lagged behind the rate of growth in the economy and the increase in overall productivity since the mid-1980s. From the late 1990s to the present, incomes for those whose formal education ended with their high school diploma and for those with some college but without a bachelor's degree stagnated or fell.

In terms of lifestyle, the likelihood of gaining the American Dream seems ever more remote to Americans. For example, fewer people are covered by pensions or other retirement plans that their employers contribute to. Jobs are less stable and predictable than during the three decades following WWII because of outsourcing, technological change, and increased trade. The costs of health care and health care insurance have risen dramatically as has the cost of a two-year or four-year college education.

Middle-aged (35–54), non-Hispanic whites whose education does not go past high school have been hit especially hard, and it is reflected in how long they live. Unlike middle-aged African Americans, Hispanics, the college-educated, and people in other rich democracies whose death rates have declined substantially and steadily since 2000, theirs has increased. That is to say, the death rate of white, middle-aged people in the United States—defined as the number of annual deaths per 100,000 people—has gotten worse rather than improved like that of other groups over the past decade and a half.[47] This may be related to the loss of stable, well-paid manufacturing jobs in the country once filled by people with only a high school education which has hit whites in the 35–54 age group especially hard. It is this group more than any other demographic that has experienced a decline in its overall living standard and an increase in behaviors associated directly or indirectly with a shorter life span: more suicides, increased drug and alcohol abuse, weight gain, and family disintegration.[48]

A troubled middle class tends to be an angry and fearful middle class, and this has important consequences for American politics.

The sense that the country and the economy are going in the wrong direction and that government leaders have ignored the American middle class may explain part of the volatility of recent elections in which one party and then the other is swept into power to "clean up the mess" in Washington or a state capital. It may partially explain why voters are increasingly prone to elect hard partisans to office who offer easily digestible explanations of who is to blame for stagnant or declining living standards. It may partially explain the rising incivility in our civic life, where angry confrontations have become more common, whether in school board meetings or town hall-type meetings in congressional districts.[49]

AMERICA'S POLITICAL CULTURE

4.3 Describe the values and beliefs that make up American political culture and how they affect politics and government.

Evidence suggests that Americans share a core set of beliefs about human nature, society, and government that is very different from the core beliefs of people in other societies.[50] To be sure, we are a vast, polyglot mixture of races, religions, ethnicities, occupations, and lifestyles, and we are increasingly riven by partisanship that some suggest will undermine in the long run Americans' broad agreement on core beliefs.[51] Nevertheless, one of the things that has always struck foreign observers of the American scene, ranging from Alexis de Tocqueville (*Democracy in America*, 1835 and 1840) to James Bryce (*The American Commonwealth*, 1888) and John Micklethwait and Adrian Wooldridge (*The Right Nation*, 2004), is the degree to which a broad consensus seems to exist on many of the core beliefs that shape our attitudes and opinions, our ways of engaging in politics, and what we expect of our government, and how different the elements of this consensus are from political cultural elements in other countries. To be sure, consensus on core beliefs does not mean that people always agree on what government should do in particular situations. Thus, people who agree that government's role should be limited might disagree on what specific things government should do (say, national defense or school lunch programs). Though people in other

political culture

The set of core beliefs in a country that help shape how people behave politically and what they believe government should do.

societies share some of the core beliefs of Americans, the package of core beliefs is truly exceptional.

Understanding our **political culture**—the set of core beliefs about human nature, society, and government—is important for understanding American politics and government. Why? Because the kinds of choices Americans make in meeting the challenges posed by a changing economy, society, and post–Cold War world depend a great deal on the core beliefs Americans hold about human nature, society, economic relations, and the role of government. In Chapter 5, we examine in some detail how Americans pass on these core beliefs to each new generation—a process called political socialization. In the remainder of this chapter, we look at the content of these core beliefs.

Individualistic

Americans believe that individuals have, as the Declaration of Independence puts it, unalienable rights, meaning that individual rights take priority over rights that might be attributed to society or government. Indeed, the very purpose of government, following John Locke's ideas in *The Second Treatise on Government* (1690) and Thomas Jefferson's in the Declaration of Independence (1776), is to protect these rights. In formal, legal terms, this has meant that Americans have worked hard to protect the constitutional rights of speech, belief, and association (among others). In a more informal sense, this has meant an abiding belief among Americans in the importance of personal ambition and choosing one's own life goals and way of life.

American individualism also is expressed as a belief that one's fate is (and ought to be) in one's own hands, rather than it being the product of impersonal social and economic forces beyond one's own control. In particular, one's fortunes are tied to one's own efforts. Those with talent, grit, and the willingness to work hard, Americans believe, are more likely than not to end up on top; those without at least some of these qualities are more likely to wind up at the bottom of the heap. Americans tend to assume that people generally get what they deserve in the long run, though the troubles hitting the middle class are beginning to erode this belief, with increasing numbers of Americans saying that hard work no longer pays off.

ALL FOR ONE, ONE FOR ALL

In Japan, commitment to the work team and the company are more important cultural values than in the United States. These Japanese supermarket workers start their day as a team.

What might be some economic advantages and disadvantages to the Japanese all-for-one, one-for-all viewpoint?

Americans also are more likely to believe that people are naturally competitive, always striving to better themselves in relation to others. Popular literature in America has always conveyed this theme, ranging from the Horatio Alger books of the late 19th century to the many contemporary self-help books with keys to "getting ahead," "making it," and "getting rich." The French have been known to refer to this celebration of the competitive individual over the community as the "Anglo-Saxon disease" (thus including the English) and profess to want no part of it in continental Europe.

This core belief about individualism affects American attitudes toward many issues, including inequality and what should be done about it.[52] Americans overwhelmingly endorse the idea of "equality of opportunity" (the idea that people ought to have an equal shot in the competitive game of life), for instance, yet they also overwhelmingly reject the idea that people should be guaranteed equal rewards, especially if this outcome comes from actions by government.[53]

Not surprisingly, Americans tend to look favorably on government programs that try to equalize opportunity—Head Start, education programs of various kinds, school lunch programs, and the like—but are less favorable to welfare-style programs that seem to redistribute income from the hard-working middle class to individuals who are considered "undeserving."[54] Not surprisingly, given this core belief, Americans are less likely to support government efforts to equalize matters than people in other rich democracies (see Figure 4.10), especially if efforts to equalize outcomes in society involve imposing limits on individual striving and achievement.[55]

FIGURE 4.10 INDIVIDUALISM

Compared to those who live in other rich democracies, Americans are the least likely to want government to play a major role in determining life's economic outcomes and the most likely to believe that individuals are mainly responsible for such outcomes.
How does this aspect of American political culture influence what people expect of the government?

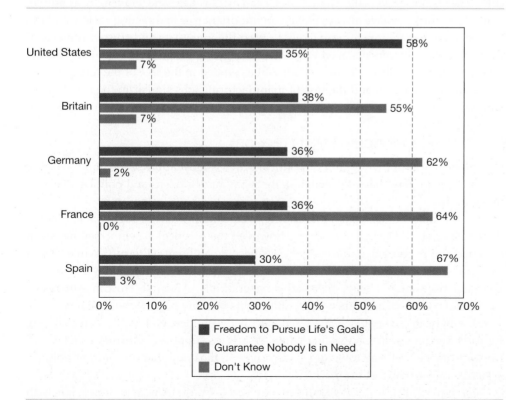

SOURCE: Pew Research Global Attitudes Project, "The American-Western European Values Gap," Pew Research Center, November 17, 2011, updated February 29, 2012.

Distrustful of Government

From the beginning, Americans have distrusted government. The framers created a republican constitutional system precisely because they distrusted government and were trying to create a set of constitutional rules that would deny government the means to act in mischievous or evil ways. Americans have long believed that when governments are imbued with too much power, they are tempted to interfere with private property, individual rights, and economic efficiency. Distrust of government remains attractive to most Americans today, even though most Americans expect government to do far more than the framers ever imagined, such as providing Social Security, Medicare, and environmental protection and trying a variety of measures to get the country out of economic recessions. In this respect—distrusting government yet supporting a range of programs that seem essential to the public's well-being—Americans are conflicted, to some extent, being what some have called ideological conservatives and operational liberals. As Ben Page and Lawrence Jacobs put it, "most Americans are philosophical conservatives but also pragmatic egalitarians. They look to government for help in ensuring that everyone has genuine equal opportunity plus a measure of economic security with which to exercise that opportunity."[56] But distrust of government increases when the help provided by government does not, in reality, seem to help or seems to help those who are already powerful and privileged, as in the bank and financial institution bailouts in the middle of the Great Recession.[57]

Distrust of government remains the "default" position of a majority of Americans. Even when they support particular government programs, they worry that government is getting too big, too expensive, and too involved in running things. During the health care debate in 2009, for example, a Pew Research Center survey discovered that a majority supported each major element of the Democrats' health care package, but only 34 percent favored the package as a whole, with widespread concern that the bill created too much government control.[58] As one commentator put it, "Americans are looking to the government for help, but they still don't like the government."[59] This core belief is not universally shared. In Germany, Sweden, and France, for example, where governments have always played an important role in directing society and the economy, people are much more likely to trust the intentions and trustworthiness of their national governments even when they disagree with political leaders on particular government policies, though this trust has eroded in the face of the refugee crisis that hit Europe in 2016 and the loss of manufacturing jobs similar to the trend in the United States.

Believers in Democracy and Freedom

Certain beliefs about what kind of political order is most appropriate and what role citizens should play shape the actual daily behavior of citizens and political decision makers alike.

At the time of the nation's founding, democracy was not highly regarded in the United States. During our history, however, the practice of democracy has been enriched and expanded, and *democracy* has become an honored term.[60] While regard for democracy is one of the bedrocks of the American belief system today, Americans have not necessarily always behaved democratically. After all, African Americans were denied the vote and other citizenship rights in many parts of the nation until the 1960s. Americans seem to see this disconnect between ideal and reality. A recent Pew Research Center survey shows that while Americans support democracy as a general principle as the best way to organize government, most say that our present political system falls way short of the mark.[61]

Foreign visitors have always been fascinated by the American obsession with individual "rights," the belief that, in a good society, government leaves people alone in their private pursuits. Studies show that freedom (also called *liberty*) is at the very top of the list of American beliefs and that it is more strongly honored here than elsewhere.[62] From the very beginning, what attracted most people to the United States was the promise of freedom in the New World. Many came for other reasons, to be sure: a great many came for strictly economic reasons, some came as convict labor, and some came in chains as slaves. But many who came to these shores seem to have done so to taste the freedom to speak and think as they chose, to worship as they pleased, to read what they might, and to assemble and petition the government if they had a mind to do so.

As in many cases, however, to believe in something is not necessarily to act consistently with that belief. There have been many intrusions on basic rights during our history. Later chapters address this issue in more detail.

Populist

The term **populism** refers to the hostility of the common person to concentrated power and the powerful. While public policy is not often driven by populist sentiments (for the powerful, by definition, exercise considerable political influence), populism has always been part of the American core belief system and has sometimes been expressed in visible ways in American politics.

populism
The belief that the common person is every bit as good as someone with wealth and power.

One of the most common targets of populist sentiment has been concentrated economic power and the people who exercise it. The Populist movement of the 1890s aimed at taming the new corporations of the day, especially the banks and the railroads. Corporations were targets of popular hostility during the dark days of the Great Depression and in the 1970s, when agitation by consumer and environmental groups made the lives of some corporate executives extremely uncomfortable. Populism is a staple of contemporary conservatism in the United States, with its attacks on Hollywood, the media, and academic elitists.[63] Members of the modern Tea Party movement directed their anger at bankers and bank bailouts, big government and taxes, and bicoastal elites who fail, they believe, to appreciate the values of ordinary Americans. Occupy Wall Street supporters also denigrated Wall Street and a government that seemed to consistently come to its aid. Donald Trump—though the latter is notoriously wealthy—based his populist appeals during his successful election campaign battle in 2016 against Washington elites, including the leaders of his own political party. Bernie Sanders's run for the Democratic nomination was focused on Wall Street greed and government policies that favored the wealthy.

Populism celebrates the ordinary person. Given this widespread belief, it behooves political candidates in America to portray themselves as ordinary folks, with tastes and lifestyles very much like everyone else's. How else might one explain private school-educated and aristocratically born-and-bred George H. W. Bush expressing his fondness for pork rinds and country and western music during the 1988 presidential campaign? His son, George W. Bush—a student at a prestigious prep school, an undergraduate at Yale, and an MBA student at Harvard—wanted to be seen (and perhaps saw himself) as a hard-working rancher on his Texas spread. Donald Trump, though very wealthy, likes to speak of himself as an ordinary guy from Queens, New York, with a fondness for fast food.

Religious

The United States is, by any measure, a strikingly religious society.[64] Polls conducted over the past three or four decades show that more Americans believe in God, regularly attend church, and say that religion is important in their lives, than people in most of the other rich democracies (see Figure 4.11), though there is mounting evidence that the category "no religious affiliation" is rising among younger Americans. This commitment to religion has existed from the beginning of the republic and is integrally related to the practice of politics in the United States—something that often baffles foreign observers.[65] Most important, political leaders in the United States have invoked religious sentiments in their public pronouncements, and Americans have come to expect religious references when leaders talk about public matters. During election contests, most American politicians at some point talk about their faith and their belief in God, something that is almost unheard of in other rich democracies. Prayer breakfasts are quite common in the White House, whether the president is a Republican or a Democrat. Such events do not occur at 10 Downing Street in Great Britain or at the Élysée Palace in France.

FIGURE 4.11   RELIGIOUS COMMITMENT

An international survey found that America is among the more religious rich democracies.
How might this affect the kinds of policies that Americans want government to create?

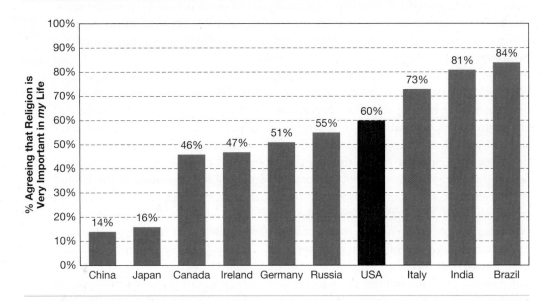

SOURCE: Win-Gallup International Global Index of Religiosity and Atheism (2012), http://www.wingia.com/web/files/news/14/file/14.pdf.

PRAYING BEFORE DOING BATTLE

Public displays of piety by political leaders are common and expected in the United States, something quite rare in other rich democracies. Here, President Obama and Republican congressional leaders John Boehner and Eric Cantor say a prayer together before holding a contentious meeting on issues dividing the president and congressional Republicans in 2013.

How does the strong religious culture of the United States affect the kinds of public policies we have here compared to other countries?

Religious faith affects politics in important ways. First, it influences which issues become part of political debate and election campaigns. For example, school prayer and the teaching of evolution have not been part of the political debate in many other democracies as they have here. Second, religious belief has been important in drawing ideological lines. While churches and religious believers have often been on the liberal side of the political divide, to be sure—note the substantial involvement of religious leaders, organizations, and believers in the civil rights and anti–Vietnam War movements—strong religious beliefs are most associated with conservative tendencies in American politics. Public opinion polls show that the most religiously committed Americans (of all denominations) are also the most conservative Americans on issues ranging from abortion to prayer in the schools, social welfare, and military spending; church attendance, in the end, is a better predictor of party affiliation than income. This suggests that conservative ideas based in religious belief have a head start over liberal beliefs on a wide range of public issues.

AMERICAN SOCIETY, ECONOMY, AND POLITICAL CULTURE: HOW DEMOCRATIC?

Throughout this book, we have examined a number of structural factors that influence American politics. This chapter examined the main features of American society, its economy, its political culture, and its place in the world and considered how each influences important aspects of politics and government in the United States. All of these structural factors are interrelated. Constitutional rules are substantially shaped by our beliefs about the nature of the individual, society, and government, which make up our political culture. Our political culture, in turn—with its celebration of the market, competitive individualism, and private property—is perfectly attuned to a capitalist economy. How the economy operates and develops has a lot to do with the American people (where people live, what kind of work they do, and so on), as does the nation's place in the world. The demographic characteristics of the American population trigger their own effects; the populace's level of education and skill has a lot to do with American economic performance, for instance.

The interplay of these factors—and the ways in which they are interpreted and played out through government policy and action—affects the quality and nature of democracy in the United States. But there is some disagreement on whether or not the American political structure, created by economics, culture, and social realities, fosters democracy.

On the one side, some argue that American society is open, diverse, and filled with opportunity for those who are ambitious and hard working. Economic growth is raising the living standards of the population (if modestly for most), which bodes well for democracy; note the evidence that high living standards and democracy seem to go together. Also, economic, technological, and social changes—including the Internet, ease of travel, medical advances, and more—are allowing more and more people to develop their unique abilities and capacities, to become informed, to link together with others who share their public concerns, to get involved in community and political affairs, and to have their voices heard by public officials. Most importantly, perhaps, these developments make it possible for Americans to shape their own lives, improving their situations and those of their families, without the help of government. In short, equality of opportunity and technological and social changes are making American society more hospitable to democracy.

Yet others counter that the American society fails to live up to the promise of equal opportunity and access to government, making it, in fact, far less democratic than other wealthy democracies. The economic system of the United States, while incredibly productive, distributes wealth and income in a highly unequal way, leaving the very few at the top with the lion's share. This leads to substantial inequalities in political power and influence among different income and wealth groups as well as dividing Americans along ethnic, racial, religious, and regional lines. Such divisions undermine democracy because economic inequality always spills over into political inequality. To make matters worse, the American political culture celebrates an extreme form of individualism and antigovernment sentiment that makes it hard for Americans to agree on a way to use government to best serve public purposes.

REVIEW THE CHAPTER

AMERICA'S POPULATION

4.1 Describe the effect of recent demographic trends on American politics.

The most important changes in the American population are its diversification along ethnic, religious, and racial lines and its relocation the Sun Belt.

These changes have enhanced the political influence of the southern and western states in Congress and in presidential elections.

Minority racial and ethnic groups have gained political influence as their numbers have grown.

Income and wealth in the United States are more unequally distributed than in any other rich democracy and are becoming more so.

Poverty increased during the 2000s and stayed there since, and median household income has been stagnant from the late 1990s to the present.

AMERICA'S ECONOMY

4.2 Discuss how the American economy shapes government and politics.

The American economy is a capitalist economy that has evolved from a highly competitive, small-enterprise form to one that is corporate-dominated and with a global reach.

The American economy has shown itself to be highly efficient and wealth producing, resulting in a high standard of living, yet it has also produced high levels of income and wealth inequality and periods of economic instability and financial difficulties.

The political responses to difficult economic times like the Great Depression of the 1930s, and the Great Recession and jobless recovery of 2008–2012, have increased the role of government in society and the economy.

Globalization, technological change, and hypercompetition between firms has transformed the American economy.

The middle class has been hard hit by emerging trends in the new American economy.

AMERICA'S POLITICAL CULTURE

4.3 Describe the values and beliefs that make up the American political culture and how they affect politics and government.

Americans believe strongly in individualism, limited government, and free enterprise. Beliefs about democracy, liberty, the primacy of the common people, and a strong religious orientation also help define the political culture.

The political culture shapes American ideas about what the good society should look like, the appropriate role for government, and the possibilities for self-government.

LEARN THE TERMS

capitalism An economic system characterized by private ownership of productive assets where most decisions about how to use these assets are made by individuals and firms operating in a market rather than by government.

demographic Pertaining to the statistical study and description of a population.

globalization The tendency of information, products, and financial capital to flow across national borders, with the effect of more tightly integrating the global economy.

gross domestic product (GDP) Monetary value of all goods and services produced in a nation each year, excluding income residents earn abroad.

labor union An organization representing employees that bargains with employers over wages, benefits, and working conditions.

median household income The midpoint of all households ranked by income.

political culture The set of core beliefs in a country that help shape how people behave politically and what they believe government should do.

populism The belief that the common person is every bit as good as someone with wealth and power.

poverty line The federal government's calculation of the amount of income families of various sizes need to stay out of poverty. In 2016, it was $24,300 for a family of four.

CHAPTER 5

AWAITING EVACUATION

A marine waits for a medical evacuation helicopter during the bloody battle for Hill 937 in Vietnam near the Laos border. Over the course of the conflict in Vietnam, rising casualties and limited success undermined public support for the war and led to an eventual change in U.S. policy and an American withdrawal. *What role should the public play in making decisions about when the country goes to war? Should we trust the president and other policy makers to make these decisions for us?*

PUBLIC OPINION

CHAPTER OUTLINE AND LEARNING OBJECTIVES

MEASURING PUBLIC OPINION

5.1   Describe public opinion research and modern methods of polling.

POLITICAL SOCIALIZATION: LEARNING POLITICAL BELIEFS AND ATTITUDES

5.2   Explain how the agents of socialization influence the development of political attitudes.

HOW AND WHY PEOPLE'S POLITICAL ATTITUDES DIFFER

5.3   Describe the forces that create and shape political attitudes.

THE CONTOURS OF AMERICAN PUBLIC OPINION: ARE THE PEOPLE FIT TO RULE?

5.4   Assess whether the public is capable of playing a meaningful role in steering public policy.

The Struggle for Democracy

VIETNAM: A MATTER OF OPINION?

On August 2, 1964, the Pentagon announced that the U.S. destroyer *Maddox*, while on "routine patrol" in international waters in the Gulf of Tonkin near Vietnam, had undergone an "unprovoked attack" by three North Vietnamese PT boats. Two days later, the Pentagon reported a "second deliberate attack." In a nationwide television broadcast, President Lyndon Johnson declared that these hostile actions required retaliation. Five days later, on August 7, the Senate passed the Tonkin Gulf Resolution by a vote of 98–2, thus approving "all necessary measures" to repel any armed attack and to assist any ally in the region. A legal basis for full U.S. involvement in the Vietnam War had been established. Surveys indicated that 48 percent of the public supported military action; only 14 percent wanted the United States to negotiate a settlement or get out of Vietnam.[1] Years later, the Pentagon Papers, a study commissioned by the Pentagon and leaked by defense analyst Daniel Ellsberg, revealed that the *Maddox* was part of a secret, large-scale effort to destabilize the North Vietnamese regime that included attacks on coastal villages and defense installations.

The number of U.S. troops in Vietnam rose rapidly, reaching more than 530,000 by the end of 1968, and casualties increased correspondingly, with just over 30,000 Americans killed by the end of that year.[2] Television news began to display weekly casualty counts in the hundreds, along with pictures of dead American soldiers arriving home in body bags. As politicians put it, the war became expensive in "American blood and treasure." Although in 1965 only 24 percent of Americans said sending troops to Vietnam had been a mistake, by December 1967, pressure to end the war was mounting. About as many people (45 percent) agreed as disagreed with the proposition that it had been a "mistake" to send troops to Vietnam.

Then catastrophe struck. In January 1968, during Vietnam's Tet holiday, the North Vietnamese launched the Tet Offensive, which comprised massive attacks throughout South Vietnam, including an assault on the U.S. embassy in Saigon. The American public was shocked by televised scenes of urban destruction, bloody corpses, and marines bogged down in the rubble in the ancient city of Hue. After Tet, criticism of the war mushroomed—by October 1968, 54 percent of Americans said the war had been a mistake, and only 37 percent said it had not. President Johnson, staggered by a surprisingly strong vote for antiwar candidate Eugene McCarthy in the New Hampshire primary, withdrew as a candidate for reelection. Anger over Vietnam continued to roil the American public throughout the remainder of the presidential campaign and contributed to the election defeat of the Democrats in November.

After taking office in January 1969, Richard Nixon began withdrawing troops from Vietnam, with the aim of gradually turning the fighting over to South Vietnamese forces. Soon, the American public called for more rapid troop reductions, telling pollsters they wanted America out of Vietnam even if it led to the collapse of the South Vietnamese government. The shift in mood was propelled, no doubt, by rising American casualties, numerous congressional hearings on the conduct of the war, and massive antiwar demonstrations. By mid-1973, most American troops were gone from Vietnam.

*   *   *   *   *

The Vietnam story shows how opinion is affected by events and their representation in the news media and how government officials can sometimes lead or manipulate opinion, especially when it concerns obscure matters in faraway lands. The story also suggests that public opinion, even on foreign policy matters, can sometimes have a strong effect on policy making. The complex interaction among public opinion, the news media, elected officials, and foreign policy on Vietnam in the 1960s is not very different from what happened with the war in Iraq. A substantial majority of the public, believing Bush administration claims about the existence of weapons of mass destruction in Iraq (since proven untrue), supported the invasion of that country in 2003 to topple Saddam Hussein. By 2006, however, a majority of Americans were telling pollsters that the war was a mistake, a shift in mood propelled by mounting American casualties, a lack of progress in achieving either democracy or stability in Iraq, and news about the mistreatment of prisoners at the Abu Ghraib prison. The shift in public attitudes on Iraq was a major factor in the Democratic Party's victory in the 2006 congressional elections and Barack Obama's first presidential win, in 2008.

THINKING CRITICALLY **ABOUT THIS CHAPTER**

This chapter is about public opinion, how it is formed, and what effect it has on American politics and government.

APPLYING THE **FRAMEWORK**

You will learn in this chapter how structural factors—including historical events, political culture, and economic and social change—as well as family and community socialization—shape public opinion. You will also learn how public opinion influences the behavior of political leaders and shapes many of the policies of the federal government.

USING THE **DEMOCRACY STANDARD**

Based on the standard of democracy, public opinion should play an important role in determining what government does. However, you will see that while there is some evidence that public opinion can affect policy outcomes, questions remain about how well public opinion can be measured, how prepared citizens are to steer policy, and how and when public officials respond to what the public thinks.

MEASURING PUBLIC OPINION

5.1 Describe public opinion research and modern methods of polling.

Public opinion is particularly important in a democracy if we understand democracy to be fundamentally about the rule of the people. For the people to rule, they must have their voice heard by those in government. Elections are one way to identify what the people want, but candidates often state their positions on a broad array of policy matters during campaigns. Thus, the fact that a voter chose one candidate over another does not necessarily mean they support all of the positions that candidate adopted during the campaign. A more direct way to figure out what policies the people want is to survey them directly.

Decades ago, people who wanted to find out anything about public opinion had to guess, based on what their barbers or taxi drivers said, on what appeared in letters to newspaper editors, or on what sorts of one-liners won cheers at political rallies. But the views of one's personal acquaintances, letter writers, or rally audiences may be quite different from those of the public as a whole. Similarly, angry people who call in to radio talk shows or rant on Reddit may hold views that are not typical of most Americans. Fortunately, social scientists have developed some fairly reliable tools for measuring the opinions of large groups of people like the American public.

Public Opinion Polls

scientific survey

A survey conducted using probability sampling to measure the attitudes of a representative sample of the public.

A **scientific survey** eliminates much of the guesswork in measuring public opinion. A scientific survey consists of systematic interviews conducted by trained professional interviewers who ask a standardized set of questions of a seemingly small number of randomly chosen Americans. A national survey usually polls between a thousand and fifteen hundred people. However, such surveys, if conducted properly, can reveal with remarkable accuracy what the broader public is thinking.

The secret of success is to make sure that the sample interviewed is representative of the entire population; that is, that the proportions of people in the sample who are young, old, female, college-educated, black, rural, Catholic, southern, western, religious, secular, liberal, conservative, Democratic, Republican, and so forth, are all about the same as in the U.S. population as a whole. If the sample is not representative of the broader population, surveys may produce inaccurate estimates of what the public wants. This potential problem was infamously illustrated by a survey conducted by *Literary Digest* before the 1936 presidential election. That survey predicted that Republican Alf Landon would defeat Franklin Delano Roosevelt in a landslide. Although *Literary Digest* surveyed millions of Americans, they surveyed a highly unrepresentative sample consisting of *Literary Digest* subscribers, automobile owners, and people with telephones. Magazine subscriptions and automobiles were luxuries at the time. As it turned out, wealthy *Literary Digest* subscribers were much more likely to support Landon than the general population. Ultimately Roosevelt defeated Landon handily, winning over 60 percent of the vote nationwide.

Survey researchers typically identify a sample of respondents that is representative by interviewing a random sample of the population; this is called **probability sampling**. This approach ensures that each member of the population has an equal chance of being selected for an interview. Then survey researchers can tally all of the responses to a given question and compute the percentages of people answering one way or another. Statisticians use probability theory to estimate how much the survey's results are likely to differ from what the whole population would say if asked the same questions. Findings from a random sample of fifteen hundred people have a 95 percent chance of accurately reflecting the views of the whole population within about two or three percentage points. When survey results are reported, this **sampling error** is typically labeled the margin of error.[3]

probability sampling

A survey technique designed so that every individual in a population of interest (e.g., the American public) has an equal chance of being included in the pool of survey respondents.

sampling error

Statistical uncertainty in estimates associated with the fact that surveys do not interview every individual in a population of interest.

Challenges of Political Polling

Those who use poll results—including citizens encountering political polls in newspapers and on television—should be aware of the following challenges researchers who conduct polls must grapple with, and what competent pollsters try to do about them.

ISSUES OF SAMPLING   One set of challenges scholars and survey professionals worry about are tied to the factors that make it difficult to draw a truly random sample that is representative of the entire population. In some cases, the problems seem to be getting worse:

- Telephone surveys are the most commonly used method for conducting surveys, but because Americans are inundated by phone calls from advertisers who may try to disguise themselves as researchers, they have become less willing to answer pollsters' questions. In addition, many Americans screen calls and refuse to pick up the phone when they do not recognize the caller's number. One study found that response rates to telephone surveys have fallen from about 36 percent in 1997 to 9 percent in 2016.[4]
- More than half of all Americans have cut their reliance on landlines and use only cell phones.[5] Many people who pay for plans with a limited number of minutes each month do not want to use up their monthly allotment talking to pollsters. In addition, federal law requires that pollsters dial cell numbers manually, so pollsters cannot use autodialing technology to make these calls. Instead, they must hire people to dial phone numbers, making cell phone calls more expensive.

- The Internet, it would seem, offers a promising new way to conduct public opinion surveys. However, most online surveys fall prey to the problem of nonrandom sampling. Not all Americans own computers and not all computer owners regularly use the Internet. Even if everyone did have a computer with Internet access, it would be difficult to identify a random sample of people to interview. Some firms are working on ways to overcome these obstacles through statistical techniques and innovative sampling procedures, but polling professionals and scholars continue to debate how to best leverage the power of the internet to measure public opinion.[6]

These days, telephone surveys are by far the most common way that professional survey firms conduct polls. The top academic and commercial polling firms use repeated callbacks and samples that combine cell and landline phone numbers to address some of the polling challenges just discussed, but the changing technology environment may mean that the challenges of surveying a random sample of people over the phone will get worse before they get better. However, the samples these organizations use appear to closely reflect how the whole population would have responded if everyone in the United States had been asked the same questions at the moment the survey was carried out. This is demonstrated by the fact that surveys conducted just before an election typically predict the outcome of the election extremely well. For example, although many pundits characterized polling in the run-up to the 2016 presidential election as a massive failure, on the eve of the election, national polls indicated that Hillary Clinton had a lead of approximately 3–4 percentage points nationwide. Although she lost the election because she failed to win enough states to prevail in the Electoral College, she won the popular vote by about 2 percentage points. In other words, the results of national polls in 2016 did quite well at predicting the share of the vote each candidate ended up winning nationally. There is no doubt that some state level polls in the 2016 election overestimated Clinton's support, but, there is reason to suspect that these errors were tied to factors such as the difficulty of predicting which respondents will actually turn out to vote, rather than fundamental problems with targeting a representative sample of the public.[7] However, it is crucial to be vigilant when reading polling results to ensure that results have been produced by quality researchers who can be relied on to use best practices, even if such practices are more expensive for them. A good rule of thumb is to see which polls public opinion scholars and other specialists in American politics rely on most.

CAN ONLINE SURVEYS "WORK"?

Some firms are working on ways to field online surveys that yield accurate estimates of public opinion. For example, YouGov is a web-based survey firm with a diverse pool of millions of panelists who have agreed to complete surveys about topics ranging from their favorite foods and companies to their attitudes about current events. When they conduct a survey they invite a pool of individuals from their panel that has characteristics that mirror those of the national public to participate. They then use statistical techniques to correct for any remaining differences between those who complete the survey and the broader public. This approach is far cheaper than telephone or face-to-face surveys and the conclusions these surveys reach about public opinion are generally similar to those found using more traditional methods. However, because respondents are not actually drawn from the public at random, some worry that respondents may not be truly representative of the broader public. For example, although an online survey may include an appropriate number of Hispanic respondents, these respondents may have characteristics or attitudes that are systematically different from those of the broader Hispanic American population.

Telephone surveys face a number of daunting challenges. Which do you think we should be more skeptical of: the results of telephone surveys or the results of carefully conducted online surveys?

ISSUES OF WORDING   The wording of questions is important because the way a question is phrased can affect the way it is answered. Consider the following issues of wording:

- Attaching the name of a president to a survey question—as in "Do you support President Trump's proposal to reduce environmental regulations?"—can affect how people respond. In this case, those who like President Trump may voice greater support for cutting environmental regulations than they would if the president were not mentioned.

- "Closed-ended" or "forced-choice" questions, which ask respondents to choose from a list of answers, do not always reveal what people are thinking on their own or what they would come up with after a few minutes of thought or discussion. So, responses to these questions may not accurately capture how people feel about political matters. Some scholars also believe that closed-ended questions create situations for people to express opinions about matters on which they really don't have opinions because they can simply choose a prepared answer from a list of options.[8] For these reasons, "open-ended" questions are sometimes asked in order to yield more spontaneous answers, and small discussion groups or "focus groups" are brought together to observe opinions that emerge when people talk among themselves about topics that a moderator introduces.

ISSUES OF INTENSITY AND TIMING   Often, while the wording of a question may be perfectly acceptable, answers may not capture the relative intensity of respondents' feelings about some policy or political issue. Pollsters attempt to address this shortcoming by building intensity measures into responses offered to survey participants. Most commonly, pollsters provide more than simple "agree or disagree" answer options, including instead a set of five to seven options ranging from "strongly agree" to "strongly disagree." At other times, surveys ask respondents to rank the importance of certain problems or policies.

The importance of considering the intensity of people's preferences can be illustrated with an example. Over the past several years, several high profile mass shootings—including the 2017 shooting at a Las Vegas music festival that left dozens dead and hundreds injured and the 2018 shooting at Stoneman Douglas High School in Parkland, Florida—have brought renewed attention to gun policy. A substantial majority of Americans support policies like background checks for gun purchases, but these policies typically fail to become law. Why? Consider the analytical framework shown in Figure 5.1, which focuses attention on *structural, political linkage,* and *government* factors that help answer that question. One explanation may be that Americans who support background checks for gun purchases are less likely to base their vote on where a candidate stands on that issue than those who oppose expanding these checks. If so, pollsters must try to account for this if they wish to understand how public opinion is likely to affect gun control policy.

The timing of a survey can also be important. For elections, in particular, polling needs to happen as close to Election Day as possible in order not to miss last-minute switches and surges. Most famously, survey organizations in 1948 predicted a comfortable victory for Republican Thomas Dewey over Democratic president Harry Truman, feeling so confident of the outcome that they stopped polling several weeks before Election Day, missing changes in public sentiments late in the campaign. Similarly, in the weeks leading up to the 2016 election, pollsters and pundits may have failed to fully appreciate late shifts in voter preferences in states such as Wisconsin and Michigan because polling in those states was relatively sparse.[9]

THE POLLSTERS GET IT WRONG

Harry Truman ridicules an edition of the *Chicago Daily Tribune* that proclaims his Republican challenger, Thomas Dewey, president. Opinion polls stopped asking questions too early in the 1948 election campaign, missing Truman's last-minute surge. Top pollsters today survey likely voters right to the end of the campaign.

Can you think of any recent examples where a candidate appeared to have a comfortable lead in the polls, only to see it melt away in the weeks leading up to Election Day?

FIGURE 5.1 APPLYING THE FRAMEWORK: WHY SO LITTLE FEDERAL GUN LEGISLATION?

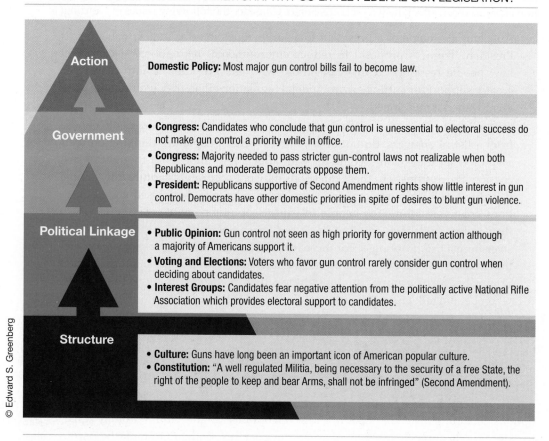

POLITICAL SOCIALIZATION: LEARNING POLITICAL BELIEFS AND ATTITUDES

5.2 Explain how the agents of socialization influence the development of political attitudes.

Most Americans share certain **core values** about the nature of human beings, society, and the political order. These core beliefs—including beliefs in individualism, limited government, and a market economy, among others—make up the American political culture. In addition to their overarching core beliefs, Americans also have **political attitudes** about the specific political issues of the day, including attitudes about government policies, public officials, political parties, and candidates. **Public opinion** refers to the political attitudes expressed by ordinary people and considered as a whole—particularly as revealed by polling surveys.

The opinions and attitudes revealed by public opinion polls do not form in a vacuum. A number of important factors—among them families, schools, churches, the news media, and social groups with which individuals are most closely associated—significantly influence our political beliefs and attitudes. Political scientists refer to the process by which individuals acquire these beliefs and attitudes as **political socialization**. The instruments by which beliefs and attitudes are conveyed to individuals in society (such as our families, schools, and so on) are called **agents of socialization**.

Political socialization is a lifetime process in the sense that people engage in political learning throughout the life-course.[10] However, childhood and adolescence seem to be particularly important times for people's incorporation of core beliefs and general outlooks about the political world, especially party identification,

core values

Individuals' views about the fundamental nature of human beings, society, the economy, and the role of government; taken together, they constitute the political culture.

political attitudes

Individuals' views and preferences about public policies, political parties, candidates, government institutions, and public officials.

public opinion

The aggregated political attitudes of ordinary people as revealed by surveys.

political socialization

The process by which individuals come to have certain core beliefs and political attitudes.

agents of socialization

The institutions and individuals that shape the core beliefs and attitudes of people.

ideological leanings, and racial and ethnic identity, though scholars are beginning to believe that early adulthood is almost as important.[11]

The *family* plays a particularly important role in shaping the outlooks of children. It is in the family—whether in a traditional or nontraditional family—that children pick up their basic outlook on life and the world around them. It is mainly from their family, for example, that children learn to trust or distrust others, something that affects a wide range of political attitudes later in life. It is from the family, and the neighborhood where the family lives, that children learn about which ethnic or racial group, social class or income group, and religion they belong to and begin to pick up attitudes that are typical of these groups.

In dinner table conversations and other encounters with parents, children also start to acquire ideas about the country—ideas about patriotism, for example—and their first vague ideological ideas: whether government is a good or bad thing, whether taxes are a good or bad thing, and whether certain people and groups in society (welfare recipients, rich people, corporations, and the like) are to be admired or not. Most important, because it represents the filter through which a great deal of future political learning takes place, many children adopt the political party identifications of their parents—especially if the parents share the same party identification and are politically engaged. One study surveyed seniors who graduated from high school in 1965 and then re-interviewed those same people in 1997. In spite of the momentous political events that occurred over those 32 years—including the Civil Rights movement, Vietnam War, Roe v. Wade decision, and end of the Cold War—almost two-thirds of seniors who shared their parents' party affiliation in 1965 reported identifying with the same party in 1997.[12]

Schools are also important as agents of political socialization. In the early grades, through explicit lessons and the celebration of national symbols—such as the flag in the classroom, recitation of the Pledge of Allegiance, pictures on the walls of famous presidents, patriotic pageants, and the like—schools convey lessons about American identity and patriotism. Schools may also teach children about the political process by sponsoring mock presidential elections and elections to student government. Most students in most school districts also take courses in American history and American government and continue learning about participation through student government.

Popular culture—movies, music, and advertising—also shapes the budding political outlooks of young people.[13] To be sure, most of the messages coming from the popular culture have more to do with style, fashion, and other matters that are not explicitly

LEARNING ABOUT DEMOCRACY

Children gain many of their initial ideas about the American political system in their elementary school classrooms. In those early grades, children gain impressions about the nation, its most important symbols (such as the flag), and its most visible and well-known presidents. They also learn the rudiments of democracy.

How might greater efforts to encourage young Americans to be active participants in the American political system change political outcomes in the United States?

political. But popular culture also can convey political messages. For example, many musicians embed political messages in their lyrics and themes of sleazy politicians and untrustworthy or corrupt elected officials are quite common in Hollywood movies.

Political socialization does not stop when children become adults. Substantial evidence shows that a *college education* affects people's outlooks about public policies and the role of government. People with a college education, for example, are more likely to support government programs to protect the environment. We know that people's political outlooks are shaped by *major events* or developments that affect the country during their young adult years. In the past, such events have included the Great Depression, World War II, the civil rights movement and the countercultural revolution of the 1960s, the Reagan Revolution of the 1980s, and the 9/11 terrorist attacks on the United States. The Great Recession and housing crash that began in late 2007 may similarly shape long-term outlooks as sustained economic troubles have derailed many people's hopes of attaining the American Dream.[14] The effect of these events and developments seems most pronounced for young people who are just coming to have a sense of political awareness. Political scientists identify this phenomenon as a **generational effect**. Thus, young people coming of age politically during the 1960s turned out to be much more liberal throughout their lives than young people coming of age during the 1950s or during the Reagan years.

generational effect

The long lasting effect of major political events—particularly those that occur when an individual is coming of age politically—on people's political attitudes.

HOW AND WHY PEOPLE'S POLITICAL ATTITUDES DIFFER

5.3 Describe the forces that create and shape political attitudes.

As we learned in the previous section, a broad range of socialization agents—from the media and popular entertainment to government leaders and the schools—reinforce one another to shape our ideas about what it means to be an American and to live in the United States. However, a variety of other forces, including how we think about who we are as individuals, where we live, and other life experiences, shape our general political outlooks and our specific attitudes in distinctive ways. In this section, we explore some of the most significant factors that define and often divide us in our political views.

Party Identification

One of the most influential political characteristics shaped by the process of socialization is party identification. More than any other factor, party identification—whether people think of themselves as Democrats, Republicans, or Independents—structures how people see the political world. Party identification also plays a powerful role in determining which government polices people support.[15] When researchers measure people's party identification in surveys, they typically first ask respondents whether they think of themselves as Democrats, Republicans, Independents, or something else. Those who do not identify as Democrats or Republicans are then asked whether they think of themselves as being closer to the Republican or Democratic Party. Researchers refer to those who say they feel closer to the Republican Party as Republican leaners and those who say they feel closer to the Democratic Party as Democratic leaners. Interestingly, these **partisan leaners** tend to behave remarkably similarly to those who unreservedly identify as Democrats or Republicans—for example, Republican leaners tend to support the same policies and vote for the same candidates as "regular" Republicans.[16]

As discussed below, political issues are often complex and few people have time to become fully informed about every issue. One of the reasons party identification is such a powerful force in American politics is that many people look to communications from members of their preferred party for guidance about how to make sense of complicated political questions. When a new political issue is being debated, people who identify as

partisan leaners

Individuals who say they do not identify as Democrats or Republicans, but say they feel closer to either the Democratic or Republican Party.

TABLE 5.1   PARTISANSHIP AND ISSUE POSITIONS

	Republicans	Democrats
% Identifying as conservative	70%	17%
% Who say the government in Washington ought to reduce the income differences between the rich and the poor	23%	69%
% Who say the government should help people with medical bills	23%	69%
% Who say the law should require a person to obtain a police permit before he or she can buy a gun	58%	80%
% Who favor legalizing marijuana	43%	66%
% Who say a woman should be able to have an abortion for any reason	30%	53%

SOURCE: General Social Survey (2016).

Democrats may rely on cues from Democratic leaders and choose to adopt the position supported by most Democrats. Similarly, a growing body of research finds that partisans are inclined to take whatever position is at odds with that taken by the opposing party. For example, Democrats are inclined to say they oppose policies that they hear Republicans support and support policies they hear Republicans oppose.[17]

Over the past several decades, Democratic and Republican politicians have taken positions that are further and further apart, and Democratic and Republican voters have largely followed suit. More than in the past, Republicans are more likely than Democrats to vote for Republican candidates, to approve of Republican presidents, and to favor policies associated with the Republican Party. Thus, Republicans are much more likely than Democrats to support big business and to oppose stem-cell research, same-sex marriage, and abortion. Democrats are much more likely than Republicans to support government programs that are designed to help the poor and racial minorities, that protect LGBTQ rights, that regulate greenhouse gas emissions, and that support abortion on demand.

There is still some debate about exactly how polarized the American public has become, but there is little doubt that Democrats and Republicans tend not to see eye to eye on many of the issues of the day.[18] Table 5.1 documents big differences between Republicans and Democrats on some of the major issues of the day, and Figure 5.2 shows that the differences between them are growing ever wider—Republicans increasingly identify as conservatives while more and more Democrats identify themselves as liberal. Today, Republicans and Democrats—particularly those who are most committed and active—face each other across a wide chasm.

Race and Ethnicity

Polling reveals significant differences in political attitudes across racial and ethnic lines. Although historically white ethnic groups like the Irish used to have distinctive political preferences, these differences between white Americans of different ethnic backgrounds have largely disappeared. In contrast, white and African Americans differ substantially in their political attitudes. Hispanics and Asian Americans also have some distinctive political opinions.

AFRICAN AMERICANS   On most core beliefs about the American system, few differences are discernible between African Americans and other Americans.[19] Similar percentages of each group believe, for example, that people can get ahead by working hard, that providing for equal opportunity is more important than ensuring equal outcomes, and that the federal government should balance its budget. Equal numbers say they are proud to be Americans and believe democracy to be the best form of government. On a range of other political issues, however, the racial divide looms large,[20] particularly with respect to what role government should play in helping people and making America more equal.

FIGURE 5.2 TRENDS IN THE RELATIONSHIP BETWEEN PARTY IDENTIFICATION AND POLITICAL IDEOLOGY

Party identification and political ideology are becoming more closely related. Republican identifiers—already more conservative than Democratic Party identifiers in the 1970s—have become dramatically more likely to identify themselves as conservative. At the same time, Democrats are becoming more liberal. This deep ideological divide between the parties has become a key feature of modern American politics and contributes to much of the incivility and intensity of public affairs in recent years. This growing gap between Democrats and Republicans shows up across a wide range of issues.

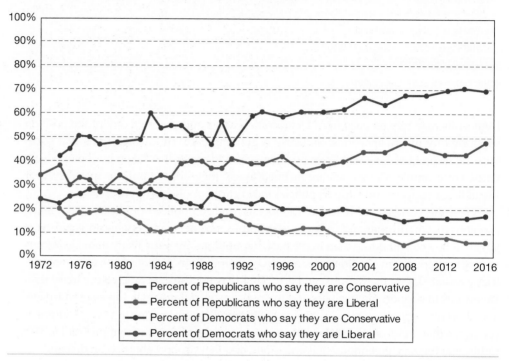

SOURCE: General Social Survey, Cumulative Data File (1972–2016).

Partisanship is one important area where African Americans differ from whites. African Americans stayed loyal to the Republican Party (the party of Lincoln and of Reconstruction) long after the Civil War. Like many Americans, they became Democrats in large proportions in the 1930s during the presidency of Franklin D. Roosevelt, whose New Deal greatly expanded the federal government's role in providing safety nets for the poor and unemployed. During the civil rights struggles of the 1960s, African Americans began to identify overwhelmingly as Democrats and continue to do so today. In 1960, about 58 percent of white Americans and 72 percent of black Americans identified as Democrats or said they leaned toward the Democratic Party—a difference of about 14 percentage points. These days, the gap in partisanship between white and black Americans is massive. In 2016, African Americans were the most solidly Democratic of any group in the population: 72 percent said they were Democrats or independents who leaned toward the Democrats, compared with only 39 percent of white Americans—a gap of over 30 percentage points (see Figure 5.3). Fewer than 10 percent of African Americans identify as Republicans or Republican "leaners." In 2016, 88 percent of African Americans voted for Democrat Hillary Clinton; only 8 percent supported Republican Donald Trump.[21]

African Americans also tend to be more liberal than whites on a range of policy matters (see Figure 5.4). More also identify themselves as liberals than as conservatives or moderates, a pattern almost exactly reversed among whites.[22] African Americans, too, are more likely than Americans in general to favor government regulation of corporations and to favor labor unions.[23] This liberalism springs, in part, from African Americans' economically disadvantaged position in American society and the still real effects of slavery and discrimination.

FIGURE 5.3 PARTY IDENTIFICATION AMONG VARIOUS DEMOGRAPHIC GROUPS, 2016

This figure displays how partisanship varies across demographic groups in the United States. We include "partisan leaners" with partisan respondents. Party identification varies across demographic groups. Most notably, black Americans overwhelmingly identify as Democrats.

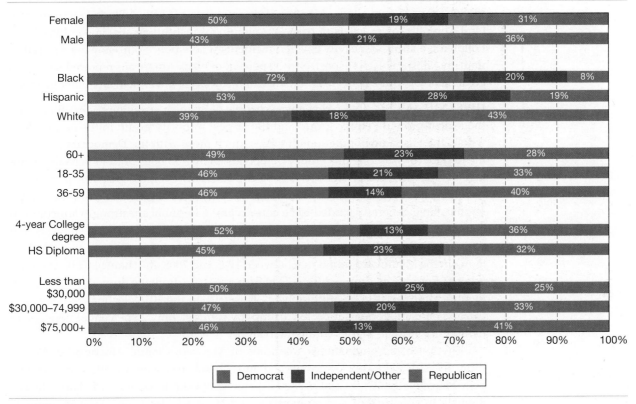

SOURCE: General Social Survey (2016).

FIGURE 5.4 THE RACIAL AND ETHNIC DIVIDE

Public opinion polls reveal substantial differences in attitudes across racial and ethnic groups on some issues, but less of a gap on others. (Figure shows percent agreeing with each statement.)

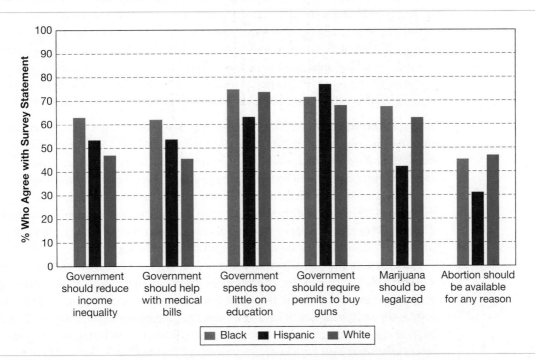

SOURCE: Data from General Social Survey (2016).

Divisions with white Americans are most apparent on matters that focus particularly on black Americans. For example, 80 percent of African Americans but only 47 percent of whites think the government spends too little on improving the conditions of Blacks in the country. Similarly, while 43 percent of black Americans say that, because of past discrimination, blacks should be given preference in hiring and promotion, only 17 percent of white Americans support this idea.[24] Black Americans also tend to report lower levels of trust in government institutions like law enforcement. Following a string of heavily covered incidents where police officers were accused of unjustly killing a black suspect, only 30 percent of black Americans reported having "a great deal" or "quite a lot" of confidence in the police—lower than any other group.[25]

HISPANIC AMERICANS Hispanics—people of Spanish-speaking background—are the fastest-growing ethnic group and the largest minority group in the nation. As a whole, the Hispanic population identifies much more with the Democrats than with the Republicans; among this group, Democrats enjoy a 53 percent to 19 percent advantage over Republicans (refer again to Figure 5.3). However, the Hispanic population itself is quite diverse. Cuban Americans, many of them refugees from the Castro regime, have generally tended to be conservative, Republican, strongly anticommunist, and skeptical of government programs. However, some evidence suggests that support for Republicans is waning among Cuban Americans. One study of Cubans living in the Miami area found that between 1995 and 2008, the share of Cubans identifying as Republican dropped from 73 to 51 percent—a dramatic drop given that party identification tends to be quite stable.[26] This said, in the 2016 election, 54 percent of Cuban voters in Florida supported Trump. By contrast, only 26 percent of non-Cuban Latinos in Florida reported voting for Trump.

The much more numerous Americans of Mexican, Central American, or Puerto Rican ancestry are mostly Democrats and quite liberal on economic matters. In 2016, exit polls indicated that 65 percent of the Hispanic vote went to Democrat Hillary Clinton. Republican sponsorship and support for laws to crack down on illegal immigrants and on people who help them in Arizona, Georgia, and Alabama, among other states, may make this group view Democrats even more favorably in the future. This said, although many speculated Donald Trump's harsh rhetoric about Mexican immigrants could do long-term damage to the Republican Party's standing among Hispanic voters, exit polls showed that he fared better among Hispanic voters than Mitt Romney did in 2012. Another factor that may be relevant is that, because Hispanics are predominantly Roman Catholic, one may expect them to be more conservative—and hence more attracted to the Republican Party—on social issues. On some issues, this is true. For example, Hispanics tend to be more conservative than Americans in general when it comes to the issue of abortion. However, on other issues—like those pertaining to homosexuality—their preferences are similar to those of the rest of the population.[27]

ASIAN AMERICANS Asian Americans, a small but growing part of the U.S. population—about 6 percent of the population as of 2017—come from quite diverse backgrounds, with origins in the Philippines, India, Vietnam, Korea, Thailand, Japan, China, or elsewhere. As a group, Asian Americans are more educated and economically successful than the general population but are less likely to vote and express an interest in politics than people of equal educational and financial status. Though there is only sparse systematic research on the politically relevant attitudes of Asian Americans, we do know the following: On social issues, Asian Americans are somewhat more conservative than are other Americans; for example, a majority supports the death penalty and opposes same-sex marriage. On the role of government, they are more liberal, however. For example, a small majority supports efforts to provide universal health care. Importantly, though once split fairly evenly between Republican and Democratic identifiers, they have been trending more Democratic in recent elections; in 2016, 65 percent voted for Clinton.[28]

Social Class

Compared with much of the world, the United States has had little political conflict among people of different income or occupational groupings. In fact, few Americans have thought of themselves as members of a social "class" at all, but when asked to place themselves in a class by survey researchers, more than half say they are middle class. Things may be changing, however, after the decades-long growth in inequality and rising popular anger with Wall Street. One survey in early 2015 reported that about 60 percent of Americans now think that the rich benefit most from government policies. Only 19 percent said policies benefit the poor most and a paltry 8 percent said the middle class benefits most from government policies.[29]

Since the time of the New Deal, low- and moderate-income people have identified much more strongly with Democrats than with Republicans. Upper-income people have typically been more likely to identify as Republicans. Surveys conducted in 2016 indicated that about 50 percent of individuals in households making less than $30,000 a year identify as Democrats or Democratic leaners, compared with only 25 percent who identify as Republicans. In contrast, individuals living in households earning more than $75,000 a year are about equally likely to identify as Republicans or Democrats.[30]

People in union households have long favored the Democrats and continue to do so. About six in ten people in union households say they favor the Democrats. However, in 2016, exit polls showed that Clinton had won only 51 percent of the vote among voters from union households, compared with 43 percent who voted for Trump. It is important to be aware that the proportion of Americans who are members of labor unions is quite low compared with the proportion of the populations of other rich countries and has been steadily declining.

Lower-income people have some distinctive policy preferences. Not surprisingly, they tend to favor more government help with jobs, housing, medical care, and the like, whereas the highest-income people, who would presumably pay more and benefit less from such programs, tend to oppose them.[31] To complicate matters, many lower- and moderate-income people favor Republican conservative positions on such social issues as abortion, law and order, religion, civil rights, education, and gay rights, doing so primarily for religious and cultural reasons. Another group, non–college-educated, moderate-income white men, are less likely than in the past to identify with Democrats. Furthermore, some high-income people—especially those with

ORGANIZED LABOR ON BOARD
Hillary Clinton and other Democrats who run for and hold elective office can generally count on the support of union members, especially public sector employees. The Service Employees International Union (SEIU) Local 1021 in San Francisco represents a large contingent of organized labor, including nurses, hospital staff, nursing home care providers, janitors, security guards, and dispatchers.
How might Republicans enhance their appeal to labor?

postgraduate degrees—tend to be very liberal on lifestyle and social issues involving sexual behavior, abortion rights, free speech, and civil rights. They also tend to be especially eager for government action to protect the environment. But on the whole, upper-income people have been more likely than others to favor Republicans and conservative economic policies, while moderate- and lower-income Americans have been more likely to favor Democrats and liberal economic policies.[32]

Geography

Region is an important factor in shaping public opinion in the United States. Each region is distinctive, with the South especially so. Although southern distinctiveness has been reduced somewhat because of years of migration by southern blacks to northern cities, the movement of industrial plants and northern whites to the Sun Belt, and economic growth catching up with that of the North, the legacy of slavery and segregation, a large black population, and late industrialization have made the South a unique region in American politics.[33]

Even now, white southerners tend to be somewhat less enthusiastic about civil rights than are northerners. Southern whites also tend to be more conservative than people in other regions on social issues, such as school prayer, crime, and abortion, and supportive of military spending and a strong foreign policy (although they remain fairly liberal on economic issues, such as government-sponsored health insurance, perhaps because incomes are lower in the South than elsewhere).

The Northeast is the most liberal of any region on social and economic issues, and people from this region tend to identify as Democrats. On most policy issues and party identification, Midwesterners, appropriately, are about in the middle between the South and the Northeast. Pacific Coast residents resemble northeasterners in many respects, but people from the Rocky Mountain states, with the exception of those in Colorado and New Mexico, tend to be quite conservative, with majorities opposed to, for example, a big government role in health insurance.[34]

These regional differences should not be exaggerated, however. Long-term trends show a narrowing in regional differences on many core beliefs and political attitudes.[35] This is the outcome of years of migration of Americans from one region to another and the rise of a media and entertainment industry that is national in scale, beaming messages and information across regional lines. In addition, a focus on differences across regions and states can lead us to overlook stark variation within states—particularly pronounced differences in attitude between those living in rural and urban areas.[36] We illustrate this important distinction in Figure 5.5.

State-level election outcomes suggest that the Northeast and West Coast are overwhelmingly Democratic, while the South and much of the middle of the country are predominantly Republican. However, although Illinois is a reliably "blue" (Democratic) state, this tendency is primarily driven by the huge number of Democratic voters in the Chicago area. Similarly, Texas is often thought of a "red state," but Houston is a liberal leaning city and was one of the first cities in the country to elect an openly gay mayor.

Education

The level of formal education that people reach is closely related to their income level because education helps people earn more and because the wealthy can pay for more and better schooling for their children. This said, a substantial education gap in party affiliation has opened up over the past few years. Americans with less than a college degree are about evenly split between identifying as Democrats and Republicans. However, 52 percent of those with a four-year college degree now

FIGURE 5.5   PRESIDENTIAL ELECTION RESULTS BY COUNTY, 2016

This map shows presidential election results from 2016 at the county level. Notice how some states that we that we often think about as liberal—e.g., California and New York—have many counties where Trump won more votes than Clinton. Conversely, Texas—often thought of as a "deep red" state—has several counties (primarily in urban areas) where Democratic candidates tend to do well.

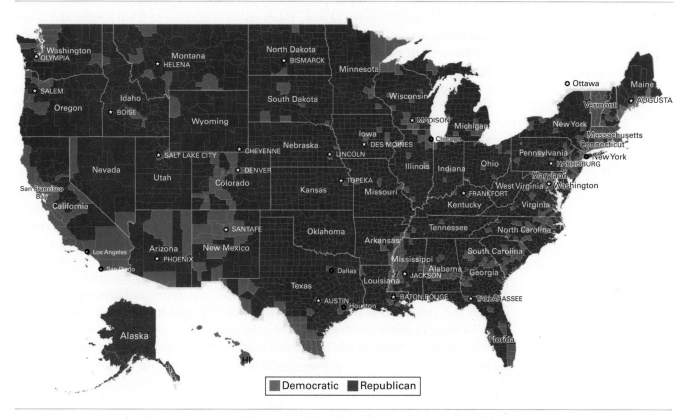

SOURCE: Data from Dave Leip, Election 2016, *Atlas of U.S. Presidential Elections*.

identify as Democrats, with only 36 percent identifying with the Republican Party. As recently as 1994 these numbers were exactly reversed, with 54 percent of college graduates identifying as Republicans and only 39 percent identifying as Democrats. Among those who pursued education beyond a four-year degree the gap is even more pronounced: 63 percent identify as Democrats and only 31 percent identify as Republicans (in 1994 this group was evenly split between Democratic and Republican identifiers).[37]

Within every income stratum of the population, college-educated people are somewhat more liberal than others on noneconomic issues such as race, gay rights, and the environment. They are also more likely than other people in their same income stratum to favor multilateralism in international affairs, favoring the use of diplomacy, multination treaties, and the United Nations to solve global problems.[38]

Education is also generally considered the strongest single demographic predictor of participation in politics. College-educated people are much more likely to say that they vote, talk about politics, go to meetings, sign petitions, and write letters to officials than people who have attained only an elementary or a high school education. The highly educated know more about politics. They know what they want and how to go about getting it—joining groups and writing letters, faxes, and e-mail messages to public officials.

Gender

A partisan "gender gap" first appeared in the 1980s and persists today, with the percentage of women who identify as Republicans or Republican leaners notably lower than the percentage of men who identify as Republicans. The differences show up in elections; in 2016, only 42 percent of women voted for Republican Donald Trump, compared with 53 percent of men. However, although the partisan gender gap is real and persistent—women identify more with the Democrats and are more likely to vote for Democratic candidates—the scale of the gap generally has not been enormous, leading some scholars to suggest that the gender gap issue has been exaggerated.[39] For example, many commentators—and many pre-election polls—suggested that the gender gap in the 2016 general election would be particularly pronounced due to some of Donald Trump's highly publicized comments about women. However, exit polls indicated that the gender gap was not dramatically different from the gap in the 2012 and 2008 elections. This said, polling data suggest that the gender gap has widened over the past few years. For example, analysis conducted by the Pew Research Center found that in 2017, 56 percent of women identified as Democrats or Democratic leaners, while only 37 percent identified as Republicans or Republican leaners. In sharp contrast, among men, Republicans hold a 48 to 44 percent advantage in party identification.[40] Exit polls showed that almost 60 percent of women (compared to 47 percent of men) voted for the Democratic candidate in the 2018 midterm elections.

Women also differ somewhat from men in certain policy preferences (see Figure 5.6). Women tend to be somewhat more supportive of spending on education and policies that protect the poor, the elderly, and the disabled. Women tend to be more opposed to violence, whether by criminals or by the state and tend to be more supportive of gun control policies than men. Over the years, women have been more likely than men to oppose capital punishment and the use of military force

FIGURE 5.6 THE GENDER GAP

Although surveys find some differences between the political attitudes of men and women, they tend to be modest and do not appear across all issues. (Figure shows percent agreeing with each statement.)

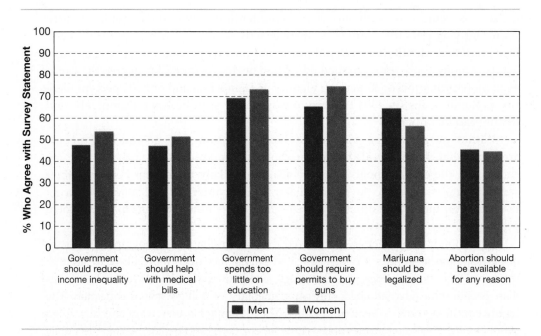

SOURCE: Data from General Social Survey (2016).

abroad and favored arms control and peace agreements.[41] Perhaps surprisingly, the gender gap on the issue of abortion is quite small.[42]

Age

Younger citizens are less likely to identify with a political party than are older cohorts, although those who do are more likely identify with the Democratic Party.[43] One particularly striking pattern that has emerged in the past few years is that the gender gap has become enormous among Millennials (those born between 1981 and 1996). Women in this age group identify as Democrats, rather than Republicans, by a margin of 70 to 23 percent. Although men in this age group are also more likely to identify as Democrats than Republicans, the gap is much smaller: 49 to 41 percent.[44] The young and the old also differ on certain matters that touch their particular interests: the draft in wartime, the drinking age, and, to some extent, Social Security and Medicare. But the chief difference between old and young has to do with the particular era in which they were raised. Those who were young during the 1960s were especially quick to favor civil rights for African Americans, for example. In recent years, young people have been especially concerned about environmental issues and income inequality and are much less supportive than other Americans of traditional or conservative social values on transgenderism, the role of women in society, and legalization of marijuana. More than any other age cohort, Americans between the ages of 18 and 35 support the idea of government-sponsored universal health insurance and permitting same-sex marriage.[45] Figure 5.7 shows the relationship between people's demographic characteristics and their political attitudes, including how younger and older Americans differ in their feelings about a number of policy matters.

America's youngest voters were particularly attracted to the Democrats' youthful presidential candidate, Barack Obama, in 2008 and 2012, with 66 percent voting for him in his first election and 60 percent voting for him in his second run for

A GENERATION EFFECT IN THE MAKING

Major political and social events that occur when young people are coming of age can leave a lasting impression. Here, two children look on as hundreds of thousands of protesters converged on Washington, D.C. in March of 2018 to demand stricter gun laws. *What current political and social events do you think will have enduring effects on young people's political attitudes and behaviors?*

FIGURE 5.7 THE AGE GAP

On some issues, like gun laws, there is little evidence of a divide between the attitudes of older and younger Americans. On others, like legalizing marijuana, surveys find huge differences. (Figure shows percent agreeing with each statement.)

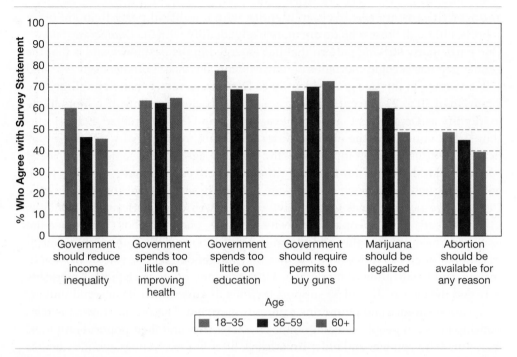

SOURCE: General Social Survey (2016).

office. In 2016, although he did not secure the Democratic nomination, presidential candidate Bernie Sanders—a self-described Democratic Socialist—was able to mount an unexpected challenge to Hillary Clinton, largely with the help of younger voters.[46]

Often social change occurs by generational replacement in which old ideas, like the Depression-era notion that women should stay at home and "not take jobs away from men," die off with old people. But it is worth noting that older Americans are not necessarily entirely fixed in their views. Like other Americans, those older than 60 have become, over the past decade or so, more tolerant of homosexuality and more supportive of the idea of women pursuing careers.[47]

Religion

Religious differences along denominational lines are and have always been important in the United States.[48] However, the differences between religiously observant people of all denominations and more secular Americans are becoming wider and more central to an understanding of contemporary American politics. Roman Catholics, who constitute about 24 percent of the U.S. population, provide a useful illustration of this pattern. Catholics were heavily Democratic after the New Deal but now resemble the majority of Americans in their party affiliations—pretty evenly split between Democrats and Republicans. Although Catholics have tended to be especially concerned with family issues and to support measures that promote law and order and morality (e.g., anti-pornography laws), many Americans who identify as Catholic disagree with long-held Church teachings on reproduction, supporting birth control and the right to have abortions in about the same proportion as other Americans.

In contrast, the extent of an individual's religious belief and practice—such as how frequently they attend religious services—is strongly associated with his or her political attitudes.[49] The religiously committed, no matter the religious denomination, are far more likely to vote Republican (see Figure 5.8) and to hold conservative views than those who are less religiously committed. The gap between the religiously committed and other Americans—particularly those who say they never or almost never go to church—on matters of party identification, votes in elections, and attitudes

FIGURE 5.8 RELIGIOUS ATTENDANCE AND THE PRESIDENTIAL ELECTION, 2016 (PERCENTAGE VOTING FOR EACH CANDIDATE)

In the 2016 presidential election, 56 percent of individuals who reported attending religious services once a week or more voted for Trump, whereas only 40 percent of these people reported voting for Clinton. In contrast, 62 percent of those who said they never attend religious services reported voting for Clinton; Trump won only 31 percent of the votes from those who never attend religious services.

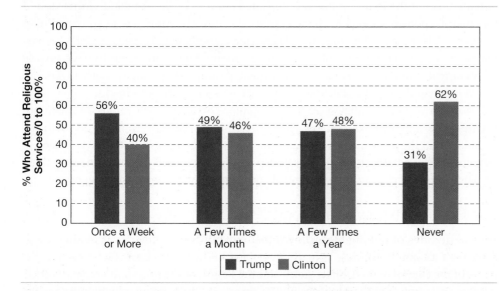

SOURCE: "Election 2016: Exit Polls." *New York Times*, November 8, 2016, accessed November 11, 2016. http://www.nytimes.com/interactive/2016/11/08/us/politics/election-exit-polls.html.

about social issues has become so wide and the debates so fierce that many have come to talk about America's culture wars. On a range of issues—including Supreme Court appointments, abortion, LGBTQ rights, prayer in the public schools, and the teaching of evolution—passions on both sides of the divide have reached what can only be called a white-hot fever pitch. To be sure, much of the noise in the culture wars is generated by leaders of and activists in religiously affiliated organizations and advocacy groups, who perhaps exaggerate the degree to which Americans disagree on core beliefs and political attitudes.[50] But, the battle between the most and least religiously observant and committed has helped heat up the passions in American politics because each group has gravitated to one or the other political party—the former to the Republicans and the latter to the Democrats—and become among the strongest campaign activists and financial contributors within them.[51]

THE CONTOURS OF AMERICAN PUBLIC OPINION: ARE THE PEOPLE FIT TO RULE?

5.4 Assess whether the public is capable of playing a meaningful role in steering public policy.

Now that we know more about how public opinion is measured and why people hold certain core beliefs and political attitudes, we can turn to the role of public opinion in a society that aspires to be a democracy. Many observers of American politics now and in the past have had little confidence in the abilities of the average person to understand vital public issues or to rationally engage in public affairs. If, as they have feared, ordinary citizens are uninformed, prone to rapid and irrational changes in their political attitudes, and easily led astray, there is not much reason to assume that public opinion can or ought to play a central role in deciding what government should do. Madison, Hamilton, and other framers of our government worried a great deal that the public's passions and opinions would infringe on liberty and be susceptible to radical and frequent shifts.[52] Journalist and statesman Walter Lippmann agreed, approvingly quoting Sir Robert Peel, who characterized public opinion as "that great compound of folly, weakness, prejudice, wrong feeling, right feeling, obstinacy and newspaper paragraphs."[53]

Modern survey researchers have not been much kinder. The first voting studies, carried out during the 1940s and 1950s, turned up appalling evidence of public ignorance, lack of interest in politics, and reliance on group and party loyalties rather than judgment about the issues of the day. Repeated surveys of the same individuals found that their responses seemed to change randomly from one interview to another. Philip Converse, a leading student of political behavior, coined the term *nonattitudes* to convey the fact that, on many issues of public policy, many Americans seem to have no real views or true opinions but simply offer "doorstep opinions" to satisfy interviewers.[54]

What should we make of this? If ordinary citizens are poorly informed and their views are based on whim, or if they have no real opinions at all, it hardly seems desirable—or even possible—that public opinion should determine what governments do. Both the feasibility and the attractiveness of democracy seem to be thrown into doubt. When we examine exactly what sorts of opinions ordinary Americans have, however, and how those opinions form and change, we will see that such fears may be somewhat exaggerated.

The People's Knowledge About Politics

Several decades of polling have shown that most ordinary Americans neither know nor care a lot about politics.[55] Nearly everyone knows some basic facts, such as the name of the capital of the United States and the length of the president's term of office, but surveys often find that only about two-thirds of adults know which party has the most members in the House of Representatives. Only about 30 percent know that the

AN ATTENTIVE PUBLIC
President Trump's first nominee to the Supreme Court—Neil Gorsuch—was confirmed by the Senate in April of 2017. Supreme Court justices play a key role in our political system and President Trump has touted his court appointments as major achievements. However, a survey conducted only a few months after he was confirmed found that only 45 percent of the public could even identify Neil Gorsuch as a Supreme Court justice.
Why might the public lack knowledge about the players in our political system? What does the public need to know in order to fulfill its role in a democracy?

term of a U.S. House member is two years, and only about one-half know that there are two U.S. senators from each state.[56] Barely one in four Americans can explain what is in the First Amendment. Furthermore, people have particular trouble with technical terms, geography, abbreviations, and acronyms like NAFTA (the North American Free Trade Agreement). Americans do not have detailed knowledge about important public policies nor about the way our economy works. Only 40 percent know that our main source of electricity comes from coal, and only 29 percent can name the federal program the government spends the most on (Medicare).[57]

People also consistently and dramatically underestimate the degree of income and wealth inequality that exists in the United States and fail to understand how tax policies affect "who gets what" in American society.[58] Many Americans do not even know if they receive benefits from particular government programs, including many young people who have federal student loans.[59] Forty-four percent of Social Security beneficiaries and 40 percent of those with Medicare do not realize these are government-run insurance programs. One recent *New York Times* poll discovered that many Americans critical of government benefit programs, such as Social Security, Medicare, food stamps, and unemployment insurance, receive benefits from these very same programs but are unable either to recognize or to explain the evident contradiction. And there has been no improvement in Americans' political knowledge over the past several decades, despite the explosion of new information sources on the Internet and on television.[60]

Some have argued what most Americans do not know may not be vital to their role as citizens. If citizens are aware that trade restrictions with Canada and Mexico have been eased, does it matter that they recognize the NAFTA acronym? How important is it for people to know about the two-year term of office for the U.S. House of Representatives, as long as they are aware of the opportunity to vote each time it comes along? Perhaps most people know as much as they need to know in order to be good citizens, particularly if they can form opinions with the help of better-informed cue givers whom they trust (experts, political leaders, media sources, informed friends, interest groups, and so on) or by means of simple rules of thumb that simplify and make the political world more coherent and understandable.[61]

To be sure, consequences flow from people's lack of political knowledge and attention. When policy decisions are made in the dark, out of public view, interest groups often influence policies that an informed public might oppose. Although organized efforts to alert and to educate the public are valuable, low levels of information and

political ideology

A coherently organized set of beliefs about the fundamental nature of good society and the role that government ought to play in achieving it.

attention are a reality that must be taken into account. Perhaps it is simply unrealistic to expect everyone to have detailed knowledge of a wide range of political matters.

By the same token, perhaps it should also not be expected that the average American have an elaborately worked-out **political ideology**, a coherent system of interlocking attitudes and beliefs about politics, the economy, and the role of government. You yourself may be a consistent liberal or conservative (or populist, or socialist, or libertarian), with many opinions that hang together in a coherent pattern, but surveys show that most people have opinions that vary from one issue to another—conservative on some issues, liberal on others. Surveys and in-depth interviews indicate that people's opinions are often linked by underlying themes and values but not necessarily in the neat ways that the ideologies of leading political thinkers would dictate.[62]

It is no surprise, then, that most individuals' expressed opinions on issues tend to be unstable. Many people give different answers to the same survey question just weeks after their first response. Scholars have disagreed about what these unstable responses mean, but uncertainty and lack of information very likely play a part.

Even if the evidence leads to the conclusion that individual Americans are politically uninformed and disengaged, it does not necessarily follow that the opinions of the public, taken as a whole, are unreal, unstable, or irrelevant. We would counter that the *collective whole* is greater than its individual parts. Even if there is some randomness in the average individual's political opinions—even if people often say things off the top of their heads to survey interviewers—the responses of thousands or millions of people tend to smooth over this randomness and reveal a stable **aggregate public opinion**. Americans' collective policy preferences are actually quite stable over time. That is, the percentage of Americans who favor a particular policy usually stays about the same, unless circumstances change in important ways, such as a major war or economic depression. In addition, even if most people form many of their specific opinions by deferring to others whom they trust rather than by compiling their own mass of political information, the resulting public opinion need not be ignorant or unwise because trusted leaders may themselves take account of the best available information. Finally, there is mounting evidence that Americans' collective policy preferences react rather sensibly to events, to changing circumstances, and to the quality of the information available to them, so that we can speak of a **rational public**. So, at the individual level, we may not be impressed with the capacities or rationality of the public. But when we aggregate individual attitudes and understandings, that is, put them together and look at averages over time, we are on somewhat firmer ground in suggesting a sort of public rationality.[63]

aggregate public opinion

The political attitudes of the public as a whole, expressed as averages, percentages, or other summaries of many individuals' opinions.

rational public

The notion that collective public opinion is rational in the sense that it is generally stable and consistent and that when it changes it does so as an understandable response to events, to changing circumstances, and to new information.

The People's Attitudes About the Political System

At the most general level, Americans are proud of their country and its political institutions. In 2017 for example, 75 percent of all Americans said they were either very or extremely proud to be an American, in spite of a sharp decline in national pride among Democrats following Donald Trump's election.[64] In 2011, about one-half of Americans said they believed "our culture is superior to others," compared to only a little more than one-fourth of the French.[65] In addition, in 2009 about seven in ten Americans said they felt that it is important to vote.[66]

THE PEOPLE'S TRUST IN THE GOVERNMENT Despite Americans' expressed pride of country, there are recent indications that people have become more pessimistic about the ability of the country to solve its problems. One indicator of the American public's rising pessimism is the steady decline in what pollsters call "trust in government." For example, at the end of 2017 the Pew Research Center, reporting results from its own polls and other leading surveys, put the level of "trust in government"—those who say they trust government to do the right thing "always" or "most of the time"—at around 19 percent, down from the 40 percent average for most of the 1980s and the 70 percent trust in government levels during the 1960s (see Figure 5.9).[67] This is perhaps no surprise given the wars in Iraq and Afghanistan, the decades-long stagnation in income for most Americans, growing income and wealth inequality, the Great Recession and slow job recovery, and persistent threats of government shutdowns.

THE PEOPLE'S OPINIONS ABOUT THE DIRECTION OF THE COUNTRY   Another way in which both pollsters and scholars assess the general mood of the country is by asking questions about whether we are moving in the right direction or the wrong direction. In October of 2018, Gallup reported that although only 38 percent of Americans were "satisfied with the way things are going in the United States at this time," this was the highest level of satisfaction recorded since the start of the financial crisis that started in the year before President Obama's election in 2008.[68] The modest uptick in satisfaction may reflect gradually improving economic conditions. Of course these results mean that most Americans are *dissatisfied* with the way things are going.

CONGRESSIONAL APPROVAL RATINGS   One more important aspect of happiness or unhappiness with government is a judgment about how well Congress is doing. For much of the past four decades or so, the proportion of Americans disapproving of the job Congress is doing has been twice as high as the proportion approving Congress's job performance. Things became especially bad in the last year of the Bush

FIGURE 5.9   PUBLIC TRUST IN GOVERNMENT

This graph shows the percentage of Americans who answered "just about always" or "most of the time" to the question: How much of the time do you trust the government in Washington?

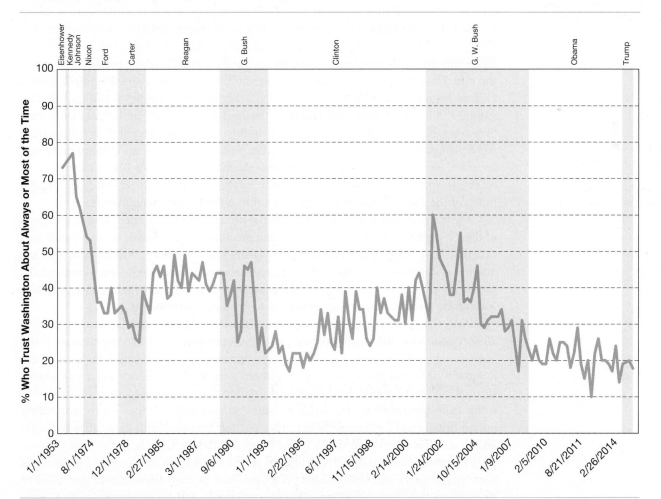

SOURCE: Data from Pew Research Center for the People & the Press, "Trust in Government, 1958–2017," Pew Research Center, November 23, 2015, based on polling by Gallup, the Pew Research Center, National Election Studies, ABC/*Washington Post*, CBS/*New York Times*, and CNN.

administration when Congress authorized unpopular bailouts of financial institutions and approval has remained low since then. In late 2018, Congress's approval was hovering just below 20 percent.[69] In fact, one poll conducted in 2013 found that Americans reported having a higher opinion of cockroaches, root canals, lice, and traffic jams than of Congress.[70]

presidential job approval rating

The percentage of Americans who believe the president is doing a good job.

PRESIDENTIAL APPROVAL RATINGS   Another indicator of government performance is the **presidential job approval rating**, or how well Americans judge the president to be doing his or her job. The public's evaluations of presidents' handling of their jobs depend on how well things are actually going. The state of the economy is especially important: when the country is prosperous and ordinary Americans are doing well and feeling confident about the future, the president tends to be popular; when there is high inflation or unemployment or when general living standards remain stagnant, the president's popularity falls.

Pollsters have been asking Americans for many decades whether they approve or disapprove of the way presidents are doing their jobs. The percentage of people saying they approve is taken as a crucial indicator of a president's popularity (see Figure 12.2 for more on presidential approval dynamics). Typically, presidents enjoy a "honeymoon period" of public good will and high approval ratings immediately after they are elected. After that, their approval fluctuates with particular events and trends. For example, Lyndon Johnson's approval fluctuated with events in Vietnam, and George H. W. Bush reached a then-record 89 percent approval in March 1991 in the aftermath of the Gulf War but fell below 30 percent by the summer, an unprecedented collapse. Oddly, Bill Clinton enjoyed the highest job approval ratings of any recent president for the final two years of the presidential term, in spite of the fact that the Republican-controlled House of Representatives impeached him. George W. Bush's job approval reached a record peak of 90 percent in the weeks following the 9/11 terrorist attacks. However, by fall 2008 his approval hovered in the mid-20s—the lowest presidential approval rating in fifty years. President Barack Obama began his term in early 2009 with a job approval rating in the mid-60s; by summer 2012, his rating had fallen to the mid-40s. In 2016, as he was preparing to leave office, his approval rating had climbed above 50 percent.[71] In a departure from past patterns, President Donald Trump entered office with a historically low approval rating—only 45 percent of respondents approved of his performance (a ceiling in approval that he had not broken by the summer of 2018)—suggesting that much of the public was not willing to grant him the traditional honeymoon.

These trends in trust in government, the direction of the country, and evaluations of the job performance of Congress and the president by the public seem sensible and rational. They reflect the difficulties many Americans have been living through, the attention of the news media to the country's economic challenges and Washington's governing problems, and the ferocious manner in which the parties have waged political combat over the causes and solutions to the nation's problems.

With the rise of the Tea Party soon after President Obama's inauguration in 2009, pessimism about government and the economy and discomfiture with the direction of the country turned into outright anger. Tea Party adherents voice anger about illegal immigrants, government deficits, bailouts and loan guarantees to financial institutions, and a growing national government involved in everything from propping up financial institutions and auto companies to mandating health insurance coverage. Much like earlier manifestations of populist-style anger, cultural, media, and academic elites are handy targets for seemingly supporting many of the disruptive changes in the country. And Tea Party supporters were particularly exercised about programs that, in their view, direct government benefits to the "undeserving," those unwilling to work or who have just come into the country.[72] Though the Tea Party movement was encouraged and partially

organized by conservative talk radio and cable television personalities such as Glenn Beck (then on Fox News), its rise reflected many people's real concerns about the state of the country. Their enthusiastic support of the Republican Party in 2010—and a lack of similar enthusiasm among groups in the Democratic Party base—helped the GOP make historic gains in that year's national, state, and local elections.

In 2011, populist anger took shape on the left of the political spectrum with the rise and rapid spread of the Occupy Wall Street protests about rising income and wealth inequality, high unemployment, and sluggish job growth, particularly for young people. Unlike the Tea Party, this movement wanted government to do more.

Widespread dissatisfaction with the government in Washington left an imprint on both of the 2016 presidential nomination contests. Republican Donald Trump and Democratic candidate Bernie Sanders each leveraged voters increasing cynicism about the political system to their advantage. Trump regularly gave voice to the sentiments of many citizens by condemning Washington elites as a corrupt class, more interested in dishing out favors to donors and friends than in stemming the flow of undocumented immigrants. On the Democratic side, Senator Bernie Sanders mounted an unexpectedly strong challenge to front-runner Hillary Clinton. Throughout the campaign he criticized Clinton for her ties to Wall Street and implied that these ties would leave her unable to serve the public rather than wealthy elites.

economic conservatives

People who favor private enterprise and oppose government regulation of business.

economic liberals

People who favor government spending for social programs and government regulation of business to protect the public.

social (or lifestyle) liberals

People who favor civil liberties, abortion rights, and alternative lifestyles.

social (or lifestyle) conservatives

People who favor traditional social values; they tend to support strong law-and-order measures and oppose abortion and gay rights.

The People's Liberalism and Conservatism

Although most Americans do not adhere to a rigid political ideology of the sort posited by political philosophers, they do divide on the role they believe government should play. To complicate matters, Americans generally divide along two dimensions when it comes to government: one related to government's role in the economy, the other related to government's role in society. Some Americans—those we usually label **economic conservatives**—tend to put more emphasis on economic liberty and freedom from government interference; they believe a free market offers the best road to economic efficiency and a decent society. Others—whom we usually label **economic liberals**—stress the role of government in ensuring equality of opportunity, regulating potentially damaging business practices, and providing safety nets for individuals unable to compete in the job market. Government regulation of the economy and spending to help the disadvantaged are two of the main sources of political dispute in America; they also make up a big part of the difference between the ideologies of liberalism and of conservatism. However, this accounts for only one of the two dimensions. It is also useful to distinguish between **social (or lifestyle) liberals** and **social (or lifestyle) conservatives**, who differ on government's role in society and have varying views on such social issues as abortion, prayer in the schools, homosexuality, pornography, crime, and political dissent. Those who favor relatively unconstrained free choices and strong protections for the rights of the accused are often said to be socially liberal, while those preferring government enforcement of order and traditional values are described as socially conservative.

It should be apparent that opinions on economic and social issues do not necessarily go together. Many people are liberal in some ways but conservative in others. A marijuana legalization activist, for example, would likely be a social liberal but might also be a small business owner and an economic conservative when it comes to taxes and regulation of business. An evangelical minister preaching in a poor community might be a social conservative on issues such as pornography but an economic liberal when it comes to government programs to help the disadvantaged. This said, as the parties have polarized over the past several decades, an increasing share of Americans have begun to report attitudes that are either consistently liberal or consistently conservative.[73]

The People's Policy Preferences

According to democratic theory, one of the chief determinants of what governments do should be what the citizens *want* them to do, that is, citizens' policy preferences. Figure 5.10 shows that public opinion on what government should do is either relatively unchanging or has changed in response to fairly well-understood developments in American society. These trends are consistent with the notion that, in the aggregate, public opinion tends to be quite stable and, perhaps, rational.

SPENDING PROGRAMS By and large, while more Americans describe themselves as conservative or moderate than as liberal, many want government to do a great deal to address societal needs. One might say that a majority of Americans are philosophical conservatives and moderates but operational liberals.

Figure 5.10 shows that over the years, Americans have been consistent in their positions on a range of things they want from government. For example, large and rather stable numbers of Americans think the government is spending "too little" on health care and improving education. By contrast, few people think too little is being spent on foreign aid or the military and defense; many more think too much is being spent. Except for disaster relief, such as for the outbreak of Ebola in West Africa, foreign aid is generally unpopular. (The reason may be, in part, that few realize how little is spent on foreign aid—only about 1 percent of the annual federal budget

FIGURE 5.10   SHARE OF PUBLIC SAYING WE SPEND TOO LITTLE IN SIX POLICY AREAS

Large, fairly stable majorities of Americans have said that the government is spending too little on health care and education, but over the years relatively few have said we spend too little on defense, welfare, or foreign aid.

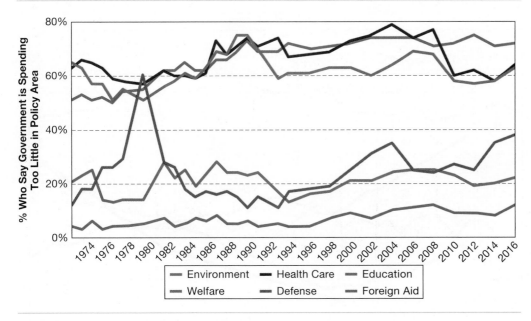

SOURCE: General Social Survey, Cumulative Data File (1972–2016).

is devoted to economic and humanitarian assistance. When the spending level is made clear, support for foreign aid rises sharply.)[74] Finally, although relatively few Americans say the government is spending too little on welfare, when surveys ask about spending on "aid to the poor" rather than "welfare," substantial majorities say we are spending too little.[75]

Many polls show that the public also gives consistent supermajority support to Social Security, Medicare, and environmental protection programs. Substantial majorities have said for many years that they want the government to pay for more research on diseases such as cancer and AIDS and to "see to it" that everyone who wants to work can find a job.

When public opinion changes, it usually does so for understandable reasons. In 2008, more Americans than before said they wanted the government to increase regulation of Wall Street, whose unregulated speculation helped bring on the Great Recession. Similarly, as Figure 5.10 illustrates, public support for defense spending spiked during the early 1980s when Cold War rhetoric was particularly prominent and the USSR was widely viewed as a serious threat to national security and again in the early years of the new century as the war on terrorism was launched in response to 9/11.

SOCIAL ISSUES   On some social issues, American public opinion has been remarkably stable; on others, the past several decades have seen massive shifts in public attitudes. As Figure 5.11 shows, views about abortion have remained quite consistent over many years, even in the face of the furious cultural war that swirls about the issue.

As the nation has become more educated and its mass entertainment culture more open to diverse perspectives and ways of life, public opinion has become more supportive of civil liberties and civil rights for women and minorities. Since the 1940s and 1950s, for example, more and more Americans have come to favor integrating

FIGURE 5.11 TRENDS IN ATTITUDES ABOUT SOCIAL ISSUES

On some issues—most notably abortion and gun policy—American attitudes have remained relatively stable for the last several decades. However, attitudes about same-sex marriage, the role of women in society, and marijuana legalization have changed rapidly.

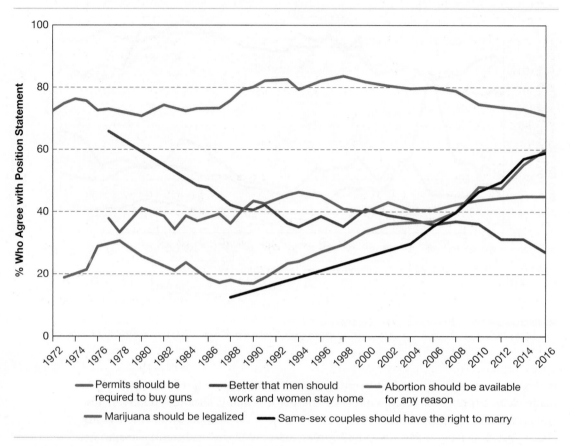

— Permits should be required to buy guns
— Better that men should work and women stay home
— Abortion should be available for any reason
— Marijuana should be legalized
— Same-sex couples should have the right to marry

SOURCE: General Social Survey, Cumulative Data File (1972–2016).

school, work, housing, and public accommodations. By 2002, less than 10 percent of Americans supported laws against interracial marriage—a dramatic drop from the early 1970s when almost 40 percent of the public supported such bans. According to the General Social Survey, over the past several decades, public support for same-sex marriage has skyrocketed, from only 12 percent supporting it in 1988 to 59 percent supporting it in 2016. By 2018, Gallup found that 67 percent of Americans supported same-sex marriage.[76] Many have cited this trend in public sentiment as playing an important role in the Supreme Court's 2015 ruling striking down state laws that banned same-sex marriage.

On a number of other issues, Americans support positions favored by social conservatives. Large majorities, for example, have consistently favored allowing organized prayer in public schools, banning pornography, preventing flag burning, punishing crimes severely, and imposing capital punishment for murder. In addition, 62 percent of Americans said in 2010 that they approved police questioning anyone they suspected of being in the country illegally, the heart of the controversial law passed in Arizona; in 2012, the Supreme Court upheld this section of that law.[77]

FOREIGN POLICY AND NATIONAL SECURITY In the realm of foreign policy and national security, public opinion sometimes changes rapidly in response to crises and other dramatic events. Major international events affect opinions, as was evident in the discussion of public reactions to the Tet Offensive during the Vietnam War, which opens the chapter. The percentage of Americans saying that the United States was wrong to invade Iraq steadily increased as the news from there got worse. Confidence in the effectiveness of American foreign and military policies declined sharply between 2005 and 2007.[78] This seems understandable, given events on the ground. But often foreign policy opinions are quite stable. Since World War II, for example, two-thirds or more of those giving an opinion have usually said that the United States should take an "active part" in world affairs. The percentage supporting a U.S. role has remained relatively high but declined somewhat by 2011.[79]

The public has generally been quite hesitant to approve the use of troops abroad, however, unless the threat to the United States is tangible. For example, in 1994, just before U.S. troops were sent as peacekeepers to Bosnia, 56 percent of the public opposed the idea and only 39 percent were in favor.[80] Opposition faded as the operation began to look less risky. The public strongly supported the use of the military to destroy Al Qaeda and the Taliban regime in Afghanistan[81] and initially supported President Bush's decision to invade Iraq in 2003, when only 23 percent of those surveyed said the United States "made a mistake sending troops to Iraq." By summer 2010, the proportion of the public who thought it was a mistake had soared to 55 percent.[82] Support for the armed conflict in Afghanistan was lower by late 2014, more than 10 years after it began; only 38 percent of Americans said it was "worth fighting."[83]

Although the American public shows some signs of being "war weary," a CBS poll conducted in late 2015 illustrates that the public is still willing to support military action overseas. Although 83 percent of respondents said they were either somewhat or very concerned "that U.S. intervention in Iraq and Syria will lead to a long and costly involvement there," 75 percent supported U.S. airstrikes against ISIS militants who occupy those countries. That same poll found that 50 percent supported sending ground troops to fight ISIS. After Donald Trump ordered airstrikes against a Syrian air force base in early 2017, polls showed that a comfortable majority of the public supported the strikes.[84]

Although relatively few Americans embrace pure **isolationism**—the view that the United States should not be involved abroad and should only pay attention to its own affairs—the public (and political and economic leaders, as well) is divided over whether its involvement in the world should take a **unilateralist** or a **multilateralist** form. Unilateralists want to go it alone, taking action when it suits our purposes and not necessarily seeking the approval or help of international organizations such as the United Nations or regional organizations such as NATO. Unilateralists are also uncomfortable with entering into too many international treaties. Multilateralists, on the other hand, believe that the protection of American interests requires continuous engagement in the world but do not think that the United States has the resources or ability to accomplish its ends without the cooperation of other nations or international and regional organizations. According to most surveys, roughly two out of three Americans are in the multilateralist camp, telling pollsters they oppose unilateral U.S. military intervention in most cases and support cooperation with the United Nations and NATO and international treaties on human rights, the environment, and arms control. In this regard, they are considerably more multilateralist than American legislative and executive branch officials.[85]

isolationism

The policy of avoiding involvement in the affairs of other countries and multilateral institutions.

unilateralist

The stance toward foreign policy that suggests that the United States should "go it alone," pursuing its national interests without seeking the cooperation of other nations or multilateral institutions.

multilateralist

The stance toward foreign policy that suggests that the United States should seek the cooperation of other nations and multilateral institutions in pursuing its goals.

The People's "Fitness to Rule" Revisited

This examination of collective public opinion, its evident stability on a wide range of issues over time, and why it sometimes changes on some issues leads us to conclude that confidence in the role of the public in the American political system is warranted. The evidence demonstrates that collective public opinion is quite stable and sensible when it comes to core beliefs and attitudes about government, the parties, and policy preferences.[86] The evidence further shows that when collective public opinion does change, it does so for understandable reasons: dramatic events, new information, or changes in perspective among American leaders. The conclusion we draw is a simple yet powerful one: the American people are fit to rule.

PUBLIC OPINION: DOES IT DETERMINE WHAT GOVERNMENT DOES?

We have argued that a crucial test of how well democracy is working is how closely a government's policies match the expressed wishes of its citizens. Some scholars claim that, yes, the government generally acts in ways that reflect public opinion. But others argue that public officials sometimes ignore public opinion; that public opinion is often heavily manipulated by government leaders so that it tends to reflect rather than influence government action; and that the public is inattentive and has no opinions on many important policy issues, leaving political leaders free to act on their own.

THE CASE FOR PUBLIC OPINION

As the opening case about the Vietnam War suggests, at least under some circumstances, public opinion significantly affects policy making. Another example that supports "government responsiveness" to public opinion is President Bush's attempt, in 2005, to privatize Social Security, which was blocked by congressional opponents and backstopped by strong public support for the current system.

Many authoritative scholarly assessments indicate a statistical correlation between public opinion and government action.[87] One assessment found that U.S. policy coincides with opinion surveys of public wants about two-thirds of the time. Another survey found that, when public opinion changes by a substantial and enduring amount and the issue is prominent, government policy moved in the same direction 87 percent of the time within a year or so afterward.[88] Yet another influential study showed that, as substantial swings in the national political mood occurred over the past half-century—from a liberal direction, to a conservative direction, and back again over the years—public policy has followed accordingly, being more activist in liberal periods and less activist in conservative periods.[89] Finally, a careful review of thirty studies concluded that public opinion almost always has some effect on what government does and is, in highly visible cases, a decisive factor in determining the substance of government policy.[90]

THE CASE AGAINST PUBLIC OPINION

A strong statistical correlation between public opinion and government policy does not, however, prove that public opinion *causes* government policies. There are a number of reasons why a correlation may not imply a "causal relationship" between public opinion and policy.[91]

- Public opinion and government policies may move in the same direction because some third factor affects them both in the same way. For example, after news networks and major newspapers highlighted the near-genocidal situation in the Darfur region of Sudan, in the mid-2000s, the public and policy makers were persuaded that action was needed.[92] Interest groups, too, may simultaneously sway public opinion and government officials, as financial industry groups did when they convinced both that deregulation, the source of disastrous losses in 2008, would be a good thing.

- It may be that political leaders shape public opinion, not the other way around, a reversal of the causal arrow wherein officials act to gain popular support for policies that they, the officials, want.[93] Such efforts can range from outright manipulation of the public—the Tonkin Gulf incident and the "weapons of mass destruction" rhetoric used to raise support for the invasion of Iraq in 2003[94]—to conventional public relations tactics carried out every day by well-equipped government communications offices, press secretaries, and public liaison personnel.

- Still another possibility, supported by several recent studies, is that policy makers only behave in accordance with the wishes of the public at large in situations where what the broader public wants is aligned with the preferences of wealthy Americans and well-funded interest groups. In other words, the public at large may often get what it wants, but only because they happen to share the policy-preferences of these elites.[95]

THE MIXED REALITY

It is probably reasonable to affirm that public opinion often plays an important role in shaping what government does and that political leaders do pay attention to public opinion, pandering, some would say, to public whims rather than exercising leadership. It is no mystery why. Spending time and money polling relevant constituencies eventually translates into votes. Staying on the right side of public opinion—giving people what they want—is how office seekers and office holders gain and keep their positions.

But, as we have seen, the public does not always have informed opinions about important matters, leading scholars to suggest that public opinion plays different roles in shaping government policy—some roles are important and some are less so, depending on conditions. Public opinion seems to matter most when issues (1) are highly visible (usually because there has been lots of political conflict surrounding the issue) and (2) are about matters that most directly affect the lives of Americans and about which reliable and understandable information is readily accessible. When economic times are tough—during a recession, for example—no amount of rhetoric from political leaders, the news media, or interest groups is likely to convince people "that they never had it so good."

By the same token, many foreign policy questions are distant from people's lives and involve issues about which information is scarce or incomplete. Under these conditions, government officials act with wide latitude and shape what the public believes rather than respond to it.

In addition, some issues, such as tax legislation and deregulation, are so obscure and complex that they become the province of interest groups and experts, with the public holding ill-formed and not very intense opinions. Many scholars convincingly argue that the combined influence of other political actors and institutions, including political parties, interest groups, the news media, and social movements, has far more of an effect than public opinion on what government does.

It is probably reasonable to say that the influence of public opinion on government is significantly less than the statistical studies suggest (e.g., the "two-thirds" rule) for the reasons given: the impact of third factors on both opinion and government and the significant amount of influence government officials have over popular opinion,[96] and the powerful influence of the wealthy and large interest groups on elected officials and the public. And it is hard to avoid noticing the many times government acts almost exactly contrary to public opinion—Congress's decision to go ahead with the impeachment and trial of Bill Clinton in late 1998 and early 1999 in the face of strong public opposition comes to mind, as does inaction on gun control alluded to earlier. More recently, the massive tax cut passed by Republicans in late 2017 was enacted in spite of public opposition to the law. Similarly, President Trump's vigorous calls to build a wall on the border with Mexico run counter to the fact that polls consistently show that most Americans oppose building the wall.

MEASURING PUBLIC OPINION

5.1 Describe public opinion research and modern methods of polling.

Public opinion consists of the core political beliefs and political attitudes expressed by ordinary citizens; it can be measured rather accurately through polls and surveys.

Today, most polling is done by telephone.

The foundation of a legitimate survey is that respondents in a sample are randomly selected.

The increased use of cell phones makes it more difficult to develop a random sample.

POLITICAL SOCIALIZATION: LEARNING POLITICAL BELIEFS AND ATTITUDES

5.2 Explain how the agents of socialization influence the development of political attitudes.

People learn their political attitudes and beliefs from their families, peers, schools, and workplaces as well as through their experiences with political events and the mass media. This process is known as political socialization.

Changes in society, the economy, and America's situation in the world affect political attitudes and public opinion.

HOW AND WHY PEOPLE'S POLITICAL ATTITUDES DIFFER

5.3 Describe the forces that create and shape political attitudes.

Opinions and party loyalties differ according to race, religion, region, urban or rural residence, social class, education level, gender, and age. Blacks, city dwellers, women, and low-income people tend to be particularly liberal and Democratic; white Protestants, suburbanites, males, and the wealthy tend to be more conservative and Republican.

THE CONTOURS OF AMERICAN PUBLIC OPINION: ARE THE PEOPLE FIT TO RULE?

5.4 Assess whether the public is capable of playing a meaningful role in steering public policy.

The democratic ideals of popular sovereignty and majority rule imply that government policy should respond to the wishes of the citizens, at least in the long run. An important test of how well democracy is working, then, is how closely government policy corresponds to public opinion.

Political knowledge among the public is low, but cue-givers allow people to make fairly rational decisions about their policy preferences.

Public opinion, considered in the aggregate as a collection of randomly selected respondents, tends to be stable, measured, and rational over the years. Some political scientists call this the "rational public."

agents of socialization The institutions and individuals that shape the core beliefs and attitudes of people.

aggregate public opinion The political attitudes of the public as a whole, expressed as averages, percentages, or other summaries of many individuals' opinions.

core values Individuals' views about the fundamental nature of human beings, society, the economy, and the role of government; taken together, they constitute the political culture.

economic conservatives People who favor private enterprise and oppose government regulation of business.

economic liberals People who favor government spending for social programs and government regulation of business to protect the public.

generational effect The long lasting effect of major political events—particularly those that occur when an individual is coming of age politically—on people's political attitudes.

isolationism   The policy of avoiding involvement in the affairs of other countries and multilateral institutions.

multilateralist   The stance toward foreign policy that suggests that the United States should seek the cooperation of other nations and multilateral institutions in pursuing its goals.

partisan leaners   Individuals who say they do not identify as Democrats or Republicans, but say they feel closer to either the Democratic or Republican Party.

political attitudes   Individuals' views and preferences about public policies, political parties, candidates, government institutions, and public officials.

political ideology   A coherently organized set of beliefs about the fundamental nature of good society and the role that government ought to play in achieving it.

political socialization   The process by which individuals come to have certain core beliefs and political attitudes.

presidential job approval rating   The percentage of Americans who believe the president is doing a good job.

probability sampling   A survey technique designed so that every individual in a population of interest (e.g., the American public) has an equal chance of being included in the pool of survey respondents.

public opinion   The aggregated political attitudes of ordinary people as revealed by surveys.

rational public   The notion that collective public opinion is rational in the sense that it is generally stable and consistent and that when it changes it does so as an understandable response to events, to changing circumstances, and to new information.

sampling error   Statistical uncertainty in estimates associated with the fact that surveys do not interview every individual in a population of interest.

scientific survey   A survey conducted using probability sampling to measure the attitudes of a representative sample of the public.

social (or lifestyle) conservatives   People who favor traditional social values; they tend to support strong law-and-order measures and oppose abortion and gay rights.

social (or lifestyle) liberals   People who favor civil liberties, abortion rights, and alternative lifestyles.

unilateralist   The stance toward foreign policy that suggests that the United States should "go it alone," pursuing its national interests without seeking the cooperation of other nations or multilateral institutions

WEAPONS OF MASS DESTRUCTION

The Bush administration sold the American people on the invasion of Iraq in 2003 on the grounds that Saddam Hussein had developed nuclear and biological weapons that threatened the region and the world. British government sources later said that the intelligence was "cooked" to support the invasion—there were no such military capabilities—but the new information failed to become important news in America's media.

Why would a story suggesting that policy-makers were not completely honest with the public receive so little attention in the media?

THE NEWS MEDIA

CHAPTER OUTLINE AND LEARNING OBJECTIVES

HOW NEWS ORGANIZATIONS OPERATE

6.1 Discuss the functions, structure, and operations of the news media.

BIAS IN THE NEWS

6.2 Evaluate news organizations' ideological and nonideological biases.

EFFECTS OF THE NEWS MEDIA ON POLITICS

6.3 Analyze the impact of the media on public opinion and political behavior.

The Struggle for Democracy

WAR WITH THE WATCHDOG

It had all the makings of a major news story that would rock Washington and trigger a major rethinking of war policies in Iraq.[1] All the pieces appeared to be in place. In an article published on April 30, 2005, the prestigious British newspaper, *The Times* of London, reported the minutes of a secret meeting between Prime Minister Tony Blair and his top military and intelligence officials that featured a report by a British intelligence operative that Washington officials had "cooked the books" to justify the invasion of Iraq in spring 2003. The operative had been at several prewar meetings with White House and Pentagon officials where it was evident, he claimed, that the decision for war already had been made and that intelligence information about Saddam Hussein's purported "weapons of mass destruction" program and ties to the 9/11 terrorists was organized and interpreted to build a case for going to war. In his words, the "facts were being fixed around the policy."[2]

As news stories go, the seeming blockbuster turned out to be a dud. The story failed to merit a lead on any of the network newscasts. While the story of the so-called Downing Street memo appeared on the front page of the *Washington Post*, it was there for only a single day. Other newspapers relegated it to the inside pages. For the most part, the story was "... treated as old news or a British politics story" rather than a story about Americans being misled into war by the Bush administration, something that might call into question the entire enterprise.[3] The liberal blogosphere jumped on the issue, but the story failed to stir more mainstream media attention or action from congressional Democrats, who were in the minority in both the House and Senate and unsure about what position to take on the war in the upcoming 2006 elections. When Representative John Conyers (D-MI) sought to bring attention to the misuse of intelligence information to encourage the Iraq war by holding an "informational hearing" (being in the minority, the Democrat Conyers could not schedule an official set of hearings), the *Washington Post* treated it as a joke; the headline read "Democrats Play House to Rally Against the War" and opened with the line, "In the Capitol basement yesterday, long suffering House Democrats took a trip to the land of make-believe."[4] Similarly, in an article published in early 2006—roughly three years after the invasion of Iraq—the *New York Times* reported a British press story, based on a memo written by a Blair aide who had attended a prewar January 2003 meeting of Prime Minister Tony Blair and President George W. Bush at the White House, where the president had made it clear to the British leader that he was determined to go to war even without evidence that Iraq was building weapons of mass destruction or had links to Al Qaeda. (At the same time, the president was making numerous statements that he had not made up his mind about an invasion and was making every effort to solve the issue diplomatically in cooperation with the United Nations and close allies.) While the revelation elicited a few comments from Democratic leaders and some blog activity, it didn't get a mention on CBS, NBC, or Fox News, and no follow-up stories appeared in the *Los Angeles Times, Wall Street Journal, Washington Post*, or *USA Today*.

Around the same time this story about the Bush–Blair meeting came and went with hardly a murmur, a feeding frenzy was swirling around an unfortunate incident in which Vice President Richard Cheney accidentally shot a long-time friend in the face while hunting. Although the friend was not seriously injured, for four or five days after the accidental shooting, every type of news media outlet—including the network and cable news networks, news magazines, local and national newspapers, news websites, and blogs—ran full coverage on the story, examining every nuance and speculating about why it happened, why an official press release about it was delayed for a few hours, and what it might all mean. Late-night comedy hosts had a field day with the story for months.

* * * * *

Many critics claim the news media are biased and cannot be relied on to tell an objective story. Other critics claim that the mainstream news media in particular are becoming irrelevant in the face of the Internet, with its multiple information and opinion sources. We suggest that the principal problems of the news media concern underreporting stories that might help American citizens better understand events and trends that affect their lives, including those involving government and political leaders, and excessive attention to stories that involve sensation, entertainment, or scandals. This chapter is about the news media and why certain things become news we pay attention to while other things, many of them very important to public conversations about government policies and the direction of the country, do not.

THINKING CRITICALLY **ABOUT THIS CHAPTER**

In this chapter, we turn our attention to the diverse news media in the United States to learn how they are organized, how they work, and what effects they have on the quality of our political life.

APPLYING THE **FRAMEWORK**

In this chapter, you will learn about the role the news media play in influencing significant actors in the political system, including citizens and elected leaders. You also will learn how the news media can shape what government does. And you will learn how the news media are influenced by changes in technology and business organization.

USING THE **DEMOCRACY STANDARD**

Using the tools introduced in Chapter 1, you will be able to evaluate the degree to which the news media advance democracy in the United States or hinder it. You will be able to judge whether the media promote popular sovereignty, political equality, and liberty. Finally, you will see how certain changes in the media may be cause for concern in terms of the health of democracy.

HOW NEWS ORGANIZATIONS OPERATE

6.1 Discuss the functions, structure, and operations of the news media.

The central idea of democracy is that ordinary citizens should control what their government does. However, citizens cannot hope to control officials, choose candidates wisely, speak intelligently with others about public affairs, or even make up their minds about which policies they favor without good information about politics and policies. Most of that information must come through the news media, whether newspapers, radio, television, or, increasingly, the Internet. How well democracy works, then, depends partly on how well the news media fulfills three essential roles or functions.

The Functions of the News Media in a Democracy

One function of the news media in a democracy is that of **watchdog**. The Founders, although not entirely enamored of democracy, nevertheless fully subscribed to the idea that a free press is essential for keeping an eye on government and for checking its excesses. The First Amendment to the Constitution ("Congress shall make no law...abridging the freedom...of the press") helps ensure that the news media will be able to expose misbehavior without fear of censorship or prosecution. That the

watchdog

The role of the media in scrutinizing the actions of government officials.

press should warn the public of official wrongdoing is fundamental to the practice of democracy. How else can citizens hold officials accountable for setting things right?

At times, news organizations' efforts to fulfill their watchdog role frustrates government officials. President Donald Trump repeatedly expressed disdain for the news media on the campaign trail. Since taking office he has continued to attack the media for what he views as unfair coverage. He has often referred to major news organizations such as CNN as "fake news," and, in a tweet on May 9, 2018, implied that any negative coverage of him was inherently "fake" saying "… despite the tremendous success we are having with the economy & all things else, 91% of the Network News about me is negative (Fake) …"[5] Notably, he has typically relied on Twitter to communicate this perspective to the public—a channel of communication that allows him to circumvent the journalists who he says are eager to attack him unfairly.

A second function of the news media in a democracy is to make the public's electoral choices clear. The media serve to clarify what the political parties stand for and how the candidates shape up in terms of personal character, knowledge, experience, and positions on the issues. Without such information, it is difficult for voters to make intelligent choices. Similarly, a third function of the news media is to present a diverse, full, and enlightening set of facts and ideas about public policy. Citizens need to know about emerging problems that will need attention and how well current policies are working, as well as the pros and cons of alternative policies that might be tried. In a democracy, government should respond to public opinion, but that opinion should be reasonably well informed.

Understanding whether news organizations provide citizens with the kinds of information they need for democracy to work properly requires an understanding of how the media are organized and function. In the remainder of this chapter, we focus on news media organizations and journalists with an eye toward better understanding the influences that affect the content of their news product and how the news shapes politics and government in the United States.

News Media Organizations

The mainstream or traditional news media are the collection of nationally prominent newspapers (such as the *Wall Street Journal, New York Times,* and *Washington Post*), national news magazines (such as *Time* and *The Week*), TV network and cable news organizations, local newspapers, and local TV news operations. These organizations gather, analyze, and report politically important events, developments, and trends. This is usually done with the help of **wire services** such as the Associated Press (AP) and Reuters—agencies that provide news outlets with news stories and accompanying photos.[6]

wire services
Organizations such as the Associated Press and Reuters that gather and disseminate news to other news organizations.

CORPORATE OWNERSHIP   Some television stations and newspapers—especially the smaller ones—are still owned locally by families or by groups of investors, although they account for a rapidly declining share of the total. Most of the biggest stations and newspapers, however, as well as television and cable networks, are owned by large media corporations, some of which, in turn, are subsidiaries of enormous conglomerates.

Mergers across media lines have accelerated in recent years, leaving a handful of giant conglomerates. Disney, for example, owns not only its theme parks, movie production and distribution operations, and sports teams, but the ABC television network, local TV and radio stations in the nation's largest cities, cable television operations, and book publishers. Rupert Murdoch's family owns News Corp. and 21st Century Fox, companies that own local TV stations in many of the nation's largest cities, cable and satellite operations (including Fox News), the 20th Century Fox film company, the *New York Post,* the *Wall Street Journal* and major newspapers in Great Britain and Australia, a stable of magazines and journals, HarperCollins and

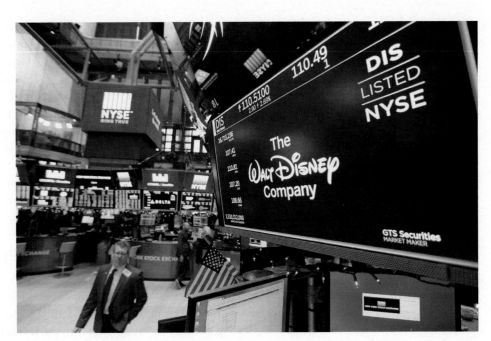

DISNEY MAKES A BID TO BUY 21ST CENTURY FOX

In late 2017, Disney announced a deal to buy much of 21st Century Fox. In addition to an array of television channels and movie franchises, the deal would give Disney a controlling stake in the streaming service Hulu.

Does the prevalence of media empires diminish the number of viewpoints that citizens get to consider when news is reported, or is there sufficient alternative information from other outlets?

Harper Morrow book companies, and radio and TV operations in Europe and Asia. In June 2018, a federal judge approved the merger of AT&T and Time Warner, giving AT&T control of an array of media properties including CNN and HBO. This ruling was expected to lead to a flurry of additional media mergers including, perhaps, an attempt by Disney to buy 21st Century Fox.[7]

So, behind the apparent proliferation of news sources—new magazines, online news and opinion operations, cable television news and commentary, handheld devices with links to the Web, and the like—is substantial concentration of ownership and dense interconnections among the vast cornucopia of news and entertainment outlets. This process of companies coming to control an increasingly large share of the media—either through buying up companies or merging—is referred to as **media consolidation**. Some have even used the term media monopoly to suggest the severity of the situation. However, most scholars are reluctant to go that far, believing that much competition remains among the giant firms.[8]

Many of the key decisions about how much media consolidation will be permitted are made by the **Federal Communications Commission (FCC)**—a federal agency set up to regulate national and international communications to ensure at least some competition between media companies. In 2015 the FCC signaled that they are concerned about excessive media consolidation by playing a key role in ending a plan for two massive media companies—Comcast and Time Warner—to merge. However, this hardly signaled an end to the trend toward greater consolidation: A year later they approved a $65 billion bid by telecommunications company Charter Communications to buy Time Warner.[9] A month later Comcast bought animation studio DreamWorks for almost $4 billion.[10] Many observers expect that recent rule change by the Federal Communications Commission (FCC) will open the door to greater consolidation by reducing limits on the number of media outlets a company can own within a single media market.[11] This said, in the summer of 2018 the FCC signaled that the Sinclair Broadcast Group would not be allowed to purchase Tribune Media Company, suggesting that there are limits to the amount of consolidation the agency is willing to tolerate.[12]

Scholars disagree about the effects of corporate ownership and increased media concentration. A few see efficiency gains and an increase in the output and availability of information. Others argue that allowing greater consolidation of media outlets is the only way smaller newspapers and TV stations can survive in an increasingly

media consolidation

The process of a small number of companies coming to own an increasingly large share of the media outlets by purchasing outlets or merging with other media companies.

Federal Communications Commission (FCC)

Federal agency set up to regulate media companies with an eye toward ensuring competition and protecting consumers.

competitive media environment. But some critics maintain that the concentrated corporate control of our media adds dangerously to the already strong business presence in American politics. They worry that media corporations are so large, powerful, and interconnected that voices that challenge the economically and politically powerful are unlikely to be aired. Others are concerned that the concentration of media ownership may lead to less diversity of news and opinion or a failure to provide citizens with substantive information about politicians and public policies, preferring instead to focus on entertaining audiences due to an excessive focus on the bottom line. Still others worry that news organizations will relinquish their watchdog role and pull their punches when reporting about the activities of their corporate parents or partners. Will ABC News go easy on problems at Disney, for example, which owns ABC? Might NBC fail to report on negative stories about its parent company General Electric? For example, although GE made more than $5 billion in profits in 2010, it paid no federal taxes—a story some noted was conspicuously absent from NBC news coverage.[13]

UNIFORMITY AND DIVERSITY   Whoever owns them, most newspapers and television stations depend largely on the same sources for news. Political scientist Lance Bennett points out that while there is a growing diversity of news outlets in the United States—more specialized magazines, television channels, and newspaper home pages on the Web—news sources are contracting. That is to say, much of what comes to us over a multitude of media avenues originates in fewer and fewer centralized sources.[14] Local radio stations increasingly buy headlines for their brief on-the-hour updates from a handful of headline service providers. Television news increasingly buys raw video footage, for in-house editing and scripting, from a handful of providers, including Independent Television News (ITN), rather than having their own reporters and film crews on the ground. The Associated Press, or AP, supplies most of the main national and international news stories for newspapers and local news (although Reuters is increasingly important)—even those that are rewritten to carry a local reporter's byline. Most of what appears on network and on cable television stations as news, too, is pulled from AP wires, although stations often take their lead on the major stories of the day from the major national newspapers such as the *New York Times, Wall Street Journal*, and *Washington Post*.[15] National and local television news organizations depend on centralized news and video suppliers, with fewer of them using their own reporters. This is why viewers are likely to see the same news (and sports) footage on different stations as they switch channels, although each station adds its own "voiceover" from a reporter or news anchor. In most cases, the person doing the voiceover has no direct relationship to the story.

Profit Motives of the News Media

Media companies, like other companies, are in business to make a profit. This is entirely appropriate in general terms but has some important and unfortunate consequences for how media companies create and disseminate the news. Generating original, in-depth reports is costly. According to one seasoned newsman, "a skilled investigative reporter can cost a news organization more than $250,000 a year in salary and expenses for only a handful of stories."[16] Thus, for many newspapers and television news organizations, pursuing profits means closing down foreign bureaus and cutting the number of reporters focused on government affairs in Washington or the economy and financial system.

INFOTAINMENT   Additionally, for many traditional news organizations, there are market pressures to alter their news coverage to appeal to audiences who are more interested in entertainment than public affairs and want their news short, snappy, and sensational. Together with the multiplication of news outlets and increasing competition for audience share, the desire to attract viewers, readers, or listeners has led to an invasion of entertainment values into political reporting and news presentation. The best way to gain and retain an audience, media executives have discovered, is to make the news more entertaining and that the worst sin one can commit is to be boring.[17] This trend toward mixing news and entertainment—often referred to as **infotainment**—is especially common in evening local news broadcasts, where coverage of politics, government, and policies that affect the public have been "crowded out by coverage of crime, sports, weather, lifestyles, and other audience-grabbing topics."[18]

infotainment
The merging of hard news and entertainment in news presentations.

In many cases, "more entertaining" means that sensation and drama replaces careful consideration of domestic politics, public policies, and international affairs. For example, in 2014, CNN was criticized by some for its relentless coverage of the fate of Malaysia Airlines Flight 370—a passenger jet that crashed somewhere in the Indian Ocean for reasons that are still not known. The *New York Times* cited a CNN network executive who "acknowledged [Flight 3370] was not really a story where reporters [had] been able to advance the known facts much. Instead, it [had] been fueled by a lot of expert analysis based on the little verifiable information that [had] been available, speculation about what might have happened to the plane and where it might be now, accompanied by all the visual pizzazz the network [could] bring to bear." Although there was little "news" to report, the story of the lost aircraft clearly entertained and engaged viewers, leading to a massive surge in CNN's ratings.[19]

Some have argued that Donald Trump's success in the 2016 Republican primaries and caucuses was, in part, a product of his ability to take advantage of media outlets' insatiable desire to attract viewers, listeners, and readers. The real estate magnate and former reality television star's often outlandish rhetoric earned him massive media attention. One report found that by the end of February 2016, candidate Jeb Bush had spent substantially more than his Republican opponents on media, devoting $82 million to television advertising. Although Trump had spent only $10 million on advertising by this stage, the report found that he had garnered almost $2 *billion* in free media in the form of extensive news coverage. His closest Republican opponent—Ted Cruz—had earned only $313 million in free media.[20]

CONFLICT When news organizations do cover political topics, they tend to prioritize stories that feature conflict. The current culture wars between liberals and conservatives over issues such as abortion, affirmative action, religious values, and teaching evolution in schools are perfect grist for the conflict-as-infotainment mill.[21] Thus, a current staple of cable and broadcast television public affairs programming is the gathering of pundits from both sides of the cultural and political divide arguing with one another for 30 or 60 minutes, often in a rather uncivil fashion. And, because bringing together shouting pundits is far cheaper than sending reporters into the field to gather hard news, this form of news coverage is becoming more and more common, especially in the world of cable TV. It is not at all clear that journalism that relies on heated exchanges of claims and counter-claims improves public understanding of candidates, political leaders, or public policies.

Conflict and contest are also evident in coverage of campaigns, where the media concentrate on the "horse-race" aspects of election contests, focusing almost exclusively on who is winning and who is losing the race and what strategies candidates are using to gain ground or to maintain a lead. When candidates talk seriously about issues, the media regularly focus on analyzing the strategy the candidate appears to have adopted, rather than the pros and cons of the policy positions they adopt.[22] The perpetual struggle between Congress and the president, built into our constitutional system, is also perfect for the profit-seeking news industry, especially if the struggle can be personalized.

NEGATIVITY AND SCANDAL Journalists are also eager to cover scandals involving political leaders and candidates of all stripes. Although the catalyst for these stories may be leaks from inside the government; negative ads aired by rival candidates, political parties, or advocacy groups; or postings to partisan and ideological blogs, they often are picked up by major news media outlets and developed further—occasionally with great gusto.[23] These stories are especially compelling to the news media when even the appearance of wrongdoing in the personal lives of prominent people creates dramatic human interest stories. Sex scandals dogged Bill Clinton for most of his presidency and contributed to his eventual impeachment. Sex or financial scandals also claimed, among others, Senator Gary Hart (D-CO), former House Speakers Jim Wright (D-TX), Newt Gingrich (R-GA), Mark Foley (R-FL), Larry Craig (R-ID), and South Carolina Governor Mark Sanford, whose staff in 2009 reported that he was hiking the Appalachian Trail while he was in Argentina visiting his mistress. More recently Senator Al Franken resigned after intense coverage of accusations that he had groped several women, as did Governor Eric Greitens of Missouri in the wake of an array of financial and sex scandals. Stories about Donald Trump authorizing payments to mistresses in the run-up to the election have also been a regular feature of the media landscape during his presidency. Identifying and sharing information about politicians' misdeeds are arguably important aspects of the media's watchdog role. On the other hand, some argue that the media sometimes overplays this role and is too quick to blow scandals out of proportion, thereby, heedlessly destroying political careers.

News-Gathering and Production Operations

The kind of news that the media report is affected by news-gathering and production operations. Much depends on where reporters are, what sources they talk to, and what sorts of video are available.

LIMITED GEOGRAPHY The vast majority of serious national news comes from surprisingly few areas of the country. A huge share of news comes from Washington, D.C., the seat of the federal government, and New York City, the center of publishing and finance in the United States. The major television networks and most newspapers cannot afford to station many reporters outside Washington, D.C. or New York.[24] The networks usually add just Chicago, Los Angeles, Miami, and Houston or Dallas. A recent analysis found that this geographic concentration of reporting has intensified with the growing importance of online reporting. Specifically, it found that "73 percent of all internet publishing jobs are concentrated in either the Boston-New York-Washington-Richmond corridor or the West Coast crescent that runs from Seattle to San Diego and on to Phoenix." When stories break in San Francisco or Seattle, news organizations can rush reporters to the area or turn to part-time "stringers" (local journalists who file occasional reports) to do the reporting. Some significant stories from outside the main media centers simply do not make it into the national news. While a few newspapers have strong regional bureaus, the majority rely heavily on wire service reports of news from elsewhere around the country for content and for cues in deciding what stories to publish.

Because so much expensive, high-tech equipment is involved, and because a considerable amount of editing is required to turn raw video into coherent stories, most television news coverage is assigned to predictable events—news conferences and the like—long before they happen, usually in one of the cities with a permanent television crew. For spontaneous news of riots, accidents, and natural disasters, special video camera crews can be rushed to the location, but they usually arrive after the main events occur and have to rely on "reaction" interviews or aftermath stories.

This is not always true; occasionally television news organizations find themselves in the middle of an unfolding series of events and can convey its texture, explore its human meaning, and speculate about its political implications in particularly meaningful ways. This was certainly true of television coverage of the Hurricane Katrina disaster and its immediate aftermath in 2005. In addition, as we discuss later in this chapter, news outlets increasingly present video footage of unfolding events submitted by citizens who happen to be at the scene of a newsworthy event.

DEPENDENCE ON OFFICIAL SOURCES Most political news is based on what public officials say. This fact has important consequences for how well the media serve democracy.

Beats and Routines A newspaper or television reporter's work is usually organized around a particular **beat**, which he or she checks every day for news stories. Most political beats center on some official government institution that regularly produces news such as a local police station or city council, the White House, Congress, the Pentagon, an American embassy abroad, or a country's foreign ministry.

beat
The assigned location where a reporter regularly gathers news stories.

Many news reports are created or originated by officials, not by reporters. Investigative reporting of the sort that Carl Bernstein and Robert Woodward did to uncover the Watergate scandal, which led to the impeachment and resignation of President Richard Nixon in 1974, is rare because it is so time-consuming and expensive. Most reporters get most of their stories quickly and efficiently from press conferences and the press releases that officials write, along with comments solicited from other officials. One pioneering study by Leon Sigal found that government officials, domestic or foreign, were the sources of nearly three-quarters of all news in the *New York Times* and the *Washington Post*. Moreover, the vast majority, 70 to 90 percent of all news stories, were drawn from situations over which the newsmakers had substantial control: press conferences (24.5 percent), interviews (24.7 percent), press releases (17.5 percent), and official proceedings (13 percent).[25] More recent research suggests that the situation described by Sigal remains relatively unchanged.[26]

Beats and news-gathering routines encourage a situation of mutual dependence by reporters (and their news organizations) and government officials. Reporters want stories; they have to cultivate access to people who can provide stories with quotes or anonymous leaks. Officials want favorable publicity and to avoid or counteract unfavorable publicity. Thus, a comfortable relationship tends to develop. Even when reporters put on a show of aggressive questioning at White House press conferences, they usually work hard to stay on good terms with officials and to avoid fundamental challenges of the officials' positions. Cozy relationships between the Washington press corps and top government officials are further encouraged by the fact that the participants know each other so well, often living in the same neighborhoods, attending the same social gatherings, and sending their children to the same private schools.[27]

A LEAKY WHITE HOUSE?

A string of highly publicized leaks frustrated President Trump during the first year of his administration. For example, in August 2017, the *Washington Post* published leaked transcripts of Trump's phone calls with the leaders of Mexico and Australia.

To what extent should there be secrecy in government? Does a democracy require complete openness?

DARNED REPORTERS

Richard Nixon resigned his presidency in August 1974 rather than face a trial in the Senate following his impeachment in the House after investigative reporters Bob Woodward and Carl Bernstein of the *Washington Post* uncovered evidence of the president's close involvement in illegal spying on his political opponents. Nixon's efforts to cover-up these activities—the political scandal that came to be known as Watergate—proved to be his undoing.

Did the news media play an important role in enhancing American democracy during Watergate, or did reporters like Woodward and Bernstein go too far?

leak

Inside or secret information given to a journalist or media outlet by a government official.

news management

The attempt by those in political power to put the presentation of news about them and their policies in a favorable light.

spin

The attempt by public officials to have a story reported in terms that favor them and their policies; see news management.

While often decried by officials hurt by a damaging revelation, the **leak** is an important part of news gathering that is useful both to journalists and officials, and so is a part of the normal currency of journalist–official working relationships. Indeed, Woodward and Bernstein's Watergate story got its start with leaks from the anonymous "Deep Throat," revealed in 2005 to be Mark Felt, deputy director of the FBI during the Nixon administration. Most commonly, leaking is a way for officials to float policy ideas, get themselves noticed and credited with good deeds, undercut rivals in other government agencies, or report real or imagined wrongdoing. President Trump has regularly complained about leaks from within his administration. His administration has also ramped up efforts to prosecute leakers that began during the Obama administration. In June 2018, it was revealed that federal law enforcement officials had seized a *New York Times* reporter's phone and e-mail records as part of an investigation into a former Senate aide accused of leaking classified information to reporters. Groups that advocate for a free press sharply criticized the seizure of the reporter's records, calling it "a fundamental threat to press freedom" and arguing that it could have a chilling effect on reporters' efforts to provide the public with accurate information about the government's actions. President Trump countered by arguing that the government cannot tolerate leaks of classified information.[28] Although the Trump administrations' efforts may reduce the frequency of leaks, because the practice is so common and useful for both reporters and leakers, it is unlikely that any administration can fully stop the flow of leaks to the press. Thus leaks are likely to remain central to how news is made.

Government News Management The news media's heavy reliance on official sources means that government officials are sometimes able to control what journalists report and how they report it—a practice often referred to as **news management**.[29] Every president and high-ranking official wants to help reporters **spin** a story in a way that is most useful or favorable to the office holder. The Reagan administration was particularly successful at picking a "story of the day" and having many officials feed that story to reporters, with a unified interpretation.[30] The Clinton administration tried to do the same but was not disciplined enough to make it work. President George W. Bush's administration pushed the news management envelope the farthest, eventually acknowledging that it had paid three journalists to write favorable stories, encouraged executive agencies to create news videos for media outlets without revealing the source of the videos, and allowed a political operative to be planted among the accredited White House press corps to ask questions at presidential news conferences.[31] President Obama's team ran an extensive news management operation using many of the same Internet-based tools honed during his nomination and election campaigns to get his administration's story out, partially bypassing the traditional news media. But he also generated a great deal of criticism when his press aides announced in 2009 that the president and his administration would have nothing more to do with Fox News because the network, in their view, failed to separate its news reporting and (strongly conservative) editorial functions. Obama later softened his stance and even agreed to be interviewed by Fox News stalwart Bill O'Reilly prior to the Super Bowl in 2011. This push and pull between President Obama and Fox News highlights the tension presidents and other political leaders face: on one hand, they want to control how their message is conveyed to the public; on the other, they must rely on news outlets to get their message out. President Trump's approach to dealing with the press has been unusually blunt. As of late 2017, out of the 39 interviews President Trump granted to major media outlets, 19 were on Fox. The runner up—the *New York Times*—had interviewed Trump only four times.[32] Additionally, when confronted with a negative story about his administration he often simply characterizes the report as "fake."

Managing images in press reports is also important. Every administration in the modern era has tried to manage public perceptions by staging events that convey strong symbolic messages. For example, George W. Bush announced that the invasion of Iraq had been successfully concluded not in a press release but from the deck of the aircraft carrier *USS Lincoln* on May 2, 2003, in front of a massive sign "Mission Accomplished," after landing in a jet on its runway. Barack Obama told Americans about his new strategy in Afghanistan not from his desk in the Oval Office but in a televised address in front of the cadets at West Point.

Of course, news management doesn't always work as planned. When the war in Iraq took a bad turn, Bush's "Mission Accomplished" came to seem false and hollow to many Americans, and the president's popularity took a dramatic plunge. With fewer American casualties in Afghanistan—by 2012, most of the fighting there was being done by Special Forces units and drone aircraft—President Obama was more insulated from the effects of bad war news.

Military Actions   Dependence on official sources is especially evident in military actions abroad. Because it is wary of the release of information that might help an adversary or undermine public support for U.S. actions—as happened during the Vietnam conflict—the Defense Department tries to restrict access of reporters to military personnel and the battlefield and provide carefully screened information for use by the news media. Information management was especially evident during the 1991 Gulf War to expel Saddam Hussein from Kuwait, with its carefully stage-managed news briefings at U.S. military headquarters in Saudi Arabia featuring video of "smart" weapons, Defense Department organization of press pools to cover parts of the war, and tight restrictions on reporters' access to the battlefields in Kuwait and Iraq.

During the rapid advance on Baghdad to topple Hussein's regime in 2003, the Defense Department encouraged coverage of combat by journalists embedded in combat units, although administration officials continued to exercise control over information about the big picture during the initial stages of the war. In the end, however, the administration was unable to control news about military and civilian casualties during the long occupation, the difficulties of helping to create a new constitution and government for that country, and the abuse of Iraqi prisoners at Abu Ghraib and other prisons. Too many journalists and news organizations from around the world were reporting on events there—and too many American soldiers and Iraqi civilians were posting what they were seeing and experiencing to blogs—for the administration and military officials to be able to control the news.

NEWSWORTHINESS Decisions about what kinds of news to print or televise depend largely on professional judgments about what is newsworthy. Exactly what makes a story newsworthy is difficult to spell out, but experienced editors make quick and confident judgments of what their audiences (and their employers) want. If they were consistently wrong, they would probably not remain in their jobs for very long.

In practice, newsworthiness seems to depend on such factors as novelty, drama and human interest, relevance to the lives of Americans, high stakes (physical violence or conflict), and celebrity. As the term news *story* implies, news works best when it can be framed as a familiar kind of narrative: an exposé of greed, sex, or corruption; conflict between politicians; or a foreign affairs crisis. On television, of course, dramatic or startling film footage helps make a story gripping. Important stories without visuals are often pushed aside for less important stories for which visuals exist. This need for visual content can often lead to missing very big stories in the making. For example, though experts had been worried for many years about the safety of New Orleans, and had been publishing their research results in specialized journals for some time, the news media did not pay much attention until the levees broke when Hurricane Katrina struck in 2005.

TEMPLATES On many important stories, a subtle "governing template" may prevail—a sense among both reporters and editors that news stories must take a generally agreed-upon slant to be taken seriously and to make it into the news broadcast or the newspaper. This is not because of censorship but because of the development of a general agreement among news reporters and editors that the public already knows what the big story looks like on a range of issues—filling in the details is what is important. Take reporting from China as an example. For many years, editors wanted to hear only about economic prosperity, emerging democratic freedoms, and happy peasants liberated from the economic and personal straightjacket of the Maoist collective farm system. After the pro-democracy demonstrations in Tiananmen Square were brutally repressed by the People's Liberation Army, however, reporters say it became almost impossible to write anything positive about China because the prevailing template about China had changed.[33] As China became a very important trading partner, stories about the Chinese economic miracle have proliferated (as well as some worrying about China as a potential economic, diplomatic, and military rival and as a source of tainted goods). The template for covering China has become more difficult

to discern since President Trump's election. Trump has repeatedly accused China of unfair trade practices and imposed substantial tariffs on Chinese imports. However, China appears to be uniquely positioned to facilitate any resolution to the challenges posed by North Korea's nuclear program.

EPISODIC FOREIGN COVERAGE   Very few newspapers other than the *New York Times* can afford to station reporters abroad. Even the *Times* and the networks and wire services cannot regularly cover most nations of the world. They keep reporters in the countries of greatest interest to Americans—those that have big effects on American interests or enjoy close economic or cultural ties with the United States, such as Great Britain, Germany, Japan, Israel, Russia, and China—and they have regional bureaus in Africa and Latin America. In many countries, however, they depend on "stringers." During major crises or big events, the media send in temporary news teams, such as the armies of reporters that swarmed to Bosnia and Kosovo during the conflicts there. The result is that most media devote the majority of their attention to limited areas of the world, dropping in only occasionally on others.

Foreign news, therefore, tends to be episodic—viewers are presented with a brief window into a foreign affairs issue but given little in the way of contextual information to help them make sense of what is going on. An unfamiliar part of the world, such as the Darfur region of the Sudan, suddenly jumps into the headlines with a dramatic story of ethnic cleansing, or elsewhere a coup, an invasion, or a famine comes as a surprise to most Americans because they have not been prepared by background reports. Strikingly, one study found that only 0.2 percent of news coverage in the United States in 2011 was about sub-Sahara Africa.[34] A story about Darfur may be covered heavily for a few days or weeks, but if nothing new and exciting happens, the story grows stale and disappears from the media. Even stories in regions of the world where the United States is directly involved are often covered episodically. For example, the civil war in Syria has been raging for several years, and the United States has been actively involved in the conflict. However, coverage of Syria has been spotty: events in Syria may be front page news one day and then receive virtually no coverage for weeks or months. Most viewers are left with little more understanding of the country than they began with. Thus, they find it difficult to form judgments about U.S. foreign policy.[35]

INTERPRETATION   Political news may not make much sense without an interpretation of what it means. Under the informal rules of **objective journalism**, taught in university journalism schools and practiced by the nation's leading newspapers and network news programs, however, explicit interpretations by journalists are to be avoided, except for commentary or editorials labeled as such. Thus, even if a reporter knows that an official is lying, he or she typically will not say so directly but will, instead, find someone else who will say so for the record.[36] In news stories, most interpretations are left implicit (so that they are hard to detect and argue with) or are given by so-called experts who are interviewed for comments. Often, particular experts are selected by print, broadcast, and telecast journalists because the position the experts will take is entirely predictable.

Experts are selected partly for reasons of convenience and audience appeal: scholars and commentators who live close to New York City or Washington, D.C., who like to speak in public, who look good on camera, and who are skillful in coming up with colorful quotations on a variety of subjects, are contacted again and again. They often show up on television to comment on the news of the day, even on issues far from the area of their special expertise. In many cases, these **pundits** are simply well-known for being on television often and are not experts on any subject at all. The experts and commentators featured in the media are often ex-officials. Their views are usually in harmony with the political currents of the day; that is, they tend to reflect a fairly narrow spectrum of opinion close to that of the party in power in Washington, D.C., or to the prevailing "conventional wisdom" inside the Beltway.

objective journalism
News reported with no evaluative language and with opinions quoted or attributed to a specific source.

pundits
Somewhat derisive term for print, broadcast, and radio commentators on the political news.

WAITING FOR HELP

These women refugees from the genocidal conflict in the Darfur region of Sudan wait for a daily food ration. The conflict in Darfur displaced almost 2 million people, with most living in dreadful conditions; however, news coverage of Darfur and the state of its people was spotty. When a celebrity or prominent politician visited refugees or when a demonstration took place in a major city in Europe or the United States, attention picked up but afterward faded into the background.

Why isn't media coverage of international crises more consistent?

Online News Media

Thus far, we have primarily focused our attention on traditional news outlets. However, in recent years, we have seen a rapid expansion of access to the Internet and use of social media, along with substantial growth in the number of online sources of political information. These dynamics have transformed the news media landscape and provide interested citizens with virtually unlimited access to information, news, and analysis as well as with opportunities to express their own views on public issues by doing things like commenting on and sharing political information on Facebook and Twitter.[37]

At the same time that Internet use has expanded at an exponential rate, there has been a decline in the audience for the most traditional news outlet: newspapers. For decades, people have consistently reported that television is their main source of news over newspapers and news magazines, but the Internet closing fast. As shown in Figure 6.1, the gap between the share of people who say they often get news online and those who say they often watch news on TV is closing rapidly. In 2016, 57 percent of Americans said they often watch TV news compared to 38 percent who said they often get news online. In just one year, this 19 percentage point gap

narrowed to only 7 percent. As Figure 6.1 illustrates, this change was driven largely by increased consumption of online news by older Americans. As more and more people choose to get their news online, some other types of outlets—especially print newspapers—have seen declines in their audiences. The collapse of the print newspaper business has been striking. Total print advertising revenue for newspapers plummeted from almost $50 billion in 2000 to less than $20 billion in 2016.[38]

Research by media scholars shows that the mainstream news organizations, taken as a whole, remain the most important set of institutions for setting the agenda of American politics and shaping how we interpret what is going on in politics and government. Despite the rapid rise and development of alternatives to the mainstream media, the mainstream news media retain their central role in the gathering and reporting of serious political and governmental news. There are a number of reasons the mainstream or traditional news organizations remain central to political news. For one thing, much of the rich and diverse information on the Internet, whether in the form of advocacy organization websites, political blogs, citizen journalism, or academic and government reports, only reach small and fragmented audiences and usually have an impact only when and to the extent they can attract the attention of the mainstream news media. Bloggers' unearthing of news anchor Dan Rather's sloppy reporting on President George W. Bush's National Guard service during the Vietnam War, for example, only mattered once the story began to run in the nation's leading newspapers and on network and cable news networks. Tens of thousands of bloggers voice their views every day, but few gain an audience. One scholar, using a vast database to chronicle the number of daily hits on blogger sites, has determined that only 10 to 20 of them have a readership of any size. Of the 5,000 most-visited political blog sites, for example, the top 5 accounted

SIGHTING POPE FRANCIS

Phones with cameras together with social media sites like Instagram and Twitter make it easy for anyone to play the role of a reporter. These technologies and services allow individual citizens to share photos and other firsthand information about politicians and public figures with their friends, followers, and acquaintances as well as with traditional news outlets.

In what ways have smartphone technologies and apps refashioned how Americans engage in political life?

FIGURE 6.1 WHERE PEOPLE GET THEIR NEWS

Surveys that ask respondents whether they "often" consume news from television and the Internet find that in recent years, people have turned increasingly to the Internet as a source of news, while decreasing somewhat in their reliance on television and newspapers. Although the Internet still trails television as people's main source of news, it is closing the gap, largely because older Americans increasingly use online news sources.

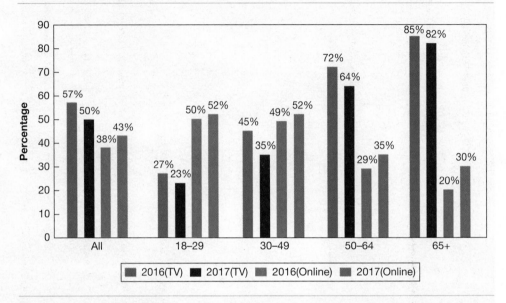

Legend: 2016(TV) · 2017(TV) · 2016(Online) · 2017(Online)

Values by age group:
- All: 57%, 50%, 38%, 43%
- 18–29: 27%, 23%, 50%, 52%
- 30–49: 45%, 35%, 49%, 52%
- 50–64: 72%, 64%, 29%, 35%
- 65+: 85%, 82%, 20%, 30%

NOTE: Bars indicate percentage of respondents who said they "often" get news online or on television.

SOURCE: Pew Research Center, "News Use Across Social Media Platforms 2017," September, 2017.

for 28 percent of all blog visits, while the top 10 accounted for almost half. Also, half of the top 10 bloggers are or were at one time professional journalists.[39]

An additional piece of evidence that traditional news outlets continue to play a central role in the contemporary news media landscape is that the most visited online news sites are overwhelmingly tied to traditional print or television outlets including CBS News, ABC News, the *New York Times, USA Today*, CNN, and Fox News.[40]

Similarly, the news that most political bloggers write about and the bits of news that get passed around on social-networking sites come mainly from material that

BLOGGING THE REPUBLICAN NATIONAL CONVENTION

Both the Republican and Democratic conventions allocate space not only to the mainstream media but also to digital journalists who produce content for the Web instantaneously.

To what extent does live reporting and instantaneous publishing enhance the quality of political information available to the public?

has been collected by reporters in the traditional news sector. The grist for commentary at the most popular political sites, including the liberal-leaning *Huffington Post* and *Salon*, and conservative-leaning sites such as *The Blaze* and *The Daily Beast*, comes mainly from traditional news organizations and the major wire services.

Unfortunately, one of the most important political consequences of the explosion of online media and social networking may be tied to the proliferation of fabricated stories—fabricated stories posted online by individuals looking to make money from online advertising by drawing traffic to a website. It is far easier to set up a website than it is to establish a print newspaper or cable news channel. Thus, in contrast to reporters at the *New York Times* or Fox News, individuals behind online outlets often have no reputation to worry about, leaving them free to post blatant falsehoods with little fear of consequences. This is not to say that traditional news outlets never make errors in their reporting. Rather, when they do they are typically quick to correct the error and apologize because they have clear incentives to maintain a reputation for conveying accurate information.

In one striking example of the ease with which false information can be spread via online sources, during the 2016 campaign, teenagers living in the small town of Veles, Macedonia—thousands of miles from the United States—made tens of thousands of dollars posting bogus stories to their websites and working to make them go viral on social media. These fake news stories and others like them were shared by millions of people during the campaign. In fact, some analysis indicates that the most popular fake news stories were shared more widely than the most popular stories from mainstream outlets.

What seems on the surface, then, to be a massive expansion in the amount of political news in reality is an expansion in the number of ways in which news is distributed and, perhaps, a proliferation of factually incorrect online information that is not news at all. An exponential growth in commentary on news from the same set of sources is not the same thing as an expansion in the size or quality of the core of political news.[41] As far as scholars have been able to tell, the bulk of original, in-depth stories is still produced by traditional news outlets.[42]

To be sure, this appears to be changing. Some mainstream media organizations have been quite aggressive in using citizen reporters to gather and submit news stories—see CNN's iReport website—while new technologies allow people to arrange Facebook posts and tweets, often of a political nature, into chronological narratives to be reposted elsewhere. Mainstream media also use new digital sources of information as sources for constructing their own news stories, as when in 2010 the *New York Times* reported about and released much of the raw diplomatic cables gathered by WikiLeaks under the leadership of its founder, Julian Assange. During the 2016 election, WikiLeaks made news again by leaking a flood of hacked e-mails from the Democratic National Committee and Clinton campaign chairman John Podesta.

Reporting from nontraditional news outlets—including satirical news programs—also appears capable of having a surprising amount of political impact if shared widely via social media. When John Oliver, the comedic host of HBO's *Last Week Tonight*, aired an in-depth story on net neutrality (the practice of Internet service providers treating all Internet traffic equally), he unleashed a tidal wave of public support that appeared to play a role in the Federal Communications Commission's (FCC) adoption of net-neutrality rules in 2015. The goal of these new net-neutrality regulations? To preserve an "open" Internet by preventing broadband providers from speeding or slowing traffic to certain locations or through certain apps based on the willingness of those providers to pay higher prices. However, other factors—outlined in Figure 6.2, where we apply our *structural-linkage-government* framework—led to the FCC rescinding these rules in June 2018. This example illustrates the potential for media to affect government actions by informing and mobilizing the public. It also shows that this influence is often limited by other forces including the power of well-funded interest groups and the changes in bureaucratic appointees that often follow presidential elections.

NEWS WITH LAUGHS

Although they are billed as comedy shows, programs like *The Daily Show* (Comedy Central), and *Last Week Tonight* with John Oliver (pictured; HBO) have become an important source of news—particularly for younger Americans. Occasionally these programs bring attention to obscure or forgotten issues. As we illustrate in Figure 6.2, in some cases these shows appear to affect which policies the government implements. However, the ability of media like this to shape policy outcomes is limited by electoral forces and the efforts of interest groups.

What role should satirical news programs play in keeping the American public informed? Should we expect them to adhere to the journalistic standards we set for traditional journalists?

The news media have changed greatly over our history and continue to change ever more rapidly. That said, while people can get their news and commentary from many different places ranging from the Internet to cable television, talk radio, and television satire and comedy programs, mainstream news organizations remain the most important set of institutions in the American political news system, even if they are fighting for their lives in an economic sense. It is the reason we mostly focus on the mainstream news media in this chapter, asking how well they play the role assigned to them by democratic theorists.

FIGURE 6.2 APPLYING THE FRAMEWORK: NET NEUTRALITY

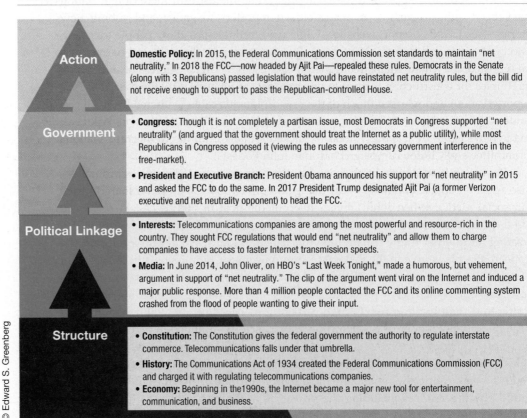

Action

Domestic Policy: In 2015, the Federal Communications Commission set standards to maintain "net neutrality." In 2018 the FCC—now headed by Ajit Pai—repealed these rules. Democrats in the Senate (along with 3 Republicans) passed legislation that would have reinstated net neutrality rules, but the bill did not receive enough to support to pass the Republican-controlled House.

Government

• **Congress:** Though it is not completely a partisan issue, most Democrats in Congress supported "net neutrality" (and argued that the government should treat the Internet as a public utility), while most Republicans in Congress opposed it (viewing the rules as unnecessary government interference in the free-market).

• **President and Executive Branch:** President Obama announced his support for "net neutrality" in 2015 and asked the FCC to do the same. In 2017 President Trump designated Ajit Pai (a former Verizon executive and net neutrality opponent) to head the FCC.

Political Linkage

• **Interests:** Telecommunications companies are among the most powerful and resource-rich in the country. They sought FCC regulations that would end "net neutrality" and allow them to charge companies to have access to faster Internet transmission speeds.

• **Media:** In June 2014, John Oliver, on HBO's "Last Week Tonight," made a humorous, but vehement, argument in support of "net neutrality." The clip of the argument went viral on the Internet and induced a major public response. More than 4 million people contacted the FCC and its online commenting system crashed from the flood of people wanting to give their input.

Structure

• **Constitution:** The Constitution gives the federal government the authority to regulate interstate commerce. Telecommunications falls under that umbrella.

• **History:** The Communications Act of 1934 created the Federal Communications Commission (FCC) and charged it with regulating telecommunications companies.

• **Economy:** Beginning in the1990s, the Internet became a major new tool for entertainment, communication, and business.

© Edward S. Greenberg

BIAS IN THE NEWS

6.2 Evaluate news organizations' ideological and nonideological biases.

Few topics arouse more disagreement than the question of whether the mass media in the United States have a liberal or conservative **bias**—or any bias at all. Researchers have found evidence that news outlets vary in the ideological slant they bring to bear when reporting a story. However, these differences in ideological leanings are not simply the product of journalists' personal political preferences. More broadly, it is difficult to pin down exactly what perfectly "unbiased" reporting would look like.

bias

Deviation from ideal standards such as representativeness or objectivity.

Ideological Bias

Many liberal critics believe the news media favor Republicans and the business establishment,[43] while many conservative critics believe the news media are unfair to Republicans and favor liberal social causes.[44] Almost half of all Americans believe there is "a great deal" of bias in news coverage and two-thirds say most news organizations fail to do a good job separating fact from opinion.[45] Much, of course, is in the eye of the beholder; experimental research shows that when people with different political allegiances are exposed to the exact same news accounts, they each believe the stories are biased against their favored positions and candidates.[46]

Partisan differences in how people evaluate the news media are also evident in polls that show a sharp divergence in Democrats' and Republicans' assessments of whether criticism from news organization "keeps leaders from doing their jobs" or "keeps them from doing things that shouldn't be done." Just a few years ago, most Democrats and Republicans said this criticism primarily fulfills a watchdog function by keeping leaders from doing things they shouldn't be done. However, in 2017 support for this view surged among Democrats (to 89 percent) and plummeted among Republicans (to 42 percent). Although the historical trend suggests that partisans are more inclined to see the media as a watchdog when the president is from the opposing party, it seems likely that the huge gap that emerged in 2017 is, at least in part, attributable to President Trump's repeated claims that news organizations attack him unfairly.[47]

STUNNED BY KATRINA

Many conservative commentators charged that the news media focused on poor African Americans in New Orleans as the main victims of Hurricane Katrina when, in fact, the range of victims was much more diverse and living across a broader swath of Gulf Coast states.
Is this photograph of Katrina's victims a fair or biased representation of the disaster?

It is quite difficult—perhaps impossible—to pinpoint what an "unbiased" story would look like. This is particularly true given that media reports are typically quite brief, while the topics they cover are complex and contentious. Should a story about a proposal to raise the minimum wage cite statistics on income inequality, or would that introduce a "liberal bias"? Should research suggesting that raising the minimum wage may increase unemployment be cited, or would that introduce a "conservative bias"? What if some studies suggest that raising the minimum wage increases unemployment, and others find that it would reduce unemployment? Journalists must make choices about what facts and perspectives to present in the limited space they are provided. Some may see a decision to include a particular fact as biased, while others may see excluding that fact as indicative of bias.

Though it is difficult to agree on what it would mean for a particular news report to be unbiased, researchers have conducted innovative studies that provide ways to assess how liberal or conservative a news outlet is *compared with other outlets*. In one fascinating study, Matthew Gentzkow and Jesse Shapiro analyzed the language used by Democratic and Republican representatives in Congress to identify words and phrases that Democrats used commonly but Republicans did not (and vice versa).[48] For example, Democrats and Republicans typically use different terms to refer to a federal tax on paid on multimillion dollar estates after the owner dies. Democrats overwhelmingly referred to this as the "estate tax," presumably to highlight the fact that the tax only applies to wealthy individuals and evoke images of homes with dozens of rooms and horse stables. In contrast, Republicans used the term "death tax," perhaps to present the tax as something that could affect everyone or to frame the policy as the government taxing people even after they are dead. The researchers then assessed how often various newspapers used these terms. This allows them to construct a measure of media slant: newspapers that use language similar to that used by Republican elected officials are considered more conservative; those that use language used by Democrats are more liberal.

Again, it is important to note that although studies like this can identify variation in newspapers' slant, they cannot point to a particular outlet as "unbiased." However, the findings from a study like this *do* suggest that news outlets vary in their ideological leanings. This raises the question of why this is the case. What factors might affect the ideological leanings of news outlets? We consider three explanations.

LIBERAL REPORTERS Surveys of reporters' and journalists' opinions suggest that these individuals tend to be somewhat more liberal than the average American on certain matters, including the environment and such social issues as civil rights and liberties, affirmative action, abortion, and women's rights.[49] This is especially true of those employed by certain elite media organizations, including the *New York Times*, *Washington Post*, and PBS. It may be that reporters' liberalism has been reflected in the treatment of issues such as global warming, same-sex marriage, and abortion. This said, in recent years more conservative reporters and newscasters have gained prominence, especially on cable news programs.

There is, however, little or no systematic evidence that reporters' personal values regularly affect what appears in the mainstream news media.[50] Journalists' commitment to the idea of objectivity helps them resist temptation, as do critical scrutiny and rewriting by editors. In any case, the liberalism of journalists may be offset by their need to rely on official sources, their reliance on experts who are either former officials or associated with centrist or conservative think tanks, and the need to get their stories past editors who are accountable to mostly conservative owners and publishers. Nonetheless, some suspect that the increasing geographic concentration of news organizations in urban areas may affect reporting. This concentration is particularly pronounced with respect to organizations that publish online. Analysis of publicly available data show that "90 percent of all Internet publishing employees work in a county where Clinton won, and 75 percent of them work in a county that she won by more than 30 percentage points." Even if journalists actively work to avoid allowing their own preferences to shape their reporting, the fact that so many live and work in heavily Democratic areas may color their perceptions of what life is like for most Americans.

NOT-SO-LIBERAL OWNERS AND CORPORATIONS The owners and top managers of most news media organizations tend to be conservative and Republican. This is perhaps not surprising. The shareholders and executives of multi-billion-dollar corporations tend not to be interested in undermining the free enterprise system, for example, or, for that matter, increasing their own taxes, raising labor costs, or losing income from offended advertisers. These owners and managers ultimately decide which reporters, newscasters, and editors to hire or fire, promote or discourage. Journalists who want to get ahead, therefore, may have to come to terms with the policies of the people who own and run media businesses.[51]

MAINTAINING A REPUTATION FOR QUALITY A final factor that may affect the ideological slant of a news outlet is closely connected to the profit motive. News organizations that do not attract and maintain an audience do not make money and, ultimately, fail. Thus, when reporting on politics, a news outlet may strive to present stories in a way that they believe their audience will interpret as being high quality. One way to convey quality to an audience may be to avoid presenting stories in a way that challenges their existing beliefs.[52] For example, a 2013 survey found that among people who cited Fox News as their primary source of news, 94 percent identified themselves as Republicans or Republican leaners, and 97 percent disapproved of President Obama's job performance.[53] If Fox News presents stories that cast a Democratic president in a favorable light, these viewers may see it as a sign that liberal bias has infiltrated what had previously been a "high-quality" outlet and tune out. Likewise, an MSNBC viewer may be put off by unflattering or critical reports about a Democratic president. Put simply, a desire to gain and retain audience—rather than the ideological preferences of reporters or owners—may be a key driver of ideological media bias.

Nonideological Bias

The questions of whether and why mainstream news outlets may be ideologically biased are not easily answered. However, other biases in reporting may also be consequential. Some of these biases include reporters' dependence on official sources and the eagerness with which journalist pursue sensational stories—matters examined earlier in this chapter. Another is the bias or set of biases generated by the marketplace. News media organizations are business enterprises or part of larger corporate entities and are in business to make a profit for themselves or their corporate parents. This may lead them to gather and present news in a way that is at odds with their role as watchdogs and providers of relevant policy information in a democratic society.

In the domain of foreign affairs, reporting typically adopts a pro-American, patriotic point of view, where the United States is presented in a favorable light and its opponents in an unfavorable light. This tendency is especially pronounced in news about military conflicts involving U.S. troops, as in Iraq and Afghanistan, but it can be found as well in a wide range of foreign affairs news reports, including those concerning conflicts with other governments on trade, arms control, immigration, and intellectual property rights (patents and copyrights).

This nationalistic perspective, together with heavy reliance on U.S. government news sources, means that coverage of foreign news generally harmonizes well with official U.S. foreign policy. Thus, the media tend to go along with the U.S. government in assuming the best about our close allies and the worst about official "enemies." When the United States was assisting Iraq in its war against Iran during the 1980s, for example, Saddam Hussein was depicted in a positive light; during the 1991 Gulf War and the Iraq War that started 12 years later, media characterizations of him turned dramatically negative.

In foreign policy crisis situations, the reliance on official news sources means that the media sometimes propagate government statements that are false or misleading, as in the announcement of unprovoked attacks on U.S. destroyers in the Gulf of Tonkin at the beginning of the Vietnam War. Secret information can also be controlled by the government. And political leaders know that the news media will be cautious in its criticism when troops are deployed and put in harm's way.

It is important to point out that when the use of American armed forces abroad drags on beyond expectations and goals are not met (as in the conflicts in Vietnam, Afghanistan, and the broader Middle East), the news media can and do become negative in their coverage. This may simply reflect the mood change among nonadministration leaders and the public, or it might be a reaction among journalists and news organizations to their own initial uncritical coverage of administration policies.

EFFECTS OF THE NEWS MEDIA ON POLITICS

6.3 Analyze the impact of the media on public opinion and political behavior.

Over time, social scientists have gone from speculating that the news media dramatically and directly influence citizens' political views to believing that media have only "minimal effects" on people's attitudes. Each of these possibilities has been discredited in favor of a more nuanced understanding of how news media affect the public. The contents of the news media do make a difference; they affect public opinion and policymaking in a number of ways, including setting the agenda for public debate, priming particular issues, and framing how issues are understood.[54] This said, it is important to bear in mind that the dramatic differences in attitudes between, say, regular viewers of Fox New and the MSNBC audience seem to be driven primarily by self-selection—a tendency for people to seek out news sources that fit with their existing political preferences—rather than the power of the media to change people's minds.[55] News reports may also affect people's broader orientation toward the political world by fostering cynicism or a fragmented understanding of the political world.

Agenda Setting

agenda setting

The way media outlets can affect people's opinions about what issues are important.

Several studies have demonstrated an effect known as **agenda setting**. The topics that get the most coverage in the news media at any point in time end up being the issues that most people tell pollsters are the most important problems facing the country. This correlation does not result just from the news media's reporting what people are most interested in; it is a real effect of what appears in the news. In controlled experiments, people who are shown doctored television news broadcasts emphasizing a particular problem (e.g., national defense) mention that problem as being important more often than people who have seen broadcasts that have not been tampered with.[56] Another line of research has shown that news media polling often is used as the basis for reporting about what the American people want regarding a certain policy (say, intervening in a civil war in Liberia) when few Americans know or care about the subject matter of the opinion survey. The polling story, if it is picked up by other news media outlets, bloggers, and pundits, however, then becomes part of the general news landscape and sparks interest among much of the public about that subject. It becomes part of the public agenda.[57]

Of course, media managers do not arbitrarily decide what news to emphasize; their decisions reflect what is happening in the world and what American audiences care about. If there is a war or an economic depression, the media report it. But some research has indicated that what the media cover sometimes diverges from actual trends in problems. Publicity about crime, for example, may reflect editors' fears or a few dramatic incidents rather than a rising crime rate. When the two diverge, it seems to be the media's emphasis rather than real trends that affects public opinion.[58]

When the media decide to highlight a human rights tragedy in "real time," such as "ethnic cleansing" in Kosovo, public officials often feel compelled to act, as Bill Clinton did when he was president. (This is sometimes called the CNN effect.) When the media ignore equally troubling human tragedies, such as the genocide in Darfur, public officials feel less pressure to intervene. One scholarly study shows that in the foreign policy area, media choices about coverage shape what presidents pay attention to.[59] But influences go in both directions. News media scholar Lance Bennett suggests that journalists and the news organizations they work for are closely attuned to the relative power balance in Washington between Democrats and Republicans, and between liberals and conservatives, and focus on matters that are of most concern to those in power at any particular time. Thus, Social Security reform becomes an important issue in the press when important political actors want to talk about it. The same is true for other issues, whether it's taxes or nuclear threats from countries such as Iran and North Korea.[60]

Priming

Beyond affecting which issues are on the public agenda, media reports can affect which considerations people give weight to when evaluating political leaders.[61] By repeatedly drawing attention to a particular issue news reports may foster a situation where matters related to that issue come to mind particularly readily when people are asked to make political judgments. This **priming** phenomenon can be illustrated with an example. Imagine a situation where news outlets are devoting substantial attention to issues related to national defense. In this context, matters related to national defense are likely to be at the top of many people's minds—that is, they are likely to be primed. When asked whether they approve or disapprove of the president's performance overall they may give particularly strong weight to their assessments of a president's handling of defense issues.[62]

priming
The way heavy media coverage of a particular topic can lead citizens to give greater weight to that topic when evaluating politicians and making other political judgments.

Framing

Experiments also indicate that how the media report a story can lead to **framing effects**. Specifically, the way a story is reported can affect how people think about political problems or who they blame for social problems.[63] Several commentators noticed during the Katrina disaster in New Orleans, for example, that TV news stories framed their reports of whites left with nothing as "foraging for food and supplies," while those of African Americans were framed as looting. There are reasons to believe that public impressions of what was going on in the city were affected by this coverage. To take another example, whether citizens ascribe poverty to the laziness of the poor or to the nature of the economy depends partly on whether the news media run stories about poor individuals (implying, through framing, that they are responsible for their own plight) or stories about the effects of economic recessions and unemployment.[64]

framing effects
The way news organizations can affect how people think about an issue by presenting it in a particular way or situating it in a particular context.

The way news media frame stories can also affect people's policy preferences. One study found, for example, that the public is more likely to favor government programs to help African Americans when the news media frame racial problems in terms of failures of society to live up to the tradition of equality in the United States. The public is less supportive of these programs when the news media frame the origins of racial problems in terms of individual failures to be self-reliant and responsible.[65] Another study found that changes in the percentages of the public that favored various policies could be predicted quite accurately by what sorts of stories appeared on network television news shows between one opinion survey and the next. News from experts, commentators, and popular presidents had especially strong effects.[66]

This is not to say that readers, viewers, and listeners blindly accept the way issues are framed in media reports. People are rarely exposed to a single way of framing a given issue or event. Different outlets and commentators, as well as friends, relatives and other discussion partners, are likely to frame an issue in different ways. This may dampen the effects of being exposed to any particular frame.[67]

Fueling Cynicism

Americans are quite cynical about the political parties, politicians, and most incumbent political leaders. To some extent, this has been true since the founding of the nation. Nevertheless, scholars and political commentators have noted a considerable increase in negative feelings about the political system over the past two decades or so. Many scholars believe that news media coverage of American politics has a great deal to do with this attitude change.[68]

As the adversarial-attack journalism style and infotainment have taken over political reporting, serious consideration of the issues, careful examination of policy alternatives, and dispassionate examination of the actions of government institutions have taken a back seat to a steady diet of charges about personal misbehavior and political conflict. In the end, the message delivered by the mass media is often that politicians' positions on policy issues are driven by special-interest maneuvering, that political leaders and aspiring political leaders never say what they mean or mean what they say, and that all of them have something in their personal lives they want to hide.

Furthermore, news reports feed the public a constant stream of messages about the failure of government: programs that don't work, wasteful spending, lazy and incompetent public employees, looming government deficits, and people receiving benefits they don't deserve. Though not entirely absent, stories about government working in a way that enhances the well-being of Americans are less common, probably because such stories are not terribly dramatic. Mail gets delivered every day into the remotest regions of the country, for example, while cars and trucks make heavy use of the interstate highway system. The Center for Disease Control stays on constant alert for dangerous pathogens, and park rangers keep watch on our national parks.

Fragmenting Comprehension

Most communications scholars agree that the media coverage of political news has certain distinctive features that result from characteristics of the mass media, including the prevailing technology and organization of news gathering, corporate ownership, and the profit-making drive to appeal to mass audiences. These characteristics of the media mean that news, especially on television, tends to be episodic and fragmented rather than sustained, analytical, or dispassionate. In other words, information comes in bits and pieces, out of context, and without historical background. This may or may not be what people want—some scholars suggest that the people, in fact, do not want hard news at all; others suggest that they want hard news, but they want it with a strong dose of entertainment.[69] Regardless, it is what they get.

However, it is important to point out that the news media often do deep and thorough investigative reporting that matters. The *Wall Street Journal, New York Times*, and *Bloomberg/Businessweek*, for example, each did in-depth stories in late 2009 and early 2010 on lobbying and big campaign contributions by large financial firms who tried, with some success, to turn back regulatory reforms in Congress not to their liking. But the pressure to stick to infotainment is relentless, and all news organizations feel it in one way or another.

THE NEWS MEDIA: DO THEY HELP OR HINDER DEMOCRACY?

The framers favored a form of government based on the consent of the governed but one in which most of the governed played only a limited and indirect role in political life. They believed government was best run by talented, educated, and broad-minded individuals who attained office through indirect elections based on a limited franchise and whose governing decisions were not directly dictated by the people. According to such an understanding of the ideal form of government, there was no pressing need for news media to educate the general public and prepare it for active participation in politics. For the framers, the purpose of the news media—newspapers, in their day—was to serve as a mechanism allowing economic, social, and political leaders to communicate with one another and to help them deliberate on the issues of the day.

For democratic theorists, the people are expected to play a more central role in governance, and the news media play an accordingly larger role in preparing the people to participate. An accurate, probing, and vigorous news media are essential building blocks for democratic life to the extent that the broad general public cannot be rationally engaged in public affairs without them. In this respect, the spread of the news media in the United States—and the penetration of millions of homes by newspapers, radio, television, and the Internet—has undoubtedly enriched democracy. It has made it much easier for ordinary citizens to form policy preferences, to judge the actions of government, and to decide whom they want to govern them. News media thus tend to contribute to political equality. When citizens, political leaders, and special-interest groups know what is going on, they can have a voice in politics. Moreover, interactive media and media-published polls help politicians hear that voice.

Scholars and media critics who want the news media to be highly informative, analytical, and issue oriented, however, are often appalled by the personalized, episodic, dramatic, and fragmented character of most news stories, which do not provide sustained and coherent explanations of what is going on. Still other critics worry that constant media exposés of alleged official wrongdoing or government inefficiency, and the mocking tone aimed at virtually all political leaders by journalists and talk-radio hosts, have fueled the growing political cynicism of the public. To the extent that this is true—that they tend to trivialize, focus on scandal and entertainment, and offer fragmented and out-of-context political and governmental information—the news media are not serving democracy as well as they might.

However, things may not be quite as bad as they appear. For one thing, for those truly interested in public affairs, there is now more readily accessible information than at any time in our history. For those willing to search for it, there is now little information relevant to public affairs that can be kept hidden, ranging from official government statistics to academic and other expert studies. Additionally, the American people have demonstrated an admirable ability on many occasions to sift the wheat from the chaff, to glean the information they need from the background noise.[70] On balance, then, the news media have probably helped advance the cause of democracy in the United States and helped transform the American republic into the American democratic republic. There is no doubt, however, that the news media could also do a considerably better job than they do at the present time.

HOW NEWS ORGANIZATIONS OPERATE

6.1 Discuss the functions, structure, and operations of the news media.

One function of the news media in a democracy is to serve as a watchdog over government, uncovering government corruption and keeping government officials accountable to the public.

Other important functions are to help citizens evaluate candidates for public office and to think about what kinds of government policies might best serve the public interest.

The shape of the news media in the United States has been determined largely by structural factors: technological developments; the growth of the American population and economy; and the development of a privately owned, corporation-dominated media industry.

New Internet-based media have not replaced traditional reporting and news organizations. For the most part, these new media use materials gathered by old media.

News gathering is limited by logistics. Most news gathering is organized around New York City, Washington, D.C., and a handful of major cities in the United States and abroad. Most foreign countries are ignored unless there are crises or other big stories to communicate.

BIAS IN THE NEWS

6.2 Evaluate news organizations' ideological and nonideological biases.

Although media outlets do vary in their ideological leanings it is usually difficult to pin down exactly what "unbiased" report would look like given the complexity of many of the political issues reporters cover.

Some scholars have argued that much of the variation in the ideological slant of news reporting can be attributed to the profit motive—outlets strive to present news in a way that will be appealing to viewers, listeners, or readers.

American news outlets tend to have a pro-American bias, particularly when it comes to reporting on foreign affairs.

EFFECTS OF THE NEWS MEDIA ON POLITICS

6.3 Analyze the impact of the media on public opinion and political behavior.

News media stories have substantial effects on the public's perceptions of problems, its interpretations of events, its evaluations of political candidates, and its policy preferences.

The news media affects the public not only by providing information but also by setting the agenda, priming, framing, fueling the public's cynicism, and fragmenting people's understanding of news and events.

agenda setting The way media outlets can affect people's opinions about what issues are important.

beat The assigned location where a reporter regularly gathers news stories.

bias Deviation from ideal standards such as representativeness or objectivity.

Federal Communications Commission (FCC) Federal agency set up to regulate media companies with an eye toward ensuring competition and protecting consumers.

framing effects The way news organizations can affect how people think about an issue by presenting it in a particular way or situating it in a particular context.

infotainment The merging of hard news and entertainment in news presentations.

leak Inside or secret information given to a journalist or media outlet by a government official.

media consolidation The process of a small number of companies coming to own an increasingly large share of the media outlets by purchasing outlets or merging with other media companies.

news management   The attempt by those in political power to put the presentation of news about them and their policies in a favorable light.

objective journalism   News reported with no evaluative language and with opinions quoted or attributed to a specific source.

priming   The way heavy media coverage of a particular topic can lead citizens to give greater weight to that topic when evaluating politicians and making other political judgments.

pundits   Somewhat derisive term for print, broadcast, and radio commentators on the political news.

spin   The attempt by public officials to have a story reported in terms that favor them and their policies; see news management.

watchdog   The role of the media in scrutinizing the actions of government officials.

wire services   Organizations such as the Associated Press and Reuters that gather and disseminate news to other news organizations.

CHAPTER
7

DISASTER IN THE GULF

Risky behavior by drilling companies, pressure from parent oil company BP, and lax government regulatory oversight all contributed to the Deepwater Horizon disaster in the Gulf of Mexico in 2010. By all accounts, it represented the most serious environmental disaster in American history, with effects still being felt in the Gulf region to this day. *What can and should be done to prevent similar disasters in the future?*

INTEREST GROUPS
AND BUSINESS POWER

CHAPTER OUTLINE AND LEARNING OBJECTIVES

INTEREST GROUPS IN A DEMOCRATIC SOCIETY: CONTRASTING VIEWPOINTS

7.1 Compare and contrast opposing viewpoints about the role of interest groups in a democracy.

THE UNIVERSE OF INTEREST GROUPS

7.2 Describe different types of interest groups.

INTEREST GROUP FORMATION AND PROLIFERATION

7.3 Explain why interest groups form and proliferate.

WHAT INTEREST GROUPS DO

7.4 Analyze the methods and activities interest groups use to influence political outcomes.

INTEREST GROUPS, CORPORATE POWER, AND INEQUALITY IN AMERICAN POLITICS

7.5 Describe the inequalities of the interest group system.

CURING THE MISCHIEF OF FACTIONS

7.6 Assess the effectiveness of regulations designed to control interest groups.

The Struggle for Democracy

DISASTER IN THE GULF

On April 20, 2010, the Deepwater Horizon drilling rig in the Gulf of Mexico was ripped apart by a series of spectacular explosions that killed eleven oil rig workers and unleashed the largest marine drilling oil spill in American history.[1] The rig, owned by the Transocean Corporation and leased to oil giant BP (British Petroleum), was finishing the final phases of drilling a well more than a mile beneath the platform when the disaster struck. The temporary cement cap that topped off the well failed, releasing an out-of-control mixture of natural gas and crude oil and setting off an inferno. By 2017, seven years after the explosion and massive oil spill, the full environmental effects had not yet been fully determined though scientists agreed that only 25 percent of the spill has been accounted for. Much of the spilled oil remains on the ocean floor and continues to adversely affect many animal and plant species.

How did it happen? We know that BP, putting cost saving before safety, insisted that platform operator Transocean take a number of risky and ill-advised operational steps. Although Transocean engineers and many workers aboard the Deepwater rig apparently expressed concerns about these decisions, production never slowed. BP executives pushed Transocean to finish on time and under budget so that it could temporarily cap the well and move on to other drilling opportunities. Oil executives who later testified at a congressional hearing on the spill agreed that BP should have done more onsite testing of critical blowout preventers at Deepwater Horizon but admitted that they were similarly negligent because of costs to suspend operations while testing—about $700 a minute.

The blowout had political origins as well. For years prior to the drilling disaster, federal and state regulations on the oil and gas industries had been rolled back, fewer people worked for government agencies with oversight responsibilities, and fewer mid-level government bureaucrats, given the deregulatory orthodoxy that held sway in the economics profession, the Republican Party and portions of the Democratic Party, and among corporate executives, were willing to take on the industry.[2] One revelation arising from congressional testimony about the spill, for example, was how few rules the Minerals Management Service (MMS) had issued regarding deep-ocean drilling and how often MMS failed to enforce the few rules that were in place.

There was also evidence of what political scientists call "agency capture." When a regulatory agency designed to regulate an industry in the public interest instead comes to act as a partner with that industry, agency capture is at work. Possible future employment for regulators, dependence of regulators on industry for the technical information, long-term relationships among regulators and firms, and overt gift-giving encourage common points of view among regulators and the regulated.

For example, congressional hearings and an Interior Department inspector general's report in 2010 revealed that energy companies paid for meals and hotel stays, elaborate vacations, and tickets to premium athletic events for MMS employees and that several MMS inspectors had examined operations at companies where they hoped to work. Also uncovered was the cozy relationship between oil rig inspectors and drilling companies. Many instances came to light of MMS inspection forms that had been filled out in pencil by industry officials but later traced over in pen by inspectors. Equally important, the MMS was entirely dependent on the technical information provided by regulated companies, having neither the personnel nor agency resources to develop information or independent testing equipment and instruments "in-house." During the Coast Guard inquiry on the failure of the various safety devices to work at the Deepwater Horizon platform, Captain Hung Nguyen was astonished when he received a simple "yes" answer from the MMS's regional supervisor for field operations to the following question: "So my understanding is that [the shear ram tool] is designed to industry standard, manufactured by industry, installed by industry, with no government witnessing oversight of the construction or the installation. Is that correct?" With such vigorous industry oversight in place, who needs more regulation?

In response to the Deepwater Horizon disaster, the Obama administration issued tough safety, financial, and environmental regulations for the offshore drilling industry. After the election of Donald Trump, however, a president committed to de-regulation as a way to unleash private enterprise, grow the economy, and bring back jobs, regulatory rollbacks on offshore drilling happened quickly. For example, under the direction of its new director Scott Angelle, the Interior Department's Bureau of Safety and Environmental Enforcement issued new rules giving drilling companies more time to replace faulty drilling equipment, eased maintenance requirements for drilling rigs, and loosened inspection requirements for blowout preventers on the ocean floor. Angelle, a long-time friend of the oil and gas industry—whose failed bid for the governorship of Louisiana was heavily funded by energy companies—said in a 2017 speech to oil and gas company executives in Houston that "help is on the way."

* * * * *

Some of what the federal government does in the United States is influenced by what the general public wants it to do. Elected and other public officials often pay attention to things such as public opinion polls and news media characterizations of popular preferences. Later chapters of this book will describe how political leaders often must be responsive to the electorate if they want to gain and retain their elected offices. But it is also the case that a wide array of private interest and advocacy groups, with business leading the way, play an enormously important, although less visible, role in determining what government does and influencing who wins and who loses from public policies. Some commentators go so far as to suggest that Washington is now run by a massive and powerful interest group industry that either clogs the governmental machinery—with a multitude of dispersed special interests vetoing government actions they oppose, whether legislation or administrative rule-making and enforcement—or gets their way most of the time on government actions that directly affect them. Conservative *New York Times* commentator David Brooks has called this system "interest group capitalism."[3]

THINKING CRITICALLY **ABOUT THIS CHAPTER**

This chapter is about the important role interest groups play in American government and politics, how they go about achieving their ends, and what effects they have in determining government policies in the United States.

APPLYING THE **FRAMEWORK**

You will see in this chapter how interest groups, in combination with other political linkage institutions, help convey the wishes and interests of people and groups to government decision makers. You will also learn how the interest group system we have in the United States is largely a product of structural factors, including our constitutional rules, political culture, social organization, and economy.

USING THE **DEMOCRACY STANDARD**

Interest groups have long held an ambiguous place in American politics. To some, interest groups are "special" interests that act without regard to the public interest and are the instruments of the most privileged parts of American society. To others, interest groups are simply another way that people and groups in a democratic society use to make their voices heard by government leaders. Using the democracy standard, you will be able to evaluate these two positions.

INTEREST GROUPS IN A DEMOCRATIC SOCIETY: CONTRASTING VIEWPOINTS

7.1 Compare and contrast opposing viewpoints about the role of interest groups in a democracy.

interest groups

Private organizations or voluntary associations that seek to influence public policy as a way to protect or advance their interests.

Interest groups are private organizations and voluntary associations that seek to advance their interests by trying to influence what government does. They are not officially a part of government. Nor are they political parties that try to place candidates carrying the party banner into government offices, though interest groups play an important role in U.S. elections. Interest groups are formed by people or firms that share an interest or cause that they are trying to protect or advance with the help of government.[4] The interests and causes they press on government range from narrowly targeted material benefits (e.g., passage of a favorable tax break or the issuance of a helpful regulation) to more broadly targeted outcomes for society at large (e.g., new rules on auto emissions or abortion availability). To do this, interest groups try to influence the behavior of public officials, such as presidents, members of Congress, bureaucrats, and judges. The framers knew that interest groups were inevitable and appropriate in a free society but were also potentially harmful, so as they wrote the Constitution the framers paid special attention to interest groups.

The Evils-of-Faction Argument

The danger posed by interest groups to good government and the public interest is a familiar theme in American politics. They are usually regarded as narrowly self-serving, out for themselves, and without regard for the public good.

factions

James Madison's term for groups or parties that try to advance their own interests at the expense of the public good.

This theme is prominent in *The Federalist* No. 10, in which James Madison defined **factions** (his term for interest groups and narrow political parties) in the following manner: "A number of citizens, whether amounting to a majority or a minority of the whole, who are united and actuated by some common impulse of passion, or of interest, adverse to the rights of other citizens or to the permanent and aggregate interests of the community."[5] The "evils-of-faction" theme recurs throughout our history, from the writings of the "muckrakers" at the turn of the 20th century to news accounts and commentary on the misdeeds of the leaders of the financial industry in the 2008 financial collapse as portrayed in the Academy Award nominated film *The Big Short* (2015).

The Pluralist Argument

pluralism

The political science position that American democracy is best understood in terms of the interaction, conflict, and bargaining of groups.

According to many political scientists, however, interest groups do not hurt democracy and the public interest but are instead an important instrument in attaining both. This way of looking at American democracy is called **pluralism** and takes the following form (also see Figure 7.1):[6]

* Free elections, while essential to a democracy, do not adequately communicate the specific wants and interests of the people to political leaders on a continuous basis. These are more accurately, consistently, and frequently conveyed to political leaders by the many groups and organizations to which people belong.

* Interest groups are easy to create; people in the United States are free to join or to organize groups that reflect their interests.

* Because of federalism, checks and balances, and the separation of powers, government power in the United States is broadly dispersed, leaving governmental institutions remarkably porous and open to the entreaties of the many and diverse groups that exist in society.

- Because of the ease of group formation and the accessibility of government, all legitimate interests in society can have their views taken into account by some public official. Farmers and business owners can make themselves heard; so, too, can consumers and workers. Because of this, the system is highly democratic and responsive.

FIGURE 7.1   THE PLURALIST VIEW OF AMERICAN POLITICS

In the pluralist understanding of the way American democracy works, citizens have more than one way to influence government leaders. In addition to voting, citizens also have the opportunity to participate in organizations that convey member views to public officials. Because of weak political parties, federalism, checks and balances, and the separation of powers, access to public officials is relatively easy.

BOSSES OF THE SENATE

In the late 19th century, many Americans thought of the Senate as the captive of large corporate trusts and other special-interest groups, as depicted in this popular cartoon, "Bosses of the Senate," with fat cat representatives of the steel, copper, iron, and coal industries, as well as Standard Oil, looming over the chamber.

How has the public's view of the Senate changed, if at all, since this cartoon was issued? Is there any basis for believing that the situation today is substantially different from that of the late 19th century?

Government Policies

Try to influence   Entrusted to decide

Interest and Advocacy Groups   Public Officials

Belong to   Citizens   Vote for

Pluralists see interest groups, then, not as a problem but as an additional tool of democratic representation, similar to other democratic instruments such as public opinion and elections. In this and other chapters, we will explore the degree to which this position is valid.

THE UNIVERSE OF INTEREST GROUPS

7.2 Describe different types of interest groups.

What kinds of interests find a voice in American politics? A useful place to start is with political scientist E. E. Schattschneider's distinction between "private" and "public" interests. Although the boundaries between the two are sometimes fuzzy, the distinction remains important. **Private interests** are organizations and associations that try to gain protections or material advantages from government for their own members rather than for society at large.[7] For the most part, these represent economic interests of one kind or another. **Public interests** are organizations and associations that try to gain protections or benefits for people beyond their own members, often for society at large. Some are motivated by an ideology or by the desire to advance a general cause—such as animal rights or environmental protection—or by the commitment to some public policy—gun control or an end to abortion. (These types of public interest groups often are called **advocacy groups**.) Some represent the nonprofit sector, and some even represent government entities, such as state and local governments.

Private and public interest groups come in a wide range of forms. Some, including AARP, are large membership organizations with sizable Washington and regional offices. Some large membership organizations have passionately committed members active in their affairs—such as the National Rifle Association (NRA)—while others have relatively passive members who join for the benefits the organization provides—such as the American Automobile Association (AAA), with its well-known trip assistance and auto buying and leasing service. Other groups are trade associations whose members are business firms. Still others are rather small organizations without members; are run by professionals and sustained by foundations and wealthy donors; and have sizable mailing, Internet, and telephone lists for soliciting contributions—the Children's Defense Fund and the National Taxpayers Union come to mind. These are examined in more detail in the sections that follow and in Table 7.1.

Private Interest Groups

Many different kinds of private interest groups are active in American politics.

BUSINESS   Because of the vast resources at the disposal of businesses and because of their strategic role in the health of local, state, and national economies, groups and associations representing businesses wield enormous power in Washington. Large corporations such as Boeing, Microsoft, Koch Industries, and Google are able to mount their own **lobbying** efforts and often join with others in influential associations, such as the Business Roundtable. Medium-sized businesses are well represented by organizations such as the National Association of Manufacturers and the U.S. Chamber of Commerce. Even small businesses have proved to be quite influential when joined in associations such as the National Federation of Independent Business, which has helped keep increases in the federal minimum wage well below the overall rate of growth in the economy and business profits for well over two decades. Agriculture and agribusinesses (fertilizer, seed, machinery, biotechnology, and food-processing companies) have more than held their own over the years through organizations such as the American Farm Bureau Federation and the Farm Machinery Manufacturer's Association and through scores of commodity groups, including the American Dairy Association and the National Association of Wheat Growers.

private interests
Interest groups that seek to protect or advance the material interests of their members.

public interests
Interest groups that work to gain protections or benefits for society at large.

advocacy groups
Interest groups organized to support a cause or ideology.

lobbying
Effort by an interest or advocacy group to influence the behavior of a public official.

TABLE 7.1 THE DIVERSE WORLD OF INTEREST ASSOCIATIONS

Interest	Interest Subtypes	Association Examples
Private Interests *(focus on protections and gains for their members)*		
Business	Corporations that lobby on their own behalf	Boeing
		Google
		Koch Industries
		Microsoft
	Trade associations	Chemical Manufacturers Association
		Health Insurance Association of America
	Peak business organizations	Business Roundtable
		Federation of Small Businesses
The professions	Doctors	American Medical Association
	Dentists	American Dental Association
	Accountants	National Society of Accountants
	Lawyers	American Bar Association
Labor	Unions	International Association of Machinists
	Union federations	AFL-CIO
Public Interests *(focus on protections and gains for a broader public or for society as a whole)*		
Ideologies and causes	Environment	Environmental Defense Fund
	Pro-choice	National Abortion Rights Action League
	Pro-life	National Right to Life Committee
	Anti-tax	Americans for Tax Reform
	Civil rights	National Association for the Advancement of Colored People
		Human Rights Campaign
Nonprofits	Medical	American Hospital Association
	Charitable	American Red Cross
Governmental entities	State	National Conference of State Legislatures
	Local	National Association of Counties

THE PROFESSIONS   Several associations represent the interests of professionals, such as doctors, lawyers, dentists, and accountants. Because of the prominent social position of professionals in local communities and their ability to make substantial campaign contributions, such associations are very influential in the policy-making process on matters related to their professional expertise and concerns. For example, the American Medical Association (AMA) and the American Dental Association (ADA) lobbied strongly against President Clinton's health care proposal and helped kill it, but they changed their tune in 2010, by backing President Obama's Affordable Care Act (perhaps because this law promised to bring health insurance coverage to an additional 32 million people.) The Trial Lawyers Association has long been a major financial contributor to the Democratic Party and has been active in blocking legislation to limit the size of personal injury jury awards.

LABOR   Although labor unions are sometimes involved in what might be called public interest activities (such as supporting civil rights legislation and pushing for an increase in the federal minimum wage), their main role in the United States has been to protect the jobs of their members and to secure good wages and benefits for them. Unlike **labor unions** in many parts of the world, which are as much political and ideological organizations as economic, American labor unions have traditionally focused on so-called bread-and-butter issues. As an important part of the New Deal coalition that dominated American politics well into the late 1960s, labor unions were influential at the federal level during the years when the Democratic Party controlled Congress and often won the presidency.

Although organized labor is still a force to be reckoned with in electoral politics, most observers believe that the political power of labor unions has eroded in dramatic

labor union

An organization representing employees that bargains with employers over wages, benefits, and working conditions.

TINA FEY ON THE PICKET LINE AT NBC HEADQUARTERS

In 2007, a long strike by television and film writers to gain concessions from the networks and film studios on use of writers' materials on the Internet was successful, partly because of the strong support it received from leading actors and performers, including actress and comedienne Tina Fey—a writer and a member of the Writers Guild of America (WGA). Despite successes such as this one, union membership has been steadily declining in the United States.

What accounts for declining union membership?

ways over the past several decades.[8] Organized labor's main long-range problem in American politics and its declining power relative to business in the workplace is its small membership base; in 2017, only 10.7 percent of American wage and salary workers—and only 6.5 percent of private-sector workers, the lowest percentage since 1916—were members of labor unions, compared with 35 percent in 1954.[9] The long but steady decline in union membership in the private sector is explained by a number of things. First, there has been a dramatic decline in the proportion of American workers in manufacturing, the economic sector in which unions have traditionally been the strongest. Fewer manufacturing workers are needed now than in the past because of outsourcing, gains in productivity (more can be manufactured with fewer workers), and pressures on companies to cut operating costs in a hypercompetitive global economy.[10] Second, business firms have become much less willing to tolerate unions and have become much more sophisticated at efforts to decertify unions and undermine union organization drives.[11] The long-term decline of private-sector labor unions was vividly on display in the successful campaign by business groups to pass so-called "right-to-work" laws in 2012 in Indiana and Michigan, historically important manufacturing states with strong labor unions. GOP control of the legislatures and governorships in both states after the 2010 elections made passage of these laws possible; right-to-work laws say that workers cannot be forced to join a union or pay dues to a union as a condition of getting or keeping a job and have long been considered anathema to organized labor.

The overall decline in labor union membership would have been more precipitous were it not for the substantial levels of unionization among public-sector workers, such as teachers, firefighters, police, and civil servants, 35 percent of whom belonged to unions in 2014. Today, there are more public-sector workers than private-sector workers in labor unions in the United States. Though stable for several decades, union density in the public sector has been undercut recently, no doubt a product of

successful efforts to pass laws weakening public-sector labor unions in Wisconsin and Michigan, historically strong union states. In 2018, in the case *Janus v. American Federation of State, County, and Municipal Workers*, in a case largely funded by conservative advocacy groups and business interest groups, the Supreme Court dealt a serious blow to public sector unions when it ruled that these unions could no longer collect dues from non-member public employees who benefit from union bargaining on wages, benefits, and working conditions. Organized labor, whether representing public sector or private sector workers, is clearly on the defensive and less influential in American politics than it has been.[12]

Public Interest Groups

Public interest groups or associations try to get government to act in ways that will serve interests that are broader and more encompassing than the direct economic or occupational interests of their own members. Such groups claim to be committed to protecting and advancing the public interest, at least as they see it.[13]

One type of public interest group is the advocacy group. People active in advocacy groups tend to be motivated by ideological concerns or a belief in a cause. Such advocacy groups have always been around, but a great upsurge in their number and influence has taken place since the late 1960s.[14] In the wake of the civil rights and women's movements, it is hardly surprising that a number of associations have been formed to advance the interests of particular racial, ethnic, and gender groups in American society. The National Organization for Women (NOW) advocates policies in Washington that advance the position of women in American society. Similarly, the NAACP and the Urban League are advocates for the interests of African Americans. The evangelical Christian upsurge led to the creation of such organizations as the Moral Majority, the Christian Coalition, the National Right to Life Committee, Focus on the Family, and the Family Research Council. The gay and lesbian movement

RECALL GOVERNOR WALKER

Teachers and other public sector workers and sympathizers took over the Wisconsin Capitol Rotunda in 2011 to protest Governor Scott Walker's plan to end collective bargaining rights for state government employees. Walker was successful in passing the new law and survived a statewide effort to recall him from office in 2012. To add insult to injury for state employees, Walker won reelection in 2014.

How might state government employees without collective bargaining rights express their interests to their supervisors and managers?

eventually led to the creation of organizations such as the Gay and Lesbian Alliance Against Defamation (GLAAD).

Most advocacy groups retain a professional, paid administrative staff and are supported by generous donors (often foundations), membership dues, and/or donations generated by direct mail campaigns. While some depend on and encourage grassroots volunteers and some hold annual membership meetings through which members play some role in making association policies, most advocacy associations are organizations without active membership involvement (other than check writing) and are run by lobbying and public education professionals.[15]

Two other types of public interest groups play a role in American politics, although usually a quieter one. First, associations representing government entities at the state and local levels of our federal system attempt to influence policies made by lawmakers and bureaucrats in Washington. The National Association of Counties is one example, as is the National Governors Association. Second, nonprofit organizations and associations try to influence policies that advance their missions to serve the public interest. Examples include the American Red Cross and the National Council of Nonprofit Associations.

INTEREST GROUP FORMATION AND PROLIFERATION

7.3 Explain why interest groups form and proliferate.

Nobody knows exactly how many interest groups exist in the United States, but there is wide agreement that the number began to mushroom in the late 1960s and grew steadily thereafter. We can see this increase along several dimensions. The number of groups listed in the *Encyclopedia of Associations*, for example, has lengthened from about 10,000 in 1968 to about 24,000 today. In addition, the number of officially registered **lobbyists** numbered more than 11,000 in 2017 and roughly double that number in Washington, D.C. are lobbyists if one includes people who lobby but have chosen not to register for one reason or another. One estimate is that about 260,000 people in Washington and its surrounding areas work in the lobbying sector in law, public relations, accounting, and technology.[16] Although lobbying Congress is only a part of what interest groups do, these associations and other lobbyists spent around $3.1 billion on lobbying efforts in Washington in 2017.[17] That amount was almost double what was spent for lobbying in 2000.

There are a number of reasons why so many interest groups exist in the United States. In the following paragraphs, we consider how constitutional rules, the country's diverse interests, its active government, and disturbances in the social, economic, and policy environment all contribute to the formation and growth of interest groups in the United States.

The Constitution

The constitutional rules of the political game in the United States encourage the formation of interest groups. For example, the First Amendment to the Constitution guarantees citizens the right to speak freely, to assemble, and to petition the government—all essential to citizens' ability to form organizations to advance their interests before government. In addition, the government is organized in such a way that officials are relatively accessible to interest groups. Because of federalism, checks and balances, and the separation of powers, there is no dominant center of decision making as there is in unitary states such as the United Kingdom and France. In unitary states, most important policy decisions are made in parliamentary bodies. In the United States, important decisions are made by many officials, on many matters, in many jurisdictions. Consequently, there are many more places where interest group pressure can be effective; there are more access points to public officials.

lobbyist
A person who attempts to influence the behavior of public officials on behalf of an interest group.

LOBBYING GRIDLOCK

The rise of the lobbying and private contractor industries in Washington has made the D.C. metropolitan area one of the fastest-growing and wealthiest regions in the United States. On the downside of this transformation, of course, are substantial increases in traffic and lengthier commuting times. *Why, one might ask, is Washington so often the scene of snarling gridlock of the political variety? Some might blame the lobbyists and a government grown too big because of them. Would you?*

Diverse Interests

Being a very diverse society, there are simply myriad interests in the United States. Racial, religious, ethnic, and occupational diversity is pronounced. Also varied are views about abortion, property rights, prayer in the schools, and environmental protection. Our economy is also strikingly complex and multifaceted and becoming more so. In a free society, these diverse interests usually take organizational forms. For example, the computer revolution spawned computer chip manufacturers, software companies, software engineers, computer magazines and blogs, Internet services, technical information providers, computer component jobbers, Web designers, social media sites, and countless others. Each has particular interests to defend or advance before government, and each has formed an association to try to do so.[18] Thus, software engineers have an association to look after their interests, as do software and hardware companies, Internet access providers, digital content providers, industry writers, and so on. After Google went public in 2004, the company opened its own Washington office to ensure its interests were protected before both Congress and important regulatory agencies against competing interests such as Microsoft and wireless phone carriers such as Verizon and Sprint.[19] Facebook opened a Washington, D.C., office in 2010, another indication that many of Silicon Valley's technology firms are actively cultivating influence in Washington.

A More Active Government

The U.S. government does far more today than it did during the early years of the republic. As government takes on more responsibilities, it quite naturally comes to have a greater effect on virtually all aspects of economic, social, and personal life. People, groups, and organizations are increasingly affected by the actions of government, so the decisions made by presidents, members of Congress, bureaucrats who write regulations, and judges are increasingly important. It would be surprising indeed if, in response, people, groups, and organizations did not try harder to influence the public officials' decisions that affect them.[20] During the long, drawn-out deliberations in Congress in 2009 and 2010 that resulted in new rules for banks and the financial industry, bank and financial industry lobbyists flooded Capitol Hill to make sure that the most onerous provisions—for example, a limit on the size of banks so they would not be "too big to fail"—did not make it into the final bill.

Some part of the growth in lobbying by business firms and industry and trade groups may be tied to the emergence of hypercompetition in the global economy, where even giant enterprises such as Microsoft must fight to protect their positions not only against competitors but against threatening actions by one or more government agencies. For many years, the Seattle-based company has been fighting antitrust actions initiated by the U.S. Justice Department and the European Union Commission and has dramatically enhanced its lobbying presence in Washington (and Brussels) and increased its campaign contributions.[21]

Some groups form around government programs to take advantage of existing government programs and initiatives. The creation of the Department of Homeland Security (DHS), with its large budget for new homeland defense technologies, stimulated the formation of new companies to serve this market, as well as new trade associations—including the Homeland Security Industries Association—to represent them. Until the Obama administration cracked down on them, for-profit higher education institutions such as the University of Phoenix received about 90 percent of their funding from the federal student loan program and other forms of federal aid, and the industry has lobbied heavily against proposals to tie federal dollars to measures of performance such as graduation rates and job placement.[22] Betsy DeVos, the Education Secretary under Donald Trump, has issued rules to ease the regulatory burden on these educational companies.

Disturbances

The existence of diverse interests, the rules of the game, and the importance of government decisions and policies enable and encourage the formation of interest groups, but formation seems to happen only when interests are threatened, usually by some change in the social and economic environment or in government policy. This is

LOBBYING FOR ETHANOL

Corn farmers and organizations that represent them have been very successful in convincing Americans and their elected officials to pass laws requiring that ethanol from corn be added to gasoline and to keep out—mainly by the imposition of high tariffs—more efficiently produced ethanol from other countries, especially Brazil, which uses sugarcane and switchgrass. Billboards along major highways such as this one near Boone, Missouri, have been very effective tools of public persuasion in this campaign by corn and domestic ethanol producers, but they also deploy many other tools.

Besides billboards, what are some other powerful tools that interest and advocacy groups use to influence public opinion?

known as the **disturbance theory** of interest group formation.[23] To take one example, Focus on the Family, a conservative religious advocacy group, was formed when many evangelical Christians began to feel threatened by what they considered to be a rise in family breakdown, an increase in the number of abortions, the sexual revolution, and the growing visibility of gay, lesbian, and transsexual people in American life. The Supreme Court's ruling upholding same-sex-marriage further spurred the activities of existing religious lobbying organizations and the formation of new ones, such as the National Organization for Marriage.

disturbance theory

A theory positing that interest groups originate with changes in the economic, social, or political environment that threaten the well-being of some segment of the population.

WHAT INTEREST GROUPS DO

7.4   Analyze the methods and activities interest groups use to influence political outcomes.

Interest groups, whether public or private in nature, are in the business of conveying the policy views of individuals and groups to public officials. There are two basic types of interest group activity: the inside game and the outside game.[24] The inside game—the older and more familiar of the two—involves direct, personal contact between interest group representatives and government officials. Some political scientists believe this inside game of influencing the actions of those who make and carry out government policy in Washington—representatives and senators, judges, and regulators—is the thing that big interest groups and business corporations care about the most in politics and where they put most of their political resources. As they put it, "For powerful groups the center of action is in Washington, not the swing states."[25] The outside game involves interest group mobilization of public opinion, voters, and important contributors to bring indirect pressure to bear on elected officials. Increasingly today, the most powerful interest groups use both inside and outside methods to influence which policies government makes and carries out.

The Inside Game

When lobbying and lobbyists are in the news, the news generally is not good. In early 2006, "super-lobbyist" Jack Abramoff pled guilty to three felony counts for fraud, tax evasion, and conspiracy to bribe public officials; he was then convicted and sentenced

inside game

The form of lobbying in which representatives of an interest or advocacy group try to persuade legislators, executive branch officials, and/or regulators to support actions favored by that group.

to ten years in prison. Prosecutors had amassed evidence that he had funneled millions on behalf of his clients to a long list of representatives and senators, mostly on the Republican side of the aisle, for campaign war chests and elaborate gifts, including vacations. The **inside game** of lobbying—so named because of the practice of interest group representatives talking to legislators in the lobbies outside House and Senate committee rooms—does not customarily involve bribing legislators. Rather, it is more the politics of insiders and the "good ol' boy" network (although, increasingly, women also are part of the network). It is the politics of one-on-one persuasion, in which the skilled lobbyist tries to get a decision maker to understand and sympathize with the interest group's point of view or to see that what the interest group wants is good for the politician's constituents. Access is critical if one is to be successful at this game.

Many of the most successful lobbyists are recruited from the ranks of retired members of the House and Senate, congressional staff, and high levels of the bureaucracy. Almost 30 percent of outgoing lawmakers, for example, are hired by lobbying firms or hang out their own lobbying shingle.[26] Eric Cantor, for example, the once-powerful Republican House Majority Leader who surprisingly lost his seat in 2014 to a Tea Party challenger, now lobbies for the investment bank Moelis & Company. In 2015, forty-eight former staffers of Senate majority leader Mitch McConnell (R-KY) were registered as lobbyists as were thirty-six who had worked for Senate minority leader Harry Reid (D-NV).[27] The promise of lucrative employment based on their skills—and especially on their many contacts—is what keeps so many of them around Washington after they leave office or quit federal employment.

The inside game seems to work best when the issues are narrow and technical, do not command much media attention or public passion, and do not stir up counter-activity by other interest groups.[28] This is not to say that interest groups play a role only on unimportant matters. Great benefit can come to an interest group or a large corporation from a small change in a single provision of the Tax Code or in a slight change in the wording of a regulation on carbon emissions or what percentage of deposits banks must keep in reserve. Enron was very successful at getting Congress to remove federal oversight on many of its energy-trading and acquisitions activities. These stayed well out of public view until they came to light after Enron's spectacular collapse in 2001.

STAFFERS TO THE RESCUE

Staffers play an important role in the life of Congress, and many go on to important careers as lobbyists, knowing as they do the ins-and-outs of the legislative branch. Here, a few of Senator Chuck Schumer's (D-NY) aides trail the senator and then-Attorney General Loretta Lynch on their way to an oversight hearing of the Senate Judiciary Committee. Schumer's staffers likely have assembled a set of questions and statements for the senator to use during the hearing.

Do you think congressional staffers should be allowed to lobby their former colleagues and acquaintances in the legislative branch after they have left public service? Why?

Lobbyists from advocacy groups also play the inside game, often with great skill and effect. For example, many environmental regulations have been strengthened because of the efforts of skilled lobbyists from the Sierra Club. The National Rifle Association (NRA) is virtually unbeatable on issues of gun control. But it is inescapably the case that lobbyists representing business and the wealthy are far more numerous and deployed on a wider range of issues than those of any other interest, as we will show later in the chapter.

Political scientist E. E. Schattschneider has pointed out that the inside game—traditional lobbying—is pretty much outside the view of the public.[29] That is to say, the day-to-day details of this form of lobbying are not the stuff of the evening news, nor the fodder of open political campaigns or conflict; such lobbying largely takes place behind closed doors.

LOBBYING CONGRESS   In Congress, lobbyists are trying to accomplish two essential tasks for those who hire them: First, have bills and provisions in bills that they favor passed; second, keep bills and provisions of bills that they do not like from seeing the light of day. The essence of this inside game in Congress is twofold. First, members of interests groups remind key actors of the electoral consequences for opposing what the group wants. No group is better at this game than the NRA, which has been deeply involved not only in blocking bills it opposes but in helping to write NRA-friendly provisions even in the few gun control bills that Congress has passed over the last two decades. After the 2012 Newtown, Connecticut, school shootings—which left twenty children and six teachers dead—prompted widespread calls for gun control, NRA lobbyists worked for a time with Democratic Senator Joe Manchin on a bill to extend background checks for those making gun purchases. The NRA refused, however, to consider bans on assault rifles and large clips for such weapons, and pressed constantly to water down background checks. Though it was successful in

PLANNING STRATEGY

Two lobbyists meet at the Capitol to talk over their inside game plan for the day. They must decide which senators, representatives, and staffers to see and which arguments to pitch in support of their clients' agendas.

Why is the inside game so central to the day-to-day operation of American government and politics?

these efforts, the NRA eventually withdrew its support, and the bill failed to break the sixty-vote threshold for Senate bills. Senators facing an election in closely contested states were reluctant in the end to provoke NRA opposition.[30]

The second key to the inside game is the cultivation of personal relationships with people who matter—Senate and House leaders, other influential and well-placed legislators, chairpersons of important committees or subcommittees, a broad swath of rank-and-file members, and key staff members.[31] Because much of the action in Congress takes place in the committees and because senators and representatives are busy with a wide range of responsibilities, cultivating relationships with important legislative and committee staff members is especially important for successful lobbyists. As one lobbyist put it, "If you have a staff member on your side, it might be a hell of a lot better than talking to the member [of Congress]."[32]

Lobbyists are also expected to make substantial contributions to the campaign war chests of representatives and senators and to persuade their clients to do the same. One influential lobbyist is reported to have said that "about one-third of my day is spent raising money from my clients to give to people I lobby."[33]

LOBBYING THE EXECUTIVE BRANCH   After bills become law, they must be carried out or implemented. This is done by the executive branch. In this process of implementation, career civil servants, political appointees in top executive branch bureaus and departments, and regulators have a great deal of discretionary authority in deciding how to transform the wishes of the president and Congress into action on the ground. This happens because Congress and the president usually legislate broad policies, leaving it to executive branch bureaus and agencies to promulgate procedures, rules, and regulations to fill in the details of how laws will actually work in practice and how the mandates of regulatory agencies will be accomplished. So, for example, while Congress appropriates monies for the Army Corps of Engineers, for the most part, decision makers in the Corps decide which specific levee and river dredging projects will be funded. Lobbyists for big contractors and for state and local governments try to make sure they have a regular presence with the Corps's top officials and staffers.

Because of the technical complexity of many of the issues that come before them, regulatory agencies such as the Securities and Exchange Commission (SEC), the Environmental Protection Agency (EPA), and the Federal Communications Commission (FCC) have been granted broad leeway in promulgating rules designed to meet the goals the president and Congress have set for them. The rules they issue have the force of law unless Congress or the courts subsequently overturn these rules (which is very hard for Congress to do). Congress rarely passes legislation involving details of television and radio broadcasting, for example, leaving regulatory decisions to the FCC. Because of this, the National Association of Broadcasters focuses its time and energies on the FCC, trying to establish stable and friendly relationships with them. The payoffs can be quite high for lobbying executive branch agencies like the FCC. In 2003, for example, large media company and news organization leaders and lobbyists met with the top staff of the FCC in a successful effort to get the agency to loosen rules on ownership so that big companies could grow even bigger. As shown in the chapter-opening story, oil and gas rig operators successfully lobbied President Trump's Interior Department to loosen economic, safety, and environmental regulations affecting their operations in the Gulf of Mexico.

The key to success in lobbying the executive branch is similar to that of lobbying Congress: personal contact and cooperative long-term relationships that a civil servant, a department or bureau leader, or a regulator finds useful.[34] Interest group representatives can convey technical information, for example, provide the results of their research, help a public official deflect criticism, and show that what the group wants is compatible with good public policy and the political needs of the official.

LOBBYING THE COURTS   Interest groups sometimes lobby the courts, although not in the same way as they lobby the other two branches. A group may find that neither Congress nor the White House is favorably disposed to its interests and will bring a **test case** to the courts. For example, during the 1940s and 1950s, the NAACP realized that improving the lot of African Americans was very low on the agenda of presidents and members of Congress, so it turned to the courts for satisfaction. The effort eventually paid off in 1954 in the landmark *Brown v. Board of Education* (1954) decision. As reported above, public employee unions were dealt a blow in 2018 when the Court ruled in *Janus v. AFSCME* that public sector unions cannot compel non-member public employees to help pay for union-led wage, benefit, and working conditions bargaining. The case was formally brought by an Illinois welfare case worker, but was backed and financed by several conservative, anti-union groups such as the National Right-to-Work Legal Foundation and the Bradley Foundation.

Interest groups sometimes lobby the courts by filing *amicus curiae* ("friends of the court") briefs in cases involving other parties. In this kind of brief, a person or an organization that is not a party to the suit may file an argument in support of one side or the other in the hope of swaying the views of the judge or judges. Major controversies before the Supreme Court on such issues as abortion, free speech, or civil rights attract scores of *amicus curiae* briefs. For example, for *District of Columbia v. Heller* (2008), in which the Court ruled that Americans have an individual right under the Constitution to own a gun, supporters and opponents of gun control filed a total of nineteen *amicus* briefs.

Interest groups also get involved in the appointment of federal judges. Particularly controversial appointments, such as the Supreme Court nominations of Robert Bork in 1987 (many women's and civil rights interests considered him too conservative), Clarence Thomas in 1992 (he was opposed by liberal and women's groups), and Samuel Alito in 2005 (Democrats and liberals considered him much too conservative on a wide range of issues), drew interest group attention and strenuous efforts for and against the nominees. Though they ultimately failed, conservative groups mobilized in 2009 to block the appointment of Sonia Sotomayor to the Court; liberal groups tried but failed to block the appointments of Neil Gorsuch in 2017 and Brett Kavanaugh in 2018.

test case

A case brought by advocacy or interest groups to try to force a ruling on the constitutionality of some law or executive action.

amicus curiae

Latin for "friend of the court"; a legal brief in which individuals not party to a suit may have their views heard in court.

CELEBRATING A HISTORIC COURT DECISION

Dick Heller—here signing his autograph on the placards of gun rights advocates in front of the Supreme Court in June 2008—won his suit against the city government of Washington, D.C., in a case that established a constitutional right to own a firearm. The legal and financial resources that made his suit possible were provided by the NRA and other anti–gun control organizations.

Why are gun lobbies such a powerful force in American politics?

The Outside Game

An interest group plays the "outside game" when it tries to mobilize local constituencies and shape public opinion to support the group's goals and to bring that pressure to bear on elected officials. Defenders of the status quo mostly depend on the inside game; those who are trying to change existing policies or create new legislation are more likely to use the outside game.[35] By all indications, the **outside game**—sometimes called **grassroots lobbying**—has been growing steadily in importance in recent years.[36] This may be a good development for democracy, and here is why. Although groups involved in the outside game often try to hide their true identities—Americans for Fair Drug Prices, for example, may well be funded by the pharmaceutical industry—and while some groups involved in the outside game have far more resources than others, it is still the case that this form of politics at least has the effect of expanding and heightening political conflict. This may serve to bring more issues out into the open and subject them to public scrutiny—what Schattschneider has called the "socialization of conflict."[37]

MOBILIZING MEMBERSHIP   Those interest groups with a large membership base try to persuade their members to send letters and to make telephone calls to senators and representatives when an important issue is before Congress. They sound the alarm, using direct mail and, increasingly, e-mail and social media. They define the threat to members; suggest a way to respond to the threat; and supply the addresses, phone numbers, and e-mail addresses of the people to contact in Washington. Members are grouped by congressional district and state and are given the addresses of their own representatives or senators. The NRA is particularly effective in mobilizing its considerable membership whenever the threat of federal gun control rears its head. Environmental organizations such as Friends of the Earth and Environmental Defense sound the alarm to people on their mailing lists whenever Congress threatens to loosen environmental protections.

ORGANIZING THE DISTRICT   Members of Congress are especially attuned to the individuals and groups in their states or districts who can affect their reelection prospects. The smart interest or advocacy group, therefore, not only will convince its own members in the state and district to put pressure on the senator or congressional representative, but it will also make every effort to be in touch with the most important campaign contributors and opinion leaders there. Republicans who have been elected to office are especially wary of groups like the Club for Growth and American Crossroads that target any in the party who support tax increases and more government spending and threaten to put money into the campaigns of their primary election opponents. Democrats who have been elected to office are wary of bucking labor unions and pro-choice groups for the same reasons.

SHAPING PUBLIC OPINION   "Educating" the public on issues that are important to the interest group is one of the central features of new-style lobbying. The idea is to shape opinion in such a way that government officials will be favorably disposed to the views of the interest group. These attempts to shape public and elite opinion come in many forms. One strategy is to produce and distribute research reports that bolster the group's position. Citizen groups such as the Environmental Defense Fund and the Food Research and Action Center have been very adept and effective in this area.[38]

Another strategy is media advertising. Sometimes this takes the form of pressing a position on a particular issue, such as the Teamsters Union raising the alarm about open borders with Mexico, focusing on the purported unsafe nature of Mexican trucks roaming American highways. Sometimes it is "image" advertising, in which some company or industry portrays its positive contribution to American life.[39] Thus, large

outside game
Similar to "grassroots lobbying"; that form of lobbying in which interest and advocacy groups try to bring outside pressure to bear on legislators, bureaucrats, and/or regulators.

grassroots lobbying
The effort by interest groups to mobilize local constituencies, shape public opinion to support the group's goals, and bring that pressure to bear on elected officials.

oil companies often feature their regard for the environment in their advertising, showing romantic forest scenes or a pristine beach, with nary a pipeline, a tanker, or a refinery in sight.

In the effort to shape public opinion, the well-heeled interest group will also prepare materials that will be of use to radio and television broadcasters and to newspaper and magazine editors. Many produce opinion pieces, magazine articles, television spots and radio "sound bites," and even television documentaries. Others stage events to be covered as news. For example, the environmentalist group Greenpeace puts the news media on full alert before attempting to disrupt a whaling operation.

Finally, interest and advocacy groups, using the latest computer technology, identify target groups to receive information on particular issues. Groups pushing for cuts in the capital gains tax rate, for instance, direct their communications to holders of the American Express card or to addresses in ZIP code areas identified as upper-income neighborhoods. Most have their own websites and publish position papers and other materials there. Many arrange postings to friendly blogs in hopes of further disseminating their message. Some will use their websites and e-mail to organize e-mails to lawmakers from their constituents.[40] Many interest and advocacy groups have made big commitments to the use of social media and smartphone apps to spread their message.

GETTING INVOLVED IN CAMPAIGNS AND ELECTIONS Interest groups try to increase their influence by getting involved in political campaigns.[41] Many interest groups issue report cards indicating the degree to which members of the House and Senate support the group's positions on a selection of key votes. Report card ratings are distributed to the members of the interest or advocacy group and to other interested parties in the hope that the ratings will influence voting behavior. To better their reelection chances, Republican members of Congress try to receive high scores from conservative groups like the National Taxpayers Union; Democrats seek high scores from liberal groups like the League for Conservation Voters. Figure 7.2 shows how a prominent Republican, Senator Jeff Sessions of Alabama, and a prominent Democratic, Senator Diane Feinstein of California, were graded by a small sample of conservative and liberal advocacy organizations.

THE FOX GUARDING THE CHICKEN COOP

Scott Pruitt, shown here at his Senate confirmation hearings in January 2017, was President Trump's first head of the Environmental Protection Agency. When he was a representative from Oklahoma, his campaigns were heavily funded by the fossil fuel industry, and as Attorney General of Oklahoma, he brought several lawsuits against the EPA for being over-zealous in issuing environmental regulations. During his short tenure as head of the EPA, he rolled back scores of environmental regulations he deemed unfriendly to oil, gas, and coal.

Is there any way to minimize the appointment of people to head regulatory agencies who are opposed to the basic missions of these agencies? Or is this simply the outcome of a democratic process where the president can appoint whomever he desires to carry out what he promised during his election campaign?

FIGURE 7.2 INTEREST GROUP REPORT CARDS, A SELECT SAMPLE

Some interest groups issue "report cards" for members of Congress. Here we show ratings for six senators from three states from the 115th Congress, three Republicans and three Democrats. Note the widely divergent scores for Democratic and Republican senators from the same states. Liberal groups like Americans for Democratic Action and the League of Conservation Voters tend to see Democratic legislators as better aligned with their group's goals and, therefore, rate them more favorably. In contrast, conservative groups like the American Conservative Union and National Taxpayers Union tend to rate Republican legislators more favorably. *If you were deciding who to vote for in a House or Senate election in your state, would you find interest and advocacy group legislative report cards useful to you? What other information would help you decide?*

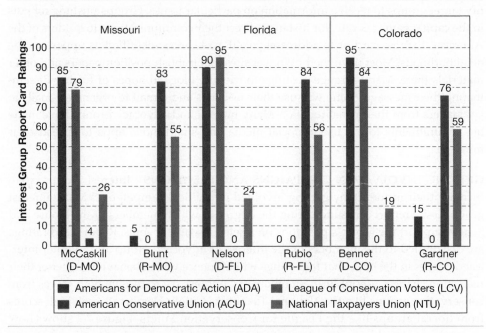

SOURCE: Data from legislative ratings of Americans for Democratic Action, the League of Conservation Voters, the American Conservative Union, and the National Taxpayers Union.

Interest and advocacy groups also encourage their members to get involved in the electoral campaigns of candidates who are favorable to their interests. Groups often assist campaigns in more tangible ways—allowing the use of their telephone banks; mail, telephone, and e-mail lists; computers; and the like. Some interest groups help with fund-raising events or ask members to make financial contributions to candidates.

Interest groups also endorse particular candidates for public office. The strategy may backfire and is somewhat risky, for to endorse a losing candidate is to risk losing access to the winner. Nevertheless, it is fairly common now for labor unions, environmental organizations, religious groups, business groups, and liberal and conservative ideological groups to make such endorsements.

Interest groups are also an increasingly important part of campaign fund-raising. The rise of super PACs and 501c organizations are especially noteworthy, injecting super-rich individuals and companies directly into the middle of electoral campaigns. For example, the energy industry played a crucial fund-raising and messaging function during the 2016 elections and helped elect a unified Republican government in Washington, D.C. One outcome was Scott Pruitt's appointment by President Trump to head the Environmental Protection Agency where he helped roll back regulations on fuel mileage requirements for cars, restrictions on waste dumping in streams by coal companies, the use of certain hazardous chemicals, and greenhouse gas emissions from plants and factories. Though Pruitt was forced out because of ethics violations, most of his regulatory decisions remained in force. We focus more on this topic in the next section and more extensively later in the book.

INTEREST GROUPS, CORPORATE POWER, AND INEQUALITY IN AMERICAN POLITICS

7.5 Describe the inequalities of the interest group system.

Overall, between the inside game and the outside game, interest groups have a diverse set of tools for influencing elected officials, bureaucrats in the executive branch, judges, and the public. The number of groups capable of deploying these tools is large and growing every year. On the surface, it might look like the proliferation of interest groups has enhanced the democratic flavor of our country, allowing more and more Americans to have their interests represented. But not all scholars and students of politics agree that this is so.

An obvious problem with the view that the interest group system enhances democracy by multiplying the number of interests whose voice is heard in the political process is that a substantial part of the American population is not organized into groups for political purposes. They do not have access to interest group organizations and resources at all. This is a critical disadvantage for the unorganized. Though some of their views might count every two to four years at election time, or occasionally when and if they become involved in social movements, for the most part the unorganized go unheard and unheeded. Not surprisingly, the unorganized tend to be the most disadvantaged among the American population: the poor, those with less education, and members of minorities.[42]

For political scientist E. E. Schattschneider, the main flaw in the pluralist (or interest group) heaven is "that the heavenly chorus sings with a strong upper class accent."[43] We would amend this, based on our reading of the evidence, in the following way: the flaw in the pluralist heaven is "that the heavenly chorus sings with a strong upper class and *corporate* accent." Figure 7.3 is a schematic of how this works in shaping what government does. If this observation about an "upper class and corporate accent" is accurate, then political equality is undermined by the interest group system, and democracy is less fully developed than it might be, even taking into account the new importance of the outside game (which, as we have said, tends to "socialize conflict"). In this section, we look at economic inequalities in the interest group system and evaluate their effects.[44]

Representational Inequality

Power in the American political system goes to the organized and to those among the organized who have the most resources and the best access to decision makers in government. We start by noting that not all segments of American society are equally represented in the interest group system. The interest group inside lobbying game in Washington, D.C., is dominated, in sheer numbers and weight of activity, by business corporations, industry trade associations, and associations of the professions, although liberal and conservative advocacy groups also lobby.[45] One group, organized labor, although still a powerful player in Washington, has lost much of its lobbying clout in recent years, mainly because of declining membership. In 2005, the passage of several pro-business bills that labor strongly opposed—namely, bills making it more difficult to declare bankruptcy and to bring class-action lawsuits in state courts—showcases labor's declining fortunes. The vast majority of advocacy groups, even those that perceive themselves as liberal and lean toward the Democrats, attract members and contributors who have much higher incomes, more elite occupations, and more education than the general public. Not surprisingly, given those whom these advocacy groups represent, they tend to focus less on issues of poverty, jobs, and income inequality—the traditional purview of labor unions—and more on "quality of life" issues such as environmental protection, consumer protection, globalization, women's rights, racial and ethnic civil rights, gay and lesbian rights, and civil liberties.[46]

FIGURE 7.3   THE MANY WAYS PRIVILEGED ACTORS INFLUENCE WHAT
GOVERNMENT DOES

Privileged groups influence all three stages of the policy process, including elections and public
opinion (arrow at left); which policies are made within the legislative, executive, and judicial branches
(arrow at bottom); and how laws, rules, and regulations are carried out (arrow at right).

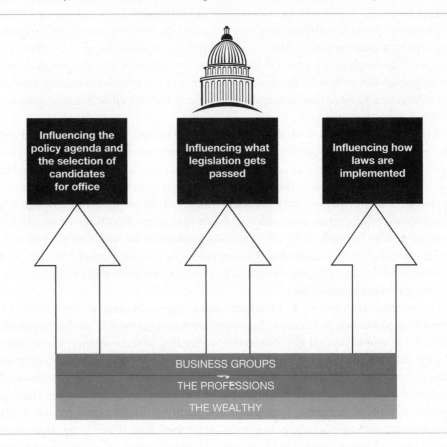

Resource Inequality

The most economically well-off parts of American society are business corporations
and financial institutions, corporate and financial institution executives and top managers, heads of private equity and hedge funds, and professionals. As firms, they are
the most important actors; as individuals, they account for a disproportionately large
share of income and wealth in the United States. It is hardly surprising that interest
groups representing them can afford to spend far more than other groups can to hire
professional lobbying firms, form their own Washington liaison office, place advertising in the media, conduct targeted mailings on issues, mobilize their members to contact government officials, and pursue all of the other activities of old- and new-style
lobbying. Lobbying in Washington is heavily dominated by lobbyists and lobbying
firms that represent business.[47] For example, registered lobbyists for the various drug
companies typically total more than the combined membership of the House and Senate; according to the Center for Responsive Politics, in 2015 there were 1,367 registered
and active lobbyists for the pharmaceutical industry.[48]

The story is the same in other industries. More than three thousand lobbyists
worked to keep provisions of the Dodd-Frank bill from being too onerous—it was
passed in 2010 to prevent a recurrence of the 2008 financial collapse—killing provisions keeping banks from becoming "too big to fail," including higher capital
requirements. After passage of the new law, financial industry lobbyists turned their
attention to the rule-making executive branch agencies charged with administering
Dodd-Frank and managed to slow down the process considerably.[49] Anger at the

**TWO-BILLION-DOLLAR
LOSING BET**

One of the leading advocates of letting
the banking industry regulate itself
is Jamie Dimon, the chairman and
CEO of JPMorgan Chase, who was
compelled to answer for the bank's
solvency problems before Congress.
Under his watch, JPMorgan Chase lost
$2 billion of its depositors' money on a
single day in May 2012 after it placed
a risky bet in the unregulated derivatives market.

*Should Congress and the executive
branch increase regulations designed to
prevent banks from taking too many risks
with depositors' assets, or are such matters best left to those running financial
institutions?*

financial community was so high, however, and enough regulators were worried
about dangerous bank practices, that the industry could not prevent adoption in 2013
of the "Volker rule" (named after the former Fed chair who advocated for it) that separated trading and commercial banking, disallowing financial institutions from speculating in the stock market with their customers' money.

In 2018, the GOP-led House and Senate, with the help of many Democrats,
exempted small to medium-sized banks from the Dodd Frank regulations, leaving
only ten giant banks subject to Dodd-Frank regulations. President Donald Trump
played a key role in undermining a central pillar of Dodd Frank when he appointed
Tea Party conservative Mike Mulvaney to head the Consumer Financial Protection
Bureau, an agency tasked with protecting consumers from predatory lenders and customer gouging by banks (secret fees imposed on their customers, and more). During
his first year, Mulvaney stopped investigations into the Equifax data breaches and
dropped on-going Bureau lawsuits against predatory payday lenders.

The lopsided lobbying situation in Washington is shown in Table 7.2, which
reports the amount of money spent by different sectors of American society on lobbying activities. It is worth noting that nonbusiness groups and associations—listed in
the table as other, ideological/single-issue, and organized labor—spent only a small
fraction of what was spent by business in 2017.

Corporate, trade, and professional associations as well as wealthy individuals can
contribute to a dizzying array of organizations that support candidates, parties, and
issues during political campaigns. Among the most important targets for politically oriented contributions are **political action committees (PACs)**, 527 and 501c social welfare
organizations, and super PACS. PACs are regulated, donations are on the public record,
and caps exist on how much can be given to candidates in federal elections and to party
committees. 527, 501c, and super PAC organizations, often labeled "outside money," are
largely unregulated and have no limits on how much money can be raised from individuals, corporations, and labor unions or spent to influence the outcome of elections. These
relatively new forms of campaign organizations were made possible by the hollowing
out of campaign finance laws by two Supreme Court cases, *Citizens United v. FEC* (2010)
and *Speechnow.org v. FEC* (2010), in which the Court ruled that many of these laws and
rules written under them violated the free speech rights of corporations, unions, and
individuals.[50] These organizations have come to play an ever-larger role in funding presidential and congressional elections and in shaping public opinion about public issues.[51]

**political action committee
(PAC)**

An entity created by an interest group
whose purpose is to collect money
and make contributions to candidates in
federal elections.

TABLE 7.2   MAJOR SPENDING ON FEDERAL LOBBYING, 2017
(BY INDUSTRY SECTOR)

Sector	Total Spending
Health	$562,953,377
Finance/Insurance/Real Estate	$522,000,556
Miscellaneous Business	$507,229,505
Communications/Electronics	$410,204,273
Energy/Natural Resources	$318,390,189
Transportation	$246,265,195
Other Business Groups	$222,872,893
Ideology/Single-Issue	$150,328,803
Agribusiness	$132,127,200
Defense	$124,891,961
Construction	$63,027,130
Labor	$47,821,117

SOURCE: Based on Center for Responsive Politics, Influence and Lobbying, Ranked Sectors, 2017.

The *Citizens United* decision turned heavily on the doctrine that corporations are "persons" with the same rights and privileges as any natural person residing in the United States, including free speech. Several scholars have pointed out that this doctrine has been pushed for a very long time in the courts by legal firms representing corporations in a broad set of cases. It need hardly be pointed out that the decades-long effort required a staying power based on access to substantial financial resources not available to most individuals, advocacy groups, or labor unions. Interestingly, corporations have managed to avoid criminal prosecution even when they have broken the law because criminal punishment is relevant only to "natural" persons. This is why none of the key players that brought about the financial collapse in 2008 have gone to jail.[52]

Corporate, trade, and professional donors have dominated all forms of campaign finance organizations during recent election cycles, though labor unions have also had a big presence.[53] PACs representing the least-privileged sectors of American society are notable for their absence. As former Senator (R-KS) and presidential candidate Bob Dole once put it, "There aren't any poor PACs or food stamp PACs or nutrition PACs or Medicaid PACs."[54] Notably, very wealthy individuals, not interest groups, have written the biggest checks for super PACs. During the 2011–2012 election cycle, the super PAC "Winning Our Future," funded entirely by gambling magnate Sheldon Adelman, contributed more than $17 million to help Newt Gingrich win the Republican nomination (it did not work). In all, super PACs spent roughly $610 million in that cycle, two-thirds on Republican and conservative candidates and causes.[55] Interestingly, though receiving less largess than Republicans, Democratic candidates for federal office also depend a great deal on contributions from business and the wealthy. This may be one reason why Democrats recently have focused more on issues such as abortion, immigration, same-sex marriage, and voting rights (where they and Republicans are deeply divided) and less on social welfare and protecting unions.[56]

Access Inequality

Inequalities of representation and resources are further exaggerated by vast inequalities in access to government decision makers. Powerful interest organizations and lobbying firms that primarily represent business, professionals, and the wealthy have the resources to employ many former regulators and staff from independent regulatory agencies, former members of Congress and congressional staff, and top employees of other federal executive departments, including many from the Department of Defense and the Internal Revenue Service (IRS). They are hired partly for their technical expertise but also for the access they can provide to those with whom they formerly worked. *Bloomberg Businessweek* reported, for example, that firms hired sixty former staffers from Congress in 2011 to work solely on successfully convincing Congress to give tax breaks to big, global companies on profits earned abroad.[57]

Access inequality may also be seen in the ability of some groups to play a central role in the formation and implementation of government policies based on their membership in informal networks within the government itself. One kind of informal network is an **iron triangle**, which customarily includes a private interest group (usually a corporation or trade association), an agency in the executive branch, and a committee or subcommittees in Congress, which act together to advance and protect certain government programs that work to the mutual benefit of their members. Most scholars believe iron triangles have become less important in American government.[58] The second type of informal network, called an issue network, is understood to be more open and inclusive than an iron triangle. **Issue networks** are said to be coalitions that form around different policy areas that include a range of public and private interest groups and policy experts as well as business representatives, bureaucrats, and legislators. Iron triangles suggest a closed system in which a small group of actors controls a policy area. Issue networks suggest a more fluid situation with more actors and visibility, where control of policy making is less predictable.

Nonetheless, corporations, trade associations, and associations of professionals not only play a prominent role in issue networks but also participate in those iron triangles that are still around.[59] These are especially prominent in shaping and carrying out public policies in the areas of agriculture, defense procurement, public lands, highway construction, and water. Large-scale water projects—dams, irrigation, and levees, for example—are supported by farm, real estate development, construction, and barge-shipping interest groups; members of key Senate and House committees responsible for these projects, who can claim credit for bringing jobs and federal money to their constituencies; and the Army Corps of Engineers, whose budget and responsibilities grow apace as it builds the projects. Another iron triangle is shown in Figure 7.4.

iron triangle

An enduring alliance of common interest among an interest group, a congressional committee, and a bureaucratic agency.

issue networks

Broad coalitions of public and private interest groups, policy experts, and public officials that form around particular policy issues; said to be more visible to the public and more inclusive than iron triangles.

FIGURE 7.4   THE IRON TRIANGLE: THE COZY POLITICS OF DEFENDING AMERICA

In an iron triangle, an alliance based on common interests, is formed among a powerful corporation or interest group, an agency of the executive branch, and congressional committees or subcommittees. In this example from the defense industry, an alliance is formed among parties that share an interest in the existence and expansion of defense industry contracts. Most scholars think iron triangles are less common today than in the past, though they are alive and well in a number of policy areas, including the one illustrated here.

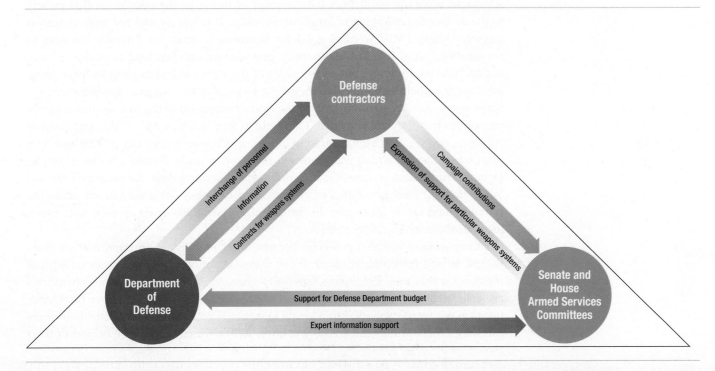

The Privileged Position of Corporations

Economist and political scientist Charles Lindblom argued that corporations wield such disproportionate power in American politics that they undermine democracy. He closed his classic 1977 book *Politics and Markets* with this observation: "The large private corporation fits oddly into democratic theory. Indeed, it does not fit."[60] Twenty years later, political scientist Neil Mitchell concluded his book *The Conspicuous Corporation*, which reported the results of careful empirical testing of Lindblom's ideas, with the conclusion that "business interests (in the United States) are not routinely countervailed in the policy process. Their political resources and incentives to participate are usually greater than other interests."[61] Two decades after Mitchell, Benjamin Page and Martin published their ground-breaking data-driven study of distortions in American democracy *Democracy in America?*, observing at one point that "...organized interest groups—especially business corporations—have much more clout [than ordinary citizens]" Let's see why these scholars reached their somber conclusion about the **privileged position of business** in American politics.

Remember that corporations and business trade associations representing groups of corporations enjoy many advantages over others in the political process. The largest corporations are far ahead of their competitors in the number of lobbyists they employ, the level of resources they can and do use for political purposes, their ability to shape public perceptions and opinions through such instruments as issue advertising and subsidization of business-oriented think tanks like the American Enterprise Institute and the CATO Institute, and the ease of access they often have to government officials.

An additional source of big-business power is the high regard in which business is held in American society and the central and honored place of business values in our culture. Faith in private enterprise gives special advantages to the central institution of private enterprise, the corporation. Any political leader contemplating hostile action against corporations must contend with business's special place of honor in the United States. To be sure, scandals involving large business enterprises such as Enron, Wells Fargo, Equifax, and BP can tarnish big business now and then, but in the long run, as President Coolidge is known to have once famously said, "The business of America is business."

Business corporations are also unusually influential because the health of the American economy—and thus the standard of living of the people—is tied closely to the economic well-being of large corporations. It is widely and not entirely unreasonably believed that what is good for business is good for America. Because of corporations' vital role in the economy, government officials tend to interpret them not as "special interests" but as the voice of the national interest and to listen more attentively to their demands than they do to those of other sectors of American society. Some companies are so important for the overall operation of the American and global economies that they are considered "too big to fail," such as AIG, Citigroup, Bank of America, and General Motors, among others, which were bailed out in 2008 and 2009 even when their downfall was from self-inflicted wounds. To take another example, Donald Trump and congressional Republicans defended their massive 2017 tax cut bill—where at least two-thirds of cuts went to business—as a way to stimulate the economy and create more jobs. In this sense, corporations enjoy an especially privileged position in American politics.

Corporations are also powerful because their mobility is an important counterweight to any government effort (local, state, or national) to raise taxes or impose regulations that business deems especially onerous. Increasingly, large corporations are able to design, produce, and market their goods and services all over the world; they are not irrevocably tied to a single location. If government threatens their interests, large corporations can credibly counter with a threat to move all or part of their

privileged position of business
The notion advanced by some political scientists that the business sector, most especially the large corporate sector, is consistently and persistently advantaged over other interests or societal actors in bringing influence to bear on government.

operations elsewhere. In this new global economic environment, political leaders are increasingly of a mind to maintain a friendly and supportive business climate.

The broad political reach of big business is illustrated by the Koch Network, a collection of groups organized by Robert and Charles Koch, the owners of the multi-billion dollar, privately-held Koch Industries.[62] The brothers Koch have founded and provide most of the funding for organizations such as the CATO Institute and the Mercatus Center at George Mason University, which propagate libertarian and small government ideas and doctrines; Citizens for a Sound Economy and the American Energy Alliance, which advocate for low taxes and deregulation and try to debunk the idea of global warming; the Koch Seminars, which annually bring together business, cultural, and government leaders to learn about the merits of private enterprise and the evils of big government; and Americans for Prosperity to organize and mobilize Republican and Republican-leaning voters at election time. The Koch Network also includes Themis/ i360 to gather voter data and Aegis Strategic to advise pro-free market, pro-small government Republican candidates. Robert and Charles Koch and Koch Industries also contribute to political campaigns of favored Republican candidates as well as to various campaign funding organizations such as 501s, 527s, and super PACs. Such a broad political operation, one that perhaps rivals the Republican Party itself, requires the inspiration and financial support of two of the richest people in the world whose combined net worth far outpaces the net worth of the richest person in the world, Bill Gates.[63]

Another way to see the influence of business corporations in our national political life is to look at the story of the increasingly business-friendly decisions of the Supreme Court under Chief Justice John Roberts. Recent research demonstrates that the Roberts Court is the most pro-business Court since the end of Second World War. In fact, five of the ten most pro-business justices since that time were members of the Roberts Court until the death of Justice Scalia (in February 2016) reduced that number to four for a short time. (The historical tilt toward business was restored in early 2017 when business-friendly conservative Neil Gorsuch joined the Court.). Even justices with consistently liberal votes on civil rights, civil liberties, and social justice matters—Stephen Breyer, Elena Kagan, and Sonia Sotomayor—have sided with business in 40 percent of the cases involving issues ranging from anti-trust and copyrights to union and employee rights.[64]

Further evidence of business success before the Court involves the U.S. Chamber of Commerce, one of our most important business advocacy associations, whose judicial success has been growing steadily. Before the Burger Court (1981–1993), the chamber was on the winning side of cases 43 percent of the time, grew to a 56 percent win rate during the Rehnquist years (1994–2004), and 70 percent during the Roberts years spanning 2006–2014.[65] In 2017, after Gorsuch joined the Court, the U.S. Chamber was on the winning side in 13 out of 17 cases, or almost 80 percent of the time.[66] The Court is likely to be even more favorable to business with Brett Kavanaugh's appointment in 2018. We can best understand the pro-business decisions on the Roberts Court, a story told in Figure 7.5, through an application of our analytical framework.

Large corporations do not, of course, run the show entirely. Although they have the most resources, for instance, these resources do not translate automatically into real political influence. For example, one interest group may have enormous resource advantages over other interest groups but may use its resources ineffectively. Or an interest group with great resources may be opposed by a coalition of other interest groups that together are able to mobilize impressive resources of their own. A powerful interest group may also find that an elected politician is not cooperative because the voters in the district are of a different mind from the interest group. So even with this immense set of resources, business power does not automatically and inevitably translate into political power.[67]

Nor does business always get its way in Washington. There are many issues of great importance on which business in general, or one corporation in particular, loses in the give-and-take of politics. There are times when business finds itself squared off

FIGURE 7.5 APPLYING THE FRAMEWORK: HOW HAS BUSINESS FARED ON THE ROBERTS COURT?

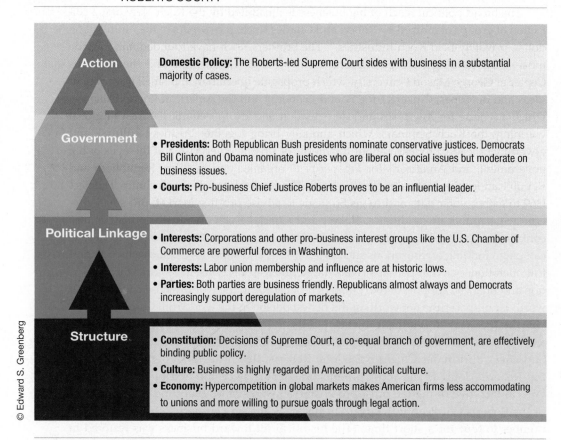

Action — **Domestic Policy:** The Roberts-led Supreme Court sides with business in a substantial majority of cases.

Government
- **Presidents:** Both Republican Bush presidents nominate conservative justices. Democrats Bill Clinton and Obama nominate justices who are liberal on social issues but moderate on business issues.
- **Courts:** Pro-business Chief Justice Roberts proves to be an influential leader.

Political Linkage
- **Interests:** Corporations and other pro-business interest groups like the U.S. Chamber of Commerce are powerful forces in Washington.
- **Interests:** Labor union membership and influence are at historic lows.
- **Parties:** Both parties are business friendly. Republicans almost always and Democrats increasingly support deregulation of markets.

Structure
- **Constitution:** Decisions of Supreme Court, a co-equal branch of government, are effectively binding public policy.
- **Culture:** Business is highly regarded in American political culture.
- **Economy:** Hypercompetition in global markets makes American firms less accommodating to unions and more willing to pursue goals through legal action.

© Edward S. Greenberg

SOURCE: Lee Epstein, William M. Landes, and Richard A. Posner, "How Business Fares in the Supreme Court," *Minnesota Law Review* 97, no. 1 (2012); Lee Epstein, William M. Landes, and Richard A Posner, "When It Comes to Business, the Right and Left Sides of the Court Agree," *University Journal of Law and Policy* 54 (September 16, 2013), pp. 33–55. Also see Tom Donnelly, "Roberts at Ten: Chief Justice Roberts and Big Business," (Washington, D.C.: The Constitutional Accountability Center, issue brief, July 30, 2015).

against powerful coalitions of other interest groups (labor, consumer, and environmentalist groups, let us say). Corporations have not gotten their way on loosening immigration controls or expanding the pool of H1-B visas, something that would have allowed them access to a larger pool of cheap labor had they won on the former and a pool of highly skilled scientific and technical workers had they won on the latter. On many occasions, corporations also find themselves at odds with one another on public policy issues. Thus, Internet service providers, computer and handheld device makers, software developers, and the music and film industries are locked in a battle over the ease of file-sharing and royalty compensation for distributed copyrighted material.

Corporations are most powerful when they can build alliances among themselves. When corporations feel that their collective interests are at stake, however—as on taxes, regulation, labor law, and executive compensation—they tend to come together to form powerful and virtually unbeatable political coalitions.[68] Large corporations and the wealthy—the vast majority of the top 1 percent derive their wealth from their positions as corporate executives, hedge fund managers, and the leaders of financial firms, so corporations and the wealthy can be understood as one and the same—recently have won some notable long-term victories:[69]

1. The long-term tax rates on the super-wealthy have declined since the 1960s (see Figure 7.6).

2. The 2017 tax cut bill's main benefits went to wealthy Americans and U.S. corporations, so long-term rates on them likely will continue to fall in the future. Indeed,

in 2018, corporate tax returns as a share of the economy was the lowest it had been in three quarters of a century.[70]

3. The minimum wage has hardly increased at all over the past three decades and trails annual increases in the cost of living.

4. The financial services industry was deregulated (with disastrous results in 2008).

5. Laws were passed shielding corporate executives from lawsuits by stockholders, thereby allowing executive compensation to skyrocket in the 1990s and 2000s.

6. IRS audits of top income earners decreased over the past three decades even as audits of the working poor recently increased (those who use the Earned Income Tax Credit).

7. The National Labor Relations Board became less willing during the 1980s, 1990s, and 2000s to penalize corporations for illegal anti-union activities.

8. Though the published corporate tax rate was 35 percent, the effective rate prior to the 2017 tax cut law (reduced to 21 percent under the new law)—what large, profitable corporations actually pay as a percentage of their earnings—was only 12.6 because of credits, exclusions, and shelters.[71]

9. Using the Congressional Review Act, which allows each new Congress the authority to rescind Executive Branch rules issued late in a president's term, the GOP Congress and President Trump in early 2017 did away with rules restricting coal company dumping in streams and requiring energy companies to disclose payments made to foreign governments.

FIGURE 7.6 INCOME TAX RATES FOR THE WEALTHIEST AMERICANS

Income tax rates for the wealthiest Americans, particularly the super-wealthy, have dropped dramatically since 1960. The drops occurred not only when Republicans were in control in Washington, but during the Democratic Carter administration and during periods when Democrats controlled Congress and Republicans held the presidency. The data suggest that the political influence of rich Americans has been fairly constant—regardless of the party heading the government. Because of cuts in estate tax and corporate tax rates in the 2017 tax cut law, average tax rates for the wealthiest Americans are likely to decline.

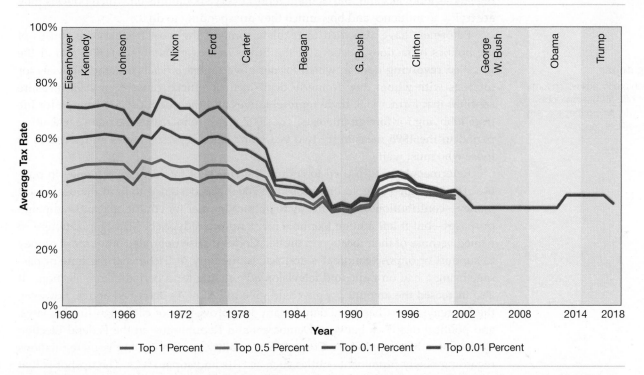

SOURCE: Data prior to 2002 are from Thomas Piketty and Emmanuel Saez, "How Progressive Is the U.S. Federal Tax System?" Working Paper 12404, National Bureau of Economic Research (July 2006), Table A3. All other data are authors' calculations based on Internal Revenue Service tax rate tables.

These "wins" on important government policies that advance corporations' interests support political scientist David Vogel's observation that "when business is both mobilized and unified, its political power can be formidable."[72] Until recently, interest group specialists in political science had not been able to empirically demonstrate links between things like money spent in lobbying or campaign contributions and specific votes in Congress or major federal policy developments.[73] But a growing body of ground-breaking empirical research shows that what the government in Washington does is overwhelmingly tied to the wishes of the wealthiest Americans and interest groups that represent our largest corporations and not to the wishes of average citizens.[74]

In our view, the best way to think about corporations in American politics is to see their power waxing and waning within their overall privileged position. Corporate power may be greater at certain times and weaker at other times, but it is always in a game in which, most of the time, corporations enjoy advantages over other groups in society. If corporations feel that their collective interests are at stake—as when labor unions are particularly aggressive or when government's regulatory burden is perceived to be too heavy—and they are able to present a united front, they are simply unbeatable. This cannot be said about any other sector of American society.[75]

CURING THE MISCHIEF OF FACTIONS

7.6 Assess the effectiveness of regulations designed to control interest groups.

Americans have worried about the "mischief of factions" ever since James Madison wrote about them in *The Federalist* No. 10. Over the years, various things have been tried to control the purported negative effects of these special interests.[76] Disclosure has been the principal tool of regulation. In 1946, Congress imposed a requirement (in the Federal Regulation of Lobbying Act) that all lobbyists working in Congress be registered. The Lobby Disclosure Act of 1995 requires a wider range of political actors to register as lobbyists and makes them report every six months on which policies they are trying to influence and how much they are spending to do it.

revolving door

The common practice in which former government officials become lobbyists for interests with whom they formerly dealt in their official capacity.

Reformers have also tried to regulate some of the most troublesome abuses of the politics of factions. Sections of the Ethics in Government Act (1978) aim at the so-called **revolving door** in which former government officials become lobbyists for interests with whom they formerly dealt in their official capacity. A 1995 measure specifies that former U.S. trade representatives and their deputies are banned for life from lobbying for foreign interests. The 2007 measure increases the one-year waiting period in the 1995 measure to two years and adds representatives and senators to those who must wait.

Reformers have also tried to control the effects of interest group money in politics. The McCain–Feingold bill, passed in 2002, was designed to limit the use of soft money—contributions made directly to political parties for educational and campaign purposes—but it left a huge loophole for nonprofit, advocacy 527 organizations—so named because of their location in the Tax Code—to use unlimited amounts of money to support or oppose candidates and issues, the only restrictions at the time of passage being a ban on radio and television advertising for a period before elections. It also increased the amount people could give to PACs. As described above, however, the Supreme Court has invalidated many key provisions of campaign finance laws, and political deadlock between Democrats and Republicans on the Federal Election Commission has crippled the Commission's ability to examine and issue regulations regarding newly prominent entities such as 501s and super PACs. The upshot is that that interest and advocacy groups have virtual free rein in financing candidates and advocating policies in federal election campaigns.

Another measure passed in 2007 requires congressional leaders to identify all **earmarks** in appropriations bills and post them to the Internet at least forty-eight hours before their consideration by the full House and Senate, along with information about their sponsors and intended purposes. The same measures require lobbyists to certify that no one in their firm or organization has provided gifts to members of Congress or their staffs and post this to a site on the Internet. In addition, the measures require lobbyists to file and post quarterly reports online of their lobbying activities in Congress.

The 2007 lobbying reform measure was passed in the wake of the corruption conviction of super-lobbyist Jack Abramoff, revelations of widespread influence peddling by lobbyists who formerly worked in Congress or the executive branch agencies, and the explosion of special interest earmarks in appropriations bills. Most keen Washington observers remain unconvinced that these rules will diminish in a major way the influence of privileged interest groups in shaping what government does. Like water seeking its own level, it may be that powerful and wealthy interests will find a way to have their needs and wishes attended to in one way or another.

earmarks
Budget items that appropriate money for specific pet projects of members of Congress, usually done at the behest of lobbyists, and added to bills at the last minute with little opportunity of deliberation.

INTEREST GROUPS: DO THEY HELP OR HINDER AMERICAN DEMOCRACY?

There is no doubt that the interest group system plays an important role in shaping what government does in the United States; elected officials pay lots of attention to them, for all the reasons explored in this chapter. Whether the interest group system advances or retards democracy, however, can only be determined by knowing which sectors of the American population are represented by interest groups and how well interest groups represent the people they claim to be representing. There is considerable disagreement regarding the role that interest groups play in American politics and governance.

Many believe the interest group system enhances democracy because it gives individuals and groups in American society another tool to keep elected and appointed officials responsible and responsive to their needs, wants, and interests. Political parties are important for making popular sovereignty work, to be sure, but being broad and inclusive umbrella organizations, they often ignore the interests of particular groups. And, although elections are essential for keeping public officials on their toes, they happen only every two to four years. Proponents of this pluralist view argue that the day-to-day work of popular sovereignty is done mainly by interest groups. In addition, pluralists point to the rise of advocacy groups—supported by thousands of ordinary people with ordinary incomes—as an indication that the interest group system is being leveled, with a wider range of groups representing a broad swath of the population now playing a key role in the political game.

However, more than ample evidence suggests that narrow, special, and privileged interests dominate the interest group world and play the biggest role in determining what government does in the United States. The powerful interest groups that play the largest role in shaping public policies in the United States represent, by and large, wealthier and better-educated Americans, corporations, and other business interests and professionals, such as doctors and lawyers. In this view, the proliferation of interest groups, mostly in the form of associations and firms that represent business, has made American politics less and less democratic. This inequality of access and influence violates the democratic principle of political equality, with less influence in the hands of ordinary Americans. Thus, some argue, the present interest group system poses a real threat to democratic ideals.

REVIEW THE CHAPTER

INTEREST GROUPS IN A DEMOCRATIC SOCIETY: CONTRASTING VIEWPOINTS

7.1 Compare and contrast opposing viewpoints about the role of interest groups in a democracy.

Americans have long denigrated special interests as contrary to the public good. Many political scientists, however, see interest groups as an important addition to the representation process in a democracy, enhancing the contact of citizens with government officials in the periods between elections.

THE UNIVERSE OF INTEREST GROUPS

7.2 Describe different types of interest groups.

Private interests are organizations and associations that try to gain protections or material advantages from government for their own members rather than for society at large. For the most part, these represent economic interests of one kind or another.

Public interests are organizations and associations that try to gain protections or benefits for people beyond their own members, often for society at large. Public interests are motivated by ideological or issue concerns.

INTEREST GROUP FORMATION AND PROLIFERATION

7.3 Explain why interest groups form and proliferate.

There has been a significant expansion in the number of public interest or citizen groups since 1968.

The United States provides a rich environment for interest groups because of our constitutional system, our political culture, and the broad responsibilities of our government.

Interests tend to proliferate in a complex and changing society, which creates a diversity of interests.

Government does more than it did in the past and affects the interests of various people, groups, and firms who organize to exert influence over laws and regulations.

WHAT INTEREST GROUPS DO

7.4 Analyze the methods and activities interest groups use to influence political outcomes.

One way interest groups attempt to influence the shape of public policy is the inside game: interest group representatives are in direct contact with government officials and try to build influence on the basis of personal relationships.

The outside game is being played when an interest group tries to mobilize local constituencies and shape public opinion to support the group's goals and to bring that pressure to bear on elected officials.

INTEREST GROUPS, CORPORATE POWER, AND INEQUALITY IN AMERICAN POLITICS

7.5 Describe the inequalities of the interest group system.

Some groups, especially corporations, trade associations, high-income professionals, and the wealthy, have more resources to put into lobbying officials and better access to them than other groups.

The business corporation enjoys what has been called a "privileged position" in American society that substantially enhances its influence on government policies.

Business corporations and the wealthy made big gains in a number of important areas of government policy during the past two decades, particularly on policies related to taxes, financial deregulation, and executive compensation.

CURING THE MISCHIEF OF FACTIONS

7.6 Assess the effectiveness of regulations designed to control interest groups.

Lobbying reform has focused on requiring interest and advocacy groups to report on their lobbying activities, trying to control the revolving door, and limiting what private and public interest groups are allowed to spend in elections.

LEARN THE TERMS

advocacy groups   Interest groups organized to support a cause or ideology.

amicus curiae   Latin for "friend of the court"; a legal brief in which individuals not party to a suit may have their views heard in court.

disturbance theory   A theory positing that interest groups originate with changes in the economic, social, or political environment that threaten the well-being of some segment of the population.

earmarks   Budget items that appropriate money for specific pet projects of members of Congress, usually done at the behest of lobbyists, and added to bills at the last minute with little opportunity for deliberation.

factions   James Madison's term for groups or parties that try to advance their own interests at the expense of the public good.

grassroots lobbying   The effort by interest groups to mobilize local constituencies, shape public opinion to support the group's goals, and bring that pressure to bear on elected officials.

interest groups   Private organizations or voluntary associations that seek to influence public policy as a way to protect or advance their interests.

iron triangle   An enduring alliance of common interest among an interest group, a congressional committee, and a bureaucratic agency.

issue networks   Broad coalitions of public and private interest groups, policy experts, and public officials that form around particular policy issues; said to be more visible to the public and more inclusive than iron triangles.

labor union   An organization representing employees that bargains with employers over wages, benefits, and working conditions.

lobbying   Effort by an interest or advocacy group to influence the behavior of a public official.

lobbyist   A person who attempts to influence the behavior of public officials on behalf of an interest group.

pluralism   The political science position that American democracy is best understood in terms of the interaction, conflict, and bargaining of groups.

political action committee (PAC)   An entity created by an interest group whose purpose is to collect money and make contributions to candidates in federal elections.

private interests   Interest groups that seek to protect or advance the material interests of their members.

privileged position of business   The notion advanced by some political scientists that the business sector, most especially the large corporate sector, is consistently and persistently advantaged over other interests or societal actors in bringing influence to bear on government.

public interests   Interest groups that work to gain protections or benefits for society at large.

revolving door   The common practice in which former government officials become lobbyists for interests with whom they formerly dealt in their official capacity.

test case   A case brought by advocacy or interest groups to try to force a ruling on the constitutionality of some law or executive action.

CHAPTER 8

DEMANDING THE RIGHT TO VOTE

Women's struggle to gain the vote blew hot and cold for more than 130 years, but persistence paid off at last in 1920 when the Nineteenth Amendment was ratified. *How might one explain why such a basic democratic right—votes for women— was so long in coming?*

SOCIAL MOVEMENTS

CHAPTER OUTLINE AND LEARNING OBJECTIVES

WHAT ARE SOCIAL MOVEMENTS?

8.1 Define social movements and who they represent.

MAJOR SOCIAL MOVEMENTS IN THE UNITED STATES

8.2 Discuss the important social movements that have shaped American society.

THE ROLE OF SOCIAL MOVEMENTS IN A DEMOCRACY

8.3 Evaluate how social movements make U.S. politics more democratic.

FACTORS THAT ENCOURAGE THE FORMATION OF SOCIAL MOVEMENTS

8.4 Identify the factors that give rise to social movements.

TACTICS OF SOCIAL MOVEMENTS

8.5 Identify tactics commonly used by social movements.

WHY DO SOME SOCIAL MOVEMENTS SUCCEED AND OTHERS FAIL?

8.6 Determine what makes a social movement successful.

The Struggle for Democracy

Meeting at Seneca Falls, New York, in 1848, a group of women who had been active in the abolitionist movement to end slavery issued a declaration written by Elizabeth Cady Stanton proclaiming that "all men and women are created equal, endowed with the same inalienable rights." The Seneca Falls Declaration, much like the Declaration of Independence on which it was modeled, then presented a long list of violations of rights. It remains one of the most eloquent statements of women's equality ever written, but it had no immediate effect because most politically active women (and men) in the abolitionist movement believed that their first order of business was to end slavery. Women's rights would have to wait.

After the Civil War destroyed the slave system, women's rights leaders such as Stanton, Susan B. Anthony, and Lucy Stone pressed for equal citizenship rights for all, white and black, male and female. They were bitterly disappointed when the Fourteenth Amendment, ratified after the war, declared full citizenship rights for all males born or naturalized in the United States, including those who had been slaves, but failed to include women. Women's rights activists realized they would have to fight for rights on their own, with their own organizations.

Women's rights organizations were formed soon after the Civil War. For more than two decades, though, the National Woman Suffrage Association (NWSA) and the American Woman Suffrage Association (AWSA) feuded over how to pressure male politicians. Susan B. Anthony (with the NWSA) and Lucy Stone (with the AWSA) were divided by temperament and ideology. Anthony favored pressing for a broad range of rights and organized dramatic actions to expose men's hypocrisy. At an 1876 centennial celebration of the United States in Philadelphia, Anthony and several other women marched onto the platform, where the emperor of Brazil and other dignitaries sat, and read the declaration aloud. Stone favored gaining the vote as the primary objective of the rights movement and used quieter methods of persuasion, such as petitions.

In 1890, the two main organizations joined to form the National American Woman Suffrage Association (NAWSA). They dropped such controversial NWSA demands as divorce reform and legalized prostitution in favor of one order of business: women's suffrage. The movement was now focused, united, and growing more powerful every year.

In 1912, NAWSA organized a march to support a constitutional amendment for suffrage. More than five thousand women paraded through the streets of Washington before Woodrow Wilson's inauguration. The police offered the marchers no protection from antagonistic spectators who pelted them with rotten fruit and vegetables and an occasional rock, despite the legal parade permit they had obtained. This lack of protection outraged the public and attracted media attention to the suffrage movement.

Almost immediately after the United States entered World War I in April 1917 with the express purpose of "making the world safe for democracy," women began to picket the White House, demanding that full democracy be instituted in America. One demonstrator's sign quoted directly from President Wilson's war message, "We shall fight . . . for the right of those who submit to authority to have a voice in their own government,"[1] and asked why women were excluded from American democracy. As the picketing at the White House picked up numbers and intensity, the police began arresting large groups of women. Other women took their places. The cycle continued until local jails were filled to capacity. When suffragists began a hunger strike in jail, authorities responded with forced feedings and isolation cells. By November, public outrage forced local authorities to relent and free the women. By this time, public opinion had shifted in favor of women's right to vote.

In the years surrounding U.S. entry into the war, other women's groups worked state by state, senator by senator, pressuring male politicians to support women's suffrage. After two prominent senators from New England were defeated in 1918 primarily because of the efforts of suffragists and prohibitionists, the political clout of the women's groups became apparent to most elected officials. In June 1919, Congress passed the Nineteenth Amendment, and the necessary thirty-six states ratified it the following year. By uniting around a common cause, women's organizations gained the right to vote for all women.

*　*　*　*　*

The struggle for women's suffrage (i.e., the right to vote) was long and difficult. The main instrument for winning the struggle to amend the Constitution to admit women to full citizenship was a powerful social movement that dared to challenge the status quo, used unconventional tactics to gain attention and sympathy, and demanded bravery and commitment from many women.[2]

Although few social movements have been as effective as the women's suffrage movement in reaching their primary goal—winning the vote for women—other social movements have also played an important role in American political life. This chapter is about what social movements are, how and why they form, what tactics they use, and how they affect American political life and what government does.

THINKING CRITICALLY **ABOUT THIS CHAPTER**

This chapter is about the important role of social movements in American government and politics.

APPLYING THE **FRAMEWORK**

You will see in this chapter how social movements are a response to structural changes in the economy, culture, and society and how they affect other political linkage actors and institutions—such as parties, interest groups, and public opinion—and government. Most important, you will learn under what conditions social movements most effectively shape the behavior of elected leaders and the content of government policies.

USING THE **DEMOCRACY STANDARD**

At first glance, because social movements are most often the political instrument of numerical minorities, it may seem that they have little to do with democracy, which is rooted in majority rule. You will see in this chapter, however, that social movements play an especially important role in our democracy, principally by broadening public debate on important issues and bringing outsiders and nonparticipants into the political arena.

WHAT ARE SOCIAL MOVEMENTS?

8.1 Define social movements and who they represent.

Social movements are loosely organized collections of ordinary people, working outside normal political channels, to get their voices heard by the public at large, the news media, leaders of major institutions, and government officials in order to promote, resist, or undo some social change. They are different from interest groups, which are longer lasting and more organized. Interest groups, for example,

social movements

Loosely organized groups with large numbers of people who use unconventional and often disruptive tactics to have their grievances heard by the public, the news media, and government leaders.

have permanent employees and budgets and are more committed to conventional and nondisruptive methods of galvanizing support, such as lobbying and issue advertising. They are different from political parties, whose main purpose is to win elective offices for candidates who campaign under the party banner and to control government and what government does across a broad range of policies. Social movements are more ephemeral in nature, coming and going as people feel they are needed, sometimes leaving their mark on public policies, sometimes not. What sets social movements apart from parties and interest groups is their focus on deeply felt causes and their tendency to act outside normal channels of government and politics, using unconventional and often disruptive tactics.[3] Some scholars call social movement politics "contentious politics."[4] When suffragists disrupted meetings, went on hunger strikes, and marched to demand the right to vote, they were engaged in contentious politics. The most important such social movement in recent times was the civil rights movement, which pressed demands for equal treatment for African Americans on the American public and elected officials, primarily during the 1960s.

This general definition of social movements requires further elaboration if we are to understand the totality of their role in American politics.[5]

- *Social movements are the political instrument of political outsiders.* Social movements often help people who are outside the political mainstream gain a hearing from the public and from political decision makers. The women's suffrage movement forced the issue of votes for women onto the public agenda. The civil rights movement did the same for the issue of equal citizenship for African Americans. Gays and lesbians forced the country to pay attention to issues that had long been left "in the closet." Insiders don't need social movements; they can rely instead on interest groups, political action committees (PACs), lobbyists, campaign contributions, and the like to make their voices heard.

  Christian conservatives, who were outsiders at one time largely ignored by the cultural and political establishment, are now a political force comprising many

STRIKING FOR JUSTICE

Farmers rarely use the protest tactic, but these poor farmers from Minnesota, facing financial ruin because of a collapse in commodity prices during the Great Depression, felt they needed to do something dramatic to call attention to their plight. The federal government, in the form of Franklin Roosevelt's New Deal, responded with a series of largely successful commodity price and relief programs that saved many family farms.

Is the federal government today as responsive as it was in the past to such protests?

well-established interest groups, such as the Family Research Council, with remarkable influence within the Republican Party. Their grassroots movement to resist the general secularization of American life and to promote their vision of religious values in American life was built at first around local churches and Bible reading groups and often took the form of protests, whether at abortion clinics or at government locations where some religious symbol (like a manger scene at Christmastime) was ordered removed by the courts because it violated the principle of separation of church and state.

- *Social movements are generally mass grassroots phenomena.* Because outsiders and excluded groups often lack the financial and political resources of insiders, they must take advantage of what they have: numbers, energy, and commitment. They depend on the participation of large numbers of ordinary people to act in ways that will move the general public and persuade public officials to address issues of concern to those in the movement. The extraordinary protests against gun violence that created the "March for our lives" demonstrations in Washington, DC, and in other American cities large and small in March, 2018, were initiated by students from Sherman Douglas High School in Florida most of whom were not old enough to vote.

- *Social movements are populated by individuals with a shared sense of grievance.* People would not take on the considerable risks involved in joining others in a social movement unless they felt a strong, shared sense of grievance against the status quo and a desire to bring about social change. Social movements tend to form when a significant number of people come to define their own troubles and problems, not in personal terms but in more general social terms (the belief that there is a common cause for all of their troubles), and when they believe that the government can be moved to take action on their behalf. Because this is a rare combination, social movements are very difficult to organize and sustain.

- *Social movements often use unconventional and disruptive tactics.* Officials and citizens almost always complain that social movements are ill-mannered and disruptive. For social movements, that is precisely the point. Unconventional

#METOO MOVEMENT ON THE MARCH

The election of Donald Trump as president of the United States in 2016—a man accused by several women of sexist behavior and sexual assault—and revelations in 2017 of the widespread sexual harassment and assault by male government, political, entertainment, and cultural leaders, helped spark the rise of the MeToo movement. Here women march in Beverly Hills, California in November 2017 to protest these behaviors and to demand equal treatment in the workplace.

In a democratic country where citizens have the right to vote, why do people sometimes resort to unconventional and disruptive behavior to try to influence politics and government policies? How can such tactics be justified?

and disruptive tactics help gain attention for movement grievances. While successful movements are ones that eventually bring many other Americans and public officials over to their side, it is usually the case that other Americans and public officials are not paying attention to the issues that are of greatest concern to movement participants, so something dramatic needs to be done to change the situation. But they do occur. For example, The "#MeToo" protests against sexual harassment and assault, going viral in late 2017 after revelations of harassment and assault by prominent men in Hollywood, corporations, and government, spurred hundreds of thousands of people across the nation to take to the streets to have their voices heard.

- *Social movements often turn into interest groups.* Although particular social movements eventually fade from the political scene, for reasons we explore later, the more successful ones create organizations that carry on their work over a longer period of time. Thus, the women's movement spawned the National Organization for Women, while the environmental movement created organizations such as the Environmental Defense Fund and the Nature Conservancy. The movement of Christian evangelicals spurred the creation of groups such as the Family Research Council and the National Right to Life Committee.

MAJOR SOCIAL MOVEMENTS IN THE UNITED STATES

8.2 Discuss the important social movements that have shaped American society.

Many social movements have left their mark on American political life and have shaped what government does in the United States.

The Abolitionist Movement

This movement, the objective of which was to end slavery in the United States, was most active in the northern states in the three decades before the outbreak of the Civil War. Its harsh condemnation of the slave system helped heighten the tensions between the North and the South, eventually bringing on the war that ended slavery. Proponents' tactics included antislavery demonstrations and resistance (sometimes violent) to enforcement of the Fugitive Slave Act, which required all states to identify, capture, and return runaway slaves to their owners.

The Populist Movement

The Populist movement was made up of disaffected farmers of the American South and West in the 1880s and 1890s who were angry with business practices and developments in the American economy that were adversely affecting them. Their main grievance was the concentration of economic power in the banking and railroad industries, both of which favored (with loans on better terms, cheaper shipping rates, and the like) larger customers. The aim of the movement was to force public ownership or regulation of banks, grain storage companies, and the railroads. Small demonstrations at banks and at foreclosed farms were part of their repertoire, but they also used the vote. For a short time, they were quite successful, winning control of several state legislatures, sending members to Congress, helping to nominate William Jennings Bryan as the Democratic candidate for president in 1896, and forcing the federal regulation of corporations (e.g., in the Interstate Commerce Act of 1887).

The Women's Suffrage Movement

This movement, active in the late nineteenth and early twentieth centuries, aimed to win women the right to vote. As discussed earlier, in the opener to this chapter, the women's suffrage movement won its objective when the Nineteenth Amendment to the Constitution was ratified in 1920. We also saw that the tactics of the movement were deliberately disruptive and unsettling to many.

The Labor Movement

In the years after it was formed, the labor movement represented efforts by working people to protect jobs, ensure decent wages and benefits, and guarantee safe workplaces. The periods of greatest militancy—when working people took to the streets and the factory floors to demand recognition of their unions—were in the 1880s, the 1890s, and the 1930s. (The movement's militancy during the Great Depression, joined with that of other groups pressing for a more activist government committed to social justice, led to the passage of the Social Security Act in 1935.) The labor movement eventually forced the federal government to recognize the right of working people to form labor unions to represent them in negotiations with management. However, labor unions, the fruit of this successful movement, have been steadily losing members, especially in the private sector, where only 6.5 percent of employees were members of unions in 2017.

The Civil Rights Movement

The civil rights movement began in the mid-1950s and reached the peak of its activity in the mid-1960s. It gradually lost steam after that (see Figure 8.1) but remains one of the most influential social movements on record, having pressed successfully for the end of formal segregation in the South and many (but not all) discriminatory practices across the nation. The primary weapons of the movement were mass demonstrations and nonviolent **civil disobedience**, a conscious refusal to obey a law considered unfair, unjust, or unconstitutional, courting arrest by the authorities and assault from others, without offering resistance, as a way to highlight injustice and gain broader public sympathy.[6] In 1968, the outbreak of violence in urban centers after the assassination of Martin Luther King Jr. and, at the same time, the rise in prominence of black power advocates like Stokely Carmichael and Malcolm X,[7] who rejected nonviolence as a basic principle, marked the end of the movement for many people.

civil disobedience
Intentionally breaking a law and accepting the consequences as a way to publicize the unjustness of the law.

Contemporary Antiwar Movements

Antiwar movements have accompanied virtually every war the United States has waged, including U.S. military interventions in Southeast Asia and the Middle East. The anti–Vietnam War movement of the late 1960s and early 1970s used a wide variety of tactics to end the war, from mass demonstrations to voting registration and nonviolent civil disobedience. Fringe elements turned to violence as the war escalated, as exemplified by the Days of Rage vandalism along Chicago's Gold Coast mounted by a radicalized wing of Students for a Democratic Society and the bombing of a research lab at the University of Wisconsin in which a graduate student was killed.

An anti–Iraq War movement quickly formed in the months leading up to the U.S. invasion of Iraq in 2003. The movement's most dramatic political act was the organization of massive demonstrations across the world on February 15, 2003. In the United States, demonstrations took place in 150 cities. In New York, the crowd converged on the headquarters of the United Nations, filling 20 city blocks along First and Second

FIGURE 8.1 TIMELINE: THE CIVIL RIGHTS MOVEMENT (1954–1968)

The civil rights movement lasted only for a decade and a half but it profoundly changed American life, influencing the passage of landmark national, state, and local legislation for equal rights; a turnabout in the judicial interpretation of the constitutionality of state-sanctioned separation of the races in schools, transportation, and public accommodations; and the opening up of channels of social mobility for many African Americans. This timeline shows landmark events in the history of this movement.

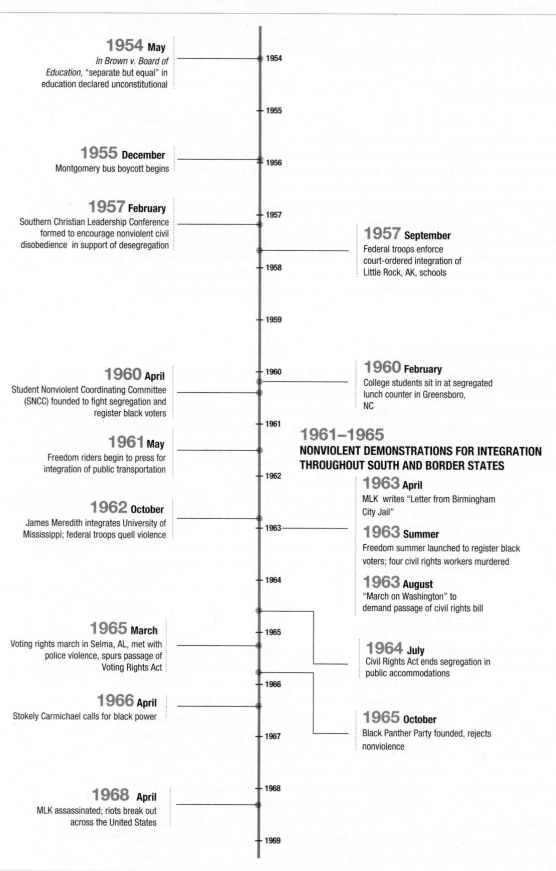

1954 May
In *Brown v. Board of Education,* "separate but equal" in education declared unconstitutional

1955 December
Montgomery bus boycott begins

1957 February
Southern Christian Leadership Conference formed to encourage nonviolent civil disobedience in support of desegregation

1957 September
Federal troops enforce court-ordered integration of Little Rock, AK, schools

1960 April
Student Nonviolent Coordinating Committee (SNCC) founded to fight segregation and register black voters

1960 February
College students sit in at segregated lunch counter in Greensboro, NC

1961 May
Freedom riders begin to press for integration of public transportation

1961–1965
NONVIOLENT DEMONSTRATIONS FOR INTEGRATION THROUGHOUT SOUTH AND BORDER STATES

1962 October
James Meredith integrates University of Mississippi; federal troops quell violence

1963 April
MLK writes "Letter from Birmingham City Jail"

1963 Summer
Freedom summer launched to register black voters; four civil rights workers murdered

1963 August
"March on Washington" to demand passage of civil rights bill

1965 March
Voting rights march in Selma, AL, met with police violence, spurs passage of Voting Rights Act

1964 July
Civil Rights Act ends segregation in public accommodations

1966 April
Stokely Carmichael calls for black power

1965 October
Black Panther Party founded, rejects nonviolence

1968 April
MLK assassinated; riots break out across the United States

1954
1955
1956
1957
1958
1959
1960
1961
1962
1963
1964
1965
1966
1967
1968
1969

Avenues.[8] Demonstrations against intervention also took place around the world, especially in western Europe (see Figure 8.2). The massive demonstrations did not convince President Bush to put off the Iraq invasion, however. The movement lost support after the invasion of Iraq in April 2003, as troops went into battle and patriotic feelings rose, but the subsequent insurgency, and the high cost to the United States of the insurgency in lives and money, rekindled the movement in late 2005. Changing public opinion on the war, some of it perhaps attributable to the antiwar demonstrations, helped set the stage for the Republicans' big losses in the 2006 congressional elections.

FIGURE 8.2 DEMONSTRATIONS AGAINST THE INVASION OF IRAQ

Roughly 16 million people worldwide gathered over the weekend of February 13–15, 2003, to protest the coming invasion of Iraq by the United States. Researchers at Worldmapper found evidence of protest demonstrations in ninety-six of the world's mapped countries and territories. The map below, which depicts each country's demonstrators as a proportion of the total number of demonstrators worldwide, shows that the largest demonstrations took place in Europe. Purple shading indicates that country's government opposed the war, while green shading indicates that country's government supported the war, with darker colors indicating that a greater percentage of the country's population protested the war. The map demonstrates the mixed effects of protests. In some of the countries with the largest protests—Italy, Spain, Portugal, Denmark, and the United Kingdom—the government supported the war in Iraq. Roll over each country to see the percentage of the population that responded positively to the statement of, "Yes, the United States plays a positive role for peace in the world." It is worth noting, however, that the map's estimates of the size of demonstrations are just that—estimates—though whenever possible, the researchers depended on more than a single source, leaning toward academic, press, and official estimates rather than those of the demonstration organizers.

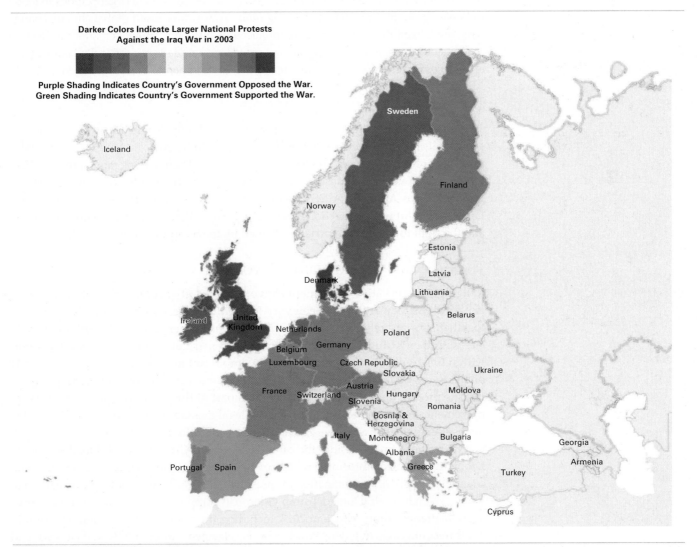

SOURCE: Worldmapper, "International Demonstrations," Map No. 361; www.worldmapper.org. Used with permission.

Equal Rights Amendment (ERA)

Proposed amendment to the U.S. Constitution stating that equality of rights shall not be abridged or denied on account of a person's gender; it failed to win the approval of the necessary number of states.

The Women's Movement

This movement has been important in American life since the late 1960s. Its aim has been to win civil rights protections for women and to broaden the participation of women in all aspects of American society, economy, and politics. Although it did not win one of its main objectives—passage of the **Equal Rights Amendment (ERA)** to the U.S. Constitution that guaranteed equal treatment for men and women by all levels of government—the broad advance of women on virtually all fronts in the United States attests to its overall effectiveness. (The movement has been sufficiently successful, in fact, that it helped trigger a countermovement among religious conservatives of all denominations who were worried about purported threats to traditional family values.) The most recent iteration of this movement has been the widespread "Me Too" demonstrations around the nation against sexual harassment and assault.

The Environmental Movement

The environmental movement has been active in the United States since the early 1970s. Its aim has been to encourage government regulation of damaging environmental practices and to raise the environmental sympathies of the public. While the vitality of the movement has waxed and waned over the years, the public's strong support for environmental regulation suggests that it has been unusually successful. Although its proponents have sometimes used disruptive and even violent tactics, the movement has depended more on legal challenges to business practices and the creation of organizations to lobby in Washington. Rising concerns among many Americans about global climate change have revitalized the movement and enhanced its influence. However, after the election of Donald Trump, many environmental protection regulations were rolled back by his appointees in the Interior Department and the Environmental Protection Agency.

The Gay and Lesbian Movements

These movements began in earnest in the late 1960s. Their aim was to gain the same civil rights protections under the law enjoyed by African Americans and other minority groups and to gain respect from the public. Their actions ranged from patient lobbying and voting to mass demonstrations and deliberately shocking actions by groups such as ACT-UP (AIDS Coalition to Unleash Power). These movements were fairly successful with protections granted to LGBTQ Americans nationally and locally and the right to same-sex marriage affirmed by the Supreme Court in 2015.

The Religious Conservative Movement

Religious conservative movements have occurred at several different moments in American history and have been very influential. These movements have brought together strongly religious people trying to infuse American society and public policies with their values. The contemporary movement of religious conservatives falls within this tradition and has become very important in American politics, especially on the issues of abortion, school prayer, educational curriculum, and marriage equality. The pro-life (anti-abortion) movement is part of this larger religious conservative movement. Its main objective is to end the legal availability of abortion in the United States. Religious conservatives have become especially influential in the Republican Party. One need only consider the candidacies of Ted Cruz, Marco Rubio, Ben Carson, Bobby Jindal, Rick Santorum, and Mike Huckabee—religious conservatives all—who sought the Republican nomination for president in 2016. Though not a particularly religious person himself, Donald Trump vigorously supported the Christian conservative agenda after assuming office in 2017, including the administration's support for religious freedom cases in federal courts. He also elevated conservatives Neil Gorsuch and Brett Kavanaugh to the Supreme Court in 2017 and 2018.

The Anti-Globalization Movement

In 1999, an emergent anti-globalization movement announced itself with demonstrations in Seattle targeted at the World Trade Organization (WTO), whose trade ministers were meeting to fashion an agreement to further open national borders to trade and foreign investment.[9] The demonstrations were mostly peaceful, but some demonstrators turned violent. The movement is extremely diverse and includes people who are worried about the effects of globalization on the environment, income inequality in the United States and elsewhere, food safety, labor rights, sweat shops, unfair trade, and national sovereignty. The movement remains intermittently active, with protesters showing up en masse at large WTO gatherings, as well as those hosted by the World Bank, the International Monetary Fund, the World Economic Forum (which meets annually in Davos, Switzerland), and the G8. Note that while the anti-globalization movement has usually been of the left-wing variety—at the presidential campaign level, think of Senator Bernie Sanders—there also are right-wing varieties embodied in Donald Trump's strongest supporters, who want to protect the borders against immigrants, remove undocumented people from the United States, and keep corporations from moving American jobs overseas.

The Tea Party Movement

The Tea Party movement exploded onto the American political scene on tax deadline day, April 15, 2009, with demonstrations in scores of locations around the country denouncing bank bailouts, the Democrats' health care reform effort, rising government deficits, taxes and regulations, illegal immigration, and, for many among the participants, the legality of the Obama presidency. Urged on by conservative talk radio hosts and the intense coverage of their activities by Fox News and funded by the energy

FIGURE 8.3 TEA PARTY PROPRONENTS ON THE ISSUES

Polls show that while Tea Party identifiers are overwhelmingly Republican, they are from the most conservative wing of the party, with stronger anti-government and anti-immigration views than mainstream Republicans. Their views diverge even farther from those of all registered voters. An opinion poll conducted right after the Tea Party's rise to prominence in the 2010 national elections demonstrates that a determined minority can be successful in very low turnout elections such as party primaries and off-year congressional elections when there is no presidential contest.

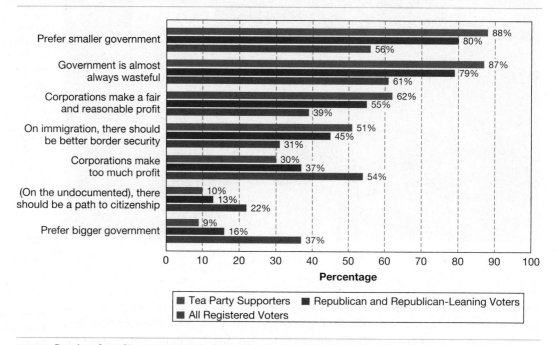

SOURCE: Data from Scott Clement and John C. Green, "The Tea Party and Religion," Pew Forum on Religion & Public Life Project, Pew Research Center, February 23, 2011.

fortune of brothers David and Charles Koch,[10] the Tea Party staged a series of demonstrations across the country and mobilized in August 2009 to flood and take over health care town hall meetings held by Democratic members of Congress. By 2010, it had become a major force within the Republican Party, defeating many establishment candidates with Tea Party adherents and helping Republicans win control of legislatures and governorships in many states and U.S. House of Representatives. The movement seems to represent a modern-day angry populism directed against an activist federal government that, in the view of movement activists and followers, has been taking too many taxes from hardworking people and saddling the country with huge debts, all for programs that support the undeserving poor (people unwilling to work) and those who are in the country illegally. (See Figure 8.3 for how Tea Party sympathizers differ from other Americans and other Republicans.)

The Occupy Wall Street Movement

Organized almost wholly through social media, Occupy Wall Street came to public attention in September 2011 when protestors staged an encampment protest at Zuccotti Park in the Wall Street section of New York City. Occupy sites rapidly spread from New York to other cities and communities across the country.

Though the message of the movement was somewhat garbled because of the many diverse groups it attracted, a common underlying theme alleged economic unfairness, asserting the failure of government to do anything about diminished job prospects, stagnant wages, crippling student loan debt, declining living standards, or rising income and wealth inequality while bailing out banks whose top executives raked in bonus upon bonus. The movement meme, "We are the 99 percent,"

OCCUPATIONAL HAZARDS
The Occupy Wall Street movement was formed not only to protest rising income inequality and dim job prospects for young workers but to highlight the possibilities of community, and all it entails. Protesters formed their own cleaning crews when public officials suggested that sanitation concerns would force occupiers out of their Zuccotti Park encampment. *Has Occupy Wall Street had a lasting or only a fleeting impact?*

contends that most of the gains of economic growth over the past two decades have flowed only up, to the top 1 percent. Some labor unions joined the protests, and many celebrities voiced support and made contributions. Because the movement believed in occupation-style action—in setting up tents, feeding stations, libraries, first-aid centers, and the like in public-space encampments—police eventually moved in to clear away demonstrators, with officials citing safety and sanitation concerns as their motivation. In New York, closing down the Occupy site was relatively peaceful; in Oakland and Berkeley evictions proved to be more violent. Though the movement has receded from view recently, its issues—from anger at Wall Street to the hollowing out of the middle class—are sufficiently consistent with the views of a substantial number of Americans to suggest that it will reappear from time to time. As the Zuccotti Park occupation moved into its second month, a Pew poll showed that 39 percent of Americans said they agreed with the movement's goals, more than said they supported the Tea Party's (32 percent).[11] Echoes of the Occupy Wall Street movement were prominent in Bernie Sanders's campaign for the Democratic presidential nomination in 2016.

The "Black Lives Matter" Movement

Black Lives Matter started in July 2013 as a hashtag tweeted by three community organizers to express their concern about a spate of high-profile acts of police violence involving white officers and African American victims.[12] The hashtag—#BlackLivesMatter—quickly evolved into a grass roots and highly decentralized social movement of significant political importance. The movement is demanding policy changes that include restrictions on the use of deadly force by the police, police training in racial bias, better recordkeeping of the incidence of police brutality, criminal justice reform, and the hiring of more police officers that reflect minority communities.[13]

Black Lives Matter has all the markings of a social movement: it is comprised of political outsiders, it leverages the numbers, energy, and commitment of those who are aggrieved, and it has used unconventional and disruptive tactics to gain attention. Black Lives Matter has held protests and marches in cities across the country, and movement leaders have not been afraid to confront political candidates directly. While the movement claims no partisan affiliation, activists have sought attention from Democratic candidates who have more potential than Republican candidates to be allies in their cause.

BLACK LIVES MATTER

Here, in 2016, demonstrators march to protest yet another shooting by police of an unarmed African American man under the banner of the Black Lives Matter movement. The movement has influenced some political leaders and police administrators to change a range of police tactics, but it has also sparked a strong counter-attack from those who believe the movement unfairly criticizes police and puts them in danger.

How do you feel about this contemporary conflict? Are movements like this good for democracy or do they disrupt daily life too much and create social divisions that make compromise less likely? Explain.

For their part, certain Democratic candidates for elective office have expressed tentative support for the movement. In a private meeting with movement leaders during her 2016 presidential campaign, Hillary Clinton acknowledged the problems that black Americans face but did not agree that the problems originate from inherently racist policies.[14] Her response reflected a concern among some liberals who sympathize with the cause but believe that the movement's rhetoric and tactics are too divisive. Alternatively, Republican candidates in the 2015–2016 election cycle used opposition to Black Lives Matter to rally their own support. In an attempt to position themselves favorably with law-and-order voters who are protective of police and with voters who don't believe that black Americans are subject to discrimination, they argued that the movement vilifies law enforcement and prioritizes the lives of black Americans over all others.

THE ROLE OF SOCIAL MOVEMENTS IN A DEMOCRACY

8.3 Evaluate how social movements make U.S. politics more democratic.

At first glance, social movements may not seem to conform very well to democratic principles. First, social movements usually start out as small minorities, whereas democracy requires majority rule. Second, social movements often use disruptive tactics—though rarely overtly violent ones—to announce their grievances when many "legitimate" democratic channels already exist (e.g., voting, petitioning, and the public expression of views). This section discusses how social movements can (and often do) help make American politics more democratic.

Encouraging Participation

Social movements may increase the level of popular involvement and interest in politics. In one sense, this is true simply by definition: social movements are the instruments of outsiders. Thus, the women's suffrage movement convinced many middle-class women that their activities need not be confined exclusively to home, family, church, and charity work and encouraged them to venture into political life by gathering petitions or joining demonstrations demanding the vote for women. In the 1960s, the civil rights movement encouraged southern African Americans, who had long been barred from the political life of their communities, to become active in their own emancipation. The religious evangelical movement spurred the involvement of previously politically apathetic evangelicals. The pro-immigration movement may yet spur increased political participation by Hispanic citizens.

Social movements also encourage popular participation by dramatizing and bringing to public attention a range of issues that have been ignored or have been dealt with behind closed doors. Their contentious actions make these movements' members highly visible because, they offer irresistible fare for the television camera. This ability to make politics more visible—called broadening the **scope of conflict** by political scientist E. E. Schattschneider[15]—makes politics the province of the many rather than the few.

Overcoming Political Inequality

Social movements also sometimes allow individuals and groups without substantial resources to enter the game of politics. Many social movements are made up of people who do not have access to the money, time, contacts, or organizational resources that fuel normal politics.[16] The ability of those without resources to disrupt the status quo by mobilizing thousands to take to the streets to voice their demands—what sociologists call **mass mobilization**—is a powerful political tool for the seemingly politically powerless. In the right circumstances, the disruptive politics of social groups can become as politically useful as other conventional resources, such as money or votes.

Creating New Majorities

When social movements, the province of numerical minorities, persuade enough citizens that what they want is reasonable, they may, over time, help create new majorities in society. Before the 1930s, for instance, only a minority of Americans may have been convinced that labor unions were a good idea. The **Great Depression** and a vigorous, militant labor movement changed the opinion of the nation, thus providing the basis for federal laws protecting the right of working people to unionize. In another example, such issues as gender-based job discrimination and pay inequity were not important to the general public until they were brought center stage by the women's movement. The anger about sexual harassment and assault that encouraged the rise of the "Me Too" phase of the women's movement increased the number of women seeking elective office at the local, state, and national levels during the 2018 election cycle.

Overcoming Constitutional Inertia

Sometimes it takes the energy and disruption of a social movement to overcome the anti-majoritarian inclinations of our constitutional system.[17] Political scientist Theodore Lowi is particularly perceptive on this issue:

> Our political system is almost perfectly designed to maintain an existing state of affairs. Our system is so designed that only a determined and undoubted majority could make it move. This is why our history is replete with social movements. It takes that kind of energy to get anything like a majority.... Change comes neither from the genius of the system nor from the liberality or wisdom of its supporters and of the organized groups. It comes from new groups or nascent groups—social movements—when the situation is most dramatic.[18]

It is important to note that many of the social reforms of which most Americans are proudest—women's right to vote, equal citizenship rights for African Americans, Social Security, collective bargaining, and environmental protection—have been less the result of "normal" politics than of social movements started by determined and often disruptive minorities.[19]

scope of conflict
Refers to the number of groups involved in a political conflict; a narrow scope of conflict involves a small number of groups, and a wide scope of conflict involves many.

mass mobilization
The process of involving large numbers of people in a social movement.

Great Depression
The period of economic crisis in the United States that lasted from the stock market crash of 1929 to America's entry into World War II.

FACTORS THAT ENCOURAGE THE FORMATION OF SOCIAL MOVEMENTS

8.4 Identify the factors that give rise to social movements.

Social movements do not appear out of nowhere. There are reasons why they form. A certain combination of factors seems necessary for a social movement to develop.[20]

Real or Perceived Distress

Safe, prosperous, respected, and contented people generally have no need of social movements. By contrast, those whose lives are difficult, unsafe, threatened, or disrespected often find social movements an attractive means of calling attention to their plight and of pressing for changes in the status quo.[21]

Social distress caused by economic, social, and technological change helped create the conditions for the rise of most of the major social movements in American history. Western and southern farmers who suffered great economic reverses during the latter part of the 19th century engendered the Populist movement. The virtual collapse of the industrial sector of the American economy during the 1930s, with historically unprecedented levels of unemployment and widespread destitution, catalyzed the labor movement. The perception that religious and family values have been declining in American life has given rise to the Christian conservative movement. For many women who were entering the job market in increasing numbers during the 1960s and 1970s, discriminatory hiring, blocked career advancement—in the form of the "glass ceiling" and the "mommy track"—and unequal pay made participation in the women's movement irresistible.[22] Discrimination, police harassment, and violence spurred gay, lesbian, and transsexual people to turn to "contentious politics."[23]

The AIDS epidemic added to their distress and stimulated further political participation.[24] The purported threat of mass illegal migration to the United States triggered the rise of the Minutemen, armed volunteers with white nationalist leanings to help control the border with Mexico, and a more general movement dedicated to stopping

ON THE BORDER

Their apparel notwithstanding, these men are not federal agents but members of the Minutemen Militia, private citizens who run freelance patrols along the southern U.S. border, claiming action is needed to counter an invading army of illegal immigrants. *Do vigilante actions of groups like the Minutemen help or hurt the anti-immigration cause?*

immigration and deporting undocumented people that contributed to the election of Donald Trump in 2016. The Great Recession, rising student loan debt, and the slow job recovery that followed sowed the seeds for the Occupy Wall Street movement on the left and the Tea Party movement on the right.

Ironically, the rise of one social movement demanding a change in how its people are regarded and treated often triggers the rise of a countermovement among people who come to feel distressed in turn. Thus, the women's and gay and lesbian movements were powerful stimulants for the rise of the Christian conservative movement, whose proponents worried that traditional family values were under assault. Civil rights advances and the diversification of the American population, much of these facilitated by or perceived to be facilitated by the federal government, contributed to the rise of scattered anti-government and anti-diversity white power groups and militias. Some of their actions have included the bombing of a federal office building in Oklahoma City in 1995 by Timothy McVeigh and associates that killed 168 people and the neo-nazi and alt-right demonstrators in Charlottesville in 2017 where counter-demonstrators were attacked with many resulting in injuries and one death.[25]

Availability of Resources for Mobilization

Although social strain and distress are almost always present in any society, social movements occur, it seems, only when aggrieved people have sufficient resources to organize.[26] A pool of potential leaders and a set of institutions that can provide infrastructure and money are particularly helpful. The grievances expressed by the labor movement had existed for a long time in the United States but not until a few unions developed—generating talented leaders like John L. Lewis and Walter Reuther and widespread media attention—did the movement take off. The nonviolent civil rights movement led by Martin Luther King Jr. found traction in the 1960s partly because network newscasts, which had just increased from fifteen to thirty minutes, filled out their programming schedules with the drama of civil rights demonstrations and the sometimes violent responses to them. The women's movement's assets included a sizable population of educated and skilled women, a lively women's press, and a broad network of meetings to talk about common problems.[27] The Christian conservative movement could build on a base of skilled clergy, an expanding evangelical church membership, religious television and radio networks, and highly developed fund-raising technologies. The

PUSHING FEMINISM

Ms. magazine, during its heyday in the 1970s, was a major force in attracting educated women to the women's movement. Gloria Steinem co-founded, edited, and wrote for the magazine. She had already established her journalism credentials before publishing *Ms.* and relied on her extensive contacts in the field to ensure a successful launch.

Could a publication like Ms. *have as much impact today in the age of the Internet as it did in the 1970s?*

anti-globalization and anti–Iraq War movements, highly decentralized and organizationally amorphous, strategically used social networking and mobile communications to spread information, raise money, and organize demonstrations here and abroad.[28]

A Supportive Environment

The rise of social movements also requires the times to be right, in the sense that a degree of support and tolerance for a movement's goals must exist among the public and society's leaders. The civil rights movement took place when support for more equality for African Americans was growing (even in parts of the then-segregated South) and the bad effects of segregation on American foreign policy worried national leaders. Christian conservatives mobilized as the Republican Party was looking at social values and practices to detach traditional Democratic voters from their party. The labor movement's upsurge during the 1930s coincided with the electoral needs of the Democratic Party.[29] The women's movement surged in the early 1970s when public opinion was becoming much more favorable toward women's equality.[30] In 1972, two out of three Americans—the same proportion that said they believed that issues raised by the women's movement were important—supported the proposal for an Equal Rights Amendment.[31] Two years before the Court's landmark decision legalizing same-sex marriage, homosexuality had become widely accepted in American society, even among self-identified Christians; large majorities of Christians in 2013 said that homosexuality should be accepted by society, including 70 percent of Catholics and 66 percent of mainline Protestants.[32] The Pew Research Center reported in 2017 that 62 percent of Americans said they supported the right of same-sex couples to marry; the percentage among Americans under the age of 30 was much higher, at 72 percent.[33] Even among self-identified Christians, large majorities now say that homosexuality should be accepted by society, including 70 percent of Catholics and 66 percent of mainline Protestants. Occupy Wall Street almost surely reflected a widespread sentiment that there is too much income inequality in the country and that government mostly helps the wealthy (54 percent of Americans agreed).[34]

Especially important for a social movement is acceptance of their concerns and demands among elites. A group of corporate leaders in the 1930s, for example, believed that labor peace was crucial for ending the Great Depression and making long-term economic stability possible and openly supported labor union efforts to organize industries and enter into labor-management contracts.[35] As noted earlier, in the 1950s and 1960s, American political leaders—concerned that widespread reports of violence and discrimination against African Americans were undermining U.S. credibility in the struggle against the Soviet Union for the loyalties of people of color in Asia, Africa, and Latin America—were ready for fundamental changes in race relations in the South and supported the civil rights movement. Leaders of the film, music, and television industries, whether for reasons of belief or economic gain, have increased the visibility of LBGT performers and experiences in their productions.

A Sense of Efficacy Among Participants

People on the outside looking in must come to believe that their actions can make a difference and that other citizens and political leaders will listen and respond to their grievances.[36] Political scientists call this I-can-make-a-difference attitude a sense of **political efficacy**. Without a sense of efficacy, grievances might explode into brief demonstrations or riots, but they would not support a long-term effort, commitment, and risk.

It may well be that the highly decentralized and fragmented nature of our political system helps sustain a sense of efficacy because movements often find places in the system where they will be heard by officials. For example, Christian conservatives have had little effect on school curricula in unitary political systems like that of Great Britain, where educational policy is made centrally, so few try to do anything about it.

political efficacy

The sense that an individual can affect what government does.

TELEVISION WITH ATTITUDE

The ensemble dramedy *Orange Is the New Black* had multiple LBGT characters in leading and support roles when it premiered in 2013. But what came first, change on television or change in society?

Did wider societal acceptance of LGBTQ people make it possible for Netflix to "green light" Orange, or have Hollywood writers and producers led society to alter its attitudes?

In the United States, however, they know they can gain the ear of local school boards and state officials where conservative religious belief is strong. For their part, LGBTQ activists have been able to convince public officials and local voters to pass antidiscrimination ordinances in accepting communities—such as San Francisco, California, and Boulder, Colorado—and to win cases in several state courts.

Some scholars have suggested that a strong sense of common identity among protest groups contributes to efficacy. Knowing that one is not alone, that others see the world in common ways and have common concerns, is often the basis for people's willingness to join social movements. Growing LGBTQ identity seems to be an important component of the rising political self-confidence of this movement. The same can be said for Christian conservatives and Tea Party activists.

A Spark to Set Off the Flames

Social movements require, as we have seen, a set of grievances, resources to form and sustain organization, a supportive environment, and a sense of political efficacy, but they also seem to require some dramatic precipitating event (or series of events)—a *catalyst*—to set them in motion. As the chapter-opening story illustrates, passage of the Fourteenth Amendment, which protects the citizenship rights of males, galvanized the early women's suffrage movement. The 1969 Stonewall rebellion—three days of rioting catalyzed by police harassment of patrons of a popular gay bar in New York City's Greenwich Village and Rosa Parks's simple refusal to give up her seat on a Montgomery, Alabama, bus in 1957 inspired countless acts of resistance afterward among gays and lesbians and African Americans. In 2006, Latinos were moved to action after the House passed a bill making illegal immigrants felons, subjecting longtime undocumented immigrants to deportation, and beefing up control of the U.S.–Mexican border. CNBC reporter Rick Santelli's rant on television about President Obama's plan to provide mortgage payment assistance to people who were about to lose their homes helped launch the Tea Party in 2009. News of movie mogul Harvey Weinstein's long history of sexual harassment and assault, coupled with news of sexual misdeeds by male leaders in government, the media, and a broad range of private corporations, was the spark for the massive "#Me Too" demonstrations in late 2017.

TACTICS OF SOCIAL MOVEMENTS

8.5 Identify tactics commonly used by social movements.

Because they often represent people and groups that lack political power, social movements tend to use unconventional tactics, disruption, and dramatic gestures to make themselves heard.[37] The women's suffrage movement, as already discussed, used mass demonstrations and hunger strikes to great effect. The labor movement invented sit-down strikes and plant takeovers as its most effective weapons in the 1930s. Pro-life activists added clinic blockades and the harassment of patients, doctors, and employees to the protest repertoire. The Occupy Wall Street movement learned to commandeer publicly prominent urban spaces such as parks and squares.

The most effective tool of the civil rights movement was nonviolent civil disobedience. Dr. Martin Luther King Jr. was the strongest advocate for and popularizer of this strategy, having borrowed it from Mahatma Gandhi, who used it as part of the campaign that ended British colonial rule in India after World War II.[38] A particularly dramatic and effective use of this tactic took place in Greensboro, North Carolina, on February 1, 1960, when four black students from North Carolina Agricultural and Technical State University sat down at a "whites only" lunch counter in a Woolworth's store and politely asked to be served. When asked to leave, they refused. They remained calm even as a mob of young white men screamed at them, squirted them with ketchup and mustard, and threatened to lynch them. Each day, more students from the college joined them. By the end of the week, more than a thousand black students had joined the sit-in to demand an end to segregation. These actions ignited the South. Within two months, similar sit-ins had taken place in nearly sixty cities across nine states; almost four thousand young people, including a number of white college students from outside the South, had spent a night in jail for their actions. Their bravery galvanized blacks across the nation and generated sympathy among many whites. The student sit-in movement also spawned a new and more impatient civil rights organization, the Student Non-Violent Coordinating Committee (SNCC).

For his part, Dr. King led a massive nonviolent civil disobedience campaign in Birmingham, Alabama, in 1963, demanding the end of segregation in the schools in addition to the **racial integration** of public services, especially public transportation. Nonviolent demonstrators, many of them schoolchildren, were assaulted by snarling police dogs, electric cattle prods, and high-pressure fire hoses that sent demonstrators sprawling. Police Commissioner Eugene "Bull" Connor filled his jails to overflowing with hundreds of young marchers, who resisted only passively, alternately praying and singing "We Shall Overcome." The quiet bravery of the demonstrators and the palpable sense among the nation's leaders that matters were quickly spinning out of control convinced President John Kennedy to introduce historic civil rights legislation for congressional consideration on June 11, 1963.

This is not to say that unconventional and disruptive tactics always work. No matter how peaceful, some tactics fail to strike the right chord. And, at times, fringe elements within movements do things so rancorous that the movement itself is discredited. In the late 1960s, urban riots and the rise of African Americans committed to black power undermined the broad popularity of the civil rights movement. The anti-globalization movement has been similarly

racial integration
Policies that encourage the interaction of different races in schools, public facilities, workplaces, and/or housing.

BIRTH OF A NEW TACTIC
The infant United Auto Workers organized a strike in early 1937 at a plant of America's top auto maker General Motors, in Flint, Michigan. Rather than put a picket line at the factory gates, which could easily be breached by police and replacement workers, the Flint UAW sat in place, daring the police to provoke violence inside the plant where irreplaceable auto-building equipment would be at risk. The sit-down strike lasted for almost six weeks and was entirely successful, with GM ultimately recognizing the UAW as the sole bargaining agent for its manufacturing workers.
Are sit-down strikes a viable tactic for people trying to form labor unions today?

undermined by its anarchist wing, which, committed to violence against property and to confrontations with police, draws attention from television cameras, whether in Seattle, Washington, or Davos, Switzerland.

WHY DO SOME SOCIAL MOVEMENTS SUCCEED AND OTHERS FAIL?

8.6 Determine what makes a social movement successful.

Social movements have had a significant effect on American politics and on what government does. Not all social movements, however, are equally successful, and here is why:[39]

- *The proximity of the movement's goals to American values.* Movements that ask for fuller participation in things that other Americans consider right and proper—such as voting and opportunities for economic advancement—are more likely to strike a responsive chord than movements that demand a redistribution of income from the rich to the poor.

- *The movement's capacity to win public attention and support.* Potential movements that fail to gain attention, either because the news media are not interested or because there is little sympathy for the cause the movement espouses, never get very far. Things become even more problematic when a social movement stimulates the formation of a counter–social movement.

- *The movement's ability to affect the political fortunes of elected leaders.* Politicians tend to pay attention to movements that can affect their electoral fortunes one way or another. If support for the aims of a movement will add to their vote totals among movement members and a broader sympathetic public, politicians likely will be more inclined to help. If opposition to the movement is a better electoral strategy, politicians are likely to act as roadblocks to the movement.

Low-Impact Social Movements

The poor people's movement, which tried to convince Americans to enact policies that would end poverty in the United States, failed to make much of a mark in the late 1960s. This social movement was never able to mobilize a large group of activists, had little support among the general public because of its fairly radical proposals for income redistribution, and was unable to disrupt everyday life significantly or to affect the electoral prospects of politicians.

The modern women's movement, while successful in a number of areas, was unable to win passage of a proposed Equal Rights Amendment (ERA) to the Constitution banning discrimination on the grounds of gender. The ERA failed to receive the votes of three-fourths of the states by the 1979 deadline, mainly because the effort to ratify it stirred up a countermovement among religious conservatives in every religious denomination.[40]

Repressed Social Movements

Social movements committed to radical change tend to threaten widely shared values and interests of powerful individuals, groups,[41] and institutions.[42] As a result, they rarely gain widespread popular support and almost always arouse the hostility of political leaders. Such movements, too, often face repression of one kind or another.[43]

COURAGE UNDER FIRE

In 1963 in Birmingham, Alabama, under the leadership of Chief of Public Safety "Bull" Connor, peaceful civil rights demonstrators protesting segregation were met with fire hoses, police billy clubs, snarling police dogs, and jail. The national and international outcry over the treatment of peaceful protestors contributed to passage of the 1964 Civil Rights Act, which ended most forms of de jure segregation in the United States.

Are there any social movements today that will have an impact as equally momentous as that of the civil rights movement of the 1960s?

In the late nineteenth and early twentieth centuries, for example, the labor movement was hindered by court injunctions forbidding strikes and boycotts, by laws against union formation, by employer-hired armed gangs, and by the National Guard and the U.S. armed forces. In 1877, sixty thousand National Guardsmen were mobilized in ten states to break the first national railroad strike. Ten thousand militiamen were called into action to break the strike against Carnegie Steel in 1892 in Homestead, Pennsylvania, which resulted in the arrest of sixteen strike leaders on conspiracy charges and the indictment of twenty-seven labor leaders for treason.

Partially Successful Social Movements

Some social movements have enough power and public support to generate a favorable response from public officials but not enough to force them to respond in more than partial or halfhearted ways.

- President Franklin D. Roosevelt responded to social movement pressures for strong antipoverty measures during the Great Depression, but the Social Security Act, ultimately, fell far short of movement expectations.[44]

- President Reagan was willing to co-opt pro-life movement rhetoric and to appoint judges sympathetic to its cause but was unwilling to submit anti-abortion legislation to Congress.

- Christian conservatives enjoyed some legislative successes during the height of their power in the 1990s, and they were important voices in the nominations of John Roberts and Samuel Alito to the Supreme Court in 2005, but they failed to achieve some of their primary objectives: enactment of a law to ban late-term (in their words, "partial birth") abortions, passage of a constitutional amendment banning same-sex marriages, and removal of Bill Clinton from the presidency.

LUDLOW MASSACRE, 1914

Siding with mine owners against striking miners in Ludlow, Colorado, the governor ordered the state's national guard to clear the camp where miners and their families were living, forced out of their tiny homes owned by the company, Colorado Fuel and Iron. Joined by company guards and security forces, the national guard attacked the camp with canon, rifles, bayonets, and fire, killing more than two dozen people, including women and children. John D. Rockefeller Jr. owned the company and was roundly criticized for the attack and was called before Congress to testify. Notwithstanding the bad publicity, the violent action worked, for it broke the back of the miners' union in the West.

Would the use of violence against strikers have been possible had the public and elites been more sympathetic to unions?

Movements can be partially successful even if no new laws are passed. Other measures of success include increased respect for members of the movement, changes in fundamental underlying values in society, and increased representation of the group in decision-making bodies. The women's movement has had some of this kind of success though much remains to be done. Although the Equal Rights Amendment (the movement's main goal) failed, women's issues came to the forefront during these years and, to a very substantial degree, the demands of the movement for equal treatment and respect made significant headway in many areas of American life though sexual harassment and assault remain a painful reality.[45] Issues such as pay equity, family leave, sexual harassment, and attention to women's health problems in medical research are now a part of the American political agenda. Women have made important gains economically and are becoming more numerous in the professions, corporate executive positions (although only 20 percent of corporate board members and 6 percent of CEOs of S&P 500 companies in the United States were female in 2017),[46] and political office. In 2016, Hillary Clinton became the first woman to win the presidential nomination of a major political party, though she later lost in the presidential race to Donald Trump. During the 2018 election cycle, a record number of women entered races for public office at all levels in the political system, local, state, and federal.

Successful Social Movements

Social movements that have many supporters, win wide public sympathy, do not challenge the basics of the economic and social orders, and wield some clout in the electoral arena are likely to achieve a substantial number of their goals. The women's suffrage movement is one of the best examples. The civil rights movement is another, yielding after years of struggle the Civil Rights Act of 1964, which banned segregation in places of public accommodations such as hotels and restaurants, and the **1965 Voting Rights Act**, which put the might of the federal government behind efforts to allow African Americans to vote and hold elected office. These enactments helped sound the death knell of the "separate but equal" doctrine enunciated in the infamous *Plessy* decision (1896) and engineered the collapse of legal segregation in the South.

The Voting Rights Act was particularly important in transforming the politics of the South. Black registration and voting turnout increased dramatically all over the region during the late 1960s and the 1970s. Elected black officials filled legislative seats, city council seats, the mayors' offices in large and small cities, and sheriffs' offices. Between 1960 and 2011, the number of elected black officials in the United States increased from a mere 40 to more than 10,500.[47] In the years after passage of the Voting Rights Act, some white politicians, tacking with the new winds of change, began to court the black vote. George Wallace, who first became famous by "standing in the schoolhouse door" to prevent the integration of the University of Alabama and who once kicked off a political campaign with the slogan, "Segregation Now, Segregation Tomorrow, Segregation Forever," actively pursued the black vote in his last run for public office.

To be sure, being successful in achieving specific policy goals may not in the end make matters better for a group across the board. Though the civil rights movement achieved its legislative goals—passage of the Civil Rights Act in 1964 guaranteeing equal treatment in public accommodations and the 1965 Voting Rights Act protecting African Americans' right to vote—the social and economic condition of African Americans today lags behind that of other Americans. This is true with respect to educational attainment, income and wealth, and life expectancy.[48] As we have seen in other places in this book, the Supreme Court has allowed the states to whittle away at African American voting rights. And the rise of the Black Lives Matter movement happened because African American males were much more likely than any other demographic group to die at the hands of the police.

1965 Voting Rights Act
A law that banned racial discrimination in voting across the United States; it gave the federal government broad powers to register voters in a set of states, mostly in the South, that had long practiced election discrimination, and required that such state pre-clear any changes in its election laws with the Department of Justice.

FIGURE 8.4 APPLYING THE FRAMEWORK: OVERTURNING THE DEFENSE OF MARRIAGE ACT (DOMA)

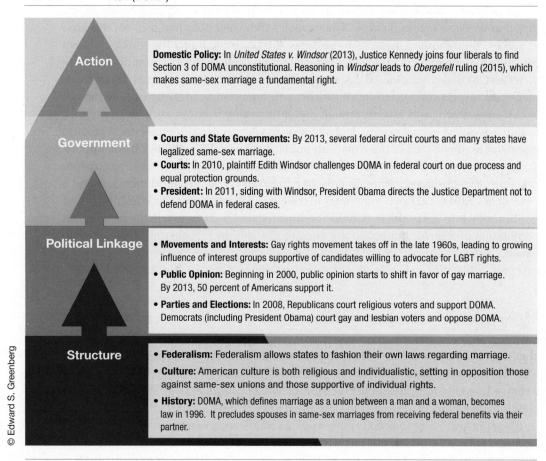

Action

Domestic Policy: In *United States v. Windsor* (2013), Justice Kennedy joins four liberals to find Section 3 of DOMA unconstitutional. Reasoning in *Windsor* leads to *Obergefell* ruling (2015), which makes same-sex marriage a fundamental right.

Government

- **Courts and State Governments:** By 2013, several federal circuit courts and many states have legalized same-sex marriage.
- **Courts:** In 2010, plaintiff Edith Windsor challenges DOMA in federal court on due process and equal protection grounds.
- **President:** In 2011, siding with Windsor, President Obama directs the Justice Department not to defend DOMA in federal cases.

Political Linkage

- **Movements and Interests:** Gay rights movement takes off in the late 1960s, leading to growing influence of interest groups supportive of candidates willing to advocate for LGBT rights.
- **Public Opinion:** Beginning in 2000, public opinion starts to shift in favor of gay marriage. By 2013, 50 percent of Americans support it.
- **Parties and Elections:** In 2008, Republicans court religious voters and support DOMA. Democrats (including President Obama) court gay and lesbian voters and oppose DOMA.

Structure

- **Federalism:** Federalism allows states to fashion their own laws regarding marriage.
- **Culture:** American culture is both religious and individualistic, setting in opposition those against same-sex unions and those supportive of individual rights.
- **History:** DOMA, which defines marriage as a union between a man and a woman, becomes law in 1996. It precludes spouses in same-sex marriages from receiving federal benefits via their partner.

© Edward S. Greenberg

Gays and lesbians reached one of their major goals in 2015 when the Supreme Court ruled in *Obergefell v. Hodges* that laws in states that banned same-sex marriage or that refused to recognize the marriages of same-sex partners performed in other states violated the due process and equal protection clauses of the Fourteenth Amendment. *Obergefell*, in short, established marriage as a fundamental right that states could not violate. The *Obergefell* decision followed an earlier ruling, *United States v. Windsor* (2013). In *Windsor*, the Supreme Court said that a piece of the Defense of Marriage Act (DOMA)—which denied federal benefits such as Social Security, Medicare, joint-return status, veterans' benefits, and inheritance rights to same-sex couples—was unconstitutional. DOMA was enacted in 1996 in response to a state Supreme Court ruling in Hawaii that same-sex marriage was legal in that state. In the *Windsor* case, dissenting justice Antonin Scalia complained that the broad language of the majority opinion, which granted homosexuals "equal liberty and basic dignity," would inevitably open the door in the future to overturning bans on same-sex marriage in all other states. He was right. *Windsor* in 2013 paved the way for the *Obergefell* decision of 2015, a case where again Scalia dissented.

Change of this magnitude is deserving of additional analysis. By applying our analytical framework to the reversal of DOMA (see Figure 8.4), we can piece together the *structural, political linkage,* and *government* factors that led first to the Supreme Court's ruling in *Windsor* and two years later to that in *Obergefell*. Especially important in this analysis is the impact of gay and lesbian activists, their increasing political influence as an organized social movement, and the transformation of public opinion on issues concerning gay and lesbian rights.

SOCIAL MOVEMENTS: DO SOCIAL MOVEMENTS MAKE AMERICA MORE OR LESS DEMOCRATIC?

The story of American democracy has been shaped by social movements—from the first stirrings of rebellion in the British colonies to the emancipation of African American slaves to the granting of the right to vote to women. But in a nation that is supposed to be governed by majority rule, expressed primarily through elections, are social movements that empower minorities truly democratic? Just what role do social movements play in a democracy?

In a perfect democratic society, social movements would be unnecessary; change would happen through political linkages like elections and public opinion and through party and interest group activity. Indeed, a democracy that depended entirely on social movements to bring needed change would not work very effectively at all. But in an imperfect and incomplete democracy like ours, social movements play a valuable and important role, creating an additional linkage between portions of the American public and their government.

Social movements affect our democracy in several ways. First, social movements represent a way—a difficult way, to be sure—by which political outsiders and the politically powerless can become players in the political game. Our constitutional system favors the status quo—federalism, separation of powers, and checks and balances make it extremely difficult to institute fundamentally new policies or to change existing social and economic conditions. Moreover, the primacy of the status quo is further entrenched by the political power of economically and socially privileged groups and individuals who generally resist changes that might undermine their positions. Movements present a way for outsiders to gain a hearing for their grievances, work to win over a majority of their fellow citizens, and persuade elected leaders to take action. Equal citizenship for women and for African Americans, for example, would not have happened at all, or would have been much longer in coming, if not for the existence of social movements demanding change. Thus, social movements are valuable tools for ensuring that popular sovereignty, political equality, and political liberty—the key ingredients in a democracy as we have defined it—are more fully realized.

In some cases, at least theoretically, social movements can pose a threat to democracy. Small minorities who credibly threaten social disruption might occasionally force elected officials to respond to their demands, even though the majority does not favor such action. Some social movements, moreover, push policies that run counter to democratic ideals, making them dangerous for democracy if they take hold. Anti-immigrant movements, for example, tried to deny citizenship rights to people from China and southern and eastern Europe earlier in our history. But threats to the fundamentals of democracy emanating from social movements seem minor compared to the persistent inequalities that arise from other quarters, including interest groups, which we considered in Chapter 7.

WHAT ARE SOCIAL MOVEMENTS?

8.1 Define social movements and who they represent.

Social movements emphasize rather dramatically the point that the struggle for democracy is a recurring feature of our political life.

Social movements are mainly the instruments of political outsiders with grievances who want to gain a hearing in American politics.

MAJOR SOCIAL MOVEMENTS IN THE UNITED STATES

8.2 Discuss the important social movements have shaped American society.

Social movements, by using disruptive tactics and broadening the scope of conflict, can contribute to democracy by increasing the visibility of important issues, encouraging wider participation in public affairs, often creating new majorities, and sometimes providing the energy to overcome the many anti-majoritarian features of our constitutional system.

THE ROLE OF SOCIAL MOVEMENTS IN A DEMOCRACY

8.3 Evaluate how social movements make U.S. politics more democratic.

Social movements often produce changes in government policies.

Social movements try to bring about social change through collective action.

Movements can also serve as a tension-release mechanism for aggrieved groups even when major policy shifts do not happen.

Social movements have had an important effect on our political life and in determining what our government does. Some of our most important legislative landmarks can be attributed to them.

Social movements do not always get what they want. They seem to be most successful when their goals are consistent with the central values of the society, have wide popular support, and fit the needs of political leaders.

FACTORS THAT ENCOURAGE THE FORMATION OF SOCIAL MOVEMENTS

8.4 Identify the factors that give rise to social movements.

Social distress caused by economic, social, and technological change often creates the conditions for the rise of social movements in the United States.

Social distress that encourages the formation of social movements comes from change that proves difficult and unsafe for people, threatens their way of life or basic values, and lessens the respect they feel from others.

Social movements can be a means for calling attention to the plight of their members and pressing for changes in the status quo.

TACTICS OF SOCIAL MOVEMENTS

8.5 Identify tactics commonly used by social movements.

Social movements use unconventional and often disruptive tactics to attract attention to their causes.

A social movement tends to be most successful when the political environment is supportive, in the sense that at least portions of the general population and some public officials are sympathetic to that movement's goals.

Movement ideas often are taken up by one of the major political parties as it seeks to add voters.

To the degree that parties attract new voters and change the views of some of their traditional voters because of social movement activities, elected officials are more likely to be receptive to responding to grievances.

Social movements sometimes spark counter–social movements, which, if strong enough, can make government leaders reluctant to address grievances.

WHY DO SOME SOCIAL MOVEMENTS SUCCEED AND OTHERS FAIL?

8.6 Determine what makes a social movement successful.

Social movements that have many supporters, win wide public sympathy, do not challenge the basics of the economic and social orders, and wield some clout in the electoral arena are most likely to achieve their goals.

LEARN THE TERMS

civil disobedience Intentionally breaking a law and accepting the consequences as a way to publicize the unjustness of the law.

Equal Rights Amendment (ERA) Proposed amendment to the U.S. Constitution stating that equality of rights shall not be abridged or denied on account of a person's gender; it failed to win the approval of the necessary number of states.

Great Depression The period of economic crisis in the United States that lasted from the stock market crash of 1929 to America's entry into World War II.

mass mobilization The process of involving large numbers of people in a social movement.

political efficacy The sense that an individual can affect what government does.

racial integration Policies that encourage the interaction of different races in schools, public facilities, workplaces, and/or housing.

scope of conflict Refers to the number of groups involved in a political conflict; a narrow scope of conflict involves a small number of groups, and a wide scope of conflict involves many.

social movements Loosely organized groups with large numbers of people who use unconventional and often disruptive tactics to have their grievances heard by the public, the news media, and government leaders.

1965 Voting Rights Act A law that banned racial discrimination in voting across the United States; it gave the federal government broad powers to register voters in a set of states, mostly in the South, that had long practiced election discrimination, and required that such state pre-clear any changes in its election laws with the Department of Justice.

CHAPTER 9

DONALD TRUMP CAMPAIGNS IN NORTH CAROLINA

In a shocking upset, Donald Trump defeated Hillary Clinton in the Electoral College, despite losing the popular vote. He won traditionally Democratic states such as Pennsylvania, Michigan, and Wisconsin, by speaking to the economic and social anxieties of disaffected white voters in rural areas.

What economic and social issues were most important to voters who supported Trump's candidacy?

POLITICAL PARTIES

CHAPTER OUTLINE AND LEARNING OBJECTIVES

POLITICAL PARTIES IN DEMOCRATIC SYSTEMS

9.1   Explain how parties can enhance popular sovereignty and political equality in democratic systems.

THE AMERICAN TWO-PARTY SYSTEM

9.2   Explain why America has a two-party system.

THE AMERICAN TWO-PARTY SYSTEM SINCE THE GREAT DEPRESSION

9.3   Trace the evolution of political parties in America since the Great Depression.

THE THREE FUNCTIONS OF TODAY'S POLITICAL PARTIES

9.4   Identify three organizational functions of today's American parties.

The Struggle for Democracy

American politics is controlled by two political parties: the more liberal Democratic Party and the more conservative Republican Party. Despite their differences, the 2016 presidential election and the first two years of the Trump presidency have revealed similar tensions within both parties, most notably, the tension between traditional party voices and populist voices. While the populist voices in the Republican and Democratic parties have different visions for America, they are both particularly frustrated with politics as usual, do not trust party leaders, want government to be more responsive to ordinary people, and are looking for more radical solutions to American economic and social problems than have traditionally been offered.

The Republican Party has long included those who prioritize fiscal conservatism (e.g., lower taxes and smaller government) and those who prioritize social conservatism (e.g., opposition to abortion and same-sex marriage). These two groups, which often overlap, have worked together as the core of the Republican Party for decades. Early in the Obama presidency, a vocal subset of Republicans emerged with socially conservative, anti-elite values, and a very strong belief that government should stay out of their lives and take less of their money. This group came to be known as the "Tea Party" and, within Congress, the "Freedom Caucus." For much of the Obama presidency, there was tension within the Republican Party between traditional Republicans and the Tea Party, with Tea Party supporters resisting any compromise with the Democrats.

The last several years have shown us that the Tea Party was merely a precursor to a larger more significant rift in Republican Party politics. Led by Donald Trump, a group we will call "Populist Nationalist Republicans" has come to be the dominant force in the Republican Party. Populist Nationalist Republicans prioritize anti-elite, anti-immigrant, anti-free-trade, and law and order principles. While Populist Nationalist Republicans may also support small government and socially conservative values, they play second fiddle to more populist concerns. Many of these people are former Tea Partiers who sympathized with Trump's message but, as an analysis by political scientist Dan Hopkins showed, Trump's core supporters are more pro-choice and less concerned about government spending than traditional Republicans.[1]

Going back to his campaign for the presidency, Trump has served as a galvanizing force for people (including some who did not think of themselves as Republicans) who have come to feel deeply abandoned by the American economy. Trump was particularly popular in cities and towns that had been hurt by the rise of automation and outsourcing that contributed to the decline of the American manufacturing industry. This alienation appears to have run deeper and been more widespread than many observers thought before election day—widespread enough for Trump to have won states such as Pennsylvania, Michigan, and Wisconsin that have supported Democrats in presidential elections for some time. The maps on the next page offer some evidence of this by comparing the 2012 and 2016 Presidential election results in the Rust Belt by county. Sliding the bar you will see that these counties were considerably more supportive of the Republican candidate in 2016 than they were in 2012.

Research by political scientist Diana Mutz has also shown that support for Trump was caused by a cultural anxiety among certain white Christian men who feel that the racial and ethnic diversification of America has put their historically dominant status at risk.[2] Trump's anti-immigrant, anti-globalization message meshed with a growing sentiment in many parts of America that the country is "not what it used to be" and that elected politicians in Washington do not care about them. According to studies done by the Pew Research Center, Trump's strongest supporters were predominantly white men without college degrees who believe that things are worse off today than they were fifty years ago. They tend not to see racial diversity as an important goal and believe that undocumented immigrants are likely to commit crimes and take jobs away from Americans.[3]

Despite these intra-party differences, at least 80 percent of Republicans have approved of the job Trump is doing since he took office and most Republicans in Congress have supported

2012 VS. 2016 ELECTION MAPS: CLOSE-UP ON THE MIDWEST

These maps compare presidential election results in 2012 and 2016 in Rust Belt states by county. Much of what was blue (signifying Democratic support) in 2012 became red (signifying Republican support) in 2016. While many of the larger Rust Belt cities like Chicago, Detroit, and Milwaukee continued to support the Democrat in 2016, more suburban counties outside these cities trended much more Republican than they had in recent elections. These suburban shifts gave Donald Trump the votes he needed to win Rust Belt states and the presidency.

Election Competitiveness by County, 2012

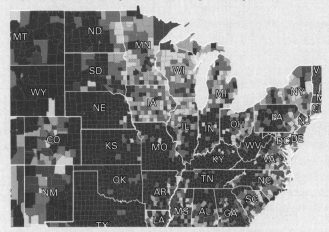

Election Competitiveness by County, 2016

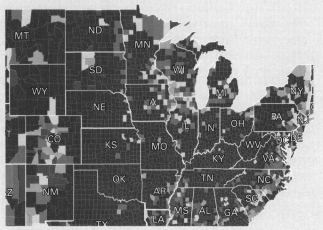

him.[4] Indeed, both sides of the party have worked together to put a conservative justice on the Supreme Court and rollback Obama-era policies such as the health insurance mandate and a wide range of environmental regulations. However, we should be careful not to let this cooperation obscure the complexities of what is going on. The rejection of certain foundational conservative ideals and expectations of presidential behavior by Trump and his supporters has left many traditional Republicans feeling like strangers in their own party. For example, after President Trump fulfilled his campaign promise to remove the United States from the Trans-Pacific Partnership trade agreement, Senator and 2008 Republican presidential nominee John McCain (R-AZ) remarked, "I just think we made a terrible mistake… These are challenging times, and I have to go my own way."[5] John Boehner, who was the Republican Speaker of the House from 2011 to 2015 remarked in 2018 that, "There is no Republican Party. There's a Trump party. The Republican Party is kind of taking a nap somewhere."[6]

While Republican control of government has brought Republican tensions to the surface, Democrats have been able to appear mostly united in opposition to the whole of the Republican Party. Nevertheless, the populist-liberal and moderate wings of the Democratic Party are at odds. More populist working-class liberal Democrats who are concerned about free trade, globalization, and under-regulation of the financial sector are facing off against more upper-middle-class Democrats and wealthy donors who are less concerned about these issues and more focused on achieving liberal social and environmental goals. This tension was most evident in the 2016 Democratic primary where Bernie Sanders, the self-described Democratic Socialist senator from Vermont, challenged Hillary Clinton for the Democratic presidential nomination. Sanders united more liberal and disaffected Democrats around his liberal platform, disgust with Wall Street, and skepticism of free trade. As 2020 approaches and the party is forced to choose a new presidential candidate, the intra-party conflicts are likely to take center stage once again.

A study conducted by *the Washington Post* in March of 2016 showed that supporters of both Bernie Sanders and Donald Trump were especially likely to agree with statements, such as "It doesn't really matter who you vote for because the rich control both political parties" and "The system is stacked against people like me." The Republican and Democratic Parties clearly have different visions for America, but they are facing some of the same challenges from within.

This chapter is about American political parties, how they evolved, what they do, how they work, and how their actions affect the quality of democracy in the United States.

You will see in this chapter how parties work as political linkages that connect the public with government leaders and institutions. You also will see how structural changes in the American economy and society have affected how our political parties function.

Political parties are, in theory, one of the most important instruments for making popular sovereignty and majority rule a reality in a representative democracy—particularly in a system of checks and balances and separated powers such as our own. Evaluating how well our parties carry out these democratic responsibilities is one of the main themes of this chapter.

POLITICAL PARTIES IN DEMOCRATIC SYSTEMS

9.1 Explain how parties can enhance popular sovereignty and political equality in democratic systems.

As we learned in previous chapters, the framers worried about the possible pernicious effects of factions, a category that included interest groups and political parties. According to noted historian Richard Hofstadter, the Founders believed that political parties "create social conflicts that would not otherwise occur, or to aggravate dangerously those that would occur."[7] And yet, political parties formed fairly quickly after the founding in response to disagreements about the role of the national government. Today, most political thinkers believe that political parties are essential to democracy. So, what are political parties and why are they essential?

A **political party** is "a group organized to nominate candidates, to try to win political power through elections, and to promote ideas about public policies."[8] In representative democracies, parties are the principal organizations that recruit candidates for public office, run their candidates in competitive elections, and try to organize and coordinate the activities of government officials under party banners and programs. In going about the business of electing people to office and running government, political parties make it possible for the people to rule by helping them to mobilize majorities and gain power.[9] As renowned political scientist E. E. Schattschnieder once put it, "If democracy means anything at all it means that the majority has the right to organize for the purpose of taking over the government."[10]

In theory, political parties can carry out a number of functions that make popular sovereignty and political equality possible:[11]

- *Parties can keep elected officials responsive.* Competitive party elections help voters choose between alternative policy directions for the future. They also allow voters to make judgments about past performance and decide whether to allow a party

political party

A group organized to nominate candidates, to try to win political power through elections, and to promote ideas about public policies.

platform

A party's statement of its positions on the issues of the day passed at the quadrennial national convention.

to continue in office. Alternatively, a party can adjust its **platform** to better reflect the preferences of voters.

- *Parties can stimulate political interest and participation.* Parties seek to win or retain power in government by mobilizing voters, bringing issues to public attention, and educating the public on issues of interest to the party.[12] By carrying out these functions, political parties can stimulate interest in politics and public affairs and increase participation. The competition that occurs between parties also attracts attention and gets people involved.[13]

- *Parties can ensure accountability.* Parties can help make office holders more accountable. When things go wrong or promises are not kept, it is important for citizens to pinpoint responsibility even when the multiplicity of government offices and branches makes it challenging to do so. Political parties can simplify this difficult task by allowing for collective responsibility. Citizens can pass judgment on the governing ability of a party as a whole and decide whether to retain party incumbents or to throw them out of office.

- *Parties can make sense of complex political issues.* Because most people lack the time or resources to learn about every candidate or every issue on the ballot at any period in time, party labels and party positions act as useful shortcuts for cutting through complexities and reaching decisions that are consistent with one's own values and interests.[14]

- *Parties can make government work.* The U.S. system of separation of powers and checks and balances was designed to make it difficult for government to act quickly. Political parties can encourage cooperation among public officials who, as members of the same party, benefit from their party's collective success. In doing so, parties have the potential to help facilitate *government action*.

The remainder of the chapter explores whether America's political parties execute these responsibilities to democracy. We will see that American political parties fulfill many of the democracy-supporting roles listed above. But we also will see that rising cohesion within America's political parties, intensified competition between them, and the influence of advocacy groups is making it more difficult to achieve the kinds of cooperation needed to allow our political system to address the most important problems facing the nation today.

BERNIE SANDERS CAMPAIGN TOURS THE COUNTRY

Bernie Sanders, running on the slogan "A Future to Believe In," offered Hillary Clinton more of a challenge for the 2016 Democratic nomination than she expected. Despite Clinton's sizable lead, Sanders' dedicated followers urged him to stay in the race and continue to press Clinton from the left. Sanders eventually bowed out and Clinton, as the presumptive nominee, was able to give Sanders a position on the DNC's Platform Committee which helps solidify the party's official position on all major issues. Sanders used this position to force more liberal platform language on trade agreements and nuclear proliferation among other issues.

How important are party platforms for shaping government action?

THE AMERICAN TWO-PARTY SYSTEM

9.2 Explain why America has a two-party system.

More than any other nation in the world, the United States comes closest to having a "pure" **two-party system**, in which two parties vie on relatively equal terms to lead a government. To understand why this is true, we need to examine the rules that structure elections and compare the American system to **multiparty systems**. Multiparty systems, which we see in most Western democracies, tend to have three or more viable parties that compete to lead government.

The Rules of the Game

The rules that organize elections are a *structural* factor in determining what kind of party system the government has. Which rules are chosen, then, have important consequences for a nation's politics. Here we look at two types of electoral systems and consider how they impact the number of major political parties in the country.

PROPORTIONAL REPRESENTATION   Although people in the United States do not use **proportional representation** (PR) to elect their representatives, people in most Western democratic nations do. In PR systems, citizens typically vote for the party rather than the candidate and parties are represented in the legislature in proportion to the percentage of the popular vote the party receives in the election. In a perfect PR system, a party winning 40 percent of the vote would get 40 seats in a 100-seat legislative body, a party winning 22 percent of the vote would get 22 seats, and so on. Because parties win seats so long as they can win a portion of the popular vote, even small parties with narrower appeals have a reason to maintain their separate identities in a PR system. Voters with strong views on an issue or with strong ideological outlooks can vote for a party that closely represents their views. Legislatures in PR systems thus tend to be made up of representatives of many parties that reflect the diverse views of the country.

Israel and the Netherlands come very close to having pure PR systems. However, most Western European nations depart in various ways from the pure form. Many, for instance, vote for slates of party candidates within multimember electoral districts, apportioning seats in each district according to each party's percentage of the vote. In Germany, seats in the Bundestag (the lower house of the national parliament) are filled by a combination of elections from single-member districts and a party's share of the nationwide vote. Most democracies that use proportional representation also have a minimum threshold (often 5 percent) below which no seats are awarded to a party. For example, 21 parties ran in the 2013 Norwegian elections with only eight of them garnering enough support to win parliamentary seats.

SINGLE-MEMBER PLURALITY ELECTIONS   Now let's look at elections in the United States, which are organized on a single-member **plurality** basis. **Single-member districts**—like House congressional districts or states for Senators—are districts where only one person is elected. A plurality election means that the winner is the person that receives the *most* votes, not necessarily a majority of the votes. Single-member plurality elections, often referred to as "winner-take-all" or "first past the post" elections, create a powerful incentive for parties to coalesce and for voters to support one of the two major parties.

A French political scientist named Duverger was the first to document that single-member plurality systems are almost always also two-party systems—we call this phenomenon "**Duverger's Law**."[15] Duverger observed two interconnected reasons that two parties dominate in single-member plurality systems. Both reasons have to do with the inability of minor parties to gain adequate support. First, in winner-take-all elections, there is no reward for coming in second (as there would be in a PR election), so minor parties gain little by running expensive campaigns that they know they are

---

two-party system

A political system in which two parties vie on relatively equal terms to win national elections and in which each party governs at one time or another.

multiparty system

A political system in which three or more viable parties compete to lead the government; because a majority winner is not always possible, multiparty systems often have coalition governments where governing power is shared among two or more parties.

proportional representation

The awarding of legislative seats to political parties to reflect the proportion of the popular vote each party receives.

plurality

Occurs when a candidate receives more votes than any other candidate in an election but still less than a majority.

single-member districts

Districts where the voters elect only one person to represent them. In single-member plurality systems, the person with the most votes (even if they do not have the majority) wins the election.

Duverger's Law

The phenomenon that electoral systems based on single-member plurality districts are almost always dominated by only two parties.

IT'S ALL ABOUT THE ELECTORAL COLLEGE

CNN anchor John King considers the potential electoral college outcomes for the 2008 presidential campaign between Barack Obama and John McCain.

How does having a single-member plurality system impact who wins the Electoral College vote for president?

unlikely to win. Second, voters are not inclined to support minor parties because they do not believe their votes will translate into actual representation—people fear that a vote for a minor party candidate is a "wasted vote" that would be better cast in support of the major party candidate they most closely align with. With little incentive to run candidates and the limited backing of voters, minor parties in single-member plurality systems have difficulty attracting enduring support.

This phenomenon also helps us to understand why disaffected factions within either the Republican or Democratic Parties are unlikely to strike out on their own. They realize that the probability of gaining political office is very low and they have a better chance of influencing change from within. The Tea Party candidates in recent elections are a good example. Knowing they had little chance on their own, they ran as Republicans and pushed the already strongly conservative Republican Party establishment in an even more conservative direction.

Note that the most important office in American government, the presidency, is elected in what is, in effect, a single-member-district (the nation). The candidate who wins a majority of the nation's votes in the Electoral College wins the presidency. A party cannot win a share of the presidency: it is all or nothing. In a parliamentary system, where the executive power is generally lodged in a cabinet and parties may have to cooperate to maintain power, several parties are more likely to be represented within the executive structure.

RESTRICTIONS ON MINOR PARTIES Once a party system is in place, the dominant parties often establish rules that make it difficult for other parties to get on the ballot.[16] These rules vary considerably by country but are particularly strict in the United States, where a number of formidable legal obstacles (such as requirements to obtain a large number of signatures and early filing deadlines) stand in the way of third parties and independent candidates getting on ballots.[17] In addition, the requirements for ballot access are different in every state. The two main parties, with party organizations in place in each state and well-heeled national party committees, are able to navigate this legal patchwork with ease while new and small parties find it quite difficult.

The federal government's partial funding of presidential campaigns has made the situation of third parties even more difficult. Major-party candidates automatically qualify for federal funding once they are nominated. Minor-party candidates must attract a minimum of 5 percent of the votes cast in the previous general election to be eligible for public funding. In recent decades, only the Reform Party, among a legion of minor parties, has managed to cross the threshold to qualify for federal funding. Because the Green Party's candidate, Ralph Nader, won only 2.74 percent of the national vote in the 2000 election, the Greens were not eligible for federal funding for the 2004 election. This hobbled its 2004 presidential candidate, David Cobb, who hardly registered at the polls, winning about 0.1 percent of the vote. Showings like this for minority parties have continued like this. In 2016, Green Party nominee Jill Stein recorded 1.07 percent of the vote, though Libertarian Party nominee Gary Johnson managed 3.28 percent.

Minor Parties in American Politics

Minor parties have played a less important role in the United States than in virtually any other democratic nation and have become even less important over time. In our

entire history, only a single minor party (the Republicans) has managed to replace one of the major parties. Only six (not including the Republicans) have been able to win even 10 percent of the popular vote in a presidential election, and only seven have managed to win a single state in a presidential election. In countries with PR systems, minor parties play a much more important role because they are likely to have at least some representation in the legislature and can work with the bigger parties to make policy.

Minor parties come in a number of forms:

- *Protest parties* sometimes arise as part of a social movement. The Populist Party, for instance, grew out of the western and southern farm protest movements in the late 19th century. The Green Party is an offshoot of the environmental and anti-globalization movements.

- *Ideological parties* are organized around coherent sets of ideas. The Socialist parties—there have been several—have been of this sort, as has the Libertarian Party and the Green Party. In 2000, the Green Party ran on an anti-corporate, anti-globalization platform.

- *Single-issue parties* are barely distinguishable from advocacy groups. What makes them different is their decision to run candidates for office. The now-defunct Prohibition Party and the Free-Soil Party were single-issue parties, as was Ross Perot's "balanced budget" Reform Party in 1996.

- *Splinter parties* form when a faction in one of the two major parties bolts to run its own candidate or candidates (e.g., the Bull Moose Progressive Party of Teddy Roosevelt formed after Roosevelt split with Republican Party regulars in 1912).

Minor parties do a number of things in American politics. Sometimes, they articulate new ideas that are eventually taken over by one or both major parties. Ross Perot's popular crusade for a balanced budget during his 1992 campaign helped nudge the major parties toward a budget agreement that, for a while, eliminated annual deficits in the federal budget. It is also the case that third parties can sometimes change the outcome of presidential contests by changing the outcome of the electoral vote contest in the various states. In 1992, a substantial portion of the Perot votes were cast by people who otherwise would have voted Republican, allowing Bill Clinton to win enough states to beat George H. W. Bush. In 2000, a substantial portion of the Ralph Nader votes in Florida were cast by people who otherwise would have voted Democratic, allowing George W. Bush to win Florida's electoral votes and the presidency over Al Gore.[18]

THE AMERICAN TWO-PARTY SYSTEM SINCE THE GREAT DEPRESSION

9.3   Trace the evolution of political parties in America since the Great Depression.

In the United States, two parties—the Democratic Party and the Republican Party—have dominated the political scene since the Civil War. But even though the same two parties have dominated for a long time, the parties are anything but static. In this section we look at how this dynamic two-party system has changed over the last several generations. Before doing so, though, it is worth briefly considering where today's parties came from. Political party scholar Marjorie Randon Hershey argues that there have really only been five major parties in the history of the United States. For a party to be "major," it must have led at least one of the branches of the national government at one time or another. The origins of those parties (including the Democrats and Republicans) are summarized in Table 9.1. However, the Democrats and Republicans have changed markedly since their births. The Democratic Party was founded in opposition to debt, government spending, and federal intervention into the affairs of the states and became the pro-slavery party before the Civil War. The Republican Party was founded in opposition to slavery and supported government intervention in the economy. As you will see, those positions largely reversed in the 20th century when the Democrats became the big government pro-civil rights party and the Republicans became the limited government party that tapped into the fears of anti-civil rights advocates.

TABLE 9.1   MAJOR POLITICAL PARTIES IN AMERICAN HISTORY

Years Active	Name of Party	Party Origins
1788–1816	Federalist Party	The champion of the new Constitution and strong national government, it was the first American political institution to resemble a political party, although it was not a full-fledged party. Its strength was rooted in the Northeast and the Atlantic Seaboard, where it attracted the support of shopkeepers, manufacturers, financiers, landowners, and other established families of wealth and status. Limited by its narrow electoral base, it soon fell before the success of the Democratic-Republicans.
1800–1832	Democratic-Republican Party	Many of its leaders had been strong proponents of the Constitution but opposed the extreme nationalism of the Federalists. This was a party of the small farmers, workers, and less privileged citizens, plus southern planters, who preferred the authority of the state governments and opposed centralizing power in the national government. Like its leader, Thomas Jefferson, it shared many of the ideals of the French Revolution, especially the extension of the right to vote and the notion of direct popular self-government.
1832–Present	Democratic Party	Growing out of the Jacksonian wing of the Democratic-Republicans, it was the first really broad-based, popular party in the United States. On behalf of a coalition of less-privileged voters, it opposed such business-friendly policies as national banking and high tariffs. It also welcomed the new immigrants (and sought their votes) and opposed nativist (anti-immigrant) sentiment.
1834–1856	Whig Party	This party, too, had roots in the old Democratic-Republican Party, but in the Clay–Adams faction and in opposition to the Jacksonians. Its greatest leaders, Henry Clay and Daniel Webster, stood for legislative supremacy and protested the strong presidency of Andrew Jackson. For its short life, the Whig Party was an unstable coalition of many interests, among them nativism, property, and business and commerce.
1854–Present	Republican Party	Born as the Civil War approached, this was the party of Northern opposition to slavery and its spread to the new territories. Therefore, it was also the party of the Union, the North, Lincoln, the freeing of slaves, victory in the Civil War, and the imposition of Reconstruction on the South. From the Whigs it also inherited a concern for business and industrial expansion.

SOURCE: Marjorie R. Hershey, *Party Politics in America*, 14th ed., © 2011, p. 15. Reprinted and electronically reproduced by permission of Pearson Education, Inc., Upper Saddle River, New Jersey.

Scholars have identified a number of party eras in the United States to help us to better understand why parties are powerful at particular moments in history and how the two-party system has changed over time. Each era is different in one or more important ways from the others. The transition from one era to the next is generally referred to as a **realignment**.[19] There is some disagreement among scholars of the American party system about exactly when party eras began and ended; however, realignments are always reflective of shifting voting coalitions in the country. Though scholars have identified several party eras before the onset of the Great Depression in the 1930s, we focus on the three party eras since then: The New Deal Party Era, the Dealignment Era, and the Polarization Era (see Figure 9.1). Taken together, these three eras tell the story of contemporary American political parties as they developed around the New Deal, reshuffled around civil rights and international conflicts, and settled into the combative ideological camps we see today.

realignment

The process by which one party supplants another as the dominant party in a two-party political system.

The New Deal Party Era

In the years leading up to the Great Depression, American government was primarily controlled by Republicans—mind you, a quite different Republican party than we see

---

FIGURE 9.1 TIMELINE: PARTY ERAS IN THE UNITED STATES, 1900–PRESENT

American politics has been characterized by a series of relatively stable political party eras punctuated by periods of transition—some sudden, others much more drawn out—from one party era to another. Since 1900, there have been four eras in party politics.

Republican Party Domination 1900–1932

In the years leading up to the Great Depression, American government was primarily controlled by Republicans. The politics of the era had moved somewhat beyond the issues of Reconstruction and the focus was largely on Progressive concerns, including the regulation of large corporations, labor practices, and women's suffrage, as well as World War II. The Great Depression, however, changed the political context.

New Deal Party Era 1932–1968

The New Deal Party Era, was marked by the ascendancy of Franklin Roosevelt. It was ushered in with voter support for New Deal policies and an expanding role for the federal government. Seven out of nine presidential elections during this period were won by Democrats.

Dealignment Era 1968–1996

The New Deal coalition began to slowly disintegrate in 1968 after the election of the Republican Richard Nixon. The Dealignment Era was characterized by divided government, with different parties controlling Congress and the presidency at different times. Party membership shifted with the Democratic embrace of civil rights and the antiwar movement. White southerners, blue-collar workers, and religious conservatives began to feel more at home in the Republican Party.

Polarization Era 1996–Present

Since the mid-1990s, American partisan politics has been characterized by a growing hostility between the parties. Democrats and Republicans have been moving farther apart on major issues while simultaneously becoming more averse to compromise.

today. The period featured politics that had moved somewhat beyond the issues of Civil War Reconstruction and the focus was largely on Progressive concerns like the regulation of large corporations, labor issues, and women's suffrage, as well as the First World War. The Great Depression, however, changed the political context and led to the **New Deal Party Era**.

Behind the leadership of President Franklin D. Roosevelt, the modern Democratic Party formed and dominated the American political landscape from 1933 until the late-1960s. During that period, Democrats won seven of nine presidential elections, controlled the Senate and the House of Representatives for all but four years, and prevailed in a substantial majority of governorships and state legislatures across the nation. Democratic dominance was built on an alliance of workers, Catholics, Jews, unionists, small- and medium-sized farmers, urban dwellers, southerners, and blacks that came to be known as the **New Deal coalition**. The New Deal coalition supported an expansion of federal government powers and responsibilities, particularly in the areas of old-age assistance, aid for the poor, encouragement of unionization, subsidies for agriculture, and regulation of business.

The Dealignment Era

The New Deal coalition began to slowly disintegrate in the 1968 election (won by Republican Richard Nixon) and finally collapsed in 1980 when the Republicans captured the presidency and the Senate.[20] What emerged was not a dominant Republican Party but, rather, two parties on relatively equal footing. This form of change in which a dominant party declines without another taking its place is called **dealignment**.

The change in the party system was triggered by three major developments. First, strong support by the Democratic Party for the civil rights movement—which brought new antidiscrimination laws, busing to achieve school integration, and, eventually, minority set-asides for government contracts and affirmative action programs in higher education—caused many white southerners to switch their loyalties from the Democrats to the Republicans. These same positions caused African Americans and Northeastern Republicans to become loyal to the Democrats. The result was that the South, long a Democratic stronghold, became a clear Republican

New Deal Party Era

The party era lasting from the Great Depression to the late 1960s during which the Democrats, originally led by President Franklin D. Roosevelt, dominated government and supported an expansion of federal government powers and responsibilities aimed at steering the economy out of the Great Depression and through the Second World War.

New Deal coalition

The informal electoral alliance of working-class ethnic groups, Catholics, Jews, urban dwellers, racial minorities, and the South that was the basis of the Democratic party dominance of American politics from the New Deal to the early 1970s.

dealignment

A gradual reduction in the dominance of one political party without another party supplanting it.

FDR ADDS TO HIS COALITION

The wealthy and patrician Franklin D. Roosevelt attracted a wide range of common people to his Democratic Party, including industrial workers, poor farmers, and farm laborers. In this photograph, he talks with Georgia farmers during his campaign for the presidency in 1932.

What are the similarities and differences between the coalition that Roosevelt built in the 1930s and the coalition that Trump built in 2016?

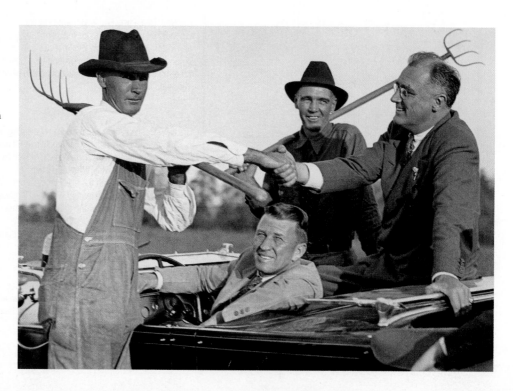

FIGURE 9.2 PRESIDENTIAL ELECTIONS, 1960 AND 2016

These maps show the results of the 1960 and 2016 presidential elections. As you can see, the electoral map has changed markedly over the last 56 years. In the 1960 election, the Democrat John F. Kennedy captured much of the conservative South and much of the liberal Northeast. In 2016, Hillary Clinton won no southern states other than Virginia (though the votes in Florida and North Carolina were very close). The change in the map reflects the shifting voting coalitions that occurred during the Dealignment Era in which rural Southerners changed their party affiliation from Democrat to Republican and many Northeast and West Coast Republicans became Democrats.
How have the changes that have come in each of the party eras impacted Presidential elections?

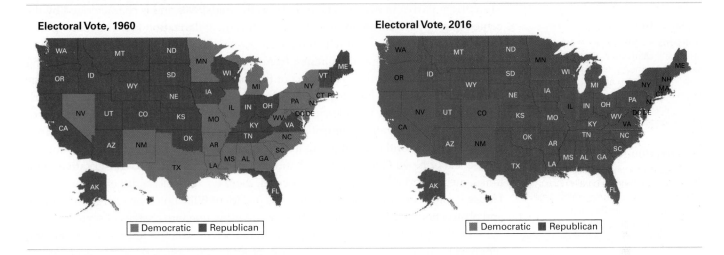

stronghold.[21] This is evidenced in Figure 9.2, which compares the results of the 1960 and 2016 presidential elections. In the 1960 election, the Democrat John F. Kennedy captured much of the conservative South and much of the liberal Northeast. In 2016, Democratic nominee Hillary Clinton won no southern states other than Virginia.

Second, as the Democratic Party became accepting of feminists, gays, and lesbians, it also supported their efforts for equal rights and a strict separation between church and state. Consequently, religious conservatives, who had embraced the Democratic Party for its support of social welfare programs, abandoned it for the Republican Party, which supported more conservative religious values and a closer relationship between church and state.

Third, while the Vietnam War was fought with the support of both Republicans and Democrats, it was the Democratic Party that embraced the anti-war sentiment toward the end of the war. In response, the Republican Party seized the opportunity to be the party that favored a strong national defense. This caused many Democrats who supported a strong military and an aggressive foreign policy to drift toward the Republicans and it set the stage for the Republican Ronald Reagan to campaign on large increases in military spending.

After 1980, the pace of Democratic decline began to pick up, with Democrats losing their big advantage in control of governorships and state legislatures, as well as in **party identification**—fewer people (most notably, in the South) were connecting and identifying with the Democratic Party. Democrats also began to lose control in Congress, first in the Senate and then the House after the 1994 elections. This period was characterized by growing parity between the parties and the existence of **divided government**—one party in control of the presidency and the other with a majority in at least the House or Senate (sometimes both). Divided government was also typical in the states, where Democrats and Republicans divided the governor's office and one or two chambers of state legislatures. Because each party contained a small wing within it open to cooperation with the other party—conservative Democrats, mainly from the South, and liberal Republicans, mainly from the Mid-Atlantic and New England states—a certain degree of **bipartisanship** was possible, especially on foreign and defense policies.

party identification

The sense of belonging to a political party; in the United States this is typically identifying as a Republican or Democrat.

divided government

Control of the executive and legislative branches by different political parties.

bipartisanship

Members of opposing political parties, usually elected officials, acting cooperatively in order to achieve a public policy goal.

Dealignment Era
The party era that lasted from the late 1960s to the early 1990s that was characterized by a gradual reduction in the dominance of the Democratic Party without another party becoming truly dominant.

Polarization Era
The party era that began in the 1990s in which the Democratic and Republican parties became increasingly ideologically different from and hostile toward each other—embracing substantially different visions for country and an unwillingness to compromise.

polarization
The process by which political parties have become more internally consistent in ideology and more ideologically distant from one another; in the U.S. the Republican party has become more conservative and the Democratic party more liberal.

The **Dealignment Era** stands out as being different from the New Deal Party Era (and those eras which preceded it) because it was *not* dominated by one party. In this case, while the dominant Democratic Party lost its overall lead, the Republican Party did not emerge as the unchallenged, across-the-board leader—the parties were fairly equal with respect to both party identification and offices held.[22]

The Polarization Era

The current party era began to take shape in the mid-1990s and is characterized by the contemporary partisan environment. We call this the **Polarization Era**. The term "polarization" refers to the way in which the Democratic and Republican parties are becoming increasingly ideologically different from and hostile toward each other—embracing substantially different visions for the country and an unwillingness to compromise. The exact date this started is hard to pin down, but two developments are particularly important. First, there was the historic victory for Republicans in the congressional elections of 1994 in which they gained control of both houses of Congress for the first time since 1946, with much of the credit going to a unified conservative surge led by Republican House leader Newt Gingrich (R-GA) and supported by an array of conservative think tanks, media, and advocacy groups. Second, there was the successful effort in 1998 by House Republicans to impeach Democratic president Bill Clinton on charges of perjury and obstruction of justice stemming from an investigation into charges of sexual harassment by the President. In a party-line vote in the Senate, Clinton fell just short of being removed from office. At the time, a majority of Americans opposed his impeachment.

By the time of the historic and disputed 2000 Bush–Gore presidential election, the Polarization Era was solidly in place. Since then, elections at all levels of government have been fought by two well-funded and strategically deft parties. The central electoral strategy of the parties has increasingly focused on using emotional appeals to turn out one's own party base voters on Election Day and gaining just enough independents to tip the balance. Adding to the divisiveness is the fact that most election outcomes in state and national races have become extremely close, with Democratic and Republican votes closely divided, and control of government seemingly hanging in the balance at every election.[23]

In the governing process, bipartisanship largely left the scene; consultations across the aisles in Congress and between the president and Congress during periods of divided government became rare. So wedded are the parties to core policy positions that compromise with the other party have come to be seen as traitorous. Underlying it all has been a fundamental settling in of a new electoral geography defined by the shift of the South to the Republicans and the Northeast and coastal West to the Democrats.

Of course, American politics is no stranger to partisanship; Democratic and Republican leaders have always been in the business of making the other party look bad. It's good politics. However, most veteran observers of American politics agree that things are getting worse.[24] Democrats and Republicans in Washington and across the country have become engaged in increasingly bitter disputes over many issues. Incivility has become the order of any day on which party leaders and elected officials deal with one another. Opponents in Congress accuse each other of being liars and cowards instead of colleagues, and, more often than not, those who try to work together are vilified by their co-partisans.

There is some debate about whether this party polarization is just an elite affair or a true reflection of the views in the mass electorate. One leading scholar has pointed out that while party office holders, activists, and advocacy groups associated with each party have become more internally unified and partisan, the public at large remains fairly moderate or middle-of-the-road on most issues that deeply divide the parties from one another.[25] Other leading scholars have simultaneously noticed that informed and active voters have become more ideologically polarized in recent years.[26]

AT THE BOILING POINT

Republican members of Congress show their displeasure with President Barack Obama during his 2009 address to Congress in which he outlined his health care reform proposal. Representative Joe Wilson of South Carolina, in the center of the photo, shocked much of the country when he shouted out "you lie" in response to the president's statement that his plan would not insure immigrants illegally in the country. While the incident was roundly criticized and Wilson later apologized, it demonstrates the poisonous level of party division that has prevailed in Washington.

Does heightened partisanship serve a useful purpose in our system of government, or does it make successful self-government less likely?

What accounts for the intense polarization of American politics today? Scholars and journalists have lots of ideas on this. Many point to the explosion in the number and influence of liberal and conservative advocacy groups that demand unity on bedrock issues such as tax rates and immigration restrictions as well as social-media bubbles that prevent exposure to alternative viewpoints. Others point to the increased number of "safe" congressional districts that allow most representatives to win elections without considering the opinions of voters from the other party. These safe congressional districts come from carefully redrawn district lines and from an increasingly sorted public where Democrats are more likely to live near Democrats and Republicans are more likely to live near Republicans.[27] Still others suggest that our presidential primary system forces candidates to play too much to their party bases. Candidates get partisans angry with the other party and fearful of a world where the other party controls government—something that has become even easier in the age of social media.[28]

The Trump presidency may eventually alter the nature of the Polarization Era. While the liberal versus conservative divide remains very strong and meaningful, the country may also be splitting along lines related to attitudes about trade and immigration. These are issues that have not traditionally fit neatly into the Democrat and Republican categories. For example, Democratic Presidents Bill Clinton and Barack Obama and Republican President George W. Bush were all supporters of free trade and paths to citizenship for undocumented immigrants. The Republican Trump, however, built his coalition on opposition to free trade and the deportation of undocumented immigrants.

THE THREE FUNCTIONS OF TODAY'S POLITICAL PARTIES

9.4 Identify three organizational functions of today's American parties.

Though our multi-branch representative system has led two major parties to be more decentralized and free-wheeling than parties in other wealthy democracies, they remain powerful, organized forces in American politics—*linkages* that help to transmit the demands of the public by taking sides on issues and supporting candidates.

However, the Republican and Democratic Parties are not "organizations" in the usual sense of the term. Rather, they are loose networks of local and state parties, campaign committees, candidates and office holders, donors, interest and advocacy groups, and, of course, voters. Unlike a corporation, a bureaucratic agency, a military organization, or even a political party in most other countries, the official leaders of major American parties cannot issue orders that get passed down a chain of command. Even popular, charismatic, and skillful presidents have had nearly as much trouble controlling the many diverse and independent groups and individuals within their own parties as they have had dealing with the opposition. George W. Bush discovered this in his second term, when a significant number of Republican members of the House and Senate, loyal followers throughout his first term, abandoned him because of his plans for a pathway to citizenship for undocumented immigrants.

Today, each party has a stable core of voters concerned about particular issues and committed to particular government policies. The result is a system where the parties are quite different from one another. We can view today's Democratic and Republican Parties as serving three related organizational purposes. The first is as an *ideological organization* that functions as a home to voters with similar political preferences. The second is as an *electoral organization* that works to get members of the party elected to office. And the third is as a *governing organization* that helps elected officials in government work together to achieve common policy goals.

Parties as Ideological Organizations

A **political ideology** is a coherently organized set of beliefs about the fundamental nature of good society and the role that government ought to play in achieving it. Today, the Republican and Democratic Parties each represent one side of the liberal–conservative ideological spectrum. While Americans of all political stripes hold a range of core beliefs about free enterprise, individualism, the Constitution, and the Bill of Rights, the differences between Democrats and Republicans are clear (see Table 9.2). The Republican Party tends to endorse economically and socially **conservative** positions. With respect to the economy, Republicans oppose the regulation of business, generous safety nets, and higher taxes. And on the social side, Republicans tend to oppose abortion and same-sex marriage. The Democratic Party, on the other hand,

political ideology

A coherently organized set of beliefs about the fundamental nature of a good society and the role government ought to play in achieving it.

conservative

The political position, combining both economic and social dimensions, that holds that the federal government ought to play a very small role in economic regulation, social welfare, and overcoming racial inequality, that abortion should be illegal, and that family values and law and order should guide public policies.

TABLE 9.2 DEMOCRATS AND REPUBLICANS ON DOMESTIC ISSUES

Issue	Democratic Party	Republican Party
Taxes	Tends to favor higher taxes (particularly on the wealthy) as a way of funding government programs and redistributing wealth to those in need	Tends to favor lower taxes as a way of keeping more money in the hands of individuals and businesses
Government Spending	Tends to favor government spending as a way of stimulating the economy and helping the poor	Tends to favor the reduction of government spending in an effort to stimulate the economy and reduce the role of government in people's lives
Social Programs	Tends to favor social programs like welfare, Social Security, Medicare, and Medicaid as a way to help the poor and prevent poverty	Tends to oppose programs like welfare, Social Security, Medicare, and Medicaid, arguing that they lead to dependency and would be better handled by the private market
Abortion	Tends to support a woman's right to an abortion and reducing obstacles to obtaining one	Tends to oppose a woman's right to abortion and supports increased obstacles to obtaining one
Same-Sex Marriage	Tends to support same-sex marriage	Tends to oppose same-sex marriage
Church-State Relationship	Tends to favor no role for religion in government matters	Tends to support religious influence in certain government matters
Immigration	Tends to favor more open immigration policies and support for illegal immigrants already in the country	Tends to favor more restrictive immigration policies and increased efforts to remove illegal immigrants from the country

tends to endorse economically and socially **liberal** positions. For example, Democrats tend to support a strong government role in guiding the economy, safeguarding the environment, and protecting the civil rights of ethnic, racial, and gay and lesbian minorities. In embracing opposing sides of the ideological spectrum, parties serve as important mental cues that help people to quickly see different sides of issues and associate themselves with the one they prefer—political psychologists often refer to these mental cues as **heuristics**.[29] This association of liberalism with the Democrats and conservatism with the Republicans is growing stronger all the time, with the gap in outlooks between the two parties growing ever larger.[30]

PARTY MEMBERSHIP AND IDENTIFICATION   What does it mean to be a Republican or a Democrat in the United States? Americans do not join parties by paying dues or carrying membership cards. To Americans, political party membership may mean nothing more than voting most of the time for the candidate of one party over the other or choosing to become a candidate of a particular party. Or membership may mean contributing money to, or otherwise helping in, a local, state, or national campaign of a party candidate. These are indeed loose criteria for membership, looser criteria than for virtually any other organization that might be imagined.

Despite the loose membership criteria, a majority of Americans say they identify with or lean toward being a Democrat or Republican. Every major polling organization asks people a form of this question: "In politics, as of today, do you consider yourself a Republican, a Democrat, or an independent?" Pollsters then typically ask people who identify as Republican or Democrat whether they consider themselves strong or weak Republicans or Democrats. Independents are asked if they generally lean toward a major party, that is, whether they tend to vote for candidates of one party or the other.

Party identification has proven to be a very powerful thing in American politics. Growing evidence suggests that many people take on a party identification *before* assessing issues or candidates. While many people may identify with the party that most closely represents their views, there are also many for whom the party they have already identified with actually shapes their views.[31] The consequences of party identification are thus very important. First, the party one identifies with impacts which candidates the person votes for. Party identifiers almost always vote for candidates who wear their preferred party's label. In 2012, for example, 93 percent of self-identified Republicans voted for Mitt Romney for president, while 92 percent of Democrats voted for Barack Obama.[32] Second, party identification helps determine people's political attitudes on a wide range of issues; for a majority of Americans, party identity is a stable and powerful shaper of one's overall political identity. People use the party label to organize their thinking about politics and to guide them in voting, in judging new policy proposals, and in evaluating the government's performance.[33] And third, how the parties stand relative to one another in the affections of the American people has a lot to do with who wins elections and, thereby, determines which party controls the presidency, Congress, and, eventually, the federal courts. This distribution, which changes over time, clearly and definitively affects what government does.

Beginning with Roosevelt's highly popular New Deal in the 1930s and continuing into the 1970s, the Democratic lead over Republicans among party identifiers was substantial, making Democrats the majority party in U.S. politics for fifty years. At times, the Democratic advantage over Republican identifiers was on the order of 35 percentage points. During the Dealignment Era of the late 1960s through the 1980s, Democrats gradually lost this big lead as Southern and religious Democrats turned to the Republican Party and an increasing number of people began identifying as Independents (no party affiliation). Since the early 2000s, the Democratic lead over the Republican identifiers has become much smaller. Democrats currently maintain a slight edge over Republicans in party identification (see Figure 9.3).

liberal

The political position, combining both economic and social dimensions, that holds that the federal government has a substantial role to play in providing economic justice and opportunity, regulating business in the public interest, overcoming racial discrimination, protecting abortion rights, and ensuring the equal treatment of gays and lesbians.

heuristics

Simple mental rules people use to make decisions and judgments quickly.

FIGURE 9.3 TRENDS IN PARTY IDENTIFICATION, 1952–2016

Over the past 65 years, the percentages of those who call themselves Democrats and those who call themselves Republicans has been getting smaller. This has happened because fewer Americans than in the 1950s were identifying as Democrats and more were identifying as Independents. While Democrats maintain an edge over Republicans in party identification, recall that there are no truly national elections in American politics. Consequently, election results are not merely a matter of which party has more people identified with it but also where those who identify with the party live.

If these trends continue, how might the landscape of American politics change?

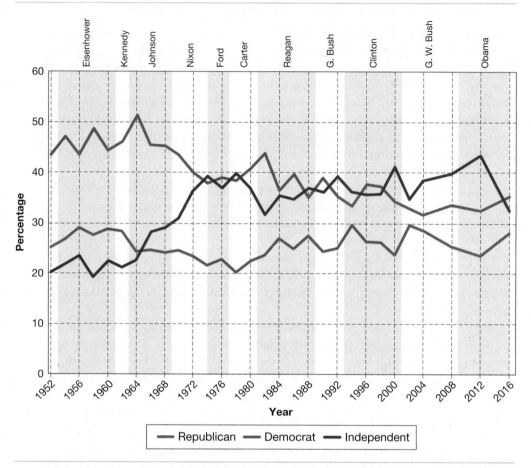

SOURCE: Data from American National Election Studies, and Stanford University. ANES Time Series Cumulative Data File (1948-2012). ICPSR08475-v15. Ann Arbor, MI: Inter-university Consortium for Political and Social Research [distributor], 2015-10-23., http://doi.org/10.3886/ICPSR08475.v15.

Figure 9.4 (see page 243) shows how Barack Obama and Mitt Romney did in each county in the 2012 presidential election. Vote choice is a good (though imperfect) measure of party identification. The redder counties indicate where Romney won by a wide margin; the bluer counties, where Obama won by a wide margin; and the purple counties, where the election was close. The strongest Republican support is found among whites (particularly in the South and in the Rocky Mountain West), conservative Christians and the most religiously committed (those who express a belief in God and say they regularly attend religious services) among all denominations, business people (whether small business owners or top executives in large corporations), economic and social conservatives, those in rural areas, and those with the highest incomes. The strongest Democratic support lies in cities and is found among African Americans, Jews, non-Cuban Hispanics, those secular in belief, those with postgraduate degrees, union households, economic and social liberals, those on the West Coast and in the Northeast, and those with lower incomes. Democrats also find strong support among teachers and other government employees at the local, state,

FIGURE 9.4 PRESIDENTIAL ELECTION RESULTS BY COUNTY, 2012

Party identification and support for presidential candidates tend to be geographically consistent. Republicans (the red counties) are concentrated in the South, lower Midwest, and the Rocky Mountain West. Democrats (the blue counties) are concentrated in the cities along the East and West Coast and the Upper Midwest. On the West Coast and in the Mid-Atlantic, the Northeast, and the upper Midwest. But the map also shows that much of the country is made up of areas that have both Democrats and Republicans (the light blue and light red areas) which tend to be in suburban areas outside major cities. In the 2016 presidential election, many of the light blue counties in the midwest turned light red, helping to lead Donald Trump to his Electoral College victory.

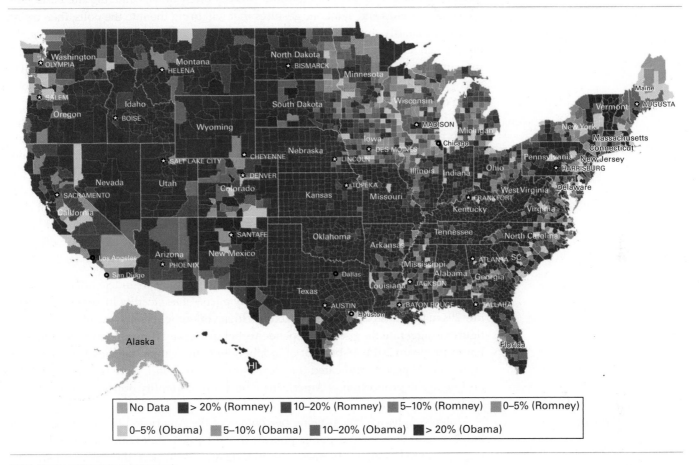

NOTE: Alaska and Hawaii are not to scale.

SOURCE: CQ Press, Voting and Elections Collection.

and national levels and among those living in university towns and in science and technology research centers such as the Silicon Valley, Austin, Seattle, Boulder, the Raleigh–Durham–Chapel Hill research triangle in North Carolina, and the Route 128 corridor around Boston and Cambridge.[34]

As you can see in Figure 9.4, large (and fairly densely populated) parts of the country are made up of more lightly shaded counties (both light red and light blue). These areas, which contain a mix of Democrats and Republicans—help to explain how small changes in voter turnout and the ability to attract independent **partisan leaners**—those who say they are independents but lean fairly consistently toward one party or another—have had big effects on who wins and loses presidential and congressional contests. To capture leaners, there has always been strong pressure on candidates to tone down matters of ideology and "get out the vote" in general elections.[35] Barack Obama's strong "get out the vote" effort among Democrats and independents helped him win in 2008 and 2012. Similar Republican efforts in 2010 led to huge GOP gains in Congress, governorships, and state legislative chambers across the country. And, as you read in the opening story, when the Republicans won the Presidency and retained control of Congress in 2016, they did so on the unexpected back of Donald

partisan leaners

Individuals who say they do not identify as Democrats or Republicans, but say they feel closer to either the Democratic or Republican Party.

Trump who brought some former Obama supporters in the blue and light blue parts of the Rust Belt into his anti-trade, anti-immigrant coalition.

Among party identifiers, some are especially strong supporters of the party and its candidates. Each party has a set of core supporters—often called the party base—and activists on which it can count for votes and campaign contributions.[36] In recent years, Republicans and Democrats have increasingly tried to win elections by first mobilizing these core supporters—in a process often called "rallying the base"—by focusing on issues and symbolic gestures that will bring them to the polls, then trying to win a majority among voters not automatically predisposed to one party or the other (such as Catholics, white mainline Protestants, and of course, independents).[37] In a situation in which Republican and Democratic core supporters are about equal in strength, winning even a small majority among these less partisan groups while mobilizing one's own partisans is the key to winning elections.

While Democratic and Republican identifiers are moving farther apart on which policies they support, the distances are even greater between Democratic and Republican active partisans, those Republican and Democratic identifiers who not only vote but are engaged in other party- and candidate-support activities, such as making campaign contributions, attending candidate meetings, making phone calls, knocking on doors to get out the party vote, and putting bumper stickers on their cars. Democratic active partisans are more likely than ordinary Democrats to hold very liberal views on issues, and Republican active partisans are more likely than ordinary Republicans to hold very conservative views on issues.[38]

INDEPENDENTS   The percentage of people who say they are independents—that is, those who say they are unaffiliated with any party—has steadily increased, from the low 20s in the 1960s to the high 30s today. However, some scholars maintain that these figures exaggerate the rise of independents because many independents are leaners.[39] For example, in 2014, 48 percent of independents indicated that they leaned Democratic and 39 percent indicated they lean Republican.[40] Still, there has clearly been a decline in the proportion of Americans who want to identify outright with either of the two major parties.

Interestingly, while a growing percentage of the American population calls itself independent, views about public policies in the United States are becoming increasingly polarized along party lines. This polarization is, in part, the result of partisans voting more often than independents; consequently, a greater number of liberal Democrats and conservative Republicans and fewer moderates in either party are elected. Independents tell journalists, pollsters, and scholars that they are fed up with the general nastiness in politics and government ineffectiveness that seems to be associated with the intensification of partisanship in the political life of the country.[41]

Parties as Electoral Organizations

Among the primary objectives of any political party is to attract as many voters as possible in order to prevail in elections. But contrary to what might be expected, each party is not a single entity dedicated to this goal. Rather, each party is a broad coalition of national, state, and local party organizations that work together to recruit and elect candidates. Parties are organizations run by a combination of elected officials, career political operatives, party activists, and loyal supporters. In addition, each party is closely allied with a network of advocacy groups that support the same causes.

Unlike a traditional organization and unlike political parties in other democracies, the American Democratic and Republican Parties have a network organization rather than a hierarchical organization. This means that various elements of the parties (including official committees, political action committees, interest groups, campaigns, and other related entities) are relatively independent from one another and act in concert on the basis of shared interests, sentiment, ideology, fund-raising, and the

FIGURE 9.5 PARTY ORGANIZATION IN THE UNITED STATES: HIERARCHICAL V. NETWORK

The graphic on the left shows a hypothetical hierarchical organizational chart of the Republican and Democratic Parties as if they were structured hierarchically. It would be a mistake, however, to think of our national parties this way. The graphic on the right, which depicts our national parties as a network of organizations with no central authority or chain of command, is closer to reality.

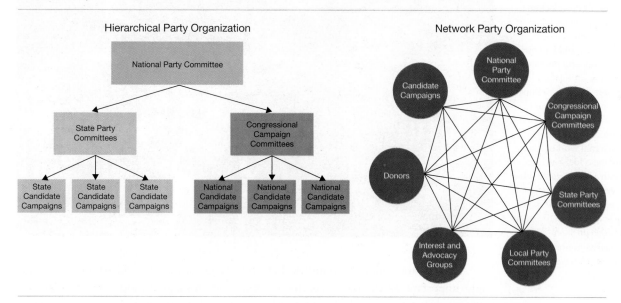

desire to win elections.[42] (See Figure 9.5 for a graphical representation of these ideas.) Critical to this is that the official party organizations neither control the nomination of candidates running under the party label, nor the flow of money that funds electoral campaigns, nor the behavior of office holders once elected. Party organizations have become, in effect, campaign machines in the service of candidates running for elected office. As such, many scholars have come to describe American political parties as "candidate-centered" (as opposed to "party-centered").[43]

Prior to World War II, party nominations were mostly controlled by major party players at state and national nominating conventions. Party elites used this power to select candidates to influence their positions and campaign strategies. Since then, nominations have become more traditionally democratic: voters voice their support for the candidate they want nominated for their party in primary elections and caucuses. The Democratic and Republican party organizations now exist to help candidates in these efforts, not to order them about. Nominations, therefore, tend to come to those best able to rally voters by raising money, gaining media access, forming crack campaign organizations, and winning the support of powerful interests and advocacy groups.[44] The 2010 and 2012 elections exemplify the extent to which American elections are candidate-centered. In these elections, Tea Party insurgents enjoyed great success in wresting nominations for congressional and gubernatorial seats away from candidates favored by Republican Party leaders.

NATIONAL PARTY COMMITTEES AND CONVENTIONS Democratic and Republican national committees conduct the official business of the parties. The national committees are made up of elected committeemen and committeewomen from each state, a sizable staff, and a chairperson, but they rarely meet. The real business of the committee is run by the party chair and their committee staff. National party committee chairs exercise little power when a president from their party is in office, because party chairs are compelled to take direction from the White House. When the opposition controls the presidency, party chairs exercise more influence in party affairs, although the extent of that power is still not very great.

BARACK OBAMA GIVES THE KEYNOTE ADDRESS AT 2004 DEMOCRATIC CONVENTION

In 2004, Barack Obama gave the keynote address at the Democratic National Convention in Boston. At the time he was in the middle of his first election to represent Illinois in the Senate. Obama was lauded for the speech in which he told his personal story and laid out his vision for a more hopeful politics: "It's the hope of slaves sitting around a fire singing freedom songs. The hope of immigrants setting out for distant shores. The hope of a young naval lieutenant bravely patrolling the Mekong Delta. The hope of a mill worker's son who dares to defy the odds. The hope of a skinny kid with a funny name who believes that America has a place for him, too." The speech launched Obama onto the national stage and set the stage for his successful 2008 presidential run.

What role do national conventions play besides serving as a forum nominating presidential candidates?

Although the national committees have little direct power, they have become increasingly important as campaign service organizations for party candidates running for national and state offices.[45] In addition to making substantial financial contributions to campaigns, they do a wide variety of things that help candidates. Their in-house TV and radio studios produce ads tailored to the particular district or state where the ads will air. They maintain large email address contact lists from which to disseminate information on party positions and to make appeals for contributions, increasingly using sophisticated data-mining techniques to target messages narrowly to different groups of people.[46] Press releases are prepared as are campaign-oriented sound bites and video clips for local broadcast. Each national party committee also produces training courses for potential candidates, complete with how-to manuals and videos. Each also publishes content for the web and for social media and solicits financial contributions for the party and for candidates. They also funnel campaign money to state and local party organizations, with the bulk going to states where competition between the parties is closest. To carry out these activities, both the national party committees have steadily increased the number of employees in their national offices in order to become highly professional campaign organization, filled with skilled people uniquely able to wage first-rate electoral campaigns.

The party committees are also responsible for organizing the national party conventions that meet every four years to nominate presidential and vice-presidential candidates, write a party platform, revise party rules, and bring together party members of varying statures and persuasions. During the 2016 Democratic presidential primary, Bernie Sanders fell short of the nomination but his strong campaign yielded him influence in the crafting of the party's platform. Conventions generate substantial media attention as they feature nationally televised speeches—including the acceptance of the party's nomination for President.

In 2016, the Republicans and Democrats put on very different conventions. The Republican convention depicted the country as being on a dangerously wrong path and post-convention analysis indicated that it was not perceived as a unifying party event. For example, in a national speech, Trump's former primary opponent Senator Ted Cruz (R-TX) took the unusual step of not endorsing the party's nominee. While the 2016 Democratic convention had its own problems (supporters of Bernie Sanders were frequently heard booing Clinton), it depicted a country that was on the right trajectory and was viewed as a more uplifting and unifying event with Sanders himself strongly endorsing Clinton for the presidency.

American parties tend to write political platforms that differ significantly from one another in both ideology and tone. Scholars discuss persistent differences in party platforms in terms of rhetoric, issues, and policies advocated. For example, Republicans tend to talk more about opportunity and freedom, whereas Democrats worry more about poverty and social welfare. A presidential nominee need not adhere either to the letter or to the spirit of a party platform, although most nominees stay fairly close to platforms most of the time (usually because a winning candidate's supporters control the platform-writing committee). State and local party organizations may nominate whomever they choose to run for public office and may or may not support key planks in the national party's platform.

CONGRESSIONAL CAMPAIGN COMMITTEES Almost as old as the national party committees, but entirely independent of them, are four congressional campaign committees—one Republican and one Democratic committee for the House and for the Senate. Congressional campaign committees help members of Congress raise money, provide media services, conduct research, and do whatever else party members in Congress deem appropriate. Increasingly, congressional campaign committees have turned their attention to identifying and encouraging quality party candidates to run in districts and states where competition between the parties is close. Rahm Emanuel (D-IL), later President Obama's chief of staff and currently mayor of Chicago, performed this function particularly well during his time as head of the Democratic House Campaign Committee. Many gave him the credit for the Democrats retaking control of the House from the Republicans in the 2005–2006 election cycle.[47] Congressional campaign committees are controlled by party members in Congress, not by party chairs, national committees, or even presidents. Much like national party committees, congressional campaign committees have become highly professionalized and well-funded.[48]

STATE PARTY ORGANIZATIONS As you would expect in a federal system, separate political party organizations exist in each state. Although tied together by bonds of ideology, sentiment, and campaign money, state party organizations are relatively independent of one another and of the national party. State parties play a particularly important role in finding and supporting candidates for state-level offices like governor, state attorney general, and state assembly.

2016 PRESIDENTIAL NOMINEES ACCEPT PARTY NOMINATIONS

The highlight of each party's presidential nominating convention comes when the presumptive nominees officially accept their party's nomination for President with a primetime speech. It signals the official end of the primary season and the beginning of the general election campaign. In 2016, Donald Trump (the Republican nominee) and Hillary Clinton (the Democratic nominee) gave very different addresses. Trump's speech depicted America as being on a dangerous path with respect to security, immigration, and globalization. Clinton offered a more optimistic message about the current state of the country—embracing a continuation of President Obama's work.

How have the messages of the Democratic and Republican parties changed in recent years? How was Trump's message in 2016 different than Republican nominees that preceded him?

INTEREST GROUPS WIELD (AND DON'T WIELD) THEIR RESOURCES

David Koch (right) and Richard Trumka (left) lead interest groups on opposite ends of the political spectrum. Billionaires David Koch and his brother Charles Koch founded Americans for Prosperity to promote fiscally conservative (and often libertarian) principles and candidates. However, the Kochs and their advocacy group remained fairly quiet during the 2016 presidential campaign owing to philosophical disagreements with Republican nominee Donald Trump. Still, Americans for Prosperity remained committed to funding down-ballot Republican campaigns. Richard Trumka is the President of the AFL-CIO, one of the largest labor unions in the country with about 12.5 million members. Unions like the AFL-CIO have typically supported Democratic candidates. And despite Donald Trump's appeal to many anti-free trade voters, Trumka and the AFL-CIO used their financial resources and membership to support Hillary Clinton and other Democrats in 2016.

How do groups like the AFL-CIO and Americans for Prosperity fit into the party networks?

interest group

A private organization or voluntary association that seeks to influence public policy as a way to protect or advance its interests.

party activist

Prominent, though often unelected, members of political parties who influence party decisions and participate in major party events.

INTEREST GROUPS AND ADVOCACY GROUPS **Interest groups** and advocacy groups are not technically part of formal party organizations but are so deeply involved in party affairs that it is hard to draw a line between them and official party organizations. Some have even argued that networks of conservative interest and advocacy groups, such as American Crossroads (founded by Republican strategist Karl Rove), the American Action Network, and Americans for Prosperity (backed by the energy billionaire Koch brothers) have taken over much of the fund-raising, campaign-messaging, and candidate-recruiting role of the Republican National Committee.[49] Organized labor (e.g., AFL-CIO, SEIU) as well as left-leaning advocacy groups such as MoveOn.org (which is heavily funded by billionaire George Soros) have a similar relationship with the Democratic Party.

In recent years, many of these groups have worked hard to push the parties and candidates into more ideological and partisan directions—something that has undoubtedly contributed to the shape of the Polarization Era. For example, MoveOn.org and the National Education Association push Democrats to be more assertive in pursuing a more liberal policy agenda and in championing the candidacy of people they favor. On the other side, conservative organizations such as the Club for Growth and the National Rifle Association (NRA) get Republican candidates to pledge to lower taxes, expand gun rights, and oppose citizenship for undocumented immigrants.

PARTY ACTIVISTS **Party activists** are the prominent, though often unelected, members of the party who influence party decisions and participate in major party events. The activists of one party are quite different in their views from activists of the other party as well as from most voters and the general public. A study of the 2004 Republican and Democratic National Conventions found that the delegates to the convention (party activists) were different than typical party voters on an array of issues including health care, the environment, abortion, social-spending programs, and same-sex marriage (see Table 9.3). For example, 40 percent of Republican voters valued universal health care over tax cuts but only 7 percent of Republican delegates felt similarly (instead, valuing tax cuts over universal health care). Likewise on the Democratic side, there was more opposition to the War in Iraq among Democratic delegates than Democratic voters.[50]

Parties as Governing Organizations

The Republican and Democratic Parties exist not only as a network of candidates, activists, contributors, and interest and advocacy groups but also as critical organizational systems in government. Parties help elected officials stay organized—primarily in Congress—so that they can work together to achieve common policy goals. Just like the electorate, however, the partisan composition of government fluctuates. These fluctuations have a major impact on the ability of government to respond to policy problems and pass new laws.

TABLE 9.3 COMPARING THE 2004 NATIONAL PARTY CONVENTION DELEGATES TO OTHER AMERICANS

	Delegates to Democratic National Convention	Democratic Voters	All Voters	Republican Voters	Delegates to Republican National Convention
Percent saying it is more important to provide health care coverage for all Americans than to hold down taxes.	94	90	67	40	7
Percent saying that the United States did the right thing in taking military action against Iraq.	2	14	37	70	80
Percent saying protecting the environment should be a higher priority for the government than developing new sources of energy.	25	30	21	9	3
Percent saying abortion not be permitted rather than available to all or limited some.	3	16	24	37	43
Percent saying gay couples be allowed to legally marry.	55	49	34	11	6

SOURCE: *New York Times*/CBS News poll, September 1, 2004.

As we discussed in the section on the Polarization Era, parties in Congress have recently become more ideologically different and increasingly concerned with ensuring that members support the party line. One veteran observer even claims that today, "Political leaders on both sides now feel a relentless pressure for party discipline and intellectual conformity more common in parliamentary systems than through most of American history."[51] Tea Party activists' pressure on Republican candidates in 2010 and 2012 helped make the GOP even more conservative than it has been. Senator Orrin Hatch (R-UT), perhaps sensing the same fate for himself as that which befell his long-time colleague and fellow conservative Robert Bennett—who was defeated by a Tea Party-backed candidate in his bid for his party's senatorial nomination in Utah in 2010—began to vote even more consistently conservative in the Senate. In 2010 and 2011, Hatch averaged a score of 99.5 from the conservative advocacy group Club for Growth, well above his lifetime score of 78 previously awarded to him by that group. During the 2012 presidential election, Mitt Romney, a fairly moderate Republican for most of his career, took on a much more conservative ideological hue in the course of gaining the GOP's presidential nomination in 2012, repudiating his previous positions on issues such as immigration, health insurance mandates, and affirmative action.

Figure 9.6 shows how moderate or extreme the parties in the House of Representatives have been going back to 1879. The higher the line, the more conservative the party was that year; the lower the line the more liberal the party was that year. Notice that since the 1980s, both parties have been becoming more extreme (the Democrats becoming more liberal and the Republicans becoming more conservative). However, the Republicans have become significantly more conservative than the Democrats have become liberal. This is the Polarization Era playing out in Congress.

DIVISIONS BETWEEN THE PARTIES   Fearful of the tyrannical possibilities of vigorous government, the framers designed a system in which power is so fragmented and competitive that effectiveness is sometimes compromised.[52] The constitutionally designed conflict between the president and Congress is more likely to be bridged when there is **unified government**—when a single party controls both houses of Congress and the presidency—as the Democrats did during much of the 1960s and the first two years of Obama's presidency, as the Republicans did between 2001 and 2006 (when Bush was in office), and as it is now during the first years of the Trump presidency. When the parties are strong and unified, this bridging can occur even when one

unified government

Control of the executive and legislative branches by the same political party.

FIGURE 9.6 POLARIZATION BETWEEN THE PARTIES IN THE U.S. HOUSE
OF REPRESENTATIVES, 1879–2015

On this graph, the farther above 0 a point appears, the more conservative the House Republicans were in that year. The farther below 0, the more liberal the House Democrats were in that year. The farther apart the plotlines, the greater the "distance," or degree of polarization, between the average Democrat and the average Republican in the House. If the plotlines were ever to meet, it would suggest that party members in those years were effectively the same. Since the 1960s, notice that both parties have been becoming more extreme. Indeed, the graph demonstrates that we are witnessing a historically polarized era in Congress, with Republicans having become significantly more conservative and Democrats having become more liberal.

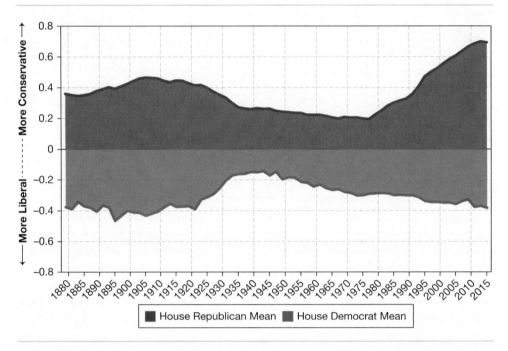

SOURCE: Data from Royce Carroll, Jeff Lewis, James Lo, Nolan McCarty, Keith Poole, and Howard Rosenthal, First Dimension DW-NOMINATE Scores, Voteview. (Voteview, a research portal of Professor Keith T. Poole, collects data on every member of the U.S. House of Representatives since the founding and uses a sophisticated formula for determining how liberal or conservative each member is.)

gridlock

A situation in which things cannot get done in Washington, usually because of divided government.

party controls the Congress with the tiniest of margins. On the other hand, periods of divided government often result in **gridlock**. When Republicans and Democrats each control a branch of the federal government, very little gets done. For example, during the last two years of President Obama's first term and all of his second term, when Republicans controlled one or both of the two chambers of Congress, the policy-making process significantly stalled.[53]

It matters a great deal whether Democrats or Republicans control the House, the Senate, and the presidency, because the public policies that parties put into effect when they win control of government have real and lasting consequences. When in power, Republicans and Democrats produce different policies on taxes, corporate regulation, scientific research, gun control, and social welfare—with Democrats favoring more liberal policies and Republicans favoring more conservative policies. Which bills become law, the composition of the federal judiciary, and the actions taken by executive branch agencies are also effected by party control of the federal government (see Figure 9.7).

The differences between both the parties became apparent to everyone in 2013 when the government failed to pass a "continuing resolution" on the federal budget. Every year, Congress must pass and the President must sign appropriations bills that fund the government. When it fails to do this, the government shuts down until it does—furloughing hundreds of thousands of federal employees. The framework pyramid below (Figure 9.8) articulates why the government could not pass something as

FIGURE 9.7   PARTY DIVISIONS IN CONGRESS, 1935–PRESENT

The chart shows partisan control of the House of Representatives and the Senate from 1935 to the present. Red periods indicate Republican control, and blue periods indicate Democratic control. The horizontal bars indicate the strength of the partisan majority in the House and Senate: the bigger the blue bar, the larger the Democratic majority; the bigger the red bar, the larger the Republican majority. Note the extended period of Democratic control of the House during much of the 20th century and the slim majorities since the middle of the Clinton administration.

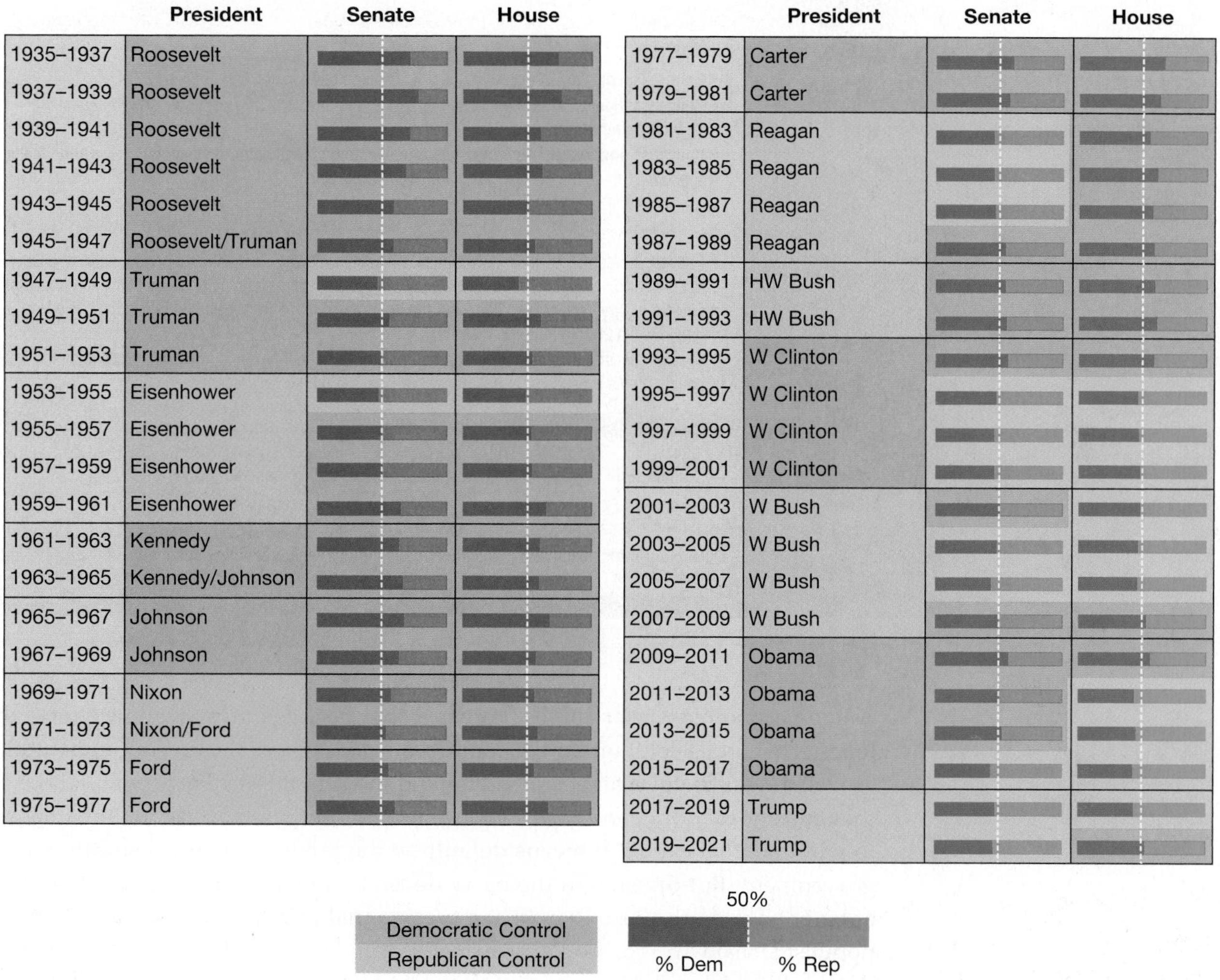

	President	Senate	House		President	Senate	House
1935–1937	Roosevelt			1977–1979	Carter		
1937–1939	Roosevelt			1979–1981	Carter		
1939–1941	Roosevelt			1981–1983	Reagan		
1941–1943	Roosevelt			1983–1985	Reagan		
1943–1945	Roosevelt			1985–1987	Reagan		
1945–1947	Roosevelt/Truman			1987–1989	Reagan		
1947–1949	Truman			1989–1991	HW Bush		
1949–1951	Truman			1991–1993	HW Bush		
1951–1953	Truman			1993–1995	W Clinton		
1953–1955	Eisenhower			1995–1997	W Clinton		
1955–1957	Eisenhower			1997–1999	W Clinton		
1957–1959	Eisenhower			1999–2001	W Clinton		
1959–1961	Eisenhower			2001–2003	W Bush		
1961–1963	Kennedy			2003–2005	W Bush		
1963–1965	Kennedy/Johnson			2005–2007	W Bush		
1965–1967	Johnson			2007–2009	W Bush		
1967–1969	Johnson			2009–2011	Obama		
1969–1971	Nixon			2011–2013	Obama		
1971–1973	Nixon/Ford			2013–2015	Obama		
1973–1975	Ford			2015–2017	Obama		
1975–1977	Ford			2017–2019	Trump		
				2019–2021	Trump		

50%

Democratic Control
Republican Control

% Dem   % Rep

essential as its budget in 2013. In short: deep policy disagreements between the parties (and within the Republican Party) could not be reconciled. Many Republicans saw a government shutdown as a way to force the Democratic Senate and President Obama into policy concessions. The Democrats never agreed to those concessions, and the government reopened 17 days later with roughly the same spending policies it had before the shutdown.

DIVISIONS WITHIN THE PARTIES   While differences between Democrats and Republicans have become more pronounced, and while ideological and policy cohesion within the parties has been increasing, especially in the GOP, important disagreements within each party remain. Parties are not perfectly unified. Fissures have existed for some time in the Republican Party, with the fault lines historically lying between economic conservatives, whose main priority is lower government spending and lower taxes, and social conservatives, who emphasize "family values" and religious beliefs. However, the Republican Party has become even more fractured in recent years with the emergence of the Tea Party and now the Populist Nationalists.

FIGURE 9.8 APPLYING THE FRAMEWORK: THE 2013 FEDERAL GOVERNMENT SHUTDOWN

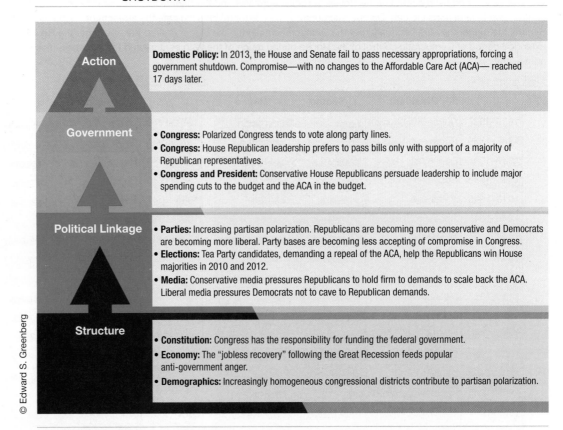

Among economic conservatives there is a split between those who recognize that a long-term budget solution for the country must involve some revenue enhancements as well as cuts in government spending and those in the Tea Party wing who believe that cutting spending and taxes is paramount and that every action must be taken to win that goal even if it means default on the public debt and a shutdown of the government. But division in the party doesn't end with the budget as was readily apparent during the 2016 Republican presidential primary in which anti-immigrant populist Donald Trump, Tea Party evangelical Ted Cruz, and more establishment candidates like Marco Rubio and Jeb Bush all had their own considerable constituencies. As was discussed in the opening story of this chapter, the populist message championed by Trump has become a strong force in the party, but many traditional Republicans remain concerned about that trajectory.

Divisions are also evident in the Democratic Party—though they are currently less pronounced—particularly between the liberal base and the more moderate office holders. The liberal wing of the party, for example, was not happy with many actions and policies of President Obama that seemed to hug the middle of the public policy spectrum: continuing many Bush-era policies on bailouts and financial industry regulation; giving in to many Republican congressional demands to cut government spending without getting much in the way of tax increases on top income groups; supporting global free trade agreements like the Trans-Pacific Partnership; failing to close the detainee facilities at Guantanamo Bay; and continuing for a number of years the wars in Iraq and Afghanistan. More recently, this division was evident in the Democratic presidential primary between the more centrist Hillary Clinton and the quite liberal Bernie Sanders. This intra-party disagreement also had consequences for the general election as it likely decreased enthusiasm for Clinton during the 2016 general election campaign.

POLITICAL PARTIES: HOW DO OUR TWO MAJOR POLITICAL PARTIES AFFECT DEMOCRACY?

You will recall that many theorists believe that vigorous and healthy political parties are essential for democracy. Parties are essential because, in theory at least, they are among the principal political institutions that help make popular sovereignty and political equality a reality. They are able to do so because they:

1. Keep elected officials responsive and responsible to the broad public.
2. Stimulate political interest and participation among ordinary Americans.
3. Embrace a broad range of groups from all economic and social levels of the population.
4. Simplify voter choices.
5. Make government work for the people by overcoming the intrinsic problems of separation of powers and checks and balances.

In contrast, the framers worried about the effects of political parties on republican government for all the same reasons. They were not at all inclined to involve all groups in political life, nor were they interested in stimulating widespread interest and participation by ordinary Americans. And they most certainly were not in favor of any institution, such as a party faction, that might overcome the constraints on national government that they had so very consciously created.

The framers might rest a bit easier knowing that our political parties have never been quite able to fulfill their democratic promise. The constitutional system the framers built does its job well, making it hard for unified parties, or even unified governments, swept into power by electoral majorities, to get their way. In the Senate, for example, a unified minority party representing a minority of Americans (because each state gets two senators no matter the size of its population) can block important bills favored by the majority party (and a majority of Americans). Today, even with the internal fights over the future of both major parties, the Democrats and Republicans are increasingly ideologically distinctive and clear on the policy alternatives they offer to the public. This means voters know what they will get when they put a party into office, even if party positions and candidates are impacted by the preferences and actions of advocacy groups and rich donors. Of course, the downside to this polarization is that it increases the likelihood of gridlock and dysfunction in the system. Despite all of this, our parties are the primary democratic mechanism we have for allowing voters to decide on a program for the government and to collectively hold elected officials responsible, even if imperfectly.

POLITICAL PARTIES IN DEMOCRATIC SYSTEMS

9.1 Explain how parties can enhance popular sovereignty and political equality in democratic systems.

Theoretically, the electoral activities of political parties facilitate popular sovereignty by making it easier for citizens to hold elected leaders accountable for their promises and actions.

While our constitutional system was designed to make it difficult for government to act decisively, political parties can offset this indecision by encouraging cooperation among public officials who benefit from their party's collective success. However, recent polarization has made cooperation between parties more infrequent.

THE AMERICAN TWO-PARTY SYSTEM

9.2 Explain why America has a two-party system.

The American party system is unique among the Western democracies because it is a relatively pure two-party system and has been since the 1830s.

America has single-member plurality elections which incentivize people to vote for major party candidates and not vote for minor party candidates (even if they support their ideas).

THE AMERICAN TWO-PARTY SYSTEM SINCE THE GREAT DEPRESSION

9.3 Trace the evolution of political parties in America since the Great Depression.

The modern Democratic Party formed during the New Deal Era. During this period Democrats, led by President Franklin D. Roosevelt, supported an expansion of federal government powers and responsibilities aimed at steering the economy out of the Great Depression. This began a period of Democratic dominance that lasted until the 1970s.

During the Dealignment Era, Democratic dominance declined and party membership resorted around civil rights, feminism, and foreign affairs. Conservative Southerners left the Democratic Party and joined the Republican Party.

The current Polarization Era is characterized by Democratic and Republican parties that are increasingly ideologically different from and hostile toward each other—embracing substantially different visions for country and an unwillingness to compromise. Neither party is dominant.

THE THREE FUNCTIONS OF TODAY'S POLITICAL PARTIES

9.4 Identify three organizational functions of today's American parties.

American parties serve as ideological organizations that function as a home to voters with similar political preferences. They help inform citizens on public policy issues and connect them with the candidates that represent their views.

American parties serve as electoral organizations comprised of career political operatives, party activists, loyal supporter, and advocacy groups. They cooperate and complete to help get their candidates in office and their concerns heard. American parties are candidate-centered. There is little power in the national party organizations to affect the behavior of individual candidates and office holders.

American parties are governing organizations that help elected officials organize so that they can work together to achieve common policy goals and remain in office.

bipartisanship Members of opposing political parties, usually elected officials, acting cooperatively in order to achieve a public policy goal.

conservative The political position, combining both economic and social dimensions, that holds that the federal government ought to play a very small role in economic regulation, social welfare, and overcoming racial inequality, that abortion should be illegal, and that family values and law and order should guide public policies.

dealignment A gradual reduction in the dominance of one political party without another party supplanting it.

Dealignment Era The party era that lasted from the late 1960s to the early 1990s that was characterized by a gradual reduction in the dominance of the Democratic Party without another party becoming truly dominant.

divided government   Control of the executive and legislative branches by different political parties.

Duverger's Law   The phenomenon that electoral systems based on single-member plurality districts are almost always dominated by only two parties.

gridlock   A situation in which things cannot get done in Washington, usually because of divided government.

heuristics   Simple mental rules people use to make decisions and judgments quickly.

interest group   A private organization or voluntary association that seeks to influence public policy as a way to protect or advance its interests.

liberal   The political position, combining both economic and social dimensions, that holds that the federal government has a substantial role to play in providing economic justice and opportunity, regulating business in the public interest, overcoming racial discrimination, protecting abortion rights, and ensuring the equal treatment of gays and lesbians.

multiparty system   A political system in which three or more viable parties compete to lead the government; because a majority winner is not always possible, multiparty systems often have coalition governments where governing power is shared among two or more parties.

New Deal Party Era   The party era lasting from the Great Depression to the late 1960s during which the Democrats, originally led by President Franklin D. Roosevelt, dominated government and supported an expansion of federal government powers and responsibilities aimed at steering the economy out of the Great Depression and through the Second World War.

partisan leaners   Individuals who say they do not identify as Democrats or Republicans, but say they feel closer to either the Democratic or Republican Party.

party activist   Prominent, though often unelected, members of political parties who influence party decisions and participate in major party events.

party identification   The sense of belonging to a political party; in the United States this is typically identifying as a Republican or Democrat.

platform   A party's statement of its positions on the issues of the day passed at the quadrennial national convention.

plurality   Occurs when a candidate receives more votes than any other candidate in an election but still less than a majority.

polarization   The process by which political parties have become more internally consistent in ideology and more ideologically distant from one another; in the U.S. the Republican party has become more conservative and the Democratic party more liberal.

Polarization Era   The party era that began in the 1990s in which the Democratic and Republican parties became increasingly ideologically different from and hostile toward each other—embracing substantially different visions for country and an unwillingness to compromise.

political ideology   A coherently organized set of beliefs about the fundamental nature of a good society and the role government ought to play in achieving it.

political party   A group organized to nominate candidates, to try to win political power through elections, and to promote ideas about public policies.

proportional representation   The awarding of legislative seats to political parties to reflect the proportion of the popular vote each party receives.

realignment   The process by which one party supplants another as the dominant party in a two-party political system.

single-member districts   Districts where the voters elect only one person to represent them. In single-member plurality systems, the person with the most votes (even if they do not have the majority) wins the election.

two-party system   A political system in which two parties vie on relatively equal terms to win national elections and in which each party governs at one time or another.

unified government   Control of the executive and legislative branches by the same political party.

CHAPTER 10

THE ELECTION OF PRESIDENT TRUMP
In a shocking upset, Donald Trump defeated Hillary Clinton in the Electoral College, despite losing the popular vote. He won traditionally Democratic states like Pennsylvania, Michigan, and Wisconsin, by speaking to the economic and social anxieties of disaffected white voters in rural areas. *What specific economic and social factors were most important to voters who preferred Trump to Clinton?*

VOTING, CAMPAIGNS, AND ELECTIONS

CHAPTER OUTLINE AND LEARNING OBJECTIVES

ELECTIONS AND DEMOCRACY

10.1 Evaluate three models of how elections can lead to popular control.

THE UNIQUE NATURE OF AMERICAN ELECTIONS

10.2 Distinguish American elections from those in other countries.

VOTING IN THE UNITED STATES

10.3 Analyze the importance of political participation in elections.

WHO VOTES?

10.4 Identify demographic factors that increase the likelihood of voting.

THE PRESIDENTIAL CAMPAIGN

10.5 Outline the process of campaigns for the presidency.

ELECTION OUTCOMES

10.6 Assess how presidential elections are decided.

The Struggle for Democracy

THE REASONS FOR TRUMP'S SUCCESS

When voting began on the morning of November 8, 2016, professional political prognosticators gave Hillary Clinton anywhere from a 65 percent to 95 percent chance of winning the election. In online futures markets, the odds were about nine to one against Trump, meaning one could have made almost $9 for every dollar invested in a Donald Trump win. On the morning of November 9, 2016, Donald Trump was the president-elect with 304[1] electoral votes—though he lost the national vote—in what will surely go down as one of the biggest political upsets in American history.

How did Trump do it? Political scientists and observers have sought to answer that question over the last two years, and a few main explanations have emerged. First, more so than other recent Republican presidential candidates, he received an enormous amount of support from working-class white voters. He also managed to hold onto more traditional Republican voters, faring well among college-educated whites and suburban voters, including suburban women (contrary to pre-election polls). 67 percent of non-college educated whites voted for Trump, an astonishing number, while 49 percent of college educated whites did so as well. In fact, in many states, he performed better among whites overall than Mitt Romney did as the Republican nominee in 2012. Older voters went for Trump, as expected, while crucially, he attracted significant support from voters in small cities and rural areas. Trump carried 62 percent of voters in these areas, and 50 percent of voters in suburbs (Clinton won only 45 percent of these voters). His anti-elite and economic populism message appeared to resonate in struggling, working-class counties in Rust Belt states. Pennsylvania, Michigan, and Wisconsin in particular, none of which had voted for a Republican since at least 1988, broke for Trump, giving him a path to an Electoral College win that virtually no one saw coming. Along with these states, he won most of the other battleground states by one or two percentage points, including Florida, North Carolina, Iowa, and Ohio. Figure 10.1 shows two maps, where states are scaled by their number of eligible voters. The top map colors states based on which candidate won, while the bottom colors states by the percentage of voters supporting Donald Trump. Dark blue indicates fewer votes for Trump and more votes for Clinton, dark red indicates the state voted heavily for Trump, and shades of purple indicate the state was closely split between the two candidates.

Clinton did not perform as well as expected among women and minorities, and suffered from lower voter turnout among Democrats in some crucial states. Though 54 percent of women supported Clinton, this was only up one point from Obama's percentage in the 2012 election, according to exit polls. This, despite numerous comments made by Trump during the campaign that were thought to alienate women, and despite the historic nature of Clinton's nomination.[2] Further, exit polls suggest that Clinton actually did eight points worse among Hispanic voters than Obama did in 2012, though some observers are suspicious that these numbers reflect the voting reality. Finally, vote tallies seem to indicate that though overall voter **turnout** was up a few percentage points from 2012, African American voters in swing states, an important part of the two Obama wins, were a slightly smaller segment of the electorate than they were in 2012.[3] This cost Clinton crucial votes in large cities in swing states such as Milwaukee, Detroit, and Philadelphia.

Not only did Donald Trump win the presidency, Republicans also performed well in the congressional elections. In the Senate, Republicans were defending nine seats considered to be competitive, while Democrats were worried only about losing retiring Senate Democratic Leader Harry Reid's in Nevada.[4] Based on these numbers alone, most thought Democrats would gain the seats necessary to become the majority. Shockingly, only two Republican senators, Mark Kirk in Illinois, and Kelly Ayotte in New Hampshire lost their seats. In the House, expected Democratic gains of up to 15 seats never materialized, with Democrats gaining fewer than 10. These results indicate that, despite pre-election polls, Donald Trump had coattails that benefited down-ballot Republicans.

* * * * *

turnout

The proportion of either eligible or all voting-age Americans who actually vote in a given election; the two ways of counting turnout yield different results.

FIGURE 10.1 2016 PRESIDENTIAL ELECTION RESULTS BY STATE

These maps of the 2016 presidential election results are called "Cartograms." Each state has been resized to reflect the voting eligible population of the state such that more populous states are made bigger and less populous states are made smaller. When you adjust the size of the states like this, states that are big in area but small in population (like Wyoming, Montana, and the Dakotas) get considerably smaller. Likewise, a geographically small but large population state like New Jersey gets bigger. The first map allows you to not only see who won the state (red for Donald Trump and blue for Hillary Clinton) but also how influential that state is in the presidential election process. In the second map, states are shaded based on how much support Trump and Clinton each got. Very red states went strongly for Trump, very blue states went strongly for Clinton, and the purple states were evenly divided. This reveals how win/lose election results can obscure just how close the 2016 election was. Note that Maine splits its electoral college votes by congressional district, with Donald Trump winning one of the four.

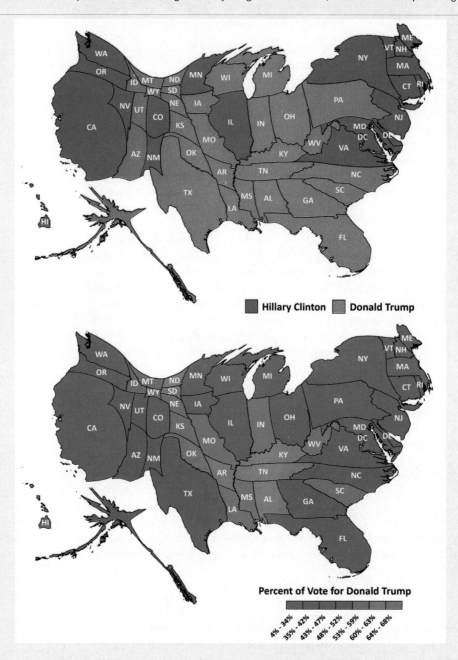

SOURCE: Cartograms produced in ArcMap 10.4.1 with the Cartogram Geoprocessing tool using the Newman-Gastner method [see details in Michael T. Gastner and Mark E. J. Newman, "Diffusion-Based Method for Producing Density-Equalizing Maps," Proceedings of the National Academy of Sciences 101 (2004): 7499–7504.]

The first two years of Trump's presidency have been tumultuous, to say the least. Republicans did manage to achieve two significant policy goals. First, they passed an enormous tax cut, a long-held priority of many Republican members of Congress, including then-Speaker Paul Ryan. At the same time, they repealed the individual mandate component of Obamacare. The effects of this are still uncertain, but it represents an important step toward weakening the law. Other attempts to repeal the entirety of the legislation, however, failed. President Trump and congressional Republicans also successfully sat Neil Gorsuch, a respected and ideologically conservative judge, to the seat left vacant by the death of Antonin Scalia in November of 2016, as well as filling Anthony Kennedy's seat on the bench with Brett Kavanaugh. On the other hand, President Trump remains historically unpopular for a new president, despite a relatively strong economy and no major foreign crisis. A number of scandals have dogged the President, most notably one conducted by Special Counsel Robert Mueller, who is looking into relationships between the Trump Campaign and Russian officials. There has been enormous turnover among President Trump's staff and executive branch officials, many of whom have had scandals of their own. With Democrats seizing control of the House, expect a slew of investigations into the president's administration and his business dealings. Democrats will have subpoena power and have already suggested they will seek the release of President Trump's tax returns, along with conducting investigations into connections between Russia and the Trump campaign in the 2016 election. Investigations will be carried out by the Intelligence and Judiciary Committees, among others, and the leaders of those committees are no fans of the president. Democrats will also seek to protect the Mueller investigation, though exactly what actions they will take remain unclear. The president's firing of Attorney General Jeff Sessions the day after the election suggests that his conflict with the FBI and the Mueller probe will only increase during the 116th Congress.

THINKING CRITICALLY **ABOUT THIS CHAPTER**

The story of the 2016 presidential election focuses our attention on the issue of democratic control of the national government through the electoral process and on the degree to which the public participates in this key activity of the representative democratic process.

APPLYING THE **FRAMEWORK**

You will see in this chapter that elections are affected by the different rates of participation of groups in American society and how structural factors such as constitutional rules, unequal access to resources, and cultural ideas help determine why some groups participate more than others. You will also learn how elections affect the behavior of public officials.

USING THE **DEMOCRACY STANDARD**

We suggest in this chapter that elections are the lynchpin of any discussion about the democratic quality of any system of government because they are, in theory, what makes popular sovereignty possible. You will see in this chapter that while elections in the United States do much to make our system democratic, they fall short of their democratic promise.

ELECTIONS AND DEMOCRACY

10.1 Evaluate three models of how elections can lead to popular control.

Elections are fundamental to democratic politics, the chief means by which citizens control elected officials, who in turn, run the government. Many important struggles for democracy in the United States have involved conflicts over the right to vote. But can elections actually ensure that elected officials do what the people want?

Democratic theorists have suggested several ways that elections in a two-party system like the one found in the United States can bring about popular control of government. We will discuss three of these ways, indicating how each works in theory and in practice.[5] The remainder of this chapter is concerned with the actual process of American elections, and with attempting to answer the question of whether elections ensure the public exercises appropriate control over elected officials.

The Prospective (or Responsible Party) Voting Model

prospective voting model
A theory of democratic elections in which voters decide what each party will do if elected and choose the party that best represents their own preferences.

responsible party model
The notion that a political party will take clear and distinct stands on the issues and enact them as policy once elected to office.

The **prospective voting model** requires that parties stake out different positions on the issues of the day and that informed voters cast ballots based on these differences. In this way, parties are **responsible** because they offer a "real choice" on important issues and once elected, they work to implement their stated policies.

THEORY For this model to work, each political party must be unified; each must take clear policy positions that differ significantly from those of the other party; citizens must accurately understand party positions and vote on them; and the winning party, when it takes office, must implement the policies it advocated. If all these conditions are met, then the party with the more popular policy positions wins, and the policies enacted into law are what the majority of the voters want.[6]

POTENTIAL PROBLEMS Responsible parties have the potential to increase the frequency and intensity of political conflict because the winning party has little reason to compromise with the losing party, even when its margin of victory is razor-thin. The party in power will try to pass the policies it wants, ignoring the objections or suggestions of the minority party. Although responsible parties make choices at the ballot box easier for voters, the result, quite often, is gridlock if one party is not able to win the presidency and a majority or supermajority in both congressional chambers (something that cannot happen in a parliamentary system but happens frequently in our presidential system).[7] In fact, parties in this country have become more polarized and are more closely approximating the responsible party model, but the political reality over the last two decades has been a dramatic increase in partisan warfare. This has made it difficult for Congress and the president to accomplish even the most mundane tasks, such as funding the government, and has led to intense fights over important issues such as health care and Supreme Court seats. American voters dislike partisan fighting and gridlock, which leads to lower trust in the other party and government overall. There is a growing perception in this country that as a result of highly "responsible" parties, Congress is unable to address major national problems.[8]

The Electoral Competition Voting Model

electoral competition voting model
A theory of elections in which parties move toward the median voter or the center of the political spectrum in order to capture the most votes.

median voter
The voter at the exact middle of the political issue spectrum.

In the **electoral competition voting model**, parties compete for votes by taking the *most popular* position on an issue. They do so by trying to appeal to the voter in the middle of the political spectrum, called the **median voter**. Both parties, according to

FIGURE 10.2 ELECTORAL COMPETITION MODEL

The electoral competition voting model suggests that, as campaigns progress, parties move toward the median voter (where most votes are to be found) in pursuit of election wins.

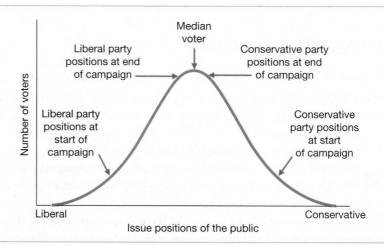

the electoral competition voting model, are therefore likely to end up standing for the *same* policies: those favored by the most voters.

THE THEORY   This theory relies on the assumption that citizens can be arranged along a single dimension from liberal to conservative as shown in Figure 10.2, that most voters are ideologically centrist, and that voters prefer the party or candidate who is closest to their own beliefs.

Different issues have been important at different times in American history, but there is substantial evidence that most of them can be placed on a single economic-social dimension.[9] (Issues having to do with race and slavery are the notable exception.) And, despite appearances, many political scientists believe that most Americans are centrists at heart (though that may be changing). Parties are thought of as vote-seeking entities without particular ideological preferences, so in order to appeal to the most number of voters, they will take positions at the *median* of the economic-social dimension, where exactly one-half the voters are more liberal and one-half are more conservative. It can be shown mathematically that the party that captures the median voter will always win the election, meaning if either party took a position even a little bit away from the median, the other party would win more votes.[10] Compare this theory to the responsible party model. According to the electoral competition model, parties are forced to move to the middle (as Figure 10.2 signifies) rather than to the extremes, as the responsible party model predicts. Also, in this theory, it should not matter which party wins the election because the policies a majority of voters want will be enacted. Democratic representation, according to the electoral competition model, is assured by the dynamics of party competition.

THE POTENTIAL PROBLEMS   The most important criticism of the electoral competition model is that a number of pressures exist which prevent parties from moving to the middle. Parties need the backing of financial contributors for campaign money, and candidates need the backing of party activists during primary elections. Both groups, contributors and activists, tend to be more extreme than the average voter and will only support the party if it too supports extreme policy positions. Individual candidates who are more ideologically extreme may win a primary election when only voters who belong to the party can participate, and these same candidates may be unwilling or unable to moderate their positions during the general election, when all voters participate. Because American political parties have little control over what individual candidates say and do, there is virtually no way a party can force its own candidates toward the center. It is quite common to see extreme candidates run in a general election, something that would not be predicted by the electoral competition model (but would be by the responsible party model). Relatedly, as the American electorate polarizes, voters may not be distributed in such a uniform fashion as depicted in Figure 10.2. Instead, they may lie more toward the ideological edges of the spectrum. This arrangement might encourage parties to become more extreme.

Still, the conditions necessary for the electoral competition voting model are close enough to the truth that the model does work, to an extent, in real elections. Extreme candidates who do manage to win a primary tend to do poorly in general elections, especially when the electorate is large and diverse (such as in senate or presidential campaigns), creating a powerful incentive for parties and their candidates to remain near the median over the long-term. Indeed, electoral competition is probably one of the main ways elected officials are influenced by public opinion.

The Retrospective (or Reward and Punishment) Voting Model

A third model by which elections might bring about popular control of government is the **retrospective voting model**, also known as the **electoral reward and punishment model**. This model suggests that voters make retrospective evaluations about how well the party in power has governed during the previous few years and then decide if they approve of the party's performance and want its members to continue in office.

retrospective voting model (or electoral reward and punishment model)

A theory of democratic elections in which voters look back at the performance of a party in power and cast ballots on the basis of how well it did in office.

FACING THE NATION

President Obama is seen shortly after addressing the nation on the 2009 global financial crisis. Voters often punish the president during periods of poor economic performance.

THE THEORY According to the model, voters simply make retrospective, or backward-looking judgments, about how well incumbents have performed. Voters reward success by reelecting officials and punish failure by voting for the other party. The result is that politicians who want to stay in office have strong incentives to promote prosperity and to address the problems that occur, such as a bad economy, rising inflation, or threats from a foreign country.[11] This reward-and-punishment model of democratic control has the advantage of simplicity. It requires very little of voters: they do not need to have well-informed policy preferences, and do not need to analyze campaign platforms. Instead, they only make a judgment of how well or poorly things have been going in the country. For example, voters seem to have punished Republicans in 2008, expressing their displeasure with George W. Bush over the wars in Iraq and Afghanistan and the bad economy, while voters punished Obama and the Democrats in 2010 for not fixing the economy and for passing a controversial health care law, the Affordable Care Act.[12]

THE POTENTIAL PROBLEMS The reward and punishment model is simple in theory, but it is also a rather blunt instrument. It removes unpopular political leaders, but only after (and not before) disasters happen, without guaranteeing that the next leaders will be any better. The retrospective voting model also requires that politicians are able to anticipate the effects of future policies and correct problems that have occurred. In fact, often when the majority party is punished and the other party takes over, it too is unable to solve the important problems of the day and is eventually voted out of office, replaced with the previous majority. This model may also encourage politicians to produce deceptively positive, but temporary results that arrive just in time for Election Day and then fade away.[13]

Imperfect Electoral Democracy

Each of the three models of popular control exists to some extent in American elections, though no model works perfectly under all conditions. On occasion, the models converge and help produce an election that is enormously consequential for the direction of the nation as in the 1932 election, which elevated Franklin Roosevelt to the presidency.

The election of 1932 was held during the Great Depression, one of the greatest crises the country has ever faced: the unemployment rate reached nearly 33 percent, banks failed, and deflation (when money becomes worth less and less) set in. At the political level, the public demanded action, but the Republican administration of Herbert Hoover was unwilling to respond to the crisis. Hoover and members of Congress believed the federal government should not be involved in fixing the economy. Franklin Roosevelt and congressional Democrats were swept into office as he laid out a clear vision of how to fix the economy which differed from the majority Republicans (responsible party government model). Voters were also extremely dissatisfied with the policies of Hoover and demanded a change (retrospective voting model). The resulting government action, as demonstrated in this chapter's Applying the Framework model (see Figure 10.3), was a large and sweeping program of public works projects and government spending meant to stimulate the economy and pull the country out of the Great Depression. The economy improved, albeit slowly, but voters responded by electing a Democratic president for the next four election cycles.

Which Party Model Works Best?

None of the three models works well enough to guarantee perfectly democratic outcomes. In certain respects, they conflict: responsible parties and electoral competition,

FIGURE 10.3 APPLYING THE FRAMEWORK: A CONSEQUENTIAL ELECTION
AND A NEW DEAL FOR AMERICA

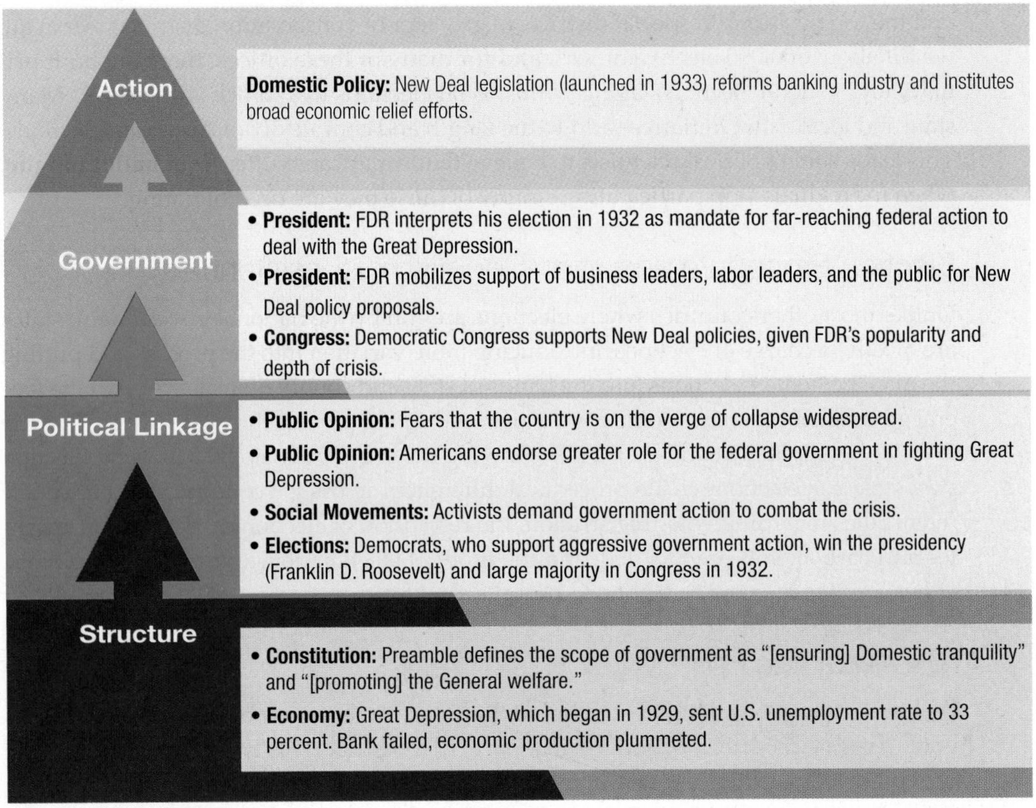

Action

Domestic Policy: New Deal legislation (launched in 1933) reforms banking industry and institutes broad economic relief efforts.

Government

- **President:** FDR interprets his election in 1932 as mandate for far-reaching federal action to deal with the Great Depression.
- **President:** FDR mobilizes support of business leaders, labor leaders, and the public for New Deal policy proposals.
- **Congress:** Democratic Congress supports New Deal policies, given FDR's popularity and depth of crisis.

Political Linkage

- **Public Opinion:** Fears that the country is on the verge of collapse widespread.
- **Public Opinion:** Americans endorse greater role for the federal government in fighting Great Depression.
- **Social Movements:** Activists demand government action to combat the crisis.
- **Elections:** Democrats, who support aggressive government action, win the presidency (Franklin D. Roosevelt) and large majority in Congress in 1932.

Structure

- **Constitution:** Preamble defines the scope of government as "[ensuring] Domestic tranquility" and "[promoting] the General welfare."
- **Economy:** Great Depression, which began in 1929, sent U.S. unemployment rate to 33 percent. Bank failed, economic production plummeted.

© Edward S. Greenberg

for example, tend to push in opposite directions. In other respects, all three models require conditions that are not met in reality.

Perhaps the most important problem with all three models is that they cannot ensure government responsiveness to all citizens unless *all* citizens have the right to vote and exercise that right. Unfortunately, tens of millions of Americans cannot or do not go to the polls and many states have recently passed laws making it *more* difficult for many citizens to vote. These stricter voting requirements demand very specific forms of identification that some types of people do not have, or impose strict residency requirements, making college students, for example, return home to vote. These laws are new and their effects are an ongoing area of research, but they are most likely to affect poor people and racial minorities. For these individuals, their voices are not heard; political equality is not achieved.

THE UNIQUE NATURE OF AMERICAN ELECTIONS

10.2 Distinguish American elections from those in other countries.

American elections differ quite dramatically from those of most other democratic countries. The differences are the result of rules—mainly found in the Constitution but also in federal statutes and judicial decisions—that define offices and describe how elections are to be conducted. The distinguishing features of elections in the United States are discussed in the sections that follow.

Elections Are Numerous and Frequent

In some sense, we are "election happy" in the United States. We not only elect the president and members of Congress (senators and representatives), but because of federalism, we also elect governors, other state officials (like attorneys general and lieutenant governors), state legislators, and (in most states) judges. In addition, all of the top officials of counties, cities, and towns are elected by the people, as are school boards and the top positions in special districts (e.g., water or conservation districts). All in all, we fill about 500,000 elective offices, and for many of these offices, there are both primary and general elections, along with special elections if an office is vacated.[14] Many state and local ballot initiatives add to the length and complexity of American elections. This leads some political scientists to believe that Americans suffer from **ballot fatigue**, when individuals stop participating simply because they are tired of voting.

ballot fatigue
The exhaustion of voter interest and knowledge in elections caused by election frequency and the length and complexity of ballots.

Election Procedure and Vote-Counting Inconsistencies

Unlike most other countries where elections are run by the national government, states are mostly in charge of elections, introducing more variation into the process and putting the management of elections into the hands of state and county officials. Though the federal government exercises some control over the voting process through laws such as the 1965 Voting Rights Act and a 2002 law allowing the use of provisional ballots on Election Day, state-run elections create procedural differences across the country. States have different rules regarding voter registration, the resolution of election disputes, how absentee and early ballots are handled, and the types of election devices used (paper ballots, either counted by hand or scanned, computerized touch screen systems, and more.)[15]

"First Past the Post" Wins

Winners in most elections in the United States are determined by who wins the most votes—not necessarily a majority—in a particular district. This type of election is often called "first-past-the-post," as in a horse race where the winner is the first past the finish line, or a single-member plurality election, so named because only one person running in each district wins. These elections include congressional elections and presidential contests for electoral votes in each of the states. We do not have proportional representation or multi-member districts (where multiple people are elected from the same district), nor do we have "run-off" elections between the top two vote-getters in presidential or congressional elections to ensure a majority winner. If no candidate wins an absolute majority (more than 50 percent of the vote), the winner is the candidate who wins a **plurality**, simply the most votes out of all the candidates. In fact, presidential candidates often win only a plurality rather than a majority. Bill Clinton won only 43 percent of the vote in 1992 because of the strong showing of a third party candidate,

plurality
Occurs when a candidate receives more votes than any other candidate in an election but still less than a majority.

PARLIAMENTARY ELECTIONS IN INDIA

Prime ministerial candidate Narendra Modi, of the opposition Bharatiya Janata Party (BJP), won the highest office in the world's largest democracy in parliamentary elections that spanned more than a month to accommodate India's hundreds of millions of eligible voters.

What factors differentiate our elections from parliamentary systems?

H. Ross Perot (who won 19 percent of the popular vote but no electoral votes). Though Bill Clinton won a plurality, consider that 56 percent of ballots were cast for Perot or the Republican nominee, incumbent president George H. W. Bush! Donald Trump won a plurality in enough states to win the Electoral College, but lost the national vote total. In France and Finland, by way of contrast, a second election is held if no candidate wins a majority in the first round of voting for the president. This type of election ensures that the person who is elected comes to office with majority support. The United States is one of the relatively few countries with a strict single-member plurality system for most offices and is an important distinguishing feature of our elections.

VOTING IN THE UNITED STATES

10.3 Analyze the importance of political participation in elections.

In this section, we turn our attention to political participation, especially voting. Individuals participate in politics in many ways: by donating time or money to a campaign, posting a yard sign, or even discussing politics with friends and family. All of these activities are important, but voting is considered the most basic act of political participation.

For elections to be democratic—whether in the prospective, electoral competition, or retrospective voting models—elections must not only have high participation, individuals in all social groups in the population (e.g., across race, gender, income, occupation, religion, ethnicity, region, and so on) must have the same ability to vote, or else the principle of political equality would be violated.

Expansion of the Franchise

Until passage of the Fourteenth and Fifteenth Amendments after the Civil War it was up to each state to determine who within its borders was eligible to vote. In the early years, many of the states limited the legal right to vote—called the **franchise**—quite severely by prohibiting many types of people, including slaves, Native Americans, women, and white men without property, from voting. One of the most important developments in the political history of the United States, an essential part of the struggle for democracy, has been the expansion of the right to vote. The extension of the franchise has been a lengthy and uneven process, spanning more than 200 years.[16]

franchise
The legal right to vote; see suffrage.

AT THE POLLS

Early U.S. elections were poorly organized and hard to get to. In addition, only a small proportion of the population was eligible to vote. In this painting (*The County Election* by George Caleb Bingham), a group of white men, the only people with the right to vote in most places in the United States at the time, wait to vote in the presidential election of 1824 at a polling station in Saline County, Missouri.
How would the demographics of eligible voters change in the United States throughout the 19th Century?

Still, more Americans now have the right to vote than ever before, though the limitations states place on exercising the right to vote continues to be an important debate.

WHITE MALES   The first barriers to fall were those concerning property and religion. So strong were the democratic currents during Thomas Jefferson's presidency (1801–1809) and in the years leading up to the election of Andrew Jackson in 1828 that by the time he assumed office in 1829, property, taxpaying, and religious requirements had been dropped in all states except North Carolina and Virginia. That left **suffrage**, or the ability to vote, firmly in place for most adult white males in the United States. Most of Europe, including Britain, did not achieve this degree of democracy until after World War I.

suffrage
The legal right to vote; see franchise.

AFRICAN AMERICANS, WOMEN, AND YOUNG PEOPLE   Despite the early expansion of the right to vote, the struggle to expand the franchise to African Americans, women, and young people proved difficult and painful. Ironically, universal white male suffrage was often accompanied by the removal of voting rights from black freedmen, even in states that did not permit slavery.[17] It took the bloody Civil War to free the slaves and the Fifteenth Amendment to the U.S. Constitution (1870) to extend the right to vote to all black males, both North and South. Southern states were still hostile to voting rights for African Americans and Congress essentially forced the South to accept all of the Civil War Amendments (the Thirteenth, Fourteenth, and Fifteenth) as a pre-condition of reentering the Union. Despite the passage of the Fifteenth Amendment, efforts by the South to disenfranchise blacks continued, and were helped by Supreme Court rulings, resulting in widespread discrimination and disenfranchisement by the end of the 19th century. These rulings allowed practices such as poll taxes and literacy tests, which were applied selectively as a way of denying the right to vote to African Americans. These limitations remained in place until the 1960s civil rights movement and the passage of the Voting Rights Act of 1965.

Though many states allowed women the right to vote, especially in the West, the passage of the Nineteenth Amendment (1920) nationalized the right for all women in all states. The franchise was granted to 18 to 20-year-olds with the passage of the Twenty-Sixth Amendment in 1971. The Twenty-Sixth Amendment was passed near the end of the Vietnam War. Support for the amendment grew out of demands that individuals old enough to fight and die for the country in war were also old enough to cast votes.

The result of these changes at the state and national levels was an enormous increase in the proportion of Americans who were legally eligible to vote: from about 23 percent of the adult population in 1788–1789 to nearly 98 percent by the beginning of the 1970s—practically all citizens above the age of 18, except people who have recently moved to another state, people in mental institutions, and incarcerated felons (and, in many states, former felons).

Direct Partisan Elections

Another voting trend has involved the direct election of government officials, replacing the old indirect methods that insulated officials from the public. At the same time, the development of a well-defined two-party system has clarified choices for citizens and increased competition between the parties, promoting democratic accountability among elected officials.

Electoral College
Representatives selected in each of the states, their numbers based on each state's total number of its senators and representatives; a majority of Electoral College votes elects the president.

The election of the president, even with the existence of the **Electoral College**, has become more directly democratic. By the time of the presidential campaign of 1800, which pitted Jefferson's Democratic-Republicans against the Federalists, most state legislatures had stopped picking the presidential electors themselves (as the Constitution permits). Instead, the legislatures allowed a popular vote for electors, most of whom were pledged to support the presidential candidate of one party or the other. The passage of the Twelfth Amendment in 1804 further clarified the process by requiring each elector to select only one candidate. By discontinuing the process in which the vice president was elected separately from the president, elections in which the vice president could belong to a party different from the party of the president ended.

This system, odd and cumbersome as it is, is very similar to the process used today and it almost always ensures that American citizens choose their president more or less directly, though two recent exceptions have left some wondering whether splits between the Electoral College and the popular vote will become more common. In the 2000 election, Democrat Al Gore won the popular vote by more than 500,000 votes, but Republican George W. Bush captured a majority of the electoral votes after the Supreme Court ruled in Bush's favor on who should receive Florida's 25 electoral votes. Again in 2016, the Republican candidate, Donald Trump, lost the popular vote (by almost 3 million ballots) but won the Electoral College. He did so by very narrowly winning a number of states while badly losing a few large population states such as California. In fact, a shift of only about 80,000 votes across three states would have resulted in the election of Hillary Clinton.

By 1840, the parties had started nominating presidential candidates in national **party conventions** instead of in congressional party caucuses. Later still, the parties began letting voters select many convention delegates directly in state primary elections or through party caucuses in which party supporters hold area meetings to vote on their preferred candidate. The result is that the presidential nominees are largely selected by voters in the states, rather than party officials. The important role of primaries and caucuses in nominating party candidates for elected office enhances democratic control of government, although we will see that some antidemocratic features remain.

Another form of direct elections occurred with the passage of the Seventeenth Amendment in 1913. Previously, U.S. senators were selected by state legislatures rather than directly by the people, leading to charges of corruption in the late 1800s when it appeared that many well-connected and wealthy individuals were "buying" senate seats from the state legislatures. Since 1913, all members of the Senate have been subject to direct election by the voters.

Taken together, the expansion of the franchise and the development of direct, two-party elections have represented major successes in the struggle for democracy. But, problems remain on the voting participation front.

party convention
A gathering of delegates who nominate a party's presidential candidate.

Barriers to Voting and Low Voter Turnout

The disturbing fact is that today proportionally fewer people vote than during most of the 19th century. Since 1912, only about 50 to 65 percent of Americans have voted in presidential elections (see Figure 10.4) and still fewer in other elections: 40 to 50 percent in off-year (non-presidential-year) congressional elections and as few as 10 to 20 percent in primaries and local elections, although the exact number depends on how turnout is measured. In addition, turnout in presidential elections remains well below turnout in other democratic countries. In Western Europe, turnout rates regularly top 75 percent, and in Australia, where voting is required by law, turnout is, unsurprisingly, over 90 percent.

Why do so few Americans vote compared to other democracies? It is not because Americans dislike participating or are inherently anti-democratic. Instead, political scientists have identified a number of possible structural factors about the way we conduct elections. It seems clear that the difficulty and effort required to vote in this country is an important cause of our relatively low turnout.[18]

REGISTRATION REQUIREMENTS   In the United States, only citizens who take the initiative to register in advance are permitted to vote in an election. Most commonly, the registration period is ten to thirty days before an election. Many people do not remember to register in advance, do not have the required paperwork, or do not understand how to go about registering. For example, people who move, either within a state or to another state, must find the appropriate election official, produce certain

FIGURE 10.4 THE RISE AND FALL OF TURNOUT IN PRESIDENTIAL ELECTIONS, 1789–2016

Turnout in presidential elections rose sharply during the 19th century—except during the "Era of Good Feelings" (1815–1825) when there was no party competition and little interest in politics among the public—but declined in the 20th century. In 2004, turnout increased dramatically, but only to a level typical of the 1950s and 1960s.

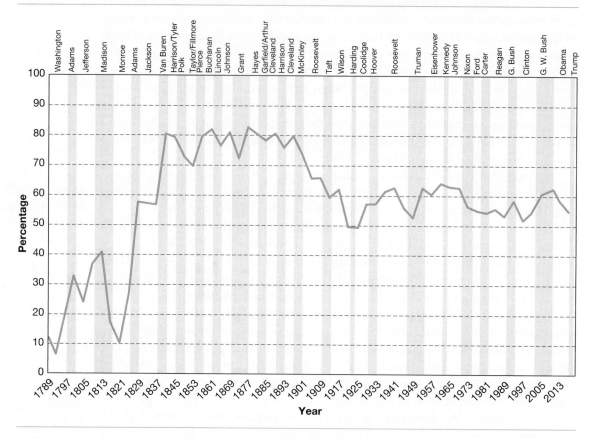

NOTE: From 1920, the Census Bureau has calculated voting turnout as the percentage of the voting-age population voting, not as a percentage of the total voting-eligible population.

SOURCE: McDonald, Michael P. 2016. "2016 General Election Turnout Rates" United States Elections Project. Accessed at: http://www.electproject.org/2016g on November 11, 2016.

documents, and complete paperwork, all months in advance of an election which they may not even be thinking about. As a result, many do not register in time, lowering turnout, according to one study, by 9 percentage points.[19] In most European countries with high turnout rates, the government, rather than individual citizens, is responsible for deciding who is listed as eligible to vote and registers them automatically.

Turnout is much higher among registered voters, so a number of states have taken steps to make registration easier. Allowing for same day registration, as seventeen states have now done, seems to be effective in increasing turnout by anywhere from three to seven percentage points.[20] In Minnesota and Wisconsin in 2016, where same-day registration is in effect, turnout was 74 percent and 69 percent, respectively, similar to turnout in other rich democracies, though these are both states with strong political cultures.[21] Other reforms designed to make registration easier include the National Voter Registration Act (known commonly as the "Motor Voter" law). The National Voter Registration Act requires states to allow people to register in places where they are already in contact with their state governments, such as at welfare offices and at motor vehicle licensing offices.

ELECTION DAY TIMING   Unlike most European countries, Election Day in the United States is held during the week and it is not a national holiday. Unfortunately, holding elections on Tuesdays when most people have to work or attend school reduces voter turnout. Further, even for those people who are able to take time off work to go vote, driving to the polling place and waiting in a long line may be too time consuming.[22] In other words, the inconvenience of voting also discourages many people from voting.

States have taken some steps to address these problems. These include allowing an extended voting period—usually called early voting—which allows voters to cast a ballot in the days leading up to Election Day (37 states now have some form of early voting).[23] Other states have experimented with mail-in ballots, which allows voters to simply fill out a ballot and mail it back to the state before Election Day. These reforms are designed to reduce the barriers to voting and increase voter turnout.

TOO MUCH COMPLEXITY As suggested earlier, when voters go to the polls in the United States, they must make voting choices for a multitude of federal, state, and local offices and often decide on constitutional and policy measures put on the ballot by state legislatures (individually called a **referendum** or collectively, **referenda**) or the public (called an **initiative**), especially in states such as California and Colorado where these are common. Research demonstrates that many potential voters are simply overwhelmed by the complexity of the issues and the number of choices they must make in the voting booth leading some to stay home.[24]

Reform Proposals and New Struggles over Voting Rights

A growing body of political science research suggests social pressures, exerted by friends on Facebook, for example, encourages individuals to vote.[25] Conversely, the risk of being exposed as a nonvoter to friends or neighbors is also successful at motivating individuals to vote.[26] Political scientists have found that voting is habit forming—when an individual votes once, they receive a positive psychological feeling and are more likely to vote again in the future.[27] Finally, for first-time voters, being reassured that their vote is private and they will not have to defend their ballot to poll workers or other officials makes it more likely they will vote.[28] This knowledge will increase the use of technology and social media as a way of encouraging voting, especially among young people, who are less likely to vote but are among the most active users of new technology.

States are also making changes to how they conduct elections. Reforms, such as same day registration, early voting, and mail-in balloting are becoming more and more common. All of these making voting less time consuming and more convenient, which improves turnout. Online voting, while not yet widely implemented, seems to be just around the corner.

NEW VOTING BARRIERS Though much has been done to make registration and voting easier, there is a countermovement that seeks to make registration and voting harder for many. The fight over registration requirements and voting access is largely a fight between the two parties. Recently, Democrats have sought an expanded electorate, believing that those least likely to vote—lower-income and less educated people, college students, and racial and ethnic minorities—are more likely to vote for them. Claiming they are interested in rooting out voter fraud in our present system, but also wishing to take away Democratic votes, Republicans have been pushing hard to more tightly regulate the voting process. In many states controlled by Republicans after their 2010 electoral landslide, Republican officials passed laws requiring government-issued photo IDs for voting, while many of them, including Ohio and Florida, also cut back the length of early voting periods. Maine ended same-day registration. Alabama and Kansas now require proof of citizenship. Florida and Iowa no longer allow ex-felons (those who have already served their time) to vote. Other states, such as Wisconsin and Tennessee, have sought to make it harder for college students to vote by not allowing the use of college identification cards as a valid form of voter identification, among other limitations. One organization counts twenty-three

referendum

Procedures available in some states by which state laws or constitutional amendments proposed by the legislature are submitted to the voters for approval or rejection.

initiative

Procedures available in some states for citizens to put proposed laws and constitutional amendments on the ballot for voter approval or rejection.

states that have passed restrictive voting laws since 2010. It remains to be seen what the turnout effects of these changes will be and many states face lawsuits over their requirements, but no one doubts that these changes will keep many eligible citizens from voting, especially those most likely to cast their ballots for Democrats.[29]

OTHER POSSIBILITIES Political scientists, journalists, and political practitioners have suggested a number of other possible reasons for low turnout. For example, it may be that the increase in negative advertising, increasing partisanship, and the growing incivility of American politics overall are adding to cynicism about the political system and politicians, causing Americans to turn away in disgust or despair. There has been some speculation that the time available to Americans for political participation has declined either because of longer working hours or because of the availability of other diversions, most especially television and the Internet. Unfortunately, scholars still are tussling with these issues; there is much disagreement among them about the extent to which these factors affect voting turnout.[30]

WHO VOTES?

10.4 Identify demographic factors that increase the likelihood of voting.

Voting in the United States varies a great deal according to people's income, education, age, and ethnicity. This means that some kinds of people have more representation and influence with elected officials than others, and, other things being equal, they are more likely to have their preferences and interests reflected in what government does.

Income and Education

For the most part, politically active people tend to be those with higher incomes and more formal education.[31] In the 2016 presidential elections, about 74.5 percent of those with incomes of $100,000 or above said they had voted, but only 46.4 percent of those with incomes under $50,000 said they had done so (see Figure 10.5). About 73.9 percent of those earning postgraduate degrees reported that they had voted, but only 47 percent of high school graduates and 29 percent of those who had not graduated from high school had done so.[32] Some statistical analyses have indicated that the

FIGURE 10.5 ELECTION TURNOUT BY SOCIAL GROUP, 2016 ELECTIONS

Age, education, race, ethnicity, income, and gender all affect voting behavior. Members of certain social groups are more likely to vote in elections than others. The Census Bureau warns that these numbers may be inflated because of people's tendency to want to report positive citizen behavior to interviewers. What is important here, however, is not necessarily the accuracy of the turnout totals but the comparison between groups of people. The relative turnout comparisons between groups fit the general picture available from other academic research and government sources.

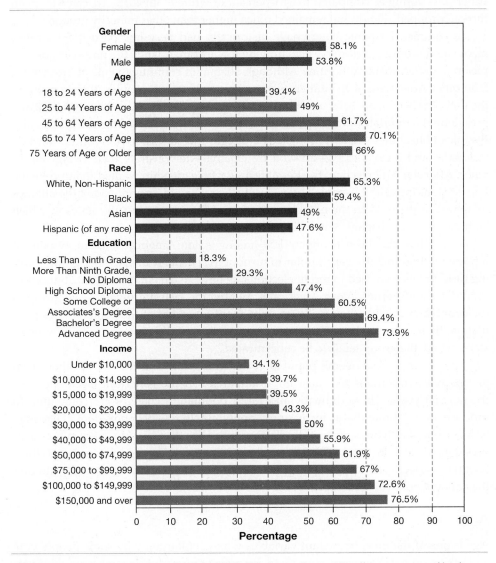

SOURCE: Voting and Registration in the Election of 2016. U.S. Census Bureau, https://www.census.gov/data/tables/time-series/demo/voting-and-registration/p20-580.html.

most important factor determining whether people vote is their level of formal education. Even when accounting for other important factors—including race, income, and gender—college-educated people are much more likely to tell interviewers that they have voted. There are several possible reasons: people with more education learn more about politics, are more interested in the political process, are less troubled by registration requirements, and are more confident in their ability to affect political life.

Looking at other important forms of political participation besides voting, citizens with lower incomes are also less likely to work in campaigns, give money, contact officials, and attend political events like town-hall meetings. Wealthier Americans have more money, stronger social ties to elected officials, and more knowledge of how to get things done. As a result, they tend to be much more active politically, and likely have more clout than poorer citizens.

Race and Ethnicity

In the past, turnout among African Americans was lower than among whites, but now the percentages have become nearly equal. In fact, African Americans are at least equally likely to vote, and sometimes more likely, than whites of similar educational and income backgrounds. The 2012 presidential election reflected this trend. For the first time ever, turnout was higher among African Americans than whites, with 66.2 percent of African Americans voting as compared to 64.1 percent of whites.[33] In 2016, African American turnout dropped slightly, but remained much higher than other minority groups.

In contrast, Hispanic voters have historically had very low participation rates; many are discouraged from participating by low incomes, language problems, or suspicion of government authorities. Although Hispanics continue to vote at lower rates than other Americans with similar incomes and educational profiles, their turnout at the polls has been increasing, reaching 48 percent in 2012.[34] In both 2008 and 2012, the presidential candidates made special efforts to win over this influential group, and the role of Hispanics in closely contested battleground states such as Florida, Nevada, Colorado, and New Mexico—all won by Obama—demonstrate their rising importance. After the 2012 election, the Republican Party leadership wanted to improve the Party's standing with Hispanic voters, but in 2016 Donald Trump made little attempt to appeal to them. With the notable exception of Florida, he lost the states in which large numbers of Hispanic voters live.

Voting has also been relatively low among Asian Americans; about 49 percent reported voting in 2016, very similar to turnout for Hispanics. Like other groups, voting turnout has increased in recent elections, as have Asian American contributions to candidates and parties. Asian Americans are now the fastest growing racial group in the country, and while they make up only about 6 percent of the United States population, their votes are becoming more important to candidates especially in western states where the group tends to be concentrated.

The decline of the overall population which is white and the rise of other racial groups will be perhaps the most important trend in the American electorate over the next 50 years. These dramatic and rapid population changes are combining to produce an electorate that is increasingly nonwhite. In the 1996 presidential election, 82.5 percent of all voters were white. That number has decreased in every subsequent presidential election, and by 2016, it was only 70 percent. Demographers and political scientists expect it to keep dropping for the foreseeable future, dramatically altering the national political landscape.[35]

Age

Age is one of the most important variables when explaining why some people vote and others do not. Younger voters go to the polls at much lower rates than older voters. This was true even in the exciting 2008 presidential election when young people played such a visible role in the Obama campaign. Though 2 million more 18- to 24-year-olds voted than in 2004, their voting turnout was still only 48.5 percent (up only 2 percent from the previous presidential election).[36] In comparison, turnout among older voters age 65 to 74 was 70 percent. In the 2016 election, turnout among 18- to 24-year-olds was only about 39 percent, while among those 65 to 74, it was about 70 percent. The reasons for low turnout among young people are that they tend to be less rooted in communities, less familiar with registration and voting procedures, not in the habit of voting, and have less time away from school and work to vote.[37]

Gender

For many years, women voted and participated in politics at lower rates than men. This gender gap in voting and other forms of political participation disappeared in the United States by the end of the 1980s, and today women actually vote at a higher

MOBILIZING THE YOUTH VOTE

College Democrats at Boston University register students to vote in the upcoming national elections, trying to match the high turnout of the youth vote that occurred in 2008 that was so helpful to Democrats.

Do low rates of voting participation matter, or are the young already well-represented by elected officials?

rate than men (by about 4 percent).[38] This dramatic change over the past two or three decades can probably be traced to the improvement in the educational attainments of women, the entrance of more women into the paid workforce, and the increased focus on socioeconomic issues important to women such as pay equity, sexual harassment, and abortion on the American political agenda.

Does It Matter Who Votes?

Some observers have argued that it doesn't matter if many people don't vote because the preferences of nonvoters, as measured by public opinion polls, aren't much different from those who do cast a ballot. Others say that few elections would have different outcomes if everyone voted as nonvoters tend to support the winning candidate at the same rate as those who actually voted.[39]

We should not be too quick to accept these arguments, just as few now accept the 19th-century view that there was no need for women to vote because their husbands could protect their interests. Even when the expressed preferences of nonvoters on surveys are similar to voters, their objective circumstances, and therefore their need for government services, may differ markedly.[40] It may not just be about the preferences of voters on certain issues, but instead about which issues politicians pay attention to when governing. For example, Hispanics, the young, and those with low incomes might want elected officials to concentrate on issues having to do with the social safety net or other government programs that are of less interest to other citizens.[41] There is a growing body of evidence, in fact, that high- and low-income people in the United States have very different preferences about what types of issues elected officials should focus on, and that elected officials are more likely to address problems thought important by higher-income groups.[42] It is also known that government redistribution programs (welfare, for example) in rich democracies are associated with the degree to which low-income people vote, with the United States, where low-income people participate at far lower rates than others, doing the least in this area of government activity when compared with most European democracies.[43]

THE PRESIDENTIAL CAMPAIGN

10.5 Outline the process of campaigns for the presidency.

Elections are the fundamental connection between voters and elected officials in republican government. The types of people who run for office, whether they take clear policy stands that differ from their opponents, and whether the candidates have beliefs that match the average voter all have important effects on the types of policies that are produced. In evaluating how democratic our elections are, we need to examine what kinds of alternatives are put before the voters in campaigns, and the processes that govern the campaign and election. We consider these issues in this section focusing on presidential elections only.

Preparing to Run and the Invisible Primary

To become president, candidates must first win the nomination of their own party through the state primaries and caucuses which occur between January and June of a presidential election year. Formally, the Republican and Democratic presidential nominees are selected at their national conventions in late August or early September before the presidential election in November, though for a variety of reasons, in 2016 the parties held their conventions in late July. In both parties, the nomination goes to the winner of a majority of delegates to the national party convention who are chosen in state primaries and caucuses. A **primary** is simply an election where voters go to the polls and cast their ballot. A **nominating caucus** is different in that voters attend local meetings which are held all over the state at the same time, with citizens casting their votes in the meeting.

For the Democrats, convention delegates are made up of those "pledged" to a candidate via an election outcome in a state primary or caucus, and **superdelegates**, party luminaries and elected officials who are not formally pledged to any candidate.[44] In 2016 about one-in-five delegates to the Democratic National Convention fell into this category, ensuring that any nominee must also have the support of the party establishment. After controversy over the role of superdelegates in Hillary Clinton's primary victory in 2016, the Democratic Party changed its rules to limit the influence of superdelegates by allowing them only to vote for a candidate at the convention if no candidate wins the nomination based strictly on the support of pledged delegates. Republicans have a few "unpledged" delegates (they are not usually referred to as superdelegates), but they are much less important because there are so few of them.

WHO RUNS In any given presidential election, only a handful of candidates are serious contenders. So far in American history, candidates have virtually always been middle-aged or elderly white men with extensive formal educations, fairly high incomes,[45] and substantial experience as public figures—usually as government officials (especially vice presidents, governors, or senators) or military heroes. The Democrats broke this mold in 2008 when Barack Obama, an African American, won the nomination in a tight race with Hillary Clinton, who herself became the nominee in 2016. Movie stars, media commentators, business executives, and others who want to run for president almost always have to perform important government service before they are seriously considered for the presidency. Ronald Reagan, for example, most of whose career was spent as actor, served as governor of California before being elected president. Donald Trump, the Republican nominee in 2016, was a notable exception, having never held prior elective office, been a high ranking military official, or been appointed to political office. No president has ever been elected without any of these prior positions. In fact, this may have been part of Trump's appeal. Most of his serious opponents for the nomination were all elected officials and many were seen as too tied into the political establishment. Ted Cruz, the least establishment of all Republicans, was the last to end his candidacy, while well-known elected officials, such as Jeb Bush, Chris Christie, and Marco Rubio had trouble generating much support.

primary election
Statewide elections in which voters choose delegates to the national party conventions.

caucus, nominating
The process in some states for selecting delegates to the national party conventions characterized by neighborhood and area-wide meetings of party supporters and activists.

superdelegates
Elected officials from all levels of government who are appointed by party committees to be delegates to the national convention of the Democratic Party; not selected in primary elections or caucuses.

The single best stepping-stone to becoming president has been the vice presidency, which is usually filled by former senators or governors. Since 1900, five of the twenty presidents have succeeded from the vice presidency after the president's death or resignation, and two others, Nixon and Bush (the elder), were former vice presidents elected in their own right.

GETTING STARTED   A person who wants to run for president usually begins at least two or three years before the election by testing the waters, asking friends and financial backers if they will support a run, and testing their national name recognition and popularity through national surveys. The potential candidate will then put together an exploratory committee to round up endorsements, advisers and consultants, and financial contributions. At this stage, if all goes well, the presidential aspirant will begin to assemble a larger group of advisers, formulate strategy, setup campaign websites, recruit campaign workers, put together organizations in key states, and officially announce his or her candidacy. Fund-raising at this stage is crucial because it finances advertising and pays for campaign workers across the country.[46] Raising serious money from donors big and small—the latter, primarily through the Internet—is a clear sign to members of the party, interest and advocacy groups, and the news media that a candidate ought to be taken seriously. If a candidate can't raise money, she or he is not taken seriously and cannot appeal to big money donors. And, with little money in the bank, the candidate cannot pay for advertising or other campaign expenditures, making failure in the first primaries and caucuses inevitable. Securing support from party elites and turning that support into financial backing is now so important to serious candidates that it is commonly called the **invisible primary**.[47] Once again, the 2016 Republican primary process was a notable exception. Part of the reason Trump's nomination shocked the political world was because he did virtually none of these things; party leaders actively campaigned against him, and he raised very little money compared to most other candidates. Whether the road to his win was an aberration of the start of a new trend is difficult to say.

Hillary Clinton took a more traditional path to the nomination, raising about $100 million by the end of 2015 despite the widespread perception that she would be the nominee and thus not need the money to fend off her only rival, Senator Bernie Sanders. However, Sanders was a stronger candidate than many expected, and Clinton ended up spending almost $300 million on the primary, while Sanders himself raised about $215 million, mostly from small donors. Having sufficient funds is seen

invisible primary

The process in which party elites and influential donors throw their support behind a candidate before any votes have been cast, giving that candidate a financial and organizational advantage during the state primaries and caucuses.

RALLYING SUPPORT

Donald Trump signs one of his trademark red hats for a supporter at a campaign rally during the Republican presidential primary. *What does Trump's victory say about the importance of raising money and winning the support of party elites?*

as a necessary condition to be a successful candidate, but money alone cannot rescue a struggling candidate. Jeb Bush raised $100 million in the first six months of 2015, but still did poorly in the primaries.[48] Bush suspended his run for the presidency after his disappointing finish in South Carolina (in February 2016). Candidates who were not able to raise much money, including Bobby Jindal, Scott Walker, and Lindsey Graham, were forced to dropout even before the first primary votes were cast. According to most estimates, the candidates, the parties, and PACs combined to spend almost $1 billion *per nominee* during the primary and general election campaigns in 2016.

Another important early decision involves how much time and energy to invest in each of the state primaries and caucuses. Candidates expect to do better in certain states because they are from the state or a neighboring one, or the primary voters in the state match the candidate's views on important issues. But, each state entry takes a lot of money, energy, and organization, and any loss is damaging. When a candidate loses in a state, voters and the media may stop taking them seriously, leading to fewer donations and less money. Bernie Sanders, who challenged Hillary Clinton from the left in the 2016 Democratic primary, expected to do well in New Hampshire because he was a well-known senator from neighboring Vermont. To win the nomination however, candidates must string together a few primary and caucus victories early in the calendar. Trump's campaign seemed to be in trouble in late March after losing to Ted Cruz in Utah, Wisconsin, and Colorado. A surprisingly strong showing by Trump in consecutive states in the northeast, then in Indiana in early April effectively ended Cruz's campaign, ensuring Trump would be the nominee.

The Presidential Primary System

Before the 1970s, the conventions were much more important, with candidates appealing to the party elite for support, often after back-room dealing. During the conventions, it could take numerous votes for the assembled delegates to agree on a candidate. Today, because the primary and caucus system ties delegates to specific candidates, the focus is on convincing voters in different states to rack up enough delegates to secure the nomination. The convention is little more than a public party and advertisement for the candidate, staged for the national television audience.

It is especially important for a candidate to establish momentum by winning early primaries and caucuses. Early winners get press attention, financial contributions, and better standings in the polls as voters and contributors decide they are viable candidates and must have some merit if people in other states have supported them. All these factors—attention from the media, money, and increased popular support—help the candidates who win early contests go on to win more and more states.[49] By tradition, Iowa holds the first caucus in early January, and New Hampshire holds the first primary shortly thereafter.

INCUMBENT PRESIDENTS AND THE PRIMARY SYSTEM　We have been focusing on how outsiders and political challengers try to win party presidential nominations. Things are very different for incumbent presidents seeking reelection, like George W. Bush in 2004 or Barack Obama in 2012. Incumbents must also enter and win primaries and caucuses, but they have the machinery of government working for them and, if times are reasonably good, a unified party behind them. They also have an easier time getting campaign contributions, especially during the primaries. As a result, when incumbent presidents only occasionally meet serious competition. They campaign on the job, taking credit for policy successes while discounting or blaming others, such as Congress, for failures. Winning renomination as an incumbent president is usually easy, except in cases of disaster such as the 1968 Vietnam War debacle for Lyndon Johnson. When no incumbent is running, the primary race tends to be much more unpredictable.

PROBLEMS WITH THE PRIMARY SYSTEM　Because the states and the parties—not Congress or the president—control the nominating process, the system is disorganized,

CLINTON AND SANDERS DEBATE DURING THE DEMOCRATIC PRIMARY

Hillary Clinton and Bernie Sanders engaged in a surprisingly close race during the 2016 Democratic Primary. Clinton was the favorite going into the contest, won the invisible primary with the support of the Democratic Party establishment, and had a significant financial advantage. Despite these advantages, Sanders' message of an unfair financial system and Clinton's ties to big banks resonated with Democratic voters. Sanders eventually conceded to Clinton and endorsed her at the Democratic Convention, but many Sanders supporters felt the contest was rigged by the Democratic Party, in favor of Clinton.

Is the primary process fair to outsider candidates with little party support, such as Bernie Sanders?

even chaotic, and changes from one election to the next. Most states have primaries or caucuses for both parties on the same day but others hold them on separate dates for each party. The first primaries and caucuses receive the most attention, and because a candidate may already have the nomination wrapped up late in the primary calendar, an increasing number of states have moved their election date forward. As a result, the primary and caucus season started to get "front-loaded" in 2004, then accelerated in 2008 when it became a stampede, with states leap-frogging over the others to position themselves earlier in the calendar. The result in 2008 was that 20 states—including big ones such as New York, New Jersey, Illinois, Missouri, and California—held their primaries on February 5, only a little more than a month after the first caucus in Iowa on January 3. Perhaps ironically, the 2008 Clinton–Obama race was so close that states with late primaries, such as North Carolina and Indiana, became very important in 2008 because neither candidate had the race locked up.

Front-loading is a big problem for candidates. It tends to favor early front-runners or those with lots of money because it requires each candidate campaign in multiple states at once, rather than moving from state to state with the primary calendar. Lesser known candidates who may do well given a little time never have a chance to build momentum, raise money, or broaden their appeal. Both parties passed rules after 2008 to slow or reverse the trend toward front-loading but states still have incentives to vote earlier. Florida, Michigan, and Arizona Republicans bucked party rules to hold their binding primaries in January and February during the 2012 nomination season even though doing so cost them one-half of their delegates to the party convention.

A second issue with the primary system has to do with the types of voters who participate and as a consequence, who the candidates appeal to during the campaign. Though presidential candidates must appeal to the average voter during the general election, this is not the case during a primary. The types of voters who participate in primary elections, months before the general election, tend to be more extreme and more partisan. This leads candidates to become more ideological and less moderate in order to win the primary. During the general election, the candidate will try to move back to the center in order to appeal to a larger cross-section of voters. However, Donald Trump was an exception to this rule, as he made little effort to move back to the center.

The substantial increase in the amount of money spent on presidential campaigns is also helping promote extreme candidates. Even candidates not taken seriously by the media or by important interest groups such as the business community can stay in the race long enough to attract attention to their ideas if they are supported by a group or even a single individual with lots of money. That happened in the 2012 Republican race when Newt Gingrich was supported by the super PAC "Winning Our Future," largely funded by Las Vegas gambling and hotel magnate Sheldon Adelson. Though he had only a handful of delegates and no chance of winning the Republican nomination, his rich backer allowed Gingrich to stay in the nomination race until late April. This problem has become more pronounced; an investigation by the *New York Times* found that by the end of 2015, only 158 wealth families contributed $176 million to presidential candidates, or about half of all donations received.[50] Simply by convincing one wealthy person to support them, an unpopular candidate can stay in the race longer and shape the policy debate. Even candidates like Ted Cruz, who had widespread support in the Republican primary, received tens of millions of dollars from just a few donors.

NOMINATION POLITICS AND DEMOCRACY   What does all this have to do with democratic control of government? Several things. On the one hand, the presidential nomination process encourages candidates to take stands with wide popular appeal, much as electoral competition theories dictate. On the other hand, as the sharp differences between Republican and Democratic convention delegates suggest (see Table 9.3), Republican and Democratic nominees tend to differ in certain systematic ways, consistent with the responsible party theory. Party platforms—the parties' official statements of their stand on issues—tend to include appeals to average voters but also distinctive appeals to each party's base constituencies. Both these tendencies are good for democracy. However, the crucial role of party activists and big money donors in selecting candidates means that nominees and their policy stands are chosen partly to appeal to these elites rather than to ordinary voters.

The General Election Campaign

The general election campaign pitting the candidates of the two major parties against one another, with an occasional third party thrown into the mix, is a very different sort of contest than the run for party nomination. It requires different things from the candidates, campaign organizations, and associated interest and advocacy groups and has an entirely different tone and set of rules, both formal and informal. The general election campaign season, much like the nomination campaign season, has also gotten much longer. For a discussion of the 2016 presidential campaign and election, please refer to the chapter-opening story.

RALLYING SUPPORT IN BATTLE-GROUND STATES

As a candidate, Donald Trump campaigned extensively in Pennsylvania. Here, a supporter attends a rally in Hershey a month before the Election Day. Hillary Clinton was criticized by some after the election for not devoting enough resources to the state.

ACTUATING THE CAMPAIGN   In the not-too-distant past, the candidates took a break over the summer and began to campaign again in earnest after the conventions around Labor Day. Today, however, the presidential nominees for both parties begin to reposition their campaigns by mid-spring. The steps a candidate must take to run in the general election include setting up a campaign organization in each state, sending aides to coordinate backers and local party leaders, and continuing the money-raising effort. In 2012, major advertising campaigns by the Obama and Romney camps were well underway in important swing states by late May, months before either was confirmed as the official nominee of his respective party.[51] The same was true in 2016, and each campaign held their convention nearly a month earlier than usual.

Once the post-convention autumn campaign begins, the nominees make speeches in six or seven media markets each week, with the pace intensifying as the November election draws closer, concentrating on so-called **battleground states**, where the contest between the presidential candidates is deemed to be very close and could go either way. In presidential elections, most states find themselves solidly in the Democratic or Republican columns, and little campaigning takes place in them. California is safely Democratic in presidential elections, for example, so Republican presidential candidates don't spend much time or money there. Democratic candidates tend to ignore places that are reliably Republican, such as Texas. In the last few elections, battleground states have included North Carolina, Nevada, Colorado, Iowa, Ohio, Pennsylvania, and Florida. Consider that in a recent presidential election, 88 percent of media ad buys in the last month of the presidential campaign were concentrated in only 10 states. If competition drives up voter turnout, as political scientists suggest, then an important reason for low turnout in the United States may be that most Americans do not live in a state where presidential elections are hotly contested.

battleground states

Those states which are highly competitive in the presidential general election.

THE PUBLIC FACE OF PARTY CONVENTIONS

The impression conveyed by political conventions can have an important impact on elections. The apparent unhappiness of many anti–Vietnam War delegates with their party's selection at the 1968 Democratic convention in Chicago severely damaged the campaign of nominee Hubert Humphrey. In contrast, the 1984 Republican convention that selected Ronald Reagan as its nominee more nearly resembled a coronation and gave Reagan and the GOP a fast start in the fall campaign.

Is the nominating and convention process still necessary? Might there be an easier or more democratic way to select each party's presidential candidate?

Besides speeches, the campaigns invest heavily in television advertising. Much of the advertising consists of "attack" ads, used to hurt the other candidate. In 2016, Clinton ran ads accusing Trump of being unfit for office, while Trump hammered Clinton on issues of corruption and scandal. Political consultants use voter focus groups to identify hot-button emotional appeals. Negative advertising, whether print, on television, or on the Internet, has been heavily criticized as simplistic and misleading, but it has often proved effective and is difficult to control or counteract. (Some scholars even argue that such ads increase voter interest and provide needed information.)[52]

Each campaign uses micro-targeting techniques to identify and communicate with base supporters and persuadable voters who might be convinced. Sophisticated software allows campaign organizations to combine surveys, census tract data, and materials from marketing research firms to tailor messages to particular groups. They deliver these messages by mail, through door-to-door canvassing, e-mail, and social-networking tools. Republican messages are directed, for example, not only to well-off people but more specifically to those who subscribe to *Golf Weekly* and shop at Saks Fifth Avenue. Democratic messages, using the same micro-targeting, might be directed to members of teachers unions and contributors to the American Civil Liberties Union.[53] Recent research in political science has cast doubt on whether micro-targeting is very effective, but campaigns see it as an important part of their arsenal.[54]

In all of these activities, presidential candidates, with help from hired pollsters and campaign consultants, coordinate campaign spending and activities. The national party organizations are there to help, running parallel advertising campaigns supporting their candidate and attacking the opponent, channeling money to state and local party organizations, and getting potential supporters registered and to the polls. Meanwhile, interest groups and advocacy organizations run their own ad campaigns and get-out-the-vote efforts. Liberal advocacy organizations such as MoveOn.org, for example, run ads in support of the Democratic presidential candidate (and House and Senate Democratic candidates), raise money, and work on turning out Democrats, while conservative Christian groups and business-oriented organizations work to help the Republican side.

INFORMING VOTERS   Presidential campaigns are important because they inform voters. Most of the time, voters do not pay close attention to the issues, or the past performance of an elected official or a party, but campaigns serve to focus voters' attention. The campaigns serve two primary purposes: activating party loyalists and persuading undecided voters. Both of these are accomplished through the information provided to voters over the course of the election. Among other things, voters get information on the candidates' stands on the issues, their past mistakes or successes, and their personal characteristics.

Candidates on the Issues   Some of the information voters get concerns issues. Consistent with the electoral competition theory, both the Republican and the Democratic candidates typically try to appeal to the average voter by taking similar, popular stands on a range of policies, whether it be support for federal student loan programs or proposals to create more jobs. In recent elections, however, intensification of partisanship has moved electoral campaigns in a more responsible party direction, where the parties take clear, distinct stands on the issues. In 2016, Hillary Clinton and Donald Trump took decidedly different stands on major issues, especially on the economy and budget, international affairs, and health care reform. On these issues, the Democratic candidate tends to take a more liberal (on both economic and social dimensions) stand than the Republican, just as Democratic Party identifiers, activists, money givers, and convention delegates tend to be more liberal than their Republican counterparts.

Past Performance of Candidates   Often, candidates focus on past performance in their campaigns consistent with the retrospective voting model. The challenger blames the incumbent for wars, recessions, and other calamities while the incumbent brags about their achievements. Both campaigns attempt to provide their own answer to the question, "Are you better off than you were four years ago?" When these issues become the overriding theme in a campaign, the result is a "retrospective," "reward–punish" type of election. Democrat Franklin Roosevelt won a landslide victory in 1932, for example, because of popular discontent with government performance under Herbert Hoover in the face of the Great Depression; Republican Ronald Reagan capitalized on economic and foreign policy troubles under Jimmy Carter to win in 1980. The state of the economy has been repeatedly shown to be one of the best ways to predict incumbent party success in presidential elections.

Personal Characteristics of Candidates   Voters also get a chance during the general election campaign to learn about the real or alleged personal characteristics of the candidates. Even when the candidates are talking about something else, they give an impression of competence, and likeability. Mitt Romney, for example, often seemed like he didn't understand the common voter, which may have hurt him in the election, while Hillary Clinton was perceived as too cozy with Wall Street and the financial industry. On the other hand, Donald Trump did not seem to care about his perceived like-ability, making controversial comments about women and minority groups during the campaign. He was also, at times, rude to Clinton during the presidential debates. His tell-it-like-it-is attitude may have actually generated more support for him among some voter groups.

Still another dimension of candidates' personalities is a candidate's presumed strength or weakness, which is especially important to voters when considering how the candidates will deal with foreign governments and enemies. George W. Bush was perceived as being better able to deal with terrorism compared to his opponent John Kerry in 2004, whom the Bush campaign sought to portray as weak on terrorism.

The Packaging of Candidates   The sparse and ambiguous treatment of policy issues in campaigns, as well as the emphasis on past performance and personal competence, fits better with ideas about electoral reward and punishment than with the responsible parties or issue-oriented electoral competition models of democratic elections. Voters can be fooled, however, by dirty tricks or slick advertising that sells presidential candidates' personalities and tears down the opponent through attack ads. Moreover, the focus on personal imagery may distract attention from substantive policy debates. If candidates who favor unpopular policies are elected on the basis of attractive personal images, democratic control of policymaking is weakened.

Money in General Elections

Money plays a crucial role in American general election campaigns and elections, especially presidential elections. Not surprisingly, parties and candidates spend much of their time and effort raising money for campaigns. The role of money has only increased in recent years as a result of some important Supreme Court decisions, especially the *Citizens United v. Federal Election Commission* (2010) ruling.

Presidential campaigns cost a great deal of money, although the system is so complex that even close observers can make only educated guesses about the total. We have good data on money coming from certain sources but not from others. For example, we know that federal candidates at all levels (president, Senate, and House of Representatives) spent $6 billion during the 2011–2012 cycle[55] and about $6.5 billion during the 2015–2016 election, but we are less sure about a wide range of other expenditures on their behalf by advocacy groups. What we do know is that, considering only monies officially reported (so-called hard money), the total that is raised and spent from one presidential election cycle to the next keeps increasing and shows no signs of slowing down (see Figure 10.6).

FIGURE 10.6 THE GROWTH IN HARD MONEY SPENDING IN PRESIDENTIAL ELECTIONS (IN MILLIONS OF DOLLARS)

Spending by candidates, party, and independent committees as reported to the Federal Election Commission. This bar chart communicates both the dollar amount spent in each year since 1976 and the accelerating rate at which spending is increasing over time.

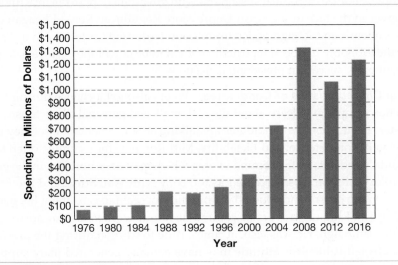

NOTE: All numbers are based on summary reports filed with the FEC.

SOURCE: Data for 1976–2004 from "Total Spending by Presidential Candidates," Center for Responsive Politics; data for 2008–2012 from "Fundraising and Spending in U.S. Presidential Elections from 1976 to 2016," Statista.

"HARD" AND "SOFT" MONEY Hard money refers to contributions made directly to the candidates and party committees that fall under the jurisdiction of the Federal Election Commission (the FEC). The rules followed by the FEC are the result of two major laws—the Federal Election Campaign Act (FECA) and its later amendments passed during the 1970s, and the Bipartisan Campaign Reform Act of 2002 (BCRA), also called the McCain–Feingold Act after its two primary sponsors in the Senate. The implementation of both laws is governed by Supreme Court rulings and administrative rules implemented by the FEC, in its role as the bureaucratic agency in charge of monitoring elections. Hard money is more difficult to raise because of regulations and limits on the sizes of donations, but it can be used for most campaign activities and can advocate for or against a certain candidate.

Soft money is money that is not as tightly regulated by the FEC because it is donated to state or local parties or candidates, rather than to a federal candidate or party. Soft money was supposed to be used only for "party-building" activities like voter drives, and the money was not allowed to be used to advocate for specific candidates. However, soft money was often used to run "issue" ads, criticizing candidates for positions taken, without actually advocating for their defeat. Increasing regulation of soft money was the major purpose of the 2002 McCain-Feingold law after both parties raised more than $500 million in soft money during the 2002 election cycle.

The largest single source of hard money funding for presidential campaigns is from individual contributors, ranging from those who made small contributions to the candidates in response to an e-mail or letter solicitation or a call from a party worker, to wealthier individuals who gave the maximum amount allowed in 2016 of $2,700 to a single candidate and $33,400 to a national party committee per year. (See Table 10.1 for FEC rules on contributions limits for the 2015–2016 election cycle.) Before passage of FECA, individuals could make contributions of unlimited size, and candidates and the parties depended on a handful of very rich individuals to fund their operations.

TABLE 10.1 HARD MONEY CONTRIBUTION LIMITS, 2015–2016

	CONTRIBUTION LIMITS FOR 2015–2016 FEDERAL ELECTIONS				
	RECIPIENTS				
DONORS	**Candidate Committee**	**PAC (SSF and Nonconnected)**	**State/District/Local Party Committee**	**National Party Committee**	**Additional National Party Committee Accounts**
Individual	$2,700 per election	$5,000 per year	$10,000 per year (combined)	$33,400 per year	$100,200 per account, per year
Candidate Committee	$2,000 per election	$5,000 per year	Unlimited Transfers	Unlimited Transfers	
PAC-Multicandidate	$5,000 per election	$5,000 per year	$5,000 per year (combined)	$15,000 per year	$45,000 per account, per year
PAC-Nonmulticandidate	$2,700 per election	$5,000 per year	$10,000 per year (combined)	$33,400 per year	$100,200 per account, per year
State/District/Local Party Committee	$5,000 per election	$5,000 per year	Unlimited	Unlimited	
National Party Committee	$5,000 per election	$5,000 per year	Unlimited	Unlimited	

SOURCE: Federal Election Commission, "Contribution Limits for 2015–2016 Federal Elections."

After limits were placed on the size of allowable contributions, both parties invented a variety of ways to attract small contributions from hundreds of thousands of people, beginning with targeted mail and telephone solicitations. The rise of Internet fund-raising has made the campaigns much more reliant on small donations from individual contributors, but has also allowed the candidates to raise much more money because of the sheer number of individuals who contribute. Indeed, Barack Obama raised approximately $233 million from small contributors in 2012, while Mitt Romney raised about $80 million.

SELF-FUNDING Candidates seeking a party's nomination will sometimes contribute or lend money to their own campaigns; both John McCain and Hillary Clinton did this during the primaries in 2007 and 2008, while Donald Trump gave some of his own money to his primary campaign in 2016, but mostly relied on the unprecedented media attention he received. Once each party chooses its nominee for the presidency, the candidates have no need to use their personal resources because of money coming in from other sources.

POLITICAL ACTION COMMITTEES (PACS) PACs are entities created by interest groups—whether business firms, unions, membership organizations, or liberal and conservative advocacy groups—to collect money from many different people (often called "bundling") and make contributions to candidates in federal elections (i.e., to candidates for the presidency, the House of Representatives, and the Senate). In 2016, PACs raised about $2.2 billion to contribute to presidential and congressional candidates, party committees, and their own electioneering activities (television, radio, and Internet advertising on the issues or candidates).[56]

POLITICAL PARTIES The political parties also play an important role in helping the party's presidential nominee. Though campaign finance laws limit the amount of money that parties can give to the candidate's official campaign committee, they are allowed to spend a regulated amount on candidate services such as polling and advertising for get-out-the-vote efforts. More importantly, as described later, parties can also run very large and mostly unregulated "independent" campaigns on behalf of candidates. For these various campaign activities, the Republican National Committee raised more than $343 million in 2015–2016, while the Democratic National Committee raised a little more than $372 million.[57]

OUTSIDE GROUPS Ironically, though the McCain-Feingold bill successfully reduced the amount of soft money coming into campaigns, other types of groups were formed to fill the soft money gap. Advocacy and advertising by corporations, unions, and rich individuals is perhaps more important now than hard money donations to campaigns.

527 Groups So named because of where they are defined in the Tax Code, 527s are entities that can use unregulated money to talk about issues, mobilize voters, and praise or criticize candidates. There are no limits on contributions to them, nor are 527s limited in what they can spend. Many of these groups devoted to liberal or conservative causes and candidates sprouted up after passage of McCain–Feingold and played a very large role in the 2004 presidential election—Swift Boat Veterans for Truth (anti-Kerry) and MoveOn.org (anti-Bush) were the most prominent. These groups sometimes depend on very large contributions from a handful of rich individuals; George Soros contributed more than $15 million to anti-Bush 527s in 2004, while Texas oilman T. Boone Pickens gave $4.6 million to anti-Kerry groups. In recent years, 527 groups have spent more of their money at the state and local level rather than the federal level.

501 Groups Although traditional 527s are still around, they have lost favor because of disclosure requirements. 527s are required to report their total receipts and expenditures to the Internal Revenue Service (IRS) and report the identity of their contributors and how much they gave. 501 groups are classified as tax-exempt organizations by the IRS because their main purpose is to encourage "civic engagement." They must also report receipts and expenditures to the IRS, but less frequently than 527s, and most importantly, they are not required to report the identities of their contributors even though, similar to 527 groups, there are no limits on how much money they can collect or spend. Not surprisingly, 501s have come to play a bigger role in the campaign finance system.

Super PACs These are nonprofit entities, usually organized as 527 organizations, that can accept unlimited amounts in donations from corporations, unions, groups, and individuals. They can use these monies to advocate issues and for and against candidates for public office, though (unlike PACs) they cannot give money directly to candidates. They must issue periodic reports to the Federal Election Commission and identify their donors, though these donors may be 501 organizations that do not report their donors. Super PACs played a major role in the 2015–2016 election cycle. They have become the favored vehicles of very rich individuals who are not worried about their

GETTING "SWIFT BOATED"

In the 2004 presidential campaign, 527 advocacy organizations became very important, mostly by running attack ads. One of the most effective was the Swift Boat group, which attacked Democratic candidate John Kerry's war record, calling his wartime awards and citations "dishonest and dishonorable." Here, one of the cofounders of the group signs autographs at a "John Kerry Lied" rally in 2004. By law, such 527 groups are not allowed specifically to ask voters to vote for a particular candidate or to not vote for a particular candidate, though they can praise or criticize them.

Is it truly possible or even reasonable for an organization to promote certain issues while not endorsing a candidate, or to praise or criticize a candidate without the same effect?

identities being known. Most famously, in 2012, Karl Rove, George W. Bush's former chief strategist, formed a super PAC called "American Crossroads" which spent nearly $105 million dollars opposing Democratic candidates. In 2016, "Priorities USA Action" as the biggest Super PAC, spending more than $133 million to support Hillary Clinton.

THE CITIZENS UNITED DECISION   The most important recent development in campaign finance law has been the Supreme Court's ruling in *Citizens United v. Federal Election Commission* (2010). The Court ruled that limits on spending for corporations and unions in favor of candidate advocacy or other election activities are unconstitutional. The Court has generally ruled that campaign giving is a form of free speech, and in *Citizens United*, the Court went a step further, saying that corporations, unions, and other groups also have rights to engage in issue and candidate advocacy as part of their free speech rights. These organizations are still not allowed to coordinate with candidates or campaigns, nor are they allowed to directly give money to campaigns, but as was seen in 2016, these distinctions are almost irrelevant. Because there are no limits on corporate or union giving, and because there are no limits on how much money 527 organizations organized as super PACs can collect and spend, the *Citizens United* decision created a system where enormous amounts of money flowed to super PACs for independent spending. This means that corporations and unions likely will play a much bigger role than in the past in financing independent, parallel campaigns, from federal elections to local races.

STEPHEN COLBERT MOCKS THE CAMPAIGN FINANCE SYSTEM

The comedian Stephen Colbert, seen here performing at a rally in Washington D.C., created his own Super PAC in 2012 to expose the silliness of the campaign finance system. His Super PAC and subsequent shell corporation (called the "Colbert Super PAC SHH Institute"), allowed him to collect over a million dollars in anonymous donations which he spent on comedic television advertisements in Iowa. His purpose was serious however, and Colbert won a prestigious Peabody Award for demonstrating to the American public the ineffectiveness of campaign finance law.
What changes, if any, should be made to the modern campaign finance system?

PUBLIC FUNDING   Since 1971, the presidential candidates have had the option of accepting campaign money from the federal treasury, paid for by taxpayers through a $3 donation on their tax return. In 2004, the Kerry and Bush campaigns each received $74.4 million in public funds for the general election in the fall and Republican John McCain accepted public funding of roughly $84 million in 2008. By accepting public funds, the candidates agree not to raise or spend any additional money on their own. This was usually a good deal for the presidential nominees however, because the federal matching funds were about the same amount of money as they would have raised anyway without requiring the candidate to spend a lot of time and effort to fund-raise.

Dramatically breaking with tradition, Democratic nominee Barack Obama chose in 2008 to reject public funding with its accompanying spending limits, primarily because of his remarkably successful fund-raising operation. He was able to raise so much money from millions of small and medium-sized donations through his online system that he realized he was better off raising his own money and not adhering to the limits the public financing system would place on his campaign. In doing so, he went back on a promise to use public funding and limit his spending, saying he needed to do so because of expected attacks from independent conservative advocacy groups and 527 and 501 organizations. In 2012, neither Democrat Barack Obama nor Republican Mitt Romney accepted public funding, effectively killing the system.

A similar system is in place for the primary campaign. Similar to the general election system, the federal government would match individual donations until the candidate had raised about $50 million. Things began to change in 2000 when George W. Bush became the first serious candidate to eschew public financing since it was first established in 1976. Since then, virtually none of the leading contenders in either party has accepted public funding with its attendant spending limits.

Public financing of presidential nomination campaigns is no longer viable for two reasons. First, the costs of running a credible campaign for the party presidential nomination have gone up much faster than the amount given to the candidates by the government. Second, most candidates do not want to limit their spending as required by the public financing system. It is much easier for campaigns to raise money now because of the growth of the Internet and the importance of individual contributions. Though Barack Obama was particularly good at raising money through email and social media in 2008 and 2012, other campaigns have adopted the same tools and strategies.

DOES MONEY TALK?   Money matters a great deal in the presidential nomination process—aspirants for party nominations who cannot raise sizable funds always drop out of the race—but it is perhaps less important in determining who wins during the post-convention run for the White House.[58] Of course, presidential campaigns are enormously expensive, and candidates do have to allocate resources carefully. Some reports of the Romney campaign in 2012 suggest it did not have enough money, especially during the summer when the Obama campaign began running attack ads that went unanswered in many states.[59] Still, generally both candidates have about the same resources, especially when accounting for the party organizations, money from interest groups, 527s, 501s, super PACS and free publicity from news organizations.

Money is likely more important at a later stage however, when elected officials begin making public policy. It is widely believed, although difficult to prove, that contributors of money often get something back.[60] After all, if they didn't see a return on their contribution, why would they continue to donate? The point is not that presidential, House, and Senate candidates take outright bribes in exchange for policy favors. Indeed, exchanges between politicians and money-givers are complex and varied, sometimes yielding little benefit to contributors. Undeniably, however, cozy relationships do tend to develop between politicians and major money-givers. Contributors gain access to, and a friendly hearing from, those whom they help to win office. One of the most important effects of money is not through the direct influence of policy outcomes, but instead through influence on the policy agenda. Though this influence is indirect rather than direct, it is surely considerable.

It is clear that money-givers are different from average citizens. They have special interests of their own. As we have indicated, a large amount of campaign money comes from large corporations, investment banking firms, wealthy families, labor unions, professional associations (e.g., doctors, lawyers, or realtors), and issue-oriented groups such as the National Rifle Association, Focus on the Family, and the National Abortion Rights Action League. Surveys show that the individuals who give money tend to have much higher incomes and more conservative views on economic issues than the average American.[61] Even wealthy individuals who contribute to Democrats (such as Silicon Valley billionaires) tend to be liberal on social issues but conservative on economic issues such as workers' rights. Because wealthy donors have easier access to politicians, elected officials might only be getting one side of the story.[62]

The result is political inequality. Those who are well organized or have a lot of money to spend on politics have a better chance of influencing policy than ordinary citizens do, and they tend to influence it in directions different from what the general public wants.[63] Citizens seem to recognize this, and surveys show that a large majority of Americans disagree with decisions such as *Citizens United*. The increasing role of money in presidential and congressional nomination and election campaigns is a major problem for democracy in the United States.

ELECTION OUTCOMES

10.6 Assess how presidential elections are decided.

After the parties and candidates have presented their campaigns, the voters decide. Exactly how people make their voting decisions affects how well or how poorly elections contribute to the democratic control of government.

How Voters Decide

Years of scholarly research have made it clear that feelings about the parties, the candidates, and the issues, as well as voters' own social characteristics, have substantial effects on how people vote.[64] Yet, despite the intense attention of the campaign, and the money spent, very few voters are truly open to hearing the appeals of both candidates. As mentioned above, the presidential campaign is as much about activating party loyalists as it is about persuading voters since most voters are reliable Republicans or Democrats.

SOCIAL CHARACTERISTICS An individual's socioeconomic status, place of residence, religion, ethnic backgrounds, gender, and age are related to how they vote (see Figure 10.7). Minorities, women, lower-income citizens, and residents living in urban areas tend to vote Democratic, while rural, religious, and white voters tend to vote Republican.

FIGURE 10.7 PRESIDENTIAL VOTE IN 2016, BY SOCIAL GROUP

Racial and ethnic minorities, young people, liberals, people with post-graduate degrees, and women voted strongly for Democrat Hillary Clinton in the 2016 election, while whites, Christians, rural residents, conservatives, older people, and men favored Republican Donald Trump.

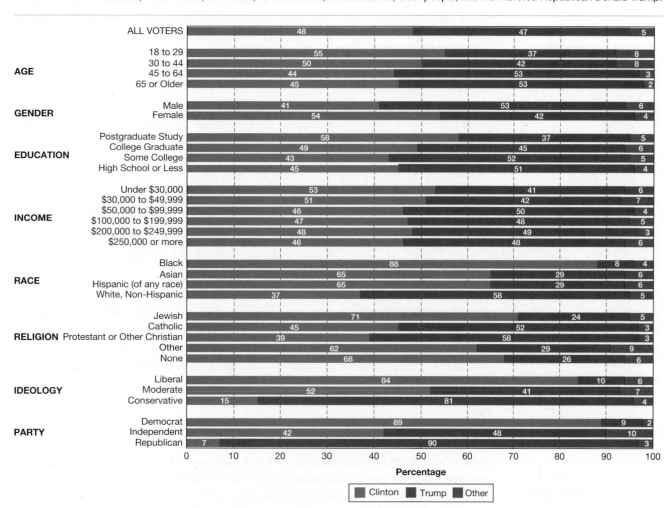

Women have voted more Democratic than men for the last 35 years or so, and most expected this pattern to be especially pronounced in the 2016 presidential elections. An audio recording of lewd comments made by Donald Trump during a 2005 interview, as well as some statements made during the campaign, seemed to indicate this gender gap would be larger than usual. An example of this is shown in the video, where Michelle Obama criticizes Trump's comments during a campaign speech. However, female support for Clinton was almost exactly the same as it was for Obama in 2012, despite her campaign's attempt to make it an important issue.

PARTY LOYALTIES   To a great extent, these social patterns of voting work through long-term attachments to the political parties. Though many Americans now self-identify as independent, most still vote consistently Republican or Democratic and party identification remains the single best predictor of how someone will vote.[65] This is especially true in congressional elections and in state and local races, where most voters have very little information about the candidates aside from their party label. Party loyalties vary among different groups of the population because of the parties' differences on economic and social issues. Party identification serves as a useful tool for choosing candidates because of the close linkage between the parties and ideology, with Democrats generally more liberal (including party identifiers, activists, and candidates) and Republicans generally more conservative. In 2016, 89 percent of Democratic identifiers voted for Clinton, and 90 percent of Republican identifiers voted for Trump.

ISSUES   Though most voters are party loyalists, a small segment of voters can swing the election based on their view of the important issues. Most often, issue voting has meant retrospective voting (the electoral reward and punishment model), based on the state of the economy and war and peace. In short, voters tend to reward the incumbent party when the economy is going well and when the country is not involved in difficult foreign conflicts.

In bad economic times, Americans tend to vote the incumbent party out of office, as they did to the Republicans during the Great Depression in 1932. In 2008, the electorate punished Republicans in the midst of the Great Recession when Obama handily beat McCain and the Democrats won big majorities in Congress. In 2012, the economy was recovering and there were no foreign crises, resulting in a win for the incumbent, Barack Obama. In 2016, the economy was better than it had been a few years earlier, but far from robust, suggesting that Democrats would neither be rewarded nor punished for its performance.

Foreign policy can be important, especially when the country is involved in wars or other military actions. Traditionally, Republican candidates have been seen as better at conducting foreign policy and projecting American strength. The bloody, expensive, and drawn-out war in Iraq undermined traditional GOP advantages in this area in 2006 and 2008, however, and voters punished Republicans accordingly. In most elections, though, foreign policy concerns take a back seat to domestic ones for most voters. Even in 2008, in the midst of war, economic troubles triggered by the sub-prime mortgage and credit crunch disasters trumped foreign policy issues for a majority of voters.

The Electoral College

When Americans vote for a presidential candidate, they are actually voting for a slate of **electors** in their state: members of each party who have promised to support their party's presidential candidate in the Electoral College. (Very rarely have electors reneged on their promises and cast ballots for someone else; there was one so-called "faithless elector" in 2000, and seven faithless electors in 2016, the most

electors

Representatives who are elected in the states to formally choose the U.S. president.

ever.) The number of electors within a state is equal to the number of House members plus Senators, so all states have at least three votes in the Electoral College (California, the most populous state, has 55 electoral votes: 53 House districts plus two senators). Nearly all states have winner-take-all systems in which the winner of the popular vote wins the state's entire allotment of electoral votes; Maine and Nebraska are the two exceptions, and allocate their electoral votes by congressional district.

The "college" of electors from the different states never actually meet together; instead, the electors meet in their respective states and send lists of how they voted to Washington, D.C. (see the Twelfth Amendment to the Constitution). There are 538 total Electoral College votes (435 members of the House, 100 members of the Senate, and 3 additional votes for Washington D.C.) so the candidate who receives a majority of all the electoral votes in the country, 270, is elected president. Notice however, that when three or more candidates run, it is possible that no one candidate could receive a majority. It is also possible for two candidates to tie at 269 electoral votes each. In either case, the Constitution says the House of Representatives chooses from among the top three candidates, by a majority vote of each state delegation, with each state receiving one vote, though this situation has not occurred since 1824. For a report of election results from 1980 to the present, see Table 10.2.

Most of the time, this peculiar system works about the same way as if Americans chose the presidents by direct popular vote, but it has certain features that are politically consequential.

Most importantly, a president can win the popular vote but lose the Electoral College vote. Such a result has occurred five times: in 1876, when Rutherford Hayes defeated Samuel Tilden; in 1888, when Benjamin Harrison beat the more popular Grover Cleveland; in 2000, when George W. Bush defeated Al Gore; and in 2016

TABLE 10.2 ELECTION RESULTS, 1980–2016

Year	Candidate	Party	Percentage of Popular Votes	Percentage of Electoral Votes
1980	Ronald Reagan	Republican	51%	91%
	Jimmy Carter	Democratic	41%	9%
	John Anderson	Independent	7%	0%
1984	Ronald Reagan	Republican	59%	98%
	Walter Mondale	Democratic	41%	2%
1988	George H. W. Bush	Republican	53%	79%
	Michael Dukakis	Democratic	46%	21%
1992	William Clinton	Republican	43%	69%
	George H. W. Bush	Democratic	37%	31%
	H. Ross Perot	Independent	19%	0%
1996	William Clinton	Democratic	49%	70%
	Robert Dole	Republican	41%	30%
	H. Ross Perot	Reform Party	8%	0%
2000	George W. Bush	Republican	48%	60.5%
	Albert Gore	Democratic	48%	49.5%
	Ralph Nader	Green Party	3%	0%
2004	George W. Bush	Republican	51%	53%
	John Kerry	Democratic	48%	47%
2008	Barack Obama	Democratic	53%	68%
	John McCain	Republican	46%	32%
2012	Barack Obama	Democratic	50%	62%
	Mitt Romney	Republican	48%	38%
2016	Hillary Clinton	Democratic	47.7%	33%
	Donald Trump	Republican	47.5%	57%

SOURCES: Data from the Federal Election Commission and Harold Stanley and Richard C. Niemi, *Vital Statistics in American Politics 2011–2012* (Washington, DC: CQ Press, 2012); *The New York Times*, Presidential Election Results.

when Hillary Clinton won the popular vote but lost the Electoral College. In 1824, John Quincy Adams defeated the very popular Andrew Jackson in the House of Representatives after an election when no candidate won a majority of electoral votes.

Another problem is that small states have more influence than they otherwise would because they are guaranteed at least three electoral votes. Finally, the winner-take-all system encourages candidates to spend almost all their time and money in the **battleground states**. Even populous states, like California and New York, are ignored during the general election because the states aren't competitive. In a popular vote system, the candidates would likely spend more time campaigning for votes all over the country, giving more attention to cities and other areas with large populations.

There have been many calls over the years to change the Electoral College system of electing the president.[66] Majorities of Americans have told pollsters repeatedly that they want a system based on direct popular vote. But, small states and **battleground states** are unlikely to support this proposal because of their outsized influence in the Electoral College system.

The popular vote system isn't without its own problems, either. What if three, four, or five candidates run and the plurality winner receives only 30 percent of the vote? Would Americans be comfortable with a president elected by so few people? One way to solve this, as they do in France, among other places, is to have a second-round run-off election between the top two candidates so that the person elected comes to office with majority support.

Another idea is to retain the Electoral College but to remove the "winner-take-all" feature. Various methods for apportioning a state's electoral votes in a way that approximates the division in the popular vote in the state have been suggested. The Constitution leaves it up to the states to choose how they determine the distribution of their Electoral College votes, so states could act on their own, without a constitutional amendment. The problem here is that unless all states acted at the same time, the first movers would be disadvantaged. If a state were to divide up its electoral votes to approximate the popular vote in the state, it would no longer be such a prize for the candidates compared to those states that were still operating on a "winner-take-all" basis. In this case, a change in the Electoral College would require national action by all the states at the same time, perhaps even through a constitutional amendment.

VOTING, CAMPAIGNS, AND ELECTIONS: DO VOTING, CAMPAIGNS, AND ELECTIONS MAKE GOVERNMENT LEADERS LISTEN TO THE PEOPLE?

Elections and citizen political participation in the United States have been substantially democratized over the years, altering some of the constitutional rules introduced by the framers. For example, the Seventeenth Amendment, adopted in 1913, transformed the Senate into an institution whose members are elected directly by voters rather than by state legislatures. The manner of electing the president is completely different from what the framers thought they had created: an independent body for presidential selection. By custom or by law, virtually all electors today are pledged to a particular candidate before the presidential election, so that, for all intents and purposes, the president is directly elected by the people (although disparities between the electoral and popular vote occasionally happen, as in 2000 and 2016). Equally important, the franchise has been so broadened—to include previously excluded racial minorities and women—that today almost all Americans 18 years and older are eligible to vote, something that few of the framers envisioned or would have found conducive to good government.

In addition to these institutional transformations, democratizing changes in the prevailing political culture have also been important. The spread of the ideas that political leaders ought to be responsible and responsive to the people, and that political leaders ought to pay attention to what the mass public wanted from them, represents a fundamental change from the prevailing view among the framers.

Elections are the most important means by which citizens can exert democratic control over their government. Although a variety of instruments help convey the people's wishes to officials—public opinion polls, interest groups, and social movements—it is ultimately the fact that officials must face the voters that keeps them in line. In terms of the responsible party idea, the fact that the Republican Party tends to be more conservative than the Democratic Party on a number of economic and social issues provides voters with a measure of democratic control by enabling them to detect differences and make choices about the future. Alternatively, through electoral punishment, voters can exercise control by reelecting successful incumbents and throwing failures out of office, thus making incumbents think ahead. Finally, electoral competition forces the parties to compete by nominating centrist candidates and by taking similar issue stands close to what most Americans want. This last force, in fact, may be the chief way in which citizens' policy preferences affect what their government does.

While U.S. elections help make the public's voice heard, they do not bring about perfect democracy. Far from it. Elections do not lead to a greater degree of democracy for a number of reasons: the low turnouts that characterize American elections at all levels, the educational and income biases in participation rates, and the role of interest groups and well-off contributors in campaign finance. Uneven participation and the influence of money on campaigns undermine political equality by giving some people much more political clout than others. Ever fiercer partisanship, moreover, increasingly is keeping candidates from choosing policies that reflect the wishes of the median voter in the electoral competition model, making this democracy-enhancing electoral mechanism less effective. So, notwithstanding the spread of democracy beyond the imaginings of the framers, those who support the democratic idea think we have some distance yet to travel.

REVIEW THE CHAPTER

ELECTIONS AND DEMOCRACY

10.1 Evaluate three models of how elections can lead to popular control.

In theory, elections are the most important means by which citizens can exert democratic control over their government by forcing elected officials to pay attention to the wishes of voters.

Three theoretical models of voting are at play in making elections a potentially democratic instrument of the people: responsible parties/prospective voting; reward and punishment/retrospective voting; and the electoral competition/median voter model. Elections matter not only when there is a clear choice but also when electoral reward or punishment occurs or when electoral competition forces both parties to take similar popular stands.

THE UNIQUE NATURE OF AMERICAN ELECTIONS

10.2 Distinguish American elections from those in other countries.

There are more elections here than in other democratic countries. They are on a fixed date and the offices voted on have a fixed term. Elections almost always are of the winner-take-all, first-past-the-post variety, encouraging a two-party system. And, elections are administered by state and local governments rather than the national government.

VOTING IN THE UNITED STATES

10.3 Analyze the importance of political participation in elections.

The right to vote, originally quite limited, was expanded in various historical surges to include nearly all adults and to apply to most major offices. The changes came about because of changes in American society and the struggle for democracy waged by various groups of Americans.

WHO VOTES?

10.4 Identify demographic factors that increase the likelihood of voting.

The higher the income and the higher the education, the more likely a person is to vote. When education and income are accounted for, the long-time differentiation between white and black turnout disappears.

Women now vote at a slightly higher rate than men.

THE PRESIDENTIAL CAMPAIGN

10.5 Outline the process of campaigns for the presidency.

Candidates for the party nomination for president start by testing the waters, raising money, and forming campaign organizations; in a series of state primaries and caucuses, they seek delegates to the national nominating conventions, which generally choose a clear front-runner or the incumbent president.

Candidates who cannot raise money or have money raised for them by others do not become serious contenders in the party nomination contests. Money differences between the candidates in the presidential contest in the general election are less important in determining the outcome because of public financing, party spending, interest and advocacy group spending, and intense and costless press coverage of the election.

The goal of presidential candidates in the fall campaign is to rally the party base and win over a substantial proportion of independent and moderate voters. Campaign activity and spending focus on battleground states.

ELECTION OUTCOMES

10.6 Assess how presidential elections are decided.

Voters' decisions depend heavily on party loyalties, the personal characteristics of the candidates, and the issues, especially the state of the economy.

The president is selected not by direct popular vote but by a majority in the Electoral College vote.

LEARN THE TERMS

ballot fatigue   The exhaustion of voter interest and knowledge in elections caused by election frequency and the length and complexity of ballots.

battleground state   Those states which are highly competitive in the presidential general election.

caucus, nominating   The process in some states for selecting delegates to the national party conventions characterized by neighborhood and area-wide meetings of party supporters and activists.

Electoral College   Representatives selected in each of the states, their numbers based on each state's total number of its senators and representatives; a majority of Electoral College votes elects the president.

electoral competition voting model   A theory of elections in which parties move toward the median voter or the center of the political spectrum in order to capture the most votes.

electors   Representatives who are elected in the states to formally choose the U.S. president.

franchise   The legal right to vote; see suffrage.

initiative   Procedures available in some states for citizens to put proposed laws and constitutional amendments on the ballot for voter approval or rejection.

invisible primary   The process in which party elites and influential donors throw their support behind a candidate before any votes have been cast, giving that candidate a financial and organizational advantage during the state primaries and caucuses.

median voter   The voter at the exact middle of the political issue spectrum.

party convention   A gathering of delegates who nominate a party's presidential candidate.

plurality   Occurs when a candidate receives more votes than any other candidate in an election but still less than a majority.

primary election   Statewide elections in which voters choose delegates to the national party conventions.

prospective voting model   A theory of democratic elections in which voters decide what each party will do if elected and choose the party that best represents their own preferences.

referendum   Procedures available in some states by which state laws or constitutional amendments proposed by the legislature are submitted to the voters for approval or rejection.

responsible party model   The notion that a political party will take clear and distinct stands on the issues and enact them as policy once elected to office.

retrospective voting model (or electoral reward and punishment model)   A theory of democratic elections in which voters look back at the performance of a party in power and cast ballots on the basis of how well it did in office.

suffrage   The legal right to vote; see franchise.

superdelegates   Elected officials from all levels of government who are appointed by party committees to be delegates to the national convention of the Democratic Party; not selected in primary elections or caucuses.

turnout   The proportion of either eligible or all voting-age Americans who actually vote in a given election; the two ways of counting turnout yield different results.

CHAPTER 11

UNPRECEDENTED VOTER ENTHUSIASM AND RECORD TURNOUT IN THE 2018 MIDTERM ELECTIONS

The 2018 midterm elections proved consequential as Democrats took control of the House while Republicans expanded their majority in the Senate. In Texas, Beto O'Rourke, the Democratic challenger who hoped to unseat Senate incumbent Ted Cruz, narrowly lost his race, but the closeness of the election results in deep-red Texas is already leading to speculation that O'Rourke may run for president in 2020.

What reasons caused the Democratic Party's success in the 2018 midterm elections?

CONGRESS

CHAPTER OUTLINE AND LEARNING OBJECTIVES

CONSTITUTIONAL FOUNDATIONS OF CONGRESS

11.1   Describe the constitutional provisions that define the Congress.

REPRESENTATION AND DEMOCRACY IN CONGRESS

11.2   Assess how well members of Congress represent their constituents.

CONGRESSIONAL ELECTIONS

11.3   Describe the process of congressional elections and the impact of incumbency on election outcomes.

THE CONGRESSIONAL LEGISLATIVE PROCESS

11.4   Outline the process by which a bill becomes a law.

VOTING IN CONGRESS

11.5   Outline the factors that influence roll-call voting in Congress.

CONGRESSIONAL OVERSIGHT OF THE EXECUTIVE BRANCH

11.6   Discuss Congress's oversight function and the relationship of oversight to party control.

The Struggle for Democracy

As expected, the 2018 midterm elections were largely a referendum on President Trump. Despite low unemployment and no major foreign policy crises, the president's approval rating hovered in the low-40s, suggesting that many Americans were not happy with the direction of the country nor with President Trump's actions in office. Democrats sought to capitalize on this dissatisfaction in the congressional elections, and most observers predicted that the Democrats would gain control of the House of Representatives, which has had a Republican majority since 2011.

The results of the election were largely positive for Democrats, though not entirely so. The party lost most of the high-profile contests, such as the Senate race in Texas (see the accompanying photo), the Senate and governorship races in Florida, the governorship race in Georgia, and four other contested Senate seats. Republicans actually expanded their Senate majority from 51 to 53 seats (at the time of printing), which will make it easier to confirm federal judges and bureaucratic officials. Still, all of these Senate seats were in Republican states. Democrat Jon Tester managed to hold on in Montana, while incumbent Republican Dean Heller, the only Republican representing a state won by Hillary Clinton in 2016 (Nevada), lost to his Democratic opponent. In Arizona, the Democratic candidate, Kyrsten Sinema, won an open seat that was previously represented by a Republican.

On the House side, Democrats made large gains, flipping more than 30 Republican-held seats. While individual House races are not as high-profile as Senate or gubernatorial races, the sheer number of wins by Democrats suggests that voters in many urban and suburban districts are dissatisfied with the policies of the Trump administration. Democrats won some surprising contests as well, flipping New York's 11th district, which encompasses Staten Island, South Carolina's 1st district, which includes parts of Charleston and Myrtle Beach, and Oklahoma's 5th district, which includes Oklahoma City. Each of these districts is urban or suburban, mostly white, and went overwhelmingly for Trump in 2016.

Nationally, Democratic House candidates won the popular vote by about 7 percent, at the low end of polling—polling having had predicted that Democrats were favored by 8 to 10 percentage points—but right around the margin Democrats needed to take control of the House of Representatives.

Many of the winning Democratic candidates reflect the growing diversity of the party. More than 100 women serve in the 116th Congress, breaking the previous record by a substantial margin. The first two Muslim women to serve in Congress were elected in Michigan and Minnesota, while the first Native American women were elected in Kansas and New Mexico. Marsha Blackburn, a Republican, will be the first woman to represent Tennessee in the Senate. Women also won Senate seats in Nevada and Arizona, though two incumbent Democratic women lost in North Dakota and Missouri.

What do the next two years hold? The answer to that question largely depends on the approach President Trump chooses to take with Congress. A party-divided Congress is nothing new for recent presidents. Both Presidents George W. Bush and Barack Obama faced at least one chamber controlled by the other party during their presidencies. President Trump might decide to seek compromise with the Democratic House and find areas of common ground on less controversial issues. On the other hand, he might decide to escalate partisan conflict in the hopes that it will energize his base for his 2020 reelection campaign. Democrats in the House, for their part, are unlikely to grant President Trump much deference. They have promised to ramp up investigations of his administration, including seeking his tax returns. The most likely outcome is that both parties dig in for a hard fight for two years, with both seeking to exploit any advantage heading into 2020. It is unlikely any significant policy changes occur during this period of divided government, and the deep ideological and partisan differences between red and blue American are likely to continue.

CONSTITUTIONAL FOUNDATIONS OF CONGRESS

11.1 Describe the constitutional provisions that define the Congress.

The framers of the Constitution recognized the legislature, Congress, as potentially the most dangerous to individual freedom. Yet, they tried to balance their worries of government tyranny with their desire to create a legislature that was both powerful and capable enough to deal with national problems. These multiple and conflicting objectives are reflected in the constitutional design of Congress.

Enumerated and Implied Powers of Congress

According to Article I, Section 1 of the Constitution, only Congress has the power to make laws: "All legislative power herein granted shall be vested in a Congress of the United States." Some powers, like the ability to declare war and the power to tax, are specifically listed in the Constitution in Article I, Section 8, and are known as **enumerated powers**.[1] Other parts of Article I, most notably the **elastic clause**, (also called the necessary and proper clause) allow Congress to pass other types of legislation "which shall be necessary and proper" to carry out its responsibilities. Through the elastic clause, Congress has additional power to legislate in other areas that are not specifically listed in the Constitution, but are instead **implied powers** of Congress. The combination of enumerated and implied powers has made Congress the most powerful branch of government for most of the country's history.

Constraints on Congress

As a result of the framers' worry about majority tyranny, a number of limitations are placed on congressional power by the Constitution. In Article I, the framers prohibited Congress from passing certain types of laws: bills of attainder, ex post facto laws, the granting of titles of nobility, and the suspension of the right of habeas corpus. Further, in the 1st Congress, additional constraints on congressional action were added in the

enumerated powers

Powers of the federal government specifically mentioned in the Constitution.

elastic clause

Article I, Section 8, of the Constitution, also called the *necessary and proper clause;* gives Congress the authority to make whatever laws are necessary and proper to carry out its enumerated responsibilities.

implied powers

Powers of the federal government not specifically mentioned in the Constitution.

form of the Bill of Rights. Note that the First Amendment, perhaps the most important constitutional provision protecting political liberty, begins with the words "Congress shall make no law …" Perhaps even more important are the ways in which the framers separated lawmaking powers and added "checks and balances" so that "ambition might check ambition" and protect the country from tyranny.

BICAMERALISM   Congress is a **bicameral** body, divided into two chambers, the House and Senate, each with its own principles of representation and constitutional responsibilities. The House, with frequent elections and small districts, is the more representative body, while the Senate, with six year terms and state constituencies, was envisioned by the chambers to be more deliberate, the "cooling saucer" of democracy according to George Washington. It is important to remember that the House and Senate must each pass the same version of a bill for it to become law, obviously making it harder to legislate than in single-chambered parliamentary systems. While we often use the word "Congress" and think of it as a single institution, it is worth remembering that the House and Senate are very different from one another and are "virtually autonomous chambers."[2]

bicameral
As applied to a legislative body, consisting of two houses or chambers.

PRESIDENTIAL VETO   Even when the House and Senate are able to agree with each other and pass the same version of a bill, it must still be approved by the president. The **veto** is the most obvious constitutional check on Congresses' power to legislate. Though vetoes can be overridden by a two-thirds vote in each chamber, this historically has been quite difficult, making the veto an important weapon against congressional overreach.

veto
Presidential disapproval of a bill that has been passed by both houses of Congress. The president's veto can be overridden by a two-thirds vote in each house.

JUDICIAL REVIEW   Finally, bills passed into law by Congress are subject to **judicial review**, the process by which the Supreme Court ensures the law does not violate the Constitution. As discussed in greater detail in Chapters 2 and 14, the power of judicial review was established by Chief Justice John Marshall in 1803 and gives the Supreme Court the ability to invalidate a portion or the entirety of a law. This has proven to be an important limitation on the power of Congress—just recently, the Supreme Court struck down parts of laws having to do with voting rights (the Voting Rights Act, in 2013), gay marriage (the Defense of Marriage Act, in 2013), and health care (the Obamacare decision in 2012 in which the Court ruled Congress could not compel states to expand the federal Medicaid program).

judicial review
The power of the Supreme Court to declare actions of the other branches and levels of government unconstitutional.

GOVERNING IN A SEPARATED SYSTEM

President Reagan confers with the powerful Speaker of the House Tip O'Neill and Senate Majority Leader Howard Baker in 1983. Presidents and leaders of the House and Senate frequently meet to discuss legislation and hammer out compromises.

Basis for Representation in Congress

During the constitutional convention, one of the most important debates to emerge was over the structure of the legislature. The delegates quickly coalesced around two competing plans. The Virginia Plan, favored by the larger population states, proposed that population be the basis for representation in the new legislature, while the New Jersey Plan adhered more closely to the Articles of Confederation and proposed each state have equal representation. In what came to be known as the **Connecticut Compromise**, also known as the Great Compromise, the framers decided to create two chambers and apportion the House of Representatives on the basis of population and the Senate on the basis of equal representation for each state. This means small population states like Wyoming have the same number of senators as large population states like California, creating important negative impacts on democracy in the United States.[3] In 2013, about one-fourth of the total population from the smallest states elected 62 senators, while three states with also one-fourth of the U.S. population—California, New York, and Texas—elected only six senators. This disparity is expected to grow as the population urbanizes and moves to more populated states.[4] The terms of office of the members of the House of Representatives were set at two years while the terms of the members of the Senate were set at six years, with only one-third of the seats up for election in each two-year election cycle. The Constitution also originally called for the election of senators by state legislatures, not by the people. This was changed by the Seventeenth Amendment, ratified in 1913.

In addition to its general grants of power to Congress, the Constitution assigns particular responsibilities to each of the legislative chambers, as Table 11.1 shows. Most importantly, only the Senate has the power to confirm presidential nominees to bureaucratic agencies and to the federal judiciary.

Is Congress Still Capable of Solving Big Problems?

The framers tried to carefully balance a Congress that could address national problems but would not become tyrannical. But today, many wonder whether Congress is powerful enough to address important national problems. The inability to craft long-term and carefully thought out solutions is a function of national trends interacting with the institutional structure of American government.

Connecticut Compromise

Also called the Great Compromise; the compromise between the New Jersey and Virginia plans formulated by the Connecticut delegates at the Constitutional Convention; called for a lower legislative house based on population size and an upper house based on equal representation of the states.

TABLE 11.1   CONSTITUTIONAL DIFFERENCES BETWEEN THE HOUSE AND THE SENATE

	Senate	House of Representatives
Length of term	6 years	2 years
Election of members	One-third elected in November of even-numbered years	Entire membership elected in November of even-numbered years
Number of members per state	2	Varies by size of state's population (minimum of 1 per state)
Total membership	100	435 (determined by Congress; at present size since 1910)
Minimum age for membership	30 years	25 years
Unique powers	Advice and consent for judicial and upper-level executive branch appointments	Origination of revenue bills
	Trial of impeachment cases	Bringing of impeachment charges
	Advice and consent for treaties	

FIGURE 11.1 APPLYING THE FRAMEWORK: CONGRESSIONAL GRIDLOCK

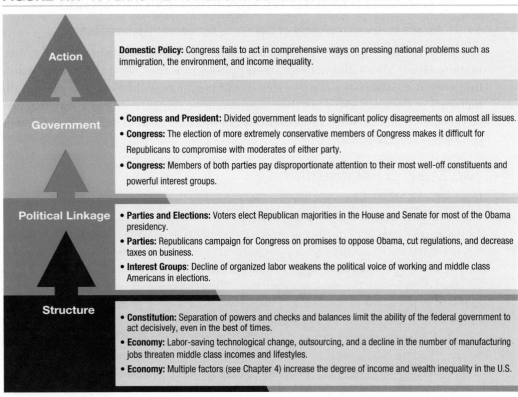

Action

Domestic Policy: Congress fails to act in comprehensive ways on pressing national problems such as immigration, the environment, and income inequality.

Government

- **Congress and President:** Divided government leads to significant policy disagreements on almost all issues.
- **Congress:** The election of more extremely conservative members of Congress makes it difficult for Republicans to compromise with moderates of either party.
- **Congress:** Members of both parties pay disproportionate attention to their most well-off constituents and powerful interest groups.

Political Linkage

- **Parties and Elections:** Voters elect Republican majorities in the House and Senate for most of the Obama presidency.
- **Parties:** Republicans campaign for Congress on promises to oppose Obama, cut regulations, and decrease taxes on business.
- **Interest Groups:** Decline of organized labor weakens the political voice of working and middle class Americans in elections.

Structure

- **Constitution:** Separation of powers and checks and balances limit the ability of the federal government to act decisively, even in the best of times.
- **Economy:** Labor-saving technological change, outsourcing, and a decline in the number of manufacturing jobs threaten middle class incomes and lifestyles.
- **Economy:** Multiple factors (see Chapter 4) increase the degree of income and wealth inequality in the U.S.

© Edward S. Greenberg

In an application of our pyramid framework (see Figure 11.1), we inspect the factors that result in congressional inaction, even as economic conditions seem to demand policy change. The last fifteen years have seen a dramatic reduction in the relative wealth of the middle class and a dramatic increase in income inequality. While no one is completely sure what is causing this shift, a number of causes are possible: the decline of labor unions, the willingness of companies to outsource jobs to other countries, a growth in companies with near-monopolies, and the rapid pace of technological advancement, which allows companies to eliminate manufacturing jobs.

The rise of the Tea Party movement in 2010 and the success of the Trump and Sanders campaigns in 2016 can be traced to fears of economic uncertainty among working-class and religious voters, but congressional representatives who identify with the Tea Party movement have made compromises between the Democrats and Republicans even more difficult because of their very conservative ideology. In spite of the dramatically different policy preferences of the wealthy as compared to lower- and middle-class Americans, members of Congress feel obligated to respond to top income earners who make up the party elites and the important donor class. Republican Party moderates, fearing losses in their primary from challengers on the right, seek to curry favor with donors by taking more conservative positions. Democratic members of Congress are beginning to feel the same pressure to conform to more liberal policy positions. The result is policy gridlock. The House, Senate, and president simply cannot agree how to address nationally pressing environmental, economic, or social issues such as immigration. Parliamentary systems, in comparison, do not have the same problems in passing legislation because (1) they are usually unicameral and (2) the executive is a member of the parliament who must also consent to passage of bills, rather than a separate institution. As many democratic theorists have suggested, when Congress is unable to act, it loses power to the president. A president who by default is the primary decision maker is not what the framers had in mind when they designed our federal system of government.

REPRESENTATION AND DEMOCRACY IN CONGRESS

11.2 Assess how well members of Congress represent their constituents.

constituent

A citizen who lives in the district of an elected official.

The job of members of Congress is to represent their **constituents** in national policy matters. Their views and actions are supposed to reflect what the people want. In theory, if members of Congress step out of line, they will be out of a job. But do members of Congress carry out their representative responsibility in a way that can be considered democratic?[5] To answer this question, we need to think about different concepts of representation.

Two Styles of Representation

delegate

According to the doctrine articulated by Edmund Burke, an elected representative who acts in perfect accord with the wishes of his or her constituents.

trustee

An elected representative who believes that his or her own best judgment, rather than instructions from constituents, should be used in making legislative decisions.

In a letter to his constituents written in 1774, English politician and philosopher Edmund Burke described two principal styles of representation. As a **delegate**, a representative tries to perfectly mirror the views of his or her constituents. As a **trustee**, a representative trusts his or her own judgment to do what's best for constituents, independent of what people might actually want.

Burke preferred the trustee approach: "Your representative owes you, not his industry only, but his judgment; and he betrays you, instead of serving you, if he sacrifices it to your opinion."[6] Campaigning for Congress in Illinois several decades later, Abraham Lincoln argued otherwise: "While acting as [your] representative, I shall be governed by [your] will, on all subjects upon which I have the means of knowing what [your] will is."[7] (If only he had had access to public opinion polls!)

In practice, most members of Congress exhibit characteristics of both a trustee and delegate, but we can think about how the rules of the House and Senate affect representation styles. Senators with six-year terms face the electorate less often than members of the House, and they represent larger, more diverse constituencies, so they are generally thought of as being more like trustees. As they get closer to the end of their terms and the prospect of facing the voters for reelection, however, senators edge toward the delegate style.[8] Members of the House must run for reelection every two years and tend to be in constant campaign mode, which, along with smaller, less diverse constituencies, pushes them toward the delegate style of representation.[9]

THE DELEGATE VERSUS THE TRUSTEE

Abraham Lincoln (left) preferred the delegate model of representation by deferring to the opinions of his constituents on important matters. Edmund Burke (right) famously articulated the trustee model of representation by saying that politicians are elected to exercise their own judgment and use their own expertise.

Is one model of representation superior to another model in democratic societies?

Member Demographics

Representation also implies that elected officials are similar to their constituents in demographic features. Even the framers worried about whether members of Congress would consist entirely of men from the upper classes, rather than a more diversified group.[10] When representatives reflect the demographic makeup of their constituents, it is called **descriptive representation**. From this perspective, a perfectly representative legislative body would be similar to the general population in terms of race, sex, ethnicity, occupation, religion, age, and other key characteristics. In this sense, the U.S. Congress is highly *unrepresentative*.[11]

RACE   Traditionally in this country, women and minorities have been significantly underrepresented in Congress, particularly in the Senate. As Figure 11.2 shows, despite recent gains, particularly for women, members of these groups serving in Congress are still significantly below their percentage in the population.

Very few African Americans were elected to Congress until the late 1960s. Since 1990, however, there has been significant improvement in the representation of African Americans in the House of Representatives—an increase in membership from 26 to over 50—and now the percentage of African Americans serving is roughly the same as the share of African Americans in the U.S. population overall. Under-representation in the Senate is still an issue, though, as only three African Americans currently serve. In fact, since 1900, only eight African Americans have held U.S. Senate seats, five of them Democrats.

descriptive representation
Sometimes called *statistical representation*; the degree to which the composition of a representative body reflects the demographic composition of the population as a whole.

FIGURE 11.2   WOMEN AND MINORITIES IN THE U.S. CONGRESS

Although their numbers in Congress have increased in recent years, women and racial minorities are still substantially under-represented in the current session of the U.S. Congress compared with their proportion in the American population.

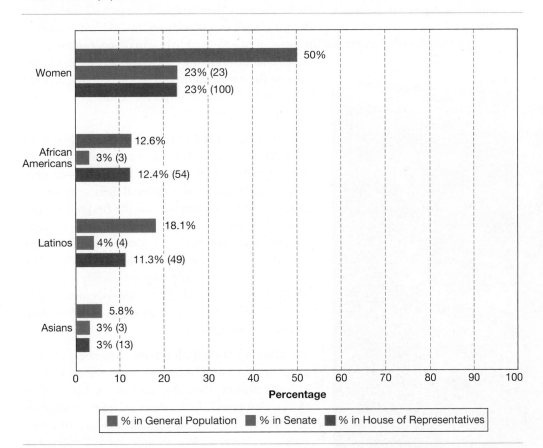

NOTE: Data not adjusted to reflect races undecided as of November 18, 2018.

SOURCE: U.S. Bureau of the Census; U.S. Senate; U.S. House of Representatives; Rutgers University, Center for Women and American Politics.

caucus, legislative interest or party

A regional, ethnic, racial, or economic subgroup within the House or Senate. Also used to name the party in the House and Senate (as in the "Republican Caucus" or the "Democratic Caucus").

GREATER DIVERSITY IN THE 116TH CONGRESS

The 2018 election produced many firsts with respect to congressional diversity. More than 100 women were elected, a new record. Many of the newly elected women also broke long-standing racial and religious barriers while attaining their positions. Shown in the photo, clockwise from top left, Sharice Davids, one of the first two Native American women elected to Congress, Ilhan Omar, one of the first two Muslim women elected to Congress, Ayanna Pressley, the first woman of color from Massachusetts elected to Congress, and Alexandria Ocasio-Cortez, the youngest woman ever elected to Congress at 29 years old.

Is electing more women to Congress important, or does the gender breakdown of congressional membership not matter for representational purposes?

While Hispanics have now replaced African Americans as the largest minority group in the population, they are less well represented in Congress than African Americans. Still, the nationally growing Hispanic population has given the Hispanic **caucus** a greater voice in legislative affairs than in the past. Thirty-nine Hispanics served in the House and five in the Senate during the 115th Congress (a record number for both chambers). Representation in Congress of other minority groups is small. Eighteen Americans of Asian descent (a record) and two Native Americans hold seats in Congress.[12]

GENDER   The number of women in Congress increased during the 1990s, with a big gain coming in the 1992 elections (often called the "year of the woman"), which sent 48 women to the House and 7 to the Senate. There were a record number of women in the 115th Congress, with 23 in the Senate and 88 in the House. Proportionally, however, female representation in Congress is still quite low, compared either with the percentage of women in the U.S. population at large (slightly more than one-half) or with the percentage of women in national legislative bodies in countries globally. On the latter point, as of late 2015, the United States ranked only 72nd on the world list of women in national legislatures.[13] Leadership posts in Congress are overwhelmingly held by men. A few women have gained important party and institutional leadership posts. Most notable among them is Nancy Pelosi (D-CA), who became the first female Speaker of the House in American history after the Democrats won a House majority in 2006. When Republicans regained control of the House in the 2010 elections, she lost the speakership but retained her position as Democratic leader. (At the time of publication, Pelosi was expected to become Speaker once again in the 116th Congress.) Unsurprisingly, given the lack of female representation in Congress, women have faced discrimination within the halls of the Capitol. Women were not allowed to use the Senate swimming pool until 2009, and until a remodel in 2013, there was only one small restroom near the Senate floor for the more than 20 female senators[14]. Things are changing, however, and an important symbolic event occurred in 2018 when Senator Tammy Duckworth became the first senator to give birth while in office. A subsequent rules change allowing her to bring her baby to the Senate floor was approved by unanimous consent as senators from both cited the realities of modern, working parents.

SEXUAL ORIENTATION   As acceptance of LGBTQ persons has become more common, so too have openly gay members of Congress—another important trend in congressional demographics. In 2012, Tammy Baldwin became the first openly gay member of the Senate. Barney Frank (now retired), a Democratic member from Massachusetts, became the first openly gay House member in 1987, but today there are seven openly gay House members, all Democrats. In 2014, there were two openly gay Republican House candidates, but both lost their election campaigns.

INCOME AND OCCUPATION   Members of Congress are far better educated than the rest of the U.S. population. They also are much wealthier than the general population—three-quarters of senators are millionaires, as are almost one-half of members of the House, though only about 2 percent of the American population earns more than $250,000

in income per year.[15] By occupational background, members lean heavily toward law and business, though many have been career politicians, and nearly all held some sort of elective or appointed office prior to their congressional career. Strikingly, about one-quarter of members in 2017 (102 in total) were former congressional staffers.[16]

Does it matter that descriptive representation is so poor in Congress and that its members are so demographically unrepresentative of the American people? Some observers of Congress think not. They suggest that the need to face the electorate forces lawmakers to be attentive to all the significant groups in their **constituency**. A representative from a rural district tends to listen to farm constituents, for example, even if that representative is not a farmer.[17]

constituency
The individuals who live in the district of a legislator.

Nevertheless, many Americans who are not well represented—especially women, minorities, and low-income groups—believe that their interests would be heard if their numbers were substantially increased in Congress. Significant evidence supports this view: female House members introduce more bills related to women's and children's issues than their male colleagues, and female representatives might be more effective overall legislators.[18] The same is true for African American legislators and issues considered important to African Americans.[19] As members of the wealthiest groups of Americans, it seems that senators and representatives don't have much in common with the daily concerns of middle- or low-income households. The demographic disparity between the American population and the makeup of Congress, then, suggests a violation of the norm of political equality, an important element of democracy.

Representation in the House: Reapportionment and Redistricting

As a result of the Great Compromise, members of the House represent relatively small districts of equal size by population within states, while senators represent states with varying population sizes. Unlike the Senate, as people move from one location to another within a state, House districts must occasionally be reapportioned and redrawn to ensure equality of size by population in House districts. Reapportionment and redistricting are two of the most controversial aspects of American politics today, and each has an enormous influence on political representation.

THE EFFECT OF REAPPORTIONMENT ON REPRESENTATION Because the American population is constantly growing in size and moving around the country, the 435 House representatives must be periodically redistributed among the states. **Reapportionment**, the technical name for redistributing districts across the states, occurs every 10 years, after each national census, as required by the Constitution, to ensure that each state gets the number of House seats to which it is entitled based on its actual population (see Figure 11.3 for a representation of the states who gained and lost seats in the U.S. House of Representatives based on the last census). Based on the official census, some states keep the same number of seats; others gain or lose them, depending on their relative population gains or losses. The big winner following the 2010 census count was Texas, which gained four additional seats in the House. Florida gained two seats, followed by Arizona, Georgia, Nevada, South Carolina, Utah, and Washington with one additional seat each. The biggest losers were New York and Ohio, which lost two seats each; Illinois, Louisiana, Massachusetts, Michigan, Missouri, New Jersey and Pennsylvania each lost one seat. These patterns reflect the general trend of the last 50 years of fewer Americans living in the upper Midwest and Northeast and more living in the South and Southwest. Those states that lose representatives have less influence in Congress on issues like securing federal funds for the state.

reapportionment
The reallocation of House seats among the states, done after each national census, to ensure that seats are held by the states in proportion to the size of their populations.

THE EFFECT OF REDISTRICTING ON REPRESENTATION All states, except for those with only a single House member (whose district therefore constitutes the entire state), must redraw their congressional district borderlines after every census.

FIGURE 11.3 REAPPORTIONED CONGRESSIONAL SEATS FOLLOWING THE 2010 CENSUS

The number of representatives for each state in the House of Representatives is based on the size of its population. Because the relative sizes of state populations change over time while the number of seats in the House is fixed, the number of representatives for each state is recalculated after each census. This process is called reapportionment.

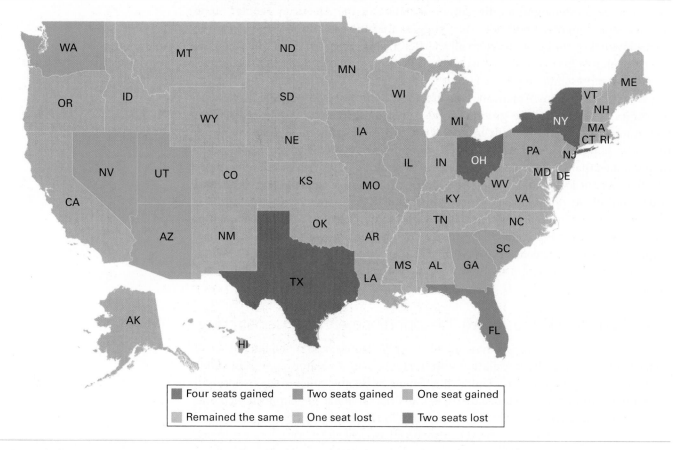

Four seats gained | Two seats gained | One seat gained

Remained the same | One seat lost | Two seats lost

SOURCE: U.S. Census Bureau, 2010 Census Apportionment Results. Apportionment Population and Number of Representatives, By State, table 1.

redistricting

The redrawing of congressional district lines within a state to ensure roughly equal populations within each district.

partisan

A committed member of a party; also, seeing issues from the point of view of the interests of a single party.

gerrymandering

Redrawing electoral district lines in an extreme and unlikely manner to give an advantage to a particular party or candidate.

Not only might a state gain or lose population, but population within a state shifts. Because people move, once-equal districts may be equal no longer.[20] Redrawing district lines is known as **redistricting**. Redistricting is managed by state legislatures in many states, though some states rely on independent commissions. In many cases, when lawsuits over redistricting plans are filed, the court system has a role to play in redistricting.

State legislatures are relatively free to draw district lines however they choose. The major limitations placed on legislatures are that districts must be of equal population and they must be contiguous (the borders of the district must be touching). Using sophisticated computer technology, the party that controls the state legislature and governorship tries to draw district borders in a way that will help its candidates win elections.[21] The results are often strange looking districts. Rather than creating compact and coherent districts, neighborhoods, towns, and counties can be pushed together in odd-looking ways in order to take full advantage of the redistricting process. Using redistricting to further **partisan** goals is known as **gerrymandering**, after Governor Elbridge Gerry of Massachusetts, who signed a bill in 1811 that created a district that looked like a salamander. It made wonderful raw material for editorial cartoonists (see the accompanying illustration).

Partisan redistricting after the 2010 Census led to four Republican losses in Illinois after a Democratic gerrymander. In Pennsylvania, thirteen of eighteen seats in the House went to Republicans, although Democrats, on a statewide level, won more votes.

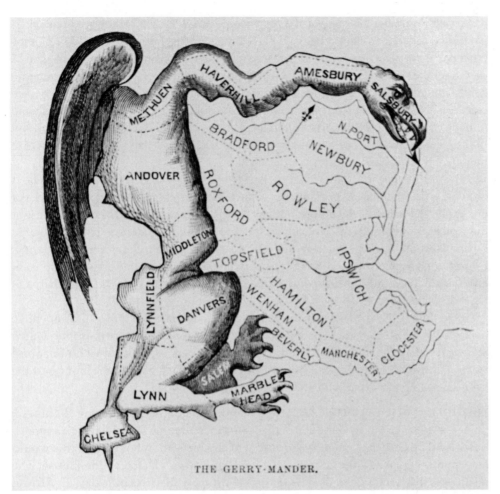

THE GERRY-MANDER.

THE "GERRY-MANDER": A NEW SPECIES OF MONSTER

The Massachusetts district created in 1812 to help the candidate supported by the Governor Elbridge Gerry, and shown here in a political cartoon from the time, was the first well-known gerrymander, but certainly not the last. *What negative effects might gerrymandering have on representation? Are there any positive effects of gerrymandering?*

A legislature usually uses two tactics to pull off an effective gerrymander: **"cracking" and "packing."** The first method, cracking, spreads one party's voters across multiple districts effectively denying them a majority in any single district. The alternative method, packing, puts voters of the rival party into one district which gives the other party a huge margin of support in one district but cuts its chances of winning seats in multiple districts.

Gerrymandering is highly controversial among the public and seems to violate most people's notions of fairness. Through the redistricting process, politicians are able to virtually ensure that one party wins the seat, which also reduces the number of competitive elections nationwide. As two political scientists put it, "politicians select voters rather than voters electing politicians."[22] One proposal to stop gerrymandering is to use independent or bipartisan commissions, made up of citizens, rather than politicians, to draw the lines. A number of states have adopted redistricting commissions, including California, Arizona, New Jersey, and Iowa. The idea is that they will draw more fair and competitive districts, rather than simply favoring one party. The evidence is mixed so far on whether independent commissions work.[23] In many states, they have simply not been around long enough to determine their effect.

Historically, the Supreme Court has been reluctant to limit flagrant redistricting abuses, unless some identifiable group of voters is disadvantaged—for example, a racial or ethnic minority. The Court, along with most politicians, seems to accept the notion that "to the victor belongs the spoils." Things may be changing as the Federal Courts have recently indicated a willingness to limit the worst excesses of gerrymandering. In 2018, the Supreme Court heard a case involving gerrymandering of state legislative seats in Wisconsin. Political scientists developed a measure of the severity of the gerrymander

"cracking" and "packing"

The act of dividing a district where the opposing party has a large majority, rendering it a minority in both parts of the redrawn districts (cracking), or concentrating all of one party's voters into a single district to dilute their influence in other districts (packing).

based on the number of votes wasted for a candidate, with each vote above or below 51 percent considered wasted. When one party draws district lines to "waste" votes of the other party, the gerrymander is more severe.[24] In the Wisconsin case, Democrats won 53 percent of the votes in 2012, but won only 39 percent of the seats. In effect, a Republican gerrymander led to a huge number of wasted Democratic votes. In the *Gill v. Whitford* case from Wisconsin, the Supreme Court ruled the plaintiffs did not have standing and sent the case back to the district court to be re-argued. That the Court did not throw out the case entirely but instead allowed for a "do-over" suggests that it may be receptive to limiting partisan abuses of gerrymandering.

Despite the negative view most observers hold of partisan gerrymanders, there is growing evidence that gerrymandering is not the cause of political polarization. For one thing, the Senate, which does not have redistricting, has polarized just as fast as the House. Many political scientists believe that residential patterns—where different types of people live—is much more important than the effects of gerrymandering. Democrats tend to cluster in urban areas, while Republicans tend to cluster in rural areas, making it hard to draw competitive districts, regardless of who is in charge of the redistricting process.

One thing is clear: whatever the cause, the decline in the number of competitive districts in House elections means that the vast majority of districts in the United States are safely Republican or safely Democratic where candidates need not appeal to the general constituency but only to members of their party, contributing to the ever-deepening partisan divide in Congress.

MAJORITY-MINORITY DISTRICTS Amendments to the 1965 Voting Rights Act passed in 1982 encouraged the states to create House districts in which racial minorities would be a district majority. Sponsors of the legislation hoped that this would lead to an increase in the number of racial minorities elected to the House. The result was the formation of 24 new **majority-minority districts**, fifteen with African American majorities and nine with Hispanic American majorities.[25] The creation of some of these districts has taken great imagination. North Carolina's Twelfth District, for instance, created after the 1990 census, linked a narrow strip of predominantly African American communities along 160 miles of Interstate 85 connecting Durham and Charlotte. The Supreme Court finally accepted a slightly redrawn North Carolina Twelfth District map, when it handed down a decision in *Hunt v. Cromartie* (2001). In its *Hunt* decision, the Court ruled that race can be a significant factor in drawing district lines "so long as it is not the dominant and controlling one." Of course, determining whether a district meets these criteria is difficult, resulting in controversy and numerous legal challenges every 10 years when new majority-minority districts are drawn.

Another example of an oddly shaped majority-minority district is the so-called "earmuff" district on the west side of Chicago. The district links two different Hispanic communities, one on the lower west side in the Pilsen, Cicero, and Lawndale neighborhoods and one on the northwest side, which includes the Logan Square and Belmont areas. To connect the two areas into one district, the boundaries run west to east, with a small north-to-south strip that bands the two areas together like a pair of thermal earmuffs.

The creation of majority-minority districts has been successful in increasing the number of racial minorities in the House as these districts nearly always elect a member of the racial group the district is intended to empower. Ironically, however, the creation of such districts has undermined Democratic Party strength in other districts by taking traditionally Democratic-oriented minority group voters away from previously

---

majority-minority districts

Districts drawn to ensure that a racial minority makes up the majority of voters.

THE EARMUFF CONGRESSIONAL DISTRICT: THE ILLINOIS FOURTH

The "earmuff" district in Chicago is an example of how creating majority-minority districts can result in odd-shaped boundaries. The district links two Hispanic communities on opposite sides of Interstate 290.

How important is it that racial minorities elect a member of Congress that is racially similar to constituents? Can racial minorities be well-represented by white members of Congress if they agree on the issues?

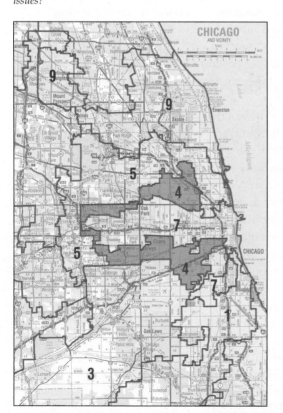

Democratic-dominated districts in order to form majority-minority ones. (One political scientist reports that after 1991, Republicans won and held every congressional seat in which redistricting had reduced the African American population by 10 percentage points or more.[26]) Naturally, Republicans have been eager to support minority group efforts to form their own districts. Concentrating black voters in certain districts—packing them, as it were—has decreased the total number of Democrats that would have been elected, leading to a reduction in the likelihood that policies favored by African Americans will be enacted into law.[27]

Representation in the Senate

Things are a lot less complicated in the Senate because a senator's district is the entire state. This means that senators usually represent a more diverse electorate and hear many different points of view. The diversity in Senate districts (the state) causes senators to be more moderate and ideologically accommodating because they must appeal to many different types of people during their reelection bids. Although members of the House are usually finely tuned into their constituents' preferences, senators represent far more people and have the latitude to behave more like trustees rather than as delegates. States that are dominated by one-party, however, enable senators to become more extreme.

How Representative Is Congress? A Look Back at the Arguments

Congress is the branch of government closest to the people, and its members are supposed to be broadly representative of the American public. But does Congress live up to this ideal? For one thing, the individuals who are elected look very different from the average American. Women and members of racial minorities and ethnic groups are vastly underrepresented in the ranks of the House and Senate, while most members of Congress are far more educated and wealthier than most Americans.

The ways in which we choose our representatives also distorts congressional representation. As we have seen, people in small-population states are disproportionately represented in the Senate because of the constitutional provision mandating two senators for each state, no matter the state's population. The necessity of redistricting after a Census creates representation problems in the House. Gerrymandering by state legislatures often produces safe districts, which discourages competition for seats. Consequently, House elections may not adequately fulfill the role assigned to elections in democratic theory: as the principle instrument for keeping elected leaders responsive and responsible.[28]

All of these problems raise concerns about whether members of Congress vote in a manner that is consistent with both national public opinion and the views of their district constituents. Some evidence suggests that they do, at least most of the time. Yet, there are clearly times when Congress seems to be too influenced by business interests, the wealthy or other groups with a large stake in a particular issue. Moreover, on many issues of high complexity or low visibility, such as securities and telecommunications regulation, the public may not have any well-formed opinions. It is in these areas that we can most fully see the influence of money and interest groups at work.

CONGRESSIONAL ELECTIONS

11.3 Describe the process of congressional elections and the impact of incumbency on election outcomes.

Congressional elections are among the most important, expensive, and competitive elections in the United States. As we learned, every member of the House must run for reelection every two years, while senators must face the voters every six years. Unlike many states legislators, members of Congress are not limited in how many times they can run for reelection. It isn't uncommon for a representative or senator to serve for decades. The longest-serving member of Congress in history, John Dingell, a Democrat from Michigan, was first elected in 1955 (in a special election) and won reelection every two years afterward, until his retirement in 2015. The longest serving member now in the House is Republican Don Young of Alaska, who has been elected every two years since 1972.

Despite the overall unpopularity of Congress, voters generally approve of their own congressional representatives and, as a result, incumbent members of Congress are reelected at a very high rate. As we will discuss, incumbents have a number of built-in advantages over challengers. Still, even powerful members of Congress have been known to lose their reelection bids. Sometimes losses follow a scandal. Sometimes dramatic change in a district's composition of voters is at fault, but most often losses occur because representatives lose touch with their constituents or take an unpopular stand on an important policy. Members work hard at winning reelection because no member wants to be the exception that proves the rule.

The Congressional Election Process

When an incumbent or challenger decides to run for a House or Senate seat, a number of steps must be taken. The candidate must ensure that voters know who they are by making speeches in the district, running advertisements, and appearing at public events. Incumbents, because they are usually better known in the state or district, are able to do this more easily than challengers. As we will see, raising money is one of the most important activities a candidate needs to engage in, but gaining name recognition through public appearances is also critical.

House members, though they have smaller districts, must spend more time focusing on their reelection. This is the direct result of having short, two-year terms. As a consequence, members of the House seem to constantly be in campaign mode, raising money, making speeches, and doing the other activities necessary to help their prospects. Some observers are concerned that representatives in the House now spend more time campaigning than they do actually governing because of the money required and the relatively short time between elections. The never-ending process of running for reelection in the House is called the **permanent campaign**. Senators, on the other hand, have six years between reelection, giving them a break from campaigning for a few years.

Both senators and House members must win a primary election (or caucus in some states) to become their party's nominee, and then win in the general election. In districts with a large majority of voters from one party, the primary election can be more important than the general election since the winner from the majority party in the district is all but assured of winning the general election. In fact, a few well known incumbents have recently lost their seat after losing the primary election to a challenger from the same party. Just like in presidential primaries, the voters who participate in primaries tend to be more extreme and ideological, and recently, some incumbents who are viewed as too moderate have been defeated in favor of a more ideological candidate.

Who Runs for Congress?

Senate seats are much more visible than House seats because senators represent an entire state, and because there are far fewer senators than House members. As a result, senators tend to face higher quality challengers who are well-known throughout the state in both the primary and general elections. House members often face underfunded and unknown challengers, or even run unopposed. Political scientists have found that candidates who previously held elected office are more successful; as a result, these individuals are called **quality challengers**. In fact, most people

permanent campaign
The idea that members of Congress are always running for reelection and focus most of their efforts on winning their seat rather than governing.

quality challengers
Individuals who run against incumbent members of Congress who have previously held elected office. They tend to be more successful in defeating incumbent members than other types of challengers.

who run for House seats are state legislators, mayors, or other local elected officials. Senators are often challenged by House members, big-city mayors, governors, or other state-wide elected officials. Quality challengers tend to do better because they understand how to run a campaign, they know prominent groups and businesses within the state or district, and they are able to raise large sums of money.

Money and Congressional Elections

Running for the House or the Senate is a very expensive proposition, and the costs keep growing. In 2016, the average House incumbent spent about $1.74 million defending their seat, while incumbent senators spent about $9 million.[29] These numbers underestimate total spending as candidates have come to rely on outside groups and organizations to spend money on their behalf. House and Senate candidate campaigns do not receive public funding and therefore face no limits on what they can spend in the general election. To fill their campaign coffers, they rely on contributions from individuals (who are limited in what they can contribute), PACs, and political party committees. In 2016, across all congressional races, the candidates and parties combined to spend an estimated $3.1 billion. These numbers are only estimates because much of the money raised and spent by outside groups, especially nonprofits (sometimes called "dark money"), cannot be directly tracked.

MONEY FROM OUTSIDE GROUPS Many congressional candidates receive campaign contributions from PACs associated with congressional party leaders such as House Speaker Nancy Pelosi (D-CA)—who was, at the time of publication, expected to become Speaker once again—and Senate Majority Leader Mitch McConnell (R-KY). Similar to presidential campaigns, contributions to PACs are dominated by business corporations and trade associations, while individual contributors to congressional campaigns come primarily from top income earners.

Not to be overlooked, parties, committees, interest groups, advocacy groups, corporations, and unions also spend lavishly on ads for issues and for candidates. Get-out-the-vote efforts funded by these organizations are extremely helpful to congressional candidates. In the 2013–2014 election cycle, following the groundbreaking *Citizen's United* (2010) decision, corporations and unions—especially the former—increased their spending in direct support of or in opposition to particular Senate and House candidates. With growing amounts of money pouring into congressional campaigns, members are relying more on super PACs to provide outside money for their race as well. Political nonprofits, sometimes called **dark money groups**, are allowed to spend unlimited amounts of money and do not need to disclose how much they raise or spend. They are not allowed to coordinate with candidates, but this is an unimportant limitation. Super PACs, which are required to disclose their donors, can receive money from dark money groups which do not, thus making it impossible to know who contributes to these groups. As you might expect, dark money is playing a more important role in campaigns.

SELF-FINANCING CONGRESSIONAL CAMPAIGNS Unlike presidential races, many candidates spend vast sums of their own money to fund campaigns. Democrat John Corzine (D-NJ) set the record in 2000 by contributing $62 million of his own money in a race which he won narrowly. In 1992, a little-known businessman named Michael Huffington spent $5.4 million to win a House seat in California. In the next election, Huffington spent $30 million of his own money in a bid to win a Senate seat, a record at the time. He lost that election by just two points.[30] Other examples abound,

THE EXCEPTION THAT PROVES THE RULE

Members of Congress, even powerful ones, tend to "run scared" and raise a lot of money, though usually their seat seems safe. Though the vast majority of members win their reelection race, inevitably some are taken by surprise and lose. Here, Eric Cantor, the powerful House majority leader, campaigns in 2014. Cantor was one such member who lost in a shocking upset during the 2014 Republican primary to a formerly unknown local professor who raised very little money. Many of Cantor's constituents believe he lost touch with the district and spent more time deal-making in Washington than he did addressing local concerns.

How important is the role of campaign money in congressional elections? Should candidates have to raise money themselves, or should the government provide campaign funds much like it used to for presidential campaigns?

dark money groups

Political advocacy groups that contribute significant sums of money in order to influence elections, but whose sources of funding, and the amount of money spent, are hidden from the public.

though perhaps surprisingly, many self-financed candidates lose. Linda McMahon, the former CEO of World Wrestling Entertainment, spent more than $50 million on her campaign in 2010 but lost to Richard Blumenthal (D-CT), who also spent more than $2.5 million of his own money. In 2012, McMahon tried again, and again spent more than $50 million on her campaign, only to lose a second time. Jeff Greene, a Democrat from Florida, spent almost $24 million on his Senate campaign, but lost in the primary.[31] Clearly, spending a lot of money on a congressional campaign is no guarantee of success, though there seems to be a new trend of extremely wealthy individuals, without prior elective experience, spending vast sums of money on congressional seats.

RAISING MONEY   Incumbents have an easier time raising money than their challengers (see Figure 11.4). The reasons are fairly obvious. Donors want access. Because incumbents are reelected at very high rates, the smart play is to give money to those in power and likely to remain in power.[32] Moreover, being a member of the majority party in Congress serves as a magnet for money because contributors generally want to be able to have access to the party in power.[33] **Open-seat elections**, in which no incumbent is involved, due to retirement, resignation, or death, attract more money, especially in the Senate, because the stakes are so high. For example, in the 2009–2010 cycle, the average open-seat candidate in House and Senate races raised 46 percent more than challengers to incumbent candidates.[34]

Even incumbents running for reelection tend to raise much larger sums of money than they seem to need. There are two reasons for this. First, they can give some of their money to other officeholders, increasing their stature within Congress. More importantly, raising large sums of money well before an election sends a signal to potential challengers—the so-called **scare-off effect**—that an incumbent will not go down without a fight. Incumbents with lots of money on hand discourage potential challengers from running against them.

open-seat election

An election in which there is no incumbent officeholder.

scare-off effect

When members of Congress raise more money than they need to signal support and resources to potential challengers, thereby discouraging others from running against them.

FIGURE 11.4   CAMPAIGN MONEY RAISED BY INCUMBENTS, CHALLENGERS, AND OPEN-SEAT CANDIDATES, 2015–2016 ELECTION CYCLE

Because campaign contributors want access to important decision makers in Congress, contributors tend to give a disproportionate share of campaign contributions to incumbents and to those open-seat candidates who have a good chance to win their elections.

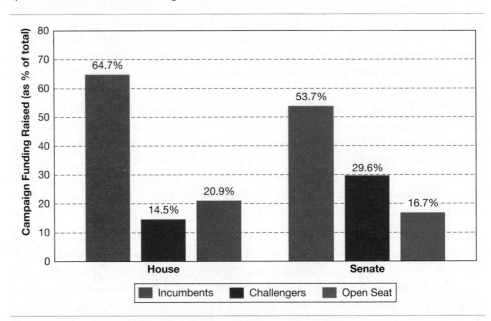

SOURCE: Center for Responsive Politics, Incumbent Advantage, Election Cycle 2016. https://www.opensecrets.org/overview/incumbs.php?cycle=2016

The Incumbency Factor

As we have seen, incumbents in Congress win at very high rates, especially in the House (see Figure 11.5), meaning that the overwhelming majority of electoral contests for Congress are not very competitive. Since the end of World War II, on average, 93 percent of House incumbents have been reelected, as have 80 percent of Senate incumbents. Incumbents won at very high rates even in the big party swing elections of 1994, 2006, 2008, and 2010. In 1994 and 2010, when Republicans took over control of Congress, incumbent losses were concentrated in Democratic districts and states; in 2006 and 2008, when the Democrats won many seats, most incumbent losses were among Republicans. In 2014, sixteen incumbent representatives or senators lost their general reelection race, while in 2016 only ten did. To be sure, there is still substantial turnover in the House and Senate. Many members retire, especially if they believe they are likely to lose an upcoming election, others lose to challengers in their party's primary, and still others take a different position or die. But, among those who choose to stay and run, most retain their seats.

Incumbents almost always win when they seek reelection for several reasons. Redistricting is an important reason, as districts are often drawn to protect incumbents. Moreover, as mentioned above, incumbents typically have an easier time raising money than challengers. But there are other reasons for the advantage of incumbency.[35] Already well known to voters because they garner so much free media coverage, incumbent members of Congress have many ways to advertise their accomplishments and keep their names before the public. For example, the **franking privilege** allows them to mail

franking privilege
Public subsidization of mail from the members of Congress to their constituents

---

FIGURE 11.5 RATES OF INCUMBENT REELECTION IN CONGRESS

The probability that an incumbent will be reelected remains at historic highs. This does not mean, however, that the membership of Congress is stagnant. Turnover in membership is substantial because of retirements and the defeat of incumbents in primary elections.

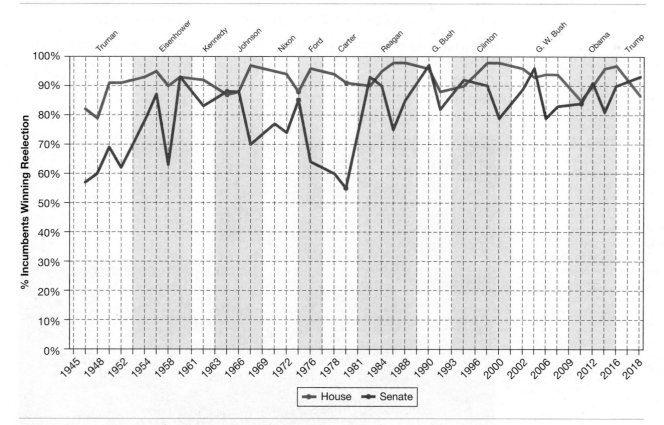

NOTE: Figure does not include races undecided as of November 18, 2018.

SOURCE: Norman J. Ornstein, Thomas E. Mann, and Michael J. Malbin, *Vital Statistics on Congress* (Washington, D.C.: Brookings Institution Press, 2013), tables 2.7–2.8; Center for Responsive Politics, OpenSecrets.org. "Reelection Rates Over the Years."

newsletters, legislative updates, surveys, and other self-promoting literature free of charge. The House and the Senate also provide travel budgets for lawmakers to make periodic visits to their states or districts. Because members believe that time spent in their districts helps their electoral chances, they spend lots of time back home meeting with constituents, attending local events, and raising money.[36] The congressional leadership helps incumbents by scheduling important legislative business only during the Tuesday-to-Thursday period, allowing members to return home four days a week.

Incumbents also use their offices to "serve the district." One way is through **casework**, helping constituents cut through the red tape of the federal bureaucracy, whether it be speeding up the arrival of a late Social Security check or expediting the issuance of a permit for grazing on public land.[37] Congress provides members budgets for establishing and staffing offices in the district to help representatives and senators do casework. Another way incumbents serve their constituents is by providing **pork**—federal dollars for various projects in the district or state. In late 2015, for example, Congress passed a massive $305 billion highway and mass transit bill that poured federal construction money into the constituencies of senators and representatives for highway and bridge projects, rail and bus improvements, urban bike paths, and more. Pork is controversial because many view it as wasteful spending, but it is also enormously important to local areas that depend on federal money to finance a project. For example, money spent in a district creating a new park, building a new highway bridge, or funding a hospital research lab benefits all members of the community. Congress has sought to limit pork through various rules, with some success. The use of the earmark, a specific line-item in a bill that directs federal spending to a district, was banned by Congress in 2011. There is now talk of bringing earmarks back; in a polarized Congress some view them as an easy way to "grease the wheels" and create bipartisan coalitions to support legislation. Further, though they spend federal tax dollars on district-specific projects, historically they were only a tiny part of the overall federal budget.[38]

Do Congressional Elections Ensure Proper Representation?

Representatives and senators pay a great deal of attention to the interests and the preferences of the people in their particular districts and states. Because they are worried about being reelected, even popular incumbents tend to run scared, knowing that some of them lose every year. As a result, members of Congress undertake a wide

casework

Services performed by members of Congress for constituents.

pork

Also called *pork barrel*; federally funded projects designed to bring to the constituency jobs and public money for which the members of Congress can claim credit.

FEDERAL SPENDING AT WORK

The American Recovery and Reinvestment Act, sometimes called the Stimulus Bill, was passed during the height of the Great Recession in early 2009. The law spent about $830 billion, much of it on construction projects like this one, meant to improve local infrastructure while also stimulating the economy and getting people back to work. Critics complained it was nothing more than pork barrel spending with little national benefit.

Is federal spending on local projects worth the benefits for the district, or is it a wasteful use of federal tax dollars?

variety of activities to ensure they can win reelection. These activities give them an advantage to be sure, as incumbents can raise more money, perform services for their constituents, and use the powers of their office to raise their profile.

Is it possible members of Congress are so successfully at winning reelection because they represent their district well? There is some support for this argument. It is almost always the case that the overall ideology of the member closely reflects the views of voters in his or her district. Conservative representatives almost always come from conservative districts, while liberal members reflect their districts. Occasionally, a conservative candidate manages to win in a liberal district (or vice-versa), but typically the member will not last long when they are not well matched to the district. Other members are famous for their ability to bring home pork or help with casework, and these practices make them popular with their voters; members who are not seen as accessible or who do not make frequent visits back home frequently lose their reelection races. All of these patterns seem to confirm the notion that most of the time, individual members do a fairly good job of representing their state or district, though there is ample room, given the complexity and near-invisibility of many issues before the Congress, to accommodate powerful interest groups as well.

As with presidential elections, however, the role of money in congressional elections is changing the connection between members and constituents. Representatives and senators now spend so much time raising money and have become so reliant on outside groups and big donors that the average constituent's voice may not get heard. There is growing evidence that wealthy individuals living in the district can speak directly to a Representative or senator about their pet issue simply by picking up the phone; most of us do not have that level of access. Money seems to be distorting the opinions members hear and the issues they care about.[39]

THE CONGRESSIONAL LEGISLATIVE PROCESS

11.4 Outline the process by which a bill becomes a law.

Congress alone, as the legislative branch, has the power to write and pass bills. Despite the strength of the modern presidency, there is no formal legislative role for presidents except the ability to sign or veto bills. The separation of powers between the executive and legislative branches of government is unique to the American system of governing—in most other countries, the executive can, independent of the national legislature, develop and propose legislation.

The path by which a bill becomes a law is not an easy one however, and the legislative labyrinth is so strewn with obstacles that few bills survive; in fact, only about 6 percent of all bills introduced are ultimately enacted. Congress is designed so that it is exceedingly difficult to make laws, but it is very easy to block a bill at each step in the passage process (see Figure 11.6). As one account of congressional lawmaking pointed out, members of the House or the Senate have "two principal functions: to make laws and to keep laws from being made. The first of these [they] perform only with sweat, patience, and a remarkable skill in the handling of creaking machinery; but the second they perform daily, with ease and infinite variety."[40]

Congress has had an even more difficult time than usual passing laws recently because of intense party **polarization**. This means that Democrats and Republicans are far apart ideologically, making compromise very difficult and increasing personal animosity between members. In turn, these factors make it much more difficult for Congress to accomplish even the simplest tasks like passing routine funding bills. Drastic changes in policy are even more difficult to achieve, especially when a different party from the president's controls at least one of the two congressional chambers, commonly called **divided government**.

polarization
The process by which political parties have become more internally consistent in ideology and more ideologically distant from one another; in the U.S. the Republican party has become more conservative and the Democratic party more liberal.

divided government
Control of the executive and the legislative branches by different political parties.

FIGURE 11.6 HOW A BILL BECOMES A LAW

This diagram shows the path by which major bills introduced in Congress become law. As explained in the text, the road that bills must travel is complex and difficult, and few bills survive it. A bill can be derailed at any stop in its passage. A subcommittee can refuse to report a bill; a bill may be defeated on the floor of each chamber; a conference committee may fail to reach an agreement on a compromise; the conference bill may be defeated in either chamber; or the president may veto the bill.

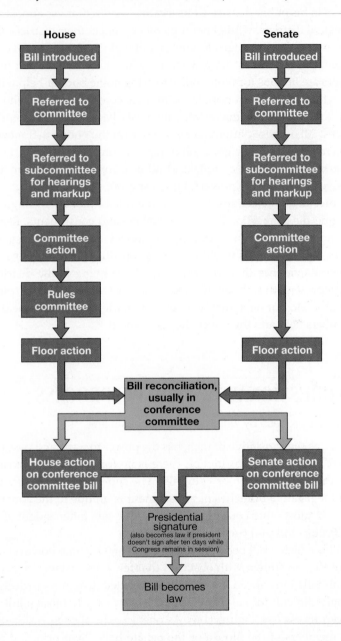

The following sections describe how major bills become law most of the time (minor or trivial bills are considered under different rules that allow shortcuts).[41] It is worth noting that the rules sometimes change for specific bills, and year to year, and that while the processes listed here are called "regular order," different procedures, commonly called "unorthodox" lawmaking are, according to some congressional observers, becoming more and more common.[42] Like all organizations, Congress is guided by both formal rules and informal norms of behavior.[43] Rules specify precisely how things should be done and what is not allowed. Norms are generally accepted expectations about how people ought to behave and how legislative business ought to proceed. Both are important in understanding how Congress works and how bills are passed into law.

Introducing a Bill

A bill can be introduced only by a member of Congress but in reality, bills are often written with the help of the executive branch or interest groups. The initial draft of the bill that became the Tax Reform Act of 1986, for instance, was fashioned in the Treasury Department by a committee headed by the department's secretary, James Baker. With the exception of tax bills (which must originate in the House according to the Constitution), a bill may be introduced in either the House or the Senate, though any bill introduced in either chamber must eventually pass both if it is to become law.

Referral to Committee

Once a bill is introduced, it is referred to one of the chamber's **standing committees** based on the issues it addresses—bills dealing with the military go to the Armed Services Committee, while bills dealing with NASA go to the Science, Space, and Technology Committee. Committees serve several useful purposes. For one thing, they allow Congress to process the huge flow of business that comes before it. The committees serve as screening devices, allowing only a small percentage of the bills put forward to take up the time of the full House and the Senate.

Committees are also islands of specialization, where members and staff develop the expertise to handle complex issues and to meet executive branch experts on equal terms. Lawmakers try to secure committee assignments that allow them to connect with their constituents and advocate for their interests, each of which enhances their chances for reelection. Members from rural districts with farming interests want to be on the Agriculture Committee, to take one example, to promote legislation beneficial to their constituents and to help direct pork to their district. That House members from different areas want to be on specific types of committees has an important collective benefit, however. It allows the most interested and knowledgeable members to work on legislation in their particular area, creating members with in-depth knowledge. In the House, standing committees are divided further into subcommittees, which perform the same tasks as committees, but are composed of fewer members.

Committees and subcommittees hold **hearings** on the bill, where those for and against the proposed law can give statements and answer questions, and committees are free to add and subtract language without any limitations. This entire process is called the **bill markup**. Committee members and their staff try to rewrite a bill that

standing committees
Relatively permanent congressional committees that address specific areas of legislation.

hearings
The taking of testimony by a congressional committee or subcommittee.

bill markup
The process of revising a bill in committee.

THE POWER OF STANDING COMMITTEES
John McCain listens to testimony in his role as chair of the Senate Armed Services Committee. Congressional committees have much of the responsibility for crafting legislation.

will attract majority support on the floors of the House and the Senate and that will gain the support of the president.

In both chambers, the party membership of the committees are appointed in proportion to the size of their party in Congress—if 55 percent of the House membership is Republican, then roughly speaking, about 55 percent of each committee will also be Republican. The leader of each committee is known as the **committee chair**, and they are generally appointed by **seniority**. As recently as the 1960s and 1970s, committee chairs alone had great power over the course of legislation, often deciding how bills would be changed and which bills would be sent to the entire chamber. They also hired and assigned staff, controlled the committee's budget, created or abolished subcommittees at will, controlled the agenda, and scheduled meetings. Committee chairs have lost much of their influence as the parties, along with their leadership, have become more powerful. Committees now frequently defer to the party leadership because of increasing polarization,[44] and committee chairs now must be attentive to the party caucus and party leaders or risk losing their positions.[45] Party leaders are taking a more active role in writing legislation too, though because the committee leadership are seen as experts in their area, they are still involved in the process.

The Rules Committee

If a standing committee decides a bill is worth considering, it will send it on to be considered by the entire chamber, commonly referred to as being reported to the "floor." The process at this point differs in the House and Senate. In the House, before a bill goes to the floor, it first must go to a special committee called the **Rules Committee**. The Rules Committee is perhaps the most important committee in the entire House because it determines the time limit for floor debate on a bill, and whether or not amendments will be allowed. No bill may be considered in the House without a rule. Thus, the Rules Committee effectively has the power to delay or prevent any bill from advancing. Closed rules prevent the full House from considering any amendments to the bill while open rules allow amendments. The minority party may want to make a change to the bill which would be supported by a majority of members, but because of a closed rule, the amendment cannot be voted on by the entire House.

The members who make up the Rules Committee are typically party loyalists appointed by the Speaker of the House, a constitutional office, but also a position held by the leader of the majority party. Members of the Rules Committee work for the Speaker in the sense that they prevent any bills from reaching the floor that are not favored by the majority party leadership. Party polarization is leading to more closed rules which shuts the minority out of the lawmaking process in the House and increases the distrust between the parties.

Floor Action on a Bill

If a bill is favorably reported from a standing committee and from the Rules Committee (if the bill is being considered in the House), congressional leaders schedule it for floor debate. There are important differences between the ways the House and Senate pass bills. Nearly all the rules in the House empower the majority party and its leadership, while the rules in the Senate generally require more cooperation between the parties, and bills must often pass with a supermajority.

THE HOUSE PASSAGE PROCESS   Passing a bill in the House is generally much easier than passing one in the Senate, simply because the rules governing debates and amendments are set by the majority party leadership through its control of the Rules Committee. Bills need only a simple majority to pass (218 votes when all members are present) so the majority party typically needs only to gather support from its own members. In theory, on close votes, the party leadership can use a variety of methods

---

committee chair

The head of a standing committee with significant power over legislation considered within the committee.

seniority

The principle that one attains a position on the basis of length of service

Rules Committee

A special committee in the House of Representatives that determines whether amendments will be allowed on a bill.

to arm twist, such as threatening to take away a member's committee assignment or denying them access to party campaign funds if they don't support the party position. There are a few more steps than described here, but generally once a bill is reported out of committee to the floor of the House, debate and amending takes place under the rules governing the bill (usually debate is allowed for one hour and is split evenly between the majority and minority parties), and then the House votes.

THE SENATE PASSAGE PROCESS   The Senate floor rules are much more complicated than in the House, and generally, it is more difficult to pass legislation in the Senate, even if the majority party leadership is supportive. The difficulty is the result of the Senate's rules and informal norms, which emphasize bipartisanship, cooperation, and tradition. The party leadership in the Senate is also much weaker than in the House, making it more difficult to twist arms.

There are fewer members in the Senate, senators are elected on a statewide basis, and a senator has more prestige, visibility, and power than a member of the House. As a result, the Senate is a much more relaxed place, one that accommodates mavericks (though less so than in the past), tolerates the foibles of its members, and pays more attention to members of the minority party. It is a place where the minority and individual senators play important roles in the legislative process.

The Senate, like the House, uses standing committees to markup legislation, though subcommittees are less important. However, unlike the House, once a bill is referred out of committee, it goes straight to the floor—the Rules Committee in the Senate does not determine how a bill shall be considered as does the Rules Committee in the House, and as a result, there are far fewer limitations on debate and amendment in the Senate. Motions to schedule a bill for consideration, to proceed to debate on a bill, and even motions on some trivial matters are open for debate in the Senate, unless all senators agree to waive debate through **unanimous consent**. The **majority leader** is the head of the majority party in the Senate and is also the de facto leader of the Senate. The majority leader negotiates unanimous consent agreements with the minority leader, which allow legislation to move forward but ensures all senators, even minority party members, are able to have their voices heard.

If all senators do not agree to waive debate, then the Senate must proceed with debate on the motion, a time consuming process, and one that allows Senate business to be delayed by a single dissenter. Outgoing Senator Jim Bunning (R-KY) blocked Senate consideration of an unemployment insurance extension for a whole week in early 2010 by responding "no" to majority leader Harry Reid's request for unanimous consent to proceed on the bill. Besides unanimous consent agreements, the most important difference between floor consideration in the House and Senate are the rules concerning time limits and amendments. There are no time limits on debate in the Senate, and there are virtually no limitations on the number or type of amendments that may be offered (the amendments do not even need to be related to the bill, unlike in the House).

Debate only ends in the Senate when all senators agree to stop talking about the bill. A vote on the legislation can only occur after debate has ended, so if the Senate wants to vote on a bill but cannot get all senators to agree to stop debating, it can vote to close off debate, called invoking **cloture**. The practice of refusing to stop debating is called the **filibuster**. In the past, senators engaged in a filibuster had to be on the floor of the Senate addressing the body, and senators trying to hold up a bill often talked for hours on end. Under Senate rules, filibustering senators did not even have to talk about the bill itself; some read from novels or quoted verse, others told stories about their children, and still others quoted long lists of sports statistics. The purpose was serious, however: to force the majority to give up the fight and move on to other business. This tactic was sometimes successful but used only occasionally because it was so hard to pull off.

Today, it is much easier to filibuster because a group of senators can simply announce a filibuster and not actually engage in the "talking" filibuster. Senate rules

unanimous consent

Legislative action taken "without objection" as a way to expedite business; used to conduct much of the business of the Senate.

majority leader

The leaders of the Senate, also the head of the majority party in the Senate. Equivalent to the House Speaker, though not a constitutional office.

cloture

A vote to end a filibuster; requires the votes of three-fifths of the membership of the Senate.

filibuster

A parliamentary device used in the Senate to prevent a bill from coming to a vote by "talking it to death," or by refusing to end debate, made possible by the norm of unlimited debate unless cloture is invoked.

require that to invoke cloture, even if no one is actually holding the floor by talking about a bill, sixty votes are required (Senate Rule XXII). Needless to say, invoking cloture with sixty votes is very hard to do in an evenly divided Senate, where a party with a small majority must attract several members of the minority party to reach the sixty-vote threshold. In the past, the Senate rarely had to muster sixty votes to end an announced filibuster which was blocking action on a bill, but today most observers believe that all important legislation is under an implicit filibuster, meaning sixty votes are almost always necessary to pass a bill.[46] The reasons for the dramatic increase in the number of cloture votes taken in the Senate are debated by political scientists but there are a few factors at play. First, an increase in party polarization makes minority parties much more willing to use their filibuster power to prevent votes on bill. Second, many believe the norms and traditions which previously governed Senate debate are gone, and along with it a sense of institutional pride. Finally, many believe that because the Senate is so busy today, with fewer days of actual legislating, the mere threat of a filibuster—and its subsequent effect of tying up the floor for hours or days—is enough to force the majority party to move onto other issues.[47] The one type of bill that may not be filibustered are those which concern budget reconciliation. These types of bills are seen as so important and need to be passed so quickly, that by law, they require only fifty-one votes. The Senate majority is now tying more and more bills to the budget process, allowing them to skip the filibuster. This was one of the steps Senate Democrats took to pass the Patient Protection and Affordable Care Act and Republicans used in 2017 to pass their tax bill over intense Democratic opposition.

What many perceive as the abuse of the filibuster is leading to calls for reform. Its use still applies for bills but also previously applied to bureaucratic and judicial nominees until recent changes removed the filibuster for these officials. In 2005, after a number of President Bush's federal court judge nominees were blocked by Democratic senators, the Republican majority threatened to change the rules through a procedural tactic requiring only a majority vote to end debate, rather than sixty votes. In response, the Democrats threatened to begin objecting to *all* unanimous consent agreements, which would have effectively slowed down Senate business to a crawl. A compromise was eventually reached and the Senate avoided what is sometimes called "the nuclear option." However, Democrats, frustrated by Senate filibusters of President Obama's nominees in 2013, changed the rules to require only fifty-one votes to invoke cloture on all non-Supreme Court judicial nominees and on bureaucratic appointees. The Democrats were tired of what they perceived as Republican abuse of the filibuster which blocked judicial nominees to very important federal appeals courts, not because the nominees weren't qualified, but because the Republicans objected to their politics. Republicans claimed that they had done nothing different than what Senate Democrats did during President Bush's administration. In a sense, Republicans are correct that Democrats also used the tactic, but the sheer number of filibusters used by Republicans against nominees increased dramatically during the Obama presidency.[48]

The battle over the filibuster escalated in the last year of Obama's presidency. In February of 2016, Supreme Court Justice Antonin Scalia died, leaving a vacancy on the Supreme Court. The Republican majority refused to confirm President Obama's nominee, saying that an appointment should not be made until after the election. Democrats argued this was an unprecedented act of obstruction for an otherwise qualified nominee, but because they were in the minority, there was little they could do. Once President Trump nominated Neil Gorsuch to Scalia's seat, Democrats filibustered because of Gorusch's conservative record, but also because of their anger over the Republicans' obstruction of Obama's nominee in 2016. Some Democrats began openly referring to the vacancy as a "stolen seat." To confirm Gorsuch, Senate Republicans changed the rules for filibustering Supreme Court nominees on April 6, 2017, from requiring sixty votes to fifty-one. The result is that today, fifty-one votes are required to approve bureaucratic officials and all federal judges, including Supreme Court nominees.

Holds, which allow an individual senator to delay consideration of a bill or a nomination, are also common, and have become more so in recent years. Holds are informal messages sent to the majority leader that indicate a senator will object to a unanimous consent request or attempt to filibuster a bill if it is brought to the floor. While the majority leader may ignore the hold and try to move forward on the bill anyway, the signal that is sent by a hold request—that another senator will attempt to block the bill at every turn—often leads the majority leader to simply avoid scheduling the bill for floor action. While holds cannot be found in the formal rules of the Senate, they have become part of the many informal customs of the body. In 2009, Senator Richard Shelby of Alabama blocked consideration of seventy nominees submitted by the president, using the hold as a tool to force the Obama administration to put a new FBI lab in his state and to award a military tanker contract to a firm in Alabama.

Advocates for the filibuster point out that it allows for more debate and consideration on the bill and that it forces the majority to compromise with at least a few members of the opposition. The framers, after all, envisioned the Senate to be a moderate and calming influence on the passions of the House. Whether future majorities will seek to further limit filibusters and holds remains to be seen, but for now it remains a highly controversial issue in the Senate. Leaders from both parties have thus far been reluctant to discuss removing the filibuster for regular legislation. If this were to occur, it would dramatically change the lawmaking process, making the Senate much more like the majority-party oriented House. Currently, garnering sixty votes to end debate is the biggest obstacle to passing legislation in the Senate. Once debate is closed, the passage of a bill requires only a simple majority, or fifty-one members.

Some of the key differences in process, rules, norms, and procedures between the House and Senate are summarized in Table 11.2.

Resolving Bicameral Differences

Nearly all important bills are passed in different forms by the House and Senate. Each chamber has different constituencies, different committee structures, different rules, and different leadership styles which result in House and Senate bills with different provisions, spending, and policies. The Constitution requires that only one bill be sent to the president for signature or veto, so before a bill can pass Congress, it must pass in identical form in each chamber. Most often, the chambers create a joint committee that irons out the differences between House and Senate versions, called a **conference committee**. A conference committee is not a permanent committee but is created as needed for each bill. Members of the conference committee are selected by the Speaker of the House and the Senate majority leader in consultation with the leaders of the committees that originally considered the bills in each chamber. Normally, most members of the conference committee are members of the standing committee with jurisdiction over the bill because these individuals are the experts in their policy areas. Again, if a bill is about agriculture, most members of the conference committee will be members from the House and Senate Agriculture Committees. Although the conference committee is supposed to reconcile the different versions of bills coming out of the House and the Senate, they are relatively free to add, subtract, or amend whatever parts of the bill they wish in order to generate agreement between the two chambers.

Much of the power of conference committees comes from the fact that once they agree on a single version of the bill, it is sent back to be voted on again by both the House and the Senate. At this stage, the chambers must vote up or down on the bill;

FILIBUSTERING TO MAKE A POINT

Ted Cruz, seen here on a television monitor in the Senate Press Gallery, spoke for about 20 hours in 2013 in opposition to the Affordable Care Act, or Obamacare, passed in 2009. Cruz sought to rally support from fellow Republicans in his mission to refuse to approve new government spending unless the health care law was also denied funding, effectively killing it. Cruz's speech demonstrates the power of a single senator to shut down Senate business for an extended period of time and the inability of a majority of Senators to control legislative action. *Is the filibuster still an important way for the minority party to ensure their voice is heard, or should the Senate be able to close off debate with a simple majority vote?*

hold

A tactic by which a single senator can prevent action on a bill or nomination; based on an implied threat of refusing to agree to unanimous consent on other Senate matters or willingness to filibuster the bill or nomination.

conference committees

Ad hoc committees, made up of members of both the Senate and the House of Representatives, set up to reconcile differences in the provisions of bills.

TABLE 11.2 DIFFERENCES BETWEEN HOUSE AND SENATE RULES AND NORMS

Senate	House
Informal, open, non-hierarchical	Rule-bound, hierarchical
Leaders have only a few formal powers	Leaders have many formal powers
Members may serve on two or more major committees	Members restricted to one major committee
Less specialized	More specialized
Unrestricted floor debate	Restricted floor debate
Unlimited time for debate unless shortened by unanimous consent or halted by invocation of cloture	Limited time for debate
Unlimited amendments possible	Only limited amendments possible
Amendments need not be germane	Amendments must be germane
More prestige for each member	Less prestige for each member
More reliance on staff	Less reliance on staff
Minority party plays a larger role; hard to put majority rule into effect	Minority party plays a smaller role; majority rule drives legislative process

no new amendments are allowed. This obviously gives conference committees enormous power—they must be careful not change the bill too much, but they can certainly exert their own influence over the final outcomes. After the bill is re-passed by the House and Senate, it can finally be sent to the president.

Like most other things in Congress, conference committees have become more partisan and divisive, resulting in less frequent use.[49] During the early and mid-2000s, Republican leaders often excluded their Democratic counterparts from conference committees considering important bills, making the conference a place to work out differences among House and Senate Republicans. This tactic is now frequently used by Democrats as well when they are in the majority in both chambers.

Presidential Action on a Bill

pocket veto

Rejection of a bill if the president takes no action on it for 10 days and Congress has adjourned during that period.

Because presidents play an important constitutional role in signing a bill into law, their advisers are usually consulted throughout the legislative process, especially if the president is of the same party that controls Congress. If presidents approve a bill, they sign it and it becomes law. If not, they can veto the bill and return it to Congress. A bill can still become law by a two-thirds vote of each house, which will override the president's veto. If presidents are not particularly favorable to the bill but do not want to block it, they can take no action and allow the bill to become law after ten days, unless the congressional session ends before the ten days pass, resulting in a **pocket veto**.

Party and Leader Influences on the Passage Process

We have now learned about the formal procedures that guide the bill passage process, but there are a number of informal influences as well. The roles of the political parties and their leadership are the two most critical. The leadership usually takes their cue from the preferences of a majority of their party and without the support of both, it is almost impossible for a bill to pass.

Political parties have a very strong presence in Congress. Most democratic theorists believe it is difficult to have a working legislature without parties because of the way they organize legislative business, assign members different tasks (in Congress through committee assignments), and ensure all members work for a collective goal rather than an individual one. The political parties work through the leadership structure of Congress because the leaders of the majority political party are, at the same time, the leaders of the House and the Senate.[50] Therefore, political parties are at the very core of legislative business in the United States and are becoming ever more important as the partisan divide between Democratic and Republican voters, activists, advocacy groups, and elected officials gets steadily wider.[51]

LEADERSHIP IN THE HOUSE   The Speaker of the House is recognized in the Constitution and stands second in the line of succession to the presidency, immediately after the vice president. Until 1910, the Speaker exercised enormous power over the House legislative process. The bases of his power were his right to appoint committees and their chairs, and his position as chair of the powerful Rules Committee, which controls the flow of legislation in the House. However, the revolt of the rank and file against Speaker "Uncle Joe" Cannon in 1910 resulted in the Speaker's removal from the Rules Committee and the elimination of the Speaker's power to appoint committees and their chairs. From 1910 until the early 1970s, the weakened Speaker competed with a handful of powerful committee chairs for leadership of the House.

The Democratic Caucus staged a revolt against the committee system after 1974 and restored some of the powers of the Speaker, especially in making committee assignments. Many liberal Democrats felt that older, southern, conservative committee chairs were blocking their progressive legislation and sought to give the Speaker more power to bypass them. The Democratic Caucus gave the Speaker more power to refer bills to committee, control the House agenda, appoint members to select committees, and direct floor debate. These changes gave more recent Democratic Speakers Tip O'Neill, Jim Wright, and Tom Foley considerable leadership resources.

In 1995, the Republican Caucus gave even more power to its first Speaker since 1954, Newt Gingrich. Some scholars suggest that Gingrich's speakership was the most powerful one since Cannon's.[52] Unexpected losses of Republican House seats in the 1998 elections, after a failed attempt to impeach the president, and a personal scandal of his own led to Gingrich's power waning and his subsequent resignation from the speakership and the House.

Democrat Nancy Pelosi (D-CA) exercised a strong hand as Speaker of the House from 2007 through 2010, when the Republicans took over. To advance the Democratic agenda, she pushed through several important rule changes in 2009, which made it difficult for minority members to obstruct legislation.[53] She is generally credited with convincing the president, several of his advisers, and other Democratic congressional leaders to make a final push for health care reform when they were wavering—and eventually prevailed.[54] When the Republicans regained their majority in the House in the 2010 elections, John Boehner (R-OH) became Speaker.

Boehner's speakership was a more difficult one and demonstrates that the power of the Speaker is not absolute. The House Republicans are divided between extremely conservative Tea Party members and other House Republicans (who are still very conservative). On several occasions from 2011 to 2015, the members of the Tea Party caucus in the Republican Party refused to support compromises that Boehner had negotiated with the Senate and the president. In 2013, largely driven by Tea Party members in the House and Senate, Republicans forced a government shutdown, a politically disastrous move for them, and one that the Speaker and most of the party leadership was opposed to. By late 2015, support for Boehner among Tea Party members was all but gone, and he resigned his speakership in frustration. Paul Ryan of Wisconsin took over, though he faced many of the same problems Boehner did, and like Boehner, resigned his position at the end of 2018.

Still, no matter which party is the majority, the Speaker has more power and influence in the legislative branch than any other representative or senator. This power and influence has come about because of House rules and political party rules that have evolved since the 1970s that give the Speaker important powers and prerogatives in determining the flow of legislative business. Aside from naming committee members and other party leaders, the Speaker also has the power to recognize (or not recognize) members to speak during floor debates and is in charge of the House's schedule, which can be used to encourage favored bills and stop others.[55] The ability

to allow certain bills to be reported out of committee and to control the schedule are the Speaker's most important powers.

Also important in the House are the majority leader and majority whip. In general, the Speaker may be likened to the chairman of the board in a business corporation, while the majority leader may be likened to the chief executive officer, responsible for the day-to-day operations of the enterprise.[56] The whip is in charge of counting votes and organizing members of the party to ensure that favored legislation passes, sometimes by threatening wavering individual members.

The minority party elects a minority leader, who acts as the chief spokesperson and legislative strategist for the opposition. The minority leader not only tries to keep the forces together but also seeks out members of the majority party who might be willing to vote against the House leadership on key issues, although this is getting more difficult to do because of rising partisanship.

LEADERSHIP IN THE SENATE   Leadership in the Senate is less visible and has less influence over whether or not a bill passes. The Senate majority leader is as close as one comes to a leader in this body, but the powers of the office pale before those of the Speaker of the House. The Senate majority leader has some influence in committee assignments, office space designation, and scheduling the calendar. The majority leader also has the right of first recognition in the Senate, meaning they are able to speak on a bill prior to other members. This gives them the power to propose their amendments first.

The degree of actual influence is based less on formal powers, however, than on skills of personal persuasion, the respect of colleagues, and visibility in the media as majority party spokesperson. In addition, campaign contributors often take the advice of the majority leader in how they allocate money for incumbents seeking reelection, giving the majority leader additional influence.

Most of the power of the position is personal and not institutional; it cannot be passed on to the next leader. The Senate remains a body of independent, relatively equal members loosely tied together by threads of party loyalty, ideology, and mutual concern about the next election. It is not an environment conducive to decisive leadership, although a few, such as Lyndon Johnson, managed to transcend the limits of the office. And, with partisanship on the rise in the Senate, it is increasingly difficult for any majority leader to push the majority party's agenda because of the filibuster requirement, and the willingness of minority party members to ignore the majority leader's requests on items such as unanimous consent agreements. The current majority leader, Mitch McConnell (R-KY), faces many of the same problems John Boehner faced with an internally divided caucus. McConnell has been fairly successful at helping guide legislation in the Senate during President Trump's first two years in office, though he suffered some failures, specifically his inability to find fifty-one votes to repeal the Patient Protection and Affordable Care Act.

The minority leader in the Senate has even less power than the majority leader but still plays an important role. The minority leader is expected to represent the party in the media and during debates on bills. The minority leader also negotiates directly with the majority leader on committee assignments, schedules, unanimous consent requests, and other items, and party members expect the minority leader to look out for their best interests.

VOTING IN CONGRESS

11.5 Outline the factors that influence roll-call voting in Congress.

The act of voting on a bill or nominee (Senate only) is the most direct way elected officials represent their constituents, and as a consequence, an enormous amount of attention is paid to how senators and representatives vote on recorded congressional votes, known as **roll-call votes**. As you can imagine, a number of factors influence roll-call voting records for different members. These include party influence, interest group and donor pressure, constituent preferences, personal beliefs, and ideology.

roll-call votes
Recorded votes taken in the House or Senate.

Procedural and Substantive Votes

On any given day, members of Congress must make voting decisions on any number of issues. They must be careful not to cast an incorrect or careless vote, lest it be used against them in the next election. There are two basic types of votes: **procedural** and **substantive**. Procedural votes are those that occur on motions or rules, like whether to proceed to a debate, approve the rule from the Rules Committee, or allow a conference committee. Substantive votes are roll calls on either the bill itself or an amendment to the bill. In other words, procedural votes are used to conduct the business of the chamber, while substantive votes are those on the actual text of a bill or amendment.

procedural votes
Roll-call votes in Congress which occur on motions or rules, used to conduct the business of the chamber. Compare to substantive votes.

substantive votes
Roll-call votes in Congress on passing a bill or adopting amendments to a bill. Compare to procedural votes.

There is substantial evidence that many of the differences between Democratic and Republican voting records come from procedural votes rather than substantive votes.[57] While members of the minority party may want to vote to pass a bill, they frequently vote "no" on motions to advance the bill or to end a filibuster. The reason this is thought to occur is because of the strength of political parties in the modern Congress. Indeed, it has been shown that party affiliation is the best predictor of voting behavior by members of the Congress and that it is becoming ever more important. In the words of several leading congressional scholars, following what party leaders and other party legislators want is the default position of most senators and representatives, especially on procedural votes.[58]

Partisan Polarization and Party-Line Voting in Congress

Political parties are the glue that holds together the decentralized fragments of Congress and the legislative process, and party labels are important cues for members of Congress as they decide how to vote on issues before committees and on the floor of the House and the Senate. But this has always been true, so why are members today so much more willing to vote with the party than they used to be?

FIGURE 11.7 PARTY VOTING IN CONGRESS

Partisanship has been growing in Congress. One indicator is the increase in the percentage of times the average Democrat and Republican in the House and Senate sided with his/her party on partisan votes—those votes when a majority of Democrats voted against a majority of Republicans.

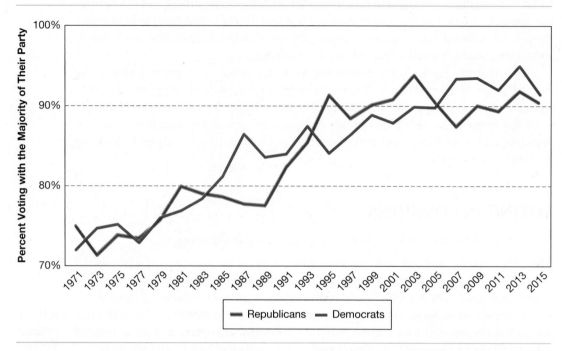

SOURCE: Data from Howard Rosenthal and Keith Poole, Party Unity Scores by Chamber for All Two-Party Systems, Voteview, May 31, 2015.

One way to track partisanship—an unshakeable adherence to party positions—is to compute a statistic that measures how often Democrats and Republicans vote with a majority of their own party (see Figure 11.7). Partisanship has been rising steadily since the early 1970s, when members voted with their parties only 60 percent of the time. Today partisan voting is evident in about nine out of ten congressional votes. In 2009, for example, Democratic leaders were able to muster only three Republican votes in the Senate for President Obama's emergency economic stimulus package and none at all in the House for the final version of the Affordable Care Act, which the House passed in 2010 by a razor thin margin along strict party lines. In 2017, not a single Democrat in either chamber voted for the Republican tax bill.

When members adhere more to the party line, the result is that reaching bipartisan agreements becomes more difficult. Former Maine Republican Senator Olympia Snowe observed, "The whole Congress has become far more polarized and partisan so it makes it difficult to reach bipartisan agreements. The more significant the issue, the more partisan it becomes."[59] There are a number of reasons why party line voting is increasing,[60] which we enumerate in the sections that follow. Now would also be a very good time to revisit our framework model (Figure 11.1) in order to re-examine the *structural, linkage,* and *government* factors that so often underlie congressional failure to act in comprehensive ways on pressing national problems.

SHIFTING REGIONALISM   One factor is the changing regional bases of the parties, particularly the historic transformation of the Deep South from a solidly Democratic region at the congressional level to a solidly Republican one.[61] From 2010 to 2016, Republicans won every contested Senate seat and virtually all competitive House seats in the South. There is currently only one Democratic senator from the South, and the only Democratic House members who remain are African Americans who represent majority-minority districts. The last white southern House Democrat, John Barrow of Georgia, lost his campaign in 2014. The rise of Republicans in the South can be traced to the Democrats' embrace of civil rights legislation during the 1960s, the breakdown of the New Deal coalition, and the increasing suburbanization of southern cities.

RISING PARTISANSHIP OF ACTIVISTS AND ADVOCATES   Another reason that party-line voting is on the rise in Congress is that partisan conflict has been on the rise nationally, especially among party activists and party-associated advocacy groups. Members of Congress are afraid of losing in primary elections where activists are the crucial voters, and they need the money and time enthusiastic activists donate to candidates. The inevitable result is that members of Congress, facing an ever-more partisan-divided electorate and interest group environment, have become more extreme in their voting behavior to satisfy these activists.

CHARACTER OF CONSTITUENCIES   It is not entirely clear whether party voting differences are caused directly by party affiliation or indirectly by the character of constituencies. As voters have become more polarized, so too have the people who represent them. Voters are also sorting themselves into certain types of areas—for example, urban areas are becoming increasingly Democratic, while rural areas are becoming increasingly Republican. Republicans generally come from districts where more people go to church on a regular basis. Democratic districts, in turn, tend to contain more union members and racial minorities or large university campuses.[62] The result is that while it appears members of Congress are voting with their party, their behavior might instead be driven by highly polarized constituents and one-party dominated districts.

IDEOLOGY   Internal party unity and conflict between the parties seems at least partially attributable to ideology. Of course, ideology is the combination of many factors like a candidate's personal beliefs, constituency pressures, and the importance the candidate attaches to different issues. It isn't exactly clear what is causing changes in ideology, but in both the electorate and among the members of Congress, Democrats have become somewhat more liberal, while Republicans have become much more consistently conservative.[63] Political scientist and former Democratic representative from Oklahoma Mickey Edwards observes the following about the ideological tendencies of members of Congress: "Most people who run for office have … [strong] feelings not only about specific issues but about general philosophical concepts, such as the proper role of government, the impact of taxation on investment and savings, and the reasons for crime and poverty."[64]

Even now, there are some important instances when members stray from the party line. Recent fights between Republicans in the House have demonstrated how hard it can be to convince members to vote for the party's preferred position, and members of Congress have to weigh many competing concerns when casting roll-call votes. Nonetheless, members of each party stick closely to one another. Rising partisanship is one of the several reasons why Congress and the president have been having great difficulty in solving our most important national problems.

CONGRESSIONAL OVERSIGHT OF THE EXECUTIVE BRANCH

11.6 Discuss Congress's oversight function and the relationship of oversight to party control.

Besides passing laws, Congress has responsibility for keeping an eye on how the executive branch carries out and enforces the law. This practice, called **oversight**, ensures the president and the bureaucracy are responsive to the public, and helps avoid abuses

oversight
Congressional responsibility for monitoring the actions of executive branch agencies and personnel to ensure conformity to federal statutes and congressional intent.

of power by executive officials. Congress has three principal tools by which it exercises its oversight responsibilities: nominee confirmations, hearings and investigations, and impeachment.

Nominee Confirmations

Even before a top bureaucratic official can take over their post, the Senate has the responsibility for ensuring they are qualified as part of its "advice and consent" responsibilities in the Constitution. The confirmation process in the Senate works very similar to the way bill passage does. Hearings are held within the relevant committee on the nominee's appropriateness for the job, and the nominee usually has to testify in front of Congress about their experience, beliefs, and qualifications, and answer questions from senators. For example, the Senate Judiciary Committee holds hearings on Supreme Court justices. Other individuals with information about the nominee might also be invited to testify. Once the committee approves the nominee, the full Senate must debate, invoke cloture, and vote on the nominee.

This process gives Congress say over the president's appointment to top bureaucratic posts and allows the Senate to exercise oversight even before a bureaucratic official begins their job. It is not uncommon for the Senate to reject a nominee if they believe the individual is unqualified or does not represent the wishes of their constituents.

Hearings and Investigations

Most other oversight is primarily the province of congressional committees and subcommittees—hearings and investigations are among Congress's most visible and dramatic roles. Guided by the wishes of House and Senate leaders and by the majority party caucus in each chamber, Congress calls witnesses, prepares reports, makes public statements, and proposes laws in response to bureaucratic failures. High-profile examples of legislative probes of alleged administrative malfeasance and incompetence include Watergate, the Iran-Contra affair, the federal response to the Hurricane Katrina disaster in New Orleans, the death of diplomats at the American embassy in Benghazi, Libya, the NSA spying scandal, and the subprime mortgage meltdown. In many cases, investigations have led to resignations, new legislation, and even criminal charges.

PUBLIC WHIPPING

John Mack, chairman of Morgan Stanley, tries to explain to members of the Senate Finance Committee why the financial collapse happened, why industry profits were soaring, and why bonuses were being paid, even as loan money for small businesses and homeowners was scarce. The chief executives of other leading financial firms wait their turns to testify.

What role in our political system do congressional hearings play? Do they lead to substantive changes in regulations and laws, or are they more often opportunities to play to the anger or frustration of the public?

In these highly partisan times, whether oversight hearings take place and the relative vigor with which they are carried out depends increasingly on which party controls which branch of government. In the years 2003 through 2006, when Republicans controlled both houses of Congress and Republican George W. Bush was president, Congress did not probe very deeply into a number of troublesome areas, including failed prewar intelligence on weapons of mass destruction in Iraq or warrantless searches and eavesdropping on American citizens. Asked why not much oversight took place during these years, representative Chris Shays (R-CT) remarked that fellow Republicans asked him, "Why do we want to embarrass the administration?"[65] After the 2006 elections, when Democrats won majorities in both chambers, oversight hearings ratcheted up on a wide range of issues, including the alleged use of harsh interrogation methods like waterboarding on terrorism detainees and access to the courts for detainees being held at Guantanamo Bay. Democrats, apparently, were not as concerned as Republicans about embarrassing a Republican administration. After Barack Obama came to office, Democrats in Congress were less aggressive in their use of congressional oversight tools, though they held hearings in 2009 on bank bailouts and the approval of lucrative bonuses to many bank executives, in 2010 on the failure of the Transportation Security Administration (TSA) and the Department of Homeland Security's to detect a suicide bomber (whose bomb failed to detonate) on a flight from Europe to the United States, and on BP's oil blowout in the Gulf of Mexico. In 2017 and 2018, Republicans in Congress proceeded cautiously when investigating ties between the Trump campaign and Russian officials. The Senate Judiciary Committee, which was charged with investigating these connections, tried to work in a bipartisan manner, while the House Intelligence Committee's investigation collapsed due to partisan bickering. Democrats are expected to aggressively pursue investigations into a wide variety of issues, and have already publicly stated that looking into Russian influence on the 2016 campaign is a top priority.

Overall, however, the number of committee hearings on executive branch performance has declined dramatically since 1980. Why? The answer probably has to do with a decline in the power of committee chairs, who have less independence from the leadership.[66] Members also spend more time raising money for reelection campaigns.[67] Still, hearings are an important part of the oversight process. Testimony is taken from agency officials, outside experts, and congressional investigatory institutions such as the Government Accounting Office and the Office of Technology Assessment. Hearings are not simply information-gathering exercises, however. As often as not, they are designed to send signals to relevant parts of the federal bureaucracy. Hearings that focus on overly aggressive efforts of Internal Revenue Service agents to collect taxes, for example, are a clear warning to IRS officials to rein in their agents before the next round of hearings on the IRS budget. Bureaucratic agencies take congressional hearings very seriously as they can sometimes result in severe sanctions, including new legislation aimed at limiting the power of the agency or a reduction in funding.

Impeachment

Congress's final instrument of oversight of the executive branch is **impeachment** (responsibility of the House) and trial and removal from office (responsibility of the Senate) of high executive officials, including the president. While the Constitution gives the power of impeachment and removal to Congress, it has only been used once against a bureaucratic official (William W. Belknap, the Secretary of War, in 1876, who was not removed from office), and only rarely against judges. No president has ever been convicted and removed from office, but the impeachment processes in the House of presidents Andrew Johnson, Nixon (though he resigned before being formally impeached), and Clinton were deeply divisive, so Congress treads very cautiously in this area.

impeachment
House action bringing formal charges against a member of the executive branch or the federal judiciary that may or may not lead to removal from office by the Senate.

CONGRESS: IS CONGRESS OUT OF TOUCH WITH THE AMERICAN PEOPLE?

Although Congress was significantly democratized by passage of the Seventeenth Amendment in 1913, which transferred the election of senators from state legislatures to voters, the institution is still largely shaped by the anti-majoritarian constitutional design of the framers. Most important in this regard is its bicameral nature, the equal representation of the states in the Senate, Senate rules on the filibuster and cloture, and its immersion in a system of checks and balances.

The framers settled on bicameralism for two reasons. First, it was the only way to break the deadlock between large and small states at the constitutional convention. Had the Connecticut Compromise not been agreed to, the convention would most likely have adjourned without completing its historic task. Second, bicameralism conformed to the framers' belief that the legislative branch—the center of policy making for government—ought to be a place where the public's business is deliberated carefully and slowly, free from the pressure of fickle public opinion. As any observer of our national legislature can report, this part of the vision was fulfilled; Congress is a place where the legislative process grinds slowly, with only a few pieces of major legislation produced in each Congress and most bills never seeing the light of day. The need for legislation to pass through two powerful chambers—one upper and one lower, each organized in different ways and each tuned to different election cycles and constituencies—is the central reason for the slow pace of this process.

As noted earlier, equal representation of the states in the Senate violates the democratic principle of political equality. Small-population states such as Wyoming, Nevada, and North Dakota have the same number of senators as large-population states such as California, New York, Texas, and Florida, meaning that the people in each of the states are unequally represented. This characteristic affects much of what the Senate does and does not do. For example, a coalition of 41 senators from the smallest population states, representing a mere 11 percent of the American population, can block any bill in the Senate (because 60 votes are needed to override a filibuster). To say that the Senate enshrines unequal representation is no exaggeration.

We must not forget, moreover, the anti-majoritarian effects of the system of checks and balances within which Congress operates. Designed by the framers as the most "popular" branch—and not very "popular" at that in its original design—Congress finds itself continually hemmed in by the other two branches. Even on those rare occasions when it acts vigorously in response to public opinion, it may not always have the support it needs from the president and the courts. Further, the balance against democracy in Congress is even more disproportionate once one takes into account the important role played by interest groups and campaign contributors in its affairs.

It appears, then, that Congress has not drifted very far from what the framers had envisioned. To be sure, senators are now elected directly by the people. Also, senators and members of the House are more prone than in the past to pay attention to public opinion. Nevertheless, it remains an institution that the framers would recognize as their own creation.

REVIEW THE CHAPTER

CONSTITUTIONAL FOUNDATIONS OF CONGRESS

11.1 Describe the constitutional provisions that define the Congress.

The framers of the Constitution granted Congress legislative power, gave it an existence independent of the executive branch, enumerated an impressive range of powers, and furnished it with elastic powers sufficient to carry out its enumerated ones. However, the framers also provisioned the other branches of government with powers to check legislative excesses, fashioned Congress as a bicameral body, and strictly denied certain powers to Congress.

REPRESENTATION AND DEMOCRACY IN CONGRESS

11.2 Assess how well members of Congress represent their constituents.

Congress is a representative institution but not necessarily fully democratic; its members are constantly balancing the preferences of the people who reside in their constituencies against important interest groups, contributors, and their own conceptions of the public interest.

CONGRESSIONAL ELECTIONS

11.3 Describe the process of congressional elections and the impact of incumbency on election outcomes.

Elections are the most important mechanism for representation in our democracy. Because elections are the way in which members of Congress attain office, elections dominate the time and energy of lawmakers and shape how Congress organizes itself and goes about its business.

THE CONGRESSIONAL LEGISLATIVE PROCESS

11.4 Outline the process by which a bill becomes a law.

To conduct its business, Congress depends on an elaborate set of norms and rules and a web of committees and subcommittees, political parties, legislative leaders, and an extensive staff.

After they are introduced, bills are referred to committee. Only a few make it out of committee for consideration by the entire membership of the House or Senate. In the House, the Rules Committee must issue a rule for a bill to reach the floor for debate.

If related bills pass each chamber, but in different forms, differences must be resolved in a conference committee. The report of the conference committee cannot be amended and must be voted up or down in the House and the Senate. If a bill makes it this far, it goes to the president for a signature or veto.

A bill becomes law if the president signs it, or absent that signature, if ten days pass while Congress is in session, or if both the House and the Senate vote by a two-thirds majority to override a veto.

Most of the business of the House and Senate takes place in committees and their subcommittees. In committees, hearings on bills and negotiations on bills take place. In committees, members of Congress can bring their subject matter expertise to bear.

Nearly every aspect of congressional organization and operations are defined by political parties. Leadership in each of the chambers, committee leadership and membership, and the agenda are determined by the majority party.

The House invests great powers in its leaders, with the Speaker of the House acting very much like a leader in a parliamentary system. Leadership in the Senate is much more elusive; each senator has a great deal of independent power and must be persuaded to side with party leaders.

VOTING IN CONGRESS

11.5 Outline the factors that influence roll-call voting in Congress.

Factors that influence roll-call voting include party influence, interest group and donor pressure, constituent preferences, personal beliefs, and ideology.

Members of Congress have to weigh many competing concerns when casting roll-call votes. Nonetheless, members of each party stick closely to one another. Rising partisanship is one of the several reasons why Congress and the president have been having great difficulty in solving our most important national problems.

CONGRESSIONAL OVERSIGHT OF THE EXECUTIVE BRANCH

11.6 Discuss Congress's oversight function and the relationship of oversight to party control.

Oversight is a way for members of Congress to bring attention to issues and to turn the spotlight on the performance of executive branch agencies. Oversight is done through committee or subcommittee hearings.

When there is unified government, Congress is reluctant to embarrass a president of its own party.

When there is divided government in today's partisan charged atmosphere, most other political actors and the media know that hearings are more about gamesmanship than about serious oversight of the executive.

LEARN THE TERMS

bicameral   As applied to a legislative body, consisting of two houses or chambers.

bill markup   The process of revising a bill in committee.

casework   Services performed by members of Congress for constituents.

caucus, legislative interest or party   A regional, ethnic, racial, or economic subgroup within the House or Senate. Also used to name the party in the House and Senate (as in the "Republican Caucus" or the "Democratic Caucus").

cloture   A vote to end a filibuster; requires the votes of three-fifths of the membership of the Senate.

committee chair   The head of a standing committee with significant power over legislation considered within the committee.

conference committees   Ad hoc committees, made up of members of both the Senate and the House of Representatives, set up to reconcile differences in the provisions of bills.

Connecticut Compromise   Also called the Great Compromise; the compromise between the New Jersey and Virginia plans formulated by the Connecticut delegates at the Constitutional Convention; called for a lower legislative house based on population size and an upper house based on equal representation of the states.

constituency   The individuals who live in the district of a legislator.

constituent   A citizen who lives in the district of an elected official.

"cracking" and "packing"   The act of dividing a district where the opposing party has a large majority, rendering it a minority in both parts of the redrawn districts (cracking), or concentrating all of one party's voters into a single district to dilute their influence in other districts (packing).

dark money groups   Political advocacy groups that contribute significant sums of money in order to influence elections, but whose sources of funding, and the amount of money spent, are hidden from the public.

delegate   According to the doctrine articulated by Edmund Burke, an elected representative who acts in perfect accord with the wishes of his or her constituents.

descriptive representation   Sometimes called *statistical representation*; the degree to which the composition of a representative body reflects the demographic composition of the population as a whole.

divided government   Control of the executive and the legislative branches by different political parties.

elastic clause   Article I, Section 8, of the Constitution, also called the *necessary and proper clause*; gives Congress the authority to make whatever laws are necessary and proper to carry out its enumerated responsibilities.

enumerated powers   Powers of the federal government specifically mentioned in the Constitution.

filibuster   A parliamentary device used in the Senate to prevent a bill from coming to a vote by "talking it to death," or by refusing to end debate, made possible by the norm of unlimited debate unless cloture is invoked.

franking privilege   Public subsidization of mail from the members of Congress to their constituents.

gerrymandering   Redrawing electoral district lines in an extreme and unlikely manner to give an advantage to a particular party or candidate.

hearings   The taking of testimony by a congressional committee or subcommittee.

hold   A tactic by which a single senator can prevent action on a bill or nomination; based on an implied threat of refusing to agree to unanimous consent on other Senate matters or willingness to filibuster the bill or nomination.

impeachment   House action bringing formal charges against a member of the executive branch or the federal judiciary that may or may not lead to removal from office by the Senate.

implied powers   Powers of the federal government not specifically mentioned in the Constitution.

judicial review   The power of the Supreme Court to declare actions of the other branches and levels of government unconstitutional.

majority leader   The leaders of the Senate, also the head of the majority party in the Senate. Equivalent to the House Speaker, though not a constitutional office.

majority-minority districts   Districts drawn to ensure that a racial minority makes up the majority of voters.

open-seat election   An election in which there is no incumbent officeholder.

oversight   Congressional responsibility for monitoring the actions of executive branch agencies and personnel to ensure conformity to federal statutes and congressional intent.

partisan   A committed member of a party; also, seeing issues from the point of view of the interests of a single party.

permanent campaign   The idea that members of Congress are always running for reelection and focus most of their efforts on winning their seat rather than governing.

pocket veto   Rejection of a bill if the president takes no action on it for 10 days and Congress has adjourned during that period.

polarization   The process by which political parties have become more internally consistent in ideology and more ideologically distant from one another; in the United States, the Republican party has become more conservative and the Democratic party more liberal.

pork   Also called *pork barrel*; federally funded projects designed to bring to the constituency jobs and public money for which the members of Congress can claim credit.

procedural votes   Roll-call votes in Congress which occur on motions or rules, used to conduct the business of the chamber. Compare to substantive votes.

quality challengers   Individuals who run against incumbent members of Congress who have previously held elected office. They tend to be more successful in defeating incumbent members than other types of challengers.

reapportionment   The reallocation of House seats among the states, done after each national census, to ensure that seats are held by the states in proportion to the size of their populations.

redistricting   The redrawing of congressional district lines within a state to ensure roughly equal populations within each district.

roll-call votes   Recorded votes taken in the House or Senate.

Rules Committee   A special committee in the House of Representatives that determines whether amendments will be allowed on a bill.

scare-off effect   When members of Congress raise more money than they need to signal support and resources to potential challengers, thereby discouraging others from running against them.

seniority   The principle that one attains a position on the basis of length of service.

standing committees   Relatively permanent congressional committees that address specific areas of legislation.

substantive votes   Roll-call votes in Congress on passing a bill or adopting amendments to a bill. Compare to procedural votes.

trustee   An elected representative who believes that his or her own best judgment, rather than instructions from constituents, should be used in making legislative decisions.

unanimous consent   Legislative action taken "without objection" as a way to expedite business; used to conduct much of the business of the Senate.

veto   Presidential disapproval of a bill that has been passed by both houses of Congress. The president's veto can be overridden by a two-thirds vote in each house.

RENEWING RELATIONS

President Obama announced in late 2014 that he would begin the process of renewing diplomatic relations with Cuba, which had been suspended for over five decades. He made good on that promise; the United States embassy reopened in Havana in 2015. Shortly after, the president visited Cuba to cement relations between the two nations. He is shown here with Cuban officials at the Jose Marti memorial in front of a depiction of revolutionary leader "Che" Guevara. After he came to office in 2017, Donald Trump put Cuba on the back burner. He not only cut U.S. embassy staff in Cuba, but made it harder for Americans to visit the island nation. In foreign policy matters, except where a formal treaty is in place, Presidents can reverse the actions of their predecessors.

Should such an important change in American policy be left mostly in the hands of the president? If you think that Congress should play a larger role, how would such a change from traditional practice be possible given provisions in Article II that seem to lodge this power in the presidential office?

THE PRESIDENCY

CHAPTER OUTLINE AND LEARNING OBJECTIVES

THE EXPANDING PRESIDENCY

12.1 Trace the expansion of presidential power.

THE POWERS AND ROLES OF THE PRESIDENT

12.2 Identify the roles and responsibilities of the president.

THE PRESIDENT'S SUPPORT SYSTEM

12.3 Describe the organization and functions of the president's advisors.

THE PRESIDENT AND CONGRESS: PERPETUAL TUG-OF-WAR

12.4 Analyze the conflict between the president and Congress.

THE PRESIDENT AND THE PEOPLE

12.5 Describe the relationship between the president and the American people.

The Struggle for Democracy

With Democratic majorities in the House and Senate in 2009 and 2010, President Barack Obama won significant legislative victories during his first two years in office. Most notable were a big economic stimulus bill to help the country get out of the Great Recession, new legislation to regulate many of the dangerous practices that led to the 2008 financial collapse, and passage of the Affordable Care Act, often referred to as Obamacare. Things got much tougher for the president after the midterm 2010 elections when Republicans won control of the House, and after the 2014 midterms when Republicans gained a majority in the Senate. With divided government, hyperpartisanship, and legislative gridlock the norm for the last six years of his presidency, Barack Obama, like many presidents before him, turned to the office's unitary powers to advance important parts of his agenda.

Candidate Donald Trump repeatedly criticized Barack Obama for his reliance on one of the several unitary powers available to presidents: executive orders. In one interview during the campaign, Trump complained that Obama was a weak leader: "We have a president that can't get anything done so he just keeps signing executive orders all over the place… I want to not use too many executive orders…. I want to do away with executive orders for the most part."

Trump was correct to point out that President Obama relied heavily on executive orders in the last six years of his presidency. So what are executive orders? As the constitutionally empowered chief executive—that is, the administrative head of the executive branch of government—presidents have the responsibility for guiding executive agencies and departments as they carry out laws specified in bills passed by Congress and signed by the president. Laws are often vague, and bureaucratic agencies often need guidance on how to carry out their provisions. Presidents have been happy to do this because it helps them move the implementation of policy in directions that are compatible with their own preferences. Here are a few of the more important ones issued by President Obama. During his first days in office, he issued orders to various bureaucratic agencies reversing Bush administration policies on stem-cell research, climate change, and the use of torture in the interrogation of enemy combatants. He instructed the Environmental Protection Agency (EPA) to issue rules to dramatically increase gas mileage requirements on cars, SUVs, and trucks. Under terms of the Clean Air Act, he allowed the EPA to order a reduction in emissions from coal-fueled power plants. He had the Department of Labor issue rules requiring financial institutions and financial advisors to act in the best interests of their clients in managing retirement accounts.

One of his most controversial actions as chief executive was his order to federal law enforcement agencies, under a program called DACA—Deferred Action for Childhood Arrivals—to stop deporting millions of undocumented people who are either the parents of U.S. citizens or children brought to the United States as young children, the so-called Dreamers. The president and his supporters claimed that these actions are within his constitutional authority and provided guidance regarding how immigration authorities should use their limited resources—an action that does not require congressional approval. Opponents, especially Republicans in Congress, argued that Obama's actions on immigration were illegal and what the president wanted to do could only be achieved through congressional legislation

Despite his promise to limit or eliminate the use of executive orders, President Trump issued fifty-seven in his first year in office, the most by any president since President Bill Clinton in 1993, even though his Republican Party controlled both houses of Congress. Among the orders were bans on entry into the United States by people from certain mostly Muslim countries, the relocation of the American embassy in Israel from Tel Aviv to Jerusalem, the termination of the DACA program by a date certain unless Congress acted to save it, In 2018, the separation from their children of illegal immigrants and asylum seekers at the southern border, the reduction in size of several national monuments (wilderness areas), rollbacks on enforcement of several important provisions in Obamacare, and the termination of a range of Obama-era environmental regulations. For example, executive orders from the president instructed the Environmental Protection Agency and the Interior Department to ease restrictions on the use of a multitude of chemicals, on power plant emissions, on off-shore drilling, and on the treatment of industrial waste. President Trump also ordered higher tariffs on imported steel and aluminum and on a wide-range of goods from China.

* * * * *

Presidents must gain the cooperation of Congress on many matters if they are to achieve the major elements of their policy agendas and fulfill the promises made during their campaigns for office, in their inauguration speeches, and in their State of the Union addresses. What many people fail to appreciate, however, is the degree to which presidents can act on their own, without Congress, on many important matters. These unitary powers encompass a broad range of tools, including executive orders, executive agreements, signing statements, presidential proclamations, national security directives, and regulatory review as well as authority over the armed forces and American foreign policy.[1] Donald Trump used these various unitary tools quite liberally when he came to the presidency despite his criticism during the 2016 election campaign that Obama had acted illegally in using them. In this chapter, we will examine the key features of the modern presidency, including the broad range of the office's unitary powers and how Congress, the courts, the American people, and domestic and international events influence what a president is able to accomplish.[2]

THINKING CRITICALLY **ABOUT THIS CHAPTER**

This chapter is about the American presidency, how it has evolved, and what role it plays in American politics and government.

APPLYING THE **FRAMEWORK**

In this chapter, you will read about how the presidential office has changed substantially from how the framers envisioned it, primarily because of changes in America's international situation, the nature of its economy, and popular expectations. You will also see how presidents interact with other governmental institutions (such as Congress and the Supreme Court) and with political linkage–level actors (such as political parties, public opinion, the mass media, and interest groups) and how these interactions influence what presidents do.

USING THE **DEMOCRACY STANDARD**

This chapter discusses how the presidential office, although not envisioned by the framers to be a democratic one, has become more directly connected to and responsive to the American people. On the other hand, you will be asked to think about whether presidents' growing ability to influence the thinking of the public and shape their perceptions of public events undermines democracy.

THE EXPANDING PRESIDENCY

12.1 Trace the expansion of presidential power.

The American presidency has grown and changed considerably since our nation's beginning. Substantial growth and changes have occurred in presidential responsibilities, burdens, power, and impact. The transformation of the office has been so considerable that two leading scholars have said that "the Constitution's framers would have great trouble recognizing today's presidency."[3]

When George Washington took office as the first president, the entire United States consisted of the thirteen original northeastern, mid-Atlantic, and southeastern states, with 864,746 square miles of land area; the population was about four million persons, most living on small farms. Consequently, the government looked very different than it does today. The new president had a total budget (for 1789–1792) of just over $4 million and a handful of federal employees. (Even by 1801, there were only about three hundred federal officeholders in the capital.) Washington's cabinet consisted of five officials: the secretaries of state, war, and the treasury; a postmaster general; and an attorney general (who acted as the president's personal attorney, rather than as head of a full-fledged Justice Department). The entire Department of State consisted of one secretary, one chief clerk, six minor clerks, and one messenger. In 1790, about seven hundred Americans were in uniform, and they had no way to project force around the world. Overall, federal government functions were few.[4]

As Donald Trump was sworn into office 225 years later, the United States had a population of almost 307 million diverse people, a gross domestic product of more than $14 trillion, and a land area of some 3.8 million square miles, stretching from Alaska to Florida and from Hawaii to Maine.[5] The federal budget then was $2.7 trillion and the federal bureaucracy numbered approximately 2.7 million civilian employees (postal workers accounted for 656,000 employees). He was commander in chief of the armed forces, with about 1.5 million men and women in active-duty service; hundreds of military bases at home and scattered throughout the world; and about 6,450 nuclear warheads, 1,600 of which were deployed and operational, enough to obliterate every medium-sized or large city in the world many times over.[6]

The Framers' Conception of the Presidency

The framers certainly had in mind a presidency more like Washington's than Obama's or Trump's. Article II of the Constitution provided for a single executive who would be strong, compared with the role under the Congress-dominated Articles of Confederation, but the Constitution's sparse language declaring that "The executive power shall be vested in a President of the United States" barely hinted at the range of things 20th- and 21st-century presidents would do.[7] For example, the Constitution made the president "commander in chief" of the armed forces without any suggestion that there would be a vast standing armed force that presidents could send abroad to fight in places such as Afghanistan, Iraq, Syria, and Panama

WASHINGTON REVIEWS THE TROOPS

The presidency has grown in scale and responsibility since George Washington was president. As commander in chief of the armed forces, President Washington, here reviewing his troops during his first year in office, commanded an army of just over seven hundred soldiers and had little to do with affairs outside the United States. Today, the president commands a force of about 1.4 million active duty personnel stationed all over the world, with 1.1 million more in the reserves. *How have changes in the role of the president, in the scale of the presidential office's responsibilities, affected the relative balance of power among the three branches of government?*

without a declaration of war. It empowered presidents to appoint and to "require the opinion in writing" of executive department heads without indicating that a huge federal bureaucracy would evolve. The Constitution provided that presidents could from time to time "recommend ... measures" to Congress without specifying that these proposals would very often come to dominate Congress's agenda. Still, the vague language of the Constitution proved flexible enough to encompass the great expansion of the presidency.[8]

The Dormant Presidency

From the time of George Washington's inauguration at Federal Hall in New York City to the end of the 19th century, the presidency, for the most part, conformed to the designs of the framers and did not dominate the political life of the nation. Presidents saw their responsibility as primarily involving the execution of policies decided by Congress. But the office changed after that.

DORMANCY STRUCTURAL FACTORS Why does the early presidency seem so weak in comparison with the contemporary presidency? Surely it is not because early presidents were less intelligent, vigorous, or ambitious; indeed, this era produced some of our greatest presidents—as well as some who are largely forgotten. A more reasonable answer is that the nation did not often require a very strong presidency before the 20th century, particularly in the key areas of foreign policy and military leadership. Only in the 20th century did the United States develop into a world power, involved in military, diplomatic, and economic activities around the globe. With that *structural* development came a simultaneous increase in the power and responsibility of the president.

It was not until the late 19th century that the economy of the United States was transformed from a simple free-market economy of farmers and small firms to a corporate-dominated economy, with units so large and interconnected that their every action had consequences for all Americans. The emergence of big banks and Wall Street finance added to the broad and consequential reach of a handful of large and interconnected firms. These transformations eventually led to demands for more government supervision of the American economic system. As this role of government grew, so did the president's role as chief executive of the federal government.

Although the presidency was largely dormant until the end of the 19th century, events and the actions of several presidents during the early period anticipated what was to happen to the office in our own time. Presidential actions created precedents for their successors; what the public and political elites expected of presidents changed; and new laws were passed that gradually enhanced presidential responsibilities and powers.

DORMANCY ERA PRESIDENTS War hero George Washington solidified the prestige of the presidency at a time when executive leadership was mistrusted.[9] Washington also affirmed the primacy of the president in foreign affairs and set a precedent for fashioning a domestic legislative program. Thomas Jefferson, although initially hostile to the idea of a vigorous central government, boldly concluded the Louisiana Purchase with France, which roughly doubled the size of the United States and opened the continent for American settlement. Andrew Jackson, elected with broader popular participation than ever before, helped transform the presidency into a popular institution, as symbolized by his vigorous opposition to the Bank of the United States (which was seen by many ordinary Americans as a tool of the wealthy).

James Polk energetically exercised his powers as commander in chief of the armed forces, provoking a war with Mexico and acquiring most of what is now the southwestern United States and California. To win the Civil War, Abraham Lincoln invoked emergency powers based on his broad reading of the Constitution: he raised and spent money and deployed troops on his own initiative, with Congress acquiescing only afterward; he temporarily suspended the right of *habeas corpus* and allowed civilians to be tried in military courts; and he unilaterally freed the slaves in the Confederate states by issuing the Emancipation Proclamation justifying it as a war measure under his commander-in-chief powers.

habeas corpus
The legal doctrine that a person who is arrested must have a timely hearing before a judge.

The Twentieth Century Transformation

More enduring changes in the presidency came in the 20th century, when new structural conditions made an expanded presidency both possible and necessary. Theodore Roosevelt vigorously pushed the prerogatives and enhanced the powers of the office as no president had done since Lincoln. Roosevelt was happiest when he was deploying troops as commander in chief or acting to protect American economic and political interests as the nation's chief diplomat. On the domestic front, Roosevelt pushed for regulation of new and powerful business corporations, especially by breaking up trusts, and he established many national parks. In Theodore Roosevelt, we see the coming together of an energetic and ambitious political leader and a new set of structural factors in the United States, particularly the nation's emergence as a world power and an industrialized economy. The interplay of these three factors expanded the power and responsibilities of the presidency.

Woodrow Wilson's presidency marked further important steps in the expansion of the federal government and the presidency. His "New Freedom" domestic program built on the Progressive Era measures of Theodore Roosevelt, including further regulation of the economy by establishment of the Federal Reserve Board (1913) and the Federal Trade Commission (1914). Under Wilson, World War I brought an enormous increase in activity: a huge mobilization of military personnel and a large, new civilian bureaucracy to oversee the production and distribution of food, fuel, and armaments by the American "arsenal of democracy."

It was Franklin D. Roosevelt, however, who presided over the most significant expansion of presidential functions and activities in American history and changed American expectations about the office. In response to the Great Depression,

TEDDY ROOSEVELT GREETS THE PEOPLE

President Teddy Roosevelt, here exuberantly greeting crowds during one of his regular tours to different parts of the country, was extraordinarily popular and accessible during his time in office. On most Sundays when he was in Washington, for example, he would spend hours greeting ordinary citizens in the White House. He was a master at using this popularity and accessibility to enhance his influence over the political agenda in Washington and to get his way with Congress in a number of policy areas. *Assuming that all presidents since Teddy Roosevelt have tried to turn personal admiration and popularity into political power, why have some been more successful at it than others?*

BUILDING THE HOOVER DAM

Franklin Roosevelt's New Deal included a multitude of federal construction projects designed to create critical infrastructure and jobs during the crisis days of the Great Depression. Here workers help build the Boulder dam, later renamed the Hoover dam, on the Colorado River.

Would large-scale federal construction projects like those in place during the New Deal be a way to create more well-paid jobs in the United States today or should job creation be left primarily in the hands of the private sector?

Roosevelt and the Democratic majority in Congress pushed into law a series of measures for economic relief that grew into vast programs of conservation and public works, farm credit, business loans, and relief payments to the destitute. Roosevelt's New Deal also established a number of independent commissions to regulate aspects of business (the stock market, telephones, utilities, airlines) and enacted programs such as Social Security, which provided income support for retired Americans, and the Wagner Act, which helped workers join unions and bargain collectively with their employers. As Congress created these and many other new agencies in the executive branch, the role of the presidency grew because of his constitutional powers as chief executive.

Even bigger changes resulted from World War II, when the government mobilized the entire population and the whole economy for the war effort. With the end of that war, the United States was established as a military superpower. Since the time of Franklin Roosevelt, all U.S. presidents have administered a huge national security state with large standing armed forces, nuclear weapons, and bases all around the world.

Although he accomplished little on the legislative front during his brief time in office—he did introduce the 1964 Civil Rights Act, passed after his death—John F. Kennedy was the first president to appreciate the importance of television as both a campaign tool and an instrument for influencing the public and political actors in Washington, the states, and other countries. His televised speeches and press conferences, where his charm, intelligence, and sense of humor were clearly evident, became one of his most effective governing tools. Succeeding presidents tried to follow his lead, but only Ronald Reagan, Bill Clinton, and Barack Obama matched Kennedy's mastery of the medium.

In the 1980s, Ronald Reagan managed to bring many of the main items of the conservative agenda to fruition: a massive tax cut to stimulate the economy, cutbacks in the number of regulations that affect business, cuts in a wide range of domestic social programs, and a substantial buildup of U.S. armed forces. Perhaps more important, he showed the American people and others around the world that a vigorous and popular presidency was still possible after the failed presidency of Richard Nixon and the relatively weak presidencies of Gerald Ford and Jimmy Carter.

After the 9/11 terrorist attacks on the United States, George W. Bush pushed
what many consider to be among the most expansive readings of presidential power
in American history. To protect the United States against future terrorist attacks,
President Bush felt it both necessary and constitutionally permissible, for example,
to advise the armed forces and the Central Intelligence Agency (CIA) to ignore the
Geneva Convention on the treatment of detainees captured in the war on terrorism.
He claimed the right to keep detainees indefinitely without trial or hearings, even if
they were American citizens. He also authorized the National Security Agency (NSA)
to surveil American citizens without first obtaining a warrant; the agency is forbidden
by law from spying on U.S. citizens without the permission of a special court.[10]

In addition to being the nation's first African American president, Barack Obama
will likely be remembered for the passage of an economic stimulus that allowed the
U.S. economy to weather the 2008 financial collapse and deep recession that followed
better than any other rich democracy in the world and the Affordable Care Act
(ACA), which was designed to extend medical insurance coverage to those who were
previously uninsured and to bring health care spending under control.

As he promised during his campaign, Donald Trump has acted in ways that are
startlingly different from presidents before him.[11] Whether the changes eventuate in
permanent changes in the presidency or prove to be fleeting remains to be seen. For
example, he depends a great deal on tweets to communicate his wishes about policies
and personnel to the American people, other political leaders in Congress and the
executive branch, and foreign leaders. He has publicly chastised and threatened by
name members of his own cabinet (for example, Jeff Sessions and Rex Tillerson), law
enforcement agencies such as the FBI and the CIA, Special Counsel Robert Mueller
looking into Russian meddling in the 2016 presidential election, and federal judges.
He has relentlessly attacked the mainstream news media—"fake news" has been his

THE WAR LEADER

President George W. Bush imposed a strong national defense orientation on nearly every aspect of American foreign policy in the wake of the 9/11 terrorist attacks. As foreign policy leader and commander in chief, the president had sufficient tools to move the United States in this direction. Secretary of Defense Donald Rumsfeld (left) and Vice President Richard Cheney (center) were strong advocates of such an orientation in foreign affairs.

Do you believe presidents should exercise such extensive national defense powers? What are the implications of such extensive powers for democracy in the United States?

favorite prerogative term—as well as particular news outlets such as the *New York Times*, the *Washington Post*, and CNN. He has refused to fill a wide range of important posts in the federal government, especially at the State Department, arguing that the federal government does not need so many employees. Unlike previous presidents, he has praised autocratic leaders around the world including Recep Erdogan of Turkey, Vladimir Putin of Russia, and Rodrigo Duterte of the Philippines, and has sharply criticized the leaders of traditional democratic American allies including Great Britain, Germany, Australia, Canada, and South Korea. It is widely reported that he refuses to read the daily brief from U.S. intelligence agencies. Unlike presidents before him, he has kept a hand in his various business enterprises—run by his children—and has never made his tax returns public. And, rather than serve as a leader devoted to inclusion of a wide range of people into American society, he often has exacerbated racial tensions and encouraged those opposed to further civil rights advances.

By these actions, he delighted many who voted for him—and alarmed many others—based on his promise to be a very different kind of president unbeholden to traditional elites and ways of doing things in Washington, and a foe of so-called political correctness. During his campaign he stated that his aim was nothing less than to make America great again by fundamentally changing the size and direction of the federal government and whom it serves and to create jobs and restore the dynamism of the American economy. His program for meeting these goals, many elements of which happened—included lifting the tax and regulatory burdens on companies, lowering taxes on the wealthy so that they might invest more in the American economy, radically slowing immigration and removing the undocumented people from the country, and leaving or renegotiating trade deals that in his view disadvantage American companies and workers. He also promised to diminish the role of the federal government in civil rights enforcement and to increase spending on national defense, both of which have happened.

How Important Are Individual Presidents?

We cannot be sure to what extent presidents themselves caused this great expansion of the scope of their office. Clearly, they played a part. For example, Lincoln, Wilson, and Franklin Roosevelt not only reacted vigorously to events but also helped create events; each had something to do with the coming of the wars that were so crucial in adding to their activities and powers. Yet these great presidents were also the product of great times; they stepped into situations that had deep historical roots and dynamics of their own.

Lincoln became president at a time when the nation was embroiled in bitter conflict over the relative economic and political power of North and South and focused on the question of slavery in the western territories; war was a likely, if not inevitable, outcome. Wilson and Franklin Roosevelt each faced a world in which German expansion threatened the perceived economic and cultural interests of the United States and in which U.S. industrial power permitted a strong response. The Great Depression fairly cried out for a new kind of presidential activism. Kennedy faced an international system in which the Soviet Union had become especially strident and menacing. George W. Bush was the president when the 9/11 terrorist attacks on the United States occurred, allowing him to make the broadest claims possible concerning the president's powers to defend the nation. Donald Trump's departure from long-accepted ways for presidents to act and his support for policies that aimed to change the country's trade patterns, international alliances, and immigration enforcement and border protection were the products, in part, as discussed in Chapter 4, of a decline in manufacturing jobs, dimming prospects for the middle class, and resentment among some Americans about the rapid ethnic and racial diversification of the country. Thus, the great upsurges in presidential power and activity were, at least in part, a result of forces at the *structural* level, stimulated by events and developments in the economy, American society, and the international system.

We see, then, that it is this mixture of a president's personal qualities (personality and character) and deeper structural factors (such as the existence of military, foreign policy, or economic crises) that determines which presidents transform the office. Most

SIGNING EXECUTIVE ORDERS

President Donald Trump came to office at a time when popular discontent with government was high, promising to turn government into an institution that would protect average working people. However, many of his executive orders undermined agencies designed to protect working people from the predatory practices of banks and financial institutions. Here, Trump signs an order in late 2017 decreasing the powers of the Consumer Financial Protection Bureau.

Should presidents, whatever his party, be permitted such sweeping powers over executive branch agencies or are such powers necessary for maintaining popular control over the bureaucracy?

of these big presidential transformations become part of the presidency as an institution. Presidents want and need the powers accumulated by their predecessors and use the precedents set by them. The American people have tended to support—and in crisis situations, demand—strong presidential leadership. Over the years, Congress has passed laws in response to new challenges that directly or indirectly increase presidential responsibilities and power. And the courts, with some notable exceptions mentioned elsewhere in this book, generally have accepted the development path the presidency has taken as it became the preeminent office in American government.

THE POWERS AND ROLES OF THE PRESIDENT

12.2 Identify the roles and responsibilities of the president.

The American presidency has assumed powers and taken on roles unimaginable to the Founders. Each touches on the daily lives of everyone in the United States and affects tens of millions of people around the world. This section examines the many roles of the president and illustrates how each role has a set of responsibilities associated with it as well as a set of powers that have become more expansive over the years.

Chief of State

The president is both the chief executive of the United States—responsible for the executive branch of the federal government—and the chief of state, a symbol of national authority and unity. In contrast to European parliamentary democracies such as Britain or Norway, where a monarch acts as chief of state while a prime minister serves as head of the government, in the United States the two functions are combined. It is the president who performs many ceremonial duties (attending funerals of important people, proclaiming official days, lighting the national Christmas tree, honoring heroes, celebrating national holidays) that are carried out by members of royal families in other nations. As one journalist once put it, "The office of President is such a bastardized thing, half royalty and half democracy, that nobody knows whether to genuflect or spit."[12] Because it adds to their prestige and standing with other government officials and the public, presidents have always found the chief of state role to be a useful tool in their political arsenal, enabling them to get their way on many important issues. Especially in times of armed conflict, criticism of the president seems to many Americans to amount to criticism of the country itself and the troops who are in harm's way, something skilled presidents can and do use to maximize support for their policies.

Domestic Policy Leader

Presidents have taken on important responsibilities on the domestic front that were probably not anticipated by the framers. These include their roles as the nation's legislative leader and manager of the economy.[13]

LEGISLATIVE LEADER While the Constitution seems to give primary responsibility for the legislative agenda of the United States to Congress, over time the initiative for proposing big policy changes and new programs has shifted significantly to the president and the executive branch. The bases of this change may be found in the Constitution, statutes passed by Congress, and the changing expectations of the American people. For example, the Constitution specifies that the president must "from time to time give the Congress

"Oh, and give the executive the right to rain down death from on high."

information on the state of the union, and recommend to their consideration such measures as he shall judge necessary and expedient." Until Woodrow Wilson's presidency, the "**State of the Union**" took the form of a written report sent every year or every two years to Congress for its consideration. These reports often gathered dust in the House and Senate clerks' offices. Wilson, a strong believer in the role of the president as chief legislative leader similar to the prime minister in a parliamentary system, began the practice of delivering the State of the Union to Congress in an address to a joint session of the House and Senate, in which presidents set out their agendas for congressional legislation. Wilson correctly sensed that the American people were in the mood for vigorous legislative leadership from the president, given the enormous technological, economic, and social changes that were happening in the United States and the problems that were being generated by these changes.

In modern times, the State of the Union address has become one of the most important tools by which presidents gain the attention of the public and other public officials for what they want to accomplish. The State of the Union is now a very dramatic and visible event, delivered before a joint session of Congress, with members of the Supreme Court, the president's cabinet, and the military joint chiefs in attendance—and a national television audience. In the State of the Union, presidents, much as Wilson did, set out what issues they hope Congress will address, with a promise that detailed proposals for legislation will be forthcoming.

The president's legislative role also was enhanced by the Budget Act of 1921, which requires the president to submit an annual federal government budget to Congress for its consideration, accompanied by a budget message setting out the president's rationale and justifications. Prior to the Act, the budget of the United States was prepared initially in Congress. Moving preliminary decisions about proposed spending for government programs and agencies from the legislative to the executive branch represented a formidable enhancement in both the responsibilities and power of the president.

Although the House and Senate often take action on their own with regard to the nation's legislative agenda, especially during times of divided government, what is striking is the degree to which Congress waits for and acts in response to presidential State of the Union addresses, budgets, and legislative proposals to meet various national problems. Indeed, the 20th century is dotted with presidential labels on broad legislative programs: Wilson's New Freedom, Roosevelt's New Deal, Truman's Fair Deal, Kennedy's New Frontier, and Johnson's Great Society. On the other hand, presidents invite trouble when they fail to lead on major pieces of legislation about which they care deeply. For example, in 2009 and 2010, Barack Obama left it almost entirely to Congress to fashion a health care reform bill, named the Affordable Care Act, without much guidance from the White House. The result was a bitter, year-and-a-half-long struggle in Congress that dismayed the public, undermined presidential and congressional popularity, and produced a bill that the president signed but satisfied few, even its supporters.[14] Donald Trump left much of the 2018 spending bill in the hands of Republican leaders in the House and Senate. He signed it, after some hesitation, because it increased military spending, which he wanted, but did not include funding for a border wall with Mexico and radically increased the sizes of the deficit and the national debt.

MANAGER OF THE ECONOMY   We now expect presidents to "do something" about the economy when things are going badly. The Great Depression taught most Americans that the federal government has a role to play in fighting economic downturns, and the example of Franklin Roosevelt convinced many that the main actor in this drama ought to be the president. Congress recognized this in 1946 when it passed the Employment Act, requiring the president to produce an annual report on the state of the economy, assisted by a new Council of Economic Advisers, with a set of recommendations for congressional action to maintain the health of the American

State of the Union
Annual report to the nation by the president, now delivered before a joint session of Congress, on the state of the nation and legislative proposals for addressing national problems.

economy. The role is now so well established that even conservative presidents like Ronald Reagan and George W. Bush felt compelled to involve the federal government in the prevention of bank failures, the stimulation of economic growth, and the promotion of exports abroad. George W. Bush supported an economic stimulus package in 2008 to fight a growing recession and the collapse of the real estate market. He also authorized the Treasury Department to work with the Federal Reserve to reorganize investment banks, provide bailouts to big commercial banks, and take over failing mortgage giants Freddie Mac and Fannie Mae to avert a financial collapse.

Chief Executive

Although presidents share influence over the executive branch of the federal government with Congress and the courts, they are the chief executive of the United States, charged by the Constitution and expected by the American people to ensure that the nation's laws are efficiently and effectively carried out by bureaucratic agencies such as the Justice, Interior, and Commerce Departments; the National Aeronautics and Space Administration (NASA); and the National Weather Service. When an agency fails, as the Federal Emergency Management Agency (FEMA) did spectacularly in the aftermath of the Katrina disaster, the president invariably takes the heat. The problem is that presidents have something less than full control over the federal bureaucracy, so they cannot be certain that agency leaders and personnel will do what they want those leaders and personnel to do.[15] Nevertheless, presidents exercise more influence over executive branch agencies than any other government actor or set of actors.

In addition to their power to nominate and appoint the topmost leaders of federal departments and agencies, presidents exercise influence over the bureaucracy mainly by the use of **executive orders**—formal directives to executive branch departments and agencies that have the force of law.[16] These orders take many specific forms, including presidential proclamations, decision memoranda, signing statements, and national security directives. The legitimacy of such orders is based sometimes on the constitutional positions of the president as chief executive and commander in chief, sometimes on discretionary authority granted to the president by Congress in statutes such as the Clean Air Act, and often on precedents set by past presidents.

Executive orders are not only about minor administrative matters; presidents have issued many of them to institute important federal policies and programs.[17] Thomas Jefferson executed the Louisiana Purchase by proclamation (though he needed Congress to appropriate money to complete the agreement with France), and Abraham Lincoln did the same during the Civil War when he ordered the emancipation of slaves held in states that were in revolt against the United States. Franklin Roosevelt ordered the internment of Japanese Americans during World War II. His successor, Harry Truman, ordered the end of racial segregation in the armed forces. Bill Clinton issued orders to set aside millions of acres of land as national monuments off-limits to logging and roads. President George W. Bush issued executive orders to use "enhanced interrogation" techniques on terrorism suspects and tap the phones and e-mail communications of American citizens. President Obama issued executive orders increasing fuel mileage requirements on cars and trucks, allowing children of illegal immigrants brought to this country at a young age to stay in the country, and closing the gun show loop hole that had blocked background checks on a significant number of gun purchasers. In the very first weeks of his presidency, President Trump ordered an end to efforts to join the Trans-Pacific Partnership (a trade agreement), that a start be made on building the wall along the U.S.–Mexico border, that construction resume on the Keystone XL pipeline, that more offshore drilling be allowed in the Atlantic and the Arctic, that a wider range of undocumented people living in the United States be subject to deportation, that federal money be withheld from so-called sanctuary cities, and that people from a number of Muslim-majority countries be

executive order

A rule or regulation for an executive agency or department issued by the president that has the force of law, based either on the constitutional powers of the presidency as chief executive or commander in chief or on congressional statutes.

denied entry into the country, a policy ruled constitutional by the U.S. Supreme Court in Spring, 2018. Some scholars worry that the use of executive orders has become so important in fashioning government policies that it amounts to unilateral presidential rule, legislating, as it were, without need of Congress or public support.[18]

Believing that in recent decades the presidency had been crippled by too much congressional and judicial interference, members of George W. Bush's administration and many conservatives revived and gave a very expansive reading to a long-dormant constitutional theory known as the **unitary executive** in an attempt to "unstymie" the office. The concept is based on Article II's "vesting" ("The executive Power shall be vested in a President of the United States of America.") and "take care" clauses ("The President shall take care that the laws be faithfully executed....") to suggest that the office is free to exercise command and authority over the executive branch in all respects, without interference from the other federal branches, including the courts.[19]

Under this doctrine, presidents have the sole authority, for example, to direct the actions of agencies such as the CIA and the NSA. They alone can interpret, in their signing statements, the meaning of laws passed by Congress for executive branch personnel and units. They alone can determine the degree to which departmental and agency personnel cooperate with Congress, such as in the release of documents or testimony before congressional committees. And they can order the review of all regulations issued by regular and independent regulatory agencies for their consistency with the law as interpreted by the president. The doctrine of the unitary executive is, to say the least, controversial, and it is not broadly accepted among constitutional scholars or by the courts. Republicans and conservatives were less enthusiastic about the need for a unitary executive when Democrat Barack Obama became president.

The reality of politics on the ground, however, is that presidents cannot entirely control what the executive branch does. In the day-to-day operations of the federal bureaucracy, direct command is seldom feasible. Too much is going on in hundreds of agencies. Presidents alone cannot keep track of each one of the millions of government officials, employees, and private contractors hired by departments and agencies. Most of the time, presidents can only issue general guidelines and pass them down the chain of subordinates, hoping that their wishes will be followed faithfully.

unitary executive

Controversial constitutional doctrine which proposes that the executive branch is under the direct control of the president, who has all authority necessary to control the actions of federal bureaucracy personnel and units without interference from the other federal branches.

CLOSE CALL

The American destroyer USS *Vesole* escorts a Soviet cargo ship carrying nuclear missiles away from Cuba after President Kennedy and Soviet Premier Nikita Khrushchev reached an agreement to end what came to be known as the Cuban Missile Crisis in 1962. The two nuclear powers came very close to war, but the two leaders managed to pull back from the brink despite a number of advisors on each side urging military action.

Are we under as great a threat today as we were during the Cuban Missile Crisis for a nuclear exchange between the United States and another military superpower such as Russia or China? Or is this less of a threat than a nuclear device being set off in the US by a smaller country or a terrorist group?

But lower-level officials, protected from job termination by civil service status, may have their own interests, their own institutional norms and practices, that lead them to do something different. President Kennedy was painfully reminded of this during the Cuban Missile Crisis of 1962, when Soviet Premier Nikita Khrushchev demanded that U.S. missiles be removed from Turkey in return for the removal of Soviet missiles from Cuba. Kennedy was surprised to learn that the missiles had not already been taken out of Turkey because he had ordered them removed a year earlier. The people responsible for carrying out this directive had not followed through.[20]

Foreign Policy and Military Leader

Although the framers gave a role to Congress in fashioning foreign and military policies—note congressional control of the federal purse strings, its role in declaring war, and the Senate's "advice and consent" responsibilities with respect to treaties and appointment of ambassadors—they wanted the president to be the major player in these areas. What they could not have anticipated was that the United States would develop into the world's superpower, with global responsibilities and commitments, a development that enormously expanded the power of the presidency.

FOREIGN POLICY LEADER   In a case decided in 1936, the Supreme Court confirmed the president's position as the nation's preeminent foreign policy maker, saying: "the president is the sole organ of the federal government in the field of international relations."[21] The president's role as foreign policy leader is rooted in the diplomatic and treaty powers sections of Article II of the Constitution as well as in the provision that designates the president as commander in chief of the armed forces.[22]

The Constitution specifies that the president shall have the power to appoint and receive ambassadors and to make **treaties**. Although these formal constitutional powers may seem minor at first glance, they confer on the president the main responsibility for fashioning American foreign policy. Take the power to appoint and receive ambassadors. From the very beginning of the American republic, presidents have used this provision as a tool for recognizing or refusing to recognize foreign governments. For example, Presidents Woodrow Wilson, Warren Harding, Calvin Coolidge, and Herbert Hoover refused to recognize the revolutionary communist government of the Soviet Union, a policy Franklin D. Roosevelt reversed in 1933. China's communist government went unrecognized by the United States for twenty-three years after

treaty

A formal international agreement between two or more countries; in the United States, requires the "advice and consent" of the Senate.

OUTREACH TO THE MUSLIM WORLD

President Donald Trump, like most presidents before him, has determined that Saudi Arabia is a key alley in the struggle against Iran. Here he is welcomed by Saudi officials on one of his first trips abroad as president.

Did the murder of Saudi dissident and journalist Jamal Khashoggi by the Saudi security services in October, 2018 do permanent damage to the alliance?

it came to power, a policy that Richard Nixon eventually reversed. The president's sole power to proclaim U.S. policy in this area is suggested by the following: neither Franklin D. Roosevelt nor Richard Nixon required the permission of any other government institution or public official—whether Congress or the courts or state legislatures, for example—to change American policy with respect to the Soviet Union or Communist China. The decision was the president's alone to make.

The power to initiate the treaty-making process is also an important tool of presidential diplomacy and foreign policy making. By virtue of this power, the president and the foreign policy officials in the State, Treasury, Commerce, and Defense Departments that report to him consult, negotiate, and reach agreements with other countries. Sometimes those agreements take the form of treaties—the Panama Canal Treaty of 1977 ceding control of the waterway to that country is an example, as are the various arms control, human rights, trade, and environmental treaties to which the United States is a party. More often, however, international agreements take the form of **executive agreements** entered into by the president and one or more foreign governments. Executive agreements appeal to presidents because they do not require the "advice and consent" of the Senate yet are understood to be lawful and binding just like treaties.[23] Originally understood to be agreements about minor or technical details associated with a treaty, executive agreements eventually began to be used for very important matters. In 2002, for example, President Bush entered into an executive agreement with Russia that committed the two countries to reducing the size of their nuclear stockpiles.[24]

COMMANDER IN CHIEF   Article II, Section 2, of the Constitution specifies that the president is the commander in chief—without saying anything at all about what that means. On the other hand, Article I, Section 8, specifies that Congress has the power to declare war. Clearly, the framers meant the president to be in charge of troops once American forces became engaged in hostilities. But they also seem to have had in mind a distinction regarding who decides whether to wage defensive war and who decides whether to wage offensive war, with the president the primary decision maker with respect to the former and Congress preeminent with respect to the latter. Thus, the president was given the power to use American forces to protect the United States against external invasions and internal insurrections; Congress was given the power to declare war against another country.[25] As president, George Washington adhered to this

executive agreement

An agreement with another country signed by the president that has the force of law, like a treaty; does not require Senate approval; originally used for minor technical matters, now an important tool of presidential power in foreign affairs.

A TOAST TO A NEW ERA

President Richard Nixon reestablished diplomatic relations with China in 1972. The two countries had been estranged since the Communists came to power in China in 1949 after defeating a long-time ally of the United States. The president did not require any action by Congress, the courts, or the American people to make this momentous change in policy, though most eventually welcomed it. Here, he joins a toast to the new era with Chinese foreign minister Zhou Enlai. *Is it a good idea in a democracy that the decision to enter diplomatic relations with other countries is solely in the hands of the president even though this is what the Framers intended when they wrote Article II of the Constitution? Would including Congress and the courts generate too much delay and too many complications into the conduct of foreign affairs?*

distinction. As he put it in 1792, "The Constitution vests the power of declaring war with Congress; therefore no offensive expedition of importance can be undertaken until after they shall have deliberated upon the subject, and authorized such a measure."

Over the years, this distinction between offensive and defensive war disappeared; American forces are now sent into hostilities abroad, deployed by presidents without a formal declaration of war by Congress, in the name of defending the United States. In fact, though the United States has been involved in many military conflicts since then, Congress last declared war—against Japan and the various Axis powers—in the months following the attack on Pearl Harbor in December 1941 that brought us into World War II. Here is what seems to have been going on: as the United States became a global power, presidents, other American leaders, and the public came to believe that defending the United States required more than simply defending against cross-border invasions from other countries. Other threats seemed to be equally dangerous, including communism, nationalist threats to American economic interests, drug trafficking, and, most recently, terrorism and cyberwarfare by groups and countries unfriendly to the United States.

Here is a sampling of how presidents have used American military power abroad since World War II. In the early 1950s, Harry Truman fought a bitter war in Korea against North Korean and Chinese forces, without a declaration of war from Congress, in the name of halting communist aggression. Presidents Eisenhower, Kennedy, Johnson, and Nixon did the same in Vietnam. Ronald Reagan used American forces in Grenada and Nicaragua to fight communism and launched an air attack against Libya to punish it for its involvement in terrorism. George H. W. Bush launched an invasion of Panama to capture its president and drug lord Manuel Noriega, and in 1991 he used more than five hundred thousand U.S. troops in Operation Desert Storm to push Iraq out of Kuwait. President Bill Clinton sent several thousand American troops as peacekeepers to Bosnia in 1995, Haiti in 1996, and Kosovo in 1999 and waged an air war against Serbia to try to prevent further "ethnic cleansing" in its province of Kosovo.

After the September 11, 2001, attacks on the United States, George W. Bush launched a military campaign against the Taliban regime and the Al Qaeda terrorist network in Afghanistan and then invaded and occupied Iraq in 2003 to protect the country against the Iraqi regime's purported weapons of mass destruction program and ties to the 9/11 terrorists (in the end, both claims proved to be untrue). President Barack Obama, as we have seen, increased the number of troops in Afghanistan, upped the number of drone attacks on terrorist targets along the Pakistani border, and used special forces in operations in Somalia and Yemen. President Donald Trump in early 2017 launched cruise missiles against Syrian military targets after President Assad used chemical weapons in his war against insurgents, and set missiles again to target chemical weapons research and storage facilities in 2018 when the Assad regime again used these outlawed weapons of war. In none of these or related cases was Congress called upon to pass a formal declaration of war, nor was Congress notified under terms of the War Powers Act that the United States was engaged in hostilities. In 2013, when President Obama asked Congress for permission to use force in Syria to protect civilians against attacks from the Assad regime, many commentators were aghast, believing that going to Congress in this way weakened the presidency and America's national defense capabilities.

President Obama's decision to use drones to attack terrorist networks in the tribal areas on the Afghanistan and Pakistan border from 2010 through 2012 as a way to help the American-backed regime in Afghanistan was done without asking permission from Congress or the American people. Like most other examples of presidential decision making, his action can be fully understood only by taking into account the relevant *structural*, *political linkage*, and *governmental* factors. To explore how and why the president was able to proceed as he did, apply the framework (see Figure 12.1).[26]

To be sure, when presidents choose to use American military power, they ordinarily consult widely with members of Congress and other government and opinion leaders. They do everything they can to enlist the support of the public. They may even ask that

FIGURE 12.1   APPLYING THE FRAMEWORK: WAGING WAR BY DRONE STRIKE IN PAKISTAN

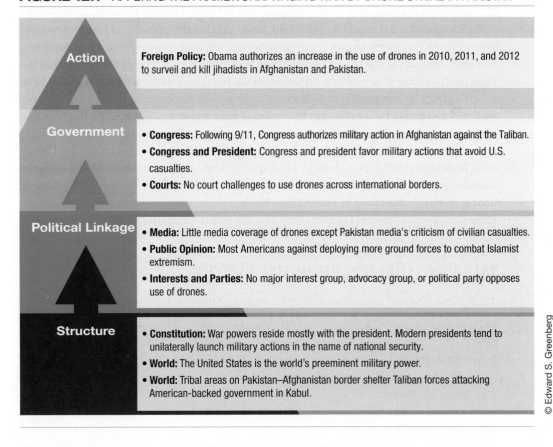

© Edward S. Greenberg

Congress pass a resolution of support authorizing presidential use of the armed forces to defend the national security of the United States, although they are not legally bound to do so. Thus, President George H. W. Bush asked Congress to pass a resolution supporting Desert Storm in 1991, which it did. Likewise, in 2002, his son, President George W. Bush, asked Congress for a resolution supporting military action against Saddam Hussein's Iraq, which it did. Tellingly, each of the Bush presidents let it be known that military action would be forthcoming no matter the outcome of congressional deliberations.

Some presidents also have claimed that the office's commander-in-chief powers allow them to take extraordinary actions on the home front that seemingly violate civil liberties of some Americans, if such actions are required to defend the nation. Thus, Abraham Lincoln used military tribunals to try a number of Southern sympathizers during the Civil War, Woodrow Wilson censored the press during World War I, Franklin Roosevelt ordered placement of Japanese Americans into internment camps during World War II, and George W. Bush detained without trial American citizens he defined as "enemy combatants" and authorized domestic eavesdropping by the NSA to find terrorists. The Supreme Court ruled in each of these cases that the president had gone beyond his constitutional authority, but the rulings were not issued until years after they had begun.

Party Leader

One of the great difficulties all presidents face is the seeming contradiction between their role as president of all the people—as commander in chief, chief diplomat, and chief executive, for example—and their role as the leader of their political party seeking partisan advantage as well as the public good.[27] Much of the apparent contradiction has been eased by the fact that presidents, like all political leaders, generally see the public good and commitment to party principles and programs as one and the same. Thus, Ronald Reagan, as leader of the Republican Party and as president, believed that the public good and his own party's prospects in upcoming elections were well served by his successful efforts to increase defense spending, deregulate the economy, and decrease domestic spending. For his part, Lyndon Johnson, as the leader of the Democratic Party and as president, believed that the public and his party would benefit from programs to end racial discrimination and reduce poverty. Sometimes, however, the public reacts negatively when a president plays the party leader role too vigorously, seeing it as perhaps unpresidential. In an oft-cited example, Franklin Roosevelt's effort to campaign for Democratic congressional candidates in 1938 was not well received, and his party won fewer seats than expected. George W. Bush's campaign involvement in the 2006 congressional elections did not prevent Democrats from winning control of both houses of Congress nor did Obama's do much for the Democrats in 2010 and 2014. President Donald Trump's intense involvement in the congressional campaigns for the 2018 elections paid off in the Senate, where the GOP added to their majority, but seemed to hurt in the House, where suburban and educated women voters helped the Democrats gain over 30 seats and the majority in that chamber.

THE PRESIDENT'S SUPPORT SYSTEM

12.3 Describe the organization and functions of the president's advisors.

Each of the president's functions is demanding; together, they are overwhelming. Of course, presidents do not face their burdens alone; they have gradually acquired many advisers and helpers. The number and responsibilities of these advisers and helpers have become so extensive—and the functions they perform so essential—that they have come to form what some call the **institutional presidency**.[28]

The White House Staff

institutional presidency
The permanent bureaucracy associated with the presidency, designed to help the incumbent of the office carry out their responsibilities.

The White House staff, which is specially formed to fit the particular needs of each president, includes a number of close advisers. One top adviser, usually designated **chief of staff**, tends to serve as the president's right hand, supervising other staff members and organizing much of what the president does. Presidents use their chiefs of staff in different ways. Franklin Roosevelt kept a tight rein on things himself, granting equal but limited power and access to several close advisers in a *competitive* system. Donald Trump had multiple advisors compete for attention and influence, including several members of his family, namely Ivanka Trump and her husband Jared Kushner. His first chiefs of staff, Reince Priebus and General John Kelly, proved unable to contain some of the president's more intemperate tweets or prevent inter-staff squabbling and leaking to the press. Dwight Eisenhower, on the other hand, used to the *hierarchical* army staff system, gave overall responsibility to his chief of staff, Sherman Adams.

chief of staff
A top adviser to the president who also manages the White House staff.

Another important staff member in most presidencies is the **national security adviser**, who is also head of the president's National Security Council, operating out of the White House. The national security adviser generally meets with the president every day to provide a briefing on the latest events that might affect the nation's security and offer advice on what to do. Several national security advisers, including Henry Kissinger (under Nixon) and Zbigniew Brzezinski (under Carter), have been strong foreign policy managers and active, world-hopping diplomats who sometimes clashed with the secretaries of the State and Defense departments. Donald Trump's first national security advisor, Michael Flynn, was forced from his position after information surfaced about his contact with Russian officials during the presidential election campaign and the transition period after the elections. H.R. McMaster followed him, though he was soon replaced by John Bolton, a long-time critic of Putin and Russia.

national security adviser
A top foreign policy and defense adviser to the president who heads the National Security Council.

Most presidents also have a top domestic policy adviser who coordinates plans for new domestic laws, regulations, and spending, although this role is often subordinate to that of the chief of staff and is not usually very visible. Close political advisers, often old comrades of the president from past campaigns, may be found in a number of White

KEY PLAYERS

Secretary of State Mike Pompeo and National Security Advisor John Bolton have been key actors supporting President Donald Trump's turn against NATO and it's key member states, especially Germany, over trade and purported underspending on national defense. Here the president answers questions at a press conference at the 2018 NATO summit. Most presidential advisors and staff are not subject to Senate approval—though the Secretary of State must be confirmed by that body—so do not receive much public scrutiny.

Should close advisors and staff be required to gain the "advise and consent" of the Senate or would that be too unwieldy and to much of an intrusion on traditional presidential prerogatives? If you believe more legislative oversight should be required, what would such an approval process look like?

House or other government posts (e.g., James Baker served as George H. W. Bush's secretary of state, while Karen Hughes served as White House counselor to the younger Bush during his first term) or may have no official position at all (such as consultant Dick Morris, who crafted Clinton's 1996 reelection strategy). Prominent in every administration is the press secretary, who holds press conferences, briefs the media, and serves as the voice of the administration. All have a legal counsel. There are also one or more special assistants who act as a liaison with Congress, deal with interest groups, handle political matters, and consult on intergovernmental relations. Facing a deep recession and continuing financial crisis when he came to office, President Obama appointed a team of economic advisers, led by Larry Summers, to try to keep him abreast of daily developments.

However, the exact composition of the White House staff changes greatly from one presidency to another, depending on the preferences and style of the president. What was particularly striking about President George W. Bush's management style was his penchant for setting overall goals and policies but giving his staffers a great deal of freedom and latitude in getting the job done.[29] Presidents Clinton and Obama were more closely involved in the day-to-day work of their staffs. President Trump famously often ignored his staff or over-ruled agreements with them on policy on the form of late-night and early morning tweets.

The Executive Office of the President

One step removed from the presidential staff, and mostly housed in the Executive Office Building next door to the White House, is a set of organizations with more than 1,800 employees that forms the **Executive Office of the President (EOP)**. Most important of these organizations is the Office of Management and Budget (OMB). The OMB advises the president on how much the administration should propose to spend for each government program and where the money will come from. The OMB also exercises legislative clearance; that is, it examines the budgetary implications of any proposed bills that will be sent to Congress and sometimes kills proposals it deems too expensive or inconsistent with the president's philosophy or goals. The OMB director often is a very powerful player in the White House and in Washington politics.

The Council of Economic Advisers (CEA) advises the president on economic policy. Occasionally, the head of the council exercises great influence, as Walter Heller did during the Kennedy administration. However, Obama economic czar Lawrence Summers and Treasury Secretary Tim Geithner, skilled bureaucratic infighters, made

Executive Office of the President (EOP)

A group of organizations that advise the president on a wide range of issues; includes, among others, the Office of Management and Budget, the National Security Council, and the Council of Economic Advisers.

sure that CEA head Christina Romer was not much of a factor in the administration's response to the Great Recession because they disagreed with her on the size of the stimulus necessary to revive the economy (she wanted a much bigger one).[30]

The Executive Office of the President also includes the National Security Council (NSC), a body of leading officials from the Departments of State and Defense, the CIA, the military, and elsewhere who advise the president on foreign affairs. The NSC has been particularly active in crisis situations and covert operations. The NSC staff, charged with various analytical and coordinating tasks, is headed by the president's national security adviser. Increasingly important in the effort to protect the United States against terrorist attacks is the Intelligence Advisory Board, which provides information and assessments to the president's director of national intelligence and to the president directly.

The Vice Presidency

In 1804, the Twelfth Amendment fixed the flaw in the original Constitution in which the person with the second most electoral votes became the vice president. Under the old rules, Aaron Burr, Thomas Jefferson's running mate in 1800, had tied Jefferson in electoral votes and tried, in the House of Representatives, to grab the presidency for himself. Since then, vice presidents have been elected specifically to that office on a party ticket with their presidents. But now, there is also another way to become vice president. The Twenty-Fifth Amendment (ratified in 1967) provides for succession in case of the temporary or permanent inability of a president to discharge the office. It also states that if the vice presidency becomes vacant, the president can nominate a new vice president, who takes office on confirmation by both houses of Congress. This is how Gerald Ford became vice president in 1973 when Spiro Agnew was forced to resign because of a scandal, and it is how Nelson Rockefeller became vice president in 1974, when Ford replaced Richard Nixon as president after Nixon resigned.

Until quite recently, the vice presidency has not been a highly regarded office. John Nance Garner, Franklin Roosevelt's first vice president, has been quoted as saying in his earthy Texan way that the office was "not worth a pitcher of warm piss."[31] Within administrations, vice presidents were considered to be fifth wheels, not fully trusted (because they could not be fired), and not personally or politically close to the president. Vice presidents used to spend much of their time running minor errands of state, attending funerals of foreign leaders not important enough to demand

A UNIQUELY POWERFUL VICE PRESIDENT

Richard Cheney is generally acknowledged to be the most engaged and influential vice president in American history, playing especially prominent roles in the development of doctrines and policies ranging from the use of American military power to the treatment of prisoners detained in the "war on terrorism" and the particulars of national energy policy. *Is it important to the nation and presidents that vice presidents play a central role in fashioning administration policies, or should vice presidents stay more in the background?*

presidential attention, or carrying out limited diplomatic missions. Some vice presidents were virtually frozen out of the policy-making process. For example, while vice president, Harry Truman was never informed of the existence of the Manhattan Project, which built the atomic bomb. He learned of the bomb only months before he was obligated to make a decision on using it to end the war against Japan, soon after he became president on the death of Franklin D. Roosevelt.

Recent presidents, however, have involved their vice presidents more.[32] Bill Clinton gave Al Gore important responsibilities, including the formulation of environmental policy, coping with Ross Perot's opposition to NAFTA, and the ambitious effort to "reinvent government." Barack Obama's vice president, Joe Biden, for many years a prominent senator, played a particularly important role in foreign policy, meeting with many foreign leaders, and in the several difficult budget negotiations with Congress during the budget crises of 2011 and 2012. More than any other vice president in American history, however, Dick Cheney was at the center of the policy-making process in the White House, serving (by all accounts) as President George W. Bush's principal adviser on both domestic and foreign policy, the key player within the administration on long-range policy planning and selection of Supreme Court justices, the main liaison to Republicans in Congress,[33] an important consumer of information from the intelligence community,[34] the chief advocate for a war against Iraq, and the leading advocate of a muscular interpretation of presidential war powers.[35] Mike Pence played an important role in explaining the Trump' vision and policy proposal to the so-called Republican establishment in Congress and across the country and to the evangelical community.

The Cabinet

The president's cabinet is not mentioned in the Constitution. No legislation designates the composition of the cabinet, its duties, or its rules of operation. Nevertheless, all presidents since George Washington have had one. It was Washington who established the practice of meeting with his top executive officials as a group to discuss policy matters. Later presidents continued the practice, some meeting with the cabinet as often as twice a week, and others paying it less attention or none at all. Today, the cabinet usually consists of the heads of the major executive departments, plus the vice president, and whichever other officials the president deems appropriate, including the director of National Intelligence and the White House chief of staff.

Presidents do not rely on the cabinet as a decision-making body. Not only is there no constitutional warrant for such a body to make policies, but presidents know that they alone will be held responsible for decisions, and they alone keep the power to make them.

A RARE CABINET MEETING

Presidents do not use their cabinets as decision making bodies. Most hardly meet with their cabinets at all. And, unlike most previous presidents, President Donald Trump has used the start of cabinet meetings to have cabinet members praise him in front of TV cameras. Here he chairs a meeting of the cabinet in June, 2018.

What do cabinet meetings tell us, if anything, about the leadership styles and effectiveness of presidents? Does it matter at all how they relate to their cabinet?

According to legend, when Abraham Lincoln once disagreed with his entire cabinet, he declared, "Eight votes for and one against; the nays have it!" Donald Trump seems to have gathered his cabinet together, with live TV present, to sing the praises of the president.

Most recent presidents have convened the cabinet infrequently and have done serious business with it only rarely. One reason is simply that government has grown large and specialized. Most department heads are experts in their own areas, with little to contribute elsewhere. It could be a waste of everyone's time to engage the secretary of Health and Human Services in discussions of military strategy. Another reason is that cabinet members occupy an ambiguous position: they are advisers to the president but also represent their own constituencies, including the permanent civil servants in their departments and the organized interests that their departments serve. They may have substantial political stature of their own—consider Hillary Clinton, at one time Obama's secretary of state—independent of the president's.

THE PRESIDENT AND CONGRESS: PERPETUAL TUG-OF-WAR

12.4 Analyze the conflict between the president and Congress.

The president and Congress are often at odds. This is a *structural* fact of American politics, deliberately intended by the framers of the Constitution.[36]

Conflict by Constitutional Design

The framers created a system of separation of powers and checks and balances between Congress and the president, setting "ambition to counter ambition" to prevent tyranny. Because virtually all constitutional powers are shared, there is a potential for conflict over virtually all aspects of government policy; our system is quite exceptional in this regard. In parliamentary systems such as those of Great Britain, Germany, Sweden, and Japan, there is no separation of powers between the executive and legislative branches. Recall that in such systems the prime minister and cabinet—who together make up the government, what we would call the executive branch—are themselves parliamentarians selected by the majority party or a majority coalition of parties in parliament. The executive and legislative functions thus are fused in such systems, not separated. So checks and balances between the executive and legislative powers do not exist because the executive and the legislative are one and the same. This is not so in the United States: separated powers and mutual checks are real and consequential for what government does, even though presidents have, as we have seen, dramatically expanded their powers by increasing their use of executive orders and executive agreements and by interpreting their war powers quite expansively.

SHARED POWERS Under the Constitution, presidents may propose legislation and can sign or veto bills passed by Congress, but both houses of Congress must pass any laws and can (and sometimes do) override presidential vetoes. Presidents can appoint ambassadors and high officials and make treaties with foreign countries, but the Senate must approve them. Presidents nominate federal judges, including U.S. Supreme Court justices, but the Senate must approve the nominations. Presidents administer the executive branch, but Congress appropriates funds for it to operate, writes the legislation that defines what it is to do, and oversees its activities.

Presidents cannot always count on the members of Congress to agree with them. The potential conflict written into the Constitution becomes real because the president and Congress often disagree about national goals, especially when there is **divided government**, that is, when the president and the majority in the House and/or the Senate belong to different parties.[37] For example, Bill Clinton was impeached by the Republican-controlled House of Representatives in late 1998,

divided government

Control of the executive and the legislative branches by different political parties.

while George W. Bush's Iraq War policies were bitterly opposed by a Democratic-dominated Congress in the last two years of his presidency. The Republican House's opposition to Barack Obama's budget plans and priorities in 2011 and 2014 was so strident that it almost led to the United States defaulting on the national debt, courting financial disaster for the country and the global economy.

It is not uncommon, however, for presidents to clash with members of Congress even if they are of the same party. George W. Bush ran into trouble with co-partisans on a number of issues during his second term, especially on the issue of a path to citizenship for undocumented immigrants, a path that Bush favored. Donald Trump struggled to get Congress to back him on budget priorities, repeal and replacement of the Affordable Care Act, funding to build a border wall, and more, even though Republicans enjoyed majorities in both the House and Senate in 2017 and 2018.

SEPARATE ELECTIONS   In other countries' parliamentary systems, the national legislatures choose the chief executives so that unified party control is ensured. But in the United States, there are separate elections for the president and the members of Congress. In addition, our elections do not all come at the same time. In presidential election years, two-thirds of the senators do not have to run and are insulated from new political forces that may affect the choice of a president. In nonpresidential, "off" years, all members of the House and one-third of the senators face the voters, who sometimes elect a Congress with views quite different from those of the president that was chosen two years earlier. For example, in 1986, halfway through Reagan's second term, the Democrats recaptured control of the Senate and caused Reagan great difficulty with Supreme Court appointments and other matters. The Republicans did the same thing to Clinton in 1994 after they gained control of Congress. In 2018, Democrats gained over 30 seats in the House ensuring control of that chamber for a party deeply opposed to President Trump's policies and actions. The Democrats used their control of House committees after taking office in January, 2019 to launch investigations into Russian involvement in the 2016 elections, state actions to suppress votes, alleged corrupt actions by several Cabinet members, and the president's business practices and finances.

OUTCOMES   In all these ways, our constitutional structure ensures that what the president can do is limited and influenced by Congress, which in turn reflects various political forces that may differ from those that affect the president. At its most extreme, Congress may even be controlled by the opposing party. This divided government situation always constrains what presidents can do and may sometimes lead to a condition called "gridlock," in which a president and Congress are locked in battle, neither able to make much headway. This is hardly surprising; presidents are not only the chief executive and commander in chief of the United States but the leaders of their party, so members of the opposition are not inclined to give them what they want on the chance that it will benefit presidential election prospects or those of the president's party in Congress. Right after the 2010 Republican landslide victory, Senate Minority Leader Mitch McConnell, explaining his party's strategy, said his goal was to ensure that Barack Obama would be a one-term president. This hardly offered the promise of compromise on important legislative issues.

What Makes a President Successful with Congress?

A number of political scientists have studied presidents' successes and failures in getting Congress to enact measures that those presidents favor. These political scientists have suggested reasons some presidents on some issues do much better than others do.[38]

PARTY AND IDEOLOGY   The most important factor is a simple one: when the president's party controls both houses of Congress, they are much more likely to get their way on legislation, approval of appointments and more gentle handling of executive branch problems by congressional oversight committees.[39] Presidential success under this condition of unified control does not come from presidents ordering party members around. Rather, presidents and the members of their party in Congress tend to be like-minded on a wide range of issues, sharing values and policy preferences and a common interest in reelection. For these reasons, members of Congress tend to go along most of the time with presidents of their own party.[40] The GOP-led Congress did not work smoothly, however, for Donald Trump in 2017. Because he was not an ideologically consistent conservative like most of his party in Congress, because he had run his nomination campaign against the Republican establishment, including the congressional leadership, and because Republicans in the House had a strong Freedom Caucus and moderate factions that agreed on very little, Donald Trump had great difficulties in advancing his legislative program in Congress.

Because the parties have become so ideologically cohesive since the mid-1990s, presidents can sometimes get their way with Congress, even when they have only a very slim party majority in the House and a small but somewhat larger majority in the Senate—where sixty votes are needed to get past the filibuster barrier. Between 2001 and 2006, for example, George W. Bush enjoyed many legislative successes though Republican majorities in the House and Senate were paper-thin. He was able to do this because the highly cohesive and disciplined Republican Party in the Senate was joined by a handful of moderate Democrats on many bills, making Democratic filibusters rare events. Because Barack Obama enjoyed bigger party majorities in Congress than George W. Bush during his first two years in office—with a 60–40 margin in the Senate (counting two independents who caucused with the Democrats)—and because the Democratic Party stayed cohesive when it came to decisive votes in Congress, he was able to put together a very substantial legislative record in his first two years. According to the *Congressional Quarterly* (CQ), Obama forged the highest presidential success score with Congress since CQ began keeping score in 1953.[41] The result was victory for the president on a wide range of matters, including a massive economic stimulus bill, a historic overhaul of health insurance in the United States, and wide-ranging regulation of the financial services industry. After the GOP gained seats in the Senate and control of the House in the 2010 elections, Obama's success with Congress sank dramatically in 2011 and 2012. Though he was reelected in 2012, congressional elections that year did not change the party balance of power in the House and Senate, and Republics won the Senate in 2014, so Obama remained stymied after that. Obama-favored legislation died in the legislative branch, as did a record number of presidential appointments to the federal courts and executive branch departments and agencies.

FOREIGN POLICY AND NATIONAL SECURITY ISSUES   Presidents tend to do better with Congress on foreign policy issues than on domestic ones mainly because Americans want to appear united when dealing with other countries and because members' constituents pay less attention to events abroad than to what is going on in the United States. Political scientist Aaron Wildavsky went so far as to refer to "two presidencies," domestic and foreign, with the latter presidency much more dominant.[42] In 2017 and 2018, for example, while President Trump was not very successful in Congress in terms of fashioning new domestic policies other than a tax cut bill (which Republicans had long advocated), House and Senate foreign policy leaders supported his cruise missile attacks on Syrian chemical weapons capability, while the chairs of important House and Senate committees tried to slow

TRYING TO FORGE A NEW RELATIONSHIP

President Donald Trump met very early in his term with Chinese leader Xi Jinping at the president's Mar-a-Lago Florida resort. Trump claimed several times after the meeting that he and Xi were good friends. Despite that claim, the president in 2018 imposed tariffs on Chinese goods coming into the United States and placed restrictions on investments in U.S. firms, especially in high tech and telecommunications.

To what extent are the personal relationships of a nation's leaders a key factor in making foreign policy decisions? Are national interests, as defined by national leaders, more important than personal relationships? Why do you believe one is more important than the other in shaping foreign policy?

Justice Department probes into Russian meddling in the 2016 elections and possible connections to the Trump campaign and businesses.

With the rise of hyperpartisanship, the House and Senate are more willing than in the past to criticize and oppose the president on foreign and military policies, especially when one or both chambers are controlled by the party other than the president's. Democrats used House and Senate hearings to air grievances about President Bush's military actions in Iraq. During the 2012 presidential campaign, House Republicans used hearings on the terrorist attacks on the American diplomatic compound in Benghazi to attack President Obama and Secretary of State Hillary Clinton. The House hauled Clinton before a hostile committee examining Benghazi once again in 2015, with the former Secretary of State more than holding her own.

VETOES   When the issue is a presidential veto of legislation,[43] the president is again very likely to prevail.[44] Vetoes have not been used often, except by certain "veto-happy" presidents, such as Franklin Roosevelt, Truman, and Ford. But when vetoes have been used, they have seldom been overridden—only 5 percent of the time for Truman and only 1.5 percent for Roosevelt. Bill Clinton did not use the veto at all during his first two years in office, when he had a Democratic majority in Congress, but he used it eleven times in 1995 alone during his budget battles with the Republican-controlled 104th Congress. Because Republicans committed to the president's agenda controlled the House from 2001 through 2006 and the Senate between 2003 and 2006, George W. Bush did not resort to the veto at all during this period. However, he used the veto several times in 2007 and 2008 on bills from the Democratic-controlled Congress. With his party in control of Congress, Barack Obama did not use the veto in 2009 and vetoed only two minor bills in 2010. With his party in control of the Senate, nothing emerged from Congress in 2011, 2012, or 2013 that generated a veto.[45] After Republicans gained control of the Senate in the 2014 national elections, Obama increased his use of the veto. In late 2015, for example, he vetoed a bill to override the EPA's new rule on carbon emissions from power plants; in early 2016, he vetoed a Republican-sponsored bill to dissolve the Affordable Care Act (Obamacare).

POPULARITY   Most scholars and observers of Washington politics, as well as elected officials and political operatives, agree that presidential effectiveness with Congress is significantly affected by how popular a president is with the American people.[46] The reasons are not hard to fathom. Voting against proposals from a very popular president may encourage quality challengers in the next election, for example, or slow the flow of campaign funds to one's war chest, whether the president is of one's party or not. On the other hand, voting with a popular president can offer protective cover for a member of Congress who favors the proposal but whose constituents may not ("This is a vote for the president").[47] When presidents' popular approval collapses—as George W. Bush's did after 2004—even members of their own party are loath to follow executive leadership. For example, Bush was unable to win his own party's approval in Congress for policies he favored on immigration, Social Security reform, and the bank bailout bill. One reason Donald Trump had difficulties advancing his legislative program in Congress may have been his historically low job approval numbers when he took office and his low ratings through 2018.

THE PRESIDENT AND THE PEOPLE

12.5 Describe the relationship between the president and the American people.

The special relationship between the president and the general public has evolved over many years to make the presidency a more powerful and perhaps more democratic office. Let's look at several aspects of this relationship.

Getting Closer to the People

The framers thought of the president as an elite leader, relatively distant from the people, interacting with Congress often but with the people only rarely. Most 19th-century presidents and presidential candidates thought the same. They seldom made speeches directly to the public, for example, generally averaging no more than ten such speeches per year.[48] In the earliest years of the American Republic, presidents were not even chosen directly by the voters but by electors chosen by state legislators or, in case no one got an Electoral College majority, by the House of Representatives. The Constitution thus envisioned very indirect democratic control of the presidency.

As we have also seen, however, this system quickly evolved into one in which the people played a more direct part. The two-party system developed, with parties nominating candidates and running pledged electors and the state legislators allowing ordinary citizens to vote on the electors. Presidential candidates began to win clear-cut victories in the Electoral College, taking the House of Representatives out of the process.

By the beginning of the 20th century, presidents began to speak directly to the public. Theodore Roosevelt embarked on a series of speech-making tours to win passage of legislation to regulate the railroads. Woodrow Wilson made appeals to the public a central part of his presidency, articulating a new theory of the office that highlighted the close connections between the president and the public. Wilson saw the desires of the public as the wellspring of democratic government: "As is the majority, so ought the government to be."[49] He argued that presidents are unique because only they are chosen by the entire nation. Presidents, he said, should help educate the citizens about government, interpret their true will, and faithfully respond to it.

Wilson's theory of the presidency has been followed more and more fully in 20th- and 21st-century thought and practice. All presidents, especially since Franklin Roosevelt, have attempted to both shape and respond to public opinion; all, to one degree or another, have attempted to speak directly to the people about policy.[50]

More and more frequently, presidents go public, using television, the Internet, and social media to bypass the print media and speak to the public directly about policy. They have held fewer news conferences with White House correspondents (where awkward questions cannot be excluded).[51] Richard Nixon pioneered prime-time television addresses, at which Ronald Reagan later excelled. Bill Clinton was more interactive with citizens, appearing on radio and TV talk shows and holding informal but televised "town hall meetings." George W. Bush liked to appear before carefully screened audiences of supporters. Barack Obama was most comfortable doing speeches and town hall–style meetings, but he also depended on the same Internet and social media–based technologies that he used so successfully in his 2008 campaign to get his message to the public, unfiltered by the news media. Donald Trump used Twitter to great effect as a way to communicate directly with the public without being filtered by the news media or his own staff.

Leading Public Opinion

Especially since the rise of television, modern presidents have enhanced their power to shape public opinion. Some studies have indicated that when a popular president takes a stand in favor of a particular policy, the public's support for that policy tends to rise.[52] But there are many cases where presidents have tried but failed to move public opinion in a favorable direction, despite strong efforts to build public support for favored programs.[53] Barack Obama repeatedly appealed to the public on television to push Congress to enact a "cap-and-trade" to control carbon emissions but failed to gain traction in a period when Republicans controlled one or both houses of Congress.

Although not as likely to happen as is often believed, the power to lead the public also implies a power to *manipulate* public opinion if a president is so inclined—that is, to deceive or mislead the public so that it will approve policies that it might oppose if it were fully informed.[54] It is useful to remember that every modern White House has had communications specialists adept at getting out the administration's views, whether through formal channels—such as press releases, the daily briefing for reporters, and materials posted on the White House website—or informal ones, including leaks to favored journalists and in-house-written but anonymous news stories and commentaries for use in newspapers, television news broadcasts, and weblogs.[55] Especially in foreign affairs, presidents can sometimes control what information the public gets, at least in the short run.

Responding to the Public

Besides trying to lead the people, presidents definitely tend to respond to public opinion. Electoral competition produces presidents who tend to share the public's policy preferences. In addition, most presidents want to be reelected or to win a favorable place in history, and they know that they are unlikely to do so if they defy public opinion on many major issues. Usually, they try to anticipate what the public will want in order to win electoral reward and avoid electoral punishment.

There is plenty of evidence that presidents pay attention to what the public is thinking. At least since the Kennedy administration, presidents and their staffs have carefully read the available public opinion surveys and now have full-blown polling operations of their own.[56] Although such polling is often deplored, it helps presidents choose policies that the American public favors and change or discard those that are unpopular. It is worth considering another view about the role of presidential polling, however: that its purpose is to uncover not what the public wants but what words and symbols can be used by a president to sell a program.[57]

Presidential Popularity

Presidential job approval ratings affect how influential a president is with Congress, the judicial branch, and elected officials at the state and local level. Since the 1930s, Gallup and other poll takers have regularly asked Americans whether they approve or disapprove of "the president's handling of the job." The percentage of people who approve varies from month to month and year to year, and as time passes, these varying percentages can be graphed in a sort of fever chart of how the public has thought the president was doing (see Figure 12.2). A number of factors seem to be especially important in determining presidential popularity, including the stage in the president's term of office, the state of the economy, and foreign policy crises.[58]

Historically, and with the exception of Donald Trump, most presidents have begun their terms of office with a majority of Americans—usually 60 percent or more—approving of how they are handling their job. Most presidents have tended to lose popularity as time passes. But this loss of popularity does not represent an inexorable working of time: Eisenhower, Reagan, and Clinton actually gained popularity during their second terms. Those who lose popularity do so in response to bad news. Good news generally makes presidents more popular.[59] Somewhat surprisingly, Donald Trump's approval rating did not improve in 2017 and 2018 despite the healthy performance of the U.S. economy.

presidential job approval rating
The percentage of Americans who believe the president is doing a good job.

BAD ECONOMY, POOR PRESIDENTIAL JOB APPROVAL

A woman in New York City in late 2009 shops for bargains before yet another retail store closure. This scene was repeated in cities and towns across the country as the nation suffered through a deep recession and jobless recovery from late 2007 through 2012.

As is almost always the case, a bad economy, especially joblessness and declining disposable income, led to blows to public approval of presidents and their parties. Is this fair? Should we judge presidents mainly on the state of the economy, or are there other matters that are equally as important?

FIGURE 12.2 TRENDS IN PRESIDENTIAL JOB APPROVAL, 1946–2018

Ratings of how well presidents are doing their jobs rise and fall in response to political, social, and economic events.

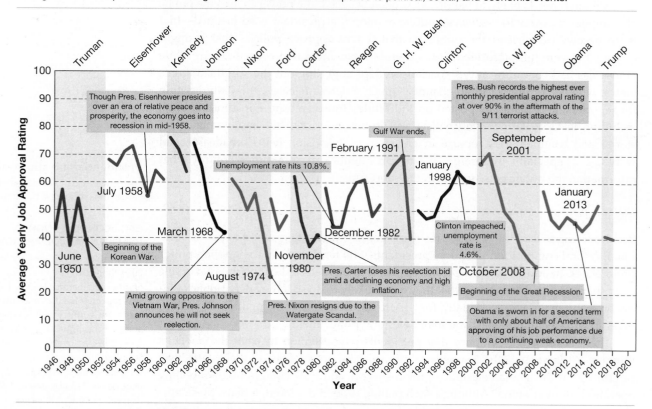

NOTE: Rating for 2018 is through August.

SOURCE: Data from Gallup surveys (graph based on average job approval for each year through August, 2018).

Successful military actions may sometimes add to presidential popularity, as Ronald Reagan happily discovered after the U.S. invasion of Grenada in 1982. The senior Bush's approval rating soared during the 1991 Gulf War, while the junior Bush's initial success in Afghanistan sustained his popularity. Conversely, an unsuccessful war is bad news for a president, as Harry Truman learned regarding the Korean War. Bad news from Iraq—perhaps in combination with the administration's apparent failures in the Hurricane Katrina disaster—steadily eroded George W. Bush's public approval after 2003. Bad news on the war and economic fronts at the same time can be especially lethal to a president's approval, as George W. Bush learned in 2008 when his rating reached a historic low in presidential polling.

THE PRESIDENCY: PRESIDENTS AND THE AMERICAN PEOPLE

When considering the role of the chief executive, the framers never intended that it be a democratic office. In creating the Electoral College, for example, they imagined an independent body whose members (or electors) would be chosen in a manner decided by state legislatures. For the most part, they understood that state legislatures would leave the responsibility of selecting electors to themselves rather than the people. The electors from the states would then meet to elect the president from among the nation's leading citizens, free from the pressures of public opinion. As Alexander Hamilton put it in *The Federalist* No. 68, "The immediate election [of the president] should be made by men most capable of analyzing the qualities adapted to the station, and acting under circumstances favorable to deliberation, and to a judicious combination of all the reasons and inducements which were proper to govern their best choice." Because presidents chosen in such a manner would not be beholden to the people for their election or reelection, they would not be overly concerned with or unduly influenced by the views of the mass public.

In addition, when designating the powers and responsibilities of the president in Article II of the Constitution, the framers evidently envisioned an office somewhat detached from national policy making, something like a constitutional monarchy, in which the officeholder would symbolize the nation but not do much in the way of running it. Although they gave the president important powers for conducting foreign affairs and defending the nation against civil unrest and invasion by foreign powers, they placed most national policy-making powers in Congress.

More than any other of the three branches of government in the Constitution created by the framers, the presidency has been democratized, with the changes so dramatic that the office would be hardly recognizable to them. As we have described this situation at various places in this chapter, the presidency has become a popular office, tied to the American people in a variety of important ways. Although the Electoral College remains in place—and can still have anti-majoritarian democratic outcomes, as in the 2000 and 2016 elections—for all intents and purposes, presidents are elected directly by the American people as a whole, the only national office (other than the vice president) carrying this distinction. As such, modern presidents are prone to claim the mandate of the people when governing, and the American people are prone, for their part, to see the president as the center of governance and the locus for their hopes and aspirations for the nation. Presidents have used these ties to the people as the foundation for expanding presidential powers in the course of responding to national problems and emergencies.

We also know that modern presidents pay close attention to what the public wants, following public opinion polls closely and commissioning their own. To be sure, presidents sometimes manipulate the public, especially in foreign and military affairs, where presidential constitutional powers are considerable and public scrutiny is lower, but in the end, presidents cannot succeed unless they enjoy strong public support.

THE EXPANDING PRESIDENCY

12.1 Trace the expansion of presidential power.

The American presidency began small; only a few 19th-century presidents (among them Jefferson, Jackson, Polk, and Lincoln) made much of a mark.

In the 20th century, however, as a result of the problems of industrialization, two world wars and the Cold War, and the Great Depression, presidential powers and resources expanded greatly. The presidency attained much of its modern design during Franklin Roosevelt's presidency.

The constitutional bases of the expansion of presidential responsibilities and power lie in the president's roles as chief executive, commander in chief, and chief diplomat.

Additional sources of presidential expansion come from public expectations, legislative grants of power, and the office's role as de facto legislative leader of the nation.

THE POWERS AND ROLES OF THE PRESIDENT

12.2 Identify the roles and responsibilities of the president.

Presidents play many roles, including chief of state, chief executive, domestic policy-making leader, foreign policy and military leader, and head of their political party.

Some of the president's roles are formally inscribed in the Constitution, but others have evolved through precedent, public expectations, and congressional actions.

THE PRESIDENT'S SUPPORT SYSTEM

12.3 Describe the organization and functions of the president's advisors.

The job of the president has become so complex and the range of the office's responsibilities are now so broad that occupants need a great deal of help carrying out their duties. The staff and agencies in the White House and the Executive Office Building that help presidents carry out their duties have grown to such an extent that they have come to be called the institutional presidency.

White House staff members are numerous and do such things as advise the president on domestic and national security policies, maintain relationships with Congress, convey the president's views to the media and the public, and help fashion legislation.

The main agencies in the Executive Office of the President advise and help the president carry out policies regarding the economy, the federal budget, and national security.

THE PRESIDENT AND CONGRESS: PERPETUAL TUG-OF-WAR

12.4 Analyze the conflict between the president and Congress.

The tug-of-war between the president and Congress is an inherent part of the constitutional design of our government as embodied in the separation of powers and checks and balances.

Presidents also have different constituencies than members of the House and Senate; the president is the only nationally elected office.

Representatives and senators often are elected at times when the president is not a candidate, so they may come to office propelled by a different public mood than what prevailed when the president was elected.

Conflict is exacerbated when there is divided government and high levels of partisanship.

THE PRESIDENT AND THE PEOPLE

12.5 Describe the relationship between the president and the American people.

The presidency has become a far more democratic office than the framers envisioned: the people play a more important role in the election of the president, and research shows that presidents listen to public opinion and respond to it most of the time (though they sometimes do not).

LEARN THE TERMS

chief of staff   A top adviser to the president who also manages the White House staff.

divided government   Control of the executive and the legislative branches by different political parties.

executive agreement   An agreement with another country signed by the president that has the force of law, like a treaty; does not require Senate approval; originally used for minor technical matters, now an important tool of presidential power in foreign affairs.

Executive Office of the President (EOP)   A group of organizations that advise the president on a wide range of issues; includes, among others, the Office of Management and Budget, the National Security Council, and the Council of Economic Advisers.

executive order   A rule or regulation for an executive agency or department issued by the president that has the force of law, based either on the constitutional powers of the presidency as chief executive or commander in chief or on congressional statutes.

habeas corpus   The legal doctrine that a person who is arrested must have a timely hearing before a judge.

institutional presidency   The permanent bureaucracy associated with the presidency, designed to help the incumbent of the office carry out their responsibilities.

national security adviser   A top foreign policy and defense adviser to the president who heads the National Security Council.

presidential job approval rating   The percentage of Americans who believe the president is doing a good job.

State of the Union   Annual report to the nation by the president, now delivered before a joint session of Congress, on the state of the nation and legislative proposals for addressing national problems.

treaty   A formal international agreement between two or more countries; in the United States, requires the "advice and consent" of the Senate.

unitary executive   Controversial constitutional doctrine which proposes that the executive branch is under the direct control of the president, who has all authority necessary to control the actions of federal bureaucracy personnel and units without interference from the other federal branches.

EXECUTIVE BRANCH ADVERSARIES

James Comey and the president he once served, Donald Trump. After Comey was fired by President Trump, he wrote an explosive book that led to public bickering between the two.

In what ways, if any, do revelations about the relationship of the president and important executive branch leaders add to the ability of the American public to hold the chief executive accountable?

THE EXECUTIVE BRANCH

CHAPTER OUTLINE AND LEARNING OBJECTIVES

HOW THE EXECUTIVE BRANCH IS ORGANIZED

13.1 Describe how the federal bureaucracy is organized.

WHAT DO BUREAUCRACIES AND BUREAUCRATS DO?

13.2 Identify the roles and responsibilities of the federal bureaucracy.

WHO ARE THE BUREAUCRATS?

13.3 Describe how the federal bureaucracy is staffed and determine how representative bureaucrats are of the American public.

POLITICAL AND GOVERNMENTAL INFLUENCES ON BUREAUCRATIC BEHAVIOR

13.4 Describe ways in which other political actors influence the federal bureaucracy.

THE AMERICAN BUREAUCRACY: CONTROVERSIES AND CHALLENGES

13.5 Describe how the unique structure of the American bureaucracy creates challenges for the implementation and enforcement of federal law.

REFORMING THE FEDERAL BUREAUCRACY

13.6 Identify ways to improve the effectiveness and responsiveness of the federal bureaucracy.

The Struggle for Democracy

Donald Trump, from the start of his presidency, has had a troubled relationship with the federal bureaucracy. Most notably, he has publicly and consistently criticized employees of the FBI, both its career officers and its leaders. In May 2017, he shocked the country by firing its director, James Comey. Comey responded by writing a revealing memoir in which he said President Trump's leadership is "ego driven and about personal loyalty." This sort of exchange between a former top-level bureaucratic official and the president is unheard of in recent administrations. There has also been unprecedented turnover among top-level appointed officials and lower-level civil servants, especially in the Department of State. Many of the appointed officials have left because of scandals or because of disagreements with President Trump. Scott Pruitt, Administrator of the Environmental Protection Agency, also recently resigned after a number of scandals came to light, including ones in which he rented a room from a lobbyist, and spent exorbitant sums on personal security. Additionally, President Trump has refused to nominate officials to serve in many key positions at various bureaucratic agencies.

Presidents have always had an uncomfortable relationship with the bureaucracy. Professional bureaucrats are only minimally accountable to the White House, while appointed officials are seen as representatives of the presidents in their departments or agencies. These people serve at the pleasure of the president and attempt to bend the actions of the bureaucracy they oversee to the preferences of the Administration. The unsettled relationship President Trump has with the bureaucracy is already having a number of important consequences. First, it is likely making it harder for the president to implement his policies because he does not have strong leaders in many important positions. Second, the federal bureaucracy is losing significant numbers of career civil servants who do not want to work in such a chaotic environment.[1] The result is that crucial, long-term institutional knowledge has been lost.

Many of the actions taken by President Trump are purposeful. Not only have many positions gone vacant, some of his most controversial bureaucratic officials are openly opposed to the mission of the agency they are leading. For example, the head of the Consumer Financial Protection Bureau requested a budget of zero dollars for his agency. This fits with the ideological orientation of the Republican Party, which is traditionally suspicious of the bureaucracy and often views it as an impediment to economic growth and the free market. Democrats see bureaucracies as a valuable tool in protecting average citizens from deception, fraud, or dangerous activities by private companies. By not appointing officials and causing resignations among career staff, the president is likely weakening the bureaucracy.

Besides the president, the bureaucracy must also answer to Congress. Because both chambers are currently controlled by Republicans, the institution has been unwilling to investigate most of the issues in the current administration or press the president on nominees. This approach is now standard—during the term of a same-party president, Congress tends to remain mostly hands-off, not wanting to embarrass the president. But, when the other party takes control of a chamber, as it inevitably does, members of the bureaucracy are typically called to account for their mistakes. Hearings are convened, investigations launched, budgets trimmed, and activities redirected. Now that Democrats control the House, expect wide-ranging and in-depth examinations of bureaucratic agencies such as the Environmental Protection Agency, the Treasury Department, and the Department of Commerce, the current and former heads of which Democrats suspect of corruption and enriching themselves through their positions. These committees have the power to call witnesses, request documents, and issue subpoenas, and most expect these investigations to proceed along party lines. After the election, President Trump initially struck a conciliatory tone, then threatened to take a "warlike posture" if Democrats were to conduct investigations into his financial dealings.

Battles over bureaucratic functions between Congress and the president, and between the parties occur because of our separated powers system. Each branch, and each chamber in Congress, fight for control, making it difficult for the bureaucracy to satisfy any of the institutions. This is one of the most important aspects that make the American bureaucracy uniquely unwieldy and difficult to control.

THINKING CRITICALLY **ABOUT THIS CHAPTER**

This chapter is about the executive branch of the federal government—often called the federal bureaucracy—responsible for carrying out programs and policies fashioned by Congress, the federal courts, and the president. We focus on how the executive branch is organized, what it does, and what effects its actions have on public policies and American democracy.

APPLYING THE **FRAMEWORK**

You will see in this chapter how the federal bureaucracy has grown over the years, primarily as a result of *structural* transformations in the economy and international position of the United States, but also because of the influence of *political linkage*–level actors and institutions, including voters, public opinion, and interest groups. Primary responsibility for many of the enduring features of the federal bureaucracy will be shown to be associated with our political culture and the Constitution.

USING THE **DEMOCRACY STANDARD**

Despite much speculation to the contrary, this chapter will demonstrate that the federal bureaucracy is fairly responsive to the American people, reacting in the long run to pressures brought to bear on it by the elected branches, the president, and Congress. On the other hand, bureaucrats in specific agencies, in specific circumstances, can be relatively insulated from public opinion, at least in the short and medium run. You will be asked to think about what this type of insulation from public opinion means, in terms of our democratic evaluative standard.

HOW THE EXECUTIVE BRANCH IS ORGANIZED

13.1 Describe how the federal bureaucracy is organized.

bureaucracy

A large, complex organization characterized by a hierarchical set of offices, each with a specific task, controlled through a clear chain of command, and where appointment and advancement of personnel is based on merit.

bureaucrat

A person who works in a bureaucratic organization.

Bureaucracy has always been a dirty word in American politics, implying red tape, inefficiency, and nonresponsiveness. To social scientists, however, **bureaucracy** and **bureaucrat** are neutral terms describing a type of social organization and the people who work in it. Bureaucracies are large organizations in which many people with specialized knowledge are organized into a clearly defined hierarchy of bureaus or offices, each of which has a specified mission. There is a clear chain of command and a set of formal rules to guide behavior. Appointment and advancement are based on merit rather than inheritance, power, or election. This is, of course, a model or "ideal type" traceable back to the German sociologist Max Weber;[2] in the real world, there are many variations.

Bureaucracy exists in a wide range of sectors, including government, private business (as in most large corporations), and the nonprofit sector, such as organizations like the Red Cross and the Girl Scouts of America. The fact that they are so common suggests that bureaucracy serves important purposes even if the popular mantra in business circles these days is to flatten hierarchies and be more nimble. One advantage of bureaucracy is its ability to organize large tasks like delivering Social Security checks, churning out automobiles from factories, delivering overnight packages, or fighting wars. Hierarchical organizations with clear chains of command are able to mobilize and coordinate the activities of thousands of people.

Another advantage of bureaucracies is the concentration of specialized talent found within them. When Apple wants to bring a new product to market, it has thousands of

Telephones

Baggage Claim

Gates 11 to 21

Security Check

Telephones

software engineers, product design specialists, and marketing experts on hand to do the necessary work, though it may at times subcontract work to other firms, many of which are also bureaucratic organizations. Similarly, when a pandemic threatens, the federal government is able to mobilize an impressively talented group of doctors and scientists at the National Institutes of Health and at the Centers for Disease Control and Prevention to find a solution and put it into effect.

The federal bureaucracy is contained within the executive branch as part of the president's constitutional role to enforce laws passed by Congress. The bureaucracy can be thought of as the mechanism through which presidents fulfill their constitutional mandate, though the Constitution neither specifies the number nor types of departments to be established. The framers apparently wanted to leave these questions to the wisdom of Congress and the president. Over the years, a large and complex bureaucracy was created to meet a wide range of needs. The most immediate reasons behind the transformation of the federal government's role and the growth of the bureaucracy have been political pressures—from public opinion, voters, parties, interest groups, business, and social movements—on government decision makers. The more fundamental reasons have been changes in such *structural factors* as the U.S. economy, the nation's population, and the role of the United States in the world, including involvement in war. We have already examined how *structural factors* have transformed the role and responsibilities of the federal government over the course of American history. The general result has been one of growth in the government's size and responsibilities with more bureaucrats overseeing increasingly complex bureaucratic agencies within different administrative agencies, creating a very complicated executive branch structure (see Figure 13.1).[3]

Cabinet-Level Departments

The most familiar and prominent bureaucracies are **departments** at the cabinet level. Currently, there are 15 cabinet level departments each headed by a secretary, with the exception of the Department of Justice, which is headed by the attorney general.

AIRPORT SECURITY

New national problems often bring new federal agencies to address them. The Transportation Security Agency (TSA) was created in the wake of the 9/11 terrorist attacks on the United States (in which airplanes were used to attack the World Trade Center and the Pentagon) to screen airline passengers. *Many critics believe the airport screening process is too expensive, intrusive, and ineffective. If this is true—it may not be, of course—how might we design bureaucratic agencies such as the TSA to be more nimble in meeting changing problems?*

departments
Generally the largest units in the executive branch, each headed by a cabinet secretary.

FIGURE 13.1 THE EXECUTIVE BRANCH OF GOVERNMENT

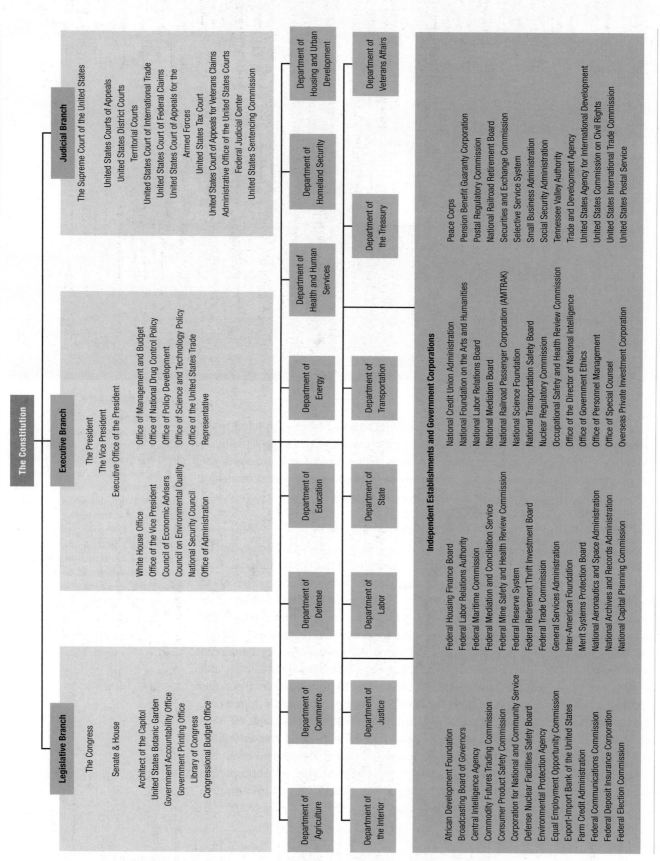

The Constitution

Legislative Branch

The Congress

Senate & House

Architect of the Capitol
United States Botanic Garden
Government Accountability Office
Government Printing Office
Library of Congress
Congressional Budget Office

Executive Branch

The President
The Vice President
Executive Office of the President

White House Office
Office of the Vice President
Council of Economic Advisers
Council on Environmental Quality
National Security Council
Office of Administration

Office of Management and Budget
Office of National Drug Control Policy
Office of Policy Development
Office of Science and Technology Policy
Office of the United States Trade
Representative

Judicial Branch

The Supreme Court of the United States

United States Courts of Appeals
United States District Courts
Territorial Courts
United States Court of International Trade
United States Court of Federal Claims
United States Court of Appeals for the
Armed Forces
United States Tax Court
United States Court of Appeals for Veterans Claims
Administrative Office of the United States Courts
Federal Judicial Center
United States Sentencing Commission

Department of Agriculture
Department of Commerce
Department of Defense
Department of Education
Department of Energy
Department of Health and Human Services
Department of Housing and Urban Development

Department of the Interior
Department of Justice
Department of Labor
Department of State
Department of Transportation
Department of the Treasury
Department of Veterans Affairs

Independent Establishments and Government Corporations

African Development Foundation
Broadcasting Board of Governors
Central Intelligence Agency
Commodity Futures Trading Commission
Consumer Product Safety Commission
Corporation for National and Community Service
Defense Nuclear Facilities Safety Board
Environmental Protection Agency
Equal Employment Opportunity Commission
Export-Import Bank of the United States
Farm Credit Administration
Federal Communications Commission
Federal Deposit Insurance Corporation
Federal Election Commission

Federal Housing Finance Board
Federal Labor Relations Authority
Federal Maritime Commission
Federal Mediation and Conciliation Service
Federal Mine Safety and Health Review Commission
Federal Reserve System
Federal Retirement Thrift Investment Board
Federal Trade Commission
General Services Administration
Inter-American Foundation
Merit Systems Protection Board
National Aeronautics and Space Administration
National Archives and Records Administration
National Capital Planning Commission

National Credit Union Administration
National Foundation on the Arts and Humanities
National Labor Relations Board
National Mediation Board
National Railroad Passenger Corporation (AMTRAK)
National Science Foundation
National Transportation Safety Board
Nuclear Regulatory Commission
Occupational Safety and Health Review Commission
Office of the Director of National Intelligence
Office of Government Ethics
Office of Personnel Management
Office of Special Counsel
Overseas Private Investment Corporation

Peace Corps
Pension Benefit Guaranty Corporation
Postal Regulatory Commission
National Railroad Retirement Board
Securities and Exchange Commission
Selective Service System
Small Business Administration
Social Security Administration
Tennessee Valley Authority
Trade and Development Agency
United States Agency for International Development
United States Commission on Civil Rights
United States International Trade Commission
United States Postal Service

SOURCE: U.S. Government Organization Manual.

All cabinet-level secretaries must be nominated by the president and confirmed by the Senate, and each department is meant to carry out the most essential government functions, as suggested by the first three to be established: War, State, and Treasury.

Departments vary greatly in size and internal organization. The Department of Agriculture, for example, has almost 50 offices and bureaus, whereas the Department of Housing and Urban Development has only a few operating agencies. They range in size from the Department of Defense, with about 742,000 employees (civilian) in 2016—not counting military contractors—to the Department of Education, with about 4,400 employees. Over the years, departments (and employees) were added as the need arose, as powerful groups demanded them, or as presidents and members of Congress wished to signal a new national need or to cement political alliances with important constituencies. The timeline in Figure 13.2 shows when each department was established. The newest department, Homeland Security, was created in the wake of the 9/11 terrorist attacks on the United States.

Subdivisions within cabinet departments are bureaus and **agencies**. Departmental bureaus and agencies are not only numerous but varied in their relative autonomy. In some departments, such as the Department of Defense, bureaus and agencies are closely controlled by the department leadership, and the entire department works very much like a textbook hierarchical model. In other cases, where the bureaus or agencies have fashioned their own relationships with interest groups and powerful congressional committees, the departments are little more than holding companies for powerful bureaucratic subunits.[4] During the long reign of J. Edgar Hoover, for example, the FBI did virtually as it pleased, even though it was (and remains) a unit within the Justice Department. Some departments have so many diverse responsibilities that central coordination is almost impossible to achieve. For example, the Department of Homeland Security has bureaus and agencies responsible for border control; immigration and citizenship; disaster relief and recovery; transportation security; and emergency preparedness against terrorist use of nuclear, biological, and other weapons. It also houses the U.S. Secret Service, for protection of the president and other high-profile public officials, and the U.S. Coast Guard, for protection and assistance for public and private maritime activities.[5]

agency
A general name used for a subunit of a cabinet department.

Independent Regulatory Commissions

Independent regulatory commissions such as the Securities and Exchange Commission, the Federal Communications Commission, and the Consumer Product Safety Commission, are responsible for regulating sectors of the economy in which it is judged that the free market does not work properly to protect the public interest. The commissions are "independent" in the sense that they stand outside the departmental structure and are protected against direct presidential or congressional control, making these agencies more removed from political pressures than other bureaucratic agencies. For some regulatory agencies, a commission made up of different individuals with long, staggered, and overlapping terms rather than a single director or agency head, is in charge. For example, the Federal Communications Commission (FCC) is headed by five commissioners, at least two of which must be from a different political party than the other three, helping to ensure the FCC does not become too partisan.

independent regulatory commission
An entity in the executive branch that is outside the immediate control of the president and Congress that issues rules and regulations to protect the public.

Independent Executive Agencies

Independent executive agencies report directly to the president rather than to a department- or cabinet-level secretary, though they typically have a head who is nominated by the president and confirmed by the Senate. They are usually created to give the president greater control in carrying out some executive function, or to highlight some particular public problem or issue that policy makers wish to address. The Environmental Protection Agency (EPA), for example, was given independent status to

independent executive agency
A unit of the executive branch outside the control of executive departments.

FIGURE 13.2   TIMELINE: CREATION OF EXECUTIVE BRANCH DEPARTMENTS AND SELECTED AGENCIES, INDEPENDENT COMMISSIONS, AND CORPORATIONS

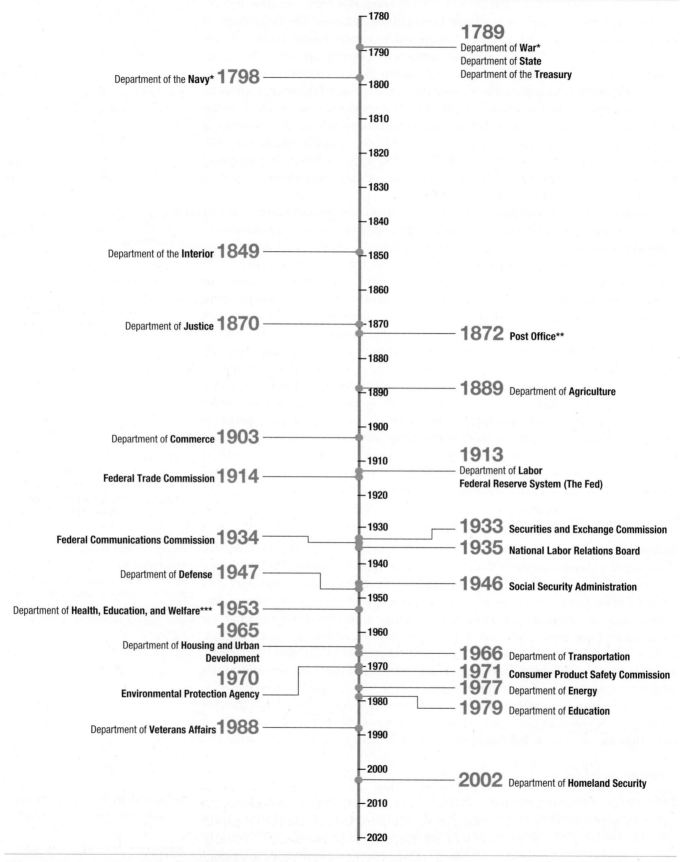

* Became part of newly formed Department of Defense in 1947

** Transformed into U.S. Postal Service, an independent agency, in 1970

*** Later split into Department of Education and Department of Health and Human Services

focus government and public attention on environmental issues and to give the federal government more flexibility in solving environmental problems. The head of the EPA is called an administrator, while the head of the Central Intelligence Agency, also an independent executive agency, is called the director.

Other Federal Bureaucracies

There are a number of other types of federal bureaucracies that exist but are less common. **Government corporations** are agencies that operate very much like private companies. They can sell stock, retain and reinvest earnings, and borrow money, for instance. They are usually created to perform some crucial economic activity that private investors are unwilling or unable to perform. The Tennessee Valley Authority, for example, was created during the Great Depression to bring electricity to most of the upper South; today it provides about 6 percent of all U.S. electrical power.[6] The U.S. Postal Service was transformed from an executive department to a government corporation in 1970 in the hope of increasing efficiency and becoming profitable (which it was, until the widespread usage of e-mail decreased the quantity of mail being sent). Amtrak is a government corporation that provides train service throughout the country.

Quasi-governmental organizations are hybrids of public and private organizations but differ from government corporations in a few ways. Most importantly, unlike government corporations, a portion of the board of directors are appointed by the private sector. Quasi-governmental organizations allow the government to be involved in a particular area of activity without exercising total control over it. The Federal Reserve Board (also called "The Fed") is the most well-known quasi-governmental organization and is composed of twelve regional banks but run by a board of governors and a chairman (all of whom serve overlapping, staggered terms) appointed by the president. The Fed is largely responsible for setting the nation's monetary policy and was a key player in preventing an economic collapse and restructuring the financial system in 2008 and 2009 during the Great Recession.

Lastly, the government runs a number of **foundations** that are separated from the rest of government to protect them from political interference with science and the arts. Most prominent are the National Foundation on the Arts and the Humanities and the National Science Foundation. Over the years, members of Congress and presidential administrations have tried on various occasions to redirect the activities of these foundations—for example, to deny grants for the support of controversial art projects or for certain areas of scientific inquiry—but such efforts, while not unimportant, have not undermined the autonomy of government foundations to the extent many critics have feared.

government corporation
A unit in the executive branch that operates like a private business but provides some public service.

quasi-governmental organization
An organization that has governmental powers and responsibilities but has substantial private sector control over its activities.

foundation
An entity of the executive branch that supports the arts or sciences and is designed to be somewhat insulated from political interference.

WHAT DO BUREAUCRACIES AND BUREAUCRATS DO?

13.2 Identify the roles and responsibilities of the federal bureaucracy.

Bureaucracies engage in a wide range of activities that are relevant to the quality of democracy in the United States and affect how laws and regulations work. Let's look at the more prominent and significant of these activities.

Executing Programs and Policies

The framers of the Constitution assumed that Congress would be the principal national policy maker and stipulated that the president and his appointees to administrative positions in the executive branch "shall take care that the laws be faithfully executed" (Article II, Section 2). For the most part, this responsibility is carried out routinely; mail is delivered, troops are trained, Social Security checks are processed, and foreign intelligence is collected. Any action taken by the executive branch bureaucracy in which it executes or carries out the law it is called **bureaucratic implementation**.

bureaucratic implementation
The actions taken by the bureaucracy in service of its mission of executing the laws of the United States.

Exercising Discretion

bureaucratic discretion

The ability of the bureaucracy to exercise its own judgment about how best to engage in implementation.

Executing the law is not as easy it sounds, however, because laws are almost always vague, incomplete, or short on details and practices the bureaucracy should use when implementing them. The lack of details in most laws gives the bureaucracy significant **discretion**, or the ability to determine how it should execute the laws passed by Congress.

It seems odd that Congress would intentionally pass ambiguous laws, but this may work to the public's advantage. Members of Congress may recognize a problem but have limited information about how to solve it, or they may disagree among themselves on the best solution and wish to delegate decision making to bureaucrats who are presumed to be experts within their policy area. This strategy also allows for greater flexibility because the bureaucracy can respond more quickly to a situation that Congress may not have foreseen when writing the bill. This perhaps is why Congress gave so much discretionary power to Bush's Treasury Secretary Henry Paulson to respond to the credit freeze and stock market collapse in fall 2008 when it passed the $700 billion Troubled Asset Relief Program (TARP). Vaguely written statutes and directives, then, leave a great deal of discretion to bureaucrats, but bureaucratic discretion is not always a good thing, as discussed below.

SIGNS OF THE TIMES

The bursting of the "housing bubble" and the subsequent wave of foreclosures led many Americans to wonder if Congress would do something to help. In a series of oversight committee hearings in 2009 and 2010, prominent Representatives and Senators pressed Fed and Treasury officials to give direct assistance to troubled homeowners from the previously passed TARP rescue package, which they did on a limited basis.

In what other circumstances might it make sense for the government to intervene in private markets, or should it always avoid doing this?

Regulating

One of the main ways bureaucracies use their discretion is through their power to write specific rules or regulations. Congress created the Environmental Protection Agency (EPA), for instance, and gave it a mission—to help coordinate the cleanup of the nation's air and water—but it left to the EPA the power to set the specific standards that communities and businesses must meet. The rules and regulations set by the EPA, and by all bureaucracies, have the force of law unless they are rescinded by Congress or overruled by the courts.

Critics of the federal bureaucracy believe there simply are too many rules and regulations. When candidates promise to "get government off our backs," they usually are referring to regulatory burdens, though taxes are also a target. Several attempts have

been made to roll back executive branch rule-making. **Cost-benefit analysis** requirements introduced under Ronald Reagan slow the rule-making process and have led to a decline in the number of rules issued. After a period of growth in federal regulations during the presidencies of George H. W. Bush and Bill Clinton, the second President Bush managed to cap further growth, consistent with his conservative philosophy (see Figure 13.3). Bush issued executive orders in 2007 mandating that agencies (1) determine and report why market forces are unable to address a problem before a new rule is issued and (2) appoint presidentially approved regulatory policy officers to review all proposed rules for compatibility with the administration's priorities. Barack Obama, more supportive of an active government, rescinded both of these Bush administration orders within the first 10 days of his new administration.[7] Today, Democrats tend to support more bureaucratic regulations, while Republicans tend to oppose them.

cost-benefit analysis
A method of evaluating rules and regulations by weighing their potential costs against their potential benefits to society.

Adjudicating

Congress has given some executive branch agencies the power to conduct quasi-judicial proceedings in which disputes are resolved. Much as in a court of law, the decisions of an administrative law judge have the force of law, unless appealed to a higher panel. The National Labor Relations Board (NLRB), for instance, adjudicates disputes between labor and management on matters concerning federal labor

FIGURE 13.3 GROWTH IN FEDERAL AGENCY RULES AND REGULATIONS

This graph shows the annual number of pages in the *Federal Register*, which is published daily and contains all new rules and changes to existing rules proposed by each and every executive branch agency. While not perfect, tracking its growth is an interesting way, widely used by scholars and journalists, to chart the course and scale of bureaucratic regulation in the United States. The graph shows the dramatic rise in regulations during the 1970s, the decline during the Reagan years, the slow increase in rule writing during the first Bush and Clinton presidencies, and a leveling out during George W. Bush's tenure in office. Rule writing increased slightly again under Barack Obama, but the first year of the Trump Administration shows a dramatic decline.

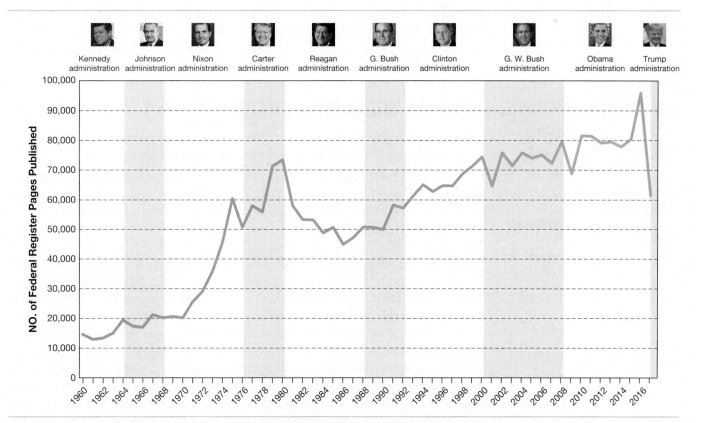

SOURCE: Office of the Federal Register, Tutorials, History, and Statistics, Federal Register Pages Published, 1936–2017.

laws. Disputes may involve claims of unfair labor practices, such as firing a labor organizer or disagreements about whether proper procedures were followed in filing for a union certification election. For example, recently, the NLRB has made decisions about whether college athletes are employees of their universities and eligible to form unions.

Often these disputes can be quite contentious, spilling over into the broader political arena. In 2011, after the Machinists Union struck at Boeing's Puget Sound plants, the company decided to open an assembly line for its new 787 Dreamliner airliner in nonunion South Carolina. The NLRB ruled that Boeing violated labor laws and ordered the company to move the work back to the state of Washington. Needless to say, political and business leaders, as well as many ordinary South Carolinians, were furious at the decision and demanded that Congress clip the wings of the NLRB. Congressional Republicans tried to do so using their legislative power, but to little effect. The NLRB later canceled its complaint when Boeing and the Machinists Union reached an agreement to move additional 787 (and 737) work back to Washington while keeping a production line in South Carolina.

Discretion and Democracy

It is quite clear, then, that bureaucrats exercise a great deal of discretion when implementing laws. There is no fixed set of orders received from Congress or the president they must follow, allowing opportunities for these unelected officials to exercise autonomy. Because bureaucrats make important decisions that have consequences for many individuals, groups, and organizations, we can say that they are policy makers. And, because they make the overwhelming majority of public policy decisions in the United States,[8] we can say they are important policy makers. They are *unelected* policy makers, however, and this fact should immediately alert us to some potential problems with regard to the practice of democracy.

Still, when the bureaucracy uses its discretion, regulatory, and adjudication powers well, it can move quickly to take important action, as when the Environmental Protection Agency forced Volkswagen to recall half a million vehicles for falsifying emissions claims, an issue we discuss in this chapter's Applying the Framework model (see Figure 13.5).

WHO ARE THE BUREAUCRATS?

13.3 Describe how the federal bureaucracy is staffed and determine how representative bureaucrats are of the American public.

There are two basic types of bureaucrats: civil service professionals and political appointees. Professional **civil service** bureaucrats work in the lower levels of the bureaucracy and obtain their jobs through a competitive application process, though this was not always the case. These professional bureaucrats often make a career of civil service and include postal workers, scientists working in government labs, or federal law enforcement agents. There are far fewer political appointees who work at the top levels of the bureaucracy and are nominated by the president and confirmed by the Senate. These individuals usually serve in the bureaucracy for a short period of time and offer direct political control over a bureaucratic agency.

Because of their importance as unelected policy makers, bureaucrats should be representative of the American public. But, because the public doesn't elect them and has no direct control over staffing, bureaucrats may be very different from the people demographically or may have very different preferences from the average American. In the sections that follow, we'll take a look at each of the different personnel systems in the executive branch and consider how well the American people are represented in their ranks.

civil service

Federal government jobs held by civilian employees, excluding political appointees.

The Merit System

Civil servants who work in the federal bureaucracy are selected on merit, on the basis of examinations, education credentials, and demonstrable skills. The merit system on which the government uses to choose employees has evolved in size and complexity in tandem with the federal bureaucracy itself.[9]

COMPETITIVE CIVIL SERVICE SYSTEM   From the election of Andrew Jackson in 1828 until the late 19th century, the executive branch was staffed through what is commonly called the **spoils system**. It was generally accepted that the "spoils of victory" belonged to the winning party. Winners were expected to clear out people who were loyal to the previous administration and to replace them with their own supporters. Bureaucrats obtained their jobs because they worked for the party and helped elect the party's candidates, not because they were qualified for the position.

Also known as **patronage**, the spoils system of appointment caused no great alarm in the beginning because of the small and relatively unimportant role of the federal government in American society. However, the shortcomings of the War Department and other bureaucratic agencies during the Civil War convinced many people that the federal personnel system needed to be reformed. Rampant corruption and favoritism in government service during the years after the Civil War gave an additional boost to the reform effort, as did the realization that the growing role of the federal government required more skilled and less partisan personnel. The final catalyst for change was the assassination in 1881 of President James Garfield by a person who, it is said, badly wanted a patronage job but could not get one.

The **Civil Service Act of 1883**, also known as the Pendleton Act, created a bipartisan Civil Service Commission to oversee a new system of appointments to certain executive branch posts on the basis of merit. Competitive examinations were to be used to determine merit. At first, the competitive civil service system included only about 10 percent of federal positions. Congress gradually extended the reach of the career civil service; today, it covers about 60 percent of roughly two million federal civilian employees (total federal employees does not include postal workers). In 1978, Congress abolished the Civil Service Commission and replaced it with two separate agencies, the Office of Personnel Management (OPM) and the Merit Systems

spoils system
The practice of distributing government offices and contracts to the supporters of the winning party; also called *patronage*.

patronage
The practice of distributing government offices and contracts to the supporters of the winning party; also called the *spoils system*.

Civil Service Act of 1883
Also known as the Pendleton Act, the law created the Civil Service Commission and began the process of changing the federal bureaucracy from the spoils or patronage system to the merit-based system.

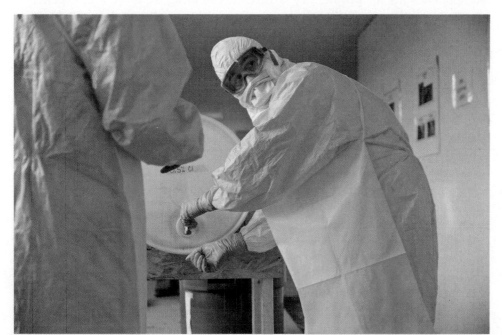

PREPARING FOR THE WORST
The federal government employs scientists, doctors, and other highly trained professionals to complete difficult and sometimes dangerous jobs. Here, a clinician sanitizes his hands after undergoing a Centers for Disease Control training on working with Ebola patients. The federal government is uniquely prepared to deal with any number of national and international crises, and depends on different types of professional bureaucrats to help carry out its mission.
Could situations which require highly trained experts, such as doctors or scientists, be better handled by private companies rather than the federal government?

Protection Board. The former administers the civil service laws, advertises positions, writes examinations, and acts as a clearinghouse for agencies that are looking for workers. The latter settles disputes concerning employee rights and obligations, hears employee grievances, and orders corrective action when needed.

AGENCY MERIT SYSTEMS Many federal agencies require personnel with particular kinds of training and experience appropriate to their special missions. For such agencies, Congress has established separate merit systems administered by each agency. The Public Health Service, for instance, recruits its own doctors and biomedical researchers. The Department of State has its own examinations and procedures for recruiting foreign service officers. The National Aeronautics and Space Administration (NASA) recruits scientists and engineers without the help of the OPM. About 35 percent of all federal civilian employees fall under these agency-specific merit systems.

Political Appointees

The highest policy-making positions in the federal bureaucracy (e.g., department secretaries, ambassadors, assistants to the president, leading officials in the agencies), about 4,000 in number, enter government service not by way of competitive merit examinations but by presidential appointment. About one-quarter of them—designated Executive Schedule appointees—require Senate confirmation.[10] These patronage positions, in theory at least, allow presidents to translate their electoral mandate into public policy by permitting him to put his people in place in key policy-making jobs. Top appointees who have the confidence of the president tend to become important policy makers and public figures in their own right. Treasury Secretary Timothy Geithner and Budget Director Peter Orszag, because of the central roles they played in President Barack Obama's economic recovery plans, achieved this status.

Most presidents use patronage not only to build support for their programs but also to firm up their political coalition by being sensitive to the needs of important party factions and interest groups. Ronald Reagan used his appointments to advance a conservative agenda for America and made conservative beliefs a prerequisite for high bureaucratic appointments.[11] President Clinton, by contrast, promised to make government "look more like America" and did so by appointing many women and minorities to top posts in his administration. Presidents also reserve important appointments for people they trust and who bring expertise and experience. John F. Kennedy appointed his brother and political confidant Robert ("Bobby") as Attorney General. George W. Bush was particularly eager to fill cabinet posts and his inner circle with people who had a great deal of experience in the upper reaches of the federal government: Donald Rumsfeld (Secretary of Defense), Colin Powell (Secretary of State in his first administration), and Condoleezza Rice (National Security Advisor) had all served in high-level positions for previous presidents. Barack Obama appointed a number of experienced Democratic operatives, and a few Republicans to his cabinet, though perhaps surprisingly, he was criticized for appointing too few women and minorities. President Trump has been slow to nominate individuals for many top-level officials. He claims this is by design, as a way to reduce the power of the bureaucracy, but it may also hinder his ability to translate his political preferences into bureaucratic action. He has also been unusually vocal about publicly criticizing his own officials, while sometimes contradicting them. One such instance occurred when Ambassador to the United Nations Nikki Haley announced new sanctions on Russia in the wake of a chemical attack by the Syrian government, only to have the White House imply she was "confused" the following day.[12] Haley disputed this, replying to reporters that she "doesn't get confused."

Presidents also want to find appointments for people who played important roles in their election, even if they are not policy experts.[13] Usually these appointments are

**THE CONSEQUENCES OF BUREAU-
CRATIC INEXPERIENCE**
Michael Brown attempts to explain his
agency's response to Hurricane Katrina
during a congressional hearing. Brown
resigned under pressure as head of
FEMA less than two weeks after the
hurricane hit.

to positions that are seen as easier or not particularly important. Ambassadorships
to wealthy European countries are particularly sought after by important campaign
donors. Appointing political friends to bureaucratic positions can be risky however, as
George W. Bush discovered when his director of the Federal Emergency Management
Agency (FEMA), Michael Brown, proved incompetent, with disastrous results for
New Orleans and the Gulf Coast following Hurricane Katrina.

In these highly partisan times, when the Senate is controlled by a different party,
it often holds up presidential nominations for executive branch positions (and judicial nominations as well) as a way to extract policy concessions from the president. In
response, presidents waited until Congress adjourned for the year in December or for
another long break to make so-called **recess appointments**, which the Constitution
allows.[14] The Senate began entering into pro forma session, where a single senator
acted as presiding officer and gaveled the Senate into business then out of business
every few days to avoid adjournment. In 2011, President Obama appointed members
of the National Labor Relations Board anyway during one of these pro forma sessions, arguing that the Senate was not in fact, in session. In 2014, the Supreme Court
rejected the president's argument, saying that pro forma sessions did not count as an
adjournment, severely limiting the president's power to make recess appointments
in the future. This ruling, combined with the new cloture precedent established by
Senate Democrats in 2013 requiring only fifty-one votes for approval of a bureaucratic nominee, means that recess appointments are likely to be less important in the
future. Presidents are more likely to get their way on their nominees and will not
need to resort to these desperate measures, especially when their party controls
the Senate.

recess appointments
Presidential action to temporarily fill
executive branch positions without
the consent of the Senate; done when
Congress is adjourned.

Top political appointees do not last very long. On average, they stay in office only
22 months; political scientist Hugh Heclo called them "birds of passage."[15] They leave
for many reasons. Most are accomplished people who see government service as only
a short-term commitment. Most make financial sacrifices. Many don't find the public notoriety appealing. Some find themselves the target of partisan campaigns that
leave them with damaged reputations. Many become frustrated by how difficult it is
to change and implement policy. Finally, important bureaucratic positions are very
difficult, and many people get burned out after a few years on the job. There has been,
by some measures, record turnover among President Trump's cabinet, with four of the
fifteen secretaries leaving their office in the first year. Scandals did in two of them, one

of them left to take a job in the White House, and the Secretary of State was fired over policy disagreements. There are controversies surrounding other secretaries as well and most observers expect additional resignations in the next year.[16]

How Different Are Civil Servants from Other Americans?

civil servants
Government workers employed under the merit system; not political appointees.

Civil servants are similar to other Americans across a wide range of characteristics.[17] Their education levels and regional origins are close to those of other Americans, for example, although they tend to be a little bit older (40 percent are over the age of 50)[18] and a little better paid (though higher-level civil servants still seriously lag behind their counterparts in the private sector), and they have better job security, retirement plans, and health insurance than most. Civil servants' political beliefs and opinions also are pretty close to those of the general American public, although they tend to favor the Democrats a bit more than the general public and are slightly more liberal on social issues than the national average, though this varies dramatically by agency.[19] Recent research in political science has shown that military oriented agencies such as the Army and Air Force are the most conservative bureaucracies, while the most liberal are agencies that serve social welfare or regulatory enforcement functions such as the EPA, NLRB, and the Department of Health and Human Services.[20] Women and minorities are very well represented (the latter are actually overrepresented), with women holding 43 percent of all nonpostal jobs and racial and ethnic minorities about 37 percent.[21] It is worth noting, however, that women and minorities are overrepresented in the very lowest civil service grades and are underrepresented in the highest. They also are far less evident in the special-agency merit systems (such as the Foreign Service and the FBI) and in the professional categories (scientists at the National Institutes of Health; doctors in the Public Health Service).[22]

POLITICAL AND GOVERNMENTAL INFLUENCES ON BUREAUCRATIC BEHAVIOR

13.4 Describe ways in which other political actors influence the federal bureaucracy.

Those who work in the bureaucracy must heed several important voices. The president's is the most important, but Congress, the courts, the public (including interest groups), and the press play a significant role in influencing what agencies do. The relationship between the president, Congress, and the bureaucracy if often called a **principal-agent relationship** where the principals, the president and Congress, give the agent, the bureaucracy, discretion to enforce federal laws, but also try to make sure the agent does not stray too far from the preferences of the principals. Figure 13.4 gives an overview of these several influences on bureaucratic behavior.

principal-agent relationship
The relationship between the president and Congress, who act as principals, with the bureaucracy, who is the agent, where the principals give the agent authority and discretion, but seek to ensure the agent still follows the wishes of the principals.

The President and the Bureaucracy

Being the nation's chief executive, the president is the formal head of the executive branch. But, the president's ability to control the executive branch is not unlimited. In fact, virtually every modern president has been perplexed by the discovery that he cannot assume that bureaucrats will do what he wants them to do.[23] Richard Nixon was so frustrated by his inability to move the federal bureaucracy that he came to think of it as an alien institution filled with Democratic Party enemies. His strategy was to intimidate bureaucrats or bypass them. He created the notorious "plumbers" unit in the White House to act as his personal domestic surveillance and espionage unit. Revelation of its activities was a factor leading the House Judiciary Committee

FIGURE 13.4 POPULAR CONTROL OF THE BUREAUCRACY: IMPERFECT
POPULAR SOVEREIGNTY

Popular control of the federal bureaucracy is complex, indirect, and only partially effective. The public does not elect government bureaucrats, and public opinion has little direct effect on their behavior. However, members of Congress and the president, both of whom are answerable to the electorate and attentive to public opinion, exercise an important influence on bureaucratic behavior. So, too, do federal judges. Because elected officials and judges often send mixed signals, however, some of the effectiveness of such controls is diminished.

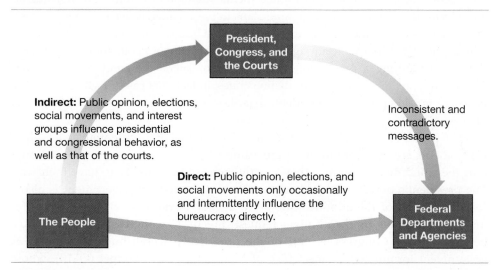

SOURCE: Federal Registry

to recommend approval of three articles of impeachment in the Watergate scandal. Thus far, President Trump's relationship with much of the bureaucracy has been combative, especially with the FBI as their investigation of Russian election-meddling has continued.

WHY PRESIDENTS OFTEN FEEL STYMIED BY THE BUREAUCRACY The sheer size and complexity of the executive branch is one reason presidents are frustrated by it. There is so much going on, in so many agencies, involving the activity of tens of thousands of people, that simply keeping abreast of it all is no easy task, even with a large White House staff to help. In addition, because of civil service regulations, presidents have no say about the tenure or salary of most federal bureaucrats beyond those they have appointed. When presidents want something to happen, they are unlikely to get instantaneous acquiescence from bureaucrats, who do not fear the president as they would fear a private employer. One of the important implications of the merit system is that it protects low-level bureaucrats from political interference from the president, but simultaneously makes it harder for the president to control the bureaucracy. Bureaucratic agencies also develop relationships with powerful interest groups and congressional committees, both of which insulate the bureaucracy from presidential control. Above all, presidents find that they are not the only ones with the authority to influence how officials and civil servants in the executive branch behave; they share this authority with Congress and often with the courts.

TOOLS OF PRESIDENTIAL LEADERSHIP Presidents do have a number of ways to encourage bureaucratic compliance.[24] Occasionally, because of a crisis or a widely shared national commitment, decisive bureaucratic action is possible, as during Roosevelt's New Deal era, Lyndon Johnson's first years as president, Ronald Reagan's first administration, and George W. Bush's war on terrorism.

Even during ordinary times, however, the president has important management tools. First, although it is difficult to measure precisely, the president's prestige as our only nationally elected political leader makes his wishes hard to ignore. When Theodore Roosevelt called the presidency a "bully pulpit," he meant that only the president can speak for the nation, set the tone for the government, and call the American people to some great national purpose. A popular president, who is willing and able to play this role, is hard to resist. Likewise, as President Trump has shown, public criticism of bureaucratic actions can bring unwanted media attention or controversy. Bureaucrats are citizens and respond like other Americans to presidential leadership. When a president chooses to become directly involved in some bureaucratic matter—for example, with a phone call to a reluctant agency head or a comment about some bureaucratic shortcoming during a press conference—most bureaucrats respond. Research done over many years in many agencies demonstrates, in fact, that career civil servants will generally go along with the president, regardless of whether they share his party or ideology.[25]

The power of appointment is also an important tool of presidential leadership.[26] If presidents are very careful to fill top administrative posts with people who support them and their programs, they greatly increase their ability to have their way. The president's power as chief budget officer of the federal government is also a formidable tool of the administration. No agency of the federal bureaucracy, for instance, can make its own budget request directly to Congress; its budget must be submitted to Congress as part of the president's overall budget for the U.S. government formulated by the Office of Management and Budget (OMB), whose director reports directly to the president. The OMB also has the statutory authority to block proposed legislation coming from any executive branch agency if it deems it contrary to the president's budget or program. But the budget process involves bargaining between the president and Congress, so although the president exercises some control through the power to submit the budget, Congress may change the president's request.

And finally, presidents have broad unitary powers to help control executive branch agencies, including regulatory review and executive orders. These tools allow the president to issue directions to the bureaucracy, which generally must be followed. Presidents who use these tools aggressively, such as George W. Bush under his theory of the **unitary executive** (see Chapter 12), are better able to control the bureaucracy.[27] Still, tight control by the president over the bureaucracy can be difficult to achieve. For example, though President Bush's staffers and agency appointees tried to edit and change the conclusion of several reports from government scientists on climate change, the information still found its way to the public through leaks to the news media and the appropriate people in Congress. Other presidents, including Barack Obama, increasingly have tried to centralize more power over the far-flung bureaucracy in the White House.[28] The White House staff has grown steadily larger and presidents, Barack Obama is a case in point, have become ever more enamored of so-called czars—as in "energy czar" or "anti-drug czar"—to oversee important policy areas that involve several departments, bureaus, and agencies. President Obama appointed Elizabeth Warren as a special advisor to oversee the creation of the new Consumer Financial Protection Bureau in 2011 as a way to bypass Senate Republican opposition to her.

unitary executive

Controversial constitutional doctrine that proposes that the executive branch is under the direct control of the president, who has complete authority control the actions of federal bureaucracy personnel and units without interference from the other federal branches.

Congress and the Bureaucracy

Some critics believe that Congress delegates entirely too much lawmaking to the executive branch.[29] As the president becomes more powerful and as the bureaucracy becomes larger, Congress has a harder and harder time exercising bureaucratic oversight. It cannot micromanage every issue; Congress lacks the time, resources, and expertise. Still Congress exercises considerable influence over the federal bureaucracy by legislating agency organization and mission, confirming or refusing to confirm presidential appointments, controlling the agency budget, and holding oversight hearings.

LEGISLATING AGENCY ORGANIZATION AND MISSION   Congress legislates the mission of bureaucratic agencies and the details of their organization. Through the law-making process, Congress alters bureaucratic structure or roles, and can undo a bureaucratic rule, though in practice, implementing any of these changes is difficult because the law must also be signed by the president or have enough support to override a veto. In 1999, for example, Congress passed a law requiring the Census Bureau to do the 2000 census by direct count, disallowing the use of statistical sampling, which the technical staff at the Bureau wanted to use. Congress also can and does create new departments, such as the Department of Homeland Security. The new department was created by Congress in 2002 after members of both parties in the House and Senate determined that the president's approach—an Office of Homeland Security in the White House Office—would not have the necessary authority and resources to coordinate the government's antiterrorism activities. After initial resistance, the president agreed and signed legislation creating the new cabinet-level department.

CONFIRMING PRESIDENTIAL APPOINTMENTS   In the past, the Senate almost always approved presidential nominations to top bureaucratic posts, but presidential success on these appointments, as you have seen, has decreased as divided government has become more common. Past or present, however, the Senate often uses the "advice and consent" process to shape policies in bureaucratic departments and agencies, not confirming the appointment until the nominee or the president promises policy changes, for example. The Senate on occasion may even reject presidential nominations or force them to be withdrawn, as it did in the case of Barack Obama's nominee for secretary of the Department of Health and Human Services. Tom Daschle,

BUDGET BLUDGEON

Republicans in the House in 2011, in a bid to roll back the power of labor unions in the airline industry, refused for a time to reauthorize the budget of the Federal Aviation Administration. This delayed scores of airport improvement projects across the country, including this near-completed airport expansion in Oakland, California.

Is controlling the budget of an agency the correct way for Congress to shape policies of executive branch agencies, or should Congress re-write laws instead?

a former Senate Minority leader, was forced to withdraw from consideration after it was discovered he had failed to properly pay his income taxes. Senate approval used to require sixty votes to invoke cloture, as is the case with the passage of bills, but delays caused by filibuster threats of nominees decreased after the Democratic-run Senate ended, in 2013, the use of the filibuster to hold up or prevent executive branch presidential nominations.

CONTROLLING THE AGENCY BUDGET   Congress can also use its control over agency budgets to influence agency behavior. In theory, Congress uses the budget process to assess the performance of each agency every year, closely scrutinizing its activities before determining its next **appropriation** (see Chapter 11), money given to the agency to operate. If a particular agency displeases Congress, its budget may be cut; if a new set of responsibilities is given to an agency, its budget is usually increased. Sometimes these agency budget actions are taken with the full concurrence of the president; often they are not. Congress sometimes lends a sympathetic ear and increases the budgets of agencies that are not favored by the president. In the 1980s, Congress consistently gave more money than President Reagan wanted given to the EPA, the National Institutes of Health, and the National Science Foundation. In 2011, in a bid to roll back airline workers' right to form labor unions, House Republicans temporarily blocked appropriations for the Federal Aviation Administration, halting airport improvement projects around the country, furloughing over four thousand FAA employees, and preventing the collection of more than $300 million in airport fees from the airlines.[30]

appropriation
Legal authority for a federal agency to spend money from the U.S. Treasury.

HOLDING OVERSIGHT HEARINGS   Oversight hearings are an important instrument for gathering information about the policies and performance of executive branch departments and agencies and a handy forum for conveying the views of the members of Congress to bureaucrats. There is a great deal of evidence that agency heads listen when the message is delivered clearly.[31]

Congress does not always speak with a single voice, however. Congress is a highly fragmented and decentralized institution, and its power is dispersed among scores of committees. Often, the activities of a particular bureaucratic agency are the province of more than a single committee or subcommittee, and the chances of receiving mixed signals from them are very high. A skilled administrator can often play these competing forces off each other and gain a degree of autonomy for his or her agency.

The Courts and the Bureaucracy

In our system of separation of powers and checks and balances, the federal judiciary also has a say in what bureaucratic agencies do.[32] It does so in a less direct manner than the president and Congress, to be sure, because the judiciary must wait for cases to reach it and cannot initiate action on its own. Nevertheless, the courts affect federal agencies on a wide range of issues. For example, executive branch agencies cannot violate the constitutional protections afforded to citizens by the Bill of Rights, so citizens who feel their rights have been violated have turned to the courts for relief on a variety of issues, including illegal searches, detentions without trials, denial of access to an attorney, harsh treatment by federal authorities, and National Security Agency (NSA) surveillance of telecommunications. Executive branch agencies are also obligated to treat citizens equally, that is, on a nondiscriminatory basis. The Small Business Administration (SBA) cannot deny loans to women or racial minorities, for example, nor can federal highway funds be denied to minority contractors.

The Administrative Procedure Act of 1946, which has been amended several times since, puts forth a set of procedures on how executive branch agencies must make their decisions.[33] Basically, the Act attempts to make sure that agencies are bound by the due process guarantees in the Fifth and Fourteenth Amendments; which means, in the end, that they cannot act capriciously or arbitrarily when carrying out their missions, whether distributing benefits, overseeing federal programs, enforcing regulations, or formulating new regulatory rules. The amended Act requires, among other things, that agencies give adequate notice of their actions, solicit comments from all interested parties, and act without bias or favoritism. Citizens, advocacy groups, and interest groups pay attention to decisions and rules from agencies that directly affect them, and it is quite common for them to turn to the courts when they feel that agencies have acted improperly. For example, the energy industry, including coal producers and other business groups, argued that the EPA did not have the authority under the Clean Air Act to regulate greenhouse gases as pollutants. The case eventually went to the Supreme Court in 2014 where a majority held the EPA could write new regulations limiting greenhouse emissions.

While the courts do not have a direct mechanism of control over the bureaucracy like the Congress and president do, and are thus not usually considered a principal of the bureaucracy, their actions can have effects on bureaucratic decisions. Bureaucracies spend significant time shaping rules and regulations in such a way as to avoid lawsuits from interested parties, or when a lawsuit is filed, to ensure that the judiciary upholds the bureaucratic action. A prominent recent example of this is the so-called travel ban, implemented by the Department of Homeland Security under direction from President Trump. The ban did not allow travelers from certain countries to enter the United States. It was repeatedly struck down by federal courts and repeatedly revised by the Department. The third version was heard by the Supreme Court in April 2018, and ruled constitutional in June by a 5–4 vote. The majority reasoned that the president's powers to secure the borders, as part of his overall national security mandate, allow him to ban immigrants from certain countries.

The Public and Press and the Bureaucracy

Usually, most Americans pay little attention to bureaucratic agencies. The public focuses mainly on the *content* of public policies rather than on their bureaucratic *implementation*. Americans have opinions about Social Security—level of benefits, eligibility, taxes, and so on—but do not concern themselves much with the Social

BERNANKE RETIRES AFTER A TUMULTUOUS EIGHT YEARS

Ben Bernanke, the Chairman of the Federal Reserve (seated), received both praise and criticism for how his agency handled the financial crisis in 2009 and 2010.

Security Administration per se. In general, then, the public does not directly know or think much about bureaucratic agencies.

There are exceptions to this generalization, however, and they usually occur when a bureaucracy fails to adequately perform its functions. The FBI and the CIA came under fire in 2005, for example, for intelligence failures relating to 9/11 and Iraq's purported weapons of mass destruction. Later in the same year, the Army Corps of Engineers and FEMA were strongly criticized during and after the Hurricane Katrina disaster, the first for its failed levee system in and around New Orleans, the second for its painfully slow and incomplete rescue and recovery operations. The Federal Reserve and Treasury were the brunt of widespread discontent in 2009 and 2010 because of a public perception that they were more interested in bailing out financial firms than in helping consumers. The NSA was widely criticized when private contractor Edward Snowden leaked details in 2013 of massive data gathering on American citizens and foreign leaders (even of close allies).

Needless to say, bureaucratic failures are pointed out to the public by the various news media and information sources. Scandals and disasters, we learned, are particularly attractive to the news media, so information about them gets to the public in short order through a variety of outlets, from television news broadcasts, blogs, and social media. The news media are also more likely to report goings-on in bureaucratic agencies when there is controversy—for example, the debate over the FBI's use of the USA Patriot Act to conduct surveillance on American citizens. The news media has an important role to play by notifying the public of bureaucratic failures, which in turn can motivate the president or Congress to fix things.

Interest Groups and the Bureaucracy

Because bureaucratic agencies make important decisions that affect many people, interest and advocacy groups pay a lot of attention to what they do and use a variety of lobbying tools to influence these decisions. Groups lobby Congress, for example, to shape the missions of executive branch departments and agencies, as environmental organizations did to give the EPA authority over development in wetland areas. Groups also lobby bureaucratic agencies directly when they appear before them to offer testimony on proposed rules. (Public comment is required in many agencies before binding rules can be issued.) Although various environmental, labor, and consumer advocacy associations regularly offer formal comment on rules, the process is dominated by businesses and economic interests that often get their way.[34] A strong body of evidence suggests that business interest groups are deeply involved in the actual process of rule-writing.[35] When Mark Zuckerberg, the founder of Facebook, testified in front of Congress about potential privacy violations at the social networking site, Senator Lindsey Graham asked Zuckerberg if he would help Congress write legislation to regulate the use of private data at Facebook and other sites.[36]

To see how the interplay between interest groups and bureaucratic agencies works, we use our pyramid framework to explore an example of a successful corrective action taken by the Environmental Protection Agency. The EPA was established in the 1970s during the Nixon administration in response to public demand for enforcement of environmental regulations. The agency used its discretion to develop rules governing car emissions and greenhouse gases. As a result of EPA requirements, car manufacturers have been forced to develop cleaner cars with lower emissions, while still responding to consumer demands for performance. Volkswagen, apparently in an effort to increase sales and become the largest car maker in the world, installed devices in many of its vehicles designed to cheat emissions tests. In Figure 13.5, we apply our framework model to the Volkswagen emissions scandal, uncovering the *structural, linkage,* and *government factors* that led the EPA, in its enforcement role, to force Volkswagen to recall its tampered-with cars.

FIGURE 13.5 APPLYING THE FRAMEWORK: EPA TAKES ACTION AGAINST VOLKSWAGEN

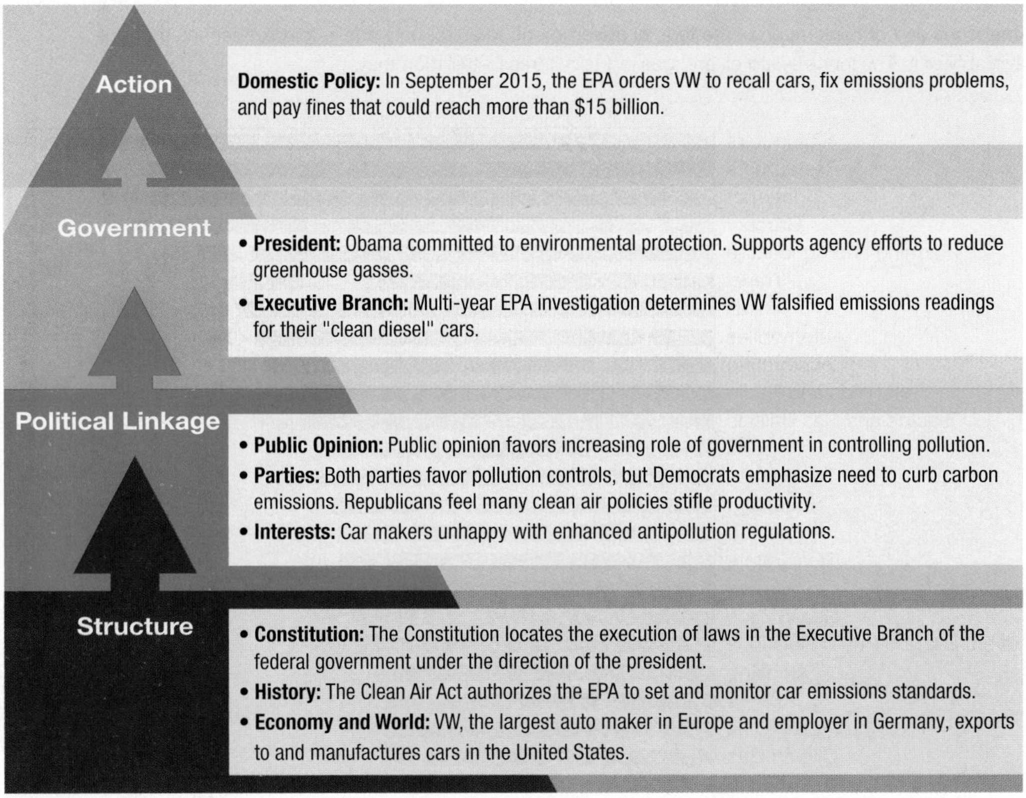

Action

Domestic Policy: In September 2015, the EPA orders VW to recall cars, fix emissions problems, and pay fines that could reach more than $15 billion.

Government

- **President:** Obama committed to environmental protection. Supports agency efforts to reduce greenhouse gasses.
- **Executive Branch:** Multi-year EPA investigation determines VW falsified emissions readings for their "clean diesel" cars.

Political Linkage

- **Public Opinion:** Public opinion favors increasing role of government in controlling pollution.
- **Parties:** Both parties favor pollution controls, but Democrats emphasize need to curb carbon emissions. Republicans feel many clean air policies stifle productivity.
- **Interests:** Car makers unhappy with enhanced antipollution regulations.

Structure

- **Constitution:** The Constitution locates the execution of laws in the Executive Branch of the federal government under the direction of the president.
- **History:** The Clean Air Act authorizes the EPA to set and monitor car emissions standards.
- **Economy and World:** VW, the largest auto maker in Europe and employer in Germany, exports to and manufactures cars in the United States.

© Edward S. Greenberg

THE AMERICAN BUREAUCRACY: CONTROVERSIES AND CHALLENGES

13.5 Describe how the unique structure of the American bureaucracy creates challenges for the implementation and enforcement of federal law.

The **federal bureaucracy** in America is different from government bureaucracies in other democratic nations. Structural influences such as the American political culture and the constitutional rules of the game have a great deal to do with these differences. Despite the complaints and jokes about federal bureaucracy, in many areas bureaucrats serve competently and with surprising efficiency. This is not to say, of course, that bureaucracy is unproblematic; it is to say that the American rhetorical distaste for bureaucracy tends to hide some of its benefits, especially when considering some of the challenges unique to the American bureaucracy.

federal bureaucracy

The totality of the departments and agencies of the executive branch of the national government.

Hostile Political Culture

Americans generally do not trust their government and government leaders, nor do they have much confidence that government can accomplish most of the tasks assigned to it. They believe on the whole that the private sector can usually do a better job and most of the time want responsibilities lodged there rather than with government. Figure 13.6 shows how poorly the federal government was regarded by the American public in 2015, compared to various private sector industries. At the same time, when difficulties or emergencies occur—whether economic recessions, natural disasters, or terrorist attacks—they want the federal government to be ready and able to respond.

FIGURE 13.6   PUBLIC PERCEPTION OF DIFFERENT INDUSTRIES (PERCENTAGE OF PUBLIC WITH POSITIVE VIEWS)

Americans do not think much of the federal government. In 2015, only one in four Americans thought favorably of it. The long-reviled oil and gas industry fares better than that.

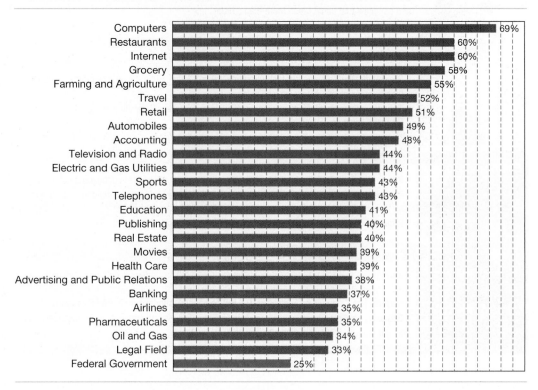

SOURCE: Jeffery M. Jones, "Americans' Views of Oil and Gas Industry Improving," Gallup, August 24, 2015.

This generally hostile environment influences the American bureaucracy in several important ways that, paradoxically, make it more difficult for it to respond when needed. For one thing, our public bureaucracy is surrounded by more legal restrictions and is subject to more intense legislative oversight than bureaucracies in other countries.[37] Because civil servants have so little prestige, moreover, many of the most talented people in our society do not aspire to work in government. In many other democratic countries, by way of contrast, civil service is highly respected and attracts talented people. In France, Britain, and Germany, for example, the higher civil service positions are filled by the top graduates of the countries' elite universities on the basis of rigorous examinations and are accorded enormous prestige. In France, the main feeder institution for higher positions in the government, the Ecole Nationale d'Administration, accepted only 80 students out of 1,352 applicants in 2009.[38] Not surprisingly, given the elite educations required for these posts and the prestige accorded to civil servants, people of decidedly upper-class and aristocratic backgrounds fill the top civil service posts in France, Great Britain, and Germany. Finally, the American system of dividing bureaucratic positions between high-level political appointees and low-level civil servants is not true in other democracies. This may make Americans more skeptical of the bureaucracy as the most high-profile positions are closely aligned with political parties and elected officials.

Incoherent Organization

Our bureaucracy is an organizational hodgepodge. It does not take the standard pyramidal form, as bureaucracies elsewhere do. There are few clear lines of control, responsibility, or accountability. Some executive branch units have no relationship at all to other agencies and departments. As one of the leading students of the federal bureaucracy once put it, other societies have "a more orderly and symmetrical, a more prudent, a more cohesive and more powerful bureaucracy," whereas we have "a more internally competitive, a more experimental, a noisier and less coherent, a less powerful bureaucracy."[39] Our bureaucracy was built piece by piece over the years in a political system without a strong central government. Bureaucracies in other democratic nations were often created at a single point in time by powerful political leaders, such as Frederick the Great in Prussia and Napoleon in France.[40]

Divided Control

Adding to the organizational incoherence of our federal bureaucracy is the fact that it has two bosses—the president and Congress—who are constantly vying with one another for control. In addition, the federal courts often constrain bureaucratic operations and decisions. No other democratic nation has opted for this arrangement. Because the executive and legislature are not separated in parliamentary democracies, civil servants are accountable to a single boss, a cabinet minister appointed by the prime minister, and to the parliamentary majority elected by the people, rather than multiple principals.[41]

REFORMING THE FEDERAL BUREAUCRACY

13.6   Identify ways to improve the effectiveness and responsiveness of the federal bureaucracy.

How can we improve the federal bureaucracy? The answer depends on what a person thinks is wrong and what needs improving. Let's look at some possibilities.

Scaling Back Its Size

If the problem with the federal bureaucracy is perceived to be its size, there are two ways to trim government activities: slimming them down and transferring activities to others, usually states and private sector contractors. Each solution has its own set of problems.

CUTTING THE FAT   For observers who worry that the federal bureaucracy is simply too big and costly, mainly due to bloat and waste, the preferred strategy is what might be called the "meat ax" approach. Virtually every presidential candidate today

WHAT IS WRONG WITH THE WATER?

The Flint Water Crisis demonstrates the importance and limitations of the federal bureaucracy. The City of Flint, Michigan changed its water supply in 2014 resulting in lead contamination in the tap water. Officials estimate from 6,000 to 12,000 children may have been exposed to lead, which causes a number of serious health effects. Officials from the local and state bureaucracies, as well as from the EPA, have been held responsible for not ensuring the water was safe.

What steps should the public take to ensure the federal bureaucracy is satisfying its mission and performing competently, especially when it comes to public health or environmental issues?

promises to "cut the fat" if elected. Bill Clinton made such a promise during the 1992 presidential campaign, and he carried through after his election. In the early weeks of his administration, he ordered that one hundred thousand federal jobs be eliminated within four years, that freezes be placed on the salaries of government workers, that cost-of-living pay adjustments be reduced, and that the use of government vehicles and planes be sharply restricted. Needless to say, this approach probably doesn't do much to enhance the morale of federal government employees, who receive the clear message in these sorts of actions that they are held in low regard by political leaders and the public. As noted earlier in the chapter, President Trump has simply refused to nominate individuals for a substantial number of appointed positions.

To some extent, recent efforts to cut the size and cost of the bureaucracy have worked; the number of federal employees has diminished since the Ford administration when considered in relationship to the size of the U.S. population (see Figure 13.7). The cuts have taken place even as the government initiated new programs. One way this has been done is to off-load many activities and their costs to the states; for example, the No Child Left Behind testing requirement forced them to hire more people in order to comply with federal law, without providing enough federal money to fully compensate the states.

There is a risk to "cutting the fat" when it goes too far. With fewer employees and money, bureaucracies are less able to provide the public goods demanded by voters: fewer campgrounds may be available in national parks, the Food and Drug

---

FIGURE 13.7 NEW GOVERNMENT EMPLOYEES AT THE FEDERAL, STATE, AND LOCAL LEVEL

While the absolute number of federal employees has been fairly constant for a long time and has actually declined as a proportion of the U.S. population, the number of state and local government employees has grown substantially. This may be one reason why such a concerted effort was made by Republican-controlled state governments to cut back the number of public employees after their anti–big government party's substantial victories across the country in the 2010 elections.

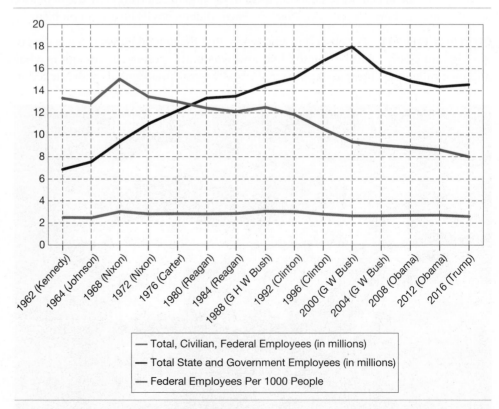

- Total, Civilian, Federal Employees (in millions)
- Total State and Government Employees (in millions)
- Federal Employees Per 1000 People

SOURCE: U.S. Census Bureau. The numbers for federal employees include those in the Postal Service.

Administration may take longer to examine and approve new drugs, and the Army Corps of Engineers may slow the pace of repairing levees along important waterways.

PRIVATIZING   A much-discussed strategy for scaling back the federal bureaucracy is to contract out some of its functions and responsibilities to the private sector.[42] This **privatization** approach is based on two beliefs:

- Private business can almost always do things better than government does.
- Competitive pressure from the private sector will force government agencies to be more efficient.

Privatization has actually been happening for many years. For example, the Defense Department does not produce its own weapons systems but uses an elaborate contracting system to design, build, and purchase fighter planes, submarines, and missiles from private corporations. In Iraq, the Defense Department depended on private contractors, including companies such as Halliburton and its subsidiary Kellogg Brown and Root, to feed and house soldiers, fight oil field fires, rebuild damaged oil pipelines, construct telephone networks, and interrogate detainees.[43] The U.S. Army Corps of Engineers uses private contractors to build and maintain levees and clear waterways. Homeland Security has contracted with Boeing to build a high-tech security system along the U.S.-Mexican border. The troubled rollout of HealthCare.gov occurred because multiple private contractors carried out portions of the job with no one in government or in the private sector closely monitoring and coordinating their activities. To fix the site's problems, the administration turned to private contractors.

While it is evident that contracting out has been expanding dramatically, the exact number of people working on a contract basis for the federal government is hard to determine. But expanded it has; money in the federal budget for private contracts rose

privatizing
The process of turning over certain government functions to the private sector.

SECURING THE PREMISES
Private contractors, such as this armed civilian providing security at an Afghan hospital during a visit from a reconstruction team, now serve roles in combat theatres formerly carried out by the U.S. armed forces. Often, they operate under different rules than regular soldiers. *How might this sometimes create problems for American foreign policy?*

37 percent between 2005 and 2010 to reach \$538 billion,[44] though the total fell back to \$445 billion in 2014 as Washington turned its attention to shrinking how much government spends. That is still a considerable amount of money for government work carried out by private-sector firms and employees. According to Paul Light, the leading expert in this area, the number of private contractor jobs done for departments and agencies of the executive branch stood at around 7.5 million in 2007, about four times more than the total of federal civilian employees.[45]

Advocates of privatizing want to expand the process, turning over to private companies functions such as the postal system, the federal prisons, and air traffic control. Critics worry that privatizing government carries significant costs.[46]

- Some matters seem so central to the national security and well-being that citizens and officials are unwilling to risk that the private sector will necessarily do the job well or at all. A good example is the transfer of the responsibility for screening airline passengers and baggage from the airlines to a new government agency, the Transportation Security Administration, after 9/11.

- Private business firms might not be willing to provide services that are unprofitable. Delivering mail to remote locations is a service that the U.S. Postal Service provides but private companies would not be able to carry out because it is too costly.

- A private business under government contract is several steps removed from political control, and the normal instruments of democratic accountability, however imperfect, might not be as effective in controlling private business as they are in controlling government agencies. The voice of the public, expressed in public opinion polls or elections, might not be heard with much clarity by private companies, particularly if they are the only supplier of some essential service.

- Private contractors may not be bound by many of the regulations and statutes that apply to other executive branch employees. For example, the military apparently has depended a great deal on private contractors to interrogate detainees in Afghanistan, Iraq, and Guantanamo Bay, believing perhaps that contractors could use methods not sanctioned for use by active service military personnel. After abuses were uncovered involving security personnel working in Iraq for Blackwater Security Consulting International, the Pentagon said it was tightening the rules under which its contractors worked.

- Citizens are not customers, and privatization tends to serve the latter. A citizen in a democracy usually requires not only satisfaction with a product or service like a customer; but also equity, transparency, and accountability as required by our constitutional rules.

Becoming More Businesslike

red tape
Overbearing bureaucratic rules and procedures.

If the problem with the federal bureaucracy is perceived to be the inefficiencies of its operations and excessive **red tape**, then the key to reform might be to reinvent governmental bureaucracy along businesslike lines. President Clinton turned over the responsibility for "reinventing government" to Vice President Al Gore at the beginning of his administration. The term "reinventing government" comes from a popular and influential book by that name written by David Osborne and Ted Gaebler,[47] although the ideas for these reforms come from advocates of what is called "the new public management."[48] "Reinventing" advocates propose transforming the federal bureaucracy not only by cutting the fat and privatizing (as discussed in the preceding section), but also by introducing business principles into the executive branch. They believe government agencies will provide better public services if they are run like private businesses: using pay-for-performance to determine salaries, for example, or focusing more on customer needs. Despite efforts to make bureaucracies more businesslike, there is little evidence that this improves government service.[49]

Protecting Against Bureaucratic Abuses of Power

Many people believe the problem with a bureaucracy the size, shape, and power of our present one is that it is potentially unresponsive to the public and a dangerous threat to individual liberty. The preferred solution has been closer control over the bureaucracy by elected political bodies and by clear legislative constraints. Accordingly, many legislative enactments have tried to keep bureaucratic activity within narrow boundaries. The Freedom of Information Act of 1966 was designed to enhance the ability of the press and private citizens to obtain information about bureaucratic policies and activities. The Ethics in Government Act of 1978 strengthened requirements of financial disclosure by officials and prohibitions against conflicts of interest. Some reformers would like to see greater protection provided for **whistle-blowers**: bureaucrats who report corruption, financial mismanagement, abuses of power, or other official malfeasance.

A potentially important innovation has been the rapid growth in what has been called e-government (and sometimes, "Google your government"), a reform based on a statute passed in 2006, that requires the OMB to make more information available online in a user-friendly database for public inspection of bureaucratic activities and expenditures. People could go, for example, to stimulus.gov to track where their economic stimulus dollars were being spent after Congress passed the bill in 2009. Data.gov is a rich source for all things related to keeping tabs on what government is doing and how well it is doing it. Then there are a legion of government employees and contractors like Edward Snowden who release information to media organizations and to online sites such as WikiLeaks.

whistle-blowers
People who bring official misconduct in their agencies to public attention.

Increasing Presidential Control

One suggestion for reform of the federal bureaucracy is to have it more closely controlled by elected representatives of the people. This suggestion follows directly from the principle of popular sovereignty, which requires that the elected representatives of the people closely oversee the bureaucracy. Popular sovereignty implies that administrative discretion should be narrowed as much as possible and that elected officials should communicate clear directions and unambiguous policies to bureaucratic agencies. (Note that this goal is very different from the one envisioned by the advocates of privatization and reinventing government.) Some advocates of popular sovereignty have argued that the president is the only public official who has an interest in seeing that the bureaucracy *as a whole* is well run and coherently organized. Accordingly, one suggestion for reform is to increase the powers of presidents so that they can be the chief executive, in fact and not just in name. This is the view of the president and the bureaucracy shared by many liberals who admire the leadership of Franklin Roosevelt during the Great Depression and World War II, and many conservatives who advocated so strongly for the concept of the unitary executive during George W. Bush's two terms. Of course, Congress tends to resist this, believing that as the elected officials closest to the people, it should be trusted with bureaucratic oversight.

THE EXECUTIVE BRANCH: DOES THE BUREAUCRACY ADVANCE OR HINDER DEMOCRACY?

The framers of the Constitution would no doubt be surprised by the great expansion in the responsibilities of the national government and the growth in the size of the bureaucracy required to carry out these responsibilities. Although they believed they had put in place constitutional provisions to restrain the size and reach of the national government—federalism, separation of powers, and checks and balances—they failed to account for the substantial democratization of the American republic or for structural changes demanding increased government involvement: urbanization, scientific and technological innovations, economic crises, the emergence of the United States as a superpower, and the need to provide national security in an interconnected world.

But as it has grown in size and reach, the federal bureaucracy has also grown more democratic in many ways. For one thing, most of what government bureaucrats do is carry out the missions defined for them by elected public officials, namely, Congress and the president, who are quite attentive to public opinion. And for the most part, civil servants are very much like other Americans, both in their demographic makeup and in what they think the government should be doing.

On the other hand, there are many ways in which the bureaucracy falls short in terms of democracy. Bureaucrats enjoy substantial discretion in carrying out their missions—much of what they do in the federal bureaucracy goes largely unnoticed, making popular control difficult. For one thing, there are so many decisions being made and rules being issued that no one could possibly keep track of them all. Moreover, many of the rules issued by bureaucrats and decisions made by them are highly technical in nature, with only specialists and experts paying very close attention. Finally, the elite and big business backgrounds of most high-level presidential appointees must cause some concern for those who care strongly about democratic responsiveness.

While democratic theorists may not be comfortable with every aspect of bureaucratic growth, the expansion of the role of government in American life, and the creation of the bureaucratic machinery associated with this expansion, is testament to the impact of democratic forces in American politics. Government has taken on new responsibilities in large part because of the demands of the people over many years. The bureaucracy that emerged to carry out these new government responsibilities has sometimes seemed inefficient and at cross purposes, probably best explained by the separation of powers and checks and balances designed by the framers.

HOW THE EXECUTIVE BRANCH IS ORGANIZED

13.1 Describe how the federal bureaucracy is organized.

The federal bureaucracy is comprised of cabinet departments, agencies and bureaus within departments, independent agencies, government corporations and foundations, independent regulatory commissions, and quasi-governmental organizations such as the Federal Reserve Board.

WHAT DO BUREAUCRACIES AND BUREAUCRATS DO?

13.2 Identify the roles and responsibilities of the federal bureaucracy.

The executive branch has grown in size and responsibility over the course of our history. This growth is a consequence of a transformation in the conception of the proper role of government because of economic and social structural changes.

Bureaucrats are involved in three major kinds of activities: executing the law, regulating, and adjudicating disputes. In each of these, they exercise a great deal of discretion.

Although bureaucracy is not a popular concept in the American political tradition, we have created a sizable one. The reason is partly that bureaucratic organizations have certain strengths that make them attractive for accomplishing large-scale tasks like preparing for war and delivering retirement checks.

WHO ARE THE BUREAUCRATS?

13.3 Describe how the federal bureaucracy is staffed and determine how representative bureaucrats are of the American public.

Bureaucrats in the merit services are very much like other Americans in terms of demographic characteristics and attitudes. Political appointees (the most important bureaucratic decision makers) are very different from their fellow citizens, coming from more elite backgrounds.

Because they are unelected policy makers, democratic theory demands that we be concerned about who the bureaucrats are.

POLITICAL AND GOVERNMENTAL INFLUENCES ON BUREAUCRATIC BEHAVIOR

13.4 Describe ways in which other political actors influence the federal bureaucracy.

Though bureaucrats are technically independent of influences beyond the bureaucratic chain of command and the rules and regulations that define their agency missions and operations, bureaucrats are in fact influenced by other political and governmental actors and institutions, including the president, Congress, and the courts as well as public opinion and interest groups.

THE AMERICAN BUREAUCRACY: CONTROVERSIES AND CHALLENGES

13.5 Describe how the unique structure of the American bureaucracy creates challenges for the implementation and enforcement of federal law.

Compared to public bureaucracies in other rich democracies, ours in the United States operates in a more hostile political/culture environment where anti–big government attitudes are widespread, it is less coherently organized, and it has several masters in addition to the chief executive (the president).

REFORMING THE FEDERAL BUREAUCRACY

13.6 Identify ways to improve the effectiveness and responsiveness of the federal bureaucracy.

Proposals to reform the executive branch are related to what reformers believe is wrong with the federal bureaucracy. Those who worry most about size and inefficiency propose budget and personnel cuts, privatization, and the introduction of business principles into government. Those who want to make democracy more of a reality propose giving more control over the bureaucracy to the president and diminishing the role of interest groups.

Problems with the bureaucracy, while real, are either exaggerated or the result of forces outside the bureaucracy itself: the constitutional rules and the struggle between the president and Congress.

LEARN THE TERMS

agency   A general name used for a subunit of a cabinet department.

appropriation   Legal authority for a federal agency to spend money from the U.S. Treasury.

bureaucracy   A large, complex organization characterized by a hierarchical set of offices, each with a specific task, controlled through a clear chain of command, and where appointment and advancement of personnel is based on merit.

bureaucratic discretion   The ability of the bureaucracy to exercise its own judgment about how best to engage in implementation.

bureaucrat   A person who works in a bureaucratic organization.

bureaucratic implementation   The actions taken by the bureaucracy in service of its mission of executing the laws of the United States.

civil servants   Government workers employed under the merit system; not political appointees.

civil service   Federal government jobs held by civilian employees, excluding political appointees.

Civil Service Act of 1883   Also known as the Pendleton Act, the law created the Civil Service Commission and began the process of changing the federal bureaucracy from the spoils or patronage system to the merit-based system.

cost-benefit analysis   A method of evaluating rules and regulations by weighing their potential costs against their potential benefits to society.

departments   Generally the largest units in the executive branch, each headed by a cabinet secretary.

federal bureaucracy   The totality of the departments and agencies of the executive branch of the national government.

foundation   An entity of the executive branch that supports the arts or sciences and is designed to be somewhat insulated from political interference.

government corporation   A unit in the executive branch that operates like a private business but provides some public service.

independent executive agency   A unit of the executive branch outside the control of executive departments.

independent regulatory commission   An entity in the executive branch that is outside the immediate control of the president and Congress that issues rules and regulations to protect the public.

patronage   The practice of distributing government offices and contracts to the supporters of the winning party; also called the *spoils system*.

principal-agent relationship   The relationship between the president and Congress, who act as principals, with the bureaucracy, who is the agent, where the principals give the agent authority and discretion, but seek to ensure the agent still follows the wishes of the principals.

privatizing   The process of turning over certain government functions to the private sector.

quasi-governmental organization   An organization that has governmental powers and responsibilities but has substantial private sector control over its activities.

recess appointments   Presidential action to temporarily fill executive branch positions without the consent of the Senate; done when Congress is adjourned.

red tape   Overbearing bureaucratic rules and procedures.

spoils system   The practice of distributing government offices and contracts to the supporters of the winning party; also called *patronage*.

unitary executive   Controversial constitutional doctrine that proposes that the executive branch is under the direct control of the president, who has all authority necessary to control the actions of federal bureaucracy personnel and units without interference from the other federal branches.

whistle-blowers   People who bring official misconduct in their agencies to public attention.

**CHANGING THE BALANCE
OF THE COURT**

When strong conservative Samuel Alito
joined the Court in 2006, replacing
moderate conservative Sandra Day
O'Connor, it changed the ideological
balance of the Court on a wide range
of issues. Because the stakes were
so high, the battle in the Senate over
his confirmation was contentious
and attracted a large audience to his
televised testimony before the Judiciary
Committee.

*Should ideology figure in at all in
presidential Supreme Court nominations
and Senate confirmation votes? Or are
ideological considerations inescapable
in appointments to the Supreme Court?
If so, how does this affect the practice of
democracy in the United States?*

THE COURTS

The Struggle for Democracy

THE BATTLE FOR THE COURTS

Tension filled the hearing room as Samuel Alito, President Bush's strongly conservative nominee for a position on the U.S. Supreme Court, began testifying before the Senate Judiciary Committee on January 9, 2006. Knowing that federal courts were deciding cases having to do with the most contentious issues of the day—including presidential powers in times of war, affirmative action, LGBTQ rights, the relationship between church and state, the role of the federal government in relationship to the states, and more—Republican and Democratic partisans and conservative and liberal advocacy groups were mobilized to fight over Alito's nomination.

Lurking in the background was the Democrats' threat to filibuster the nomination, meaning that Alito's confirmation would need sixty votes, not a simple majority of fifty-one. Republicans claimed the filibuster could not be used when the Senate was exercising its constitutional "advice and consent" duty on judicial nominations. Most Democrats believed it was the only way to prevent the accession of judges to the federal bench who would threaten hard-won rights and protections, particularly a woman's right to terminate her pregnancy.

Partisan tensions over the judicial filibuster had been festering for years. In 2003, Republicans fell seven votes short of the sixty votes needed to end Democratic filibusters blocking Senate votes on several very conservative Bush federal judicial nominees. Republicans were furious, saying they were ready to proceed with the so-called nuclear option ending filibusters on judicial nominations.[1] Tensions grew in 2005 after Democrats announced they would use the filibuster to block the nomination of conservative jurist Priscilla Owen for the Fifth Circuit Court of Appeals. Republican Majority Leader Bill Frist (R-TN) again warned he would begin the process of outlawing the filibuster for judicial confirmation votes. Democrats countered with a threat to tie up the business of the Senate for the foreseeable future if Frist took this step.

Into the fray stepped the so-called gang of fourteen, a group of Republican and Democratic moderates who worked out a compromise. Wielding enormous power because their fourteen votes would be decisive on any vote related to this issue, they agreed that the judicial filibuster could be used only in undefined "extraordinary circumstances" when considering nominations to federal district and circuit courts. Under the agreement, the Senate confirmed the long-delayed nominations of Priscilla Owen and two additional nominees but took no action on two other nominees who presumably fit the "extraordinary circumstances" requirement that would allow Democrats to use the filibuster. Crucially, the compromise agreement left the filibuster in place for Supreme Court nominations.

Talk of a filibuster circulated among Democrats and liberal advocacy groups on the nomination to the Supreme Court of Samuel Alito because he was to replace the retiring Sandra Day O'Connor, a relatively moderate voice and swing vote on the Court who played an important role in protecting abortion rights and affirming the use, under certain circumstances, of affirmative action in higher education admissions. In the end, however, perhaps exhausted by years of struggle over the issue in the Senate and Alito's skilled testimony before the Judiciary Committee, the Democrats were unable to mount much of a challenge and he was confirmed on January 31, 2006.

As predicted by almost everyone, Alito's ascension to the Court swung it sharply in a conservative direction on issues ranging from civil rights to environmental protection, regulation of abortions, class-action lawsuits, and the role of corporations in campaign finance,[2] all matters examined in this and later chapters. The fundamental balance on the Court was not affected much when Obama nominee Sonia Sotomayor joined the Court in 2009 because she was a liberal replacing a liberal, David Souter, who retired. The same thing was true regarding the appointment of Elena Kagan in 2010; she was a liberal replacing a liberal stalwart, John Paul Stevens, so the balance on the Court was unaffected. The key appointment in determining the balance of power on the

Court remained that of Alito replacing O'Connor in 2006, which created a solid conservative 5–4 majority under the able leadership of Chief Justice Roberts.

When conservative stalwart Antonin Scalia died in early 2016, it seemed likely that the Court would change direction.[3] An appointment by President Barack Obama would have created a 5–4 liberal majority, something Republicans were loath to let happen. Various Republican senators announced they would refuse to even consider Obama's widely respected nominee, Merrick Garland, during an election year (a concern that is nowhere mentioned in the Constitution) and Senate Majority Leader Mitch McConnell refused to even schedule a hearing for him. Their hope was that the 2016 election would produce a Republican president and maintain a GOP majority in the Senate, both of which happened. The end of the filibuster on all federal judicial nominees, including those to the Supreme Court, came with the nomination by President Trump of conservative jurist Neil Gorsuch. Believing that the Garland seat was stolen by the Republicans, Democrats invoked the filibuster to block Gorsuch. As expected, McConnell then invoked the nuclear option, ending the use of the filibuster for Supreme Court appointments. The Gorsuch nomination was approved by the Senate on April 7, 2017, by a vote of 54–45. Had the filibuster not been set aside, he would not have taken his seat on the Court.

*   *   *   *   *

In the system of separated powers and federalism created by the framers, the judicial branch, most especially the Supreme Court, assesses, in cases that come before it, the legitimacy of actions taken by the other two branches and by the states in light of the Constitution. It also can decide disputes on the meaning of laws passed by Congress. Although the Supreme Court does not legislate or regulate on its own, its decisions strongly influence the overall shape of federal and state policies in a number of important areas. As such, the Supreme Court is a key national policy maker, and an important political actor in Washington, every bit as much a part of the governing process as the president and Congress.[4]

THINKING CRITICALLY **ABOUT THIS CHAPTER**

This chapter is about the judicial branch of the federal government, with a special focus on the Supreme Court. We examine how the federal judiciary and Supreme Court are organized, what they do in the American political and government systems, and what effects their actions have on public policies and American democracy.

APPLYING THE **FRAMEWORK**

You will see in this chapter that the Supreme Court is embedded in a rich *governmental–political linkage–structural environment* that shapes its behavior. The other branches of government impinge on and influence its composition, deliberations, and rulings; *political linkage institutions* such as elections, interest groups, and social movements matter; and structural factors such as economic and social change influence its agenda and decisions.

USING THE **DEMOCRACY STANDARD**

This chapter describes how an unelected Supreme Court makes important decisions about public policies, raising questions about the degree to which popular sovereignty and majority rule prevail in our system. You will see that the Court often turns its attention to cases that involve issues of political equality and liberty, so essential to the existence of a healthy representative democracy.

THE FOUNDATIONS OF JUDICIAL POWER

14.1 Describe the constitutional and political foundations of federal judicial power in the United States.

> The judicial Power of the United States shall be vested in one supreme Court, and in such inferior Courts as the Congress may from time to time ordain and establish.
> —U.S. CONSTITUTION, ARTICLE III, SECTION 1

> We are under a Constitution, but the Constitution is what the judges say it is, and the judiciary is the safeguard of our liberty and our property under the Constitution.
> —CHIEF JUSTICE CHARLES EVANS HUGHES (1907)

The place of the Court in our system of separation of powers and checks and balances is the result of constitutional provisions, Court interpretations, and the actions and reactions of other political actors. Following is a discussion of the foundations of its most important power, judicial review.

Constitutional Design

The Constitution speaks only briefly about the judicial branch and doesn't provide much guidance about what it is supposed to do or how it is supposed to go about its job. The document says little about the powers of the judicial branch in relationship to the other two federal branches or about its responsibilities in the area of constitutional interpretation. Article III, which establishes the federal judicial branch, is considerably shorter than Articles I and II, which focus on Congress and the president. It creates the office of "chief justice of the United States," it states that judges shall serve life terms, it specifies the jurisdiction of the Supreme Court (to be explained later), and it grants Congress the power to create additional federal courts as needed.

Article III of the Constitution is virtually devoid of detail,[5] but the few requirements that are stated are very important. For example, the Constitution requires that federal judges serve "during good behavior," which means, in practice, until they retire or die in office, as Chief Justice William Rehnquist did in 2005 at the age of 81. Because impeachment by Congress is the only way to remove federal judges, the decision about who will be a judge is an important one because they are likely to serve for a very long time. Article III also states that Congress cannot reduce the salaries of federal judges once they are in office. This provision was designed to maintain the independence of the judiciary by protecting it from legislative intimidation.

Judicial Review

judicial review

The power of the Supreme Court to declare actions of the other branches and levels of government unconstitutional.

Extremely interesting is the Constitution's silence about **judicial review**, the long-established power of the Supreme Court to declare state and federal laws and actions null and void when they conflict with the Constitution.[6] Debate has raged for many years over the question of whether the framers intended that the Court should have this power.[7]

The framers surely believed that the Constitution ought to prevail when other laws were in conflict with it. But did they expect the Supreme Court to make the decisions in this matter? Jefferson and Madison thought that Congress and the president were capable of rendering their own judgments about the constitutionality of their actions. Alexander Hamilton, however, believed that the power of judicial review was inherent in the notion of the separation of powers and was essential to balanced government. As he suggested in *The Federalist* No. 78, the very purpose of constitutions is to place limitations on the powers of government, and only the Court can ensure such limits in the United States. The legislative branch, in particular, is unlikely to restrain itself without the helping hand of the judiciary.

There is reason to believe that Hamilton's view was the prevailing one for a majority of the framers.[8] They were firm believers, for instance, in the idea that there was a "higher law" to which governments and nations must conform. Their enthusiasm for written constitutions was based on their belief that governments must be limited in what they could do in the service of some higher or more fundamental law, such as that pertaining to individual rights. The attitudes of the time, then, strongly supported the idea that judges, conversant with the legal tradition and free from popular pressures, were best able to decide when statutory and administrative laws were in conflict with fundamental law.[9]

JUDICAL REVIEW ESTABLISHED: *MARBURY V. MADISON*   Chief Justice John Marshall boldly claimed the power of judicial review for the U.S. Supreme Court in the case of *Marbury v. Madison* in 1803.[10] The case began with a flurry of judicial appointments by President John Adams in the final days of his presidency, after his Federalist Party had suffered a resounding defeat in the election of 1800. The apparent aim of these so-called midnight appointments was to establish the federal courts as an outpost of Federalist Party power (federal judges are appointed for life) in the midst of rising Jeffersonian sentiment. After the 1800 election, control of the presidency and the Congress was firmly in Republican hands.

William Marbury was one of Adams's midnight appointments, but he was less lucky than most. His judgeship commission was signed and sealed, but it had not been delivered to him before the new administration took office. Jefferson, knowing what Adams and the Federalists had been up to, ordered Secretary of State James Madison not to deliver the commission. Marbury sued Madison, claiming that the secretary of state was obligated to deliver the commission and asked the Supreme Court to issue a *writ of mandamus,* a legal order commanding Madison to do so.

Marshall faced a quandary. If the Court decided in favor of Marbury, Madison would almost surely refuse to obey, opening the Court to ridicule for its weakness. The fact that Marshall was a prominent Federalist might even provoke the Jeffersonians to take more extreme measures against the Court. But if the Court ruled in favor of Madison, it would suggest that an executive official could defy without penalty the clear provisions of the law.

Marshall's solution was worthy of Solomon. The Court ruled that William Marbury was entitled to his commission and that James Madison had broken the law in failing to deliver it. By this ruling, the Court rebuked Madison. However, the Court simultaneously ruled that it could not compel Madison to comply with the law because the Judiciary Act of 1789, which granted the Court the power to issue writs of mandamus, was unconstitutional. The act was unconstitutional, Marshall said, because it expanded the **original jurisdiction** of the Supreme Court, as defined in Article III.

original jurisdiction
The authority of a court to be the first to hear a particular kind of case.

ADVOCATES OF JUDICIAL REVIEW
Although the Constitution is silent on the issue of judicial review, many of the Founders probably agreed with Alexander Hamilton (right), who argued that the Supreme Court's power to interpret the Constitution and declare state and federal laws and actions unconstitutional is inherent in the notion of the separation of powers. However, it was not until the Supreme Court's 1803 *Marbury v. Madison* decision that Chief Justice John Marshall (left) affirmed the Court's power of judicial review.
How might the absence of the power of judicial review hinder the classic American system of checks and balances?

On the surface, the *Marbury* decision was an act of great modesty. It suggested that the Court could not force the action of an executive branch official. Beneath the surface, however, the Court's decision in *Marbury*, in claiming that judicial review was the province of the judicial branch alone, was not modest in the least. In Marshall's written opinion, "It is emphatically the province and duty of the judicial department to say what the law is." In making this claim, he was following closely Hamilton's argument in *The Federalist* No. 78.

JUDICIAL REVIEW INVOKED Until quite recently, the Supreme Court used the power of judicial review with great restraint, perhaps recognizing that its regular use would invite retaliation by the other two branches. Judicial review of a congressional act was not exercised again until 54 years after *Marbury* and was used to declare acts of Congress unconstitutional only about 241 times from then through 2013. However, the Court has been much less constrained about overruling the laws of states and localities; it did so more than 1,100 times during this same period.[11]

During the 1990s and early 2000s, the Rehnquist Court was much more inclined to review and overturn congressional actions, especially in cases involving federalism and the powers of Congress under the commerce clause, trimming back the power of the federal government relative to the states. Indeed, it invalidated congressional actions at a rate double that of the Warren Court of the 1960s, considered by many to be the most "activist" Court since the early 1930s.[12]

The Court has been less inclined to exercise judicial review on presidential actions, though some important ones have occurred during our history.[13] In recent years, however, the Court seems more willing to do so. On four occasions between 2004 and 2006, when George W. Bush was president and Sandra Day O'Connor had yet to leave the Court, it invalidated presidential actions pertaining to the treatment of detainees designated as enemy combatants.[14] With a conservative 5–4 majority in control of the Court and a Democratic president in office, it issued a number of rulings curbing presidential powers. In 2014, it ruled that President Obama had abused his power to make recess appointments to the executive branch. In 2015, it halted the EPA's action

DETENTION

Though the Court initially deferred to the president, military authorities, and Congress on how such detainees should be treated and how long they can be held in custody, it has since 2004 allowed greater access of suspected terrorism detainees to certain legal protections and to the American judicial system. In this photograph, a detainee captured in the first months on the war against the Taliban in Afghanistan is "escorted" to his cell at Guantanamo Bay, Cuba, by military police.

Did the Court go too far in allowing a range of legal protections for terrorism detainees? Should presidents be given wide latitude in providing national security or should Congress and the Court act as checks on presidential actions?

to limit toxic emissions from coal-fired power plants under provisions of the Clean Air Act, dealing a blow to one of President Obama's most cherished initiatives.

JUDICIAL REVIEW AND DEMOCRACY Judicial review involves the right of a body shielded from direct accountability to the people—federal judges are appointed, not elected, and serve for life (barring impeachment for unseemly, unethical, or illegal behavior)—to set aside the actions of government bodies whose members are elected. Many believe that judicial review has no place in a democratic society. One prominent democratic theorist has described the issue this way:

> But the authority of a high court to declare unconstitutional legislation that has been properly enacted by the coordinate constitutional bodies ... in our system, the Congress and the president—is far more controversial.... The contradiction remains between imbuing an unelected body—or in the American case, five out of nine justices on the Supreme Court—with the power to make policy decisions that affect the lives and welfare of millions of Americans. How, if at all, can judicial review be justified in a democratic order?[15]

Political scientists and legal scholars use the phrase the "counter-majoritarian difficulty," coined by Alexander Bickel in 1962, to describe this enduring problem in the American political system; Bickel described judicial review as a "deviant institution in American democracy."[16] On the other hand, some observers believe that judicial review is the only way to protect the rights of political and racial minorities, to check the potential excesses of the other two government branches and the states, and to preserve the rules of the democratic process.

Many political scientists believe that the problem of democratic accountability of a nonelected judiciary with life tenure is less dire than it seems on the surface because the Supreme Court and other federal courts are influenced, directly and indirectly, by elected officials, public opinion, and other important actors in American society.[17] We will revisit this issue later in the chapter.

THE FEDERAL COURT SYSTEM: JURISDICTION AND ORGANIZATION

14.2 Describe the structure of the federal judiciary.

Our country has one judicial system for the national government (the federal court system) and another in each of the states. The federal court system is comprised of district courts, circuit courts of appeal, and the Supreme Court, and each state has a similar system. In each state, courts adjudicate cases on the basis of the state's own constitution, statutes, and administrative rules.[18] In total, the great bulk of laws, legal disputes, and court decisions (roughly 99 percent) are located in the states. Most important political and constitutional issues, however, eventually reach the federal courts. This chapter focuses on the federal courts. The following sections look at the jurisdiction of the federal courts and the organization of the federal court system.

The Jurisdiction of the Federal Courts

The jurisdiction of the federal judiciary—that is, the kinds of cases they have the authority to hear and make rulings about—include the following:

- The Constitution, including cases involving disputes about the meaning of some clause or provision in the document such as freedom of speech in the First Amendment, the scope of the commerce clause, or the power of the president to make recess appointments to the executive branch

- Federal statutes, including disputes about the meaning of a law passed by Congress and signed by the president, such as the extent to which the EPA can require gas mileage standards for automobiles
- Ambassadors and diplomats, including disputes about the meaning and extent of diplomatic immunity
- Treaties such as hearing cases about the extent to which states must follow the provisions of a treaty that the United States signs with a foreign government
- Admiralty and maritime issues, that is, disputes between parties that involve shipping and commerce on the high seas
- Controversies in which the U.S. government is a party, including suits brought against a government agency for a perceived violation of some fundamental freedom such as speech or ownership and use of private property
- Disputes between the states, including cases involving the proper location of borders between states or the split of sales taxes between states when products are bought, sold, and shipped across state lines
- Disputes between a state and a citizen of another state, including cases like those involving same-sex marriage in which a person claims that he or she has not been accorded equal protection when travelling to or moving to a different state.
- Disputes between a state (or citizen of a state) and foreign states or citizens, including most usually, claims that a person or firm in another country is infringing on a copyright or patent.

The Organization of the Federal Court System

The only court specifically mentioned in the Constitution's Article III is the U.S. Supreme Court. The framers left to Congress the tasks of designing the details of the Supreme Court and establishing "such inferior courts as the Congress may from time to time ordain and establish." Beginning with the Judiciary Act of 1789, Congress has periodically reorganized the federal court system. The end result is a three-tiered pyramidal system (see Figure 14.1), with a handful of offshoots. At the bottom are ninety-four U.S. district courts, with at least one district in each state. In the middle are thirteen U.S. courts of appeals. At the top of the pyramid is the U.S. Supreme Court. These courts are called **constitutional courts** because they were created by Congress under Article III. Congress has also created a number of courts to adjudicate cases in highly specialized areas of concern, such as taxes, monetary claims against the government, and maritime law. These courts were established under Article I, which specifies the duties and powers of Congress, and are therefore called **legislative courts**.

U.S. DISTRICT COURTS   Most cases in the federal court system are first heard in one of the ninety-four U.S. district courts. District courts are courts of original jurisdiction, that is, courts where cases are first heard. U.S. district courts do not hear appeals from other courts. They are also trial courts; some use juries—either **grand juries**, which bring indictments, or **petit (trial) juries**, which decide cases—and in some, cases are heard only by a judge.

Most of the business of the federal courts takes place at the district level. In 2017, more than 374,000 cases were filed; roughly 80 percent of them were civil cases, and 20 percent were criminal cases.[19] Civil cases include everything from antitrust cases brought by the federal government, to copyright infringement suits (as when Apple sued Amazon for its use of the term "Appstore" on the Amazon website), and commercial and contract disputes between citizens (or businesses) of two or more states. Criminal cases include violations of federal criminal laws such as bank robbery, interstate drug trafficking, and kidnapping.

---

constitutional courts

Federal courts created by Congress under the authority of Article III of the Constitution.

legislative courts

Highly specialized federal courts created by Congress under the authority of Article I of the Constitution.

grand juries

Groups of citizens who decide whether there is sufficient evidence to bring an indictment against accused persons.

petit (trial) juries

Juries that hear evidence and sit in judgment on charges brought in civil or criminal cases.

FIGURE 14.1 THE FEDERAL COURT SYSTEM

The federal court system is a three-tiered pyramidal system, with the Supreme Court at the top. Below it are thirteen U.S. courts of appeals and ninety-four U.S. district courts, with at least one district in each state. Additional courts hear cases in highly specialized areas such as taxes, international trade, and financial claims against the U.S. government.

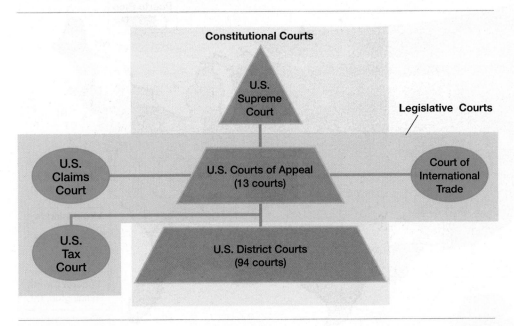

SOURCE: Administrative Office of the U.S. Courts, "About Federal Courts: Court Role and Structure," *Annual Report 2015.*

Most civil and criminal cases are concluded at this level. In a relatively small number of disputes, however, one of the parties to the case may feel that a mistake has been made in trial procedure or in the law that was brought to bear in the trial, or one of the parties may feel that a legal or constitutional issue is at stake that was not taken into account at the trial stage or was wrongly interpreted. In such cases, one of the parties may appeal to a higher court—a U.S. Court of Appeals.

U.S. COURTS OF APPEALS (CIRCUIT COURTS) The United States is divided into twelve geographic **circuit courts** (see the map in Figure 14.2) that hear appeals from U.S. district courts. The U.S. Court of Appeals for the District of Columbia (the Twelfth Circuit), not only hears appeals from the U.S. district court but also is charged with hearing cases arising from rule making by federal agencies like the Securities and Exchange Commission and the National Labor Relations Board. A thirteenth circuit court, also located in Washington, D.C.—the U.S. Court of Appeals for the Federal Circuit—hears appeals from U.S. district courts from all over the nation on patents and government contracts.

In 2017, almost 50,000 cases were filed in federal appeals courts, although only about 8,000 reached the formal hearing stage (most cases end in negotiated settlements without going to trial).[20] Cases cannot originate in appeals courts but must come to them from district courts. Because they exist only to hear appeals, they are referred to as **appellate courts**. At the appellate level, lawyers do not examine witnesses or introduce new evidence; instead, they submit **briefs**, which set out the legal issues at stake. Judges usually convene as panels of three (on important cases, there are more—sometimes seven members) to hear oral arguments from the lawyers on each side of the case and to cross-examine them, not witnesses, on points of law. Weeks or even months later, after considerable study, writing, and discussion among the judges, the panel issues a ruling. In important cases, the ruling is usually accompanied by an **opinion** that sets forth the majority side's reasoning for the decision.

circuit courts
The twelve geographical jurisdictions and one special court that hear appeals from the federal district courts.

appellate courts
Courts that hear cases on appeal from other courts.

briefs
Documents setting out the arguments in legal cases, prepared by attorneys and presented to courts.

opinion
The explanation of the majority's and the minority's reasoning that accompanies a court decision.

FIGURE 14.2 GEOGRAPHIC LOCATIONS OF U.S. CIRCUIT COURTS

The United States is divided into twelve geographic regions, each housing one U.S. court of appeals. One additional circuit, the U.S. Court of Appeals for the Federal Circuit, is located in Washington, D.C.

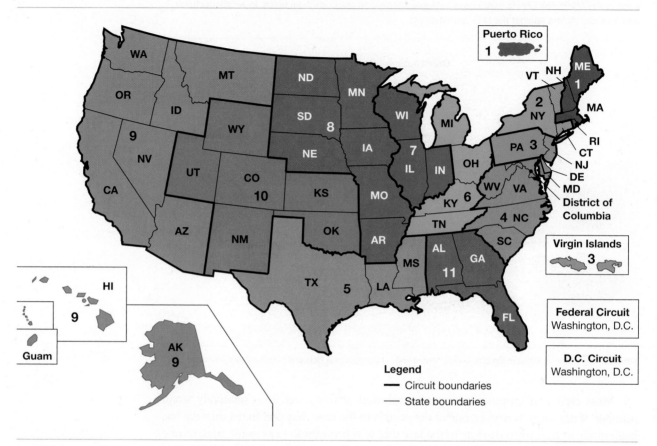

SOURCE: Administrative Office of the U.S. Courts, "About Federal Courts: Court Role and Structure," *Annual Report 2015.*

precedents

Past rulings by courts that guide judicial reasoning in subsequent cases.

stare decisis

The legal doctrine that says precedent should guide judicial decision making.

Once appellate decisions are published, they become **precedents** that guide the decisions of other judges in the same circuit. Although judges do not slavishly follow precedents, they tend to move away from them only when necessary and only in very small steps. This doctrine of closely following precedents as the basis for legal reasoning is known as **stare decisis**.

It is important to know that the decisions of each circuit court determines the meaning of laws for people who live in all of the states covered by that circuit. They have become more important as they have ruled on more cases recently, without review by the Supreme Court, which decides fewer than eighty cases each year.

Sometimes particular circuits play a more important role than others in changing constitutional interpretation. For example, the Fourth Circuit Court, based in Richmond, Virginia, was a leader in the trend toward reasserting the power of the states in the federal system.[21] The Ninth Circuit Court, which sits in San Francisco, is known to be especially liberal on civil rights and civil liberties cases. Because the Supreme Court considers only a relative handful of cases from the appeals courts each term, the rulings of the Fourth Circuit are binding for almost thirty-three million people in the southeastern United States, while the rulings of the Ninth Circuit Court of Appeals hold for roughly sixty-four million people in the western United States, including California. Although it has had several of its rulings reversed in recent years by the more conservative U.S. Supreme Court and has drawn President Trump's criticism on more than one occasion, the Ninth Circuit's rulings, nevertheless, cover about 18 percent of the American population.

THE U.S. SUPREME COURT Congress decides how many judges sit on the U.S. Supreme Court. The first Court had six members. The Federalists, however, reduced the number to five in 1801 to prevent newly elected president Thomas Jefferson from filling a vacancy. In 1869, Congress set the number at its present nine members (eight associate justices and the chief justice). It has remained this way ever since, weathering the failed effort by President Franklin Roosevelt to "pack" the Court with more politically congenial justices by expanding its size to fifteen.

The Supreme Court is both a court of original jurisdiction and an appellate court. That is, some cases are first heard in the Supreme Court, though most heard there are on appeal. Disputes involving ambassadors and other diplomatic personnel, as well as disputes between two or more states, originate in the Supreme Court rather than in some other court, though the Court is not obliged to hear such cases.[22]

In its most important role, the Supreme Court also serves as an appellate court for the U.S. courts of appeals and for the highest courts in each of the states. Cases in which a state or federal law has been declared unconstitutional can be heard by the Supreme Court, as can cases in which the highest state court has denied a claim that a state law violates federal law or the Constitution (see Figure 14.3). It also takes appeals that involve the interpretation of the meaning of federal statutes and regulations.

This last point is worth emphasizing. There is a popular misconception that the Supreme Court only takes cases having to do with constitutional questions. This is not correct. The Court takes both constitutional and statutory cases; it can rule on issues related to the constitutionality of actions by federal, state, and local governments, but it can also rule on disputes centered on the meaning of statutes and regulations.[23] For example, in *Grove City College v. Bell* (1984), the Court ruled that Title IX of the Federal Education Act did not mean that institutions of higher education receiving

FIGURE 14.3 HOW CASES GET TO THE U.S. SUPREME COURT

The vast majority of cases that reach the Supreme Court come to it from within the federal court system. Most of the others come on appeal from the highest state courts. A handful originate in the Supreme Court itself.

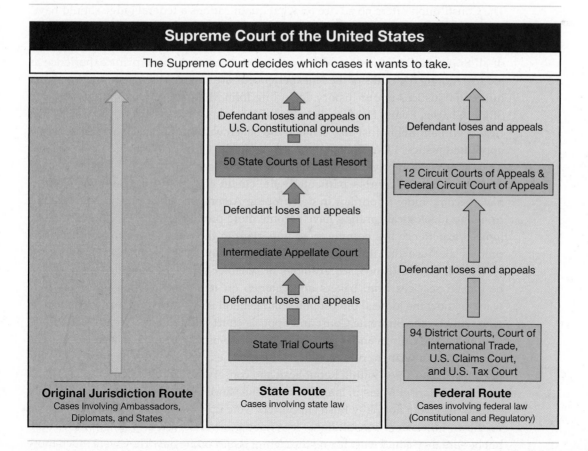

federal funds would lose all federal funding if they practiced gender discrimination (as Congress clearly intended). Rather, it ruled that only the discriminating program or department—such as an athletic department or a physics department—would lose funding. Congress cannot ignore a constitutional ruling about a law it has passed. It can and does amend statutes to satisfy the concerns of the Court—or to get around the Court—when the meaning of a law to the Court is not consistent with Congress's understanding.

Congress determines much of the appellate jurisdiction of the Supreme Court. In 1869, following the Civil War, a Congress controlled by radical Republicans removed the Court's power to review cases falling under the Reconstruction program for the South. In 1995, responding to a plea from Chief Justice Rehnquist to lighten the Court's caseload, Congress dropped the requirement that the Supreme Court *must* hear cases in which a state court declares a federal statute unconstitutional. It can choose to do so.

Because it is the highest appellate court in the federal court system, the decisions and opinions of the Supreme Court become the main precedents for federal and constitutional questions for courts at all other levels. For this reason, Supreme Court decisions receive so much attention from other political actors, the media, and the public.

APPOINTMENT TO THE FEDERAL BENCH

14.3 Describe the background of appointees to the federal bench and the process by which they are appointed.

Because federal judges are appointed for life and make important decisions, it matters who they are and how they get to the bench. If they are isolated from popular influence, democracy is at risk. If they are too responsive, they ignore their judicial role to act as neutral arbiters of the meaning of the Constitution in political and government affairs.

Who Are the Appointees?

The Constitution offers no advice on what qualifications a federal judge should have. By custom and tradition, appointees to the federal bench must be lawyers, but until quite recently, they did not have to have judicial experience. Indeed, almost one-half of all Supreme Court justices during the 20th century had no prior experience as judges. Among the ranks of the "inexperienced" are some of the most prominent and influential justices in our history, including John Marshall, Louis Brandeis, Harlan Stone, Charles Evans Hughes, Felix Frankfurter, and Earl Warren.[24] Former Chief Justice William Rehnquist also came to the bench without judicial experience, as did appointed justice, Elena Kagan, who served in the Clinton White House in the late 1990s after years in private practice and law school teaching.

As the federal courts—particularly the circuit courts and the Supreme Court—have become more important in determining American public policies, and as partisan and ideological conflicts have become more pronounced in the country, having judicial experience has become more important in the nomination and confirmation process. Because the stakes seem so high to many people—whether *Roe v. Wade* (1973) will be overturned, for example, or whether same-sex marriage partners can be denied services from bakers and caterers on religious freedom grounds—they want to know the judicial philosophies and general ideological outlooks of the people who will become Supreme Court and appeals court judges. One way to know this is to examine the rulings and written opinions of nominees who have been judges. The new, though unwritten, rules about prior judicial experience became apparent in the firestorm that erupted within Republican and conservative circles after President Bush nominated Harriet Miers in late 2005 to fill the Sandra Day O'Connor vacancy. Many people who were normally Bush supporters were upset by the fact that Miers was an unknown in terms of constitutional law, having never served as a judge. They could not be sure they could trust her on the central issues of the day. They were much more

Chief Justice John Roberts
Born: 1955
Sworn In: 2005
Appointed By: George W. Bush

Clarence Thomas
Born: 1948
Sworn In: 1991
Appointed By: George H. W. Bush

Ruth Bader Ginsburg
Born: 1933
Sworn In: 1993
Appointed By: Bill Clinton

Stephen G. Breyer
Born: 1938
Sworn In: 1994
Appointed By: Bill Clinton

Samuel A. Alito Jr.,
Born: 1950
Sworn In: 2006
Appointed By: George W. Bush

Sonia Sotomayor
Born: 1954
Sworn In: 2009
Appointed By: Barack Obama

Elena Kagan
Born: 1960
Sworn In: 2010
Appointed By: Barack Obama

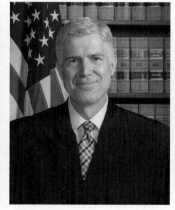

Neil Gorsuch
Born: 1967
Sworn in: 2017
Appointed By: Donald Trump

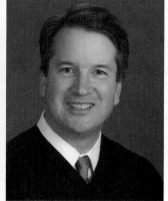

Brett M. Kavanaugh
Born: 1965
Sworn In: 2018
Appointed By: Donald Trump

comfortable with Bush nominees John Roberts and Samuel Alito, who had established extensive conservative records on the federal bench.[25]

Like most lawyers, federal judges tend to come from privileged backgrounds. In addition, federal judges, and particularly Supreme Court justices, come from the most elite parts of the legal profession. For most of our history, they have been white male Protestants from upper-income or upper-middle-class backgrounds who attended the

KENNEDY MAKES WAY FOR KAVANAUGH

Here Supreme Court justices Anthony Kennedy (center), Stephen Breyer (left), and Chief Justice John Roberts (right) attend a joint session of Congress in early 2017 to listen to President Donald Trump's State of the Union Address. Justice Kennedy's retirement in 2018 allowed the president to nominate Brett Kavanaugh for the ninth seat on the Supreme Court. He was approved by the Senate in one of the closest, most contentious, and decidedly partisan confirmation votes in American history. *What will be the likely long term effects of the replacement on the Court of moderate conservative Kennedy by ultra conservative Kavanaugh on issues such as abortion, business regulation, civil rights, environmental protection, and labor union power?*

most selective and expensive undergraduate and graduate institutions.[26] The current Supreme Court has moved entirely away from the almost exclusive Protestant membership that marked its history. Indeed, three current members—Ginsburg, Breyer, and Kagan—are Jewish, and five—Thomas, Kavanaugh, Roberts, Alito, and Sotomayor—are Catholic. Gorsuch has not stated his religion; he was born and raised in the Catholic faith but for years was a member of St. John's Episcopal Church in Boulder, Colorado. The current Court is also more diverse in terms of race and gender than at any time in its history. On the current Supreme Court, there is one African American (Clarence Thomas), one Hispanic (Sotomayor), and three women (Ginsburg, Sotomayor, and Kagan). The racial and gender representativeness of judicial appointees at the circuit and district court levels is better, and improving rapidly, but it is still a long way from reflecting the composition of the legal profession, much less the American people as a whole.

The Appointment Process

Federal judges assume office after they have been nominated by the president and confirmed by the Senate in a process that has become ever more contentious as national politics have become more partisan.[27] Presidents pay special attention to judicial appointments because those appointments are a way for presidents to affect public policy long after their terms are up.[28] Senators who are not in the president's party or who are ideologically opposed to the president often seek to block the nomination and deny the president a hold on future policy.

Presidents take many things into consideration besides merit.[29] For example, no president wants a nomination rejected by the Senate so the president and presidential advisers consult with key senators, especially those on the Judiciary Committee, before forwarding nominations. Nominations for district court judgeships are subject to **senatorial courtesy**, the practice of allowing the senior senator from the president's party to approve nominees from the state where the district court is located. Senatorial courtesy does not operate, however, in appointments to the circuit courts, whose jurisdictions span more than a single state, or to the Supreme Court, whose jurisdiction is the entire nation. There is also the blue slip, the informal Senate practice in which the Judiciary Committee solicits the opinions on the nominee from the two senators from the state where the nominee resides (submitted on blue slips of paper). Holds are also widely used. A hold is an informal practice in which a member of the majority party can inform the majority leader that he or she wishes to keep a judicial nomination from coming to the floor for a vote. (Majority leaders can choose to go along or not.) So,

senatorial courtesy

The tradition that a judicial nomination for a federal district court seat be approved by the senior senator of the president's party from the state where a district court is located before the nominee is considered by the Senate Judiciary Committee.

BORK REJECTED

The Democratic Senate's rejection in 1987 of conservative legal scholar Robert Bork, President Reagan's nominee for a vacant seat on the Supreme Court, helped trigger the long ideological and partisan battle over the composition of the Supreme Court that persists to the present day. Here, Bork explains his judicial philosophy to members of the Senate Judiciary Committee.

Should senators base their vote for federal judicial nominees on their own personal ideological outlooks and partisan loyalties, on their best judgments about the qualifications of the nominee, or should they defer to the president on the grounds that he or she is the only nationally elected official in the government?

presidents must be extremely mindful of the views of key senators, even those in the opposing party, especially when the opposing party controls the Senate.

On occasion, despite presidential efforts to placate it, the Senate has refused to give its consent. Of the 143 nominees for the Supreme Court since the founding of the Republic, the Senate has refused to approve 28 of them, although only 5 of these refusals have occurred since 1900. Rejection of nominees has usually happened when the president was weak or when the other party was in control of the Senate. The defeat of Ronald Reagan's nominee, Robert Bork, was the product of deep ideological differences between a Republican president and a Democratic-controlled Senate. There have also been several near-defeats. George H. W. Bush's nominee, Clarence Thomas, was confirmed by a margin of only 4 votes after questions were raised about his legal qualifications and about sexual harassment charges brought by law professor Anita Hill. As you saw in the chapter-opening story, President Obama nominated Merrick B. Garland, the chief judge of the U.S. Court of Appeals for the D.C. Circuit, to fill the seat of deceased justice Antonin Scalia, but the Republican-led Senate refused to hold hearings or vote on his nomination.

As the opening story on Justice Alito's Senate confirmation illustrates, judicial nominees, especially for the federal circuit courts and the Supreme Court, have become very contentious, partisan battles.[30] Fights over presidential judicial nominees raged during the Clinton presidency and during the Bush presidency, culminating in the use of the filibuster by the Democrats to block several judicial nominations and the threat by Republicans to use the nuclear option to end filibusters against conservative nominees and send their nominations to a floor vote. In 2013, frustrated by the record low rate of confirmation of President Obama's judicial (and executive branch) nominees despite a Democratic majority status in the Senate, Democrats finally exercised the nuclear option by outlawing the use of the filibuster on nominations for federal district and circuit court judgeships. This change allowed President Obama to appoint a large number of federal district and circuit judges in 2013 and 2014 when his party had a majority in the Senate, but the Republican capture of the Senate in the 2014 elections radically reduced his success rate on judicial appointments for the remainder of his term in office. Because of the end of the filibuster for all federal judicial nominations and a big backlog of unfilled positions, President Donald Trump set a record pace in 2017 for the appointment of federal district and circuit court judges primarily from lists prepared for him by the conservative Federalist Society.[31] All of this was in addition to Trump's adding Neil Gorsuch and Brett Kavanaugh to the Supreme Court.

Although presidents must be concerned about the merit of their candidates and their acceptability to the Senate, they also use appointments to try to make their mark on the future. Presidents go about this in different ways.

standing

Authority to bring legal action because one is directly affected by the issues at hand.

For the most part, presidents, naturally concerned about their historical legacy, are interested in nominating judges who share their ideological and public policy commitments.[32] John Adams nominated John Marshall and a number of other judges to protect Federalist principles during the ascendancy of the Jeffersonians. Franklin Roosevelt tried to fill the courts with judges who favored the New Deal. Ronald Reagan favored conservatives who were committed to rolling back affirmative action and other civil rights claims, abortion rights, protections for criminal defendants, and broad claims of **standing** in environmental cases. Both George H. W. Bush and his son George W. Bush carried on the Reagan tradition of nominating conservative judges to the federal courts. Donald Trump promised during his campaign to nominate very conservative judges in the Anton Scalia mold, a promise he kept in 2017 and 2018 with Gorsuch and Kavanaugh joining the High Court and others of similar judicial philosophy added to district and circuit courts.[33]

In the first years of his administration, Bill Clinton nominated two judges with reputations as moderates for the high court: Ruth Bader Ginsburg and Stephen Breyer. Clinton was eager to avoid a bitter ideological fight in the Senate, where he was trying to forge a bipartisan coalition to support the North American Free Trade Agreement and a national crime bill. The Ginsburg nomination was also indicative of Clinton's apparent commitment to diversifying the federal court system. (More than one-half of federal court nominees during his presidency were women and minorities.)

Diversity was also important to President Barack Obama. During his first year in office, he nominated twelve people for federal circuit court positions; nine of the twelve were women and/or minorities. He also was anxious to appoint the first Hispanic to the Supreme Court and did so in 2009, choosing Sonia Sotomayor.[34] He added another woman to the Court when he nominated Elena Kagan in 2010. Both were liberal on social issues but relatively favorable to business.

Presidents are often disappointed in how their nominees behave once they reach the Court. Dwight Eisenhower was dumbfounded when his friend and nominee, Earl Warren, led the Court in a liberal direction by transforming constitutional law regarding civil rights and criminal procedure. Richard Nixon was no doubt surprised by the odyssey of his nominee Harry Blackmun, who, despite a conservative judicial record before joining the Court, had become one of its most liberal justices by the time of his retirement in 1994 (he wrote the majority opinion in *Roe v. Wade* [1973]). The elder George Bush may have been shocked when his nominee, David Souter, refused to vote for the overturn of *Roe* in *Planned Parenthood v. Casey* (1992). Despite these dramatic examples, the past partisan and ideological positions of federal court nominees are a fairly reliable guide to their later behavior on the bench.[35] Few were surprised when five Republican justices ruled in favor of Republican George W. Bush in the disputed election of 2000 (*Bush v. Gore*, 2000). Few were surprised when the Court moved in an even more conservative direction after Bush nominees Roberts and Alito joined the Court, given the record of their past partisan activities and judicial opinions.

THE SUPREME COURT IN ACTION

14.4 Outline the process by which the Supreme Court makes decisions and the factors that influence judicial decision making.

The Supreme Court meets from the first Monday in October until late June or early July, depending on the press of business. Let's see how it goes about accepting, processing, and deciding cases.[36]

The Norms of Operation

A set of unwritten but clearly understood rules of behavior—*norms*—shapes how the Court operates.

SECRECY One norm is *secrecy,* which keeps the conflicts between justices out of the public eye and elevates the stature of the Court as an institution. Justices do not grant interviews very often, though several recently have authored books. Reporters are not allowed to stalk the corridors for a story. Law clerks are expected to keep confidential all memos, draft opinions, and conversations with the justices they work for. Justices are not commonly seen on the frantic Washington, D.C., cocktail party circuit. When meeting in conference to argue and decide cases, the justices meet alone, without secretaries or clerks. Breaches of secrecy have occurred only occasionally. As a result, we know less about the inner workings of the Court than about any other branch of government.

SENIORITY *Seniority* is another important norm. Seniority determines the assignment of office space, the seating arrangements in open court (the most junior are at the ends), and the order of speaking in conference (the chief justice, then the most senior, and so on down the line). Speaking first often allows the senior members to set the tone for discussion.

PRECEDENT Finally, the justices are expected to stick closely to *precedent* when they decide cases. When the Court departs from a precedent, it is essentially overruling its own past actions, in effect, exercising judicial review of itself. In most cases, departures from precedent come in small steps over many years. For example, several decisions chipped away at the **separate but equal doctrine** of *Plessy v. Ferguson* (1896) before it was decisively reversed in *Brown v. Board of Education of Topeka* (1954) to end state and local laws requiring racial segregation. Times may be changing, however, as the Court has become more sharply divided along ideological lines. For example, in 2010, when ruling on *Citizens United,* which allows corporations to spend unlimited money in funding issue advertising during election campaigns, the Roberts Court showed no inclination to move slowly; it simply overruled a series of its previous rulings, one of which was only three years old.

separate but equal doctrine
The principle articulated in *Plessy v. Ferguson* (1896) that laws prescribing separate public facilities and services for nonwhite Americans are permissible if the facilities and services are equal to those provided for whites.

Control of the Agenda

The Court has a number of screening mechanisms to control which cases it will hear so that it can focus on cases that involve important federal or constitutional questions.[37]

TECHNICAL RULES Several technical rules help keep the numbers down. Cases must be *real* and *adverse;* that is, they must involve a real dispute between two parties. The disputants in a case must have *standing;* that is, they must have a real and direct interest in the issues that are raised. The Court sometimes changes the definition of *standing* to make access for **plaintiffs** easier or more difficult. The Warren Court (1956–1969) favored an expansive definition, while the Rehnquist Court (1986–2005) favored a restricted one. Cases must also be *ripe;* that is, all other avenues of appeal must have been exhausted, and the injury must already have taken place (the Court will not accept hypothetical cases). Appeals must also be filed within a specified time limit, the paperwork must be correct and complete, and a filing fee of $300 must be paid. The fee may be waived if a petitioner is poor and files an affidavit *in forma pauperis* ("in the manner of a pauper"). One of the most famous cases in American history, *Gideon v. Wainwright* (1963), which established the right of all defendants to have lawyers in criminal cases, was submitted *in forma pauperis* on a few pieces of lined paper by Clarence Earl Gideon, a Florida State Penitentiary inmate.

plaintiff
One who brings suit in a court.

in forma pauperis
Describing a process by which indigents may file a suit with the Supreme Court free of charge.

Though the Supreme Court can only take cases that come to it, there is considerable evidence that justices, in rulings in previous cases, often signal what kinds of cases they would like to hear in the future. Thus, in *Abood v. Detroit Board of Education* (1975), Justice Samuel Alito wrote in his majority opinion that the constitutionality of public sector unions requiring nonunion members to pay fees for union bargaining on wages, benefits, and working conditions. The Center for Individual Rights, a conservative anti-union advocacy group, filed a suit challenging such fees on behalf of a group of nonunion California teachers in a case that the Court decided to take up: *Friedrichs v. California Education Association* (2015).[38] After the death of Anton Scalia, the Supreme Court deadlocked 4–4 on the case, leaving in place the ruling of the Ninth Circuit Court of Appeals in favor of the teachers' union. After conservative Neil Gorsuch joined the Court, it ruled against the union on a 5–4 vote.

CERTIORARI The most powerful tool the Court has for controlling its own agenda is the power to grant or not to grant a **writ of certiorari**. A grant of "cert" is a decision of the Court that an appellate case raises an important federal or constitutional issue it is prepared to consider.[39] Under the **rule of four**, petitions are granted cert if at least four justices vote in favor. There are several reasons a petition may not command four votes, even if the case involves important constitutional issues: it may involve a particularly controversial issue that the Court would like to avoid, or the Court may not yet have developed a solid majority and may wish to avoid a split decision. Few petitions survive all of these hurdles. Of the 7,000 to 8,000 new cases filed with the Court each term, the Court today grants cert for about 80 of them for plenary review, that is, where the justices hear oral arguments from lawyers on both sides in a case. (This number varies a bit year to year.) In the 1970s and 1980s, by way of comparison, the Court granted cert to about 150 cases per term. In cases denied cert, the decision of the federal appeals court or the highest state court stands.

Deciding how freely to grant cert is a tricky business for the Court. Granted too often, it threatens to inundate the Court with cases. Granted too sparingly, it leaves in place the decisions of thirteen different federal appeals courts on substantial federal and constitutional questions as well as the decisions of state supreme courts, which often leads to inconsistent constitutional interpretations across the country. Because the Court now takes so few cases, more influence than ever is being exercised by the thirteen federal circuit courts. For many important cases, the federal circuit courts have become the judicial forum of last resort. However, when the Supreme Court wants to reach out and settle differences in decisions in lower federal courts or among the states, it is entirely free to do so; it controls its own agenda. This is what the Court did in 2015 in *Obergefell v. Hodges* when, confronted with conflicting federal district and circuit court rulings on whether or not states could ban same-sex marriage, it struck down all state bans on such unions.

Deciding Cases

Almost all cases granted cert are scheduled for oral argument (about ten to fifteen are decided without oral argument, depending on the session). Lawyers on each side are alerted to the key issues that the justices wish to consider, and new briefs are invited.

BRIEFS Briefs are also submitted on important cases by other parties who may be interested in the disputes. These "friend of the court," or *amicus curiae*, briefs may be submitted by individuals, interest groups, or an agency of the federal government, including the Justice Department or even the president.

ORAL ARGUMENTS Each case is argued for one hour, with thirty minutes given to each side in the dispute. Oral argument is not so much a presentation of arguments, however, as it is a give-and-take between the lawyers and the justices and among the justices. When the federal government is a party to the case, the solicitor general or one of his or her deputies presents the oral arguments. Some justices—Chief Justice John Roberts, for example—are famous for their relentless grilling of lawyers. Ruth Bader Ginsburg often asks that lawyers skip abstract legal fine points and put the issues in terms of their effect on ordinary people. Neil Gorsuch is quite active in oral exchanges though he is relatively new to the Court. Justice Clarence Thomas famously hardly speaks at all.

CONFERENCE After hearing oral arguments and reading the briefs in the case, the justices meet in conference to reach a preliminary decision. The custom is for each justice to state his or her position, starting with the chief justice and moving through

---

writ of certiorari

An announcement that the Supreme Court will hear a case on appeal from a lower court; its issuance requires the vote of four of the nine justices.

rule of four

An *unwritten* practice that requires at least four justices of the Supreme Court to agree that a case warrants review by the Court before it will hear the case.

amicus curiae

Latin for "friend of the court"; a legal brief in which individuals not party to a suit may have their views heard in court.

the ranks in order of seniority. Chief justices of great stature and intellect, such as John Marshall and Charles Evans Hughes, used the opportunity to speak first as a way of structuring the case and of swaying votes. Those who did not command much respect from the other justices (e.g., Warren Burger) were less able to shape the decision process.[40]

DECISION FACTORS Political scientists have tried to determine what factors are most important in predicting how the justices will vote.[41] One approach looks at the ideological predilections of the justices and manages to explain a great deal about their voting behavior that way.[42] Another approach looks at the strategic behavior of judges, using the diaries and personal papers of retired justices to show that a great deal of negotiating and "horse trading" goes on, with justices trading votes on different cases and joining opinions they do not like so that they can have a hand in modifying them.[43] Another approach tries to link voting behavior to social background, types of previous judicial experience, and the political environment of family upbringing.[44] Still another believes that justices often vote to maintain the influence and standing of the Court in American society even if it means departing from their own ideological preferences,[45] None of these approaches has been totally successful in explaining decision making by justices, though the ideological model seems to do the best job in explaining judicial behavior over the long term.[46] Because Democrats in office and in the electorate have become more liberal and because Republicans in office and in the electorate have become much more conservative, we can conclude that the most decisive dividing lines in today's Court are partisan; appointees of Republican presidents vote in a conservative direction on most issues before the Court, while appointees of Democratic presidents vote in a liberal direction.

About all one can say is that the justices tend to form relatively stable voting blocs over time, with ideology and party increasingly the most important factor.[47] For example, on many cases involving federalism and the rights of criminal defendants during the 1990s and early 2000s, the Rehnquist Court divided into two blocs, a five-member conservative bloc (Justices Scalia, Thomas, Rehnquist, Kennedy, and O'Connor) and a four-member liberal bloc (Justices Stevens, Breyer, Ginsburg, and Souter). The Roberts Court has been dominated by a solid Republican conservative majority, with Neil Gorsuch taking Anton Scalia's place in 2017 and Brett Kavanaugh taking Anthony Kennedy's seat, even taking into account the action of the Chief Justice when he surprisingly sided with his liberal colleagues in upholding the Affordable Care Act in 2012.

OPINIONS The vote in conference is not final, however. As Justice John Harlan once explained, "The books on voting are never closed until the decision finally comes down."[48] The justices have an opportunity to change their votes in response to the opinion supporting the majority decision. Some conservative commentators have reported that Chief Justice Roberts initially voted in favor of declaring the Affordable Care Act unconstitutional in 2012 before switching sides.[49] He then wrote the ruling opinion in the case that upheld Obamacare but included a section calling into question the Congress's use of the commerce clause to justify federal government actions, something that might endanger an entire range of laws favored by liberals and Democrats.

An opinion is a statement of the legal reasoning that supports the decision of the Court. There are three kinds of opinions. The **opinion of the Court** is the written opinion of the majority. A **concurring opinion** is the opinion of a justice who supports the majority decision but has different legal reasons for doing so. A **dissenting opinion** presents the reasoning of the minority. Dissenting opinions sometimes become the basis for future Court majorities.

If he votes with the majority in conference, the chief justice assigns the writing of the opinion. He can assign it to any justice in the majority; chief justices often write majority opinions themselves. John Roberts, for example, has chosen to write the majority opinion on many of the most important decisions on First Amendment cases, striking

opinion of the Court
The majority opinion that accompanies a Supreme Court decision; also called the majority opinion.

concurring opinion
The opinion of one or more judges who vote with the majority on a case but wish to set out different reasons for their decision.

dissenting opinion
The opinion of the judge or judges who are in the minority on a particular case before the Supreme Court.

down restrictions on campaign financing (with *Citizens United* the most well-known and perhaps consequential of recent cases) and commercial speech.[50] Some jurists and scholars believe that this power to assign is the most important role of the chief justice, and it is guarded jealously. Warren Burger was so eager to play a role in opinion assignments that, much to the distress of his colleagues, he would often delay announcing his vote so that he could place himself with the majority. Justice William Douglas angrily charged that Burger voted with the majority in *Roe* only so that he could assign the case to a justice who was closer to the minority view.[51] If the chief justice's opinion is with the minority, the opinion is assigned by the most senior member of the majority.

The justice assigned to write the opinion does not work in isolation. He or she is assisted by law clerks and other justices, who helpfully provide memoranda suggesting wording and reasoning. Justices also consider the legal reasoning presented to the Court in *amicus curiae* briefs.[52] Most opinions go through numerous revisions and are subject to a considerable amount of bargaining among the justices.

FINAL VOTE   Only when an opinion is completed is a final vote taken in conference. The justices are free to change their earlier votes: they may join the majority if they are now persuaded by its reasoning, or a concurring opinion may be so compelling that the majority may decide to replace the original majority opinion with it.

Outside Influences on Supreme Court Decisions

CLERKING FOR JUSTICE THOMAS
Law clerks play an extremely important role at the Supreme Court, with each justice selecting his or her own clerks from among graduates of the nation's leading law schools. Here, Justice Clarence Thomas relaxes with three of his clerks after a long day.
What is the importance of clerks to the effectiveness of the justices? Should each justice be allowed to hire more clerks so that they can decide more cases each term?

The Supreme Court makes public policy when it issues its rulings and will continue to do so, but it does not do so in isolation; many other *governmental and political linkage actors and institutions* influence what it does. Indeed, many scholars suggest that what the Supreme Court does reflects the prevailing politics and opinion of the day. After all, justices are nominated by presidents and confirmed by senators whose views are known to the public and who are elected by them. As new coalitions come to power in American politics, they make appointments to the federal courts in general and the Supreme Court in particular that are in tune with the electoral coalition supporting the president and a majority of the Senate. A highly politicized judiciary, whose

decisions become entangled in and engaged with the prevailing issues of the day and whose decisions reflect the views of the winners, in this view, is not to be lamented but celebrated as a reflection of democratic politics. In the view of several leading scholars, aggressive use of judicial review by the Supreme Court is simply a way for the new majority in the country to clear the way for its own policies.[53] Critics of this view would point out, however, that the courts might be out of touch with the mood of the country for long periods of time because judges on federal district and circuit courts and justices on the Supreme Court serve life terms and are slow to be replaced.

Government and political influences on the Court come not only during times of partisan realignment and the appearance of new electoral coalitions but on an everyday basis. Here are important ways this happens.

GOVERNMENTAL INFLUENCES   The Supreme Court must coexist with other governmental bodies that have their own powers, interests, constituencies, and visions of the public good.[54] Recognizing this, the Court usually tries to stay somewhere near the boundaries of what is acceptable to other political actors. Being without "purse or sword," as Alexander Hamilton put it in *The Federalist* No. 78, the Court cannot force others to obey its decisions. It can only hope that respect for the law and the Court will cause government officials to do what it has mandated in a decision. If the Court fails to gain voluntary compliance, it risks a serious erosion of its influence, for it then appears weak and ineffectual.[55]

The President   The president, as chief executive, is supposed to carry out the Court's decrees. However, presidents who have opposed particular decisions or have been lukewarm to them have dragged their feet, as President Eisenhower did on school desegregation after the Court's *Brown* decision in 1954.

Presidents have constitutional powers that give them some degree of influence over the Court. In addition to the Court's dependence on presidents to carry out its decisions (when the parties to a dispute do not do it voluntarily), presidents influence the direction of the Court by their power to nominate judges when there are vacancies. They can also file suits through the Justice Department, argue cases before the Court, or convince Congress to consider legislation to alter the Court's organization or jurisdiction (as Franklin Roosevelt did with his Court-packing proposal).

Congress   Congress's main influence on the Court is the Senate's responsibility to give its "advice and consent" to presidential judicial nominees, that is, vote to confirm or to reject. The Senate can also delay consideration of presidential nominations, or even refuse to meet and hold hearings on a nominee as it did during most of 2016 with respect to Merrick Garland whose name President Obama put forward to fill the vacancy caused by Justice Scalia's death.

Congress also can alter the size, organization, and appellate jurisdiction of the federal courts, including the Supreme Court, but it rarely does so.[56] The size of the Court has not changed since 1860. Nor, since that time, has Congress changed its jurisdiction as a reaction to its decisions, despite the introduction of many bills over the years to do so. In 2003, for example, a bill was introduced by Republicans in the House to take away the Court's jurisdiction to hear cases challenging the inclusion of the phrase "under God" in the Pledge of Allegiance. In 2004, a resolution was introduced in the House decrying the citation of the opinions of foreign and international courts and international law in U.S. judicial pronouncements—something Justice Kennedy had done in his majority opinion in a case overturning the state of Texas's antisodomy statute in *Lawrence v. Texas* (2003)—and threatening impeachment for any federal judge doing so. (Neither bill passed.) Congress is more likely to bring pressure to bear on the courts by being unsympathetic to pleas from the justices for pay increases or for a suitable budget for clerks or office space. The Senate also plays a role in the appointment process, as we have learned, and can convey its views to the Court during the course of confirmation hearings. Finally, Congress can change statutes or pass new laws that specifically challenge Supreme Court decisions, as it did when it legislated the Civil Rights Act of 1991 to make it easier for people to file employment discrimination suits. All of this matters. There is evidence that throughout American history, the Supreme Court has exercised a great deal of restraint in its judicial review of congressional actions when Congress was clearly hostile to the Court.[57]

POLITICAL LINKAGE INFLUENCES The Supreme Court is influenced not only by other government officials and institutions, but also by what we have termed *political linkage factors.*

Groups and Movements Interest groups, social movements, and the public not only influence the Court indirectly through the president and Congress but often do so directly. An important political tactic of interest groups and social movements is the **test case**. A test case is an action brought by a group that is designed to challenge the constitutionality of a law or an action by government. Groups wishing to force a court determination on an issue that is important to them will try to find a plaintiff on whose behalf they can bring a suit. When Thurgood Marshall was chief counsel for the NAACP in the 1950s, he spent a long time searching for the right plaintiff to bring a suit that would drive the last nail into the coffin of the *Plessy* separate-but-equal doctrine that was the legal basis for southern segregation. He settled on a fifth-grade girl named Linda Brown who was attending a segregated school in Topeka, Kansas. Several years later, he won the landmark case *Brown v. Board of Education of Topeka* (1954). A network of conservative advocacy organizations and wealthy donors largely financed suits against public sector unions' practice of collecting agency fees from government employees; it all paid off when the Supreme Court ruled against public sector union practices in *Janus v. AFSCME* 2018.[58]

Many test cases take the form of **class-action suits**. These are suits brought by an individual on behalf of a class of people who are in a similar situation. A suit to prevent the dumping of toxic wastes in public waterways, for example, may be brought by an individual in the name of all the people living in the area who are adversely affected by the resulting pollution. Class-action suits were invited by the Warren Court's expansion of the definition of *standing* in the 1960s. The Rehnquist Court later narrowed the definition of *standing,* making it harder to bring class-action suits. As you learned above, the Roberts Court further limited the ability of similarly situated people to bring such suits.

Interest groups often get involved in suits brought by others by filing *amicus curiae* briefs.[59] Pro-abortion and anti-abortion groups submitted seventy-eight such briefs in *Webster v. Reproductive Health Services* (1989), a decision that allowed states to regulate and limit abortion availability.[60] These briefs set out the group's position on the constitutional issues or talk about some of the most important consequences of deciding the case one way or the other. In a sense, this activity is a form of lobbying. Some scholars believe that the Court finds such briefs to be a way to keep track of public and group opinion on the issues before it, which is helpful to its work.[61]

Leaders The Supreme Court does not usually stray very far from the opinions of public- and private-sector leaders when a consensus exists among them.[62] Social and economic leaders use their influence in a number of ways. As we learned in earlier chapters, their influence is substantial in the media, the interest group system, party politics, and elections at all levels. It follows,

test case

A case brought by advocacy or interest groups to try to force a ruling on the constitutionality of some law or executive action.

class-action suit

A suit brought on behalf of a group of people who are in a situation similar to that of the plaintiffs.

CIVIL RIGHTS CHAMPION

Social movements often use test cases to challenge the constitutionality of laws and government actions. After a long search, NAACP attorney Thurgood Marshall—shown here in front of the Supreme Court, where he would later sit as a justice—selected Linda Brown, a fifth grader from Topeka, Kansas, who was not permitted to attend the school closest to her house because it was reserved for whites, as the principal plaintiff in *Brown v. Board of Education of Topeka,* the historic case that successfully challenged school segregation. *How else has the Court been a vehicle for social change?*

then, that elites play a substantial role in the thinking of presidents and the members of Congress as they, in turn, deal with the Court.

On the other hand, when there is no elite consensus but rather deep divisions among them, as in our current period, the Court has more freedom to operate and is likely to swing back-and-forth between liberal and conservative rulings decided by 5–4 votes where a single justice often decide the outcome. Today, as we have learned, party, business, media, and advocacy group leaders are split along partisan and ideological lines. During the 1950s, to take a counter-example, elites were generally agreed that the United States, for both domestic and foreign policy reasons, had to end the legal segregation of the races in education. One result was the unanimous decision of the Court in *Brown v. Board of Education* (1954) that de jure segregation of schools was unconstitutional.[63]

In addition to this powerful but indirect influence, the Court is also shaped by developments on issues and doctrine within the legal profession as these are expressed by bar associations, law journals, and law schools. For example, Justice O'Connor, in her opinion in the 2004 Michigan Law School affirmative action case, justified her vote by pointing out that the use of race as one criterion among many in law school admission decisions was now widely accepted in the university and legal communities, as was the legitimacy of the goal of "diversity" in higher education. The conservative Federalist Society has become increasingly influential over the years among law school faculty and students and among practicing attorneys in both the public and private sectors. Recall that Donald Trump asked the Federalist Society to prepare a list for him of potential Supreme Court nominees should he win the presidency. His appointees to the Court, Neil Gorsuch and Brett Kavanaugh, were both on the final list.

Public Opinion   We might think that the Supreme Court is immune from public opinion because the justices are appointed for life and do not face the electorate. There is reason to believe, however, that what the Court does and what the public wants—at least as expressed in public opinion polls—are in fact highly correlated. A substantial body of research shows that Court rulings and public opinion are consistent with one another about two-thirds of the time, about the same level of consistency with the public as the president and Congress.[64] There does not seem to be a yawning gap, then, between the public and the Supreme Court. We cannot say for sure, however, that public opinion causes the Court to act in particular ways when making decisions.[65] Indeed, it is just as likely that third factors—such as major events, political developments, and cultural changes conveyed in the media—shape the perceptions of judges and citizens alike. Nevertheless, the close association between Court decisions and public opinion is good news in a society that aspires to be democratic.

However, it also is important to point out that there have been times during our history when the Court was so influenced by other political actors that it set aside, if only for a short while, its responsibility to protect the rights and liberties of all citizens. Although the Court has played an important role in advancing rights and liberties in the United States, it has not been entirely immune from pressure brought to bear by the public, other government officials, and private-sector leaders to punish suspect groups. For example, the Court went along with local, state, and federal actions to punish dissident voices during the McCarthy era's anticommunist hysteria of the 1950s. It also approved in *Korematsu v. United States* (1944) the forced relocation and internment of 112,000 Japanese Americans during World War II, when Franklin Roosevelt, on the advice of his top military command, issued orders as commander in chief to relocate them into camps in the interior West, away from the Pacific coast. To gain a holistic account of how this was possible, examine the analytical framework shown in Figure 14.4. A broad overview of the decision in *Korematsu*, taking into account the influence of *structural, political linkage, and governmental factors,* helps explain why the Supreme Court upheld the legality of internment.

FIGURE 14.4 APPLYING THE FRAMEWORK: UPHOLDING THE LEGALITY OF INTERNMENT

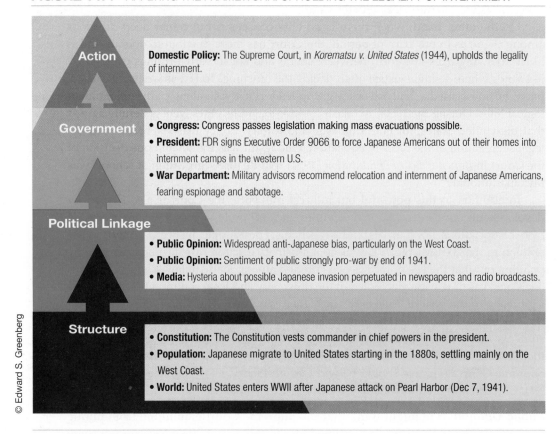

© Edward S. Greenberg

Action

Domestic Policy: The Supreme Court, in *Korematsu v. United States* (1944), upholds the legality of internment.

Government

- **Congress:** Congress passes legislation making mass evacuations possible.
- **President:** FDR signs Executive Order 9066 to force Japanese Americans out of their homes into internment camps in the western U.S.
- **War Department:** Military advisors recommend relocation and internment of Japanese Americans, fearing espionage and sabotage.

Political Linkage

- **Public Opinion:** Widespread anti-Japanese bias, particularly on the West Coast.
- **Public Opinion:** Sentiment of public strongly pro-war by end of 1941.
- **Media:** Hysteria about possible Japanese invasion perpetuated in newspapers and radio broadcasts.

Structure

- **Constitution:** The Constitution vests commander in chief powers in the president.
- **Population:** Japanese migrate to United States starting in the 1880s, settling mainly on the West Coast.
- **World:** United States enters WWII after Japanese attack on Pearl Harbor (Dec 7, 1941).

THE SUPREME COURT AS A NATIONAL POLICY MAKER

14.5 Evaluate the role of the Supreme Court in national policy making.

People often say the Court should settle disputes and not make policy. But because the disputes it settles involve contentious public issues (such as abortion rights and affirmative action) and fundamental questions about the meaning of our constitutional rules (such as the extent of presidential powers in wartime), the Court cannot help but make public policy.

It seems likely that the Court recognizes and cultivates its policy-making role. In the main, the Court does not see itself as a court of last resort, simply righting routine errors in the lower courts or settling minor private disputes. It sees itself instead as the "highest judicial tribunal for settling policy conflicts" and constitutional issues and chooses its cases accordingly.[66] The fact that decisions are not simply handed down but come with an opinion attached for the purpose of guiding the actions of other courts, litigants, and public officials is another demonstration that the Court recognizes its policy-making role. Let's look at judicial policy making—which takes the form of the Court's constitutional interpretations as revealed in its decisions—and see how it has evolved over time.

Structural Change and Constitutional Interpretation

Scholars generally identify three periods in the history of constitutional interpretation by the Supreme Court in the United States, one stretching from the early 1800s to the Civil War, the next from the end of the Civil War to the Great Depression, and the last from World War II to the mid-1980s.[67] We would add a fourth, covering the years from 1991 to the present (see Figure 14.5). We will see how changes in constitutional law have been influenced by structural factors, particularly economic change.

FIGURE 14.5 TIMELINE: CHIEF JUSTICES OF THE SUPREME COURT AND ERAS OF CONSTITUTIONAL INTERPRETATION, 1789–2018

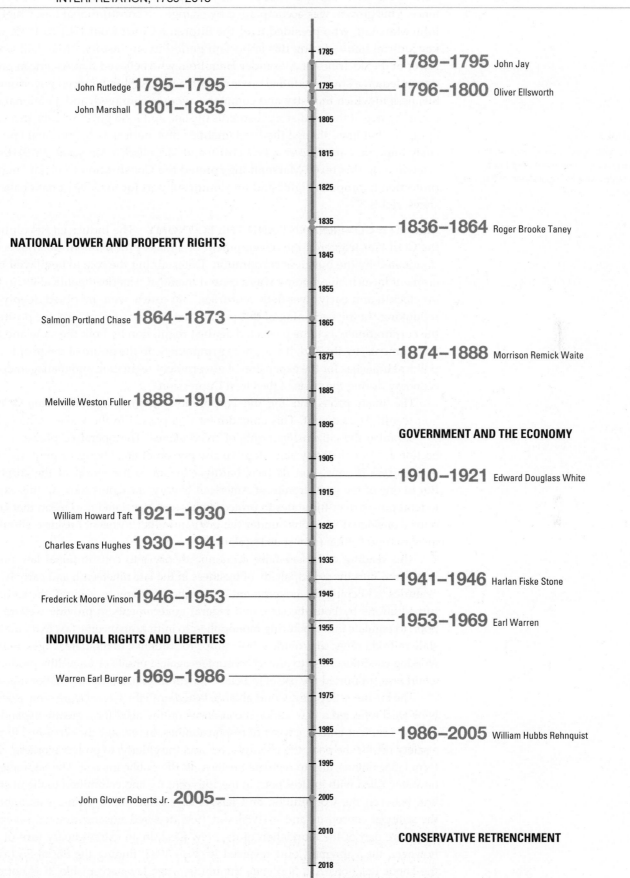

1789–1795 John Jay

John Rutledge **1795–1795**

1796–1800 Oliver Ellsworth

John Marshall **1801–1835**

NATIONAL POWER AND PROPERTY RIGHTS

1836–1864 Roger Brooke Taney

Salmon Portland Chase **1864–1873**

1874–1888 Morrison Remick Waite

Melville Weston Fuller **1888–1910**

GOVERNMENT AND THE ECONOMY

1910–1921 Edward Douglass White

William Howard Taft **1921–1930**

Charles Evans Hughes **1930–1941**

1941–1946 Harlan Fiske Stone

Frederick Moore Vinson **1946–1953**

1953–1969 Earl Warren

INDIVIDUAL RIGHTS AND LIBERTIES

Warren Earl Burger **1969–1986**

1986–2005 William Hubbs Rehnquist

John Glover Roberts Jr. **2005–**

CONSERVATIVE RETRENCHMENT

1785, 1795, 1805, 1815, 1825, 1835, 1845, 1855, 1865, 1875, 1885, 1895, 1905, 1915, 1925, 1935, 1945, 1955, 1965, 1975, 1985, 1995, 2005, 2010, 2018

SOURCE: United States Supreme Court.

laissez-faire

The political-economic doctrine that holds that government ought not interfere with the operations of the free market.

PERIOD 1: NATIONAL POWER AND PROPERTY RIGHTS   The United States experienced significant growth and change during the first seventy-five years of its existence. This growth was accompanied by changes in constitutional law. Chief Justice John Marshall, who presided over the Supreme Court from 1801 to 1835, was the key judicial figure during this important period in our history.[68] Marshall was a follower of the doctrines of Alexander Hamilton, who believed that American greatness depended on a strong national government, a partnership between government and business in which industry and commerce were encouraged, and a national market economy free of the regulatory restraints of state and local governments. In a string of opinions that have shaped the fundamentals of American constitutional law—especially important are *Fletcher v. Peck* (1810) and *McCulloch v. Maryland* (1819) discussed elsewhere in this text—Marshall interpreted the Constitution to mean "maximum protection to property rights and maximum support for the idea of nationalism over states' rights."[69]

PERIOD 2: GOVERNMENT AND THE ECONOMY   The Industrial Revolution and the Civil War triggered the development of a mass-production industrial economy dominated by the business corporation. Determining the role to be played by government in such an economy was a central theme of American political life in the late nineteenth and early twentieth centuries. The courts were involved deeply in this rethinking. At the beginning of this period, the Supreme Court took the position that the corporation was to be protected against regulation by both the state and federal governments; by the end, it was more sympathetic to the desire of the people and the political branches for the expansion of government regulation and management of the economy during the crisis of the Great Depression.

The main protection for the corporation against regulation came from the Fourteenth Amendment. This amendment was passed in the wake of the Civil War to guarantee the citizenship rights of freed slaves. The operative phrase was from Section 1: "Nor shall any state deprive any person of life, liberty, or property without due process of law"—on its face, hardly relevant to the world of the corporation. But in one of the great ironies of American history, the Court took up this expanded federal power over the states to protect rights and translated it to mean that corporations (considered "persons" under the law) and other forms of business should have increased protection from state regulation.

This reading of **laissez-faire** economic theory into constitutional law made the Supreme Court the principal ally of business in the late nineteenth and early twentieth centuries.[70] Keeping the government out of the economy in general, the Court overturned efforts by both the state and federal governments to provide welfare for the poor; to regulate manufacturing monopolies; to initiate an income tax; to regulate interstate railroad rates; to provide scholarships to students; to regulate wages, hours, and working conditions; and to protect consumers against unsafe or unhealthy products. The Court also supported the use of judicial injunctions to halt strikes by labor unions.

The business–Supreme Court alliance lasted until the Great Depression. Roosevelt's New Deal reflected a new national consensus on the need for a greatly expanded federal government with a new set of responsibilities: to manage the economy; to provide a safety net for the poor, the unemployed, and the elderly; to protect workers' rights to form labor unions; and to regulate business in the public interest. The Supreme Court, however, filled with justices born in the 19th century and committed to the unshakable link between the Constitution and laissez-faire economic doctrine, was opposed to the national consensus and in 1935 and 1936 declared unconstitutional several laws that were part of the foundation of the New Deal. In an extraordinary turn of events, however, the Supreme Court reversed itself in 1937, finding the Social Security Act, the Labor Relations Act, and state minimum wage laws acceptable. It is not entirely clear why the so-called switch-in-time-that-saved-nine occurred, but surely Roosevelt's landslide reelection in 1936, the heightening of public hostility toward the Court, and Roosevelt's threat to expand and "pack the Court" all played a role. Whatever the reason, the Court abandoned its effort to prevent the government from playing a central role in the management of the economy and the regulation of business, and it came to defer to the political linkage branches of government on such issues by the end of the 1930s. In doing so, it brought another constitutional era to a close.

PERIOD 3: INDIVIDUAL RIGHTS AND LIBERTIES Three fundamental issues of American constitutional law—the relationship of the states to the nation, the nature and extent of private property rights, and the role of government in the management of the economy—were essentially settled by the time World War II broke out. From then until the mid- to late 1980s, the Court turned its main attention to the relationship between the individual and government.[71]

Later chapters tell the story on civil liberties and civil rights. For now, it is sufficient to point out that the Court—especially during the tenure of Chief Justice Earl Warren—decided cases that expanded protections for free expression and association, religious expression, fair trials, and civil rights for minorities. In another series of cases dealing with the apportionment of electoral districts, the Court declared for political equality, based on the principle of "one person, one vote." In many of its landmark decisions, the Court applied the Bill of Rights to the states. Although the Court's record was not without blemishes during and after World War II (see Figure 14.6), it made significant strides in expanding the realm of individual freedom.

PERIOD 4: CONSERVATIVE RETRENCHMENT A new conservative majority emerged on the Supreme Court in the early 1990s, fashioned by the judicial nominations of Presidents Ronald Reagan and George H. W. Bush, and the patient efforts of conservative Chief Justice William Rehnquist. This new majority—with O'Connor and Kennedy usually, but not always, joining the three most consistently conservative justices, Scalia, Thomas, and Rehnquist—moved the Court to reconsider many of its long-established doctrines in the areas of rights and liberties and the relationship between the national and state governments. Its steady restriction of Congress's use of the commerce clause to underpin national laws in favor of "states' rights" was particularly noteworthy. In a string of landmark cases, the Court said Congress had gone too far in its efforts to ban guns from the area immediately around public schools, requiring background checks for gun buyers, and barring age discrimination in employment.

After moderate justice Sandra Day O'Connor retired in 2006 and Samuel Alito joined the Court, and with the strong leadership of Chief Justice John Roberts, the 5–4 conservative majority became even more cohesive, even overcoming the death of Justice Scalia in early 2016.[72] Here are some representative rulings: In 2007, the Court ruled that school districts could not use racial criteria to promote school integration, and it upheld federal restrictions on very late-term abortions (called "partial birth abortions" by abortion opponents). In 2008, in *District of Columbia v. Heller*, the Court for the first time ruled that Americans have a constitutional right to own guns for their personal use under terms of the Second Amendment; the Court later ruled in 2010 that state and local regulations that effectively banned guns were unconstitutional. In 2009, it ruled in favor of a group of New Haven firefighters (nineteen white and one Hispanic) in a reverse discrimination case that bodes ill for the constitutional acceptability of local, state, and national affirmative action programs. In 2013, in *Shelby County v. Heller*, the Court's 5–4 conservative majority struck down a key provision of the 1965 Voting Rights Act, which had been instrumental in protecting the equal citizenship of African Americans.

The Roberts Court has been especially friendly to business interests and large corporations. In a stunningly broad ruling in 2010, the Court said that Congress could not restrict the campaign activities of corporations as specified by the McCain–Feingold reforms of 2002—*Citizens United v. FEC*—in the process overturning three of its own

FIGURE 14.6 SUPREME COURT IDEOLOGY, 1938–2016

The data represented in this line graph confirms that the Supreme Court has tended to be a fairly conservative branch of government over the last 75 years, with only brief periods of ideological liberalism. Decisions of conservative-leaning Courts tend to reflect stricter readings of the Constitution and a preference for states' rights over federal power, while decisions of liberal-leaning Courts reflect the opposite tendencies. The farther distant a point on the graph above zero, the more conservative the median ideology of the Supreme Court for that year; the farther distant a point on the graph below zero, the more liberal the median ideology. "Median justices"—those in the ideological center of the nine-member Court—are frequently in a position to determine the outcome of cases.

How can a president's opportunity to nominate a new Supreme Court justice impact the trajectory of American public policy?

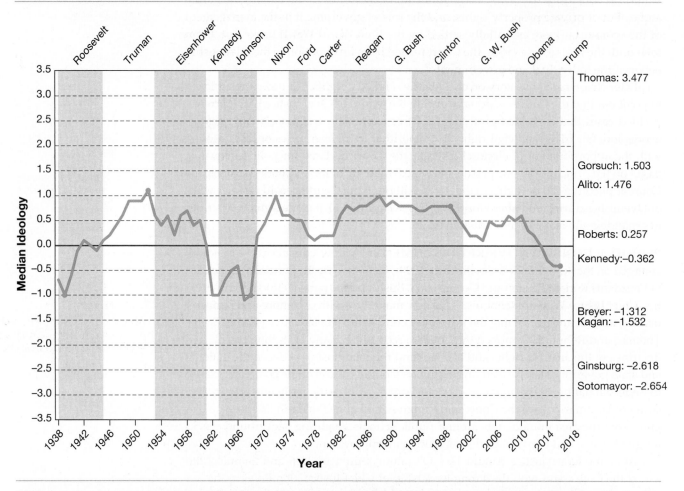

NOTE: Justice Neil Gorsuch replaced Justice Antonin Scalia in 2016. His conservative judicial philosophy is similar to Scalia's so the median of the Court probably did not change much in 2017. However, Brett Kavanaugh, by every indication is a much more conservative justice than Anthony Kennedy who he replaced, so the median score for the Court probably will have shifted to the right after 2018.

SOURCE: Andrew D. Martin and Kevin M. Quinn, "Dynamic Ideal Point Estimation via Markov Chain Monte Carlo for the U.S. Supreme Court, 1953–1999," *Political Analysis* 10 (2002), pp. 134–153. [Scores updated through 2016: http://mqscores.lsa.umich.edu/measures.php]; and Adam Liptak and Alicia Parlapiano, "Conservatives in Charge, the Supreme Court Moved Right," *The New York Times* (June 28, 2018) online at https://www.nytimes.com/interactive/2018/06/28/us/politics/supreme-court-2017-term-moved-right.html

past rulings (precedents) on the same issue in which it had upheld restrictions on corporation campaign activity in the statutes of twenty-one states. In a 2011 case involving Walmart, the Court issued a ruling making it more difficult for consumers and employees to bring class-action lawsuits against businesses. In 2012, it made a ruling making it more difficult for public-sector unions to raise money to use in political campaigns. In 2018 it dealt a crippling blow to public employee unions when it ruled in *Janus v. AFCME* that nonunion members cannot be forced to pay to support union efforts to improve wages, benefits, and working conditions. In a series of cases in 2013, the Court made it more difficult to bring class-action suits against large corporations. In 2018 it ruled that employees could not bring class-action suits against their employers for alleged wage theft. In 2016, it placed a stay on the EPA's rules to limit emissions from coal-fired power plants. Perhaps the best indicator of the ideological leaning of the Roberts Court is the mounting success of the U.S. Chamber of Commerce before the Court. As we pointed out in Chapter 7, in the many cases supported by it, the Chamber was on the winning side 43 percent of the time before the Burger Court (1981–1993), 56 percent of the time during the Rehnquist years (1994–2004), and 69 percent of the time during the Roberts years (2006–2016). As you saw in Chapter 7, the Chamber won almost 80 percent of the time after Gorsuch joined the Court in 2017.

There were two exceptions to the ever-more conservative drift of the Court while Kennedy was on the Court. First, the Court proved to be a strong defender of gay and lesbian rights, even ruling that state and federal laws against same-sex marriage are unconstitutional. For whatever reason, Justice Kennedy, normally part of the five-member majority conservative coalition during these years, swung to the liberal side on this issue. Many LGBTQ activists worry that the accession of Brett Kavanaugh to the Court to fill Kennedy's seat will put these advances in jeopardy. Second, and, for reasons that have stumped liberals and conservatives, and Democrats and Republicans, Chief Justice John Roberts provided the winning vote on the ruling that upheld the Affordable Care Act in 2012. It may be that the Chief Justice was worried about the standing of the Court were it to rule against such a massive program, with its millions of enrollees and scores of health insurance companies involved in its implementation and which had changed much of the landscape of the health care sector of the American economy. Of course, there is no way to know with any certainty. And, recall that he rejected Congress's use of the commerce clause to justify the Act and that this part of his opinion may represent a booby-trap for liberal legislation in the future.

The Debate over Judicial Activism

Has the Court become too involved in national policy making? Many people think so; others think not. Let us examine several of the ways in which **judicial activism** is expressed.[73]

JUDICIAL REVIEW We have already seen how, under John Marshall's leadership, the Court claimed the right of judicial review in the case of *Marbury v. Madison* (1803). Still, the Court did not exercise that power to any great extent until the late 19th century. The use of judicial review increased during the 20th century, however, with most of the Court's adverse attention being paid to the states. As described earlier, the Rehnquist Court was fairly aggressive in overturning federal statutes, averaging almost six per term from 1994 to 2005, compared with one every two years from the end of the Civil War to the early 1990s.[74] Oddly, given the tendency of conservative activists and organizations to be the most vociferously concerned about an overly activist judiciary, it was the most conservative members of the Court who most frequently voted to overturn congressional statutes during these years.[75] The Roberts Court seems to be even more aggressively moving in this direction with the conservative majority most often ruling against the actions of the political bodies, Congress and the president.[76] These trends in the use of judicial review suggest that over time the Court has become more willing to monitor the activities of the other branches of the federal government.

REVERSING THE DECISIONS OF PAST SUPREME COURTS Despite the norm of precedent (*stare decisis*) that guides judicial decision making, the Warren, Burger, Rehnquist, and Roberts Courts all overturned previous Court decisions. The most dramatic instance was the Warren Court's reversal of *Plessy v. Ferguson* (1896), which had endorsed legal segregation in the South, with *Brown v. Board of Education* (1954), which removed segregation's legal underpinnings. The Rehnquist Court overturned a number of previous Court decisions that had expanded the rights of criminal defendants and that had supported the extension of federal government power, reviewed earlier. When the Roberts Court upheld the federal Partial-Birth Abortion Ban Act, it reversed its own position on an identical Nebraska law it had declared unconstitutional in 2000. In *Citizens United v. Federal Election Commission* (2010), the Court overturned three of its

judicial activism
Actions by the courts that purportedly go beyond the role of the judiciary as interpreter of the law and adjudicator of disputes.

REDUCED DAMAGES

The *Exxon Valdez* oil spill in Prince William Sound in Alaska in 1989 caused substantial environmental damage and hurt the area's fishing- and tourist-based economy. After a long legal battle, the Roberts Court in 2008 dramatically reduced the money the big energy company owed in punitive damages for its negligence, overturning the actions of lower federal courts.

With Congress and the president often gridlocked, does it make sense for both liberal and conservative groups to turn to the federal courts to fashion the sorts of public policies they support?

remedy

An action that a court determines must be taken to rectify a wrong done by government.

own precedents, including cases from 1990, 2003, and 2007. In his dissent in this case, read from the bench as a sign of his deep displeasure with the majority, Justice John Paul Stevens lamented what he took to be the overly broad and ambitious reach of the majority, saying "essentially, five justices were unhappy with the limited nature of the case before us, so they changed the case to give themselves an opportunity to change the law." In 2018, the Court again reversed one of its long-standing precedents—this one stretching back over four decades and reaffirmed on several occasions since—when it ruled against public sector unions collecting fees from nonunion member state employees protected by union agreements with state and local governments.

DECIDING "POLITICAL" ISSUES   Critics claim that the Court is taking on too many matters best left to the elected branches of government. An oft-cited example is the Court's willingness to become increasingly involved in the process of drawing congressional electoral district boundaries in the states. Defenders of the Court argue that when such basic constitutional rights as equality of citizenship are at peril, the Court is obligated to protect these rights, no matter what other government bodies may choose to do. The Court's intervention in the 2000 presidential election generated widespread criticism for its meddling in politics, although its many defenders insist that the Court's decision in *Bush v. Gore* saved the nation from a constitutional crisis.

REMEDIES   The most criticized aspect of judicial activism is the tendency for federal judges to impose broad remedies on states and localities. A **remedy** is what a court determines must be done to rectify a wrong. Since the 1960s, the Court has been more willing than in the past to impose remedies that require other governmental bodies to take action. Some of the most controversial of these remedies include court orders requiring states to build more prison space and mandating that school districts bus students to achieve racial balance. Such remedies often require that governments spend public funds for things they do not necessarily want to do. Critics claim that the federal judiciary's legitimate role is to prevent government actions that threaten rights and liberties, not to compel government to take action to meet some policy goal.

STRICT CONSTRUCTION   Many conservative legal scholars and judges believe that the Constitution is not, as we suggested in Chapter 2, a "living" document whose meaning does and should change as the United States evolves, but one that must be

DECIDING THE 2000 PRESIDENTIAL ELECTION
The outcome of the closely fought 2000 presidential election was not finally decided until the Supreme Court stopped the recount in Florida, giving the state's electoral votes to George W. Bush. Here, passionate supporters of Bush and Al Gore demonstrate in front of the Supreme Court building while awaiting its decision.
Do you think the Court's intervention was in the nation's best interest?

true to its beginnings, a position often called **strict construction**. Strict construction takes two very closely related forms: Advocates of **original intention** believe the Court must be guided by the original intentions of the framers when they wrote the document in Philadelphia in 1787 and ratified it in 1788; advocates of **originalism** like the late Antonin Scalia, believe judges should interpret the Constitution in light of the original meaning of the text (words and phrases) as understood by the people who wrote and ratified it.[77] Strict constructionists believe the expansion of rights that has occurred since the mid-1960s—such as the new right to privacy that formed the basis of the *Roe v. Wade* decision and rights for criminal defendants—is illegitimate, having no foundation in the framers' intentions or the text of the Constitution.

Critics of **strict construction** believe that the intentions of the framers and the meaning of the text at the time of the founding are not only impossible to determine but also unduly constricting. They point out that original intent cannot be known, mostly because the only record of the debates at the constitutional convention are Madison's[78] notes, which incorporated only about 10 percent of what was said, according to scholars. Moreover, it is not entirely clear how to define the framers. Is it all who attended the convention? All who signed the document? And what about the ratification conventions in the states? Do we include them among what we might call the Founders, knowing that there were several states that voted against the Constitution and many who dissented from the majority in those state conventions that voted to ratify? Other critics wonder why we ought to be bound by late-18th-century interpretations of the meaning of words, even if it were possible to uncover what the words meant to people at the time.[79] Most importantly, strict construction, according to its many critics, is unduly constricting in light of the great transformations that have occurred in American society in the years since ratification. What seems more reasonable in this view is to have jurists try to reconcile the fundamental principles of the Constitution with changing conditions in the United States and the democratic aspirations of the American people.[80]

Clearly, the modern Supreme Court is more activist than it was in the past; most justices today hold a more expansive view of the role of the Court in forging national policy than their predecessors. And because the Court is likely to remain activist under Chief Justice John Roberts or any future chief justice, the debate about judicial activism is likely to remain important in American politics.

original intent
The doctrine that the courts must interpret the Constitution in ways consistent with the intentions of the framers rather than in light of contemporary conditions and needs.

originalism
The doctrine that judges must interpret the Constitution based on the exact meaning of the words and phrases in the document as understood by the Framers.

strict construction
The doctrine that the provisions of the Constitution have a clear meaning and that judges must stick closely to this meaning when rendering decisions.

THE COURTS: DOES THE SUPREME COURT ENHANCE AMERICAN DEMOCRACY?

The framers designed the Supreme Court as an institution that would serve as a check on the other branches, most especially on Congress, the only semi-democratic institution of the lot in their original design. They also structured the Court to be the least democratic of the branches in the new federal government, with justices appointed rather than elected and serving for life rather than for a fixed term of office. The framers wanted the judiciary to function as a referee who stands above the fray, preserving the rules, overseeing the orderly changing of some rules when the situation demands it, protecting minorities against the potentially tyrannical behavior of the majority, and protecting individuals in the exercise of their constitutionally guaranteed rights. From the perspective of democratic theory, however, it is unacceptable that one of the three main branches of the federal government in the United States—with the power to override the decisions of presidents, Congress, and state legislatures and to make binding decisions for the nation as a whole—is staffed with members who never face the judgment of the voters. It also is troubling how the Court has often sided with the business community against other sectors of American society, over-ruling laws and regulations passed by the popular branches of government. And the Court recently has been unwilling to tackle extreme partisan gerrymandering of House districts that result in the underrepresentation of the views of the majority of voters in a wide swath of states.

Although designed as an antimajoritarian institution, the Supreme Court has sometimes been more responsive to majoritarian political actors and to the public than the framers ever imagined would be the case. For example, we have seen that the Supreme Court does not often stray very far from what is acceptable to the president and Congress or to private elites; we have seen, also, that the Court acts consistently with public opinion about as often as Congress and the president do. In addition, as the chapters on civil rights and civil liberties will show, the Court has sometimes played an important and positive role in the protection of minority rights and liberties in the United States, although it has been inconsistent and slow in doing so.

The overall view suggests that, whatever the intention of the framers or the original meaning of the Constitution, the Court has not acted consistently as an antimajoritarian institution, though it has sometimes done so. It is a mixed picture. The Court has sometimes been the protector of democracy and individual rights and liberties, and sometimes not. The Court, being a creature of the Constitution, the political process, social and cultural trends, and the proclivities of individual justices, is hard to unambiguously categorize in terms of its democratic character.

THE FOUNDATIONS OF JUDICIAL POWER

14.1 Describe the constitutional and political foundations of federal judicial power in the United States.

Despite the fact that Article III of the Constitution is quite vague about the powers and responsibilities of the U.S. Supreme Court, the Court has fashioned a powerful position for itself in American politics, coequal with the executive and legislative branches.

Under Justice John Marshall in the early 19th century, the Court first claimed its right to rule on the constitutionality of state and federal legislation. The Court exercised its power of judicial review in the 19th century primarily over state actions, with particular regard to preventing regulation of business.

The Rehnquist and Roberts Courts regularly overruled Congress and, beginning in the 2000s, the president as well.

THE FEDERAL COURT SYSTEM: JURISDICTION AND ORGANIZATION

14.2 Describe the structure of the federal judiciary.

The federal court system is made up of three parts. At the bottom are ninety-four federal district courts, in which most cases originate. In the middle are thirteen appeals courts. At the top is the Supreme Court, with both original and appellate jurisdiction. Only a relative handful of the thousands of cases filed in the federal district courts make it to the Supreme Court.

APPOINTMENT TO THE FEDERAL BENCH

14.3 Describe the background of appointees to the federal bench and the process by which they are appointed.

Until quite recently, the federal judiciary was dominated by white Protestant men from top law firms and law schools or from government service.

Today, many more women and racial and ethnic minorities serve in the federal judiciary, with one African American man and three women, one of whom is Hispanic, on the Supreme Court. A majority of the justices on the current Court are Catholic.

The appointment process is highly political and increasingly contentious, with presidents trying to leave their mark on the Court, the political parties bringing ideological views to the process, and interest and advocacy groups fully engaged.

THE SUPREME COURT IN ACTION

14.4 Outline the process by which the Supreme Court makes decisions and the factors that influence judicial decision making.

The Supreme Court operates on the basis of several widely shared norms: secrecy, seniority, and adherence to precedent. The Court controls its agenda by granting or not granting a writ of certiorari to cases filed.

Cases before the Court wend their way through the process in the following way: submission of briefs, oral argument, initial consideration in conference, opinion writing, and final conference consideration by the justices.

Published opinions serve as precedents for other federal courts and future Supreme Court decisions.

The decisions of the Court are influenced not only by the judicial philosophies of the justices, but also by the actions and preferences of other political actors such as the president and Congress as well as by interest groups and public and elite opinion.

Increasingly, the ideological predispositions and partisan identifications of the justices determine how they vote on cases. The Supreme Court was dominated by a conservative majority appointed by Republican presidents until the death of Justice Scalia in early 2016.

THE SUPREME COURT AS A NATIONAL POLICY MAKER

14.5 Evaluate the role of the Supreme Court in national policy making.

The Supreme Court is a national policy maker of considerable importance. Its rulings not only settle disputes between political actors on critical matters and help define the meaning of the Constitution for others in the political system, but it also is quite active in pushing its own policy agenda.

The Court often serves as the referee of the democratic process and the rights of minorities, although it has sometimes failed to do this.

LEARN THE TERMS

amicus curiae   Latin for "friend of the court"; a legal brief in which individuals not party to a suit may have their views heard in court.

appellate courts   Courts that hear cases on appeal from other courts.

briefs   Documents setting out the arguments in legal cases, prepared by attorneys and presented to courts.

circuit courts   The twelve geographical jurisdictions and one special court that hear appeals from the federal district courts.

class-action suit   A suit brought on behalf of a group of people who are in a situation similar to that of the plaintiffs.

concurring opinion   The opinion of one or more judges who vote with the majority on a case but wish to set out different reasons for their decision.

constitutional courts   Federal courts created by Congress under the authority of Article III of the Constitution.

dissenting opinion   The opinion of the judge or judges who are in the minority on a particular case before the Supreme Court.

grand juries   Groups of citizens who decide whether there is sufficient evidence to bring an indictment against accused persons.

in forma pauperis   Describing a process by which indigents may file a suit with the Supreme Court free of charge.

judicial activism   Actions by the courts that purportedly go beyond the role of the judiciary as interpreter of the law and adjudicator of disputes.

judicial review   The power of the Supreme Court to declare actions of the other branches and levels of government unconstitutional.

laissez-faire   The political-economic doctrine that holds that government ought not interfere with the operations of the free market.

legislative courts   Highly specialized federal courts created by Congress under the authority of Article I of the Constitution.

opinion   The explanation of the majority's and the minority's reasoning that accompanies a court decision.

opinion of the Court   The majority opinion that accompanies a Supreme Court decision; also called the majority opinion.

original intent   The doctrine that the courts must interpret the Constitution in ways consistent with the intentions of the framers rather than in light of contemporary conditions and needs.

original jurisdiction   The authority of a court to be the first to hear a particular kind of case.

originalism   The doctrine that judges must interpret the Constitution based on the exact meaning of the words and phrases in the document as understood by the Framers.

petit (trial) juries   Juries that hear evidence and sit in judgment on charges brought in civil or criminal cases.

plaintiff   One who brings suit in a court.

precedents   Past rulings by courts that guide judicial reasoning in subsequent cases.

remedy   An action that a court determines must be taken to rectify a wrong done by government.

rule of four   An *unwritten* practice that requires at least four justices of the Supreme Court to agree that a case warrants review by the Court before it will hear the case.

senatorial courtesy   The tradition that a judicial nomination for a federal district court seat be approved by the senior senator of the president's party from the state where a district court is located before the nominee is considered by the Senate Judiciary Committee.

separate but equal doctrine   The principle articulated in *Plessy v. Ferguson* (1896) that laws prescribing separate public facilities and services for nonwhite Americans are permissible if the facilities and services are equal to those provided for whites.

standing   Authority to bring legal action because one is directly affected by the issues at hand.

stare decisis   The legal doctrine that says precedent should guide judicial decision making.

strict construction   The doctrine that the provisions of the Constitution have a clear meaning and that judges must stick closely to this meaning when rendering decisions.

test case   A case brought by advocacy or interest groups to try to force a ruling on the constitutionality of some law or executive action.

writ of certiorari   An announcement that the Supreme Court will hear a case on appeal from a lower court; its issuance requires the vote of four of the nine justices.

CHAPTER 15

WHERE IS MY PRIVACY?

WHERE IS MY PRIVACY?

Although most government officials describe Edward Snowden as a traitor, civil liberties advocates view him as a hero for revealing government surveillance practices they see as violations of citizens' freedom from government interference. *How should we find the appropriate balance between protecting citizens' privacy and ensuring that the public is safe?*

CIVIL LIBERTIES: THE STRUGGLE FOR FREEDOM

CHAPTER OUTLINE AND LEARNING OBJECTIVES

CIVIL LIBERTIES IN THE CONSTITUTION

15.1 Discuss the constitutional basis for civil liberties, and trace the process by which these liberties have gradually been applied to the states.

FIRST AMENDMENT FREEDOMS

15.2 Identify the freedoms enumerated in the First Amendment.

RIGHTS OF THE ACCUSED

15.3 Enumerate the constitutional rights of the accused, and discuss the impact of terrorism on these rights.

RIGHT TO PRIVACY

15.4 Outline the constitutional justification for the right to privacy.

The Struggle for Democracy

DIGITAL SURVEILLANCE AND THE WAR ON TERROR

On June 13, 2013, the British newspaper *The Guardian* revealed that it had obtained documents exposing a secret spy program operated by the National Security Agency (NSA), a bureaucracy within the United States Department of Defense. The source of the leaks was later discovered to be Edward Snowden, a former computer technician working for a private contractor with access to the NSA's computers. Snowden's revelations led the U.S. government to charge him with espionage, while others called him a hero for exposing massive (and unprecedented) government-sanctioned spying on private citizens.

The most prominent NSA spying program, called PRISM, seems to have scooped up millions of phone records, e-mails, and other information on Internet usage through sophisticated technology, with the cooperation of the largest telecom firms in the country, including Verizon, AT&T, and Sprint. In the wake of 9/11 and the War on Terror, the government sought new ways to gather digital data, and Congress passed changes to existing laws in 2001, 2007, and 2008 to enable such data mining. PRISM and other programs were apparently authorized by these amendments.[1]

The sheer size and scope of PRISM was controversial once exposed to the American public. Additional details revealed since Snowden's initial revelations outraged many and forced Congress to reassess. For example, documents revealed that the NSA collected information about the phone usage of American citizens, such as the phone number called and the length of the call, though not what was actually said. The data was also used to create social network maps, allowing the NSA to see potential targets' friends and frequent contacts. Further, the NSA tapped the personal cell phones of foreign leaders like German Chancellor Angela Merkel and listened in on private conversations held in foreign embassies—tactics typically reserved for hostile governments, not important European allies.

Despite denials from the NSA, *The Guardian* reported that the agency taps into fiber optic cables and then stores metadata, which *The Guardian* describes as "a record of almost anything a user does online, from browsing history—such as map searches and websites visited—to account details, e-mail activity, and even some account passwords."[2] Finally, various newspapers have reported that the NSA can't even keep track of the data it collects and frequently violates its own rules about data collection. The *Wall Street Journal* reported that NSA officers sometimes used technology to spy on love interests.[3]

*   *   *   *   *

Proponents of the NSA's data collection programs say they are necessary to find terrorists and prevent future attacks. Many believe it is crucial for the government to do everything possible to seek out, investigate, and prevent destructive acts. One of the primary goals of government is, after all, to protect its citizens. But the framers were well aware that governments may use their police power to tyrannize individuals and groups. To balance these competing goals, the framers enshrined **civil liberties** into the Constitution, especially through the Bill of Rights. Civil liberties are freedoms granted to citizens which protect them from certain types of government interference and prevent the government from becoming too powerful.

On the surface, the liberties outlined in the Constitution may appear to be relatively straightforward. However, the broad language used in the Constitution means that there is often no clear way of determining the limits of government action. Over time, the boundaries between government actions and our rights have been redrawn in response to changing technology, social circumstances, and other dynamics. For example, the framers could have never imagined spying programs as sophisticated as those done by the NSA, but we must still use the Constitution to decide whether government storage of citizens' private e-mails violates an individual's civil liberties. Determining appropriates uses of government power is done through the Supreme Court, through the lawmaking process, and through the public's changing perceptions of what civil liberties mean.

civil liberties

Freedoms found primarily in the Bill of Rights, the enjoyment of which are protected from government interference.

THINKING CRITICALLY **ABOUT THIS CHAPTER**

This chapter is about civil liberties in the United States, with special attention on how historical developments, politics, and government policies have influenced the degree to which Americans can and do exercise their freedoms.

APPLYING THE **FRAMEWORK**

You will see in this chapter how *structural, political linkage, and governmental factors* influence the meaning and practice of civic freedoms. Although the decisions of the Supreme Court are particularly important in determining the status of civil liberties at any particular moment in American history, you will learn how they are also the product of influences from a wide range of actors, institutions, and social processes.

USING THE **DEMOCRACY STANDARD**

You will see in this chapter how the expansion of the enjoyment of civil liberties in the United States has been a product of the struggle for democracy and how civil liberties are fundamental to the democratic process itself.

CIVIL LIBERTIES IN THE CONSTITUTION

15.1   Discuss the constitutional basis for civil liberties, and trace the process by which these liberties have gradually been applied to the states.

The framers were particularly concerned about establishing a society in which liberty might flourish. While government was necessary to protect liberty from the threat of anarchy, the framers believed government might threaten liberty if it became too powerful and used that power to unfairly jail citizens or impose excessive restrictions on how people could live their daily lives. Political liberty is essential to both popular sovereignty and political equality. Popular sovereignty cannot be guaranteed if people are prevented from criticizing the government and political equality is violated if some people can speak out but others cannot.

Explicit Protections in the Constitution

In the Preamble to the Constitution, the framers wrote that they aimed to "secure the Blessings of Liberty to ourselves and our Posterity." But the Constitution, as originally ratified, protected few liberties from the national government and almost none from state governments. Rather than listing specific prohibitions against certain kinds of government action, the framers believed a republican constitutional design that separated powers, allowed for checks and balances, and distributed power across federal and state levels of government through federalism would best protect liberty. Still, the framers singled out a few freedoms as too crucial to be left unmentioned. For example, the Constitution prohibits Congress and the states from suspending the writ of *habeas corpus*, which prohibits the government from arresting an individual and holding that person without a trial or hearing on their guilt. The Constitution also prohibits the legislature from passing **bills of attainder**, laws that declare a person or a group of people guilty of a crime or punish them without a trial. Finally, Article I prohibits **ex post facto laws**, acts passed by Congress outlawing a previously legal activity, allowing the government to arrest someone for doing something that was legal at the time they did it (see Table 15.1 for an enumeration of civil liberties in the U.S. Constitution).

habeas corpus

The legal doctrine that a person who is arrested must have a timely hearing before a judge.

bill of attainder

A law that declares a person or a group of people guilty of a crime or punishes them without a trial.

ex post facto law

A law that retroactively declares some action illegal.

TABLE 15.1 CIVIL LIBERTIES IN THE U.S. CONSTITUTION

The exact meaning and extent of civil liberties in the Constitution are matters of debate, but this table presents the principal freedoms either spelled out in the text of the Constitution and its amendments or clarified by early court decisions.

Constitution		
Article I	Section 9	Congress may not suspend habeas corpus.
		Congress may not pass bills of attainder or ex post facto laws.
Article I	Section 10	States may not pass bills of attainder or ex post facto laws.
		States may not impair obligation of contracts.
Article III	Section 2	Criminal trials in federal courts must be jury trials in the state in which the defendant is alleged to have committed the crime.
Article III	Section 3	No one may be convicted of treason unless there is a confession in open court or testimony of two witnesses to the same overt act.

The Bill of Rights	
First Amendment	Congress may not make any law with respect to the establishment of religion.
	Congress may not abridge the free exercise of religion.
	Congress may not abridge freedom of speech or of the press.
	Congress may not abridge the right to assemble or to petition the government.
Second Amendment	Congress may not infringe the right to keep and bear arms.
Third Amendment	Congress may not station soldiers in houses against their owners' will, except in times of war.
Fourth Amendment	Citizens are to be free from unreasonable searches and seizures.
	Federal courts may issue search warrants based only on probable cause and specifically describing the objects of the search.
Fifth Amendment	Citizens are protected against double jeopardy (being prosecuted more than once for the same crime) and self-incrimination.
	Citizens are protected against the deprivation of life, liberty, or property without due process of law.
	Citizens are guaranteed just compensation for public use of their private property.
Sixth Amendment	Citizens have the right to a speedy and public trial before an impartial jury.
	Citizens have the right to face their accuser and to cross-examine witnesses.
Seventh Amendment	Citizens have right to trial by jury in civil cases.
	Judges cannot overrule judgments of fact made by juries.
Eighth Amendment	Excessive bail and fines are prohibited.
	Cruel and unusual punishments are prohibited.

During the debate over the ratification of the Constitution, many citizens were concerned that the new government was too powerful and not enough rights were included in the Constitution. Many Anti-Federalists criticized the lack of specific protections for the rights of individuals, and their arguments were persuasive. As a result, the Federalists promised a "bill of rights," amendments to the Constitution to be passed during the first congressional term, as a condition for ratifying the Constitution. The Bill of Rights was passed by Congress in 1789 and was ratified by the required number of states by 1791 (though twelve amendments were proposed, only ten were actually ratified). Passage of the Bill of Rights made the Constitution more democratic by specifying new limits on the types of laws the national government could implement. These limits were meant to ensure that the new national government could not infringe on freedoms that many view as crucial to ensuring popular sovereignty.

Reading the Constitution and its amendments, however, reveals how decisions by government officials and changes brought about by political leaders, interest groups, social movements, and individuals have remade the Constitution over time; hence many of the freedoms we expect today are not explicitly spelled out there. A variety of dynamics led to the extensions of civil liberties, including evolving interpretations of laws by judges and other officials, the passage of new constitutional amendments, and changes stemming from the American people's willingness to accept novel and even once-threatening ideas. Still other liberties have secured a place in the Republic through partisan and ideological combat. It is also important to remember that many of the rights listed in the Constitution, and those which have developed over the years through all these forces, are often poorly defined, vague, and controversial. In addition, the liberties outlined in the Constitution initially only placed limits on the federal government, not the state governments. Thus, many of the most important debates about civil liberties in our country today involve the appropriate interpretation and application of different provisions in the Constitution. The key to understanding civil liberties in the United States, then, is to follow their evolution over the course of our nation's history.

Incorporation of the Bill of Rights

After the Bill of Rights was added, the most important change to the language of the Constitution regarding civil liberties was the ratification of the Fourteenth Amendment in 1868. The Thirteenth (ending slavery), Fourteenth, and Fifteenth (the right to vote regardless of race or previous condition of servitude) Amendments were passed in the aftermath of the Civil War, pushed by northern Reconstructionists as a way to end slavery and bring about more equal treatment for blacks. The Fourteenth Amendment has proven hugely consequential for a number of reasons, but one of the most important consequences of this amendment is the legal framework that has been used to apply the civil liberties protections laid out in the Constitution to the states. As noted above, when the Bill of Rights was originally passed, the protections against government interference applied only to the federal government, not the states. Most of the states, after all, had bills of rights in their own constitutions, and the framers believed that because they were closer to the people, state governments would be less likely to intrude on the people's freedom. However, the experience of slaves in southern states demonstrates that states can also violate individual liberties just as readily as the federal government. That the Bill of Rights prohibits certain actions only by the national government seems explicit in the language of many of the first ten amendments. The First Amendment, for instance, starts with the words *"Congress shall make no law...."* This view of the Bill of Rights, as not applying to the states, was confirmed by Chief Justice John Marshall in *Barron v. Baltimore* (1833). As he put it:

> The Constitution was ordained and established by the people of the United States for themselves, for their own government, and not for the government of the individual states.

SLAVES HARVESTING THE COTTON CROP

Before passage of the Thirteenth and Fourteenth Amendments after the Civil War, slaves in the states of the American South where slavery was allowed by state constitutions were considered to be nothing more nor less than the private property of their owners. Here slaves on a large plantation, who enjoyed no rights to life or liberty under state laws, bring cotton to a cotton gin for processing. *Are there some decisions about people's civil rights and liberties that are so fundamental that they should not be left to the individual states?*

Three parts (or clauses) of the Fourteenth Amendment have each played a significant role in the expansion of civil liberty protections in the United States because they include language saying that there are some fundamental liberties that not only policy makers in the federal government, but also those in state governments, are bound to protect.

privileges or immunities clause

The portion of the Fourteenth Amendment that says states may not make laws that abridge the rights granted to people as citizens of the United States.

due process clause

The section of the Fourteenth Amendment that prohibits states from depriving anyone of life, liberty, or property "without due process of law," a guarantee against arbitrary or unfair government action.

equal protection clause

The section of the Fourteenth Amendment that provides for equal treatment by government of people residing within the United States and each of its states.

selective incorporation

The gradual and piecemeal spread of the protections of the Bill of Rights to the states by the U.S. Supreme Court.

1. The **privileges or immunities clause** specifies that no *state* "shall make or enforce any law which shall abridge the privileges or immunities of citizens of the United States."

2. The **due process clause** specifies that no *state* shall "deprive any person of life, liberty, or property, without due process of law."

3. The **equal protection clause** requires states to provide equal treatment for all persons within their boundaries.

The Supreme Court has interpreted these three clauses as limiting the ability of states to deny the civil liberties described elsewhere in the Constitution to its residents, but it has done so slowly over time by ruling on each liberty separately. In other words, although the Court could have simply applied all civil liberties in the Bill of Rights to the states, liberties have been nationalized on a case-by-case basis through a process called **selective incorporation**.[4] Although most liberties described in the Constitution have been incorporated to the states, several liberties have not. These include the Third Amendment ban on government quartering of troops, the Fifth Amendment guarantee of the right to a grand jury hearing, the Seventh Amendment right to a jury trial in civil suits, and the Eighth Amendment prohibition against excessive fines. Refer to Figure 15.1, for a timeline of Supreme Court cases that have had the effect of extending the Bill of Rights to the states.

The most recent liberty to be incorporated to the states is the right to bear arms. The dynamics surrounding this incorporation also illustrate how interpretations of the text of the Constitution can change over time. The Second Amendment reads: "A well regulated Militia, being necessary to the security of a free State, the right of the people to keep and bear Arms, shall not be infringed." The Second Amendment was not explicitly interpreted as protecting an individual right of gun ownership until 2008 in *District of Columbia v. Heller* when the Supreme Court struck down a handgun ban in the District of Columbia, a city under the jurisdiction of the federal government. Two years later, the right to gun ownership was incorporated, that is, interpreted as applying to the states (in *McDonald v. Chicago*, 2010). The prevailing view in the courts until *McDonald* had been that the Second Amendment protects a collective right to form militias rather than an individual right to gun ownership. Gun advocates, the National Rifle Association, and libertarian organizations like the Cato Institute, on the other hand, having long held that the Second Amendment is a fundamental individual right, felt vindicated by the Supreme Court's affirmation in *Heller* and *McDonald*. The issue of gun rights is not entirely settled, however. Exactly how much state and local regulation of gun ownership the Court will allow remains an open question.

FIRST AMENDMENT FREEDOMS

15.2 Identify the freedoms enumerated in the First Amendment.

The First Amendment protects the rights of Americans to freedom of speech, freedom of the press, and freedom of religion. But these freedoms are not unlimited. Under what conditions should free speech, freedom of the press, and religious freedom be restricted?

FIGURE 15.1 TIMELINE: MILESTONES IN INCORPORATION OF THE BILL OF RIGHTS

Over time the Supreme Court has extended protections enshrined in the Bill of Rights to the states on a case-by-case basis. Originally these rights were understood only as protections from the actions of the national government.

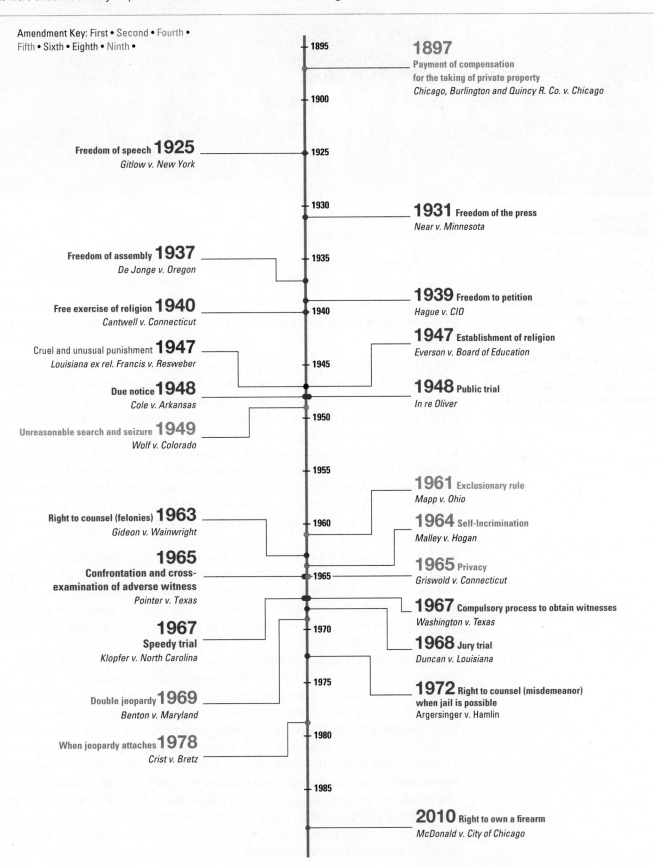

Amendment Key: First • Second • Fourth •
Fifth • Sixth • Eighth • Ninth •

1897
Payment of compensation
for the taking of private property
Chicago, Burlington and Quincy R. Co. v. Chicago

Freedom of speech **1925**
Gitlow v. New York

1931 Freedom of the press
Near v. Minnesota

Freedom of assembly **1937**
De Jonge v. Oregon

1939 Freedom to petition
Hague v. CIO

Free exercise of religion **1940**
Cantwell v. Connecticut

1947 Establishment of religion
Everson v. Board of Education

Cruel and unusual punishment **1947**
Louisiana ex rel. Francis v. Resweber

Due notice **1948**
Cole v. Arkansas

1948 Public trial
In re Oliver

Unreasonable search and seizure **1949**
Wolf v. Colorado

1961 Exclusionary rule
Mapp v. Ohio

Right to counsel (felonies) **1963**
Gideon v. Wainwright

1964 Self-Incrimination
Malley v. Hogan

1965
Confrontation and cross-
examination of adverse witness
Pointer v. Texas

1965 Privacy
Griswold v. Connecticut

1967 Compulsory process to obtain witnesses
Washington v. Texas

1967
Speedy trial
Klopfer v. North Carolina

1968 Jury trial
Duncan v. Louisiana

Double jeopardy **1969**
Benton v. Maryland

1972 Right to counsel (misdemeanor)
when jail is possible
Argersinger v. Hamlin

When jeopardy attaches **1978**
Crist v. Bretz

2010 Right to own a firearm
McDonald v. City of Chicago

SOURCE: United States Supreme Court.

**THE FRAMERS OF
THE CONSTITUTION**

The Framers of the Constitution were wary of a tyrannical central government. The Bill of Rights was intended to ensure that the new national government could not interfere excessively in people's personal lives or punish those who were critical of the government. *Over two centuries have passed since the Bill of Rights was ratified. Are these protections still needed or can the government today be trusted to ensure that people are allowed to speak freely and practice religion as they choose?*

Freedom of Speech

> Congress shall make no Law … abridging the freedom of speech.
> —First Amendment to the U.S. Constitution

Speech can take many forms. The Supreme Court has had to consider which forms of speech are protected under the Constitution and exactly how far these protections extend.

POLITICAL SPEECH For many people, the right to speak one's mind is the first principle of a free and democratic society. Democratic theorists have argued, by and large, that a democratic society is based not only on popular sovereignty but on the existence of a range of freedoms that allow unrestricted conversations about the kind of government and the sorts of public policies that people consider good and appropriate. Central among these freedoms is speech, the idea being that public discourse about government and politics depends on the ability and willingness of people to express their views, even if it means saying unpopular, even inflammatory things. Justice Oliver Wendell Holmes described the centrality of this "marketplace of ideas" in a free society in his famous and influential dissenting opinion in *Abrams v. United States* (1919).

Given the centrality of free speech to democracy, it is perhaps odd that free speech was not nationalized by the Supreme Court until *Gitlow v. New York* (1925). Benjamin Gitlow, who had published *The Left Wing Manifesto*, embraced a militant and revolutionary socialism. Gitlow did not advocate any specific action that might break the law, but he was nonetheless convicted of a felony under the New York Criminal Anarchy Law (1902).

The Supreme Court majority held that New York was bound by the First Amendment—thus nationalizing the First Amendment and making it binding on all other states. But the Court simultaneously argued that the First Amendment did not prohibit New York from incarcerating Gitlow for publishing his incendiary pamphlet. It represented a danger to peace and order for which, said Justice Edward Sanford, "A single revolutionary spark may kindle a fire that, smoldering for a time, may burst into a sweeping and destructive conflagration. It cannot be said that the State is acting … unreasonably when … it seeks to extinguish the spark without waiting until it has enkindled the flame or blazed into the conflagration." In his famous dissent, Justice Oliver Wendell Holmes said, "Every idea is an incitement…. Eloquence may set fire to reason. But whatever may be thought of the redundant discourse before us, it had no chance of starting a present conflagration."

Freedom of speech has grown in the ensuing years so that far more speech is protected than is not. In general, no U.S. government today—whether federal, state, or local—can regulate or interfere with the content of speech without a compelling reason. For a reason to be compelling, a government must show that the speech poses a "clear and present danger" that it has a duty to prevent—the standard formulated by Holmes in *Schenck v. United States* (1919). However, this is not sufficient. The danger must also be substantial, and the relationship between the speech and the danger must be direct, such as falsely yelling "Fire!" in a crowded theater. The danger must also be so immediate that the people responsible for maintaining order cannot afford to tolerate the speech. As the Court put it in *Brandenburg v. Ohio* (1969), in a case involving an appeal of the conviction of a leader of the Ku Klux Klan under Ohio's criminal syndicalism law, "… the constitutional guarantees of free speech … do not permit a State to forbid or proscribe advocacy of the use of force or of law violation except where such advocacy is directed to incitement or producing imminent lawless action and is likely to incite or produce such action." In establishing this **imminent lawless action test**, the Court ruled that abstract advocacy of ideas, even ideas considered dangerous by police, politicians, or popular majorities, cannot be prohibited simply because the government argues that it may cause problems or violence at some point in the future. In order for the government to be allowed to prohibit speech, it must be likely to lead directly and immediately to law breaking.

In the name of free speech, the Court has also been gradually taking down legislative efforts to restrict campaign spending in federal elections. In *Buckley v. Valeo* (1976), it invalidated a restriction of the Federal Election Campaign Act on how much money a candidate for federal office might put into his or her own campaign. Other important cases, including *Citizens United v. FEC* (2010) and

imminent lawless action test
Supreme Court standard that in order for the government to be allowed to prohibit speech, it must be likely to lead directly and immediately to law breaking.

FREE SPEECH ON CAMPUS

Milo Yiannopoulos spoke to a group at the University of California–Berkeley in September 2017. A scheduled speech by Yiannopoulos in February of that year was canceled after protests turned violent. Protesters said that Yiannopoulos' views are racist and misogynistic and that the university should not provide a platform for speakers who promote intolerance.
What kinds of limits should be put on student protests and speech on college campuses?

Speechnow.org v. FEC (2010), struck down various other laws limiting the ability of corporations and unions to collect and spend money on elections, giving rise to super PACs (see Chapter 10). The foundation for the Court's decisions in these cases was that money spent in campaigns expressing political ideas is speech that must be protected and that corporations and unions are "persons" under the Constitution with the same liberties as an individual citizen.

Not all political speech is protected from government restriction. The Supreme Court has allowed governments to restrain and punish speakers whose words can be shown to lead or to have led directly to acts of violence or vandalism, interfered with the constitutional rights of others (e.g., blocking access to an abortion clinic), disrupted a legitimate government function (e.g., a sit-in demonstration in the House chambers), or improperly divulged information contained in classified documents.

The Court has also allowed some restrictions on speech during time of war. But over the years, the Court has been careful to keep the leash tight on government officials who have tried to quiet the voice of citizens. Laws that restrict political speech typically must be content neutral (i.e., cannot favor some views over others), serve a legitimate government purpose, be narrowly tailored to address a specific problem, and not have a chilling effect on other people's willingness to exercise their free speech rights. All in all, freedom of speech has gained powerful legal foundations over the years and, as a result, remains a central component of democracy in the United States.[5]

ACTIONS AND SYMBOLIC SPEECH   Difficult questions about free expression persist, of course. Speech mixed with *conduct* may be restricted if the restrictions are narrowly and carefully tailored to curb the conduct while leaving the speech unmolested. Symbolic expressions (such as wearing armbands or picketing) may also receive less protection from the Court. Still, despite these limits, the right of free speech has grown in the United States to the point at which contenders now wrestle with relatively peripheral issues. In *Texas v. Johnson* (1989), Gregory Johnson challenged a Texas state law against flag desecration. Johnson had been convicted by the State of Texas for burning an American flag at the 1984 Republican convention in Dallas. Although dominated by a conservative majority, the Rehnquist Court overturned the Texas law and Johnson's conviction, affirming that flag burning, unless it is likely to incite imminent violence, falls under the free expression protections of the Constitution. In response to the Court's ruling in *Texas*, some members of Congress have tried on several occasions to pass a constitutional amendment banning flag desecration. Although polls typically find that most Americans think burning the flag should be illegal, efforts to ban flag burning through a Constitutional amendment have failed, highlighting how difficult it can be for elected officials to clarify the boundaries of the civil liberties protections.

SUPPRESSION OF FREE EXPRESSION   A major exception to the trending expansion of freedom of expression has been the periodic concern about internal security and national defense.[6] Fearing a rise of radicalism inflamed by the French Revolution, Congress passed the Sedition Act of 1798 to forbid criticism of the government and its leaders. Some states put restrictions on speech during the Civil War, although the national government remained surprisingly lenient on this score. (The Lincoln administration did, however, jail some rebel sympathizers without trial and used military tribunals to try civilians accused of actively helping the Southern cause.) Censorship of dissent and protests occurred during and after World War I; thirty-two states enacted laws to suppress dangerous ideas and talk, and local, state, and national officials led raids on the offices of "radicals." Hoping to become president, Attorney General A. Mitchell Palmer conducted raids on the headquarters of suspect organizations in 1919 and 1920, sending the young J. Edgar Hoover out to collect information on suspected anarchists and communists.

A similar period of hysteria followed World War II. Its foundations were laid when the Democrat-controlled House of Representatives impaneled the House Un-American

Activities Committee (generally referred to as the HUAC). When the Republicans won control of the Congress in 1952, they professed to see security risks in the Truman administration, labor unions, and Hollywood. Soon Democrats and Republicans alike were exploiting the "Red scare" for political gain. The greatest gain (and, subsequently, the hardest fall) was for Senator Joseph McCarthy (R-WI). McCarthy brandished lists of purported communists and denounced all who opposed him as traitors.[7]

More recently, many observers worry about the possible chilling effect on free speech and privacy violations stemming from new laws passed to combat terrorism. The Court has granted broad leeway to the government in fighting terrorism. For example, in *Holder v. Humanitarian Law Project* (2010)—the first test of the constitutionality of the PATRIOT Act's "material support" provision, the Court ruled that the government has very broad authority and can prosecute people for providing legal services and expert advice to government-designated terrorist organizations seeking to overturn their designation.

Freedom of the Press

> Congress shall make no law … abridging the freedom … of the press.
> —First Amendment to the U.S. Constitution

In its opinion in *Gitlow v. New York* (1925), the Supreme Court specified freedom of the press as a freedom guaranteed against state interference under the Fourteenth Amendment. This ruling was in line with the idea that the unencumbered flow of information is essential in a society that aspires to freedom and democracy.

PRIOR RESTRAINT   In *Near v. Minnesota* (1931), the Court made good on the promise of *Gitlow* by invalidating the Minnesota Public Nuisance Law as a violation of freedom of the press.[8] Jay Near published the *Saturday Press*, a scandal sheet that attacked public officials, Jews, Catholics, blacks, unions, and a few other groups he disliked. Near and his associates were ordered by a state court not to publish, sell, or possess the *Saturday Press*. This sort of state action is called **prior restraint** because it prevents publication before it has occurred. Freedom of the press is not necessarily infringed if publishers are sued or punished for harming others after they have published, but

SOUNDING THE ALARM ON THE COMMUNIST THREAT

Senator Joseph McCarthy made his reputation and career sounding the alarm bell about communists and communist sympathizers in every nook and cranny of the federal government. Though he was almost always wrong in his assertions and ruined the lives and careers of many, he did not stir the wrath of other elites until he took on the Army in 1954. Army counsel Joseph Welch listens in disbelief as the junior senator from Wisconsin points out the location of the latest threats during a committee hearing.
How might politicians today take advantage of the public's fears to justify restricting free expression or improve their own standing in the eyes of voters?

prior restraint
A government action prohibiting publication or broadcast of materials (rather than punishing publication afterward).

Minnesota was trying to keep Near and his associates from publishing in the future. The prohibition of prior restraint on publication is at the core of freedom of the press.[9]

Freedom of the press and freedom of speech tend to be considered together as freedom of expression, so the general principles applicable to free speech apply to freedom of the press as well. Thus, the Court will allow the repression of publication only if the state can show some "clear and present danger" that publication poses, similar to its position on free speech. In *New York Times v. United States* (1971), the Court ruled that the U.S. government could not prevent newspapers from publishing portions of the Pentagon Papers, secret government documents revealing how policy-makers had misled the public to justify involvement in the Vietnam War. A major expansion of freedom of the press was also established in *New York Times v. Sullivan* (1964), a ruling that protects newspapers against punishment for trivial or incidental errors when they are reporting on public persons. *New York Times v. Sullivan* limits the use or threat of libel prosecutions by officials because they can recover damages only by showing that the medium has purposely reported untruths or has made no effort to find out if what is being reported is true.

OFFENSIVE MEDIA   Pornography is a nonlegal term for offensive sexual materials; the legal term is obscenity. Although the courts have held that "obscenity" is not protected by the First Amendment, the definition of obscenity has provoked constitutional struggles for half a century. Early disputes concerned the importation and mailing of works that we regard today as literary classics: James Joyce's *Ulysses* and D. H. Lawrence's *Lady Chatterley's Lover*, for example.[10] Although justices have admitted that principled distinctions sometimes elude them (Justice Potter Stewart once famously said that he did not know how to define hard-core pornography but that he knew it when he saw it), a reasonably clear three-part test for obscenity emerged from *Miller v. California* (1973):

1. The average person, applying contemporary community standards, must find that the work as a whole appeals to the prurient interest (lust).

2. The state law must specifically define what depictions of sexual conduct are obscene.

3. The work as a whole must lack serious literary, artistic, political, or scientific value.

If the work survives even one part of this test, it is not legally obscene and is protected by the First Amendment. Community standards, applied by juries, are used to judge whether the work appeals to lust and whether the work is clearly offensive. However, literary, artistic, political, and scientific value (the *LAPS test*) is *not* judged by community standards but by the jury's assessment of the testimony of expert witnesses. If, and only if, all three standards are met, the Supreme Court allows local committees to regulate the sale of obscene materials. Because these tests are not easily met in practice, the *Miller* ruling has done little to stem the tide of sexually explicit material in American popular culture.[11] The Court has ruled, however, in *New York v. Ferber* (1982), that states can prohibit the production, distribution, and sale of child pornography.

Recently, many Americans have begun to worry about the availability to minors of sexually offensive material on the Internet. Responding to this concern, Congress and President Clinton cooperated in 1996 to pass the Communications Decency Act, which would have made it a crime to transmit over the Internet or to allow the transmission of indecent materials to which minors might have access. The Supreme Court, in *Reno, Attorney General of the United States v. American Civil Liberties Union* (1997), however, ruled unanimously that the legislation was an unconstitutional violation of the First Amendment, being overly broad and vague and violating the free speech rights of adults to receive and send information (the Court reaffirmed this ruling in 2004). The strong and unambiguous words of the opinion of the Court make it clear that government efforts to regulate the content of the Internet, as well as cable television, will not get very far.

Because the government licenses a limited number of airwaves (there are only so many frequencies available at any one time) and they are considered public property, broadcast television falls under different rules. Thus, the Court has allowed the

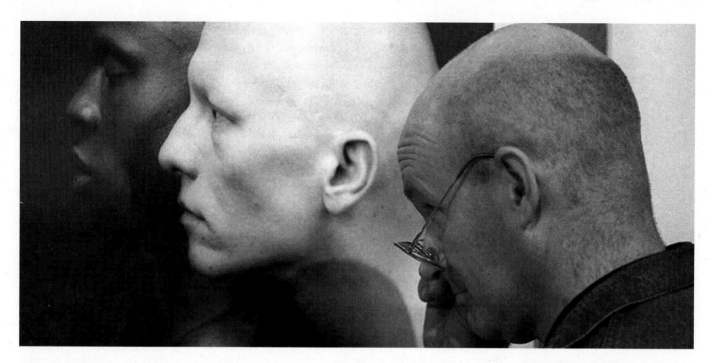

Federal Communications Commission to ban cursing and nudity on broadcast TV, something it cannot do with respect to other electronic or print media or cable television. The Court went further in affirming new media press freedoms in 2011 when it ruled that efforts by governments to ban violent video games are constitutionally unacceptable. As Justice Scalia wrote in *Brown v. Entertainment Merchants Association* (2011), "Like the protected books, plays and movies that preceded them, video games communicate ideas—and even social messages—through familiar literary devices (such as characters, dialogue, plot and music) and through features distinctive to the medium (such as the player's interaction with the virtual world). That suffices to confer First Amendment protection."[12]

Religious Freedom

> Congress shall make no law respecting an establishment of religion, or prohibiting the free exercise thereof.
>
> —First Amendment to the U.S. Constitution

For much of our history, Congress did not impede the exercise of religion because it did not legislate much on the subject. Because the states were not covered by the First Amendment, the free exercise of religion was protected by state constitutions or not at all. The Supreme Court was content to defer to the states on issues of religious freedom.

As late as 1940, in *Minersville School District v. Gobitis*, the Supreme Court upheld the expulsion of two schoolchildren who refused to salute the flag because it violated their faith as Jehovah's Witnesses. Justice Harlan Stone wrote a stinging dissent:

> The Constitution expresses more than the conviction of the people that democratic processes must be preserved at all costs. It is also an expression of faith and a command that freedom of mind and spirit must be preserved, which government must obey, if it is to adhere to that justice and moderation without which no free government can exist.

Stone's dissent, as well as a series of decisions deferring to state restrictions on Jehovah's Witnesses in 1941 and 1942, eventually moved other justices to Stone's side. In *West Virginia v. Barnette* (1943), the Court reversed *Gobitis* and firmly established free exercise of religion as protected against infringement by the states.

free exercise clause

The portion of the First Amendment to the Constitution that prohibits Congress from impeding religious observance or impinging on religious beliefs.

FREE EXERCISE OF RELIGION   The core of the **free exercise clause** is that neither the federal government nor state governments may interfere with religious *beliefs*. This is one of the few absolutes in U.S. constitutional law. Religious *actions*, however, are not absolutely protected. In general, people are free in the United States to practice their religious beliefs as they wish. However, there are some exceptions where the free exercise of religion violates general statutes that serve some compelling public purpose, such as state and federal drug laws or local public health ordinances (which in most locales do not permit such religious practices as animal sacrifice). The Court has upheld state laws, for instance, outlawing the use of peyote (an illegal hallucinogen) in Native American religious ceremonies (*Employment Division v. Smith*, 1990). Although Congress and President Clinton tried to overturn this decision, in 1993, with the Religious Freedom Restoration Act, the Act was declared unconstitutional in *City of Boerne v. Flores* (1997) because the act, in view of the Court majority, unduly extended national government power over the states.

The passage of the Patient Care and Affordable Care Act (PCACA; often referred to as Obamacare) has brought with it a thorny question about free exercise of religion. The PCACA requires that health insurance policies that employers—excluding explicitly religious employers like churches—provide to their employees cover basic preventive care, including contraception. Some employers argue that they are opposed to birth control for religious reasons and that the government should not be permitted to force them to effectively pay for birth control for their employees. In *Burwell v. Hobby Lobby Stores, Inc.* (2014), the Supreme Court ruled that the federal government cannot require closely held corporations—those primarily owned by a small group of people—to take actions that violate the owners' religious beliefs. In a subsequent case—*Zubik v. Burwell*—the Court considered whether the liberties of religious nonprofits are violated by the birth control mandate and a government "work around" where the government, rather than the organization itself, would provide contraceptive access (institutions requesting this exemption needed to submit a one-page letter to the government). However, in a step that many speculated was driven by the fact that Justice Scalia's seat on the bench had not been filled and a desire to avoid issuing a split (4–4) ruling, the Court sent the case back to the lower courts for further consideration.

In 2018, the Court handed down a ruling in *Masterpiece Cakeshop v. Colorado Civil Rights Commission*. The core questions in the case involved how far the right to free expression and free exercise of religion extend when they seem to conflict with the fundamental rights of other people. Colorado's Anti-Discrimination Act prohibits businesses from refusing service to customers based on their sexual orientation. However, Jack Phillips—a Christian baker—refused to make a custom wedding cake for a gay couple. He argued that he should not be forced to use his artistic expression to create a cake that would celebrate an event that is at odds with his religious commitments. Although this was expected to be a landmark ruling, the Court opted not to rule on whether the U.S. Constitution protected Phillips' decision. Instead, they issued a narrower 7–2 ruling finding that some members of the Colorado Civil Rights Commission, which had ruled that Phillips could not refuse to provide this type of service, made statements that were openly hostile to religion during his hearing. Thus, the majority found that Phillips' rights had been violated by religious bias in the enforcement agency. The federal Courts will continue to be called upon to resolve tricky questions about where to draw the line between individuals' expressive and religious liberties and other citizens' rights to equal treatment.

ESTABLISHMENT OF RELIGION   Many countries in the world have an official state religion. Sometimes this means that religious law trumps secular law in almost every instance, as in Saudi Arabia and Iran. Sometimes this means that religious law takes precedence in a narrow range of matters, usually involving family, marriage, and divorce, as in Israel. Often, a state church will exist but not affect everyday life

NO SEPARATION OF CHURCH AND STATE
Eighteen-year-old Hajara Ibrahim was sentenced to death by stoning by a Sharia Islamic court in Nigeria for committing adultery. The man in the adulterous relationship was not charged with a crime. Her sentence was overturned by Nigerian authorities after the case sparked international outrage and censure.
What might our country look like if the majority's religious preferences became the basis for constitutional law and statutes?

in many ways, playing more of a symbolic role. In most Western European democracies that have monarchies, for example, the king or queen must be a member in good standing of the state church. The monarchs of Great Britain, for instance, must be members of the Church of England.

There is no state church in the United States but many churches (and mosques and synagogues and temples) and many religious people. What allows them to peacefully coexist, in the view of many, is not only the broad freedom to worship or not worship as one pleases under the terms of the "free exercise" clause of the First Amendment, but keeping religion and government at arm's length from one another. Freedom of conscience, it is often argued, requires that government not favor one religion over another by granting it special favors, privileges, or status, or interfering in the affairs of religious institutions. It requires, in Jefferson's famous terms, "a wall of separation between church and state."

Nevertheless, despite general support for the doctrine of "separation of church and state," incorporation of the **establishment clause** by the Court proved to be a particularly messy matter. In *Everson v. Board of Education* (1947), Justice Hugo Black for the Supreme Court determined that no state could use revenues to support an institution that taught religion, thus incorporating the First Amendment's establishment clause to the states. But the majority in that case upheld the New Jersey program that reimbursed parents for bus transportation to parochial schools. A year later, Justice Black wrote another opinion regarding how the establishment clause applied to the states in *McCollum v. Board of Education* (1948). This time, a program for teaching religion in public schools was found unconstitutional. In *Zorach v. Clauson* (1952), however, the Court upheld a similar program in New York State that let students leave school premises early for religious instruction. The establishment clause had been incorporated, but the justices have had a difficult time determining what "separation of church and state" means in practice.

THE LEMON TEST The Warren Court (1953–1969) brought together a solid church–state separationist contingent whose decisions the early Burger Court (1969–1973) distilled into the major doctrine of the establishment clause: the **"Lemon test."** In *Lemon v. Kurtzman* (1971), Chief Justice Warren Burger specified three conditions that every law must meet to avoid "establishing" religion:

establishment clause

The part of the First Amendment to the Constitution that prohibits Congress from establishing an official religion; the basis for the doctrine of the separation of church and state.

Lemon test

Supreme Court standard that in order for a law with a religious element to be constitutional it must have a secular purpose, its primary effect cannot be to advance or impede religion, and it must not foster excessive entanglements between government and religion.

1. The law must have a secular *purpose*. That secular purpose need not be the only or primary purpose behind the law. The Court requires merely some plausible non-religious reason for the law.

2. The *primary effect* of the law must be neither to advance nor to impede religion. The Court will assess the probable effect of a governmental action for religious neutrality.

3. Government must never foster *excessive entanglements* between the state and religion.

While the *Lemon* test would seem to have erected substantial walls that bar mixing church and state, the Court has not consistently struck down laws where religion and government mix.[13] In *Rosenberger v. University of Virginia* (1995), it ruled that the university (a state-supported institution) must provide the same financial subsidy to a student religious publication that it provides to other student publications. In other cases, the Court ruled that public monies can go to parochial schools if they are for programs that are similar to ones in public schools and not used to advance religious instruction. This would include things such as funds to purchase science books or support drug education programs.[14] However, the Court has been unwilling to depart too far from the principle of separation of church and state; in 2004, for example, the Court ruled that the state of Washington had done no constitutional harm when it denied a state-funded scholarship to a student studying for the ministry.

With regard to religious displays in courthouses and other public buildings, the Rehnquist Court seemingly adopted Justice Sandra Day O'Connor's somewhat vague proposition that the establishment clause does not forbid religious displays in courthouses and other public buildings unless a "reasonable observer would view them as endorsing religious beliefs or practices."[15] The Court seems to have decided that it will need to look at such things as religious displays—lights, manger scenes, and the like—at public buildings on a case-by-case basis. In 2005, it ruled in one instance that hanging framed copies of the Ten Commandments in a courthouse in Kentucky went too far in promoting a particular set of religious beliefs (*McCreary County, Kentucky, et al. v. ACLU*). As Justice David Souter put it in his majority opinion, "The reasonable observer could only think that the counties meant to emphasize and celebrate the religious message…. The display's unstinting focus was on religious passages [posted with the Commandments], showing that the counties posted the Commandments precisely because of their sectarian content." In another ruling handed down the same day (*Van Orden v. Perry*), the Court allowed a display of a six-foot-high monument of the Ten Commandments in front of the state capitol in Austin because it was one of 40 monuments and historical markers that, in the words of Justice Stephen Breyer, "… served a mixed but primarily nonreligious purpose." Similarly, in *Town of Greece v. Galloway* (2014), the Court considered whether a town council's practice of beginning meetings with a prayer was unconstitutional. Although the town claimed that the prayers were not exclusively nor overtly Christian, the town residents who challenged the practice argued that most prayers were "uniquely Christian" and often referred explicitly to Jesus. In a 5–4 decision, the Supreme Court overturned a decision by a lower court and found that this practice did not violate the establishment clause because meeting attendees were not required to participate nor did the practice discriminate against minority religious groups.

In 2012, in *Hosanna-Tabor Church v. Equal Employment Opportunity Commission*, the Court ruled unanimously that employees of religious organizations who carry out some religious duties—leading services, teaching bible classes, and the like—cannot bring job discrimination suits under federal law. Arguing for a "ministerial exception" to federal employment laws, the justices said their enforcement would be an unconstitutional intrusion of government into the affairs of religious institutions, breaking the wall of separation between church and state. Religious organizations from virtually all denominations in the United States hailed the decision, though worries were expressed by many others that this might mean that teachers of theology in religious-affiliated colleges, for example, might not be able to bring suits under federal law for age discrimination or sexual harassment at work.[16] Such issues no doubt will be litigated in the years ahead.

Waiting in the wings are a range of issues involving the separation of church and state that the Court may be asked to consider in the years ahead. These include the legitimacy of the words "one nation under God" in the Pledge of Allegiance, and the acceptability of the nondenominational prayers that open the daily sessions in Congress. The point here is fairly straightforward: the debate over where to draw the line that separates church and state is a continuing one in America and is unlikely to ever be resolved once and for all.

RELIGION IN PUBLIC SCHOOLS   One of the most controversial aspects of constitutional law regarding the establishment of religion concerns school prayer. Although a majority of Americans support allowing a nondenominational prayer or a period of silent prayer in the schools, the Court has consistently ruled against such practices since the early 1960s, perhaps believing that children in school settings, as opposed to adults in other areas of life, are more likely to feel pressure from those conveying religious messages. In *Engel v. Vitale* (1962), the Court ordered the state of New York to suspend its requirement that all students in public schools recite a nondenominational prayer at the start of each school day. In *Stone v. Graham* (1980), the Court ruled against posting the Ten Commandments in public school classrooms. In *Lee v. Weisman* (1992), it ruled against allowing school-sponsored prayer at graduation ceremonies. In *Santa Fe Independent School District v. Doe* (2000), the Court ruled that student-led prayers at school-sponsored events such as football games are not constitutionally permissible because they have the "improper effect of coercing those present to participate in an act of religious worship." In these and other cases, the Court has consistently ruled against officially sponsored prayer in public schools as a violation of the separation of church and state.

An important battle about religion in the schools concerns attempts by some committed believers to either exclude Darwinian evolutionary biology from the school curriculum or to balance it with alternative interpretations such as "creationism" (the idea that God created the earth as described in the Bible) or "intelligent design" (the idea that the natural world is so complex that it could not have evolved as scientists propose and a higher being must have designed it). Because courts at all levels have rejected the teaching of "creationism" in the science curriculum as an improper intrusion of religion into public education, many religious activists have pushed "intelligent design" as an alternative approach that might pass court muster. The Dover, Pennsylvania, school board tried this strategy but lost in federal court. As District Court Judge John Jones put it in his opinion in *Kitzmiller v. Dover Area School District* (2005), "… we conclude that the religious nature of ID [intelligent design] would be readily apparent to an objective observer, adult, or child…. The overwhelming evidence at trial established that ID is a religious view, a mere relabeling of creationism, and not a scientific theory."

With no sign that the tide of religious feeling is about to recede in the United States, debates over school prayer, religious displays in school, and the teaching of evolution will continue for the foreseeable future. The main reason these issues will linger is that neither the courts nor the American people are entirely certain where the line between church and state should be drawn.

PRAY AND PLAY

A high school coach leads his team in prayer before a game. This practice, quite common across America, raises important questions about the "establishment" clause, especially the degree to which local school authorities in many communities are willing to comply with the doctrine of "separation of church and state."

Should the federal government take a harder line against expressions of religious belief in the schools, or should schools be exempt from federal scrutiny as long as no one complains?

RIGHTS OF THE ACCUSED

15.3 Enumerate the constitutional rights of the accused, and discuss the impact of terrorism on these rights.

The framers were so concerned about protections for individuals suspected, accused, or convicted of a crime that they included important protections in the main body of the Constitution. Article I, as you have learned, prohibits Congress, and by implication, the federal government, from issuing bills of attainder, passing ex post facto laws, or suspending the right of habeas corpus. As further indication of their concern for the rights of those accused of a crime, consider that five of the ten amendments that make up the Bill of Rights focus on such protections. The framers were worried about the ability of the new government to accuse and imprison individuals it didn't like or who criticized the government's actions, so these rights offer significant protections for individuals. Most Americans today treasure the constitutional rights and liberties that protect innocent individuals—what are generally termed *due process* protections—from wrongful prosecution and imprisonment. But most Americans also want to control crime as much as possible. The rise of "tough on crime" measures has significantly increased the number of people in American jails; although the United States accounts for a little less than 5 percent of the world's population, it has almost one-fourth of the world's total prison population.[17] Balancing concerns about safety with a desire to protect the rights of the accused is still an issue the Supreme Court and society, struggle with.

As with most other civil liberties, the Court has alternatively expanded and narrowed the rights of those accused of crimes. The more liberal Warren Court (1953–1969) greatly expanded protections, the Burger Court (1969–1986) rulings trimmed protections for defendants, and the Rehnquist Court (1987–2004) quickened the pace of favoring prosecutors. Early assessments suggest that the Roberts Court is continuing to tilt the balance in favor of prosecutors, though there have been notable exceptions.[18]

Unreasonable Searches and Seizures

The Fourth Amendment secures the right of all persons against unreasonable searches and seizures and allows the granting of search warrants only if the police have **probable cause** to conduct the search. In other words, they must be able to specify evidence of serious lawbreaking that they reasonably expect to find when they conduct the search. Until the Warren Court compelled the states to abide by the Fourth Amendment in 1961, they had frequently used searches and seizures that the federal courts would consider "unreasonable" in an effort to control crime. In *Mapp v. Ohio* (1961), the Supreme Court said that evidence gathered through a warrantless and unreasonable search may not be used at trial, even if the evidence is incriminating. This **exclusionary rule** now applies to states, and the justices hoped it would force the police to play by the constitutional rules while conducting their investigations.

Generally, the Warren Court required police to obtain a warrant whenever the person subjected to a search had a "reasonable expectation of privacy."[19] However, exactly how far the exclusionary rule extends is a matter of on-going debate. The Supreme Court is periodically asked to clarify exceptions to the exclusionary rule and standards under which searches are legal without a valid warrant. The Burger Court authorized a "good-faith" exception to the exclusionary rule, under which prosecutors may introduce evidence obtained illegally if they can show that the police had relied on a warrant that appeared valid but later proved to be invalid.[20] The Court allowed another exception for situations where illegally gathered evidence would have been discovered eventually without the illegal search.[21] The Rehnquist Court went beyond these exceptions. In *Murray v. United States* (1988), it allowed prosecutors to use products of illegal searches if other evidence unrelated to the illegal evidence would have justified a search warrant. The combination of "good faith," "inevitable discovery," and "retroactive probable cause" considerably narrowed the exclusionary rule.

In general, the Court has been more willing to protect individuals inside their homes from searches than inside their car or in a public place where the Court has consistently ruled there is a lower expectation of privacy. In *Kyllo v. United States* (2001)—a case pertaining to searches of private homes—the Court ruled that police could not use high-technology thermal devices to search through the walls of a house to check for the presence of high-intensity lights used for growing marijuana. Justice Scalia was especially incensed by the practice, saying in his opinion that to allow such searches "would leave the homeowner at the mercy of advancing technology..." Similarly, in 2013, the Court ruled in *Florida v. Jardines* that bringing drug sniffing dogs to the front door of a house without a warrant was an unreasonable search as, in that case, there was no probable cause to justify the search.

Although the Court generally finds that people have less of an expectation of privacy when they are driving, or otherwise away from home, the Court has drawn boundaries around the government's ability to gather information about people outside of the confines of their home. For example, in one recent case (*Collins v. Virginia*, 2018), the Court ruled that police who found a stolen motorcycle under a tarp in a suspect's driveway needed a warrant to search that area because people have a reasonable expectation to privacy not only within their home, but in the area of their property that is immediately outside of their home.[22] In another case (*United States v. Jones*, 2012), the Court unanimously ruled that the police had conducted a "search" when it attached a GPS device to a suspect's car without a warrant in order to track his movements. In 2018, the Court considered the case of *Carpenter v. United States*. At issue was the question of whether the police needed a warrant in order to use cell-site location information (CSLI) as part of an investigation. This data, which is gathered by cellphone companies such as T–Mobile, can provide a detailed picture of a cell phone user's movements over time. A critical question in this case was tied to the fact that CSLI is provided by third

probable cause
Legal doctrine that refers to a reasonable belief that a crime has been committed.

exclusionary rule
A standard established by the Supreme Court that prevents police and prosecutors from using evidence against a defendant that was obtained in an illegal search.

parties (the cellphone providers): the government did not directly gather information on the suspect, but rather had relied on data that private companies had gathered legally. In a 5–4 decision Chief Justice Roberts pointed to the "unique nature of cell phone location records" and argued that "[w]hether the government employs its own surveillance technology... or leverages the technology of a wireless carrier... an individual maintains a legitimate expectation of privacy in the record of his physical movements as captured through CSLI." In short, the government could not use these detailed records without a warrant even though they did not gather the data themselves.[23]

Court rulings regarding limits on when and how the government can gather information on individuals and use that information to prosecute people do not always impose stricter limits on the government. For example, the Rehnquist Court (1986–2005) narrowed the exclusionary rule when it held in *Wyoming v. Houghton* (1999) that police who have probable cause to search an automobile for illegal substances may also search personal possessions (in this case, a purse) of passengers in the car. This said, the Court has also ruled that police could not search every driver or car involved in petty traffic offenses. Thus, in *Knowles v. Iowa* (1998) the Court ruled that a bag of marijuana discovered in a search when an individual was simply being issued a speeding ticket must be excluded as the product of an illegal search.

In *Utah v. Strieff* (2016) the Court issued a 5-3 ruling that also narrowed the exclusionary rule. The police had received an anonymous tip that a particular house was involved in "narcotics activity." Although legally he had no probable cause to do so, an officer stopped Strieff for questioning after seeing him walk out of the house. During this illegal stop he found that Strieff had an outstanding warrant tied to a minor traffic offense, arrested him, searched him, and found methamphetamine in his pockets. In their decision the majority argued that the discovery of the outstanding warrant legitimized the search and, thus, the illegal drugs the officer found was admissible evidence. They wrote that "errors in judgment hardly rise to a purposeful or flagrant violation of... Fourth Amendment rights."

In a strongly worded dissent, Justice Sotomayor argued that this ruling gave police incentives to conduct illegal stops saying: "This case allows the police to stop you on the street, demand your identification, and check it for outstanding traffic warrants—even if you are doing nothing wrong. If the officer discovers a warrant for a fine you forgot to pay, courts will now excuse his illegal stop and will admit into evidence anything he happens to find by searching you after arresting you on the warrant." This cases illustrates the difficult balance the Courts are asked to find between protecting people from "unreasonable" searches and ensuring that those who have committed crimes do not escape punishment. On the one hand, Strieff had clearly broken the law; on the other, there may be reason to worry about the implications of police being able to stop people without cause and fish around for evidence of wrongdoing.

Right to Counsel and Protections Against Self-Incrimination

The Sixth Amendment's right to counsel was incorporated in two landmark cases. In *Powell v. Alabama* (1932)—the famed Scottsboro Boys prosecution—the Court ruled that legal counsel must be supplied to all indigent defendants accused of a **capital crime** (any crime in which the death penalty can be imposed). Before this decision, many poor people in the southern states, especially African Americans, had been tried for and convicted of capital crimes without the benefit of an attorney. Thirty-one years later, in *Gideon v. Wainwright* (1963), the Warren Court ruled that defendants accused of any felony in state jurisdictions are entitled to a lawyer and that the states must supply a lawyer when a defendant cannot afford to do so. Justice Black wrote the following for a unanimous Court:

capital crime

Any crime for which death is a possible penalty.

Not only … precedents but also reason and reflection require us to recognize that in our adversary system of criminal justice, any person hauled into court, who is too poor to hire a lawyer, cannot be assured of a fair trial unless counsel is provided for him. This seems to be an obvious truth.

Gideon, who had been convicted of burglary, had taken the extraordinary step of writing his own appeal to the Supreme Court from his prison cell using pencil and paper. When he was retried, with the assistance of counsel, Gideon was acquitted. By incorporating the Sixth Amendment's guarantee of legal counsel, the Court has ensured that every criminal defendant in the United States can, at least in theory, mount a defense regardless of socioeconomic status.

Still, problems persist. State governments have little incentive to fund public defenders resulting in many offices being understaffed, with attorneys who have too

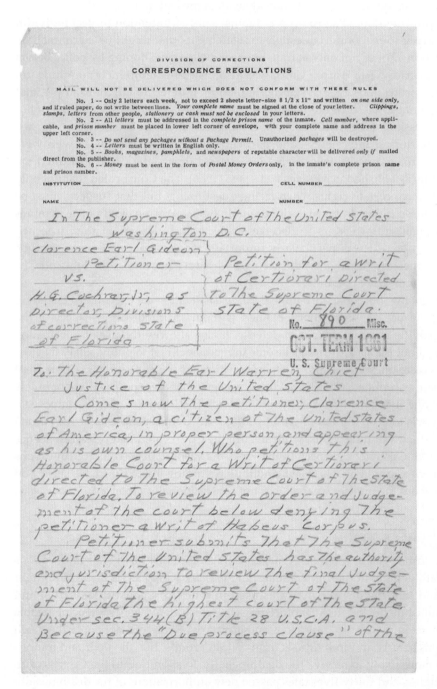

GIDEON'S PETITION

Before Clarence Gideon won his case before the Supreme Court in 1963, states did not have to provide attorneys for people accused of a felony. Gideon wrote his appeal letter—shown here—from his prison cell in Florida. The Court agreed with Gideon, incorporating this part of the Sixth Amendment.

Should the government have to provide defendants with a lawyer at trial?

many clients and too little time to offer vigorous representation. For example, in 2016, the American Civil Liberties Union (ACLU) filed a class action lawsuit alleging that Louisiana's public defender system was so underfunded that defendants were effectively being put on "waiting lists" because there were not enough lawyers to take their cases. The case was dismissed by a federal judge on the grounds that ordering the state to remedy funding shortfalls would "inevitably lead this court to engage in an ongoing audit of the criminal cases in Orleans Parish"—a task the court did not have the means to carry out. This said, in his ruling the judge agreed that "the Louisiana legislature is failing miserably at upholding its obligations" and that "[b]udget shortages are no excuse to violate the United States Constitution."[24] In other cases, attorneys have been shown to be incompetent or inexperienced, and there are even occasional cases of attorneys being drunk or sleeping throughout trials. The result is often an inadequate defense, and though the Supreme Court has generally been reluctant to set standards for public defenders, it has sometimes supported lower court opinions which throw out convictions based on inadequate representation.

The Fifth Amendment's protections against self-incrimination protect individuals from having to respond to questions or statements that might be incriminating. This protection applies not only at trial, but also during questioning by police before or during an arrest. The Warren Court was also instrumental in incorporating Fifth Amendment protections against self-incrimination. It determined, for example, that the privilege not to be forced to incriminate oneself was useless at trial if the police coerced confessions long before the trial took place. To bar police from forcing suspects to talk during interviews—and particularly to ensure that those who were not aware of their constitutional rights understood them—the Court instituted the famous rights established in *Miranda v. Arizona* (1966). The Court ruled that not only do suspects have certain rights when facing questioning, but that suspects must be *informed* of these rights. In his majority opinion, Justice Warren cited police manuals that encouraged interrogators to deceive suspects and play off of their insecurities. He also noted it was particularly important for less educated suspects to be informed of their rights, saying "the accused who does not know his rights may be the one most in need of counsel."

Although the Burger Court upheld *Miranda*, it allowed exceptions including permitting the use of information obtained without "Mirandizing" suspects if the suspects took the stand in their own defense. It also allowed the use of information obtained without *Miranda* warnings if some immediate threat to public safety had justified immediate questioning and postponing warnings.[25] The Rehnquist Court went beyond these exceptions when it held that a coerced confession may be "harmless error" that does not constitute self-incrimination.[26] The Roberts Court has imposed a few new restrictions on Miranda rights. In 2010, it ruled that suspects have the burden of invoking their Miranda rights, while in 2013 the Court ruled that pre-arrest silence could be used to convict a suspect. In that case, the suspect answered some questions but not others prior to being arrested, and thus, according to the Court, his silence on a question about the murder weapon was not constitutionally protected.

Capital Punishment

The Eighth Amendment's ban on "cruel and unusual punishment" has implications for the death penalty in the United States. In *Furman v. Georgia* (1972), a split Burger Court found that the death penalty, as used in the states, constituted "cruel and unusual punishment" because the procedures by which states were sentencing people to death were, in its words, "capricious and arbitrary." States did not apply the death penalty consistently and individuals from certain groups, like the poor and minorities, were more likely to receive the death penalty. Responding to the Court's criticisms, Congress and thirty-five states passed new authorizations of the death penalty

"YOU HAVE THE RIGHT TO REMAIN SILENT"

An Occupy Wall Street demonstrator in 2012 is arrested and read his rights as defined by the landmark Supreme Court ruling *Miranda v. Arizona* (1966). Though the requirement that arrestees be notified of their rights has been challenged by police departments ever since the ruling, Miranda remains in place. *How have police adjusted to the restrictions on their actions required by Miranda?*

aimed at rectifying procedural problems identified by the Court. The Burger Court held, in *Gregg v. Georgia* (1976), after states had changed their sentencing procedures, that capital punishment was not inherently cruel nor unusual so long as procedures were nonarbitrary and nondiscriminatory. However, the Court tended to create an "obstacle course" of standards the states had to meet if they wanted to use the death penalty. Basically, the Court insisted defendants be given every opportunity to show mitigating circumstances so that as few convicts as possible would be killed.

Later, the Rehnquist Court expedited the use of the death penalty. In *McCleskey v. Kemp* (1987), the Court said that statistical evidence that blacks who kill whites are four times more likely to be sentenced to death than whites who kill blacks—even after accounting for aggravating circumstances and defendants' criminal history—cannot be used to prove racism in a particular death penalty case. Individual defendants, it ruled, must show that racism played a role in their specific cases. In *Penry v. Lynaugh* (1989), the Court allowed the execution of a mentally disabled convicted murderer who had the intelligence of a seven-year-old. In *Stanford v. Kentucky* (1989), it allowed the execution of a minor who had been convicted of murder. The Rehnquist Court also limited avenues of appeal and delay in death penalty cases. In *McCleskey v. Zant* (1991), it made delays much less likely by eliminating many means of challenging capital convictions. In *Keeney v. Tamayo-Reyes* (1992), the Court limited the ability of "death row" inmates to appeal to the Supreme Court.

Part of the reason for the Court's decisions on the death penalty has to do with the political environment in the country from the middle of the 1960s to the late 1990s. During this period, urban decay increased along with the crime rate, and political leaders, driven by public opinion, were only too happy to get "tough on crime" through strict sentencing laws and increased use of the death penalty. In this environment, the Court removed most of the obstacles to its use. It is hardly surprising, then, that the number of people executed in the United States in 1999 reached its highest level (98) since 1976, when the Court reinstated the death penalty, with Texas accounting for more than one-third of those executions (see Figure 15.2).[27]

The crime rate began to drop in the mid-1990s (and has continued to drop), leading to diminished support for the death penalty—from 80 percent support in 1994 to 55 percent in 2017.[28] Much to the surprise of observers, the Rehnquist Court began in

FIGURE 15.2 EXECUTIONS IN THE UNITED STATES, 1977–2017

Fueled by fear of violent crime, executions in the United States increased dramatically from the early 1980s to the late 1990s but declined significantly after that as public concerns rose about how fairly the death penalty is used.

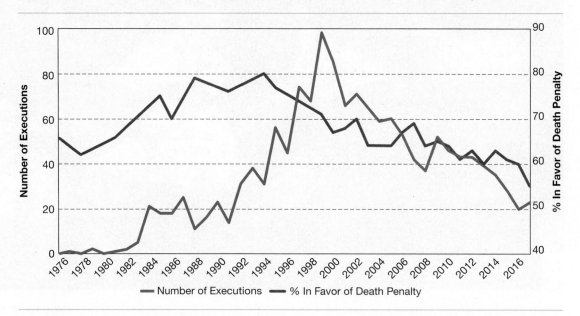

— Number of Executions — % In Favor of Death Penalty

SOURCE: Data from Bureau of Justice Statistics, "Prisoners Executed under Civil Authority in the United States, by Year, Region, and Jurisdiction, 1977–2014"; Death Penalty Information Center, Facts About the Death Penalty, October 11, 2018; "Death Penalty," In Depth: Topics A to Z, Gallup Polls, April 1976–May 2018.

2002 to pull back from its unstinting support for the death penalty. In *Atkins v. Virginia* (2002), the Court followed the lead of 18 states in banning the use of the death penalty for mentally disabled defendants, saying, in Justice John Paul Stevens's majority opinion, that "a national consensus now rejects such executions as excessive and inappropriate" and that "society views mentally retarded offenders as categorically less culpable than the average criminal." In *Ring v. Arizona* (2002), the Court overruled the death sentences of more than 160 convicted killers, declaring that only juries, not judges, can decide on the use of the death penalty for those convicted of capital crimes. In 2005, the Supreme Court struck down death penalty convictions in cases in which it was convinced that a defendant had inadequate legal defense, another in which a defendant was brought to a death penalty sentencing hearing in shackles (terming it "inherently prejudicial"), and yet another in which the defendant was under the age of 18.

The Roberts Court has sent mixed signals about how it views the death penalty. Two characteristics of contemporary American society will likely affect the Court's decisions. First, the continued decline in crime and—if it continues—the public's declining support for the death penalty.[29] The second trend is the more frequent use of DNA testing, which has exonerated hundreds of individuals convicted of murders and other serious crimes. In 2011, Illinois banned the use of the death penalty after 13 inmates on death row were found to have been wrongly convicted, joining 19 other states (7 of which have abolished it since 2000).[30] According to the Innocence Project, an organization which advocates for prisoners who claim to have been wrongly convicted, 362 convictions have been overturned since 1989, 20 of these were for individuals who had served time on death row.[31] These results have led to a rethinking about the death penalty, based on concerns about the quality of legal defense for those accused of murder, and the fairness of the judicial system toward racial minorities.

The Court has sent mixed signals about allowing prisoners to gain access to DNA evidence. In 2009, the Court ruled that state and federal governments should determine the circumstances under which a prisoner could view DNA tests, though the Court did not make it entirely clear whether or not there is a constitutional right to DNA testing.[32] But, in 2011, in a very narrow ruling, the Supreme Court seemed to allow those convicted of crimes slightly greater access to DNA testing.[33] The issue is far from settled, and the Court's rulings have arguably only served to complicate matters. As a result, future rulings in this area are likely.

Other death penalty rulings illustrate how the Court has attempted to strike a balance between prisoner's rights and the ability of the state to execute inmates. In 2008, the Roberts Court ruled in a case involving the state of Kentucky that the most widely used method of execution by lethal injection was constitutionally permissible, rejecting the argument that it caused unacceptable pain, as many medical professionals have claimed. Similarly, in a 5–4 decision handed down in 2015, the court ruled that the drugs Oklahoma used in lethal injection procedures—drugs critics said could cause immense pain—did not violate the Eighth Amendment. In 2006, the Court ruled unanimously that states cannot deny the introduction of evidence in capital cases that suggests a person other than the defendant had committed the crime. However, in 2007, a Court ruling made it easier for prosecutors to exclude people from juries who were unsure about the appropriateness and morality of the death penalty.

It is well known that the United States has more prisoners on death row and executes more prisoners annually than any other rich democratic country. It is also well known that some states are far more likely than others to use the death penalty. Some of these differences may be tied to variation in the frequency of violent crime—including murder—from state to state. However, the response of the public, prosecutors, and juries to violent crimes also appears to vary a great deal across states. That is to say, key actors in some states may simply be more inclined to impose the ultimate penalty than those in other states. The map in Figure 15.3 illustrates how the use of the death penalty varies across states.

FIGURE 15.3 EXECUTIONS IN THE UNITED STATES BY STATE (SINCE 1976)

This map shows the number of people each state has executed since 1976—the year the Supreme Court effectively opened the door for states to resume using the death penalty. In some states, the death penalty has not been legal at any point since 1976. Others allowed it for some of this period but have since outlawed the practice. States that do have the death penalty vary a great deal in terms of how much they have used it. Three states—Texas, Oklahoma, and Virginia—have carried out more than half of the executions in the United States since 1976. At the other end of the spectrum are states like Kansas and New Hampshire, where the death penalty is legally permitted but has not actually been used since 1976.

SOURCE: "Death Penalty Information Center," July 18, 2018, and "States and Capital Punishment," National Council of State Legislatures, June 6, 2018.

Although the United States remains among the world's leaders in the use of the death penalty (along with China, Iran, Yemen, and North Korea), as discussed above, the number of executions has declined substantially from the highs of the late 1990s.[34] Between the reinstatement of the death penalty by the Supreme Court in 1976 and the end of 2001, 737 inmates were executed in the United States. Of the total, 619 (84 percent) took place in the 1990s. In 1999, 98 executions were carried out, the highest total since 1951, with Texas and Virginia carrying out half of the executions that year. During the first decade of the 21st century, however, the number of executions declined. In 2017, only 23 executions were carried out in the United States.

Four of the 23 executions carried out in 2017 were done within the span of eight days in Arkansas. This unusual wave of executions illustrates another factor that has contributed to the recent decline in executions: pharmaceutical companies are increasingly unable or unwilling to provide the drugs used to carry out lethal injections. The authorities in Arkansas carried out these four executions on a strikingly rapid schedule—executing two inmates in a single day—because one of the drugs used in their lethal injection process was nearing its expiration date. In response to pharmaceutical companies' reluctance to provide drugs to use in lethal injections, in 2018, some states approved the use of an alternative method of execution: nitrogen gas. Nitrogen makes up most of the earth's atmosphere (and thus is widely available), but if inhaled in isolation, causes death within minutes. Other states plan to use fentanyl (a synthetic opioid) as an alternative method for carrying out executions. Each of these methods in certain to face legal challenges.[35] We can understand recent trends in capital punishment more completely by using the analytical framework to consider how *structural, political linkage, and governmental factors* have influenced the death penalty issue (see Figure 15.4).

Terrorism and the Rights of the Accused

As we discussed earlier in this chapter, threats to national security can alter how people think about the balance between protecting civil liberties and keeping the public safe. In the wake of the terrorist attacks of September 11, 2001, the Bush administration took a number of steps that worried and continue to worry civil liberties advocates. However, most Americans believed at the time that the actions of the Bush administration were reasonable measures to take in perilous times.[36]

USA PATRIOT ACT   The USA PATRIOT Act, passed soon after the 9/11 attacks, gave the federal government expanded powers to use wiretapping and electronic surveillance, impose stricter penalties for harboring or financing terrorists, monitor the bank accounts and e-mail of suspect individuals and organizations, and detain any noncitizens living in the United States whom the attorney general deemed to be a threat to national security without a hearing. Despite strong criticism of the USA PATRIOT Act by civil libertarians, it was renewed by Congress in 2006, and again in 2015, with only modest changes in its original provisions.

NATIONAL SECURITY LETTERS   The Bush administration also expanded the use of a little-known and little-used law created in the 1970s to give the FBI secret authorization to access personal information about U.S. citizens, including phone and financial records and information from businesses' customer databases. Between 2002 and 2005, almost 150,000 "national security letters" were issued.[37] Under terms of the law, suspects were given no notice of these requests for information, firms were obligated to comply, and no one was permitted to make public the fact that such requests had been made. Issuance of these letters required approval

FIGURE 15.4 APPLYING THE FRAMEWORK: WHY HAVE SOME STATES ABOLISHED THE DEATH PENALTY?

Action

State Policy: Over the last decade, several states have abolished the death penalty.

Government

- **Courts and Civil Liberties:** String of Supreme Court rulings starting in the 1970s affirmed that the death penalty was constitutional except in cases involving the mentally disabled, the young, or methods of execution judged "cruel or unusual."
- **Courts:** Juries have increasingly chosen "life without parole" even when the death penalty is available. Prosecutors are also less willing to ask for the death penalty.
- **State Governments:** Many state governments have rethought the death penalty given its financial cost.

Political Linkage

- **Public Opinion:** Long history of public support for the death penalty undermined by DNA exonerations and botched executions.
- **Interests:** Advocacy and religious groups rallied against the death penalty in the 1990s as executions rose.
- **Corporations:** Pharmaceutical companies now unwilling to supply drugs for lethal-injections.

Structure

- **Federalism:** Under federalism, states, not the federal government, author most criminal statutes and prosecute criminals.
- **Constitution:** "Cruel and unusual" punishment forbidden. Scant evidence that framers viewed capital punishment to be "cruel and unusual."
- **World:** Virtually all other rich democracies have abolished the death penalty.
- **Science:** Advances in DNA science have identified cases where an individual was wrongly sentenced to death.

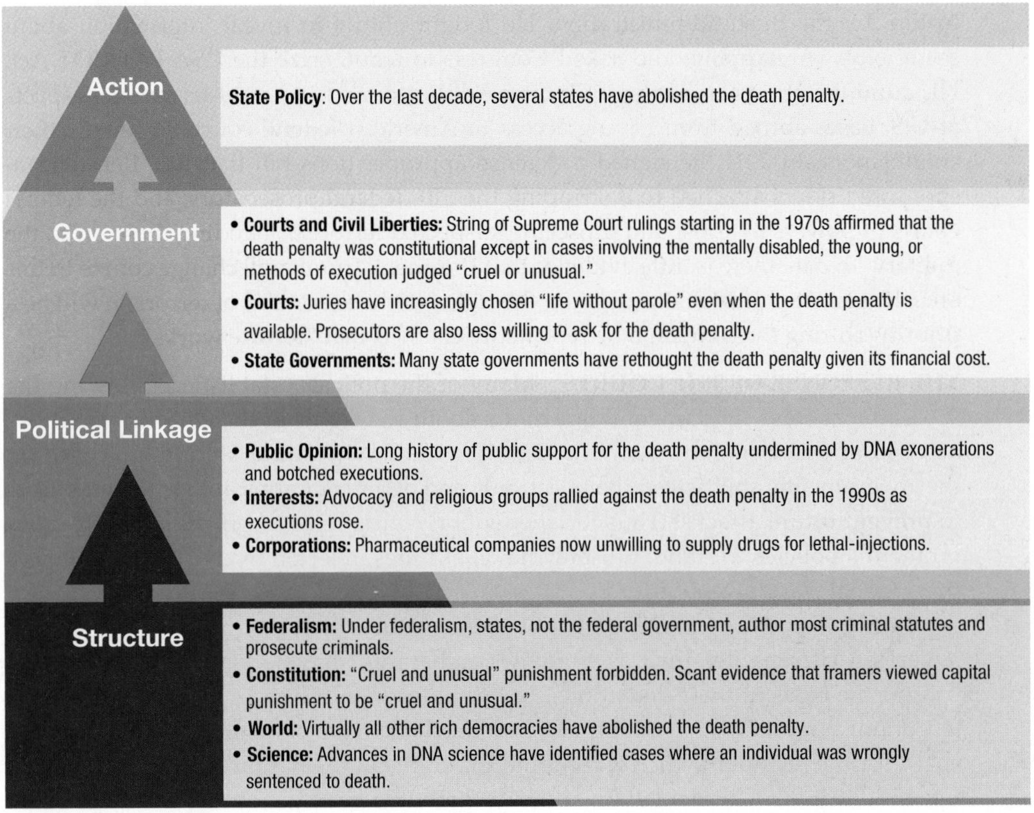

© Edward S. Greenberg

by the Office of Intelligence Policy and Review in the Justice Department; there was no judicial oversight.[38]

NATIONAL SECURITY ADMINISTRATION (NSA) EAVESDROPPING   Finally, President Bush authorized a vast eavesdropping and data-mining operation by the National Security Agency on the electronic and wire communications of American citizens. Under terms of the Foreign Intelligence Surveillance Act (FISA), NSA eavesdropping on American citizens requires a warrant granted by a special court. When it was revealed in late 2005 that the NSA had been doing this without warrants, the president claimed he had the power to do so as the commander in chief charged with protecting the country and by post-9/11 legislation passed by congress that authorized him to pursue terrorists. In 2008, Congress passed a bill proposed by President Bush that allowed more latitude in the use of wiretaps and immunized phone companies against lawsuits for their cooperation with the government. The fact that the USA PATRIOT Act was renewed with so few changes in 2006 and that a Democratic Congress gave a Republican president more authority to use wiretaps are probably a testament to the public's strong support for government actions aimed at preventing terrorist attacks.

Barack Obama campaigned against many Bush-era policies and altered some policies in this area—he released some documents related to the treatment of detainees, dropped the designation "enemy combatants" for people held without trial, drastically cut back the use of national security letters to gather information, and ended the use of most harsh interrogation techniques. He also took steps to close the prison at Guantanamo and to try 9/11 conspirators in civilian courts, but these efforts were blocked by congressional Republicans.

However, ultimately Obama ended up continuing many of the policies bequeathed to him by the Bush administration. He fought efforts to reveal information about secret NSA wiretapping, and asked Congress to reauthorize the USA PATRIOT Act. His administration also successfully pressed the courts to prevent terrorism suspects at U.S. bases abroad from having access to American federal courts to review their confinement. In 2011, he signed a defense appropriations bill that had Republican-sponsored riders attached to it stripping the FBI, federal prosecutors, and the federal courts of powers to arrest and prosecute suspected terrorists, handing these off to the military. To date there is little evidence that President Trump will change course in this area. It seems unlikely that protecting the rights of those accused of terrorism will be a priority. During the campaign he repeatedly claimed that "torture works."

THE RESPONSE OF THE COURTS Many of the policies established following the 9/11 attacks raise fundamental questions about the rights of the accused. Do those accused of terrorism have a right to a public trial? What limits should be placed on the government's ability to gather electronic and other communications in their efforts to prevent future attacks? Thus far, the federal courts have mostly allowed the government's policies to stand, but they have, at times, rejected overly broad claims of presidential war powers.

In *Hamdi v. Rumsfeld* (2004), the Supreme Court ruled that both foreigners and American citizens detained as "enemy combatants" have a right to a hearing to contest the basis of their detentions. In her opinion in the case, Justice Sandra Day O'Connor wrote, "We have long since made clear that a state of war is not a blank check for the president when it comes to the rights of the nation's citizens." In 2007, the Ninth Circuit Court ruled that enemy combatants could not be held indefinitely in military detention in the United States. The Roberts Court has also been troubled by the legal treatment of foreign detainees. In 2006, the Court ruled that all detainees held at Guantanamo Bay and elsewhere are entitled to protections guaranteed under the Geneva Convention. It also ruled that the military tribunal-style hearings used at Guantanamo were unacceptable because they had not been authorized by Congress. In response, Congress passed the Military Commissions Act of 2006, which set up a system of tribunals but, almost provocatively, added language to the effect that no court would be allowed to consider habeas corpus petitions from foreigners held as enemy combatants. Perhaps seeing this "habeas" provision as a direct challenge by the legislative branch to the independent powers of the judiciary, the Court rejected this provision in 2008 when it ruled that foreign detainees held at Guantanamo have a constitutional right to challenge their detentions in the federal courts.

So far, the United States has not taken as harsh a line as several other rich democracies including Australia, Canada, and Great Britain, which have instituted the practice of preventive detention—incarceration of terrorism suspects who are citizens or otherwise legally in the country without charges or hearings—and placed strict limits on subversive speech.[39]

RIGHT TO PRIVACY

15.4 Outline the constitutional justification for the right to privacy.

The freedoms addressed so far—speech, press, and religion—are listed in the First Amendment. The freedom to be left alone in our private lives—what is referred to as the *right to privacy*—is not explicitly mentioned in the First Amendment nor in any of the other amendments that make up the Bill of Rights. Nevertheless, most Americans consider the right to privacy to be one of our most precious freedoms. Americans believe, in most cases, that citizens should be able to make their own personal decisions regarding our own health and welfare, for example, and that we should be free from too much government monitoring of what we say and do in our everyday lives.

Many (though not all) constitutional scholars believe, moreover, that a right to privacy is inherent in the Bill of Rights, even if it is not explicitly stated. Examples abound in the Constitution of an implied right to privacy, including the prohibitions against illegal searches and seizures and against quartering of troops in our homes, as well as the right to free expression and conscience. Scholars also point to the Ninth Amendment as evidence that the framers believed in the existence of liberties not specifically mentioned in the Bill of Rights: "The enumeration in the Constitution of certain rights, shall not be construed to deny or disparage others retained by the people."

Most jurists and legal scholars have come to accept that a fundamental right to privacy exists, though a group of "**original intent**" conservatives like Justice Clarence Thomas do not agree. Even among those who accept the fundamental right to privacy, there is disagreement on its specific applicability in wide variety of areas. Of course, we aren't free to do what we want at all times because the government frequently has a compelling interest in protecting individuals and society from dangerous actions. Drawing the line on the right to privacy encompasses many of the most controversial issues in American society including abortion, LGBTQ rights, and the security of interpersonal communications.

original intent
The doctrine that the courts must interpret the Constitution in ways consistent with the intentions of the framers rather than in light of contemporary conditions and needs.

Private Decisions

The Supreme Court's first important right to privacy case was *Griswold v. Connecticut* (1965), in which it ruled that a law banning the sale of contraception by the state of Connecticut was unconstitutional. The Supreme Court said that although the right to privacy does not appear in the Constitution, it is included in the penumbra of other rights found in the Constitution, meaning it exists in the shadow or emanations of other rights. As suggested above, the Court pointed to the rights outlined in the First, Third, Fourth, Fifth, Ninth, and Fourteenth Amendments as all implying a right to privacy.

ABORTION   *Griswold's* right to privacy doctrine became the basis for Justice Harry Blackmun's majority opinion in the landmark case *Roe v. Wade* (1973), in which the Court ruled in favor of a woman's right to terminate her pregnancy. Prior to the ruling, some states banned abortions, while others allowed them, but typically restricted the availability of abortion to cases of rape and incest, or situations where the woman's life was in danger. The *Roe* case transformed abortion from a legislative issue into a constitutional issue, from a matter of policy into a matter of rights. According to the Court, the right to an abortion is constitutionally protected and states could not prohibit a woman from having an abortion in the first trimester of her pregnancy and could only restrict abortion up to the point of fetal viability in order to protect the health of the mother.

The Court's decision hardly resolved matters. Many states began to place restrictions on abortion, ranging from parental notification to waiting periods, counselling about alternatives to abortion, and prohibitions on the use of public money for the procedure. In *Webster v. Reproductive Health Services* (1989), the Court seemed to invite these restrictions. A subsequent ruling in *Planned Parenthood v. Casey* by a conservative court in 1992 declared that states could regulate abortion to protect the health and safety of women, just like any other medical procedure, but the state could not adopt an "undue burden" on a woman's right to terminate her pregnancy. The case involved regulations established by the state of Pennsylvania that included a 24-hour waiting period and a requirement that women notify their husbands. The notification requirement was the only part of the Pennsylvania law that failed the "undue burden" test.

As a result of *Casey*, many states have adopted more aggressive regulations that have had the intended effect of making it much more difficult or uncomfortable for women to terminate pregnancies. A 2011 North Carolina law included a provision that required doctors to conduct an ultrasound and describe the characteristics of the fetus to women seeking an abortion. The Fourth Circuit Court struck down the law, finding that "[t]his compelled speech... is ideological in intent and in kind" and, thus, impinged on doctors' free speech. The case was appealed, but the Supreme Court refused to hear it, allowing the Circuit Court ruling to stand.[40] In 2013, Texas passed a very restrictive abortion law, known has House Bill 2, that required doctors performing abortions, among other things, to have admitting privileges at hospitals within 30 miles of their clinics, a requirement many rural doctors are unable to meet. In *Whole Woman's Health v. Hellerstedt* (2016), the Supreme Court heard a challenge to the Texas bill. The plaintiffs argued that the law imposed an undue burden on women's access to abortion and did not better protect women's health. They argued that the law was designed, in fact, with the sole intent of limiting access to abortions. The Court ruled that the Texas law did constitute an undue burden and rejected Texas' claims that the law was sincerely intended to protect women's health, rather than impede access to abortion. In May of 2018, Iowa passed a law prohibiting abortion once a fetal heartbeat can be detected—usually around 6 weeks into a pregnancy. The state legislators who supported the bill fully expected the law to be challenged in the courts and viewed it as providing an opportunity for the Supreme Court to overturn *Roe v. Wade*. Similar laws passed in other states have been struck down as unconstitutional.[41] However, legislators in states like Iowa are hoping that President Trump's Supreme Court appointees will be more willing to allow strict abortion restrictions to stand.

PRIVATE SEXUAL ACTIVITY   The Supreme Court had ruled as recently as 1986 in *Bowers v. Hardwick* that private sexual activity between consenting adults was not a protected right under the Constitution. The case involved two gay men found having sex by police and subsequently arrested under Georgia's anti-sodomy law. According to the Court, states could continue to outlaw certain sexual acts, particularly those involving homosexuals, as the state of Georgia did after winning *Bowers*. The ruling was an important one because it was the first time the Court reduced, rather than expanded, the right to privacy doctrine described in the *Griswold* case.

A subsequent case, *Lawrence v. Texas* (2003) overturned the decision in *Bowers* as the Court ruled that state anti-sodomy laws prohibiting consensual gay and lesbian sexual relations are unconstitutional. The result is that states can no longer regulate consensual sex between adults, regardless of their sexuality. "Private lives in matters pertaining to sex," declared Justice Anthony Kennedy in his majority opinion, "are a protected liberty."

Private Communications

Finally, there are issues relating to government intrusion on private communications. Although many of these issues are closely related to the Fourth Amendment's prohibition of unreasonable searches and seizures, policies instituted in the name of preventing terrorism have raised broader questions about citizens' right to privacy.

PRIVACY IN THE CLOUD

The government is explicitly forbidden from entering a person's home without a warrant to search through their personal communications. However, our personal communications are increasingly transmitted through third-party companies or stored in "the cloud"—on servers housed by private businesses.

Should the government have to use the same procedures that they use to access documents in a person's home in order to access personal communications and documents stored "in the cloud" or do people who use these services forfeit the right to keep their communications private?

As noted above, the USA PATRIOT Act grants the federal government a great deal of access to Americans' private and business records. Revelations that the FBI and the NSA had been conducting secret and warrantless searches of phone conversations (land lines and cell phones), financial transactions, and Internet communications ever since 9/11 led to intense press scrutiny, public condemnation, and congressional probes in early 2006, but the opposition was unable to block renewal of the PATRIOT Act. In 2007, in a disclosure that came too late to affect congressional deliberations on renewal, FBI director Robert Mueller reported to Congress that, since 2001, his agents had improperly and sometimes illegally obtained personal information on thousands of American citizens by overzealously using tools authorized by the Act.[42]

Debates about the government's ability to access private information—particularly information that is transmitted electronically—are unlikely to be resolved any time soon. In 2016, Microsoft took the unusual step of suing the Justice Department. Microsoft argued that the Justice Department's policy of secrecy orders that prohibit Microsoft from informing users when the government obtains a warrant and searches their electronic information is unconstitutional.[43] As an increasing share of citizens' private information comes to be stored digitally on computers that are not in their homes or offices (i.e., in "the cloud") the courts will be pushed to address thorny questions about the appropriate balance between individuals' rights to communicate privately and the government's interest in preventing terrorist attacks.

CIVIL LIBERTIES: SO, HAS THE STATE OF AMERICAN FREEDOM IMPROVED?

Both the framers and more recent democratic theorists are committed to civil liberties, but each has taken a somewhat different approach concerning how civil liberties might be enjoyed by Americans. Recall that the framers focused their attention on the potential for violations of liberty by the national government and paid little attention to the states, believing that freedom in the states was well protected. Civil liberties, broadly understood, became widely available to Americans only in the 20th century in response to the spread of democratic aspirations in politics and of democratic ideas in the culture, the efforts of individuals and groups to struggle for liberty, and a federal judiciary that finally agreed to nationalize most of the protections of the Bill of Rights.

There has been an enormous expansion of freedom in the United States; the freedoms of speech, association, press, conscience, and religion, as well as the rights of those accused of a crime, are far more extensively developed and protected in the United States today than they were in the past. However, it is important to recognize that although civil liberties today are fairly well protected against intrusions by government, not all people have the same capacity to use their liberties effectively. Substantial income and wealth inequality means that only a small segment of the public can express themselves by making substantial campaign contributions, forming lobbying organizations, and running ads for their favorite candidates, parties, and issues.

We cannot say with total confidence, moreover, that civil liberties will not face new government restrictions at some point in the future. In the past, waves of hysteria among political leaders and the public have led to the violation of civil liberties. Given the right conditions—war, civil unrest, economic depression—the same might happen again. Many worry, with some justification, that government efforts to combat terrorism may represent just such a setting for the suppression of civil liberties. What makes the possibility especially troubling is that, unlike a war that eventually ends, the fight against terrorism is unlikely to have a clear endpoint.

CIVIL LIBERTIES IN THE CONSTITUTION

15.1 Discuss the constitutional basis for civil liberties and trace the process by which these liberties have gradually been applied to the states.

The formal foundation of American liberties is found in the Constitution and its amendments, particularly the Bill of Rights and the Fourteenth Amendment, but the degree to which civil liberties have been enjoyed in practice during our history has depended on the actions of courts, the behavior of government officials, and the struggle for democracy by the American people. In addition, over time the Supreme Court has gradually incorporated the liberties granted in the Bill of Rights to the states, based on its reading of the Fourteenth Amendment.

FIRST AMENDMENT FREEDOMS

15.2 Identify the freedoms enumerated in the First Amendment.

The First Amendment specifies a number of protections often thought of as being at the heart of American civil liberties: the right to free speech, freedom of the press, and religious freedoms. Over the past two centuries, the exact meaning and extent of these protections has evolved—in some cases substantially. These changes are, in large part, the product of changing social conditions and evolving interpretations of the language written into the Constitution.

RIGHTS OF THE ACCUSED

15.3 Enumerate the constitutional rights of the accused, and discuss the impact of terrorism on these rights.

The expansion of the rights of the accused was always a hotly disputed political issue, and the conservative orientation of the Rehnquist and Roberts Courts resulted in the reversal of many of the due process innovations of the Warren and Burger Courts. Recently, the fight against terrorism has raised new questions about how much flexibility the government should be afforded in its efforts to combat terrorism.

RIGHT TO PRIVACY

15.4 Outline the constitutional justification for the right to privacy.

The Constitution does not explicitly specify that Americans have a right to privacy. However, in the wake of the Supreme Court's 1965 *Griswold* ruling, many have come to believe that this right is implied by the other rights stated explicitly in the Constitution. The notion that the Constitution provides a right to privacy has played a key role in an array of Court rulings—perhaps most notably in the rulings regarding the government's ability to regulate abortion.

bill of attainder A law that declares a person or a group of people guilty of a crime or punishes them without a trial.

capital crime Any crime for which death is a possible penalty.

civil liberties Freedoms found primarily in the Bill of Rights, the enjoyment of which are protected from government interference.

due process clause The section of the Fourteenth Amendment that prohibits states from depriving anyone of life, liberty, or property "without due process of law," a guarantee against arbitrary or unfair government action.

equal protection clause The section of the Fourteenth Amendment that provides for equal treatment by government of people residing within the United States and each of its states.

establishment clause The part of the First Amendment to the Constitution that prohibits Congress from establishing an official religion; the basis for the doctrine of the separation of church and state.

ex post facto law A law that retroactively declares some action illegal.

exclusionary rule A standard established by the Supreme Court that prevents police and prosecutors from using evidence against a defendant that was obtained in an illegal search.

free exercise clause The portion of the First Amendment to the Constitution that prohibits Congress from impeding religious observance or impinging on religious beliefs.

habeas corpus The legal doctrine that a person who is arrested must have a timely hearing before a judge.

imminent lawless action test Supreme Court standard that in order for the government to be allowed to prohibit speech, it must be likely to lead directly and immediately to law breaking.

Lemon Test Supreme Court standard that in order for a law with a religious element to be constitutional it must have a secular purpose, its primary effect cannot be to advance or impede religion, and it must not foster excessive entanglements between government and religion.

original intent The doctrine that the courts must interpret the Constitution in ways consistent with the intentions of the framers rather than in light of contemporary conditions and needs.

prior restraint A government action prohibiting publication or broadcast of materials (rather than punishing publication afterward).

privileges or immunities clause The portion of the Fourteenth Amendment that says states may not make laws that abridge the rights granted to people as citizens of the United States.

probable cause Legal doctrine that refers to a reasonable belief that a crime has been committed.

selective incorporation The gradual and piecemeal spread of the protections of the Bill of Rights to the states by the U.S. Supreme Court.

STOP THE VIOLENCE

Demonstrations—mostly peaceful, but occasionally violent—followed the police shooting of an unarmed African American man in Ferguson, Missouri on August 14, 2014. A string of police shootings of young Black men followed, leading to the creation of the Black Lives Matter movement. *Do these incidents suggest that not much progress has been made in advancing the civil rights of African Americans or do you see progress in other areas of American life for African Americans?*

CIVIL RIGHTS: THE STRUGGLE FOR POLITICAL EQUALITY

CHAPTER OUTLINE AND LEARNING OBJECTIVES

THE STATUS OF CIVIL RIGHTS BEFORE 1900

16.1 Trace the evolution of civil rights protections for racial minorities and women before 1900.

THE CONTEMPORARY STATUS OF CIVIL RIGHTS FOR RACIAL AND ETHNIC MINORITIES

16.2 Assess the evolving status of civil rights protections for racial and ethnic minorities since 1900.

THE CONTEMPORARY STATUS OF CIVIL RIGHTS FOR WOMEN

16.3 Assess the evolving status of civil rights protections for women since 1900.

BROADENING THE CIVIL RIGHTS UMBRELLA

16.4 Assess the evolving status of civil rights protections for the elderly, people with disabilities, and LGBTQ individuals.

The Struggle for Democracy

CIVIL RIGHTS, AFRICAN AMERICANS, AND THE POLICE

From 2014 to 2018, there were a number of high-profile incidents where interactions between the police and members of the public ended in the deaths of unarmed young African American men. Although data indicate that overall killings by police officers are not on the rise,[1] evidence does suggest that African American men are, nevertheless, far more likely than other groups to die in police confrontations, even when they are unarmed.[2] The factors that lead to fatalities are hotly debated, but many see police shootings as reminders that African Americans in the United States are treated unequally by government authorities.

In one especially notable incident, Michael Brown—an unarmed 18-year-old black man—was shot and killed in Ferguson, Missouri, by a white police officer.[3] After the shooting, Ferguson became a hotbed of racial tension and protest, pitting citizens of this predominantly black St. Louis suburb against its predominantly white police force. A grand jury investigation into Brown's death ultimately decided not to press charges against the shooter. Peaceful protests and vigils followed both the shooting and the grand jury decision as did looting and vandalism. The Ferguson Police Department's heavy-handed response to the protests, including the use of heavy-duty military equipment, further inflamed tensions and was seen by many as more evidence that the police are all too ready to view African Americans as an enemy to vanquish rather than as a community to protect.

Other incidents followed. Here are a few of the most notable ones. On Staten Island in New York City in 2014, Eric Garner was detained on suspicion of selling cigarettes illegally. After Garner resisted arrest, the officer put him in a chokehold—contrary to New York Police Department policy—and pressed him to the ground where he died while repeatedly saying, "I can't breathe." As with Michael Brown, the city decided not to indict the officer. In 2015, Freddie Gray, also African American, died in police custody from the extreme use of force by officers during his arrest and detention, riots erupted in Baltimore, where Gray had been stopped on suspicion that he possessed an illegal switchblade (the knife he had turned out to be legal). Unlike the incident in Ferguson, the six officers involved in Gray's death were charged by a grand jury, but all charges were dropped against the police officers after the state's attorney failed to win convictions for the first three brought to trial. In 2016, just outside Minneapolis, a police officer, on a routine traffic stop, shot and killed Philando Castile. He was unarmed, in the driver's seat, with his girlfriend and her child in the car. Charges were brought against the officer who fired her gun, but she was acquitted. In 2017, while the numbers of unarmed black men killed by the police dropped—national publicity of shootings captured on mobile phone cameras and dashboard cams in police cars led to numerous reforms by police departments across the country to ease tensions and lower deadly incidents in police-suspect encounters—the problem has not disappeared. In March, 2018, in Sacramento, California, for example, Stephon Clark, a 22-year-old unarmed African American man, was shot and killed by police in his own fenced-in backyard.

While there has certainly been major progress on racial equality issues over the last half-century, it is also the case that the ideal of racial equality has not been fully realized in the United States. Protests in response to these recent deaths are rooted in frustrations with persistent racial inequality and a sense that racial biases continue to lead to unequal treatment. On average, African and Hispanic Americans make far less money, have lower life expectancies, are far more likely to be jailed than white Americans, and are less likely now than a few decades ago to be in schools with whites.[4] Furthermore, some of America's most racially diverse cities, such as Chicago, St. Louis, Baltimore, and New York City, are also among the most racially segregated.[5] People may occupy the same cities but they are not necessarily living together.

* * * * *

As this chapter demonstrates, the struggle for civil rights is about more than laws that promise equal treatment. It is also about how public officials act to ensure that those promises are kept. One of the factors that will make this difficult to do is the perception among white Americans, a large majority of voters, that racism has largely been overcome and that African Americans focus too much on race-based grievances. Pew research reported after the Ferguson incident, for example, that blacks thought racial issues were at the heart of what happened in Ferguson and that the police had gone too far. Whites, on the other hand, reported that race had little to do with the shooting of Michael Brown and that the police had not overreacted.[6]

Civil rights are government guarantees of equality for people in the United States regarding judicial proceedings, the exercise of political rights, treatment by public officials, and access to and enjoyment of the benefits of government programs. (The terms *equal citizenship* and *civil rights* often are used interchangeably, which is our practice in this textbook.) The expansion of civil rights protections for African Americans, as well as for other racial, ethnic, and religious minorities, for women, and for LGBTQ individuals, is one of the great achievements of American history. These changes on the civil rights front have not come easily or quickly; it took the struggle of millions of Americans to force change from political leaders and government institutions. The result has been a significant democratization of the republican constitutional system of the framers. As the above story suggests, however, the expansion of civil rights protection in the United States is neither complete nor free of problems and controversy. And there continue to be setbacks.

THINKING CRITICALLY **ABOUT THIS CHAPTER**

This chapter is about civil rights in the United States and how politics and public policies have affected the status of equal protection and equal treatment for all Americans.

APPLYING THE **FRAMEWORK**

In this chapter, you will see that the meaning of civil rights has changed over the course of American history, and you will learn how *structural, political linkage, and governmental factors,* taken together, explain that change.

USING THE **DEMOCRACY STANDARD**

You will learn how civil rights are at the very center of our understanding of democracy in the United States. You will see how the struggle for democracy helped expand civil rights protections and how the expansion of civil rights has enhanced formal political equality in the United States, one of the basic foundations of a democratic political order.

THE STATUS OF CIVIL RIGHTS BEFORE 1900

16.1 Trace the evolution of civil rights protections for racial minorities and women before 1900.

The attainment of **civil rights** by racial minorities and women has been a comparatively late development in U.S. history, with most major advances not evident until well into the 20th century. This section looks at the period in U.S. history before 1900, when the expansion of civil rights to citizens of African descent, Native Americans, and other racial and ethnic minorities and to women was bitter, contentious, and prolonged.

civil rights

Guarantees of equal treatment by government officials regarding political rights, the judicial system, and public programs.

An Initial Absence of Civil Rights in the Constitution

Neither the original Constitution nor the Bill of Rights said anything about equality beyond insisting that all Americans are equally entitled to due process in the courts.[7] Indeed, the word *equality* does not appear in the Constitution at all. Nor did state

ADVOCATING FOR WOMEN'S RIGHTS

In 1848, Elizabeth Cady Stanton helped organize the Seneca Falls Convention on women's rights. The resulting Declaration of Sentiments and Resolutions was patterned after the Declaration of Independence, including a statement that "all men and women are created equal" and a list of the injustices of men against women. Stanton remained an activist for many years, helping to found the National Woman Suffrage Association in 1869 to press for the vote for women, and became the first president of the National American Woman Suffrage Association in 1890. *Why did it take so many years of outspoken activism for women finally to be granted the right to vote?*

constitutions offer much in the way of guaranteeing equality other than equality before the law. Americans in the late 18th and early 19th centuries, when the republic was new, seemed more interested in protecting individuals against the encroachment of government rather than guaranteeing certain political rights through government.[8] For their part, Native Americans were considered citizens of tribal nations, with no legal standing as equal citizens of the United States (they were not granted U.S. citizenship until 1924). In short, for the most numerous racial and ethnic minorities and women—to say nothing of LGBTQ individuals—equality eluded constitutional protection until the 20th century, although the groundwork was laid earlier.

The inequality of African Americans and women before the Civil War is quite striking. In the South, African Americans lived in slavery, with no rights at all. In the North, the few states that allowed African Americans to vote declined in number as the Civil War approached, even as universal white male suffrage was spreading. In many places outside the slave South, African Americans were denied entry into certain occupations, were required to post bonds guaranteeing their good behavior, were denied the right to sit on juries, and were occasionally threatened and harassed by mobs whenever they tried to vote or to petition the government for redress. In *Dred Scott v. Sandford* (1857), Chief Justice Roger Taney went so far as to claim that the Founders intended that blacks have no rights that whites nor the government were bound to honor or respect. As for women, no state allowed them to vote, few allowed them to sit on juries, and a handful even denied them the right to own property or to enter into contracts.

Many African Americans and women refused to play passive political roles, however. Although pre–Civil War society was not conducive to their participation in politics, African Americans voted in elections wherever allowed, helped organize the Underground Railroad to smuggle slaves out of the South, and were prominent in the movement to abolish slavery. Both black and white women played important roles in the abolitionist movement. The antislavery speaking tours of Angelina and Sarah Grimké caused something of a scandal in the 1840s when women's participation in public affairs was considered improper. Other women began to write extensively on the need for women's emancipation and their legal and political equality. In 1848, Elizabeth Cady Stanton issued a call for a convention on women's rights to be held at the village of Seneca Falls, New York. The Declaration of Sentiments and Resolutions issued by the delegates to the convention stands as one of the landmarks in women's struggle for political equality in the United States:

> All men and women are created equal … but the history of mankind is a history of repeated injuries and usurpations on the part of man toward woman, having in direct object the establishment of a direct tyranny over her…. [We demand] that women have immediate admission to all the rights and privileges which belong to them as citizens of the United States.

Civil Rights After Ratification of the Civil War Amendments

In the years following the Civil War, Congress passed three constitutional amendments—known collectively as the Civil War amendments—that created, in essence, the constitutional foundation for civil rights as we understand them today.

1. The Thirteenth Amendment to the Constitution, ratified in 1865, outlawed slavery throughout the United States, settling once and for all the most divisive issue of our early history as a nation.

2. The Fourteenth Amendment (1868) reversed *Dred Scott* by making all people citizens, both of the United States and of the states in which they reside, whether native born or naturalized, black or white.

To secure the rights and liberties of recently freed slaves, Congress articulated several new freedoms in Article I of the Fourteenth Amendment. The **privileges or immunities clause** guarantees that "no State shall make or enforce any law which shall abridge the privileges or immunities of citizens of the United States." The **due process clause** forbids "any State [from depriving] any person of life, liberty, or property, without due process of law." The **equal protection clause** bans states "[from denying] to any person within its jurisdiction the equal protection of the laws." As imposing as this constitutional language sounds, the Supreme Court would soon transform it into protections, not for the civil rights of African Americans, women, or Native Americans, but for business firms.

3. The Fifteenth Amendment (1870) said states could not prevent people from voting on the grounds of "race, color, or previous condition of servitude" (former slaves).

UNDERMINING THE CIVIL WAR AMENDMENTS   In the two decades following their passage, the Supreme Court blocked the promise of equal citizenship for African Americans found in the Civil War amendments. During this time, when many Americans in the North had grown weary of efforts to reconstruct the South and uplift and protect former slaves, white supremacists were regaining control in many areas of the South, and racist attitudes were widespread across the nation, the Supreme Court struck against key provisions of the amendments. The *Slaughterhouse Cases* (1873) rendered the privileges and immunities clause of the Fourteenth Amendment virtually meaningless. Writing for the Court, Justice Samuel Miller found that the clause did not guarantee citizenship rights against violations by state governments, only against violations by the federal government. The Court ruled that it was powerless to protect African Americans against abuses by state governments, including barriers to voting and office holding. Within five years of its passage, the Court had seriously compromised this key clause of the Fourteenth Amendment, foiling the work of the post–Civil War radical Republican Congress to amend the Constitution in favor of racial equality.

Though the equal protection clause of the Fourteenth Amendment survived the *Slaughterhouse Cases*, it too soon lost all practical meaning as a guarantor of equality for African Americans. First, the Court ruled in the *Civil Rights Cases* (1883) that the Fourteenth Amendment gave Congress no power to prohibit discrimination unless it was practiced by a state government. "Equal protection of the laws" did not, therefore, preclude race discrimination by nonstate entities such as private owners or managers of restaurants, theaters, hotels, and other public accommodations. Then the Court made government-sponsored discrimination constitutional. In *Plessy v. Ferguson* (1896), the Court said that states could separate the races on intrastate railways if they provided "equal" facilities. The *Plessy* ruling gave the doctrine of "separate but equal" full constitutional status and legitimacy and provided the legal underpinnings for segregation in nearly every area of life throughout the South. This state-sanctioned system of racial segregation—usually referred to as **Jim Crow**—would remain in force until *Plessy* was overturned in *Brown v. Board of Education of Topeka* (1954) more than half a century later.

The Fifteenth Amendment's voting guarantees were also rendered ineffectual—this time by a variety of devices invented to prevent African Americans from voting in the former states of the Confederacy. The **poll tax** was a tax required of all voters in many states, and it kept many African Americans away from the polls, given their desperate economic situation in the South in the late nineteenth and early twentieth centuries. Several states required voters to pass a **literacy test** devised and administered by local officials (see Table 16.1). The evaluation of test results was entirely up to local officials, who rarely passed blacks, even those with college educations or PhDs. If white voters failed the literacy test, many states allowed them to vote under a **grandfather clause**, which provided that anyone whose ancestors had voted before 1867 could also vote. Because the ancestors of African Americans in the South had been slaves, the grandfather clause was no help to them at all.

privileges or immunities clause
The portion of the Fourteenth Amendment that says states may not make laws that abridge the rights granted to people as citizens of the United States.

due process clause
The section of the Fourteenth Amendment that prohibits states from depriving anyone of life, liberty, or property "without due process of law," a guarantee against arbitrary or unfair government action.

equal protection clause
The section of the Fourteenth Amendment that provides for equal treatment by government of people residing within the United States and each of its states.

Jim Crow
Popular term for the system of legally sanctioned racial segregation that existed in the American South from the end of the 19th century until the middle of the 20th century.

poll tax
A tax to be paid as a condition of voting; used in the South to keep African Americans away from the polls.

literacy test
A device used by the southern states to prevent African Americans from voting before the passage of the Voting Rights Act of 1965, which banned its use; usually involved interpretation of a section of a state's constitution.

grandfather clause
A device that allowed whites who had failed the literacy test to vote anyway by extending the franchise to anyone whose ancestors had voted before 1867.

JIM CROW

For more than half a century, until the Court's 1954 *Brown* decision, the civil rights movement, and the 1964 Civil Rights Act ended it, the Jim Crow system of racial segregation of public facilities was virtually universal in the southern states.

Should states have been left alone to address how to change Jim Crow, or was federal intervention essential?

white primaries

Primary elections open only to whites in the one-party South, where the only elections that mattered were the Democratic Party's primaries; this effectively disenfranchised blacks.

Several states instituted **white primaries**, which excluded African Americans from the process of nominating candidates for local, state, and national offices. The states argued that excluding blacks from primaries was acceptable because political parties were private associations that could define their own membership requirements, including skin color. In the one-party (Democratic) South at the time, the actual election of public officials happened in the state Democratic primaries, leaving those few African Americans who voted in the November general elections without any voice at all. And, for those African Americans who might try to vote anyway in the

---

TABLE 16.1   ITEMS FROM THE ALABAMA LITERACY TEST

These questions, part of the sixty-eight-question Alabama Literacy Test, still in use in the 1950s and early 1960s, were used to decide the eligibility of voters in that state. The test and others like it were declared illegal by the 1965 Voting Rights Act. Most white voters who were unable to pass this or similar tests in the states of the Deep South were protected by "grandfather clauses," which authorized people to vote if their grandfathers had done so whether or not they could pass the "literacy" requirement.

1. A person appointed to the U.S. Supreme Court is appointed for a term of _____.
2. If a person is indicted for a crime, name two rights which he has.
3. Cases tried before a court of law are of what two types: civil and _____.
4. If no candidate for president receives a majority of the electoral vote, who decides who will become president?
5. If no person receives a majority of the electoral vote, the vice president is chosen by the Senate. True or False?
6. If an effort to impeach the President of the United States is made, who presides at the trial?
7. If the two houses of Congress do not agree to adjournment, who sets the time?
8. A president elected in November takes office the following year on what date?
9. Of the original 13 states, the one with the largest representation in the first Congress was _____.
10. The Constitution limits the size of the District of Columbia _____.

Answers: (1) good behavior; life; (2) jury trial, protection against self-incrimination, right to counsel, speedy trial, protection against excessive bail; (3) criminal; (4) the House of Representatives; (5) true; (6) The Chief Justice of the Supreme Court; (7) the president; (8) before 1933, March 4; after 1933, January 20; (9) Virginia; (10) not to exceed ten miles square

SOURCE: Alabama Literacy Test (1965), Kids Voting USA 9–12 Classroom Activities. Retrieved from http://www.socialstudies.org/system/files/publications/se/6006/600604.html. Used with permission from Kids Voting USA, Inc.

face of the poll tax, the literacy test, and the white primary, there was always the use of terror as a deterrent: night riding, bombings, and lynchings were used with regularity, especially during times when blacks showed signs of assertiveness.

The statutory devices for keeping African Americans away from the polls were consistently supported by state and federal courts until well into the 20th century. Terror as a means of preventing voting remained a factor until the 1960s, when the civil rights movement and federal intervention finally put an end to most of it.

WOMEN AND THE FIFTEENTH AMENDMENT   Politically active women in 19th-century America were stung by their exclusion from the Fifteenth Amendment's extension of the right to vote; the amendment said only that no state could exclude voters on the grounds of "race, color, or previous condition of servitude," not gender. These women quickly turned their attention to winning the vote for women. Once the Supreme Court had decided, in *Minor v. Happersett* (1874), that women's suffrage was not a right inherent in the national citizenship guarantees of the Fourteenth Amendment, many women abandoned legal challenges and turned to more direct forms of political agitation: petitions, marches, and protests. The fruits of their labors, however, would not be realized for another forty-six years.

THE CONTEMPORARY STATUS OF CIVIL RIGHTS FOR RACIAL AND ETHNIC MINORITIES

16.2   Assess the evolving status of civil rights protections for racial and ethnic minorities since 1900.

At the turn of the 20th century, the struggle of racial minorities for equality seemed very bleak indeed. The *Plessy* doctrine of separate but equal and Jim Crow seemed firmly and immutably established, but change, ever on the horizon, would come.

The Supreme Court, using the guidelines written by Justice Harlan Fiske Stone in *United States v. Carolene Products Company* (1938), gradually extended the protections of the Bill of Rights to the states, based on the Fourteenth Amendment. Among the state actions that would trigger **strict scrutiny** under the *Carolene* guidelines were those that either "restricted the democratic process" or "discriminated against racial, ethnic, or religious minorities." The application of the Fourteenth Amendment in *Carolene*, particularly the equal protection clause, lent judicial support to the gradual advance of civil rights guarantees for African Americans and other minorities and eventually (although less so) for women, and LGBTQ individuals.

strict scrutiny

The assumption that actions by elected bodies or officials violate the Constitution.

The following sections look at the extension of civil rights to racial and ethnic minorities and, later in the chapter, to women and other groups, including the LGBTQ community.[9] Though the focus is mainly (although not exclusively) on Supreme Court decisions, the actions of other branches of government regarding civil rights also were important in improving the standing of these groups in American society. Most important, recall the important role that protest and social movements played in improving the civil rights of a broad range of Americans. Without these movements and the pressures they brought to bear on public opinion, elected officials, and the courts, many of the changes we now take for granted would surely not have happened.

The End of Government-Sponsored Segregation and Discrimination

We reviewed earlier how the Constitution was long interpreted to condone slavery and segregation. In the 20th century, however, legal and political challenges to segregation and the battles waged by the civil rights movement eventually pushed the Supreme Court, the president, Congress, and the American people to take seriously the equal protection clause of the Fourteenth Amendment.

GRUDGING INTEGRATION

The erosion of official segregation in education came slowly and reluctantly in many parts of the nation. When ordered by a federal court in 1948 to admit a qualified black applicant to its Ph.D. program in education, the University of Oklahoma did so but forced the lone student to sit separated from other students.

Would a college or university today be able to discriminate against racial minorities in a similar manner? If not, can you think of other ways that discrimination continues in higher education but in more subtle and less obvious ways, or are we pretty much past that?

suspect classification

The invidious, arbitrary, or irrational designation of a group for special treatment by government, whether positive or negative; historically, used in laws to discriminate against visible minorities without the power to protect themselves.

It is worth noting at first, however, that the federal government itself played an important role in creating segregated housing in cities outside the South where Jim Crow prevailed. The first housing the government built for defense industry workers near defense factories and bases during World War I, for example, excluded African Americans.[10] Also, when Franklin Roosevelt's New Deal established a public housing program for the poor and middle class, it built separate projects for whites and blacks for the most part, and where projects were racially mixed, it segregated the population by having "whites only" and "blacks only" buildings. For its part, the Federal Housing Administration, established in 1934 to encourage homeownership by making it easier for people to obtain home mortgage loans, tended to deny mortgages to African American applicants, virtually shutting them off from suburban, single-family homes.[11]

However, in mid-century, changes in the status of legally sanctioned segregation and discrimination in the United States began to change. In 1944, amid World War II (a war aimed, in great part, at bringing down the racist regime of Adolf Hitler) and an NAACP campaign to rid the nation of segregation, the Supreme Court finally declared that race was a **suspect classification** that demanded strict judicial scrutiny. As a result of this declaration, any local ordinances and state and national statutes that used racial criteria were presumed to be unconstitutional, unless, under judicial investigation, they could be shown as both necessary and compelling for achieving some legitimate government goal. Pressed by the legal efforts of the NAACP, the Court gradually chipped away at the *Plessy* "separate but equal" doctrine and the edifice of segregation it helped create. In *Smith v. Allwright* (1944), the Court declared that the practice of excluding nonwhites from political party primary elections was unconstitutional. Then the Court ruled that the practice of setting up separate all-white and all-black law schools to circumvent integration was unacceptable. Thurgood Marshall—later a justice of the Supreme Court—argued many of the key cases that the NAACP brought before the Court for the purpose of eroding the official structure of segregation.[12]

The great legal breakthrough for racial equality came in 1954, in *Brown v. Board of Education of Topeka*, which was also argued on the plaintiffs' side by Thurgood Marshall. In *Brown*, the Court declared that "separate but equal" was inherently contradictory and that segregation imposed by state and local laws was constitution-ally unacceptable in public schools because it violated guarantees of equal protection. Speaking for a unanimous Court, Chief Justice Earl Warren said that education was "perhaps the most important function of state and local governments" and that segregation in education communicated the message that blacks were inferior and deserving of unequal treatment; in Warren's words, "In the field of education the doctrine of 'separate but equal' has no place."[13] *Brown* was a constitutional revolution, destined to transform racial relations law and practices in the United States because it struck down the foundations of segregation and discrimination.[14]

The white South did not at first react violently to *Brown*, but it did not peacefully desegregate either. Once recognition spread that the Court was going to demand that the states *enforce* the civil rights of African Americans, however, massive resistance to racial integration gripped the South. All-white Citizens Councils, com-mitted to imposing economic sanctions and boycotts on support-ers of desegregation, had more than 250,000 members by 1956. Membership in the Ku Klux Klan (KKK) increased dramatically, along with beatings, cross-burnings, and the murders of blacks and their white supporters.[15] In opposition, a movement of orga-nized activists, led by Dr. Martin Luther King Jr. and others, began working (and dying) to overcome Southern white resistance to *Brown*. The Court—even with many follow-up cases after *Brown*—was able to accomplish little until the president and Congress backed its decisions with legislation. The civil rights movement—examined in Chapter 8—and supportive changes in American public opinion helped spur legislative and presidential action in favor of protections for blacks. Ten years after *Brown*, Congress passed and Lyndon Johnson signed into law the Civil Rights Act of 1964 and the 1965 Voting Rights Act. (See Chapter 1 for a further elaboration of how the Voting Rights Act happened).

The Beginning of Government-Sponsored Remedies to Right Past Wrongs

Two basic trends have dominated the story of the extension of civil rights for African Americans since the mid-1960s:

1. The ending of legally sanctioned discrimination, separation, and exclusion from citizenship.
2. The debate over what actions to take to remedy past discrimination.

DE JURE VERSUS DE FACTO DISCRIMINATION   The prevailing legal doctrine on racial discrimination today is straightforward: Any use of race in law or government regulations to discriminate—sometimes called **de jure discrimination**—triggers strict scrutiny (a presumption of unconstitutionality) by the courts. A state or the federal gov-ernment can defend its acts under strict scrutiny only by proving a *compelling* govern-ment interest for which the act in question is a *necessary* means. Almost no law survives this challenge; laws that discriminate on the basis of race are dead from the moment of passage. In *Loving v. Virginia* (1967), for example, the Court ruled that Virginia's law against interracial marriage served no compelling government purpose that would jus-tify unequal treatment of the races. Needless to say, other racial minority groups in addi-tion to African Americans—Hispanics, Asian Americans, and Native Americans—have benefited from the constitutional revolution that has occurred since *Brown*.[16]

THE NAACP

The National Association for the Advancement of Colored People (NAACP) was founded in 1909 in New York City for the purpose of ending Jim Crow in the South, making lynching a federal crime, and advancing the interests of African Americans across the country. Its most important gains came from its legal defense arm, which brought and won many cases in the courts, cases that gradually moved the country toward providing equal protection of the law for African Americans, though it took a long time. This poster for an NAACP conference was published in 1946, a time when the organization, energized by black veterans of World War II, expanded its membership and redoubled its efforts to challenge racism in the United States. *Is there still a need for such organizations to push for the end of discrimination in the United States or should we depend on voting and contacting elected representatives to do the job?*

de jure discrimination

Unequal treatment based on government laws and regulations.

THE MARCH ON WASHINGTON

Dr. Martin Luther King Jr. waves to a crowd of an estimated half-million people who had just heard his "I Have a Dream" speech, delivered at the Lincoln Memorial on August 28, 1963, during the March on Washington. This event, one of the high points of the civil rights movement, helped convince Congress to pass and President Lyndon Johnson to sign into law the Civil Rights Act of 1964 and the 1965 Voting Rights Act.

Many Americans, including leading officials in the Kennedy administration, vehemently opposed the March on Washington, saying that it would stir racial emotions and hinder progress in gaining civil rights protections for African Americans. Do you believe such advances would have been made absent the March?

Passage of the Civil Rights Act of 1964 and the 1965 Voting Rights Act were incredibly consequential. The 1964 law outlawed racial discrimination in businesses that were engaged in interstate commerce in any way (including restaurants, hotels, theaters, and transit systems), prohibited denial of access to public facilities on the basis of race, allowed the federal government to sue school districts that refused to desegregate, and required all recipients of federal funds as well as businesses employing 250 or more people to act in a racially nondiscriminatory manner. As you learned in Chapter 1, the 1965 Voting Rights Act outlawed many practices that had kept African Americans from the polls in the South—literacy tests, poll taxes, and the like—sent federal employees to register African American voters in counties in the South with the most egregious histories of blocking blacks from voting, and required Southern states that had long records of discrimination to seek Justice Department approval for any changes in its voting rules and procedures. The Fair Housing Act of 1968 banned racial discrimination in the sale and rental of housing.

The results of judicial, congressional, and presidential actions helped transform race relations in the United States and the legal and political standing of African Americans. At this writing, de jure segregation of the races no longer exists in the United States, whether in schools, courts, or entertainment venues, to take but a few examples, and African Americans and other racial minorities are no longer formally barred from participation as voters and officeholders in local, state, or national politics. In the South, where the 1965 Voting Rights Act had its greatest effects—as intended—African Americans became an important voting block and filled many offices, from county sheriffs and city councils, to mayors of cities of all sizes. By 2012, the number of registered African American voters exceeded the number of registered non-Hispanic Whites in Louisiana, Mississippi, North Carolina, and South Carolina.[17] Voting participation and office holding increased dramatically for Hispanics as well in places such as Florida, Texas, New Mexico, Arizona, and California as formal mechanisms denying them access to the political sphere fell.

In 2013, however, the Supreme Court declared the preclearance provision of the 1965 Voting Rights Act unconstitutional. "Preclearance" required states and counties with a history of discrimination against African American and other minority voters to obtain federal approval, or preclearance, before altering laws that regulated voting within their borders. This preclearance provision gave the federal government the authority to block changes to state voting laws, including the redrawing of voting district boundaries, if those changes might have a discriminatory effect on racial minorities. In *Shelby County v. Holder*, the Court held, by a 5 to 4 vote, that the standards used to determine if states were engaged in discriminatory voting practices were no longer valid and that preclearance itself was a violation of the constitutional requirement that states be treated equally. As a result, all states are now free to change their voting laws as they see fit (within other established federal and constitutional requirements).

In the aftermath of *Shelby*, many Republican-controlled states, claiming they were fighting voter fraud, enacted changes to their voting requirements, making it more difficult to register to vote, mostly by requiring particular kinds of documentary proof to establish place of residence or citizenship status. If, for example, potential voters do not have permanent addresses, driver's licenses, or birth certificates, their access to the ballot box can be denied.[18] In October 2015, Alabama raised the barrier to voting even higher when it closed 31 Department of Motor Vehicle offices in rural counties, claiming budget problems.[19] This decision makes it more difficult for many people to obtain a driver's license or a state-issued ID, one of which is required to vote. The rural counties in question are primarily ones with African American majorities so the impact of the closings is likely to be a reduction in the size of the African American electorate in Alabama, though only time will tell. Before *Shelby*, the Justice Department would surely have not allowed the state to institute such a change in voting rules. In fact, using other parts of the 1965 Voting Rights Act, the Justice Department under President Obama brought suit against several states over voter ID laws and other new laws that might diminish the votes of minority groups, such as curtailing early voting. The administration and civil rights organizations enjoyed some successes in the courts. The following rulings happened in July 2016 alone: the Fourth Circuit ruled that North Carolina's law was enacted with "racially discriminatory intent"; the conservative Seventh Circuit Court ruled that Wisconsin must find ways to ease the burdens on minorities of its Voter ID laws; and the Sixth Circuit ruled that Ohio's roll-back of early voting was unconstitutional. In 2018, a three-judge panel of the Fifth Circuit ruled that Texas's voter ID law did not discriminate against African Americans and Hispanics and could go into effect.[20] Given contradictory rulings in district and circuit courts, the matter of state-level Voter ID laws is likely to reach the Supreme Court.

Even in light of the Shelby County decision and continuing efforts in some states to make it difficult for some people to vote—including not only Voter ID laws but also closing off of the voting booth for convicted felons who have served their time (disproportionally, African Americans and Hispanic Americans)—racial discrimination in law is less and less evident in the United States. This is not to say, however, that racial discrimination is a thing of the past in the United States. **De facto discrimination**—unequal treatment of racial or ethnic minority groups based on practices rather than statutes and regulations mandating discrimination (as in Jim Crow laws)—remains a fact of life, although its exact extent is hard to measure accurately. In 2016, for example, 49 percent of African Americans said that in the previous year, they had been treated unfairly in stores and restaurants because of their race (for whites, it was 21 percent).[21]

de facto discrimination
Unequal treatment by private individuals, groups, and organizations.

Complaints from African Americans and other minorities about discriminatory treatment by public officials also abound. For example, 70 percent of African Americans report feeling that police treat them less well than they treat others, and 68 percent say the same about the courts. For Hispanics, the numbers are 51 percent and 40 percent for the police and the courts.[22] Young black and Hispanic men are especially prone to experiencing specific instances of negative contact with police.

States and localities have instituted many laws and practices that can have discriminatory effects without any explicit reference to race or ethnicity. Thus, the self-described "toughest sheriff in America," Joe Arpaio of Maricopa County, Arizona, claimed that his policy of stopping suspicious automobiles—with Hispanics four to nine times more likely to be stopped than whites—was aimed only at stopping illegal immigration and was not targeted at Hispanics. A federal court in 2013 found these actions to be unconstitutional and appointed a monitor to oversee changes in these policies, but compliance has proved difficult to enforce even though Sheriff Joe was removed from office. Several states, including Arizona, require that police ask about the immigration status of anyone stopped for a routine traffic stop if police have a "reasonable suspicion" that the person stopped may be undocumented. The Supreme Court ruled in 2013 that while states could require police to make such inquiries, they would need to do so on a nondiscriminatory basis. In New York City, during the tenure of Mayor Michael Bloomberg, police depended heavily on "stop and frisk" tactics in an effort to find illegal weapons, get dangerous felons off the streets, and decrease gang violence. In 2012, the practice resulted in more than two hundred thousand stop and frisks, with 53 percent of those stopped being African Americans and 34 percent Hispanic.[23] A federal judge ruled in 2013 that the practice was discriminatory and must cease in its present form and appointed a federal monitor to oversee changes in police department practices. In 2016, the federal monitor reported that the police were having difficulty putting rule changes in the program into practice. By 2017, the number of "stops" had decreased significantly from the peaks that occurred prior to the 2013 court ruling, but African Americans and Hispanics were still being disproportionally targeted.[24]

American Muslims and Americans of Arab descent have faced significant hostility since the 9/11 terrorist attacks on the United States in 2001. There have been a number of mosque defacements over the years since 9/11 even as several proposed projects to build additional mosques failed to gain approval from local authorities in various cities around the nation. Anti-Muslim posters appeared in early 2016 at UCLA, American University, Virginia Tech, and other campuses, while defacements of Islamic centers happened at the University of Arizona and elsewhere.[25] During the 2016 presidential campaign, Donald Trump aimed much of his ire at Muslim Americans and Arab Americans. After winning the presidency, he issued a number of executive orders temporarily banning entry into the United States of people from several Muslim majority nations (the first two were overturned in federal court;

STOP AND FRISK

In New York, as well as in many other cities, the policy of police stopping and frisking people acting suspiciously led to the arrests of mainly African American and Hispanic men. Advocates of the policy claim it has led to a dramatic drop in crime as many individuals with arrest warrants have been caught, as was the case for this man arrested in New York's Chinatown. Critics claim the policy is discriminatory, with mostly innocent people caught up in a humiliating experience.

Can you suggest other ways that crime might be reduced without discriminatory outcomes?

the third was upheld by the Supreme Court). It is not surprising that a Republican president felt free to take this action because attitudes toward Muslims living in the United States break sharply along partisan lines, with conservative Republicans the most distrustful of them and liberal Democrats most supportive; in 2017, 65 percent of Republicans said they believed there is a fundamental contradiction between Islam and democracy, a position endorsed by only 30 percent of Democrats.[26]

AFFIRMATIVE ACTION   Despite these examples of real or perceived mistreatment by governments, it is now widely accepted that the Constitution protects racial minorities against any discrimination or disadvantage that is sanctioned or protected by law or government action. The issues are not as clear-cut, however, in the area of government actions that *favor* racial and ethnic minorities (and women) in **affirmative action** programs designed to rectify past wrongs.[27]

Origins of Affirmative Action   The main goal of the civil rights movement of the 1950s and 1960s was to remove barriers to equal citizenship for black Americans. This goal was largely accomplished by Court decisions, passage of the 1964 Civil Rights Act and the Voting Rights Act of 1965, and broad changes in public attitudes about race. But even with these important changes, the economic and social situations of African Americans did not appear to be improving much. It seemed to an increasing number of people that ending government-sponsored discrimination was a start but that more proactive government actions might be required if African Americans were to escape the conditions caused by years of discrimination. President Lyndon Johnson, Senator Robert Kennedy, and Martin Luther King Jr., among others, eventually came to believe that the advancement of black Americans could happen only if there was a broad societal effort to eradicate poverty by equipping the poor, both black and white, with the tools for success. This led to the founding of the Johnson administration's Great Society and War on Poverty and programs such as Head Start.

After Martin Luther King's assassination in 1968 and the urban riots that followed, many people in government, the media, higher education, and the major foundations began to support the notion that progress for African Americans would happen only if government encouraged proactive efforts to increase the levels of black representation in private- and public-sector jobs and contracting and in colleges and

affirmative action

Programs of private and public institutions favoring minorities and women in hiring and contracting, and in admissions to colleges and universities, in an attempt to compensate for past discrimination or to create more diversity.

OPENING THE CONSTRUCTION TRADES

For many years, African Americans found it difficult to gain entry into high-paying jobs in the construction trades because of discriminatory union and construction company policies. Though the Supreme Court has barred affirmative action in city and state construction contracts to increase diversity, it does allow affirmative action to compensate for past discrimination practiced by specific unions, companies, and local governments. As a result, a substantial number of African Americans have gained entry and worked on major construction projects, like this man working on the Freedom Tower building next to the site of the Twin Towers in New York City.
Do you believe that affirmative action should be used to increase diversity in all areas of American life or only as a tool to compensate for specific discriminatory practices? Or do you believe that affirmative action programs are never justifiable because they discriminate against people today who are not in a "protected class?" Defend your answer.

universities.[28] Somewhat surprisingly, it was Richard Nixon—who was not generally thought of as a booster of civil rights—who took the most important step, requiring in his 1969 Philadelphia Plan that construction companies with federal contracts and the associated construction trade unions hire enough blacks and other minorities to achieve "racial balance" (a proportion roughly equal to the racial distribution in the community).

Although initially skeptical of racial preferences, Justices William Brennan, Byron White, Thurgood Marshall, and Harry Blackmun supported temporary programs to remedy the effects of past discrimination. Joined by Justice Lewis Powell, they formed the majority in *Regents v. Bakke* (1978), in which the Court authorized a compromise on affirmative action programs. The Constitution and federal law prohibited employers and admissions committees from using strictly racial quotas, the Court said, but it saw no problem with the use of race as one factor among several in hiring or college admissions.

Since *Bakke*, government and higher education racial outreach programs, which were preferred at that time, have become relatively permanent rather than temporary, and their aim has shifted from providing remedies for past discrimination to enhancing diversity. The proliferation of diversity programs, diversity training, and diversity offices has become commonplace in colleges and universities, in government, and in the corporate world, but they now are in great jeopardy.

Why Affirmative Action? Proponents offer the following justifications for affirmative action:[29]

- The effects of past discrimination disadvantage, to one degree or another, all members of discriminated-against groups, so simply removing barriers to advancement is insufficient. When government policies themselves have had profound and lasting effects—slavery being the most obvious, but also state-sanctioned segregation and racial discrimination in major benefit programs such as the post–World War II GI Bill[30]—the proper remedy is to prefer members of such groups in hiring, contracts, and education until such time as they reach parity with the majority. For example, despite big gains since passage of the Civil Rights Act in 1964, African Americans are a long way from reaching economic parity with whites, lagging significantly in educational attainment, annual income, and wealth (net worth for white households was seventeen times that of African American households in 2012).[31]

- In a diverse society such as the United States, tolerance and a sense of community can develop only if we work together in educational, workplace, and government institutions that are diverse.

- People from disadvantaged and discriminated-against groups will improve themselves only if they have experience with successful role models in important institutions.

Critics of affirmative action are not convinced by these arguments. They believe:

- Affirmative action violates one of the most basic American principles: that people be judged, rewarded, and punished as individuals, not because they are members of one group or another.

- Affirmative action benefits those within each preferred group who are already advantaged and need little help. Thus, the main beneficiaries of affirmative action in higher education have been middle-class African Americans, not the poor.

- Affirmative action seeks to remedy the effects of past discrimination by discriminating against others today—most notably, white males—simply because they belong to nonpreferred groups.

- Affirmative action increases intergroup and interracial tension by heightening the saliency of group membership. That is, social friction is increased by encouraging people to think of themselves and others as members of groups and to seek group advantages in a zero-sum game in which one group's gain is another group's loss.

Public Opinion on Affirmative Action   In survey after survey, a vast majority of Americans say they approve of the diversity goals of affirmative action—special programs to help those who have been discriminated against get ahead; outreach programs to hire minority workers and find minority students—but disapprove of racial preferences in hiring, awarding of government contracts, and admission to colleges.[32] Not surprisingly, perhaps, there is a wide gap between the races on the issue of preferential treatment are wide; 66 percent of African Americans and 59 percent of Latinos in 2013 supported racial preferences compared to only 22 percent of whites.[33]

American discomfort with affirmative action programs can perhaps be best seen in actions in several of the states. For example, referenda banning affirmative action in any state and local government activity were passed in California (1996), Washington (1997), and Michigan (2006)—three very liberal states—and other states have severely restricted affirmative action by executive order of their governors.[34] In 2008, Nebraska voters approved a measure that bans government use of affirmative action; Colorado voters narrowly rejected a ban, the first time affirmative action bans at the state level had failed at the polls.

The Supreme Court on Affirmative Action   The Supreme Court has been grappling for years with the issue of which forms of affirmative action, if any, are constitutionally permissible. Since the mid-1980s, the Supreme Court has been moving gradually toward the position that laws and other government actions that are not colorblind should be subject to strict scrutiny. State and local statutes that use racial preferences to increase diversity have been ruled constitutionally unacceptable in government hiring and contracting, and their use in higher education admissions has been substantially restricted. In the University of Michigan cases in 2003, the Court ruled by a 5–4 vote that universities could take race into consideration when considering applications for admission, so long as the consideration of race was not done in a mechanically quantitative manner or used as part of a racial and ethnic quota system, reaffirming, as it were, its position in the 1978 *Bakke* decision. The Court rejected the University of Michigan's undergraduate admissions affirmative action program—because it automatically assigned extra points to each minority applicant—but accepted the law school's—whose admissions process uses race as but one among several factors in a holistic examination of each applicant's file.

Remember that the balance on the Court swung dramatically in a conservative direction after Samuel Alito replaced the retiring Sandra Day O'Connor, who favored affirmative action in higher education under certain not-too-difficult to achieve conditions. With Alito anchoring a 5–4 conservative majority, the Court radically narrowed how race could be used in higher education admissions. Most important was *Fisher v. Texas* (2013) in which the Court set out standards for universities to meet that were more stringent than ever, leading many observers to suggest that few institutions could meet them. The Court suggested that such admissions programs would be subject to strict scrutiny and could only be justified if all other possible non-race–based methods had been used to try to achieve diversity and if a college or university could show that a critical mass of minority students had not already been achieved.

In 2014, the Court ruled in *Schuette v. Coalition to Defend Affirmative Action* that the Michigan constitutional amendment to ban affirmative action in higher education was permissible. By extension, it lent support to seven other states that also had such bans in place and seemed to suggest that affirmative action in higher education would soon be gone.

In 2016, however, and much to the surprise of nearly everyone, the Court put on the brakes on its seemingly inexorable drive to severely limit or end affirmative action programs in higher education admissions. In yet another consideration of the University of Texas's admissions program—one in which most students at the university are admitted if they are in the top ten percent of their Texas high school class with a much smaller number admitted by means of a holistic consideration of an applicant's qualifications and attributes, including race—the Court ruled 4–3 that the University of Texas program was constitutionally acceptable (the uncharacteristic vote was because Justice Scalia had died and Justice Kagan recused herself because of prior involvement in the case before she joined the Court). In his opinion for the majority, Justice Kennedy said that student body diversity is central to many universities' identity and educational mission but in meeting that goal they must be careful not to impinge on the promise of equal treatment guaranteed by the "equal protection" clause of the Fourteenth Amendment. With Kennedy's retirement and Brett Kavanaugh's accession to the Court, advocates of affirmative action worry that its future is not bright.[35]

Here is where affirmative action programs stand after the three *Fisher* rulings and taking into account all of the Court's rulings on racial preferences since *Bakke*:

- Any program by a government entity that uses race to define who receives or does not receive benefits or services is subject to strict scrutiny—that is, considered unconstitutional unless compelling and necessary reasons for the policies are proved. This holds whether or not such policies are designed to discriminate against or to favor racial minorities.

- Affirmative action programs are acceptable in the awarding of government contracts and government hiring—whether federal, state, or local—only if those programs are narrowly tailored to rectify past discriminatory actions by that particular government agency. Such programs, however, must be temporary efforts to transcend past practices and not a permanent feature of hiring and contracting. Affirmative action in hiring and contracting is not valid if it is designed simply to increase diversity or to decrease racism in society.

- Actions to rectify past discriminatory admissions policies by a particular higher education institution are compelling and necessary and are permitted.

- Higher education's goal of achieving a diverse student body is a compelling reason to have affirmative action programs. However, race can only be used if it is one among several factors in a holistic consideration of each applicant's file, if other non-race–based methods to increase diversity have been tried, and if the college or university has not already achieved a critical mass of minority students.

Affirmative action programs in the United States have been designed to help not only African Americans, of course, but other racial and ethnic minorities as well, including Hispanics, Asian Americans, and Native Americans. Most of the programs also have included women as beneficiaries. The present Supreme Court guidelines on affirmative action described here apply to all of these groups, not only African Americans, so the extreme narrowing of the acceptability by the Court of affirmative action affects each of these groups in one way or another. Figure 16.1, an application of our analytical framework, examines the interaction *of structural, political linkage, and governmental factors* to explain why the Supreme Court has become less friendly to affirmative action.

FIGURE 16.1 APPLYING THE FRAMEWORK: WHY HAS THE SUPREME COURT DRAMATICALLY NARROWED THE SCOPE OF AFFIRMATIVE ACTION PROGRAMS?

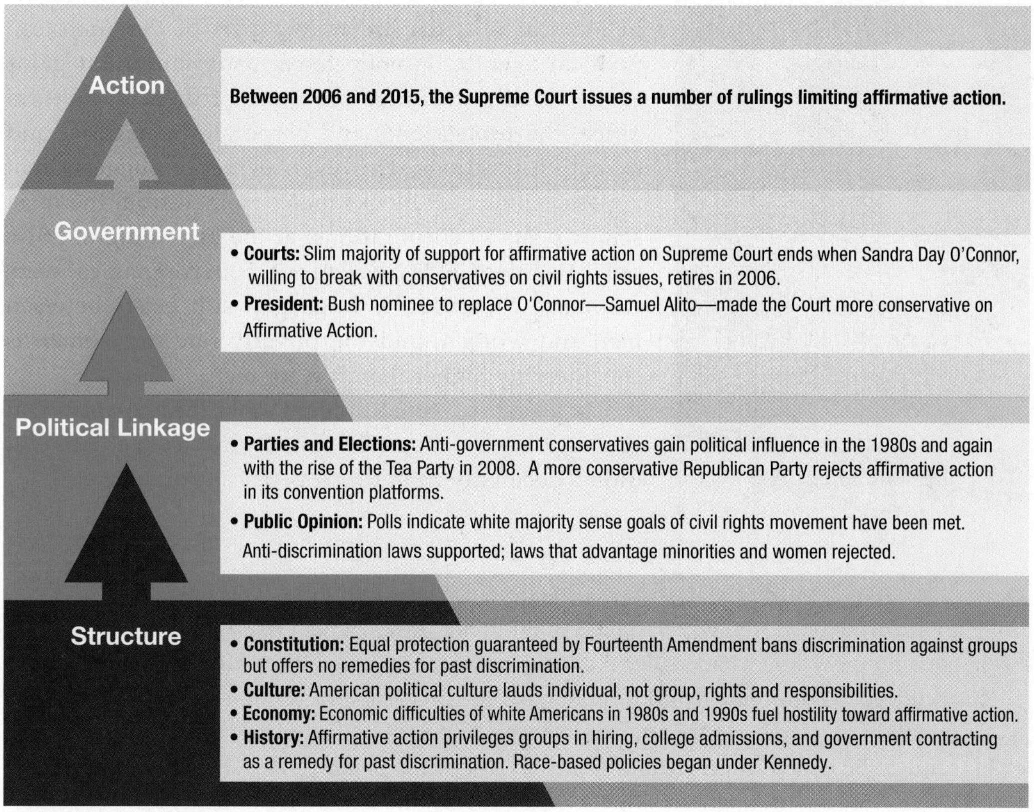

Action

Between 2006 and 2015, the Supreme Court issues a number of rulings limiting affirmative action.

Government

- **Courts:** Slim majority of support for affirmative action on Supreme Court ends when Sandra Day O'Connor, willing to break with conservatives on civil rights issues, retires in 2006.
- **President:** Bush nominee to replace O'Connor—Samuel Alito—made the Court more conservative on Affirmative Action.

Political Linkage

- **Parties and Elections:** Anti-government conservatives gain political influence in the 1980s and again with the rise of the Tea Party in 2008. A more conservative Republican Party rejects affirmative action in its convention platforms.
- **Public Opinion:** Polls indicate white majority sense goals of civil rights movement have been met. Anti-discrimination laws supported; laws that advantage minorities and women rejected.

Structure

- **Constitution:** Equal protection guaranteed by Fourteenth Amendment bans discrimination against groups but offers no remedies for past discrimination.
- **Culture:** American political culture lauds individual, not group, rights and responsibilities.
- **Economy:** Economic difficulties of white Americans in 1980s and 1990s fuel hostility toward affirmative action.
- **History:** Affirmative action privileges groups in hiring, college admissions, and government contracting as a remedy for past discrimination. Race-based policies began under Kennedy.

© Edward S. Greenberg

THE CONTEMPORARY STATUS OF CIVIL RIGHTS FOR WOMEN

16.3 Assess the evolving status of civil rights protections for women since 1900.

After years of struggle, the efforts of the women's suffrage movement bore fruit when the Nineteenth Amendment, which gave women the vote, was ratified in 1920: "The right of citizens of the United States to vote shall not be denied or abridged by the United States or by any State on account of sex." At first, women did not vote in the same proportion in elections as men. But they gradually caught up. Indeed, women now vote at higher rates than men in U.S. elections. As their turnout increased over the years, not only did male elected officials need to pay more attention to the interests of women, but women increasingly became office-holders themselves.

Voting was not the only avenue to advance equality, however. As the civil rights movement of the 1950s and 1960s helped put the issue of equality for African Americans on the nation's political agenda, so did several women's rights movements advance civil rights protections for women. Fifty years after the adoption of the Nineteenth Amendment, the women's movement of the 1970s and 1980s helped win additional civil rights protections for women and broaden the participation of women in all aspects of American society, economy, and politics. Although the movement did not win one of its main objectives—passage of the Equal Rights Amendment (ERA) to the U.S. Constitution—the broad advance of women in

gaining equal treatment and respect on virtually all fronts in the United States attests to its overall effectiveness.[36] Issues such as pay equity, family leave, sexual harassment, and attention to women's health problems in medical research are now a part of the American political agenda. Women have made important gains economically, and there are more of them in political office, the professions, and corporate managerial and executive positions. However, evidence suggests that a glass ceiling still blocks many women from the most senior posts in corporations; at the beginning of 2016, only twenty CEOs of *Fortune* 500 companies were women.[37] Moreover, a wage gap still exists between men and women, and the poverty rate for women is considerably higher than it is for men.

In terms of constitutional law, the expansion of civil rights protections for women has taken a path that differs decidedly from that for African Americans.[38]

LEANING IN

Sheryl Sandberg, the COO of Facebook, is one of the most powerful and visible corporate executives in the world, widely acknowledged as second in importance only to Mark Zuckerberg in the fantastic growth of the company. In her controversial book *Lean In: Women, Work, and the Will to Lead*, she suggests that it is not only discrimination that holds back the rise of women in various institutions in the U.S., including business and politics, but their tendency to defer to men. Her advice to women: "Lean in" and be more assertive.
What do you make of Sandberg's argument? Is she right? Is it relevant to all women or only to highly-educated professional women as her critics claim?

intermediate scrutiny

A legal test falling between ordinary and strict scrutiny relevant to issues of gender; under this test, the Supreme Court will allow gender classifications in laws if they are *substantially* related to an *important* government objective.

Intermediate Scrutiny

By 1976, the proposed Equal Rights Amendment (ERA), which would guarantee full legal equality for women, had stalled, falling short of the required three-fourths of the states. In addition, the Supreme Court did not have the necessary votes for a strict scrutiny interpretation of gender classification. There was support, however, for the new doctrine that came to be called **intermediate scrutiny**. In *Craig v. Boren* (1976), six justices supported Justice William Brennan's compromise, which created a more rigorous scrutiny of gender as a *somewhat* suspect classification. In the view of the justices, the use of strict scrutiny would endanger traditional gender roles, while the use of ordinary scrutiny would allow blatant discrimination to survive. The Burger Court defined a test that it believed to be "just right." Under intermediate scrutiny, government enactments that relied on gender would be constitutional if the use of gender were *substantially related* to an *important government interest*.[39] The test in *Craig* was refined in *United States v. Virginia* (1996), when the Court ruled that a male-only admissions policy at the state-supported Virginia Military Institute was unacceptable in that it discriminated against women. In this case, the standard to be met when men and women are treated differently in statutes and state government practices became "an exceedingly persuasive justification." Intermediate scrutiny defines a legal test, then, somewhere between strict and lax. Thus, for example, certain laws protecting pregnant women from dangerous chemicals in the workplace have passed this test. Unlike race, then, gender is not considered a suspect classification by which laws and government practices are reviewed under the strict scrutiny standard, and assumed to be unconstitutional, but only a semi-suspect classification, less likely to be declared unconstitutional. The improvement of women's rights under the doctrine of intermediate scrutiny is less than what many in the women's movement have wanted.

Thus, women's rights have not followed the path of other rights and liberties. The nation has not restructured civil rights for women based on the courts' expansive reading of the equal protection clause of the Fourteenth Amendment. Rather, advances have come by virtue of changing societal attitudes about the role of women in society, increased involvement of women in politics (see Figure 16.2), and new statutes designed to equalize women's opportunities. In the private sector, women have made important advances in the corporate world and in the professions. Women now outnumber men among law school and medical school students, and more women than men go to college and graduate. However, significant wage disparities

FIGURE 16.2   PERCENTAGE OF ELECTIVE OFFICES HELD BY WOMEN, 1979–2018

Although accounting for more than one-half the American population, women hold a much smaller proportion of elected federal, state, and local offices across the nation than men. However, the percentage of offices held by women has increased significantly since the 1970s. Given rising education and incomes among women, as well as changing social attitudes toward women's role in society, it may be that the proportion of elected offices held by women will increase.

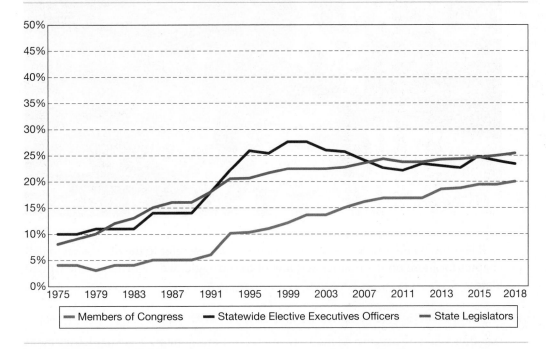

SOURCE: Data from Center for American Women and Politics, Rutgers University.

still exist between men and women in every occupation, at every level of education, and in every area of the country, though the gap has narrowed somewhat for college graduates between the ages of 25 and 34.[40]

Women have also successfully pushed for laws that compensate for past injustices. One example of such a law is Title IX of the Civil Rights Act of 1964, which prohibits discrimination against women at federally funded institutions, including universities. Title IX is generally credited with enhancing funding for women's sports programs in colleges and dramatically improving the quality of women's athletics in the United States. Another example is the Lilly Ledbetter Fair Pay Restoration Act, signed into law by President Barack Obama in January 2009 only days after his inauguration, which makes it easier for women and others to sue companies over pay discrimination, a remedy that may serve to narrow the pay gap between men and women. The new law was designed to override the Supreme Court's ruling in *Ledbetter v. Goodyear Tire & Rubber Co.* (2007), which made pay discrimination lawsuits exceedingly difficult to mount.

Abortion Rights

For many women (and men), the right of women to terminate an unwanted pregnancy is a central element of the civil rights agenda falling under the equal protection clause of the Fourteenth Amendment. (To be sure, many others are against abortion on religious and other grounds.) That may well be, but the Supreme Court, in a number of important cases beginning with *Roe v. Wade* (1973), has based a woman's right to terminate a pregnancy on privacy grounds rather than equal protection grounds. It is for this reason that we have addressed the abortion issue, with its contentious politics and string of Supreme Court rulings revising and refining *Roe*, in Chapter 15 on

NOTRE DAME WINS

The Department of Education's interpretation of Title IX of the Civil Rights Act is widely credited with opening up opportunities for women to take part, on increasingly equal footing with men, in high school and college-level varsity sports. One result has been the emergence of world-class women's teams in soccer, volleyball, basketball, and several other sports. Here action from the finals of the 2018 NCAA championship is shown, won by Notre Dame.

Would something analogous to Title IX be useful to women's advancement in other areas of American life or does it seem appropriate only to sports?

civil liberties where privacy issues are discussed. Please refer to the discussion in that chapter for more on the politics and law of the struggle over abortion in the United States.

Sexual Harassment and Hostile Environments

Another issue of concern to many women (and many men) is sexual harassment in the workplace. People disagree about what kinds of behavior constitute sexual harassment, although the courts, regulatory agencies, and legislative bodies are gradually defining the law in this area. In 1980, the Equal Employment Opportunity Commission (EEOC) ruled that making sexual activity a condition of employment or promotion violates the 1964 Civil Rights Act, a ruling upheld by the Supreme Court. The EEOC also ruled that creating "an intimidating, hostile, or offensive working environment" is contrary to the law. The U.S. Supreme Court took a major step in defining sexual harassment when it ruled unanimously, in *Harris v. Forklift Systems Inc.* (1993), that workers do not have to prove that offensive actions make them unable to do their jobs or cause them psychological harm, only that the work environment is hostile or abusive. In a pair of rulings in June 1998, the Court broadened the definition of sexual harassment by saying that companies were liable for the behavior of supervisors even if top managers were unaware of harassing behavior. However, the Court offered a measure of protection to companies by ruling that companies with solid and well-communicated harassment policies could not be held liable if victims failed to report harassment in a reasonable period of time.

An increase in public awareness about sexual harassment has triggered an increase in lawmaking by state legislatures to erase sexual harassment in the workplace. In addition, most major corporations and state and local government entities (including public colleges and universities) have sexual harassment and hostile environment prohibitions in place and require their employees to participate in training programs to lessen the incidence of harassment. Surely, however, the United States has a very long way to go on this front as recent revelations show that sexually offensive behavior on the job by powerful men in government, journalism, entertainment, and education. The list of sexual offenders grows daily; it includes liberals and conservatives, Republicans and Democrats, and men of all races. A credible list, at this writing in Summer, 2018, would include at a minimum FoxNews CEO Roger Ailes and popular conservative talk show host on that network Bill O'Reilly. But it also includes Matt Lauer of the Today show, Charlie Rose of PBS and CBS, and Mark Halperin of CNN. In Hollywood, award-winning producer Harvey Weinstein was revealed to have been a serial sexual predator as was Academy Award winning actor Kevin Spacey. Louis C. K., comedian and actor, fell to charges from many women, and Bill Cosby was convicted at trial of using drugs to break down the resistance of female colleagues to his sexual advances. In government, liberal Democratic Senator Al Franken was forced to resign in light of revelation of objectionable sexual conduct. New York Attorney General Eric Schneiderman resigned his post in May, 2018, after multiple woman accused him of sexual and physical abuse. Many Americans were appalled by Donald Trump's bragging about how easy it was to assault women in the Access Hollywood Tapes. His second nominee to the Court, Brett Kavanaugh, faced allegations of sexual assault.

Troubled by the election of Donald Trump, women responded with a massive Women's March after the president's inauguration. Appalled over and over by revelations of sexual harassment and abuse, as discussed above, women created the #MeToo movement on social media, for the purpose of encouraging others to tell their own stories and empowering women to push for change. Only time will tell how much political and social change will come from this activism.

PROTESTING THE NEW PRESIDENT

Closely following Donald Trump's inauguration as President of the United States—Trump had pledged during his campaign to appoint judges who would reverse *Roe v. Wade* and was elected despite the fact that he was caught on tape bragging about sexual assault—a massive women's march took place in Washington, D.C. and other cities on January 21, 2017.

Do marches of this sort have important long range effects on American politics? Has this march, in particular, raised awareness among the public about sexual harassment, sexual assault, and women's rights?

EVEN CHARLIE ROSE?

Television star and journalist-author Charlie Rose was dropped by CBS This Morning and PBS after sexual harassment charges were leveled against him by eight women in 2017.

In your view, how might we best lower the incidence of sexual harassment in the country? What should the role of government be in this effort? Or are matters best left to the private sector?

American Women by Comparison

Despite the significant progress that American women have made in both the private and public sectors, they have not fared very well when compared with women in other rich democracies. American women rank only 17th according to a glass-ceiling index created by the statistical research team at *The Economist* (see Figure 16.3). *The Economist* index calculates male and female differences across a variety of life situations, including higher education, participation in the labor force, representation in senior jobs and corporate boards, wages and salaries, access to abortion services, the extent of paid maternity leave, child care costs, representatives in national legislatures, and applications to business schools. The United States ranks at just the OECD average, with a score well below that of leaders Iceland, Finland, Norway, and Sweden. (The OECD, the Organization of Economic Co-Operation and Development, is an organization whose members incorporate all the world's rich democracies). Many Americans might see its glass-ceiling score as reason to redouble efforts to improve the position of women in the United States; other Americans may not agree that the index is valid because they do not believe that paid maternity leave, for example, is good for the business community or that the availability of abortion services is acceptable as an indicator of women's equality.

FIGURE 16.3 THE GLASS-CEILING INDEX

The Economist, a well-respected pro-business, pro-market magazine of economic and political affairs, has created a measure that purports to compare the status and well-being of women across the world's rich democracies. Using a variety of indicators—described in the text and on the magazine's website—*The Economist* shows that the United States ranks seventeenth out of twenty-seven countries. While the status of women in the United States is well below that of Iceland, Norway, Finland, and Sweden among others, it is, according to the measure, about average for the world's rich democracies. No measure, however, is without controversy. For example, the "glass ceiling" index includes access to abortion as one of the main indicators of female status and well-being. People who opposed abortion might not see this component of the index as valid.

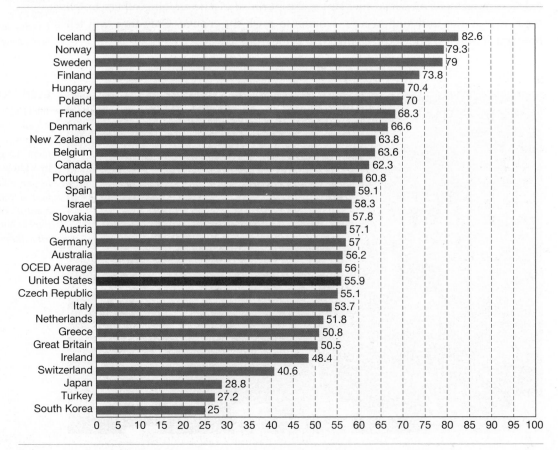

SOURCE: Data from *The Economist*, "The best—and worst—places to be a working woman," March 3, 2016.

BROADENING THE CIVIL RIGHTS UMBRELLA

16.4 Assess the evolving status of civil rights protections for the elderly, people with disabilities, and the LGBTQ community.

The expansion of civil rights protections for women and racial minorities encouraged other groups to press for expanded rights protections.

The Elderly and People with Disabilities

Interest groups for the elderly have pressed for laws barring age discrimination and have enjoyed some success in recent years.[41] Several federal and state laws, for instance, now bar mandatory retirement. And, the Age Discrimination in Employment Act passed in 1967, modeled on the Civil Rights Act of 1964, prohibits employers from discriminating against employees who are older than 40 in terms of pay, benefits, promotions, and working conditions. The courts also have begun to strike down hiring practices based on age unless a compelling reason can be demonstrated. But problems persist; downsizing companies often lay off older workers first because the pay and benefits of older workers are almost always higher than those of younger workers. And, because people are living longer and are worried about the size of their retirement savings along with the rising costs of medical care (even with Medicare), many more Americans say they want to work, at least part time, beyond the normal retirement age.

People with disabilities have also pushed for civil rights and other protections and have won some notable victories, including passage of the Americans with Disabilities Act (ADA) in 1990. The act prohibits employment discrimination against persons with disabilities and requires that reasonable efforts be made to make places of employment and public facilities (such as concert halls and restaurants) accessible. The proliferation of wheelchair ramps and wheelchair-accessible toilet facilities is a sign that compliance with the legislation is widespread, although advocates for the people with disabilities claim that the act depends too much on voluntary compliance.

In 2001, the Supreme Court dramatically narrowed the reach of the ADA when it ruled that state employees cannot sue states for damages arising from violations of the act, as provided for in the legislation. Critics worried that this judicial ruling would doom other sections of the ADA, including the requirement that state governments make their services and offices accessible to people with disabilities. Others feared that a wide range of civil rights laws that require nondiscriminatory behavior by state agencies, such as schools and hospitals, would also be at risk because the basis of the Court's decision in expanding the scope of state immunity from congressional action was that Congress had exceeded its authority under the interstate commerce clause.[42] If states are immune from the requirements of the ADA, the reasoning goes, why should they not be immune from the provisions of other civil rights laws? The Supreme Court, perhaps concerned about the backlash from its 2001 decision, ruled in *Tennessee v. Lane* (2004) that those with disabilities could sue a state for money damages in federal court if the state fails to make its courts fully accessible. Congress pushed back against the Court's 2001 ruling even more in 2008 when it renewed and amended the ADA, extending antidiscrimination protections to those with a disability to a wider range of private and public settings.

Gay, Lesbian, and Transgender People

The gay and lesbian civil rights movement began in earnest following the 1969 "Stonewall rebellion"—three days of rioting set off by police harassment of the patrons of a popular gay bar in Greenwich Village, New York.

BETTER ACCESS?

Since passage of the Americans with Disabilities Act in 1990, increasing numbers of public and private buildings have become more accessible to people in wheelchairs like this wounded veteran of the war in Iraq. In spite of the Act, accessibility for the disabled remains less widespread than many of its proponents had hoped for when it was signed into law by President George H.W. Bush. *Why, even with passage of the ADA, are so many public and private buildings not accessible for many people? Do governments at all levels need to be more forceful in gaining compliance or is there too much government interference in such matters already, as some Americans believe?*

The movement picked up steam over the next two decades as the gay community organized to confront AIDS and the Supreme Court's decision in *Bowers v. Hardwick* (1986), which upheld Georgia's ban against homosexual sexual relations. The movement, inspired by the civil rights and women's movements, borrowed many of their tactics to gain the same civil rights protections under the law enjoyed by racial minorities and women and to gain respect from the public. These tactics have ranged from patient lobbying, voting, mass demonstrations, and direct action. Substantial gains have been made by the gay and lesbian movement, often in conjunction with other actors encompassed by the broader label, LGBTQ, from their advocacy for antidiscrimination legislation targeting employment and housing, the right to adopt children, and same-sex marriage. The strong counterattacks over the years by conservative religious groups such as the American Family Association, Concerned Women for America, and Focus on the Family, and by most Republican office-holders and candidates, failed in the end to stop major advances, including eventually, the right to same-sex marriage.

CONGRESSIONAL AND PRESIDENTIAL ACTION ON GAY AND LESBIAN RIGHTS   The gay and lesbian movement at first suffered a series of setbacks. In the 1990s, Congress passed several bills that denied equal treatment for gays and lesbians. In 1993—responding to decisions by several major universities to bar military recruiters from campus because the military would not allow openly practicing homosexuals to serve—Congress passed the Solomon Amendment to the defense appropriations act; the amendment barred federal money to colleges and universities that deny military recruiters the same campus access as other private and public employers. In 1996, in response to the decision of Hawaii's Supreme Court in 1991 that denying same-sex couples the right to marry violated the state's constitution, Congress passed the Defense of Marriage Act (referred to as DOMA). This act defined marriage as a union of a man and a woman and declared that states are under no legal obligation to recognize same-sex marriages performed in other states. It also barred same-sex couples in civil unions or marriages from receiving federal benefits like Social Security in the same way as heterosexual couples. Former president Bill Clinton, who had signed DOMA, later renounced his action and called for its repeal. In 2011, with many challenges to DOMA making their way forward in the federal courts, President Obama issued an executive order directing the Justice Department to stop defending DOMA. Finally, the Supreme Court ruled DOMA unconstitutional in 2013.

It took time, but progress on equal treatment for gays and lesbians in the military also happened. For most of the 20th century, openly gay people were not allowed to serve in the military. Discovery of one's homosexual orientation was grounds for a dishonorable discharge, with loss of all veteran's benefits. Under pressure from LGBTQ activists and organizations, which generally supported Democrats, candidate Bill Clinton promised during his presidential campaign in 1992 to lift the ban on gays and lesbians in the military. Because of the hostile reaction from Congress and from the top brass in the armed services, he introduced a compromise measure called "don't ask, don't tell, don't pursue," a policy that pleased few people but stayed in place through George W. Bush's presidency. True to his campaign promise, President Barack Obama persuaded Congress in late 2010 to repeal the policy, allowing gays and lesbians to openly serve in the military. After considerable Pentagon study and preparation, the new policy went into effect in September 2011.

Despite claiming on the campaign trail that his presidency would be great for the LGBTQ community, Donald Trump reneged almost immediately. In a tweet on July 26, 2017, he announced that transgendered people would henceforth not be allowed to serve in the U.S. military. In March 2018, he issued an executive order barring almost all transgendered people from serving, adding exceptional circumstances in which a few might serve. Some speculated that this conditional ban rather than an outright ban was more likely to pass judicial muster when challenged in court.[43]

THE SUPREME COURT ON GAY AND LESBIAN RIGHTS Gays and lesbians rights were also aided by actions of the Supreme Court. This may seem surprising given the conservative majority on the Court for the whole of this period. Whatever the reason may be, long-time conservative justice Anthony Kennedy became the leading voice on the Court in favor of equal treatment for gays and lesbians, joining the four liberal justices on major rulings. He wrote the opinion of the Court on each of its three most important rulings in this area of the law. In *Romer v. Evans* (1996), for example, the Court ruled that state laws designed to deny basic civil rights to gays and lesbians are unconstitutional. In this case, the Court looked at Colorado's provision (known as Amendment 2) prohibiting local communities from passing gay antidiscrimination ordinances. The Court ruled that the law was constitutionally unacceptable because not only was there was no rational basis for the law but, as Justice Anthony Kennedy declared in his opinion, "a state cannot so deem a class of persons [gays and lesbians] a stranger to its laws."

In a stunning and highly unexpected decision in 2003, the Supreme Court overturned its own *Bowers* decision from 1986 and ruled in *Lawrence v. Texas* that state antisodomy laws designed to make homosexual sexual relations illegal were unconstitutional. Justice Kennedy again gave the ruling a very expansive reading, declaring that gay people "were entitled to freedom, dignity, and respect for their private lives."

In *United States v. Windsor* (2013), which overturned DOMA, Kennedy declared in his opinion that "the federal statute is invalid, for no legitimate purpose overcomes the purpose and effect [of DOMA] to disparage and injure those whom the state, by its marriage laws, sought to protect in personhood and dignity... . By seeking to displace this protection and treating those persons as living in marriages less respected than others, the federal statute is in violation of the Fifth Amendment."

Note that the Court did not base its ruling on the "equal protection" clause of the Fourteenth Amendment. That is, its ruling made no claim that the Constitution prohibited states from denying marriage licenses to same-sex couples. Kennedy's opinion for the Court did not declare lesbians and gays (or bisexuals and transvestites) a protected class like racial minorities, requiring "strict scrutiny," nor did it declare them to be a semi-protected class, like women, requiring "intermediate scrutiny." Instead, Kennedy said that overturning DOMA was based on the "deprivation of equal liberty of persons protected by the Fifth Amendment," which referred only to the federal government. A Fifth Amendment foundation for advancing equality has rarely been used, something that Justice Scalia, writing for the minority, found utterly mystifying.

LGBTQ PEOPLE IN THE MILITARY

After a long period when homosexuals were not allowed to serve in the military at all, and an almost two-decade-long period of "don't ask, don't tell, don't pursue" during which gays and lesbians could serve so long as their sexual orientation stayed hidden, President Obama and Congress agreed on a bill in late 2010 that allowed homosexuals to serve their country without having to hide their orientation. Here, two active-duty sailors demonstrate their feelings during a Gay Pride parade in San Diego.

Do you believe that more friendly Pentagon policies toward lesbian and gay personnel was a result of the LGBT movement outside the military or was it a contributing factor in pushing civil rights protections for these Americans in society at large?

Windsor had a number of important effects. In his capacity as Chief Executive, President Obama moved quickly to make federal programs consistent with the overturn of DOMA. He directed the Veterans Administration to distribute benefits to gay married couples. Under his direction, the Social Security Administration announced that it would treat partners in same-sex marriages the same way that it treats spouses in opposite-sex marriages when distributing Social Security checks, no matter where the same-sex couple might reside. The IRS acted similarly, stating that beginning with the 2013 tax year, people in same-sex marriages could no longer file their tax returns as two single individuals.

The *Windsor* decision also had an immediate effect on the federal courts. Beginning in late 2013, federal judges used the reasoning in that ruling to, among other things, overturn bans on same-sex marriage in several states, told the state of Ohio that it must recognize same-sex marriages performed in other states, and set aside bans on jury service based on sexual orientation.

Defenders of laws banning same-sex marriage had been almost uniformly defeated in federal courts following *Windsor*. By late 2014, same-sex marriage was permitted in thirty-two states. Then, in November 2014, the Sixth Circuit Court issued a split ruling by upholding bans on same-sex marriage in four states under its jurisdiction: Ohio, Tennessee, Michigan, and Kentucky. The Sixth Circuit argued that the U.S. Constitution did not prohibit bans on same-sex marriage.

This Sixth Circuit ruling forced the Supreme Court's hand. The Supreme Court is charged with interpreting the law—including the U.S. Constitution—and lower federal courts now disagreed on what the Constitution said about an important issue. In January 2015, the Supreme Court agreed to hear appeals from litigants in the Sixth Circuit's jurisdiction (consolidated into a single case, *Obergefell v. Hodges*) to decide, once and for all, whether states can deny marriage licenses to same-sex couples and refuse to recognize same-sex marriages performed in other states. On June 26, 2015, the Court handed down a closely divided 5–4 ruling that struck down all state bans on same-sex marriage.

In his dissent, Chief Justice John Roberts argued that the Court was overstepping its bounds and that the Constitution, as it is written, does not guarantee a freedom to marry. Though he, at times, seemed to imply that he personally believed that states should permit same-sex couples to marry, he said the Court should have left this decision to individual states and that the majority of the Court had "seize[d] for itself a question the Constitution leaves to the people, at a time when the people are engaged in a vibrant debate on that question."

However, Justice Kennedy and four other justices saw it differently, and the majority opinion concluded with a paragraph of soaring rhetoric:

"No union is more profound than marriage, for it embodies the highest ideals of love, fidelity, devotion, sacrifice, and family. In forming a marital union, two people become something greater than once they were. As some of the petitioners in these cases demonstrate, marriage embodies a love that may endure even past death. It would misunderstand these men and women to say they disrespect the idea of marriage. Their plea is that they do respect it, respect it so deeply that they seek to find its fulfillment for themselves. Their hope is not to be condemned to live in loneliness, excluded from one of civilization's oldest institutions. They ask for equal dignity in the eyes of the law. The Constitution grants them that right. The judgment of the Court of Appeals for the Sixth Circuit is reversed."[44]

PUBLIC OPINION ON GAY AND LESBIAN RIGHTS   Though one cannot know which is cause and which is effect, the change in federal and state policies concerning gays and lesbians has been accompanied by a dramatic change in public opinion. The move from low tolerance to high tolerance in so short a time for gay and lesbian civil rights may well be unique in U.S. history. Any number of factors may have been at work. There is of course, the gay rights movement itself which made the rights issue more prominent. There was also the increasingly sympathetic treatment of gays and lesbians in the arts and entertainment, including televisions shows and movies.

Rising educational levels may have played a role, as support for gay and lesbian rights, as well as support for the rights of racial and ethnic minorities, increases with education. Whatever the cause or set of causes, public attitudes about gays and lesbians have become more tolerant and accepting. Today, according to Gallup, more Americans than in the past think that gay and lesbian relationships should be accepted and legal; indeed, the percentage has increased dramatically, from 43 percent support in 1977, to 52 percent in 2002, to 69 percent in 2015.[45] Pew Research Center surveys show similar results; in 1906, 51 percent of Americans said homosexual relations were acceptable, but by 2016, the percentage jumped to 63 percent.[46] Substantial majorities also favor ending discrimination against gays and lesbians in jobs, housing, and education and favor passing hate-crime legislation. Fully 58 percent of Americans believe that same-sex couples should be allowed to marry, up from 27 percent in 1996, a remarkable change in public attitudes in so short a time[47]—a finding that is reflected in other polling reports (see Figure 16.4). Among Millennials (born after 1980), fully 73 percent say they favor extending equality of marriage rights to same-sex couples.[48] In addition, members of the LGBTQ community have experienced and apparently liked the changes that have occurred in public attitudes, with 92 percent of people in this group in 2013 agreeing with the statement that "compared with 10 years ago, society is now more accepting of people who are LGBT." Only 5 percent of respondents reported "being treated unfairly by an employer in the past year" because of their sexual orientation or gender identity or "receiving poor service in a restaurant, hotel, or place of business in the past year."[49]

FIGURE 16.4 PUBLIC OPINION ABOUT SAME-SEX MARRIAGE, 2003–2017

Public sentiment about same-sex marriage has changed dramatically over a very short period of time. In less than a decade, public opinion moved from being opposed to same-sex marriage to being in favor of it, in each case by substantial margins. Given young adults' favorable views of such unions, there is every reason to believe that public opinion will become even more supportive in the future. Politicians no doubt will pay attention.

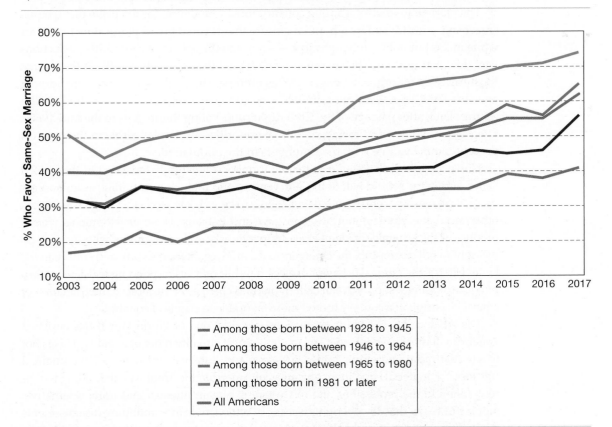

Legend:
— Among those born between 1928 to 1945
— Among those born between 1946 to 1964
— Among those born between 1965 to 1980
— Among those born in 1981 or later
— All Americans

SOURCE: Pew Research Center, "Changing Attitudes on Gay Marriage," June 26, 2017.

CIVIL RIGHTS: IS EQUAL CITIZENSHIP A REALITY IN THE UNITED STATES?

With respect to civil rights—guarantees of equality for people in the United States with regard to judicial proceedings, the exercise of political rights, treatment by public officials, and access to and enjoyment of the benefits of government programs—the differences between the ideas of the framers and the demands of democratic theory are most evident. Also with respect to civil rights is that democratic aspirations and the struggle for democracy have most altered the original Constitution of the United States. Recall that the framers not only paid scant attention to guarantees of equality but accepted and sustained the institution of slavery as well as the noncitizen status of Native Americans in a number of provisions in the Constitution. Further, in leaving voting and office-holding requirements largely to the states, the framers implicitly endorsed prevailing state practices that, among other things, excluded women from political life and put property qualifications and religious tests on voting and office holding. For the framers, civil rights guarantees—other than equality in the courts—were not among the first principles of good government. In fact, the framers worried a great deal about "leveling tendencies" that might lead to too much equality and a system of governance in which people of virtue, character, and education would not be in control. In democratic theory, on the other hand, equal citizenship—another way of saying civil rights—is the very essence of good government, one of the three essential pillars of democracy, joining popular sovereignty and liberty. Absent equal citizenship, democracy cannot be said to exist.

The glaring absence of a strong constitutional foundation for the principle of equal citizenship—buttressed by a popular culture that favored broad political inclusion for white males but not for other groups—meant that the spread of civil rights protections was slow and uneven. Thus, women were denied the vote well into the 20th century. Most African Americans, who were slaves until passage of the Thirteenth Amendment after the Civil War, were not admitted into full citizenship across the nation until a century later, after passage of the Civil Rights and Voting Rights Acts in the mid-1960s. Even today, women and racial and ethnic minorities fail to play a role in the political process commensurate with their numbers in the population.

However, it is undeniably true that civil rights dramatically increased in the United States during the second half of the 20th century and into the twenty-first, as guarantees of equal citizenship were extended—unevenly to be sure—to women, African Americans, other racial and ethnic minorities, and gays and lesbians. These developments were a product of the struggle for democracy by previously excluded groups who insisted on the right to full citizenship, the emergence of a more egalitarian society and culture in the United States, the rational behavior of elected public officials responding legislatively to a public increasingly supportive of civil rights, and changes in the judicial interpretation of equal citizenship in a country turned more favorable to claims of equality.

The advance of civil rights protections since the end of World War II has enriched American democracy because it has made political equality more of a reality. This is not to say that racial and ethnic minorities, gays and lesbians, and women have attained full social or material equality; many areas of American life, from wealth holding to representation in the professions and in Congress, remain unequal and unrepresentative. Nor is this to say that all civil rights issues are settled; note the continuing disagreements over affirmative action and police treatment of African American men. Nevertheless, the attainment of enjoyment of more political equality is real and something about which many Americans take a great deal of pride.

THE STATUS OF CIVIL RIGHTS BEFORE 1900

16.1 Trace the evolution of civil rights protections for racial minorities and women before 1900.

The original Constitution and the Bill of Rights were relatively silent on equality other than providing for equality before the law.

The Fourteenth Amendment, which was adopted after the Civil War, was a foundation for later civil rights advances.

Although the Court paid little attention to civil rights during the 19th century, structural changes in society, the transformation of attitudes about race and gender, and the political efforts of racial and ethnic minority group members and women of all races finally prompted the Court to begin to pay attention by the middle of the 20th century. These contributed to important civil rights gains for racial and religious minorities and women.

THE CONTEMPORARY STATUS OF CIVIL RIGHTS FOR RACIAL AND ETHNIC MINORITIES

16.2 Assess the evolving status of civil rights protections for racial and ethnic minorities since 1900.

It is now settled law that discrimination of any kind against racial minorities in the statutes and administrative practices of federal, state, or local government is unconstitutional. It is also settled law that governments may use affirmative action to rectify the past discriminatory practices of a particular public entity, such as a fire department in its hiring practices or county government in awarding road-building contracts. The status of affirmative action programs meant to achieve general societal progress for minorities (or women) or to enhance diversity also is largely settled with the Court against the former but allowing the latter in higher education admissions where no other method is effective in achieving the diversity goal.

THE CONTEMPORARY STATUS OF CIVIL RIGHTS FOR WOMEN

16.3 Assess the evolving status of civil rights protections for women since 1900.

The Court has taken the position that laws mentioning gender fall under the doctrine of "intermediate scrutiny," signaling that it will allow more latitude than it does to race to federal, state, and local governments that wish to give gender special attention.

Recent political, social, and economic gains by women are the result of changes in social attitudes, the political efforts of women, and the changing occupational needs of the American economy, rather than the product of a series of favorable Court rulings about gender equality. Despite advances, the overall status of women in the United States lags behind many other rich democracies.

BROADENING THE CIVIL RIGHTS UMBRELLA

16.4 Assess the evolving status of civil rights protections for the elderly, people with disabilities, and the LGBTQ community.

The civil rights movement gave impetus not only to the women's movement but also to a range of other groups of Americans who felt they were discriminated against, including the elderly, people with disabilities, and gays and lesbians. Statutes have been passed at all levels of government addressed to the equal protection needs of the elderly and those with disabilities, though compliance has been very uneven.

The question of whether lesbians and gay men can be discriminated against in housing, employment, and education has been largely settled in law and, increasingly, in social practice. Gays and lesbians can now serve in the military without hiding their orientation. And, in a series of recent rulings, the Supreme Court has recognized same-sex marriage as a fundamental right incumbent on the states to recognize.

LEARN THE TERMS

affirmative action   Programs of private and public institutions favoring minorities and women in hiring and contracting, and in admissions to colleges and universities, in an attempt to compensate for past discrimination or to create more diversity.

civil rights   Guarantees of equal treatment by government officials regarding political rights, the judicial system, and public programs.

de facto discrimination   Unequal treatment by private individuals, groups, and organizations.

de jure discrimination   Unequal treatment based on government laws and regulations.

due process clause   The section of the Fourteenth Amendment that prohibits states from depriving anyone of life, liberty, or property "without due process of law," a guarantee against arbitrary or unfair government action.

equal protection clause   The section of the Fourteenth Amendment that provides for equal treatment by government of people residing within the United States and each of its states.

grandfather clause   A device that allowed whites who had failed the literacy test to vote anyway by extending the franchise to anyone whose ancestors had voted before 1867.

intermediate scrutiny   A legal test falling between ordinary and strict scrutiny relevant to issues of gender; under this test, the Supreme Court will allow gender classifications in laws if they are *substantially* related to an *important* government objective.

Jim Crow   Popular term for the system of legally sanctioned racial segregation that existed in the American South from the end of the 19th century until the middle of the 20th century.

literacy test   A device used by the southern states to prevent African Americans from voting before the passage of the Voting Rights Act of 1965, which banned its use; usually involved interpretation of a section of a state's constitution.

poll tax   A tax to be paid as a condition of voting; used in the South to keep African Americans away from the polls.

privileges or immunities clause   The portion of the Fourteenth Amendment that says states may not make laws that abridge the rights granted to people as citizens of the United States.

strict scrutiny   The assumption that actions by elected bodies or officials violate the Constitution.

suspect classification   The invidious, arbitrary, or irrational designation of a group for special treatment by government, whether positive or negative; historically, used in laws to discriminate against visible minorities without the power to protect themselves.

white primaries   Primary elections open only to whites in the one-party South, where the only elections that mattered were the Democratic Party's primaries; this effectively disenfranchised blacks.

DEREGULATING ENVIRONMENTAL PROTECTION AT THE EPA

President Trump's first Environmental Protection Agency Administrator, Scott Pruitt, meets with coal industry executives after Trump signed executive orders rolling back ten Obama-era environmental regulations. Pruitt, a climate change skeptic, viewed the job as an opportunity to reduce the federal government's role in protecting the environment. Pruitt resigned in July 2018 amidst several scandals and was replaced by his deputy and former coal industry lobbyist, Andrew Wheeler. *When it comes to environmental regulation, what are the primary differences between the Republican Party and Democratic Party positions?*

DOMESTIC POLICIES

CHAPTER OUTLINE AND LEARNING OBJECTIVES

WHY DOES THE FEDERAL GOVERNMENT DO SO MUCH?

17.1 Explain the reasons for federal involvement in economic and societal affairs.

ECONOMIC POLICY

17.2 Analyze the goals and tools of economic policy making.

THE FEDERAL BUDGET

17.3 Identify the components of the federal budget, and analyze the problems associated with the national debt.

REGULATION

17.4 Explain government regulation and why regulations change.

FEDERAL SAFETY NET PROGRAMS

17.5 Describe the major federal safety net programs, and assess their effectiveness.

HEALTH CARE POLICY

17.6 Explain the key provisions of the Affordable Care Act and the challenges it has faced.

THE AMERICAN SAFETY NET IN CONTEXT

17.7 Compare and contrast systems of social safety nets across countries.

The Struggle for Democracy

ENVIRONMENTAL REGULATION IN A POLARIZED ERA

The Clean Air and Clean Water Acts were monumental pieces of environmental legislation passed in the early 1970s. They were responses to new scientific evidence that the effects of industry and human activity were severely damaging to the natural world and negatively impacting public health. The effort was bipartisan. For example, the Clean Air Act of 1970 passed the Senate by a vote of 73–0 and the House 374–1. Democratic Senator Edmund Muskie (ME) took the lead in developing the legislation, while Republican President Richard Nixon helped to create the Environmental Protection Agency (EPA) to enforce environmental protection laws. Up through 1980, the United States continued to pass key laws aimed at protecting the environment in a bipartisan fashion. And they were effective. Between its passage in 1970 and 1990, the Clean Air Act is estimated to have prevented 184,000 premature deaths and 674,000 cases of chronic bronchitis. And the Clean Water Act has dramatically reduced the amount of toxic pollutants being dumped into water bodies increasing the number of lakes, rivers, and estuaries suitable for fishing from less than one-third before the law passed to more than two-thirds today.[1]

Since the 1980s, the politics of environmental regulation have become increasingly partisan with Democrats pushing a pro-environment agenda with increased environmental regulation and Republicans pushing a pro-industry agenda that calls for scaled-back environmental regulation and continued reliance on fossil fuels. Despite the scientific consensus on the devastating long-term effects of global climate change, recent legislative efforts to shift the country in a more environmentally sustainable direction have failed. One of the consequences of environmental policy being such a partisan issue is that much of the related policy making and the degree of enforcement gets left to the executive branch and the political appointees that control it. President Obama faced a Republican majority in Congress for six of his eight years in office and, despite campaigning on a pro-environment platform, was unable to get any legislative traction on new environmental or energy policies. To pursue his environmental agenda, President Obama and his administration turned to making reforms through executive orders and the regulatory process in which government agencies enact policies under the broad authority delegated to them by Congress (see Chapter 13). In June 2014, President Obama issued a major executive order called the "Clean Power Plan." The Plan required states to develop actions to achieve significant carbon emissions reductions from primarily coal and gas-fired power plants. The goal was to bring carbon emissions from energy plants well below 2005 levels by 2030.[2] The EPA also developed rules during the Obama administration that protected wetlands from fracking, increased monitoring of methane gas leaks from power plants, and reduced carbon emissions from cars among other environmental protections.[3]

Much of the environmental regulation instituted during the Obama administration has been (or is in the process of being) rolled back by the Trump administration. Arguing that these regulations are a barrier to economic growth, President Trump and his EPA Administrators have eliminated the Clean Power Plan and many of the other regulations mentioned above. They have also increased access to oil fields and scaled back efforts to enforce existing environmental regulations. Since taking office, President Trump's EPA has pursued about 30 percent fewer cases against polluters than the Obama administration, sought 60 percent less in financial penalties, and 90 percent less in forced compliance for factories that are emitting too much pollution.[4] Because the environmental regulations enacted during the Obama administration were done through the bureaucratic rule-making process, they are subject to much easier repeal than had they been enacted through the law-making process. Trump campaigned on dramatically reducing regulation and his administration was able to move forward on this quickly after taking office.

The political polarization that has been discussed in previous chapters has made it incredibly difficult for Congress and the president to agree on new environmental and energy laws. The result is that action in this policy area has shifted with the election of each new president as new administrations use flexibility in existing laws to bend bureaucratic rules and actions to fit with their own policy preferences.

In this chapter we explore major American domestic policies with an eye toward developing a better understanding of how the government came to have such a vast array of responsibilities. In particular, we consider the role the American government has in managing the economy and ensuring minimum living standards for all citizens.

THINKING CRITICALLY **ABOUT THIS CHAPTER**

This chapter offers an overview of major American economic and social policies focusing on what the policies do, how they came to be, and whether they are effective.

APPLYING THE **FRAMEWORK**

This chapter discusses how our analytical framework can be used to examine what government does in the domestic policy sphere. You will use what you learned in previous chapters about *structural, political linkage, and government factors* to better understand policy actions such as spending, taxing, regulating, subsidizing, and income and medical support decisions.

USING THE **DEMOCRACY STANDARD**

In previous chapters, you used the democracy standard to examine the extent to which American political and government institutions have enhanced popular sovereignty, political equality, and liberty. You will use the democracy standard in this chapter to ask whether the American people get the sorts of policies and performance they want from government.

WHY DOES THE FEDERAL GOVERNMENT DO SO MUCH?

17.1 Explain the reasons for federal involvement in economic and societal affairs.

It is hard to imagine any activity in our daily lives that is not touched in one way or another by government intervention. Government policies have an impact on the food supply, energy, health care, transportation, education, public safety, environmental quality, and the economy, to name just a few examples. Why does the government have such broad involvement in a country that has long been committed to the idea of limited government? Remember that the Constitution empowers the government to do a great many things. The power to regulate interstate commerce, coin money, establish post offices and post roads, create a system to protect intellectual property (patents), borrow money and collect taxes to meet its many responsibilities, and many more powers and responsibilities emanate directly from the Constitution. However, it has historically been the American people, using the political tools available to them in a democracy, who have pressed elected officials to institute policies and programs that improve and protect their safety and well-being. In the face of profound economic and social change, Americans have regularly asked government to do more. An enduring theme in our recent politics is the question of whether the role of government has expanded too far.

THE FEDERAL GOVERNMENT HAS OVER 2.5 MILLION NON-MILITARY EMPLOYEES

The US Department of Health and Human Services (HHS) is one of the many federal departments with large office buildings in DC. In 2017, HHS had over 79,000 full time employees, some of whom work in the Hubert H. Humphrey building (pictured). Other HHS employees work in regional offices across the country and in other agency buildings.

What is the value of having federal offices in DC and spread throughout the country?

Governments in all rich democracies, not just in the United States, play a substantial role in managing economic affairs and in providing a safety net for citizens who experience hardship. Let's see why this is so.

Managing the Economy

Today, no government would dare leave stagnant economic growth, unemployment, trade imbalances, inflation, or financial collapse to work themselves out "naturally," though that is what free-market purists ordinarily recommend. History shows that free-market economies, left to themselves, are subject to periodic bouts of **inflation**, financial bubbles that inevitably burst, and occasional sustained periods of deep unemployment and declining economic output (or **depressions**). The worldwide trauma of the Great Depression in the 1930s etched this lesson into the minds of virtually everyone and changed the role of government in economic affairs in rich democracies the world over.

Government responsibility for the state of the national economy is now so widely accepted that national elections are often decided by the voters' judgment of how well the party in power is carrying out this responsibility. When times are good, the party or president in power is very likely to be reelected; when times are bad, those in power have an uphill battle to stay in office.[5] Witness the election defeats of Jimmy Carter in 1980, George H. W. Bush in 1992, and John McCain (a Republican running on the record of Republican president George W. Bush) in 2008.

Providing a Safety Net

All rich democracies have safety net programs that help to ensure minimum standards of living and protect against loss of income from economic instability, old age, illness, disability, and family disintegration.[6] The reason is simple: demand. Even when working at peak efficiency, market economies do not guarantee a decent living for all nor offer protection against economic disruption.[7] Long-term unemployment affects people who have been regularly employed, not just the chronically unemployed, and contributes to serious physical and mental illness, shortened life spans, family tensions, higher rates of divorce, and educational underachievement among their children.[8]

inflation

A condition of rising prices and reduced purchasing power.

depression

A severe and persistent drop in economic activity.

ECONOMIC POLICY

17.2   Analyze the goals and tools of economic policy making.

Government economic policies have a number of goals. This section considers these goals in detail and then explores the fiscal and monetary tools American government has as its disposal to try and achieve these goals.

The Goals of Economic Policy

Although economic policy goals sometimes conflict and involve important trade-offs, they are consistently driven by six key concerns: (1) maintaining economic growth, (2) controlling inflation, (3) maintaining a healthy balance of trade, (4) budgetary discipline, (5) avoiding negative externalities, and (6) ensuring economic vibrancy.[9]

MAINTAINING ECONOMIC GROWTH   The quintessential goal of economic policy makers is sustained economic growth—generally defined by economists and policy makers as an annual increase in the **gross domestic product (GDP)**.[10] GDP is a measure of the total value of goods and services produced in a nation on an annual basis. A growing economy means more jobs, more products, and higher incomes, so most Americans support this policy goal. Economic growth is also the basis for increased profits, so business tends to support it. For political leaders, economic growth, accompanied by rising standards of living, brings public popularity and heightened prospects for reelection as well as more revenues for government programs.

CONTROLLING INFLATION   Inflation refers to the purchasing power of money— when inflation rises, people's wages, salaries, savings accounts, and retirement pensions diminish in value. So, too, do the holdings of banks and the value of their loans. To nobody's surprise, political leaders seek to enact policy solutions that dampen

gross domestic product (GDP)
Monetary value of all goods and services produced in a nation each year, excluding income residents earn abroad.

ELECTED IN TOUGH TIMES
Tough economic times have political consequences. Both Bill Clinton and Barack Obama were elected in part because the parties they were running against in their first presidential election campaigns were in power when the nation's economy turned sour. President Obama's Democrats suffered big election losses in the 2010 congressional elections because of ongoing high unemployment and a slow recovery from the Great Recession.
How accountable should voters hold presidents for the state of the economy?

Federal Reserve Board (The Fed)

The body responsible for deciding the monetary policies of the United States.

inflation and keep prices stable (though low inflation rates for too long can get in the way of economic growth). In the United States, the **Federal Reserve Board (The Fed)** manages inflation by adjusting certain interest rates that impact the supply of money in circulation.

One way to combat inflation is to slow down the economy by having the Fed raise interest rates. Higher interest rates make it harder and more expensive for consumers to borrow for purchases and for businesses to fund expansion. Conversely, when the economy is stagnant or declining, pumping money into the hands of consumers and businesses by lowering interest rates or by increasing government spending (or by doing both) acts as an economic stimulant. Too much stimulus, however, can lead to too much inflation as too many dollars chase too few goods and services.

MAINTAINING A HEALTHY BALANCE OF TRADE   All nations, including the United States, strive to maintain a healthy **balance of trade**. This typically means exporting more goods and services than they import (a positive trade balance). Sustained and sizable negative trade balances—a situation in which more money leaves the country than is brought in—can lead to declines in the value of a nation's currency in international markets. As a result, businesses and consumers would find that their dollars buy less, all other things being equal. However, it is often not as simple as having a positive or negative balance of trade. With such a globalized world economy, imported items may be essential to the production of goods in the United States. Maurice Obstfeld, Director of Research at the International Monetary Fund, has noted that the United States' importing of aluminum contributes to its trade deficit but that lower-cost aluminum is essential to the production of aircraft, which is one of America's biggest exports.[11]

The United States has run substantial balance-of-trade deficits for most of the past two decades. Trade was a hotly debated issue during the 2016 Presidential election with both Republican Donald Trump and Democrat Bernie Sanders arguing that America's trade imbalances were hurting the American economy. More moderate candidates on both sides argued that America's trade deals are good for the country on the whole as they open the American economy up to international markets and reduce prices for American consumers on certain goods.

balance of trade

The annual difference between payments and receipts between a country and its trading partners.

CHINA RISING

One of the most important developments in the global economy is the emergence of China as a major player—reflected in this scene depicting a sewing factory. China is the destination for many U.S. exports, while the United States is the destination for many Chinese exports. But the trade is heavily unbalanced in favor of China. Addressing this trade imbalance is a continuing concern of American policy makers, though little progress has been made to date.

To what extent are policy makers smart to concern themselves with trade imbalances with China and with other U.S. trading partners?

BUDGETARY DISCIPLINE   All nations try—or claim to try—to keep budgets in rough balance between revenues (primarily taxes) and expenditures. Since the end of World War II, the budgets of rich democracies have tilted into deficit most of the time, with spending outpacing revenues by a few percentage points. Small budget deficits can help spur economic growth because spending, whether on infrastructure, like roads and harbors, or on human capital, like education, training, and research and development (R&D), can improve long-range economic prospects by creating jobs and employable citizens. Big budget deficits spell trouble, however, because excessive spending is funded by borrowing. The government borrows money from people (here and abroad) and from foreign governments by selling U.S. government bonds and Treasury notes. Budget deficits grew dramatically in 2009 and 2010 in the United States and in Europe when, because of the **recession** (a period of two or more quarters of declining GDP), stimulus spending increased and tax revenues plummeted (see Figure 17.1).

recession
A slowing of the economy defined by two quarters or more of declining gross domestic product.

AVOIDING NEGATIVE EXTERNALITIES   Most people also want to avoid **negative externalities**, the harmful side effects that often accompany normal economic activity. A growing manufacturing economy, for example, often produces air and water pollution, toxic wastes, workplace injuries, and health hazards. High demand for oil and the decline of easily drilled areas on and near shore drove companies (such as British Petroleum) to drill in very deep waters, increasing the risk of blowouts and environmental catastrophes. In response to these negative externalities, the public has pressed the government to take actions that compensate those who have been negatively impacted and, hopefully, prevent future problems. After British Petroleum's Deep Water Horizon oil rig exploded in 2010, the company wound

negative externalities
The harmful effects of economic activities on third parties.

FIGURE 17.1   FEDERAL BUDGET SURPLUS OR DEFICIT (AS A % OF GDP), 1929–2017

This graph shows whether the government was running a surplus or deficit going back to 1929 (the beginning of the Great Depression). When the line is above zero, the government is running a surplus. When the line is below zero, the government is running a deficit. As you can see, for most of the last century, the American government has spent more than it brought in.

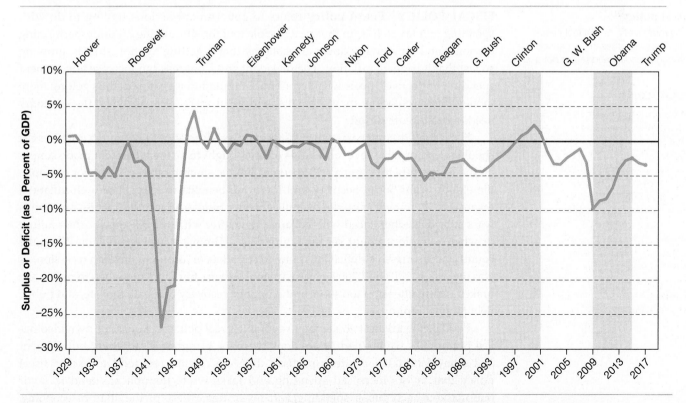

SOURCE: Data from Federal Reserve Bank of St. Louis, Federal Surplus or Deficit [–] as Percent of Gross Domestic Product, March 25, 2016.

up paying billions of dollars in damages to compensate those whose lives and businesses were hurt by the resulting oil spill.[12] More long-term efforts to prevent negative externalities include environmental laws like the Clean Air Act and the Clean Water Act.

ENSURING ECONOMIC VIBRANCY   Finally, there are economic activities that are essential for the health of the national economy but unlikely to be provided by private firms. For example, the United States and all European countries subsidize farmers, who are vital to the nation's food supply. The subsidies ensure that farmers grow enough of the necessary crops regardless of how economic forces impact the cost of production. Also, the federal government encourages business activity in America's inner cities by using enterprise zone tax incentives and supports the defense industry by directly purchasing weapons systems and subsidizing research. In the aftermath of the Great Recession, and the long jobless recovery from it, the government intervened to save the American auto industry, bailing out, taking temporary ownership, and encouraging the reorganization of General Motors (which reported record profits in 2011, just three years after the bailout).[13] Economic vibrancy also requires good roads, airports, and harbors, something the private sector does not always provide on its own. Governments in rich democracies have filled this void by providing support for such vital activities and services with subsidies and tax breaks and, occasionally, direct public ownership.

The Tools of Economic Policy

The government's main tools for dealing with inflation, unemployment, and national output are fiscal policy and monetary policy. However, government action is complicated by the considerable disagreement that exists about which tool works best for solving particular economic problems. The multidimensional phenomenon of globalization also increasingly intensifies the complexity of national policy-making choices as policies enacted abroad impact the economy at home (and vice versa).[14]

fiscal policy

Government efforts to affect overall output and incomes in the economy through spending and taxing policies.

FISCAL POLICY   **Fiscal policy** refers to government actions having to do with spending and taxes. It is, in theory, a flexible tool for stimulating an underperforming economy and for slowing down an economy that is getting too hot—that is, growing so fast that it triggers inflation. The president and Congress can increase government spending or decrease taxes when economic stimulation is required, thus getting more money into circulation; they can cut spending or increase taxes when the economy needs a cooling-off period.

Fiscal tools are not easy to use, however. Decisions about how much government should spend or what level and kinds of taxes ought to be levied are not made simply on the basis of their potential effects on economic stability and growth. For example, the elderly want Social Security and Medicare benefits to keep pace with inflation, regardless of their effect on the overall economy. Similarly, auto companies and banks want subsidies when faced with collapse, no matter what the reasons for their failure or what example it might set for future crises. Timing is also a problem. When the country needs massive deficit spending to stimulate an economy in deep recession, as was the case in 2008 and 2009, it is easy enough to do, but knowing when to put on the brakes is difficult—stop too soon, and economic recovery can stall; too late, and public debt mounts rapidly.

Perhaps the greatest challenge to a nimble fiscal policy is America's own ideological politics. As we learned in previous chapters, Congress is anything but efficient and often debilitated by deep partisan divisions. Democrats tend to back a fiscal policy that favors increased spending and taxes while Republicans tend to favor one marked by reduced spending and taxes. Regardless of the state of economy, these partisan divisions often stand in the way of fiscal reforms—even those reached by way of compromise.

MONETARY POLICY   **Monetary policy** refers to policies carried out by the Federal Reserve Board (the "Fed") that affect how much money is available to businesses and individuals from banks and how much it costs to borrow that money. The more money that is available and the lower the interest rates at which money can be borrowed, the higher overall consumer and business spending are likely to be. For example, if the Fed wants to increase total spending in the economy, it increases the money supply by using the money in its reserve funds to buy government securities from the private sector. When it does this, it puts more money into circulation. The Fed can also lower the discount rate, which reduces the interest banks pay to borrow money from the Fed. This in turn reduces the interest rates at which these banks are willing to lend to consumers and firms.

The Fed is managed by a board of governors that is nominated by the president and approved by the Senate. Jerome Powell, who previously served on the Federal Reserve Board of Governors and as an Under Secretary of Treasury, became Fed Chair in 2018 after being nominated by President Trump. Powell replaced Janet Yellen, President Obama's selection for the position in 2014 and the first women to have the role. The Chair of the Fed has long been considered among the most powerful people in the world economy.[15] However, the Fed's influence on interest rates and the availability of credit is not unlimited. Interest rates are also affected by the value of the dollar and the willingness of foreign investors to put their money into American firms, properties, and government bonds. Furthermore, the Fed has limited impact on many factors that affect long-term economic performance, such as productivity growth and the price of commodities like oil.

THE FISCAL VERSUS MONETARY POLICY DEBATE   People may agree that government has a role to play in the management of the economy, but they disagree about how it should be done.[16] **Keynesians**—who trace their roots to English economist John Maynard Keynes's classic work, *The General Theory of Employment, Interest, and Money*—have one view. They believe that in an economy where the tools of production (labor, equipment, factories, and the like) are not being used to full capacity, government must stimulate economic activity by increasing government spending

monetary policy
Government efforts to affect the supply of money and the level of interest rates in the economy.

Keynesians
Advocates of government programs to stimulate economic activity through tax cuts and government spending.

FEDERAL RESERVE CHAIR JEROME POWELL
Jerome Powell became Chair of the Federal Reserve Board in 2018. One of the key questions the Fed faces is whether to raise interest rates. If the economy is growing too fast, the Fed may raise rates to slow it down. On the other hand, if the economy is growing too slowly, the Fed may lower rates to give it a push.
What are the differences between the role the Fed plays in the economy and the role that Congress and the President play in the economy?

or by cutting taxes (or both). Most Keynesians would prefer to see increased spending rather than lower taxes, and they are associated with an activist conception of the role of government most favored by Democrats. Keynesian economics went out of fashion with the election of Ronald Reagan in 1980 and the ascendancy of the Chicago school of free-market economics associated with Milton Friedman. However, in the midst of the Great Recession, the governments of many capitalist countries, ranging from the United States to Germany, China, and Japan, stimulated their economies with increased government spending and reduced taxes. The results of such efforts have been mostly positive as these countries continue on a track of steady (if sometimes lackluster) economic recovery. Alternatively, harsh austerity budgets—that is, those with deep cuts in spending—instituted in such places as Greece, Spain, and the UK appear to have led to the increases in unemployment and continued economic stagnation that Keynesians predicted.[17]

monetarists

Advocates of a minimal government role in the economy, limited to managing the growth of the money supply.

Monetarists, such as the late Nobel Prize winning economist Milton Friedman, believe that government (e.g., the Federal Reserve in the United States or, in the case of the European Union, the European Central Bank) should confine its activity to managing the growth in the supply of money and credit so that it closely tracks the growth in productivity in the economy as a whole. In the monetarist view, this will stimulate private investment, which in turn will allow slow but steady economic growth without inflation. Balanced federal budgets are essential in the monetarist position because, in their view, unbalanced budgets make it difficult for central banks to control the money supply properly. Monetarism is the economic policy, then, of those who believe in a minimal federal government and the virtues of the free market most associated with conservatives and Republicans. Monetarists are closely associated with "efficient market" economists who believe that, if left alone, markets tend toward efficiency and the rational allocation of resources, reducing the need for regulation by government.[18] These economists have dominated their discipline for several decades now and have massively influenced public policies on regulation, including the financial and energy industries.

STIMULATING SOLAR POWER

A construction worker installs solar panels on the roof of a home in San Ramon, California. The 2009 stimulus package created a tax credit for homeowners that install solar power systems. Though they have become controversial, the credits are still available today.
Why would tax credits be an ineffective way to encourage energy savings? Why would they be controversial?

THE FEDERAL BUDGET

17.3 Identify the components of the federal budget, and analyze the problems associated with the national debt.

America's fiscal policy is the outcome of decisions made by the president and Congress on spending and taxes. These matters are settled in the budget and in separate tax and spending bills.

Each year, the U.S. federal budget is prepared by the president and his or her staff (and the **Office of Management and Budget, or the OMB**) but then considered, amended (typically dramatically), and passed by Congress. After being passed, the budget and the associated spending bills are put into effect by the president and the executive branch. The budget takes the form of line items, with funds allocated for specific activities of federal programs such as salaries, supplies, travel, and the like rather than a lump sum given to an agency or department that might be used more flexibly.

The Budgeting Process

From start to finish, preparation of the annual budget takes longer than a year. It is a complex and often harrowing process that must result in Congress passing and the president signing all of the appropriations bills necessary to fund the government. Failure to do so leads to a government shutdown where non-emergency government operations stop and many government workers are put on unpaid leave. In each budgeting process, the stakes are high and so are the political tensions.[19]

THE PRESIDENT'S BUDGET PROPOSAL   Each spring, the president and staff (principally the Office of Management and Budget or OMB) prepare a broad budget outline that is sent to all federal departments and agencies, proposing total government spending, the revenues that will be available to fund this spending, and the spending limits that will apply to each department and agency. A process of negotiation then begins among executive branch departments and agencies, the OMB, and presidential staffers about these proposals. Because economic conditions and the business climate will affect how the budget works out in practice—for example, the level of government receipts that flow into government coffers from taxes will depend on how well the government is performing—the Council of Economic Advisers and the Treasury Department are active participants in the discussions surrounding the formulation of the budget.

Office of Management and Budget (OMB)

Part of the Executive Office of the President charged with helping the president prepare the annual budget request to Congress; also performs oversight of rule making by executive branch agencies.

THE FEDERAL BUDGET

The 2019 Federal Budget as produced by the Office of Management and Budget is presented for public consideration. The Federal Budget outlines all the planned expenditures for the federal government in the upcoming year. Ultimately, it is up to Congress to craft the appropriations laws necessary for spending taxpayer dollars. Because the Budget is only a plan, the government does not always end up staying within its limits.

If the budget is not binding, what is its value to Congress?

The executive branch agencies whose budgets are ultimately being determined by this process also have a say. Like most organizations, executive branch agencies try to gain more money and personnel to fulfill their missions, although they generally try not to be too unreasonable, given the competing demands of other agencies and the president's concern with staying under the federal government's planned budget ceiling.[20] These requests are filtered through the OMB, whose job it is to examine department and agency requests, negotiate changes, and package the requests into a final budget proposal that fits the president's priorities. The director of the OMB then reviews the budgets for each department and agency and passes them on to the White House for consideration. After some adjustments are made to accommodate new needs, changing economic forecasts, pleas from some departments and agencies, and the president's political agenda, a final budget is prepared in the White House for presentation to Congress within fifteen days of when it first convenes each January.

THE CONGRESSIONAL BUDGET   After receiving the budget request from the president, both the House and the Senate go through a process of developing their own versions of a budget with technical advice from the Congressional Budget Office (Congress's counterpart to the OMB). Like the president, Congress strives to pass a budget resolution that specifies broad budget boundaries for the year. The budget that Congress eventually passes, however, does not guarantee that agencies or programs will be funded at budgeted levels. The budget is not a law; rather, it serves as a blueprint for Congress as it makes its official funding decisions throughout the remainder of the year.

The process by which the government officially funds federal departments, agencies, and programs is called the appropriations process. Decisions about funding levels are first the responsibility of House and Senate **appropriations committees**, with subcommittees generally focusing on appropriations for individual departments (e.g., Department of Defense, Department of Education). Subcommittees hold hearings, taking testimony from department and agency officials as well as friends and critics of particular programs. Each chamber then considers the appropriations committees' spending bills—which hopefully have been written with the larger budget in mind—and, like any other bill, these must be signed by the president. The thirteen or fourteen appropriations bills that make their way to the floor of each chamber must be enacted by the end of the fiscal year. Failure to do so leads to government shutdown. A final process—budget reconciliation—allows the House and Senate to pass a law that brings already-passed funding levels into closer alignment with the annual budget.

An additional complication is that money cannot be spent unless standing committees pass funding authority bills, which create and maintain the programs that government spends on. Some programs must be authorized annually; others are authorized every few years (or longer).

Budget making in Congress is never easy, even when revenues are plentiful, when economic prospects are good, and when Republicans and Democrats are willing to settle differences amicably through compromise. Absent these conditions, the processes by which annual appropriations bills work their way through Congress can be a torturous, conflict-laden, blame-apportioning business. In recent years, as partisanship has increased, the budget process has become fraught with difficulties, delays, and debt-ceiling crises.

appropriations committees

The committees in the House and Senate that set specific spending levels in the budget for federal programs and agencies.

Federal Spending

The federal government spent almost $3.98 trillion in 2017, just over 20 percent of GDP. Figure 17.2 shows the change over time in federal outlays as a percentage of GDP.

Several things about the trend in government spending charted in Figure 17.2 should be apparent. First, the most dramatic increases in federal government spending are associated with involvement in major wars. Note the big spike in the graph for the years associated with World War II. Second, the relative spending level of the

FIGURE 17.2 FEDERAL GOVERNMENT SPENDING (IN BILLIONS OF 2017 DOLLARS AND AS A % OF GDP), 1940–2017

This graph shows the scale of federal government spending in constant 2009 dollars and relative to the size of the U.S. economy. While federal spending has been steadily increasing since the end of World War II, the amount of spending as a share of the total U.S. economy has been more stable.

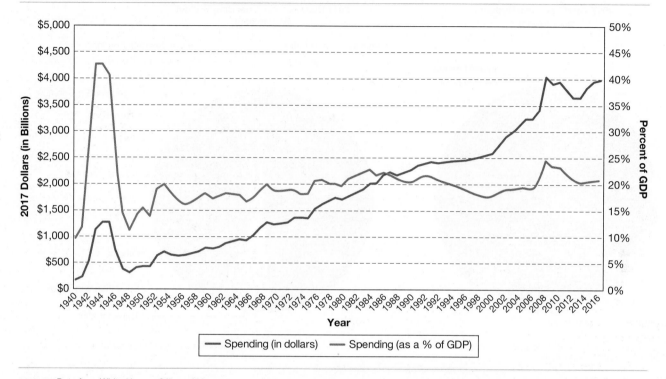

SOURCE: Data from White House, Office of Management and Budget, Historical Tables, Table 1.3, Summary of Receipts, Outlays, and Surpluses or Deficits (–) in Current Dollars, Constant (FY 2009) Dollars, and as Percentages of GDP: 1940–2021. 2016 data from Congressional Budget Office "The Budget and Economic Outlook: 2017 to 2027.

federal government increased steadily through the 1980s as a percentage of GDP then leveled off and declined. This decrease was caused, in large part, by a substantial decrease in the relative size of the national defense budget after the end of the Cold War. Third, the wars in Afghanistan and Iraq, the Medicare prescription drug program, and stimulus and bailout spending to fight the Great Recession again increased federal government spending as a percentage of the economy in the 2000s.

As detailed in Figure 17.3, the largest portion of the federal budget—roughly 63 percent in 2017—is for mandatory spending, over which Congress and the president exercise little real control. **Mandatory spending** is automatic and not impacted by the annual appropriations bills. Spending on mandatory programs such as Social Security retirement benefits, Medicare, and Medicaid are determined based on the formulas included in the laws that authorize the programs. For example, Medicare benefits go automatically to Americans who are older than 65. Medicaid is distributed to the states according to a formula based on the number of poor people in each state. Expenditures on these programs happen outside the annual appropriations process and are triggered by changes in, for example, the number of elderly or poor people. About 7.5 percent of the federal budget for 2017 was for payment of interest on the national debt; such payments are required, as well. The result is that only 30 percent of the 2017 budget was discretionary (that is, open to changes in funding through the annual appropriations process). And because the costs of mandatory programs are increasing rapidly—particularly Social Security and Medicare—elected leaders have less and less discretion over spending decisions.

In addition, a majority of the **discretionary spending** budget was taken up by national defense in 2017 ($590 billion). The share of defense spending was, therefore,

mandatory spending
Government spending that does not go through the annual appropriations process because it is tied to a formula that determines the amount to be spent. Primarily includes Social Security and Medicare.

discretionary spending
That part of the federal budget that is not tied to a formula that automatically provides money to some program or purpose.

FIGURE 17.3 2017 FEDERAL BUDGET: MANDATORY AND DISCRETIONARY SPENDING

These two graphs break down federal spending for 2017. The first graph breaks down all of government spending into mandatory spending, discretionary spending, and interest on the federal debt. The second graph breaks down only the 30 percent of federal spending that is discretionary into 14 categories of spending (including defense, transportation, education, and others).

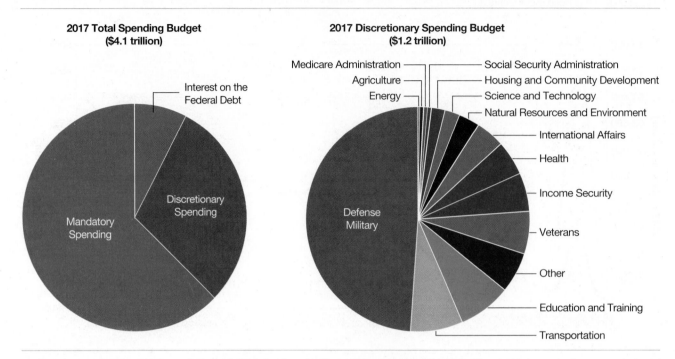

SOURCE: White House Historical Tables, Table 3.1—Outlays by Superfunction and Function: 1940–2023, https://www.whitehouse.gov/wp-content/uploads/2018/02/hist03z1-fy2019.xlsx.

14 percent of all federal spending and 48 percent of all discretionary spending. Taking defense, interest on the national debt, and mandatory programs together, only about 17 percent (or $710 billion) was left in the 2017 budget for all other federal programs and activities, such as education, scientific and medical research, transportation, energy, agriculture, housing, national parks, the administration of justice, environmental protection, international affairs, the space program, public works projects, and everything else.

Federal Revenues

Government can spend money only if it has a stream of revenues coming in. Such revenues are raised by various kinds of taxes.[21] The national government depends primarily on **income taxes** (both personal and corporate) and **payroll taxes** to fund its activities. The states get most of their revenues from sales taxes, although many also have income taxes. Local governments depend most heavily on property taxes.

Americans from all walks of life report feeling squeezed by taxes, but the total of all taxes levied by all government jurisdictions in the United States as a proportion of GDP is relatively low when compared to in other rich democracies (see Figure 17.4). Moreover, what individual Americans pay in income taxes as a percentage of their overall income has remained about the same for the last thirty years.[22]

The American income tax code is based on marginal tax rates. Congress passed a major tax overhaul in 2017 that sets marginal rates through 2026; these rates are presented in Table 17.1. Marginal tax rates treat segments of a person's income differently. Because the U.S. tax code is progressive, higher segments of a person's income are taxed at higher rates. For example, if a person makes $80,000 per year in 2018, the first $9,525 of their income is taxed at rate of 10 percent, the next $9,526 to $38,700 of their income is taxed at 12 percent, and their remaining $38,701 to $80,000 of income is taxed at 22 percent. Marginal tax rates ensure that no one has an incentive to earn less money.

income tax

Taxes levied on the annual incomes of individuals and corporations. In the United States those who make more money pay a higher tax rate than those who make less money.

payroll tax

Tax levied on salaries and wages for Social Security and Medicare.

FIGURE 17.4 TAX REVENUE AS A PERCENT OF GDP IN THE UNITED STATES AND OTHER RICH DEMOCRACIES, 2016

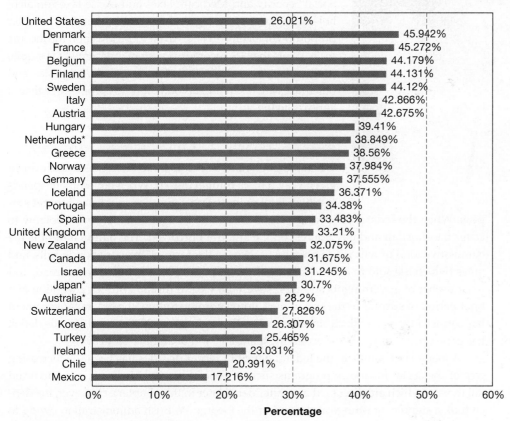

*Most recent data are from 2013.

SOURCE: Data from Organization for Economic Cooperation and Development, OECD. Stat, Revenue Statistics, Comparative Tables, Tax Revenue as a % of GDP, 2016.

NOTE: *Data from 2015.

The American tax system is uniquely complex. The voluminous U.S. Tax Code is filled with endless exceptions to the rules and with special exemptions that are usually the product of influence peddling of one kind or another. For instance, hedge fund and private equity managers make the bulk of their income from hefty fees, which are taxed not as normal income but as capital gains. Capital gains have a lower tax rate than normal income. Few people besides accountants and tax attorneys fully understand the intricacies of the tax code, and their services are available mainly to those who can afford them.

Analyses show that the median American paid a tax rate of about 13.6 percent in 2017, with the top fifth of earners paying about 26.1 percent.[23] However, many very wealthy Americans end up paying significantly lower income tax rates than would be expected

TABLE 17.1 MARGINAL INCOME TAX RATES: 2018–2026

Individuals	Married Filing Jointly	Rate (%)
Up to $9,525	Up to $19,050	10
$9,526 to $38,700	$19,051 to $77,400	12
38,701 to $82,500	$77,401 to $165,000	22
$82,501 to $157,500	$165,001 to $315,000	24
$157,501 to $200,000	$315,001 to $400,000	32
$200,001 to $500,000	$400,001 to $600,000	35
Over $500,000	Over $600,000	37

SOURCE: United States Internal Revenue Service.

GETTING READY FOR TAX DAY

The American tax system is complex. Before filing taxes every April 15, Americans must determine their income, consider their potential tax deductions, and complete forms. American politicians frequently campaign on making the tax code simpler but never seem to succeed. *Why do you think that Congress has continually failed to make the tax code simpler?*

progressive taxation

A tax system in which higher-income individuals are taxed at a higher rate than those who make less.

regressive taxation

A tax system in which lower-income individuals are taxed at a higher rate than those who make more.

budget deficit

Occurs when the government is bringing in less money than it is spending.

budget surplus

Occurs when the government is bringing in more money than it is spending.

national debt

The total outstanding debt of the federal government; the sum total of all annual budget deficits and surpluses.

Great Recession

The economic crisis that officially began in December 2007. The recession was triggered by the bursting of a housing bubble that led to a financial crisis and cuts in consumer spending. Though it officially ended in June 2009, its after effects have been long-lasting.

after all deductions, exclusions, credits, and tax shelters are taken into account. Furthermore, other federal taxes, such as Social Security and Medicare taxes and excise taxes on alcohol and cigarettes, are **regressive**—that is, they take a higher proportion of income in taxes from those lower on the income scale. While the U.S. income tax system is designed to be quite **progressive,** the reality is that after exceptions, loopholes, and other taxes are taken into account, it is less progressive than it appears on the surface.

Budget Deficits and the National Debt

When the government spends more than it takes in during a given year, it has a **budget deficit**. When government spends less than it takes in during a given year, it has a **budget surplus**. When the federal government runs an annual budget deficit, it must borrow to cover the shortfall and pay interest on the amount borrowed. The **national debt** is the cumulative total of what the government owes in the form of Treasury bonds, bills, and notes (which are sold to individuals and financial institutions at home and abroad, and to a number of governments and their sovereign wealth funds).With the exception of a brief period of surplus at the end of the Clinton administration, the federal government has consistently run a deficit since the 1970s. Throughout the 2000s and 2010s, the deficit has gone up and down as the economy, spending, and taxes have shifted.

A major contributor to the federal deficit in recent decades has been the increasing cost of the social insurance programs such as Social Security, Medicare, and Medicaid (all three of which are discussed in greater detail later in this chapter). However, the deficit took a significant plunge at the end of the George W. Bush administration owing to a combination of tax cuts and the onset of the **Great Recession,** the economic crisis that was triggered by the bursting of a housing bubble that led to a financial crisis and cuts in consumer and business spending. The deficit grew more at the beginning of the Obama administration mostly because of the $787 billion stimulus package that was passed to jump start the economy. The stimulus was a combination of tax cuts, unemployment benefit extensions, and, perhaps most importantly, new expenditures on programs that funded new research and development in alternative energy sources, school construction, and increased spending on infrastructure (roads, bridges, canals, etc.). Nevertheless, the federal deficit declined over the remainder of the Obama's term in office. The economy was slowly improving leading to increased tax revenues. Additionally, budget negotiations between President Obama and the Republican Congress resulted in overall spending decreases. After Obama's first year as president, the deficit stood at $1.4 trillion but it was down to a third of that by the time he left office.

The early years of the Trump presidency have the deficit increasing again. Major tax cuts and spending bills with no major cuts passed by the Republican Congress and signed by the president, have the Congressional Budget Office (CBO) projecting that the federal deficit will exceed $1 trillion by 2020.[24]

Are annual deficits necessarily bad? Is having a national debt a bad thing? It depends. Economists generally agree that running a budget deficit in a slow economy helps stimulate economic activity. It puts money into the economy when individuals and firms have cut back on their own spending leaving government to fill the gap. They also agree that a national debt that grows larger to meet emergencies—such as waging a war or fighting a recession—is unavoidable and that borrowing to make investments that will have positive long-term effects on society and the economy—such as building schools and roads, modernizing ports and airports, and funding research and development—is a good thing. However, borrowing to pay current operating expenses is dangerous, something akin to living on one's credit card to buy groceries and pay the mortgage. When outlays are greater than revenues, the federal government runs a deficit and accumulates debt.

As you can see in Figure 17.5, which shows the U.S. national debt as a percentage of GDP, the Great Recession caused the size of the debt relative to the economy to increase, but debt levels still remain below the historic highs of World War II. At the end of 2017, the federal debt stood at just over $20 trillion or about 103 percent of GDP. Eminent economists such as the Nobel Prize winning Paul Krugman have consistently maintained that the country is able to handle a fairly high level of debt without problem—particularly during recessionary times, though more conservatively oriented economists disagree.[25]

As a math problem, solving the deficit and debt problems is a simple matter: increase revenues and decrease expenditures. But this is unlikely for a number of reasons. First, Americans do not agree about what they want or are willing to sacrifice. Hardly anyone wants his or her taxes increased—nor do recipients of government program dollars want fewer coming in, whether they are farmers receiving agricultural subsidy payments or older Americans receiving Medicare benefits.

In addition, one of the central obstacles to solving the long-term debt problem is the extreme partisanship in Washington and across the country. Pushed by their base,

---

FIGURE 17.5   THE NATIONAL DEBT AS A PERCENTAGE OF GDP, 1940–2017

After a long period of decline, the relative national debt—that is, the size of the debt compared with the total size of the American economy (GDP)—grew dramatically during the 1980s and early 1990s but fell after 1993. The relative size of the debt is again increasing, quite dramatically from 2008 forward because of the increase in the size of annual deficits and the decline of GDP during the Great Recession. Even at its worst, however, the size of the relative national debt in recent decades is nowhere near the historic high point it reached during World War II.

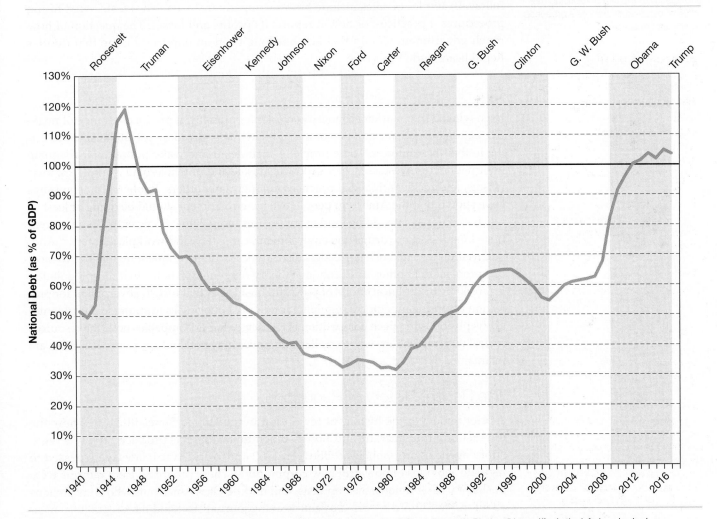

SOURCE: Federal Reserve Bank of St. Louis, "Federal Debt: Total Public Debt as Percent of Gross Domestic Product," https://fred.stlouisfed.org/series/GFDEGDQ188S.

Republicans now stand firmly against tax increases of any sort, even as they oppose cuts in spending for national defense and the military and for energy industry and agricultural subsidies. Democrats, while willing to raise taxes on high earners, also have pushed for increased government spending on a range of existing and new programs and strongly support stimulus spending during recessions to try to generate economic growth. For example, when President Obama asked Congress to create a bipartisan commission to make recommendations on how to tackle the debt problem, Republicans blocked the measure. In February 2010, President Obama issued an executive order creating the commission and appointed moderate Republican Alan Simpson and moderate Democrat Erskine Bowles to head it. After the commission made its report in December 2011, President Obama ignored many of its recommendations.[26] It is not clear whether American political leaders of either political party will be willing and able to do what must be done to solve the long-term debt problem. Partisanship is not the only roadblock; the other one is the mixed message coming from the American people. As a liberal-leaning columnist put it: Americans are "in favor of Medicare, Social Security, good schools, wide highways, a strong military—and low taxes."[27]

REGULATION

17.4 Explain government regulation and why regulations change.

regulation

The issuing of rules by government agencies with the aim of reducing the scale of negative externalities produced by private firms.

Regulation is one of the most visible and important activities of the federal government. For example, federal agencies issue rules that private businesses must follow. Examples of rules include how a company treats its toxic waste, what hiring procedures it practices, or how it reports its profits and losses. The question of how much government should regulate has long been an important issue that divides Republicans and Democrats.

The Role of Regulation

Even when a free-market economy is working optimally, it produces a range of negative externalities that cannot be or are unlikely to be solved by private businesses acting in their best interest. These problems include air and water pollution, inadequate information for investors, unsafe products, unsafe and unwholesome workplaces, toxic wastes, and reckless financial practices among many others. Public opinion surveys have shown that the American people believe government should be doing at least as much as it is currently doing (and in some cases more than it is currently doing) to regulate business, food, drugs, the environment, car safety, and workplace safety.[28] And, odd as it may seem, business leaders also advocate for government regulations to meet one problem or another. The economic theory of regulation holds that most regulation is caused by the political efforts of powerful businesses that turn to government for protection against competitors. Regulation often puts businesses in strategically advantageous positions in which competition is restricted (larger companies have the resources to deal with regulations while smaller companies may not) and above-market prices are maintained.[29]

The Recent History of Regulation

A brief review of the history of regulation in the United States illustrates how the interaction of democratic and non-democratic factors has produced today's regulatory agencies and policies.[30] Between 1900 and World War I, laws were passed to regulate activities of powerful new corporations. These progressive era reforms were pushed by labor unions, the Populists, and middle-class Americans who were anxious about the conditions reported by muckraking journalists. Landmark regulatory measures included the Federal Trade Commission Act, the Meat Inspection Act, the Pure

Food and Drug Act, and the Federal Reserve Act. These measures dealt with problems such as monopolies, unstable financial institutions, and unsafe products and working conditions.

Franklin Roosevelt's New Deal in the 1930s focused on speculative and unsafe practices in the banking and securities industries that had contributed to the onset of the Great Depression. The goal was to restore stability to financial markets and important industries. Legislation focused on such issues as federal bank inspection, federal deposit insurance, the prohibition of speculative investments by banks, and the creation of the Securities and Exchange Commission (SEC) to regulate stock market operations. The linkage factors that led to New Deal regulation were mixed. Some came from popular pressures,[31] but some also came from the business community, seeking stability in its various industries.[32]

The successes of the consumer, environmental, and civil rights movements of the late 1960s to the late 1970s resulted in a substantial increase in the federal government's regulation of business. The aim of these regulatory efforts was to protect against health and environmental hazards, to provide equal opportunity, and to allow more public access to regulatory rule making. Under the authority of new laws, agencies such as the Environmental Protection Agency (EPA), the Equal Opportunity Employment Commission (EOEC), the Food and Drug Administration (FDA), and the Occupational Safety and Health Administration (OSHA) issued numerous rules that affected business operations and decisions. It was one of the only times in U.S. history when business was almost entirely on the defensive, unable to halt the imposition of laws and regulations to which it was strongly opposed.[33]

By the end of the 1970s, the mood of opinion leaders had turned against regulation in the name of economic efficiency. Many blamed excessive regulation for forcing inefficient practices on American companies, contributing to sluggish economic growth, low productivity, and disappointing competitiveness in the global economy. Many found fault with the government for imposing uniform national standards, strict deadlines for compliance with regulations, and detailed instructions.[34] The deregulatory mood was spurred by a political offensive by businesses that funded think tanks, foundations that favored the business point of view, and electoral campaigns of sympathetic candidates.[35] From then until as recently as the 2008 financial crisis, the watchword was **deregulation**: the attempt to loosen the hand of government in a variety of economic sectors, including banking and finance, transportation, and telecommunications.

deregulation
The process of diminishing regulatory requirements for business.

The rollback in federal regulation has been a bipartisan affair. Early reforms such as the deregulation of the airline and trucking industries occurred at the end of the Carter administration and were followed by the deregulation of the financial and oil industries during the Reagan administration—Reagan was perhaps deregulation's most stalwart advocate. In 1999, President Bill Clinton signed the Gramm-Leach-Bliley Act, which allowed commercial banks, insurance companies, and investment banks to compete in the same markets and innovate new financial products (such as the highly risky mortgage-backed securities and credit default swaps that contributed to the 2008 financial collapse) relatively free from government oversight. During George W. Bush's administration, the SEC allowed Wall Street investment banks to regulate themselves and to dramatically lower the amount of money they had to keep on hand as back-up. In a speech in early 2010, then-Federal Chairman Ben Bernanke placed responsibility for the financial collapse in the United States on weak government regulation of the industry's underwriting and risk management practices as well as on the lax ratings standards on the quality and safety of mortgage-backed securities and derivatives given by private agencies such as Standard and Poor's, Moody's, and Fitch.[36]

Americans generally want a smaller and less expensive government in the abstract, but they also want government to protect them against the bad practices of firms and other externalities. As economic activity and technological change generate new problems, and when firms take advantage of their market power, people demand that government intervene. Thus, when people become ill from tainted beef, the public demands higher standards of meat inspection and tracking. When companies collapse, taking with them the retirement savings of their employees, or when accounting firms allow companies to mislead investors, Americans demand that government protect them against similar behavior by other companies. When American companies import dangerous products from abroad—children's toys, for example—people demand closer scrutiny of manufacturing practices abroad and testing of imported products. When an unregulated, little understood, and highly leveraged "shadow banking" system collapses and triggers a deep and long-lasting recession, as it did in 2008, the public, leaders of other industries, and elected officials push for increased regulation to diminish dangerous financial practices.[37] The Dodd–Frank Wall Street Reform and Consumer Protection bill that passed in 2010 imposes a range of requirements on financial institutions—including greater transparency in their operations, higher reserve requirements, and clearer language for consumers on mortgage loans and credit cards—and new powers to regulatory agencies to enforce them (though some of those regulatory powers were rolled back by Congress in 2018).

This dynamic of the appearance of new problems, public pressures to institute regulations that prevent future problems, and industry pushback is typical of American politics. Some periods see a wave of new regulatory initiatives; some periods experience a rollback of government regulation. Yet, the need for regulation over a wide range of activities is frequently evident to the public, political leaders, and many business leaders. New technologies and a dynamic economy cannot help but generate new regulatory demands. Government's regulatory role is here to stay as is the contentious political debate that surrounds the question of how extensive this role should be.

FEDERAL SAFETY NET PROGRAMS

17.5 Describe the major federal safety net programs, and assess their effectiveness.

Safety net programs protect Americans from ruinous losses of income stemming from unemployment, poverty, physical and mental illness, disability, family disintegration, and old age by assuring them of a minimum standard of living. Federal safety net programs account for the largest share of the annual federal budget, considerably outstripping spending in all other areas, including national defense and homeland security. In 2017, total federal expenditures on safety net programs were about $2.5 trillion, a little less than two-thirds of total federal outlays.[38]

Types of Federal Safety Net Programs

There are two basic types of federal safety net programs. The first type is **social insurance**, typified by Social Security and Medicare, in which Americans contribute some of their own money to an insurance trust fund by way of payroll taxes on earnings. They then receive benefits based on their lifetime contributions when they reach a certain age or become disabled. The second type of federal safety net program is **means-tested**, meaning that benefits are distributed on the basis of need to those who can prove that their income is low enough to qualify and those who receive benefits do not pay anything for them. The food stamp program is an example, as is the **Temporary Assistance to Needy Families (TANF)** program, which provides federal grants-in-aid to the states to help support the very poor.

Some safety net programs are administered directly by the federal government; others are administered jointly by the federal government and the states. Social Security is an example of a social insurance program run by the federal government. Payroll taxes for Social Security are levied directly on wages and salaries by the

social insurance
Government programs that provide services or income support in proportion to the amount of mandatory contributions made by individuals to a government trust fund.

means-tested programs
Social insurance programs that require recipients demonstrate need before getting benefits.

Temporary Assistance to Needy Families (TANF)
Federal welfare program that provides income and services to poor families via state block grants. The program has benefit time limits and a work requirement.

federal government, and the Social Security Administration issues benefit checks to the elderly and persons with disabilities. By contrast, **Medicaid**, a means-tested program, is jointly funded and administered by the states and the federal government, as is the unemployment compensation system. Each state, consequently, has its own Medicaid and its own unemployment compensation systems, with wide variation in benefit levels from state to state.

Some safety nets are designated as **entitlement** programs; that is, payments are made automatically to people who meet certain eligibility requirements once the relevant criteria are met. For example, citizens whose incomes are under a certain level are entitled to food stamps and Medicaid. People older than 65 are entitled to Medicare and those older than 62 are entitled to Social Security benefits. Because payments are made automatically, these expenditures are locked into the federal budget, and Congress can do little to change their cost without revising the underlying laws—a steep challenge given the hurdles of federal policy making.

Social Insurance Programs

The main social insurance programs in the United States are **Social Security** and **Medicare**. Both programs are primarily aimed at ensuring a baseline standard of living for those who are retired or disabled. Social Security provides seniors with an income, and Medicare provides them with health insurance. By almost any measure, both of these programs have been very successful. Although the benefits do not allow people to live luxuriously, they provide an income floor for the retired and pay for medical services that before 1965 were likely to impoverish many of those who had serious illnesses and long hospital stays. Social Security and Medicare, by many accounts, are the federal government's most effective tools at fighting poverty and reducing inequality.[39] Below, we take a closer look at both.

SOCIAL SECURITY   Social Security was created in 1935 in the midst of the Great Depression to provide income to seniors. Within a year, however, benefits were added for widows and their children, and coverage for those with disabilities was added in 1956. Today, the system is funded by a payroll tax on employees and employers—this means that employers deduct the tax from your paycheck for you. Social Security (and Medicare) work by having today's workers pay for today's retirees, so the net effect is to redistribute income across generations.

Social Security was never meant to fund the full cost of retirement for Americans. Planners had always assumed that the program was part of a three-legged stool that also included private workplace pensions and individual savings. Unfortunately, most Americans do not earn enough to save a substantial amount of money on their own for retirement, and workplace pensions are less generous today and fewer in number than they once were. In recent years, 36 percent of retirees have been relying on Social Security payments for more than 90 percent of their income.[40] Nevertheless, Social Security continues to play an essential role in keeping the elderly out of poverty. According to a report by the Center for Budget and Policy Priorities, Social Security keeps 14.7 million retirees out of poverty every year.[41]

Experts have long been concerned about the long-term solvency of the Social Security Trust Fund—the account that workers pay into to fund today's social security payment. The post-World War II baby boom has resulted in the United States having more retirees now (and for the near future) than it has had with previous generations. Consequently, there are and will continue to be fewer working people to pay the benefits for additional elderly recipients—so a time will come when the fund will be paying out at a faster clip than it is being replenished.

Current projections indicate that the trust fund will move into the red in 2034, but the well will not run completely dry. Given a continued inflow of payroll taxes even after the fund goes into deficit, the current system will be able to pay about

Medicaid
Program administered by the states that pays for health care services for the poor; jointly funded by the federal government and the states.

entitlement
Government benefits distributed automatically to citizens who qualify on the basis of a set of guidelines set by law; for example, Americans older than 65 are entitled to Medicare coverage.

Social Security
Social insurance program that provides income support for the elderly, those with disabilities, and family survivors of working Americans.

Medicare
Federal health insurance program for the elderly and the disabled.

75 percent of full benefits for the foreseeable future.[42] The system may also stay viable for a longer period of time if trends continue in which healthier and more active seniors choose not to retire at 65.

Some changes to the system could help to alleviate Social Security's solvency problems. Policy options include:[43]

- Raising the payroll tax rate. One study shows that raising the payroll tax on earning by 2 percent would solve the system's fiscal shortfall.
- Raising the ceiling on taxable income subject to the payroll tax ($128,400 in 2018).
- Taxing all income rather than the current practice of only taxing income from wages and salaries.
- Cutting back recipient benefits. For example, cutting benefits by 13 percent would fully fund the system.
- Taxing the benefits of the wealthy at higher rates.
- Raising the retirement age.

None of these changes would be politically popular or easy to achieve. The political challenges to reform are both demographic and partisan.[44] Americans approaching retirement would be unlikely to appreciate having to wait longer to retire, and elected leaders are likely to listen to them because older Americans vote at higher rates than other groups and have the support of powerful groups like the AARP. On the other side, younger Americans are unlikely to be enthusiastic about the prospect of paying more in payroll taxes or having to retire later.

Meanwhile, Democrats oppose raising the retirement age and Republicans oppose tax increases of any kind so finding a solution in this polarized era will not be easy. Indeed, there is even partisan disagreement about the health of the program. Democrats have argued that the system is in reasonably good health and requires only some tinkering to solve emerging problems. Many Republicans, on the other hand, believe the system is seriously flawed and that the only way to save it is with major overhauls such as using a portion of the payroll tax to set up individual investment private accounts for retirement. President George W. Bush emphasized this after his reelection in 2004, but it gained little traction and is probably off the table for the foreseeable future in the wake of the Great Recession.[45]

PRESIDENT GEORGE W. BUSH PITCHES HIS SOCIAL SECURITY PRIVATIZATION PLAN

After his reelection in 2004, President George W. Bush sought to privatize social security and used the bully pulpit of the presidency to convince Congress to pass legislation. The reform effort never gained the necessary political traction to become law and was completely knocked off the table when the Great Recession hit.

What are the pros and cons of privatizing social security? What about increasing the social security retirement age?

MEDICARE   Medicare was created in 1965 to provide all senior citizens with very affordable health insurance. Presidents Franklin Roosevelt and Harry Truman both sought to create a health insurance program for seniors but were unsuccessful. Roosevelt feared that it would prevent the passage of Social Security and Truman faced anti-communist forces that labeled it "socialized health care." Thus, the enactment of Medicare and Medicaid (health insurance for the poor, discussed below) were major legislative achievements for President Johnson—following a huge Democratic victory in 1964—as strong evidence mounted that health care costs were a leading cause of poverty. These programs fell well short of covering all Americans, but they were a significant step toward guaranteeing health care for those who were most in danger of becoming sick and least equipped to afford it.

Medicare dramatically transformed access to health care for the elderly in the United States. Millions of people who at one time would have been priced out of the health care market now have quality care available to them. In 2017, there were just over 55 million people enrolled in Medicare.[46] Everyone age 65 or older is automatically enrolled in Medicare Part A, which pays for a portion of the bill for most hospital-related health care costs. But people need to buy additional insurance coverage—Medicare Part B—to help pay for physician, nursing, and mental health services, including wellness visits and X-rays. And, because there are many gaps in coverage and significant co-pays under Parts A and B, many who are older than 65 choose to buy Medicare Advantage (Part C) insurance, which fills in these holes with added coverage. Medicare Part D went into effect in 2006 and pays a substantial portion of prescription drug costs for seniors.

Most experts agree that the Medicare program has been extremely successful. People older than 65 have more access to health care services today than at any time in American history, and it shows; people are living longer and have healthier lives.[47] But, like Social Security, there are widespread concerns about the program's costs. Paying for Medicare over the long term is a problem. First, the American population is, on average, getting older so there are not going to be enough people in the work-force to pay for all the people who receive Medicare in the future. Second, health care costs—doctors, hospitals, tests, and prescription drugs—have been rising much faster than the tax revenues that support Medicare. The Medicare program is growing so fast that it will pass Social Security as the federal government's most expensive endeavor somewhere around the year 2035.

Means-Tested Anti-Poverty Programs

Means-tested programs are designed to provide income support and services for those with very low means who fall below certain income thresholds. One scholar suggests that these programs might more accurately be called "absence of means" programs.[48] Rather than being paid for by payroll taxes, means-tested programs are paid for with government's general revenues. While accounting for a much smaller portion of the federal budget than social insurance programs, means-tested programs have tradi-tionally attracted the bulk of the criticism directed at the safety net programs. While Social Security and Medicare enjoy widespread support, welfare (a popular term for means-tested programs) has long been the object of scorn.

Most Americans report wanting government to help the poor,[49] but almost everyone disliked the long-lasting but now defunct public assistance program, Aid to Families with Dependent Children (AFDC). A consensus existed that something was wrong with AFDC—which provided direct cash assistance primarily to single-parent families with needy children.[50] For most Americans, AFDC and other means-tested programs seemed to contradict such cherished cultural values as independence, hard work, stable families, and responsibility for one's own actions. Public opinion polls consistently showed that Americans believed that AFDC kept people dependent; didn't do a good job of helping people support themselves; and encouraged divorce, family disintegration, and out-of-wedlock births.[51] AFDC was replaced by the more limited Temporary Assistance to Needy Families program (TANF) in 1996 (see Chapter 3, but much of the public sentiment about means-tested programs and public assistance recipients remains unchanged.

Since the 1970s, means-tested programs (such as Medicaid, Food Stamps, and TANF block grants to the states) constitute a substantially smaller portion of the federal budget but have also been growing in size (see Figure 17.6).[52] As a result, the non-poor and the elderly (rather than the poor and the young) are the main benefi-ciaries of American safety net spending. This is because social insurance, the largest federal safety net, goes mainly to those who are retired, have been employed the longest, have had the highest incomes, and have paid the maximum level of payroll taxes. Let's take a look at the five most important mean-tested programs.

TEMPORARY ASSISTANCE FOR NEEDY FAMILIES   Temporary Assistance to Needy Families (TANF) is America's primary welfare assistance program for those living below the poverty level. Each state runs its own program using a combination of block grant funds from the federal government and their own money. The funds are used by states to provide direct cash assistance to families as well as money for child care, education, job training, and other services to encourage recipients to enter paid employment. Some

FIGURE 17.6 FEDERAL SPENDING ON MEANS-TESTED PROGRAMS, 1972–2012

Though it still represents a fairly small portion of the social safety net in total, spending on means-tested safety-net programs has increased since the 1970s. Means-tested benefits are distributed only to those who can prove that their income is low enough to qualify for assistance. Means tested programs include such programs as Medicaid, Temporary Assistance for Needy Families (TANF), and food stamps (SNAP).

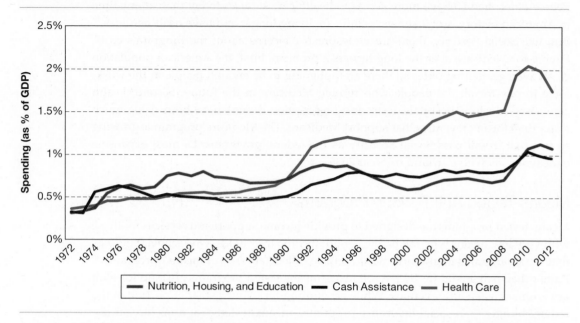

SOURCE: Congressional Budget Office, Growth in Means-Tested Programs and Tax Credits for Low-Income Households, February 2013.

poverty line

The federal government's calculation of the amount of income families of various sizes need to stay out of poverty. In 2018 it was $25,100 for a family of four.

states spend much more generously than others. In the vast majority of states, monthly cash benefits are less than $600 per month. The head of every family receiving assistance is required to work within two years of receiving benefits and is limited to a total of five years of benefits. States are allowed to impose even more stringent requirements if they want. States are also allowed to use their own funds (not federal block grant money) to extend the two-year and five-year limits—though most have not been willing to do so.

When TANF was enacted in 1996, proponents of welfare reform believed that the program would end dependency, reestablish the primacy of the family in poor communities, improve the income situation of the poor, and help balance the federal budget. Opponents believed that TANF would lead to more poverty, homelessness, and hunger—especially among children—once recipients reached their five-year time limit.

Research tells us that welfare rolls dropped dramatically after the new law was passed; many people trained for jobs and entered the paid workforce, and many raised their incomes, especially during the latter part of the 1990s and from 2004 until the financial collapse in 2008. However, the law's more stringent requirements also meant that many people who were previously eligible for assistance were no longer eligible. Because pay levels for entry-level jobs are so low, only a small percentage of former welfare recipients were able to cross the official **poverty-line** threshold in the first years of the program. And, while the poverty rate decreased among former welfare recipients between 1996 and 2000, it slowly increased after that.[53] According to a study by the Center for on Budget and Policy Priorities, only 23 percent of families living below the poverty were receiving welfare benefits in 2016. In 1996, the final year of AFDC, it was 68 percent.[54] This decline is the result of a host of factors including the stigma of being on welfare, the complexities of signing up, time limits on benefits, and an overall decreased commitment to maintaining this kind of safety net in many states.[55]

NUTRITIONAL ASSISTANCE The **Supplemental Nutrition Assistance Program (SNAP)**, which has historically been referred to as "food stamps," is funded through the Department of Agriculture and state budgets. It helps Americans that fall below a certain income (roughly 133 percent of the poverty line) to buy food for themselves and their families. The United States has other nutritional assistance programs, such as the free or reduced-price school lunch program and the Women, Infants, and Children nutrition program, but the SNAP program is the largest of these. About forty-two million people (that is, roughly one in eight Americans) received nutritional assistance in 2018.[56]

SNAP benefits are modest; a family of four with an income of less than $24,000 per year can expect no more than $650 per month in SNAP benefits (or less than $2.00 per meal). SNAP assistance can be used only for food, not alcohol, cigarettes, beauty care products, or even household goods such as toilet paper. Despite the modest benefits, nutritional assistance has made a significant dent in the prevalence of malnutrition in the United States and by allowing families to concentrate resources elsewhere it helps lift them out of poverty.[57]

MEDICAID AND THE CHILDREN'S HEALTH INSURANCE PROGRAM The federal government allocates money to the states to help them pay for medical services for many of their needy adult citizens and children in two big and rapidly growing programs: **Medicaid** and the **Children's Health Insurance Program (CHIP)**. Medicaid is now the nation's second-largest public assistance program. More than 22 percent of Americans (almost 74 million people) were enrolled in Medicaid and CHIP in 2018.[58]

Medicaid is quite complicated and varies a great deal by state. States are required to provide a specific range of medical services for people who are defined as "medically indigent" or are below certain income thresholds. Medicaid pays for hospital, physician, and nursing services; home health care; diagnostic screenings and tests; and nursing home costs—provided that recipients do not exceed the income ceilings for the program. Some states also provide prescription drug coverage. In addition to providing medical services for the very poor, it has become increasingly common for Medicaid to be used to pay for nursing home care for those who have exhausted their savings, including many people who had been longtime members of the middle class. Indeed, about 60 percent of nursing home residents in the United States receive aid from Medicaid to pay for their housing and care.[59] States have some latitude in determining who receives benefits and who does not—federal statutes identify around fifty categories of people potentially eligible for Medicaid benefits—and how much service providers receive in compensation, so benefits vary widely across the states.

Medicaid is funded by both the states and the federal government; states receive from 50 to 80 percent (in 2016) of the cost of their state-designed and administered Medicaid programs from Washington, with the poorest states receiving the highest percentage of reimbursements.[60] President Obama's ACA (discussed in more detail in the next section) helped states to significantly increase the number of Americans eligible for Medicaid by funding an expansion that covers Americans whose incomes are less than 138 percent of the poverty line—prior to the ACA many states had Medicaid eligibility levels set at the poverty level or lower. The ACA had originally made this expansion of eligibility effectively mandatory for states; however, in *NFIB v. Sebelius* (2012) the Supreme Court ruled that the federal government lacked the power to compel states to expand their programs. Consequently, many (mostly conservative) states have elected not to expand their Medicaid coverage (see Figure 3.7 for a map of states that accepted and rejected the Medicaid expansion). Red state or blue, funding Medicaid and CHIP has become one of the most difficult fiscal problems for state governments, especially during tough economic times when state tax revenues decline and the need for assistance increases.

CHIP is a program that pays for medical care for children whose families make too much money to be eligible for Medicaid and can't afford private health

Supplemental Nutritional Assistance Program (SNAP)
Federal program that helps Americans that fall below a certain income to buy food for themselves and their families. Frequently referred to as "food stamps."

Children's Health Insurance Program (CHIP)
Program that pays for health care services for children in households above the poverty line but below 133 percent to 400 percent of the poverty line, depending on the state.

insurance. First enacted in 1997, the program is also funded jointly by the states and the federal government, with states having significant discretion in determining benefit levels and covered services. In terms of coverage, CHIP has been an unqualified success. In the three years following its enactment in 1997, for example, the number of medically uninsured poor and near-poor children in the United States dropped by more than a third, down to 15.4 percent among poor children.[61]

THE EARNED INCOME TAX CREDIT   The working poor benefit greatly from a provision in the U.S. Tax Code that allows low-income individuals with at least one child to claim a credit against taxes owed or, for some, to receive a direct cash transfer from the IRS. The **Earned Income Tax Credit (EITC)** benefited more than twenty-eight million low-income families in 2015 without much bureaucratic fuss.[62] Families eligible for the EITC make between $15,000 and $54,000, and the tax credit is based on family size and income. A family of four with an income of $40,000 could expect a tax credit of about $2,800.[63]

Poverty in the United States

It is important for the government to know how many Americans are living in poverty. These numbers help to determine the size, cost, and effectiveness of the means-tested safety-net programs discussed above. Knowing these numbers also gives us an indication of how well we are doing as a society. *But how do we measure poverty?* While most would probably agree that poverty involves living in dire circumstances (inadequate shelter, food, and health care), measuring this is difficult. The best test we have is to use income as a proxy. Rather than collect information about how people live—what our homes are like, for example—the Census Bureau collects information about how much money people earn. However, identifying the dividing line between who is and is not living in poverty is a challenge.

Earned Income Tax Credit (EITC)

A provision in the U.S. Tax Code that allows low-income individuals with at least one child to claim a credit against taxes owed or, for some, to receive a direct cash transfer from the IRS.

THE POOR ARE AMONG US

However poverty is measured, it is clear that the percentage of the population living in poverty in the United States is higher than in any other rich democracy. Although the United States arguably has the least generous set of safety nets among these countries, families like this one can usually depend on food stamps, some income support, and Medicaid to maintain a minimum standard of living.

Why are so many people in the United States living at or below the poverty line?

In 1964, the Department of Agriculture calculated how much it would cost a family of four to buy enough food to survive. Then, because the assumption was that the average American family spent one-third of its budget on food, they multiplied the number by three and adjusted it for family size. Since then, the U.S. government has merely adjusted this number for inflation.[64] In 2018, a family of four making less than $25,100 was officially living in poverty.[65]

This measure of poverty has its critics. Some argue that the various costs of living have changed over the years, thus requiring new calculations and different, more all-encompassing approaches.[66] Others point out that the measure does not take into account the substantial differences in the cost of living that exist across the country. For example, a family of four earning $17,000 can stretch its income further in rural Alabama than it can in San Francisco. The Census Bureau is aware of these concerns and has developed a "supplemental poverty measure"—but this measure is not always used for the implementation of policy.[67]

Figure 17.7 shows the rate of Americans living in poverty from 1959 to 2016 by race. Based on this measure, the United States made good progress during the 1990s—the poverty rate fell to 11.3 in 2000, its lowest point in twenty-one years—but increased again as the nation went through a recession and a recovery that had not included adequate job growth. According to the Census Bureau, by 2010, at the height of the Great Recession, 15.3 percent of Americans—more than forty-six million people—were living below the poverty line. It is critical to note that the poverty rate for African Americans and Hispanics remains considerably higher than for whites and Americans of Asian descent. In 2016, 11 percent of whites in the United States were living in poverty while the rate for African Americans and Hispanics was roughly double that.

FIGURE 17.7 POVERTY RATE BY RACE/ETHNICITY, 1959–2016

The poverty rate in the United States has hovered between 10 and 15 percent since the early 1970s. Owing to the financial crisis, Great Recession, and jobless economic recovery, the poverty rate has been on a disconcerting uptick in recent years. In 2014, about 15 percent of Americans were living in poverty. Poverty is also connected to race and ethnicity with a much larger percentage of African Americans and Hispanics living in poverty than whites.

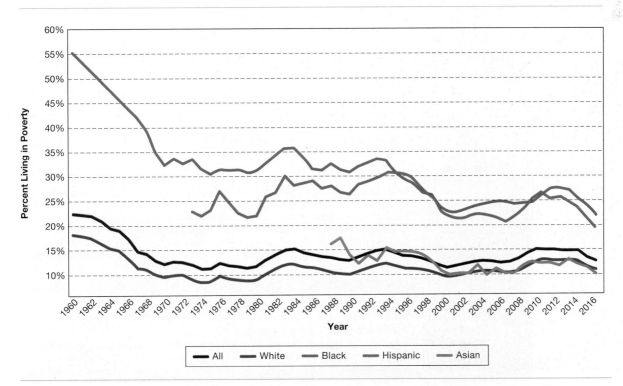

SOURCE: Data from U.S. Census Bureau, Historical Poverty Tables, Table 2, Poverty Status, by Family Relationship, Race, and Hispanic Origin.

HEALTH CARE POLICY

17.6 Explain the key provisions of the Affordable Care Act and the challenges it has faced.

Affordable Care Act (ACA)

The far-reaching health care reform law passed in 2010. The Act was aimed at increasing access to health insurance for all Americans and driving down the rising, burdensome cost of health care in the United States.

On March 23, 2010, President Barack Obama signed the **Affordable Care Act (ACA)** into law; it was the most far-reaching reform of the nation's health care system since the passage of Medicare in 1965. The Act was aimed at increasing access to health insurance for all Americans and driving down the rising, burdensome cost of health care in the United States. Since that day in 2010, the ACA has been the subject of near endless controversy, litigation, and change.

As you can see in Figure 17.8, an application of our analytical framework to the adoption of the ACA, comprehensive health care reform was a long-time in the making. The root causes of the reform lie in the *structure* of the American health care system which depended (and still depends) heavily on employers to provide health insurance before retirement. Millions of Americans in jobs that did not provide insurance found it too expensive to purchase on their own. The U.S. health care system is the most costly in the world. Rising sentiment among the public that government needed to do something to bring down the costs of health care and increase access to insurance, eventually led the Congress, in conjunction with the White House, to propose a reform plan that garnered the support (albeit tepid) of much of the existing health care industry (a critical *linkage* factor). Many of the profitable elements of the American health care system were left in place; namely, a private insurance system without a competing government plan. Through a series of legislative maneuvers, Democrats in Congress were ultimately able to garner barely enough support to pass the law.

FIGURE 17.8 APPLYING THE FRAMEWORK: THE AFFORDABLE CARE ACT (2010)

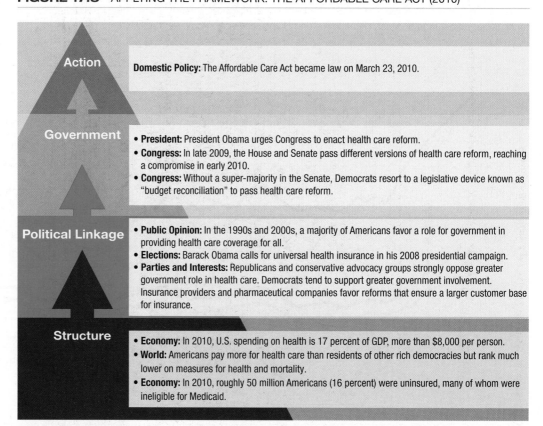

Action

Domestic Policy: The Affordable Care Act became law on March 23, 2010.

Government

- **President:** President Obama urges Congress to enact health care reform.
- **Congress:** In late 2009, the House and Senate pass different versions of health care reform, reaching a compromise in early 2010.
- **Congress:** Without a super-majority in the Senate, Democrats resort to a legislative device known as "budget reconciliation" to pass health care reform.

Political Linkage

- **Public Opinion:** In the 1990s and 2000s, a majority of Americans favor a role for government in providing health care coverage for all.
- **Elections:** Barack Obama calls for universal health insurance in his 2008 presidential campaign.
- **Parties and Interests:** Republicans and conservative advocacy groups strongly oppose greater government role in health care. Democrats tend to support greater government involvement. Insurance providers and pharmaceutical companies favor reforms that ensure a larger customer base for insurance.

Structure

- **Economy:** In 2010, U.S. spending on health is 17 percent of GDP, more than $8,000 per person.
- **World:** Americans pay more for health care than residents of other rich democracies but rank much lower on measures for health and mortality.
- **Economy:** In 2010, roughly 50 million Americans (16 percent) were uninsured, many of whom were ineligible for Medicaid.

Key Components of the ACA

Although the law is long and complex, its goals are not. The authors of the ACA aimed to extend health insurance coverage to a substantial share of the more than 40 million Americans that were uninsured prior, improve the quality of health insurance coverage, and bring down the overall cost of health care. They also aimed to do this without dramatically changing the American health care system. Rather than creating a new single-payer or socialized system like in Canada and much of Europe, the ACA continued a system in which health care is provided by private practitioners, insurance is primarily provided by private companies, Medicare, and Medicaid, and those without employer or government health insurance purchase coverage on their own.

To accomplish these goals, the ACA includes provisions that created online marketplaces (also known as "exchanges") for people to compare and purchase health insurance and set rules for insurance companies to keep people covered in a variety of circumstances in which they would have lost coverage in the past. For example, the ACA forbids insurance companies from rejecting people for preexisting conditions (such as diabetes or cancer) or from placing annual or lifetime limits on benefits. The ACA also sets baseline standards for what health care plans must cover (including emergency services, maternity and newborn care, mental health care, and wellness services among others).

The health insurance companies had long contended that they could not afford to insure those with expensive preexisting medical conditions, so another provision in the ACA mandated that every American have health insurance either through their workplaces, through government (Medicare, Medicaid, CHIP), or purchased on their own. Those who did not have health insurance were forced to pay a penalty. Those who cannot afford insurance get government subsidies or, in many states, access to Medicaid. Under the ACA, the federal government helped states increase access to Medicaid by providing them with most of the funds necessary to expand eligibility up to 138 percent of the poverty line. The idea behind the health insurance mandate was that more people having insurance helps to bring down the cost for everyone by spreading health care costs more evenly across the population of healthy and unhealthy people. Without the threat of a penalty, there is less incentive for healthy people to purchase health insurance. And without a large healthy customer base, health insurance companies cannot afford to cover those with preexisting conditions.

HEALTH INSURANCE MARKET-PLACES ALLOW CONSUMERS TO COMPARE PLANS

One of the key components of the Affordable Care Act was the creation of online health insurance marketplaces that allow customers to easily compare plans and select the one that is right for them. States were asked to create their own marketplace, but if they elected not to the federal government would do it instead. Here we see the opening screen to the federal health insurance marketplace: HealthCare.gov.

How can health insurance marketplaces like HealthCare.gov help bring down the cost of health insurance?

However, the mandate was removed in 2017 by the Republican-led Congress and President Trump who argued that it was unfair to force people to buy insurance.[68] Health care experts remain uncertain about what will happen to the health insurance market with the mandate removed. If health insurance enrollment by healthy people declines significantly in the coming years, it could make other parts of the ACA (like the requirement that insurers cover preexisting conditions) unsustainable.

Challenges and Changes to the ACA

The ACA's complexity means that it has lots of moving parts, which became apparent as the Obama administration began rolling out its major provisions in 2014. To reduce the cost of individually purchased health insurance plans, the law mandated that states either set up online marketplaces where people compare and purchase plans or allow the federal government to do so for them. When the federal exchange website, healthcare.gov, came online on October 1, 2013 (providing the marketplace for seventeen states), it proved largely incapable of handling the Internet traffic or complex information necessary for people to sort through and purchase plans at the correct price. The failure to successfully launch the website was a major obstacle in the way of getting uninsured Americans to sign up. Over the ensuing several months, the Obama administration was able to get the site up and running, but the failure was a public relations catastrophe for the Obama administration and a black mark on the government's ability to administer the ACA.[69]

The implementation of the program has also been marked by lawsuits and controversies over its expansion of Medicaid and requirements and the essential services that all health insurance plans must cover. During the Obama administration, several religious organizations (primarily ones connected to the Catholic Church) and companies took exception to a rule instituted by the Department of Health and Human Services requiring that all plans cover contraception—which includes the plans that religious organizations provide to their employees. The Obama administration stood fast in its belief that all plans should cover contraception as a matter of public health, but in *Burwell v. Hobby Lobby* (2014), the Supreme Court ruled that the federal government cannot force private companies to cover services that they object to on religious grounds. While most companies and organizations continued to cover contraception, the *Hobby Lobby* decision was a blow to both ACA supporters and women's rights advocates. The Trump administration has sought to roll back the requirement insurers cover contraception entirely.

SEVEN YEARS AFTER PASSAGE: A PIVOTAL VOTE FOR THE ACA

Senator John McCain (R-AZ) walks to the Senate chamber where he is about to cast the deciding vote against a Republican proposal to repeal the Affordable Care Act. While McCain has been a critic of the ACA, he took issue with the process the Senate was using to change the law. His vote created a dramatic scene on the floor of the Senate as his Republican colleagues hung their heads in disappointment and Democrats expressed relief that ACA would remain alive. *Why do you think that the Affordable Care Act has been such a controversial law?*

The ACA has also served as core point of opposition for conservatives. The Republican-controlled chambers of Congress have voted more than 60 times to repeal the ACA in entirety but never succeeded at turning those votes into law. Americans have been consistently split on their approval of the law along party lines: a 2018 poll, for example, indicated that nearly 80 percent of Democrats have a favorable view of the ACA but only about 15 percent of Republicans feels similarly.[70]

THE AMERICAN SAFETY NET IN CONTEXT

17.7 Compare and contrast systems of social safety nets across countries.

The American safety net system is quite different than those found in most other rich democracies.[71] For one, it covers fewer people. Most of the Western European nations blanket their entire populations with benefits. The American system also favors the elderly, while others distribute benefits more evenly across age groups. Medicare and Social Security, aimed at people 65 and older, make up the largest parts of the federal government's social safety net spending, far larger than programs whose benefits go to the nonelderly poor, especially children. In most other systems, family allowances and universal health care coverage keep benefit distributions more balanced. All of this means that the American system is less redistributive than what we see in many other Western countries. Research on wealthy countries has shown that redistributive safety net policies help to alleviate income inequality. But even with the expansion of Medicaid under the ACA, the United States' safety net policies have remained relatively constant since the 1970s.[72]

Another difference between the U.S. safety net system and those of many other Western democracies is that the American system asks less of private employers. Western European countries require employers to offer significant maternity and paternity leave (German mothers receive six weeks' paid leave before giving birth and eight to twelve weeks' paid leave after) and require flexibility for parental schedules. The United States mandates only three months of unpaid leave for firms of fifty employees or more.

And last, the American system does not have universal health insurance coverage. Many other rich countries either provide health services directly to their populations (the National Health Service in Great Britain is an example), offer universal health insurance coverage (e.g., the Canadian system), or use some combination of the two.

Factors That Have Shaped the American Safety Net

Here we identify structural and political linkage factors that have shaped the American safety net.

CONSTITUTIONAL RULES   Federalism is one reason safety net programs were introduced here later than other rich democracies. Until the 1930s, it was not clear where the main responsibility for social safety nets was constitutionally lodged. In fact, it was not generally accepted that the national government had any authority at all on these matters until the U.S. Supreme Court accepted the New Deal.[73] Federalism means that many of the needs and interests of states are accounted for, but this in turn leads to incredible administrative complexity and great unevenness in program coverage. The result is great variation among the states in benefits, eligibility requirements, and rules.

RACIAL DIVISIONS   It is often argued that Europe's greater propensity toward welfare states with universal coverage is a result of the ethnic and racial homogeneity in their societies when they first created them. In homogeneous societies, the argument goes, voters are willing to support generous welfare programs because they believe recipients are very much like themselves—neighbors, down on their luck.[74]

Whether or not this argument holds up—the growing diversity within European countries, especially their large and growing Muslim populations, will eventually make it possible to test this idea—it is apparent that racial tensions influenced the shape of the American safety net system.[75] Some of the hostility toward AFDC, for instance, was likely related to the fact that African Americans made up a disproportionately large share of AFDC recipients (although less than a majority of all recipients) and that media stories about welfare recipients focused almost entirely on African Americans.[76] In fact, research conducted in the mid-1990s found that racial attitudes are the most important driver of how white Americans view welfare.[77]

POLITICAL CULTURE   Almost every aspect of the American political culture works against a generous and comprehensive safety net system. The belief in competitive individualism is especially important. Voters who believe that people should stand on their own two feet and take responsibility for their lives are not likely to be sympathetic to appeals for helping able-bodied, working-age people.[78] Anti-government themes in the political culture also play a role. Generous and comprehensive safety net programs are almost always in large and centralized states supported by high taxes, and many Americans are deeply suspicious of politicians and centralized government and resistant to high taxes.

THE POWER OF BUSINESS   Business plays a powerful role in American politics. Almost without exception, the business community has been a voice for low taxes, limited government benefits, and the flexibility to provide the employee benefits they want. There are many points where legislation can be stopped in the American lawmaking process and business is quite adept at using this system to stop laws that they view as not in their interest. Scholars generally believe that business is a more powerful actor in the United States than it is in other rich democracies where more generous benefits are more common.[79]

WEAK LABOR UNIONS   Countries where workers are organized into unions and exercise significant political power have extensive and generous social safety net systems; countries where this is not the case tend to have less extensive and generous systems.[80] American labor unions have never been as strong or influential as labor unions in most of the other rich democracies, partly because the proportion of American workers who belong to labor unions has always been and remains smaller than in comparable countries. Today, union membership is at historically low levels, with only about 12 percent of employed workers in unions (compared to its peak of 28.3 percent in 1954).[81]

DOMESTIC POLICIES: DO AMERICANS GET THE ECONOMIC POLICIES AND SAFETY NET PROGRAMS THEY WANT FROM GOVERNMENT?

It is difficult to draw firm conclusions about the relative weight democracy has in determining what sorts of economic policies exist in the United States, partly because the government does so many different things. Economic policies that encompass spending and taxing, control of the money supply, and regulation are more often than not the result of the combined influences of popular pressures on elected political leaders and business and interest group influence. Business regulation is a good example of a set of policies that resulted from this joint influence.

The American public gets at least part of what it wants in terms of economic policies from government. For example, people tell pollsters that they distrust big government and don't want to pay high taxes—which they don't, compared with other rich democracies. And, they want government to control and help clean up some of the bad effects of economic activity like air and water pollution—which it has done with varying degrees of enthusiasm and success over the years.

Even if the American people get the sorts of economic policies they want, it is also the case that the hand of special interests can be found in abundance in the details of many of our economic policies. First, this is the case for spending where commitments to specific priorities and projects, from weapons systems procurement to direct business subsidies, are hammered out in a legislative process dominated by special interests. Second, this is the case for taxation, where the detailed provisions of the tax code come from the efforts of special interests—who are also the main beneficiaries.[82] Third, this is the case in regulatory policy, where far too many regulatory agencies remain heavily influenced by those they are charged with regulating.

It is also difficult to determine if Americans get the kinds of safety net programs they want from government. On the one hand, we might argue that the size and types of programs fit what Americans say they want. For example, surveys show that strong majorities support Social Security and Medicare—a fact confirmed on numerous occasions by voters' punishment of candidates who have dared to threaten either program. The public's desire for government to do something about lessening or eliminating poverty has borne some fruit, as programs such as the Earned Income Tax Credit, food stamps, CHIP, and Medicaid have helped to halve the poverty rate over the past five decades—although the poverty rate in the United States remains among the highest of the rich democracies.

The most obvious hole in America's safety net has been the absence of universal health insurance coverage. For years, Americans have told pollsters that they wanted better and more affordable coverage—though there was a great deal of disagreement among people about what type of program would be best. As such, health care reform efforts have been on the platforms of presidential candidates since the end of World War II, but these efforts have been undermined by powerful interest groups that elected officials were loath to cross, including doctors' and hospital associations, insurance companies, and pharmaceutical companies. For the Affordable Care Act to happen, these powerful interests had to be brought on board. By accommodating their needs, however, the primary objective of bringing overall health care costs under control perhaps has been undermined. What is more, the divisiveness of the polarization era has made health care reform so contentious that the ACA has remained subject to constant litigation, inconsistent administration, and ceaseless partisan acrimony.

REVIEW THE CHAPTER

WHY DOES THE FEDERAL GOVERNMENT DO SO MUCH?

17.1 Explain the reasons for federal involvement in economic and societal affairs.

The Constitution provides that the government is responsible for providing for "the general welfare."

The normal operations of a market economy produce an abundance of problems that people want government to alleviate.

Wealthy democracies have safety net programs that help to ensure minimum standards of living and protect against loss of income from economic instability, old age, illness, disability, and family disintegration.

ECONOMIC POLICY

17.2 Analyze the goals and tools of economic policy making.

Policy makers try to achieve a number of objectives with economic policy, including stimulating economic growth, controlling inflation, maintaining a positive balance of trade, budgetary discipline, avoiding negative externalities, and ensuring a vibrant economy.

Fiscal policy refers to the overall spending and taxing impact of the federal government. Policy makers can use spending and taxing to stimulate economic activity—by increasing spending and/or cutting taxes—or slow it down—by cutting spending and/or increasing taxes. Fiscal policy, however, is not very flexible.

Monetary policy refers to Federal Reserve policies that influence the availability and cost of credit in the overall economy. The Fed uses these tools to expand credit when the economy is stalled or in decline and to shrink credit when inflation becomes a problem.

THE FEDERAL BUDGET

17.3 Identify the components of the federal budget, and analyze the problems associated with the national debt.

The federal budget is the detailed accounting of how government spends and receives money. It includes expenditures on all government programs and revenues from taxes and other sources.

Federal government outlays cover a very broad range of programs, including national defense, social insurance such as Social Security and Medicare, safety net programs for the poor such as Medicaid and food stamps, subsidies to various businesses such as agriculture and oil and natural gas, scientific research and higher education, food and drug safety regulation, and more. Government receipts mainly come from income, payroll, corporate, and excise taxes.

The deficit is the annual difference between government outlays and government receipts. Annual deficits have grown dramatically in recent years. The national debt is the total of what the U.S. government owes to individuals, firms, and governments to pay for the sum total of annual deficits. The national debt has grown most dramatically during war and economic crises, including the recent Great Recession.

More than half of the federal budget is taken up by mandatory spending—spending that occurs based on formulas and not annual decisions by Congress.

REGULATION

17.4 Explain government regulation and why regulations change.

The federal government plays an important regulatory role where markets do not operate to protect the public; these include things like food, drug, and product safety; the many unsafe and exploitative practices of financial institutions; air and water pollution; deep-water oil drilling; and regulation of utility rates where companies have monopoly power.

The deregulation fervor of the 1980s and 1990s was halted by the reaction to the flood of unsafe products from abroad, the collapse of the financial system because of the unregulated practices of many of its leading firms, and the oil spill disaster in the Gulf of Mexico, and the demand that government do more to protect the public. In the Trump era we are seeing renewed pushes for deregulation.

FEDERAL SAFETY NET PROGRAMS

17.5 Describe the major federal safety net programs and assess their effectiveness.

The major distinction among safety net programs is between programs that are based on insurance principles (Social Security and Medicare) and means-tested programs (SNAP and Medicaid) that are based on need.

Social insurance programs like Social Security, Medicare, and unemployment compensation are funded by a payroll tax on the earnings of individuals who may receive benefits; such benefits are based on their lifetime contributions.

Social Security and Medicare have proven very successful and are highly popular. Both programs primarily benefit older Americans.

Means-tested programs distribute benefits on the basis of need to those who can prove that their income is low enough to qualify. These programs are funded by general income tax revenues.

The United States reformed its welfare program in 1996. TANF has been successful in shrinking the welfare rolls, but the degree to which it has helped lift former recipients out of poverty has not been impressive.

HEALTH CARE POLICY

17.6 Explain the key provisions of the Affordable Care Act and the challenges it has faced.

The ACA was a major reform of the U.S. health care system that originally required everyone to have health insurance (either from the employer, the government, or purchased on their own). The insurance mandate was removed in 2017.

To help make insurance more affordable to many, the ACA subsidizes individuals and small businesses who cannot afford to buy private health insurance and funded the expansion of Medicaid.

The ACA made it so that insurance companies are no longer allowed to deny coverage to people with preexisting conditions or to place lifetime limits on benefits.

Since its passage, the ACA has faced a number of obstacles including constitutional challenges to the insurance mandate, the Medicaid expansion, and its coverage requirements. The Republican controlled congress in concert with the Trump administration, have worked to limit the effectiveness of the ACA.

THE AMERICAN SAFETY NET IN CONTEXT

17.7 Compare and contrast systems of social safety nets across countries.

The American welfare system is considerably different from those of other rich democracies. The United States system is smaller, less comprehensive, less redistributive, and tilted more toward the benefit of the elderly.

Structural and political linkage factors explain most of the differences. Federalism and the decentralization of power in our constitutional system are important in this story, as is the prevailing political culture that celebrates individualism and is uncomfortable with big government. The power of business and the weakness of organized labor are also important.

LEARN THE TERMS

Affordable Care Act (ACA) The far-reaching health care reform law passed in 2010. The Act was aimed at increasing access to health insurance for all Americans and driving down the rising, burdensome cost of health care in the United States.

appropriations committees The committees in the House and Senate that set specific spending levels in the budget for federal programs and agencies.

balance of trade The annual difference between payments and receipts between a country and its trading partners.

budget deficit Occurs when the government is bringing in less money than it is spending.

budget surplus Occurs when the government is bringing in more money than it is spending.

Children's Health Insurance Program (CHIP) Program that pays for health care services for children in households above the poverty line but below 133 percent to 400 percent of the poverty line, depending on the state.

depression A severe and persistent drop in economic activity.

deregulation The process of diminishing regulatory requirements for business.

discretionary spending That part of the federal budget that is not tied to a formula that automatically provides money to some program or purpose.

Earned Income Tax Credit (EITC) A provision in the U.S. Tax Code that allows low-income individuals with at least one child to claim a credit against taxes owed or, for some, to receive a direct cash transfer from the IRS.

entitlement Government benefits distributed automatically to citizens who qualify on the basis of a set of guidelines set by law; for example, Americans older than 65 are entitled to Medicare coverage.

Federal Reserve Board (The Fed) The body responsible for deciding the monetary policies of the United States.

fiscal policy Government efforts to affect overall output and incomes in the economy through spending and taxing policies.

Great Recession The economic crisis that officially began in December 2007. The recession was triggered by the bursting of a housing bubble that led to a financial crisis and cuts in consumer spending. Though it officially ended in June 2009, its after effects have been long-lasting.

gross domestic product (GDP) Monetary value of all goods and services produced in a nation each year, excluding income residents earn abroad.

Income Tax Taxes levied on the annual incomes of individuals and corporations. In the United States those who make more money pay a higher tax rate than those who make less money.

inflation A condition of rising prices and reduced purchasing power.

Keynesians Advocates of government programs to stimulate economic activity through tax cuts and government spending.

mandatory spending Government spending that does not go through the annual appropriations process because it is tied to a formula that determines the amount to be spent. Primarily includes Social Security and Medicare.

means-tested programs Social insurance programs that require recipients demonstrate need before getting benefits.

Medicaid Program administered by the states that pays for health care services for the poor; jointly funded by the federal government and the states.

Medicare Federal health insurance program for the elderly and the disabled.

monetarists Advocates of a minimal government role in the economy, limited to managing the growth of the money supply.

monetary policy Government efforts to affect the supply of money and the level of interest rates in the economy.

national debt The total outstanding debt of the federal government; the sum total of all annual budget deficits and surpluses.

negative externalities The harmful effects of economic activities on third parties.

Office of Management and Budget (OMB) Part of the Executive Office of the President charged with helping the president prepare the annual budget request to Congress; also performs oversight of rule making by executive branch agencies.

payroll tax Tax levied on salaries and wages for Social Security and Medicare.

poverty line The federal government's calculation of the amount of income families of various sizes need to stay out of poverty. In 2018 it was $25,100 for a family of four.

progressive taxation A tax system in which higher-income individuals are taxed at a higher rate than those who make less.

recession A slowing of the economy defined by two quarters or more of declining gross domestic product.

regressive taxation A tax system in which lower-income individuals are taxed at a higher rate than those who make more.

regulation The issuing of rules by government agencies with the aim of reducing the scale of negative externalities produced by private firms.

social insurance Government programs that provide services or income support in proportion to the amount of mandatory contributions made by individuals to a government trust fund.

Social Security Social insurance program that provides income support for the elderly, those with disabilities, and family survivors of working Americans.

Supplemental Nutritional Assistance Program (SNAP) Federal program that helps Americans that fall below a certain income to buy food for themselves and their families. Frequently referred to as "food stamps."

Temporary Assistance to Needy Families (TANF) Federal welfare program that provides income and services to poor families via state block grants. The program has benefit time limits and a work requirement.

SYRIAN DISASTER

The Syrian civil war has killed hundreds of thousands of Syrians and displaced millions inside Syria and into Lebanon, Turkey, Jordan, and Europe. It will take a very long time to sort out the differences between Sunnis and Shiites, Iran and Saudi Arabia, Israel and Iran (and Hezbollah), Turkey and the Assad regime in Syria, and the United States and Russia, and to diminish the threat of ISIS before a settlement can be reached that will make rebuilding possible. *Should the United States stick to its current strategy in Syria, change it, or simply withdraw from the conflict?*

FOREIGN AND NATIONAL DEFENSE POLICIES

CHAPTER OUTLINE AND LEARNING OBJECTIVES

FOREIGN AND NATIONAL SECURITY POLICIES AND DEMOCRACY

18.1 Assess the extent to which foreign and national defense policy making can be democratic.

DIMENSIONS OF AMERICA'S SUPERPOWER STATUS

18.2 Examine the foundations of America's status as a world superpower.

AMERICAN SUPERPOWER: STRATEGIC ALTERNATIVES

18.3 Assess the goals and strategies of American foreign and national defense policies.

PROBLEMS OF THE POST–COLD WAR WORLD

18.4 Evaluate problems facing the United States in the post–Cold War world.

WHO MAKES FOREIGN AND NATIONAL DEFENSE POLICIES?

18.5 Describe the roles of the principal architects of U.S. foreign and national defense policies.

The Struggle for Democracy

THE SYRIAN NIGHTMARE

President Obama ran for office in 2008 and again in 2012 pledging that he would end substantial U.S. military involvement in Afghanistan and Iraq where two wars he inherited from George W. Bush languished. Most American troops were indeed gone by the end of 2015, as promised, though neither Iraq nor Afghanistan were anywhere near stable by then. The resurgence of the Taliban in 2015 and 2016 slowed troop withdrawals, leaving close to 10,000 soldiers in Afghanistan in early 2016, primarily in support, training, and advisory roles. Fearful of being drawn into another military quagmire where the goals of the intervention would likely be elusive, as in Vietnam, Afghanistan, and Iraq, President Obama resisted calls from many quarters to intervene in the Syrian civil war that broke out after President Bashar al-Assad's army attacked peaceful anti-regime protestors during the late summer and fall of 2011. Some believed then and still believe today that had President Obama provided safe refuge for anti-regime forces by deploying U.S. aircraft to enforce a "no fly zone" against Assad, the civil war would not have spun out of control. Assad would not have remained the leader of Syria, and Russia and Iran would not have been able to gain bigger military and political footholds in Syria, which they eventually did. There is no way of knowing.

But spin out of control it did, with terrible human consequences. It is estimated that more than 500,000 Syrians have died so far in the conflict through the end of 2017—with the war still raging—that almost 7 million have become internally displaced from their homes in Syria and living in terrible conditions, and that over 5.5 million have become refugees, fleeing to neighboring countries, mainly Lebanon, Jordan, and the Kurdish-controlled areas of Syria and Iraq, with hundreds of thousands desperately seeking refuge in Europe as well, with most wanting to reach Germany or Scandinavia.[1]

The brutality of the Assad regime—overwhelmingly made up of Alawites, part of Syria's Shia minority—and its Shiite allies Hezbollah and Iran, who supplied weapons, fighters, and battlefield leadership, and Russia, which used airstrikes to pulverize rebel groups, pushed many Sunnis into the ranks of extremist groups, including al-Qaeda-affiliated Jabhat al-Nusra and the Islamic State (ISIS or ISIL). ISIS had seized large swaths of Iraqi and Syrian territory in an attempt to create a self-proclaimed Sunni Islamic caliphate. Non-ISIS anti-Assad rebel groups turned to Turkey, Saudi Arabia, and the Gulf states for assistance, but these countries never matched the level of commitment or effectiveness of Iran and Russia.

For its part, ISIS—skilled in the use of television, film, and social media—spread its ideology of hatred for the West. As "protector" of Sunnis against Shiite apostates (the vast majority of Muslims in the world are Sunni), ISIS attracted thousands of fighters from all regions of the world and gained sympathizers and followers almost everywhere, including in western democracies such as France, Britain, Germany, Belgium, and the United States. Unfortunately, ISIS did not confine its activities to Iraq and Syria, as its recruits and sympathizers carried out devastating terrorist attacks in Iraq, Paris, Nice, Berlin, London, Istanbul, Barcelona, and the United States, including San Bernardino, California, New York City, and Orlando, Florida.

The Syrian civil war has not only become a nightmare for the Syrian people, but highlights many of the enduring conflicts and problems that will challenge the United States and its national security and foreign policy leaders—most especially, American presidents—in the years ahead. How deeply should the United States get involved at all in these kinds of civil war situations? President Obama wanted Assad gone but did not create a "no fly" zone to protect civilians, gave some aid to rebel groups, and used airpower to shrink ISIS and damage the Assad regime, but would not put American boots on the ground except for special operations units to help rebel groups. President Trump has been even less willing than Obama to become deeply engaged. He continued to hit ISIS positions with airpower and twice attacked Syrian chemical weapons facilities after Assad used internationally outlawed chemical weapons against rebellious Syrian citizens, but to little effect. Nor did he insist that Russia decrease its role of protecting the Assad regime.

The war has pitted Sunni against Shiite in Iraq and Syria and more broadly throughout the Muslim world. It has increased tensions between Saudi Arabia, the principle Sunni power in the Middle East, and a close ally of the United States and Iran, the leading Shiite power, tensions which have spilled over into yet another brutal civil war in desperately poor Yemen. Having backed the winning side in the Syrian civil war and adding to and expanding its military bases there, Russia has increased its influence in the Middle East and will likely be as important as the United States in shaping the future of the region. Hezbollah, mortal enemy of Israel and the de facto leader of Lebanon, emerges from Syria with more battle-hardened and well-equipped troops on the Jewish state's northern border. With the United States seemingly less and less interested in involvement in Syria, except for bombing runs against the few ISIS targets remaining there, Turkey has increased its footprint in Syria near its border with Syria and taken military action against Kurdish fighters supported in the past by the United States. Each of these conflicts adds to the humanitarian crises of civilian deaths, internal displacements, and refugees and what to do about them.

*　*　*　*　*

What American policy should be in the face of all of this is the subject of increasingly intense debate in the United States, which has not only pitted Democrats against Republicans in Congress and on the presidential campaign trail but exposed differences within each of the parties about the best way forward: withdrawal, limited engagement, escalation of the air campaign, or American "boots on the ground." Presidents are constitutionally in charge of U.S. foreign and defense policies, but they do not always get their way as events and the interests of other actors overtake the best of intentions and carefully crafted policies, or hastily tweeted ones.

In this chapter, we examine American foreign and national security goals and policies, the nation's resources for achieving them, the constraints on America's freedom of action, and how policies in these areas are made. As always, we remain interested in whether the processes of making and carrying out these policies arise from democratic processes and whether Americans get the sorts of policies they want.

THINKING CRITICALLY **ABOUT THIS CHAPTER**

This chapter is about American foreign and military policies, how these policies are made, and how they affect Americans and others.

APPLYING THE **FRAMEWORK**

You will see in this chapter how foreign and military policies are the product of the interaction of *structural factors* (such as American economic and military power, and globalization); political *linkage factors* (such as the choices the media make about foreign news coverage, public opinion about what the U.S. role in the world ought to be, and what various interest groups want the government to do); and *governmental factors* (such as the objectives and actions of presidents, members of Congress, and important executive branch agencies such as the Central Intelligence Agency and the Joint Chiefs of Staff).

USING THE **DEMOCRACY STANDARD**

Using the evaluative tools you learned in Chapter 1, you will see that foreign policy is not always made with the members of the public being as fully informed or as involved as they are in domestic affairs. You will see why this is so, ask whether policies would be better if they were made more democratically, and investigate how the members of the public might play a larger role.

FOREIGN AND NATIONAL SECURITY POLICIES AND DEMOCRACY

18.1 Assess the extent to which foreign and national defense policy making can be democratic.

Unlike domestic policy making, presidents and the executive branch tend to play a much more important part in foreign and defense policy formulation and implementation than Congress primarily because the Constitution lodges most responsibilities and powers for foreign and military affairs there. The Constitution makes the president commander in chief of the nation's armed forces as well as its chief diplomat. Consequently, in the perpetual tug-of-war between presidents and Congress, presidents usually prevail in national defense and foreign policy matters, especially during crises.

Groups and actors such as interest groups and the public are sometimes set aside in favor of the **national interest** as defined by a small number of national security advisors, intelligence officials, military leaders, other executive branch officials, and, most especially, the president. While public opinion can have an important influence on foreign and national defense policy matters, in the short run and medium run, it often is simply ignored. In crisis situations, citizens, whose opinions are sometimes reshaped by government leaders,[2] often "rally 'round the flag," similarly accepting a president's actions, at least as long as the results seem good and little dissent is heard. When things go wrong or seem to be going wrong in the foreign and defense policy sphere, domestic politics can return with a vengeance to the national stage, as when, in the cases of both the Vietnam and the Iraq wars, public support eventually dwindled.

Involvement by ordinary citizens in foreign and defense policy is also diminished by the sheer complexity of international matters, their remoteness from day-to-day life, and the unpredictability of other countries' actions. Also, much of foreign policy is influenced by fundamental factors that are continually in flux, such as the relative power and resources of the United States and its economic interests abroad. All these aspects of foreign and defense policy, taken together, tend to make the public's

national interest

What is of benefit to the nation as a whole.

STOP THE WAR

Here are two demonstrations, each part of a larger anti-war movement, that had very different impacts on American policy. The anti-Vietnam War movement—here demonstrators are shown in Washington, D.C. in 1972 in the photo on the left—eventually forced American withdrawal from that country. The movement to block the invasion of Iraq in 2003, despite the urgent pleas of these demonstrators in New York City in the photo on the right, had no impact on George W. Bush and his advisors. *Should democratically elected leaders like President Bush pay much attention to demonstrators? Or, would doing so violate the wishes of the majority that elected the president?*

convictions about foreign and military affairs less certain and more subject to revision. In military matters, in particular, the need for speed, unity, and secrecy in decision making often argue for the exclusion of the public.

At the same time, however, the exclusion of the public from foreign and defense policy is far from total. The American public has probably always played a larger part in the making of foreign policy than some observers have imagined, and its role has become increasingly important in the areas of trade, economic crisis management, immigration, and global environmental protection, where government actions have noticeable impacts on Americans' economic well-being. When the International Monetary Fund (IMF) asked its most important members, including the United States, to increase contributions to a rescue fund to fight the European debt crisis in 2011 and 2012, President Obama declined, knowing full well that the American public, which was suffering through its own economic troubles, would be disinclined to do so.

DIMENSIONS OF AMERICA'S SUPERPOWER STATUS

18.2 Examine the foundations of America's status as a world superpower.

In the autumn of 1990, the United States sent more than half a million troops, twelve hundred warplanes, and six aircraft carriers to the Persian Gulf region to roll back Iraq's invasion of Kuwait. In 1999, the United States supplied almost all the pilots, airplanes, ordnance, supplies, and intelligence for a NATO-led (North Atlantic Treaty Organization) bombing campaign to force the Serbian military out of Kosovo province in the former Yugoslavia. American armed forces were again called into action in Afghanistan in very short order following the 9/11 terrorist attacks on the United States. In 2003, the United States invaded Iraq, where, in less than four weeks, Iraq's regular army and its Republican Guard had been routed, nominal control of all its major cities, including Baghdad, had been secured, and the Saddam Hussein regime had been removed from power. In 2011, while still fighting in Iraq and Afghanistan—where initial victories had turned into long counterinsurgency wars—the United States supplied intelligence, mid-air refueling, missiles, munitions, and air support for the NATO "no-fly zone" and for "civilian protection" missions that supported the overthrow of the brutal regime of Muammar Gaddafi. (A cruel civil war followed Gaddafi's ouster). Additionally, U.S. special forces have ongoing operation against jihadist groups Boko Haram in Nigeria, ISIS in Iraq and Syria, al-Shabab in Somalia, and Ansar al-Dine in Mali.

For many years, the United States was the world's reigning **superpower**, the only nation strong enough militarily and economically to project its power into any area of the globe. (American armed forces have been used abroad with a frequency that might surprise most Americans; see the timeline in Figure 18.1.) To a large extent, this remains true today, though a newly aggressive Russia and a rising China are posing serious challenges to this long-term dominance. Russia has been modernizing its military and using it more frequently in places such as Georgia, Chechnya, Crimea, Eastern Ukraine, and Syria. China is modernizing its military even more aggressively than Russia and is seeking to bring close neighbors under its wing and claiming for its own huge portions of the South China Sea. To be sure, neither Russia nor China yet approaches the global scale and scope of U.S. military bases, alliances, and operations. This section examines the foundations of American superpower status and how some of these foundations are beginning to erode.

superpower
A nation with the military, economic, and political resources to project force anywhere in the world.

American Superpower: Structural Foundations

A nation's place in the international system is largely determined by its *relative* economic, military, and cultural power in the world. Since the end of World War II in 1945, the United States has enjoyed strong advantages over other countries in all three areas, although, for reasons explored below, U.S. advantages have diminished in recent years.[3]

FIGURE 18.1 TIMELINE: SIGNIFICANT AMERICAN FOREIGN MILITARY OPERATIONS AND CONFLICTS, 1940–PRESENT

Timeline does not include foreign interventions by agencies such as the CIA that have not involved the armed forces of the United States.

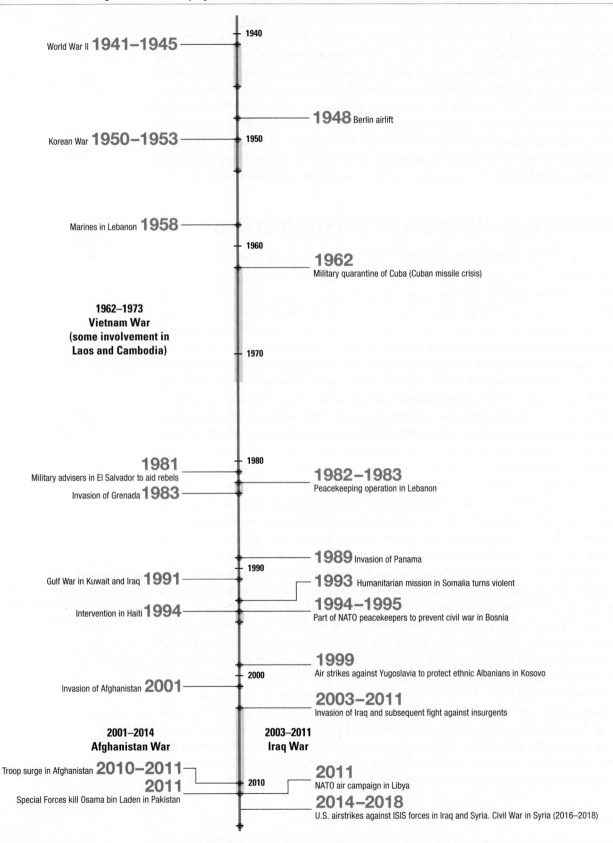

SOURCE: Data from Pearson Education, publishing on Infoplease.com.

ECONOMIC POWER   For seven decades following the end of World War II in 1945, the United States has been the largest and most dynamic economy in the world. In 2016, the United States had a population of a little more than 322 million people—considerably fewer than China's 1.40 billion or India's roughly 1.32 billion— but enough to support the world's largest economy, measured by exchange rates, with an annual gross domestic product (GDP) of $18.6 trillion. U.S. GDP is just a little less than the GDP of the next three largest economies of the world combined: China, Japan, and Germany (see Figure 18.2) though slightly smaller than the GDP of the 28-member European Union ($19.0 trillion). U.S. GDP in 2016, measured in U.S. dollars, was about 60 percent larger and seven times larger on a per-capita basis than fast-rising China. However, when GDP is measured in purchasing price power, which takes into account the relative price of goods and services in a country, China became the world's largest economy in 2015 and lengthened its lead over the United States in 2016.[4] Another measure of economic clout—a combination of GDP, trade, and net foreign investment—had the United States and China about even in 2015.[5]

Starting in the 1990s, U.S.-headquartered companies established preeminence in the economic sectors that count the most in the new global economy: telecommunications, mass entertainment, biotechnology, software, finance, e-commerce, business services, transportation, and computer chips. Despite the financial sector's 2008 disaster and the Great Recession associated with it, many U.S.-headquartered companies have continued to prosper globally, even as European-, Russian-, Chinese-, and Indian-based companies have improved their competitive positions. Still, American corporations lead the pack, with Apple, Google, Microsoft, Coca-Cola, and Amazon at the top, with seven of the world's top ten "best brands" headquartered in the United States.[6]

The United States also remains the top player in global financial markets. The global market share of Wall Street firms, for example, has actually expanded in recent years. American fund managers in 2015, moreover, controlled about 55 percent of all assets under management in the world. The U.S. Federal Reserve remains the top

FIGURE 18.2   ECONOMIC LEADERS RANKED BY GDP, 2016 (IN TRILLIONS OF CONSTANT U.S. DOLLARS)

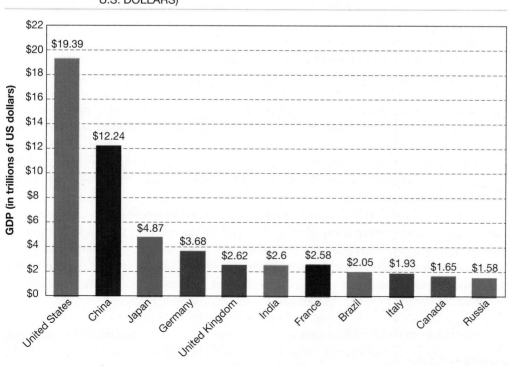

SOURCE: Data from Economy Watch, GDP (Current Prices, U.S. Dollars) Data for Year 2015, All Countries.

CELEBRATING CHINA'S POWER

The Chinese leadership used the 2008 Beijing Olympic Games to announce the emergence of China as a power on the world stage. Although the government squelched domestic and foreign dissidents, many of whom were protesting Chinese actions in Tibet and Sudan, the games had the intended effect. The spectacular opening and closing ceremonies were held in the stunning "bird's nest" stadium pictured here. *Do you believe that the grandeur of the opening and closing ceremonies of the Beijing Olympics and the excitement of the games worked to make Chinese people forget the controversy and outcry leading up to them? Do other countries, even democracies like Brazil, use the Olympics to turn attention away from national problems?*

terrorism

The use of deadly violence against civilians to further some political goal.

player in the global monetary system and the dollar continues, despite recent challenges from the Euro and the Chinese renminbi, to be the main currency of international trade and commercial transactions.[7]

The fact that major American corporations are increasingly global affects U.S. foreign policy. For the largest of those corporations, a substantial portion of their revenues comes from sales abroad, much of their manufacturing takes place in other countries, and many of the parts for products manufactured domestically are imported. And in industries such as oil and petrochemicals, many of the sources of raw materials are outside our borders (though the natural gas boom and new oil recovery methods have turned the United States into a net exporter of these primary products.) Because American businesses can be found almost anywhere, American national interests can also be said to exist almost anywhere. It follows that American officials are attentive to potential trouble spots and threats around the globe. **Terrorism**—whether the threat is to embassies and consulates or to private American companies and their employees—is certainly a worrisome menace. But economic threats also include actions of other governments that challenge U.S. access to resources and markets or that violate the intellectual property rights of American companies. Alone or in combination, fines levied by the European Union on American producers; cyber spying on the plans of U.S. firms; and the counterfeit production of American movies, software, and pharmaceuticals—often tainted—in China have the potential to damage American economic interests.

MILITARY POWER   Enormous economic strength and a commitment to preserving the global order that emerged after World War II allowed the United States to field the most powerful armed forces in the world. The scale of American military superiority as well as the nation's ability to deploy and use these resources is orders of magnitude

FIGURE 18.3 EXPENDITURES FOR NATIONAL DEFENSE, 2017 (IN BILLIONS OF CURRENT U.S. DOLLARS)

The national defense budget of the United States is multiples greater than those of friends and potential foes alike. There is no reason to suspect this will change, although China and Russia are rapidly modernizing their military forces.

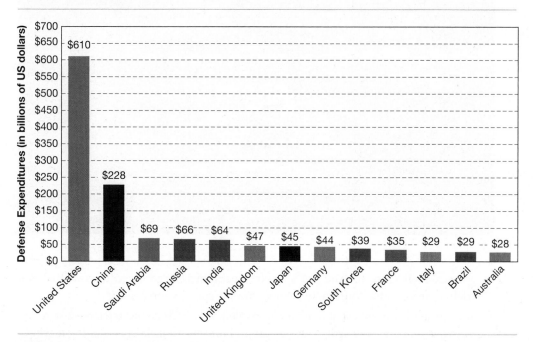

NOTE: The graph does not include costs for combat operations in Iraq or Afghanistan nor spending on nuclear weapons.

SOURCE: Stockholm International Peace Research Institute, 2018 Fact Sheet.

beyond that of any existing or potential rival, though China is making up ground. Indicators of the disproportionality of U.S. military power[8] are numerous and convincing:

- The U.S. defense budget exceeds that of all other NATO countries (including the United Kingdom, France, Germany, Italy, and others), Russia, Saudi Arabia China, Japan, India, Brazil, South Korea, and Australia combined (see Figure 18.3) and accounts for about 35 percent of all military spending in the world. The United States has maintained this vast lead despite the ramping up of defense spending by China and Russia. America's lead will actually increase over the next few years. Donald Trump's budget request for Fiscal Year 2018, passed by Congress, proposed that the United States spend almost $750 billion a year on national defense from 2019 to 2023.

- U.S. naval power is unrivaled, especially its ability to project military power all over the globe with aircraft carriers. In 2018, it has nineteen aircraft carriers in operation, including ten nuclear powered super-carriers. France has five carriers; Japan has three; Britain, Italy, and India have two each. Potentially hostile powers Russia and China, each have two carriers. China has several in the pipeline.[9] The United States has more submarines than any other country—including the stealthy Seawolf-class, nuclear-powered submarine—one reason China is focusing on anti-submarine missiles and building its own submarine fleet. And, the United States has three of the latest Zumwalt-class stealth destroyers deployed in the Asia-Pacific region, called by some "the world's most advanced surface ship."[10]

- U.S. air power is unrivaled. It has more advanced fighter aircraft and bombers, many of the stealth variety, than the rest of the world combined. Its aerial tanker fleet allows these aircraft to reach any target in the world. These aircraft also have the advantage of carrying a varied arsenal of "smart" munitions. In addition, the United States leads the world in the number, variety, and lethality of unmanned drone aircraft, though other countries are closing the gap. No other country

DOMINATING THE SEAS

The United States deploys ten carrier groups similar to this one supporting the *USS Ronald Reagan*; no other nation has a single carrier group. Despite the disproportionate naval strength, many private sector and government leaders have been demanding that the United States increase its naval capabilities in this area.

Does this make sense to you? Do we have sufficient naval strength to guard against most threats to American interests? Can we increase naval strength without adverse effects on funding for other important national priorities?

comes even close to America's airlift capabilities; large cargo aircraft that can deliver troops and equipment to most trouble spots when needed.

- U.S. ground warfare capabilities are unrivaled. While China has the largest standing army, it is not as well armed as U.S. ground forces and lacks many of the logistical and technological capabilities of American forces, though it is being modernized rapidly. In addition, no other nation comes close to matching America's armored forces, which include approximately 9,000 M1 Abrams tanks firing smart munitions.

- U.S. electronic warfare capabilities are considerable. These capabilities include, among other things, global positioning systems to guide smart weapons to their targets, self-guided anti-tank missiles that seek out enemy tanks, sophisticated jamming systems to confuse anti-aircraft guns and missiles, and underwater sensing systems to track submarines. Russia and China are working furiously to close the gap.

- The United States and Russia have the world's largest strategic nuclear arsenals, with each having 1,548 deployed warheads. Each also has large non-deployed nuclear weapons, the United States with 4,000, and Russia with 4,500. Each can deliver these warheads to their targets by strategic bombers, land-based intercontinental ballistic missiles, and submarines, the so-called nuclear triad. France has 300 warheads; China, 270; and the UK, 120. Though they are not members of the Nuclear Nonproliferation Treaty—and don't report on their stockpile of nuclear weapons—arms control experts estimate that Pakistan has 140 nuclear warheads; India, 130; and Israel, 80.[11]

- The United States has by far the largest permanent and sizeable military-base network deployed in nearly every part of the world,[12] though it is closing some bases because of changes in strategic doctrine, tighter budgets, the end of military operations in Iraq, and the rapid drawdown of forces in Afghanistan and Syria. Still, as of 2015, the United States had more than 800 bases in eighty countries, according to the Pentagon.[13] Russia has nine overseas bases, including a recently expanded one in Syria, while China opened its first overseas base in 2017 in Djibouti in the Horn of Africa. China also has been extended its practice of expanding islands in the South China Sea and placing small bases on several of them.

- As evidenced by the Stuxnet computer virus that damaged equipment and software used in Iran's uranium-enrichment program and significantly set back that country's nuclear weapons program, the United States has powerful cyber-warfare capabilities; Stuxnet is widely credited to be the product of a joint U.S.–Israel effort.

WARNING RUSSIA

A U.S. tank crew awaits the start of joint military exercises with units from the nation of Georgia in 2016. The exercises are part of a strategy by the U.S. and NATO warning Russia not to attack countries on its border over which it once held sway. President Donald Trump has shown his displeasure with NATO on numerous occasions and has often said how much he admires President Vladimir Putin, so it is unclear how much longer exercises of the type shown in this photo will go on. *What do you think of the U.S. playing such a role in the world? Do policies like these advance the national interest and the well-being of Americans, or would we be better off retreating from some of these global responsibilities?*

Most experts believe the United States and Israel rank first and second in cyber war capabilities, with Russia, China, Iran, and North Korea important players as well.[14]

NATO and Allies as Force Multipliers   The United States would be the world's strongest military power, even without the assistance of others. However, the United States is part of the NATO military alliance of 28 European and North American countries. Though the United States supplies three-fourths of the NATO budget and spends the largest portion of its GDP on defense—a fact that has displeased a succession of American presidents, but most especially Donald Trump—NATO includes such significant military powers as Great Britain, France, and Italy, all of whom are nuclear powers with substantial navies, sophisticated weaponry, and well-trained combat personnel. Japan, South Korea, and Australia have highly regarded armed forces. Though not members of NATO, they are close allies who have long cooperated with the American military. These partnerships enhance the military capabilities lead of the United States over potential foes. It is not yet apparent whether Trump's verbal and tweeted criticisms of U.S. allies will have long-term effects on the strength of these military alliances.

Beyond Military Capabilities   The superiority of U.S. weapons systems and troops does not always result in attainment of national defense and foreign policy goals nor the ability to prevail in all conflicts, in all places, at all times. Here are a few factors that affect U.S. military outcomes:

- The president may be unwilling to fully commit the U.S. military in situations where the costs might far outweigh the benefits. President Obama, for example, decided to conduct very limited airstrikes in Syria and against ISIS. He sent only 250 ground troops into Iraq and Syria in spring 2016, hoping to avoid entanglement in another long war in the Middle East where American casualties might be high. He also refused to commit armed forces to the defense of Ukraine when Russia invaded it, first taking the Crimea, then large swaths of the eastern parts of the country. President Donald Trump promised during his campaign to focus on reviving the American economy and lifting the middle class and eschewing unnecessary foreign military entanglements. True to his word, he did not use America's military might to turn back Russian aggression in Ukraine or China's expansion of militarized islands in the South China Sea. Though he twice launched cruise missile attacks on Syrian military targets after the Assad regime used chemical weapons against rebel groups in 2017 and 2018, the attacks were limited in scale and scope, carefully avoiding targeting Russian troops in Syria, and doing little to set back Assad's chemical weapons capabilities.

asymmetric warfare
Unconventional tactics used by a combatant against an enemy with superior conventional military capabilities.

- The size and quality of America's armed forces almost guarantee that the United States will prevail in any large and protracted conventional war. However, we have learned that resourceful enemies, using **asymmetric warfare** tactics and weapons—roadside bombs, rocket-propelled grenades, sniper rifles, cyber warfare, and AK-47 assault rifles—can inflict tremendous damage on U.S. conventional forces and on forces allied with us, as happened in Iraq and Afghanistan. Iran has threatened on several occasions to take on American naval forces in the Persian Gulf, for example, with swarms of rocket-firing speedboats.

- Defense policies can fail no matter what resources are mobilized. For years, the United States sent billions of dollars and military personnel to train and equip forces fighting against jihadists. Almost without exception, these forces failed at key moments when confronted by a determined enemy. American-backed militias disintegrated against ISIS fighters in Anbar Province in Iraq in 2015. In Kunduz Province in Afghanistan in 2015 and 2016, American-backed forces did little to stop the advance of Taliban fighters. American efforts to arm moderate, anti-Assad rebels in Syria produced few fighters and few effective units during the long Syrian civil war.[15]

- Conventional and strategic military power may not be terribly useful in rooting out terrorists. A terrorist enemy is not a country—though the Islamic State once controlled considerable territory in Iraq and Syria and claimed to be one—but instead comprises loosely organized shadow cells that may best be uprooted by police investigations, intelligence-gathering operations in cooperation with other countries, and perhaps special forces operations like the one that killed Osama bin Laden in Pakistan in 2011. Nuclear submarines and high-tech tanks are unlikely to be useful against such enemies.

- Though militarily much weaker on paper than the United States, countries can attempt to even the odds by focusing on narrower goals than attaining victory in an all-out war and developing technologies to support these goals. China, for example, has been developing a strategy to keep the mighty American navy well away from Chinese shores, with an emphasis on long-range, land-based anti-ship missiles, a big buildup of its naval forces equipped with anti-surface ship weaponry, and a rapid expansion in its submarine fleet equipped with smart ordinance.[16]

So military capabilities matter a great deal but do not guarantee that foreign policy and national security goals will always be met.

soft power
Influence in world affairs that derives from the attractiveness to others of a nation's culture, products, and way of life.

SOFT POWER In assessing superpower status and capabilities, we should not underestimate the influence of what some have called America's **soft power**: the attractiveness of its culture, ideology, values, institutions, and way of life for many people living in other countries.[17] As political scientist Joseph Nye has pointed out, it is important for the U.S. position in the world that more than a half million foreign students study in American colleges and universities every year (the number is now over 1 million); that people in other countries flock to American entertainment and cultural products; that English has become the language of the Internet, business, science, and technology; and that the openness and opportunity of American society are admired by many people around the world.[18] It also helps that seventeen of the top twenty-five universities in the world are here and that the United States remains the center of scientific and technological research and development.[19] If this very openness and opportunity place the United States in a good position to prosper in the new global, information-based economy, then U.S. soft power enhances its harder-edged economic and military powers.

Soft power is no easy thing to measure, though *Portland Strategic Communications consultancy* has a highly regarded index called "The SoftPower30," which it compiles using a panel of experts from a variety of fields, rates countries on fifty indicators—everything from the effectiveness and openness of its governance and the standard of living of its population to the appeal of its cuisine, popular culture, architecture, companies, and attractiveness as a tourist destination. In 2017, the United States was third in the world on the SoftPower30 index, just behind France and Britain, and slightly ahead of Germany, a very high mark indeed, and substantially higher than any of its diplomatic or military rivals. China and Russia ranked twenty-fifth and twenty-sixth, respectively.[20]

Though considerable, the U.S.'s soft power has taken some hits. The invasion of Iraq was extremely unpopular, even among our allies in the conflict, and revelations of torture on detainees in Iraq, Afghanistan, and Guantanamo—called enhanced interrogation by the Bush administration—further undermined admiration of the United States, particularly in Muslim countries such as Turkey, Jordan, and Pakistan. In addition, U.S. popularity was undermined at the perceived unilateralist tendencies of the United States under President George W. Bush, especially his renunciation of several international treaties and the proclamation of the right of the United States to take preemptive/preventive military action when the president considered it appropriate.[21]

President Barack Obama made restoring America's image and standing in the world a top priority. Both his popularity abroad[22] and changes in presidential language about America's place in the world—more negotiations with adversaries and increased collaboration with allies and international bodies—gave a big boost to U.S. favorability around much of the world compared to the George W. Bush years as did the drawdown of U.S. military action in Iraq and Afghanistan. President Donald Trump's denigration of long-time allies, NATO, and the Iran nuclear deal, as well as his executive orders to temporarily ban entry to people from seven predominantly Muslim countries, has hurt regard for the United States abroad, but it is too early to tell how lasting these developments will be. The Pew Research Center, for example, reported a drop of 15 percent points in favorable views of the United States from the end of the Obama Administration to the first months of the Trump Administration, as well as 32 percentage point decline worldwide in confidence in the U.S. President.[23] American colleges and universities have reported a drop-off in applications for admission from non-U.S. students, with higher education officials saying that potential students are feeling less welcome in the United States after Donald Trump became president.[24]

America's soft power advantages as a responsible and trusted leader of the world's trade and financial system has also taken hits. Most important was the financial collapse in 2008, which most political and economic leaders around the world blamed on the reckless behavior of U.S. financial firms. The prevalence of gridlock in Washington, especially on budget issues, also alarmed many as did the perceived declining influence of the United States on the International Monetary Fund and the World Bank.[25] Slow economic growth in the United States compared to China's double-digit growth from 2008 to 2014, and its continued relatively rapid growth since then, has increased for many around the world the appeal of China's state capitalism model (a society in which the economy is guided by the state), compared to the free market or free enterprise capitalism model of the American and British variety.[26]

President Donald Trump's withdrawal from the Trans-Pacific Partnership trade agreement, his threats to leave the North American Free Trade Agreement, his trade disputes with the European Union, and his insistence that the United States is being taken advantage of by other players in the global trading system, has raised doubts about American leadership of the global system. The Pew Research Center reported, for example, that favorable views of the United States across the 37 countries it periodically surveys fell from a median approval score of 67 percent in Barack Obama's final year in office to 49 percent a year-and-a-half into Donald Trump's presidency.[27]

Figure 18.4 shows how favorably selected countries view the United States as of 2017. Note that even among American allies, perceptions of the United State vary widely. Approval of the United States in Germany is only 35 percent while approval in Israel is 81 percent. This reflects the complex and changing role the United States is playing in the world as well as the differing views of American influence abroad.

FIGURE 18.4 FAVORABLE VIEWS OF THE UNITED STATES, 2017 (SELECTED COUNTRIES)

Favorable views of the United States are found among many (though not all) NATO members and close allies but also are quite high in Africa. Not surprisingly, given U.S. military involvement in many parts of their world, America is not viewed very favorably in Muslim countries. The rise of Great Power competition between the United States and China and the United States and Russia has undermined favorable attitudes among their populations, especially the latter.

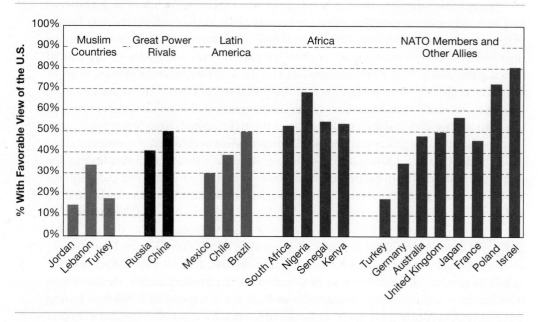

NOTE: Turkey is both a Muslim country and a member of NATO. China data are from 2016, data for all other countries from 2017.

SOURCE: Pew Research Center, Global Indicators Database: Opinion of the United States, http://www.pewglobal.org/database/indicator/1/survey/all/

AMERICAN SUPERPOWER: STRATEGIC ALTERNATIVES

18.3 Assess the goals and strategies of American foreign and national defense policies.

The United States must make a number of decisions about how to use its considerable power.

What Goals for American Power?

Like the leaders of any other country in the international system, foreign and military policy makers, and most especially the president, take as one of their primary duties the defense of the nation against real or potential attacks. This goes almost without saying. And like the leaders of any other country in the international system, American leaders try to first define and then advance and protect the **national interest**. Components of the national interest are hard to clearly define, to be sure, and people disagree about what they might be, but at a minimum they include such things as protecting American citizens when they are living or traveling abroad and ensuring that American firms are treated fairly when operating in other countries, that vital raw materials are available to consumers and firms, and that markets remain open to American goods and services.

But what about the goal of spreading American values? Many Americans, including many political leaders, have believed that the United States has a special mission to improve the world by spreading liberty and representative democracy; many others have said that improving the world also involves spreading free enterprise and open markets. While President George W. Bush perhaps more clearly articulated these goals as essential elements of American foreign policy than other recent presidents have, his aspirations for American foreign policy would not have been unfamiliar to Thomas Jefferson (who referred to the United States as "the empire of liberty"), Woodrow Wilson ("the world must be made safe for democracy"), Franklin Roosevelt (the "four freedoms"), or John F. Kennedy (whose inaugural address pledged to "oppose any foe to assure the survival and success of liberty"). One scholar suggests, in fact, that while President Bush's rhetoric may have been different, "the U.S. quest for an international order based on freedom, self-determination, and open markets has changed astonishingly little."[28] President Barack Obama expressed more modest goals, bringing accusations from Republican politicians and elected officials that he wanted to diminish America's place in the world. President Donald Trump holds to an almost pure "transactional" understanding of American goals, meaning that he has endeavored to make a series of bilateral trade, diplomatic, and military deals that put American national security and economic interests first, with no apparent regard for spreading American values or institutions globally.

Finally, it has long been argued by foreign policy experts and political leaders that the dominant global power—political scientists call such countries **hegemons**[29]— must provide a range of services to the international system if the world is to enjoy any degree of stability. The hegemon does this not necessarily for altruistic reasons but because global instability may threaten the economic, military, or political position of the dominant power itself. These services have included using one's power to put down states that upset the global order, protecting the international trading system, and providing economic leadership. The Ottoman Empire played this role in the 16th century for large swatches of the known world. Before the 19th century, France and Spain played this role, with the UK playing it for much of the 19th century. Until quite recently, many believed it was the turn of the United States to play the role of hegemon.[30] It must not only protect itself from attack and pursue its own interests, but it must use its power to prevent the outbreak of regional wars (India and Pakistan, perhaps), stop the spread of **weapons of mass destruction (WMD)**, coordinate the effort to prevent pandemics, provide protection for a wide range of countries important for the world economy, protect and maintain the international trading and financial systems (i.e., patrol key shipping lanes, provide the world's reserve currency, act as the world's banker—for the most part, through the World Bank and the International Monetary Fund), and help make and enforce trade rules.

Do Americans and their leaders believe U.S. foreign policy goals should include more than national defense and a strict focus on defending national interests? Donald Trump and his supporters say they do not think so. America, in this view, has been played for a sucker, providing expensive services for countries that do not pay their fair share. It's time, in this view, to put America first. Even before Trump's election, 57 percent of Americans told Pew Research Center researchers that they want the government to deal with its own problems first, not the world's. A plurality of Americans said that the United States does too much rather than too little to help solve world problems.[31]

Nor is it certain that the United States could take on the role of hegemon even if it wanted to do so; it is not as powerful relative to other nations as it was in 1945 or 1990. Nor is it clear that rising global powers such as China, Turkey, Indonesia, Brazil, Russia, the European Union, and India want the United States to fill the role of hegemon.

hegemon
Term used to refer to the dominant power during various historical periods that takes on responsibilities for maintaining and protecting a regional or global system.

weapons of mass destruction
Nuclear, biological, or chemical weapons with the potential to cause vast harm to human populations.

How to Use American Power? Competing Viewpoints

American leaders and citizens must decide not only what goals to pursue as a **superpower** but how best to go about using America's power. The opposing viewpoints in the debate about how to use American power mainly belong to the unilateralists and the multilateralists.

unilateralists

Those who believe that the United States should "go it alone," pursuing its national interests without seeking the cooperation of other nations or multilateral institutions.

multilateralists

Those who believe the United States should use its military and diplomatic power in the world in cooperation with other nations and international organizations.

global climate change

The upset of historical climate patterns, with rising temperatures and more extreme climate events, tied to the increase in atmospheric carbon, whether caused by human activities or naturally occurring cycles.

Cold War

The period of tense relations between the United States and the Soviet Union from the late 1940s to the late 1980s.

UNILATERALISTS **Unilateralists** would have the United States pursue American national interests in the world on a "go it alone" basis, if necessary. While it might often act in concert with others, unilateralists would have the United States act on the international stage on its own terms, without asking the permission of others, or binding itself to restrictive international agreements, or following the lead of international organizations such as the United Nations. President Donald Trump has voiced strong support for this orientation to foreign affairs. Unilateralists tend to believe the United States has the capacity to maintain its position as the world's leading superpower and it need not accommodate rivals or allies if it is not in our national interest. Some unilateralists—though not President Trump—are interested in using American power to spread American values such as liberty, free enterprise, and democracy, believing these values to be universally valid and appealing. Such unilateralists do not see a contradiction between power and principle. Indeed, they believe they are inextricably woven together.[32]

MULTILATERALISTS **Multilateralists** believe American interests are compatible with the interests of others in the world and that protecting U.S. national interests requires cooperation and collaboration with other nations and international organizations. Although the United States is undeniably the most powerful nation in the world, the thinking goes, it cannot solve every important problem on its own.[33] Problems such as **global climate change**, pollution, the wider availability of the means to make weapons of mass destruction, the spread of infectious diseases, and terrorism threaten virtually every country in the world, and multilateralists insist that solving these problems will require broad cooperation and collaboration by many countries and international organizations.[34]

The multilateralist view is consistent with the idea that the needs and interests of rising powers in the developing world must be taken into consideration and accommodated on a wide range of issues. In a world characterized by what commentator Fareed Zakaria calls "the rise of the others," the United States, the argument goes, cannot and should not go it alone.[35] The others have the capacity to resist American pressures at any rate, so cooperation and collaboration seem the more sensible course.

PROBLEMS OF THE POST–COLD WAR WORLD

18.4 Evaluate problems facing the United States in the post–Cold War world.

With the end of the **Cold War**, the main concerns of that era—the possibility of global thermonuclear war, a land war in Europe against the Soviet Union, and communist takeovers of Third World countries—have disappeared from the list of foreign policy problems that concern Americans and their leaders. But a host of problems remain and new ones have arisen. We review these issues in the next several sections, keeping in mind that the debate among unilateralists and multilateralists will help shape our response to each one.

Security Issues

Traditional security concerns like the threat of direct attack by large-scale forces on American territory, the proliferation of weapons of mass destruction, political instability, and regional and interethnic conflicts are important elements on U.S. policy agendas in the post–Cold War world, but other threats, including terrorism and cyberattacks, also loom large.

POSSIBLE GREAT POWER CONFLICTS World War I, often referred to as the Great War, was a not a war waged between ideologies or ways of life, but one in which major world powers were brought to the battlefield by competition over land, resources, colonies, and national prestige. It was not a war between Christianity

and Islam, for example, or Communism and capitalism, or democracy and autocracy. Rather, in the beginning, it pitted the so-called Triple Entente of Great Britain, France, and Czarist Russia against the so-called Triple Alliance of Germany, and Austria-Hungary. Later, the United States, Italy, and Japan joined the Entente while the Ottoman Empire and Bulgaria joined the Triple Alliance. Today, many speculate that we have entered a new stage of great power rivalry that mainly pits the United States against Russia and China.[36]

Russia After the breakup of the Soviet Union left Russia's economy and once-proud military in disarray, the country avoided foreign adventures for a time and cut its nuclear and conventional arms under international treaties. In 2008, however, Russia invaded the small country of Georgia (a former Soviet Republic), serving notice that it could cause trouble if Georgia or Ukraine were allowed to join NATO. It also reminded Europe that it was eager to use its considerable reserves of oil and natural gas to wield diplomatic power in Europe and the world and cut deliveries several times to Ukraine and several European nations between 2010 and 2016.

The terrible performance of its military forces against tiny Georgia convinced Vladimir Putin to reform and modernize Russia's military, bolstered by a tripling of its defense budget since 2007, even as European NATO members decreased theirs.[37] Russia showed off its new military sophistication and aggressive new foreign and national defense posture in a number of ways. It seized Ukrainian Crimea in 2014, for example, then soon after encouraged Russian separatists in the southeastern part of the country to revolt against Ukraine, providing them with ample supplies of weapons, intelligence, and disguised Russian troops. It waged cyber warfare against Ukraine and several Baltic states once in the USSR but now NATO members. Russia also sent military jets on several occasions into NATO member airspace and has held large military exercises close to NATO borders. Western military officials claim that the number of subs Russia has deployed in the North Atlantic now rivals the numbers at the height of the Cold War, and these are part of a revamped and improved Russian submarine fleet.[38] It also has rapidly built military outposts and bases in the Arctic to make more convincing claims on the region's natural resources increasingly accessible because of global warming. Russia also intervened quite aggressively with air power in the Syrian civil war—even striking rebel groups supported by the United States—and considerably strengthened the position of its ally, President Assad. There is mounting evidence that it used its hacking prowess and clever use of social media to influence the 2016 U.S. presidential election.

Though it has cooperated with the United States in a number of areas, Russia under Putin seems determined to reassert its once great power status. Though its economy is in shambles—inefficient crony and gangster capitalism; low foreign investment; a collapse in the price of its main export commodity, oil; and an aging and shrinking population—and experts wonder how much of a military capability it can afford to maintain over the long run, Putin has shown an eagerness to use what power his nation has to advance Russian interests, even risking military conflict with NATO.[39] The dangers of such a conflict are self-evident: Russia is the leader, with the United States, in deliverable nuclear weapons and is reported to have considerable cyber-warfare capabilities.

China   If Russia may be considered a declining but dangerous power trying perhaps to relive its golden age through military means, China may be considered a rising power looking to take its place economically, culturally, and militarily alongside the United States and the West. With its huge population, fast-growing economy—for three decades, it had the fastest-growing economy in modern times, and its recent slowdown to 5 or 6 percent per annum is still much greater than that of the EU and the United States—and modernizing military, China someday may pose a security threat to the United States in the Asia-Pacific region or even globally. Some Americans have warned of a great "clash of civilizations" between the West and "Confucian" China.[40]

This seems a bit overblown, given the strong economic ties between China and the United States, but tensions do exist. Disputes over trade, the imposition of tariffs, intellectual property rights protections (on software, movies, and so on), Taiwan, Tibet, and human rights periodically cloud U.S.–Chinese relations. For years, China had been reluctant to help in reining in North Korea's nuclear program, though it played a role in setting up the Singapore meeting in 2018 of President Trump and North Korean leader Kim Jong Un on denuclearizing the Korean peninsula. It succeeded, despite American efforts to stop it, in establishing the Asian Infrastructure Development Bank to counter the World Bank, which is heavily influenced by the United States. Fifty-seven countries have joined, including Britain, Germany, Australia, and South Korea, but not Japan or the United States. Additionally, China seems to be the key player in cyberattacks on American firms, including defense

A RISING TIDE

A Filipino fisherman watches a Chinese warship patrolling disputed sections of the South China Sea.

Does it matter to American national security that China is seeking to extend its influence in areas where the United States has been dominant politically and militarily? Why?

contractors and government agencies such as the Office of Personnel Management, in an attempt to gain access to technology and other information that will aid its economic and military rise.[41]

In addition, as discussed earlier, China has been pressing its claims over territories in its region that are rich in oil and natural gas reserves, as well as fishing grounds, creating disputes with American allies including Vietnam, Taiwan, Indonesia, South Korea, and Japan. China has been transforming rock piles in the South China Sea into small artificial islands, some with military outposts and air strips to create "facts on the ground." China unsettled these and other countries further when it unilaterally extended into international waters its so-called Air Defense Identification Zone, requiring all commercial aircraft to ask China's permission to enter the zone.

Despite these many friction points, China and the United States are strong trading and manufacturing partners and their financial systems are deeply entwined, making them economically dependent on one another. Also, China is the most important purchaser of America's public and private debt in the form of Treasury bills and notes and corporate bonds. China also is where much of the manufacturing for American-based companies, such as Apple, occurs, and China exports much of what it produces to the United States. President Trump has vowed to reverse some of these trends; he successfully pushed changes in the corporate tax code to encourage some corporations to set up shop at home, and imposed large tariffs on a wide range of Chinese goods exported to the U.S.in an attempt to rebalance the trade deficit. So the U.S.–Chinese relationship is a complicated one, both rival and partner, with China becoming more economically and militarily significant with each passing year. Inescapably, among the most important questions for American foreign policy makers in the years ahead will be how to respond to China's rise. Will we try to resist it or try to accommodate it in some way?

TERRORISM   The issue of terrorism moved front and center on the American political agenda after the September 11, 2001, attacks on the World Trade Center and the Pentagon and has remained there ever since though both presidents Obama and Trump have tried to shift focus to relationships with Russia and China. The retaliatory U.S. attacks on the Taliban regime and Al Qaeda in Afghanistan were the first of many steps that have been taken and will be taken in terms of a military response to terrorist attacks and threats. Responses include a wide range of overt and covert activities, some undertaken in cooperation with others, some undertaken unilaterally. At a minimum, American policy makers will try to improve

ISIS SHOOTS A RECRUITING AD

Here, ISIS fighters in Syria pose for photos and videos to be used to recruit people on the Internet and via social media. ISIS was very effective in using these tools to recruit foreign fighters to join its cause in Syria and Iraq where it once held substantial territory. As it began to lose territory, the group's online postings increasingly focused on the damage believers in the cause might do in their home countries, especially in the U.S., Europe, and Turkey. *Do you think that ISIS's success depends on its ability to control territory, or can it be just as effective in advancing radical jihadism by encouraging terrorist actions away from its geographical center?*

TERROR AT HOME

One of the continuing challenges faced by the United States is how to prevent terrorist attacks on home soil, such as the Boston Marathon bombing of April 15, 2013. Especially troubling are attacks by American citizens who have connections to terrorist organizations abroad, seemingly the case for the Boston bombers, one of whom, Tamerlan Tsarnaev, had close ties to radical Islamic groups in Chechnya. *Is the threat of terrorism in the United States more likely to emanate from jihadist-directed operations or from self-radicalized Americans, inspired by jihadist postings on the Internet and social media?*

intelligence gathering, create rapid-strike armed forces to attack terrorist cells and kill their leaders, and increase the use of drone aircraft surveillance and missile strikes as President Obama did in Yemen and in the Afghanistan–Pakistan border regions and as he did with special forces operations against the Islamic State in Iraq and Syria in 2016.

Sunni extremist jihadists, many educated in madrassas funded by the government and citizens of Saudi Arabia—a U.S. ally—formed the core of the Islamic State, which seized large Sunni areas of Iraq and Syria. Two other presumptive allies of the United States played a central role in the rise of ISIS: Pakistan is reported to have allowed the free movement of fighters into Iraq and Syria; Qatar is reported to have provided ISIS fighters with passports and funding to join the fight. ISIS, of course, though largely defeated on the battlefield now, threatened the entire region, escalated the fight between Sunni and Shia across the Muslim world, mounted terrorist attacks against the West, and encouraged others to perform terrorist attacks in the countries where they live (in San Bernardino and Orlando, in Brussels, in Marseille). ISIS-inspired attacks pose a dilemma for American policy makers who find much to dislike about the Sunni extremism of Al Qaeda and ISIS, among others, and the Shia extremism localized in Iran, Lebanon (Hezbollah), and various Shia militias in Iraq and Syria. Both Sunni and Shia extremists pose threats to populations in their own region and to Israel, Europe, and the United States.

Other nations are more skeptical of a purely military response to the threat of terrorism, believing that solid policing and intelligence operations offer better protection, though Britain and France increased their military operations against ISIS after the attacks on Paris in 2015. Nevertheless, purely military responses are unlikely to improve America's and the West's security against large-scale cyberattacks on economic, military, energy, or communications infrastructure, for example. Nor do purely military responses do much to control highly effective jihadist websites and social media recruitment of sympathizers in the United States and other western nations. It would seem, then, that policing and intelligence may be the only way to address a possible increase in the number of homegrown terrorists as in San Bernardino and at the Boston Marathon. In the long run, then, it is likely that military, policing, and intelligence methods to counter terrorism will all be necessary, the choice of methods depending on circumstances.

WEAPONS OF MASS DESTRUCTION   A high-priority task for American foreign policy makers since the presidency of John F. Kennedy has been to slow the arms race between the Soviet Union and the United States and to prevent **nuclear proliferation**, the spread of nuclear weapons throughout the world, including terrorist organizations. The first goal has been achieved. In a series of agreements reached first with the Soviet Union and then with its successor Russia, the two powers' stockpiles of deployed nuclear weapons have shrunk from about seventy-five thousand at their peak in the early 1980s to a little more than three thousand today.[42] Citing Russian cheating, President Trump has threatened to withdraw from these treaties.

Nuclear proliferation results are more mixed. France, Great Britain, and China also have nuclear weapons but are members of the Nuclear Non-Proliferation Treaty that commits these countries to measures that prevent the further spread of those weapons (the United States and Russia are also signatories to the treaty). India, Israel, and Pakistan also are nuclear powers but have not signed the Nuclear Non-Proliferation Treaty. After the breakup of the Soviet Union in 1991, Belarus, Kazakhstan, and Ukraine, Soviet republics but independent countries after the breakup, agreed to give up their nuclear arsenals. In 2003, Libya agreed to destroy its nuclear weapons. In 2015, members of the EU, Russia, and the United States reached a formal agreement with Iran, which did not yet have a weapon but apparently was working on one, to stop its nuclear program for at least a decade in exchange for relief from crippling sanctions. The agreement with Iran was deeply contested by Republicans inside and outside Congress. Donald Trump withdrew the United States from the agreement in 2018, much to chagrin of the other signatories including our European allies. It remains to be seen whether Iran will restart its nuclear program.

For many in the U.S. defense establishment, Pakistan represents the most significant proliferation threat, given its history and the turmoil that exists in the country. Lone Pakistani scientist A. Q. Khan was responsible for facilitating development of nuclear weapons programs in North Korea, Iran, and Libya, although he probably had help from parts of Pakistan's state security services. In addition, Pakistan is itself a nuclear power, has regions under the control of jihadists, and has a state security service riddled with people who have long-term ties to the Taliban and terrorists operating in Kashmir. And, Kashmir is in India, another nuclear power.

nuclear proliferation
The spread of nuclear weapons to additional countries or to terrorist groups.

NOW THEY MUST TREAT ME AS AN EQUAL

North Korean ruler Kum Jong-un inspects a nuclear warhead designed for delivery by mid-range and long-range missiles in 2017. With his missile and nuclear capabilities now well developed, Kim pressed for talks with President Trump ostensibly to "denuclearize" the Korean peninsula.

Is there any reason to believe that Kim will give up his nuclear weapons in trade for sanctions relief? How confident are you that North Korea will live up to its commitments if a deal is reached?

North Korea, a highly militarized totalitarian state run by Kim Jong-un and a secretive state leader Kim Jong-un moved with great speed to produce nuclear warheads and mid-range and intercontinental missiles, a goal they reached in 2018. The North Korean regime has threatened to use these weapons against close neighbors such as South Korea and Japan, as well as the American military base on Guam and the United States homeland. President Trump has tweeted on several occasions that the United States will not allow North Korea to deploy long-range nuclear-tipped missiles and even was willing to meet with the North Korean leader. The two leaders met in Singapore in June, 2018. Though short on details and with no inspection and verification tools in place, President Trump and Kim Jong Un reached a tentative agreement in 2018 to reduce or eliminate North Korean nuclear weapons. It is too soon to tell whether this agreement will bear fruit.

THE MIDDLE EAST AND THE PERSIAN GULF Although some countries there have huge oil wealth, the Middle East is home to some of the least-advanced nations in the world in terms of economic development, democracy and freedom, women's rights, and education.[43] It is also a veritable tinderbox, with a number of conflicts festering. There is the one between Shiite and Sunni Muslims, intensified by the war in Iraq and the brutal civil war in Syria but tied in the long run to Shiite Iran's growing power and regional ambitions and discomfort with these developments on the part of the Sunni governments of Saudi Arabia, Jordan, Egypt, and the Persian Gulf states.

There is also the long conflict between Turkey and the Kurds, with Turkey conducting cross-border incursions into Syria to battle anti-Turkish PKK (the Kurdish Workers Party) guerillas and other elements yearning for an independent Kurdistan (which would include portions of Turkey). In this conflict, the United States is caught in the middle. Turkey is a NATO ally and has a long-standing military alliance with the United States, but over the years a vibrant Kurdistan has emerged in the north of Iraq with the full support of the United States and which was an ally in the fight against the Islamic State group. Donald Trump stopped military and humanitarian assistance to northwest Syria in summer, 2018, seemingly leaving the field to Turkey.

Adding to the tinderbox is the seemingly unending conflict between Israel and the Palestinians, which stirs passions in the Arab and Muslim worlds and feeds anti-Americanism. What to do about this conflict is a matter of intense debate.

WELCOME TO THE NEW AMERICAN EMBASSY

Ivanka Trump and Secretary of the Treasury Steven Mnuchin officially open the U.S. embassy in Jerusalem in 2018, an action that most experts believe will cripple the ability of Israel and the Palestinian Authority to reach a peace agreement establishing two states.
Why did President Trump take this action? Will it advance the peace process or hinder it? And, why should Americans care?

Although groups such as Hamas and Hezbollah are committed to the destruction of Israel, as is Iran, most of the Arab states in the region support some sort of two-state solution in which Israel and Palestine live side by side as independent countries. The United States and the European Union have been committed historically to this outcome, though it is not entirely clear whether a majority of the Israeli and Palestinian publics still believe that such an outcome is attractive or possible.[44] President Donald Trump, fulfilling a campaign promise, officially moved the U.S. embassy in Israel to Jerusalem in 2018, neither asking or getting concessions from Israel nor making any promises to the Palestinians. To many, this signaled that the United States was no longer interested in investing in a two-state solution but was openly siding with Israel for now and in the future.

The Arab Middle East has been a region where people were long saddled with unelected and corrupt governments, near-useless educational systems, stagnant economies, and mass unemployment. The popular and largely peaceful uprising known as the Arab Spring toppled autocratic governments in Tunisia and Egypt and brought elected governments to power, generating great hope at first among people in the Middle East and forcing rulers in other places—Morocco, Jordan, and even Saudi Arabia—to pay more attention to popular aspirations. However, in other places, the Arab Spring was brutally crushed (in Libya, before Muammar Gaddafi was killed, and in Saudi-backed Bahrain). In Egypt, elections brought to power the Muslim Brotherhood, which ruled for only about a year before a military coup removed it from power and put its leaders and activists in prison. In Syria in 2011, Arab Spring-like reformers took to the streets to demand that Assad step down. The largely peaceful movement was violently put down by the regime, and a terrible civil war unfolded, gradually taking on the form of a conflict between Sunnis and Shias within Syria supported by regional powers Saudi Arabia, the Gulf States, Jordan, and Turkey (Sunni) and Iran (Shia), as well as Russia and the United States.

THE INDIAN SUBCONTINENT   U.S. policy makers also must be concerned about the possible outbreak of war between India and Pakistan, each armed with nuclear weapons. The issues between the two will not be easily resolved, given the history of enmity between them, past military conflicts, and the struggle over the fate of the future of Muslim-majority Kashmir. Indeed, the two countries mobilized for war in late 2001 and 2002, and each implied it would use nuclear weapons, if necessary. The

HAMAS SUPPORTERS BURN THE U.S. FLAG

Here Hamas sympathizers burn the U.S. flag in 2012 to display their displeasure with the United States, which Hamas believes is too closely aligned diplomatically and militarily with Israel.

Do you agree or disagree with this position? What policies do you favor that might help bring the two parties together? Or do you believe we should let the two sides settle the matter themselves without our help?

TERROR ATTACK ON MUMBAI
Smoke pours from the Taj Hotel after a coordinated attack on multiple locations in the city was carried out by Islamic extremists from Pakistan. How to keep the enduring conflict between India and Pakistan—both American allies with nuclear weapons—from getting out of hand remains a daunting puzzle for the people of the area and for U.S. foreign policy makers.

How much influence does the United States have in managing the tensions between India and Pakistan? Should affairs on the Indian subcontinent be an American foreign policy concern?

globalization
The tendency of information, products, and financial capital to flow across national borders, with the effect of more tightly integrating the global economy.

General Agreement on Tariffs and Trade (GATT)
An international agreement that requires the lowering of tariffs and other barriers to free trade.

World Trade Organization (WTO)
An agency designed to enforce the provisions of the General Agreement on Tariffs and Trade and to resolve trade disputes between nations.

situation is complicated for the United States by the fact that Pakistan is deemed crucial in the fight against the Taliban and Al Qaeda, yet elements of its security and military forces openly aid and protect the leadership of those groups in Pakistan. For example, when Navy Seals killed Osama bin Laden, he was living in a compound not far from Pakistan's elite military training academy. At the same time, the United States is forming a stronger strategic alliance with India, partly as a counter to the rising power of China, the increasing ties between the American and Indian economies, and sympathy with India as a target of terrorist attacks widely thought to be encouraged by Pakistan.

Economic and Social Issues

In addition to national security concerns, a number of other international issues have drawn the attention of American policy makers and the public. **Globalization** is particularly important in this regard. Recall that globalization is the integration of much of the world into a single market and production system in which the United States plays a leading role. It raises a number of new issues for American policy makers and citizens to address in addition to those raised about globalization's impact on the strategic behavior of American-based corporations and financial institutions and how their actions have affected jobs and economic prospects for Americans.

TRADE From 1945 until 2014, the United States was the leading trading nation in the world when totaling together all imports and exports.[45] China assumed the lead in 2014, although the United States remains a very close second. Moreover, the United States was the leading player in the design and management of the global trading system. Since the end of World War II, the United States has been the leading advocate for the freer and more open trading system that has evolved. President Donald Trump, breaking with the long-term bipartisan consensus, has said that this system has been unfair to the United States, with others taking advantage of the system and causing a decline in the number of good-paying manufacturing jobs for American workers. He promised he would get the United States out of trade agreements that disadvantage the United States.

In 1948, under American leadership, the most important trading nations adopted the **General Agreement on Tariffs and Trade (GATT)**, an agreement designed to lower, then eliminate, tariffs on most traded goods and to end nontariff trade restrictions. Periodically, members of GATT enter into talks (called *rounds*) and reach new agreements designed to refine and expand the system. Delegates at the Uruguay Round in 1994 agreed to replace GATT with the **World Trade Organization (WTO)**, which came

NO MORE TAKING ADVANTAGE OF THE UNITED STATES

President Trump announced that he was imposing tariffs on imported steel and aluminum in March, 2018. Here he tells workers at US Steel how his actions were saving high paying jobs in their company.

Though steel and aluminum companies—as well as their employees—have benefited from these tariffs, most economists believe that the tariffs will hurt other industries and businesses who use these materials because they will cost more. Are tariffs the best way to generate good jobs? Are there other tools that would be more effective in your opinion?

into being the following year. U.S. negotiators hoped that the new agreement eventually would open more markets to American agricultural products and services and halt the piracy of patented and copyrighted goods such as software and films. The Doha Round (2001–2008) focused on helping developing nations gain better access for their agricultural products to developed nations' markets, but the talks failed.

Most economists believe trade is generally good for all countries involved, whether rich or poor, and eventually for all members of society,[46] though not all agree, and increasing numbers of pro-free trade economists admit that some parts of American society gain more than others from free trade and some are badly hurt by it.[47] Many Americans believe the loss of manufacturing jobs can be traced to free trade and trade agreements such as the **North American Free Trade Agreement (NAFTA)** with Canada and Mexico because goods manufactured abroad using cheap labor and by firms that have few labor protections or environmental requirements can enter the United States tariff-free. Most economists, however, believe the majority of manufacturing job loss can be linked to technological change and rising productivity. Organized labor begs to differ, passionately believing that free trade costs American jobs. Others worry that a flood of cheap, yet high-quality goods and services threatens firms that are important for the health of the American economy and point to the decline of the American auto, steel, and consumer electronics industries as examples. Still others believe the threat of trade sanctions—a violation of free trade agreements—should be used to improve environmental standards, human rights practices, and religious tolerance in other countries. Trade, then, is likely to remain an important political issue for a long time to come. People do not agree on what the costs and benefits are from free trade, nor do they agree on whether free trade helps or hurts ordinary working people and companies, nor do they agree on whether trade agreements can be made to advance labor rights and environmental protections.

Though trade may generally be beneficial, it is also the case, as liberal commentator Fareed Zakaria put it in an op-ed piece, "Trump is right: China's a trade cheat," that China has been cheating, not playing by the rules others play by, as shown in a detailed report by the Office of the U.S. Trade Representative.[48] The report highlights the many ways the Chinese government helps its companies compete at home and abroad, the many ways products and services from the United States and Europe are kept completely out of the vast Chinese market or are crippled by regulations. Most egregiously,

North American Free Trade Agreement (NAFTA)

An agreement among the United States, Canada, and Mexico to eliminate nearly all barriers to trade and investment among the three countries.

Chinese law encourages western high technology companies—in AI, software, robotics, materials science, and biotechnology—to take on Chinese partner companies that more often than not steal western intellectual property. While many, including President Trump, worry about the size of the Chinese–U.S. trade deficit,[49] large American, Japanese, and European companies worry more about these intellectual property issues.

These are among the reasons why President Obama's signature trade agreement, the Trans-Pacific Partnership (TPP), was so controversial. The TPP was an agreement among twelve Pacific Rim nations, including the United States, Canada, Mexico, Australia, Vietnam, and Japan (but not China) that would have open TPP partner countries to more American products and services while increasing environmental and labor standards across the group. Because many groups in the Democratic base opposed TPP, including environmentalists, labor unions, and Bernie Sanders supporters, President Obama never submitted the agreement to the Senate for confirmation. One of its original authors when she was Secretary of State, Hillary Clinton disavowed the TPP during her 2016 run for the presidency. Though Republicans in Congress and state and local governments traditionally favored free trade, they mostly reversed their positions when Donald Trump's anti- free trade positions gained traction among voters during the 2016 presidential campaign. One of his first actions as president on assuming office in early 2017 was to formally withdraw from the TPP. He also forced a renegotiation in 2018 of NAFTA with provisions, he claimed, that are more favorable to the U.S. It remains to be seen how much this new United States, Mexico, Canada Agreement substantially changes the terms of trade between the three countries.

ECONOMIC STABILITY   The United States has been the leading player in the global economy since the end of World War II, and its leaders have been involved in trying to ensure the health and vitality of the overall global economy. In addition to encouraging free trade—until Donald Trump tried a different approach—American leaders have been concerned with stabilizing global financial markets when necessary and in rescuing countries on the verge of economic collapse. They have done so because the health of our own economy is closely tied to the health of the global economy. A strong American role is guaranteed by our leadership of and large financial contributions to the International Monetary Fund (IMF, charged with rectifying and preventing currency collapses) and the World Bank (charged with financing projects to assist economic development and poverty reduction). Ironically, perhaps, given its traditional financial leadership role, the U.S. housing bubble, credit crunch, investment bank collapse,

GLOBAL PRODUCTION AND SALES

In a globalized economy, many products consumed by Americans are manufactured abroad. The consumers in this photograph scrutinize flat-screen televisions, manufactured in China on spec for a Japanese electronics company, in a Costco store in California. *How difficult is it to buy products made entirely in the United States? Why does it matter where products are made for American consumers?*

and stock market decline in 2008 imperiled the world's financial system. With its own economy in a stall, its reputation hurt by the financial collapse, the Great Recession, and political gridlock on the national budget, the United States increasingly is being forced to share global financial and economic leadership with others, particularly with China and the European Union and its economic leaders, Germany and France. President Trump has expressed his low regard for shared global economic and financial arrangements and has promised to find ways for the United States to go it alone.

THE GLOBAL ENVIRONMENT AND CLIMATE CHANGE   Most Americans realize that environmental problems cross national borders and have been willing to support international agreements to tackle them. Thus, the United States and Canada have worked out a joint approach to reduce acid rain, and the United States has signed on to agreements on the prevention and cleanup of oil spills, the use of Antarctica, the protection of fish species, and the protection of the ozone layer. The United States is also a signatory to the biodiversity treaty.

Regarding climate change, it took the United States some time to reach an understanding with other countries. Although the Clinton administration was involved in hammering out the details of the Kyoto Protocol to limit greenhouse gases, Clinton, fearing rejection, never submitted the treaty to the Senate for its "advice and consent." In 2001, George W. Bush pulled out of the treaty entirely, citing his concern that strict controls on developed countries coupled with no controls on large, fast-growing economies in developing countries, such as China and India, would do irreparable harm to the American economy. President Obama professed a strong interest in bringing the United States into a new international agreement with mandatory targets for greenhouse gas reductions with China, India, and Brazil included, but no agreement could be worked out at the Copenhagen climate summit in late 2009. China's reluctance to agree to mandatory measures and lack of confidence in Obama's ability to deliver a "cap and trade" climate bill in Congress were major issues in the Copenhagen failure. Conferees were correct in their predictions; a "cap and trade" bill died in the U.S. Senate in 2010.

However, in 2015, President Obama signed an agreement in Paris with 186 other countries to cut carbon emissions sufficient to slow the rise in global temperature to less than 2 degrees centigrade above pre-industrial levels. Big polluters India and China, holdouts at previous climate summits, this time signed on to the agreement. The commitments by each country to cut carbon emissions are in the form of pledges, however, and do not mean that full compliance is guaranteed. In the United States, though much can be achieved by executive action on the part of the president and the EPA, emissions targets will require changes in existing law as well as new legislation. Given hyper-partisanship in Congress, deep divisions between Republicans and Democrats across the country on the issue of climate change, and President Trump's general skepticism that climate change is caused by human activity, neither executive action nor legislation on emissions are likely to happen any time soon. In fact, one of Donald Trump's most important actions in the first year of his presidency was to withdraw the United States from the Paris Climate Agreement.

WHO MAKES FOREIGN AND NATIONAL DEFENSE POLICIES?

18.5   Describe the roles of the principal architects of U.S. foreign and national defense policies.

The president is the key player in making foreign and national security policies and is especially powerful during international crises and in times of war. But Congress has always been involved in making foreign and national defense policies, especially with regard to decisions about international trade, foreign aid, military

FIGURE 18.5   APPLYING THE FRAMEWORK: WHY DID THE UNITED STATES INVADE IRAQ IN 2003?

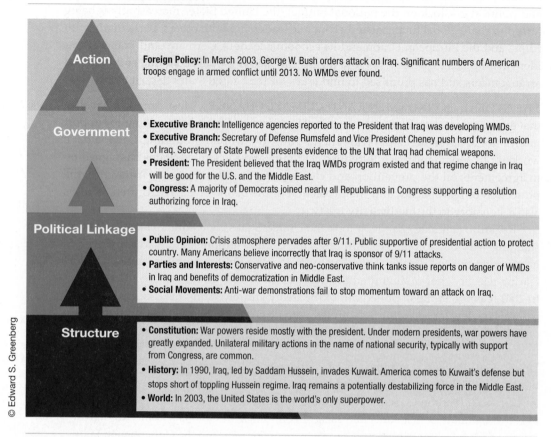

© Edward S. Greenberg

Action

Foreign Policy: In March 2003, George W. Bush orders attack on Iraq. Significant numbers of American troops engage in armed conflict until 2013. No WMDs ever found.

Government

- **Executive Branch:** Intelligence agencies reported to the President that Iraq was developing WMDs.
- **Executive Branch:** Secretary of Defense Rumsfeld and Vice President Cheney push hard for an invasion of Iraq. Secretary of State Powell presents evidence to the UN that Iraq had chemical weapons.
- **President:** The President believed that the Iraq WMDs program existed and that regime change in Iraq will be good for the U.S. and the Middle East.
- **Congress:** A majority of Democrats joined nearly all Republicans in Congress supporting a resolution authorizing force in Iraq.

Political Linkage

- **Public Opinion:** Crisis atmosphere pervades after 9/11. Public supportive of presidential action to protect country. Many Americans believe incorrectly that Iraq is sponsor of 9/11 attacks.
- **Parties and Interests:** Conservative and neo-conservative think tanks issue reports on danger of WMDs in Iraq and benefits of democratization in Middle East.
- **Social Movements:** Anti-war demonstrations fail to stop momentum toward an attack on Iraq.

Structure

- **Constitution:** War powers reside mostly with the president. Under modern presidents, war powers have greatly expanded. Unilateral military actions in the name of national security, typically with support from Congress, are common.
- **History:** In 1990, Iraq, led by Saddam Hussein, invades Kuwait. America comes to Kuwait's defense but stops short of toppling Hussein regime. Iraq remains a potentially destabilizing force in the Middle East.
- **World:** In 2003, the United States is the world's only superpower.

spending, immigration, and other matters that clearly and directly touch constituents' local interests. Congress also is more likely to get involved when presidential foreign policy and national security decisions lead to bad outcomes as happened during the Vietnam War. Public opinion, the mass media, political parties, and interest and advocacy groups also affect what both Congress and the executive branch do.

Figure 18.5 applies the analytical framework to the U.S. decision to invade Iraq in 2003 and demonstrates that, while the president is central to fashioning matters of war and peace, many other factors, actors, and institutions also play important roles. Recall that Operation "Iraqi Freedom" began on March 20, 2003, when American and British forces were supported by very small contingents from other countries in a so-called coalition of the willing. Aerial bombardments were launched across Iraq, with initial strikes aimed at air defenses and at command-and-control facilities. The stated goal of the invasion was to shut down Iraq's weapons of mass destruction (WMD) program, which was later proved nonexistent. After the initial air strikes, American and British ground forces struck from the south through Kuwait. Baghdad fell on April 9. Rather than the short war that the Bush administration had promised, however, U.S. forces stayed in Iraq for an additional ten years, sustaining thousands of casualties as it fought a fierce Sunni insurgency.

The President and the Executive Branch

Presidents have broad discretion and sometimes exercise extraordinary powers in foreign and national security matters derived from their status as commander in chief and from constitutionally assigned diplomatic powers. Over the years, broad deference has been given to presidents in the vigorous use of these powers by the public, Congress, and the courts.[50] Thus, President John F. Kennedy made the decision to impose a naval blockade on Cuba in 1962 that brought the United States and the Soviet Union to the brink of nuclear war. President Richard Nixon decided to expand the Vietnam conflict into neighboring Cambodia, and Nixon decided to recognize Communist China by opening diplomatic relations. President George H. W. Bush made the decision to invade Panama to capture its president and drug lord Manuel Noriega in 1989. In 1999, President Bill Clinton made the decision to wage an air war against Serbia to prevent its ethnic cleansing of Kosovo. President Obama decided to increase the use of drone attacks inside Pakistan, authorized cyberattacks on Iran's nuclear weapons program, decreed a "pivot to Asia" in U.S. military strategy, and restored diplomatic relations with Cuba. President Trump twice launched cruise missiles against Syrian chemical weapons facilities, withdrew the United States from trade agreements, the Paris Climate Accord, and the Iran nuclear agreement, and changed Obama's Cuba policy, all without seeking congressional approval.

Though they have the final word in foreign and military policy decisions, presidents rely on many people and several government agencies to assist and advise them. By most accounts, during George W. Bush's presidency and with his backing, Vice President Richard Cheney was the key architect of the invasion of Iraq and policies on the harsh treatment of enemy combatants and detainees, partnering with Secretary of Defense Donald Rumsfeld in these efforts.

MINGLING WITH THE TROOPS

Presidents have broad powers to deploy and use American armed forces. President George W. Bush mingled with troops from Fort Benning, Georgia, whom he ordered deployed to Iraq. *Should presidents have broad powers to deploy American armed forces? If not, how might presidential powers be constrained without undermining national security?*

The national security adviser plays a prominent role in every administration, informing the president daily on foreign and national security matters. The Department of State, headed by the secretary of state, is the president's chief arm for carrying out diplomatic affairs. Some secretaries of state have been extremely important in helping presidents make foreign policy—such as Henry Kissinger in the Nixon and Ford administrations and Hillary Clinton in the Obama administration—although others have not been in the inner circle, such as Rex Tillerson, Trump's first Secretary of State. Department of State itself is organized along both functional lines—economic affairs, human rights, counterterrorism, and refugees—and geographic lines, with "country desks" devoted to each nation of the world. It also oversees three hundred embassies, consulates, and missions around the world that carry out policy and advise. As issues of trade, U.S. corporate investment in other countries, and protection of intellectual property rights (patents and copyrights) become more important in the global economy, both the cabinet-level Department of Commerce and the Office of the U.S. Trade Representative, part of the Executive Office of the President, have become more important in advising the president on foreign policy.

The Department of Defense (DOD) and its civilian head, the Secretary of Defense, are particularly influential in shaping foreign and military policies. The Secretary of Defense has authority over the entire department and reports directly to the president. Strong defense secretaries who enjoy the confidence of the president, such as Robert McNamara under Presidents Kennedy and Johnson and Donald Rumsfeld under President George W. Bush, often impose policies about which the military services are not keen. Several Army leaders insisted that the light and technologically advanced fighting forces favored by Rumsfeld ignored the fact that holding and exploiting battlefield gains in places like Iraq and Afghanistan would require a larger military than Rumsfeld had planned. Robert Gates, who succeeded Rumsfeld—and who continued as defense secretary to President Obama—was instrumental in convincing President Bush to increase troop levels in Iraq in 2007 and convincing President Obama to do the same in Afghanistan in 2009.

Civilian secretaries are also in charge of the Departments of the Army, Navy, and Air Force and report to the secretary of defense. Each service also has a military command structure headed by people in uniform: the Army and Air Force chiefs of staff, the chief of naval operations, the commandant of the Marine Corps, and their subordinates.

BENGHAZI AGAIN?

Hillary Clinton was a particularly visible and influential Secretary of State during President Obama's first term. When it became clear that Clinton would be the Democratic nominee for president in 2016, the Republican-controlled House and Senate mounted several investigations into her performance at State, with a special focus on the terrorist attack on the American diplomatic compound in Benghazi, Libya in 2012. Here she testifies before the Foreign Relations Committee.
Were these investigatory hearings useful for the American people? Did they help the administration and Congress formulate better policies regarding State Department personnel?

The uniformed chiefs of each branch serve together in the **Joint Chiefs of Staff (JCS)**, headed by the chairman of the Joint Chiefs, who reports not only to the secretary of defense but also directly to the president.

A large intelligence community is also involved in fashioning and implementing foreign and military policy. This community is made up of a number of specific agencies. The National Security Agency (NSA) is responsible for intercepting and monitoring electronic messages from around the world, including, as we know from the massive leaks by Edward Snowden, American citizens, citizens of foreign countries, and the leaders of friendly allies. The National Reconnaissance Office (NRO) is responsible for satellite reconnaissance. Each of the armed services also has a separate tactical intelligence unit.

The Central Intelligence Agency (CIA) was established in 1947 to advise the National Security Council, to coordinate all U.S. intelligence agencies, to gather and evaluate intelligence information, and to carry out such additional functions as the NSC directs. Congress, the press, and the public subjected the CIA to intense scrutiny in 2004 because of its failure to alert the nation to the September 11, 2001, terrorist attacks and its misreading of the existence of weapons of mass destruction in Iraq before the U.S. invasion. In 2005, a presidential commission excoriated the CIA for these failures. In response to these failures, Congress and President Bush established a new cabinet-level post of Director of National Intelligence (DNI) to coordinate the intelligence-gathering and interpretation activities of fifteen scattered agencies, thus taking over some important responsibilities from the CIA. It remains to be seen how effective this change will be in intelligence gathering and dissemination.

Oddly, because of its conclusion that Russia had interfered in the 2016 presidential campaign with the intention of helping him beat Hillary Clinton, President Donald Trump has been at war with his own intelligence agencies since becoming president. He does not trust them nor does he read the daily intelligence brief put together by the DNI and designed to give the president an overview of developments around the world affecting U.S. foreign policy and national security.[51] It remains to be seen whether or not this tension within the executive branch will lead to bad policy decisions with troubling consequences.

Congress

Congress generally plays a less active role in foreign and military policy than in domestic policy. Members of Congress recognize the strong constitutional foundations of the president's preeminence in these areas but generally believe their constituents care more about policies that are close to home than about those that are far away. Of course, the exception is when wars go badly, as in Vietnam and Iraq; then, Congress becomes more assertive.

As Congress has become increasingly hyperpartisan, it also has become more intrusive in foreign policy and military affairs, especially during periods of divided government when the president is of a different party. In the last two years of the Obama administration, for example, Republicans in Congress tried to block the Iran nuclear deal. GOP leaders, in a shocking breach of protocol, invited the

Joint Chiefs of Staff (JCS)
The military officers in charge of each of the armed services.

SNOWDEN UNMASKS THE NSA
Until former National Security Agency contractor Edward Snowden stole and released files on NSA activities to *The Guardian* newspaper in the UK and *The Washington Post*, very few people knew the true extent of NSA surveillance of the communications of ordinary citizens, leaders in the public and private sectors in the United States, and even foreign leaders like German Chancellor Angela Merkel.
Do you consider Snowden to be a criminal and a traitor? Or a whistle-blowing hero? How did you come to your conclusion?

Israeli Prime Minister, a fervent opponent of the agreement, to address a joint session of Congress. Following that, a group of forty-seven Republican senators sent a letter to Iran, in which it was suggested that the agreement would last no longer than Obama's remaining days in office. President Obama endorsed the agreement and bypassed Congress entirely. Chapter 12 on the presidency addressed how he was able to do this. Note, however, that using similar executive powers, Donald Trump reversed Obama's actions and withdrew the United States from the Iran nuclear agreement.

In national defense emergencies, Congress tends to take a back seat to the president. This was the case, for example, in the immediate aftermath of the terrorist attacks on the United States in 2001. No congressional leader or political party was about to take on George W. Bush's broad assertion of powers, given the crisis situation and the president's extraordinary popularity at the time. However, as the occupation of Iraq dragged on and the president's popularity plummeted, and after Democrats gained control of the House and Senate following the 2006 elections, Congress reasserted itself, focusing especially on the decision to invade Iraq and the management of the aftermath by the president and his team. However, because Democrats did not have enough votes to break Republican filibusters in the Senate, Congress failed on several occasions in 2007 and 2008 to pass legislation setting a date for withdrawal of troops from Iraq. It may not have mattered that much because President Bush had already announced plans for an end to combat missions in Iraq. President Obama moved the withdrawal of combat troops to an earlier date, though not early enough to satisfy the antiwar elements in the Democratic Party.

The Constitution gives Congress the power to declare war—which it has not been asked to do since the beginning of World War II—and to decide about defense expenditures. It also gives the Senate the power to approve or disapprove treaties and the appointment of ambassadors. At times, Congress has used its treaty or spending powers to challenge the president on important issues, such as when Congress tried to force an end to the Vietnam War, resisted the Reagan administration's aid to the Nicaraguan Contras, and barely acquiesced to military and peacekeeping operations in Bosnia and Kosovo.

Congress has probably exerted its greatest foreign and military policy influence on issues that involve spending money, all of which must pass through the regular congressional appropriations process. It has tended to resist calls to increase foreign aid, for example, but has more often than not heeded calls by the president and the DOD for increased defense spending and procurement of new weapons systems. Military contracts are a special focus of attention because each has powerful interest group backers and a great economic effect on many congressional districts.

FOREIGN AND NATIONAL DEFENSE POLICIES: WHAT ROLE DO THE PEOPLE PLAY IN FOREIGN AND DEFENSE POLICY MAKING?

Democracy is less evident in the process of making foreign and national defense policies than in making domestic policies. For one thing, Americans generally care more about what is going on in the United States and how it affects them directly than they do about issues and developments in distant places. They also know more about what is going on inside U.S. borders—whether it is health care, living standards, or the environment—than they do about what is happening elsewhere, particularly in the poor countries that get very little media news coverage. In addition, to be effective, many foreign and military policies must be made in secret, so citizens often do not have the information necessary to be politically effective. And political leaders have sometimes misled or ignored the public.[52] Given this, Americans are clearly more competent citizens when faced with domestic matters than with military and foreign affairs and are more interested in playing a role in shaping domestic policies. The result is that Americans give political, diplomatic, and military leaders a relatively free hand in making foreign and military policy. This is very much what the framers had in mind when they fashioned the Constitution.

Americans are not powerless in the foreign and military policy arenas, however. Although they give their leaders a great deal of latitude in this area, the leaders are ultimately answerable to the people, and they know it. Presidents and members of Congress pay very close attention to public opinion and worry about the next election, so they are careful to avoid actions that may eventually prove unpopular.

Furthermore, Americans seem to be becoming more informed about other places in the world—whether through the mass media or the Internet—and are coming to recognize the interconnectedness of our fate with the fates of others. **Globalization**, perhaps, has forced Americans to be more attentive to how they are connected to other parts of the world, whether the issues are trade, outsourcing, climate change, human rights violations, or disasters like the earthquake, tsunami, and nuclear plant meltdown in Japan, which adversely affected the U.S. economy. It may well be that Americans are increasing their capacities to be attentive and effective citizens when it comes to foreign and national defense issues.

Nonetheless, it is still the case that the framers put the major responsibility for foreign and military affairs in the hands of the president and, by extension, the executive branch. Although Congress has control over the budget and the constitutional power to declare war against other nations, it is usually at a great disadvantage relative to the president in these areas, primarily because of the president's "war powers." The war powers represent a broad grant of constitutional power that presidents have used over the years to expand their responsibilities for national security, a concept that now involves a wide range of potential threats to the United States and its interests, ranging from direct military attacks on the nation (nuclear, conventional, terrorist) to attacks on U.S. citizens and business firms abroad. In addition, in the president's treaty powers and in the responsibility for naming and receiving ambassadors, the Constitution gives the president working control over most other aspects of foreign policy making. In crisis situations, such as existed after the 1941 attack on Pearl Harbor, and in 2001 after the attacks on the World Trade Center and the Pentagon, the president fashions foreign and military policies without much interference from Congress or the public. In such cases, the Constitution, historical precedents of strong leadership in crisis times by the chief executive, and public opinion all contribute to the broad powers and responsibilities of the president, with little scope, however, for conventional democratic processes.

REVIEW THE CHAPTER

FOREIGN AND NATIONAL SECURITY POLICIES AND DEMOCRACY

18.1 Assess the extent to which foreign and national defense policy making can be democratic.

Democratic theorists tend not to make distinctions between domestic policy and foreign and national security policies, believing that democratic processes are relevant to each; it is argued that the people can and should be sovereign in all areas.

In reality, however, democracy plays a less central role in foreign and national security policy making. The reasons are varied: the public, for the most part, knows and cares more about domestic policies; foreign and national security policy making often require secrecy and speed and are less amenable to full deliberation; and the constitutional powers of the president to act independently are considerable.

DIMENSIONS OF AMERICA'S SUPERPOWER STATUS

18.2 Examine the foundations of America's status as a world superpower.

The superpower status of the United States rests on three pillars: its large and innovative economy, the world's most powerful military, and widespread admiration for its national culture and way of life.

The United States is the world's military superpower. U.S. advantages in high-tech and smart weapons, aerial reconnaissance, and the ability to deploy large forces to world trouble spots are particularly important.

The United States also possesses a good deal of soft power, as American culture and ideology wield a fair amount of influence around the world. But the war in Iraq, the 2008 financial collapse, the Great Recession, and budget gridlock have taken a toll on our soft power advantage.

U.S. policies during its superpower era have combined unilateralist and multilateralist tendencies. In certain periods, it has tilted toward unilateralism. At other periods, it has tilted toward a less "go it alone" stance, depending more on cooperation with allies, negotiations with antagonists, and collaboration with international institutions. Each administration faces the choice of what stance it will take toward the world in its foreign and national security policies.

American policy makers also must decide on what goals to pursue. At the two extremes are policies to extend and protect a set of values or an ideology and policies that are more pragmatic, such as providing for the material well-being and safety of the nation's people.

U.S. superpower preeminence will likely be challenged at some point by the rise of China as an economic and military power.

AMERICAN SUPERPOWER: STRATEGIC ALTERNATIVES

18.3 Assess the goals and strategies of American foreign and national defense policies.

Foreign and national defense policy makers, starting with the president but including many others primarily from the Executive Branch of the federal government, usually have a number of goals in mind as they plan and act. First, all presidents, and defense and intelligence officials must necessarily be concerned with attacks on the U.S. homeland by states or terrorist groups. Though it has been a very long time since the U.S. has been threatened by a land invasion across its borders, policy makers pay attention to and try to counter threats from nuclear, chemical, and biological attacks by states and terrorist groups. Second, presidents and other executive officials pay attention to advancing what has been called the national interest in conducting foreign affairs, though this can mean very different things as presidents and officials have not formed a consensus on what this might be. It could mean, for example, protection of raw materials the United States needs for its economy, or it could mean protecting the intellectual property rights of American corporations operating abroad, or any number of other things, including acting as the hegemon for the international system. Finally, some presidents and executive branch officials have wanted to advance American values abroad whether these be the rule of law or democratic governance.

American policy makers have differed over how they propose the United States meets some or all of the goals. Unilateralists believe America has sufficient power and foresight to "go it alone," acting on the world stage without the permission of other countries or international institutions such as the UN. Multilateralists believe most problems in the world require the cooperation of others and going it alone not only is less likely to succeed but becomes prohibitively expensive in the long run.

PROBLEMS OF THE POST–COLD WAR WORLD

18.4 Evaluate problems facing the United States in the post–Cold War world.

The collapse of the Soviet Union in the early 1990s changed the nature of American foreign and national security policy, which had been focused on fighting communism for more than forty years.

National security has expanded to include not only the threat of direct attack by large-scale forces on American territory—the main concern during the **Cold War** years—but other threats including terrorism, global economic and financial instability, the rapid spread of infectious diseases, poverty in less-developed countries, global climate change, and cyberattacks on the government and private firms.

Traditional concerns like possible proliferation of weapons of mass destruction and regional and interethnic conflicts that might lead to global instability remain important elements on the agenda of policy makers.

China is both an important economic partner of the United States and a potential rival whose interests are not always aligned with America's. Knowing how to balance these opposite tendencies will remain an important problem for American policy makers.

WHO MAKES FOREIGN AND NATIONAL DEFENSE POLICIES?

18.5 Describe the roles of the principal architects of U.S. foreign and national defense policies.

Foreign policy has traditionally been made mostly in the executive branch, where the president is assisted by a large national security bureaucracy, including the National Security Council, the Department of Defense, the Department of State, and various intelligence agencies, including the NSA.

Congress has been little involved in crises or covert actions and has generally gone along with major decisions on defense policy; it has asserted itself chiefly on matters of foreign trade and aid, military bases, and procurement contracts.

Public opinion affects policy makers, perhaps increasingly so, but this influence is limited by the executive branch's centralization of decision making, secrecy, and control of information. How large a part interest groups play is disputed but is probably substantial in limited areas.

LEARN THE TERMS

asymmetric warfare   Unconventional tactics used by a combatant against an enemy with superior conventional military capabilities.

Cold War   The period of tense relations between the United States and the Soviet Union from the late 1940s to the late 1980s.

General Agreement on Tariffs and Trade (GATT)   An international agreement that requires the lowering of tariffs and other barriers to free trade.

global climate change   The upset of historical climate patterns, with rising temperatures and more extreme climate events, tied to the increase in atmospheric carbon, whether caused by human activities or naturally occurring cycles.

globalization   The tendency of information, products, and financial capital to flow across national borders, with the effect of more tightly integrating the global economy.

hegemon   Term used to refer to the dominant power during various historical periods that takes on responsibilities for maintaining and protecting a regional or global system.

Joint Chiefs of Staff (JCS)   The military officers in charge of each of the armed services.

multilateralists   Those who believe the United States should use its military and diplomatic power in the world in cooperation with other nations and international organizations.

national interest   What is of benefit to the nation as a whole.

North American Free Trade Agreement (NAFTA)   An agreement among the United States, Canada, and Mexico to eliminate nearly all barriers to trade and investment among the three countries.

nuclear proliferation   The spread of nuclear weapons to additional countries or to terrorist groups.

soft power   Influence in world affairs that derives from the attractiveness to others of a nation's culture, products, and way of life.

superpower   A nation with the military, economic, and political resources to project force anywhere in the world.

terrorism   The use of deadly violence against civilians to further some political goal.

unilateralists   Those who believe that the United States should "go it alone," pursuing its national interests without seeking the cooperation of other nations or multilateral institutions.

weapons of mass destruction   Nuclear, biological, or chemical weapons with the potential to cause vast harm to human populations.

World Trade Organization (WTO)   An agency designed to enforce the provisions of the General Agreement on Tariffs and Trade and to resolve trade disputes between nations.

THE DECLARATION OF INDEPENDENCE

When in the Course of human events, it becomes necessary for one people to dissolve the political bands which have connected them with another, and to assume among the Powers of the earth, the separate and equal station to which the Laws of Nature and of Nature's God entitle them, a decent respect to the opinions of mankind requires that they should declare the causes which impel them to the separation.

We hold these truths to be self-evident, that all men are created equal, that they are endowed by their Creator with certain unalienable Rights, that among these are Life, Liberty and the pursuit of Happiness. That to secure these rights, Governments are instituted among Men, deriving their just powers from the consent of the governed, That whenever any Form of Government becomes destructive of these ends, it is the Right of the People to alter or to abolish it, and to institute new Government, laying its foundation on such principles and organizing its powers in such form, as to them shall seem most likely to effect their Safety and Happiness. Prudence, indeed, will dictate that Governments long established should not be changed for light and transient causes; and accordingly all experience hath shown, that mankind are more disposed to suffer, while evils are sufferable, than to right themselves by abolishing the forms to which they are accustomed. But when a long train of abuses and usurpations, pursuing invariably the same Object evinces a design to reduce them under absolute Despotism, it is their right, it is their duty, to throw off such Government, and to provide new Guards for their future security.—Such has been the patient sufferance of these Colonies; and such is now the necessity which constrains them to alter their former Systems of Government. The history of the present King of Great Britain is a history of repeated injuries and usurpations, all having in direct object the establishment of an absolute Tyranny over these States. To prove this, let Facts be submitted to a candid world.

He has refused his Assent to Laws, the most whole-some and necessary for the public good.

He has forbidden his Governors to pass Laws of immediate and pressing importance, unless suspended in their operation till his Assent should be obtained; and when so suspended, he has utterly neglected to attend to them.

He has refused to pass other Laws for the accommodation of large districts of people, unless those people would relinquish the right of Representation in the Legislature, a right inestimable to them and formidable to tyrants only.

He has called together legislative bodies at places unusual, uncomfortable, and distant from the depository of their Public Records, for the sole purpose of fatiguing them into compliance with his measures.

He has dissolved Representative Houses repeatedly, for opposing with manly firmness his invasions on the rights of the people.

He has refused for a long time, after such dissolutions, to cause others to be elected; whereby the Legislative Powers, incapable of Annihilation, have returned to the People at large for their exercise; the State remaining in the mean time exposed to all the dangers of invasion from without, and convulsions within.

He has endeavoured to prevent the population of these States; for that purpose obstructing the Laws of Naturalization of Foreigners; refusing to pass others to encourage their migration hither, and raising the conditions of new Appropriations of Lands.

He has obstructed the Administration of Justice, by refusing his Assent to Laws for establishing Judiciary Powers.

He has made Judges dependent on his Will alone, for the tenure of their offices, and the amount and payment of their salaries.

He has erected a multitude of New Offices, and sent hither swarms of Officers to harass our People, and eat out their substance.

He has kept among us, in times of peace, Standing Armies without the Consent of our legislature.

He has affected to render the Military independent of and superior to the Civil Power.

He has combined with others to subject us to a jurisdiction foreign to our constitution, and unacknowledged by our laws; giving his Assent to their acts of pretended legislation:

For quartering large bodies of armed troops among us:

For protecting them, by a mock Trial, from Punishment for any Murders which they should commit on the Inhabitants of these States:

For cutting off our Trade with all parts of the world:

For imposing taxes on us without our Consent:

For depriving us in many cases, of the benefits of Trial by Jury:

For transporting us beyond Seas to be tried for pretended offences:

For abolishing the free System of English Laws in a neighbouring Province, establishing therein an Arbitrary government, and enlarging its Boundaries so as to render it at once an example and fit instrument for introducing the same absolute rule into these Colonies:

For taking away our Charters, abolishing our most valuable Laws, and altering fundamentally the Forms of our Governments:

For suspending our own Legislature, and declaring themselves invested with Power to legislate for us in all cases whatsoever.

He has abdicated Government here, by declaring us out of his Protection and waging War against us.

He has plundered our seas, ravaged our Coasts, burnt our towns, and destroyed the lives of our people.

He is at this time transporting large armies of foreign mercenaries to compleat the works of death, desolation and tyranny, already begun with circumstances of Cruelty & perfidy scarcely paralleled in the most barbarous ages, and totally unworthy the Head of a civilized nation.

He has constrained our fellow Citizens taken Captive on the high Seas to bear Arms against their Country, to become the executioners of their friends and Brethren, or to fall themselves by their Hands.

He has excited domestic insurrections amongst us, and has endeavoured to bring on the inhabitants of our frontiers, the merciless Indian Savages, whose known rule of warfare, is an undistinguished destruction of all ages, sexes and conditions.

In every stage of these Oppressions We have Petitioned for Redress in the most humble terms: Our repeated Petitions have been answered only by repeated injury. A Prince, whose character is thus marked by every act which may define a Tyrant, is unfit to be the ruler of a free People.

Nor have We been wanting in attention to our British brethren. We have warned them from time to time of attempts by their legislature to extend an unwarrantable jurisdiction over us. We have reminded them of the circumstances of our emigration and settlement here. We have appealed to their native justice and magnanimity, and we have conjured them by the ties of our common kindred to disavow these usurpations, which, would inevitably interrupt our connections and correspondence. They too have been deaf to the voice of justice and of consanguinity. We must, therefore, acquiesce in the necessity, which denounces our Separation, and hold them, as we hold the rest of mankind, Enemies in War, in Peace Friends.

We, therefore, the Representatives of the united States of America, in General Congress, Assembled, appealing to the Supreme Judge of the world for the rectitude of our intentions, do, in the Name, and by Authority of the good People of these Colonies, solemnly publish and declare, That these United Colonies are, and of Right ought to be Free and Independent States; that they are Absolved from all Allegiance to the British Crown, and that all political connection between them and the State of Great Britain, is and ought to be totally dissolved; and that as Free and Independent States, they have full Power to levy War, conclude Peace, contract Alliances, establish Commerce, and to do all other Acts and Things which Independent States may of right do. And for the support of this Declaration, with a firm reliance of the Protection of Divine Providence, we mutually pledge to each other our Lives, our Fortunes and our sacred Honor.

John Hancock,

Josiah Bartlett, Wm Whipple, Saml Adams, JohnAdams, Robt Treat Paine, Elbridge Gerry, Steph. Hopkins, William Ellery, Roger Sherman, Samel Huntington, Wm Williams, Oliver Wolcott, Matthew Thornton, Wm Floyd, Phil Livingston, Frans Lewis, LewisMorris, Richd Stockton, Jno Witherspoon, Fras Hopkinson, John Hart, Abra Clark, Robt Morris, Benjamin Rush, BenjaFranklin, John Morton, Geo Clymer, Jas Smith, Geo. Taylor, James Wilson, Geo. Ross, Caesar Rodney, Geo Read, Thos M:Kean, Samuel Chase, Wm Paca, Thos Stone, Charles Carroll of Carrollton, George Wythe, Richard Henry Lee, Th. Jefferson, Benja Harrison, Thos Nelson, Jr., Francis Lightfoot Lee, Carter Braxton, Wm Hooper, Joseph Hewes, John Penn, Edward Rutledge, Thos Heyward, Junr., Thomas Lynch, Junor., Arthur Middleton, Button Gwinnett, Lyman Hall, Geo Walton.

SOURCE: Worthington C. Ford et al., eds., *Journals of the Continental Congress, 1774–1789*, vol. 5, *June 5–Oct. 8, 1776* (Washington, D.C., 1906), 510.

THE CONSTITUTION OF THE UNITED STATES

We the people of the United States, in Order to form a more perfect Union, establish Justice, insure domestic Tranquility, provide for the common defence, promote the general Welfare, and secure the Blessings of Liberty to ourselves and our Posterity, do ordain and establish this constitution for the United States of America.

Article I

SECTION 1 All legislative Powers herein granted shall be vested in a Congress of the United States, which shall consist of a Senate and House of Representatives.

SECTION 2 The House of Representatives shall be composed of Members chosen every second Year by the People of the several States, and the Electors in each State shall have the Qualifications requisite for Electors of the most numerous Branch of the State Legislature.

No person shall be a Representative who shall not have attained to the Age of twenty-five Years, and been seven Years a Citizen of the United States, and who shall not, when elected, be an Inhabitant of that State in which he shall be chosen.

Representatives and direct Taxes shall be apportioned among the several States which may be included within this Union, according to their respective Numbers, which shall be determined by adding to the whole Number of free Persons, including those bound to Service for a Term of Years, and excluding Indians not taxed, three fifths of all other Persons. The actual Enumeration shall be made within three Years after the first Meeting of the Congress of the United States, and within every subsequent Term of ten Years, in such Manner as they shall by Law direct. The Number of Representatives shall not exceed one for every thirty Thousand, but each State shall have at Least one Representative; and until such enumeration shall be made, the State of New Hampshire shall be entitled to chuse three, Massachusetts eight, Rhode-Island and Providence Plantations one, Connecticut five, New-York six, New Jersey four, Pennsylvania eight, Delaware one, Maryland six, Virginia ten, North Carolina five, South Carolina five, and Georgia three.

When vacancies happen in the Representation from any State, the Executive Authority thereof shall issue Writs of Election to fill such Vacancies.

The House of Representatives shall chuse their Speaker and other Officers; and shall have the sole Power of Impeachment.

SECTION 3   The Senate of the United States shall be composed of two Senators from each State, chosen by the Legislature thereof, for six Years; and each Senator shall have one Vote.

Immediately after they shall be assembled in Consequence of the first Election, they shall be divided as equally as may be into three Classes. The Seats of the Senators of the first Class shall be vacated at the Expiration of the second Year, of the second Class at the Expiration of the fourth Year, and of the third Class at the Expiration of the sixth Year, so that one-third may be chosen every second Year; and if Vacancies happen by Resignation, or otherwise, during the Recess of the Legislature of any State, the Executive thereof may make temporary Appointments until the next Meeting of the Legislature, which shall then fill such Vacancies.

No Person shall be a Senator who shall not have attained to the Age of thirty Years, and been nine Years a Citizen of the United States, and who shall not, when elected, be an Inhabitant of that State in which he shall be chosen.

The Vice President of the United States shall be President of the Senate, but shall have no vote, unless they be equally divided.

The Senate shall chuse their other Officers, and also a President pro tempore, in the absence of the Vice President, or when he shall exercise the Office of the President of the United States.

The Senate shall have the sole Power to try all Impeachments. When sitting for that purpose, they shall be on Oath or Affirmation. When the President of the United States is tried, the Chief Justice shall preside: And no person shall be convicted without the Concurrence of two thirds of the Members present.

Judgment in Cases of Impeachment shall not extend further than to removal from Office, and disqualification to hold and enjoy any Office of honor, Trust, or Profit under the United States: but the Party convicted shall nevertheless be liable and subject to Indictment, Trial, Judgment, and Punishment, according to Law.

SECTION 4   The Times, Places and Manner of holding Elections for Senators and Representatives, shall be prescribed in each state by the Legislature thereof; but the Congress may at any time by Law make or alter such Regulations, except as to the Places of Chusing Senators.

The Congress shall assemble at least once in every Year, and such Meeting shall be on the first Monday in December, unless they shall by Law appoint a different Day.

SECTION 5   Each House shall be the Judge of the Elections, Returns and Qualifications of its own Members, and a Majority of each shall constitute a Quorum to do

Business; but a smaller number may adjourn from day to day, and may be authorized to compel the Attendance of absent Members, in such Manner, and under such Penalties, as each House may provide.

Each House may determine the Rules of its Proceedings, punish its Members for disorderly Behavior, and, with the Concurrence of two thirds, expel a Member.

Each House shall keep a Journal of its Proceedings, and from time to time publish the same, excepting such Parts as may in their Judgment require Secrecy; and the Yeas and Nays of the Members of either House on any question shall, at the Desire of one fifth of those Present, be entered on the Journal.

Neither House, during the Session of Congress, shall, without the Consent of the other, adjourn for more than three days, nor to any other Place than that in which the two Houses shall be sitting.

SECTION 6   The Senators and Representatives shall receive a Compensation for their Services, to be ascertained by Law, and paid out of the Treasury of the United States. They shall in all Cases, except Treason, Felony, and Breach of the Peace, be privileged from arrest during their Attendance at the Session of their respective Houses, and in going to and returning from the same; and for any Speech or Debate in either House, they shall not be questioned in any other Place.

No Senator or Representative shall, during the Time for which he was elected, be appointed to any civil Office under the Authority of the United States, which shall have been created, or the Emoluments whereof shall have been increased, during such time; and no Person holding any Office under the United States shall be a Member of either House during his continuance in Office.

SECTION 7   All Bills for raising Revenue shall originate in the House of Representatives; but the Senate may propose or concur with Amendments as on other bills.

Every Bill which shall have passed the House of Representatives and the Senate, shall, before it become a Law, be presented to the President of the United States; If he approve he shall sign it, but if not he shall return it, with his Objections, to that House in which it shall have originated, who shall enter the Objections at large on their Journal, and proceed to reconsider it. If after such Reconsideration two thirds of that House shall agree to pass the bill, it shall be sent, together with the objections, to the other House, by which it shall likewise be reconsidered, and if approved by two thirds of that House, it shall become a Law. But in all such Cases the Votes of both Houses shall be determined by Yeas and Nays, and the Names of the Persons voting for and against the Bill shall be entered on the Journal of each House respectively. If any Bill shall not be returned by the President within ten Days (Sundays excepted) after it shall have been presented to him, the Same shall be a Law, in like Manner as if he had signed it, unless the Congress by their Adjournment prevent its Return, in which Case it shall not be a Law.

Every Order, Resolution, or Vote to which the Concurrence of the Senate and House of Representatives may be necessary (except on a question of Adjournment) shall be presented to the President of the United States; and before the Same shall take Effect, shall be approved by him, or being disapproved by him, shall be repassed by two thirds of the Senate and House of Representatives, according to the Rules and Limitations prescribed in the Case of a Bill.

SECTION 8   The Congress shall have Power

To lay and collect Taxes, Duties, Imposts and

Excises, to pay the Debts and provide for the common Defence and general Welfare of the United States; but all Duties, Imposts and Excises shall be uniform throughout the United States;

To borrow money on the credit of the United States;

To regulate Commerce with foreign Nations, and among the several States, and with the Indian Tribes;

To establish a uniform Rule of Naturalization, and uniform Laws on the subject of Bankruptcies throughout the United States;

To coin Money, regulate the Value thereof, and of foreign Coin, and fix the Standard of Weights and Measures;

To provide for the Punishment of counterfeiting the Securities and current Coin of the United States;

To establish Post offices and post Roads;

To promote the Progress of Science and useful Arts, by securing for limited Times to Authors and Inventors the exclusive Right to their respective Writings and Discoveries;

To constitute Tribunals inferior to the Supreme Court;

To define and punish Piracies and Felonies committed on the high Seas, and Offences against the Law of Nations;

To declare War, grant Letters of Marque and Reprisal, and make Rules concerning Captures on Land and Water;

To raise and support Armies, but no Appropriation of Money to that Use shall be for a longer Term than two Years;

To provide and maintain a Navy;

To make Rules for the Government and Regulation of the land and naval forces;

To provide for calling forth the Militia to execute the Laws of the Union, suppress Insurrections and repel Invasions;

To provide for organizing, arming, and disciplining the Militia, and for governing such Part of them as may be employed in the Service of the United States, reserving to the States respectively, the Appointment of the Officers, and the Authority of training the Militia according to the discipline prescribed by Congress;

To exercise exclusive Legislation in all Cases whatsoever, over such District (not exceeding ten Miles square) as may, by Cession of particular States, and the acceptance of Congress, become the Seat of Government of the United States, and to exercise like Authority over all Places purchased by the Consent of the Legislature of the State in which the Same shall be, for the Erection of Forts, Magazines, Arsenals, dock-Yards, and other needful Buildings;—And

To make all Laws which shall be necessary and proper for carrying into Execution the foregoing Powers, and all other Powers vested by this Constitution in the government of the United States, or in any Department or Officer thereof.

SECTION 9   The Migration or Importation of such Persons as any of the States now existing shall think proper to admit, shall not be prohibited by the Congress prior to the Year one thousand eight hundred and eight, but a tax or duty may be imposed on such Importation, not exceeding ten dollars for each Person.

The privilege of the Writ of Habeas Corpus shall not be suspended, unless when in Cases of Rebellion or Invasion the public Safety may require it.

No Bill of Attainder or ex post facto Law shall be passed.

No capitation, or other direct, Tax shall be laid unless in Proportion to the Census or Enumeration herein before directed to be taken.

No Tax or Duty shall be laid on Articles exported from any State.

No Preference shall be given by any Regulation of Revenue to the Ports of one State over those of another: nor shall Vessels bound to, or from, one state, be obliged to enter, clear, or pay Duties in another.

No Money shall be drawn from the Treasury, but in Consequence of Appropriations made by Law; and a regular Statement and Account of the Receipts and Expenditures of all public Money shall be published from time to time.

No Title of Nobility shall be granted by the United States: And no Person holding any Office of Profit or Trust under them, shall, without the Consent of the Congress, accept of any present, Emolument, Office, or Title, of any kind whatever, from any King, Prince, or Foreign State.

SECTION 10 No state shall enter into any Treaty, Alliance, or Confederation; grant Letters of Marque and Reprisal; coin Money; emit Bills of Credit; make any Thing but gold and silver Coin a Tender in Payment of Debts; pass any Bill of Attainder, ex post facto Law, or Law impairing the Obligation of Contracts, or grant any Title of Nobility.

No State shall, without the Consent of the Congress, lay any Imposts or Duties on Imports or Exports, except what may be absolutely necessary for executing its inspection Laws: and the net Produce of all Duties and Imposts, laid by any State on Imports or Exports, shall be for the Use of the Treasury of the United States; and all such Laws shall be subject to the Revision and Control of the Congress.

No State shall, without the Consent of Congress, lay any duty of Tonnage, keep Troops, or Ships of War in time of Peace, enter into any Agreement or Compact with another State, or with a foreign Power, or engage in War, unless actually invaded, or in such imminent Danger as will not admit of delay.

Article II

SECTION 1 The executive Power shall be vested in a President of the United States of America. He shall hold his Office during the Term of four years, and, together with the Vice President, chosen for the same Term, be elected, as follows:

Each State shall appoint, in such Manner as the Legislature thereof may direct, a Number of Electors, equal to the whole Number of Senators and Representatives to which the State may be entitled in the Congress; but no Senator or Representative, or Person holding an Office of Trust or Profit under the United States, shall be appointed an Elector.

The Electors shall meet in their respective States, and vote by Ballot for two persons, of whom one at least shall not be an Inhabitant of the same State with themselves. And they shall make a List of all the Persons voted for, and of the Number of Votes for each; which List they shall sign and certify, and transmit sealed to the Seat of the Government of the United States, directed to the President of the Senate. The President of the Senate shall, in the Presence of the Senate and House of Representatives, open all the Certificates, and the Votes shall then be counted. The Person having the greatest Number of Votes shall be the President, if such Number be a Majority of the whole Number of Electors appointed; and if there be more than one who have such Majority, and have an equal Number of Votes, then the House of Representatives shall immediately chuse by Ballot one of them for President; and if no Person have a Majority, then from the five highest on the List the said House shall in like Manner chuse the President. But in chusing the President, the votes shall be taken by States, the Representation from each State having one Vote; a quorum for this Purpose shall consist of a Member or Members from two-thirds of the States, and a Majority of all the States shall be necessary to a Choice. In every Case, after the Choice of the President, the Person having the greatest Number of Votes of the Electors shall be the Vice President. But if there should remain two or more who have equal votes, the Senate shall chuse from them by Ballot the Vice President.

The Congress may determine the time of chusing the Electors, and the Day on which they shall give their Votes; which Day shall be the same throughout the United States.

No person except a natural-born Citizen, or a Citizen of the United States, at the time of the Adoption of this Constitution, shall be eligible to the Office of President; neither shall any Person be eligible to that Office who shall not have attained to the Age of thirty-five years, and been fourteen Years a Resident within the United States.

In Case of the Removal of the President from Office, or of his Death, Resignation, or Inability to discharge the Powers and Duties of the said Office, the same shall devolve on the Vice President, and the Congress may by Law provide for the Case of Removal, Death, Resignation, or Inability, both of the President and Vice President, declaring what Officer shall then act as President, and such Officer shall act accordingly, until the disability be removed, or a President shall be elected.

The President shall, at stated Times, receive for his Services a Compensation, which shall neither be increased nor diminished during the Period for which he shall have been elected, and he shall not receive within that Period any other Emolument from the United States, or any of them.

Before he enter on the execution of his Office, he shall take the following Oath or Affirmation:—"I do solemnly swear (or affirm) that I will faithfully execute the Office of President of the United States, and will, to the best of my Ability, preserve, protect, and defend the Constitution of the United States."

SECTION 2 The President shall be Commander in Chief of the Army and Navy of the United States, and of the Militia of the several States, when called into the actual Service of the United States; he may require the Opinion, in writing, of the principal Officer in each of the executive Departments, upon any subject relating to the Duties of their respective Offices, and he shall have Power to Grant Reprieves and Pardons for Offences against the United States, except in Cases of Impeachment.

He shall have Power, by and with the Advice and Consent of the Senate, to make Treaties, provided two thirds of the Senators present concur; and he shall nominate, and by and with the Advice and Consent of the Senate, shall appoint Ambassadors, other public Ministers and Consuls, Judges of the supreme Court, and all other Officers of the United States, whose Appointments are not herein otherwise provided for, and which shall be established by Law: but the Congress may by Law vest the Appointment of such inferior Officers, as they think proper, in the President alone, in the Courts of Law, or in the Heads of Departments.

The President shall have Power to fill up all Vacancies that may happen during the Recess of the Senate, by granting Commissions which shall expire at the End of their next Session.

SECTION 3 He shall from time to time give to the Congress Information of the State of the Union, and recommend to their Consideration such Measures as he shall judge necessary and expedient; he may, on extraordinary occasions, convene both Houses, or either of them, and in Case of Disagreement between them, with respect to the Time of Adjournment, he may adjourn them to such Time as he shall think proper; he shall receive Ambassadors and other public Ministers; he shall take Care that the Laws be faithfully executed, and shall Commission all the Officers of the United States.

SECTION 4 The President, Vice President and all civil Officers of the United States, shall be removed from Office on Impeachment for, and Conviction of, Treason, Bribery, or other high Crimes and Misdemeanors.

Article III

SECTION 1 The judicial Power of the United States, shall be vested in one supreme Court, and in such inferior Courts as the Congress may from time to time ordain and establish. The Judges, both of the supreme and inferior Courts, shall hold their Offices during good Behaviour, and shall, at stated Times, receive for their Services, a Compensation, which shall not be diminished during their Continuance in Office.

SECTION 2 The judicial Power shall extend to all Cases, in Law and Equity, arising under this Constitution, the Laws of the United States, and treaties made, or which shall be made, under their Authority;—to all Cases affecting ambassadors, other public ministers and consuls;—to all cases of admiralty and maritime Jurisdiction;—to Controversies to which the United States shall be a Party;—to Controversies between two or more States;—between a State and Citizens of another State;—between Citizens of different States,—between Citizens of the same State claiming Lands under

Grants of different States, and between a State, or the Citizens thereof, and foreign States, Citizens or Subjects.

In all Cases affecting Ambassadors, other public Ministers and Consuls, and those in which a State shall be Party, the supreme Court shall have original Jurisdiction. In all the other Cases before mentioned, the supreme Court shall have appellate Jurisdiction, both as to Law and Fact, with such Exceptions, and under such Regulations as the Congress shall make.

The trial of all Crimes, except in Cases of Impeachment, shall be by Jury; and such Trial shall be held in the State where the said Crimes shall have been committed; but when not committed within any State, the Trial shall be at such Place or Places as the Congress may by Law have directed.

SECTION 3 Treason against the United States, shall consist only in levying War against them, or in adhering to their Enemies, giving them Aid and Comfort. No Person shall be convicted of Treason unless on the testimony of two Witnesses to the same overt Act, or on Confession in open Court.

The Congress shall have power to declare the Punishment of Treason, but no Attainder of Treason shall work Corruption of Blood, or Forfeiture except during the Life of the Person attained.

Article IV

SECTION 1 Full Faith and Credit shall be given in each State to the public Acts, Records, and judicial Proceedings of every other State. And the Congress may by general Laws prescribe the Manner in which such Acts, Records and Proceedings shall be proved, and the Effect thereof.

SECTION 2 The Citizens of each State shall be entitled to all Privileges and Immunities of Citizens in the several States.

A Person charged in any State with Treason, Felony, or other Crime, who shall flee from Justice, and be found in another State, shall on demand of the executive Authority of the State from which he fled, be delivered up, to be removed to the State having Jurisdiction of the crime.

No Person held to Service or Labour in one State, under the Laws thereof, escaping into another, shall, in Consequence of any Law or Regulation therein, be discharged from such Service or Labour, but shall be delivered up on Claim of the Party to whom such Service or Labour may be due.

SECTION 3 New States may be admitted by the Congress into this Union; but no new State shall be formed or erected within the Jurisdiction of any other State; nor any State be formed by the Junction of two or more States, or parts of States, without the Consent of the Legislatures of the States concerned as well as of the Congress.

The Congress shall have Power to dispose of and make all needful Rules and Regulations respecting the Territory or other Property belonging to the United States; and nothing in this Constitution shall be so construed as to Prejudice any Claims of the United States, or of any particular State.

SECTION 4 The United States shall guarantee to every State in this Union a Republican Form of Government, and shall protect each of them against Invasion; and on Application of the Legislature, or the Executive (when the Legislature cannot be convened) against domestic Violence.

Article V

The Congress, whenever two-thirds of both Houses shall deem it necessary, shall propose Amendments to this Constitution, or, on the Application of the Legislatures of two-thirds of the several States, shall call a Convention for proposing

Amendments, which, in either Case, shall be valid to all Intents and Purposes, as part of this Constitution, when ratified by the Legislatures of three-fourths of the several States, or by Conventions in three-fourths thereof, as the one or the other Mode of Ratification may be proposed by the Congress; Provided that no Amendment which may be made prior to the Year One thousand eight hundred and eight shall in any Manner affect the first and fourth Clauses in the Ninth Section of the first Article; and that no State, without its Consent, shall be deprived of its equal Suffrage in the Senate.

Article VI

All Debts contracted and Engagements entered into, before the Adoption of this Constitution, shall be as valid against the United States under this Constitution, as under the Confederation.

This Constitution, and the Laws of the United States which shall be made in Pursuance thereof; and all Treaties made, or which shall be made, under the Authority of the United States, shall be the supreme Law of the Land; and the Judges in every State shall be bound thereby, any Thing in the Constitution or Laws of any State to the Contrary notwithstanding.

The Senators and Representatives before mentioned, and the Members of the several State Legislatures and all executive and judicial Officers, both of the United States and of the several States, shall be bound by Oath or Affirmation to support this Constitution; but no religious Test shall ever be required as a qualification to any Office or public Trust under the United States.

Article VII

The Ratification of the Conventions of nine States shall be sufficient for the Establishment of this Constitution between the States so ratifying the same.

Done in Convention by the Unanimous Consent of the States present the Seventeenth Day of September in the Year of our Lord one thousand seven hundred and Eighty seven, and of the Independence of the United States of America the Twelfth. In Witness whereof We have here-unto subscribed our Names.

Go. Washington, President and deputy from Virginia; Attest William Jackson, Secretary; Delaware: Geo. Read,* Gunning Bedford, Jr., John Dickinson, Richard Basset, Jaco. Broom; Maryland: James McHenry, Daniel of St. Thomas' Jenifer, Danl. Carroll; Virginia: John Blair, James Madison, Jr.; North Carolina: Wm. Blount, Richd. Dobbs Spaight, Hu Williamson; South Carolina: J. Rutledge, Charles Cotes worth Pinckney, Charles Pinckney, Pierce Butler; Georgia: William Few, Abr. Baldwin; New Hampshire: John Langdon, Nicholas Gilman; Massachusetts: Nathaniel Gorham, Rufus King; Connecticut: Wm. Saml. Johnson, Roger Sherman,* New York: Alexander Hamilton; New Jersey: Wil. Livingston, David Brearley, Wm. Paterson, Jona. Dayton; Pennsylvania: B. Franklin,* Thomas Mifflin, Robt. Morris,* Geo. Clymer,* Thos. Fitz Simons, Jared Ingersoll, James Wilson, Gouv. Morris.

SOURCE: Library of Congress, *Constitution of the United States of America: Analysis and Interpretation*, https://www.congress.gov/constitution-annotated/.

AMENDMENTS TO THE CONSTITUTION OF THE UNITED STATES

Articles in Addition to, and Amendment of, the Constitution of the United States of America, Proposed by Congress, and Ratified by the Legislatures of the Several States, Pursuant to the Fifth Article of the Original Constitution.

Amendment I [1791]

Congress shall make no law respecting an establishment of religion, or prohibiting the free exercise thereof; or abridging the freedom of speech, or of the press; or the right of the people peaceably to assemble, and to petition the Government for a redress of grievances.

Amendment II [1791]

A well regulated Militia, being necessary to the security of a free State, the right of the people to keep and bear Arms shall not be infringed.

Amendment III [1791]

No Soldier shall, in time of peace, be quartered in any house, without the consent of the Owner, nor in time of war, but in a manner to be prescribed by law.

Amendment IV [1791]

The right of the people to be secure in their persons, houses, papers, and effects, against unreasonable searches and seizures, shall not be violated, and no Warrants shall issue, but upon probable cause, supported by Oath or affirmation, and particularly describing the place to be searched, and the persons or things to be seized.

Amendment V [1791]

No person shall be held to answer for a capital or otherwise infamous crime, unless on a presentment or indictment of a Grand Jury, except in cases arising in the land or naval forces, or in the Militia, when in actual service in time of War or public danger; nor shall any person be subject for the same offence to be twice put in jeopardy of life or limb; nor shall be compelled in any criminal case to be a witness against himself, nor be deprived of life, liberty, or property, without due process of law; nor shall private property be taken for public use, without just compensation.

Amendment VI [1791]

In all criminal prosecutions, the accused shall enjoy the right to a speedy and public trial, by an impartial jury of the State and district wherein the crime shall have been committed, which district shall have been previously ascertained by law, and to be informed of the nature and cause of the accusation; to be confronted with the witnesses against him; to have compulsory process for obtaining witnesses in his favor, and to have the Assistance of Counsel for his defence.

Amendment VII [1791]

In suits at common law, where the value in controversy shall exceed twenty dollars, the right of trial by jury shall be preserved, and no fact tried by a jury, shall be otherwise reexamined in any Court of the United States, than according to the rules of the common law.

Amendment VIII [1791]

Excessive bail shall not be required, nor excessive fines imposed, nor cruel and unusual punishments inflicted.

Amendment IX [1791]

The enumeration in the Constitution, of certain rights, shall not be construed to deny or disparage others retained by the people.

Amendment X [1791]

The powers not delegated to the United States by the Constitution, nor prohibited by it to the States, are reserved to the States respectively, or to the people.

Amendment XI [1798]

The Judicial power of the United States shall not be construed to extend to any suit in law or equity, commenced or prosecuted against one of the United States by Citizens of another State, or by Citizens or Subjects of any Foreign State.

Amendment XII [1804]

The Electors shall meet in their respective States and vote by ballot for President and Vice President, one of whom, at least, shall not be an inhabitant of the same State with themselves; they shall name in their ballots the person voted for as President, and in distinct ballots the person voted for as Vice President, and they shall make distinct lists of all persons voted for as President, and of all persons voted for as Vice President, and of the number of votes for each, which lists they shall sign and certify, and transmit sealed to the seat of the government of the United States, directed to the President of the Senate;—The President of the Senate shall, in the presence of the Senate and House of Representatives, open all the certificates and the votes shall then be counted;—The person having the greatest number of votes for President, shall be the President, if such number be a majority of the whole number of Electors appointed; and if no person have such majority, then from the persons having the highest numbers not exceeding three on the list of those voted for as President, the House of Representatives shall choose immediately, by ballot, the President. But in choosing the President, the votes shall be taken by states, the representation from each state having one vote; a quorum for this purpose shall consist of a member or members from two-thirds of the states, and a majority of all the states shall be necessary to a choice. And if the House of Representatives shall not choose a President whenever the right of choice shall devolve upon them, before the fourth day of March next following, then the Vice President shall act as President, as in the case of the death or other constitutional disability of the President.—The person having the greatest number of votes as Vice President, shall be the Vice President, if such number be a majority of the whole number of Electors appointed, and if no person have a majority, then from the two highest numbers on the list, the Senate shall choose the Vice President; a quorum for the purpose shall consist of two-thirds of the whole number of Senators, and a majority of the whole number shall be necessary to a choice. But no person constitutionally ineligible to the office of President shall be eligible to that of Vice President of the United States.

Amendment XIII [1865]

SECTION 1   Neither slavery nor involuntary servitude, except as a punishment for crime whereof the party shall have been duly convicted, shall exist within the United States, or any place subject to their jurisdiction.

SECTION 2   Congress shall have power to enforce this article by appropriate legislation.

Amendment XIV [1868]

SECTION 1   All persons born or naturalized in the United States, and subject to the jurisdiction thereof, are citizens of the United States and of the State wherein they reside. No State shall make or enforce any law which shall abridge the privileges or immunities of citizens of the United States; nor shall any State deprive any person of life, liberty, or property, without due process of law; nor deny to any person within its jurisdiction the equal protection of the laws.

SECTION 2 Representatives shall be apportioned among the several States according to their respective numbers, counting the whole number of persons in each State, excluding Indians not taxed. But when the right to vote at any election for the choice of electors for President and Vice President of the United States, Representatives in Congress, the Executive and Judicial officers of a State, or the members of the Legislature thereof, is denied to any of the male inhabitants of such State, being twenty-one years of age, and citizens of the United States or in any way abridged, except for participation in rebellion, or other crime, the basis of representation therein shall be reduced in the proportion which the number of such male citizens shall bear to the whole number of male citizens twenty-one years of age in such State.

SECTION 3 No person shall be a Senator or Representative in Congress, or elector of President and Vice President, or hold any office, civil or military, under the United States, or under any State, who, having previously taken an oath, as a member of Congress, or as an officer of the United States, or as a member of any State legislature, or as an executive or judicial officer of any State, to support the Constitution of the United States, shall have engaged in insurrection or rebellion against the same, or given aid or comfort to the enemies thereof. But Congress may by a vote of two-thirds of each House, remove such disability.

SECTION 4 The validity of the public debt of the United States, authorized by law, including debts incurred for payment of pensions and bounties for services in suppressing insurrection or rebellion, shall not be questioned. But neither the United States nor any State shall assume or pay any debt or obligation incurred in aid of insurrection or rebellion against the United States, or any claim for the loss or emancipation of any slave; but all such debts, obligations, and claims shall be held illegal and void.

SECTION 5 The Congress shall have the power to enforce, by appropriate legislation, the provisions of this article.

Amendment XV [1870]

SECTION 1 The right of citizens of the United States to vote shall not be denied or abridged by the United States or by any State on account of race, color, or previous condition of servitude.

SECTION 2 The Congress shall have power to enforce this article by appropriate legislation.

Amendment XVI [1913]

The Congress shall have power to lay and collect taxes on incomes, from whatever source derived, without apportionment among the several States, and without regard to any census or enumeration.

Amendment XVII [1913]

The Senate of the United States shall be composed of two Senators from each State, elected by the people thereof, for six years; and each Senator shall have one vote. The electors in each State shall have the qualifications requisite for electors of the most numerous branch of the State legislatures.

When vacancies happen in the representation of any State in the Senate, the executive authority of such State shall issue writs of election to fill such vacancies: Provided, That the legislature of any State may empower the executive thereof to make temporary appointments until the people fill the vacancies by election as the legislature may direct. This amendment shall not be so construed as to affect the election or term of any Senator chosen before it becomes valid as part of the Constitution.

Amendment XVIII [1919]

SECTION 1   After one year from the ratification of this article the manufacture, sale, or transportation of intoxicating liquors within, the importation thereof into, or the exportation thereof from the United States and all territory subject to the jurisdiction thereof for beverage purposes is hereby prohibited.

SECTION 2   The Congress and the several States shall have concurrent power to enforce this article by appropriate legislation.

SECTION 3   This article shall be inoperative unless it shall have been ratified as an amendment to the Constitution by the legislatures of the several States, as provided in the Constitution, within seven years from the date of the submission hereof to the States by the Congress.

Amendment XIX [1920]

The right of citizens of the United States to vote shall not be denied or abridged by the United States or by any State on account of sex.

Congress shall have power to enforce this article by appropriate legislation.

Amendment XX [1933]

SECTION 1   The terms of the President and Vice President shall end at noon on the 20th day of January, and the terms of Senators and Representatives at noon on the 3d day of January, of the years in which such terms would have ended if this article had not been ratified; and the terms of their successors shall then begin.

SECTION 2   The Congress shall assemble at least once in every year, and such meeting shall begin at noon on the 3d day of January, unless they shall by law appoint a different day.

SECTION 3   If, at the time fixed for the beginning of the term of the President, the President elect shall have died, the Vice President elect shall become President. If a President shall not have been chosen before the time fixed for the beginning of his term, or if the President elect shall have failed to qualify, then the Vice President elect shall act as President until a President shall have qualified; and the Congress may by law provide for the case wherein neither a President elect nor a Vice President elect shall have qualified, declaring who shall then act as President, or the manner in which one who is to act shall be selected, and such person shall act accordingly until a President or Vice President shall have qualified.

SECTION 4   The Congress may by law provide for the case of the death of any of the persons from whom the House of Representatives may choose a President whenever the right of choice shall have devolved upon them, and for the case of the death of any of the persons from whom the Senate may choose a Vice President whenever the right of choice shall have devolved upon them.

SECTION 5   Sections 1 and 2 shall take effect on the 15th day of October following the ratification of this article.

SECTION 6   This article shall be inoperative unless it shall have been ratified as an amendment to the Constitution by the legislatures of three-fourths of the several States within seven years from the date of its submission.

Amendment XXI [1933]

SECTION 1 The eighteenth article of amendment to the Constitution of the United States is hereby repealed.

SECTION 2 The transportation or importation into any State, Territory, or possession of the United States for delivery or use therein of intoxicating liquors, in violation of the laws thereof, is hereby prohibited.

SECTION 3 This article shall be inoperative unless it shall have been ratified as an amendment to the Constitution by conventions in the several States, as provided in the Constitution, within seven years from the date of the submission hereof to the States by the Congress.

Amendment XXII [1951]

No person shall be elected to the office of the President more than twice, and no person who has held the office of President, or acted as President, for more than two years of a term to which some other person was elected President shall be elected to the office of the President more than once.

But this Article shall not apply to any person holding the office of President when this Article was proposed by the Congress, and shall not prevent any person who may be holding the office of President or acting as President, during the term within which this Article becomes operative from holding the office of President or acting as President during the remainder of such term.

Amendment XXIII [1961]

SECTION 1 The District constituting the seat of Government of the United States shall appoint in such manner as the Congress may direct:

A number of electors of President and Vice President equal to the whole number of Senators and Representatives in Congress to which the District would be entitled if it were a State, but in no event more than the least populous State; they shall be in addition to those appointed by the States, but they shall be considered, for the purposes of the election of President and Vice President, to be electors appointed by a State; and they shall meet in the District and perform such duties as provided by the twelfth article of amendment.

SECTION 2 The Congress shall have power to enforce this article by appropriate legislation.

Amendment XXIV [1964]

SECTION 1 The right of citizens of the United States to vote in any primary or other election for President or Vice President, for electors for President or Vice President, or for Senator or Representative in Congress, shall not be denied or abridged by the United States or any State by reason of failure to pay any poll tax or other tax.

SECTION 2 The Congress shall have the power to enforce this article by appropriate legislation.

Amendment XXV [1967]

SECTION 1 In case of the removal of the President from office or his death or resignation, the Vice President shall become President.

SECTION 2 Whenever there is a vacancy in the office of the Vice President, the President shall nominate a Vice President who shall take the office upon confirmation by a majority vote of both houses of Congress.

SECTION 3 Whenever the President transmits to the President pro tempore of the Senate and the Speaker of the House of Representatives his written declaration that he is unable to discharge the powers and duties of his office, and until he transmits to them a written declaration to the contrary, such powers and duties shall be discharged by the Vice President as Acting President.

SECTION 4 Whenever the Vice President and a majority of either the principal officers of the executive departments, or of such other body as Congress may by law provide, transmit to the President pro tempore of the Senate and the Speaker of the House of Representatives their written declaration that the President is unable to discharge the powers and duties of his office, the Vice President shall immediately assume the powers and duties of the office as Acting President.

Thereafter, when the President transmits to the President pro tempore of the Senate and the Speaker of the House of Representatives his written declaration that no inability exists, he shall resume the powers and duties of his office unless the Vice President and a majority of either the principal officers of the executive departments, or of such other body as Congress may by law provide, transmit within four days to the President pro tempore of the Senate and the Speaker of the House of Representatives their written declaration that the President is unable to discharge the powers and duties of his office. Thereupon Congress shall decide the issue, assembling within 48 hours for that purpose if not in session. If the Congress, within 21 days after receipt of the latter written declaration, or, if Congress is not in session, within 21 days after Congress is required to assemble, determines by two-thirds vote of both houses that the President is unable to discharge the powers and duties of his office, the Vice President shall continue to discharge the same as Acting President; otherwise, the President shall resume the powers and duties of his office.

Amendment XXVI [1971]

SECTION 1 The right of citizens of the United States, who are 18 years of age or older, to vote shall not be denied or abridged by the United States or any state on account of age.

SECTION 2 The Congress shall have the power to enforce this article by appropriate legislation.

Amendment XXVII [1992]

No law varying the compensation for the service of Senators and Representatives shall take effect until an election of Representatives shall have intervened.

SOURCE: Library of Congress, *Constitution of the United States of America: Analysis and Interpretation*, https://www.congress.gov/constitution-annotated/

THE FEDERALIST NO. 10, NO. 51, AND NO. 78

The Federalist Papers is a collection of eighty-five essays written by Alexander Hamilton, John Jay, and James Madison under the pen name Publius. They were published in New York newspapers in 1787 and 1788 to support ratification of the Constitution. *Federalist* Nos. 10, 51, and 78 are reprinted here.

James Madison: *The Federalist* No. 10

Among the numerous advantages promised by a well constructed Union, none deserves to be more accurately developed than its tendency to break and control the violence of faction. The friend of popular governments never finds himself so much alarmed for their character and fate as when he contemplates their propensity to this dangerous vice. He will not fail, therefore, to set a due value on any plan which, without violating the principles to which he is attached, provides a proper cure for it. The instability, injustice, and confusion, introduced into the public councils, have, in truth been the mortal diseases under which popular governments have everywhere perished; as they continue to be the favorite and fruitful topics from which the adversaries to liberty derive their most specious declamations. The valuable improvements made by the American constitutions on the popular models, both ancient and modern, cannot certainly be too much admired; but it would be an unwarrantable partiality, to contend that they have as effectually obviated the danger on this side, as was wished and expected. Complaints are everywhere heard from our most considerate and virtuous citizens, equally the friends of public and private faith, and of public and personal liberty, that our governments are too unstable; that the public good is disregarded in the conflicts of rival parties; and that measures are too often decided, not according to the rules of justice, and the rights of the minor party, but by the superior force of an interested and overbearing majority. However anxiously we may wish that these complaints had no foundation, the evidence of known facts will not permit us to deny that they are in some degree true. It will be found, indeed, on a candid review of our situation, that some of the distresses under which we labor, have been erroneously charged on the operation of our governments; but it will be found, at the same time, that other causes will not alone account for many of our heaviest misfortunes; and, particularly, for the prevailing and increasing distrust of public engagements, and alarm for private rights, which are echoed from one end of the continent to the other. These must be chiefly, if not wholly, effects of the unsteadiness and injustice, with which a factious spirit has tainted our public administrations.

By a faction, I understand a number of citizens, whether amounting to a majority or minority of the whole, who are united and actuated by some common impulse of passion, or of interest, adverse to the rights of other citizens, or to the permanent and aggregate interests of the community.

There are two methods of curing the mischiefs of faction: The one, by removing its causes; the other, by controlling its effects.

There are again two methods of removing the causes of faction: the one, by destroying the liberty which is essential to its existence; the other, by giving to every citizen the same opinions, the same passions, and the same interests.

It could never be more truly said, than of the first remedy, that it was worse than the disease. Liberty is to faction what air is to fire, an aliment, without which it instantly expires. But it could not be a less folly to abolish liberty, which is essential to political life because it nourishes faction, than it would be to wish the annihilation of air, which is essential to animal life, because it imparts to fire its destructive agency.

The second expedient is as impracticable, as the first would be unwise. As long as the reason of man continues fallible, and he is at liberty to exercise it, different opinions will be formed. As long as the connection subsists between his reason and his self-love, his opinions and his passions will have a reciprocal influence on each other; and the former will be objects to which the latter will attach themselves. The diversity in the faculties of men, from which the rights of property originate, is not less an insuperable obstacle to a uniformity of interests. The protection of those faculties is the first object of government. From the protection of different and unequal faculties of acquiring property, the possession of different degrees and kinds of property immediately results; and from the influence of these on the sentiments and views of the respective proprietors, ensues a division of the society into different interests and parties.

The latent causes of faction are thus sown in the nature of man; and we see them everywhere brought into different degrees of activity, according to the different circumstances of civil society. A zeal for different opinions concerning religion, concerning government, and many other points, as well of speculation as of practice;

an attachment to different leaders, ambitiously contending for preeminence and power; or to persons of other descriptions, whose fortunes have been interesting to the human passions, have, in turn, divided mankind into parties, inflamed them with mutual animosity, and rendered them much more disposed to vex and oppress each other, than to cooperate for their common good. So strong is this propensity of mankind, to fall into mutual animosities, that where no substantial occasion presents itself, the most frivolous and fanciful distinctions have been sufficient to kindle their unfriendly passions, and excite their most violent conflicts. But the most common and durable source of factions has been the various and unequal distribution of property. Those who hold, and those who are without property, have ever formed distinct interests in society. Those who are creditors, and those who are debtors, fall under a like discrimination. A landed interest, a manufacturing interest, a mercantile interest, a moneyed interest, with many lesser interests, grow up of necessity in civilized nations, and divide them into different classes, actuated by different sentiments and views. The regulation of these various and interfering interests forms the principle task of modern legislation, and involves the spirit of party and faction in the necessary and ordinary operations of government.

No man is allowed to be a judge in his own cause; because his interest will certainly bias his judgment, and, not improbably, corrupt his integrity. With equal, nay, with greater reason, a body of men are unfit to be both judges and parties at the same time; yet what are many of the most important acts of legislation, but so many judicial determinations, not indeed concerning the rights of single persons, but concerning the rights of large bodies of citizens? And what are the different classes of legislators, but advocates and parties to the cause which they determine? Is a law proposed concerning private debts? It is a question to which the creditors are parties on one side, and the debtors on the other. Justice ought to hold the balance between them. Yet the parties are, and must be, themselves the judges; and the most numerous party, or, in other words, the most powerful faction, must be expected to prevail. Shall domestic manufactures be encouraged, and in what degree, by restrictions on foreign manufactures? are questions which would be differently decided by the landed and the manufacturing classes; and probably by neither with a sole regard to justice and the public good....

It is in vain to say, that enlightened statesmen will be able to adjust these clashing interests, and render them all subservient to the public good. Enlightened statesmen will not always be at the helm; nor, in many cases, can such an adjustment be made at all, without taking into view indirect and remote considerations, which will rarely prevail over the immediate interest which one party may find in disregarding the rights of another, or the good of the whole.

The inference to which we are brought is, that the causes of faction cannot be removed; and that relief is only to be sought in the means of controlling its effects.

If a faction consists of less than a majority, relief is supplied by the republican principle, which enables the majority to defeat its sinister views, by regular vote. It may clog the administration, it may convulse the society; but it will be unable to execute and mask its violence under the forms of the constitution. When a majority is included in a faction, the form of popular government, on the other hand, enables it to sacrifice to its ruling passion or interest, both the public good and the rights of other citizens. To secure the public good, and private rights, against the danger of such a faction, and at the same time to preserve the spirit and the form of popular government, is then the great object to which our inquiries are directed. Let me add, that it is the great desideratum, by which alone this form of government can be rescued from the opprobrium under which it has so long labored, and be recommended to the esteem and adoption of mankind.

By what means is this object attainable? Evidently by one of two only. Either the existence of the same passion or interest in a majority, at the same time must be prevented; or the majority, having such coexistent passion or interest, must be rendered, by their number and local situation, unable to concert and carry into effect schemes of oppression. If the impulse and the opportunity be suffered to coincide, we well know, that neither moral nor religious motives can be relied on as an adequate control. They are not found to be such on the injustice and violence of individuals, and lose their efficacy in proportion to the number combined together; that is in proportion as their efficacy becomes needful.

From this view of the subject, it may be concluded, that a pure democracy, by which I mean a society consisting of a small number of citizens, who assemble and administer the government in person, can admit of no cure from the mischiefs of faction. A common passion or interest will, in almost every case, be felt by a majority of the whole; a communication and concert, results from the form of government itself; and there is nothing to check the inducements to sacrifice the weaker party, or an obnoxious individual. Hence it is, that such democracies have ever been spectacles of turbulence and contention; have ever been found incompatible with personal security, or the rights of property; and have, in general been as short in their lives, as they have been violent in their deaths. Theoretic politicians, who have patronized this species of government, have erroneously supposed that by reducing mankind to a perfect equality in their political rights, they would, at the same time, be perfectly equalized and assimilated in their possessions, their opinions, and their passions.

A republic, by which I mean a government in which the scheme of representation takes place, opens a different prospect, and promises the cure for which we are seeking. Let us examine the points in which it varies from pure democracy, and we shall comprehend both the nature of the cure and the efficacy which it must derive from the union.

The two great points of difference, between a democracy and a republic, are, first, the delegation of the government, in the latter, to a small number of citizens elected by the rest; secondly, the greater number of citizens, and greater sphere of country, over which the latter may be extended.

The effect of the first difference is on the one hand, to refine and enlarge the public views, by passing them through the medium of a chosen body of citizens, whose wisdom may best discern the true interest in their country, and whose patriotism and love of justice, will be least likely to sacrifice it to temporary or partial considerations. Under such a regulation, it may well happen, that the public voice, pronounced by the representatives of the people, will be more consonant to the public good, than if pronounced by the people themselves, convened for the purpose. On the other hand, the effect may be inverted. Men of factious tempers, of local prejudices, or of sinister designs, may by intrigue, by corruption, or by other means, first obtain the suffrages, and then betray the interests, of the people. The question resulting is, whether small or extensive republics are most favorable to the election of proper guardians of the public weal; and it is clearly decided in favor of the latter by two obvious considerations.

In the first place, it is to be remarked, that however small the republic may be, the representatives must be raised to a certain number, in order to guard against the cabals of a few; and that however large it may be, they must be limited to a certain number, in order to guard against the confusion of a multitude. Hence, the number of representatives in the two cases not being in proportion to that of the constituents, and being proportionally greatest in the small republic, it follows that if the proportion of fit characters be not less in the large than in the small republic, the former will present a greater option, and consequently a greater probability of a fit choice.

In the next place, as each representative will be chosen by a greater number of citizens in the large than in the small republic, it will be more difficult for unworthy candidates to practice with success the vicious arts, by which elections are too often carried; and the suffrages of the people being more free, will be more likely to center in men who possess the most attractive merit, and the most diffusive and established characters....

The other point of difference is, the greater number of citizens, and extent of territory, which may be brought within the compass of republican, than of democratic government; and it is this circumstance principally which renders factious combinations less to be dreaded in the former, than in the latter. The smaller the society, the fewer probably will be the distinct parties and interests composing it; the fewer the distinct parties and interests, the more frequently will a majority be found of the same party; and the smaller the number of individuals composing a majority, and the smaller the compass within which they are placed, the more easily they will concert and execute their plans of oppression. Extend the sphere, and you take in a greater variety of parties and interests; you make it less probable that a majority of the whole will have a common motive to invade the rights of other citizens; or if such a common motive exists, it will be more difficult for all who feel it to discover their own strength, and to act in unison with each other....

Hence, it clearly appears, that the same advantage, which a republic has over a democracy, in controlling the effects of faction, is enjoyed by a large over a small republic—is enjoyed by the union over the states composing it. Does this advantage consist in the substitution of representatives, whose enlightened views and virtuous sentiments render them superior to local prejudices, and to schemes of injustice? It will not be denied, that the representation of the union will be most likely to possess these requisite endowments. Does it consist in the greater security afforded by a greater variety of parties, against the event of any one party being able to outnumber and oppress the rest? In an equal degree does the increased variety of parties, comprised within the union, increase this security? Does it, in fine, consist in the greater obstacles opposed to the concert and accomplishment of the secret wishes of an unjust and interested majority? Here, again, the extent of the union gives it the most palpable advantage. The influence of factious leaders may kindle a flame within their particular states, but will be unable to spread a general conflagration through the other states; a religious sect may degenerate into a political faction in a part of the confederacy; but the variety of sects dispersed over the entire face of it, must secure the national councils against any danger from that source; a rage for paper money, for an abolition of debts, for an equal division of property, or for any other improper or wicked project, will be less apt to pervade the whole body of the union, than a particular member of it; in the same proportion as such a malady is more likely to taint a particular country or district, than an entire state.

In the extent and proper structure of the union, therefore, we behold a republican remedy for the diseases most incident to republican government. And according to the degree of pleasure and pride we feel in being republicans, ought to be our zeal in cherishing the spirit, and supporting the character of Federalists.

James Madison: *The Federalist* No. 51

To what expedient then shall we finally resort, for maintaining in practice the necessary partition of power among the several departments, as laid down in the constitution? The only answer that can be given is, that as all these exterior provisions are found to be inadequate, the defect must be supplied, by so contriving the interior structure of the government, as that its several constituent parts may, by their mutual relations, be the means of keeping each other in their proper places....

In order to lay a due foundation for that separate and distinct exercise of the different powers of government, which, to a certain extent, is admitted on all hands to be essential to the preservation of liberty, it is evident that each department should have a will of its own; and consequently should be so constituted, that the members of each should have as little agency as possible in the appointment of the members of the others....

It is equally evident, that the members of each department should be as little dependent as possible on those of the others, for the emoluments annexed to their offices. Were the executive magistrate, or the judges, not independent of the legislature in this particular, their independence in every other would be merely nominal.

But the great security against a gradual concentration of the several powers in the same department, consists in giving to those who administer each department, the necessary constitutional means, and personal motives, to resist encroachments of the others. The provision for defense must in this, as in all other cases, be made commensurate to the danger of attack. Ambition must be made to counteract ambition. The interest of the man must be connected with the constitutional rights of the place. It may be a reflection on human nature, that such devices should be necessary to control the abuses of government. But what is government itself, but the greatest of all reflections on human nature? If men were angels, no government would be necessary. If angels were to govern men, neither external nor internal controls on government would be necessary. In framing a government, which is to be administered by men over men, the great difficulty lies in this: You must first enable the government to control the governed; and in the next place, oblige it to control itself. A dependence on the people is, no doubt, the primary control on the government; but experience has taught mankind the necessity of auxiliary precautions.

This policy of supplying by opposite and rival interests, the defect of better motives, might be traced through the whole system of human affairs, private as well as public. We see it particularly displayed in all the subordinate distributions of power; where the constant aim is, to divide and arrange the several offices in such a manner, as that each may be a check on the other; that the private interest of every individual, may be a sentinel over the public rights. These interventions of prudence cannot be less requisite to the distribution of the supreme powers of the state.

But it is not possible to give to each department an equal power of self-defense. In republican government, the legislative authority necessarily predominates. The remedy for this inconvenience is, to divide the legislature into different branches; and to render them by different modes of election, and different principles of action, as little connected with each other, as the nature of their common functions, and their common dependence on the society will admit. It may even be necessary to guard against dangerous encroachments, by still further precautions. As the weight of the legislative authority requires that it should be thus divided, the weakness of the executive may require, on the other hand, that it should be fortified. An absolute negative on the legislature, appears, at first view, to be the natural defense with which the executive magistrate should be armed. But perhaps it would be neither altogether safe, nor alone sufficient. On ordinary occasions, it might not be exerted with the requisite firmness; and on extraordinary occasions, it might be perfidiously abused. May not this defect of an absolute negative be supplied by some qualified connection between this weaker department, and the weaker branch of the stronger department, by which the latter may be led to support the constitutional rights of the former, without being too much detached from the rights of its own department?

There are, moreover, two considerations particularly applicable to the federal system of America, which place that system in a very interesting point of view.

FIRST In a single republic, all the power surrendered by the people is submitted to the administration of a single government, and the usurpations are guarded against by a division of the government into distinct and separate departments. In the compound republic of America, the power surrendered by the people is first divided between two distinct governments, and then the portion allotted to each subdivided among distinct and separate departments. Hence a double security arises to the rights of the people. The different governments will control each other, at the same time that each will be controlled by itself.

SECOND It is of great importance in a republic not only to guard the society against the oppression of its rulers, but to guard one part of the society against the injustice of the other part. Different interests necessarily exist in different classes of citizens. If a majority be united by a common interest, the rights of the minority will be insecure.

There are but two methods of providing against this evil: the one by creating a will in the community independent of the majority—that is, of the society itself; the other, by comprehending in the society so many separate descriptions of citizens as will render an unjust combination of a majority of the whole very probable, if not impracticable. The first method prevails in all governments possessing an hereditary or self-appointed authority. This, at best, is but a precarious security; because a power independent of the society may as well espouse the unjust views of the major, as the rightful interests of the minor party, and may possibly be turned against both parties. The second method will be exemplified in the federal republic of the United States. Whilst all authority in it will be derived from and dependent on the society, the society itself will be broken into so many parts, interests and classes of citizens, that the rights of individuals, or of the minority, will be in little danger from interested combinations of the majority. In a free government the security for civil rights must be the same as that for religious rights. It consists in the one case in the multiplicity of interests, and in the other in the multiplicity of sects. The degree of security in both cases will depend on the number of interests and sects; and this may be presumed to depend on the extent of country and number of people comprehended under the same government. This view of the subject must particularly recommend a proper federal system to all the sincere and considerate friends of republican government, since it shows that in exact proportion as the territory of the Union may be formed into more circumscribed Confederacies, or States, oppressive combinations of a majority will be facilitated; the best security, under the republican forms, for the rights of every class of citizens, will be diminished; and consequently the stability and independence of some member of the government, the only other security, must be proportionately increased. Justice is the end of the government. It is the end of civil society. It ever has been and ever will be pursued until it be obtained, or until liberty be lost in the pursuit. In a society under the forms of which the stronger faction can readily unite and oppress the weaker, anarchy may as truly be said to reign as in a state of nature, where the weaker individual is not secured against the violence of the stronger; and as, in the latter state, even the stronger individuals are prompted, by the uncertainty of their condition, to submit to a government which may protect the weak as well as themselves; so, in the former state, will the more powerful factions or parties be gradually induced, by a like motive, to wish for a government which will protect all parties, the weaker as well as the more powerful. It can be little doubted that if the State of Rhode Island was separated from the Confederacy and left to itself, the insecurity of rights under the popular form of government within such narrow limits would be displayed by such reiterated oppressions of factious majorities that some power altogether independent of the people would soon be called for by the voice of the very factions whose misrule had proved the necessity of it. In the extended republic of the United States, and among the great variety of interests, parties, and sects which it embraces, a coalition of a majority of the whole society could seldom take place on any other principles than those of justice and the general good; whilst there being thus less danger to a minor from the will of a major party, there must be less pretext, also, to provide for the security of the former, by introducing into the government a will not dependent on the latter, or, in other words, a will independent of the society itself. It is no less certain than it is important, notwithstanding the contrary opinions which have been entertained, that the larger the society, provided it lie within a practical sphere, the more duly capable it will be of self-government. And happily for the republican cause, the practicable sphere may be carried to a very great extent, by a judicious modification and mixture of the federal principle.

Alexander Hamilton: *The Federalist* No. 78

We proceed now to an examination of the judiciary department of the proposed government.

In unfolding the defects of the existing confederation, the utility and necessity of a federal judicature have been clearly pointed out. It is the less necessary to recapitulate the considerations there urged; as the propriety of the institution in the abstract is not disputed; the only questions which have been raised being relative to the manner of constituting it, and to its extent. To these points, therefore, our observations shall be confined.

The manner of constituting it seems to embrace these several objects: 1st. The mode of appointing the judges; 2nd. The tenure by which they are to hold their places; 3rd. The partition of the judiciary authority between courts, and their relations to each other.

FIRST As to the mode of appointing the judges: This is the same with that of appointing the officers of the union in general, and has been so fully discussed...that nothing can be said here which would not be useless repetition.

SECOND As to the tenure by which the judges are to hold their places: This chiefly concerns their duration in office; the provisions for their support; the precautions for their responsibility.

According to the plan of the convention, all the judges who may be appointed by the United States are to hold their offices during good behavior; which is conformable to the most approved of the state constitutions.... . The standard of good behavior for the continuance in office of the judicial magistracy is certainly one of the most valuable of the modern improvements in the practice of government. In a monarchy, it is an excellent barrier to the despotism of the prince; in a republic, it is a no less excellent barrier to the encroachments and oppressions of the representative body. And it is the best expedient which can be devised in any government, to secure a steady, upright, and impartial administration of the laws.

Whoever attentively considers the different departments of power must perceive, that, in a government in which they are separated from each other, the judiciary, from the nature of its functions, will always be the least dangerous to the political rights of the constitution; because it will be at least in a capacity to annoy or injure them. The executive not only dispenses the honors, but holds the sword of the community. The legislature not only commands the purse, but prescribes the rules by which the duties and rights of every citizen are to be regulated. The judiciary, on the contrary, has no influence over either the sword or the purse; no direction either of the strength or of the wealth of the society; and can take no active resolution whatever. It may truly be said to have neither force nor will, but merely judgment; and must ultimately depend upon the aid of the executive arm for the efficacious exercise even of this faculty.

This simple view of the matter suggests several important consequences: It proves incontestably, that the judiciary is beyond comparison, the weakest of the three departments of power, that it can never attack with success either of the other two: and that all possible care is requisite to enable it to defend itself against their attacks. It equally proves, that, though individual oppression may now and then proceed from the courts of justice, the general liberty of the people can never be endangered from that quarter; I mean so long as the judiciary remains truly distinct from both the legislature and executive. For I agree, that "there is no liberty, if the power of judging be not separated from the legislative and executive powers." It proves, in the last place, that as liberty can have nothing to fear from the judiciary alone, but would have everything to fear from its union with either of the other departments; that, as all the effects of such a union must ensue from a dependence of the former on the latter, notwithstanding a nominal and apparent separation; that as, from the natural feebleness of the judiciary, it is in continual jeopardy of being overpowered, awed or influenced by its coordinate branches; that, as nothing can contribute so much to its firmness and independence as permanency in office, this quality may therefore be justly regarded as an indispensable ingredient in its constitution; and, in a great measure, as the citadel of the public justice and the public security.

The complete independence of the courts of justice is peculiarly essential in a limited constitution. By a limited constitution, I understand one which contains certain specified exceptions to the legislative authority; such, for instance, as that it shall pass no bills of attainder, no ex post facto laws, and the like. Limitations of this kind can be preserved in practice no other way than through the medium of the courts of justice, whose duty it must be to declare all acts contrary to the manifest tenor of the constitution void. Without this, all the reservations of particular rights or privileges would amount to nothing.

Some perplexity respecting the right of the courts to pronounce legislative acts void, because contrary to the constitution, has arisen from an imagination that the doctrine would imply a superiority of the judiciary to the legislative power. It is urged that the authority which can declare the acts of another void, must necessarily be superior to the one whose acts may be declared void. As this doctrine is of great importance in all the American constitutions, a brief discussion of the grounds on which it rests cannot be unacceptable.

There is no position which depends on clearer principles than that every act of a delegated authority, contrary to the tenor of the commission under which it is exercised, is void. No legislative act, therefore, contrary to the constitution, can be valid. To deny this would be to affirm, that the deputy is greater then his principal; that the servant is above his master; that the representatives of the people are superior to the people themselves; that men, acting by virtue of powers, may do not only what their powers do not authorize, but what they forbid.

If it be said that the legislative body are themselves the constitutional judges of their own powers, and that the construction they put upon them is conclusive upon the other departments, it may be answered, that this cannot be the natural presumption, where it is not to be collected from any particular provisions in the constitution. It is not otherwise to be supposed that the constitution could intend to enable the representatives of the people to substitute their will to that of their constituents. It is far more rational to suppose that the courts were designed to be an intermediate body between the people and the legislature, in order, among other things, to keep the latter within the limits assigned to their authority. The interpretation of the laws is the proper and peculiar province of the courts. A constitution is, in fact, and must be, regarded by the judges as a fundamental law. It must therefore belong to them to ascertain its meaning, as well as the meaning of any particular act proceeding from the legislative body. If there should happen to be an irreconcilable variance between the two, that which has the superior obligation and validity ought, of course, to be preferred; in other words, the constitution ought to be preferred to the statute, the intention of the people to the intention of their agents.

Nor does this conclusion by any means suppose a superiority of the judicial to the legislative power. It only supposes that the power of the people is superior to both; and that where the will of the legislature declared in its statutes, stands in opposition to that of the people declared in the constitution, the judges ought to be governed by the latter, rather than the former. They ought to regulate their decisions by the fundamental laws, rather than by those which are not fundamental... .

It can be of no weight to say, that the courts, on the pretense of a repugnancy, may substitute their own pleasure to the constitutional intentions of the legislature. This might as well happen in the case of two contradictory statutes; or it might as well happen in every adjudication upon any single statute. The courts must declare the sense of the law; and if they should be disposed to exercise will instead of judgment, the consequence would equally be the substitution of their pleasure to that of the legislative body. The observation, if it proved anything, would prove that there ought to be no judges distinct from the body.

If then the courts of justice are to be considered as the bulwarks of a limited constitution, against legislative encroachments, this consideration will afford a strong argument for the permanent tenure of judicial officers, since nothing will contribute so much as this to that independent spirit in the judges, which must be essential to the faithful performance of so arduous a duty.

This independence of the judges is equally requisite to guard the constitution and the rights of individuals, from the effects of those ill-humors which are the arts of designing men, or the influence of particular conjunctures, sometimes disseminate among the people themselves, and which, though they speedily give place to better information, and more deliberate reflection, have a tendency, in the meantime, to occasion dangerous innovations in the government, and serious oppressions of the minor party in the community.... Until the people have, by some solemn and author-itative act, annulled or changed the established form, it is binding upon themselves collectively, as well as individually; and no presumption, or even knowledge of their sentiments, can warrant their representatives in a departure from it, prior to such an act. But it is easy to see, that it would require an uncommon portion of fortitude in the judges to do their duty as faithful guardians of the constitution, where legislative invasions of it had been instigated by the major voice of the community.

But it is not with a view to infractions of the constitution only, that the indepen-dence of the judges may be an essential safeguard against the effects of occasional ill-humors in the society. These sometimes extend no farther than to the injury of the private rights of particular classes of citizens, by unjust and partial laws. Here also the firmness of the judicial magistracy is of vast importance in mitigating the severity, and confining the operation of such laws. It not only serves to moderate the immedi-ate mischiefs of those which may have been passed, but it operates as a check upon the legislative body in passing them; who, perceiving that obstacles to the success of an iniquitous intention are to be expected from the scruples of the courts, are in a manner compelled by the very motives of the injustice they meditate, to qualify their attempts....

That inflexible and uniform adherence to the rights of the constitution, and of individuals, which we perceive to be indispensable in the courts of justice, can cer-tainly not be expected from judges who hold their offices by a temporary commis-sion. Periodical appointments, however regulated, or by whomsoever made, would, in some way or other, be fatal to their necessary independence. If the power of making them was committed either to the executive or legislature, there would be danger of an improper compliance to the branch which possessed it; if to both, there would be an unwillingness to hazard the displeasure of either; if to the people, or to persons chosen by them for the special purpose, there would be too great a disposition to con-sult popularity to justify a reliance that nothing would be consulted but the constitu-tion and the laws.

There is yet a further and a weighty reason for the permanency of judicial offices, which is deducible from the nature of the qualifications they require. It has been fre-quently remarked, with great propriety, that a voluminous code of laws is one of the inconveniences necessarily connected with the advantages of a free government. To avoid an arbitrary discretion in the courts, it is indispensable that they should be bound down by strict rules and precedents, which serve to define and point out their duty in every particular case that comes before them; and it will readily be conceived, from the variety of controversies which grow out of the folly and wickedness of mankind, that the records of those precedents must unavoidably swell to a very considerable bulk, and must demand long and laborious study to acquire a competent knowledge of them. Hence it is, that there can be but few men in the society, who will have suffi-cient skill in the laws to qualify them for the stations of judges. And making the proper deductions for the ordinary depravity of human nature, the number must be still smaller, of those who unite the requisite integrity with the requisite knowledge ...

SOURCE: Alexander Hamilton, James Madison, and John Jay, *The Federalist Papers*, ed. Clinton Rossiter (New York: New American Library, 1961; originally published 1787–1788)

PRESIDENTS AND CONGRESSES, 1789–PRESENT

Year	President and Vice President	Party of President	Congress	Majority Party	
				House	Senate
1789–1797	**George Washington**	None	1st	Admin. Supporters	Admin. Supporters
	John Adams		2nd	Federalist	Federalist
			3rd	Democratic-Republican	Federalist
			4th	Federalist	Federalist
1797–1801	**John Adams**	Federalist	5th	Federalist	Federalist
	Thomas Jefferson		6th	Federalist	Federalist
1801–1809	**Thomas Jefferson**		7th	Democratic-Republican	Democratic-Republican
	Aaron Burr (to 1805)		8th	Democratic-Republican	Democratic-Republican
	George Clinton (to 1809)		9th	Democratic-Republican	Democratic-Republican
			10th	Democratic-Republican	Democratic-Republican
1809–1817	**James Madison**	Democratic- Republican	11th	Democratic-Republican	Democratic-Republican
	George Clinton (to 1813)		12th	Democratic-Republican	Democratic-Republican
	Elbridge Gerry (to 1817)		13th	Democratic-Republican	Democratic-Republican
			14th	Democratic-Republican	Democratic-Republican
1817–1825	**James Monroe**	Democratic-Republican	15th	Democratic-Republican	Democratic-Republican
	Daniel D. Tompkins		16th	Democratic-Republican	Democratic-Republican
			17th	Democratic-Republican	Democratic-Republican
			18th	Democratic-Republican	Democratic-Republican
1825–1829	**John Quincy Adams**	National-	19th	Admin. Supporters	Admin. Supporters
	John C. Calhoun	Republican	20th	Jacksonian Democrats	Jacksonian Democrats
1829–1837	**Andrew Jackson**	Democratic	21st	Democratic	Democratic
	John C. Calhoun (to 1833)		22nd	Democratic	Democratic
	Martin Van Buren (to 1837)		23rd	Democratic	Democratic
			24th	Democratic	Democratic
1837–1841	**Martin Van Buren**	Democratic	25th	Democratic	Democratic
	Richard M. Johnson		26th	Democratic	Democratic
1841	**William H. Harrison** (died a month after inauguration)	Whig			
	John Tyler				
1841–1845	**John Tyler**	Whig	27th	Whig	Whig
	(VP vacant)		28th	Democratic	Whig
1845–1849	**James K. Polk**	Democratic	29th	Democratic	Democratic
	George M. Dallas		30th	Whig	Democratic
1849–1850	**Zachary Taylor** (died in office)	Whig	31st	Democratic	Democratic
	Millard Fillmore				
1850–1853	**Millard Fillmore**	Whig	32nd	Democratic	Democratic
	(VP vacant)				
1853–1857	**Franklin Pierce**	Democratic	33rd	Democratic	Democratic
	William R. King		34th	Republican	Democratic
1857–1861	**James Buchanan**	Democratic	35th	Democratic	Democratic
	John C. Breckinridge		36th	Republican	Democratic
1861–1865	**Abraham Lincoln** (died in office)	Republican	37th	Republican	Republican
	Hannibal Hamlin (to 1865)		38th	Republican	Republican
	Andrew Johnson (1865)				

Year	President and Vice President	Party of President	Congress	Majority Party	
				House	Senate
1865–1869	**Andrew Johnson** (VP vacant)	Republican	39th	Unionist	Unionist
			40th	Republican	Republican
1869–1877	**Ulysses S. Grant** Schuyler Colfax (to 1873) Henry Wilson (to 1877)	Republican	41st	Republican	Republican
			42nd	Republican	Republican
			43rd	Republican	Republican
			44th	Democratic	Republican
1877–1881	**Rutherford B. Hayes** William A. Wheeler	Republican	45th	Democratic	Republican
			46th	Democratic	Democratic
1881	**James A. Garfield** (died in office) Chester A. Arthur	Republican	47th	Republican	Republican
1881–1885	**Chester A. Arthur** (VP vacant)	Republican	48th	Democratic	Republican
1885–1889	**Grover Cleveland** Thomas A. Hendricks	Democratic	49th	Democratic	Republican
			50th	Democratic	Republican
1889–1893	**Benjamin Harrison** Levi P. Morton	Republican	51st	Republican	Republican
			52nd	Democratic	Republican
1893–1897	**Grover Cleveland** Adlai E. Stevenson	Democratic	53rd	Democratic	Democratic
			54th	Republican	Republican
1897–1901	**William McKinley** (died in office) Garret A. Hobart (to 1901) Theodore Roosevelt (1901)	Republican	55th	Republican	Republican
			56th	Republican	Republican
1901–1909	**Theodore Roosevelt** (VP vacant, 1901–1905) Charles W. Fairbanks (1905–1909)	Republican	57th	Republican	Republican
			58th	Republican	Republican
			59th	Republican	Republican
			60th	Republican	Republican
1909–1913	**William Howard Taft** James S. Sherman	Republican	61st	Republican	Republican
			62nd	Democratic	Republican
1913–1921	**Woodrow Wilson** Thomas R. Marshall	Democratic	63rd	Democratic	Democratic
			64th	Democratic	Democratic
			65th	Democratic	Democratic
			66th	Republican	Republican
1921–1923	**Warren G. Harding** (died in office) Calvin Coolidge	Republican	67th	Republican	Republican
1923–1929	**Calvin Coolidge** (VP vacant, 1923–1925) Charles G. Dawes (1925–1929)	Republican	68th	Republican	Republican
			69th	Republican	Republican
			70th	Republican	Republican
1929–1933	**Herbert Hoover** Charles Curtis	Republican	71st	Republican	Republican
			72nd	Democratic	Republican
1933–1945	**Franklin D. Roosevelt** (died in office) John N. Garner (1933–1941) Henry A. Wallace (1941–1945) Harry S Truman (1945) 77th	Democratic	73rd	Democratic	Democratic
			74th	Democratic	Democratic
			75th	Democratic	Democratic
			76th	Democratic	Democratic
		Democratic	77th	Democratic	Democratic
			78th	Democratic	Democratic
1945–1953	**Harry S Truman** (VP vacant, 1945–1949) Alben W. Barkley (1949–1953)	Democratic	79th	Democratic	Democratic
			80th	Republican	Republican
			81st	Democratic	Democratic
			82nd	Democratic	Democratic

Year	President and Vice President	Party of President	Congress	Majority Party	
				House	Senate
1953–1961	**Dwight D. Eisenhower** Richard M. Nixon	Republican	83rd	Republican	Republican
			84th	Democratic	Democratic
			85th	Democratic	Democratic
			86th	Democratic	Democratic
1961–1963	**John F. Kennedy** (died in office) Lyndon B. Johnson	Democratic	87th	Democratic	Democratic
1963–1969	**Lyndon B. Johnson** (VP vacant, 1963–1965) Hubert H. Humphrey (1965–1969)	Democratic	88th	Democratic	Democratic
			89th	Democratic	Democratic
			90th	Democratic	Democratic
1969–1974	**Richard M. Nixon** (resigned office) Spiro T. Agnew (resigned office) Gerald R. Ford (appointed vice president)	Republican	91st	Democratic	Democratic
			92nd	Democratic	Democratic
1974–1977	**Gerald R. Ford** Nelson A. Rockefeller (appointed vice president)	Republican	93rd	Democratic	Democratic
			94th	Democratic	Democratic
1977–1981	**Jimmy Carter** Walter Mondale	Democratic	95th	Democratic	Democratic
			96th	Democratic	Democratic
1981–1989	**Ronald Reagan** George H. W. Bush	Republican	97th	Democratic	Republican
			98th	Democratic	Republican
			99th	Democratic	Republican
			100th	Democratic	Democratic
1989–1993	**George H. W. Bush** J. Danforth Quayle	Republican	101st	Democratic	Democratic
			102nd	Democratic	Democratic
1993–2001	**Bill Clinton** Albert Gore Jr.	Democratic	103rd	Democratic	Democratic
			104th	Republican	Republican
			105th	Republican	Republican
			106th	Republican	Republican
2001–2009	**George W. Bush** Richard Cheney	Republican	107th	Republican	Democratic
			108th	Republican	Republican
			109th	Republican	Republican
			110th	Democratic	Democratic
2009–2017	**Barack Obama** Joseph Biden	Democratic	111th	Democratic	Democratic
			112th	Republican	Democratic
			113th	Republican	Democratic
			114th	Republican	Republican
2017–2020	**Donald Trump** Michael Pence	Republican	115th	Republican	Republican
			116th	Democratic	Republican

NOTES

1. During the entire administration of George Washington and part of the administration of John Quincy Adams, Congress was not organized in terms of parties. This table shows that during these periods, the supporters of the respective administrations maintained control of Congress.
2. This table shows only the two dominant parties in Congress. Independents, members of minor parties, and vacancies have been omitted.

Glossary

1965 Voting Rights Act   A law that banned racial discrimination in voting across the United States; it gave the federal government broad powers to register voters in a set of states, mostly in the South, that had long practiced election discrimination, and required that such state pre-clear any changes in its election laws with the Department of Justice.

A

advocacy groups   Interest groups organized to support a cause or ideology.

affirmative action   Programs of private and public institutions favoring minorities and women in hiring and contracting, and in admissions to colleges and universities, in an attempt to compensate for past discrimination or to create more diversity.

Affordable Care Act (ACA)   The far-reaching health care reform law passed in 2010. The Act was aimed at increasing access to health insurance for all Americans and driving down the rising, burdensome cost of health care in the United States.

agency   A general name used for a subunit of a cabinet department.

agenda setting   The way media outlets can affect people's opinions about what issues are important.

agents of socialization   The institutions and individuals that shape the core beliefs and attitudes of people.

aggregate public opinion   The political attitudes of the public as a whole, expressed as averages, percentages, or other summaries of many individuals' opinions.

amicus curiae   Latin for "friend of the court"; a legal brief in which individuals not party to a suit may have their views heard in court.

anarchist   One who believes that people are natural cooperators capable of creating free and decent societies without the need for government.

Anti-Federalists   Opponents of the Constitution during the fight over its ratification; the orientation of people like Patrick Henry.

appellate courts   Courts that hear cases on appeal from other courts.

appropriation   Legal authority for a federal agency to spend money from the U.S. Treasury.

appropriations committees   The committees in the House and Senate that set specific spending levels in the budget for federal programs and agencies.

Articles of Confederation   The first constitution of the United States, adopted during the last stages of the Revolutionary War, created a system of government with most power lodged in the states and little in the central government.

asymmetric warfare   Unconventional tactics used by a combatant against an enemy with superior conventional military capabilities.

autocracy   General term that describes all forms of government characterized by rule by a single person or by a group with total power, whether a monarchy, a military tyranny, or a theocracy.

B

balance of trade   The annual difference between payments and receipts between a country and its trading partners.

ballot fatigue   The exhaustion of voter interest and knowledge in elections caused by election frequency and the length and complexity of ballots.

battleground state   Those states which are highly competitive in the presidential general election.

beat   The assigned location where a reporter regularly gathers news stories.

bias   Deviation from ideal standards such as representativeness or objectivity.

bicameral   As applied to a legislative body, consisting of two houses or chambers.

bill markup   The process of revising a bill in committee.

bill of attainder   A law that declares a person or a group of people guilty of a crime or punishes them without a trial.

Bill of Rights   The first ten amendments to the U.S. Constitution, concerned with the protection of basic liberties.

bipartisanship   Members of opposing political parties, usually elected officials, acting cooperatively in order to achieve a public policy goal.

block grants   Federal grants to the states to be used for general activities.

briefs   Documents setting out the arguments in legal cases, prepared by attorneys and presented to courts.

budget deficit   Occurs when the government is bringing in less money than it is spending.

budget surplus   Occurs when the government is bringing in more money than it is spending.

bureaucracy   A large, complex organization characterized by a hierarchical set of offices, each with a specific task, controlled through a clear chain of command, and where appointment and advancement of personnel is based on merit.

bureaucrat A person who works in a bureaucratic organization.

bureaucratic discretion The ability of the bureaucracy to exercise its own judgment about how best to engage in implementation.

bureaucratic implementation The actions taken by the bureaucracy in service of its mission of executing the laws of the United States.

C

capital crime Any crime for which death is a possible penalty.

capitalism An economic system characterized by private ownership of productive assets where most decisions about how to use these assets are made by individuals and firms operating in a market rather than by government.

casework Services performed by members of Congress for constituents.

categorical grants Federal aid to states and localities clearly specifying what the money can be used for.

caucus, legislative interest or party A regional, ethnic, racial, or economic subgroup within the House or Senate. Also used to name the party in the House and Senate (as in the "Republican Caucus" or the "Democratic Caucus").

caucus, nominating The process in some states for selecting delegates to the national party conventions characterized by neighborhood and area-wide meetings of party supporters and activists.

checks and balances The constitutional principle that each of the separate branches of government has the power to hinder the unilateral actions of the other branches as a way to restrain an overreaching government and prevent tyranny.

chief of staff A top adviser to the president who also manages the White House staff.

Children's Health Insurance Program (CHIP) Program that pays for health care services for children in households above the poverty line but below 133 percent to 400 percent of the poverty line, depending on the state.

circuit courts The 12 geographical jurisdictions and one special court that hear appeals from the federal district courts.

civil disobedience Intentionally breaking a law and accepting the consequences as a way to publicize the unjustness of the law.

civil liberties Freedoms found primarily in the Bill of Rights, the enjoyment of which are protected from government interference.

civil rights Guarantees of equal treatment by government officials regarding political rights, the judicial system, and public programs.

The **Civil Rights Act of 1964** A law that banned discrimination based on race, sex, or national origin in public accommodations such as hotels, restaurants, and conveyances and gave the Attorney General the power to sue local and state governments that maintained racially segregated schools.

civil servants Government workers employed under the merit system; not political appointees.

civil service Federal government jobs held by civilian employees, excluding political appointees.

Civil Service Act of 1883 Also known as the Pendleton Act, the law created the Civil Service Commission and began the process of changing the federal bureaucracy from the spoils or patronage system to the merit-based system.

Civil War Amendments The Thirteenth, Fourteenth, and Fifteenth Amendments to the Constitution, adopted immediately after the Civil War, each of which represented the imposition of a national claim over that of the states.

class-action suit A suit brought on behalf of a group of people who are in a situation similar to that of the plaintiffs.

cloture A vote to end a filibuster; requires the votes of three-fifths of the membership of the Senate.

Cold War The period of tense relations between the United States and the Soviet Union from the late 1940s to the late 1980s.

committee chair The head of a standing committee with significant power over legislation considered within the committee.

concurrent powers Powers under the Constitution that are shared by the federal government and the states.

concurring opinion The opinion of one or more judges who vote with the majority on a case but wish to set out different reasons for their decision.

conditional grants Federal grants with provisions requiring that state and local governments follow certain policies in order to obtain funds.

confederation A loose association of states or territorial units in which very little or no power is lodged in a central government.

conference committees Ad hoc committees, made up of members of both the Senate and the House of Representatives, set up to reconcile differences in the provisions of bills.

Connecticut Compromise Also called the Great Compromise; the compromise between the New Jersey and Virginia plans formulated by the Connecticut delegates at the Constitutional Convention; called for a lower legislative house based on population size and an upper house based on equal representation of the states.

conservative The political position, combining both economic and social dimensions, which holds that the federal government ought to play a very small role in economic regulation, social welfare, and overcoming racial inequality, that abortion should be illegal, and that family values and law and order should guide public policies.

constituency The individuals who live in the district of a legislator.

constituent A citizen who lives in the district of an elected official.

constitution The basic framework of law for a nation that prescribes how government is to be organized, how government decisions are to be made, and what powers and responsibilities government shall have.

constitutional courts Federal courts created by Congress under the authority of Article III of the Constitution.

cooperative federalism Federalism in which the powers and responsibilities of the states and the national government are intertwined and in which they work together to solve common problems; said to have characterized the 1960s and 1970s.

core values Individuals' views about the fundamental nature of human beings, society, the economy, and the role of government; taken together, they constitute the political culture.

cost-benefit analysis A method of evaluating rules and regulations by weighing their potential costs against their potential benefits to society.

"cracking" and "packing" The act of dividing a district where the opposing party has a large majority, rendering it a minority in both parts of the redrawn districts (cracking), or concentrating all of one party's voters into a single district to dilute their influence in other districts (packing).

D

dark money groups Political interest and advocacy groups that contribute significant sums of money in order to influence elections, but whose sources of funding, and the amount of money spent, are hidden from the public.

de facto discrimination Unequal treatment by private individuals, groups, and organizations.

de jure discrimination Unequal treatment based on government laws and regulations.

dealignment A gradual reduction in the dominance of one political party without another party supplanting it.

Dealignment Era The party era that lasted from the late 1960s to the early 1990s that was characterized by a gradual reduction in the dominance of the Democratic Party without another party becoming truly dominant.

delegate According to the doctrine articulated by Edmund Burke, an elected representative who acts in perfect accord with the wishes of his or her constituents.

democracy A system of government in which the people rule; rule by the many as opposed to rule by one, or rule by the few.

demographic Pertaining to the statistical study and description of a population.

departments Generally the largest units in the executive branch, each headed by a cabinet secretary.

depression A severe and persistent drop in economic activity.

deregulation The process of diminishing government regulatory requirements for business.

descriptive representation Sometimes called *statistical representation*; the degree to which the composition of a representative body reflects the demographic composition of the population as a whole.

devolution The delegation of authority over government programs from the federal government down to state and/or local governments.

direct democracy A form of political decision making in which policies are decided by the people themselves, rather than by their representatives, acting either in small face-to-face assemblies or through the electoral process as in initiatives and referenda in the American states.

discretionary spending That part of the federal budget that is not tied to a formula that automatically provides money to some program or purpose.

dissenting opinion The opinion of the judge or judges who are in the minority on a particular case before the Supreme Court.

disturbance theory A theory positing that interest groups originate with changes in the economic, social, or political environment that threaten the well-being of some segment of the population.

divided government Control of the executive and the legislative branches by different political parties.

dual federalism A system of federalism in which state and national powers are neatly divided between the national and state governments. Most powers of the national government are not shared with the states, and most powers of the states are not shared with the national government.

due process clause The section of the Fourteenth Amendment that prohibits states from depriving anyone of life, liberty, or property "without due process of law," a guarantee against arbitrary or unfair government action.

Duverger's law The phenomenon that electoral systems based on single-member plurality districts are almost always dominated by only two parties.

E

earmarks Budget items that appropriate money for specific pet projects of members of Congress, usually done at the behest of lobbyists, and added to bills at the last minute with little opportunity of deliberation.

Earned Income Tax Credit (EITC) A provision in the U.S. Tax Code that allows low-income individuals with at least one child to claim a credit against taxes owed or, for some, to receive a direct cash transfer from the IRS.

economic conservatives People who favor private enterprise and oppose government regulation of business.

economic liberals People who favor government spending for social programs and government regulation of business to protect the public.

elastic clause Article I, Section 8, of the Constitution, also called the necessary and proper clause; gives Congress the authority to make whatever laws are necessary and proper to carry out its enumerated responsibilities.

Electoral College Representatives selected in each of the states, their numbers based on each state's total number of its senators and representatives; a majority of Electoral College votes elects the president.

electoral competition voting model A theory of elections in which parties move toward the median voter or the center of the political spectrum in order to capture the most votes.

electoral reward and punishment model The tendency to vote for incumbents when times are good and against them when times are bad; same as retrospective voting.

electors Representatives who are elected in the states to formally choose the U.S. president.

entitlement Government benefits that are distributed automatically to citizens who qualify on the basis of a set of guidelines set by law; for example, Americans over the age of 65 are entitled to Medicare coverage.

enumerated powers Powers of the federal government specifically mentioned in the Constitution.

equal protection clause The section of the Fourteenth Amendment that provides for equal treatment by government of people residing within the United States and each of its states.

Equal Rights Amendment (ERA) Proposed amendment to the U.S. Constitution stating that equality of rights shall not be abridged or denied on account of a person's gender; it failed to win the approval of the necessary number of states.

establishment clause The part of the First Amendment to the Constitution that prohibits Congress from establishing an official religion; the basis for the doctrine of the separation of church and state.

ex post facto law A law that retroactively declares some action illegal.

exclusionary rule A standard established by the Supreme Court that prevents police and prosecutors from using evidence against a defendant that was obtained in an illegal search.

executive agreement An agreement with another country signed by the president that has the force of law, like a treaty; does not require Senate approval; originally used for minor technical matters, now an important tool of presidential power in foreign affairs.

Executive Office of the President (EOP) A group of organizations that advise the president on a wide range of issues; includes, among others, the Office of Management and Budget, the National Security Council, and the Council of Economic Advisers.

executive order A rule or regulation for an executive agency or department issued by the president that has the force of law, based either on the constitutional powers of the presidency as chief executive or commander in chief or on congressional statutes.

F

factions James Madison's term for groups or parties that try to advance their own interests at the expense of the public good.

federal bureaucracy The totality of the departments and agencies of the executive branch of the national government.

Federal Communications Commission (FCC) Federal agency set up to regulate media companies with an eye toward ensuring competition and protecting consumers.

Federal Reserve Board (The Fed) The body responsible for deciding the monetary policies of the United States.

federalism A system in which significant governmental powers are divided between a central government and smaller territorial units, such as states.

Federalist No 10 One of a series on essays written by James Madison (others were written by Alexander Hamilton and John Jay), urging the people of New York to support ratification of the Constitution. In No. 10, Madison defended republican government for large states with heterogeneous populations and expressed his fear of majorities and his abhorrence of political parties.

Federalists Proponents of the Constitution during the ratification fight; also the political party of Hamilton, Washington, and Adams.

filibuster A parliamentary device used in the Senate to prevent a bill from coming to a vote by "talking it to death," or by refusing to end debate, made possible by the norm of unlimited debate unless cloture is invoked.

fiscal federalism That aspect of federalism having to do with federal grants to the states.

fiscal policy Government efforts to affect overall output and incomes in the economy through spending and taxing policies.

foundation An entity of the executive branch that supports the arts or sciences and is designed to be somewhat insulated from political interference.

framing effects The way news organizations can affect how people think about an issue by presenting it in a particular way or situating it in a particular context.

franchise The legal right to vote; see suffrage.

franking privilege Public subsidization of mail from the members of Congress to their constituents.

free enterprise An economic system characterized by competitive markets and private ownership of a society's productive assets; a form of capitalism.

free exercise clause The portion of the First Amendment to the Constitution that prohibits Congress from impeding religious observance or impinging on religious beliefs.

full faith and credit clause   The provision in Article IV, Section 1 of the Constitution which provides that states must respect the public acts, laws, and judicial rulings of other states.

G

General Agreement on Tariffs and Trade (GATT)   An international agreement that requires the lowering of tariffs and other barriers to free trade.

generational effect   The long lasting effect of major political events—particularly those that occur when an individual is coming of age politically—on people's political attitudes.

gerrymandering   Redrawing electoral district lines in an extreme and unlikely manner to give an advantage to a particular party or candidate.

global climate change   The upset of historical climate patterns, with rising temperatures and more extreme climate events, tied to the increase in atmospheric carbon, whether caused by human activities or naturally occurring cycles.

globalization   The tendency of information, products, and financial capital to flow across national borders, with the effect of more tightly integrating the global economy.

government corporation   A unit in the executive branch that operates like a private business but provides some public service.

grand juries   Groups of citizens who decide whether there is sufficient evidence to bring an indictment against accused persons.

grandfather clause   A device that allowed whites who had failed the literacy test to vote anyway by extending the franchise to anyone whose ancestors had voted prior to 1867.

grants-in-aid   Funds from the national government to state and local governments to help pay for programs created by the national government.

grassroots lobbying   The effort by interest groups to mobilize local constituencies, shape public opinion to support the group's goals, and bring that pressure to bear on elected officials.

Great Depression   The period of economic crisis in the United States that lasted from the stock market crash of 1929 to America's entry into World War II.

Great Recession   The economic crisis that officially began in December 2007. The recession was triggered by the bursting of a housing bubble that led to a financial crisis and cuts in consumer spending. Though it officially ended in June 2009, its after effects have been long-lasting.

gridlock   A situation in which things cannot get done in Washington, usually because of divided government.

gross domestic product (GDP)   Monetary value of all goods and services produced in a nation each year, excluding income residents earn abroad.

H

habeas corpus   The legal doctrine that a person who is arrested must have a timely hearing before a judge.

hearings   The taking of testimony by a congressional committee or subcommittee.

hegemon   Term used to refer to the dominant power during various historical periods that takes on responsibilities for maintaining and protecting a regional or global system.

heuristics   Simple mental rules people use to make decisions and judgments quickly.

hold   A tactic by which a single senator can prevent action on a bill or nomination; based on an implied threat of refusing to agree to unanimous consent on other Senate matters or willingness to filibuster the bill or nomination.

horizontal federalism   Term used to refer to relationships among the states.

I

imminent lawless action test   Supreme Court standard that in order for the government to be allowed to prohibit speech, it must be likely to lead directly and immediately to law breaking.

impeachment   House action bringing formal charges against a member of the executive branch or the federal judiciary that may or may not lead to removal from office by the Senate.

implied powers   Powers of the federal government not specifically mentioned in the Constitution.

in forma pauperis   Describing a process by which indigents may file a suit with the Supreme Court free of charge.

income tax   Taxes levied on the annual incomes of individuals and corporations. In the United States those who make more money pay a higher tax rate than those who make less money.

independent executive agency   A unit of the executive branch outside the control of executive departments.

independent regulatory commission   An entity in the executive branch that is outside the immediate control of the president and Congress that issues rules and regulations to protect the public.

inflation   A condition of rising prices and reduced purchasing power.

infotainment   The merging of hard news and entertainment in news presentations.

initiative   Procedures available in some states for citizens to put proposed laws and constitutional amendments on the ballot for voter approval or rejection.

inside game   The form of lobbying in which representatives of an interest or advocacy group try to persuade legislators, executive branch officials, and/or regulators to support actions favored by that group.

institutional presidency The permanent bureaucracy associated with the presidency, designed to help the incumbent of the office carry out his responsibilities.

interest groups Private organizations or voluntary associations that seek to influence public policy as a way to protect or advance their interests.

intermediate scrutiny A legal test falling between ordinary and strict scrutiny relevant to issues of gender; under this test, the Supreme Court will allow gender classifications in laws if they are *substantially* related to an *important* government objective.

interstate compacts Agreements among states to cooperate on solving mutual problems; requires approval by Congress.

invisible primary The process in which party elites and influential donors throw their support behind a candidate before any votes have been cast, giving that candidate a financial and organizational advantage during the state primaries and caucuses.

iron triangle An enduring alliance of common interest among an interest group, a congressional committee, and a bureaucratic agency.

isolationism The policy of avoiding undue involvement in the affairs of other countries and multilateral institutions.

issue networks Broad coalitions of public and private interest groups, policy experts, and public officials that form around particular policy issues; said to be more visible to the public and more inclusive.

J

Jim Crow Popular term for the system of legally sanctioned racial segregation that existed in the American South from the end of the 19th century until the middle of the 20th century.

Joint Chiefs of Staff (JCS) The military officers in charge of each of the armed services.

judicial activism Actions by the courts that purportedly go beyond the role of the judiciary as interpreter of the law and adjudicator of disputes.

judicial review The power of the Supreme Court to declare actions of the other branches and levels of government unconstitutional.

K

Keynesians Advocates of government programs to stimulate economic activity through tax cuts and government spending.

L

laboratories of democracy The ability of states in the U.S. federal system to experiment with policy ideas; the success or failure of state policies can then be a template for national policy action.

labor unions An organization representing employees that bargains with employers over wages, benefits, and working conditions.

laissez-faire The political-economic doctrine that holds that government ought not interfere with the operations of the free market.

leak Inside or secret information given to a journalist or media outlet by a government official.

legislative courts Highly specialized federal courts created by Congress under the authority of Article I of the Constitution.

Lemon Test Supreme Court standard that in order for a law with a religious element to be constitutional it must have a secular purpose, its primary effect cannot be to advance or impede religion, and it must not foster excessive entanglements between government and religion.

liberal The political position, combining both economic and social dimensions, which holds that the federal government has a substantial role to play in providing economic justice and opportunity, regulating business in the public interest, overcoming racial discrimination, protecting abortion rights, and ensuring the equal treatment of gays and lesbians.

liberal democracy Representative democracy characterized by popular sovereignty, liberty, and political equality.

literacy test A device used by the southern states to prevent African Americans from voting before the passage of the Voting Rights Act of 1965, which banned its use; usually involved interpretation of a section of a state's constitution.

lobbying Effort by an interest or advocacy group to influence the behavior of a public official.

lobbyist A person who attempts to influence the behavior of public officials on behalf of an interest group.

M

majority leader The leaders of the Senate, also the head of the majority party in the Senate. Equivalent to the House Speaker, though not a constitutional office.

majority rule The form of political decision making in which policies are decided on the basis of what a majority of the people want.

majority tyranny Suppression of the rights and liberties of a minority by the majority.

majority-minority districts Districts drawn to ensure that a racial minority makes up the majority of voters.

mandate A formal order from the national government that the states carry out certain policies.

mandatory spending Government spending that does not go through the annual appropriations process because it is tied to a formula that determines the amount to be spent. Primarily includes Social Security and Medicare.

mass mobilization   The process of involving large numbers of people in a social movement.

means-tested programs   Social insurance programs that require recipients demonstrate need before getting benefits.

media consolidation   The process of a small number of companies coming to own an increasingly large share of the media outlets by purchasing outlets or merging with other media companies.

median household income   The midpoint of all households ranked by income.

median voter   The voter at the exact middle of the political issue spectrum.

Medicaid   Program administered by the states that pays for health care services for the poor; jointly funded by the federal government and the states.

Medicare   Federal health insurance program for the elderly and the disabled.

monarchy   Rule by the one, such as where power rests in the hands of a king or queen.

monetarists   Advocates of a minimal government role in the economy, limited to managing the growth of the money supply.

monetary policy   Government efforts to affect the supply of money and the level of interest rates in the economy.

multilateralist   The stance toward foreign policy that suggests that the United States should seek the cooperation of other nations and multilateral institutions in pursuing its goals.

multilateralists   Those who believe the United States should use its military and diplomatic power in the world in cooperation with other nations and international organizations.

multiparty system   A political system in which three or more viable parties compete to lead the government; because a majority winner is not always possible, multiparty systems often have coalition governments where governing power is shared among two or more parties.

N

national debt   The total outstanding debt of the federal government; the sum total of all annual budget deficits and surpluses.

national interest   What is of benefit to the nation as a whole.

national security adviser   A top foreign policy and defense adviser to the president who heads the National Security Council.

nationalist position   The view of American federalism that holds that the Constitution created a system in which the national government is supreme, relative to the states, and that it granted that government a broad range of powers and responsibilities.

necessary and proper clause   Article I, Section 8, of the Constitution, also known as the *elastic clause*; gives Congress the authority to make whatever laws are necessary and proper to carry out its enumerated powers and the responsibilities mentioned in the Constitution's preamble.

negative externalities   The harmful effects of economic activities on third parties.

New Deal   The social and economic programs of the administration of President Franklin D. Roosevelt in response to the Great Depression.

New Deal Coalition   The informal electoral alliance of working-class ethnic groups, Catholics, Jews, urban dwellers, racial minorities, and the South that was the basis of the Democratic party dominance of American politics from the New Deal to the early 1970s.

New Deal Party Era   The party era lasting from the Great Depression to the late 1960s during which the Democrats, originally led by President Franklin D. Roosevelt, dominated government and supported an expansion of federal government powers and responsibilities aimed at steering the economy out of the Great Depression and through the Second World War.

New Jersey Plan   Proposal of the smaller states at the Constitutional Convention to create a government with slightly more power in a central government than under the Articles, with the states equally represented in a unicameral national legislature.

news management   The attempt by those in political power to put the presentation of news about them and their policies in a favorable light.

North American Free Trade Agreement (NAFTA)   An agreement among the United States, Canada, and Mexico to eliminate nearly all barriers to trade and investment among the three countries.

nuclear proliferation   The spread of nuclear weapons to additional countries or to terrorist groups.

nullification   An attempt by states to declare national laws or actions null and void.

O

objective journalism   News reported with no evaluative language and with opinions quoted or attributed to a specific source.

Office of Management and Budget (OMB)   Part of the Executive Office of the President charged with helping the president prepare the annual budget request to Congress; also performs oversight of rule making by executive branch agencies.

oligarchy   Rule by the few, where a minority holds power over a majority, as in an aristocracy or a clerical establishment.

open-seat election   An election in which there is no incumbent officeholder.

opinion   The explanation of the majority's and the minority's reasoning that accompanies a court decision.

opinion of the Court   The majority opinion that accompanies a Supreme Court decision; also called the majority opinion.

original intent The doctrine that the courts must interpret the Constitution in ways consistent with the intentions of the framers rather than in light of contemporary conditions and needs.

original jurisdiction The authority of a court to be the first to hear a particular kind of case.

originalism The doctrine that judges must interpret the Constitution based on the exact meaning of the words and phrases in the document as understood by the Framers.

outside game Similar to "grassroots lobbying"; that form of lobbying in which interest and advocacy groups try to bring outside pressure to bear on legislators, bureaucrats, and/or regulators.

oversight Congressional responsibility for monitoring the actions of executive branch agencies and personnel to ensure conformity to federal statutes and congressional intent.

P

partisan A committed member of a party; also, seeing issues from the point of view of the interests of a single party.

partisan leaners Individuals who say they do not identify as Democrats or Republicans, but say they feel closer to either the Democratic or Republican Party.

party activist Prominent, though often unelected, members of political parties who influence party decisions and participate in major party events.

party convention A gathering of delegates who nominate a party's presidential candidate.

party identification The sense of belonging to a political party; in the United States this is typically identifying as a Republican or Democrat.

patronage The practice of distributing government offices and contracts to the supporters of the winning party; also called the *spoils system*.

payroll tax Tax levied on salaries and wages primarily for Social Security and Medicare.

permanent campaign The idea that members of Congress are always running for reelection and focus most of their efforts on winning their seat rather than governing.

petit (trial) juries Juries that hear evidence and sit in judgment on charges brought in civil or criminal cases.

plaintiff One who brings suit in a court.

platform A party's statement of its positions on the issues of the day passed at the quadrennial national convention.

pluralism The political science position that American democracy is best understood in terms of the interaction, conflict, and bargaining of groups.

plurality Occurs when a candidate receives more votes than any other candidate in an election but still less than a majority.

pocket veto Rejection of a bill if the president takes no action on it for 10 days and Congress has adjourned during that period.

polarization The process by which political parties have become more internally consistent in ideology and more ideologically distant from one another; in the U.S., the Republican party has become more conservative and the Democratic party more liberal.

Polarization Era The party era that began in the 1990s in which the Democratic and Republican parties became increasingly ideologically different from and hostile toward each other—embracing substantially different visions for country and an unwillingness to compromise.

police powers Powers of a government to protect the health, safety, and general well-being of its people.

political action committee (PAC) An entity created by an interest group whose purpose is to collect money and make contributions to candidates in federal elections.

political attitudes Individuals' views and preferences about public policies, political parties, candidates, government institutions, and public officials.

political culture The set of core beliefs in a country that help shape how people behave politically and what they believe government should do.

political efficacy The sense that an individual can affect what government does.

political equality The principle that each person carries equal weight in the conduct of the public business.

political ideology A coherently organized set of beliefs about the fundamental nature of good society and the role that government ought to play in achieving it.

political liberty The principle that citizens in a democracy are protected from government interference in the exercise of a range of basic freedoms, such as the freedoms of speech, association, and conscience.

political party A group organized to nominate candidates, to try to win political power through elections, and to promote ideas about public policies.

political socialization The process by which individuals come to have certain core beliefs and political attitudes.

poll tax A tax to be paid as a condition of voting; used in the South to keep African Americans away from the polls.

popular sovereignty The basic principle of democracy that the people are the ultimate source of government authority and of the policies that government leaders make.

populism The belief that the common person is every bit as good as those with wealth and power.

pork Also called *pork barrel*; federally funded projects designed to bring to the constituency jobs and public money for which the members of Congress can claim credit.

poverty line The federal government's calculation of the amount of income families of various sizes need to stay out of poverty. In 2018 it was $25,100 for a family of four.

precedents Past rulings by courts that guide judicial reasoning in subsequent cases.

preemption Exclusion of the states from actions that might interfere with federal authority or statutes.

presidential job approval rating The percentage of Americans who believe the president is doing a good job.

primary election Statewide elections in which voters choose delegates to the national party conventions.

priming The way heavy media coverage of a particular topic can lead citizens to give greater weight to that topic when evaluating politicians and making other political judgments.

principal-agent relationship The relationship between the president and Congress, who act as principals, with the bureaucracy, who is the agent, where the principals give the agent authority and discretion, but seek to ensure the agent still follows the wishes of the principals.

prior restraint A government action prohibiting publication or broadcast of materials (rather than punishing publication afterward).

private interests Interest groups that seek to protect or advance the material interests of their members.

privatizing The process of turning over certain government functions to the private sector.

privileged position of business The notion advanced by some political scientists that the business sector, most especially the large corporate sector, is consistently and persistently advantaged over other interests or societal actors in bringing influence to bear on government.

privileges or immunities clause The portion of the Fourteenth Amendment that says states may not make laws that abridge the rights granted to people as citizens of the United States.

probability sampling A survey technique designed so that every individual in a population of interest (e.g., the American public) has an equal chance of being included in the pool of survey respondents.

probable cause Legal doctrine that refers to a reasonable belief that a crime has been committed.

procedural votes Roll-call votes in Congress which occur on motions or rules, used to conduct the business of the chamber. Compare to substantive votes.

progressive taxation A tax system in which higher-income individuals are taxed at a higher rate than those who make less.

property rights The freedom to use, accumulate, and dispose of a valuable asset subject to rules established by government.

proportional representation The awarding of legislative seats to political parties to reflect the proportion of the popular vote each party receives.

prospective voting model A theory of democratic elections in which voters decide what each party will do if elected, and choose the party that best represents their own preferences.

public interests Interest groups that work to gain protections or benefits for society at large.

public opinion The aggregated political attitudes of ordinary people as revealed by surveys.

pundits Somewhat derisive term for print, broadcast, and radio commentators on the political news.

Q

quality challengers Individuals who run against incumbent members of Congress who have previously held elected office. They tend to be more successful in defeating incumbent members than other types of challengers.

quasi-governmental organization An organization that has governmental powers and responsibilities but has substantial private sector control over its activities.

R

racial integration Policies that encourage the interaction of different races in schools, public facilities, workplaces, and/or housing.

rational public The notion that collective public opinion is rational in the sense that it is generally stable and consistent and that when it changes it does so as an understandable response to events, to changing circumstances, and to new information.

realignment The process by which one party supplants another as the dominant party in a two-party political system.

reapportionment The reallocation of House seats among the states, done after each national census, to ensure that seats are held by the states in proportion to the size of their populations.

recess appointments Presidential action to temporarily fill executive branch positions without the consent of the Senate; done when Congress is adjourned.

recession A slowing of the economy defined by two quarters or more of declining gross domestic product.

red tape Overbearing bureaucratic rules and procedures.

redistricting The redrawing of congressional district lines within a state to ensure roughly equal populations within each district.

referendum Procedures available in some states by which state laws or constitutional amendments proposed by the legislature are submitted to the voters for approval or rejection.

regressive taxation A tax system in which lower-income individuals are taxed at a higher rate than those who make more.

regulation The issuing of rules by government agencies with the aim of reducing the scale of negative externalities produced by private firms.

remedy An action that a court determines must be taken to rectify a wrong done by government.

representative democracy Indirect democracy in which the people rule through elected representatives; see liberal democracy.

republicanism A political doctrine advocating limited government based on popular consent but protected against majority tyranny.

reservation clause Part of the Tenth Amendment to the Constitution that says those powers not given to the federal government and not prohibited to the states by the Constitution are reserved for the states and the people.

responsible party model The notion that a political party will take clear and distinct stands on the issues and enact them as policy once elected to office.

retrospective voting model (or electoral reward and punishment model) A theory of democratic elections in which voters look back at the performance of a party in power and cast ballots on the basis of how well it did in office.

revolving door The common practice in which former government officials become lobbyists for interests with whom they formerly dealt in their official capacity.

roll-call votes Recorded votes taken in the House or Senate.

rule of four An *unwritten* practice that requires at least four justices of the Supreme Court to agree that a case warrants review by the Court before it will hear the case.

Rules Committee A special committee in the House of Representatives that determines whether amendments will be allowed on a bill.

S

sampling error Statistical uncertainty in estimates associated with the fact that surveys do not interview every individual in a population of interest.

scare-off effect When members of Congress raise more money than they need to signal support and resources to potential challengers, thereby discouraging others from running against them.

scientific survey A survey conducted using probability sampling to measure the attitudes of a representative sample of the public.

scope of conflict Refers to the number of groups involved in a political conflict; a narrow scope of conflict involves a small number of groups, and a wide scope of conflict involves many.

selective incorporation The gradual and piecemeal spread of the protections of the Bill of Rights to the states by the U.S. Supreme Court.

senatorial courtesy The tradition that a judicial nomination for a federal district court seat be approved by the senior senator of the president's party from the state where a district court is located before the nominee is considered by the Senate Judiciary Committee.

seniority The principle that one attains a position on the basis of length of service.

separate but equal doctrine The principle articulated in *Plessy v. Ferguson* (1896) that laws prescribing separate public facilities and services for nonwhite Americans are permissible if the facilities and services are equal to those provided for whites.

separation of powers The distribution of government legislative, executive, and judicial powers to separate branches of government.

signing statement A document sometimes issued by the president in connection with the signing of a bill from Congress that sets out the president's understanding of the new law and how executive branch officials should carry it out.

single-member districts Districts where the voters elect only one person to represent them. In single-member plurality systems, the person with the most votes (even if they do not win a majority) wins the election.

social (or lifestyle) conservative People who favor traditional social values; they tend to support strong law-and-order measures and oppose abortion and gay rights.

social (or lifestyle) liberals People who favor civil liberties, abortion rights, and alternative lifestyles.

social contract The idea that government is the result of an agreement among people to form one, and that people have the right to create an entirely new government if the terms of the contract have been violated by the existing one.

social insurance Government programs that provide services or income support in proportion to the amount of mandatory contributions made by individuals to a government trust fund.

social movements Loosely organized groups with large numbers of people who use unconventional and often disruptive tactics to have their grievances heard by the public, the news media, and government leaders.

Social Security Social insurance program that provides income support for the elderly, those with disabilities, and family survivors of working Americans.

soft power Influence in world affairs that derives from the attractiveness to others of a nation's culture, products, and way of life.

spin The attempt by public officials to have a story reported in terms that favor them and their policies; see news management.

spoils system The practice of distributing government offices and contracts to the supporters of the winning party; also called *patronage.*

standing Authority to bring legal action because one is directly affected by the issues at hand.

standing committees Relatively permanent congressional committees that address specific areas of legislation.

stare decisis   The legal doctrine that says precedent should guide judicial decision making.

State of the Union   Annual report to the nation by the president, now delivered before a joint session of Congress, on the state of the nation and his legislative proposals for addressing national problems.

states' rights position   The view of American federalism that holds that the Constitution created a system of dual sovereignty in which the national government and the state governments are sovereign in their own spheres.

strict construction   The doctrine that the provisions of the Constitution have a clear meaning and that judges must stick closely to this meaning when rendering decisions.

strict scrutiny   The assumption that actions by elected bodies or officials violate the Constitution.

substantive votes   Roll-call votes in Congress on passing a bill or adopting amendments to a bill. Compare to procedural votes.

suffrage   The legal right to vote; see franchise.

superdelegates   Elected officials from all levels of government who are appointed by party committees to be delegates to the national convention of the Democratic Party; not selected in primary elections or caucuses.

superpower   A nation with the military, economic, and political resources to project force anywhere in the world.

Supplemental Nutritional Assistance Program (SNAP)   Federal program that helps Americans that fall below a certain income to buy food for themselves and their families. Frequently referred to as "food stamps."

supremacy clause   The provision in Article VI of the Constitution that states that the Constitution and the laws and treaties of the United States are the supreme law of the land, taking precedence over state laws and constitutions when they are in conflict.

suspect classification   The invidious, arbitrary, or irrational designation of a group for special treatment by government, whether positive or negative; historically, used in laws to discriminate against visible minorities without the power to protect themselves.

T

Temporary Assistance to Needy Families (TANF)   Federal welfare program that provides income and services to poor families via state block grants. The program has benefit time limits and a work requirement.

terrorism   The use of deadly violence against civilians to further some political goal.

test case   A case brought by advocacy or interest groups to try to force a ruling on the constitutionality of some law or executive action.

treaty   A formal international agreement between two or more countries; in the United States, requires the "advice and consent" of the Senate.

trustee   An elected representative who believes that his or her own best judgment, rather than instructions from constituents, should be used in making legislative decisions.

turnout   The proportion of either eligible or all voting-age Americans who actually vote in a given election; the two ways of counting turnout yield different results.

two-party system   A political system in which two parties vie on relatively equal terms to win national elections and in which each party governs at one time or another.

tyranny   The abuse of the inalienable rights of citizens by government.

U

unanimous consent   Legislative action taken "without objection" as a way to expedite business; used to conduct much of the business of the Senate.

unfunded mandates   Requirements imposed by the federal government on the states to perform certain actions, with not enough money provided to fulfill the requirements.

unified government   Control of the executive and legislative branches by the same political party.

unilateralist   The stance toward foreign policy that suggests that the United States should "go it alone," pursuing its national interests without seeking the cooperation of other nations or multilateral institutions.

unitary executive   Controversial constitutional doctrine which proposes that the executive branch is under the direct control of the president, who has all authority necessary to control the actions of federal bureaucracy personnel and units without interference from the other federal branches.

unitary system   A system in which a central government has complete power over its constituent units or states.

V

veto   Presidential disapproval of a bill that has been passed by both houses of Congress. The president's veto can be overridden by a two-thirds vote in each house.

Virginia Plan   Proposal by the large states at the Constitutional Convention to create a strong central government with power in the government apportioned to the states on the basis of population.

W

watchdog   The role of the media in scrutinizing the actions of government officials.

weapons of mass destruction   Nuclear, biological, or chemical weapons with the potential to cause vast harm to human populations.

whistle-blowers   People who bring official misconduct in their agencies to public attention.

white primaries Primary elections open only to whites in the one-party South, where the only elections that mattered were the Democratic Party's primaries; this effectively disenfranchised blacks.

wire services Organizations such as the Associated Press and Reuters that gather and disseminate news to other news organizations.

World Trade Organization (WTO) An agency designed to enforce the provisions of the General Agreement on Tariffs and Trade and to resolve trade disputes between nations.

writ of certiorari An announcement that the Supreme Court will hear a case on appeal from a lower court; its issuance requires the vote of four of the nine justices.

Endnotes

Chapter 1

1. William H. Chafe, *The Unfinished Journey: America Since World War II* (New York: Oxford University Press, 1986), p. 304; Howard Zinn, *SNCC: The New Abolitionists* (Boston: Beacon Press, 1964), p. 64.

2. Pei-te Lien, Dianne M. Pinderhughes, Carol Hardy-Fanta, and Christine M. Sierra, "The Voting Rights Act and the Election of Non-white Officials," *PS: Political Science and Politics* 40, no. 3 (July 2007), pp. 489–494.

3. On the recent decline of democracy in many parts of the world, including the United States, see "Freedom in the World, 2018," Freedom House, https://freedomhouse.org/report/freedom-world/freedom-world-2018#fiw-key-findings; Steven Levitsky and Daniel Ziblatt, *How Democracies Die* (New York: Crown Publishers, 2018); Adam Przeworski, "Democracy: A Never-Ending Quest," *Annual Review of Political Science* 19 (2016), https://www.annualreviews.org/doi/10.1146/annurev-polisci-021113-122919; and Roberto Stefan Foa and Yascha Mounk, "The Signs of Deconsolidation," *Journal of Democracy* 28, no. 1 (2017), pp. 5–15. Project MUSE, doi:10.1353/jod.2017.0000.

4. Michael Coppedge and John Gerring, "Conceptualizing and Measuring Democracy," *Perspectives on Politics* 9, no. 2 (June 2011), pp. 247–267.

5. See a summary of polls at Latinobarómetro, www.latinobarometro.org; AsiaBarometer, www.asiabarometer.org; and the PEW Center for the People and the Press, www.pewresearch.org.

6. See the Freedom House report, *Freedom in the World, 2015* (Washington, DC: Freedom House, 2012), www.freedomhouse.org.

7. Again, see "What's Gone Wrong With Democracy?" *The Economist*, www.economist.com/news/essays, (September 13, 2014), pp. 1–18; *Freedom in the World, 2018*; and Levitsky and Ziblatt, *How Democracies Die*.

8. James Surowiecki, *The Wisdom of Crowds* (New York: Doubleday, 2004).

9. Daron Acemoglu, Suresh Naidu, Pascual Restrepro, and James A. Robinson, "Democracy Does Cause Growth" (National Bureau of Economic Research, Cambridge, MA, Working Paper 20004, March, 2014), pp. 1–64; and Klaus Grundler and Tommy Krieger, "Democracy and Growth" (University of Wurzburg, Working Paper No. 131, April, 2015), pp. 1–29.

10. For a fuller treatment of the claims in this paragraph, as well as supporting evidence, see Robert A. Dahl, *Democracy and Its Critics* (New Haven, CT: Yale University Press, 1989), and Robert A. Dahl, *On Democracy* (New Haven, CT: Yale University Press, 1998). Also see Benjamin Radcliff, "Politics, Markets, and Life Satisfaction: The Political Economy of Human Happiness," *American Political Science Review* 95 (December 2001), pp. 939–952.

11. Robert A. Dahl, "James Madison: Republican or Democrat?" *Perspectives on Politics* 3, no. 3 (September 2005), pp. 439–448.

12. John Dewey, *The Public and Its Problems* (New York: Holt, 1927).

13. Charles Tilly, *Democracy* (Cambridge, UK: Cambridge University Press, 2007), p. 59.

14. Przeworski, "Democracy: A Never-Ending Quest."

15. Tilly, *Democracy*, pp. 26–28. Also see Josiah Ober, "What the Ancient Greeks Can Tell Us About Democracy," *Annual Review of Political Science* 11 (2008), pp. 67–91.

16. Dahl, *Democracy and Its Critics*, p. 13.

17. On deliberation and democracy, see Jason Barabas, "How Deliberation Affects Policy Opinions," *American Political Science Review* 98 (2004), pp. 687–701; Seyla Benhabib, "Toward a Deliberative Model of Democratic Legitimacy," in *Democracy and Difference*, ed. Seyla Benhabib (Princeton, NJ: Princeton University Press, 1996); John Dryzek, *Discursive Democracy* (Cambridge, UK: Cambridge University Press, 1990); Nancy Fraser, "Rethinking the Public Sphere," in *Habermas and the Public Sphere*, ed. Craig Calhoun (New Brunswick, NJ: Rutgers University Press, 1992), pp. 109–142; Amy Guttman and Dennis Thompson, *Democracy and Disagreement* (Cambridge, UK: Belknap Press, 1996); and Jurgen Habermas, *The Structural Transformation of the Public Sphere* (Cambridge, MA: MIT Press, 1989).

18. See Robert A. Dahl, *After the Revolution: Authority in the Good Society* (New Haven, CT: Yale University Press, 1970); Dahl, *Democracy and Its Critics*; and Jane Mansbridge, *Beyond Adversary Democracy* (New York: Basic Books, 1980). Also see Kevin O'Leary, *Saving Democracy* (Stanford, CA: Stanford University Press, 2006), ch. 1.

19. Christian Welzel and Ronald Inglehart, "The Role of Ordinary People in Democratization," *Journal of Democracy* 19, no. 1 (2008), p. 126.

20. On deliberation and democracy, see Jason Barabas, "How Deliberation Affects Policy Opinions," *American Political Science Review* 98 (2004), pp. 687–701; Seyla Benhabib, "Toward a Deliberative Model of Democratic Legitimacy," in *Democracy and Difference*, ed. Seyla Benhabib (Princeton, NJ: Princeton University Press, 1996); John Dryzek, *Discursive Democracy* (Cambridge, UK: Cambridge University Press, 1990); Nancy Fraser, "Rethinking the Public Sphere," in *Habermas and the Public Sphere*, ed. Craig Calhoun (New Brunswick, NJ: Rutgers University Press, 1992), pp. 109–142; Amy Guttman and Dennis Thompson, *Democracy and Disagreement* (Cambridge, UK: Belknap

Press, 1996); and Jurgen Habermas, *The Structural Transformation of the Public Sphere* (Cambridge, MA: MIT Press, 1989).

21. Kenneth May, "A Set of Independent, Necessary, and Sufficient Conditions for Simple Majority Decision," *Econometrical* 20 (1952), pp. 680–684, shows that only majority rule can guarantee popular sovereignty, political equality, and neutrality among policy alternatives. See also Douglas W. Rae, "Decision Rules and Individual Values in Constitutional Choice," *American Political Science Review* 63 (1969), pp. 40–53; and Phillip D. Straffin Jr., "Majority Rule and General Decision Rules," *Theory and Decision* 8 (1977), pp. 351–360. On the other hand, Hans Gersbach argues in *Designing Democracy* (New York: Springer Publishers, 2005) that larger majorities ought to be required for more important decisions.

22. Mark Warren, "Democracy and the State," in *The Oxford Handbook of Political Theory*, ed. John S. Dryzek, Bonnie Honig, and Ann Phillips (Oxford, UK: Oxford University Press, 2006), pp. 385–386; and Gordon S. Wood, *The Idea of America: Reflections on the Birth of the United States* (New York: Penguin Press, 2011), pp. 189–212.

23. For a review of contemporary research on this issue, see Larry M. Bartels, *Unequal Democracy: The Political Economy of the New Gilded Age* (New York: Russell Sage Foundation, 2008); Seymour Martin Lipset and Jason M. Lakin, *The Democratic Century* (Norman, OK: University of Oklahoma Press, 2004); and Tilly, *Democracy*.

24. Dahl, *A Preface to Economic Democracy*, p. 68. Also see Benjamin I. Page and Martin Gilens, *Democracy in America? What Has Gone Wrong and What We Can Do to Fix It* (Chicago: University of Chicago Press, 2017).

25. The definitive works establishing this relationship are by Gilens and Page. See especially Martin Gilens and Benjamin I. Page, "Testing Theories of American Politics: Elites, Interest Groups, and Average Citizens," *Perspectives on Politics* 12, no. 3 (September 2014); and Martin Gilens, *Affluence and Influence: Economic Inequality and Political Power in America* (New York and Princeton, NJ: Russell Sage Foundation and Princeton University Press, 2012).

26. Robert A. Dahl, "On Removing Certain Impediments to Democracy in the United States," *Political Science Quarterly* 92, no. 1 (Spring 1977), p. 14; Elaine Spitz, *Majority Rule* (Chatham, NJ: Chatham House, 1984), p. 83; Dahl, *Democracy and Its Critics*, p. 170.

27. See Marc Plattner, "Liberalism and Democracy," *Foreign Affairs* (March–April 1998), pp. 171–180. On the inevitability of tension between and the necessity of balancing the claims of liberty and majority rule, see Adam Przeworski, "Self-Government in Our Times," *Annual Review of Political Science* 12 (2009), pp. 88–90; and Coppedge and Gerring, "Conceptualizing."

28. David Caute, *The Great Fear* (New York: Simon & Schuster, 1978); Victor Navasky, *Naming Names* (New York: Viking, 1980); and Michael Rogin, *The Intellectuals and McCarthy* (Cambridge, MA: MIT Press, 1967).

29. Fareed Zakaria, *The Future of Freedom: Illiberal Democracy at Home and Abroad* (New York: Norton, 2004).

30. See Bartels, *Unequal Democracy*; Bernard R. Berelson, Paul F. Lazarsfeld, and William N. McPhee, *Voting* (Chicago: The University of Chicago Press, 1954); V. O. Key Jr., *Public Opinion and American Democracy* (New York: Knopf, 1961); Herbert McClosky and Alida Brill, *Dimensions of Tolerance: What Americans Believe About Civil Liberties* (New York: Russell Sage Foundation, 1983); Robert Weissberg, *Polling, Policy, and Public Opinion: The Case Against Heeding the Voice of the People* (New York: Palgrave Press, 2003); Robert Weissberg, "Politicized Pseudo Science," *PS: Political Science and Politics* 39, no. 1 (January 2006), pp. 39–42; and Alan Wolfe, *Does American Democracy Still Work?* (New Haven, CT: Yale University Press, 2006). But see, in rebuttal, James L. Gibson, "Political Intolerance and Political Repression During the McCarthy Red Scare," *American Political Science Review* 82 (1988), pp. 511–529; and Benjamin I. Page and Robert Y. Shapiro, *The Rational Public: Fifty Years of Trends in Americans' Policy Preferences* (Chicago: The University of Chicago Press, 1992).

31. Katherine Brandt, "Madisonian Majority Tyranny, Minority Rights, and American Democracy: A New Defense of the Electoral College" (paper, Midwest Political Science Association, Chicago, IL, April 2004); Dahl, *A Preface to Democratic Theory*; and Desmond S. King and Rogers M. Smith, *Still a House Divided: Race and Politics in Obama's America* (Princeton, NJ: Princeton University Press, 2011).

32. Dahl, *Democracy and Its Critics*, p. 161.

33. Thanks to Professor Larry Martinez of the California State University, Long Beach, for this insight.

34. Philip A. Klinkner and Rogers M. Smith, *The Unsteady March: The Rise and Decline of Racial Equality in America* (Chicago: The University of Chicago Press, 1999).

Chapter 2

1. Richard Bushman, "Revolution," in *The Reader's Companion to American History*, eds. Eric Foner, and John A. Garraty (Boston: Houghton Mifflin, 1991), p. 936; and Gordon S. Wood, *The Creation of the American Republic* (New York: Norton, 1972), p. 12.

2. Joseph J. Ellis, *Founding Brothers: The Revolutionary Generation* (New York: Alfred A. Knopf, 2001), pp. 212–213; and Roger Wilkins, *Jacob's Pillow: The Founding Fathers and the Dilemma of Black Patriotism* (Boston: Beacon Press, 2002).

3. Sarah M. Evans, *Born for Liberty: A History of Women in America* (New York: Free Press, 1997); and John Hope Franklin and Alfred A. Moss Jr., *From Slavery to Freedom* (New York: Knopf, 1967).

4. See Hannah Arendt, *On Revolution* (New York: Viking, 1965).

5. Page Smith, *The Shaping of America: A People's History of the Young Republic*, vol. 3 (New York: McGraw-Hill, 1980).

6. Richard Hofstadter, *The American Political Tradition* (New York: Vintage Books, 1948), p. 4.

7. For a review of thinking about relevance of republicanism in our own time, see Frank Lovett and Philip Pettit, "Neo-

republicanism: A Normative and Institutional Research Program," *Annual Review of Political Science* 12 (2009), pp. 11–29.

8. Kevin O'Leary, *Saving Democracy* (Stanford, CA: Stanford University Press, 2006), ch. 3; and Gordon S. Wood, *The Idea of America: Reflections on the Birth of the United States* (New York: Penguin Press, 2011), ch. 4.

9. Alexander Hamilton, James Madison, and John Jay, *The Federalist Papers*, ed. Clinton Rossiter (New York: New American Library, 1961; originally published 1787–1788), No. 10.

10. See Gordon S. Wood, *The Radicalism of the American Revolution* (New York: Knopf, 1992).

11. Wood, *Creation of the American Republic*, pp. 311–318.

12. *Ibid.*, ch. 8.

13. Samuel Eliot Morison, *The Oxford History of the American People* (New York: Oxford University Press, 1965), p. 274.

14. See Wood, *Creation of the American Republic*, p. 400.

15. Smith, *Shaping of America*, pp. 24–26.

16. Quoted in Jackson Turner Main, *The Anti-Federalists* (Chapel Hill: University of North Carolina Press, 1961), p. 62.

17. David Brian Robertson, "Madison's Opponents and Constitutional Design," *American Political Science Review* 99 (May 2006), pp. 225–243.

18. Melvin I. Urofsky, *A March of Liberty* (New York: Knopf, 1988), p. 89.

19. Al Kamen, "Marshall Blasts Celebration of Constitution Bicentennial; Justice Calls Document 'Defective From Start,'" *Washington Post*, May 7, 1987. See also Lee Epstein and Thomas G. Walker, *Constitutional Law for a Changing America* (Washington, DC: CQ Press, 2000), p. 6.

20. Charles Beard, *An Economic Interpretation of the Constitution* (New York: Macmillan, 1913). For a more recent work broadly supporting Beard's interpretation, see Robert A. McGuire, *To Form a More Perfect Union: A New Economic Interpretation of the United States Constitution* (New York: Oxford University Press, 2003).

21. See Robert Brown, *Charles Beard and the Constitution* (Princeton, NJ: Princeton University Press, 1956); Hofstadter, *American Political Tradition*; Leonard Levy, *Constitutional Opinions* (New York: Oxford University Press, 1986); Robert A. McGuire and Robert L. Ohsfeldt, "An Economic Model of Voting Behavior Over Specific Issues at the Constitutional Convention of 1787," *Journal of Economic History* 66 (March 1986), pp. 79–111; James A. Morone, *The Democratic Wish* (New York: Basic Books, 1990); Forrest McDonald, *We the People: The Economic Origins of the Constitution* (Chicago: The University of Chicago Press, 1958); Gordon S. Wood, *The Convention and the Constitution* (New York: St. Martin's Press, 1965); and Wood, *Creation of the American Republic*.

22. Wood, *Idea of America*, p. 131.

23. Quoted in Wood, *Creation of the American Republic*, p. 473.

24. *Ibid.*, p. 432.

25. Charles Stewart, "Congress and the Constitutional System," in *The Legislative Branch*, eds. Paul J. Quirk and Sarah A. Binder (New York: Oxford University Press, 2005).

26. See Robertson, "Madison's Opponents and Constitutional Design," for more information on how the Great Compromise shaped the Constitution as a whole.

27. Ellis, *Founding Brothers*, p. 110.

28. Hamilton, Madison, and Jay, *The Federalist Papers*, No. 10.

29. "The Invention of Centralized Federalism," in *The Development of Centralized Federalism*, ed. William H. Riker (Boston: Kluwer Academic, 1987).

30. Robert A. Dahl, "On Removing the Impediments to Democracy in the United States," *Political Science Quarterly* 92 (Spring 1977), p. 5.

31. Sanford Levinson, "Democracy in Peril," *Democracy: A Journal of Ideas* 8 (Spring 2017), https://democracyjournal.org/magazine/48/democracy-in-peril.

32. Akhil Reed Amar, *America's Constitution: A Biography* (New York: Random House, 2005), p. 14.

33. Hamilton, Madison, and Jay, *The Federalist Papers*, No. 51.

34. Jefferson wrote this in a letter to James Madison dated November 18, 1788, quoted in *The Life and Selected Writings of Thomas Jefferson*, ed. Adrienne Koch and William Peden (New York: Random House/The Modern Library, 1944), p. 452.

35. See Main, *Anti-Federalists*; Wood, *Creation of the American Republic*; Smith, *Shaping of America*, p. 99; Herbert Storing, *What the Anti-Federalists Were For* (Chicago: The University of Chicago Press, 1981), p. 71; and Robertson, "Madison's Opponents and Constitutional Design."

36. Sanford Levinson, *Our Undemocratic Constitution: Where the Constitution Goes Wrong* (New York: Oxford University Press, 2006).

37. See Cass R. Sunstein, *A Constitution of Many Minds: Why the Founding Document Doesn't Mean What It Meant Before* (Princeton, NJ: Princeton University Press, 2009), for a particularly compelling statement of this idea.

38. On the undemocratic Constitution, see Levinson, *Our Undemocratic Constitution*; and Sanford Levinson, "How I Lost My Constitutional Faith," *Maryland Law Review* 71, no. 4 (2012), pp. 955–977. Also see Edward S. Greenberg, "Class Rule and the Constitution," in *How Capitalistic Is the Constitution?* eds. Robert Goldwin and William Schambra (Washington, DC: The American Enterprise Institute, 1982), pp. 22–48.

Chapter 3

1. Sources for this chapter opening story include Colorado Department of Revenue, "Marijuana Sales Report," https://www.colorado.gov/pacific/revenue/colorado-marijuana-sales-reports; Abigail Geiger, "About Six-In-Ten Americans Support Marijuana Legalization," Pew Research Center, January 5, 2018, http://www.pewresearch.org/fact-tank/2018/01/05/americans-support-marijuana-legalization; Evan Halper, "Trump Administration Abandons Crackdown on Legal Marijuana," Los Angeles Times, April 13, 2018, http://www.latimes.com/politics/la-na-pol-marijuana-trump-20180413-story.html; The White House, "Statement by President Trump on the Paris Climate Accord,"

June 1, 2017, https://www.whitehouse.gov/the-press-office/2017/06/01/statement-president-trump-paris-climate-accord; Hiroko Tabuchi and Henry Fountain, "Bucking Trump, These Cities, States and Companies Commit to Paris Accord," New York Times, June 1, 2017, https://www.nytimes.com/2017/06/01/climate/american-cities-climate-standards.html; Hiroko Tabuchi, "U.S. Climate Change Policy: Made in California," New York Times, September 27, 2017, https://www.nytimes.com/2017/09/27/climate/california-climate-change.html; Nadja Popvich and Livia Albeck-Ripka, "52 Environmental Rules on the Way Out Under Trump," New York Times, Updated October 6, 2017, https://www.nytimes.com/interactive/2017/10/05/climate/trump-environment-rules-reversed.html; Robinson Meyer, "The Coming Clean-Air War Between Trump and California," The Atlantic, March 6, 2017, https://www.theatlantic.com/science/archive/2017/03/trump-california-clean-air-act-waiver-climate-change/518649.

2. William H. Riker, *The Development of American Federalism* (Boston: Kluwer Academic, 1987), pp. 56–60.

3. Mark Rush, "Voting Power in Federal Systems: Spain as a Case Study," *PS: Political Science & Politics* 40, no. 4 (2007), pp. 715–720.

4. See "Symposium: Congress, Preemption, and Federalism," *PS: Political Science and Politics* 38, no. 3 (July 2005), pp. 359–378.

5. Stephen Wermiel, "SCOTUS for Law Students: The Defense of Marriage Act and the Constitution (sponsored by Bloomberg Law)," *SCOTUSblog*, March 23, 2013, http://www.scotusblog.com/2012/03/scotus-for-law-students-the-defense-of-marriage-act-and-the-constitution–sponsored-by-bloomberg-law.

6. For more on the nationalist position, see Samuel H. Beer, *To Make a Nation: The Rediscovery of American Federalism* (Cambridge, MA: Belknap Press, 1993).

7. For more on the states' rights position, see Martha Derthick, *Keeping the Compound Republic: Essays on American Federalism* (Washington, DC: Brookings Institution Press, 2001), pp. 11.

8. The study of the complex constitutional, legal, fiscal, and political links between states and the national government is often called the study of *intergovernmental relations* (the ever-changing constitutional, legal, fiscal, and political linkages among the states and the national government). For more on this, see B. Guy Peters and Jon Pierre, "Developments in Intergovernmental Relations: Towards Multi-Level Governance," *Policy and Politics* 29, no. 2 (April 2001), pp. 131–141.; Alberta M. Sbragia, "American Federalism and Intergovernmental Relations," in *The Oxford Handbook of Political Institutions*, eds. Sarah A. Binder, R. A. W. Rhodes, and Bert A. Rockman, Binder, Sarah A., et al. (New York: Oxford University Press, 2008), http://www.oxfordhandbooks.com/view/10.1093/oxfordhb/9780199548460.001.0001/oxfordhb-9780199548460-e-13.

9. Thomas Gais and James Fossett, "Federalism and the Executive Branch," in *The Executive Branch*, eds. Joel D. Aberbach and Mark A. Peterson (New York: Oxford University Press, 2005), pp. 486–524.

10. Robert G. McCloskey, *The American Supreme Court*, 5th ed., ed. Sanford Levinson (Chicago: The University of Chicago Press, 2010), pp. 104–119.

11. David P. Currie, *The Constitution in the Supreme Court: The First Hundred Years, 1789–1888* (Chicago: The University of Chicago Press, 1992), pp. 65–73.

12. McCloskey, *The American Supreme Court*, pp. 49–51.

13. Paul E. Peterson, *The Price of Federalism* (Washington, DC: Brookings Institution, 1995).

14. Pew Research Center for the People & the Press, "A Partisan Public Agenda: Opinion of Clinton and Congress Improves," January 16, 1997, http://www.people-press.org/1997/01/16/a-partisan-public-agenda; Pew Research Center for the People & the Press, "How Americans View Government: Deconstructing Distrust," Pew Research Center, March 10, 1998, http://www.people-press.org/1998/03/10/how-americans-view-government; "National Omnibus Survey" (Cambridge, MA: Cambridge Reports/Research International, 1982).

15. Tim Conlan and John Dinan, "Federalism, the Bush Administration, and the Transformation of American Conservatism," *Publius: The Journal of Federalism* 37, no. 3 (Summer 2007), pp. 279–303.

16. Michael Cooper, "More U.S. Rail Funds for 13 States as 2 Reject Aid," New York Times, December 9, 2010; Timothy Williams, "Florida's Governor Rejects High-Speed Rail Line, Fearing Cost to Taxpayers," New York Times, February 16, 2011.

17. *NFIB v. Sebelius*, https://www.supremecourt.gov/opinions/11pdf/11-393c3a2.pdf.

18. Kevin Quealy and Margot Sanger-Katz, "Who Would Have Health Insurance if Medicaid Expansion Weren't Optional," *New York Times*, November 3, 2014, http://www.nytimes.com/interactive/2014/11/03/upshot/map-if-medicaid-expansion-were-not-optional.html.

19. Dale Krane, "The middle tier in American federalism: State government policy activism during the Bush presidency," Publius: *The Journal of Federalism* 37.3 (2007): 453–477.

20. Ann O'M. Bowman and George A. Krause, "Power Shift: Measuring Policy Centralization in U.S. Intergovernmental Relations, 1947–1998," *American Politics Research* 31, no. 3 (May 2003), pp. 301–313; B. Guy Peters, *American Public Policy: Promise and Performance* (Washington, DC: CQ Press, 2009), pp. 24–29; Robert Nagel, *The Implosion of American Federalism* (New York: Oxford University Press, 2002).

21. Morton Grodzins, *The American System* (New Brunswick, NJ: Transaction Books, 1983), p. 8.

22. Riker, *Development of American Federalism*, pp. 157–190; David B. Walker, *Toward a Functioning Federalism* (Cambridge, MA: Winthrop, 1981), pp. 60–63.

23. Paul E. Peterson, Barry G. Rabe, and Kenneth Wong, *When Federalism Works* (Washington, DC: Brookings Institution Press, 1986), p. 2.

24. Gamkhar and Pickerill, "State of American Federalism," p. 363.

25. Timothy Conlan, *From New Federalism to Devolution: Twenty-Five Years of Intergovernmental Reform* (Washington, DC: Brookings Institution Press, 1998), p. 71.

26. Ed Gillespie and Bob Schellhas, eds., *Contract with America: The Bold Plan by Rep. Newt Gingrich, Rep. Dick Armey and the House Republicans to Change the Nation* (New York: Random House, 1994), p. 125.

27. William H. Riker, *Federalism: Origin, Operation, Significance* (Boston: Little, Brown, 1964), ch. 6.

28. Environmental Protection Agency, "EPA and NHTSA Finalize Historic National Program to Reduce Greenhouse Gases and Improve Fuel Economy for Cars and Trucks," April 2010, https://nepis.epa.gov/Exe/ZyPDF.cgi/P100AKHW.PDF?Dockey=P100AKHW.PDF.

29. Kristin Gross, "Gun Laws Being Reformed, Just Not on Capitol Hill," *The Conversation*, https://theconversation.com/gun-laws-are-being-reformed-just-not-on-capitol-hill-51850.

30. Paul E. Peterson, *City Limits* (Chicago: The University of Chicago Press, 1981), pp. 17–38; Paul E. Peterson, *The Price of Federalism* (Washington, DC: Brookings Institution Press, 1995), pp. 16–49.

Chapter 4

1. See Roger Bybee, "Boeing Holds Jobs Hostage in Two-Pronged Fight with State Government and Machinists," *In These Times*, November 25, 2013, http://inthesetimes.com/working/entry/15922/boeing_holds_jobs_hostage_in_two_pronged_fight_with_state_government_and_ma. See also Timothy Egan, "Under My Thumb," *New York Times*, November 14, 2013, http://www.nytimes.com/2013/11/15/opinion/egan-under-my-thumb.html?_r=0; Dominic Gates, "Boeing Picks 15 Potential Sites Nationwide to Build 777X," *Seattle Times*, November 23, 2013, http://seattletimes.com/html/businesstechnology/2022318847_boeing777xrfpxml.html; and Edward S. Greenberg, Leon Grunberg, Sarah Moore, and Pat Sikora, *Turbulence: Boeing and the State of American Workers and Managers* (New Haven, CT: Yale University Press, 2010).

2. Erik Brynjolfsson and Adrew McAfee, *The Second Machine Age: Work, Progress, and Prosperity in a Time of Brilliant Technologies* (New York: Norton, 2015); and Martin Ford, *Rise of the Robots: Technology and the Threat of a Jobless Future* (New York: Basic Books, 2015).

3. Thomas B. Edsall, "Industrial Revolutions Are Political Wrecking Ball," *New York Times*, May 3, 2018, https://www.nytimes.com/2018/05/03/opinion/trump-industrial-revolutions.html.

4. However, the United States fell slightly below replacement level during the Great Recession. See J.A. Martin, "Births: Final Data for 2016," Centers for Disease Control and Prevention, National Center for Health Statistics, January 21, 2018.

5. For a history of immigration and government policies regarding immigration, see Aristide R. Zolberg, *A Nation by Design: Immigration Policy in the Fashioning of America* (Cambridge, MA: Harvard University Press, 2006).

6. Julia Preston, "Share of Immigrants in U.S. Nears Highs of Early 20th Century, Report Finds," *New York Times*, September 29, 2015, p. A1.

7. Michael Lipka, "Muslims and Islam: Key Findings in the U.S. and Around the World," *Fact Tank*, December 7, 2015, http://www.pewresearch.org.

8. Preston, "Share of Immigrants in U.S.....," based on data from the Pew Research Center.

9. D'Vera Cohn, "It's Official: Minority Babies Are the Majority Among the Nation's Infants, But Only Just," Pew Research Center, Factank, June 23, 2016, http://www.pewresearch.org/fact-tank/2016/06/23/its-official-minority-babies-are-the-majority-among-the-nations-infants-but-only-just.

10. Sandra L. Colby and Jennifer M. Ortman, *Projections of the Size and Composition of the U.S. Population: 2014 to 2060* (Washington, DC: U.S. Census Bureau, March, 2015), Table 2, http://www.census.gov/population/projections/data/national/2015/summarytables.html.

11. Paul Taylor and D'Vera Cohn, "A Milestone En Route to a Majority Minority Nation," Pew Research Center, September 24, 2013, http://www.pewsocialtrends.org/2012/11/07/a-milestone-en-route-to-a-majority-minority-nation.

12. "Modern Immigration Wave Brings 59 Million to U.S., Driving Population Growth and Change Through 2065," Pew Research Center, Hispanic Trends, September 28, 2015, www.pewhispanic.org/2015/09/28.

13. "Modern Immigration Wave Brings 59 Million to U.S., Driving Population Growth and Change Through 2065," Pew Research Center, Hispanic Trends, September 28, 2015, www.pewhispanic.org/2015/09/28. Figure 8.

14. CNN/ORC Poll, July 22–25, 2015, www.pollingreport.com.

15. CBS News Poll, March 8–11, 2018.

16. Tim Malloy and Pat Smith Rubenstein, "Stop Taking the Kids," Quinnipiac University Poll Press Release, June 18, 2018, https://poll.qu.edu/images/polling/us/us06182018_uwsf18.pdf.

17. "Trump Takes a Hard Turn on Immigration," *The Economist*, April 5, 2018, https://www.economist.com/news/united-states/21740005-fox-news-tv-helped-fire-him-up-donald-trump-takes-hard-turn-immigration?frsc=dg%7Ce; "America Is On Track to Admit the Fewest Refugees in Four Decades," *The Economist*, April 21, 2018, https://www.economist.com/news/united-states/21740774-muslim-refugees-are-set-decline-85-america-track-admit-fewest-refugees?frsc=dg%7Ce.

18. Lindsay M. Howden and Julie A. Meyer, "Age and Sex Composition, 2010," in *2010 Census Briefs* (Washington, DC: U.S. Census Bureau, May 2011), http://www.census.gov/prod/cen2010/briefs/c2010br-03.pdf; and Colby and Ortman, "Projections of the Size...."

19. Pew Research Social & Demographic Trends, "Recession Turns a Graying Office Grayer," Pew Research Center, September 3, 2009, http://www.pewsocialtrends.org/2009/09/03/recession-turns-a-graying-office-grayer.

20. "World Population Ageing: 1950–2050," United Nations, Population Division, http://www.un.org/esa/population/publications/worldageing19502050.

21. "Purchasing Power GDP per capita," the World Bank, data.worldbank.org/indicator/NY.GDP.PCAP.CD.

22. Selim Jahan, *Human Development Report, 2015* (New York: United Nations, 2015).

23. For the most part, income and poverty data in this section are from Jessica L. Semega, Kayla R. Fontenot, and Melissa A. Kollar, "Income and Poverty in the United States, 2016," (Washington, DC: U.S Census Bureau, September, 2017), https://www.census.gov/data/tables/2017/demo/income-poverty/p60-259.htm.

24. See Max Roser and Esteban Ortiz-Ospina, 2018, "Income Inequality," Published online at OurWorldInData.org. Retrieved from https://ourworldindata.org/income-inequality.

25. Emmanuel Saez, "Striking It Richer: The Evolution of Top Incomes in the United States" (working paper, updated with 2015 preliminary estimates, University of California–Berkeley, June 30, 2016).

26. U.S. Census Bureau, reported in Conor Dougherty, "Income Slides to 1996 Levels," *Wall Street Journal*, September 14, 2014.

27. Thomas Piketty and Emmanuel Saez, "Income Inequality in the United States, 1913–1998," *Quarterly Journal of Economics* 118, no. 1 (2003), pp. 1–39 (Tables and figures updated to 2015, June 2016).

28. Bernadette D. Proctor, Jessica L. Semega, and Melissa A. Kollar, *Income and Poverty in the United States* (Washington, DC: US Census Bureau, *Current Population Reports*), September 2016; DeNavas-Walt, Bernadette D. Proctor, and Jessica C. Smith, *Income, Poverty, and Health Insurance Coverage in the United States: 2012* (Washington, DC: U.S. Census Bureau, September 2013).

29. Proctor, Semega, and Kollar, *Income and Poverty in the United States*.

30. *Ibid.*

31. *Ibid.*

32. CBS News Poll (October 6–11, 2016) as reported in Polling Report at www.pollingreport.com.

33. William Julius Wilson, *When Work Disappears: The World of the New Urban Poor* (New York: Vintage, 1997).

34. David Coen, Wyn Grant, and Graham Wilson, "Perspectives on Business and Government (Political Science)," in *The Oxford Handbook of Business and Government*, eds. David Coen, Wyn Grant, and Graham Wilson (New York: Oxford University Press, 2010).

35. Steven Pinker, *Enlightenment Now: The Case for Reason, Science, Humanism, and Progress* (New York: Viking/Penguin, 2018).

36. Piketty, *Capitalism in the Twenty-First Century*.

37. On the different forms of capitalism in the modern world, see William J. Baumol, Robert E. Litan, and Carl J. Schramm, *Good Capitalism, Bad Capitalism and the Economics of Growth and Prosperity* (New Haven, CT: Yale University Press, 2007); Gosta Esping-Andersen, "The Three Political Economies of the Welfare State," *Canadian Review of Sociology and Anthropology* 26 (1989), pp. 10–36; Jonas Pontusson, "The American Welfare State in Comparative Perspective," *Perspectives on Politics* 4, no. 2 (June 2006), pp. 315–326; Harold L. Wilensky, *Rich Democracies: Political Economy, Public Policy, and Performance* (Berkeley, CA: University of California Press, 2002).

38. Edward S. Greenberg, "Capitalism and the American Political Ideal" (M.E. Sharpe, Inc: New York and London, 1985), Chapter 6.

39. U.S. Department of Commerce, *International Direct Investment* (Washington, DC: U.S. Government Printing Office, 1984), p. 1.

40. For entertaining yet highly informative critiques of extreme pro-globalization advocates and extreme anti-globalization advocates, see Michael Veseth, *Selling Globalization: The Myth of the Global Economy* (Boulder, CO: Lynne Rienner, 1998); and Michael Veseth, *Globaloney: Unraveling the Myths of Globalization* (Lanham, MD: Rowman & Littlefield, 2005).

41. Robert B. Reich, *Supercapitalism: The Transformation of Business, Democracy, and Everyday Life* (New York: Alfred A. Knopf, 2007).

42. Pinker, *Enlightenment Now*.

43. See John Markoff, "Google Puts Money on Robots, Using Man Behind Android," *New York Times*, December 4, 2013.

44. Brynjolfsson and McAfee, *The Second Machine Age*; Ford, *Rise of the Robots*; and Schumpeter, "The Age of Smart Machines," *Economist*, May 25, 2013, pp. 22–24.

45. Shobhana Chandra and Steve Matthews, "Having a Job Ain't All It's Cracked Up to Be," *Bloomberg BusinessWeek*, October 12, 2011.

46. For citations to the research used in this section on the middle class see Jacob S. Hacker and Paul Pierson, *Winner-Take-All Politics* (New York: Simon and Schuster, 2010); Robert B. Reich, *Aftershock: The Next Economy and America's Future* (New York: Knopf, 2010), ch. 7; and Benjamin I. Page and Martin Gilens, *Democracy in America?: What Has Gone Wrong and What We Can Do About It* (Chicago: University of Chicago Press, 2017), ch. 2. Semega, Fontenot, and Kollar, *Income and Poverty in the United States, 2016*; David Leonhardt, "The American Dream, Quantified, At Last," *New York Times*, Sunday Review, December 8, 2016.

47. Anne Case and Angus Deaton, "Rising Morbidity and Mortality in Midlife Among White Non-Hispanic Americans in the 21st Century," *Proceedings of the National Academy of Sciences* 112 (2015), pp. 1–6; and Andrew Gelman, "Is the Death Rate Really Increasing for Middle-Aged White Americans?" *Slate Online*, November 11, 2015, www.slate.com/articles/health_and_science/science/2015.

48. As for people in other rich democracies hit hard by the relative decline in manufacturing employment, it is worth pointing out the widespread existence of fairly generous, government provided safety nets, including more fulsome unemployment insurance, job retraining, health care, and housing subsidies, that might serve to moderate the impact of job losses. We will have more to say about the nature of our safety net programs in Chapter 17.

49. Reich, *Aftershock*, Part II, "Backlash." Also see "Angling for the Hopping Mad," *New York Times*, January 5, 2016, p. A22. This piece is based on a survey conducted by NBC News and *Esquire Magazine*.

50. See Seymour Martin Lipset, *American Exceptionalism: A Double-Edged Sword* (New York: Norton, 1996); Jennifer L. Hochschild, *Facing Up to the American Dream* (Princeton, NJ: Princeton University Press, 1995), ch. 1; and John Micklethwait and Adrian Wooldridge, *The Right Nation: Conservative Power in America* (New York: Penguin Press, 2004), part IV. For a contrary view—namely, that America is divided into distinct political cultural traditions—see Rogers M. Smith, *Civic Ideals: Conflicting Visions of Citizenship in U.S. History* (New Haven, CT: Yale University Press, 1997). For an answer to Smith that defends the idea that the American political culture is of a single large cloth, see Marc Stears, "The Liberal Tradition and the Politics of Exclusion," *Annual Review of Political Science* 10 (2007), pp. 85–101.

51. Robert P. Jones, "The Collapse of American Identity," *New York Times*, May 2, 2017, https://www.nytimes.com/2017/05/02/opinion/the-collapse-of-american-identity.html?_r=0.

52. For a contrary view of the place of individualism in American life, see Desmond King, *The Liberty of Strangers: Making the American Nation* (New York: Oxford University Press, 2004).

53. See Jennifer L. Hochschild, *What's Fair? American Beliefs About Distributive Justice* (Cambridge, MA: Harvard University Press, 1981); Herbert McClosky and John R. Zaller, *The American Ethos: Public Attitudes Toward Capitalism and Democracy* (Cambridge, MA: Harvard University Press, 1984); and Sidney Verba and Gary R. Orren, *Equality in America* (Cambridge, MA: Harvard University Press, 1985). However, see Benjamin I. Page and Lawrence R. Jacobs, *Class War: What Americans Really Feel About Inequality* (Chicago: The University of Chicago Press, 2009), which shows that public support exists for programs to lessen inequality.

54. See Joel F. Handler and Yeheskel Hasenfeld, *Blame Welfare, Ignore Poverty and Inequality* (Cambridge, UK: Cambridge University Press, 2007). For arguments suggesting that Americans are uncomfortable with income inequality and are willing to let government do something about making it less extreme, see Page and Jacobs, *Class War*.

55. Verba and Orren, *Equality in America*, p. 255.

56. Page and Jacobs, *Class War*, pp. 96–97.

57. Frank Newport, "Americans' Views on Bank Takeovers Appear Fluid," The Gallup Poll, February 24, 2009, http://www.gallup.com/poll/116065/americans-views-bank-takeovers-appear-fluid.aspx.

58. Pew Research Center for the People & the Press, "Support for Health Care Principles, Opposition to Package," news release, October 8, 2009, http://www.people-press.org/files/legacy-pdf/551.pdf.

59. John Judis, "Anti-Statism in America," *New Republic*, November 11, 2009, p. 2.

60. Russell Hanson, *The Democratic Imagination in America* (Princeton, NJ: Princeton University Press, 1985).

61. "Democracy in America: Ideal vs. Reality," The Pew Research Center, April 25, 2018, http://www.people-press.org/2018/04/26/the-public-the-political-system-and-american-democracy/overview_1-6.

62. McClosky and Zaller, *American Ethos*, p. 18; Pew Research Center for the People & the Press, "Views of a Changing World 2003," Pew Research Center, June 3, 2003, http://www.people-press.org/2003/06/03/views-of-a-changing-world-2003.

63. Alan Wolfe, *Does American Democracy Still Work?* (New Haven, CT: Yale University Press, 2006).

64. Gary Wills, *Under God: Religion and American Politics* (New York: Simon and Schuster, 1991); Micklethwait and Wooldridge, *Right Nation*; and Kevin Phillips, *American Theocracy: The Peril and Politics of Radical Religion, Oil, and Borrowed Money in the 21st Century* (New York: Viking, 2006).

65. Micklethwait and Wooldridge, *Right Nation*.

Chapter 5

1. All public opinion polls cited in this chapter-opening story are from John E. Mueller, *War, Presidents and Public Opinion* (New York: Wiley, 1973).

2. U.S. Department of Defense, OASD (Comptroller), *Selected Manpower Statistics* (Washington, DC: Government Printing Office, June 1976), pp. 59–60.

3. Robert S. Erikson and Kent L. Tedin, *American Public Opinion: Its Origins, Content, and Impact*, 9th ed. (New York: Routledge, 2016); Herbert Asher, *Polling and the Public: What Every Citizen Should Know*, 9th ed. (Washington, DC: CQ Press, 2016), offers an excellent introduction to how surveys are done.

4. Scott Keeter, Nick Hatley, Courtney Kennedy and Arnold Lau, "What Low Response Rates Mean for Telephone Surveys," Pew Research Center, May 15, 2017, http://www.pewresearch.org/2017/05/15/what-low-response-rates-mean-for-telephone-surveys.

5. Stephen J. Blumberg, Ph.D., and Julian V. Luke, "Wireless Substitution: Early Release of Estimates From the National Health Interview Survey, July–December 2016," National Center for Health Statistics. May 2017. https://www.cdc.gov/nchs/data/nhis/earlyrelease/wireless201705.pdf.

6. A 2016 report by the Pew Research Center provides a useful primer on the accuracy of online surveys. Courtney Kennedy, Andrew Mercer, Scott Keeter, Nick Hatley, Kyley McGeeney, and Alejandra Gimenez, "Evaluating Online Nonprobability Surveys," Pew Research Center, May 2, 2016, http://www.pewresearch.org/2016/05/02/evaluating-online-nonprobability-surveys.

7. Scott Keeter and Ruth Igielnik, "Can Likely Voter Models Be Improved? Evidence from the 2014 U.S. House Elections," Pew Research Center, January 7, 2016, http://www.pewresearch.org/2016/01/07/can-likely-voter-models-be-improved. "An Evaluation of 2016 Election Polls in the U.S.," American Association of Public Opinion Research, May 4, 2017. https://www.aapor.org/Education-Resources/Reports/An-Evaluation-of-2016-Election-Polls-in-the-U-S.aspx.

8. George F. Bishop, *The Illusion of Public Opinion: Fact and Artifact in American Public Opinion Polls* (Lanham, MD: Rowman & Littlefield, 2004); Herbert Asher, *Polling and the*

Public: What Every Citizen Should Know, 9th ed. (Washington, DC: CQ Press, 2016).

9. "An Evaluation of 2016 Election Polls in the U.S.," American Association of Public Opinion Research, May 4, 2017. https://www.aapor.org/Education-Resources/Reports/An-Evaluation-of-2016-Election-Polls-in-the-U-S.aspx.

10. For a review of the research literature on political socialization, see Erikson and Tedin, *American Public Opinion,* ch. 5.

11. M. Kent Jennings, "Political Socialization," in *The Oxford Handbook of Political Behavior,* eds. Russell Dalton and Hans-Dieter Klingman (Oxford, UK: Oxford University Press, 2004); M. Kent Jennings, Laura Stoker, and Jake Bowers, "Politics Across Generations: Family Transmission Reexamined," *Journal of Politics* 71, no. 3 (July 2009), pp. 782–799; and Laura Stoker and Jackie Bass, "Political Socialization," in *The Oxford Handbook of Public Opinion and the Media,* eds. Robert Shapiro and Lawrence R. Jacobs (Oxford, UK: Oxford University Press, 2011).

12. Jennings et al., "Politics Across Generations."

13. Doris A. Graber, *Mass Media and American Politics,* 8th ed. (Washington, DC: CQ Press, 2010), pp. 161–166.

14. For data on how the economic prospects of young people have changed for the worse and on how their political attitudes differ from other age cohorts, see Richard Fry, D'Vera Cohn, Gretchen Livingston, and Paul Taylor, "The Rising Age Gap in Economic Well-Being," Pew Research Social & Demographic Trends, Pew Research Center, November 7, 2011, http://www.pewsocialtrends.org/2011/11/07/the-rising-age-gap-in-economic-well-being; and Richard Fry, "Gen X Rebounds as the Only Generation to Recover the Wealth Lost After the Housing Crash," Pew Research Center, July 23, 2018, http://www.pewresearch.org/fact-tank/2018/07/23/gen-x-rebounds-as-the-only-generation-to-recover-the-wealth-lost-after-the-housing-crash.

15. Erikson and Tedin, *American Public Opinion,* pp. 83–84; Gabriel S. Lenz, "Learning and Opinion Change, Not Priming: Reconsidering the Priming Hypothesis," *American Journal of Political Science* 53 (2009), pp. 821–837; but see Cheryl Boudreau and Scott A. MacKenzie, "Informing the Electorate? How Party Cues and Policy Information Affect Public Opinion About Initiatives," *American Journal of Political Science* 58 (2014), pp. 48–62.

16. Bruce E. Keith, David B. Magleby, Candice J. Nelson, Elizabeth A. Orr, Mark C. Westlye, and Raymond E. Wolfinger, *The Myth of the Independent Voter* (Oakland, CA: University of California Press, 1992).

17. Stephen P. Nicholson, "Polarizing Cues," *American Journal of Political Science* 56 (2012), pp. 52–66. doi:10.1111/j.1540-5907.2011.00541.x.

18. Morris P. Fiorina, Samuel J. Abrams, and J. C. Pope, *Culture War? The Myth of a Polarized America,* 2nd ed. (New York: Pearson Longman, 2006); Alan I. Abramowitz and Kyle L. Saunders, "Is Polarization a Myth?" *Journal of Politics* 70 (2008), pp. 542–555; Matthew Levendusky, *How Liberals Became Democrats and Conservatives Became Republicans* (Chicago: University of Chicago Press, 2009).

19. Paul Sniderman and Thomas Piazza, *Black Pride and Black Prejudice* (Princeton, NJ: Princeton University Press, 2002), pp. 175–179; Erikson and Tedin, *American Public Opinion,* pp. 199–200; William G. Jacoby, "Is There a Culture War? Conflicting Value Structures in American Public Opinion," *American Political Science Review* 108 (2014), pp. 754–771.

20. Pew Research Center for the People & the Press, "Trends in Political Values and Core Attitudes: 1987–2009," news release, May 21, 2009, http://www.people-press.org/files/legacy-pdf/517.pdf; and Laura R. Olson and John C. Green, *Beyond Red State, Blue State: Electoral Gaps in the Twenty-First Century American Electorate* (New York: Pearson Prentice-Hall, 2009).

21. This and the votes of other groups reported in this section are from the General Social Survey (2016).

22. Pew Research Center for the People & the Press, "Trends."

23. *Ibid.,* sec. 9; and Erikson and Tedin, *American Public Opinion,* pp. 200–201.

24. General Social Survey 2016.

25. Jeffrey M. Jones, "In U.S., Confidence in Police Lowest in 22 Years," Gallup, June 19, 2015, http://www.gallup.com/poll/183704/confidence-police-lowest-years.aspx.

26. Chris Girard, Guillermo J. Grenier, and Hugh Gladwin, "Exile Politics and Republican Party Affiliation: The Case of Cuban Americans in Miami," *Social Science Quarterly* 93 (2012), pp. 42–57.

27. Paul Taylor, Mark Hugo Lopez, Jessica Martínez, and Gabriel Velasco, "When Labels Don't Fit: Hispanics and Their Views of Identity," Pew Research Hispanic Trends Project, Pew Research Center, April 4, 2012, http://www.pewhispanic.org/2012/04/04/when-labels-dont-fit-hispanics-and-their-views-of-identity. Hispanic Protestants, however, are more consistently conservative on social issues, according to research reported by Rodolfo O. de la Garza and Seung-Jin Jang, "Latino Public Opinion," in *The Oxford Handbook of American Public Opinion and the Media,* eds. Robert Y. Shapiro and Lawrence R. Jacobs. (Oxford, UK: Oxford University Press).

28. "Election 2016: Exit Polls," *New York Times,* November 8, 2016, accessed November 11, 2016, http://www.nytimes.com/interactive/2016/11/08/us/politics/election-exit-polls.html.

29. Sarah Dutton, Jennifer De Pinto, Anthony Salvanto, and Fred Backus, "How Americans Are Feeling About the Fight Against ISIS, Economy," CBS News, February 19, 2015, http://www.cbsnews.com/news/how-americans-are-feeling-about-the-fight-against-isis-economy.

30. See Pew Research Center for the People & the Press, "Trends," p. 24. For pre-2009 data, see Erikson and Tedin, *American Public Opinion,* pp. 191–199, using overtime reports from the National Election Study surveys; and Nolan McCarty, Keith T. Poole and Howard Rosenthal, Polarized America: The Dance of Ideology and Unequal Riches (Cambridge, MA: MIT Press, 2006).

31. Pew Research Center for the People & the Press, "Trends," sec. 2.

32. Leslie McCall and Jeff Manza, "Class Differences in Social and Political Attitudes in the United States," in *The Oxford Handbook of American Public Opinion and the Media,* eds. Robert Y. Shapiro and Lawrence R. Jacobs.

33. Earl Black and Merle Black, *The Rise of Southern Republicans* (Cambridge, MA: Harvard University Press, 2002); and Earl Black and Merle Black, *Divided America: The Ferocious Power Struggle in American Politics* (New York: Simon and Schuster, 2007).

34. Erikson and Tedin, *American Public Opinion,* pp. 213–218.

35. Morris P. Fiorina, *Culture War: The Myth of a Polarized America* (New York: Pearson Longman, 2005); and Morris P. Fiorina and Samuel J. Abrams, "Political Polarization in the American Public," *Annual Review of Political Science* 11 (2008), pp. 563–588; and Erikson and Tedin, *American Public Opinion,* pp. 214–215.

36. James G. Gimpel and Kimberly A. Karnes, "The Rural Side of the Urban-Rural Gap," *PS: Political Science & Politics* 39 (2006), pp. 467–472.

37. Pew Research Center, "Wide Gender Gap, Growing Educational Divide in Voters' Party Identification," March 2018, http://assets.pewresearch.org/wp-content/uploads/sites/5/2018/03/20113922/03-20-18-Party-Identification.pdf.

38. Erikson and Tedin, *American Public Opinion,* pp. 195–197.

39. Fiorina, *Culture War,* pp. 34–35, 66–76; and Karen M. Kaufman, "The Gender Gap," *PS: Political Science and Politics* 39, no. 3 (2006), pp. 447–453. For a contrary view, see Janet M. Box-Steffensmeier, Suzanna De Boef, and Tse-Min Lin, "The Dynamics of the Partisan Gender Gap," *American Political Science Review* 98, no. 3 (August 2004), pp. 515–528.

40. Pew Research Center, "Wide Gender Gap."

41. Mark Schlesinger and Caroline Heldman, "Gender Gap or Gender Gaps?" *Journal of Politics* 63, no. 1 (February 2001), pp. 59–92; Erikson and Tedin, *American Public Opinion,* pp. 219–223; General Social Survey, 2008; and Leonie Huddy and Erin Cassese, "On the Complex and Varied Political Effects of Gender," in *The Oxford Handbook of American Public Opinion and the Media,* eds. Robert Y. Shapiro and Lawrence R. Jacobs.

42. Fiorina, *Culture War,* pp. 66–69.

43. Pew Research Center for the People & the Press, "Trends."

44. Pew Research Center, "Wide Gender Gap."

45. ABC News/*Washington Post* poll, March 2011.

46. William Jordan, "Age and Race in the 2016 Democratic Primary," YouGov, June 07, 2016, https://today.yougov.com/topics/politics/articles-reports/2016/06/07/age-and-race-democratic-primary; The Economist, "Young v. old votes for Bernie and Hillary in the 2016 Primaries," April 27, 2016, https://www.economist.com/graphic-detail/2016/04/27/young-v-old-votes-for-bernie-and-hillary-in-the-2016-primaries.

47. Pew Research Center for the People & the Press, "Trends," sec. 4; and Nicholas L. Danigelis, Melissa Hardy, and Stephen J. Cutler, "Population Aging, Intracohort Aging, and Sociopolitical Attitudes," *American Sociological Review* 72 (2007), pp. 812–830.

48. For detailed information on the size, beliefs, and political attitudes of various religious denominations in the United States, see Pew Research Religion & Public Life Project, "U.S. Religious Landscape Survey," Pew Research Center, November 9, 2009. All of the survey data in this section, unless otherwise noted, comes from this source.

49. David E. Campbell, "Religious 'Threat' in Contemporary Presidential Elections," *Journal of Politics* 68: 104–115.

50. Fiorina, *Culture War;* Fiorina and Abrams, "Political Polarization."

51. King and Smith, *Still a House Divided;* Mason, Lilliana, *Uncivil Agreement: How Politics Became Our Identity,* (Chicago: University of Chicago Press, 2018).

52. Alexander Hamilton, James Madison, and John Jay, *The Federalist Papers,* ed. Clinton Rossiter (New York: New American Library, 1961; originally published 1787–1788). See Benjamin I. Page and Robert Y. Shapiro, *The Rational Public: Fifty Years of Trends in Americans' Policy Preferences* (Chicago: The University of Chicago Press, 1992), chs. 1 and 2.

53. Walter Lippmann, *Public Opinion* (New York: Macmillan, 1922), p. 127.

54. Philip E. Converse, "The Nature of Belief Systems in Mass Publics," in *Ideology and Discontent,* ed. David Apter (New York: Free Press, 1964), pp. 206–261; and Philip E. Converse, "Attitudes and Non-Attitudes: Continuation of a Dialogue," in *The Quantitative Analysis of Social Problems,* ed. Edward R. Tufte (Reading, MA: Addison-Wesley, 1970), pp. 168–189. See also Bartels, *Unequal Democracy,* for an argument that people find it hard to understand whether public policies are consistent with their values and wishes.

55. Michael X. Delli Carpini and Scott Keeter, *What Americans Know About Politics and Why It Matters* (New Haven, CT: Yale University Press, 1996); and Alan Wolfe, *Does American Democracy Still Work?* (New Haven, CT: Yale University Press, 2006).

56. For full details, see Erikson and Tedin, *American Public Opinion,* Table 3.1. See also Benjamin I. Page and Robert Y. Shapiro, *Rational Public,* pp. 9–14; Wolfe, *Does American Democracy Still Work?* pp. 24–30.

57. Pew Research Center for the People & the Press, "Well Known: Clinton and Gadhafi; Little Known: Who Controls Congress," Pew Research Center, March 31, 2011, http://www.people-press.org/2011/03/31/well-known-clinton-and-gadhafi-little-known-who-controls-congress.

58. Jacob S. Hacker and Paul Pierson, *Winner-Take-All Politics* (New York: Simon and Schuster, 2010), pp. 154–155; and Bartels, *Unequal Democracy.*

59. Suzanne Mettler, *The Submerged State: How Invisible Government Policies Undermine American Democracy* (Chicago: The University of Chicago Press, 2011).

60. Michael X. Delli Carpini and Scott Keeter, "Stability and Change in the US Public's Knowledge of Politics," Public Opinion Quarterly, 55, no. 4 (August 1991).

61. Paul M. Sniderman, Richard A. Brody, and Philip E. Tetlock, *Reasoning and Choice: Explorations in Political Psychology* (New York: Cambridge University Press, 1991). See also Carpini and Keeter, *What Americans Know About Politics*; and Samuel Popkin, *The Reasoning Voter* (Chicago: The University of Chicago Press, 1991). For the view that it matters a great deal that Americans don't know many of the details about what is going on in Washington, see Bartels, *Unequal Democracy*; Bryan Caplan, *The Myth of the Rational Voter: Why Democracies Choose Bad Policies* (Princeton, NJ: Princeton University Press, 2008); and Wolfe, *Does American Democracy Still Work?*

62. Robert E. Lane, *Political Ideology: Why the American Common Man Believes What He Does* (New York: Free Press, 1962); Jennifer L. Hochschild, *What's Fair? American Beliefs About Distributive Justice* (Cambridge, MA: Harvard University Press, 1986); and Carroll J. Glynn, Susan Herbst, Garrett O'Keefe, and Robert Y. Shapiro, *Public Opinion* (Boulder, CO: Westview Press, 1999), ch. 8.

63. Binyamin Appelbaum and Robert Gebeloff, "Even Critics of Safety Net Increasingly Depend on It," *New York Times*, February 11, 2012. Robert Y. Shapiro and Lawrence R. Jacobs, "The Democratic Paradox," in *The Oxford Handbook of American Public Opinion and the Media*, eds. Robert Y. Shapiro and Lawrence R. Jacobs, pp. 720–722.

64. Art Swift, "Smaller Majority 'Extremely Proud' to Be an American," *Politics*, Gallup, July 2, 2015, http://www.gallup.com/poll/183911/smaller-majority-extremely-proud-american.aspx.

65. Pew Research Global Attitudes Project, "The American-Western European Values Gap," Pew Research Center, November 17, 2011, updated February 29, 2011, http://www.pewglobal.org/2011/11/17/the-american-western-european-values-gap.

66. Pew Research Center for the People & the Press, "Trends," p. 78.

67. Pew Research Center, "Public Trust in Government: 1958–2017," December 14, 2017, http://www.people-press.org/2017/12/14/public-trust-in-government-1958-2017.

68. Jim Norman, "Satisfaction with U.S. Direction Reaches 12-Year High," Gallup, June 18, 2018, https://news.gallup.com/poll/235739/satisfaction-direction-reaches-year-high.aspx.

69. Justin McCarthy, "Snapshot: U.S. Congressional Job Approval at 18%," Gallup, April 18, 2018, https://news.gallup.com/poll/232553/snapshot-congressional-job-approval.aspx

70. "Congress Less Popular than Cockroaches, Traffic Jams," Public Policy Polling, January 8, 2013, http://www.publicpolicypolling.com/main/2013/01/congress-less-popular-than-cockroaches-traffic-jams.html.

71. "Gallup Daily: Obama Job Approval," The Gallup Poll, http://www.gallup.com/poll/113980/gallup-daily-obama-job-approval.aspx.

72. Vanessa Williamson, Theda Skocpol, and John Coggin, "The Tea Party and the Remaking of Republican Conservatism," *Perspectives on Politics* 9, no. 1 (2011), pp. 25–43.

73. Pew Research Center, "Political Polarization, 1994–2017," October 20, 2017, http://www.people-press.org/interactives/political-polarization-1994-2017.

74. Steven Kull, *Americans and Foreign Aid: A Study of American Public Attitudes* (Washington, DC: Program on International Policy Attitudes, 1995).

75. Tom W. Smith, "That Which We Call Welfare by Any Other Name Would Smell Sweeter: An Analysis of the Impact of Question Wording on Response Patterns," *Public Opinion Quarterly* 51 (1987), pp. 75–83.

76. Gallup, "In Depth: Topics A to Z: Marriage," http://news.gallup.com/poll/117328/marriage.aspx.

77. Pew Research Center for the People & the Press, "Broad Approval for New Arizona Immigration Law," Pew Research Center, May 12, 2010, http://www.people-press.org/2010/05/12/broad-approval-for-new-arizona-immigration-law.

78. Scott Bittle, Jonathan Rochkind, and Amber Ott, "Confidence in U.S. Foreign Policy Index," PublicAgenda.org and Foreign Affairs 7 (Spring 2010), http://www.publicagenda.org/pages/foreign-policy-index-2010.

79. William Caspary, "The 'Mood Theory': A Study of Public Opinion and Foreign Policy," *American Political Science Review* 64 (1970), pp. 536–547; John E. Reilly, ed., *American Public Opinion and U.S. Foreign Policy, 1995* (Chicago: Chicago Council on Foreign Relations, 1995), p. 13; Lydia Saad, "Growing Minority Wants Minimal U.S. Role in World Affairs," The Gallup Poll, February 21, 2011, http://www.gallup.com/poll/146240/growing-minority-wants-minimal-role-world-affairs.aspx. See also Pew Research Center for the People & the Press, "Trends," sec. 6.

80. Survey by Time, Cable News Network. Methodology: Conducted by Yankelovich Partners on April 21, 1994 and based on 600 telephone interviews. Sample: National adult.

81. Survey by Cable News Network, USA Today. Methodology: Conducted by Gallup Organization, September 21–22, 2001 and based on 1,005 telephone interviews. Sample: National adult.

82. Gallup Poll, August 5–8, 2010 (*N*=1,013 adults nationwide, margin of error ± 4).

83. Washington Post-ABC News poll, December 11–14, 2014, https://www.washingtonpost.com/politics/polling/afghanistan-united-states-united/2015/01/04/3905e062-9409-11e4-8385-866293322c2f_page.html.

84. Steven Shepard, "Majority supports Syrian airstrikes," Politico, April, 18, 2018.

85. Summary of polls on American foreign policy reported at PublicAgenda.org, http://www.publicagenda.org; and Benjamin I. Page and Marshall M. Bouton, *The Foreign Policy Disconnect: What Americans Want from Our Leaders But Don't Get* (Chicago: The University of Chicago Press, 2006).

86. This seems to be the case in foreign and national defense issues as well. See John H. Aldrich, Christopher Gelpi, Peter Feaver, Jason Reifler, and Kristin Tompson Sharp, "Foreign Policy and the Electoral Connection," *Annual Review of Political Science* 9 (2006), pp. 477–502.

87. For a summary of the evidence, see Erikson and Tedin, *American Public Opinion*, pp. 305–312.

88. Alan D. Monroe, "Consistency Between Public Preferences and National Policy Decisions," *American Politics Quarterly* 7 (January 1979), pp. 3–19; and Benjamin I. Page and Robert Y. Shapiro, "Effects of Public Opinion on Policy," *American Political Science Review* 77 (1983), pp. 175–190.

89. James A. Stimson, *Public Opinion in America: Moods, Cycles and Swings* (Boulder, CO: Westview Press, 1991).

90. Paul Burstein, "The Impact of Public Opinion on Public Policy: A Review and an Agenda," *Political Research Quarterly* 56, no. 1 (March 2003). See also Vincent L. Hutchings, *Public Opinion and Democratic Accountability: How Citizens Learn About Politics* (Princeton, NJ: Princeton University Press, 2003).

91. The various arguments for this are summarized in Benjamin I. Page, "The Semi-Sovereign Public," in *Navigating Public Opinion: Polls, Policy, and the Future of American Democracy*, eds. Jeff Manza, Fay Lomax Cook, and Benjamin I. Page (New York: Oxford University Press, 2002); and in Robert Y. Shapiro and Lawrence R. Jacobs, "The Democratic Paradox," in *The Oxford Handbook of American Public Opinion and the Media*, eds. Robert Y. Shapiro and Lawrence R. Jacobs.

92. For the argument that public opinion is largely a media creation, see W. Lance Bennett, "News Polls: Constructing an Engaged Public," in *The Oxford Handbook of American Public Opinion and the Media*, eds. Robert Y. Shapiro and Lawrence R. Jacobs.

93. Lawrence R. Jacobs and Robert Y. Shapiro, *Politicians Don't Pander: Political Manipulation and the Loss of Democratic Responsiveness* (Chicago: The University of Chicago Press, 2000); Shapiro and Jacobs, "The Democratic Paradox," in *The Oxford Handbook of American Public Opinion and the Media*, eds. Robert Y. Shapiro and Lawrence R. Jacobs; John Zaller, *The Nature and Origins of Mass Opinion* (New York: Cambridge University Press, 1992); and Wolfe, *Does American Democracy Still Work?*

94. W. Lance Bennett, Regina G. Lawrence, and Steven Livingston, *When the Press Fails: Political Power and the News Media from Iraq to Katrina* (Chicago: The University of Chicago Press, 2007), ch. 5.

95. Martin Gilens, *Affluence and Influence: Economic Inequality and Political Power in America* (Princeton, NJ: Princeton University Press, 2012); Larry M. Bartels, *Unequal Democracy: The Political Economy of the New Gilded Age* (Princeton, NJ: Princeton University Press, 2008); Martin Gilens and Benjamin I. Page, "Testing Theories of American Politics: Elites, Interest Groups, and Average Citizens," *Perspectives on Politics* 12, pp. 564–581.

96. Public opinion scholar Larry Bartels suggests that the 2001 tax cut (the largest in two decades, with tax relief going overwhelmingly to upper-income people) was supported by the public out of sheer ignorance and confusion about the impact of changes in the Tax Code. See Larry M. Bartels, "Homer Gets a Tax Cut: Inequality and Public Policy in the American Mind," *Perspectives on Politics* 3, no. 1 (March 2005), pp. 15–29. In the same issue (pp. 33–53), Jacob Hacker and Paul Pierson disagree; in their article "Abandoning the Middle: The Bush Tax Cuts and the Limits of Democratic Control," they suggest that manipulation and deception were prominent in the successful effort to raise public support for the 2001 tax cuts.

Chapter 6

1. Material for this chapter opener is from W. Lance Bennett, Regina G. Lawrence, and Steven Livingston, *When the Press Fails: Political Power and the News Media from Iraq to Katrina* (Chicago: University of Chicago Press, 2007), pp. 13–45.

2. Adam Schiffer, "Blogswarms and Press Norms: News Coverage of the Downing Street Memos" (paper, American Political Science Association, August 31–September 3, 2006, Washington, DC).

3. Bennett, Lawrence, and Livingston, *When the Press Fails*, p. 27.

4. Dana Milbank, "Democrats Play House to Rally Against the War," *Washington Post*, June 6, 2005, p. 17.

5. Donald Trump (@realDonaldTrump), "The Fake News is working overtime. Just reported that, despite the tremendous success we are having with the economy & all things else, 91% of the Network News about me is negative (Fake). Why do we work so hard in working with the media when it is corrupt? Take away credentials?" May 9, 2018, 4:38 AM. Tweet. https://twitter.com/realDonaldTrump/status/994179864436596736?

6. Bennett, Lawrence, and Livingston, *When the Press Fails*, pp. 57–59.

7. Cecilia Kang, Edmund Lee, and Emily Cochrane, "AT&T Wins Approval for $85.4 Billion Time Warner Deal in Defeat for Justice Dept.," *New York Times*, June 12, 2018, https://www.nytimes.com/2018/06/12/business/dealbook/att-time-warner-ruling-antitrust-case.html.

8. W. Lance Bennett, *News: The Politics of Illusion* (New York: Pearson Longman, 2011), pp. 231–246, reviews the debate. The term *media monopoly* is from University of California–Berkeley journalism professor Ben Bagkikian's book, *Media Monopoly*, 5th ed. (Boston: Beacon Press, 1997).

9. Cecilia Kang and Emily Steel, "Regulators Approve Charter Communications Deal for Time Warner Cable," *New York Times*, April 25, 2016, http://www.nytimes.com/2016/04/26/technology/charter-time-warner-cable-bright-house-cable-deal.html?_r=0.

10. Anousha Sakoui, "Comcast to Acquire DreamWorks Animation for $3.8 Billion," *Bloomberg*, April 28, 2016, http://www.bloomberg.com/news/articles/2016-04-28/comcast-to-acquire-dreamworks-animation-for-3-8-billion.

11. Cecilia Kang, "F.C.C. Opens Door to More Consolidation in TV Business," *New York Times*, November 16, 2017, https://www.nytimes.com/2017/11/16/business/media/fcc-local-tv.html.

12. David Shepardson, "FCC Votes to Refer Sinclair Tribune Merger to Administrative Judge," *Reuters*, July 18, 2018, https://www.reuters.com/article/us-tribune-media-m-a-sinclair-ma/fcc-votes-to-refer-sinclair-tribune-merger-to-administrative-judge-idUSKBN1K81OU.

13. Paul Farhi, "On NBC, The Missing Story About Parent Company General Electric," *Washington Post,* March 29, 2011, https://www.washingtonpost.com/lifestyle/style/on-nbc-the-missing-story-about-parent-company-general-electric/2011/03/29/AFpRYJyB_story.html.

14. Bennett, *News,* pp. 242–244.

15. *Ibid.,* p. 241.

16. Alex Jones, *Losing the News: The Future of the News that Feeds Democracy* (New York: Oxford University Press, 2009).

17. Bennett, *News,* pp. 238–241; Doris Graber, *Mass Media and American Politics* (Washington, DC: CQ Press, 2014), pp. 97–100; Jones, *Losing the News,* p. 51; and James Fallows, "Learning to Love the (Shallow, Divisive, Unreliable) New Media," *Atlantic Monthly,* April, 2011.

18. Doug Underwood, "Market Research and the Audience for Political News," in *The Politics of News: The News of Politics,* eds. Doris Graber, Denis McQuail, and Pippa Norris (Washington, DC: CQ Press, 1998), p. 171; also see Bennett, *News,* ch. 7.

19. Bill Carter, "CNN's Ratings Surge Covering the Mystery of the Missing Airliner," *New York Times,* March 17, 2014, http://www.nytimes.com/2014/03/18/business/media/cnns-ratings-surge-with-coverage-of-the-mystery-of-the-missing-airliner.html?_r=1.

20. Nicholas Confessore and Karen Yourish, "$2 Billion Worth of Free Media for Donald Trump," *New York Times,* March 15, 2016, http://www.nytimes.com/2016/03/16/upshot/measuring-donald-trumps-mammoth-advantage-in-free-media.html.

21. Alan Wolfe, *Does American Democracy Still Work?* (New Haven, CT: Yale University Press, 2006), pp. 108–110.

22. Joseph N. Cappella and Kathleen Hall Jamieson, *Spiral of Cynicism: The Press and the Public Good* (New York: Oxford University Press, 1997).

23. John Zaller, *A Theory of Media Politics* (Chicago: University of Chicago Press, 2004).

24. Graber, *Mass Media and American Politics,* pp. 87–91.

25. Leon V. Sigal, *Reporters and Officials: The Organization and Politics of News Reporting* (Lexington, MA: Heath, 1973), p. 124.

26. Bennett, *News,* pp. 112–114; Steven Livingston and W. Lance Bennett, "Gatekeeping, Indexing, and Live Event News," *Political Communication* 20, no. 4 (October–December 2003), pp. 363–380; Graber, *Mass Media and American Politics,* pp. 79–82.

27. Bennett, *News,* pp. 164–167.

28. Eileen Sullivan and Katie Benner, "Trump Praises Arrest of Former Senate Committee Aide in Leaks Inquiry," *New York Times,* June 8, 2018, https://www.nytimes.com/2018/06/08/us/politics/trump-leak-investigation.html.

29. Bennett, *News,* pp. 127–134.

30. Mark Hertsgaard, *On Bended Knee* (New York: Farrar, Straus & Giroux, 1988), p. 5.

31. Anne E. Kornblut, "Administration Is Warned About Its News Videos," *New York Times,* January 19, 2005, p. A9; Anne E. Kornblut, "Third Journalist Was Paid to Promote Bush Policies," *New York Times,* January 29, 2005, p. A13; Charlie Savage and Alan Wirzbicki, "White House-Friendly Reporter Under Scrutiny," *Boston Globe,* February 2, 2005, p. A1; "Source Watch," *Center for Media and Democracy,* February 2005, http://www.prwatch.org/cmd/index.html.

32. Brian Stelter, "Trump Has Granted Fox News 19 Interviews Since Inauguration," *CNN,* October 25, 2017, http://money.cnn.com/2017/10/25/media/fox-news-president-trump-interviews/index.html.

33. David Murray, Joel Schwartz, and S. Robert Lichter, *It Ain't Necessarily So: How Media Make and Unmake the Scientific Picture of Reality* (Lanham, MD: Rowman & Littlefield Publishers, 2001), pp. 29–30.

34. Journalism.org, November 30, 2011.

35. Graber, *Mass Media and American Politics,* ch. 11.

36. For excellent analysis of why and how this happens and its unfortunate impact on the democratic process, see Bennett, Lawrence, and Livingston, *When the Press Fails.*

37. For a description and a review of a group of thinkers celebrating the birth of a new journalism see Dean Starkman, *Confidence Game: The Limited Vision of the News Gurus* (Columbia Journalism Review Books, November 9, 2011), www.cjr.org, accessed February 20, 2012.

38. Jordan Weissmann, "The Decline of Newspapers Hits a Stunning Milestone," April 28, 2014, http://www.slate.com/blogs/moneybox/2014/04/28/decline_of_newspapers_hits_a_milestone_print_revenue_is_lowest_since_1950.html; Pew Research Center, "State of the News Media 2015," April 2015, http://assets.pewresearch.org/wp-content/uploads/sites/13/2017/05/30142603/state-of-the-news-media-report-2015-final.pdf.

39. Matthew Hindman, *The Myth of Digital Democracy* (Princeton, NJ: Princeton University Press, 2009), ch. 6.

40. Pew Research Center, "State of the News Media 2015."

41. Amy Mitchell and Dana Page, "State of the News Media," Pew Research Center, March 2014.

42. Graber, *Mass Media and American Politics,* pp. 36–37.

43. Eric Alterman, *What Liberal Media?* (New York: Basic Books, 2003). Also see the website FAIR (Fairness and Accuracy in Reporting) at www.fair.org for a liberal point of view about press bias.

44. Bernard Goldberg, *Bias in the News* (Washington, DC: Regnery, 2001); and the online conservative site AIM (Accuracy in Media) at www.aim.org.

45. Jeffrey M. Jones and Zacc Ritter, "Americans See More News Bias; Most Can't Name Neutral Source," Gallup, January 17, 2018, https://news.gallup.com/poll/225755/americans-news-bias-name-neutral-source.aspx.

46. Glenn J. Hansen and Hyunjung Kim. "Is the Media Biased Against Me? A Meta-Analysis of the Hostile Media Effect Research," *Communication Research Reports* 28 (2011), pp. 169–179.

47. Pew Research Center, "Americans' Attitudes About the News Media Deeply Divided Along Partisan Lines," May 2017, http://assets.pewresearch.org/wp-content/uploads/sites/13/2017/05/09144304/PJ_2017.05.10_Media-Attitudes_FINAL.pdf.

48. Matthew Gentzkow and Jesse M. Shapiro, "What Drives Media Slant? Evidence from U.S. Daily Newspapers," *Econometrica* 78 (2010), pp. 35–71.

49. Neal Hickey, "Is Fox News Fair?" *Columbia Journalism Review* 31 (March/April 1998), pp. 30–35; David Weaver and G. Cleveland Wilhoit, *The American Journalist* (Mahwah, NJ: Lawrence Erlbaum, 1996); Graber, *Mass Media and American Politics*, pp. 86–89; and Erikson and Tedin, *American Public Opinion*, pp. 233–234.

50. Bennett, *News*, pp. 34–35; Graber, *Mass Media and American Politics*, pp. 76–77; Thomas E. Patterson and Wolfgang Donsbach, "News Decisions: Journalists as Partisan Actors," *Political Communications* 13 (October–December 1996), pp. 455–468.

51. Martin Gilens and Craig Hertzman, "Corporate Ownership and News Bias: Newspaper Coverage of the 1996 Telecommunications Act," Journal of Politics 62 (2000), pp. 369–386.

52. Matthew Gentzkow and Jesse M. Shapiro, "Media Bias and Reputation," *Journal of Political Economy* 114 (2006), pp. 280–316; Gentzkow and Shapiro, 2010.

53. Lydia Saad, "TV Is Americans' Main Source of News," Gallup, July 8, 2013, http://www.gallup.com/poll/163412/americans-main-source-news.aspx.

54. David L. Paletz, "The Media and Public Policy," in *The Politics of News: The News of Politics*, eds. Doris Graber, Denis McQuail, and Pippa Norris (Washington, DC: CQ Press, 1998); Dietram A. Scheufele and David Tewksbury, "Framing, Agenda Setting, and Priming: The Evolution of Three Media Effects Models," *Journal of Communication* 57 (2007), pp. 9–20.

55. Kevin Arceneaux and Martin Johnson, *Changing Minds or Changing Channels? Partisan News in an Age of Choice* (Chicago: University of Chicago Press, 2013).

56. Shanto Iyengar and Donald R. Kinder, *News That Matters* (Chicago: University of Chicago Press, 1987); also see Erikson and Tedin, *American Public Opinion*, pp. 247–248, for a review of the research on news media agenda setting.

57. W. Lance Bennett, "News Polls: Constructing an Engaged Public," in *The Oxford Handbook of American Public Opinion and the Media*, eds. Robert Y. Shapiro and Lawrence R. Jacobs (Oxford: Oxford University Press, 2011).

58. G. Ray Funkhauser, "The Issues of the Sixties: An Exploratory Study in the Dynamics of Public Opinion," *Public Opinion Quarterly* 37 (Spring 1973), pp. 62–75.

59. George C. Edwards, "Who Influences Whom? The President, Congress and the Media," *The American Political Science Review* 93 (June 1999), pp. 327–344.; for more on debates about the "CNN effect" see: Eytan Gilboa, "The CNN Effect: The Search for a Communication Theory of International Relations," *Political Communication* 22 (2005), pp. 27–44; Piers Robinson, "The CNN Effect Reconsidered:

60. Bennett, Lawrence, and Livingston, *When the Press Fails*.

61. Shanto Iyengar, Mark D. Peters, and Donald R. Kinder, "Experimental Demonstrations of the "Not-So-Minimal" Consequences of Television News Programs," *American Political Science Review* 76 (1982), pp. 848–858.

62. Austin Hart and Joel A. Middleton, "Priming Under Fire: Reverse Causality and the Classic Media Priming Hypothesis," *Journal of Politics* 76 (2014), pp. 581–592.

63. On framing, see Thomas E. Nelson, "Issue Framing," in *The Oxford Handbook of American Public Opinion and the Media*, eds. Shapiro and Jacobs.

64. Shanto Iyengar, *Is Anyone Responsible? How Television News Frames Political Issues* (Chicago: University of Chicago Press, 1991); Kathleen Hall Jamieson and Paul Waldman, *The Press Effect* (Washington, DC: CQ Press, 2002).

65. Paul M. Kellstedt, *The Mass Media and the Dynamics of American Racial Attitudes* (Cambridge, UK: Cambridge University Press, 2003).

66. Benjamin I. Page, Robert Y. Shapiro, and Glenn R. Dempsey, "What Moves Public Opinion?" *American Political Science Review* 81 (1987), pp. 23–43.

67. James N. Druckman and K. R. Nelson, "Framing and Deliberation: How Citizens' Conversations Limit Elite Influence," *American Journal of Political Science* 47, no. 4 (2003), pp. 729–746; Dennis Chong and James N. Druckman, "A Theory of Framing and Opinion Formation in Competitive Elite Environments," *Journal of Communication* 57 (2007), pp. 99–118.

68. Joseph Cappella and Kathleen Jamieson, *Spiral of Cynicism: The Press and the Public Good* (New York: Oxford University Press, 1997); Stephen C. Craig, ed., *Broken Contract: Changing Relations Between Americans and Their Government* (Boulder, CO: Westview Press, 1996); Mark J. Hetherington, "Declining Trust and Shrinking Policy Agenda," in *Communications in U.S. Elections*, eds. Robert Hart and Daron R. Shaw (Lanham, MD: Rowman & Littlefield, 2001); Bennett, *News*; Thomas E. Patterson, "Bad News, Period," *PS* (March 1996), pp. 17–20.

69. For a review of the literature on the subject, see Samuel L. Popkin, "Changing Media, Changing Politics," *Perspectives on Politics* (June 2006), pp. 327–341; Wolfe, *Does American Democracy Still Work?* ch. 5.

70. John A. Ferejohn and James H. Kuklinski, eds., *Information and Democratic Processes* (Urbana, IL: University of Illinois Press, 1990); Benjamin I. Page, *Who Deliberates? Mass Media in Modern Democracy* (Chicago: University of Chicago Press, 1996).

Chapter 7

1. Results of scientific studies five years after the spill are reported in "An Oil Spill's Aftermath," *Science News* (April 18, 2015). Information surrounding the blowout is from the following sources: David Barstow, Laura Dodd, James Glanz, Stephanie Sauo, and Ian Urbina, "Regulators Failed to Address Risks in Oil Rig Fail-Safe Device," *New York*

Mapping a Research Agenda for the Future," *Media, War & Conflict* 4 (2011), pp. 3–11.

Times, June 20, 2010; Ian Urbina, "Inspector General's Inquiry Faults Regulators," *New York Times,* May 24, 2010; "The Oil Well and the Damage Done," *Economist Online,* June 17, 2010, http://www.economist.com/node/16381032; "How Did This Happen and Who Is to Blame?" *Bloomberg Businessweek,* June 14–20, 2010, pp. 60–64; and "BP Oil Spill," *Guardian,* 2014, http://www.theguardian.com/environment/bp-oil-spill.

2. On the most recent deregulation movement in American politics and the thinking behind it, see Richard Harris and Sidney Milkis, *The Politics of Regulatory Change* (New York: Oxford University Press, 1989); and John Cassidy, *How Markets Fail* (New York: Farrar, Straus and Giroux, 2009). See also Marver Bernstein, *Regulation by Independent Commission* (Princeton, NJ: Princeton University Press, 1955); Grant McConnell, *Private Power and American Democracy* (New York: Vintage Books, 1966); James Buchanan and Gordon Tullock, "Polluters, Profits and Political Responses: Direct Control Versus Taxes," *American Economic Review* 65 (1975), pp. 139–147; Murray Weidenbaum, *The Costs of Government Regulation of Business* (Washington, DC: Joint Economic Committee of Congress, 1978); and Kevin P. Phillips, *The Politics of Rich and Poor: Wealth and the American Electorate in the Reagan Aftermath* (New York: Random House, 1990).

3. David Brooks, "Strengthen the Presidency," *New York Times,* December 12, 2013, http://www.nytimes.com/2013/12/13/opinion/brooks-strengthen-the-presidency.html?_r=0. For other books on the growth and dominance of interest groups and how their effect on the governing process and the distribution of political power, see Francis Fukuyama, "The Decay of American Political Institutions," *American Interest,* December 8, 2013, http://www.the-american-interest.com/articles/2013/12/08/the-decay-of-american-political-institutions/; Jacob S. Hacker and Paul Pierson, *Winner-Take-All Politics* (New York: Simon & Schuster, 2010); and Hedrick Smith, *Who Stole the American Dream* (New York: Random House, 2012).

4. Jeffrey M. Berry and Clyde Wilcox, *The Interest Group Society,* 5th ed. (New York: Pearson Longman, 2009), pp. 4–6.

5. Alexander Hamilton, James Madison, and John Jay, *The Federalist Papers,* ed. Clinton Rossiter (New York: New American Library, 1961; originally published 1787–1788), No. 10.

6. The classics of the pluralist tradition include Arthur F. Bentley, *The Process of Government* (Chicago: The University of Chicago Press, 1908); David Truman, *The Governmental Process* (New York: Knopf, 1951); V. O. Key Jr., *Politics, Parties, and Pressure Groups* (New York: A. Crowell, 1952); Robert A. Dahl, *A Preface to Democratic Theory* (Chicago: The University of Chicago Press, 1956); and Robert A. Dahl, *Who Governs?* (New Haven, CT: Yale University Press, 1961). For a summary treatment of the pluralist tradition and its thinking about interest groups, see Berry and Wilcox, *Interest Group Society,* ch. 1.

7. E. E. Schattschneider, *The Semi-Sovereign People* (New York: Holt, Rinehart & Winston, 1960).

8. John S. Ahlquist and Margaret Levi, *In the Interest of Others: Organizations and Social Activism* (Princeton, NJ: Princeton University Press, 2013); Michael Goldfield, *The Decline of Organized Labor in the United States* (Chicago: The University of Chicago Press, 1987); Edward S. Greenberg, Leon Grunberg, Sarah Moore, and Patricia B. Sikora, *Turbulence: Boeing and the State of American Workers and Managers* (New Haven, CT: Yale University Press, 2010); Robert B. Reich, *Supercapitalism: The Transformation of Business, Democracy, and Everyday Life* (New York: Knopf, 2007), pp. 80–86; Jake Rosenfeld, *What Unions No Longer Do* (Cambridge, MA: Harvard University Press, 2014); and David Vogel, *Fluctuating Fortunes: The Political Power of Business in America* (New York: Basic Books, 1989), ch. 8.

9. U.S. Department of Labor, Bureau of Labor Statistics, "Union Members Summary," news release, January 23, 2015.

10. Reich, *Supercapitalism.* A country's institutional and legal structure also matter. The proportion of workers in labor unions actually increased over the past several decades in the Scandinavian countries. See Lyle Scruggs and Peter Lange, "Where Have All the Workers Gone? Globalization, Institutions, and Union Density," *Journal of Politics* 64, no. 1 (February 2002), pp. 126–153.

11. Kenneth McLennan, "What Do Unions Do? A Management Perspective," in *What Do Unions Do? A Twenty-Year Perspective,* eds. James T. Bennett and Bruce E. Kaufman (New Brunswick, NJ: Transaction Publishers, 2007).

12. For the broader context in which the assault on labor unions has taken place, see Michael Goldfield and Amy Bromsen, "The Changing Landscape of US Unions in Historical and Theoretical Perspective," *Annual Review of Political Science* 16 (May 2013), pp. 231–257; and Rosenfeld, *What Unions No Longer Do.*

13. Jeffrey M. Berry, *Lobbying for the People* (Princeton, NJ: Princeton University Press, 1977), p. 7; Berry and Wilcox, *Interest Group Society,* pp. 24–26; and Berry, *New Liberalism,* p. 2.

14. Ronald Brownstein, *The Second Civil War: How Extreme Partisanship Has Paralyzed Washington and Polarized America* (New York: The Penguin Press, 2007), pp. 106–112; Berry, *Lobbying for the People;* David Broder, *Changing the Guard* (New York: Simon & Schuster, 1980); Hugh Heclo, "Issue Networks and the Executive Establishment," in *The New American Political System,* ed. Anthony King (Washington, DC: American Enterprise Institute, 1978); Kay Lehman Schlozman and John A. Tierney, *Organized Interests and American Democracy* (New York: Harper and Row, 1986); Jack L. Walker Jr., "The Origins and Maintenance of Interest Groups in America," *American Political Science Review* 77 (1983), pp. 390–406; and Theda Skocpol, *Diminished Democracy: From Membership to Management in American Civil Life* (Norman, OK: University of Oklahoma Press, 2003).

15. Skocpol, *Diminished Democracy;* Theda Skocpol, "Associations Without Members," *American Prospect* 10, no. 4 (July/August 1999), pp. 66–73; Theda Skocpol, "Voice and Inequality: The Transformation of American Civil Democracy," *Perspectives on Politics* 2, no. 1 (March 2004), pp. 3–20.

16. The numbers above are from Roger H. Davidson, Walter J. Oleszek, and Francis E. Lee, *Congress and Its Members,* 15th ed. (Washington, DC: CQ Press, 2015), p. 369.

17. The Center for Responsive Politics, "Lobbying Database," OpenSecrets.org, 2016, http://www.opensecrets.org/

lobby/, which is based on required reports to the House and Senate.

18. David Coen, Wyn Grant, and Graham Wilson, "Political Science Perspectives on Business and Government," in *The Oxford Handbook of Business and Government,* eds. David Coen, Wyn Grant, and Graham Wilson (Oxford, UK: Oxford University Press, 2010), pp. 18–37.

19. Reich, *Supercapitalism,* pp. 143–148; and Ken Auletta, "The Search Party," *New Yorker,* January 14, 2008, pp. 30–37.

20. Gary J. Andres, *Lobbying Reconsidered* (New York: Pearson Longman, 2009), ch. 4.

21. Reich, *Supercapitalism,* pp. 144–146.

22. Joseph E. Stiglitz, *The Price of Inequality: How Today's Divided Society Endangers Our Future* (New York: Norton, 2012), p. 196.

23. Truman, *Governmental Process.*

24. Jack L. Walker Jr., *Mobilizing Interest Groups in America* (Ann Arbor, MI: University of Michigan Press, 1991).

25. Jacob S. Hacker and Paul Pierson, "Winner-Take-All Politics: Public Policy, Political Organization, and the Precipitous Rise of Top Incomes in the United States," *Politics & Society* 38, no. 2 (2010), p. 172.

26. See the Center for Public Integrity, "Revolving Door," at www.publicintegrity.org.

27. For these and other former members of Congress and congressional staffers now registered as lobbyists, see "Revolving Door," *Open Secrets.org* at http://www.opensecrets.org/revolving.

28. Mark A. Smith, *Business and Political Power: Public Opinion, Elections and Democracy* (Chicago: The University of Chicago Press, 2000). Also see Pepper D. Culpepper, *Quiet Politics and Business Power* (New York: Cambridge University Press, 2011), ch. 1.

29. Schattschneider, *Semi-Sovereign People.*

30. Robert Draper, "Inside the Power of the N.R.A.," *New York Times Magazine,* December 12, 2013, http://www.nytimes.com/2013/12/15/magazine/inside-the-power-of-the-nra.html.

31. Frank R. Baumgartner, Jeffrey M. Berry, Marie Hojnacki, David C. Kimball, and Beth L. Leech, *Lobbying and Policy Change: Who Wins, Who Loses, and Why* (Chicago: The University of Chicago Press, 2009), pp. 150–155; and Davidson, Oleszek, and Lee, *Congress and Its Members,* pp. 377–386.

32. Berry and Wilcox, *Interest Group Society,* p. 138.

33. Peter Katel, "The Lobbying Boom," *CQ Researcher,* July 22, 2005, p. 1.

34. Berry and Wilcox, *Interest Group Society,* pp. 142–145.

35. Baumgartner et al., *Lobbying and Policy Change,* pp. 155–157.

36. Berry and Wilcox, *Interest Group Society,* pp. 118–120.

37. Schattschneider, *Semi-Sovereign People.*

38. Berry, *New Liberalism.*

39. Schlozman and Tierney, *Organized Interests,* p. 175.

40. Bruce Bimber, *Information and American Democracy* (New York: Cambridge University Press, 2003).

41. For a comprehensive examination of interest group involvement in campaigns, see Michael M. Franz, *Choices and Changes: Interest Groups in the Electoral Process* (Philadelphia: Temple University Press, 2008).

42. Schattschneider, *Semi-Sovereign People*; Fukuyama, "Decay"; Hacker and Pierson, *Winner-Take-All Politics*; and Smith, *Who Stole the American Dream.*

43. Schattschneider, *Semi-Sovereign People,* p. 2.

44. For the most sweeping claim for this state of affairs as well as solid empirical evidence for the claim, see Benjamin I. Page and Martin Gilens, *Democracy in America?: What Has Gone Wrong and What Can We Do About It* (Chicago: University of Chicago Press, 2017).

45. Timothy Werner and Graham Wilson, "Business Representation in Washington," in Coen, Grant, and Wilson, *The Oxford Handbook of Business and Government* (Oxford, UK : Oxford University Press, 2012), pp. 87–109.

46. Berry, *Lobbying for the People*; Skocpol, "Voice and Inequality"; Dara Strolovitch, "Do Interest Groups Represent the Disadvantaged? Advocacy at the Intersections of Race, Class, and Gender," *Journal of Politics* 68, no. 4 (November 2006), pp. 894–910; and Hacker and Pierson, "Winner-Take-All Politics," pp. 180–181.

47. Werner and Wilson, "Business Representation"; and Hacker and Pierson, *Winner-Take-All Politics.*

48. Center for Responsive Politics, "Pharm/Health Prod 2015," *OpenSecrets.org,* March 23, 2016, http://www.opensecrets.org/lobby/indusclient_lobs.php?id=H04&year=2015.

49. Eric Dash and Nelson D. Schwartz, "As Reform Takes Shape, Some Relief on Wall St.," *New York Times,* May 23, 2010.

50. Adam Liptak, "Justices, 5–4, Reject Corporate Spending Limit," *New York Times,* January 21, 2010; "Unbound: The Supreme Court Undermines Convoluted Campaign Finance Rules," *Economist,* January 30, 2010.

51. For a lively and controversial examination of the role of David and Charles Koch—whose combined wealth is greater than that of Bill Gates—in funding pro-business, anti-government, and anti-tax advocacy organizations and candidates at all levels in the political system see Jane Mayer, *Dark Money: The Hidden History of the Billionaires Behind the Rise of the Radical Right* (New York: Doubleday, 2016). Also see Page and Gilens, *Democracy in America?* ch. 4.

52. For elaboration of the points made here and the supporting scholarly evidence, see Gregory C. Shaffer, "Law and Business," in *The Oxford Handbook of Business and Government,* eds. Coen, Grant, and Wilson, pp. 66–70.

53. Davidson, Oleszek, and Lee, *Congress and Its Members,* pp. 383–386.

54. "Money Talks, Congress Listens," *Boston Globe,* December 12, 1982.

55. Russ Choma, "The 2012 Election: Our Price Tag (Finally) for the Whole Ball of Wax," *OpenSecretsblog*, The Center for Responsive Politics, March 13, 2013, http://www.opensecrets.org/news/2013/03/the-2012-election-our-price-tag-fin.html.

56. Thomas B. Edsall, "How Did the Democrats Become Favorites of the Rich?" *The New York Times, op ed* (October 7, 2015).

57. "The Trillion-Dollar Tax Holiday," *Bloomberg Businessweek*, October 3–9, 2011, pp. 66–67.

58. The term *issue networks* is from Heclo, "Issue Networks." For a review and evaluation of the scholarly debate over sub-governments and issue networks, see Baumgartner et al., *Lobbying and Policy Change*, pp. 57–67. See also Berry and Wilcox, *Interest Group Society*, pp. 163–165; Berry, *New Liberalism*; Scott H. Ainsworth, *Analyzing Interest Groups: Group Influence on People and Policies* (New York: Norton, 2002); Allan J. Cigler, "Interest Groups," in *Political Science: Looking to the Future*, ed. William Crotty, vol. 4 (Evanston, IL: Northwestern University Press, 1991); Robert H. Salisbury, John P. Heinz, Edward O. Laumann, and Robert L. Nelson, "Triangles, Networks, and Hollow Cores," and Mark P. Petracca, "The Rediscovery of Interest Group Politics," both in *The Politics of Interests: Interest Groups Transform*, ed. Mark P. Petracca (Boulder, CO: Westview Press, 1992); and Robert M. Stein and Kenneth Bickers, *Perpetuating the Pork Barrel: Policy Subsystems and American Democracy* (Cambridge, UK: Cambridge University Press, 1995).

59. Shaffer, "Law and Business," pp. 66–67.

60. Charles Lindblom, *Politics and Markets* (New York: Basic Books, 1977), p. 356.

61. Neil J. Mitchell, *The Conspicuous Corporation: Business, Public Policy and Representative Democracy* (Ann Arbor, MI: University of Michigan Press, 1997), p. 167.

62. Theda Skocpol and Alexander Hertel-Fernandez, "The Koch Network and the Rightward Shift in U.S. Politics" (paper, Midwest Political Science Association, Chicago, Illinois, April 8, 2016).

63. "The World's Billionaires," *Forbes*, http://www.forbes.com/billionaires/list/.

64. Lee Epstein, William M. Landes, and Richard A Posner, "When It Comes to Business, the Right and Left Sides of the Court Agree," *University Journal of Law and Policy* 54 (September 16, 2013), pp. 33–55.

65. Tom Donnelly, "The U.S. Chamber of Commerce Continues Its Winning Ways," (Washington, DC: The Constitutional Accountability Center, Issue Brief, June 30, 2014).

66. Lee Epstein, William M. Landes, and Richard A Posner, "When it comes to business, the Right and Left sides of the Court Agree, University Journal of Law and Policy, Volume 54: 33–55.

67. Dan Clawson, Alan Neustadt, and Mark Weller, *Dollars and Votes* (Philadelphia: Temple University Press, 1998), pp. 26–28, 64–71, 97–99; and Berry and Wilcox, *Interest Group Society*, pp. 184–185.

68. Jeffrey A. Winters and Benjamin I. Page, "Oligarchy in the United States?" *Perspectives on Politics* 7, no. 4 (December 2009), pp. 731–751.

69. The full story of what has happened is told in Hacker and Pierson, "Winner-Take-All Politics."

70. "Overview of the Federal Tax System as in Effect for 2018," Washington, DC: The Joint Budget Committee of the United States Congress, February 7, 2018, https://www.jct.gov/publications.html?func=startdown&id=5060; and *An American Budget: Mid-Session Review* (Washington, DC: Office of Management and Budget, 2018), https://www.whitehouse.gov/wp-content/uploads/2018/07/19msr.pdf.

71. Government Accounting Office, 2013.

72. Vogel, *Fluctuating Fortunes*, p. 291.

73. Coen, Grant, and Wilson, "Political Science Perspectives on Business and Government," and Werner and Wilson, "Business Representation in Washington, DC," both in Coen, Grant, and Wilson, *The Oxford Handbook of Business and Government*.

74. See, especially, Martin Gilens, *Affluence and Influence: Economic Inequality and Political Power in America* (New York and Princeton, NJ: Russell Sage Foundation and Princeton University Press, 2012); and Martin Gilens and Benjamin I. Page, "Testing Theories of American Politics: Elites, Interest Groups, and Average Citizens," *Perspectives on Politics* 12, no. 3 (September 2014). The Gilens-Page assessment of business power is rejected by Robert S. Erikson, "Income Inequality and Policy Responsiveness," *Annual Review of Political Science* 18 (May 2015), pp. 11–29.

75. Hacker and Pierson, *Winner-Take-All Politics*.

76. For a comparison of U.S. lobbying rules with those of other democracies, see Raj Chari, Gary Murphy, and John Hogan, "Regulating Lobbyists: A Comparative Analysis of the United States, Canada, Germany, and the European Union," *Political Quarterly* 78, no. 3 (July–September 2007), pp. 422–438.

Chapter 8

1. Woodrow Wilson, "Declaration of War Message to Congress, April 2, 1917," Records of the United States Senate, Record Group 46, National Archives, http://www.ourdocuments.gov/doc.php?flash=true&doc=61.

2. James MacGregor Burns and Stewart Burns, *A People's Charter: The Pursuit of Rights in America* (New York: Knopf, 1991), ch. 5; E. McGlen and Karen O'Connor, *Women's Rights* (New York: Praeger, 1983), ch. 3; and Sarah M. Evans, *Born for Liberty: A History of Women in America* (New York: Free Press, 1997).

3. Sidney Tarrow, *Power in Movement* (New York: Cambridge University Press, 1998); David S. Meyer and Sidney Tarrow, eds., *The Social Movement Society* (Lanham, MD: Rowman & Littlefield Publishers, 1997); Doug McAdam, John D. McCarthy, and Mayer N. Zald, "Social Movements," in *Handbook of Sociology*, ed. Neil J. Smelser (Newbury Park, CA: Sage, 1994); Doug McAdam, *Political Process and the Development of Black Insurgency* (Chicago: The University of Chicago Press, 1982); and Doug McAdam, Sidney Tarrow, and Charles Tilly, *Dynamics of Contention* (Cambridge, UK: Cambridge University Press, 2001).

4. Sidney Tarrow, "Social Movements as Contentious Politics," *American Political Science Review* 90 (1996), pp. 853–866; Ronald R. Aminzade, Jack A. Goldstone, Doug McAdam, Elizabeth J. Perry, William H. Sewell Jr., and Sidney Tarrow, eds., *Silence and Voice in the Study of Contentious Politics* (New York: Cambridge University Press, 2001).

5. Our focus is on social movements in politics and their impact on public policies. For a review of the scholarly literature on social movements more broadly considered, see Edwin Amenta, Neal Caren, Elizabeth Chiarello, and Yang Su, "The Political Consequences of Social Movements," *Annual Review of Sociology* 36 (2010), pp. 287–307; Elizabeth A. Armstrong and Mary Bernstein, "Culture, Power, and Institutions: A Multi-Institutional Approach to Social Movements," *Sociological Theory* 26, no. 1 (March 2008), pp. 74–99.

6. The philosophy of non-violent civil disobedience is spelled out in Martin Luther King, *Why We Can't Wait* (New York: Signet Classic, 2000).

7. Malcolm X was a complex and compelling character who changed political course during his active political lifetime. See Manning Marable, *Malcolm X: A Life of Redefinition* (New York: Viking Press, 2011).

8. CBS News telecast, February 16, 2003.

9. Jackie Smith, "Globalizing Resistance: The Battle of Seattle and the Future of Social Movements," *Mobilization: An International Journal* 6, no. 1 (2000), pp. 1–19.

10. For a compelling and deeply researched study of the role of the Koch brothers broad political influence, see Jane Mayer, *The Hidden History of the Billionaires Behind the Rise of the Radical Right* (New York: Doubleday, 2016).

11. Pew Research Center for the People & the Press, "Public Divided Over Occupy Wall Street," Pew Research Center poll, October 24, 2011, http://www.people-press.org/2011/10/24/public-divided-over-occupy-wall-street-movement.

12. Herbert Ruffin, "Black Lives Matter: The Growth of a New Social Justice Movement," *Blackpast.org,* http://www.blackpast.org/perspectives/black-lives-matter-growth-new-social-justice-movement#sthash.qbfU05b5.dpuf.

13. Campaign Zero, http://www.joincampaignzero.org.

14. Jamil Smith, "Black Lives Matter Arrives on Hillary Clinton's Doorstep," *The New Republic,* August 11, 2015, https://newrepublic.com/article/122524/blacklivesmatter-activists-disrupt-hillary-clinton-event.

15. E. E. Schattschneider, *The Semi-Sovereign People* (New York: Holt, Rinehart & Winston, 1960), p. 142.

16. Richard Polenberg, *One Nation Divisible* (New York: Penguin Press, 1980), p. 268; and Craig A. Rimmerman, *From Identity to Politics: The Lesbian and Gay Movements in the United States* (Philadelphia, PA: Temple University Press, 2002), ch. 1.

17. Frances Fox Piven, *When Movements Matter: How Ordinary People Change America* (Lanham, MD: Rowman & Littlefield, 2006).

18. Theodore J. Lowi, *The Politics of Disorder* (New York: Basic Books, 1971), p. 54.

19. Piven, *When Movements Matter.*

20. Aminzade et al., *Silence and Voice;* Meyer and Tarrow, *Social Movement Society;* McAdam, McCarthy, and Zald, "Social Movements"; and Sidney Tarrow, *Social Movements, Collective Action, and Politics* (New York: Cambridge University Press, 1994).

21. Neil J. Smelser, *Theory of Collective Behavior* (New York: Free Press, 1962); and Elaine Walker and Heather J. Smith, *Relative Deprivation: Specification, Development, and Integration* (Cambridge, UK: Cambridge University Press, 2001).

22. Barbara Sinclair Deckard, *The Women's Movement* (New York: Harper & Row, 1983); and Ethel Klein, *Gender Politics: From Consciousness to Mass Politics* (Cambridge, MA: Harvard University Press, 1984), ch. 2.

23. Donald P. Haider-Markel, "Creating Change—Holding the Line," in *Gays and Lesbians in the Political Process,* eds. Ellen D. B. Riggle and Barry L. Tadlock (New York: Columbia University Press, 1999), pp. 38–59.

24. Rimmerman, *From Identity to Politics.*

25. Kathleen Belew, "The History of White Power," *New York Times,* April 18, 2018, https://www.nytimes.com/2018/04/18/opinion/history-white-power.html.

26. William Gamson, *The Strategy of Social Protest* (Homewood, IL: Dorsey, 1975); and John D. McCarthy and Mayer N. Zald, "Resource Mobilization and Social Movements: A Partial Theory," *American Journal of Sociology* 82 (1977), pp. 1212–1241.

27. Jo Freeman, *The Politics of Women's Liberation* (New York: McKay, 1975); and Nancy Burns, "Gender: Public Opinion and Political Action," in *Political Science: The State of the Discipline,* eds. Ira Katznelson and Helen V. Milner (New York: Norton, 2002), pp. 472–476.

28. Bruce Bimber, *Information and American Democracy: Technology and the Evolution of Political Power* (New York: Cambridge University Press, 2003), chs. 3 and 5.

29. Amenta, Caren, Chiarello, and Su, "Political Consequences," p. 299; McAdam, *Political Process;* Tarrow, *Social Movements;* and Peter K. Eisenger, "The Conditions of Protest Behavior in American Cities," *American Political Science Review* 67 (1973), pp. 11–28.

30. Frances Fox Piven and Richard A. Cloward, *Poor People's Movements: Why They Succeed, How They Fail* (New York: Vintage, 1979), ch. 3.

31. Klein, *Gender Politics,* pp. 90–91.

32. Pew Research Center for the People & the Press, "Support for Same-Sex Marriage at Record High, but Key Segments Remain Opposed," Pew Research Center, June 6, 2013, http://www.people-press.org/2015/06/08/support-for-same-sex-marriage-at-record-high-but-key-segments-remain-opposed.

33. Pew Research Center for the People & the Press, "Support for Same-Sex Marriage Grows, Even Among Groups That Had Been Skeptical," Pew Research Center, June 26, 2017, http://www.people-press.org/2017/06/26/support-for-same-sex-marriage-grows-even-among-groups-that-had-been-skeptical.

34. Pew Research Center for the People & the Press, "Trends in Political Values and Core Attitudes: 1987–2009," news release, May 21, 2009, http://www.people-press.org/files/legacy-pdf/517.pdf.

35. G. William Domhoff, *The Higher Circles* (New York: Random House, 1970); Edward S. Greenberg, *Capitalism and the American Political Ideal* (Armonk, NY: Sharpe, 1985); Gabriel Kolko, *The Triumph of Conservatism* (Chicago: Quadrangle, 1967); and James Weinstein, *The Corporate Ideal in the Liberal State* (Boston: Beacon Press, 1968).

36. Rimmerman, *From Identity to Politics.*

37. Piven, *When Movements Matter.*

38. Taylor Branch, *Parting the Waters: America in the King Years* (New York: Simon and Schuster, 1986); and William H. Chafe, *The Unfinished Journey: America Since World War II* (New York: Oxford University Press, 2003).

39. Amenta, Caren, Chiarello, and Su, "Political Consequences," pp. 294–298.

40. Jane Mansbridge, *Why We Lost the ERA* (Chicago: The University of Chicago Press, 1986).

41. Christian Davenport, Hank Johnson, and Carol Mueller, eds., *Mobilization and Repression* (Minneapolis: University of Minnesota Press, 2005).

42. See David Caute, *The Great Fear* (New York: Simon & Schuster, 1978); Robert Justin Goldstein, *Political Repression in Modern America* (Cambridge, MA: Schenkman, 1978); and Alan Wolfe, *The Seamy Side of Democracy* (New York: McKay, 1978).

43. Greenberg, *Capitalism and the American Political Ideal.*

44. *Ibid.*

45. Chafe, *Unfinished Journey,* pp. 430–468; Deckard, *Women's Movement*; Klein, *Gender Politics,* ch. 2; Freeman, *Politics of Women's Liberation.* See also debates on the relative progress of women in the United States collected in Dorothy McBride Stetson, *Women's Rights in the United States: Policy Debates and Gender Roles* (London: Routledge, 2004).

46. "Knowledge Center: Women in S & P 500 Companies," Catalyst.org, 2015, http://www.catalyst.org/knowledge/women-sp-500-companies.

47. *National Roster of Black Elected Officials, Fact Sheet* (Washington, DC: Joint Center for Political and Economic Studies, 2013), p. 1.

48. Desmond S. King and Rogers M. Smith, *Still a House Divided: Race and Politics in Obama's America* (Princeton, NJ: Princeton University Press, 2011), pp. 268–280; "A Dream Examined," *New York Times,* August 23, 2013, http://www.nytimes.com/interactive/2013/08/24/us/a-dream-examined.html?action=click&module=Search&region=searchResults%230&version=&url=http%3A%2F%2Fquery.nytimes.com%2Fsearch%2Fsitesearch%2F%23%2F-Dream%2Bexamined%2F&_r=0; and "Fifty Years After Martin Luther King's Death: A Divided America," *The Economist,* April 4, 2018, https://enterprise.chaucercloud.com/bookeditor/?v=4.45.5#/3545/619/track-changes-edit.

Chapter 9

1. Dan Hopkins, "What Trump Supporters Were Doing Before Trump," *Five Thirty Eight,* March 14, 2016, http://fivethirtyeight.com/features/what-trump-supporters-were-doing-before-trump/.

2. "Presidential Approval Ratings—Donald Trump," Gallup, http://news.gallup.com/poll/203198/presidential-approval-ratings-donald-trump.aspx.

3. Samantha Smith, "6 Charts that Show Where Clinton and Trump Supporters Differ," Pew Research Center, October 20, 2016, http://www.pewresearch.org/fact-tank/2016/10/20/6-charts-that-show-where-clinton-and-trump-supporters-differ/.

4. Diana Mutz, "Status Threat, Not Economic Hardship, Explains the 2016 Presidential Vote," Proceedings of the National Academy of Sciences of the United States of America, April 23, 2018, http://www.pnas.org/content/early/2018/04/18/1718155115.

5. Gabriel Sherman, "How Many Chances Do you Get to Be a Hero?" *New York Magazine,* February 18, 2017, http://nymag.com/daily/intelligencer/2017/02/john-mccain-takes-on-donald-trump.html.

6. Marilyn Icsman, "John Boehner Slams Republicans: 'There Is No Republican Party. There's a Trump Party'," *USA Today,* May 31, 2018, https://www.usatoday.com/story/news/politics/onpolitics/2018/05/31/former-speaker-john-boehner-criticizes-republican-party/661544002/.

7. Richard Hofstadter, *The Idea of a Party System: The Rise of Legitimate Opposition in the United States, 1780–1840* (Berkeley: University of California Press, 1969), p. 12.

8. Marjorie Randon Hershey, *Party Politics in America,* 14th ed. (New York: Pearson Longman, 2011), p. 7.

9. Robert A. Dahl, *On Democracy* (New Haven, CT: Yale University Press, 1998); Hershey, *Party Politics,* pp. 1–2; and E. E. Schattschneider, *Party Government* (Portsmouth, NH: Praeger, 1977), p. 208. See also Jonathan White and Lea Ypi, "On Partisan Political Justification," *American Political Science Review* 105, no. 2 (May 2011), pp. 381–396.

10. Schattschneider, *Party Government,* p. 208.

11. Marjorie Randon Hershey, *Party Politics in America,* 14th ed. (New York: Pearson Longman, 2011); A. James Reichley, *The Life of the Parties: A History of American Political Parties* (Lanham, MD: Rowman & Littlefield, 2002).

12. Steven J. Rosenstone and John Mark Hansen, *Mobilization, Participation, and Democracy in America* (New York: Macmillan, 1993).

13. E. E. Schattschneider, *The Semi-Sovereign People* (New York: Holt, Rinehart & Winston, 1960).

14. John H. Aldrich and John D. Griffin, "Parties, Elections, and Democratic Politics," in *The Oxford Handbook of American Elections and Political Behavior,* ed. Jan E. Leighley (Oxford, UK: Oxford University Press, 2010). See also John H. Aldrich, *Why Parties? A Second Look* (Chicago: The University of Chicago Press, 2011).

15. Maurice Duverger, *Political Parties: Their Organization and Activity in the Modern State* (London: Methuen, 1959).

16. Marjorie Randon Hershey, "Like a Bee: Election Law and the Survival of Third Parties," in *Election Law and Electoral Politics,* ed. Matthew J. Streb (Boulder, CO: Lynn Rienner, 2004); and Hershey, *Party Politics,* pp. 37–38.

17. James T. Bennett, *Not Invited to the Party: How the Demopublicans Have Rigged the System and Left Independents Out in the Cold* (New York: Springer, 2009); and Elisabeth Carter, *The Extreme Right in Western Europe: Success or Failure?* (Oxford: Oxford University Press, 2011).

18. Much of this discussion is drawn from Steven J. Rosenstone, Roy L. Behr, and Edward H. Lazarus, *Third Parties in America,* 2nd ed. (Princeton, NJ: Princeton University Press, 1996). See also Paul S. Herrnson and John C. Green, *Multiparty Politics in America* (Lanham, MD: Rowman & Littlefield, 2002); Hershey, *Party Politics,* pp. 37–40; John F. Bibby and L. Sandy Maisel, *Two Parties or More?* (Boulder, CO: Westview Press, 2003); and Shigeo Hirano and James M. Snyder Jr., "The Decline of Third-Party Voting in the United States," *Journal of Politics* 69, no. 1 (February 2007), pp. 1–16.

19. On realignment, see Walter Dean Burnham, *Critical Elections and the Mainsprings of American Politics* (New York: Norton, 1970); Jerome Clubb, William H. Flanigan, and Nancy H. Zingale, *Partisan Realignment* (Newbury Park, CA: Sage, 1980); V. O. Key Jr., "A Theory of Critical Elections," *Journal of Politics* 17 (1955), pp. 3–18; Hershey, *Party Politics,* ch. 7; James L. Sundquist, *Dynamics of the Party System* (Washington, DC: Brookings Institution Press, 1973); and Samuel Merrill, Bernard Grofman, and Thomas L. Brunnell, "Cycles in American National Electoral Politics, 1854–2006," *American Political Science Review* 102, no. 1 (February 2008), pp. 1–17. David R. Mayhew, *Electoral Realignments* (New Haven, CT: Yale University Press, 2004); Hershey, *Party Politics*; Peter F. Nardulli, "The Concept of a Critical Realignment, Electoral Behavior, and Political Change," *American Political Science Review* 89 (1995), pp. 10–22; Gary Miller and Norman Schofield, "The Transformation of the Republican and Democratic Party Coalitions in the U.S.," *Perspectives on Politics* 69, no. 3 (September 2008), pp. 433–450; and Matt Bai, "The Great Unalignment," *New York Times Sunday Magazine,* January 24, 2010, pp. 13–15.

20. John Aldrich and Richard Niemi, "The Sixth American Party System," in *Broken Contract: Changing Relationships Between Americans and Their Government,* ed. Stephen C. Craig (Boulder, CO: Westview Press, 1996); and Walter J. Stone and Ronald B. Rapoport, "It's Perot Stupid! The Legacy of the 1992 Perot Movement in the Major-Party System, 1994–2000," *PS: Political Science and Politics* XXXIV, no. 1 (March 2001), pp. 49–56.

21. Larry M. Bartels, *Unequal Democracy: The Political Economy of the Guided Age* (New York and Princeton, NJ: Russell Sage Foundation and Princeton University Press, 2008); Thomas Byrne Edsall and Mary D. Edsall, *Chain Reaction: The Impact of Race, Rights and Taxes on American Politics* (New York: Norton, 1991); Stanley B. Greenberg, *Middle Class Dreams: The Politics and Power of the New American Majority* (New Haven, CT: Yale University Press, 1996); and Desmond S. King and Rogers M. Smith, *Still a House Divided: Race and Politics in Obama's America* (Princeton, NJ: Princeton University Press, 2011).

22. James L. Sundquist, *Dynamics of the Party System: Alignment and Realignment of Political Parties in the United States* (Washington, DC: Brookings Institution Press, 2011), ch. 17; Martin P. Wattenberg, *The Decline of American Political Parties, 1952–1996* (Cambridge: Harvard University Press, 2009).

23. Morris Fiorina, *Unstable Majorities: Polarization, Party Sorting, and Political Stalemate* (Stanford: Hoover Press, 2017). John Sides and Daniel J. Hopkins, eds. *Political Polarization in American Politics* (New York: Bloomsbury Publishing, 2015). Marc J. Hetherington and Thomas J. Rudolph, *Why Washington Won't Work: Polarization, Political Trust, and the Governing Crisis* (Chicago: University of Chicago Press, 2015). Geoffrey C. Layman Thomas M. Carsey, and Juliana Menasce Horowitz, "Party Polarization in American Politics: Characteristics, Causes, and Consequences," *Annual Review of Political Science* 9 (2006), pp. 83–110. James A. Thurber and Antoine Yoshinaka, eds. *American Gridlock: The Sources, Character, and Impact of Political Polarization* (Cambridge: Cambridge University Press, 2015).

24. Ronald Brownstein, *The Second Civil War: How Extreme Partisanship Has Paralyzed Washington and Polarized America* (New York: Penguin Press, 2007); Nicol C. Rae, "Be Careful What You Wish For: The Rise of Responsible Parties in American National Politics," *Annual Reviews, Political Science* 10 (2007), pp. 169–191; and Thomas E. Mann and Norman J. Ornstein, *It's Even Worse Than It Looks: How the American Constitutional System Collided with the New Politics of Extremism* (New York: Basic Books, 2012).

25. Morris P. Fiorina, *Disconnect: The Breakdown of Representation in American Politics* (Norman: University of Oklahoma Press, 2009). Alan Abramowitz disagrees with Fiorina, arguing that the politically attentive mass public is deeply polarized. See his *The Disappearing Center: Engaged Citizens, Polarization, and American Democracy* (New Haven, CT: Yale University Press, 2010). Bill Bishop joins Abramowitz's position in his book *The Big Sort: Why the Clustering of Like-Minded Americans Is Tearing Us Apart* (New York: Houghton Mifflin, 2008).

26. Alan I. Abramowitz and Kyle L. Saunders, "Is Polarization a Myth?" *Journal of Politics* 70, no. 2 (2008), pp. 542–555.

27. Ian McDonald, "Migration and Sorting in the American Electorate: Evidence from the 2006 Cooperative Congressional Election Study," *American Politics Research* 39, no. 3 (2011), pp. 512–533; Bishop, *The Big Sort.*

28. Geoffrey C. Layman, Thomas M. Carsey, and Juliana Menasce Horowitz, "Party Polarization in American Politics: Characteristics, Causes, and Consequences," *Annual Review of Political Science* 9 (2006), pp. 83–110; and Sean M. Theriault, *Party Polarization in Congress* (New York: Cambridge University Press, 2008). Sunstein, Cass R. Republic: Divided Democracy in the Age of Social Media. Princeton: Princeton University Press, 2018.

29. Alan Lewis, *The Cambridge Handbook of Psychology and Economic Behaviour* (Cambridge: Cambridge University Press), p. 43.

30. Lydia Saad, "Conservatives Hang On to Ideology Lead by a Thread," Gallup, January 11, 2016, http://news.gallup.com/poll/188129/conservatives-hang-ideology-lead-thread.aspx.

31. M. S. Lewis-Beck, H. Norpoth, W. G. Jacoby, H. F. Weisberg, and P. E. Converse, *The American Voter Revisited* (Ann Arbor: University of Michigan Press, 2008).

32. *Washington Post*, "Exit Polls 2012: How the Vote Has Shifted," http://www.washingtonpost.com/wp-srv/special/politics/2012-exit-polls/table.html.

33. Donald Green, Bradley Palmquist, and Eric Schickler, *Partisan Hearts and Minds: Political Parties and the Social Identity of Voters* (New Haven, CT: Yale University Press, 2002); Robert S. Erikson and Kent L. Tedin, *American Public Opinion* (New York: Pearson Longman, 2011), pp. 85–89; Hershey, *Party Politics*, pp. 118–136; and Pew Research Center for the People & the Press, "Trends," pp. 97–110.

34. Richard Florida, *The Rise of the Creative Class: How It's Transforming Work, Leisure, Community, and Everyday Life* (New York: Basic Books, 2002); and Richard Florida, *The Flight of the Creative Class* (New York: Harper Business, 2005).

35. Marjorie Randon Hershey, *Party Politics in America*, 14th ed. (New York: Pearson Longman, 2011); A. James Reichley, *The Life of the Parties: A History of American Political Parties* (Lanham, MD: Rowman & Littlefield, 2002).

36. On the "great sorting out" of groups and regions along party lines in the United States, see Ronald Brownstein, *Second Civil War*, ch. 6.

37. John Sides, Daron R. Shaw, Matthew Grossmann, and Keena Lipsitz et al., *Campaigns & Elections: Rules, Reality, Strategy, Choice: 2012 Election Update* (New York: WW Norton, 2014). Thomas M. Holbrook and Scott D. McClurg, "The Mobilization of Core Supporters: Campaigns, Turnout, and Electoral Composition in United States Presidential Elections," *American Journal of Political Science* 49, no. 4 (2005), pp. 689–703.

38. Pew Research Center, "Political Polarization in the American Public," http://assets.pewresearch.org/wp-content/uploads/sites/5/2014/06/6-12-2014-Political-Polarization-Release.pdf.

39. Bruce E. Keith, David B. Magleby, Candice J. Nelson, Elizabeth Orr, Mark C. Westlye, and Raymond E. Wolfinger, *The Myth of the Independent Voter* (Berkeley, CA: University of California Press, 1992). See also Hershey, *Party Politics*, pp. 113–115.

40. Carroll Doherty and Rachel Weisel, "A Deep Dive into Party Affiliation," Pew Center for People and the Press, April 7, 2015.

41. Ronald Brownstein, *Second Civil War*; Rae, "Be Careful What You Wish For"; and Layman, Carsey, and Horowitz, "Party Polarization."

42. Gregory Koger, Seth Masket, and Hans Noel. "Partisan Webs: Information Exchange and Party Networks," *British Journal of Political Science* 39, no. 3 (2009), pp. 633–653. Kathleen Bawn, Martin Cohen, David Karol, Seth Masket, Hans Noel, and John Zaller, "A Theory of Political Parties: Groups, Policy Demands and Nominations in American Politics," *Perspectives on Politics* 10, no. 3 (2012), pp. 571–597.

43. Brian Arbour, *Candidate-Centered Campaigns: Political Messages, Winning Personalities, and Personal Appeals* (New York: Springer, 2016). Martin P. Wattenberg, "From a Partisan to a Candidate-Centered Electorate," In *The New American Political System*, ed. Anthony King, 2nd ed. (Washington, DC: The AEI Press, 1990).

44. J. A. Schlesinger, "The New American Political Party," *American Political Science Review* 79 (1985), pp. 1152–1169; and Aldrich, *Why Parties?*

45. David Menefee-Libey, *The Triumph of Campaign-Centered Politics* (New York: Chatham House Publishers, 2000); and Hershey, *Party Politics*, pp. 75–78.

46. Sasha Issenberg, *The Victory Lab: The Secret Science of Winning Campaigns* (Broadway Books, 2012).

47. Alan D. Monroe, "American Party Platforms and Public Opinion," *American Journal of Political Science* 27 (February 1983), p. 35; Layman, Carsey, and Horowitz, "Party Polarization"; and Maisel, *American Political Parties*, pp. 73–76.

48. Naftali Bendavid, "The House Rahm Built," *Chicago Tribune*, November 12, 2006, http://www.chicagotribune.com/news/local/politics/chi-0611120215nov12-story.html.

49. Norman Schofield and Gary Miller, "Elections and Activist Coalitions in the United States," *American Journal of Political Science* 51, no. 3 (July 2007), pp. 518–531.

50. Nicholas Confessore, "Outside Groups Eclipsing G.O.P. as Hub of Campaigns," *New York Times*, November 1, 2011. *New York Times*/CBS News, "Republican Convention Delegate Poll," news release, July 18, 2004, and *New York Times*/CBS News, "Democratic Convention Delegate Poll," news release, August 24, 2004.

51. Lewis L. Gould, *Grand Old Party: A History of the Republicans* (New York: Random House, 2003); "When American Politics Turned European," *Economist*, October 25, 2005, p. 74; Nils Gilman, "What the Rise of the Republicans as America's First Ideological Party Means for the Democrats," Forum 2, no. 1 (2004), pp. 1–4; Brownstein, *Second Civil War*; and Layman, Carsey, and Horowitz, "Party Polarization."

52. Ronald Brownstein, *The Second Civil War: How Extreme Partisanship Has Paralyzed Washington and Polarized America* (Penguin, 2008), p. 12.

53. James MacGregor Burns, *Deadlock of Democracy* (Englewood Cliffs, NJ: Prentice Hall, 1967). Sarah A. Binder, Stalemate: Causes and consequences of legislative gridlock. (Washington, DC: Brookings Institution Press, 2004.) On the pernicious effects of divided government, see Benjamin Ginsberg and Martin Shefter, *Politics by Other Means: The Declining Significance of Elections in America* (New York: Basic Books, 1990). For the contrary view, see Morris P. Fiorina, *Divided Government* (New York: Macmillan, 1992); Gary Jacobson, *The Electoral Origins of Divided Government: Competition in U.S. House Elections* (Boulder, CO: Westview Press, 1990); David R. Mayhew, *Divided We Govern: Party Control, Lawmaking, and Investigations, 1946–1990* (New Haven, CT: Yale University Press, 1991); and Layman, Carsey, and Horowitz, "Party Polarization," pp. 88–101.

Chapter 10

1. Though Trump won states worth 306 electoral votes, there were two so-called faithless electors who cast their votes for other candidates.

2. "Election 2016: Exit Polls," *New York Times,* November 9, 2016, http://www.nytimes.com/interactive/2016/11/08/us/politics/election-exit-polls.html.

3. "How Clinton Lost." Cnn.com, November 9, 2016, http://www.cnn.com/2016/11/09/politics/clinton-votes-african-americans-latinos-women-white-voters.

4. Prior to the election, observers considered Republican seats in Ohio, Illinois, Wisconsin, Missouri, New Hampshire, North Carolina, Pennsylvania, Florida, and Indiana to be competitive.

5. For further discussion, see Benjamin I. Page, *Choices and Echoes in Presidential Elections: Rational Man and Electoral Democracy* (Chicago: University of Chicago Press, 1978), ch. 2; Robert A. Dahl, *Democracy and Its Critics* (New Haven, CT: Yale University Press, 1989); Robert A. Dahl, *On Democracy* (New Haven, CT: Yale University Press, 1998); Hans Gersbach, *Designing Democracy* (New York: Springer Publishers, 2005).

6. See Russell Muirhead, "A Defense of Party Spirit," *Perspectives on Politics* 4, no. 4 (December 2006), pp. 713–727; Austin Ranney, *The Doctrine of Responsible Party Government: Its Origins and Present State* (Urbana, IL: University of Illinois Press, 1962); E. E. Schattschneider, *Party Government* (New York: Holt, Rinehart & Winston, 1942); and Jonathan White and Lea Ypi, "On Partisan Political Justification," *American Political Science Review* 105, no. 2 (May 2011), pp. 381–396.

7. Marjorie Randon Hershey, *Party Politics in America* (New York: Pearson Longman Publishers, 2011), pp. 263–269.

8. Nicol C. Rae, "Be Careful What You Wish For: The Rise of Responsible Parties in American National Politics," *Annual Reviews, Political Science* 10 (2007), pp. 169–191.

9. Keith Poole and Howard Rosenthal, *Congress: A Political-Economic History of Roll Call Voting* (New York: Oxford University Press, 1997).

10. Anthony Downs, *An Economic Theory of Democracy* (New York: Harper & Row, 1957); Otto Davis, Melvin Hinich, and Peter Ordeshook, "An Expository Development of a Mathematical Model of the Electoral Process," *American Political Science Review* 64 (1970), pp. 426–448.

11. See V. O. Key Jr., *Public Opinion and American Democracy* (New York: Knopf, 1961); Morris P. Fiorina, *Retrospective Voting in American National Elections* (Cambridge, MA: Harvard University Press, 1981).

12. Gary C. Jacobson, "The 2008 Presidential and Congressional Elections: Anti-Bush Referendum and Prospects for the Democratic Majority," *Political Science Quarterly* 124, no. 1 (2009), pp. 1–30.

13. Robert J. Franzese, "Electoral and Partisan Cycles in Economic Policies and Outcomes," *Annual Review of Political Science* 5 (2002), pp. 369–421.

14. L. Sandy Maisel, *American Political Parties and Elections: A Very Short Introduction* (New York: Oxford University Press, 2007), p. 5.

15. Mary Fitzgerald, "Greater Convenience but Not Greater Turnout: The Impact of Alternative Voting Methods on Electoral Participation in the United States," *American Politics Research* 33, no. 6 (2005), pp. 842–867.

16. Chilton Williamson, *American Suffrage* (Princeton, NJ: Princeton University Press, 1960), pp. 223, 241, 260; and Gordon S. Wood, *The Idea of America* (New York: Penguin, 2011), ch. 6, and "The Making of American Democracy." Also see Hershey, *Party Politics in America,* pp. 140–144; Maisel, *American Political Parties and Elections,* pp. 47–51.

17. See John Hope Franklin, *From Slavery to Freedom* (New York: Knopf, 1967); Leon Litwack, *North of Slavery* (Chicago: University of Chicago Press, 1961); Alexander Keyssar, *The Right to Vote: The Contested History of Democracy in the United States* (New York: Basic Books, 2001); and Wood, "The Making of American Democracy," pp. 209–210.

18. For a brief but excellent discussion of the scholarly literature on the cause of low voting turnout, see Daniel M. Shea, *Let's Vote: The Essentials of the American Electoral Process* (New York: Longman, 2013), pp. 169–178; Kay Lehman Schlozman, "Citizen Participation in America: What Do We Know? Why Do We Care?" in *Political Science: The State of the Discipline,* eds. Ira Katznelson and Helen V. Milner (New York: W. W. Norton, 2002), pp. 439–443; Martin P. Wattenberg, *Where Have All the Voters Gone?* (Cambridge, MA: Harvard University Press, 2002); Andre Blais, "What Affects Voter Turnout?" *Annual Reviews, Political Science* 9 (2006), pp. 111–125.

19. Peverill Squire, Raymond E. Wolfinger, and David P. Glass, "Residential Mobility and Voter Turnout," *American Political Science Review* 81 (1987), pp. 45–65.

20. National Conference of State Legislatures, "Same Day Voter Registration," December 28, 2015, http://www.ncsl.org/research/elections-and-campaigns/same-day-registration.aspx.

21. U.S. Bureau of the Census, 2007; Hershey, *Party Politics in America,* p. 140.

22. John E. McNulty, Conor Dowling, and Margaret Ariotti, "Driving Saints to Sin: Increasing the Difficulty of Voting Dissuades Even the Most Motivated Voters," *Political Analysis* 17, no. 4 (2009), pp. 435–455.

23. National Conference of State Legislatures, "Absentee and Early Voting," December 28, 2015, http://www.ncsl.org/research/elections-and-campaigns/absentee-and-early-voting.aspx.

24. Wattenberg, *Where Have All the Voters Gone?* ch. 6.

25. Robert M. Bond, Christopher J. Fariss, Jason J. Jones, Adam D. I. Kramer, Cameron Marlow, Jaime E. Settle, and James H. Fowler, "A 61-Million-Person Experiment in Social Influence and Political Mobilization," *Nature* 489, no. 7415 (2012), pp. 295–298.

26. Alan S. Gerber, Donald P. Green, and Christopher W. Larimer, "Social Pressure and Voter Turnout: Evidence from a Large-Scale Field Experiment," *American Political Science Review* 102, no. 1 (2008), pp. 33–48.

27. Alan S. Gerber, Donald P. Green, and Ron Shachar. "Voting May Be Habit-Forming: Evidence From a Randomized Field Experiment," *American Journal of Political Science* 47, no. 3 (2003), pp. 540–550.

28. Alan S. Gerber, Gregory A. Huber, David Doherty, Conor M. Dowling, and Seth Hill, "Do Perceptions of Ballot Secrecy Influence Turnout? Results from a Field Experiment," *American Journal of Political Science* 57 (2013), pp. 537–551.

29. Ari Berman, "The GOP War on Voting," Rolling Stone Online (posted August 30, 2011), accessed June 12, 2012; and Wendy R. Weiser and Lawrence Norden, *Voting Law Changes in 2012* (New York: The Brennan Center, New York University School of Law, 2011).

30. Shea, *Let's Vote*, pp. 169–178, for a summary of the research on voter turnout.

31. Sidney Verba, Kay Lehman Schlozman, and Henry E. Brady, *Voice and Equality: Civic Volunteerism in American Politics* (Cambridge, MA: Harvard University Press, 1995); Sidney Verba and Norman H. Nie, *Participation in America* (New York: Harper & Row, 1972); Hershey, *Party Politics in America*, pp. 150–153.

32. United States Census Bureau, "Voting and Registration in the Election of November 2016—Detailed Tables."

33. Thom File, "The Diversifying Electorate—Voting Rates by Race and Hispanic Origin in 2012 (and Other Recent Elections)," The United States Census Bureau, May 2013.

34. John A. Garcia, "Latinos and Political Behavior," in *The Oxford Handbook of American Elections and Political Behavior,* ed. Jan E. Leighley (New York: Oxford University Press, 2010).

35. John B. Judis and Ruy Teixeira, *The Emerging Democratic Majority* (New York: Simon and Schuster, 2004).

36. Mark Hugo Lopez and Paul Taylor, *Dissecting the 2008 Electorate: Most Diverse in U.S. History* (Washington, DC: Pew Research Center, April 30, 2009), p. 6.

37. Susan A. MacManus, *Young v. Old* (Boulder, CO: Westview Press, 1996), ch. 2; and Martin P. Wattenberg, *Is Voting for Young People?* (New York: Pearson, 2012).

38. Margaret M. Conway, *Political Participation in the United States,* 3rd ed. (Washington, DC: CQ Press, 2000), p. 37; and Julie Dolan, Melissa Deckman, and Michele L. Swers, *Women and Politics: Paths to Power and Political Influence* (New York: Pearson Longman, 2011), pp. 55–72.

39. E. J. Dionne, "If Nonvoters Had Voted: Same Winner, but Bigger," *New York Times,* November 21, 1988, p. B16.

40. Sidney Verba, Kay Lehman Schlozman, Henry E. Brady, and Norman H. Nie, "Citizen Activity: Who Participates? What Do They Say?" *American Political Science Review* 87 (1993), pp. 303–318; Robert S. Erikson and Kent L. Tedin, *American Public Opinion* (New York: Pearson Longman Publishers, 2007), ch. 7; Eric Shiraev and Richard Sobel, *People and Their Opinions* (New York: Pearson Longman Publishers, 2006), chs. 7–9.

41. Wattenberg, *Is Voting for Young People?*

42. Martin Gilens, "Preference Gaps and Inequality in Representation," *PS* (April 2009), pp. 331–335; Lawrence R. Jacobs and Theda Skocpol, eds., *Inequality and American Democracy: What We Know and What We Need to Learn* (New York: Russell Sage Foundation, 2005); Larry M. Bartels, Hugh Keclo, Rodney E. Hero, and Lawrence Jacobs, "Inequality and American Government," *Perspectives on Politics* 2, no. 4 (20), pp. 651–668; and Larry M. Bartels, *Unequal Democracy: The Political Economy of the Gilded Age* (New York and Princeton, NJ: The Russell Sage Foundation and Princeton University Press, 2008).

43. Jacob Hacker and Paul Pierson, *Off Center* (New Haven, CT: Yale University Press, 2005); Larry M. Bartels, "Is the Water Rising: Reflections on Inequality and American Democracy," *PS* (January 2006), pp. 39–42; Kay Lehman Schlozman, "On Inequality and Political Voice," *PS* (January 2006), pp. 55–57.

44. For an overview of the Democratic superdelegates and the 2008 race, see Josh M. Ryan, "Is the Democratic Party's Superdelegate System Unfair to Voters?" *Electoral Studies* 30, no. 4 (2011), pp. 756–770.

45. David D. Kirkpatrick, "Wealth Is a Common Factor Among 2008 Hopefuls," *New York Times,* May 17, 2007, p. A1.

46. Nelson W. Polsby and Aaron Wildavsky, *Presidential Elections,* 12th ed. (Lanham, MD: Rowman & Littlefield, 2007) pp. 53–55, 57.

47. Hershey, *Party Politics in America*, pp. 181–182.

48. Chris Cillizza, "The 5 Big Lessons I Learned in 2015," *Washington Post,* December 20, 2015. Accessed on December 27, 2015, https://www.washingtonpost.com/politics/five-biggest-political-lessons-that-2015-taught/2015/12/20/4278634e-a75a-11e5-bff5-905b92f5f94b_story.html.

49. Larry Bartels, *Presidential Primaries and the Dynamics of Public Choice* (Princeton, NJ: Princeton University Press, 1988); John H. Aldrich, *Before the Convention* (Chicago: University of Chicago Press, 1980); Wayne, *The Road to the White House.*

50. Nicholas Confessore, Sarah Cohen, and Karen Yourish, "The Families Funding the 2016 Presidential Election," *New York Times,* October 10, 2015, accessed on December 27, 2015, http://www.nytimes.com/interactive/2015/10/11/us/politics/2016-presidential-election-super-pac-donors.html.

51. Jeremy W. Peters, "Campaigns Blitz 9 Swing States in a Battle of Ads," *New York Times,* June 8, 2012, p. 1.

52. John G. Geer, *In Defense of Negativity* (Chicago: University of Chicago Press, 2006); Ken Goldstein and Paul Freedman, "Campaign Advertising and Voter Turnout: New Evidence for a Stimulation Effect," *Journal of Politics* 64 (2002), pp. 721–740; and Caterina Gennaioli, "Go Divisive or Not: How Political Campaigns Affect Turnout" (London: London School of Economics and Political Science, Working Paper 3298, December 30, 2010).

53. Anna Greenberg, "Targeting and Electoral Gaps," in *Beyond Red State, Blue State: Electoral Gaps in the Twenty-First Century American Electorate,* eds. Laura R. Olson and John C. Green (Upper Saddle River, NJ: Pearson Prentice Hall, 2009); Magleby, "How Barack Obama Changed Presidential Campaigns;" also see D. Sunshine Hillygus

and Todd G. Shields, *The Persuadable Voter: Wedge Issues in Presidential Campaigns* (Princeton, NJ: Princeton University Press, 2008).

54. Eitan Hersh, *Hacking the Electorate* (New York, NY: Cambridge University Press, 2015).

55. "The 2012 Election Will Cost $6 Billion," *Bloomberg/ Businessweek*, October 3–9, 2011, pp. 32–34.

56. Center for Responsive Politics, OpenSecrets 2016.

57. *Ibid.*

58. Polsby and Wildavsky, *Presidential Elections*, pp. 62–67.

59. Mark Halperin and John Heilemann, *Double Down: Game Change 2012* (New York, NY: Penguin Press, 2013).

60. On this research, see Thomas E. Mann, "Linking Knowledge and Action: Political Science and Campaign Finance Reform," *Perspectives on Politics* 1, no. 1 (2003), pp. 69–83.

61. See Verba, Schlozman, and Brady, *Voice and Equality*.

62. Benjamin I. Page and Martin Gilens, *Democracy in America? What Has Gone Wrong and What We Can Do About It* (Chicago, IL: The University of Chicago Press, 2017).

63. Benjamin I. Page, Larry M. Bartels, and Jason Seawright, "Democracy and the Policy Preferences of Wealthy Americans," *Perspectives on Politics* 11, no. 1 (2013), pp. 51–73.

64. Efforts to sort out their relative contributions include Benjamin I. Page and Calvin Jones, "Reciprocal Effects of Policy Preferences, Party Loyalties, and the Vote," *American Political Science Review* 73 (1979), pp. 1071–1089; Gregory B. Markus and Philip E. Converse, "A Dynamic Simultaneous Equation Model of Public Choice," *American Political Science Review* 73 (1979), pp. 1066–1070; and William G. Jacoby, "The American Voter," in *The Oxford Handbook of American Elections and Political Behavior*, ed. Leighley.

65. Larry M. Bartels, "Partisanship and Voting Behavior, 1952–1996," *American Journal of Political Science* 44 (January 2000), pp. 35–50; Hershey, *Party Politics in America*, pp. 108–111; D. Sunshine Hillygus and Simon Jackman, "Voter Decision Making in Election 2000: Campaign Effects, Partisan Activation, and the Clinton Legacy," *American Journal of Political Science* 47 (2003), pp. 583–596; Stephen A. Jessee, "Spatial Voting in the 2004 Presidential Election," *American Political Science Review* 103, no. 1 (February 2009), pp. 59–81; and Jacoby, "The American Voter," pp. 263–265.

66. Maisel, *American Political Parties and Elections*, pp. 107–112.

Chapter 11

1. Roger H. Davidson, Walter J. Oleszek, and Frances E. Lee, *Congress and Its Members*, 13th ed. (Washington, DC: CQ Press, 2012), pp. 19–28.

2. *Ibid.*, pp. 27–28. Also see Walter J. Oleszek, *Congressional Procedures and the Policy Process*, 8th ed. (Washington, DC: CQ Press, 2010), pp. 23–28.

3. Sanford Levinson, *Our Undemocratic Constitution: Where the Constitution Goes Wrong* (New York: Oxford University

Press, 2006); Robert A. Dahl, *How Democratic Is the American Constitution?* (New Haven, CT: Yale University Press, 2001).

4. Adam Liptak, "Smaller States Find Outsize Clout Growing in Senate," *New York Times*, March 11, 2013, http://www.nytimes.com/interactive/2013/03/11/us/politics/democracy-tested.html#/#smallstate.

5. On this general question, see Jane Mansbridge, "Rethinking Representation," *American Political Science Review* 97, no. 4 (2003), pp. 515–528; Nadia Urbinati and Mark E. Warren, "The Concept of Representation in Contemporary Democratic Theory," *The Annual Review of Political Science* 11 (2008), pp. 387–412. Also see Davidson, Oleszek, and Lee, *Congress and Its Members*, pp. 140–141.

6. Quoted in Charles Henning, *The Wit and Wisdom of Politics* (Golden, CO: Fulcrum, 1989), p. 235.

7. Abraham Lincoln, announcement in the *Sagamo Journal*, New Salem, Illinois, June 13, 1836.

8. Kenneth A. Shepsle, Robert P. Van Houweling, Samuel J. Abrams, and Peter C. Hanson, "The Senate Electoral Cycle and Bicameral Appropriations Politics," *American Journal of Political Science* 53, no. 2 (2009), pp. 343–359.

9. Davidson, Oleszek, and Lee, *Congress and Its Members*, pp. 122–124. For a dissenting view, one that suggests that senators, facing much more competitive elections than representatives, are just as likely as House members to lean toward the delegate style throughout their six-year term of office, see Charles Stewart III, "Congress and the Constitutional System," in *The Legislative Branch*, eds. Paul J. Quirk and Sarah A. Binder (New York: Oxford University Press, 2005).

10. See for example, Anti-Federalist #3, Brutus III. *The Complete Anti-Federalist Papers*, Vol. III, ed. Herbert J. Strong (Chicago, IL: University of Chicago Press, 1981).

11. Davidson, Oleszek, and Lee, *Congress and Its Members*, pp. 110–115.

12. Jennifer E. Maning, "Membership of the 115th Congress: A Profile." Congressional Research Service Report, April 12, 2018.

13. The Inter-Parliamentary Union, "Women in National Parliaments," April 2016, www.ipu.org/wmn-e/world.htm.

14. Liza Mundy, "The Secret History of Women in the Senate." *Politico.com*, February, 2014.

15. Andrew Ross Sorkin, "Rich and Sort of Rich," *New York Times*, May 14, 2011.

16. Davidson, Oleszek, and Lee, *Congress and Its Members*, pp. 127–128.

17. The distinction between descriptive and substantive representation—the latter meaning that legislators act in the interests of their constituents irrespective of the demographic makeup of the constituency—is made by Hanna Pitkin in her classic work *The Concept of Representation* (Berkeley, CA: University of California Press, 1967).

18. Arturo Vega and Juanita Firestone, "The Effects of Gender on Congressional Behavior and the Substantive Representation of Women," *Legislative Studies Quarterly* 20 (May 1995), pp. 213–222. Also see Michele L. Swers, *The*

Difference Women Make (Chicago: University of Chicago Press, 2002); the collection of research on women's impact on the legislative process in Cindy Simon Rosenthal, ed., *Women Transforming Congress* (Norman, OK: University of Oklahoma Press, 2002).

19. Datina L. Gamble, "Black Political Representation," *Legislative Studies Quarterly* 32 (2007), pp. 421–448.

20. For a review of research on the political impacts of redistricting, see Raymond La Raja, "Redistricting: Reading Between the Lines," *The Annual Review of Political Science* 12 (2009), pp. 202–223.

21. Gary W. Cox and Jonathan Katz, "The Reapportionment Revolution and Bias in U.S. Congressional Elections," *American Journal of Political Science* 43 (1999), pp. 812–840; Davidson, Oleszek, and Lee, *Congress and Its Members*, pp. 48–58; Steven S. Smith, Jason M. Roberts, and Ryan J. Vander Wielen, *The American Congress* (New York, NY: Cambridge University Press, 2007), pp. 62–64.

22. Michael McDonald and Micah Altman, "Pulling Back the Curtain on Redistricting," *Washington Post*, July 9, 2010.

23. See Josh M. Ryan and Jeffrey Lyons, "The Effect of Redistricting Commissions on District Partisanship and Member Ideology," *Journal of Elections, Public Opinion, and Parties* 25, no. 2 (2015), pp. 234–263, for more information about the effects of independent commissions.

24. Measuring Partisan Bias in Single-Member District Electoral Systems. Eric McGhee, *Legislative Studies Quarterly*, 2014, pp. 55–85.

25. Davidson, Oleszek, and Lee, *Congress and Its Members*, pp. 53–58.

26. Charles S. Bulloch, "Affirmative Action Districts: In Whose Face Will They Blow Up?" *Campaigns and Elections*, April 1995, p. 22.

27. Charles Cameron, David Epstein, and Sharon O'Halloran, "Do Majority-Minority Districts Maximize Black Representation in Congress?" *American Political Science Review* 90 (1996), pp. 794–812; David Epstein and Sharon O' Halloran, "A Social Science Approach to Race, Districting and Representation," *American Political Science Review* 93 (1999), pp. 187–191; David Lublin, *The Paradox of Representation: Racial Gerrymandering and Minority Interests* (Princeton, NJ: Princeton University Press, 1997); David T. Canon, "Representing Racial and Ethnic Minorities," in *The Legislative Branch*, eds. Paul J. Quirk and Sarah A. Binder (New York: Oxford University Press, 2005), pp. 185–186.

28. Alan Wolfe, *Does American Democracy Still Work?* (New Haven, CT: Yale University Press, 2006), ch. 3.

29. OpenSecrets.org, "2014 Election Overview," https://www .opensecrets.org/overview/index.php?cycle=2014& display=A&type=R.

30. Ronald B. Turovsky, "To Michael Huffington: You Lost, Move On," *Los Angeles Times*, December 9, 1994.

31. Center for Responsive Politics, "Self-Financed Candidates Spreadsheet," 2012, http://www.opensecrets.org/ news/2010/11/biggest-losers-on-election-night-se.html.

32. Richard Hall and Frank W. Wayman, "Buying Time: Moneyed Interests and the Mobilization of Bias in Congressional Committees," *American Political Science Review* 84 (1990), pp. 797–820.

33. Gary W. Cox and Eric Magar, "How Much Is Majority Status in the U.S. Congress Worth?" *American Political Science Review* 93 (1999), pp. 299–309.

34. Davidson, Oleszek, and Lee, *Congress and Its Members*, pp. 75–77.

35. See the classic work on this subject, David R. Mayhew, *Congress: The Electoral Connection* (New Haven, CT: Yale University Press, 1974). Also see Davidson, Oleszek, and Lee, *Congress and Its Members*, ch. 4; Smith, Roberts, and Vander Wielen, *The American Congress*, pp. 97–104.

36. Richard F. Fenno Jr., *Home Style: House Members and Their Districts* (New York: Pearson Longman, 2003); Richard F. Fenno Jr., *Senators on the Home Trail* (Norman: University of Oklahoma Press, 1996).

37. Bruce Cain, John A. Ferejohn, and Morris P. Fiorina, *The Personal Vote: Constituency Service and Electoral Independence* (Cambridge, MA: Harvard University Press, 1987); Glenn Parker, *Homeward Bound: Explaining Change in Congressional Behavior* (Pittsburgh: University of Pittsburgh Press, 1986); Fenno, *Home Style*.

38. See The Brookings Institute, "Earmarks: The One Thing Trump Gets Right About Congress," https://www .brookings.edu/blog/fixgov/2018/01/17/earmarks-the- one-thing-trump-gets-right-about-congress.

39. Martin Gilens and Benjamin I. Page, "Testing Theories of American Politics," *Perspectives on Politics* 12, no. 3 (2014), pp. 564–581.

40. Robert Bendiner, *Obstacle Course on Capitol Hill* (New York: McGraw-Hill, 1964), p. 15.

41. Oleszek, *Congressional Procedures and the Policy Process*, ch. 1.

42. Barbara Sinclair, *Unorthodox Lawmaking: New Legislative Processes in the U.S. Congress* (Washington, DC: CQ Press, 2007).

43. Davidson, Oleszek, and Lee, *Congress and Its Members*, ch. 8; Donald R. Matthews, *U.S. Senators and Their World* (Chapel Hill, NC: University of North Carolina Press, 1960).

44. Davidson, Oleszek, and Lee, *Congress and Its Members*, pp. 210–211; Smith, Roberts, and Vander Wielen, *The American Congress*, pp. 163–164; Ronald Brownstein, *The Second Civil War: How Extreme Partisanship Has Paralyzed Washington and Polarized America* (New York: Penguin, 2008), pp. 124–127.

45. Brownstein, *The Second Civil War*, p. 157.

46. Interview with Ezra Klein, *Washington Post Online*, December 28, 2009, http://voices.washingtonpost.com /ezra-klein/2009/12/the_right_of_the_filibuster_ an.html.

47. For competing views on the rise of filibustering, see Gregory J. Wawro and Eric Schickler, *Filibuster: Obstruction and Lawmaking in the U.S. Senate* (Princeton, NJ: Princeton

University Press, 2006); Sarah A. Binder, *Politics or Principle? Filibustering in the United States Senate* (Washington, DC: Brookings Institution Press, 1997); and Gregory Koger, *Filibustering: A Political History of Obstruction in the House and Senate* (Chicago, IL: University of Chicago Press, 2010).

48. "Graphic: The Filibuster's Power to Block Nominees," *New York Times*, November 21, 2013, http://www.nytimes.com/interactive/2013/11/21/us/politics/senate-filibusters.html?_r=0.

49. Josh M. Ryan, "The Disappearing Conference Committee: The Use of Procedures by Minority Coalitions to Prevent Conferencing," *Congress & the Presidency* 38, no. 1 (2011), pp. 101–125.

50. See John J. Kornacki, ed., *Leading Congress: New Styles, New Strategies* (Washington, DC: Congressional Quarterly Press, 1990); David W. Rohde, *Parties and Leaders in the Postreform Congress* (Chicago: University of Chicago Press, 1991); Randall Strahan, *Leading Representatives: The Agency of Leaders in the Politics of the U.S. House* (Baltimore, MD: The Johns Hopkins University Press, 2007); Hershey, *Party Politics in America*, pp. 244–249.

51. Hershey, *Party Politics in America*, pp. 243–244; Davidson, Oleszek, and Lee, *Congress and Its Members*, ch. 6; Garry W. Cox and Keith T. Poole, "On Measuring Partisanship in Roll-Call Voting," *American Journal of Political Science* 46 (2002), pp. 477–489; Keith T. Poole and Howard Rosenthal, "On Party Polarization in Congress," *Daedalus* 136, no. 3 (2007), pp. 104–107; Gerald D. Wright and Brian F. Schaffner, "The Influence of Party," *American Political Science Review* 96 (2002), pp. 367–379; Smith, Roberts, and Vander Wielen, *The American Congress*, pp. 23–24.

52. Oleszek, *Congressional Procedures and the Policy Process*, pp. 160–161.

53. Davidson, Oleszek, and Lee, *Congress and Its Members*, pp. 157–159.

54. Sheryl Gay Stolberg, Jeff Zeleny, and Carl Hulse, "Health Vote Caps a Journey Back from the Brink," *New York Times*, March 20, 2010, p. 1.

55. Smith, Roberts, and Vander Wielen, *The American Congress*, p. 137.

56. This analogy is that of Congressman Tom DeLay reported in Jonathan Kaplan, "Hastert, DeLay: Political Pros Get Along to Go Along," *The Hill*, July 22, 2003, p. 8.

57. Sean M. Theriault, *Party Polarization in Congress* (New York: Cambridge University Press, 2008).

58. Davidson, Oleszek, and Lee, *Congress and Its Members*, pp. 266–267.

59. *Ibid.*, p. 193.

60. For the fullest review of the scholarly literature, see Geoffrey C. Layman, Thomas M. Carsey, and Julianna Menasce Horowitz, "Party Polarization in American Politics: Characteristics, Causes and Consequences," *Annual Review of Political Science* 9 (2006), pp. 83–110.

61. On the transformation of the South in American politics and how it has affected Congress, see Nelson W. Polsby, *How Congress Evolves: Social Bases of Institutional Change* (New York: New York University Press, 2004); Earl Black

and Merle Black, *The Rise of Southern Republicans* (Cambridge, MA: Harvard University and Belknap Press, 2003); Earl Black and Merle Black, *Divided America: The Ferocious Power Struggle in American Politics* (New York: Simon and Schuster, 2007); Stanley B. Greenberg, *The Two Americas* (New York: St. Martin's Griffin, 2005).

62. Dante Chinni and James Gimpel, *Our Patchwork Nation* (New York: Penguin, Gotham Publishers, 2010).

63. Alan I. Abramowitz and Kyle L. Saunders, "Ideological Realignment in the U.S. Electorate," *Journal of Politics* 60 (1998), pp. 634–652; Nolan McCarty, Keith T. Poole, and Howard Rosenthal, *Polarized America: The Dance of Ideology and Unequal Riches* (Cambridge, MA: MIT Press, 2006); *Evenly Divided and Increasingly Polarized: The 2004 Political Landscape* (Washington, DC: Pew Research Center, 2003); *Trends in Political Values and Core Attitudes: 1987–2007* (Washington, DC: The Pew Research Center for the People and the Press, report released March 22, 2007); Nils Gilman, "What the Rise of the Republicans as America's First Ideological Party Means for the Democrats," *The Forum* 2, no. 1 (2004), pp. 1–4.

64. Mickey Edwards, "Political Science and Political Practice," *Perspectives on Politics* 1, no. 2 (June 2003), p. 352.

65. Brownstein, *The Second Civil War*, p. 277.

66. Suzy Khimm, "The Decline of Congressional Oversight, in One Chart," *Washington Post*, December 2, 2011, http://www.washingtonpost.com/blogs/ezra-klein/post/the-decline-of-congressional-oversight-in-one-chart/2011/11/29/gIQAwq078N_blog.html.

67. Lawrence Lessig, *Republic Lost, Version 2.0* (New York: Twelve, 2011).

Chapter 12

1. On President Trump's enthusiastic embrace of executive orders as well as the source of the quote in the above paragraph, see Andrew Rudalevige, "Candidate Trump Attacked Obama's Executive Orders. President Trump Loves Executive Orders," *Washington Post*, October 17, 2017, https://www.washingtonpost.com/news/monkey-cage/wp/2017/10/17/candidate-trump-attacked-obamas-executive-orders-president-trump-loves-executive-orders/?noredirect=on&utm_term=.bce2449d23a2. For a list of Trump's executive orders during his first year in office, see "2017 Donald Trump Executive Orders," (Washington, DC: The Federal Register, 2018), https://www.federalregister.gov/executive-orders/donald-trump/2017.

2. For the argument that Congress and the Courts as well as public opinion influence how freely presidents use their unitary powers, see Fang-Yi Chiou and Lawrence S. Rothenberg, "The Elusive Search For Presidential Power," *American Journal of Political Science* 58, no. 3 (July 2014), pp. 653–668.

3. Lee Epstein and Thomas G. Walker, *Constitutional Law for a Changing America: Institutional Powers and Constraints* (Los Angeles and Washington, DC: SAGE Publications and CQ Press, 2014), p. 183.

4. U.S. Department of Commerce, *Historical Statistics of the United States, Colonial Times to 1970* (Washington, DC: U.S. Government Printing Office, 1971), pp. 8 and 1143.

5. "Current Population Reports, 2009" (Washington, DC: U.S. Census Bureau, 2010).

6. Hans M. Dristensen and Robert S. Norris, "Status of World Nuclear Forces" (Washington, DC: Federation of American Scientists, 2018), https://fas.org/issues/nuclear-weapons/status-world-nuclear-forces.

7. George C. Edwards III and Stephen J. Wayne, *Presidential Leadership: Politics and Policy Making* (Belmont, CA: Cengage Wadsworth, 2009), pp. 2–9; and James P. Pfiffner and Roger H. Davidson, eds., *Understanding the Presidency* (New York: Pearson, 2013), pp. 1–6.

8. For more on the role of the Supreme Court in this development, see Epstein and Walker, *Constitutional Law,* pp. 183–256.

9. On the contributions of particular presidents in shaping today's presidency, see Scott C. James, "The Evolution of the Presidency," in *The Executive Branch,* eds. Joel D. Aberbach and Mark A. Peterson (New York: Oxford University Press, 2005).

10. James P. Pfiffner, "Constraining Executive Power: George W. Bush and the Constitution," and Andrew Rudalevige, "A New Imperial Presidency?" both in *Understanding the Presidency,* eds. James P. Pfiffner and Roger H. Davidson (New York: Pearson Longman, 2013).

11. Peter Baker, "For Trump, A Year of Reinventing the Presidency," *New York Times,* December 31, 2017, https://www.nytimes.com/2017/12/31/us/politics/trump-reinventing-presidency.html.

12. Jimmie Breslin, quoted in Laurence J. Peter, *Peter's Quotations* (New York: Morrow, 1977), p. 405.

13. See Edwards and Wayne, *Presidential Leadership,* ch. 12.

14. Ron Suskind, *Confidence Men: Wall Street, Washington, and the Education of a President* (New York: HarperCollins, 2011).

15. Richard E. Neustadt, *Presidential Power and the Modern Presidents: The Politics of Leadership from Roosevelt to Reagan* (New York: Free Press, 1990); and David E. Lewis and Terry M. Moe, "The Presidency and the Bureaucracy: The Levers of Presidential Control," in *The Presidency and the Political System,* ed. Michael Nelson (Washington, DC: CQ Press, 2010).

16. Roger H. Davidson, Walter J. Oleszek, Frances E. Lee, and Eric Schickler, *Congress and Its Members,* 16th ed. (Washington, DC: CQ Press, 2018), pp. 298–299.

17. Howell, *Power Without Persuasion;* Phillip J. Cooper, *By Order of the President: The Use and Abuse of Executive Direct Action* (Lawrence: University of Kansas Press, 2002); Adam L. Warber, *Executive Orders and the Modern Presidency* (Boulder, CO: Lynne Rienner Publishers, 2006); and Andrew Rudalevige, "The Presidency and Unilateral Power: A Taxonomy," in *Presidency and the Political System,* ed. Nelson.

18. Matthew Crenson and Benjamin Ginsberg, *Presidential Power, Unchecked and Unbalanced* (New York: Norton, 2007); Pfiffner, "Constraining Executive Power: George W. Bush and the Constitution," Rudalevige, "A New Imperial Presidency?" and Richard Pious, "Prerogative Power and the War on Terrorism," all in Pfiffner and Davidson, *Understanding the Presidency.*

19. See John Yoo, *The Powers of War and Peace: The Constitution and Foreign Affairs After 9/11* (Chicago: The University of Chicago Press, 2005). In contrast, see Crenson and Ginsberg, *Presidential Power,* and Waterman, "Assessing the Unilateral Presidency."

20. Graham T. Allison, *Essence of Decision: Explaining the Cuban Missile Crisis* (Boston: Little, Brown, 1971), pp. 141–142.

21. *United States v. Curtiss-Wright* (1936). For more on judicial interpretations of presidential powers in foreign policy and war, see R. Shep Melnick, "The Courts, Jurisprudence, and the Executive Branch," in *Executive Branch,* eds. Aberbach and Peterson; Richard A. Brisbin Jr., "The Judiciary and the Separation of Powers," in *The Judicial Branch,* eds. Kermit L. Hall and Kevin T. McGuire (New York: Oxford University Press, 2005).

22. Melnick, "Courts, Jurisprudence, and the Executive Branch."

23. Epstein and Walker, *Constitutional Law,* pp. 255–256.

24. Edwards and Wayne, *Presidential Leadership,* p. 480.

25. Arthur Schlesinger Jr., *The Imperial Presidency* (New York: Popular Library, Atlantic Monthly Press, 1973).

26. David Nather and Anna Palmer, "Bushies Fear Obama Weakening Presidency," *Politico,* September 1, 2013, http://www.politico.com/story/2013/09/bushies-fear-obama-weakening-presidency-96143.html.

27. Marjorie Randon Hershey, *Party Politics in America* (New York: Pearson, 2012), pp. 266–272; and Sidney M. Milkis and Jesse H. Rhodes, "George W. Bush, the Republican Party, and the New American Party System," *Perspectives on Politics* 5, no. 3 (September 2007), pp. 461–488.

28. James P. Pfiffner, *The Modern Presidency* (New York: St. Martin's Press, 1998), ch. 4. See also Edwards and Wayne, *Presidential Leadership,* ch. 6; Pfiffner and Davidson, *Understanding the Presidency,* pp. 222–252.

29. Edwards and Wayne, *Presidential Leadership,* p. 209.

30. Suskind, *Confidence Men.*

31. Nathan Miller, *FDR: An Intimate History* (Lanham, MD: Madison Books, 1983), p. 276.

32. Thomas E. Cronin and Michael A. Genovese, *The Paradoxes of the American Presidency* (New York: Oxford University Press, 2004), ch. 10; and Joseph A. Pika, "The Vice Presidency: Dick Cheney, Joe Biden, and the New Vice Presidency," in *Presidency and the Political System,* ed. Nelson.

33. Edwards and Wayne, *Presidential Leadership,* p. 216.

34. Elisabeth Bumiller and Eric Schmitt, "In Indictment's Wake, a Focus on Cheney's Powerful Role in the White House," *New York Times,* October 20, 2005.

35. Stephen F. Hayes, *Cheney: The Untold Story of the Nation's Most Powerful and Controversial Vice President* (New York: HarperCollins, 2007); and Barton Gellman, *Angler: The Cheney Vice Presidency* (New York: Penguin Press, 2008).

36. Charles O. Jones, *Separate but Equal: Congress and the Presidency* (New York: Chatham House, 1999); Davidson, Oleszek, Lee, and Schickler, *Congress and Its Members*, pp. 301–306; and Roger H. Davidson, "Presidential Relations with Congress," in *Understanding the Presidency*, eds. Pfiffner and Davidson.

37. On the tendency for presidents to rely on unitary actions more in their second terms and when there is divided government, see Michelle Bellco and Brandon Rottinghaus, "In Lieu of Legislation," *Political Research Quarterly* 67, no. 2 (June 2014), pp. 413–425.

38. Andrew Rudalevige, "The Executive Branch and the Legislative Process," in *Executive Branch*, eds. Aberbach and Peterson, pp. 432–445; and Davidson, Oleszek, Lee, and Schickler, *Congress and Its Members*, ch. 10.

39. Edwards and Wayne, *Presidential Leadership*, pp. 336–348; Jon R. Bond and Richard Fleisher, eds., *Polarized Politics: Congress and the President in a Partisan Era* (Washington, DC: CQ Press, 2000); and Glen Biglaiser, David J. Jackson, and Jeffrey S. Peake, "Back on Track: Support for Presidential Trade Authority in the House of Representatives," *American Politics Research* 32 (November 2004), pp. 679–697.

40. Terry Sullivan, "Headcounts, Expectations and Presidential Coalitions in Congress," *American Journal of Political Science* 32 (1988), pp. 657–689; Davidson, Oleszek, Lee, and Schickler, *Congress and Its Members*, pp. 300–302; and Hershey, *Party Politics*, pp. 266–270.

41. "2009 Was the Most Partisan Year Ever," *Congressional Quarterly Weekly Report*, January 11, 2010.

42. Aaron Wildavsky, "The Two Presidencies," in *Perspectives on the Presidency*, ed. Aaron Wildavsky (Boston: Little, Brown, 1975), pp. 448–461.

43. For a review of the leading scholarship on the various uses and consequences of the presidential veto, see Charles M. Cameron, "The Presidential Veto," in *Oxford Handbook of the American Presidency*, eds. Edwards and Howell.

44. Roger H. Davidson, "Presidential Relations with Congress," in *Understanding the Presidency*, eds. Pfiffner and Davidson.

45. Gerhard Peters, "Presidential Vetoes," in *The American Presidency Project*, eds. John T. Woolley and Gerhard Peters (Santa Barbara, CA: University of California, 1999–2014), http://www.presidency.ucsb.edu/data/vetoes.php.

46. For the most sophisticated analysis of the effects of presidential approval on a president's success with Congress, see George C. Edwards III, "Presidential Approval as a Source of Influence in Congress," in *Oxford Handbook of the American Presidency*, eds. Edwards and Howell. See also Richard Brody, *Assessing the President: The Media, Elite Opinion, and Public Support* (Stanford, CA: Stanford University Press, 1991); George C. Edwards III, *At the Margins: Presidential Leadership of Congress* (New Haven, CT: Yale University Press, 1989); and George C. Edwards III, "Aligning Tests with Theory: Presidential Approval as a Source of Influence in Congress," *Congress and the Presidency* 24 (Fall 1997), pp. 113–130.

47. Edwards and Wayne, *Presidential Leadership*, pp. 348–350.

48. Jeffrey K. Tulis, *The Rhetorical Presidency* (Princeton, NJ: Princeton University Press, 1987), chs. 2 and 3, esp. p. 64.

49. Woodrow Wilson, *Leaders of Men*, ed. T. H. Vail Motter (Princeton, NJ: Princeton University Press, 1952), p. 39; quoted in Tulis, *Rhetorical Presidency*, ch. 4, which analyzes Wilson's theory at length and expresses some skepticism about it.

50. Tulis, *Rhetorical Presidency*, pp. 138, 140.

51. Samuel Kernell, *Going Public: Strategies of Presidential Leadership*, 3rd ed. (Washington, DC: CQ Press, 1997), p. 92 and ch. 4.

52. Benjamin I. Page and Robert Y. Shapiro, "Presidents as Opinion Leaders: Some New Evidence," *Policy Studies Journal* 12 (1984), pp. 649–661; and Benjamin I. Page, Robert Y. Shapiro, and Glenn R. Dempsey, "What Moves Public Opinion," *American Political Science Review* 81 (1987), pp. 23–43. For a counter-argument, see Donald L. Jordan, "Newspaper Effects on Policy Preferences," *Public Opinion Quarterly* 57 (1993), pp. 191–204.

53. For an examination of the complexities of the scholarly literature on the effects of presidential opinion leadership, see George C. Edwards III, "Leading the Public," in *Oxford Handbook of the American Presidency*, eds. Edwards and Howell.

54. Lawrence R. Jacobs and Robert Y. Shapiro, *Politicians Don't Pander: Political Manipulation and the Loss of Democratic Responsiveness* (Chicago: The University of Chicago Press, 2000); and Jacob Hacker and Paul Pierson, *Off Center* (New Haven, CT: Yale University Press, 2005).

55. Doris Graber, *Mass Media and American Politics*, 8th ed. (Washington, DC: CQ Press, 2010), ch. 9; Lawrence R. Jacobs, "Communicating from the White House," in *Executive Branch*, eds. Aberbach and Peterson, pp. 189–205.

56. Lawrence Jacobs and Robert Y. Shapiro, "The Rise of Presidential Polling: The Nixon White House in Historical Perspective," *Public Opinion Quarterly* 59 (1995), pp. 163–195; and Jacobs, "Communicating from the White House," pp. 178–189.

57. W. Lance Bennett, Regina G. Lawrence, and Steven Livingston, *When the Press Fails: Political Power and the News Media from Iraq to Katrina* (Chicago: The University of Chicago Press, 2007), ch. 5; Jacobs and Shapiro, *Politicians Don't Pander*; and James M. Druckman and Lawrence R. Jacobs, "Presidential Responsiveness to Public Opinion," in *Oxford Handbook of the American Presidency*, eds. Edwards and Howell.

58. Edwards and Wayne, *Presidential Leadership*, pp. 112–123.

59. Brody, *Assessing the President*. Also see Edwards and Wayne, *Presidential Leadership*, pp. 112–123; John E. Mueller, "Presidential Popularity from Truman to Johnson," *American Political Science Review* 64 (1970), pp. 18–34; Samuel Kernell, "Explaining Presidential Popularity," *American Political Science Review* 72 (1978), pp. 506–522; and George C. Edwards III, *Presidential Approval* (Baltimore, MD: Johns Hopkins University Press, 1990).

Chapter 13

1. Tracy Lee, "Influence Diplomat Steps Down Among Large-Scale Exodus at State Department." Newsweek, February 1, 2018.

2. Max Weber, *Economy and Society,* vol. 1 (London: Owen, 1962).

3. Jay M. Shafritz, E. W. Russell, and Christopher P. Borick, *Introducing Public Administration* (New York: Pearson Longman, 2007), pp. 87–94; and Peters, *American Public Policy,* pp. 114–121.

4. Peters, *American Public Policy,* p. 116.

5. Daniel Carpenter, "The Evolution of National Bureaucracy in the United States," in *The Executive Branch,* eds. Joel D. Aberbach and Mark A. Peterson (New York: Oxford University Press, 2005), pp. 55–57.

6. Peters, *American Public Policy,* p. 118.

7. Roger H. Davidson, Walter J. Oleszek, Frances E. Lee, and Eric Schickler, *Congress and Its Members,* 14th ed. (Washington, DC: CQ Press, 2014), pp. 289–290.

8. Charles R. Shipan, "Congress and the Bureaucracy," in *The Legislative Branch,* eds. Paul J. Quirk and Sarah A. Binder (New York: Oxford University Press, 2005).

9. David Lewis, "Presidential Appointments and Personnel," *Annual Review of Political Science* 14 (2011), p. 52.

10. Lewis, "Presidential Appointments," p. 48.

11. Richard P. Nathan, *The Administrative Presidency* (New York: Wiley, 1983).

12. Sabrina Siddiqui, " 'I Don't Get Confused': Nikki Haley Hits Back After White House Contradicts Her on Russia Statements," *The Guardian,* April 17, 2018.

13. David E. Rosenbaum and Stephen Labaton, "Amid Many Fights on Qualifications, a Nomination Stalls," *New York Times,* September 24, 2005.

14. Lewis, "Presidential Appointments," p. 56.

15. Hugh Heclo, *A Government of Strangers* (Washington, DC: Brookings Institution Press, 1977), p. 103.

16. Tamara Keith, "Trump Cabinet Turnover Sets Record Going Back 100 Years," NPR.org, March 29, 2018.

17. See Samuel Krislov and David H. Rosenbloom, *Representative Bureaucracy and the American Political System* (New York: Praeger, 1981); Goodsell, *Case for Bureaucracy*; and Ingraham, "Federal Service."

18. Organisation for Economic Co-operation and Development (OECD), 2005, as reported on a graph in "Public Service Careers: A Tough Search for Talent," *Economist,* October 31, 2009, p. 71.

19. Goodsell, *Case for Bureaucracy,* pp. 84–90; and Stanley Rothman and S. Robert Lichter, "How Liberal Are Bureaucrats?" *Regulation* (November–December 1983), pp. 35–47.

20. Joshua D. Clinton, Anthony Bertelli, Christian R. Grose, David E. Lewis, and David C. Nixon, "Separated Power in the United States: The Ideology of Agencies, Presidents, and Congress," *American Journal of Political Science* 56, no. 3 (2102), pp. 341–354.

21. Office of Personnel Management, 2018, "Executive Branch Employment by Gender and Race/National Origin."

22. Ingraham, "Federal Service," pp. 291–294.

23. Richard E. Neustadt, *Presidential Power* (New York: Wiley, 1960); and George C. Edwards III and Stephen J. Wayne, *Presidential Leadership: Politics and Policy Making* (Wadsworth, CA: Thomson Wadsworth, 2009), ch. 9.

24. Terry M. Moe, "Control and Feedback in Economic Regulation," *American Political Science Review* 79 (1985), pp. 1094–1116; David Lewis and Terry M. Moe, "The Presidency and the Bureaucracy: The Levers of Presidential Control," in *The Presidency and the Political System,* ed. Michael Nelson (Washington, DC: CQ Press, 2010); Richard W. Waterman, *Presidential Influence and the Administrative State* (Knoxville: University of Tennessee Press, 1989); and Edwards and Wayne, *Presidential Leadership,* pp. 295–303.

25. Richard W. Waterman and Kenneth J. Meier, "Principal-Agent Models: An Expansion?" *Journal of Public Administration Research and Theory* 8 (April 1998), pp. 173–202; and Edwards and Wayne, *Presidential Leadership,* pp. 305–307.

26. For a review of research on the president's appointment powers, see Joel D. Aberbach and Bert A. Rockman, "The Appointments Process and the Administrative Presidency," *Presidential Studies Quarterly* 39, no. 1 (January 2009), pp. 38–59.

27. James P. Pfiffner, "Constraining Executive Power: George W. Bush and the Constitution," in *Understanding the Presidency,* eds. James P. Pfiffner and Roger H. Davidson (New York: Pearson Longman, 2009); and Andrew Rudalevige, "The Presidency and Unilateral Power," in *Presidency and the Political System,* ed. Nelson.

28. Lewis, "Presidential Appointments," pp. 54–55; and Robert F. Durant and William G. Resh, " 'Presidentializing' the Bureaucracy," in *The Oxford Handbook of American Bureaucracy,* ed. Robert F. Durant (New York: Oxford University Press, 2011).

29. Theodore J. Lowi, *The End of Liberalism,* 2nd ed. (New York: Norton, 1979); and Christian Hunold and B. Guy Peters, "Bureaucratic Discretion and Deliberative Democracy," in *Transformation in Governance,* eds. Matti Malkia, Ari-Veikko Anttiroiko, and Reigo Savolainen (London: Idea Group. 2004), pp. 131–149.

30. "Wings Clipped: A Working Example of the Effects of Congressional Stupidity," *Economist,* August 6, 2011, p. 40.

31. John A. Ferejohn and Charles R. Shipan, "Congressional Influence on Administrative Agencies: A Case Study of Telecommunications Policy," in *Congress Reconsidered,* 4th ed., eds. Lawrence C. Dodd and Bruce I. Oppenheimer (Washington, DC: CQ Press, 1989); and Davidson, Oleszek, Lee, and Schickler, *Congress and Its Members,* pp. 331–332.

32. See Jerry L. Mashaw, "Bureaucracy, Democracy, and Judicial Review," in *The Oxford Handbook of American Bureaucracy,* ed. Durant.

33. Barry R. Weingast, "Caught in the Middle: The President, Congress, and the Political-Bureaucratic System," in *Executive Branch,* eds. Aberbach and Peterson, pp. 322–325.

34. Cornelius M. Kerwin, *Rulemaking: How Government Agencies Write Law and Make Policy* (Washington, DC: CQ Press, 2003), p. 183.

35. See especially Cornelius Kerwin, Scott Furlong, and William West, "Interest Groups, Rulemaking, and American Bureaucracy," in *The Oxford Handbook of American Bureaucracy*, ed. Durant, pp. 602–607. See Derek Bok, *The Trouble with Government* (Cambridge, MA: Harvard University Press, 2001), ch. 9.

36. Ian Sherr, Abrar Al-Heeti, Erin Carson, "Zuckerberg Faces Harder Questions in Second Round of Testimony," CNet.com, April 11, 2018.

37. B. Guy Peters, *American Public Policy: Policy and Performance*, 9th ed. (New York: CQ Press, 2012), p. 43.

38. "A Tough Search for Talent," *Economist*, October 31, 2011, p. 71.

39. Wallace Sayre, "Bureaucracies: Some Contrasts in Systems," *Indian Journal of Public Administration* 10 (1964), p. 223. For contemporary evidence in support of this claim, see Gabriel A. Almond, G. Bingham Powell Jr., Kaare Strom, and Russell J. Dalton, *Comparative Politics Today* (New York: Pearson Longman, 2010), pp. 120–124.

40. John A. Rohr, *Civil Servants and Their Constitutions* (Lawrence: University of Kansas Press, 2002); and Richard J. Stillman II, *The American Bureaucracy* (Chicago: Nelson-Hall, 1987), p. 18.

41. On the problem of government accountability in our system of separated powers and checks and balances in an environment characterized by growing interest group influence and rising partisanship, see Francis Fukuyama, "The Ties That Used to Bind: The Decay of American Political Institutions," *American Interest*, December 8, 2013, http://www.the-american-interest.com/articles/2013/12/08/the-decay-of-american-political-institutions.

42. Emanuel S. Savas, *Privatization: The Key to Better Government* (Chatham, NJ: Chatham House, 1987); Sheila B. Kamerman and Alfred J. Kahn, eds., *Privatization and the Welfare State* (Princeton, NJ: Princeton University Press, 1989); and Lester M. Salamon, ed., *The Tools of Government: A Guide to the New Governance* (Oxford, UK: Oxford University Press, 2002).

43. Moshe Schwartz, *Department of Defense Contractors in Iraq and Afghanistan: Background and Analysis* (Washington, DC: The Congressional Research Service, December 14, 2009).

44. John Cranford, "Job Creation: The Engine in Chief," *Roll Call*, September 29, 2011, http://www.rollcall.com/features/Outlook_Job-Creation/outlook/-209070-1.html.

45. Bernard Wysocki Jr., "Is U.S. Government Outsourcing Its Brain?" *Wall Street Journal*, March 30, 2007.

46. Bok, *Trouble with Government*, pp. 233–234; Roberta Lynch and Ann Markusen, "Can Markets Govern?" *American Prospect* (Winter 1994), pp. 125–134; and Dan Guttman, "Governance by Contract," *Public Contract Law Journal* 33 (Winter 2004), pp. 321–360.

47. David Osborne and Ted Gaebler, *Reinventing Government* (Reading, MA: Addison-Wesley, 1992).

48. Bok, *Trouble with Government*, pp. 234–239; Joel D. Aberbach and Bert A. Rockman, eds., *In the Web of Politics: Three Decades of the U.S. Federal Executive* (Washington, DC: Brookings Institution Press, 2000); Lester M. Salamon,

"The New Governance and the Tools of Public Administration," in *The Tools of Government*, ed. Lester M. Salamon (Oxford, UK: Oxford University Press, 2002); and Steven G. Koven, "Bureaucracy, Democracy, and the New Public Management," in *Bureaucracy and Administration*, ed. Ali Farazmand (Boca Raton, FL: CRC Press, 2009); Carpenter, "Evolution," pp. 63–64; and Shafritz, Russell, and Borick, *Introducing Public Administration*, pp. 112–114.

49. Terry M. Moe, "The Politics of Bureaucratic Structure," in *Can the Government Govern?* eds. John E. Chubb and Paul E. Peterson (Washington, DC: Brookings Institution Press, 1989), p. 280; John E. Chubb and Paul E. Peterson, "American Political Institutions and the Problem of Governance," in *Can the Government Govern?* eds. Chubb and Peterson, p. 41; and James L. Sundquist, *Constitutional Reform and Effective Government* (Washington, DC: Brookings Institution Press, 1986).

Chapter 14

1. All quotes are from Neil A. Lewis, "Bitter Senators Divided Anew on Judgeships," *Washington Post*, November 15, 2003.

2. Jan Crawford Greenburg, *Supreme Conflict: The Inside Story of the Struggle for Control of the United States Supreme Court* (New York: Penguin Press, 2007); Jess Bravin, "Top Court Hands Conservatives Victories," *Wall Street Journal*, June 26, 2007; Linda Greenhouse, "In Steps Big and Small, Supreme Court Moves Right," *New York Times*, July 1, 2007; "Supreme Success," *Economist*, July 7, 2007, p. 36; "Conservatives Resurgent," *Economist*, April 21, 2007, p. 34; and David M. O'Brien, *Storm Center: The Supreme Court in American Politics*, 10th ed. (New York, Norton, 2014), pp. 28–29.

3. For strong empirical confirmation of the emergence of a strong conservative majority on the Court with the arrival of Samuel Alito and under the leadership of John Roberts, see Stephen A. Jessee and Alexander M. Tahk, "What Can We Learn About the Ideology of the Newest Supreme Court Justices?" *PS: Political Science and Politics* 44, no. 3 (July 2011), pp. 524–529; Linda Greenhouse, "The Real John Roberts Emerges," *New York Times*, June 28, 2013; and Adam Liptak, "Roberts Pulls the Supreme Court to the Right Step by Step," *New York Times*, June 27, 2013.

4. O'Brien, *Storm Center*, ch. 1.

5. Akhil Reed Amar, *America's Constitution: A Biography* (New York: Random House, 2005), ch. 6.

6. For a review of the theory and practice of judicial review in the United States and in other democratic countries, see Georg Vanberg, "Constitutional Courts in Comparative Perspective," *Annual Review of Political Science* 18 (2015), pp. 167–185.

7. J. M. Sosin, *The Aristocracy of the Long Robe: The Origins of Judicial Review in America* (Westport, CT: Greenwood Press, 1989); William E. Nelson, "The Historical Foundations of the American Judiciary," Kermit L. Hall, "Judicial Independence and the Majoritarian Difficulty," and Cass R. Sunstein, "Judges and Democracy: The Changing Role of the United States Supreme Court," in *The Judicial Branch*, eds. Kermit L. Hall and Kevin T. McGuire (New York: Oxford University Press, 2005).

8. Lee Epstein and Thomas G. Walker, *Rights, Liberties, and Justice* (Washington, DC: CQ Press, 2010), pp. 47, 53; and Mark A. Graber, "Establishing Judicial Review? *Schooner Peggy* and the Early Marshall Court," *Political Research Quarterly* 51 (1998), pp. 221–239.

9. Robert G. McCloskey, *The American Supreme Court*, 4th ed. (Chicago: The University of Chicago Press, 2005), pp. 12–13.

10. On *Marbury*, see Sylvia Snowmiss, *Judicial Review and the Law of the Constitution* (New Haven, CT: Yale University Press, 1990).

11. David M. O'Brien, *Constitutional Law and Politics*, vol. 2 (New York: Norton, 2008), p. 36; and Adam Liptak, "How Activist Is the Supreme Court?" *New York Times*, October 12, 2013, http://www.nytimes.com/2013/10/13/sunday -review/how-activist-is-the-supreme-court.html?- pagewanted%3Dall%26_r%3D0.

12. Linda Greenhouse, "The Imperial Presidency vs. the Imperial Judiciary," *New York Times*, March 2, 2000; and Paul Gewirtz and Chad Golder, "So Who Are the Activists?" *New York Times*, July 6, 2005.

13. See *Ex parte Milligan* (1866) and *Youngstown Sheet and Tube Co. v. Sawyer* (1952).

14. See Keith E. Whittington, "Judicial Checks on the President," in *The Oxford Handbook of the American Presidency*, eds. George C. Edwards III and William G. Howell (New York: Oxford University Press, 2009).

15. Robert A. Dahl, *How Democratic Is the American Constitution?* (New Haven, CT: Yale University Press, 2001), pp. 54–55. See also Lawrence D. Kramer, *The People Themselves: Popular Constitutionalism and Judicial Review* (New York: Oxford University Press, 2004).

16. Alexander M. Bickel, *The Least Dangerous Branch: The Supreme Court at the Bar of Politics* (Indianapolis, IN: Bobbs-Merrill, 1962), pp. 16–18.

17. Robert A. Dahl, "Decision-Making in a Democracy: The Supreme Court as a National Policy Maker," *Journal of Public Law* 6 (1957), pp. 279–295; and Mark A. Graber, "Constructing Judicial Review," *Annual Review of Political Science* 8 (2005), pp. 425–451.

18. Richard S. Randall, *American Constitutional Development* (New York: Longman, 2002), pp. 488–489.

19. "United States District Courts—National and Judicial Caseload Profile," *Federal Court Management Statistics*, 2017, http://www.uscourts.gov/sites/default/files/data _tables/fcms_na_distprofile1231.2017.pdf.

20. http://www.uscourts.gov/sites/default/files/fcms_na _appprofile1231.2017.pdf.

21. Neil Lewis, "An Appeals Court That Always Veers to the Right," *New York Times*, May 24, 1999; and Deborah Sontag, "The Power of the Fourth," *New York Times Sunday Magazine*, March 9, 2003, pp. 38–44.

22. Lawrence Baum, *The Supreme Court* (Washington, DC: CQ Press, 2010), pp. 6–10.

23. Roger H. Davidson, Walter J. Oleszek, Frances E. Lee, and Eric Schickler, *Congress and Its Members*, 16th ed. (Washington, DC: CQ Press, 2018), pp. 355–357.

24. O'Brien, *Storm Center*, pp. 34–39. See also Joel B. Grossman, "Paths to the Bench," in *Judicial Branch*, eds. Hall and McGuire, p. 162; and Lee Epstein, Jack Knight, and Andrew D. Martin, "The Norm of Judicial Experience," *University of California Law Review* 91 (2003), pp. 938–939.

25. Greenburg, *Supreme Conflict*.

26. Robert A. Carp and Ronald Stidham, *Judicial Process in America*, 6th ed. (Washington, DC: CQ Press, 2004), ch. 8; Grossman, "Paths to the Bench," pp. 160–161.

27. Baum, *Supreme Court*, pp. 27–50; Ronald Brownstein, *The Second Civil War: How Extreme Partisanship Has Paralyzed Washington and Polarized America* (New York: Penguin Press, 2007); Greenburg, *Supreme Conflict*; Alan Wolfe, *Does American Democracy Still Work?* (New Haven, CT: Yale University Press, 2006), ch. 5.

28. Lee Epstein and Jeffrey A. Segal, "Nominating Federal Judges and Justices," in *The Oxford Handbook of the American Presidency*, eds. Edwards and Howell.

29. Lee Epstein and Jeffrey A. Segal, *Advice and Consent: The Politics of Judicial Appointments* (New York: Oxford University Press, 2005), ch. 3; Baum, *Supreme Court*, pp. 27–50; Davidson, Oleszek, Lee, and Schickler, *Congress and Its Members*, pp. 362–369; and O'Brien, *Storm Center*, pp. 34–39.

30. On the rising importance of ideology and partisanship in nominating and confirming federal judges, see Mark A. Graber, "The Coming Constitutional Yo-Yo? Elite Opinion, Polarization, and the Direction of Judicial Decision Making," *Howard Law Journal* 56, no. 3 (2013), pp. 661–719.

31. Charlie Savage, "Trump Is Rapidly Reshaping the Judiciary. Here's How," *New York Times online*, November 11, 2017, https://www.nytimes.com/2017/11/11/us/politics/ trump-judiciary-appeals-courts-conservatives.html?_r=0; and "Donald Trump's Judicial Appointments May Prove His Most Enduring Legacy," *Economist online*, January 13, 2018, https://www.economist.com/news/united- states/21734409-everything-else-could-theory-be-reversed- his-effect-law-will-be-profound-donald?frsc=dg%7Ce; Jeremy W. Peters, "Trump's New Judicial Litmus Test: Shrinking the Administrative State," *New York Times online*, March 26, 2018, https://www.economist.com/news/unit- ed-states/21734409-everything-else-could-theory-be- reversed-his-effect-law-will-be-profound-donald?- frsc=dg%7Ce.

32. Epstein and Segal, "Nominating Federal Judges," pp. 629–630 and 634–635.

33. Thomas Kaplan, "Trump Is Putting Indelible Conservative Stamp on Judiciary," *New York Times*, July 31, 2018, https://www.nytimes.com/2018/07/31/us/politics/ trump-judges.html.

34. Charlie Savage, "Obama Backers Fear Opportunities to Reshape Judiciary Are Slipping Away," *New York Times*, November 14, 2009.

35. Epstein and Segal, *Advice and Consent*, ch. 3; Epstein and Segal, "Nominating Federal Judges," pp. 634–635; Lee Epstein and Thomas G. Walker, *Constitutional Law for a Changing America: Institutional Powers and Constraints* (Los Angeles and Washington, DC: SAGE and CQ Press, 2014),

pp. 34–39; Baum, *Supreme Court*, pp. 123–125; Grossman, "Paths to the Bench"; Lawrence Baum, "The Supreme Court in American Politics," in *Annual Review of Political Science*, ed. Nelson W. Polsby (Palo Alto, CA: Annual Reviews, 2003), pp. 161–180; Dahl, "Decision-Making in a Democracy"; Ronald Stidham and Robert A. Carp, "Judges, Presidents, and Policy Choices," *Social Science Quarterly* 68 (1987), pp. 395–404; and Carp and Stidham, *Judicial Process in America*, ch. 9.

36. See Epstein and Walker, *Constitutional Law*, pp. 11–23; Bernard Schwartz, *Decision: How the Supreme Court Decides Cases* (New York: Oxford University Press, 2005).

37. Jeffrey A. Segal, Harold J. Spaeth, and Sara C. Benesh, *The Supreme Court in the American Legal System* (New York: Cambridge University Press, 2005), ch. 11; Epstein and Walker, *Rights, Liberties, and Justice*, pp. 57–63.

38. Adam Liptak, "With Subtle Signals, Supreme Court Justices Request the Cases They Want to Hear," *New York Times*, July 6, 2015, http://nyti.ms/1KLaZVG.

39. For details, see H. W. Perry Jr., *Deciding to Decide: Agenda Setting in the United States Supreme Court* (Cambridge, MA: Harvard University Press, 2005).

40. John Paul Stevens, *Five Chiefs: A Supreme Court Memoir* (New York: Little, Brown, 2011).

41. Perry, *Deciding to Decide*. For a current review of the extensive scholarly literature, see Lee Epstein and Jack Knight, "Reconsidering Judicial Preferences," *Annual Review of Political Science* 16 (2013), pp. 11–31, and Thomas M. Keck, "Party, Policy, or Duty: Why Does the Supreme Court Invalidate Federal Statutes?" *American Political Science Review* 101 (May 2007), pp. 321–338. Also see Epstein and Segal, *Advice and Consent*, ch. 5.

42. Segal, Spaeth, and Benesh, *Supreme Court in the American Legal System*, pp. 318–323; David Adamany, "The Supreme Court," in *The American Courts*, eds. John B. Gates and Charles A. Johnson (Washington, DC: CQ Press, 1991), pp. 111–112; Baum, "Supreme Court in American Politics," pp. 162–168; Glendon Schubert, *The Judicial Mind* (Evanston, IL: Northwestern University Press, 1965); Jeffrey A. Segal and Harold J. Spaeth, *The Supreme Court and the Attitudinal Model* (New York: Cambridge University Press, 1993); John D. Sprague, *Voting Patterns of the United States Supreme Court* (Indianapolis, IN: Bobbs-Merrill, 1968); Tom S. Clark, "Measuring Ideological Polarization on the United States Supreme Court," *Political Research Quarterly* 20, no. 10 (May 2008), pp. 1–12; and Jessee and Tahk, "What Can We Learn About the Ideology?"; and Donald Michael Gooch, "Ideological Polarization on the Supreme Court," *American Politics Research* 43, no. 6 (January 20, 2015), pp. 999–1040.

43. Walter Murphy, *Elements of Judicial Strategy* (Princeton, NJ: Princeton University Press, 1964); and Lee Epstein and Jack Knight, *The Choices Justices Make* (Washington, DC: CQ Press, 1997).

44. Joel B. Grossman, "Social Backgrounds and Judicial Decision-Making," *Harvard Law Review* 79 (1966), pp. 1551–1564; S. Sidney Ulmer, "Dissent Behavior and the Social Background of Supreme Court Justices," *Journal of Politics* 32 (1970), pp. 580–589.

45. L. Epstein, J. Knight, and J. Martin, "The Supreme Court as a Strategic National Policy-Maker," *Emory Law Review* 50 (2001), pp. 583–610.

46. Epstein and Walker, *Constitutional Law for a Changing America*, pp. 23–44; Jessee and Tahk, "What Can We Learn About the Ideology"; Adam Liptak, "'Politicians in Robes?' Not Exactly, But …," *New York Times*, November 26, 2012; Segal and Spaeth, *Supreme Court and the Attitudinal Model*.

47. Nicholas Wade, "A Mathematician Crunches the Supreme Court's Numbers," *New York Times*, August 4, 2003; Segal, Spaeth, and Benesh, *Supreme Court in the American Legal System*, pp. 318–323; and Epstein and Segal, "Nominating Federal Judges," pp. 629–630 and 634–635.

48. The Honorable John M. Harlan, "A Glimpse of the Supreme Court at Work," *The Law School Record* 11, no. 2 (1951), p. 7.

49. Linda Greenhouse, "A Justice in Chief," *Opinionator* (blog), *New York Times*, June 28, 2012, http://opinionator.blogs.nytimes.com/2012/06/28/a-justice-in-chief/.

50. Amelia Thomson-DeVeaux, "Chief Justice John Roberts Is Reshaping the First Amendment," *FiveThirty Eight*, March 20, 2018, https://fivethirtyeight.com/features/chief-justice-roberts-is-reshaping-the-first-amendment/?ex_cid=538email.

51. Bob Woodward and Scott Armstrong, *The Brethren: Inside the Supreme Court* (New York: Simon & Schuster, 1979).

52. Lee Epstein and Jack Knight, "Mapping Out the Strategic Terrain: The Informational Role of Amici Curiae," in *Supreme Court Decision-Making*, eds. Cornell Clayton and Howard Gillman (Chicago: The University of Chicago Press, 1999); Segal, Spaeth, and Benesh, *Supreme Court in the American Legal System*, chs. 12 and 13.

53. Graber, "Constructing Judicial Review"; Thomas M. Keck, *The Most Activist Supreme Court in History: The Road to Modern Judicial Conservatism* (Chicago: The University of Chicago Press, 2004); George I. Lovell, *Legislative Deferrals: Statutory Ambiguity, Judicial Power, and American Democracy* (New York: Cambridge University Press, 2003); Kevin K. McMahon, *Reconsidering Roosevelt on Race: How the Presidency Paved the Way for Brown* (Chicago: The University of Chicago Press, 2004); and Keith E. Whittington, *Political Foundations of Judicial Supremacy: The Presidency, the Supreme Court, and Constitutional Leadership in U.S. History* (Princeton, NJ: Princeton University Press, 2007). See also Bruce Ackerman, *We the People: Transformations* (Cambridge, MA: Harvard University Press, 2000); and McCloskey, *American Supreme Court*.

54. Davidson, Oleszek, Lee, and Schickler, *Congress and Its Members*, pp. 357–369; and Epstein and Walker, *Constitutional Law*, pp. 39–44.

55. Epstein and Knight, "Reconsidering Judicial Preferences"; Vanberg, "Constitutional Courts in Comparative Perspective," pp. 179–181; and Brian Christopher Jones, *Disparaging the Supreme Court: Is SCOTUS in Serious Trouble?* 2015 Wis. L. Rev. Forward 53, http://wisconsinlawreview.org/disparaging-the-supreme-court-is-scotus-in-serious-trouble/.

56. Baum, "Supreme Court in American Politics," p. 167; and Davidson, Oleszek, Lee, and Schickler, *Congress and Its Members*, pp. 354–355.

57. Tom S. Clark, "The Separation of Powers, Court Curbing, and Judicial Legitimacy," *American Journal of Political Science* 53, no. 4 (October 2009), pp. 971–989.

58. Noam Scheiber and Kenneth P. Vogel, "Behind a Key Labor Case, A Web of Conservative Donors," *New York Times*, February 25, 2018, https://www.nytimes.com/2018/02/25/business/economy/labor-court-conservatives.html.

59. Lisa A. Solowiej and Paul M. Collins Jr., "Counteractive Lobbying in the U.S. Supreme Court," *American Politics Research* 37, no. 4 (2009), pp. 670–699.

60. Edward Lazarus, *Closed Chambers* (New York: Penguin Press, 1999), pp. 373–374.

61. Epstein and Knight, "Mapping Out the Strategic Terrain."

62. Dahl, "Decision-Making in a Democracy," pp. 279–295; Thomas R. Marshall, "Public Opinion, Representation, and the Modern Supreme Court," *American Politics Quarterly* 16 (1988), pp. 296–316; McCloskey, *American Supreme Court*, p. 22; O'Brien, *Storm Center*, p. 337; and Baum, *Supreme Court*, pp. 142–144.

63. Graber, "The Coming Constitutional Yo-Yo?," pp. 693–696.

64. G. Caldeira, "Courts and Public Opinion," in *The American Courts*, eds. John B. Gates and Charles A. Johnson (Washington, DC: CQ Press, 1991); Jay Casper, "The Supreme Court and National Policy Making," *American Political Science Review* 70 (1976), pp. 50–63; Marshall, "Public Opinion"; William Mishler and Reginald S. Sheehan, "The Supreme Court as a Counter-Majoritarian Institution: The Impact of Public Opinion on Supreme Court Decisions," *American Political Science Review* 87 (1993), pp. 87–101; and Benjamin I. Page and Robert Y. Shapiro, "Effects of Public Opinion on Policy," *American Political Science Review* 77 (1983), p. 183.

65. Segal, Spaeth, and Benesh, *Supreme Court in the American Legal System*, pp. 326–328; and Baum, *Supreme Court*, pp. 140–142.

66. Herbert Jacob, *Justice in America*, 3rd ed. (Boston: Little, Brown, 1978), p. 245. See also Keith E. Whittington, "Judicial Review and Interpretation," in *Judicial Branch*, eds. Hall and McGuire.

67. McCloskey, *American Supreme Court*. See also James H. Fowler and Sangick Jeon, "The Authority of Supreme Court Precedent" (working paper, University of California, Davis, June 29, 2005).

68. Carp and Stidham, *Judicial Process in America*, p. 28.

69. *Ibid.*, p. 57.

70. Mark A. Graber, "From Republic to Democracy: The Judiciary and the Political Process," in *Judicial Branch*, eds. Hall and McGuire.

71. McCloskey, *American Supreme Court*. See also H. W. Perry Jr., *The Transformation of the Supreme Court's Agenda: From the New Deal to the Reagan Administration* (Boulder, CO: Westview Press, 1991); Charles R. Epp, "The Supreme Court and the Rights Revolution," in *Judicial Branch*, eds.

Hall and McGuire; and Sunstein, "Judges and Democracy."

72. Jessee and Tahk, "What Can We Learn About the Ideology."

73. Steven Vago, *Law and Society* (New York: Prentice Hall, 2012), pp. 166–170.

74. Gewirtz and Golder, "So Who Are the Activists?"

75. *Ibid.*

76. Epstein and Walker, *Constitutional Law*, p. 37.

77. Epstein and Walker, *Rights, Liberties, and Justice*, pp. 22–28.

78. James V. Calvi and Susan Coleman, *American Law and Legal Systems* (New York: Longman, 2012), pp. 148–150.

79. Sanford Levinson, "How I Lost My Constitutional Faith" *Maryland Law Review* 71, no. 4 (2012), pp. 955–977.

80. Stephen Breyer, *Active Liberty: Interpreting Our Democratic Constitution* (New York: Knopf, 2005); and Cass Sunstein, *A Constitution of Many Minds: Why the Founding Document Doesn't Mean What It Meant Before* (Princeton, NJ: Princeton University Press, 2009).

Chapter 15

1. For more information, see "Timeline: Controversies Over Spy Programs, Privacy," *USA Today*, June 9, 2013, https://www.usatoday.com/story/news/nation/2013/06/09/timeline-spy-programs-nsa-data-surveillance/2405549.

2. James Ball, "NSA Stores Metadata of Millions of Web Users for Up to a Year, Secret Files Show," *Guardian*, September 30, 2013.

3. Siobhan Gorman, "NSA Officers Spy on Love Interests," *Wall Street Journal*, August 23, 2013.

4. Lee Epstein and Thomas G. Walker, *Rights, Liberties, and Justice* (Washington, DC: CQ Press, 2010), pp. 67–87, 93–94.

5. Lucius J Barker, Michael Combs, Kevin Lyles, H. W. Perry Jr., and Twiley Barker, *Civil Liberties and the Constitution: Cases and Commentaries*, 9th ed. (London: Routledge, 2010); Lee Epstein and Thomas G. Walker, *Constitutional Law for a Changing America: Rights, Liberties, and Justice*, 9th ed. (Washington, DC: CQ Press, 2014); Anthony Lewis, *Freedom for the Thought That We Hate: A Biography of the First Amendment* (New York: Basic Books, 2007); John C. Domino, *Civil Rights and Liberties in the 21st Century* (New York: Pearson Longman, 2010), ch. 2.

6. See Geoffrey R. Stone, *Perilous Times: Free Speech in Wartime* (New York: W. W. Norton, 2004).

7. See Stanley I. Kutler, *The American Inquisition: Justice and Injustice in the Cold War* (New York: Hill & Wang, 1982).

8. See Fred W. Friendly, *Minnesota Rag* (New York: Vintage, 1981).

9. See Barker et al., *Civil Liberties and the Constitution*, pp. 169–178; Epstein and Walker, *Rights, Liberties, and Justice*, pp. 292–295; and Alpheus Thomas Mason and Donald Grier Stephenson Jr., *American Constitutional Law* (New York: Longman, 2012), pp. 463–467.

10. See Charles Rembar, *The End of Obscenity* (New York: Harper & Row, 1968).

11. Richard H. Fallon Jr., *The Dynamic Constitution: An Introduction to American Constitutional Law* (New York: Cambridge University Press, 2013).

12. *Supreme Court of the United States, Syllabus, Brown, Governor of California, et al. v. Entertainment Merchants Association et al.,* No. 08–1448, Argued November 2, 2010—Decided June 27, 2011.

13. Epstein and Walker, *Rights, Liberties, and Justice,* pp. 145–192.

14. Fallon, *The Dynamic Constitution,* pp. 61–67.

15. *Ibid.,* p. 63.

16. Adam Liptak, "Religious Groups Given 'Exception' to Work Bias Law," *New York Times,* January 11, 2012, p. 1.

17. Roy Walmsley, "World Prison Population List," 11th ed., *International Centre for Prison Studies, 2016,* http://www.prisonstudies.org/sites/default/files/resources/downloads/world_prison_population_list_11th_edition_0.pdf.

18. Erwin Chemerinsky, "The Roberts Court and Criminal Procedure at Age Five," *Texas Tech Law Review* 43 (2010), pp. 13–27.

19. *Katz v. United States* (1967).

20. *United States v. Leon* (1984); *Massachusetts v. Sheppard* (1984).

21. *Nix v. Williams* (1984).

22. *Supreme Court of the United States, Syllabus, Collins v. Virginia,* No. 16–1027, Argued January 9, 2018—Decided May 29, 2018.

23. *Supreme Court of the United States, Syllabus, Carpenter v. United States,* No. 16–402, Argued November 29, 2017—Decided June 22, 2018.

24. Richard Fausset "New Orleans Puts Poor on 'Waiting List' for Lawyers, Suit Alleges," *New York Times,* January 15, 2016; Ken Daley, "Federal Judge Dismisses ACLU Lawsuit Aimed at Boosting New Orleans' Indigent Defense Funding," *Times-Picayune,* February 1, 2017.

25. *Harris v. New York* (1971); *New York v. Quarles* (1984).

26. *Arizona v. Fulminate* (1991).

27. Jim Yardley, "A Role Model for Executions," *New York Times,* January 9, 2000, pp. A1, IV–5.

28. "Gallup, In-Depth: Topics A to Z: Death Penalty," Accessed: October 28, 2018. http://www.gallup.com/poll/1606/death-penalty.aspx.

29. Gallup, In-Depth: Topics A to Z: Death Penalty," Accessed: October 28, 2018. http://www.gallup.com/poll/1606/death-penalty.aspx.

30. See the "Death Penalty Information Center," http://www.deathpenaltyinfo.org/states-and-without-death-penalty.

31. The Innocence Project, "DNA Exonerations in the United States," http://www.innocenceproject.org/dna-exonerations-in-the-united-states.

32. Robert Barnes, "Supreme Court Opens Way for Prisoners to Try to Gain Access to DNA Evidence," *Washington Post,* March 7, 2011.

33. *Ibid.*

34. For all data in this paragraph, see the Death Penalty Information Center, "Facts About the Death Penalty," http://www.deathpenaltyinfo.org/documents/FactSheet.pdf.

35. Denise Grady and Jan Hoffman, "States Turn to an Unproven Method of Execution: Nitrogen Gas," *New York Times,* May 7, 2018.

36. "Security Trumps Civil Liberties" (report, National Public Radio, the Kennedy School of Government of Harvard University, and the Kaiser Family Fund, November 30, 2001).

37. David Stout, "FBI Head Admits Mistakes in Use of Security Act," *New York Times,* March 10, 2007, p. A1.

38. Barton Gellman, "The FBI's Secret Scrutiny," *Washington Post,* November 6, 2005, p. A1.

39. Kent Roach, *The 9/11 Effect: Comparative Counter-Terrorism* (New York: Cambridge University Press, 2011); and Adam Liptak, "Civil Liberties Today," *New York Times,* September 11, 2011, p. 14.

40. *United States Court of Appeals for the Fourth Circuit, Syllabus, Gretchen Stuart v. Paul Camnitz,* No. 14–1150, December 22, 2014. https://www.ca4.uscourts.gov/Opinions/Published/141150.P.pdf.

41. Julie Bosman and Mitch Smith, "Iowa Lawmakers Pass Abortion Bill With Roe v. Wade in Sights," *New York Times,* May 2, 2018.

42. David Stout, "FBI Head Admits Mistakes in Use of Security Act," *New York Times,* March 10, 2007, p. A1; "FBI Underreported Patriot Act Use," *Wall Street Journal,* March 9, 2007, p. 1.

43. Steve Lohr, "Microsoft Sues Justice Department to Protest Electronic Gag Order Statute," *New York Times,* April 14, 2016.

Chapter 16

1. Machel Wines and Sarah Cohen, "Police Killings Rise Slightly, Though Increased Focus May Suggest Otherwise," *New York Times,* April 30, 2015, http://www.nytimes.com/2015/05/01/us/no-sharp-rise-seen-in-police-killings-though-increased-focus-may-suggest--otherwise.html. For statistics on fatal shootings by the police—in the vast number of cases, it should be noted, the people who were shot had lethal weapons when they were confronted by the police—see the data base and graphics at "Fatal Force," *Washington Post online,* https://www.washingtonpost.com/graphics/national/police-shootings-2017. The data at this site are updated annually.

2. Jaeah Lee, "Exactly How Often Do Police Shoot Unarmed Black Men?" *Mother Jones,* August 15, 2014, http://www.motherjones.com/politics/2014/08/police-shootings-michael-brown-ferguson-black-men.

3. U.S. Department of Justice, "Department of Justice Report Regarding the Criminal Investigation into the Shooting Death of Michael Brown by Ferguson, Missouri Police Officer Darren Wilson," March 4, 2015, http://www.justice.gov/sites/default/files/opa/press-releases/attachments/2015/03/04/doj_report_on_shooting_of_michael_brown_1.pdf.

4. "Schools in U.S. Growing More Separate, Still Unequal," The UCLA Civil Rights Project, May 16, 2014, http:// www.universityofcalifornia.edu/news/schools-us-growing-more-separate-still-unequal. Also see "Fifty Years After Martin Luther King's Death: A Divided America," *The Economist,* April 4, 2018.

5. Nate Silver, "The Most Diverse Cities Are Often the Most Segregated," *FiveThirtyEight,* May 1, 2015, http://fivethir-tyeight.com/features/the-most-diverse-cities-are-often-the-most-segregated; and "Fifty Years After Martin Luther King's Death."

6. "Ferguson Highlights Deep Divisions Between Blacks and Whites in America," Pew Research Center, November 26, 2014, http://www.pewresearch.org/fact-tank/2014/11/26 /ferguson-highlights-deep-divisions-between-blacks-and -whites-in-america.

7. Lucius J. Barker, Twiley W. Barker Jr., Michael W. Combs, Kevin L. Lyles, and H. W. Perry Jr., *Civil Liberties and the Constitution,* 9th ed. (New York: Pearson, 2011), pp. 446–447; Richard H. Fallon, *The Dynamic Constitution: An Introduction to Constitutional Law* (New York: Cambridge University Press, 2004), pp. 109–110; and John C. Domino, *Civil Rights and Liberties in the 21st Century,* 3rd ed. (New York: Pearson, 2010), pp. 2–3.

8. James MacGregor Burns and Stewart Burns, *A People's Charter: The Pursuit of Rights in America* (New York: Knopf, 1991), p. 37.

9. On why the courts were such an attractive target for people seeking to expand civil rights, see Charles R. Epp, "The Courts and the Rights Revolution," in *The Judicial Branch,* eds. Kermit L. Hall and Kevin T. McGuire (New York: Oxford University Press, 2005).

10. Richard Rothstein, *The Color of Law: A Forgotten History of How Our Government Segregated America* (New York: Liveright-W.W. Norton, 2017).

11. Douglass Massey and Nancy Denton, *American Apartheid: Segregation and the Making of the Underclass* (Cambridge, MA: Harvard University Press, 1998).

12. William H. Chafe, *The Unfinished Journey: America Since World War II* (New York: Oxford University Press, 1986), p. 149.

13. Fallon, *Dynamic Constitution,* pp. 118–120.

14. *Ibid.,* pp. 119–122. See also Lee Epstein and Thomas G. Walker, *Rights, Liberty, and Justice* (Washington, DC: CQ Press, 2010), pp. 593–601.

15. Domino, *Civil Rights and Liberties,* p. 297; Chafe, *Unfinished Journey,* pp. 79–110.

16. Epp, "Courts and the Rights Revolution."

17. "Black America," *The Economist,* August 24, 2013, www .economist.com/news/briefing/21584003.

18. Wendy Underhill, "Voter Identification Laws | Voter ID Laws," National Conference of State Legislatures, http:// www.ncsl.org/research/elections-and-campaigns/voter-id .aspx.

19. Brian Lyman, "Alabama Will Reopen Closed DMV Offices in Black Counties," *Governing Magazine Web Site,* October 20, 2015, www.governing.com. Governor Robert Bentley, responding to the national outcry over this change, later allowed these rural motor vehicle offices to reopen for one day a month.

20. Political scientists have not reached a consensus on whether or to what degree state Voter ID laws suppress turnout among racial and ethnic minorities or lower income Americans. See, for example, Zoltan Hajnal, Nazita Lajevardi, and Lindsay Nielson, "Voter Identification Laws and the Suppression of Minority Votes," *Journal of Politics* 79, no. 2 (January 5, 2017), pp. 363–379; and Justin Grimmer, Eitan Hersh, Marc Meredith, Jonathan Mummolo, and Clayton Nall, "Obstacles to Estimating Voter ID Laws' Effect on Turnout," *Journal of Politics* (April 18, 2018), https://www.journals.uchicago.edu/doi/abs/10.1086/696618.

21. "On Views of Race and Inequality, Blacks and Whites Are Worlds Apart," Pew Research Center, June 27, 2016, http:// www.pewsocialtrends.org/2016/06/27/on-views-of-race-and-inequality-blacks-and-whites-are-worlds-apart.

22. Pew Research Social & Demographic Trends, "King's Dream Remains an Elusive Goal: Many Americans See Racial Disparities," Pew Research Center, August 22, 2013, http:// www.pewsocialtrends.org/2013/08/22/kings -dream-remains-an-elusive-goal-many-americans-see-racial -disparities. These numbers have been confirmed in a number of subsequent surveys. See, for example, Giovanni Russonello, "Race Relations Are at Lowest Point in Obama Presidency, Poll Finds," July 13, 2016, https://www.nytimes .com/2016/07/14/us/most-americans-hold-grim-view -of-race-relations-poll-finds.html. For confirmation of practices by police and other public officials contributing to the development of these attitudes, see *Investigation of the Baltimore City Police Department* (Washington, DC: The U.S. Department of Justice, Civil Rights Division, August 10, 2016).

23. Federal Bureau of Investigation, "Uniform Crime Reports, 2014," https://www.fbi.gov/about-us/cjis/ucr/ucr.

24. Peter Zimroth, "Federal Monitor Says NYPD Faces Challenge Putting Stop-Frisk Changes into Practice," *CBSNewYork/AP,* February 16, 2016, http://newyork. cbslocal.com/2016/02/16/nypd-stop-frisk-policy-changes -practice. There is evidence to suggest, moreover, that police in New York have been systematically under-reporting "stops." See "Federal Monitor Submits Status Report in Court-Ordered NYPD Stop-and-Frisk Reforms, Advocates Raise Concerns," *The Center for Constitutional Rights,* December 13, 2017, https://ccrjustice.org /home/press-center/press-releases/federal-monitor -submits-status-report-court-ordered-nypd-stop-and.

25. Fernanda Santos, "University of Arizona Students Hurl Insults, and Litter, at Mosque in Tucson," *New York Times,* February 16, 2016, http://www.nytimes. com/2016/02/17/us/mosque-near-university-of-arizona-endures-scorn-of-students-next-door.html? smprod=nytcore-ipad&smid=nytcore-ipad-share.

26. Michael Lipka, "Muslims and Islam: Key Findings in the U.S. and Around the World," Pew Research Center, August 9, 2017, http://www.pewresearch.org/fact-tank/ 2017/08/09/muslims-and-islam-key-findings-in -the-u-s-and-around-the-world.

27. This section is based on Richard D. Kahlenberg, *The Remedy: Class, Race, and Affirmative Action* (New York: Basic Books, 1996); and Fallon, *Dynamic Constitution*, ch. 5.

28. Ira Katznelson, *When Affirmative Action Was White: An Untold Story of Racial Inequality in Twentieth-Century America* (New York: Norton, 2005), pp. 145–149.

29. Barker et al., *Civil Liberties and the Constitution*, pp. 514–517.

30. Katznelson, *When Affirmative Action*.

31. "Black America," *Economist*, August 24, 2013, p. 27.

32. Martin Gilens, Paul M. Sniderman, and James H. Kuklinski, "Affirmative Action and the Politics of Realignment," *British Journal of Political Science* 28 (January 1998), pp. 159–184; Jack Citrin, David O. Sears, Christopher Muste, and Cara Wong, "Multiculturalism in American Public Opinion," *British Journal of Political Science* 31 (2001), pp. 247–275; and Drew DeSilver, "As Supreme Court Defers Affirmative Action Ruling, Deep Divides Persist," *Fact Tank* (blog), Pew Research Center, June 24, 2013, http://www.pewresearch.org/fact-tank/2013/06/24/as-supreme-court-defers-affirmative-action-ruling-deep-divides-persist.

33. DeSilver, "As Supreme Court Defers Affirmative Action"; "Public Backs Affirmative Action, But Not Minority Preferences," Pew Research Center, June 2, 2009, http://www.pewresearch.org/2009/06/02/public-backs-affirmative-action-but-not-minority-preferences/; Pew Research Center for the People & the Press, "Trends in Political Values and Core Attitudes: 1987–2007," Pew Research Center, March 22, 2007, http://www.people-press.org/2007/03/22/trends-in-political-values-and-core-attitudes-1987-2007.

34. George M. Fredrickson, "Still Separate and Unequal," *New York Review of Books*, November 17, 2005, p. 13.

35. *Fisher v. University of Texas at Austin* (2016).

36. A. Judith Baer and Leslie Friedman Goldstein, *The Constitutional and Legal Rights of Women* (Belmont, CA: Roxbury Publishing, 2006); Chafe, *Unfinished Journey*; Barbara Sinclair Deckard, *The Women's Movement* (New York: Harper and Row, 1975); Ethel Klein, *Gender Politics* (Cambridge, MA: Harvard University Press, 1984), ch. 2; and J. Freeman, *Politics of Women's Liberation* (New York: McKay, 1975).

37. "Women CEOs of the Fortune 1000," Catalyst.org, February 3, 2016, http://www.catalyst.org/knowledge/women-ceos-fortune-1000.

38. See Epp, "Courts and the Rights Revolution"; Fallon, *Dynamic Constitution*, pp. 129–133; and Barker et al., *Civil Liberties and the Constitution*, pp. 689–691.

39. Epstein and Walker, *Rights, Liberties, and Justice*, p. 629.

40. Caitlin Peterkin, "Male-Female Pay Gap Persists and Starts Early, Study Finds," *Chronicle of Higher Education*, October, 24, 2012, http://chronicle.com/article/Male-Female-Pay-Gap-Persists/135270. For sharply conflicting views on the seriousness of the wage gap, see Marcia Greenberger's testimony on the Paycheck Fairness Act before the House Committee on Education and Labor on July 11, 2007, at http://www.nwlc.org/sites/default/files/pdfs/071107marcia-greenbergertestimony.pdf, and Barbara Berish Brown's testimony before the Senate Committee on Health, Labor and Pensions on April 12, 2007, at http://www.help.senate.gov/imo/media/doc/Brown4.pdf.

41. For a compelling introduction to "ageism" and its growth in an economy and culture tilted toward youth, see Tad Friend, "Why Ageism Never Gets Old," *New Yorker*, November 2017, http://www.pewresearch.org/fact-tank/2017/06/13/5-key-findings-about-lgbt-american.

42. Linda Greenhouse, "Justices Give the States Immunity from Suits by Disabled Workers," *New York Times*, February 22, 2001.

43. "5 Key Findings About LGBT Americans," Pew Research Center, survey results from June 13, 2017, http://www.pewresearch.org/fact-tank/2017/06/13/5-key-findings-about-lgbt-americans.

44. Supreme Court of the United States, Slip Opinion, *Obergefell et al. v. Hodges, Director, Ohio Department of Health, et al.*, No. 14–556, Argued April 28, 2015—Decided June 26, 2015, www.supremecourt.gov/opinions/14pdf/14-556_3204.pdf.

45. "Gay and Lesbian Rights," *Gallup Historical Statistics*, http://www.gallup.com/poll/1651/Gay-Lesbian-Rights.aspx.

46. "5 Key Findings About LGBT Americans," Pew Research Center, survey results from June 13, 2017, http://www.pewresearch.org/fact-tank/2017/06/13/5-key-findings-about-lgbt-americans.

47. "Gay and Lesbian Rights," *Gallup Historical Statistics*.

48. "Growing Support Across Generations for Same-Sex Marriage," Pew Research Center Survey, May 12–18, 2015, http://www.pewresearch.org/fact-tank/2015/06/26/same-sex-marriage.

49. Pew Research Social & Demographic Trends, "A Survey of LGBT Americans," Pew Research Center, June 13, 2013, http://www.pewsocialtrends.org/2013/06/13/a-survey-of-lgbt-americans/9.

Chapter 17

1. Alan H. Lockwood, "How the Clean Air Act Has Saved $22 Trillion in Health Care Costs," *Atlantic*, September 7, 2012, https://www.theatlantic.com/health/archive/2012/09/how-the-clean-air-act-has-saved-22-trillion-in-health-care-costs/262071; United States Environmental Protection Agency, "National Water Quality Inventory: Report to Congress," 2004 Reporting Cycle, January 2009, https://www.epa.gov/sites/production/files/2015-09/documents/2009_01_22_305b_2004report_2004_305breport.pdf.

2. Jonathan L. Ramseur and James E. McCarthy, "EPA's Clean Power Plan: Highlights of the Final Rule," Congressional Research Service, September 27, 2016, https://fas.org/sgp/crs/misc/R44145.pdf.

3. Marianne Lavelle, "Here Are 9 Obama Environmental Regulations in Trump's Crosshairs," *Inside Climate News*, November 22, 2016, https://insideclimatenews.org/news/22112016/donald-trump-obama-environmental-regulations-deregulation-epa.

4. Eric Lipton and Danielle Ivory, "Under Trump, EPA Has Slowed Actions Against Polluters, and Put Limits on Enforcement Officers," *New York Times,* December 10, 2017, https://www.nytimes.com/2017/12/10/us/politics/pollution-epa-regulations.html; Coral Davenport and Hiroko Tabuchi, "EPA Prepares to Roll Back Rules Requiring Cars to Be Cleaner and More Efficient," *New York Times,* March 29, 2018, https://www.nytimes.com/2018/03/29/climate/epa-cafe-auto-pollution-rollback.html; "Climate Deregulation Tracker," Columbia Law School Sabin Center for Climate Change Law, http://columbiaclimatelaw.com/climate-deregulation-tracker/epa-issues-advance-notice-of-proposed-rulemaking-to-replace-clean-power-plan.

5. Robert S. Erikson and Kent L. Tedin, *American Public Opinion* (New York: Longman, 2011), pp. 121–122.

6. Fred C. Pampel, *Age, Class, Politics, and the Welfare State* (New York: Cambridge University Press, 1989), p. 16; and Harold Wilensky, *The Welfare State and Equality* (Berkeley, CA: University of California Press, 1975).

7. Robert E. Goodin, "Reasons for Welfare," in *Responsibility, Rights, and Welfare: The Theory of the Welfare State,* ed. J. Donald Moon (Boulder, CO: Westview Press, 1988); and Wilensky, *Welfare State and Equality.* Also see Clark Kerr, John T. Dunlop, Frederick H. Harbison, and Charles A. Myers, *Industrialism and Industrial Man* (New York: Oxford University Press, 1964).

8. Dean Baker and Kevin Hassett, "The Human Disaster of Unemployment," *New York Times,* May 12, 2012.

9. This discussion is based largely on B. Guy Peters, *American Public Policy: Promise and Performance,* 8th ed. (New York: CQ Press, 2010), pp. 202–213.

10. William J. Baumol, Robert E. Litan, and Carl J. Schramm, *Good Capitalism, Bad Capitalism, and the Economics of Growth and Prosperity* (New Haven, CT: Yale University Press, 2007), ch. 2; and Gregg Easterbrook, *The Progress Paradox* (New York: Random House, 2003).

11. Maurice Obstfeld, "Targeting Specific Trade Deficits Is a Game of Whack-a-Mole," *Financial Times,* April 22, 2018, https://www.ft.com/content/1cbc63c4-432c-11e8-97ce-ea0c2bf34a0b.

12. Michael Kunzelman and Chevel Johnson, "Court Upholds Approval of BP Oil Spill Settlement," Associated Press, January 10, 2014.

13. Sharon Terlep, "Target at Post-Bailout GM: Earning $10 Billion a Year," *Wall Street Journal,* February 6, 2012.

14. Zachary Karabell, "Does Government Matter?" *Bloomberg Businessweek,* July 4–July 10, 2011, pp. 10–11.

15. William Greider, *Secrets of the Temple: How the Federal Reserve Runs the Country* (New York: Simon and Schuster, 1989).

16. See David Coen, Wyn Grant, and Graham Wilson, "Political Science: Perspectives on Business and Government," in *The Oxford Handbook of Business and Government,* eds. David Coen, Wyn Grant, and Graham Wilson (New York: Oxford University Press, 2010), pp. 20–24.

17. Paul Krugman, "How the Case for Austerity Has Crumbled," *New York Review of Books,* June 6, 2013.

18. John Cassidy, *How Markets Fail: The Logic of Economic Calamities* (New York: Farrar, Straus and Giroux, 2009).

19. Roger H. Davidson, Walter J. Oleszek, and Frances E. Lee, *Congress and Its Members,* 13th ed. (Washington, DC: CQ Press, 2012); Allen Schick, *The Federal Budget: Politics, Policy, Process* (Washington, DC: Brookings Institution Press, 2008).

20. William A. Niskanen, *Bureaucracy and Representative Government* (Chicago: Aldine, 1971).

21. For a concise and stimulating discussion of forms of taxation and their effects, as well as the politics surrounding them, see B. Guy Peters, "Tax Policy," in *Handbook of Public Policy,* eds. B. Guy Peters and Jon Pierre (Thousand Oaks, CA: Sage, 2006), pp. 281–292; and Bruce Bartlett, *The Benefit and the Burden* (New York: Simon & Schuster, 2012).

22. Peters, B. Guy, "Tax Policy," in Handbook of Public Policy, eds. B. Guy Peters and Jon Pierre (Thousand Oaks, CA: Sage, 2006), pp. 281–292.

23. Congressional Budget Office, *The Distribution of Household Income and Federal Taxes, 2011* (Washington, DC: Congressional Budget Office, December 4, 2013). (2014 is the most recent year in which Congressional Budget Office released an analysis of overall tax burdens. Tax Policy Center, Urban Institute and Brookings Institution, "T16-0094—Average Effective Federal Tax Rates—All Tax Units by Expanded Cash Income Percentile, 2017," https://www.taxpolicycenter.org/model-estimates/baseline-average-effective-tax-rates-july-2016/t16-0094-average-effective-federal).

24. "The Budget and Economic Outlook for 2018–2028," Congressional Budget Office, April 2018, https://www.cbo.gov/system/files/115th-congress-2017-2018/reports/53651-outlook.pdf.

25. Paul Krugman, "Addicted to the Apocalypse," *New York Times,* October 24, 2013.

26. Jackie Calms, "Obama's Deficit Dilemma," *New York Times,* February 27, 2012, https://www.nytimes.com/2012/02/27/us/politics/obamas-unacknowledged-debt-to-bowles-simpson-plan.html; Ezra Klein, "The Reason the White House Didn't Embrace Simpson-Bowles," *Washington Post,* February 27, 2012, https://www.washingtonpost.com/blogs/ezra-klein/post/the-reason-the-white-house-didnt-embrace-simpson-bowles/2011/08/25/gIQAq1j2dR_blog.html.

27. David Leonhardt, "In Greek Debt Crisis, Some See Parallels to U.S.," *New York Times,* May 12, 2010.

28. Pew Research Center for the People & the Press, "Public Support for Environmental Regulations Varies by State," February 26, 2016, Pew Research Center, http://www.pewresearch.org/fact-tank/2016/02/25/public-support-for-environmental-regulations-varies-by-state; Samantha Smith, "Public Remains Divided Over Role of Government in Financial Regulation," Pew Research Center, March 2, 2017, http://www.pewresearch.org/fact-tank/2016/02/25/public-support-for-environmental-regulations-varies-by-s.

29. George J. Stigler, "The Theory of Economic Regulation," *Bell Journal* 2 (Spring 1971), pp. 3–21. See also Gabriel Kolko, *The Triumph of Conservatism* (Chicago: Quadrangle, 1967); and James Weinstein, *The Corporate Ideal in the Liberal State* (Boston: Beacon Press, 1968).

30. See Marc Allen Eisner, *Regulatory Politics in Transition* (Baltimore: Johns Hopkins University Press, 2000); Richard Harris and Sidney Milkis, *The Politics of Regulatory Change* (New York: Oxford University Press, 1989); and Michael Moran, "The Rise of the Regulatory State," in *The Oxford Handbook of Business and Government,* eds. Coen, Grant, and Wilson, pp. 383–403. Also see Gary Gerstle, *Liberty and Coercion: The Paradox of American Government from the Founding to the Present* (Princeton, NJ: Princeton University Press, 2015).

31. Frances Fox Piven and Richard A. Cloward, *Poor People's Movements* (New York: Vintage, 1979).

32. Marver H. Bernstein, *Regulation by Independent Commission* (Princeton, NJ: Princeton University Press, 1955); Grant McConnell, *Private Power and American Democracy* (New York: Vintage Books, 1966); and Theodore J. Lowi, *The End of Liberalism* (New York: Norton, 1979).

33. David Vogel, *Fluctuating Fortunes: The Political Power of Business in the United States* (New York: Basic Books, 1989), pp. 59, 112.

34. James Buchanan and Gordon Tullock, "Polluters, Profits and Political Responses: Direct Control Versus Taxes," *American Economic Review* 65 (1975), pp. 139–147; L. Lave, *The Strategy of Social Regulation* (Washington, DC: Brookings Institution Press, 1981); and Murray Weidenbaum, *The Costs of Government Regulation of Business* (Washington, DC: Joint Economic Committee of Congress, 1978).

35. Thomas Byrne Edsall, *The New Politics of Inequality* (New York: Norton, 1984); Vogel, *Fluctuating Fortunes*; Kevin P. Phillips, *The Politics of Rich and Poor: Wealth and the American Electorate in the Reagan Aftermath* (New York: Random House, 1990); and Thomas Ferguson and Joel Rogers, *Right Turn: The Decline of the Democrats and the Future of American Politics* (New York: Farrar, Straus & Giroux, 1986).

36. Catherine Rampell, "Lax Oversight Caused Crisis, Bernanke Says," *New York Times,* January 6, 2001.

37. For accessible descriptions of this shadow banking system and its risky practices, see Simon Johnson and James Kwak, *13 Bankers: The Wall Street Takeover and the Next Financial Meltdown* (New York: Pantheon, 2010); Michael Lewis, *The Big Short: Inside the Doomsday Machine* (New York: Norton, 2010); and Roger Lowenstein, *The End of Wall Street* (New York: Penguin Press, 2010).

38. "White House Historical Tables, Table 3.1—Outlays by Superfunction and Function: 1940–2023," https://www .whitehouse.gov/wp-content/uploads/2018/02 /hist03z1-fy2019.xlsx.

39. Theodore R. K. Marmor, Jerry L. Mashaw, and Philip L. Harvey, *America's Misunderstood Welfare State* (New York: HarperCollins, 1990), ch. 4; Carmen DeNavas-Walt, Bernadette D. Proctor, Jessica C. Smith, *Income, Poverty, and Health Insurance Coverage in the United States: 2012* (Washington, DC: U.S. Census Bureau, September 2013). Center on Budget and Policy Priorities, "Policy Basics: Top Ten Facts About Social Security," August 13, 2015, http:// www.cbpp.org/research/social-security/policy-basics -top-ten-facts-about-social-security.

40. Social Security Administration, "Income of Population 55 or Older, 2012," April 2016, https://www.ssa.gov/policy /docs/statcomps/income_pop55/index.html.

41. Center on Budget and Policy Priorities, "Policy Basics."

42. Social Security Administration, *The 2017 OASDI Trustees Report* (Washington, DC: Social Security Administration, 2017).

43. *The Social Security Fix-It Book* (Boston: Boston College Center for Retirement Research, 2010).

44. Benjamin I. Page and James R. Simmons, *What Government Can Do: Dealing with Poverty and Inequality* (Chicago: The University of Chicago Press, 2000), ch. 3; Edmund L. Andrews, "4 Ways That Might Save the Government Trillions," *New York Times,* February 4, 2006; and Peters, *American Public Policy*, pp. 300–311.

45. Robert Pear, "AARP Opposed Bush Plan to Reduce Social Security with Private Accounts," *New York Times,* November 12, 2004. William A. Galston, "Why the 2005 Social Security Initiative Failed, and What It Means for the Future," *Brookings,* September 21, 2007, https://www .brookings.edu/research/why-the-2005-social-security -initiative-failed-and-what-it-means-for-the-future.

46. Centers for Medicare and Medicaid Services, "Medicare Enrollment Dashboard," https://www.cms.gov /Research-Statistics-Data-and-Systems/Statistics-Trends -and-Reports/CMSProgramStatistics/Dashboard.html.

47. Diana M. DiNitto, *Social Welfare: Politics and Public Policy,* 7th ed. (New York: Pearson, 2010), pp. 310–318.

48. B. Guy Peters, *American Public Policy,* 9th ed. (Thousand Oaks, California: CQ Press), p. 327.

49. Pew Research Center, "Majorities Say Government Does Too Little for Older People, the Poor and the Middle Class," January 30, 2018, http://www.people-press .org/2018/01/30/majorities-say-government-does-too -little-for-older-people-the-poor-and-the-middle-class.

50. Hugh Heclo, "The Political Foundations of Anti-Poverty Policy," in *Fighting Poverty: What Works and What Doesn't?* eds. Sheldon Danziger and Daniel Weinberg (Cambridge, MA: Harvard University Press, 1986); and Fay Lomax Cook and Edith J. Barrett, *Support for the American Welfare State: The Views of Congress and the Public* (New York: HarperCollins, 1990), ch. 4.

51. Joel F. Handler and Yeheskel Hasenfeld, *Blame Welfare, Ignore Poverty and Inequality* (Cambridge, UK: Cambridge University Press, 2007); and Martin Gilens, *Why Americans Hate Welfare: Race, Media, and the Politics of Antipoverty Policy* (Chicago: The University of Chicago Press, 1999).

52. Congressional Budget Office, "Growth in Means-Tested Programs and Tax Credits for Low-Income Households," February 11, 2013, https://www.cbo.gov/publication/43934.

53. "From Welfare to Work," *Economist,* July 29, 2006, pp. 27–30; Lauren Etter, "Welfare Reform: Ten Years Later," *Wall Street Journal,* August 26, 2006; and Robert Pear and Erik Eckholm, "A Decade After Welfare Reform," *New York Times,* August 21, 2006.

54. Ife Floyd, Ladonna Pavettie, and Liz Schott, "TANF Reaching Few Poor Families," Center on Budget and Policy Priorities, December 13, 2017, https://www.cbpp.org /research/family-income-support/tanf-reaching-few- poor-families.

55. Jordan Weissman, "The Failure of Welfare Reform," *Slate,* June 1, 2016, http://www.slate.com/articles/news_and_politics/moneybox/2016/06/how_welfare_reform_failed.html; Liz Schott, Ife Floyd, and Ashley Burbside, "Policy Brief: How States Use Funds Under the TANF Block Grant," Center on Budget and Policy Priorities, April 3, 2018, https://www.cbpp.org/research/family-income-support/policy-brief-how-states-use-funds-under-the-tanf-block-grant.

56. United States Department of Agriculture, "Supplemental Nutrition Assistance Program (SNAP)," SNAP Tables, https://www.fns.usda.gov/pd/supplemental-nutrition-assistance-program-snap.

57. Center on Budget and Policy Priorities, "Chart Book: SNAP Helps Struggling Families Put Food on the Table," February 14, 2018, https://www.cbpp.org/research/food-assistance/chart-book-snap-helps-struggling-families-put-food-on-the-table.

58. The Henry J. Kaiser Family Foundation, "Total Monthly Medicaid and CHIP Enrollment," December 2015, http://kff.org/health-reform/state-indicator/total-monthly-medicaid-and-chip-enrollment.

59. Center on Budget and Policy Priorities, "Policy Basics: Introduction to Medicaid," June 19, 2015, http://www.cbpp.org/research/health/policy-basics-introduction-to-medicaid.

60. The Henry J. Kaiser Family Foundation, "Federal and State Share of Medicaid Spending: FY2014," http://kff.org/medicaid/state-indicator/federalstate-share-of-spending.

61. Carmen DeNavas-Walt, Bernadette D. Proctor, and Jessica C. Smith, *Income, Poverty, and Health Insurance Coverage in the United States: 2010* (Washington, DC: U.S. Census Bureau, September 2011).

62. National Conference of State Legislatures, "Tax Credits for Working Families: Earned Income Tax Credit (EITC)," April 17, 2018, http://www.ncsl.org/research/labor-and-employment/earned-income-tax-credits-for-working-families.aspx.

63. Center on Budget and Policy Priorities, "Policy Basics: The Earned Income Tax Credit," January 15, 2016, http://www.cbpp.org/research/federal-tax/policy-basics-the-earned-income-tax-credit; Peters, *American Public Policy,* p. 320; and Christopher Howard, *The Hidden Welfare State: Tax Expenditures and Social Policy in the United States* (Princeton, NJ: Princeton University Press, 1999), ch. 3. Internal Revenue Service, "Due I Qualify for EITC?" https://www.irs.gov/credits-deductions/individuals/earned-income-tax-credit/do-i-qualify-for-earned-income-tax-credit-eitc.

64. U.S. Census Bureau, "How Census Measures Poverty," *Measuring America,* http://www.census.gov/how/infographics/poverty_measure-how.html.

65. US Department of Health and Human Services, "US Federal Poverty Guidelines Used to Determine Financial Eligibility for Certain Programs," https://aspe.hhs.gov/poverty-guidelines.

66. Mark Greenberg, "It's Time for a Better Poverty Measure," Center for American Progress, August 25, 2009, https://aspe.hhs.gov/poverty-guidelines.

67. Liana Fox, "The Supplemental Poverty Measure: 2016," The United States Census Bureau, September 2017, https://www.census.gov/content/dam/Census/library/publications/2017/demo/p60-261.pdf.

68. Christiano Lima, "Trump Boasts of Individual Mandate Repeal in GOP Tax Bill," *Politico,* December 20, 2017, https://www.politico.com/story/2017/12/20/trump-individual-mandate-repeal-tax-bill-308286.

69. John Dickerson, "System Malfunction: How Politics, Partisanship, and Spin Doomed healthcare.gov," *Slate,* November 4, 2013, http://www.slate.com/articles/news_and_politics/politics/2013/11/healthcare_gov_doomed_by_partisanship_and_spin_obamacare_s_failed_launch.html.

70. Kaiser Family Foundation, "Kaiser Health Tracking Poll: The Public's Views on the ACA," May 10, 2018, https://www.kff.org/interactive/kaiser-health-tracking-poll-the-publics-views-on-the-aca.

71. Gosta Esping-Andersen, "The Three Political Economies of the Welfare State," *Canadian Review of Sociology and Anthropology* 26 (1989), pp. 10–36; and Jonas Pontusson, "The American Welfare State in Comparative Perspective," *Perspectives on Politics* 4, no. 2 (June 2006), pp. 315–326.

72. Andrea Brandolini and Timothy M. Smeeding, "Patterns of Economic Inequality in Western Democracies: Some Facts on Levels and Trends," *PS* 39, no. 1 (January 2006), pp. 21–26; and Lee Kenworthy and Jonas Pontusson, "Rising Inequality and the Politics of Redistribution in Affluent Countries," *Perspectives on Politics* 3, no. 3 (September 2005), pp. 449–472; Thomas Piketty, *Capital in the Twenty-First Century* (Cambridge, MA: Harvard University Press, 2014).

73. Gary Gerstle, *Liberty and Coercion: The Paradox of American Government from the Founding to the Present* (Princeton, NJ: Princeton University Press, 2017).

74. Alberto Alesina and Edward L. Glaeser, *Fighting Poverty in the US and Europe: A World of Difference* (New York: Oxford University Press, 2004); and Nathan Glazer, *The Limits of Social Policy* (Cambridge, MA: Harvard University Press, 1988), pp. 187–188. Also see W. Sombart, *Why There Is No Socialism in the United States* (Armonk, NY: M. E. Sharpe, 1976).

75. Douglas S. Massey, "Globalization and Inequality: Explaining American Exceptionalism," *European Sociological Review* 25, no. 1 (2009), pp. 9–23.

76. Gilens, *Why Americans Hate Welfare*; and Jeff Manza, "Race and the Underdevelopment of the American Welfare State," *Theory and Society* 29 (2000), pp. 819–832. See also Alesina and Glaeser, *Fighting Poverty in the US and Europe*; Carol A. Horton, *Race and the Making of American Liberalism* (New York: Oxford University Press, 2005); and Desmond S. King and Rogers M. Smith, *Still a House Divided: Race and Politics in Obama's America* (Princeton, NJ: Princeton University Press, 2011).

77. Martin Gilens, "'Race Coding' and White Opposition to Welfare," *American Political Science Review* 90, no. 3 (1996), pp. 593–604.

78. Wilensky, *Welfare State and Equality;* John Micklethwait and Adrian Wooldridge, *The Right Nation: Conservative Power*

in America (New York: Penguin Press, 2004); and Handler and Hasenfeld, *Blame Welfare.*

79. Koen Caminada and Megan C. Martin, "Differences in Anti-Poverty Approaches in Europe and the United States," *Poverty and Public Policy* 3, no. 2 (2011), pp. 1–14.

80. Francis G. Castles, *The Impact of Parties: Politics and Policies in Democratic Capitalist States* (Newbury Park, CA: Sage, 1982); Gosta Esping-Andersen, *Politics Against Markets* (Princeton, NJ: Princeton University Press, 1985); Walter Korpi, *The Democratic Class Struggle* (New York: Routledge, 1983); and John Stephens, *The Transition from Capitalism to Socialism* (London: Macmillan, 1979).

81. U.S. Department of Labor, Bureau of Labor Statistics, "Union Members—2015," January 28, 2017, https://www.bls.gov/news.release/union2.t01.htm; Gerald Mayer, "Union Membership Trends in the United States," *CRS Report for Congress,* RL 32553, August 31, 2004.

82. Martin Gillens, *Affluence and Influence: Economic Inequality and Political Power in America* (Princeton: Princeton University Press, 2012); Benjamin I. Page and Martin Gilens, *Democracy in America?: What Has Gone Wrong and What We Can Do About It* (Chicago: University of Chicago Press, 2017).

Chapter 18

1. See Megan Specia, "How Syria's Death Toll Is Lost in the Fog of War," *New York Times,* April 13, 2018, https://www.nytimes.com/2018/04/13/world/middleeast/syria-death-toll.html, on the difficulties of calculating war deaths in a complex and brutal civil war that involves not only the Syrian government but a set of ever-changing rebel groups and countries and groups with a stake in the future of the region. For estimates of internally displaced persons and refugees, see "Syria," Internally Displaced Monitoring Center, Geneva Switzerland, http://www.internal-displacement.org/countries/syria.

2. Benjamin I. Page and Marshall M. Bouton, *The Foreign Policy Disconnect: What Americans Want From Our Leaders But Don't Get* (Chicago: University of Chicago Press, 2006).

3. For opposing views on just how much America's relative advantage has slipped or grown more pronounced, see, for the former view, Fareed Zakaria, *The Post-American World* (New York: Norton, 2008). For the latter view, see Robert Kagan, *The World America Made* (New York: Knopf, 2012).

4. Statistics in this paragraph are from "Economy Watch, Econ Stats: The Economic Statistics and Indicators Database," *Economy Watch,* http://www.economywatch.com/economic-statistics; and the World Bank, https://data.worldbank.org/indicator/NY.GDP.MKTP.CD?end=2016&start=2016&view=map.

5. Arvind Subramanian, quoted in Patrick Foulis, "The Sticky Superpower," *Economist,* October 23, 2015, http://www.economist.com/econ2015.

6. Best Global Brands, *Interbrand,* 2017, http://interbrand.com/best-brands/best-global-brands/2017/ranking.

7. Foulis, "The Sticky Superpower."

8. Global Firepower (GFP), http://www.globalfirepower.com. This site gathers data from the CIA Factbook and other publically available sources. It calculates country standings on conventional war-making capacities and does not include nuclear weapons.

9. "Naval Strength," *Global Firepower,* http://www.globalfirepower.com/navy-ships.asp.

10. "Sea Power: Who Rules the Waves," *Economist,* October 17, 2015, http://www.economist.com/news/international/21674648-china-no-longer-accepts-america-should-be-asia-pacifics-dominant-naval-power-who-rules.

11. "Nuclear Weapons: Who Has What at a Glance," *Arms Control Association,* March, 2018, https://www.armscontrol.org/factsheets/Nuclearweaponswhohaswhat.

12. Chalmers Johnson, *The Sorrows of Empire: Militarism, Secrecy, and the End of the Republic* (New York: Metropolitan Books, 2004).

13. David Vine, "The United States Probably Has More Foreign Military Bases Than Any Other People, Nation, or Empire in History," *The Nation,* September 14, 2015, http://www.thenation.com/article/the-united-states-probably-has-more-foreign-military-bases-than-any-other-people-nation-or-empire-in-history. Also see Jules Dufour, "The Worldwide Network of US Military Bases," *Center for Research on Globalization,* September 20, 2015, http://www.globalresearch.ca/the-worldwide-network-of-us-military-bases/5564.

14. Bob Mason, "Who Has the Most Advanced Cyber Warfare Technology?" *Nasdaq,* October 19, 2017, https://www.nasdaq.com/article/so-who-has-the-most-advanced-cyber-warfare-technology-cm861979.

15. Eric Schmitt and Tim Arango, "Billions From U.S. Fails to Sustain Foreign Policies," *New York Times,* October 3, 2015, http://www.nytimes.com/2015/10/04/world/middleeast/uss-billions-fail-to-sustain-foreign-forces.html?action=click&pgtype=Homepage&module=first-column-region&region=top-news&WT.nav=top-news&_r=0.

16. "The Odds on a Conflict Between the Great Powers," *Economist,* January 25, 2018, https://www.economist.com/special-report/2018/01/25/the-odds-on-a-conflict-between-the-great-powers.

17. For definitions of the different forms of power in international affairs, see Joseph S. Nye, "Hard, Soft and Smart Power," in *The Oxford Handbook of Modern Diplomacy,* eds. Andrew F. Cooper, Jorge Heine, and Ramesh Thakur (New York: Oxford University Press, 2013).

18. Joseph S. Nye Jr., *Soft Power: The Means to Success in World Politics* (New York: Public Affairs Press, 2005).

19. "Rankings," *Center for World Class Universities of Shanghai Jiao Tong University* (2015), http://www.shanghairanking.com/ARWU2015.html.

20. "Soft Power Survey 2015–16," *Monocle,* 2016, .at https://monocle.com/film/affairs/soft-power-survey-2015-16.

21. Pew Research Center for the People & the Press, "War with Iraq Further Divides Global Publics," Pew Research

Center, June 3, 2003; Pew Research Center for the People & the Press, "A Year After Iraq War: Mistrust of America in Europe Ever Higher, Muslim Anger Persists," Pew Research Center, March 16, 2004, http://www.people-press.org/2004/03/16/a-year-after-iraq-war; and Pew Research Global Attitudes Project, "Global Unease with Major World Powers: Rising Environmental Concern in 47-Nation Survey," June 27, 2007, http://www.pewglobal.org/files/pdf/2007%20Pew%20Global%20Attitudes%20Report%20-%20June%2027.pdf.

22. Pew Research Global Attitudes Project, "Obama More Popular Abroad Than at Home, Global Image of U.S. Continues to Benefit," Pew Research Center, June 17, 2010, http://www.pewglobal.org/2010/06/17/obama-more-popular-abroad-than-at-home.

23. Richard Wike, Bruce Stokes, Jacob Poushter, and Janell Fetterolf, "U.S. Image Suffers as Publics Around World Question Trump's Leadership," Pew Research Center, June 26, 2017, http://www.pewglobal.org/2017/06/26/u-s-image-suffers-as-publics-around-world-question-trumps-leadership.

24. Elizabeth Redden, "Will International Students Stay Away?" Inside Higher Ed, March 13, 2017, https://www.insidehighered.com/news/2017/03/13/nearly-4-10-universities-report-drops-international-student-applications.

25. Jonathan Weisman, "At Global Economic Gathering, U.S. Primacy Is Seen as Ebbing," *New York Times*, April 17, 2015, http://www.nytimes.com/2015/04/18/business/international/at-global-economic-gathering-concerns-that-us-is-ceding-its-leadership-role.html?_r=0.

26. Steven Rattner, "Is China's Version of Capitalism Winning?" *New York Times*, March 27, 2018, https://www.nytimes.com/2018/03/27/opinion/china-economy-state-capitalism-winning.html.

27. Richard Wike, Bruce Stokes, Jacob Poushter, and Janell Ferrerolf, "U.S. Image Suffers as Publics Around the World Question Trump's Leadership," Pew Research Center press release, June 26, 2017, http://www.pewglobal.org/2017/06/26/tarnished-american-brand.

28. Melvyn P. Leffler, "Bush's Foreign Policy," *Foreign Policy* (September/October 2004), p. 23.

29. Robert O. Keohane and Joseph S. Nye Jr., *Power and Interdependence: World Politics in Transition* (Boston: Little, Brown, 1977); and Robert Gilpin, *The Political Economy of International Relations* (Princeton, NJ: Princeton University Press, 1987).

30. Michael Mandelbaum, *The Case for Goliath* (New York: Public Affairs, 2005); Niall Ferguson, *Colossus: The Rise and Fall of the American Empire* (New York: Penguin Press, 2004); and William E. Odom and Robert Dujarric, *America's Inadvertent Empire* (New Haven: Yale University Press, 2004). See also Robert Gilpin, *The Challenge of Global Capitalism: The World Economy in the 21st Century* (Princeton, NJ: Princeton University Press, 2000).

31. Bruce Drake and Carroll Doherty, "Key Findings on How Americans View the U.S. Role in the World," Pew Research Center survey press release, May 5, 2016, http://www.pewresearch.org/fact-tank/2016/05/05/key-findings-on-how-americans-view-the-u-s-role-in-the-world.

32. John Lewis Gaddis, "A Grand Strategy," *Foreign Policy* (November/December 2002), pp. 50–57; and Ivo H. Daalder and James M. Lindsay, *America Unbound: The Bush Revolution in Foreign Policy* (Washington, DC: Brookings Institution Press, 2003).

33. Roger Cohen, "Obama's Implicit Foreign Policy," *New York Times*, February 25, 2016, http://www.nytimes.com/2016/02/26/opinion/obamas-implicit-foreign-policy.html.

34. Zbigniew Brzezinski, *The Choice: Global Domination or Global Leadership* (New York: Basic Books, 2004); Al Gore, *The Path to Survival* (New York: Rodale Books, 2008); and Fareed Zakaria, *The Post-American World* (New York: Norton, re-release and update, 2012).

35. Zakaria, *Post-American World*.

36. Lamont Colucci, "Great Power Conflict: Will It Return?" *World Affairs*, January/February, 2015, http://www.worldaffairsjournal.org/article/great-power-conflict-will-it-return.

37. "What Russia Wants: From Cold War to Hot War, *Economist*, February 14, 2015, http://www.economist.com/news/briefing/21643220-russias-aggression-ukraine-part-broader-and-more-dangerous-confrontation.

38. Thomas Gibbons-Neff, "Russian Sub Activity Returns to Cold War Levels," *Washington Post*, February 4, 2016, https://www.washingtonpost.com/news/checkpoint/wp/2016/02/04/report-russian-sub-activity-returns-to-cold-war-levels.

39. Eric Schmitt and Steven Lee Myers, "NATO Refocuses on the Kremlin, It's Original Foe," *New York Times*, June 23, 2015, http://www.nytimes.com/2015/06/24/world/europe/nato-returns-its-attention-to-an-old-foe-russia.html?action=click&pgtype=Homepage&module=first-column-region&region=top-news&WT.nav=top-news; and "The Odds on a Conflict Between the Great Powers," *Economist*.

40. Martin Jacques, *When China Rules the World: The End of the Western World and the Birth of a New Order* (New York: Penguin Press, 2009); and Christopher A. Preble, "Adapting to American Decline," *New York Times*, April 21, 2018, https://www.nytimes.com/2018/04/21/opinion/sunday/adapting-to-american-decline.html.

41. Tabassum Zakaria, "U.S. Blames China, Russia for Cyber Espionage," *Reuters*, November 3, 2011. See also Sanger, "U.S. Directly Blames China's Military."

42. "Nuclear Weapons: Who Has What at a Glance," Arms Control Association.

43. *Arab Human Development Report 2016* (New York: United Nations, 2016).

44. Shibley Telhami, "The 2011 Public Opinion Poll of Jewish and Arab Citizens of Israel," Brookings Institution, December 1, 2011, http://www.brookings.edu/research/reports/2011/12/01-israel-poll-telhami; and Zogby Research Services, "ZRS Releases 2013 Israel/Palestine Poll," news release, January 30, 2014, http://www.zogbyresearchservices.com/blog/2014/1/30/israel-and-palestine-20-years-after-oslo. However, one poll in

early 2016 shows that a small but significant Palestinian majority continues to support a two-state solution though few are confident that it will happen. See "Poll: 54% of Palestinians Support a Two-State Solution," *Jerusalem Post*, March 2, 2016, http://www.jpost.com/Middle-East/Poll-54-percent-of-Palestinians-support-two-states-330637. Another recent poll shows bare majorities support a two-state solution, with support for that position lower than just a few years ago. See "Joint Israeli Palestinian Poll–56," *Policy and Survey Research*, June 2–14, 2015, http://www.pcpsr.org/en/node/611.

45. "International Trade Statistics, 2015," *World Trade Organization* (2015), Table 1.7, p. 44, https://www.wto.org/english/res_e/statis_e/its2015_e/its15_toc_e.htm.

46. See "Somewhere Over the Rainbow," *Economist*, January 26, 2008, pp. 27–29; "Liberty's Great Advance," *Economist*, June 28, 2003, pp. 5–9; Jagdish Bhagwati, *In Defense of Globalization* (New York: Oxford University Press, 2004); Jagdish Bhagwati and Marvin H. Kosters, eds., *Trade and Wages: Leveling Down Wages?* (Washington, DC: AEI Press, 1994); Martin Wolf, *Why Globalization Works* (New Haven, CT: Yale University Press, 2004); and Michael Veseth, *Globaloney: Unraveling the Myths of Globalization* (Lanham, MD: Rowman and Littlefield, 2005). Dani Rodrik, among others, disagrees. See his *Has Globalization Gone Too Far?* (Washington, DC: The Institute of International Economics, 1997). See also E. Stiglitz, *Globalization and Its Discontents* (New York: Norton, 2003).

47. "Economists Rethink Free Trade," *Businessweek*, February 11, 2008, pp. 32–34.

48. Fareed Zakaria, "Trump Is Right: China's a Trade Cheat," *Washington Post*, April 5, 2018, https://www.washingtonpost.com/opinions/global-opinions/trump-is-right-chinas-a-trade-cheat/2018/04/05/6cd69054-390f-11e8-8fd2-49fe3c675a89_story.html?utm_term=.cf271e39ada5; and "2017 Report to Congress on China's WTO Compliance," Washington, DC: United States Trade Representative, 2017, https://ustr.gov/sites/default/files/files/Press/Reports/China%202017%20WTO%20Report.pdf.

49. For the argument from a conservative point of view that trade deficits with particular countries are both unavoidable and very often a good thing for the United States, see Veronique de Rugy, "How Trump Misunderstands Trade," *New York Times*, April 10, 2018, https://www.nytimes.com/2018/04/10/opinion/trump-china-trade-deficit.html.

50. Matthew Crenson and Benjamin Ginsberg, *Presidential Power: Unchecked and Unbalanced* (New York: Norton, 2007).

51. Carol D. Leonnig, Shane Harris, and Gregg Jaffe, "Breaking with Tradition, Trump Skips President's Written Intelligence Report," *Washington Post,* February 9, 2018, https://www.washingtonpost.com/politics/breaking-with-tradition-trump-skips-presidents-written-intelligence-report-for-oral-briefings/2018/02/09/b7ba569e-0c52-11e8-95a5-c396801049ef_story.html?utm_term=.1d03b9769a2d.

52. On the gap in outlooks between American leaders and the American public on issues of foreign and national security policies, see Page with Bouton, *Foreign Policy Disconnect*.

Chapter 1   Page 1: Walter Sanders/The LIFE Picture Collection/Getty Images; 4: Tim Graham/Alamy Stock Photo; 4: Rusheng Yao/Alamy Stock Photo; 5: Morteza Nikoubazl/SIPA/Newscom; 6: James Leynse/Corbis Historical/Getty Images; 7: S. Sabawoon/epa european pressphoto agency b.v./Alamy Stock Photo; 8: Everett Collection Historical/Alamy Stock Photo; 8: Gerry Broome/AP Images; 9: Spencer Platt/Getty Images North America/Getty Images; 10: Niday Picture Library/Alamy Stock Photo

Chapter 2   Page 17: Carlos Barria/Reuters; 20: Library of Congress Rare Book and Special Collections Division Washington, D.C. 20540 USA [LC-USZ62-10658]; 20: Gift of Marian B. Maurice/National Gallery of Art; 22: Bilderbuch/Getty Images; 23: General George Washington leading the Continental Army to Valley Forge winter camp; 24: Pictorial Press Ltd/Alamy Stock Photo; 27: Shays's Mob in Possession of a Courthouse, illustration from 'The Birth of a Nation' by Thomas Wentworth Higginson, pub. in Harper's Magazine, January 1884 (engraving), Pyle, Howard (1853-1911) (after) / Private Collection/Bridgeman Images; 28: Michael Ventura/Alamy Stock Photo; 31: Library of Congress Prints and Photographs Division Washington, D.C. 20540 USA [LC-DIG-ds-05506]; 37: East View of Philadelphia, Pennsylvania, and part of Camden, New Jersey," ca. 1836. Lithograph. A. Koliner, Philadelphia. 208-PR-10E-6; 38: Library of Congress Prints and Photographs Division, Popular Graphic Arts [LC-DIG-ppmsca-30581]; 40: Mark Peterson/Corbis/Getty Images; 41: George W. Bush Presidential Library and Museum/US National Archives and Records Administration 41: White House Photo/Alamy Stock Photo

Chapter 3   Page 44: Henning Kaiser/dpa picture alliance/Alamy Stock Photo; 52: Sean Pavone/Alamy Stock Photo; 54: Alex Wong/ Getty Images News/Getty Images; 54: Andrew Harrer/Bloomberg via Getty Images; 56: Classic Image/Alamy Stock Photo; 60: Cecil Stoughton/LBJ Presidential Library; 62: B Christopher/Alamy Stock Photo; 63: White House Photo/Alamy Stock Photo; 66: Everett Collection Inc/Alamy Stock Photo; 66: Scott Olson/Getty Images News/Getty Images; 67: Haraz N. Ghanbari/AP Images; 69: Zoonar GmbH/Alamy Stock Photo

Chapter 4   Page 73: Kevin P. Casey/Bloomberg/Getty Images; 79: Seth Wenig/AP Images; 80: Ross D. Franklin/AP Images; 89: Brennan Linsley/AP Images; 90: Fabian Bimmer/Reuters; 91: Geoffrey Robinson/Alamy Stock Photo; 93: Matt Cardy/Getty Images News/Getty Images; 94: Fujifotos/The Image Works; 98: Saul Loeb/AFP/Getty Images

Chapter 5   Page 102: Hugh Van Es/AP Images; 106: SkyLine/Fotolia; 107: Bettmann/Getty Images; 109: Ramin Talaie/Getty Images News/Getty Images; 115: David Paul Morris/Bloomberg/Getty Images; 119: J.M. Giordano/SOPA Images/ZUMA Press, Inc./Alamy Stock Photo; 121: Melina Mara/The Washington Post/Getty Images; 123: Ken Cedeno/ZUMA Press, Inc./Alamy Stock Photo; 127: Jim West/Alamy Stock Photo

Chapter 6   Page 137: Romeo Gacad/AFP/Getty Images; 141: Xinhua/Alamy Stock Photo; 145: dpa picture alliance/Alamy Stock Photo; 146: Bill Pierce/The LIFE Images Collection/Getty Images; 148: Roberto Westbrook/Blend Images/Newscom; 150: Christine Nesbitt/africanpictures.net/The Image Works; 151: Alberto Pizzoli/AFP/Getty Images; 152: Mario Tama/Getty Images News/Getty Images; 154: dpa picture alliance/Alamy Stock Photo; 155: Gerardo Mora/epa european pressphoto agency b.v./Alamy Stock Photo; 161: Jim Damaske/Tampa Bay Times/AP Images

Chapter 7   Page 165: US Coast Guard Photo/Alamy Stock Photo; 169: Nawrocki/ClassicStock/Alamy Stock Photo; 172: Brian Zak/Sipa Press/AP Images; 173: Paul Damien/National Geographic/Getty Images; 175: Jason Reed/Reuters; 176: Dustin Cunningham/The Booneville Daily News/AP Images; 177: Nicholas Kamm/AFP/Getty Images; 178: Bill Clark/CQ-Roll Call Group/Getty Images; 179: Moodboard Stock Photography Ltd./Canopy/Getty Images; 181: Jose Luis Magana/AP Images; 183: Mark Reinstein/Alamy Stock Photo; 187: Chip Somodevilla/Getty Images News/Getty Images

Chapter 8   Page 188: American Press Association/Library of Congress Prints and Photographs Division Washington, D.C. 20540 USA; 202: George E. Luxton/Minnesota Historical Society; 203: Gabriel Olsen/WireImage/Getty Images ; 209: REUTERS/Alamy Stock Photo; 209: Brooks Kraft LLC/Corbis via Getty Images; 211: Emmanuel Dunand/AFP/Getty Images; 212: Janine Wiedel Photolibrary/Alamy Stock Photo; 214: Scott J. Ferrell/Congressional Quarterly/Getty Images; 215: Jill Freedman/Premium Archive/Getty Images; 217: Pictorial Press Ltd/Alamy Stock Photo; 218: Tom Watson/New York Daily News Archive/Getty Images; 219: Black Star/Alamy Stock Photo; 220: Niday Picture Library/Alamy Stock Photo

Chapter 9   Page 226: Jim West/Alamy Stock Photo; 230: Gino's Premium Images/Alamy Stock Photo; 232: Ralf-Finn Hestoft/Corbis via Getty Images; 233: Lisa Poole/AP Images; 236: Bettmann/Getty Images; 239: Chip Somodevilla/Getty Images News/Getty Images; 246: Charlie Neibergall/AP Images; 247: Richard Ellis/Alamy Stock Photo; 247: Tannen Maury/epa european pressphoto agency b.v./Alamy Stock Photo; 248: Jim West/Alamy Stock Photo; 248: Phelan M. Ebenhack/AP Images

Chapter 10   Page 256: Yaacov Dagan/Alamy Stock Photo; 262: Pete Marovich/ZUMA Press, Inc./Alamy Stock Photo; 264: Saurabh Das/AP Images; 265: Francis G. Mayer/Corbis Historical/VCG/Getty Images; 270: Eric Gay/AP Images; 273: David L Ryan/Boston Globe/Getty Images; 275: Matt Slocum/AP Images; 277: Anna Sergeeva/ZUMA Press, Inc./Alamy Stock Photo; 278: Bastiaan Slabbers/Alamy Stock Photo; 279: Bettmann/Getty Images; 279: Everett Collection Historical/Alamy Stock Photo; 284: Alex Wong/Getty Images News/Getty Images; 285: EPA/Jim Lo Scalzo/Newscom

Chapter 11   Page 294: michelmond/Alamy Stock Photo; 297: Everett Collection Inc/Alamy Stock Photo; 300: North Wind

Picture Archives/Alamy Stock Photo; 302: Nancy Pelosi/democraticleader.gov; 305: Bettmann/Getty Images; 306: © 2012 Issued by the State Board of Elections, Prepared with the assistance of the Illinois Department of Transportation; 309: ZUMA Press,Inc./Alamy Stock Photo; 312: Charles Dharapak/AP Images; 315: National Geographic Image Collection/Alamy Stock Photo; 319: Charles Dharapak/AP Images; 322: dpa picture alliance/Alamy Stock Photo; 326: Jay Mallin/Bloomberg/Getty Images

Chapter 12 Page 332: Dennis Rivera/AP Images; 335: The Metropolitan Museum of Art/Art Resource, NY.; 337: Library of Congress Prints and Photographs Division Washington, D.C. 20540 USA; 338: Everett Collection Historical/Alamy Stock Photo; 339: IraSchwartz/AP Images; 340: Ron Edmons/AP Images; 341: Archistoric/Alamy Stock Photo; 342: Paul Noth/The New Yorker Collection/The Cartoon Bank; 345: Carl Mydans/The LIFE Picture Collection/Getty Images; 346: White House Photo/Alamy Stock Photo; 347: John Dominis/The LIFE Picture Collection/Getty Images; 351: Sean Gallup/Getty Images News/Getty Images; 352: Evan Vucci/AP Images; 353: Win McNamee/Getty Images News/Getty Images; 356: Xinhua/Alamy Stock Photo; 359: ANDREW HOLBROOKE/Corbis via Getty Images

Chapter 13 Page 364: Andrew Harrer/dpa picture alliance/Alamy Stock Photo; 367: Yoon S.Byun/Boston Globe/Getty Images; 372: Jacob Kepler/Bloomberg/Getty Images; 373: The White House; Michael Stewart/WireImage/Getty Images; 375: Brynn Anderson/AP Images; 377: Scott J. Ferrell/Congressional Quarterly/Getty Images; 381: Justin Sullivan/Getty Images News/Getty Images; 383: Federal Reserve/Alamy Stock Photo; 387: Jim West/Alamy Stock Photo; 389: Marco Di Lauro/Getty Image Sport/Getty Images

Chapter 14 Page 395: Charles Dhapak/AP Images; 399: 4X5 Collection/SuperStock; 399: North Wind Picture Archives/Alamy Stock Photo; 400: Shane McCoy/WireImage/Getty Images; 407: The Supreme Court of the United States; 407: WDC Photos/Alamy Stock Photo; 408: Chris Kleponis/CNP /MediaPunch Inc/Alamy Stock Photo; 409: James K.W. Atherton/The Washington Post via Getty Images; 414: David Hume Kennerly/ 3rd Party - Misc/Getty Images; 416: Everett Collection Historical/Alamy Stock Photo; 424: John Gaps III/AP Images; 425: Reuters Photographer/Reuters

Chapter 15 Page 429: Adam Berry/AFP/Getty Images; 433: Bettmann/Getty Images; 436: WS Collection/Alamy Stock Photo; 437: Elijah Nouvelage/Getty Images News/Getty Images; 439: akg-images/The Image Works; 441: David Thomson/AFP/Getty Images; 443: Pius Utomi Ekpei/AFP/Getty Images; 446: Stan Grossfeld/Boston Globe/Getty Images; 449: AP Images; 449: National Archives, Records of the Supreme Court of the United States; 451: EMMANUEL DUNAND/AFP/GettyImages; 459: Sergey Nivens/Shutterstock

Chapter 16 Page 463: Raffe Lazarian/ZUMA Press, Inc./Alamy Stock Photo; 466: Library of Congress Prints and Photographs Division Washington, D.C. 20540 USA; 468: Marion Post Wolcott/Library Of Congress/Getty Images; 470: Bettmann/Getty Images; 471: Library of Congress Prints and Photographs Division Washington, D.C. 20540 USA [LC-DIG-ppmsca-24950]; 472: Francis Miller/The LIFE Picture Collection/Getty Images; 474: Michael Matthews - Police Images/Alamy Stock Photo; 475: Spencer Platt/Getty Images News/Getty Images; 480: epa european pressphoto agency b.v./Alamy Stock Photo; 482: Tim Nwachukwu/NCAA Photos via Getty Images; 483: Mario Tama/Getty Images News/Getty Images; 483: Michele Crowe/CBS via Getty Images; 485: Charles Rex Arbogast/AP Images; 487: Gregory Bull/AP Images

Chapter 17 Page 493: EPA/Alamy Stock Photo; 496: B Christopher/Alamy Stock Photo; 497: SAUL LOEB/AFP/Getty Images; 498: Meritzo/Alamy Stock Photo; 501: Ron Sachs/CNP/ZUMA Press, Inc./Alamy Stock Photo; 502: Robert Nickelsberg/Getty Images News/Getty Images; 503: Bill Clark/CQ Roll Call/AP Images; 508: Jochen Tack/Alamy Stock Photo; 514: BRENDAN SMIALOWSKI/AFP/Getty Images; 518: Margot Granitsas/The Image Works; 521: sjscreens/Alamy Stock Photo; 522: Alex Edelman/ZUMA Press, Inc./Alamy Stock Photo

Chapter 18 Page 529: Pan Chaoyue/Xinhua/Alamy Stock Photo; 532: US National Archives and Records Administration; 532: Frank Franklin II/AP Images; 536: Lars Baron/Bongarts/Getty Images; 538: Stocktrek Images, Inc./Alamy Stock Photo; 539: Artur Widak/Sipa/AP Images; 545: John Gaps III/AP Images; 546: The Asahi Shimbun via Getty Images; 547: Handout/Alamy Stock Photo; 548: John Tlumacki/The Boston Globe via Getty Images; 549: STEPHEN SHAVER/UPI/Newscom; 550: Ilia Yefimovich/picture alliance via Getty Images; 551: Hatem Moussa/AP Images; 552: Punit Paranjpe/Reuters; 553: SAUL LOEB/AFP/Getty Images; 554: Daniel Acker/Bloomberg via Getty Images; 557: Jason Reed/Reuters; 558: Christy Bowe/Globe Photos/ZUMAPress, Inc./Alamy Stock Photo; 559: ADAM BERRY/AFP/Getty Images